This is Volume 7 of WEST'S NEW YORK PRACTICE SERIES

―――

West's New York Practice Series

Vol. 1 Walker, et al., New York Limited Liability Companies and Partnerships: A Guide to Law and Practice

Vols. 2–4 Haig, et al., Commercial Litigation in New York State Courts

Vol. 5 Barker and Alexander, Evidence in New York State and Federal Courts

Vol. 6 Greenberg, Marcus, et al., New York Criminal Law

Vol. 7 Marks, et al., New York Pretrial Criminal Procedure

Vol. 8 Davies, Stecich and Gold, et al., New York Civil Appellate Practice

Vol. 9 Ginsberg, Weinberg, et al., Environmental Law and Regulation in New York

COORDINATED RESEARCH IN NEW YORK FROM WEST

WEST'S McKINNEY'S FORMS

Civil Practice Law and Rules
Uniform Commercial Code
Business Corporation Law
Matrimonial and Family Law
Real Property Practice
Estates and Surrogate Practice

Criminal Procedure Law
Not-For-Profit Corporation Law
Tax Practice and Procedure
Local Government Forms
Selected Consolidated Law Forms

McKinney's Consolidated Laws of New York Annotated
West's New York Legal Update
New York Digest
New York Law Finder

New York Estate Administration
Margaret V. Turano and
C. Raymond Radigan

Handling the DWI Case in New York
Peter Gerstenzang

New York Practice 2d
David D. Siegel

New York State Administrative Procedure and Practice
Patrick J. Borchers and
David J. Markell

PAMPHLETS

New York Civil Practice Law and Rules

New York Sentence Charts

WESTLAW®

WESTCheck® and WESTMATE®

West CD–ROM Libraries™

To order any of these New York practice tools, call your West Representative or 1–800–328–9352.

NEED RESEARCH HELP?
If you have research questions concerning WESTLAW or West Publications, call West's Reference Attorneys at 1–800–733–2889.

NEW YORK PRETRIAL CRIMINAL PROCEDURE

By

LAWRENCE K. MARKS
ROBERT S. DEAN
MARK DWYER
ANTHONY J. GIRESE
HON. JAMES A. YATES

Bancroft-Whitney • Banks-Baldwin • Clark Boardman Callaghan
Lawyers Cooperative Publishing • WESTLAW® • West Publishing

1996

NEW YORK PRETRIAL CRIMINAL PROCEDURE FORMS ON DISK™

The **Forms on Disk**™ which accompany this volume provide instant access to DOS text versions of the forms included in *New York Pretrial Criminal Procedure*. These electronic forms will save you hours of time drafting legal documents. Each electronic form includes text and punctuation identical to the forms in this volume. The electronic forms can be loaded into your word processing software and formatted to match the document style of your law firm. These electronic forms become templates for you to use over and over without having to retype them each time.

The forms in Volume 7 that are included on the accompanying disk are marked with the following disk icon for easy identification. 💾

COPYRIGHT © 1996 By WEST PUBLISHING CO.
610 Opperman Drive
P.O. Box 64526
St. Paul, MN 55164-0526
1-800-328-9352

All rights reserved
Printed in the United States of America
Library of Congress Catalog Card Number: 96-060314
ISBN 0-314-09764-3

PREFACE

This book provides an in-depth guide to pretrial procedure in New York criminal proceedings. Its primary focus is on the Criminal Procedure Law—the extensive statutory compilation governing criminal actions and proceedings in New York's courts. Enacted a quarter century ago, the CPL is a continually evolving code that is the subject of yearly amendment by the New York Legislature and daily interpretation by trial and appellate courts throughout the State. This book's analysis of the CPL's pretrial provisions and the extensive body of case law applying those statutes is unprecedented in its scope and reach. Moreover, because the vast number of criminal actions in New York are disposed of prior to trial, this work should prove useful to practitioners in virtually every criminal case.

Shortly after the enactment of the CPL, the New York State Judicial Conference established an advisory committee of leading judges, practitioners and academics to monitor the effectiveness of the new code's provisions and to propose statutory amendments where they were needed. The work of that group, now known as the Chief Administrative Judge's Advisory Committee on Criminal Law and Procedure, continues today and has resulted in a number of important statutory reforms. I am privileged to serve the advisory committee as its counsel, and several of the other authors of this book are among the committee's most active members.

It is our hope that special features provided in the book, such as the "Practice Summary" included at the end of each chapter, will render it of particular value to practitioners. Readers should note, however, that although the book takes a comprehensive and thorough approach to its subject, a few procedures that rarely, if ever, arise in everyday pretrial criminal practice are not addressed. In addition, except when necessary to explain suppression procedures, the book does not seek to address the "substantive" law relating to suppression motions; indeed, treatment of that topic could fill an entire separate book, or series of separate books.

It has been an honor for me to work on this project with some of the most knowledgeable and experienced persons in this area of New York law. My collaboration with these authors has been a distinct pleasure as well as a singular learning experience. I also want to express my appreciation to Marilyn Minzer of West Publishing Company, whose participation in this project greatly facilitated the development and completion of the book.

LAWRENCE K. MARKS

May 1996

ABOUT THE EDITOR-IN-CHIEF

LAWRENCE K. MARKS (Author of Chapters 3, 7, 8) is Deputy Counsel-Criminal Justice for the New York State Office of Court Administration. In that capacity, he advises court administrators on criminal justice matters, participates in the development of criminal justice programs for the State court system, and drafts, advocates and comments on criminal justice legislation. The author of numerous governmental reports, he serves as counsel to several State judicial committees, including the Chief Administrative Judge's Advisory Committee on Criminal Law and Procedure and the Chief Judge's Committee on Alternatives to Incarceration. Mr. Marks previously served as Senior Supervising Attorney with the Criminal Appeals Bureau of New York City's Legal Aid Society, as a litigation associate with a New York City law firm, and as law clerk to United States District Judge Thomas C. Platt. He received his undergraduate degree in 1979 from the State University of New York at Albany and his law degree in 1982 from the Cornell Law School, where he served as an editor of the law review.

ABOUT THE AUTHORS

ROBERT S. DEAN (Chapters 9, 11) is Senior Supervising Attorney for the Criminal Appeals Bureau of New York City's Legal Aid Society, where for the past 18 years he has briefed and argued criminal appeals in the Appellate Division, the Court of Appeals, the Second Circuit and the United States Supreme Court. Mr. Dean is a member of the adjunct faculty at New York University School of Law, from which he graduated in 1977. He is an active member of the Association of the Bar of the City of New York and the New York County Lawyers' Association. He received his undergraduate degree from Northwestern University in 1973.

MARK DWYER (Chapters 6, 10 (Suppression Proceedings)) has been Chief of the Appeals Bureau of the New York County District Attorney's Office since 1985. In that capacity, he supervises a staff of over 50 attorneys who represent the District Attorney in the Appellate Division, the Court of Appeals and the federal courts. Prior to working in the District Attorney's Office, which he joined in 1977, Mr. Dwyer was an instructor at New York University School of Law and law clerk to United States District Judge Thomas C. Platt. He is a member of the Chief Administrative Judge's Advisory Committee on Criminal Law and Procedure and an active participant in the New York State District Attorneys Association. Mr. Dwyer received his undergraduate degree in 1972 from Princeton University and his law degree in 1975 from the Yale Law School.

ANTHONY J. GIRESE (Chapters 1, 2, 4) is Counsel to the Bronx County District Attorney. He previously served as Chief of the Appeals Bureau of the Nassau County District Attorney's Office and as a prosecutor in the New York County District Attorney's Office. Mr. Girese is a fre-

ABOUT THE AUTHORS

quent writer and lecturer on a variety of criminal law topics. He is the chief legislative secretary of the New York State District Attorneys Association, a member of the Chief Administrative Judge's Advisory Committee on Criminal Law and Procedure, and a past member of several criminal justice committees of the Association of the Bar of the City of New York. He received his undergraduate degree in 1968 from City College of the City University of New York and his law degree in 1971 from the Columbia University Law School.

THE HONORABLE JAMES A. YATES (Chapter 5) is Judge of the New York State Court of Claims, and sits as Acting Justice in the criminal term of the Supreme Court, New York County. Prior to his appointment to the bench, he was employed for 13 years in the New York State Assembly, where he served as Senior Counsel to the Codes Committee, as Counsel to the Majority and as Legislative Counsel to the Speaker. During that period, he participated in the drafting and negotiation of hundreds of laws, including virtually all criminal justice legislation enacted by the State Legislature. Judge Yates has served on the adjunct faculty of four New York law schools, as a member of the New York State Committee on Sentencing Guidelines and the New York State Commission on Uniform Laws. Among his many current affiliations, he is a member of the Chief Administrative Judge's Advisory Committee on Criminal Law and Procedure, the IOLA board of directors, and the Association of the Bar of the City of New York's Criminal Law Committee, which he chairs. Judge Yates received his undergraduate degree in 1967 from Princeton University and his law degree in 1973 from Rutgers University School of Law.

* * *

BARRY STENDIG (Chapter 10 (Search Warrants)) practices criminal law in New York City. Prior to entering private practice, he was employed for 20 years with New York City's Legal Aid Society, first as a trial attorney with the Criminal Defense Division and then as Senior Supervising Attorney with the Criminal Appeals Bureau. Mr. Stendig received his undergraduate degree in 1972 from the Johns Hopkins University and his law degree in 1975 from Boston University School of Law. He also received a master of laws degree in criminal justice from New York University School of Law in 1980.

WESTLAW® ELECTRONIC RESEARCH GUIDE

Coordinating Legal Research With WESTLAW

The *New York Practice Series* is an essential aid to legal research. WESTLAW provides a vast, online library of over 7000 collections of documents and services that can supplement research begun in this publication, encompassing:

- Federal and state primary law (statutes, regulations, rules, and case law), including West's editorial enhancements, such as headnotes, Key Number classifications, annotations

- Secondary law resources (texts and treatises published by West Publishing Company and by other publishers, as well as law reviews)

- Legal news

- Directories of attorneys and experts

- Court records and filings

- Citators

Specialized topical subsets of these resources have been created for more than thirty areas of practice.

In addition to legal information, there are general news and reference databases and a broad array of specialized materials frequently useful in connection with legal matters, covering accounting, business, environment, ethics, finance, medicine, social and physical sciences.

This guide will focus on a few aspects of WESTLAW use to supplement research begun in this publication, and will direct you to additional sources of assistance.

Databases

A database is a collection of documents with some features in common. It may contain statutes, court decisions, administrative materials, commentaries, news or other information. Each database has a unique identifier, used in many WESTLAW commands to select a database of interest. For example, the database containing New York cases has the identifier NY-CS.

The WESTLAW Directory is a comprehensive list of databases with information about each database, including the types of documents each contains. The first page of a standard or customized WESTLAW Directory is displayed upon signing on to WESTLAW, except when prior, saved

WESTLAW ELECTRONIC RESEARCH GUIDE

research is resumed. To access the WESTLAW Directory at any time, enter DB.

A special subdirectory, accessible from the main WESTLAW Directory, lists databases applicable to Criminal Justice research.

Databases of potential interest in connection with your research include:

NY-CS	New York Case Law
NYETH-CS	New York Legal Ethics & Professional Responsibility Cases
NY-JLR	New York Journals and Law Reviews
LAWPRAC	The Legal Practice Database
WLD-CJ	West Legal Directory - Criminal
FCJ-CS	Federal Cases - Criminal Justice
MCJ-CS	Multistate Cases - Criminal Justice
CJ-CJA	Criminal Justice Abstracts
ULA-MPC	ULA Model Penal Code
LAFAVE1	Search and Seizure
CJ-CJAREP	Criminal Justice Act Reports
CJ-SCJ	ABA Standards for Criminal Justice (American Bar Assoc.)
CJ-PI	Criminal Justice Periodical Index (DIALOG)
NCJRS	National Criminal Justice Reference Service (DIALOG)

For information as to currentness and search tips regarding any WESTLAW database, enter the SCOPE command SC followed by the database identifier (e.g., SC NY-CS). It is not necessary to include the identifier to obtain scope information about the currently selected database.

WESTLAW Highlights

Use of this publication may be supplemented through the WESTLAW Bulletin (WLB), the WESTLAW New York State Bulletin (WSB-NY) and various Topical Highlights, including Criminal Justice Highlights (WTH-CJ). Highlights databases contain summaries of significant judicial, legislative and administrative developments and are updated daily; they are searchable both from an automatic list of recent documents and using general WESTLAW search methods for documents accumulated over time. The full text of any judicial decision may be retrieved by entering FIND.

Consult the WESTLAW Directory (enter DB) for a complete, current listing of highlights databases.

Retrieving a Specific Case

The FIND command can be used to quickly retrieve a case whose citation is known. For example:

FI 616 A.2d 1336

Updating Case Law Research

There are a variety of citator services on WESTLAW for use in updating research.

WESTLAW ELECTRONIC RESEARCH GUIDE

Insta-Cite® may be used to verify citations, find parallel citations, ascertain the history of a case, and see whether it remains valid law. References are also provided to secondary sources, such as Corpus Juris Secundum®, that cite the case. To view the Insta-Cite history of a displayed case, simply enter the command IC. To view the Insta-Cite history of a selected case, enter a command in this form:

IC 574 A.2d 502

Shepard's® Citations provides a comprehensive list of cases and publications that have cited a particular case, with explanatory analysis to indicate how the citing cases have treated the case, e.g., "followed," "explained." To view the Shepard's Citations about a displayed case, enter the command SH. Add a case citation, if necessary, as in the prior Insta-Cite example.

For the latest citing references, not yet incorporated in Shepard's Citations, use Shepard's PreView® (SP command) and QuickCite™ (QC command), in the same way.

To see a complete list of publications covered by any of the citator services, enter its service abbreviation (IC, SH, SP or QC) followed by PUBS. To ascertain the scope of coverage for any of the services, enter the SCOPE command (SC) followed by the appropriate service abbreviation. For the complete list of commands available in a citator service, enter its service abbreviation (IC, SH, SP or QC) followed by CMDS.

Retrieving Statutes, Court Rules and Regulations

Annotated and unannotated versions of the New York statutes are searchable on WESTLAW (identifiers NY-ST-ANN and NY-ST), as are New York court rules (NY-RULES) and New York Administrative Code (NY-ADC).

The United States Code and United States Code - Annotated are searchable databases on WESTLAW (identifiers USC and USCA, respectively), as are federal court rules (US-RULES) and regulations (CFR).

In addition, the FIND command may be used to retrieve specific provisions by citation, obviating the need for database selection or search. To FIND a desired document, enter FI, followed by the citation of the desired document, using the full name of the publication, or one of the abbreviated styles recognized by WESTLAW.

If WESTLAW does not recognize the style you enter, you may enter one of the following, using US, NY, or any other state code in place of XX:

FI XX-ST	Displays templates for codified statutes
FI XX-LEGIS	Displays templates for legislation
FI XX-RULES	Displays templates for rules
FI XX-ORDERS	Displays templates for court orders

Alternatively, entering FI followed by the publication's full name or an accepted abbreviation will normally display templates, useful jump possibilities, or helpful information necessary to complete the FIND process. For example:

FI USCA	Displays templates for United States Code - Annotated
FI FRAP	Displays templates for Federal Rules of Appellate Procedure
FI FRCP	Displays templates for Federal Rules of Civil Procedure
FI FRCRP	Displays templates for Federal Rules of Criminal Procedure
FI FRE	Displays templates for Federal Rules of Evidence
FI CFR	Displays templates for Code of Federal Regulations
FI FR	Displays templates for Federal Register

To view the complete list of FINDable documents and associated prescribed forms, enter FI PUBS.

Updating Research in re Statutes, Rules and Regulations

When viewing a statute, rule or regulation on WESTLAW after a search or FIND command, it is easy to update your research. A message will appear on the screen if relevant amendments, repeals or other new material are available through the UPDATE feature. Entering the UPDATE command will display such material.

Documents used to update New York statutes are also searchable in New York Legislative Service (NY-LEGIS). Those used to update rules are searchable in New York Orders (NY-ORDERS).

Documents used to update federal statutes, rules, and regulations are searchable in the United States Public Laws (US-PL), Federal Orders (US-ORDERS) and Federal Register (FR) databases, respectively.

When documents citing a statute, rule or regulation are of interest, Shepard's Citations on WESTLAW may be of assistance. That service covers federal constitutional provisions, statutes and administrative provisions, and corresponding materials from many states. The command SH PUBS displays a directory of publications which may be Shepardized on WESTLAW. Consult the WESTLAW manual for more information about citator services.

Using WESTLAW as a Citator

For research beyond the coverage of any citator service, go directly to the databases (cases, for example) containing citing documents and use standard WESTLAW search techniques to retrieve documents citing specific constitutional provisions, statutes, standard jury instructions or other authorities.

Fortunately, the specific portion of a citation is often reasonably distinctive, such as 22:636.1, 301.65, 401(k), 12-21-5, 12052. When it is, a search on that specific portion alone may retrieve applicable documents without any substantial number of inapplicable ones (unless the number happens to be coincidentally popular in another context).

WESTLAW ELECTRONIC RESEARCH GUIDE

Similarly, if the citation involves more than one number, such as 42 U.S.C.A. § 1201, a search containing both numbers (e.g., 42 +5 1201) is likely to produce mostly desired information, even though the component numbers are common.

If necessary, the search may be limited in several ways:

A. Switch from a general database to one containing mostly cases within the subject area of the cite being researched;

B. Use a connector (&, /S, /P, etc.) to narrow the search to documents including terms which are highly likely to accompany the correct citation in the context of the issue being researched;

C. Include other citation information in the query. Because of the variety of citation formats used in documents, this option should be used primarily where other options prove insufficient. Below are illustrative queries for any database containing New York cases:

> N.Y.Const.! Const.! Constitution /s 6 VI +3 3

will retrieve cases citing the New York State Constitution, Art. 6, § 3; and

> "Criminal Procedure Law" CPL /s 30.30

will retrieve cases citing Criminal Procedure Law § 30.30.

Alternative Retrieval Methods

WIN® (WESTLAW Is Natural™) allows you to frame your issue in plain English to retrieve documents:

> Exclusion of witness as sanction for late (untimely) disclosure.

Alternatively, retrieval may be focused by use of the Terms and Connectors method:

> DI(EXCLU**** /P WITNESS /P DISCLOS*** /P UNTIM*** LATE)

In databases with Key Numbers, either of the above examples will identify Criminal Law ⟺629.5 as a Key Number collecting headnotes relevant to this issue if there are pertinent cases.

Since the Key Numbers are affixed to points of law by trained specialists based on conceptual understanding of the case, relevant cases that were not retrieved by either of the language-dependent methods will often be found at a Key Number.

Similarly, citations in retrieved documents (to cases, statutes, rules, etc.) may suggest additional, fruitful research using other WESTLAW databases (e.g., annotated statutes, rules) or services (e.g., citator services).

Key Number Search

Frequently, case law research rapidly converges on a few topics, headings and Key Numbers within West's Key Number System that are likely to contain relevant cases. These may be discovered from known, relevant reported cases from any jurisdiction; Library References in West publications; browsing in a digest; or browsing the Key Number System on WESTLAW using the JUMP feature or the KEY command.

Once discovered, topics, subheadings or Key Numbers are useful as search terms (in databases containing reported cases) alone or with other search terms, to focus the search within a narrow range of potentially relevant material.

For example, to retrieve cases with at least one headnote classified to Criminal Law ⟜629.5, sign on to a caselaw database and enter

> 110k629.5 [use with other search terms, if desired]

The topic name (Criminal Law) is replaced by its numerical equivalent (110) and the ⟜ by the letter k. A list of topics and their numerical equivalents is in the WESTLAW Reference Manual and is displayed in WESTLAW when the KEY command is entered.

Other topics of special interest are listed below.

Adulteration (18)
Adultery (19)
Arrest (35)
Arson (36)
Assault and Battery (37)
Bigamy (55)
Breach of the Peace (62)
Bribery (63)
Burglary (67)
Compounding Offenses (88)
Conspiracy (91)
Convicts (98)
Counterfeiting (103)
Criminal Law (110)
Disorderly Conduct (129)
Disorderly House (130)
Disturbance of Public Assemblage (133)
Double Jeopardy (135H)
Drugs and Narcotics (138)
Embezzlement (146)
Escape (151)
Extortion and Threats (165)
Extradition and Detainers (166)
False Personation (169)
False Pretenses (170)
Fines (174)
Fires (175)
Forfeitures (180)
Forgery (181)
Fraud (184)
Grand Jury (193)

Habeas Corpus (197)
Homicide (203)
Incest (207)
Indictment and Information (210)
Insurrection and Sedition (218)
Kidnapping (232)
Larceny (234)
Lewdness (236)
Malicious Mischief (248)
Mayhem (256)
Neutrality Laws (273)
Obscenity (281)
Obstructing Justice (282)
Pardon and Parole (284)
Perjury (297)
Prisons (310)
Prostitution (316)
Racketeer Influenced and Corrupt Organizations (319H)
Rape (321)
Receiving Stolen Goods (324)
Rescue (337)
Riot (341)
Robbery (342)
Searches and Seizures (349)
Sodomy (357)
Suicide (368)
Treason (384)
Unlawful Assembly (396)
Vagrancy (399)
Weapons (406)
Witnesses (410)

Using JUMP

WESTLAW's JUMP feature allows you to move from one document to another or from one part of a document to another, then easily return

WESTLAW ELECTRONIC RESEARCH GUIDE

to your original place, without losing your original result. Opportunities to move in this manner are marked in the text with a JUMP symbol (▶). Whenever you see the JUMP symbol, you may move to the place designated by the adjacent reference by using the Tab, arrow keys or mouse click to position the cursor on the JUMP symbol, then pressing Enter or clicking again with the mouse.

Within the text of a court opinion, JUMP arrows are adjacent to case cites and federal statute cites, and adjacent to parenthesized numbers marking discussions corresponding to headnotes.

On a screen containing the text of a headnote, the JUMP arrows allow movement to the corresponding discussion in the text of the opinion,

▶ (3)

and allow browsing West's Key Number System beginning at various heading levels:

- ▶ 110   CRIMINAL LAW
- ▶ 110XX   Trial
- ▶ 110XX(A)   Preliminary Proceedings
- ▶ 110k629   List of Witnesses and Disclosure of Other Matters
- ▶ 110k629.5   Effect of Failure to Make Proper Disclosure
- ▶ 110k629.5(2)   k. Exclusion of evidence or witnesses.

To return from a JUMP, enter GB (except for JUMPs between a headnote and the corresponding discussion in opinion, for which there is a matching number in parenthesis in both headnote and opinion). Returns from successive JUMPs (e.g., from case to cited case to case cited by cited case) without intervening returns may be accomplished by repeated entry of GB or by using the MAP command.

General Information

The information provided above illustrates some of the ways WESTLAW can complement research using this publication. However, this brief overview illustrates only some of the power of WESTLAW. The full range of WESTLAW search techniques is available to support your research.

Please consult the WESTLAW Reference Manual for additional information or assistance or call West's Reference Attorneys at 1-800-REF-ATTY (1-800-733-2889).

For information about subscribing to WESTLAW, please call 1-800-328-0109.

*

SUMMARY OF CONTENTS

Chapter	Page
1. Jurisdiction and Removal	1
2. Double Jeopardy	50
3. Preliminary Proceedings in Local Criminal Courts	97
4. Bail and Recognizance	176
5. Grand Jury and Indictment	215
6. Competency Proceedings	367
7. Discovery	405
8. The Omnibus Motion	471
9. Timeliness of Prosecution and Speedy Trial	483
10. Search Warrants and Suppression Proceedings	554
11. Pleas	650
Table of Statutes	689
Table of Rules	717
Table of Cases	719
Index	785

*

TABLE OF CONTENTS

CHAPTER 1. JURISDICTION AND REMOVAL

Sec.
1.1 Jurisdiction—In General.
1.2 ——— Courts.
1.3 Geographical Jurisdiction of Offenses—New York State.
1.4 ——— Counties.
1.5 Geographical Jurisdiction of Local Criminal Courts Within a County—Filing of Accusatory Instruments.
1.6 Removal—In General.
1.7 ——— From One Local Criminal Court to Another.
1.8 ——— From a Local Criminal Court to a Superior Court.
1.9 ——— From One Superior Court to Another.
1.10 ——— To Family Court.
1.11 Practice Summary.
1.12 Forms
    1.12.1 Notice of Motion to Remove Action to Another Local Criminal Court of the County.
    1.12.2 Affirmation in Support of Motion to Remove Action to Another Local Criminal Court of the County.
    1.12.3 Notice of Motion by Prosecutor in Support of Motion to Adjourn Proceedings in Local Criminal Court on Misdemeanor Charge to Present Charge to a Grand Jury.
    1.12.4 Affirmation in Support of Prosecutor's Motion to Adjourn Proceedings on Misdemeanor Charge in Local Criminal Court to Present Charge to a Grand Jury.
    1.12.5 Notice of Motion by Defendant to Remove Proceedings on Misdemeanor Charge to Superior Court.
    1.12.6 Affirmation in Support of Motion by Defendant to Remove Proceedings on Misdemeanor Charge to Superior Court.
    1.12.7 Notice of Motion in Appellate Division for Change of Venue.
    1.12.8 Affirmation in Support of Motion in the Appellate Division for Change of Venue.

CHAPTER 2. DOUBLE JEOPARDY

2.1 Introduction.
2.2 Attachment of Jeopardy—In General.
2.3 Lack of Jurisdiction and "Procurement" Exceptions to Attachment of Jeopardy.
2.4 Nullified Proceedings—Mistrials, Hung Juries, Vacated Pleas, and Appellate Reversals.
2.5 "Same Offense" Constitutional Double Jeopardy.
2.6 "Same Criminal Transaction" Statutory Double Jeopardy.
2.7 Mandatory Joinder.
2.8 Collateral Estoppel.
2.9 Enterprise Corruption Double Jeopardy.
2.10 Miscellaneous Issues—Multiple Punishment, Civil Proceedings and Juvenile Proceedings.

TABLE OF CONTENTS

Sec.
2.11 Procedure for Raising a Double Jeopardy Claim.
2.12 Practice Summary.
2.13 Forms
    2.13.1 Notice of Motion to Dismiss Accusatory Instrument on Ground That Prosecution Is Barred by Previous Prosecution.
    2.13.2 Affirmation in Support of Motion to Dismiss Accusatory Instrument on Ground That Prosecution Is Barred by Previous Prosecution.
    2.13.3 Petition in Article 78 Proceeding to Prohibit Prosecution on Ground that it is Barred by Previous Prosecution.

CHAPTER 3. PRELIMINARY PROCEEDINGS IN LOCAL CRIMINAL COURTS

3.1 Introduction.
3.2 Local Criminal Court Accusatory Instruments—Types.
3.3 _____ Form and Content.
3.4 _____ Supporting Depositions.
3.5 _____ Supporting Depositions Filed in Connection With Simplified Informations.
3.6 _____ Verification.
3.7 _____ Facial Sufficiency.
3.8 _____ Severance, Consolidation, Amendment and Bill of Particulars.
3.9 _____ Superseding Informations and Prosecutor's Informations.
3.10 Means of Compelling a Defendant's Appearance for Arraignment—In General.
3.11 The Arrest Warrant.
3.12 Arrest Warrant—Form and Content.
3.13 _____ Additional Procedural Requirements.
3.14 _____ Execution.
3.15 _____ Post-Arrest Procedure.
3.16 The Summons.
3.17 Warrantless Arrests—In General.
3.18 _____ Authorization and Execution.
3.19 _____ Post-Arrest Procedure.
3.20 Appearance Ticket—In General.
3.21 _____ Pre-arraignment Bail and Post-Issuance Procedures.
3.22 _____ Marihuana Violations.
3.23 Fingerprinting.
3.24 Arraignment on Non-felony Accusatory Instrument.
3.25 Conversion or Replacement of Misdemeanor Complaint to Information.
3.26 Motion to Dismiss—In General.
3.27 _____ Defective Accusatory Instrument.
3.28 _____ In Furtherance of Justice.
3.29 Adjournment in Contemplation of Dismissal.
3.30 Arraignment on Felony Complaints.
3.31 Return of Felony Complaint to Local Criminal Court.
3.32 Reduction of Felony Charges.
3.33 The Preliminary Hearing.
3.34 Release of Defendant in Custody.
3.35 Practice Summary.

TABLE OF CONTENTS

Sec.
3.36 Forms
    3.36.1 Supporting Deposition.
    3.36.2 Defendant's Request for Supporting Deposition.
    3.36.3 Supporting Deposition for Simplified Information.
    3.36.4 Notice of Motion to Amend Prosecutor's Information.
    3.36.5 Affirmation in Support of Motion to Amend Prosecutor's Information.
    3.36.6 Notice of Motion to Amend Information.
    3.36.7 Affirmation in Support of Motion to Amend Information.
    3.36.8 Petition for Writ of *Habeas Corpus* on Behalf of Person Arrested Without Warrant Who Has Not Been Produced for Arraignment.
    3.36.9 Notice of Motion to Dismiss Local Criminal Court Accusatory Instrument (or a count thereof).
    3.36.10 Affirmation in Support of Motion to Dismiss Local Criminal Court Accusatory Instrument (or a count thereof).
    3.36.11 Notice of Motion to Dismiss Local Criminal Court Accusatory Instrument in Furtherance of Justice.
    3.36.12 Affirmation in Support of Motion to Dismiss Local Criminal Court Accusatory Instrument in Furtherance of Justice.
    3.36.13 Notice of Motion to Restore Proceedings on Local Criminal Court Accusatory Instrument that were Adjourned in Contemplation of Dismissal.
    3.36.14 Affirmation in Support of Motion to Restore Proceedings on Local Criminal Court Accusatory Instrument That Were Adjourned in Contemplation of Dismissal.
    3.36.15 Notice of Motion for Order Releasing Defendant From Custody for Failure to Replace Misdemeanor Complaint With Information.
    3.36.16 Affirmation in Support of Motion for Order Releasing Defendant From Custody for Failure to Replace Misdemeanor Complaint With Information.
    3.36.17 Notice of Motion for Order Releasing Defendant From Custody for Lack of Timely Disposition of Felony Complaint.
    3.36.18 Affirmation in Support of Motion for Order Releasing Defendant From Custody for Lack of Timely Disposition of Felony Complaint.

CHAPTER 4. BAIL AND RECOGNIZANCE

4.1 Introduction.
4.2 Definitions.
4.3 Acceptable Varieties of Bail.
4.4 Fixing of Bail—In General.
4.5 Bail Applications and General Criteria.
4.6 Fixing of Bail by Local Criminal Courts.
4.7 Fixing of Bail by Superior Courts.
4.8 "Stationhouse" Pre-arraignment Bail.
4.9 Bail After Conviction and on Appeal.
4.10 Bail and Recognizance Conditions and Modification.
4.11 Examination of Sufficiency of Bail.
4.12 Forfeiture of Bail and Remission.
4.13 Procedure for Challenges to Excessive Bail.

TABLE OF CONTENTS

Sec.
4.14 Practice Summary.
4.15 Forms
    4.15.1 Notice of Application for Recognizance or Bail in Superior Court When Action Pending in Local Criminal Court.
    4.15.2 Affirmation in Support of Application for Recognizance or Bail in Superior Court When Action Pending in Local Criminal Court.
    4.15.3 Petition for Writ of *Habeas Corpus* on Ground That Bail Fixed by Trial Court Is So Excessive as to Constitute an Abuse of Discretion.
    4.15.4 Notice of Application for Remission of Forfeiture of Bail.
    4.15.5 Affidavit in Support of Application for Remission of Forfeiture of Bail.

CHAPTER 5. GRAND JURY AND INDICTMENT

5.1 Grand Jury—In General.
5.2 ____ Formation and Organization.
5.3 ____ Secrecy and Attendance.
5.4 ____ Legal Advisors.
5.5 ____ Legal Instructions.
5.6 ____ Applicability of Rules of Evidence.
5.7 ____ Exculpatory Evidence.
5.8 ____ Appearance of Witnesses.
5.9 Compelled Testimony.
5.10 Waiver of Indictment and Superior Court Informations.
5.11 Indictment—In General.
5.12 ____ Form and Content.
5.13 ____ Purpose.
5.14 ____ Adequate Notice.
5.15 ____ Date of Offense.
5.16 ____ Jurisdictional Defects.
5.17 ____ Duplicitous Counts.
5.18 ____ Curing Defects.
5.19 ____ Bill of Particulars.
5.20 ____ Lesser Offenses Prosecuted by Indictment.
5.21 ____ Joinder of Offenses.
5.22 ____ Joinder of Defendants.
5.23 ____ Securing Defendant's Appearance.
5.24 ____ Arraignment.
5.25 ____ Motion to Dismiss—In General.
5.26 ____ Motion to Dismiss—Procedure.
5.27 ____ Motion to Dismiss or Reduce Indictment—Grounds.
5.28 ____ Disposition Following Dismissal.
5.29 ____ Disposition Following Order Reducing Count.
5.30 Practice Summary—Grand Jury.
5.31 ____ Waiver of Indictment (*See* § 5.10).
5.32 ____ Indictment.
5.33 Forms
    5.33.1 Notice of Motion in Superior Court to Release Defendant Due to Failure of Timely Grand Jury Action.

TABLE OF CONTENTS

Sec.
5.33 Forms—Continued
- 5.33.2 Affirmation in Support of Motion in Superior Court to Release Defendant Due to Failure of Timely Grand Jury Action.
- 5.33.3 Notice of Motion to Dismiss Indictment Because Defendant Not Afforded Opportunity to Testify Before Grand Jury.
- 5.33.4 Affirmation in Support of Motion to Dismiss Indictment Because Defendant Not Afforded Opportunity to Testify Before Grand Jury.
- 5.33.5 Notice of Motion for Severance of Counts.
- 5.33.6 Affirmation in Support of Motion for Severance of Counts.
- 5.33.7 Notice of Motion to Consolidate Indictments Against the Same Defendant.
- 5.33.8 Affirmation in Support of Motion to Consolidate Indictments Against the Same Defendant.
- 5.33.9 Notice of Motion for Severance of Trials of Jointly Indicted Defendants.
- 5.33.10 Affirmation in Support of Motion for Severance of Trials of Jointly Indicted Defendants.
- 5.33.11 Notice of Motion to Consolidate Indictments Against Different Defendants.
- 5.33.12 Affirmation in Support of Motion Consolidating Indictments Against Different Defendants.
- 5.33.13 Notice of Motion to Amend Indictment.
- 5.33.14 Affirmation in Support of Motion to Amend Indictment.
- 5.33.15 Notice of Motion to Amend Bill of Particulars.
- 5.33.16 Affirmation in Support of Motion to Amend Bill of Particulars.
- 5.33.17 Notice of Motion to Dismiss Indictment (or Count(s) of Indictment) as Defective.
- 5.33.18 Affirmation in Support of Motion to Dismiss Indictment (or Count(s) of Indictment) as Defective.
- 5.33.19 Notice of Motion to Dismiss Indictment (Grand Jury Immunity).
- 5.33.20 Affirmation in Support of Motion to Dismiss Indictment (Grand Jury Immunity).
- 5.33.21 Notice of Motion to Dismiss Indictment in Furtherance of Justice.
- 5.33.22 Affirmation in Support of Motion to Dismiss Indictment in Furtherance of Justice.
- 5.33.23 Notice of Motion by Prosecutor to Submit Charge(s) to a New Grand Jury.
- 5.33.24 Affirmation in Support of Prosecutor's Motion to Submit Charge(s) to a New Grand Jury.

CHAPTER 6. COMPETENCY PROCEEDINGS

- 6.1 In General.
- 6.2 Order of Examination.
- 6.3 Effect on Case of Order of Examination.
- 6.4 Initial Examination—By Whom Conducted.
- 6.5 _____ How and When Conducted.
- 6.6 Post-Examination Procedure in Superior Court.
- 6.7 Post-Examination Procedure in Local Criminal Court.
- 6.8 The 1980 Amendments.

TABLE OF CONTENTS

Sec.
6.9 Hearing Procedure.
6.10 Additional Considerations.
6.11 Practice Summary.
6.12 Forms
    6.12.1 Notice of Motion for Order of Examination.
    6.12.2 Affirmation in Support of Motion for Order of Examination.

CHAPTER 7. DISCOVERY

7.1 Introduction.
7.2 Criminal Discovery in New York.
7.3 Demand Disclosure—In General.
7.4 _____ By Defendant.
7.5 _____ By Prosecution.
7.6 _____ Refusal of Demand.
7.7 Defense Motion for Discovery—Statutory Basis.
7.8 _____ Subpoenas.
7.9 _____ Identity of Prosecution Witnesses.
7.10 _____ Identity of Informant.
7.11 Prosecution Motion for Discovery.
7.12 *Brady*—In General.
7.13 _____ Materiality.
7.14 _____ Other Issues.
7.15 Disclosure of Uncharged Prior Bad Acts.
7.16 *Rosario*—In General.
7.17 _____ Specific Issues.
7.18 Witness Criminal History Information.
7.19 Protective Orders.
7.20 Sanctions—In General.
7.21 _____ Belated Disclosure.
7.22 _____ Complete Failure to Disclose.
7.23 _____ Loss or Destruction of Discoverable Material.
7.24 _____ Against the Defense.
7.25 Pretrial Notices of Defenses—In General.
7.26 _____ Psychiatric Evidence.
7.27 _____ Alibi.
7.28 _____ Computer-Related Offenses.
7.29 Prosecution's Notice of Intent to Seek Death Penalty.
7.30 Discovery of Privileged and Confidential Material.
7.31 The Work Product Exemption.
7.32 Defendant's Right to Test of Physical Evidence.
7.33 Miscellaneous Issues.
7.34 Practice Summary—Defense.
7.35 _____ Prosecution.
7.36 _____ Court.
7.37 Forms
    7.37.1 Demand to Produce (Made by Defendant).
    7.37.2 Demand to Produce (Made by Prosecutor).
    7.37.3 Refusal of Demand to Produce (Either Party).
    7.37.4 Notice of Motion by Defendant for Disclosure in Response to Refusal of Prosecution to Comply With Demand to Produce.

TABLE OF CONTENTS

Sec.

7.37 Forms—Continued
    7.37.5 Affirmation in Support of Defendant's Motion for Disclosure After Refusal of Prosecutor to Comply With Demand to Produce.
    7.37.6 Notice of Motion by Defendant for Discovery Beyond That Required Under Demand to Produce.
    7.37.7 Affirmation in Support of Defendant's Motion for Discovery Beyond That Required Under Demand to Produce.
    7.37.8 Notice of Motion by Prosecutor for Discovery of Non-testimonial Evidence.
    7.37.9 Affirmation of Prosecutor in Support of Motion for Discovery of Non-testimonial Evidence.
    7.37.10 Notice of Motion for Protective Order.
    7.37.11 Affirmation in Support of Motion for Protective Order.
    7.37.12 Demand for Notice of Alibi.
    7.37.13 Notice of Alibi.

CHAPTER 8. THE OMNIBUS MOTION

8.1 The Omnibus Motion.
8.2 Forms
    8.2.1 Notice of Omnibus Motion in Felony Case.
    8.2.2 Affirmation in Support of Omnibus Motion in Felony Case.

CHAPTER 9. TIMELINESS OF PROSECUTION AND SPEEDY TRIAL

9.1 CPL Article 30—Introduction.
9.2 Statute of Limitations—Introduction.
9.3 _____ Relevant Time Periods.
9.4 _____ Extensions.
9.5 _____ Tolling.
9.6 _____ How and When to Raise; Burden of Proof.
9.7 _____ Waiver of Defense by Guilty Plea.
9.8 Federal Constitutional Speedy Trial.
9.9 State Speedy Trial and Due Process Guarantees—In General.
9.10 _____ *Taranovich* Factors.
9.11 Preference of Criminal Over Civil Cases.
9.12 Constitutional Speedy Trial/Due Process Claims—Procedural Requirements.
9.13 Prosecutorial Readiness Rule—In General.
9.14 Nonapplicability to Some Criminal Actions.
9.15 "Commencement" of the Criminal Action Starts the Clock Ticking.
9.16 Special Recommencement Rule—Plea Withdrawal, Mistrial, or Order for New Trial.
9.17 Desk Appearance Tickets.
9.18 Reduction of Original Charges—Reduction of Felony Complaint.
9.19 _____ Inspection and Reduction of Indicted Felony.
9.20 _____ Other Reductions.
9.21 Prosecutor's "Readiness" Stops the Clock—"Readiness" Defined.
9.22 _____ Genuine "Readiness" Defined.
9.23 _____ Valid Communication of "Present" Readiness Defined.
9.24 Time Within Which Prosecution Must Be Ready to Avoid Dismissal.

TABLE OF CONTENTS

Sec.
- 9.25 Time Within Which Prosecution Must Be Ready to Avoid Release of Jailed Defendant on Bail or Recognizance.
- 9.26 Excludable Periods—In General.
- 9.27 ____ Other Proceedings Concerning the Defendant.
- 9.28 ____ ____ Competency.
- 9.29 ____ ____ Discovery.
- 9.30 ____ ____ Pre-trial Motions.
- 9.31 ____ ____ Appeals.
- 9.32 ____ ____ Trial of Other Charges.
- 9.33 ____ ____ The Period During Which Such Matters Are Under Consideration by the Court.
- 9.34 ____ Continuances.
- 9.35 ____ Absence or Unavailability of the Defendant.
- 9.36 ____ ____ Cause of Prosecution's Unreadiness.
- 9.37 ____ ____ Bench Warrants.
- 9.38 ____ ____ Absent.
- 9.39 ____ ____ Unavailable.
- 9.40 ____ Co-defendant Joinder.
- 9.41 ____ Incarcerated Defendants.
- 9.42 ____ Defendant Without Counsel.
- 9.43 ____ Exceptional Circumstances.
- 9.44 ____ Adjournments in Contemplation of Dismissal.
- 9.45 ____ Prosecutor's Direction to Appear at Arraignment.
- 9.46 ____ Family Offenses.
- 9.47 Post-Readiness Delay.
- 9.48 Procedural Considerations—Calculating Time.
- 9.49 ____ Motion Practice Requirements.
- 9.50 ____ Sufficiency of Motion Papers and Burden of Proof.
- 9.51 ____ Sufficiency of Motion Papers.
- 9.52 ____ Burden of Proof.
- 9.53 Interstate Agreement on Detainers (CPL § 580.20).
- 9.54 Interstate Agreement on Detainers—The Prisoner's Request (Article III).
- 9.55 ____ The Receiving State's Request (Article IV).
- 9.56 Practice Summary—Defense.
- 9.57 ____ Prosecution.
- 9.58 Forms
  - 9.58.1 Notice of Motion to Dismiss for Statute of Limitations Violation.
  - 9.58.2 Affirmation in Support of Motion to Dismiss for Statute of Limitations Violation.
  - 9.58.3 Notice of Motion to Dismiss Indictment for Violation of Right to Speedy Trial (Constitutional/CPL 30.20).
  - 9.58.4 Affirmation in Support of Motion to Dismiss Indictment for Violation of Right to Speedy Trial (Constitutional/CPL § 30.20).
  - 9.58.5 Notice of Motion to Dismiss Indictment for Failure of the Prosecution to Timely Announce Readiness for Trial (CPL § 30.30(1) Only).
  - 9.58.6 Affirmation in Support of Motion to Dismiss Indictment for Failure of the Prosecution to Timely Announce Readiness for Trial (CPL § 30.30(1) Only).

TABLE OF CONTENTS

Sec.
9.58 Forms—Continued
    9.58.7 Notice of Motion for Bail/Recognizance for Failure of the Prosecution to Timely Announce Readiness for Trial (CPL § 30.30(2) Only).
    9.58.8 Affirmation in Support of Motion for Bail/Recognizance for Failure of the Prosecution to Timely Announce Readiness for Trial (CPL § 30.30(2) Only).

CHAPTER 10. SEARCH WARRANTS AND SUPPRESSION PROCEEDINGS

10.1 Search Warrants—In General.
10.2 _____ Application for and Issuance of Search Warrant.
10.3 _____ Facial Sufficiency of Warrant and Warrant Application.
10.4 _____ Controverting the Warrant.
10.5 _____ Execution of Warrant.
10.6 _____ Extent of Search Allowed Under Proper Warrant.
10.7 Suppression Proceedings—Introduction.
10.8 Suppressible Evidence—In General.
10.9 _____ Indirect Fruits.
10.10 _____ Attenuation.
10.11 Standing.
10.12 Motion to Suppress—Court.
10.13 _____ Time Of Motion.
10.14 _____ Time of Decision.
10.15 _____ Renewal.
10.16 The Defendant's Motion Papers—In General.
10.17 _____ Factual Allegations.
10.18 The Prosecution's Motion Papers.
10.19 Suppression Hearings—In General.
10.20 _____ Burden of Proof.
10.21 _____ Decision.
10.22 Implications for Subsequent Proceedings.
10.23 Notice—In General.
10.24 _____ Timing and Content of Notice.
10.25 _____ Statements Within and Without the Rule.
10.26 _____ Identifications Within and Without the Rule.
10.27 _____ Good Cause for Lateness.
10.28 _____ Scope of Preclusion.
10.29 _____ Waiver and Appeal.
10.30 Practice Summary.
10.31 Forms
    10.31.1 Forms—Notice of Motion to Suppress Statements.
    10.31.2 Forms—Affirmation in Support of Motion to Suppress Statements.
    10.31.3 Forms—Notice of Motion to Suppress Identification Evidence.
    10.31.4 Forms—Affirmation in Support of Motion to Suppress Identification.
    10.31.5 Forms—Notice of Motion to Suppress Physical Evidence.
    10.31.6 Forms—Affirmation in Support of Motion to Suppress Physical Evidence.

TABLE OF CONTENTS

CHAPTER 11. PLEAS

Sec.
11.1 Introduction.
11.2 Pleading Guilty as of Right.
11.3 Guilty Pleas by Permission of the Court and the Consent of the Prosecutor.
11.4 Pleas of Not Responsible by Reason of Mental Disease or Defect.
11.5 Statutory Plea Bargaining Restrictions.
11.6 Withdrawal of Not Guilty Plea by the Defendant.
11.7 Entry of the Guilty Plea—Knowing and Voluntary Waiver of Rights.
11.8 _____ Competency of Defendant.
11.9 _____ Defendant's Understanding of Collateral Consequences of the Plea.
11.10 _____ Factual Basis for the Plea.
11.11 Sentence Promises—In General.
11.12 _____ Conditional Nature of Promise.
11.13 _____ Special Conditions for Defendants at Liberty Between Plea and Sentence.
11.14 _____ Specific Performance.
11.15 Rights Automatically Relinquished by a Defendant Upon Pleading Guilty.
11.16 Claims That Ordinarily Survive a Guilty Plea.
11.17 Bargained-for Waivers of the Right to Appeal.
11.18 Withdrawal of Guilty Plea—Defendant.
11.19 _____ Court or Prosecutor.
11.20 Practice Summary—Defense.
11.21 _____ Prosecution.
11.22 _____ Court.
11.23 Forms
    11.23.1 Notice of Motion to Withdraw Guilty Plea.
    11.23.2 Affirmation of Attorney Upon Motion to Withdraw Guilty Plea.
    11.23.3 Affidavit of Defendant Upon Motion to Withdraw Guilty Plea.

	Page
Table of Statutes	689
Table of Rules	717
Table of Cases	719
Index	785

Chapter 1

JURISDICTION AND REMOVAL

Table of Sections

1.1 Jurisdiction—In General.
1.2 ___ Courts.
1.3 Geographical Jurisdiction of Offenses—New York State.
1.4 ___ Counties.
1.5 Geographical Jurisdiction of Local Criminal Courts Within a County—Filing of Accusatory Instruments.
1.6 Removal—In General.
1.7 ___ From One Local Criminal Court to Another.
1.8 ___ From a Local Criminal Court to a Superior Court.
1.9 ___ From One Superior Court to Another.
1.10 ___ To Family Court.
1.11 Practice Summary.
1.12 Forms.
    1.12.1 Notice of Motion to Remove Action to Another Local Criminal Court of the County.
    1.12.2 Affirmation in Support of Motion to Remove Action to Another Local Criminal Court of the County.
    1.12.3 Notice of Motion by Prosecutor in Support of Motion to Adjourn Proceedings in Local Criminal Court on Misdemeanor Charge to Present Charge to a Grand Jury.
    1.12.4 Affirmation in Support of Prosecutor's Motion to Adjourn Proceedings on Misdemeanor Charge in Local Criminal Court to Present Charge to a Grand Jury.
    1.12.5 Notice of Motion by Defendant to Remove Proceedings on Misdemeanor Charge to Superior Court.
    1.12.6 Affirmation in Support of Motion by Defendant to Remove Proceedings on Misdemeanor Charge to Superior Court.
    1.12.7 Notice of Motion in Appellate Division for Change of Venue.
    1.12.8 Affirmation in Support of Motion in the Appellate Division for Change of Venue.

WESTLAW Electronic Research
See WESTLAW Electronic Research Guide preceding the Summary of Contents.

§ 1.1 Jurisdiction—In General

In its most general sense, the "jurisdiction," of a court is "the power residing in such court to determine judicially a given action, controversy, or question which has been presented to it."[1] In the criminal context,

---

1. Tonnele v. Wetmore, 195 N.Y. 436, 443, 88 N.E. 1068, 1071 (1909)(citation omitted).

jurisdiction may be said to involve three separate concepts. Geographical or "territorial" jurisdiction, as the term implies, is concerned with the authority of the state itself, or a particular subdivision of the state such as a county, to entertain in its courts a prosecution for an offense that occurred in a particular place or places. This sort of jurisdiction is governed largely by Article 20 of the CPL, and is concerned with such matters as interstate and intercounty criminal behavior, crimes committed in vehicles, vessels and aircraft or over the telephone, and crimes that take place in one jurisdiction but have certain effects in another. A related question involves jurisdiction over crimes committed in federal enclaves or on reservations located within New York.

The two remaining forms of jurisdiction are jurisdiction of offenses, also known as "jurisdiction of courts" or "subject matter jurisdiction," and jurisdiction over the person of the defendant, also known as *in personam* jurisdiction," "jurisdiction over the particular case," and "personal jurisdiction." While there appears to be a good deal of loose terminology in this area,[2] the difference between these concepts is clear enough. Subject matter jurisdiction of offenses is concerned with the statutory allocation of jurisdiction over different levels of offenses among different courts, and is governed by Article 10 of the CPL, which sets forth rules applicable to entire classes of cases. By contrast, jurisdiction

---

2. In the criminal context terms describing jurisdiction appear to be promiscuously and imprecisely used. The CPL addresses "geographical jurisdiction" in one Article, in the course of which it defines a concept, "geographical jurisdiction of counties" (also known as "venue"), which, as noted in the text, in many respects is not truly "jurisdictional." CPL § 20.40; see § 1.4, infra. Another provision refers to a court's "control over [the defendant's] person." CPL § 1.20(9)(defining "arraignment"). Otherwise, the CPL, when speaking of subject matter jurisdiction of offenses, either simply refers generally to "jurisdiction," or speaks of "jurisdiction of offenses." See, e.g., CPL §§ 10.20, 10.30. In the courts, there has been some debate about the meaning of "subject matter jurisdiction," which seems to be used in two senses. The Court of Appeals has noted generally that "subject matter jurisdiction ... embraces the competence of a court to entertain a particular kind of litigation." Gager v. White, 53 N.Y.2d 475, 485 n. 2, 442 N.Y.S.2d 463, 466 n. 2, 425 N.E.2d 851, 854 n. 2 (1981). In the criminal context, this essentially means jurisdiction over a particular class of offenses, such as misdemeanors as opposed to felonies, and many courts have used "subject matter jurisdiction" to mean just that. See, e.g., People v. Harper, 137 Misc.2d 357, 361 n. 2, 520 N.Y.S.2d 892, 895 n. 2 (N.Y.C.Crim.Ct.1987)("subject matter jurisdiction, i.e. the general power of a particular court to adjudicate all cases of a certain class" as opposed to "in personam jurisdiction, in this particular case, the power to sentence this defendant to punishment"); see also People v. Brabbush, 150 Misc.2d 174, 566 N.Y.S.2d 475 (Sup.Ct., N.Y. County, 1991); People v. Fysekis, 164 Misc.2d 627, 625 N.Y.S.2d 861 (N.Y.C.Crim.Ct.1995); People v. Gross, 148 Misc.2d 232, 560 N.Y.S.2d 227 (N.Y.C.Crim.Ct.1990)(all distinguishing between the two). However, some courts, in the context of dealing with issues involving the filing of valid accusatory instruments, use the term subject matter jurisdiction when referring to jurisdiction over the particular offense with which the particular defendant is charged. See, e.g., People v. Consolidated Edison Co., 161 Misc.2d 907, 909 n. 3, 615 N.Y.S.2d 978, 980 n. 3 (N.Y.C.Crim.Ct.1994)("The term 'subject matter jurisdiction' connotes the court's power to hear and determine the particular case in question, and not the general competence of a court, derived from constitution or statute, to hear and determine specific categories of cases.")(citations omitted). In this latter usage, subject matter jurisdiction over the particular offense is different from in personam jurisdiction. It is regrettable that clear and uniform terminology, such as "subject matter jurisdiction of offenses" and "jurisdiction over the person," is neither statutorily prescribed nor used in common practice.

over the person is case-specific, deals with the court's authority over the particular defendant, and is concerned with the filing of a jurisdictionally sufficient accusatory instrument and the defendant's physical presence before the court.

Although the CPL deals extensively with the two other forms of criminal jurisdiction, it is largely silent on the subject of jurisdiction over the person. In general, a criminal court acquires jurisdiction over a defendant's person by the filing of an accusatory instrument and an appearance by the defendant.[3] As the CPL does recognize, the usual point of appearance is the arraignment of the defendant, and in the overwhelming majority of cases, that is the point at which jurisdiction over the person of the defendant is acquired.[4] It is sometimes said that "where the court has jurisdiction over the offense, the manner or means by which the defendant is brought before the court is immaterial and of little importance."[5] Aside from some fairly esoteric questions involving appearance tickets and corporate defendants,[6] most problems in this area involve jurisdictional defects in the particular accusatory instrument, a point covered elsewhere in this publication.[7]

Library References:

West's Key No. Digests, Criminal Law ⊜83–105.

3. People v. Grant, 16 N.Y.2d 722, 723, 262 N.Y.S.2d 106, 107, 209 N.E.2d 723, 724 (1965)("[T]he trial court had jurisdiction of the offense charged and acquired jurisdiction of defendant's person by the filing of an information and an appearance by defendant.").

4. CPL § 1.20(9) provides that arraignment "means the occasion upon which a defendant against whom an accusatory instrument has been filed appears before the court in which the criminal action is pending for the purpose of having such court *acquire and exercise control over his person* with respect to the accusatory instrument and of setting the course of further proceedings in the action." (emphasis supplied).

5. People v. Sessa, 43 Misc.2d 24, 26, 250 N.Y.S.2d 193, 196 (N.Y.C.Crim.Ct. 1964). Although securing the defendant's person through improper means may not be relevant on the question of jurisdiction, it might support a motion to dismiss the accusatory instrument in the interests of justice. See CPL §§ 170.40(1)(e), 210.40(1)(e).

6. In the area of appearance tickets issued against corporate defendants, there appears to be a lively debate concerning whether failure to file an accusatory instrument in a timely fashion deprives the court of jurisdiction. Cf. People v. Consolidated Edison Co., 161 Misc.2d 907, 615 N.Y.S.2d 978 (N.Y.C.Crim.Ct.1994)(jurisdictional impediment) with People v. Consolidated Edison Co., 159 Misc.2d 354, 604 N.Y.S.2d 482 (N.Y.C.Crim.Ct.1993); People v. Consolidated Edison Co., 153 Misc.2d 595, 582 N.Y.S.2d 614 (N.Y.C.Crim.Ct.1992)(not jurisdictional impediment). Corporate defendants appear by counsel. CPL § 600.20. It has also been held that in criminal law, there is no such thing as a limited appearance to contest jurisdiction. People v. Causeway Const. Co., 164 Misc.2d 393, 625 N.Y.S.2d 856 (Sup.Ct., Bronx County, 1995).

7. See Chapter 3, § 3.7; Chapter 5, § 5.16. At this point, it might be noted that not every defect in an accusatory instrument renders it jurisdictionally defective. As the Court of Appeals has noted: "In essence, an indictment is jurisdictionally defective only if it does not effectively charge the defendant with the commission of a particular crime. For example, an indictment will be jurisdictionally defective if the acts it accuses defendant of performing simply do not constitute a crime ... or if it fails to allege that a defendant committed acts constituting every material element of the crime charged. Insufficiency in the factual allegations alone, as opposed to a failure to allege every material element of the crime, does not constitute a nonwaivable jurisdictional defect." People v. Iannone, 45 N.Y.2d 589, 600–01, 412 N.Y.S.2d 110, 117–18, 384 N.E.2d 656, 664 (1978)(citations omitted).

§ 1.2 Jurisdiction—Courts

The CPL divides courts exercising criminal jurisdiction into two general categories, "superior courts" and "local criminal courts."[8] The former consist of the Supreme Court and the County Court. In New York criminal proceedings, these courts essentially exercise concurrent jurisdiction, except within New York City, where by constitutional provision the county court has been abolished[9] and the Supreme Court has exclusive jurisdiction over indictment prosecutions.[10] Elsewhere in the state, grand juries may be impaneled by either court, and resulting indictments may be tried in the impaneling court or transferred from one superior court to another.[11]

Two kinds of subject matter jurisdiction are defined in the CPL: "preliminary jurisdiction" and "trial jurisdiction." The former exists when, regardless of whether the court in question has trial jurisdiction over the matter, a "criminal action"[12] may be commenced in such court, and the court may conduct proceedings that lead or may lead to prosecution and final disposition of the action in a court having trial jurisdiction.[13] "Trial jurisdiction" exists when, following the filing of an appropriate accusatory instrument, the court has authority to accept a plea, try, or otherwise dispose of the charges contained in the accusatory instrument.[14]

Superior courts have exclusive trial jurisdiction of felonies, trial jurisdiction of misdemeanors concurrent with that of the local criminal courts, and trial jurisdiction of petty offenses that are charged in an indictment that also charges a crime.[15] However, only offenses charged in an indictment or superior court information are prosecutable in a superior court.[16] Superior courts also have "preliminary jurisdiction of all offenses,[17] but they exercise such jurisdiction only by reason of and

---

8. CPL § 1.20(19),(20) and (21); CPL § 10.10(1).

9. N.Y. Const., Art. 6, § 35.

10. N.Y. Const., Art. 6, § 7.

11. 22 NYCRR §§ 200.13, 200.14 (Uniform Rules for Courts Exercising Criminal Jurisdiction). Outside of New York City, local practice varies throughout the state. Although the Supreme Court continues to exercise considerable criminal jurisdiction in some counties, it has been observed that the county courts have been "long recognized as the primary [superior] courts of criminal jurisdiction." People v. Rupp, 75 Misc.2d 683, 685, 348 N.Y.S.2d 649, 651 (Sup.Ct., Sullivan County, 1973).

12. CPL § 1.20(16), (17), and (18), respectively define the terms "criminal action," "commencement of a criminal action" and "criminal proceeding." In the usual case, a criminal action begins with the filing of an accusatory instrument in a court, and continues until the imposition of sentence or some other final disposition of a criminal case. A criminal proceeding is more broadly defined to include any part of a criminal action, matters relating thereto, or a criminal investigation.

13. CPL § 1.20(25).

14. CPL § 1.20(24).

15. CPL § 10.20(1). The term "indictment" includes the superior court information. CPL § 200.10. See P.L. § 10.00(4), (5) and (6) for definitions of "misdemeanor," "felony,", and "crime," and CPL § 1.20(39) and Penal Law § 10.00(2) and (3) for a definition of "petty offense."

16. See CPL § 210.05 ("The only methods of prosecuting an offense in a superior court are by an indictment filed therewith by a grand jury or by a superior court information filed therewith by a district attorney.").

17. "Offenses" is essentially an all-inclusive term for any conduct that has criminal consequences. P.L. § 10.00(1).

through the agency of their grand juries."[18]

Local criminal courts[19] consist of (a) district courts; (b) the New York City Criminal Court; (c) other city courts;[20] (d) town courts;[21] (e) village courts;[22] or (f) a Supreme Court justice or a county court judge sitting as a local criminal court.[23] They have trial jurisdiction over all offenses other than felonies, which, in the case of misdemeanors, is concurrent with that of superior courts, and, in the case of petty offenses, is exclusive.[24] Local criminal courts have preliminary jurisdiction over all offenses, including felonies, subject to divestiture by action of the superior court or grand jury.[25]

A court that possesses both civil and criminal jurisdiction—*e.g.*, the Supreme Court—"does not act as a criminal court when acting solely in the exercise of its civil jurisdiction," and an order or determination made in that civil capacity is not part of a criminal proceeding, even though, as a practical matter, it may substantially affect or even determine the

18. CPL § 10.20(2). In People v. Middleton, 54 N.Y.2d 42, 444 N.Y.S.2d 581, 429 N.E.2d 100 (1981), it was held that this authority—or, alternatively, the court's authority to sit as a local criminal court pursuant to CPL § 10.30(3)—allowed a superior court to issue an order directing the defendant to furnish bite impressions in furtherance of a grand jury investigation even though the case against the defendant was still pending in the local criminal court.

19. CPL § 10.10(3).

20. This is further refined by CPL § 10.10(4) to mean "any court for a city, other than New York City, having trial jurisdiction of offenses of less than felony grade only committed within such city, whether such court is entitled a city court, a municipal court, a police court, a recorder's court or is known by any other name or title." Note that the New York City Criminal Court is separately defined and excluded from the general definition of "city court."

21. Specified by CPL § 10.20(5) to be "comprised of all the town justices of a town."

22. CPL § 10.20(6) provides that "a 'village court' is comprised of the justice of a village, or all the justices thereof if there be more than one, or, at a time when he or they are absent, an acting justice of a village who is authorized to perform the functions of a village justice during his absence."

23. CPL § 10.30(3) provides that superior court judges may sit as local criminal courts for the purpose of conducting arraignments, issuing arrest warrants, or issuing search warrants. However, it must be noted that in the case of the Supreme Court, which has "general original jurisdiction in law and equity," N.Y. Const., Art. 6, § 7, it appears unlikely that this should be construed as a limit on the powers of that court. Cf. People v. Darling, 50 A.D.2d 1038, 377 N.Y.S.2d 718 (3d Dep't 1975)(Supreme Court justice sitting as such may arraign and accept plea to various minor offenses). The County Court does not enjoy the same constitutional status. See N.Y. Const., Art. 6, § 11.

24. CPL § 10.30(1). See Michelson v. Clyne, 84 A.D.2d 883, 444 N.Y.S.2d 331 (3d Dep't 1981)(Supreme Court justice, even sitting as local criminal court, has no trial jurisdiction to hear a suppression hearing in a case involving a violation). However, if a petty offense is charged in an indictment that also charges a crime, it may be tried in a superior court. CPL §§ 10.20(1)(c), 10.30(1)(a).

25. CPL § 10.30(2). For the constitutional provisions underpinning the jurisdiction of local criminal courts, see N.Y. Const., Article 6, §§ 15(c)(New York City Criminal Court); 16(d)(district courts); and 17(b)(town, village and city courts). It should be noted that the authority of some local courts to issue processes such as search warrants "is regulated by statute and is confined to matters of which the court has jurisdiction." People v. Hickey, 40 N.Y.2d 761, 762, 390 N.Y.S.2d 42, 44, 358 N.E.2d 868, 869 (1976); See CPL §§ 20.50, 100.55 (principles of jurisdiction for certain local courts); People v. Epstein, 47 A.D.2d 661, 364 N.Y.S.2d 38 (2d Dep't 1975)(suppressing search warrant issued by local court without jurisdiction). Cf. CPL § 690.20(2)(limits on area of execution of search warrant issued by certain local courts).

outcome of such a proceeding.[26] Whether a proceeding is civil or criminal in nature is not always as obvious as it appears, particularly when it involves litigation over subpoenas, and the answer may have practical consequences, such as the potential appealability of adverse rulings.[27]

It bears noting that where a court is authorized by statute to review a process such as a search warrant previously issued by another court, it does not matter if the court that issued the warrant was of higher rank than the court that reviews it.[28]

A criminal defendant has a fundamental right to have all critical stages of a criminal trial conducted by a person with jurisdiction to preside.[29] Thus, where a jury, with the defendant's consent, was supervised by a judge's law secretary during deliberations, the ensuing conviction was reversed,[30] and the same result obtained where an unavailable judge directed a court officer to inform a deliberating jury that had reached an impasse to continue to deliberate.[31] However, the CPL permits a court to refer any pretrial motion, including suppression motions, to a judicial hearing officer, who may entertain it in the same manner as a court, and who then files with the court a report setting forth findings of fact and conclusions of law. The court thereafter

---

26. CPL § 10.10(7). Cf. CPL § 1.20(1), General Construction Law § 18–a (criminal action prosecuted in the name of the "people of the state of New York").

27. Codey on Behalf of New Jersey v. Capital Cities, 82 N.Y.2d 521, 605 N.Y.S.2d 661, 626 N.E.2d 636 (1993)(CPL § 640.10 application for attendance of witness in out-of-state criminal proceeding was civil in nature); Matter of Abrams, 62 N.Y.2d 183, 476 N.Y.S.2d 494, 465 N.E.2d 1 (1984)(application to quash subpoena issued was civil in nature); see Cunningham v. Nadjari, 39 N.Y.2d 314, 383 N.Y.S.2d 590, 347 N.E.2d 915 (1976)(application to quash grand jury subpoena was civil in nature). Cf. People v. Santos, 64 N.Y.2d 702, 485 N.Y.S.2d 524, 474 N.E.2d 1192 (1984) (application to quash a subpoena for production of police reports, issued in the course of prosecution of a criminal action, is criminal in nature). See also CPL § 1.20(18)(defining "criminal proceeding"). In addition to subpoena litigation, forfeiture actions may be either civil or criminal, depending on the theory upon which forfeiture is sought. Criminal forfeiture is relatively rare in New York. There are two sorts: enterprise corruption (OCCA or state RICO) forfeiture (P.L. § 460.30), and felony controlled substances forfeiture (Penal Law Article 480). These are imposed as an integral part of the criminal action that leads to conviction for the offense underlying the forfeiture. All of the remaining forfeiture statutes, including CPLR Article 13–A, the state's comprehensive civil forfeiture statute, are civil in nature and are brought separate and apart from any criminal action; indeed, forfeiture under some theories may proceed even if no criminal action is ever brought.

28. People v. P.J. Video, 65 N.Y.2d 566, 568–69, 493 N.Y.S.2d 988, 990–91, 483 N.E.2d 1120, 1122–23 (1985), rev'd on other grounds 475 U.S. 868, 106 S.Ct. 1610, 89 L.Ed.2d 871 (1986), on remand 68 N.Y.2d 296, 508 N.Y.S.2d 907, 501 N.E.2d 556 (1986)(village justice, who may or may not be a lawyer, may review search warrant issued by Supreme Court justice). See generally People v. Liberatore, 79 N.Y.2d 208, 581 N.Y.S.2d 634, 590 N.E.2d 219 (1992)(judge who issues warrant is neither prohibited from reviewing nor mandated to do so). Cf. People v. Davis, 162 Misc.2d 662, 618 N.Y.S.2d 194 (Sup.Ct., Kings County, 1994)(where a Supreme Court justice exercising preliminary jurisdiction makes an evidentiary ruling relating to a grand jury presentment, another such justice should not review that decision on a motion to dismiss the indictment).

29. Gomez v. United States, 490 U.S. 858, 109 S.Ct. 2237, 104 L.Ed.2d 923 (1989)(holding that harmless error analysis is inapplicable where federal magistrate improperly presided over jury selection).

30. People v. Ahmed, 66 N.Y.2d 307, 496 N.Y.S.2d 984, 487 N.E.2d 894 (1985).

31. People v. Torres, 72 N.Y.2d 1007, 534 N.Y.S.2d 914, 531 N.E.2d 635 (1988).

decides the motion.[32]

Under some circumstances, based upon the supremacy clause of the United States Constitution, which invalidates state laws that interfere with, or are contrary to, federal statutes and regulations, the federal government may preempt the criminal jurisdiction of the New York courts. This usually occurs when the conduct in question takes place in a context that is the subject of pervasive federal regulation.[33] Another form of preemption, rarely encountered in practice, arises when federal officers and certain other persons who act under color of federal authority are charged with a state criminal offense related to their duties, and the case is removed to a federal court pursuant to the "Federal Officer Removal Statute."[34]

Library References:

West's Key No. Digests, Action ⊜18; Constitutional Law ⊜75; Criminal Law ⊜85–90; Double Jeopardy ⊜23.

§ 1.3 Geographical Jurisdiction of Offenses—New York State

Article 20 of the CPL addresses the subject of geographical jurisdiction of offenses. This implicates two separate topics: the jurisdiction of New York State itself and the jurisdiction of the various counties within New York State. A third provision, which governs jurisdiction of minor offenses among cities, towns and villages within a county, is also contained within this article, and is separately discussed.

At the outset, it is important to recognize the crucial difference between the two primary concepts of Article 20. Although the statute characterizes both as "geographical jurisdiction," and both are ultimately issues of fact if disputed at trial, the jurisdiction of the state, which evolved from the "territorial principle" of the common law, involves "the power of the sovereign to prosecute and punish an accused for conduct which is allegedly criminal." This form of geographical jurisdiction is fundamental, non-waivable, and, when put in issue, must be

---

32. CPL § 255.20(4), found constitutional in People v. Scalza, 76 N.Y.2d 604, 562 N.Y.S.2d 14, 563 N.E.2d 705 (1990).

33. See, e.g., Massachusetts v. Morash, 490 U.S. 107, 109 S.Ct. 1668, 104 L.Ed.2d 98 (1989)(federal ERISA does not preempt state criminal payment of wages statute); People v. Pymm, 76 N.Y.2d 511, 561 N.Y.S.2d 687, 563 N.E.2d 1 (1990)(federal OSHA does not preempt state enforcement of general criminal law against employer conduct committed in the workplace); People v. Calandra, 164 A.D.2d 638, 565 N.Y.S.2d 467 (1st Dep't 1991)(federal regulation of national banks preempts state prosecution for misapplication of funds under state Banking Law); People v. Cannon, 194 A.D.2d 496, 599 N.Y.S.2d 809 (1st Dep't 1993)(agreeing with Calandra regarding Banking Law offense, but holding that general larceny charge is not preempted); People v. Abedi, 156 Misc.2d 904, 595 N.Y.S.2d 1011 (Sup.Ct., N.Y. County, 1993)(no federal preemption of false statements charge involving a different sort of bank). Another type of "preemption," involving federal jurisdiction over crimes committed in federal enclaves within New York State (e.g., courts, military bases, etc.) is discussed in § 1.3, infra.

34. 28 U.S.C.A. § 1442(a). See Mesa v. California, 489 U.S. 121, 109 S.Ct. 959, 103 L.Ed.2d 99 (1989)(removal of postal drivers charged with traffic offenses). A third form of preemption, concerned with crimes committed on federal enclaves within New York State, is discussed in § 1.3, infra.

§ 1.3 JURISDICTION & REMOVAL Ch. 1

proved by the prosecution beyond a reasonable doubt. By contrast, the geographical jurisdiction of counties, often called "venue,"[35] refers only to the proper place of trial, is waivable, and, if disputed, may be established by a preponderance of the evidence.[36]

In practice, situations that implicate the state's jurisdiction are much rarer than disputes over venue, and tend to involve offenses committed at or near the state's borders or multi-state conspiracy-type offenses.[37] However, those in search of guidance in either area should be aware that the statutes defining state jurisdiction and county venue are similar in many respects, and accordingly when investigating any given statutory subdivision or theory, it is often profitable to check both, while remaining aware of the fundamental difference between them. There is considerably more interpretative precedent in the area of venue.

As for the geographical jurisdiction of New York State, "[t]he general rule in New York is that, for the state to have criminal jurisdiction, either the alleged conduct or some consequence of it must have occurred within the state."[38] The CPL breaks this down into two main premises, one governing situations where all or at least a portion of the conduct constituting the offense in question is committed inside the state, while the other, "extraterritorial" provisions apply when the conduct in question occurs outside the state but certain consequences occur or may occur therein. In either situation, jurisdiction may attach either through a defendant's own actions or through the actions of an accomplice.[39] Of course, in the vast majority of ordinary criminal cases

---

35. This is another illustration of the confusing terminology of jurisdiction, although in this instance the argot of common practice is perhaps better than strict adherence to the statutory language. Despite the use of the term "jurisdiction" in the title of CPL § 20.40 ("Geographical jurisdiction of offenses; jurisdiction of counties"), courts have continued to adhere to "venue" when wrestling with inter-county jurisdictional problems, because doing so avoids the misleading implications of confusing this concept with the true "jurisdiction" of the state. See, e.g., People v. Ebron, 116 Misc.2d 774, 778, 456 N.Y.S.2d 308, 311 (Sup.Ct., N.Y. County, 1982)("Although the terms 'venue' and 'jurisdiction' are often used interchangeably, 'jurisdiction' relates to the general power or competence of a court to try the accused. By contrast, venue in [criminal cases] means merely the place where the crime occurred.")(citations omitted).

36. People v. McLaughlin, 80 N.Y.2d 466, 591 N.Y.S.2d 966, 606 N.E.2d 1357 (1992).

37. New York extends statutory double jeopardy protection to offenders who were previously prosecuted in another jurisdiction, such as a neighboring state (CPL § 40.30(1)), and also takes a broad view of the scope of such protection where there has been a previous prosecution. Neither is constitutionally required. This may preclude some multi-state prosecutions that would otherwise be permissible. See Chapter 2, § 2.2.

38. People v. McLaughlin, 80 N.Y.2d 466, 471, 591 N.Y.S.2d 966, 968, 606 N.E.2d 1357, 1359 (1992).

39. CPL § 20.20 provides, as a preamble, that "a person may be convicted in the criminal courts of this state of an offense defined by the laws of this state, committed either by his own conduct or by the conduct of another pursuant to section 20.00 of the Penal Law." The reference is to the definition of "criminal liability for conduct of another," conventionally known as accomplice liability. See People v. Nieves, 205 A.D.2d 173, 617 N.Y.S.2d 751 (1st Dep't 1994)(New York has jurisdiction to prosecute defendant for felony murder where defendant and confederates committed underlying felony in Connecticut, and death occurred when car driven by confederate struck victim during getaway attempt in New York.)

all of the defendant's conduct takes place wholly within New York State, and the state's jurisdiction is not at issue.

Initially, the state has geographical jurisdiction of an offense when conduct occurs *within* New York that is sufficient to establish either (a) an element of the offense;[40] (b) an attempt to commit the offense,[41] or (c) a conspiracy or criminal solicitation to commit the offense "or otherwise to establish the complicity of at least one of the persons liable therefor."[42] The latter bases for the state's geographical jurisdiction have not been frequently applied.[43]

Alternatively, by statute[44] New York has geographical jurisdiction of an offense when conduct occurs *outside* of the state's borders under any

---

40. CPL § 20.20(1)(a). See People v. Nieves, 205 A.D.2d 173, 617 N.Y.S.2d 751 (1st Dep't 1994)(New York may prosecute for felony murder where underlying felony occurred in Connecticut); People v. Quackenbush, 98 A.D.2d 875, 470 N.Y.S.2d 855 (3d Dep't 1983)(New York may prosecute for rape where then-required element of forcible compulsion occurred in New York, although crime consummated in Pennsylvania); People v. Winley, 105 Misc.2d 474, 432 N.Y.S.2d 429 (Sup.Ct., N.Y. County, 1980)(New York may prosecute defendant who received money in New York for unauthorized sound recordings offense, although recordings were to be made in New Jersey). Cf. People v. Axentiou, 158 Misc.2d 19, 598 N.Y.S.2d 928 (Sup.Ct., N.Y. County, 1993)(New York may not prosecute defendant who failed to remit payment to a New York insurance company after collecting and embezzling premiums in New Jersey).

41. CPL § 20.20(1)(b). Under this provision, the conduct within the state must have advanced far enough to constitute an attempt to commit a crime. See Borzuko v. New York Police Department Prop. Clerk, 136 Misc.2d 758, 519 N.Y.S.2d 491 (Sup.Ct., N.Y. County, 1987)(conduct in New York intended to advance drug transaction "did not proceed beyond mere preparation," and was accordingly insufficient to supply jurisdiction). See generally Penal Law § 110.00 (statutory definition of attempt); People v. Di Stefano, 38 N.Y.2d 640, 382 N.Y.S.2d 5, 345 N.E.2d 548 (1976)(crime must advance to a point very near to accomplishment).

42. CPL § 20.20(1)(c). A proviso adds that geographical jurisdiction extends only to those persons "whose conspiratorial or other conduct of complicity occurred within this state." Accordingly, those conspirators who refrain from such conduct within New York State are apparently exempted from the reach of this provision. It is important to remember that this is a jurisdictional statute only, and because New York does not follow the so-called "Pinkerton" rule, membership in a conspiracy does not, as a matter of substantive law, establish accessorial guilt for a substantive crime that is the object of the conspiracy. People v. McGee, 49 N.Y.2d 48, 424 N.Y.S.2d 157, 399 N.E.2d 1177 (1979).

43. See Borzuko v. New York Police Department Prop. Clerk, 136 Misc.2d 758, 519 N.Y.S.2d 491 (Sup.Ct., N.Y. County, 1987)(sufficient conduct in New York based on telephonic drug conversations plus other acts within New York). Cf. People v. Puig, 85 Misc.2d 228, 378 N.Y.S.2d 925 (Sup.Ct., N.Y. County, 1976)(mere agreement between seller and buyer of drugs insufficient).

44. "Broadly speaking, a state's criminal law is of no force beyond its territorial limits, and local criminal statutes have no extraterritorial operation." 21 Am. Jur.2d § 344, p. 597. It seems reasonable to assume that there are some limits, perhaps constitutional in nature, to a state's authority to exert criminal jurisdiction over extraterritorial acts. See Pearson v. Northeast Airlines, 309 F.2d 553, 563 (2d Cir.1962) (noting that in the context of civil jurisdiction "the Due Process Clause prevents an arbitrary application of a state's jurisdiction to an out of state event"); People v. Puig, 85 Misc.2d 228, 378 N.Y.S.2d 925 (Sup.Ct., N.Y. County, 1976)(suggesting such a limit in a criminal context). Cf. U.S. Const., Article III, § 2 (providing that the "[t]rial shall be held in the State where the said Crimes shall have been committed."); U.S. Const., Amend. VI (according an accused the right to trial by "an impartial jury of the State and district wherein the crime shall have been committed"). Although the extent, if any, to which these provisions jointly or separately operate to limit state legislation in this area is vague, the CPL extraterritoriality provisions appear constitutionally sound. Cf. People v. Goldswer, 39 N.Y.2d 656, 385 N.Y.S.2d 274, 350 N.E.2d 604 (1976)(rejecting constitutional attack on inter-county transfer of venue, and providing historical analysis).

of several conditions: (1) if the offense was a "result offense," and the result occurred within the state; (2) if New York law defines an offense designed to prevent a particular "effect" from occurring, and the conduct that constituted the offense was performed with the intent that the effect occur in New York; (3) if the offense committed was an attempt to commit a crime in New York; or (4) if the offense committed was conspiracy and an overt act in furtherance of the conspiracy occurred within New York.[45] Finally, extraterritorial jurisdiction may also be based upon a failure to perform a legal duty within New York.[46]

Analysis of the concept of a "result offense" begins with a statutory definition: "When a specific consequence, such as the death of the victim in a homicide case, is an element of an offense, the occurrence of such consequence constitutes the 'result' of such offense. An offense of which a result is an element is a 'result offense'."[47] If the offense committed by the defendant was a "result offense," and the result occurs within New York, the state has geographical jurisdiction to prosecute.[48]

It should be noted that to satisfy the test, the "result" in New York must be an element of the offense in question. The classic result offense is homicide, and there is a statutory presumption that the death of the victim occurred in New York if the victim's body or a part thereof was found within the state.[49] Crimes such as aggravated harassment[50] and criminal facilitation[51] have been held to be result offenses. On the other hand, sale and possession of narcotics[52] and forgery[53] have been held not to qualify as result offenses. Larceny prosecutions have presented the courts with particularly complex problems. For example, where an insurance agent in New Jersey collected and embezzled premiums on behalf of a New York company, failing to remit the monies to New York, it was held that the embezzlement larceny was complete at the point of the taking with larcenous intent in New Jersey, and accordingly the resulting loss to the New York company was not an element of the offense, thus failing to satisfy the statutory test for result offense

---

45. CPL § 20.20(2)(a)-(d).
46. CPL § 20.20(3).
47. CPL § 20.10(3).
48. CPL § 20.20(2)(a). Note that this statute is meant to operate when none of the defendant's conduct constituting the offense occurs within New York, whereas CPL § 20.20(1)(a) provides jurisdiction when conduct constituting an element of the offense does occur within New York. Thus, where a defendant, with the requisite intent to kill, shoots someone in New York, who then staggers over the border into New Jersey and dies, New York's jurisdiction to prosecute for murder may be predicated upon the defendant's commission of an element of the offense within the state (CPL § 20.20(1)(a)). In the converse situation, where the defendant shoots to kill and remains in New Jersey while the victim crosses into and dies in New York, the defendant may be prosecuted for murder in New York on the "result offense" theory (CPL § 20.20(2)(a)) even though he or she did not engage in any conduct within New York. Of course, in any given scenario more than one theory of jurisdiction may be applicable.

49. CPL § 20.20(2)(a).
50. People v. Hunt, 65 A.D.2d 246, 412 N.Y.S.2d 208 (3d Dep't 1979).
51. People v. Puig, 85 Misc.2d 228, 378 N.Y.S.2d 925 (Sup.Ct., N.Y. County, 1976).
52. Id.
53. People v. Schlatter, 55 A.D.2d 922, 390 N.Y.S.2d 441 (2d Dep't 1977).

jurisdiction.[54] However, in the context of inter-county geographical jurisdiction, which may also be premised upon the result offense concept, it has also been held that the payment of a fraudulently procured check by a bank in Westchester County established the situs of the loss to the victim as Westchester and supported result offense jurisdiction, although all of the defendant's conduct was in another county.[55]

The next basis of extraterritorial jurisdiction is the concept of "effect," "protective," or "injured forum" jurisdiction, which is premised upon the idea that the state may properly exercise jurisdiction upon conduct committed outside of its borders when such conduct was intended to have a deleterious effect within the state. The CPL provides that the state may exercise jurisdiction, even though none of the conduct in question occurs within New York, when "the statute defining the offense is designed to prevent the occurrence of a particular effect within this state and the conduct constituting the offense committed was performed with intent that it would have such effect" in New York.[56]

The definition of "particular effect" is as follows: "When conduct constituting an offense produces consequences which, though not necessarily amounting to a result or element of such offense, have a materially harmful impact upon the governmental processes or community welfare of a particular jurisdiction, or result in the defrauding of persons in such jurisdiction, such conduct and offense have a 'particular effect' upon such jurisdiction."[57]

In general, the courts have been cautious in their approach to effect jurisdiction, which has been interpreted to be more limited than the statutory text would appear to suggest. In several decisions, the Court of Appeals has emphasized that the particular effect intended by the criminal conduct must be to cause a materially harmful effect, not to any particular individual, but to the well being of the community as a whole, and that the conduct must be intended to impact "upon one particular jurisdiction"—e.g., New York State or one of its counties, rather than the region or country in general.[58] Further, the nature of the effect—that is, the injury within the state—must be "perceptible and of the character and type which can be demonstrated by proof before a Grand Jury," rather than "amorphous" or "nebulous" in nature.[59] Thus, it

---

54. People v. Axentiou, 158 Misc.2d 19, 598 N.Y.S.2d 928 (Sup.Ct., N.Y. County, 1993).

55. People v. Crean, 115 Misc.2d 996, 454 N.Y.S.2d 943 (Sup.Ct., Westchester County, 1982). The reasoning of this case is contrary to the later decision in People v. Axentiou, supra; the latter appears to make the more convincing case. See also People v. Zaccaro, 132 A.D.2d 589, 517 N.Y.S.2d 567 (2d Dep't 1987)(accomplishment of an extortionate threat is not an element of attempted grand larceny by extortion for purposes of geographical jurisdiction).

56. CPL § 20.20(2)(b).

57. CPL § 20.10(4).

58. People v. Fea, 47 N.Y.2d 70, 77–78, 416 N.Y.S.2d 778, 781–82, 390 N.E.2d 286, 289–90 (1979)(in the context of venue, assault committed in Rockland County with intent that victim resume usurious loan payment to Bronx County lender "was not intended to cause harmful impact upon the community as a whole, but rather only upon the recalcitrant debtor," who might be repaid anywhere; thus, effect jurisdiction inapplicable).

59. Steingut v. Gold, 42 N.Y.2d 311, 317, 397 N.Y.S.2d 765, 769, 366 N.E.2d 854, 857 (1977)(in the context of venue, the fact that discussions in Manhattan giving rise to Election Law violations concerning an elec-

§ 1.3 JURISDICTION & REMOVAL Ch. 1

has been held that an attempt, in mid-Atlantic air space, to blow up an aircraft headed for New York could not be prosecuted in the New York courts, because there was no potential impact on the community as a whole and no intent to have the consequences of the conduct occur in New York.[60]

Where the offenses in question involve interference with judicial or governmental proceedings, the courts have been more willing to invoke effect jurisdiction. Thus, effect jurisdiction has been found when there was an attempt in another jurisdiction to bribe a witness in a New York administrative proceeding;[61] in the jurisdiction that issued a protective order, where the actual act of violation occurred elsewhere;[62] in the jurisdiction where a falsely made supporting deposition, composed elsewhere, was to be filed in court;[63] and in the jurisdiction where documents were required to be filed, although the omission of material information contained in the documents was done elsewhere.[64]

The remaining bases for the state's extraterritorial jurisdiction have been infrequently invoked. The third and fourth involve attempts and conspiracies; although all of the conduct constituting the offense occurs outside the state, New York has jurisdiction if the offense committed was an attempt to commit a crime within New York,[65] or a conspiracy to commit a crime within New York. In the latter instance, an overt act in furtherance of the conspiracy must occur within the state.[66] Finally, if the offense in question is "one of omission to perform within this state a duty imposed by the laws of this state," jurisdiction exists regardless of the situs of the offender at the time of the offense.[67]

In situations where the conduct constituting the offense in question is committed partially in this state and partially elsewhere, New York's jurisdiction under the foregoing provisions is subject to the rarely

---

tion in Kings County was insufficient to establish effect jurisdiction: "If the injured forum jurisdictional statute were to be triggered by the amorphous fact that the voters of the county would be called upon to vote in an election allegedly tainted by criminal activity localized in a single county, then if the election was one for a state-wide office *any* county within the state would be able to assert jurisdiction.")(emphasis in original).

60. People v. Costa, 121 Misc.2d 864, 469 N.Y.S.2d 545 (Sup.Ct., Queens County, 1983); but see People v. Corsino, 91 Misc.2d 46, 397 N.Y.S.2d 342 (N.Y.C.Crim.Ct.1977)(assault on aircraft bound for New York may be prosecuted there on effect theory). See also People v. Axentiou, 158 Misc.2d 19, 598 N.Y.S.2d 928 (Sup.Ct., N.Y. County, 1993)(New York has no effect jurisdiction to prosecute defendant who failed to remit payment to New York company after embezzlement in New Jersey).

61. People v. Cox, 127 Misc.2d 336, 486 N.Y.S.2d 143 (Sup.Ct., N.Y. County, 1985).

62. People v. Ortega, 152 Misc.2d 84, 575 N.Y.S.2d 247 (N.Y.C.Crim.Ct.1991)(inter-county geographical jurisdiction).

63. People v. Morbelli, 144 Misc.2d 482, 544 N.Y.S.2d 442 (N.Y.C.Crim.Ct.1989)(dicta only).

64. People v. Abedi, 156 Misc.2d 904, 595 N.Y.S.2d 1011 (Sup.Ct., N.Y. County, 1993).

65. CPL § 20.20(2)(c).

66. CPL § 20.20(2)(d); Penal Law § 105.25(3). Overt acts may include telephone calls connecting a person within the state to a person outside of it. See People v. Weaver 157 A.D.2d 983, 550 N.Y.S.2d 467 (3d Dep't 1990); People v. Kellerman, 102 A.D.2d 629, 479 N.Y.S.2d 815 (3d Dep't 1984).

67. People v. Ortega, 152 Misc.2d 84, 575 N.Y.S.2d 247 (N.Y.C.Crim.Ct.1991)(geographical jurisdiction of county where protective order, violated elsewhere, was issued).

applicable limitation of CPL § 20.30, which precludes prosecution where the consummation of the conduct in another jurisdiction is not an offense therein.[68]

Finally, some locations that are geographically within New York State's boundaries[69] are nevertheless not within New York State's criminal jurisdiction. Under the United States Constitution,[70] the federal government enjoys criminal jurisdiction over federal enclaves such as military bases, courthouses, and other facilities. However, federal ownership of a facility does not, in and of itself, establish exclusive federal jurisdiction; rather, either the federal government must have asserted exclusive jurisdiction or the state must have agreed to surrender its own jurisdiction over the premises.[71] If this is the case, crimes committed on such premises are prosecuted in federal court, albeit often under substantive New York law.[72] As for Indian reservations, it has been held that the federal government has generally delegated back to the states its exclusive criminal jurisdiction over crimes committed on reservation

---

68. CPL § 20.30 contains two provisions. The first, CPL § 20.30(1), limits the reach of New York's jurisdiction in situations where the out-of-state consummation of certain conduct within New York is not a crime in the jurisdiction of consummation. See also P.L. § 105.25(2) (conspiracy). A good illustration is provided in the CPL Practice Commentary: a group that plans, in New York, to open a casino in a jurisdiction where casinos are legal may not be prosecuted for conspiracy in New York, although it may be prosecuted if the situs of the proposed establishment is either New York or another jurisdiction where casinos are illegal. Preiser, "Practice Commentary" to CPL § 20.30, McKinney's Cons. Laws of New York, Book 11A, at 101 (1992)(repeating Judge Denzer's original comments). On the other hand, in the reverse situation, CPL § 20.30(2) allows New York to prosecute those whose out-of-state conduct—which must otherwise satisfy the provisions of CPL § 20.20—will result in an illegal consummation in New York. Thus, an agreement reached in a jurisdiction where casinos are legal to open an illegal casino in New York is not insulated from prosecution in New York. Interpretive precedent is scarce. See People v. Cox, 127 Misc.2d 336, 486 N.Y.S.2d 143 (Sup.Ct., N.Y. County, 1985); People v. Winley, 105 Misc.2d 474, 432 N.Y.S.2d 429 (Sup.Ct., N.Y. County, 1980)(no bar found). These provisions do not apply if the offense in question is completed in New York—that is, if all of the elements are committed within the state, even if the in-state conduct will have consequences outside of New York. See People v. Frankel, 129 Misc.2d 95, 492 N.Y.S.2d 671 (Sup.Ct., Queens County, 1985)(sale within state of an illegal cable TV decoder completes crime; that ultimate objective might have been used in New Jersey is irrelevant).

69. CPL § 20.10(1) defines "this state" to essentially mean the area within the state's boundaries and the space over it.

70. Article I, § 8.

71. See People v. Kobryn, 294 N.Y. 192, 61 N.E.2d 441 (1945)(purchase of land alone "does not of itself oust state sovereignty over such land"); People v. Tate, 128 A.D.2d 652, 513 N.Y.S.2d 38 (2d Dep't 1987)(state has jurisdiction over crime committed in federal prison within New York); People v. Materon, 107 A.D.2d 408, 487 N.Y.S.2d 334 (2d Dep't 1985)(state has jurisdiction over possession of drugs in customs area at JFK Airport); People v. Fisher, 97 A.D.2d 651, 469 N.Y.S.2d 187 (3d Dep't 1983)(state has jurisdiction over crime committed in customs facility at Canadian border). However, if the federal government follows the procedure set forth in General Municipal Law § 211 and files certain documents with New York's Secretary of State, federal jurisdiction is exclusive. People v. Williams, 136 Misc.2d 294, 518 N.Y.S.2d 751 (N.Y.C.Crim.Ct.1987)(exclusive federal jurisdiction over harassment committed in federal office building).

72. The Assimilative Crimes Act (18 U.S.C.A. § 13), which operates in the absence of a specific federal criminal statute, makes conduct punishable by a state's criminal law a violation of federal law if committed on a federal enclave within the state in question. See, e.g., United States v. Vaughan, 682 F.2d 290 (2d Cir.1982)(burglary within Manhattan federal courthouse tried in federal court).

property.[73]

Library References:

West's Key No. Digests, Criminal Law ⚖97, 737(2).

§ 1.4 Geographical Jurisdiction of Offenses—Counties

As noted, although the CPL refers to "geographical jurisdiction" in connection with the criminal jurisdiction of counties within New York State, this terminology can be somewhat misleading. This form of geographical jurisdiction, also known as venue, stands on a very different theoretical foundation than the geographical jurisdiction of the state itself. The most glaring practical difference between the two is that objections to the geographical jurisdiction of a county can be waived. In the words of the Court of Appeals, "The vital distinction between these often interchangeably, albeit imprecisely, used terms is at once demonstrated by operation of the principle that although venue may be waived by a defendant, jurisdiction, where absent, cannot be conferred upon a court by a defendant's waiver.... Whereas a court's jurisdictional limits must be strictly construed, venue statutes permitting prosecution of a crime in more than one county are remedial in nature and should be liberally construed."[74] The issue may be waived by a failure to raise the point by pretrial motion,[75] failure to request the appropriate charge to the jury,[76] or by guilty plea.[77] Venue must also be preserved as an appellate issue by an appropriate motion[78] and may be subjected to harmless error analysis by an appellate court.[79] However, as is the case with other forms of jurisdiction, a challenge to venue may be brought by means of an Article 78 proceeding.[80]

73. See People v. Edwards, 64 N.Y.2d 658, 485 N.Y.S.2d 252, 474 N.E.2d 612 (1984); People v. Boots, 106 Misc.2d 522, 434 N.Y.S.2d 850 (Franklin Co.Ct. 1980)(both finding state criminal jurisdiction).

74. People v. Moore, 46 N.Y.2d 1, 9–10, 412 N.Y.S.2d 795, 800–01, 385 N.E.2d 535, 539–40 (1978). In the absence of an applicable statute, the State Constitution and the common law provide defendants with the right to be tried in the county where the crime was committed. People v. Moore, supra; People v. Giordano, 87 N.Y.2d 441, 640 N.Y.S.2d 432, 663 N.E.2d 588 (1995).

75. People v. Lowen, 100 A.D.2d 518, 473 N.Y.S.2d 22 (2d Dep't 1984).

76. People v. Pilgrim, 52 N.Y.2d 730, 436 N.Y.S.2d 265, 417 N.E.2d 559 (1980); People v. Hernandez, 198 A.D.2d 375, 603 N.Y.S.2d 187 (2d Dep't 1993).

77. People v. Ianniello, 156 A.D.2d 469, 548 N.Y.S.2d 755 (2d Dep't 1989); People v. Hinestrosa, 121 A.D.2d 469, 503 N.Y.S.2d 155 (2d Dep't 1986). Cf. People v. Kellerman, 102 A.D.2d 629, 479 N.Y.S.2d 815 (3d Dep't 1984)(in case that appears to involve a question of state jurisdiction, a guilty plea does not waive "a geographical jurisdiction challenge."). Cf. People v. Williams, 14 N.Y.2d 568, 248 N.Y.S.2d 659, 198 N.E.2d 45 (1964)(guilty plea waives failure of indictment to plead venue).

78. People v. Chaitin, 61 N.Y.2d 683, 472 N.Y.S.2d 597, 460 N.E.2d 1082 (1984).

79. Cf. People v. Ribowsky, 77 N.Y.2d 284, 567 N.Y.S.2d 392, 568 N.E.2d 1197 (1991)(error harmless if it appears from the instructions given or by necessary implication from the verdict that the jury made a finding of proper venue) with People v. Sosnik, 77 N.Y.2d 858, 568 N.Y.S.2d 340, 569 N.E.2d 1019 (1991)(error not harmless).

80. See, e.g., Steingut v. Gold, 42 N.Y.2d 311, 397 N.Y.S.2d 765, 366 N.E.2d 854 (1977).

If disputed, venue is a question of fact that must be proved by the prosecution at trial by a preponderance of the evidence.[81] Where a defendant, in a pretrial motion, challenges venue, it must be established before the grand jury.[82]

The basic structure of the statute allocating geographical jurisdiction among counties resembles its "state" counterpart, although there are some additional special rules applicable only in specific circumstances. Again, the statute begins by establishing a basic division between a set of rules applicable when certain conduct occurs within the county[83] and another set that applies when none of the conduct occurred within the county. And the conduct in question may be committed by the defendant or by an accomplice.[84]

Initially, a county is accorded geographical jurisdiction when conduct occurs within that county sufficient to establish "an element" of the offense in question.[85] In situations where criminal behavior touches upon more than one county, this is the most commonly applied, and the most commonly upheld, theory of venue. For example, it has been found that if the intent to kill is formulated in one county, that county has jurisdiction to prosecute for murder even if the actual killing occurred elsewhere.[86] For purposes of a kidnapping charge, it has been found that a county where the restraint continued until the victim escaped has jurisdiction to prosecute, although the initial abduction occurred else-

---

81. People v. Tullo, 34 N.Y.2d 712, 356 N.Y.S.2d 861, 313 N.E.2d 340 (1974)(preponderance standard); see also People v. Moore, 46 N.Y.2d 1, 412 N.Y.S.2d 795, 385 N.E.2d 535 (1978)(questions of where the county boundary lies are for the court). Cf. People v. Davis, 194 A.D.2d 473, 599 N.Y.S.2d 559 (1st Dep't 1993)(no need to submit question to jury where essential fact admitted. Where there is testimony at trial identifying the specific place where a crime occurred within a particular county, failure to specify the name of the county itself is not fatal. People v. Peterson, 194 A.D.2d 124, 127, 605 N.Y.S.2d 542 (3d Dep't 1993)("based upon the testimony that the (drug) sales occurred at Dell's bar in Binghamton, the jury could reasonably have concluded that the crime occurred in Broome County without that fact being explicitly stated").

82. Steingut v. Gold, 42 N.Y.2d 311, 397 N.Y.S.2d 765, 366 N.E.2d 854 (1977).

83. "County" means "any of the sixty-two counties of this state as its boundaries are prescribed by law, and the space over it." CPL § 20.10(2).

84. The Court of Appeals has noted that "whenever a defendant commits an act in a county sufficient to establish an element of a charged offense, codefendants may likewise be tried in that county." People v. Guidice, 83 N.Y.2d 630, 635, 612 N.Y.S.2d 350, 352, 634 N.E.2d 951, 953 (1994). See, e.g., People v. Johnson, 213 A.D.2d 791, 623 N.Y.S.2d 418 (3d Dep't 1995) (accomplice's actions, directed by defendant, constituted element of the crime in county of prosecution). However, in assessing venue based on the actions of another, a word of caution is in order. New York takes a fairly stringent view of accomplice liability (see Penal Law § 20.20), and careful attention must be paid to: (1) that principle; (2) the particular theory upon which venue is grounded; and (3) the charged offense. Two people can be accomplices in one or more offenses without possessing that status with regard to all of the offenses committed by both of them, and venue in a particular county may be only partial with respect to the totality of those offenses. See generally Greenberg, Marcus, et al., New York Criminal Law § 2.7 (West 1996).

85. CPL § 20.40(1)(a).

86. People v. Tullo, 34 N.Y.2d 712, 356 N.Y.S.2d 861, 313 N.E.2d 340 (1974); People v. Seifert, 113 A.D.2d 80, 495 N.Y.S.2d 543 (4th Dep't 1985)(restoring dismissed indictment), appeal after remand 152 A.D.2d 433, 548 N.Y.S.2d 971 (1989)(on direct appeal); People v. Lovacco, 147 A.D.2d 592, 537 N.Y.S.2d 886 (2d Dep't 1989). Cf. People v. Guidice, 83 N.Y.2d 630, 612 N.Y.S.2d 350, 634 N.E.2d 951 (1994)(assault).

where.[87] Taking property in one county and transporting it to another usually attaches jurisdiction for theft-type offenses in either county.[88] Finally, it has been held that the county in which negotiations concerning a transfer of illegal drugs occurred has jurisdiction over the resulting sale, although the money and drugs were actually exchanged elsewhere.[89] However, when the crime in question is drug possession, the element of "knowledge" cannot be separated from the element of "possession," and will not support an argument that venue attaches in the jurisdiction where the defendant first learns of the character of the drugs in question, if that differs from the jurisdiction of possession.[90]

Next, a county may prosecute for an offense when conduct occurs within it sufficient to establish "an attempt or a conspiracy to commit such offense."[91] This echoes the comparable provision of state geographical jurisdiction.[92]

Next, a series of rules is applicable to the situation in which none of the conduct constituting the offense occurred within a particular county. Notwithstanding that, the county may prosecute: where the offense was a "result offense" and the result occurred within the county;[93] where the offense committed was one of homicide and the victim's body or a part thereof was found in the county;[94] where the conduct had or was likely to have a "particular effect" upon the county or a political subdivision within it, and was performed with the intent or knowledge that this would occur;[95] or where the offense committed was attempt, conspiracy, or criminal solicitation to commit a crime in the county[96] or criminal facilitation of a felony in the county.[97]

Finally, where the offense is one of omission to perform a legal duty, which was required to be or could be performed within a county, the location of the actor at the time of omission is irrelevant.[98] These rules

87. People v. Danielson, 184 A.D.2d 723, 585 N.Y.S.2d 78 (2d Dep't 1992).

88. People v. Colon, 28 N.Y.2d 1, 318 N.Y.S.2d 929, 267 N.E.2d 577 (1971); People v. Davis, 194 A.D.2d 473, 599 N.Y.S.2d 559 (1st Dep't 1993); People v. Danielson, 184 A.D.2d 723, 585 N.Y.S.2d 78 (2d Dep't 1992).

89. People v. Pilgrim, 52 N.Y.2d 730, 436 N.Y.S.2d 265, 417 N.E.2d 559 (1980).

90. People v. Cullen, 50 N.Y.2d 168, 428 N.Y.S.2d 456, 405 N.E.2d 1021 (1980). Cf. People v. Giordano, 87 N.Y.2d 441, 640 N.Y.S.2d 432, 663 N.E.2d 588 (1995)(holding that "laying off" bets was a separate element of the crime promoting gambling, and doing so by telephone established venue in the county in which the calls were received).

91. CPL § 20.40(1)(b).

92. CPL § 20.40(1)(b). See also P.L. § 105.25(3)(conspiracy offense itself may be prosecuted in any county in which an overt act occurs). It should be noted that, with regard to conspiracy, the comparable state provision, CPL § 20.20(1)(c), contains a limitation, not extant in the venue provision, that limits jurisdiction to those who engage in certain conduct within the state. Again, it is well to remember that this section deals with geographical jurisdiction, and mere membership in a conspiracy does not establish substantive liability for crimes committed in furtherance of that conspiracy. People v. McGee, 49 N.Y.2d 48, 424 N.Y.S.2d 157, 399 N.E.2d 1177 (1979).

93. CPL § 20.40(2)(a).

94. CPL § 20.40(2)(b).

95. CPL § 20.40(2)(c).

96. CPL § 20.40(2)(d). See also P.L. § 105.25(1)(conspiracy itself may be prosecuted in any county in which an overt act occurs).

97. CPL § 20.40(2)(e).

98. CPL § 20.40(3).

essentially echo the comparable provisions of inter-state jurisdiction, discussed in the previous section.

Apart from the general principles, there are also eleven special rules, applicable in a variety of narrower circumstances.[99] These may be roughly grouped into three categories: those dealing with particular offenses, those dealing with particular geographical features, and those involving offenses committed on board moving vehicles, common carriers, and the like. As to the first category, the first special rule provides that an offense of "abandonment of a child or non-support of a child" may be prosecuted in any one of three places: the county wherein the child resided when abandoned or unsupported; the county wherein the defendant resided when these acts took place; or any county where the defendant can be found, provided that the defendant is arrested in that county or the criminal action in question was commenced while he or she was present in that county.[100] Similarly broad is the special rule for bigamy, which may be prosecuted in the county in which the offense was committed, in any county in which "bigamous cohabitation subsequently occurred," or in any county in which the defendant was present, again provided that the defendant is arrested therein or present when the criminal action was commenced.[101] Given the nature of these offenses, the obvious intent of the statute is to provide a very broad venue for prosecution.

Two other offense-based special rules apply in certain forgery and larceny cases. A prosecution for forgery may be brought in any county in which either the defendant, or an accomplice, possessed the instrument.[102] A prosecution for the crime of offering a false instrument for filing,[103] or of larceny by means of a false pretense therein,[104] may be prosecuted in any county in which the instrument in question was wholly or partly executed, or in any county in which any goods or services for which payment or reimbursement is sought by means of the instrument were purported to have been provided.[105]

99. CPL § 20.40(4)(a)-(k).

100. CPL § 20.40(4)(a). The substantive offenses in question are P.L. §§ 260.00 (abandonment of a child) and 260.05 (non-support of a child).

101. CPL § 20.40(4)(b). See P.L. § 255.15 for the offense of bigamy.

102. CPL § 20.40(4)(j). See P.L. Article 170 for forgery offenses, and P.L. § 20.00 for the standard for accomplice liability.

103. P.L. §§ 175.30, 170.35.

104. Although once defined as a separate crime, under the modern Penal Law larceny by false pretense is now defined within the general definition of larceny. P.L. § 155.05(2)(a). The gist of the crime is the obtaining of property by means of a false representation of a past or present fact. People v. Churchill, 47 N.Y.2d 151, 155–56, 417 N.Y.S.2d 221, 223–24, 390 N.E.2d 1146, 1148–49 (1979). Note that for purposes of jurisdiction, the CPL provision reference to a larceny by false pretense contained "therein" apparently limits the reach of this provision to false representations contained within the instrument that the defendant offers for filing.

105. CPL § 20.40(4)(k).

Another "offense-based" special venue rule is found in an entirely separate statute—Article 5–B of the Judiciary Law, which governs "special narcotics parts" in New York City. This article provides that the New York City Special Narcotics Prosecutor may prosecute a felony drug offense in a "special narcotics part" in any of the five counties of New York City, regardless of where the offense allegedly was committed and regardless of where the indictment was returned. Judiciary Law § 177–d. In practice, the Special Narcotics Prosecutor prosecutes cases only in the Supreme Court

§ 1.4 JURISDICTION & REMOVAL Ch. 1

The next category of special venue rules deals with peculiar geographical features. The broadest and most generally applicable of these provides that an offense committed within 500 yards of a border between New York State counties may be prosecuted in the county on either side of that border.[106] A second provision allows prosecution in any New York City county of an offense committed anywhere on the Hudson River southward of New York City's northern border, or anywhere on New York bay between Staten Island and Long Island.[107] A third provides rules governing offenses committed in the Atlantic Ocean.[108] Finally, a fourth provision allows an offense committed on a bridge or tunnel between New York State counties to be prosecuted in either such county.[109]

The final category involves offenses committed on board moving vehicles, vessels, and aircraft. Three special rules exist. The most important ostensibly provides that an offense committed in a private vehicle during a trip that passes through more than one county "may be prosecuted in any county through which such vehicle passed in the course of such trip."[110] However, the Court of Appeals has limited this rule by finding it inapplicable in situations where the exact place—and hence county—where the crime was committed can be identified.[111] Further, the prosecution must, "in good faith, elicit all facts tending to show the exact location where the crime was committed,"[112] and will be entitled to the benefit of this provision only after such an effort fails to identify the specific location.[113]

in New York County, where his office is located.

106. CPL § 20.40(4)(c). In People v. Moore, 46 N.Y.2d 1, 6–7, 412 N.Y.S.2d 795, 798, 385 N.E.2d 535, 538 (1978), the Court of Appeals held that although questions as to where the boundary lies should generally be decided by the court, this provision, like other venue provisions, presents a question of fact that, upon a proper request by the defendant, must ultimately be decided by the jury. At least one court has held that under this provision, unlike the provisions dealing with moving vehicles (discussed infra), it is irrelevant whether the precise location of the criminal act—that is, the actual county situs of the crime—can be precisely determined. People v. Berg, 101 Misc.2d 726, 421 N.Y.S.2d 968 (Dist.Ct., Nassau County, 1979). See also People v. Riley, 58 A.D.2d 816, 396 N.Y.S.2d 271 (2d Dep't 1977)(jurisdiction to prosecute burglary committed less than 500 yards from border of adjoining county).

107. CPL § 20.40(4)(d).

108. CPL § 20.40(4)(i). In essence, the provision directs that offenses committed less than two nautical miles from the shore at high water mark be prosecuted in the county that has the closest shore to the offense, while offenses committed over two nautical miles from shore, but within the state boundary, must be prosecuted in the Supreme Court of the closest such county.

109. CPL § 20.40(4)(e). One court, utilizing the definition of "bridge" contained in the Highway Law, has held that the provision includes offenses committed upon the roadway leading up to the bridge itself. People v. Kaminski, 151 Misc.2d 664, 573 N.Y.S.2d 394 (Rhinebeck Village Ct.1991).

110. CPL § 20.40(4)(g).

111. People v. Moore, 46 N.Y.2d 1, 7–8, 412 N.Y.S.2d 795, 798–99, 385 N.E.2d 535, 538–39 (1978).

112. People v. Cullen, 50 N.Y.2d 168, 174, 428 N.Y.S.2d 456, 459, 405 N.E.2d 1021, 1024 (1980).

113. Again, this remains ultimately a question of fact. Accordingly, if the prosecution's proof is inexact as to the specific situs of the crime, while the defendant claims that the place can be ascertained, the jury should settle the issue. Cf. People v. Ebron, 116 Misc.2d 774, 456 N.Y.S.2d 308 (Sup.Ct., N.Y. County, 1982)(where prosecution, trying defendant in county A, claims crime occurred in county A, defendant not entitled to dismissal on grounds that his proof shows crime occurred in county B). For examples of appropriate application of the private vehicle provision,

Two other similar provisions concern offenses committed on other sorts of vehicles. One provides that an offense committed on a train, aircraft, or omnibus operating as a common carrier may be prosecuted in any county through or over which the vehicle or craft operated, or in the county where the trip terminated or was scheduled to terminate.[114] The other provides rules for offenses committed on vessels navigating or lying on rivers, canals, and lakes within the state.[115] It is not clear whether these provisions are subject to the same limitation as the private vehicle provision.[116]

It should be noted that these special rules are neither mutually exclusive nor limitations on the more general venue rules, which themselves are not mutually exclusive. In other words, venue may be, and frequently is, established by more than one provision. For example, if a person in county A forms the intent in county A to commit a robbery at a bridge toll booth that is located in county B, but within 500 yards of the border between A and B, county A can argue that it may properly prosecute for the ensuing robbery at the booth under at least three separate provisions.[117]

Another special rule, concerning communications and transportation of property between jurisdictions, is separately promulgated, and, unlike the above, applies to state jurisdiction as well as county venue. The provision actually contains three rules. The first declares that for purposes of geographical jurisdiction, an oral or written statement made by a person in one jurisdiction to a person in another jurisdiction by telecommunication, mail, or any other method of communication is deemed to be made in each jurisdiction—that is, in that of both the sender and the receiver of the communication.[118] The second rule establishes that one who transports property by mail, common carrier, or any other method from one jurisdiction to another is deemed personally

---

see, People v. Bailey, 133 A.D.2d 462, 519 N.Y.S.2d 676 (2d Dep't 1987); People v. Francine CC, 112 A.D.2d 531, 491 N.Y.S.2d 470 (3d Dep't 1985).

114. CPL § 20.40(4)(f).

115. CPL § 20.40(4)(h). Such offenses may be prosecuted in any county bordering the body of water in question, in which it is located, or through which it passes. If the vessel is operating as a common carrier, venue may be found in any county through which the vessel navigated or passed during that particular trip.

116. One court has held that the common carrier provision (CPL § 20.40(4)(f)) is not subject to this limitation, reasoning that passengers on board such a vehicle are less likely to be aware of their precise location, and also invoking "public policy." People v. Ebron, 116 Misc.2d 774, 456 N.Y.S.2d 308 (Sup.Ct. N.Y. County, 1982). While there is obvious truth to that reasoning in some situations, such as cases involving aircraft, it is debatable in the case of the subway train involved in Ebron, and in any event it might be said that this merely means that the level of proof required under Moore, see footnote 111, supra, will be more readily met under these subdivisions. As previously noted, the Moore limitation has also been held not to apply to the provision concerned with offenses committed within 500 yards of a county border. People v. Berg, 101 Misc.2d 726, 421 N.Y.S.2d 968 (Dist.Ct., Nassau County, 1979). On the other hand, it has been recently applied to certain cases involving telecommunications under CPL § 20.60 (see above).

117. To wit: CPL § 20.40(1)(a)("element of the offense" in county A); CPL § 20.40(4)(c)(offense within 500 yards of A–B border); and CPL § 20.40(4)(e)(special bridge provision).

118. CPL § 20.60(1).

to have transported it in each jurisdiction, and if delivery is made, he or she is deemed personally to have made the delivery.[119] The final rule provides that a person who causes by any means the use of a computer or computer service in one jurisdiction from another jurisdiction is deemed to have personally used the computer in each jurisdiction.[120]

Unlike the rules referred to above, this provision does not in itself confer venue; rather, it defines the place where certain conduct took place, which may, under another part of Article 20, be determinative of the question. For example, it has been held that where intercounty phone conversations concerning gambling activity were sufficient to establish an element of a gambling offense, a defendant who was outside the county of trial could nevertheless be prosecuted therein.[121]

One court has limited this provision, suggesting that it should apply only if the defendant's location at the time he or she made the communication cannot be determined, or in situations where "the requirements of venue are otherwise satisfied by a sufficient criminal connection or effect in the county of prosecution."[122] While the facts of that case are compelling,[123] no such limitation has been applied by any higher court.[124]

Library References:

West's Key No. Digests, Criminal Law ⬅106–114, 564, 1033.2, 1166(4).

119. CPL § 20.60(2).

120. CPL § 20.60(3).

121. People v. Botta, 100 A.D.2d 311, 474 N.Y.S.2d 72 (2d Dep't 1984) (CPL § 20.40(1)(a) plus CPL § 20.60 equals venue). See also People v. Giordano, 87 N.Y.2d 441, 640 N.Y.S.2d 432, 663 N.E.2d 588 (1995); accord Matter of Machado v. Donalty, 107 A.D.2d 1079, 486 N.Y.S.2d 544 (4th Dep't 1985); People v. Kellerman, 102 A.D.2d 629, 479 N.Y.S.2d 815 (3d Dep't 1984)(venue found in telephone conversations concerning illegal drugs).

122. People v. R., 160 Misc.2d 142, 148, 607 N.Y.S.2d 887, 891 (Sup.Ct., Kings County, 1994). The limitation is premised upon People v. Moore, 46 N.Y.2d 1, 412 N.Y.S.2d 795, 385 N.E.2d 535 (1978), and appears to suggest a constitutional limit upon extraterritoriality in the inter-county venue context in cases where the defendant's contacts with the county of prosecution are minimal.

123. The case involved an investigation into false accident claims. An chiropractor acting as an undercover agent placed a telephone call from Kings County, the county of trial, to the defendant, a lawyer in New York County, whereupon the defendant solicited the crime. Although there was correspondence between the agent and the defendant as well as the falsification of medical records, all such activity took place either in New York County or in a third county where the agent had an office; thus the only contact with Kings County was the telephone call.

124. The court in People v. R. distinguished People v. Botta, 100 A.D.2d 311, 474 N.Y.S.2d 72 (2d Dep't 1984) on the theory that the defendant—or at least a co-conspirator—had more significant contacts with the county of prosecution. The court also ignored at least two other post-Moore appellate holdings applying CPL § 20.60 in similar circumstances without any such limitation. Matter of Machado v. Donalty, 107 A.D.2d 1079, 486 N.Y.S.2d 544 (4th Dep't 1985); People v. Kellerman, 102 A.D.2d 629, 479 N.Y.S.2d 815 (3d Dep't 1984). Most tellingly, however, although the Appellate Division dissenter in People v. Giordano, 211 A.D.2d 814, 622 N.Y.S.2d 89 (2d Dep't 1995) noted People v. R. with apparent approval, in its subsequent affirmance the Court of Appeals applied CPL § 20.60 without limitation in a case in which the telephone caller was clearly and exclusively in a different county from where the calls were received, which was the county of trial. People v. Giordano, 87 N.Y.2d

§ 1.5 Geographical Jurisdiction of Local Criminal Courts Within a County—Filing of Accusatory Instruments

The court structure of New York includes a diverse collection of local criminal courts. Apart from the previously discussed grant of jurisdiction to local criminal courts in general,[125] two additional provisions of the CPL allocate prosecution of offenses among the courts of political subdivisions within the same county. One specifies in which local criminal court a particular accusatory instrument should be filed, and the other, classified as a rule of geographic jurisdiction, provides that the principles set forth elsewhere in CPL Article 20 are applicable unless the situation is governed by another statute.

The first provision[126] is essentially a "laundry list" of rules applicable to the different local criminal courts that exist in various parts of the state. Initially, any "local criminal court accusatory instrument"[127] may be filed with a district court of a particular county when the offense charged was committed in the county or the part of the county over which the court has jurisdiction;[128] any such instrument may be filed with the New York City Criminal Court when the offense was committed in New York City;[129] and any such instrument may be filed with a city court when the offense was committed within the city in question.[130]

The rules governing town and village courts are more complex, and differentiate between the various sorts of accusatory instruments. An information, a simplified information, a prosecutor's information or a misdemeanor complaint may be filed in a village court when the offense was committed in the village;[131] or in a town court when the offense was committed in the town, unless it was in a village contained therein that has a village court.[132] On the other hand, a felony complaint may be filed in any town or village court of a county if a felony charged therein was committed in some town of such county, not necessarily the town or village that is the situs of the court. Finally, an information, a simplified information, a misdemeanor complaint or a felony complaint may be filed with a superior court judge sitting as a local criminal court when the charged offense was committed in a county in which the judge is present and resides or holds court.[133]

441, 640 N.Y.S.2d 432, 663 N.E.2d 588 (1995).

125. CPL § 10.30 (see § 1.2, supra). Since the two "superior courts" with trial jurisdiction over felony prosecutions—the Supreme Court and the County Court—enjoy concurrent and (at least) county-wide jurisdiction, the question of competing jurisdictional claims within a county does not arise on that level, although in busy jurisdictions with many court parts, perhaps in several courthouses, administrative difficulties may arise.

126. CPL § 100.55.

127. See CPL § 1.20(2)(defining "local criminal court accusatory instrument" as "any accusatory instrument other than an indictment or superior court information)." See Chapter 3, § 3.2.

128. CPL § 100.55(1).

129. CPL § 100.55(2).

130. CPL § 100.55(3).

131. CPL § 100.55(5).

132. CPL § 100.55(5). See, People v. Miller, 120 Misc.2d 30, 465 N.Y.S.2d 120 (Stukey Town Ct.1983)(information filed in town court charging offense committed in village, contained in town, that has village court is defective).

133. CPL § 100.55(7).

§ 1.5　　　　　　JURISDICTION & REMOVAL　　　　　　Ch. 1

Other provisions allow for the substitution of courts when the court normally designated to act in particular situations is unavailable.[134] Additionally, a statutory escape clause operates where it is otherwise expressly provided by law that a particular kind of accusatory instrument may be filed with a particular court,[135] and in any case where two or more courts are authorized as proper courts to receive the accusatory instrument, in the absence of an express statutory prohibition, the instrument can be filed in either, but not both, of such courts.[136]

For purposes of the above, an offense is "committed in" a particular county, city, town or village not only when it actually takes places therein, but also when it occurs in a manner that places it within the geographical jurisdiction of the particular political subdivision in question.[137] Essentially, unless there is a specific prohibition in some other body of law, the geographical jurisdiction of cities, towns, and villages may be expanded within a county in the same manner as the county and state's jurisdiction may be invoked pursuant to Article 20.[138] Further, outside New York City, offenses committed within 100 yards of two political subdivisions of the county may be prosecuted in either such subdivision.[139]

Library References:
West's Key No. Digests, Indictment and Information ⚖6, 38.

§ 1.6　Removal—In General

A number of provisions of the CPL deal with the subject of "removal"[140]—the transfer of criminal actions between different courts. These include the well-known application for a change of venue as well as other provisions that are rarely encountered in practice. Roughly speaking, removals can be said to fall into four categories: removal from one local criminal court to another local criminal court; removal from a local criminal court to a superior court; removal from one superior court to

---

134. See Chapter 3, § 3.19.
135. CPL § 100.55(8) essentially provides that this section of the CPL is not a bar in such situations.
136. CPL § 100.55(2). Where local criminal courts have overlapping boundaries, disputes may arise as to which court can try which offenders. Resolution may require examination of both state court acts and local law. See, e.g., Beach v. Kunken, 162 Misc.2d 381, 616 N.Y.S.2d 721 (Sup.Ct., Suffolk County, 1994)(jurisdiction of village court vs. district court within same geographical area of Suffolk County).
137. CPL § 100.55(10); CPL § 20.50.
138. CPL § 20.50(1). See, e.g., People v. Wright, 163 Misc.2d 139, 142–44, 619 N.Y.S.2d 525, 527 (Mount Vernon City Ct.1994)(city court has jurisdiction over violation of order of protection issued therein but violated in neighboring city via, inter alia, "effect jurisdiction" theory).

139. CPL § 20.50(2). The 100 yards applies only to political subdivisions within a county when there is no question of county jurisdiction; when there is such a question, the 500 yard provision of CPL § 20.40(4)(c) governs. The exclusion for New York City reflects the fact that there are no city, town, or village courts within that city, and does not limit the jurisdiction of the counties bordering New York City. People v. Griffin, 99 Misc.2d 874, 875–76, 420 N.Y.S.2d 824, 825 (App. Term., 2d Dep't, 1979)(act committed within New York City 18 feet from Westchester border may be prosecuted in an appropriate court in either county); but see People v. Thomas, 93 Misc.2d 961, 404 N.Y.S.2d 254 (Mount Vernon City Ct.1978).
140. Although it is addressed in many sections of the CPL, "removal" is not a term defined in any statute.

§ 1.7 Removal—From One Local Criminal Court to Another

Initially, removal from one local criminal court to another local criminal court essentially involves two situations. The first arises when a defendant is arrested by a police officer, charged in a specified accusatory instrument with an offense of less than felony grade,[141] but "owing to special circumstances and pursuant to law" is brought before a local criminal court other than the one having trial jurisdiction over the situs of the offense.[142] This usually occurs when the court that has ultimate jurisdiction over the offense is not available.[143] The statute allows the defendant to be arraigned before an available substitute local criminal court, and, in the interests of judicial economy and convenience to the defendant, further allows that court to accept an immediate plea of guilty to the charges. Failing that, the local criminal court conducting the arraignment must remit the action, and all appropriate papers, to the local criminal court that has trial jurisdiction. If the defendant is brought in the first instance before a superior court judge who is sitting as a substitute local criminal court, the defendant must be arraigned and the action remitted to the appropriate local criminal court. In this situation, the statute does not authorize the taking of a plea.[144]

The second situation occurs when a criminal action of the kind noted above is pending[145] before a local criminal court with the requisite jurisdiction to try it, but the defendant or the prosecution moves to transfer it for disposition to another designated local criminal court of the same county. The motion, which must be made in the County Court of the county in question within 45 days of arraignment and before

---

141. The accusatory instruments in question are an information, a simplified information, a prosecutor's information or a misdemeanor complaint. A separate statute, CPL § 180.20 (discussed infra), governs the situation where a felony complaint is filed in a local criminal court.

142. CPL § 170.15(1).

143. See, e.g., CPL §§ 120.90(5)(arrest on warrant where issuing court unavailable); CPL § 140.20(1)(arrest without a warrant where issuing court unavailable). These statutes provide lists of appropriate substitute town, village, and city courts. See generally Chapter 3, §§ 3.15, 3.19. While the primary purpose of the statute is to provide an alternative arraignment court for minor offenses in smaller jurisdictions where local courts are frequently not in session, the phrase "owing to special circumstances" has been construed, for example, to allow removal from a local justice court that lacked subject matter jurisdiction over the offense in question to a court which possessed such jurisdiction. People v. Caltabiano, 154 Misc.2d 860, 586 N.Y.S.2d 714 (Lindenhurst Vill.Ct.1992).

144. CPL § 170.15(2). However, in People v. Darling, 81 Misc.2d 487, 366 N.Y.S.2d 982 (Sup.Ct., Rensselaer County, 1975), the court held that because of the constitutional powers of the Supreme Court this restriction was ineffective as to that court, and it accepted the plea.

145. If the action is not properly pending in the first court, there appears to be no authority to transfer it to another court. People v. Myles, 107 Misc.2d 960, 436 N.Y.S.2d 134 (Schoharie Co.Ct.1981).

commencement of trial,[146] must be upon the ground that "disposition ... within a reasonable time" in the original court is unlikely, owing either to "death, disability or other incapacity or disqualification" of all of the judges of the original court,[147] or, in cases where the defendant is entitled to a jury trial,[148] and has requested one, to the "inability" of the original court "to form a jury."[149]

Obviously, the statute is most concerned with smaller jurisdictions. The first prong of the statute might come into play when the sole judge of a local criminal court falls ill, or is legally disqualified from presiding by virtue of a relationship with the defendant or the case that would amount to a conflict of interest, while the second prong addresses situations in which the court lacks the resources, physical or human, to form a jury. Thus, removals have been ordered where the judge who would otherwise preside over the action in the original court was to appear as a witness,[150] and where the original court had a public policy against plea bargaining in cases involving the offense for which the defendant was charged.[151] Notably, unlike the provisions governing the transfer of felony prosecutions in superior courts,[152] there is no reference to a transfer on the theory that a fair trial cannot be had in the original local criminal court owing to such circumstances as community prejudice or extensive publicity, and there is a split of opinion as to whether the language of the statute is sufficiently broad to include this concept.[153]

A separate statute, rarely controversial, governs the removal of felony complaints from one local criminal court to another.[154] The accusatory instrument, when filed in a local criminal court, commences a

---

146. CPL § 255.10(1)(e); CPL § 255.20(1). The specification of the County Court in CPL § 170.15(3) rather than the more-inclusive "superior court," which includes the Supreme Court, is puzzling and, if constitutional (see footnote 144, supra) might make for some administrative problems in areas where both the County and Supreme Courts are involved in criminal actions. Further, it appears that such motions are occasionally decided in the Supreme Court. See People v. Glendenning, 127 Misc.2d 880, 487 N.Y.S.2d 952 (Sup.Ct., Westchester County, 1985). Of course, in New York City there is no County Court, but because there is only one large local criminal court, these removal provisions are inapplicable in that city.

147. CPL § 170.15(3)(a).

148. See CPL § 340.40(2)(right to misdemeanor jury trial). Outside New York City—where this removal provision applies—a defendant prosecuted by information for any misdemeanor has the right to a jury trial. There is no right to a jury trial for offenses of less than misdemeanor grade.

149. CPL § 170.15(3)(b).

150. People v. Keneston, 105 Misc.2d 440, 432 N.Y.S.2d 355 (Fulton Co.Ct.1980).

151. People v. Glendenning, 127 Misc.2d 880, 487 N.Y.S.2d 952 (Sup.Ct., Westchester County, 1985).

152. Cf. CPL § 230.20(2)(removal of indictments for "reasonable cause to believe that a fair and impartial trial cannot be had" in the original court).

153. Cf. People v. Mundhenk, 141 Misc.2d 795, 534 N.Y.S.2d 843 (Rockland Co.Ct.1988); People v. Roberts, 95 Misc.2d 41, 406 N.Y.S.2d 432 (Tompkins Co.Ct. 1978) with People v. Capuano, 68 Misc.2d 481, 327 N.Y.S.2d 17 (Monroe Co.Ct.1971)(restrictive view). The question is problematical. In the abstract the statutory language—with a little judicious stretching—does appear broad enough to include a transfer on this basis, and, as these cases note, there are sound constitutional reasons for preferring this interpretation. However, the specific use of restrictive language here—e.g.,"inability of such court to form a jury"—provides a striking contrast with the "fair and impartial" jury standard of the felony statute, and thus precludes an easy answer.

154. CPL § 180.20.

felony criminal action but cannot serve as the basis for a felony prosecution;[155] rather, for that prosecution to continue, it must be replaced by an indictment issued by a grand jury, or, with the defendant's consent, a superior court information.

The felony complaint removal statute is aimed at the same general concept as the first part of the more general removal statute—allowing for the defendant's arraignment in a local criminal court other than the one situated in the area where the crime occurred.[156] Initially, there are two similar provisions, one operable where the defendant is brought before a court of a town or village other than the one wherein the felony was committed,[157] while the other governs when one who commits a felony in a city is brought, not to the city court in question, but to the local criminal court of an adjoining town or village.[158] In both cases, the substitute court must either dispose of the felony complaint itself[159]—which, if there is a reduction to a non-felony offense includes adjudicating all stages of the case through the final disposition—or remit the case to the appropriate court. The final part of the statute, applicable where the defendant is brought before a superior court judge sitting as a local criminal court for purposes of arraignment, is similar, except that the judge, if he or she reduces the charge to a non-felony, is statutorily required to remit the case to the appropriate local criminal court having trial jurisdiction over the charges.[160]

Library References:
West's Key No. Digests, Criminal Law ⟐101.

§ 1.8 Removal—From a Local Criminal Court to a Superior Court

Two statutes allow for the removal of a misdemeanor[161] action to a superior court at the request of either the prosecution or the defense. The first provision[162] allows the prosecutor, at any time prior to the entry of a plea of guilty to or commencement of trial of an appropriate misdemeanor accusatory instrument,[163] to apply to the local criminal

---

155. CPL § 1.20(8).

156. CPL § 170.15(1) and (2). Because a felony complaint is essentially a temporary accusatory instrument, that in the usual case will be replaced with an indictment if not dismissed, pleaded to, or otherwise disposed of, there is no need for a separate "change of venue" provision here, as that application can be made when the action is pending for trial in a superior court.

157. CPL § 180.20(1). Under CPL § 100.55(6), a felony complaint can be filed in any town or village court of the county in which the felony was committed.

158. CPL § 180.20(1–a).

159. In essence, the court must either hold the defendant for the action of a grand jury, reduce the charge to a non-felony offense, or dismiss the charge. CPL §§ 180.50, 180.70.

160. CPL § 180.20(2). However, see footnote 144, supra (Supreme Court may have constitutional power to proceed further).

161. Instruments charging offenses of less than misdemeanor grade are not removable.

162. CPL § 170.20.

163. The statute is applicable in cases involving a "local criminal court accusatory instrument containing a misdemeanor." CPL § 170.20(1). This means "any accusatory instrument other than an indictment or superior court information." CPL § 1.20(2). However, it has been held inapplicable—so as not to bar a grand jury

court for an adjournment of the case on the grounds that he or she intends to present the charge to a grand jury. The court must grant the initial adjournment, and may grant subsequent adjournments for this purpose. Thereafter, the grand jury has all of its usual options, which include dismissing the case, indicting the defendant, or in effect returning the matter to the local criminal court as a misdemeanor by directing the prosecutor to file the necessary information. Indictment or dismissal divests the local criminal court of jurisdiction.[164] Further, if the charge is not presented to the grand jury within the designated period, the proceedings must continue in the local criminal court. If the grand jury dismisses the case, nothing seems to prevent the prosecutor from simply filing a new information in the local criminal court and continuing with the prosecution.[165]

The statute essentially affords the prosecutor an absolute right to present a misdemeanor case to a grand jury, limited only by available resources. It is often used in situations where the prosecutor believes that an original misdemeanor charge should be recast as a felony, either because of a subsequently-discovered factor such as the existence of a predicate enhancement crime or the extent of injury to a victim, or simply because a closer look at the case reveals that the drafters of the original accusatory instrument mischarged it. Since the felony must be prosecuted in the superior court, but there is a valid misdemeanor accusatory instrument in the local criminal court—that, prior to the removal application, can be pleaded to—prosecutors must move quickly to avoid the potential double jeopardy bar to a felony prosecution.[166]

presentment—where a misdemeanor charge was contained in a felony complaint after the original charges in that instrument were reduced to a misdemeanor. People v. Blount, 156 Misc.2d 489, 593 N.Y.S.2d 962 (Sup.Ct., Kings County, 1993). Moreover, it has also been held that where such an application is made, the accusatory instrument removed to the grand jury is not in effect converted to a felony complaint for the purpose of making the release provisions of CPL § 180.80 applicable. People v. Rodriguez, 152 Misc.2d 501, 577 N.Y.S.2d 760 (N.Y.C.Crim.Ct.1991).

164. CPL § 170.20(2)(a) specifies that the local criminal court is divested of jurisdiction if the charge is presented within the designated period "and either an indictment or dismissal results." If the grand jury votes to continue with a misdemeanor prosecution, see CPL §§ 190.60(2), 190.70, those statutes require that the prosecutor must thereafter "file a prosecutor's information" in the local criminal court. Presumably, throughout this process the local criminal court never loses jurisdiction. See People v. Rivera, 144 Misc.2d 1007, 545 N.Y.S.2d 455 (N.Y.C.Crim.Ct.1989)(so holding, for speedy trial purposes). Cf. CPL § 1.20(16)(criminal action "includes the filing of all accusatory instruments directly derived from the initial one").

165. See People v. Nuccio, 78 N.Y.2d 102, 571 N.Y.S.2d 693, 575 N.E.2d 111 (1991)(proper to file new information after dismissal for failure to supply necessary supporting deposition). Although this strategy allows prosecution of the case as a misdemeanor to continue, absent judicial permission the case cannot again be presented to a grand jury. CPL § 190.75(3).

166. Moreover, there is another danger as well. The first adjournment, "to a date which affords the district attorney reasonable opportunity" to pursue the matter in the grand jury, CPL § 170.20(2), is mandatory, and the defendant has no right to plead guilty to the misdemeanor charge in the local criminal court if the prosecutor makes such an application. People v. Barkin, 49 N.Y.2d 901, 428 N.Y.S.2d 192, 405 N.E.2d 674 (1980). However, following the initial adjournment, the same provision specifies that the court "*may* subsequently grant such further adjournments for that purpose as are reasonable under the circumstances" (emphasis supplied). Thus, additional adjournments are discretionary, and a plea of guilty may be accepted in the local criminal court at a point subsequent

However, because of the absence of criteria or limitations in the provision, it can be used for other purposes as well, such as removing a notorious or complex case from a small town or village court to a superior court of wider jurisdiction perhaps more capable of dealing with it.[167]

Two separate clauses in the statute divest the local criminal court of jurisdiction. The first[168] does so if, at any time before entry of a plea of guilty or commencement of trial, an indictment is "filed" in a superior court, while the second operates when the case is presented to a grand jury and an indictment or dismissal "results."[169] The Court of Appeals has construed the two as separate rather than conjoined in effect, and therefore has held that a local criminal court was divested of jurisdiction at the point that the grand jury voted to indict the defendant, rather than the subsequent filing date of the indictment.[170]

The statute addressing removal at the defendant's request[171] is considerably different. At any time before a plea of guilty or commencement of trial on a local criminal court accusatory instrument containing a misdemeanor, or within 30 days of arraignment, whichever comes first, the defendant may apply to the local criminal court for an adjournment of the proceedings therein on the ground that he or she intends to make a motion in the appropriate superior court for an order that the case be prosecuted by indictment. He or she must receive an adjournment for that purpose.[172] Thereafter, the defendant, on notice to the prosecutor, may so move in an appropriate superior court, upon a showing of "good cause to believe that the interests of justice so require."[173] If the superior court issues the order, the prosecutor must present the case to a grand jury.

to the first adjournment, but before a divestiture of jurisdiction. Matter of Johnson v. Andrews, 179 A.D.2d 417, 579 N.Y.S.2d 332 (1st Dep't 1992).

167. In this sense, the statute provides a possible alternative to removing such a case from one local criminal court of a county to another such court pursuant to CPL § 170.05, although at the price of a grand jury presentment.

168. CPL § 170.20(1).

169. CPL § 170.20(2)(a). Adjourning the case in the local criminal court does not divest that court of jurisdiction. People v. Rivera, 144 Misc.2d 1007, 545 N.Y.S.2d 455 (N.Y.C.Crim.Ct.1989).

170. People v. Brancoccio, 83 N.Y.2d 638, 612 N.Y.S.2d 353, 634 N.E.2d 954 (1994). As illustrated in this case, the point of divestiture is important because a guilty plea to the lesser charge taken in the local criminal court subsequent to the divestiture is, for double jeopardy purposes, a nullity that will not bar prosecution of the higher charge.

171. CPL § 170.25.

172. CPL § 170.25(3). The statute does not actually require a motion for adjournment in the lower court as a precondition of the removal motion in the superior court, but, of course, the danger here is that the defendant will be forced to trial in the lower court while the superior court considers the motion. As in the case of the prosecutor's request under CPL § 170.20, the court must grant the initial adjournment, and may grant subsequent adjournments. Proceedings in the local criminal court are stayed once the motion is "made" (e.g. filed) in the superior court, and the stay continues if that court grants the removal motion. CPL § 170.25(2), (3)(b) and (3)(c). If the defendant does not make the motion in a timely fashion, the proceedings in the local criminal court continue, and the same ensues if the superior court denies the removal motion. CPL § 170.25(3)(a) and (d).

173. CPL § 170.25(1).

In this instance, the grand jury may not direct the filing of a prosecutor's information in the local criminal court.[174] If the grand jury indicts, proceedings in the local criminal court terminate and the case is prosecuted in superior court. If the grand jury dismisses, those proceedings also terminate, and, unlike the comparable situation in the prosecutorial removal scenario, here the prosecutor cannot ignore the dismissal and file a new information in the local criminal court. If the grand jury does not act within 45 days, a confined defendant must be released, unless the inaction was at the defendant's request or based upon other "good cause."[175]

The differences between this statute and the comparable prosecutorial removal statute are obvious. The defendant must ask court permission to remove the case, and make a required showing. The practical consequences of making the application can be considerable: most obviously, a defendant who has been charged only with a misdemeanor runs the risk of initiating a course of action that could result in an indictment for a felony. Nevertheless, although virtually non-existent in urban areas, such motions appear to be made from time to time in smaller jurisdictions of the state. There may be several reasons for this. Some may believe that town or village courts in very small jurisdictions possess insufficient resources to determine some misdemeanors. Also, in places where a misdemeanor prosecution is an unusual and therefore significant event, some may wish the larger jury pool or relative anonymity of a superior court's jurisdiction, or simply prefer that court's location. In this regard, it should be noted that unless there is some compelling tactical reason to prefer to have the action tried in a superior court,[176] if sufficient grounds exist it might be wise to first apply to remove the action to another local criminal court,[177] because doing so avoids the possibility of felony prosecution. Of course, the two removal statutes can often be pleaded as alternatives in a single motion.

The statutory standard of "good cause to believe that the interests of justice so require" is vague, perhaps deliberately so. Clearly, however, the decision is discretionary, and accordingly an Article 78 proceeding is not available to compel removal.[178] The burden of proof is on the

---

174. Because the superior court has ordered prosecution by indictment, CPL § 190.70 contains a specific restriction to this effect. Of course, the grand jury may indict for the misdemeanor, which is then prosecuted in the superior court. It is interesting to note that because an indictment must contain at least one "crime," CPL § 200.10, the effect of this is to prevent the grand jury from charging only a non-criminal petty offense, while had the case been removed at the prosecutor's insistence pursuant to CPL § 170.20, the grand jury could have directed the filing of a prosecutor's information charging such an offense.

175. CPL § 170.30(4).

176. One might be that the trial of a misdemeanor prosecuted by indictment is, by operation of the State Constitution, before a jury of twelve, rather than six. N.Y. Const., Article 6, § 18(a); People v. Griffin, 142 Misc.2d 41, 536 N.Y.S.2d 386 (Sup.Ct., Monroe County, 1988).

177. See CPL § 170.15(3). See § 1.7, infra. Losing such a motion does not bar an application to remove the case to a superior court.

178. Matter of Legal Aid Society v. Scheinman, 53 N.Y.2d 12, 439 N.Y.S.2d 882, 422 N.E.2d 542 (1981).

defendant to establish the need for the removal.[179] Given the posture of the application, appellate guidance is minimal.[180] However, a set of general criteria of historic origins appears to have evolved in the lower courts. It is said that the motion should be granted if: (1) the case presents intricate and complicated questions of fact, rendering a jury trial proper; (2) it presents difficult questions of law; (3) a property right is involved; (4) a decision may be far reaching in its effects, and will become a precedent; and (5) the case is of exceptional character and the defendant, for some special reason, cannot have a fair trial in lower court.[181] It should be noted, however, that since this formulation was created, the nature of New York's lower courts has evolved considerably, and many of these criteria may now be somewhat insulting to local criminal courts.

In any event, some grounds for removal have included: the inability of the local criminal court to hold a trial because of a lack of proper physical facilities;[182] extensive publicity or the possibility of other local bias in the community of the local criminal court;[183] or unusually severe potential economic consequences to the defendant, such as the loss of a professional license or pension.[184] Courts seem somewhat reluctant to grant removal on the basis of a "difficult question of law," perhaps because of the implication for the local criminal court.[185] The Court of Appeals has held that there is no absolute right to trial before a judge who has legal training, and accordingly "the mere allegation that a

---

179. See, e.g., People v. Prisco, 68 Misc.2d 493, 326 N.Y.S.2d 758 (Suffolk Co. Ct.1970)(pre-CPL).

180. Not only is Article 78 relief unavailable to compel removal, but the court's decision, being an interlocutory order in a criminal action, is not appealable by either side. See Application of Cross, 275 App. Div. 719, 87 N.Y.S.2d 338 (2d Dep't 1949), app. dismissed 299 N.Y. 680, 87 N.E.2d 68 (1949). Moreover, if the defendant is subsequently convicted before the local criminal court in otherwise fair and proper proceedings, raising the issue of an improper denial of removal on direct appeal would appear to be extremely difficult.

181. Apparently, these criteria were first formulated in People v. Rosenberg, 59 Misc. 342, 344, 112 N.Y.S. 316, 318 (Gen. Sess., N.Y. County, 1908), and have been applied by the courts more recently. See, e.g., In re Application of Hewitt, 81 Misc.2d 202, 203, 365 N.Y.S.2d 760, 761 (Tompkins Co.Ct.1975).

182. People v. Rose, 82 Misc.2d 429, 368 N.Y.S.2d 387 (Rockland Co.Ct.1975).

183. See, e.g., People v. Prisco, 68 Misc.2d 493, 326 N.Y.S.2d 758 (Suffolk Co.Ct.1970)(pretrial publicity); People v. Graydon, 59 Misc.2d 330, 298 N.Y.S.2d 555 (Sup.Ct., Nassau County, 1969) (local community activist involved in controversial activities). Note that in this area, this procedure can be most obviously seen as an alternative to removal to another local criminal court. See CPL § 170.15(3). As discussed in the previous section, that statute lacks a specific reference to removal on this basis.

184. This is apparently what is meant in the general criteria by "property rights." See People v. Galamison, 42 Misc.2d 387, 248 N.Y.S.2d 358 (Sup.Ct., Kings County, 1964)(potential for pension or license loss by hospital demonstrators justifies removal). Cf. People v. Lovejoy, 66 Misc.2d 1003, 323 N.Y.S.2d 95 (Tompkins Co.Ct. 1971)(granting removal on other grounds, but opining that the loss of a driver's license is a "property right," albeit insufficient); People v. Harris, 148 Misc.2d 408, 560 N.Y.S.2d 926 (N.Y.C.Crim.Ct.1990)(argument that suspended employment of public employee defendant qualifies).

185. See People v. Mossow, 118 Misc.2d 522, 524, 461 N.Y.S.2d 191, 193 (Oswego Co.Ct.1983)(case involving "two simple crimes arising out of the Vehicle and Traffic law"; no removal). Cf. People v. Lovejoy, 66 Misc.2d 1003, 323 N.Y.S.2d 95 (Tompkins Co.Ct.1971)(granting removal on basis of blood alcohol evidence) with In re Application Hewitt, 81 Misc.2d 202, 203, 365 N.Y.S.2d 760, 761 (Tomkins Co.Ct.1975)(denying removal in breathalyzer case).

Judge lacks legal training does not mandate removal."[186] However, it should remain possible to argue that this should be considered in conjunction with some of the other factors, such as a claim that the case presents a difficult question of law, or might have far-reaching implications as precedent.

Library References:
West's Key No. Digests, Criminal Law ⚖101.

§ 1.9 Removal—From One Superior Court to Another

Article 230 governs removals from one superior court to another superior court.[187] The most important part of the Article[188] deals with what is perhaps the best known of all removal procedures, the "motion for a change of venue,"[189] which is technically an application by either

---

186. People v. Charles F., 60 N.Y.2d 474, 477, 470 N.Y.S.2d 342, 343, 458 N.E.2d 801, 802 (1983). Prior to this case, there was something of a controversy on this issue, as the Court of Appeals had previously ruled that New York's system of employing non-lawyer judges to staff some local criminal courts was constitutional, in part because of the existence of this removal statute. People v. Skrynski, 42 N.Y.2d 218, 221, 397 N.Y.S.2d 707, 708, 366 N.E.2d 797, 799 (1977), and some courts had accordingly opined that removal was mandatory under these circumstances. See, e.g., People v. Dean, 96 Misc.2d 781, 409 N.Y.S.2d 647 (Sup.Ct., Chemung County, 1978).

187. These provisions were held to be constitutional, in the context of a defendant's assertion of a right to trial in the locality of the crime, in People v. Goldswer, 39 N.Y.2d 656, 385 N.Y.S.2d 274, 350 N.E.2d 604 (1976). However, it should be noted that, in the context of a defendant's application, there is a constitutional component to this issue. See People v. Quartararo, 200 A.D.2d 160, 162, 612 N.Y.S.2d 635, 637 (2d Dep't 1994)("In a criminal case, a change of venue will be warranted as a matter of due process ... when it is proved that the assembly of an impartial jury in the venue to which a transfer is sought is possible, whereas the assembly of an impartial jury in the original venue is not.")(citations omitted). See also Irvin v. Dowd, 366 U.S. 717, 81 S.Ct. 1639, 6 L.Ed.2d 751 (1961)(pretrial publicity violates defendant's right to impartial jury); Patton v. Yount, 467 U.S. 1025, 104 S.Ct. 2885, 81 L.Ed.2d 847 (1984)(right not violated under instant circumstances.)

188. The other topic treated in the article is removal between County and Supreme Courts of the same county (outside New York City, where there is no County Court). The first of these provisions, CPL § 230.10, which allows a court itself to remove a criminal action from one of these superior courts to another, is now essentially unnecessary and obsolete, as the subject is now being handled administratively. See Preiser, "Practice Commentary" to CPL § 230.10, McKinney's Cons. Laws of New York, Book 11A, at 190 (1993). Otherwise, sections 230.20(1) and 230.30(1) permit a party to ask the Appellate Division to remove an action from the County to the Supreme Court of the same county (but not the reverse) "for good cause shown"—a standard that appears similar to that of CPL § 170.25(1)(see § 1.7, supra). Although these provisions, which were originally aimed at bias or prejudice on the part of a single judge, may be largely obsolete because of the existence of the administrative remedy, there may yet be some residual force to them in very unique situations. See footnote 197, infra.

189. It is interesting to note that CPL Article 230, which is generally entitled "removal of action," frequently speaks of "removal" when referring to a transfer of actions between the County and Supreme Courts of a county, but often, but not invariably, uses "change of venue" when referring to a transfer from one county to another. The Article is inconsistent in this regard. See, e.g., § 230.30(1)(although entitled "Removal of action; stay of trial pending motion therefor," it begins: "At any time when a timely motion for removal of an action from the county court to the supreme court *or for a change of venue* may be made.... ")(emphasis supplied); cf. CPL § 230.20(2)(a)(core provision permitting a change of venue speaks of action being "removed"). The reason for this dichotomy is unclear, although "change of venue" is perhaps a better known term than "removal," which, as previously noted, is not defined by statute.

the prosecutor or the defense[190] to remove a criminal action prosecuted by indictment (typically a felony[191]) from a superior court to another superior court in another county.

The motion is addressed to the Appellate Division of the judicial department containing the county in which the action is pending. Although the statute on its face provides that the motion may be made within the same time period as any other pre-trial motion—that is, "within forty-five days after arraignment and before commencement of trial"[192]—"[t]he courts have consistently held that except in exceptional circumstances change of venue motions made prior to the voir dire are premature."[193]

The court preference makes sense in the usual case, where the basis of the motion is pre-trial publicity or some other form of local notoriety, because it may still be possible to assemble an untainted jury panel and thus avoid the inconvenience and expense of changing the venue or expanding the jury pool. This rule, however, may be practically troublesome, since making the motion at this last stage of the pre-trial proceedings does entail a certain amount of inconvenience and even unnecessary expense in the original court, and many movants will feel uneasy about waiting so long before making the initial application. Further, some courts have been willing to find "exceptional circumstances" to grant the relief before the jury voir dire.[194] In this regard, it should be noted that there is no statutory limit to the number of such motions,[195] and denial of the motion as premature does not bar its renewal after voir dire or at some other appropriate time. If an initial motion for a change of venue is denied as premature, in the course of the jury voir dire counsel should do everything possible to explore further the effects of the publicity.[196] It should also be noted that there are potential grounds for

---

190. Applications by the defendant are of course far more common. If the Appellate Division grants an application by the prosecutor, the court may "impose such conditions as it deems equitable and appropriate to insure that the removal does not subject the defendant to an unreasonable burden in making his defense." CPL § 230.20(2)(b). A defendant opposing such a motion should ask for such conditions.

191. It is possible to move under this Article for a change of venue in a misdemeanor case prosecuted by indictment.

192. CPL §§ 230.20(2) and (3), 255.20(1). The motion must made be on five days' notice to the other party, returnable at either the instant or next term of the Appellate Division. CPL § 230.20(3). It is always advisable to consult the rules governing motion practice in the particular Appellate Division in question.

193. People v. Brensic, 136 A.D.2d 169, 172, 526 N.Y.S.2d 968, 970 (2d Dep't 1988).

194. See People v. Boudin, 90 A.D.2d 253, 457 N.Y.S.2d 302 (2d Dep't 1982)("exceptional circumstances" for early motion in very notorious case, based on continuing "unabated" publicity, plus a survey of local community attitudes towards the case).

195. Cf. CPL § 255.20(3)(allowing determination of tardy pre-trial motions if there is, inter alia, "good cause" for the delay). See People v. Parker, 60 N.Y.2d 714, 715, 468 N.Y.S.2d 870, 871, 456 N.E.2d 811, 812 (1983).

196. See, e.g, People v. Parker, supra ("Proper procedure after denial of a motion for change of venue requires that a defendant attempt to select an impartial jury and that the proceedings be stenographically transcribed. At that time counsel could have attempted to establish by his questions and the answers to them that the extensive publicity made it impossible to select an impartial jury, if such was the fact, and upon such record the motion for change of venue could have been renewed and given proper consideration."). People v. Jones, 214 A.D.2d 1051, 626 N.Y.S.2d 617, 618 (4th Dep't 1995)(denying application as premature, but noting that "[i]f it develops during voir dire that a fair and

the motion that will not be affected by a jury voir dire, and there may be reasons that would justify transferring the case at an early stage.[197]

The CPL also permits, but does not require, that "at any time when a timely motion for a change of venue ... may be made,"[198] a party seeking a change of venue ask either a justice of the Appellate Division or a justice of the Supreme Court in the district in which the indictment is pending to order a stay of the trial to allow the party to make the change of venue motion. The application must be in writing and the other party must be afforded reasonable notice and an opportunity to be heard.[199] After such an application has been made and denied, no other such application can be made to another justice.[200] Upon such an application, as a matter of discretion and "for good cause shown," the justice may issue a stay of the trial of the indictment "for a designated period, not to exceed thirty days from the issuance of [the stay order]."[201] Once the stay order has been filed with the clerk of the court in which the indictment is pending, no further proceeding can take place in the trial court until either the change of venue motion is decided, or, if no such motion is made, the designated period for making one has expired.[202]

Substantively, the standard for a motion to change the venue is "reasonable cause to believe that a fair and impartial trial cannot be had" in the original county.[203] If that standard is met, the Appellate Division may either order the action removed to a superior court in another county or order the appropriate administrative judge to expand the original county's juror pool by drawing from contiguous counties within the judicial department.[204] In making that determination, the

impartial jury cannot be drawn, an appropriate application can be made at that time").

197. An example might be where the basis of the motion is bias or prejudice on the part of one or more of the superior court judges of a particular county, such that it would be inappropriate for those court(s) to conduct such important pre-trial procedures as a review of the sufficiency of the grand jury evidence or a suppression hearing. In People v. Blake, 133 A.D.2d 549, 520 N.Y.S.2d 92 (4th Dep't 1987), the court denied a motion for removal to the Supreme Court from the County Court on this ground, opining that the proper procedure is not a motion under CPL § 230.20, but a motion for disqualification in the trial court. However, the cited authority in that case, People v. Capuano, 68 Misc.2d 481, 483, 327 N.Y.S.2d 17, 20 (Monroe Co.Ct. 1971), actually holds that "before bringing this [removal] motion, the petitioner should have first requested [disqualification]." Accordingly, this provision may still offer a viable option in such circumstances if disqualification is refused. Depending on whether the disqualification is unique to a single judge of the County Court, or extends to all of the superior court judges of a particular county, it might be cast as either removal to the Supreme Court or an application to change the venue.

198. CPL § 230.30(1). This should be read as referring to the statutorily prescribed period, "within forty-five days after arraignment and before commencement of trial," CPL §§ 230.20(2) and (3), 255.20(1), and not to the judicially preferred post-jury voir dire application. Otherwise, the practical difficulties and dangers of moving for the relief without a stay at such a late stage of the proceedings are obvious.

199. CPL § 230.30(2).

200. CPL § 230.30(4). Note, however, that the statute does not forbid a second application to the same justice.

201. CPL § 230.30(1).

202. CPL § 230.30(3).

203. CPL § 230.20(2).

204. CPL § 230.20(2)(a) and (b).

court is directed to consider, among other factors, the hardship resulting from the latter alternative.[205]

Motions to change the venue tend to be resisted by the courts, probably because of the inconvenience and expense to the criminal justice system, coupled with the popular belief that it is almost always possible to find a sufficient number of untainted jurors. By far the most common ground for the motion is pretrial publicity. Applications on this basis are frequently denied.[206] In one case, the Second Department was confronted with a statistical argument that, even after numerous jurors who had knowledge of a notorious murder had been excluded from the case, 52 percent of the remaining jurors had expressed a disqualifying prejudice, and of the jurors actually selected, only two knew nothing of the case. Nevertheless, the court refused to adopt a "bright line" test: "[The] propriety of this remedy [changing the venue] does not hinge solely on proof of the extent to which the original venue has been saturated with pretrial publicity. Instead, the propriety of this remedy hinges on proof of the extent to which, as between the original venue and the venue to which a transfer is sought, significantly different levels of 'saturation' have been reached, thus rendering the selection of a fair jury impossible in one place and possible in another."[207] Noting that the jurors' simple knowledge of the publicity was not determinative[208] and that a temporal lapse between the peak publicity and the trial was also important, the court held that denial of the application was not error. Although it will be very difficult to meet the standard of this case, it should be noted that it involved a large suburban county with a large jury pool, and local conditions in a smaller jurisdiction might favor a different result.

If the motion to change the venue is granted, a certified copy of the order must be filed with the clerk of the court in which the action is pending, who will then transmit the papers to the new court.[209] After removal, the new court will conduct all proceedings; however, removal does not void pre-removal determinations and rulings made in the original court.[210]

---

205. Although the alternative of expanding the jury pool was added in 1985 (L.1985, c.257) in an effort to provide what was thought to be a less onerous alternative to a change of venue, perhaps because of this cautionary language, a change of venue seems to remain the judicial preference.

206. See, e.g., People v. Keefer, 197 A.D.2d 915, 602 N.Y.S.2d 268 (4th Dep't 1993); People v. Solomon, 172 A.D.2d 781, 569 N.Y.S.2d 101 (2d Dep't 1991); People v. Zehner, 112 A.D.2d 465, 490 N.Y.S.2d 879 (3d Dep't 1985).

207. People v. Quartararo, 200 A.D.2d 160, 162, 612 N.Y.S.2d 635, 637 (2d Dep't 1994).

208. 200 A.D.2d at 167, 612 N.Y.S.2d at 640 ("there will always be people who form strong opinions based on a minimum of information; however, there will fortunately always be others who, even if possessed of a great amount of information, will wisely hold off judgment knowing that there may be more to learn. The key is to identify those persons who will make good jurors and those who will not. This is a task which can be accomplished anywhere, if enough care is taken.").

209. CPL § 230.20(4).

210. CPL § 230.40. The statute further provides that the new court "is deemed to have control of the grand jury minutes underlying the indictment for the purpose of determining post-removal motions addressed to the legal sufficiency of the grand jury evidence or the validity of the grand jury proceeding."

It has been held that a failure to renew a motion for a change of venue after an initial denial may waive the issue on direct appeal from an ensuing conviction.[211] Accordingly, if the common pattern is followed—an early motion, initially denied pending jury voir dire—and the results of the voir dire are not to counsel's satisfaction, care should be taken to renew the issue. Although it may seem unlikely that the Appellate Division that denies the renewed motion will be inclined to differ with its previous decision on direct appeal,[212] circumstances may change, and in any event a failure to renew the motion may ultimately preclude Court of Appeals or collateral review.

Library References:
West's Key No. Digests, Criminal Law ⟜101.

§ 1.10 Removal—To Family Court

In 1978,[213] the Legislature created the concept of a "juvenile offender," in essence a person of 13 to 15 years of age who is criminally responsible for certain specified crimes, but not all crimes.[214] Previously, those under 16 had not been considered criminally responsible, and were dealt with in Family Court as "juvenile delinquents."[215] Juvenile offenders are now treated as criminally responsible adults, and the criminal courts are given exclusive original jurisdiction over their cases. However, to ameliorate what might otherwise be considered draconian treatment, in the course of time numerous provisions were added to allow for the removal of these youths to the Family Court system, where they would be treated as juvenile delinquents, which would have been their status had the juvenile offender concept never been created.[216] This result is accomplished in a series of eight separate CPL sections,[217] plus one CPL article[218] that is intended to supply a common procedural

---

211. People v. Pepper, 59 N.Y.2d 353, 465 N.Y.S.2d 850, 452 N.E.2d 1178 (1983); People v. Keefer, 197 A.D.2d 915, 602 N.Y.S.2d 268 (4th Dep't 1993).

212. In People v. Quartararo, 200 A.D.2d 160, 163, 612 N.Y.S.2d 635, 637 (2d Dep't 1994), it was held that the "law of the case" doctrine does not prevent the Appellate Division from changing its mind.

213. L.1978, c.481.

214. CPL § 1.20(42) and P.L. § 10.00(18) define the concept, listing the crimes and what each age group is criminally responsible for. A corresponding amendment was made to P.L. § 30.00, which now broadly defines 16 as the age of general criminal responsibility, see P.L. § 30.00, except as to the crimes specified in the juvenile offender definition. See P.L. § 30.00(2). Not to be confused with the juvenile offender is the "youthful offender," a somewhat older young person who is tried as an adult for a criminal offense but who is eligible, upon conviction, to have the conviction replaced by a youthful offender adjudication. See CPL Article 720.

215. Family Court Act § 301.2(1). Under present law, a "juvenile delinquent" is either a 7 to 15–year–old who commits an act that otherwise would be criminal if committed by adults, but who is not a "juvenile offender" (i.e., a person excluded from that definition either by age or the nature of the crime), or a "juvenile offender" whose case has been removed to Family Court under the provisions discussed in this section.

216. The present section is concerned only with removals and can only sketch the outlines of the substantive and procedural law in this area, which is complex. See Warner, "The Juvenile Offender Handbook" (Looseleaf Law Publications 1995), for fuller treatment.

217. CPL §§ 180.75, 190.71, 210.20(5), 210.30(7), 210.43, 220.10, 310.85, and 330.25.

218. CPL Article 725.

framework for all of these provisions.[219]

When a juvenile offender is arraigned on a felony complaint before a local criminal court, a special provision supersedes the usual statutes applicable to adults in that situation.[220] The provision contains three separate removal procedures. Initially, as with adults, the court is empowered to accept a waiver of a preliminary hearing and transmit the documents in the case to the superior court. However, if a hearing is held, the court may either dismiss the felony complaint entirely, order that the defendant be held for grand jury action, or, as a third alternative, if it finds that there is reasonable cause to believe that the defendant juvenile has not committed an act for which he or she is criminally liable, but which would make the defendant a "juvenile delinquent," order a removal of the case to Family Court.[221]

The remaining removals are at the request of the parties. The next subdivision mandates a removal at the prosecutor's request "if it is determined that to do so would be in the interests of justice."[222] The third provision allows the defendant to move for removal in a superior court.[223] There are certain preconditions: the defendant must not have waived a preliminary hearing and the hearing must not have already commenced. The statute allows the superior court to sit as a local criminal court and exercise the requisite preliminary jurisdiction to entertain all necessary procedures, including a hearing[224] for the purpose of determining whether there should be a removal, for which the same criteria apply that would be employed on a post-indictment motion to

---

219. However, as is noted in Warner, "The Juvenile Offender Handbook," supra at p. 77, CPL § 725.00, which defines the applicability of that article, omits two of these sections—CPL §§ 210.20(5) and 210.30(7)—which were added in 1980, although the latter is referenced elsewhere in the Article. See § 725.05(4–a). This appears to be an oversight.

220. CPL § 180.75(1), which supersedes CPL §§ 180.30, 180.50, and 180.70.

221. CPL § 180.75(3). Removal to Family Court under this provision would normally occur if, for example, a 13-year-old defendant was arrested for a juvenile offender offense such as murder, but, after the hearing, was found to have committed only a lesser, non-juvenile offense such as manslaughter.

222. CPL § 180.75(4). Although the section is cast in mandatory terms—"the court shall, at the request of the district attorney, order removal"—this is modified by the interests of justice requirement, for which a set of criteria is provided by cross-reference to CPL § 210.43(2) (the superior court removal motion, discussed infra). However, where the defendant is charged with one of a number of specified egregious crimes—first degree murder, first degree rape, first degree sodomy or certain, but not all, armed felonies—in addition to the other requirements the court must find one or more of the following: "(1) mitigating circumstances that bear directly upon the manner in which the crime was committed; (ii) where the defendant was not the sole participant in the crime, the defendant's participation was relatively minor, though not so minor as to constitute a defense to the prosecution; or (iii) possible deficiencies in proof of the crime."

223. CPL § 180.75(5). The statute, by cross-reference, adopts the criteria and procedures of CPL § 210.43 (removal motion in superior court), but modifies them slightly, so that the exception in the latter statute that requires the prosecutor's consent in cases involving certain serious crimes is eliminated if the court finds no reasonable cause to believe that such a crime had been committed.

224. A hearing is not mandated. Vega v. Bell, 47 N.Y.2d 543, 419 N.Y.S.2d 454, 393 N.E.2d 450 (1979). Moreover, as that case further holds, the prosecutor may circumvent this entire procedure by presenting the case to a grand jury and obtaining an indictment, unless a defendant's removal motion has been *granted*, in which case a statutory bar is operative. CPL § 180.75(6)(f).

remove the case to Family Court.[225] There is, however, a statutory bar to making two such motions, or a motion both at this stage and after indictment;[226] thus, a defendant who moves at this early stage, before the grand jury has had a chance to consider the matter, relinquishes an important opportunity if he or she is indicted. The bar, however, does not prevent an attempt at this stage to persuade either the court or the prosecution to exercise its removal powers.

Other noteworthy features include a provision allowing the receipt of any evidence that is not legally privileged at a hearing held on a motion by either party; if the defendant testifies at such a proceeding, that testimony thereafter may be used only for impeachment purposes.[227] Finally, both the court and the prosecutor are mandated to state on the record, "in detail and not in conclusionary terms," their reasons for consenting to or ordering removal.[228]

The grand jury is also provided a somewhat limited power to remove the case to Family Court. Under the relevant provisions,[229] the grand jury is authorized to direct removal only when it is presented with a juvenile offender charge and finds insufficient evidence of that charge, but sufficient evidence of criminal act(s) that would support a juvenile delinquency proceeding in the Family Court. Under those circumstances, the grand jury may vote to remove the case to Family Court.[230] In other words, the statute clearly does not allow the grand jury, in the exercise of its so-called "mercy" function,[231] to ask for removal as a matter of discretion.[232] However, in juvenile offender situations, as in all other situations, the grand jury retains its customary non-reviewable discretion to dismiss the charges.

Special problems arise when there is more than one charge, but not all are juvenile offender offenses. To avoid the potential problems of multiple proceedings in different courts, the grand jury is authorized to indict for all offenses pursuant to a special joinder provision, subject to certain restrictions.[233]

In 1980,[234] two additional interlocking removal provisions were added to address post-indictment review of a juvenile offender grand jury indictment. One of these[235] provides that if a court, upon reviewing the sufficiency of the evidence before the grand jury, finds that the evidence

---

225. CPL § 180.75(5) cross-references CPL § 210.43.
226. CPL § 180.75(6)(d).
227. CPL § 180.75(6)(c).
228. CPL § 180.75(6)(a) and (b).
229. CPL §§ 190.60(3), 190.71.
230. Mechanically, after the vote the grand jury must file a request for removal, which must contain certain specified information, with the impaneling court. Upon the filing of such a request, the court must, unless the request is "improper or insufficient on its face," order the removal. CPL § 190.71(c) and (d).
231. Whether the grand jury possesses any such power is a matter of historic debate. Clearly, under the relevant New York statutes, no such function exists as a matter of law. CPL § 190.75(1).

232. See People v. Rios, 78 A.D.2d 642, 432 N.Y.S.2d 120 (2d Dep't 1980) (where grand jury indicted for juvenile offender crime, it may not direct removal).
233. CPL §§ 190.71(1), 200.20(6). If an ensuing conviction does not include a juvenile offender offense, removal then occurs post-verdict pursuant to CPL § 310.85.
234. L.1980, c.136.
235. CPL § 210.30(7).

is insufficient to establish either the charged juvenile offender offense or any other lesser included offenses for which the defendant is criminally responsible, the court may allow resubmission to the grand jury or, as a matter of discretion, and if there is sufficient evidence of juvenile delinquency, direct removal to Family Court. No standard for the exercise of that discretion is provided.[236]

The other provision[237] directs that if a court dismisses the juvenile offender count(s) of an indictment, but does not also dismiss non-juvenile offender count(s)—*i.e.*, any counts for which the defendant, in the absence of the juvenile offender charges, could not be indicted, and which were joined solely pursuant to the special joinder provision noted above—then the remaining counts must be removed to Family Court.

The next, and probably most important of these removal statutes, is the general motion for removal made in the superior court. The statute,[238] which in many respects resembles the more familiar motion to dismiss an indictment in furtherance of justice,[239] is more limited in one crucial regard: the court may not order removal without the prosecutor's consent where the defendant is charged with certain serious crimes.[240] Otherwise, in making the determination that removal is "be in the interests of justice," the court is directed to examine, "individually and collectively," the following factors: (a) the seriousness and circumstances of the offense; (b) the extent of harm caused by the offense; (c) the evidence of guilt, whether admissible or inadmissible at trial; (d) the history, character, and condition of the defendant; (e) the purpose and effect of imposing upon the defendant a sentence authorized for the offense; (f) the impact of a removal of the case to the Family Court on the safety and welfare of the community; (g) the impact of a removal of the case to Family Court upon the confidence of the public in the criminal justice system; (h) where the court deems it appropriate, the attitude of the complainant or victim with respect to the motion; and (i) any other relevant fact indicating that a judgment of conviction in the criminal court would serve no useful purpose.[241]

---

236. Unlike CPL § 180.75(5)(motion for removal in local criminal court), this section contains no explicit cross-reference to the criteria of CPL § 210.43 (motion for removal in superior court). Nevertheless, those criteria are certainly useful, and should be consulted.

237. CPL § 210.20(5).

238. CPL § 210.43. Prior to the passage of this statute, the Court of Appeals had opined that a trial court's power to dismiss in the interests of justice pursuant to CPL § 210.40 "impliedly" provided the power to remove. Vega v. Bell, 47 N.Y.2d 543, 552, 419 N.Y.S.2d 454, 460, 393 N.E.2d 450, 455 (1979).

239. CPL § 210.40.

240. CPL § 210.43(b). The crimes in question are murder in the second degree, rape or sodomy in the first degree, or certain armed felonies defined elsewhere (see CPL § 1.20(41)(a); note that not all "armed felonies are within this definition"). Even with prosecutorial consent, the court must still find certain mitigating factors. See footnote 222, supra. The prosecutorial consent restriction does not render the statute unconstitutional. People v. Murphy, 70 N.Y.2d 969, 525 N.Y.S.2d 834, 520 N.E.2d 552 (1988).

241. CPL 210.43(2). These are slight modifications of the interests of justice dismissal criteria of CPL § 210.40(1), with one exception—the "misconduct of law enforcement" dismissal criterion is omitted. See CPL § 210.40(1)(e).

§ 1.10 JURISDICTION & REMOVAL Ch. 1

Procedurally, the motion follows the same path as other pre-trial motions, but as with removal in the local criminal court, special provisions allow for the receipt of evidence that is not legally privileged at any hearing; if the defendant testifies at such a proceeding, that testimony may thereafter be used only for impeachment purposes, and both the court and the prosecutor are mandated to state on the record, "in detail and not in conclusionary terms," their reasons for consenting to or ordering removal.[242]

Minimal interpretive precedent currently exists. The relief is said to be discretionary and only proper in "exceptional cases."[243] A guilty plea waives any complaint about denial of the removal motion.[244] Removal has been granted where, among other factors, it was found that a youthful defendant charged with assault had been provoked and teased by older victims, who initiated the confrontation.[245] It should be noted that, in an appropriately sympathetic case, removal under this statute might be pleaded as an alternative to dismissal in furtherance of justice, thus allowing the court to choose what seems like a middle course between outright dismissal and a criminal prosecution.

The remaining removal provisions involve plea bargaining[246] or post-verdict procedures beyond the scope of this book.[247]

Finally, a separate CPL article is intended to provide a common framework for all of these removal provisions.[248] The primary purpose of many of its provisions is to avoid duplication of effort and save time in the Family Court by insuring that an order of removal issued by a criminal court will be sufficient for a number of purposes in the new court.[249] Other provisions allow for the transfer to and appearance of the juvenile in Family Court,[250] for the transfer of records to Family Court[251] and for the sealing of previous records of the case[252] and the creation of certain other records for monitoring purposes.[253]

---

242. CPL § 210.43(4) and (5).

243. People v. Woods, 143 A.D.2d 1068, 533 N.Y.S.2d 888 (2d Dep't 1988); People v. Sanchez, 128 A.D.2d 816, 513 N.Y.S.2d 521 (2d Dep't 1987).

244. People v. Woods, 143 A.D.2d 1068, 533 N.Y.S.2d 888 (2d Dep't 1988).

245. People v. Gregory C., 158 Misc.2d 872, 602 N.Y.S.2d 492 (Sup.Ct., Erie County, 1993). See also Matter of John G. v. Dubin, 89 A.D.2d 839, 452 N.Y.S.2d 907 (2d Dep't 1982)(factors discussed).

246. CPL § 220.10(5)(g) allows the prosecutor in the case of some, but not all, juvenile offenders, to recommend removal to Family Court at that stage. A list of mitigating factors is provided. The court may then accept a plea to what would normally not be a juvenile offender offense in the interests of justice; thereafter, in the interests of judicial economy this becomes a juvenile delinquency fact determination and the case is removed to Family Court.

247. CPL §§ 310.85, 330.25. The first of these deals with the situation in which a defendant is convicted of crimes for which he or she is not criminally responsible. The second is yet another provision allowing a discretionary removal of some, but not all, juvenile offender offenses to Family Court, in this case after a jury verdict.

248. As previously noted, however, several provisions are not specifically cross-referenced in § 725.00, which establishes the applicability of the Article. See footnote 219, supra.

249. CPL § 725.05(1)-(5); see Preiser, "Practice Commentary" to CPL § 725.05, McKinney's Cons. Laws of New York, Book 11A, at 429 (1995).

250. CPL § 725.05(6) and (7).

251. CPL § 725.05(8).

252. CPL § 725.20.

253. Id.

The core jurisdictional provision of the Article[254] has two subdivisions. The first directs the Family Court to "assume jurisdiction" when the criminal court's order of removal is filed with the Family Court and to conduct all further proceedings. The second subdivision provides that upon the filing of the order in a criminal court, the criminal action upon which it was based shall be terminated, no further criminal proceedings shall occur, and prior proceedings in the criminal court will in effect become proceedings of the Family Court. In other words, the criminal court is divested of jurisdiction at the filing of the removal motion and cannot, for example, change its mind and deny a removal motion it has previously granted,[255] or allow for re-presentation of the case to a grand jury after it has been removed.[256]

Library References:
West's Key No. Digests, Infants ⇔68.6.

§ 1.11 Practice Summary

A. Jurisdiction of Courts (*See* § 1.2)

1. This form of jurisdiction is concerned with which courts have authority over different stages of different levels of offenses. The CPL divides courts exercising criminal jurisdiction into two categories—"superior courts" (County and Supreme court), and "local criminal courts" (city, town, village, and district courts and the New York City Criminal Court)—and specifies which of these courts has "trial jurisdiction" and "preliminary jurisdiction" over the various levels of offenses. Preliminary jurisdiction involves such early steps in the criminal process as the arraignment of the defendant. In very general terms, local criminal courts exercise preliminary jurisdiction over all offenses, and trial jurisdiction over offenses of less than felony grade, while superior courts have exclusive trial jurisdiction over felonies. Superior court judges may sit as local criminal courts for some purposes, with certain restrictions.

2. In some instances, such as a proceeding involving the validity of a subpoena or a crime-linked forfeiture action, whether a proceeding is civil or criminal in nature may not be immediately apparent. That determination may affect questions of appealability of adverse rulings or even double jeopardy protection.

3. A criminal defendant has the right to have all critical stages of the trial conducted by an official with jurisdiction to preside; judicial delegation of trial tasks to law secretaries and other court personnel has occasionally produced reversals of convictions.

---

254. CPL § 725.10.

255. Matter of John G. v. Dubin, 89 A.D.2d 839, 452 N.Y.S.2d 907 (2d Dep't 1982).

256. Matter of Rodriguez v. Grajales, 188 A.D.2d 474, 591 N.Y.S.2d 66 (2d Dep't 1992). In the context of removal motions in the local criminal court, a special statutory bar, rather than this general section, governs, which prevents further criminal proceedings when the removal motion is *granted*. CPL § 180.75(6)(f). However, if the prosecution divests the local criminal court of jurisdiction by filing an indictment prior to this point, the local criminal court would appear to be powerless to order removal.

4. In unusual circumstances, typically involving areas of activity that are the subject of intensive federal regulation such as OSHA or banking, the federal government may preempt the criminal jurisdiction of the New York courts. Another, extremely rare, form of such preemption occurs when a federal officer is charge with a state criminal offense related to his or her duties.

B. Geographical jurisdiction

1. Geographical jurisdiction is concerned with where the crime took place. There are two primary concepts: the jurisdiction of the state itself and the jurisdiction of the counties within the state (referred to as "venue"). Although the statutes defining these concepts seem quite similar, it is important to recognize the difference between the two. The jurisdiction of the state is fundamental, non-waivable, and, if at issue, must be proved by the prosecution beyond a reasonable doubt. The jurisdiction of the counties within the state is not fundamental, may be waived by a plea of guilty or otherwise, must be preserved for appeal, and, if disputed, may be proved by a preponderance of evidence. However, either form of geographical jurisdiction may be challenged by a special proceeding pursuant to CPLR Article 78, and because the statutes governing both are substantially similar, precedent interpreting one may be relevant on a question involving the other (*see* § 1.3).

2. Situations implicating the jurisdiction of the state are quite rare, and usually, but not invariably, involve complex crimes such as conspiracy, RICO, or interstate schemes involving fraud or larceny. The governing statute establishes two main premises. There is state jurisdiction if:

(1) sufficient conduct occurs within the state to establish either (a) an element of the offense; (b) an attempt to commit the offense; or (c) a conspiracy or criminal solicitation to commit the offense (with certain restrictions); or

(2) even if none of the conduct occurred within the state, (a) the offense committed was a "result offense" and the result occurred in New York; (b) the conduct outside the state was violative of a statute designed to prevent a particular effect in this state and was performed with the intent that it have that "effect"; (c) the offense committed was an attempt to commit a crime in this state; (d) the offense committed was conspiracy to commit a crime in this state and an overt act occurred in this state; or (e) the offense was failure to perform a legal duty in this state.

In interpreting these rules, several things should be kept in mind. First, the conduct in question may be committed either by the defendant personally or by an accomplice, as New York stringently defines that status (*see* Penal Law § 20.00). Second, particularly in situations involving "result" or "effect" jurisdiction, the case law has limited these concepts beyond what the face of the statute seems to suggest. Third, a separate statute (CPL § 20.30) limits some of these provisions in situations where a particular form of conduct, such as gambling, is legal in one state and not legal in another. Fourth, these provisions are not mutually exclusive, and jurisdiction may be predicated on more than one basis (*see* § 1.3).

3. Certain areas within the state, such as federal facilities and Indian reservations, may pose special jurisdictional problems. Federal ownership of the facility is not in itself dispositive of the question (*see* § 1.3).

4. The general statutory rules governing county geographical jurisdiction are similar to the state rules, but the issue arises much more often, and should be considered whenever any part of a criminal act takes place in more than one county. Again, the governing statute establishes two main premises. Jurisdiction exists in a county if:

> (1) sufficient conduct occurs within the county to establish either (a) an element of the offense (this is the most common theory—make sure the conduct consists of an "element" and is not merely proof of an element); or (b) an attempt or conspiracy to commit the offense; or
>
> (2) even if none of the conduct occurred within the county, (a) the offense committed was a "result offense" and the result occurred in the county; (b) the offense was homicide and the victim's body was found in the county; (c) the conduct outside the county was violative of a statute designed to prevent a particular effect in this state and was performed with the intent that it have that "effect"; (d) the offense committed was an attempt, conspiracy, or criminal solicitation to commit a crime in the county; (e) the offense committed was criminal facilitation to commit a crime in the county; or (f) the offense was failure to perform a legal duty in the county (*see* § 1.4).

In addition to these general rules, there are also eleven special rules, narrowly focused on particular offenses (abandonment or non-support of a child, bigamy, and certain forgery and larceny offenses); particular geographical features (offenses committed within 500 yards of a county border, on bridges, on certain rivers, or on the ocean); or offenses committed on vehicles, vessels, and aircraft. A final special provision deals with offenses committed by mail, telecommunication, or computer (*see* § 1.4).

Again, the conduct in question may be committed either by the defendant personally or by an accomplice, and these provisions are not mutually exclusive—venue is often asserted on more than one basis. Remember that venue is waivable, and must be challenged. If there is reason to believe that a venue problem exists, a request should be made to charge the jury on this issue (*see* § 1.4).

5. Other statutes govern the geographical jurisdiction of local criminal courts within a county and provide for the filing of certain accusatory instruments in certain courts (*see* § 1.5).

C. Removal

1. Two situations involve removal from one local criminal court to another local criminal court: (1) where a defendant is arraigned before a

substitute local criminal court because the court that will ultimately try the case is unavailable; and (2) where a case is pending before the local criminal court with trial jurisdiction, but the parties seek to transfer it, either because disposition within a reasonable time therein is unlikely owing to death, incapacity, or disqualification of the original court, or because of the inability of the original court to form a jury. A motion to transfer the case must be made in the County Court, in writing and within 45 days of arraignment and before commencement of trial. The courts are divided on whether this procedure may be used in cases involving excessive publicity (*see* § 1.7).

2. Removal is also permitted in certain situations from a local criminal court to a superior court. A prosecutor may ask a local criminal court to adjourn a case because he or she intends to present it to a grand jury. No grounds are necessary. The court must grant the initial adjournment for this purpose, and may grant subsequent adjournments. The local criminal court is divested of jurisdiction at the point the indictment is voted. If the grand jury dismisses the case, the prosecutor may nevertheless file another misdemeanor accusatory instrument with the local criminal court.

A defendant may move a superior court to order that a pending misdemeanor charge charged in a local criminal court accusatory instrument be prosecuted by indictment in a superior court, and may obtain an adjournment in the local criminal court for that purpose. The defendant must show good cause to believe that the interests of justice require removal. A set of historic criteria have evolved. This is a risky procedure—the grand jury may vote to indict for a felony. It may be an option where other remedies for bias or prejudice have failed, or in very complex or important cases. If appropriate, disqualification motions in the original court, administrative remedies or a motion for removal to another local criminal court might be tried first (*see* § 1.8).

3. Removal from one superior court to another superior court may arise in two situations: removal of an action from a County to a Supreme Court within one county, or transfer to a superior court of another county (commonly known as a change of venue). The County to Supreme Court removal now may be accomplished administratively, although the CPL provision may still be useful in some situations where a motion for recusal or attempt at administrative relief has failed. A motion to change the venue is made in the Appellate Division, upon reasonable grounds to believe that a fair trial cannot be held in the original jurisdiction. A stay of proceedings in the original court while the motion is being considered is available, but must be requested. By far the most common ground for the motion is pretrial publicity. Generally, the Appellate Division will deny a motion made prior to jury voir dire. If this happens, counsel should fully explore the matter at the voir dire, make an appropriate record, and renew the motion at that time if the results of the voir dire are unsatisfactory (*see* § 1.9).

4. In cases involving a "juvenile offender"—a 13 to 15–year–old who can be held criminally responsible for some, but not all, crimes, a variety

of statutory provisions allow for removal to Family Court at virtually every stage of a criminal prosecution (see § 1.10).

In a local criminal court, a case involving a juvenile offender arraigned on a felony complaint may be removed at the court's own order, if the court finds reasonable cause to believe that the juvenile committed an act for which he or she cannot be criminally responsible. Removal may also be made on the prosecutor's request, in the interests of justice, or by motion of the defendant, made in a superior court under certain limitations and conditions. If a defendant makes such a motion here, it bars a post-indictment motion in the superior court. Hence, delay may be preferable in the hope that the grand jury will not indict.

The grand jury may not indict a juvenile offender and then direct removal to Family Court in the exercise of a mercy function, but it may direct such removal if it only finds evidence of an offense for which the juvenile is not criminally responsible. If the grand jury does indict for a juvenile offender offense, it may also indict for other offenses for which the defendant would not otherwise be criminally responsible.

A superior court, upon reviewing the evidence before the grand jury, may, if it finds the evidence of all juvenile offender crimes insufficient, either allow resubmission to the grand jury or direct removal to Family Court. If it dismisses all juvenile offender crimes, leaving only non-juvenile offender crimes in the indictment, it must direct removal.

The defendant may also move in the superior court for removal, although in the case of certain very serious offenses the prosecutor's consent is required. A series of criteria, similar to those governing a motion for dismissal in the interests of justice, are provided in the statute. In an appropriate case, a motion for removal can be pleaded as an alternative to dismissal, upon the same facts.

Other Family Court removal provisions relate to plea bargaining or post-verdict relief. A separate article of the statute provides the procedural framework for these provisions. In cases where a court grants a removal motion, care should be taken to file the removal order in the criminal court as soon as possible so as to divest that court of jurisdiction.

§ 1.12 Forms

§ 1.12.1 Notice of Motion to Remove Action to Another Local Criminal Court of the County

[Caption]

COUNSEL:

PLEASE TAKE NOTICE, that upon the annexed affirmation and all the prior papers and proceedings herein, the undersigned will move this Court, at the Courthouse at _____, New York, on the __ day of _____, 199__, at __ in the forenoon, or as soon thereafter as counsel can be heard, for an order pursuant to section 170.15 [(3)(a) or (3)(b)] of the Criminal Procedure Law for an order removing the trial of the above-named defendant from the [specify local criminal court in which action is pending] to the [specify local criminal court to which action is sought to be removed], and for such other relief as the Court deems proper.

Dated: _____, 19__
_____, New York

[Name of defense attorney]
Attorney for Defendant
Address
Tel. No.

TO: HON. _____
District Attorney
_____ County

HON. _____
Clerk of the Court

§ 1.12.2 Affirmation in Support of Motion to Remove Action to Another Local Criminal Court of the County

[Caption]

_____, an attorney duly admitted to practice in the Courts of this State, hereby affirms under penalty of perjury that the following statements are true, and as to those made upon information and belief he [she] believes them to be true:

1. I am the attorney for the defendant herein.

2. On _____, 19__, a [specify accusatory instrument] was filed in the [specify local criminal court in which action is pending] charging defendant with commission of the following offense(s): [specify offense(s) charged]. A copy of the [specify accusatory instrument] is attached hereto as Exhibit A.

3. No plea of guilty has been entered with respect to the [specify accusatory instrument], nor has a trial been commenced thereon.

4. This affirmation is made in support of defendant's application for an order pursuant to section 170.15 [(3)(a) or (3)(b)] of the Criminal Procedure Law, removing this action from the [specify local criminal court in which action is pending] to the [specify local criminal court to which removal is sought].

5. Removal is sought on the ground that disposition of this action within a reasonable time in the [specify local criminal court in which action is pending] is unlikely because of [the death, other incapacity or disqualification of all the judges of such court; or the inability of such court to form a jury in this action, despite defendant's request for and legal right to a jury trial].

6. [specify facts in support of ground for removal]

7. No prior application for the relief sought herein has been made.

WHEREFORE, defendant respectfully requests that this Court issue an order removing the aforesaid criminal action to the [specify local criminal court to which removal is sought].

Dated: _____, 19__
_____, New York

[Signature]

_____
Name of Defense Attorney

§ 1.12.3 Notice of Motion by Prosecutor in Support of Motion to Adjourn Proceedings in Local Criminal Court on Misdemeanor Charge to Present Charge to a Grand Jury

[Caption]

COUNSEL:

PLEASE TAKE NOTICE, that upon the annexed affirmation and all the prior papers and proceedings herein, the undersigned will move this Court, at the Courthouse at _____, New York, on the __ day of _____, 19__, at __ in the forenoon, or as soon thereafter as counsel can be heard, for an order pursuant to section 170.20(2) of the Criminal Procedure Law removing the proceedings concerning the misdemeanor charge(s) against the above-named defendant so that said charge(s) may be presented to a grand jury, and for such other relief as the Court deems proper.

Dated: _____, 19__
_____, New York

HON. _____
District Attorney
_____ County

TO: [Name of defense attorney]
    Attorney for Defendant

HON. _____
Clerk of the Court

§ 1.12.4 Affirmation in Support of Prosecutor's Motion to Adjourn Proceedings on Misdemeanor Charge in Local Criminal Court to Present Charge to a Grand Jury

[Caption]

_____, an attorney duly admitted to practice in the Courts of this State, hereby affirms under penalty of perjury that the following statements are true, and as to those made upon information and belief he [she] believes them to be true:

§ 1.12 JURISDICTION & REMOVAL Ch. 1

1. I am an assistant district attorney in the office of _____, the District Attorney for _____ County.

2. On _____, 19__, a [specify accusatory instrument] was filed in this Court charging the above-named defendant with the following misdemeanor offense(s): [specify misdemeanor offense(s) charged]. A copy of the [specify accusatory instrument] is attached hereto as Exhibit A.

3. No plea of guilty has been entered with respect to the [specify accusatory instrument], nor has a trial been commenced thereon.

4. The District Attorney intends to present the misdemeanor charge(s) against the defendant to a grand jury with a view to prosecuting by indictment in a superior court.

5. No prior application for the relief sought herein has been made.

WHEREFORE, the District Attorney requests that this Court issue an order adjourning the proceedings of the aforesaid misdemeanor charge(s) so that said charge(s) may be presented to a grand jury with a view to proceeding by indictment in superior court.

Dated: _____, 19__
_____, New York

[Signature]

_____
[Name of Assistant District Attorney]

§ 1.12.5 Notice of Motion by Defendant to Remove Proceedings on Misdemeanor Charge to Superior Court

[Caption]

COUNSEL:

PLEASE TAKE NOTICE, that upon the annexed affirmation and upon all the prior papers and proceedings herein, the undersigned will move this Court, at the Courthouse at _____, New York, on the ___ day of _____, 19__, at ___ in the forenoon, or as soon thereafter as counsel can be heard, for an order pursuant to section 170.25 of the Criminal Procedure Law directing that the misdemeanor charge(s) pending against the above-named defendant in the [specify local criminal court in which action is pending] be prosecuted by indictment in this Court and that the District Attorney present such misdemeanor charge(s) to a grand jury for such purpose, and for such other relief as the Court deems proper.

Dated: _____, 19__
_____, New York

[Name of defense attorney]
Attorney for Defendant
Address
Tel. No.

TO: HON. _____
District Attorney
_____ County

HON. _____
Clerk of the Court

§ 1.12.6 Affirmation in Support of Motion by Defendant to Remove Proceedings on Misdemeanor Charge to Superior Court

[Caption]

_____, an attorney duly admitted to practice in the Courts of this State, hereby affirms under penalty of perjury that the following statements are true, and as to those made upon information and belief he [she] believes them to be true:

1. I am the attorney for the above-named defendant.

2. On _____, 19__, a [specify accusatory instrument] was filed against defendant in the [specify local criminal court in which action is pending] charging defendant with commission of the following misdemeanor offense(s): [specify misdemeanor charge(s)]. A copy of the [specify accusatory instrument] is attached hereto as Exhibit A.

3. No plea of guilty has been entered with respect to the [specify accusatory instrument], nor has a trial been commenced thereon.

4. This application is made in support of defendant's application pursuant to section 170.25 of the Criminal Procedure Law for an order directing that the aforesaid misdemeanor charge(s) be prosecuted by indictment in this Court and that the District Attorney be directed to present such charge(s) to a grand jury for that purpose.

5. Prosecution of such charge(s) by indictment in this Court would be in the interests of justice because [specify reasons].

6. No prior application for the relief sought herein has been made.

WHEREFORE, defendant requests that this Court issue an order directing that the aforesaid misdemeanor charge(s) be prosecuted by indictment in this Court and that the District Attorney be directed to present such charge(s) to a grand jury for that purpose.

Dated: _____, 19__
_____, New York

[Signature]

_____
[Name of defense attorney]

§ 1.12.7 Notice of Motion in Appellate Division for Change of Venue

[Caption]
COUNSEL:

PLEASE TAKE NOTICE, that upon the annexed affirmation and upon all the prior papers and proceedings herein, the undersigned will move this Court, at the Courthouse at _____, New York, on the ___ day of _____, 19__, at ___ in the forenoon, or as soon thereafter as counsel can be heard, for an order pursuant to section 230.20 of the Criminal Procedure Law removing the trial of the indictment against the above-named defendant pending in the [specify superior court in which action is pending] to a term of a superior court of another county, and for such other relief as the Court deems proper.

Dated: _____, 19__
_____, New York

[Name of defense attorney]
Attorney for Defendant
Address
Tel. No.

TO: HON. _____
District Attorney
_____ County

HON. _____
Clerk of the Court

§ 1.12.8 Affirmation in Support of Motion in the Appellate Division for Change of Venue

[Caption]

_____, an attorney duly admitted to practice in the Courts of this State, hereby affirms under penalty of perjury that the following statements are true, and as to those made upon information and belief he [she] believes them to be true:

1. I am the attorney for the above-named defendant.

2. On _____, 19__, an indictment was filed with the [specify superior court in which action is pending] charging defendant with the following offense(s): [specify charges]. A copy of the indictment is attached hereto as Exhibit A.

3. No plea of guilty has been entered with respect to the indictment, nor has a trial been commenced thereon.

4. This affirmation is made in support of defendant's motion pursuant to section 230.20(2) of the Criminal Procedure Law for a change of venue of the trial on the aforesaid indictment on the ground that a fair and impartial trial cannot be had in _____ County.

5. [specify reasons in support of motion, such as why public opinion in the county in which the action is pending is particularly biased against defendant]

6. No prior application for the relief sought herein has been made.

WHEREFORE, defendant requests that this Court issue an order removing the trial of the indictment pending against him [her] in _____ County to the superior court of another county.

Dated: _____, 19__
_____, New York

[Signature]
_____
[Name of defense attorney]

Chapter 2

DOUBLE JEOPARDY

Table of Sections

2.1   Introduction.
2.2   Attachment of Jeopardy—In General.
2.3   Lack of Jurisdiction and "Procurement" Exceptions to Attachment of Jeopardy.
2.4   Nullified Proceedings—Mistrials, Hung Juries, Vacated Pleas, and Appellate Reversals.
2.5   "Same Offense" Constitutional Double Jeopardy.
2.6   "Same Criminal Transaction" Statutory Double Jeopardy.
2.7   Mandatory Joinder.
2.8   Collateral Estoppel.
2.9   Enterprise Corruption Double Jeopardy.
2.10 Miscellaneous Issues—Multiple Punishment, Civil Proceedings and Juvenile Proceedings.
2.11 Procedure for Raising a Double Jeopardy Claim.
2.12 Practice Summary.
2.13 Forms.
    2.13.1 Notice of Motion to Dismiss Accusatory Instrument on Ground That Prosecution Is Barred by Previous Prosecution.
    2.13.2 Affirmation in Support of Motion to Dismiss Accusatory Instrument on Ground That Prosecution Is Barred by Previous Prosecution.
    2.13.3 Petition in Article 78 Proceeding to Prohibit Prosecution on Ground That It Is Barred by Previous Prosecution.

WESTLAW Electronic Research

See WESTLAW Electronic Research Guide preceding the Summary of Contents.

§ 2.1 Introduction

Most people have heard the phrase "double jeopardy" and are at least vaguely aware that there is a constitutional guarantee that prevents a defendant from being tried twice for the same crime. In fact, the double jeopardy clause of the Fifth Amendment of the United States Constitution simply provides: "Nor shall any person be subject for the same offense to be twice put in jeopardy of life or limb." The provision is binding on the states via the Fourteenth Amendment.[1] As the Supreme Court has stated:

> The underlying idea, one that is deeply ingrained in at least the Anglo–American system of jurisprudence, is that the State with

---

1. Benton v. Maryland, 395 U.S. 784, 89 S.Ct. 2056, 23 L.Ed.2d 707 (1969).

all its resources and power should not be allowed to make repeated attempts to convict an individual for an alleged offense, thereby subjecting him to embarrassment, expense, and ordeal and compelling him to live in a continuing state of anxiety and insecurity, as well as enhancing the possibility that even though innocent he may be found guilty.[2]

The New York Constitution also provides that "no person shall be subject to be twice put in jeopardy for the same offense."[3] Further, Article 40 of the CPL sets forth a complex set of statutory double jeopardy principles designed to effectuate and, in many cases, exceed the constitutional protection. In addition, a few double jeopardy statutes applicable to narrow, specific situations are defined outside CPL Article 40.

Although the constitutional language is deceptively simple, the law in this area is not. Justice Rehnquist once noted that "[w]hile the Clause itself simply states that no person shall 'be subject for the same offense to be twice put in jeopardy of life or limb' the decisional law in the area is a veritable Saragasso Sea which could not fail to challenge the most intrepid judicial navigator."[4] Indeed, some commentators have called for wholesale revision and simplification.[5]

In attempting to chart a course through these murky depths, two general principles should always be kept in mind. First, in New York the law of double jeopardy emanates from two—or, more precisely, three—separate sources: the Constitutions, federal and state,[6] and the statutes. The latter are primarily contained in CPL Article 40, but bits and pieces can also be found in other places both within and outside of the CPL. Often, different rules of interpretation are applicable, and different substantive results will follow, depending on whether constitutional or statutory principles are being considered. In particular, as will be seen, in many instances the double jeopardy statutes were deliberately written to confer greater protection than the Constitutions require. Therefore, any given problem should always be considered from both the constitutional and statutory perspectives, and, when dealing with precedent, care should be taken to avoid assuming that a decision interpreting, for example, the federal Constitution, settles all of the ramifications

---

2. Green v. United States, 355 U.S. 184, 187–88, 78 S.Ct. 221, 223–24, 2 L.Ed.2d 199 (1957).

3. N.Y.Const., Article 1, § 6.

4. Albernaz v. United States, 450 U.S. 333, 343, 101 S.Ct. 1137, 1144, 67 L.Ed.2d 275 (1981).

5. See, e.g., Richardson, "Eliminating Double Talk from the Law of Double Jeopardy," 22 Fla. State Univ. Law Rev. 119 (1994).

6. While the New York Court of Appeals could interpret the state constitutional guarantee against double jeopardy in a different manner from the federal guarantee, as interpreted by the United States Supreme Court, so far this does not appear to have happened. See Preiser, "Practice Commentary" to CPL § 40.10, McKinney's Cons. Laws of N.Y., Book 11A, at 303 (1992)("[T]he New York Court of Appeals has not construed this state's constitutional counterpart as vouchsafing any broader protection than the federal requirement."). Accordingly, at least for the present, constitutional double jeopardy can be treated as a single issue rather than a bifurcated one.

of the issue.[7]

Second, when considering whether a given situation raises double jeopardy implications, it might be well to keep the underlying purposes of the protection in mind. Both the United States Supreme Court and the New York Court of Appeals have recognized that the prohibition against double jeopardy actually has three different purposes:

> It protects against a second prosecution for the same offense after acquittal. It protects against a second prosecution for the same offense after conviction. And it protects against multiple punishments for the same offense. Each "protection" serves different purposes and is surrounded by its own exceptions thereby complicating exposition of which rule attaches in different procedural situations.[8]

Library References:

West's Key No. Digests, Constitutional Law ⟜260; Double Jeopardy ⟜1–20.

§ 2.2 Attachment of Jeopardy—In General

"An accused must suffer jeopardy before he can suffer double jeopardy."[9] Initially, CPL § 40.30 establishes the general rule as to when jeopardy "attaches"—*i.e.*, when a prior proceeding has sufficiently advanced to constitute a "previous prosecution" that precludes another prosecution. The statute essentially duplicates the federal constitutional definition of a previous prosecution, which is binding on the states, and which replaced the previous New York definition.[10] It provides that a person "is prosecuted" for an offense when he or she is charged by an accusatory instrument filed in a court of this state or of any jurisdiction within the United States, and when that action either terminates in a conviction upon a plea of guilty, or proceeds to the trial stage and a jury has been impaneled and sworn or, in the case of a trial by the court without a jury, where a witness is sworn.[11]

In the context of a plea of guilty, jeopardy attaches when the accusatory instrument terminates in a conviction upon a plea of guilty. "Conviction" is defined to mean "the entry of a plea of guilty to, or a verdict of guilty upon, an accusatory instrument other than a felony

---

7. Particularly dangerous is reliance on a federal or other state case, which of course will usually make no mention of a New York statute that may compel an entirely opposite result. For example, although the federal Constitution does not bar a second prosecution in a federal court for conduct that has been the subject of a previous prosecution in a state court, as is discussed above, the CPL does bar New York from prosecuting an offense previously prosecuted in a federal court.

8. People v. Brown, 40 N.Y.2d 381, 386, 386 N.Y.S.2d 848, 851, 353 N.E.2d 811, 814 (1976)(citations omitted).

9. Matter of Lockett v. Juviler, 65 N.Y.2d 182, 187, 490 N.Y.S.2d 764, 768, 480 N.E.2d 378, 382 (1985), quoting Serfass v. United States, 420 U.S. 377, 393, 95 S.Ct. 1055, 1065, 43 L.Ed.2d 265 (1975).

10. See Matter of Chang v. Rotker, 155 A.D.2d 49, 55, 552 N.Y.S.2d 676, 679 (2d Dep't 1990) "Pursuant to the Double Jeopardy Clause of the New York State Constitution (N.Y. Const., Art. 1, § 6) which was controlling until [Benton v. Maryland, 395 U.S. 784, 89 S.Ct. 2056, 23 L.Ed.2d 707 (1969)] jeopardy did not 'attach' until after a jury was sworn and evidence was actually presented."

11. CPL § 40.30(1)(a) and (b).

complaint, or to one or more counts of such instrument."[12] Thus, literally it is "entry" of the guilty plea that constitutes the significant event for purposes of double jeopardy. Historically, "entry" was "frequently used as synonymous with 'recorded' in the law books."[13] However, in practice a court's acceptance of a defendant's proffered guilty plea is usually done on the record in open court, and promptly followed by the ministerial act of noting the plea in the court record. This routine should present few practical problems or ambiguities, and the acceptance of the plea on the record in open court should suffice to attach jeopardy.[14]

It should be noted that a "conviction" upon a plea of guilty is not synonymous with a "judgment." The latter "is comprised of a conviction and the sentence imposed thereon and is completed by imposition and entry of the sentence."[15] Accordingly, whether a person was sentenced upon a plea should make no difference for jeopardy purposes.[16]

An exception to the general rule concerning the double jeopardy effect of pleas of guilty is the special plea of not responsible by reason of mental disease or defect.[17] The Court of Appeals has held that acceptance of such a plea does not attach jeopardy, because it is not the functional equivalent of a conviction or acquittal on criminal charges, but rather subjects the defendant to a somewhat modified form of civil

---

12. CPL § 1.20(13).

13. Lent et al. v. N.Y. & M.R. Co., 130 N.Y. 504, 509, 29 N.E. 988, 989 (1892); see CPLR 5016(a)("A judgment is entered when, after it has been signed by the clerk, it is filed by him.").

14. However, at least one court has apparently held that "entry" and acceptance of the plea on the record are different events. People v. D'Amico, 147 Misc.2d 731, 556 N.Y.S.2d 456 (Sup.Ct., Suffolk County, 1990), aff'd 179 A.D.2d 671, 578 N.Y.S.2d 610 (2d Dep't 1992). The court, after approving defendant's plea allocution and accepting the plea on the record, withheld "entry" of the plea—which was apparently interpreted as separately recording the plea in the court file—at the defendant's request in order to avoid immediate mandatory incarceration. Following the death of a crucial witness prior to sentencing, the defendant sought a declaration that no plea had ever occurred. The court treated the application as a motion to withdraw the plea and denied it.

15. CPL § 1.20(15). See also Matter of Gunning v. Codd, 49 N.Y.2d 495, 427 N.Y.S.2d 209, 403 N.E.2d 1208 (1980)(history and evolution of the term "conviction" in the context of a forfeiture of public office following criminal conviction).

16. It should be noted that in Matter of Corbin v. Hillery, 74 N.Y.2d 279, 286–87, 545 N.Y.S.2d 71, 74, 543 N.E.2d 714, 717 (1989), aff'd 495 U.S. 508, 110 S.Ct. 2084, 109 L.Ed.2d 548 (1990)(later overruled by United States v. Dixon, 525 U.S. 688, 113 S.Ct. 2849, 125 L.Ed.2d 556 (1993)), the Court of Appeals stated, "[t]he District Attorney's office was represented at the sentencing, the final step in what CPL 40.30(1)(a) defines as a 'prior prosecution' for purposes of the statutory double jeopardy rules." Insofar as the court suggested that in a plea situation, jeopardy does not attach until sentencing, that is contradicted by (1) the plain meaning of the defined terms of the statutes involved; (2) comparison with CPL § 40.30(1)(b), which attaches jeopardy in trial situations at a point well before any potential sentence, and (3) the logical imperatives of the situation. Prior to sentencing, an accepted guilty plea is a "binding factual finding of the defendant's guilt." Matter of Lockett v. Juviler, 65 N.Y.2d 182, 187, 490 N.Y.S.2d 764, 768, 480 N.E.2d 378, 382 (1985). Absent a court's inability to keep a sentence promise or other unusual circumstances, it may not be withdrawn by a defendant. See, e.g., People v. Dixon, 29 N.Y.2d 55, 323 N.Y.S.2d 825, 272 N.E.2d 329 (1971); People v. Selikoff, 35 N.Y.2d 227, 360 N.Y.S.2d 623, 318 N.E.2d 784 (1974). Accordingly, it is an appropriate point for the attachment of jeopardy.

17. See CPL § 220.15.

§ 2.2   DOUBLE JEOPARDY   Ch. 2

commitment.[18]

In the case of a trial, jeopardy attaches when the proceeding advances to the trial stage and either a jury has been impaneled and sworn or, in a trial by the judge without a jury, when a witness is sworn.[19] In jury trials, jeopardy attaches once 12 jurors (6 in misdemeanor trials) have been sworn, regardless of whether the swearing is done individually or in groups. Moreover, jeopardy attaches as soon as a complete jury is sworn even though alternate jurors have not been selected or sworn.[20]

In non-jury trials, the crucial point occurs when a witness is sworn. Under prior law, in an era when jeopardy was said to attach in a trial only when "evidence is taken," it was held that the preliminary questioning of a child witness by the court to determine whether the child could be sworn did not advance the proceedings far enough to attach jeopardy.[21] It has also been held that a stipulation between the parties as to what certain witnesses would testify to if called is not the functional equivalent of swearing a witness.[22]

Under these rules, if a prior proceeding has not advanced to the entry of a guilty plea, the swearing of a jury, or the swearing of a witness in a non-jury trial, then jeopardy has not attached and the prior proceeding is not a previous prosecution that bars another prosecution. Thus, for example, multiple accusatory instruments charging the same offense may be filed in both state and federal court, without double jeopardy effect.[23]

It is essential to note that the New York statutory definition of a prior proceeding specifies one that has sufficiency advanced "in a court of this state *or of any jurisdiction within the United States.*"[24] This is a significant extension of double jeopardy protection beyond what is constitutionally required. For constitutional purposes, the Supreme Court has held that double jeopardy only precludes repeated prosecution by the same jurisdiction—the so-called "dual sovereignty" doctrine.[25] For example, federal prosecutions for acts that have been previously prosecuted

---

18. Matter of Lockett v. Juviler, 65 N.Y.2d 182, 187, 490 N.Y.S.2d 764, 480 N.E.2d 378, 382 (1985). ("Under the statute governing this special plea, there were only two options available to the court. First, the court could accept the plea, thus terminating the criminal proceedings and initiating the civil commitment proceedings.... Second, the court could reject the petitioner's plea offer and allow the criminal proceeding to continue in its normal course. In no event could the court make a binding factual finding of the defendant's guilt.")(citations omitted).

19. CPL § 40.30(1)(b).

20. People v. Innis, 182 A.D.2d 641, 642, 582 N.Y.S.2d 245, 246 (2d Dep't 1992).

21. People v. Pearl, 272 App.Div. 563, 74 N.Y.S.2d 108 (1st Dep't 1947).

22. People v. Gingello, 84 Misc.2d 63, 374 N.Y.S.2d 276 (Monroe Co.Ct.1975).

23. See Matter of Altman v. Bradley, 184 A.D.2d 131, 135, 591 N.Y.S.2d 403, 405 (1st Dep't 1992)("Although there is currently outstanding both a New York County indictment and a District of Columbia Federal indictment, each stemming from alleged[ly] [the same] criminal activity, petitioner has not been 'prosecuted' under the Federal indictment in this case, and accordingly jeopardy has not attached.").

24. CPL § 40.30(1)(emphasis supplied).

25. See, e.g., Heath v.Alabama, 474 U.S. 82, 106 S.Ct. 433, 88 L.Ed.2d 387 (1985); Bartkus v. Illinois, 359 U.S. 121, 79 S.Ct. 676, 3 L.Ed.2d 684 (1959).

in state courts are not prohibited by the constitutional guarantee, and do take place from time to time, although as a matter of federal policy they are not routine.[26] As a matter of statutory grace, however, New York prohibits subsequent prosecution in New York for acts that have been the subject of previous prosecutions in the courts of other states or the federal government, as well as those previously brought in New York. One practical consequence of this variance is that a case may be brought in a federal court even if the same charges have been previously prosecuted in a New York court, although the reverse is barred by the CPL. The Court of Appeals has held that a military court-martial proceeding is the equivalent of a federal district court within the meaning of New York's additional and broader statutory double jeopardy protection.[27]

Library References:

West's Key No. Digests, Double Jeopardy ⊜51–80.

§ 2.3 Lack of Jurisdiction and "Procurement" Exceptions to Attachment of Jeopardy

There are a number of exceptions to the general rule that a "previous prosecution" bars another. The first involves the absence of appropriate jurisdiction in the court in which the prior proceeding occurred.[28] The issue can arise in a number of ways. Initially, if the court in which the first prosecution was heard lacked geographical or subject matter jurisdiction, the exception will be applicable.[29] In addition, the case may have been removed from one court to another at a critical point. For example, in *People v. Brancoccio*,[30] the defendant pleaded guilty to a misdemeanor complaint in a local criminal court after the prosecutor had requested an adjournment to present the case to the grand jury, and after the grand jury had voted to indict but before the indictment was filed. The Court of Appeals held that the local criminal court had been divested of jurisdiction by operation of law and that prosecution under the indictment that replaced the misdemeanor complaint, which of course involved the same incident, was therefore not barred by double jeopardy. Finally, it should be remembered that "under New York law, if an accusatory instrument 'is so radically

---

26. Courts interpreting the constitutional doctrine have sometimes wrestled with the question of whether the two prosecuting jurisdictions are in fact "dual." Cf. United States v. Wheeler, 435 U.S. 313, 98 S.Ct. 1079, 55 L.Ed.2d 303 (1978)(previous prosecution in Navajo tribal court does not bar prosecution in federal district court) with Waller v. Florida, 397 U.S. 387, 90 S.Ct. 1184, 25 L.Ed.2d 435 (1970)(city and state of which it is a political subdivision may not bring successive prosecutions).

27. Booth v. Clary, 83 N.Y.2d 675, 613 N.Y.S.2d 110, 635 N.E.2d 279 (1994).

28. CPL § 40.30(2)(a).

29. See Steingut v. Gold, 54 A.D.2d 481, 485, 388 N.Y.S.2d 622, 625 (2d Dep't 1976), aff'd 42 N.Y.2d 311, 397 N.Y.S.2d 765, 366 N.E.2d 854 (1977)("a defendant who either was convicted or acquitted in a court which lacked geographical jurisdiction over him, or over the offense charged, may be retried in another forum without the constitutional or statutory ban against double jeopardy being violated").

30. 83 N.Y.2d 638, 612 N.Y.S.2d 353, 634 N.E.2d 954 (1994).

defective that it would not support a judgment of conviction,' jeopardy never attaches under the instrument, and retrial upon correction of the defect is not barred."[31]

The second exception applies where a prosecution for a lesser offense is "procured by the defendant, without the knowledge of the appropriate prosecutor, for the purpose of avoiding prosecution for a greater offense."[32] The statute has not been liberally interpreted. The prime illustration is *Matter of Corbin v. Hillery*.[33] The defendant was involved in a traffic fatality, and was served with two traffic tickets returnable in a town court charging him with driving while intoxicated and driving on the wrong side of the road. Through a mix-up, prosecutorial paperwork on the traffic offenses did not mention the fatality. Appearing with an attorney on the return date of the tickets, on a night when the district attorney was not present in the town court, the defendant, after advising the court simply that he had been in "contact" with the prosecutor's office, pleaded guilty to the traffic offenses without mentioning the fatality. He was ultimately sentenced to pay a fine, and his driver's license was revoked for six months. Subsequently, when a grand jury indicted the defendant for homicide, he sought to dismiss the indictment on the basis of double jeopardy, and the prosecution countered with the procurement exception.

The Court of Appeals held that the statutory exception was not applicable. According to the court, the primary situation that the exception was intended to reach occurs when a defendant or attorney, before the District Attorney has entered the picture, induces a local criminal court to accept a guilty plea and enter a conviction for a relatively minor offense as a means of foreclosing the possibility of a prosecution for a more serious offense in superior court. In such a situation, because the responsible prosecutorial authority does not have an opportunity to be heard or to apprise the court of the aggravating factors before a conviction for a minor offense is entered, the court reasoned that it makes sense to withhold double jeopardy protection. Here, however, because the District Attorney's office was said to have actively participated in the traffic infraction prosecution by filing paperwork, the court ruled that the requirement that the prosecution be procured without the knowledge of the appropriate prosecutor was not met. The court also noted that although the defendant's counsel was "less than forthcoming" with the town court,[34] even evasive engineering of the town prosecution by the defendant might not be enough to satisfy the terms of the statute.

31. People v. Key, 45 N.Y.2d 111, 117, 408 N.Y.S.2d 16, 20, 379 N.E.2d 1147, 1150 (1978)(citations omitted).

32. CPL § 40.30(2)(b).

33. 74 N.Y.2d 279, 545 N.Y.S.2d 71, 543 N.E.2d 714 (1989), aff'd 495 U.S. 508, 110 S.Ct. 2084, 109 L.Ed.2d 548 (1990). The Supreme Court subsequently overruled its decision in this case in United States v. Dixon, 525 U.S. 688, 113 S.Ct. 2849, 125 L.Ed.2d 556 (1993). Of course, only that part of the Court of Appeals decision which deals with the federal Constitution was affected by the Supreme Court action.

34. 74 N.Y.2d at 287 n.6, 545 N.Y.S.2d at 75 n.6.

Other interpretations of the exception have been similarly strict.[35] Given this rather stringent construction, it is evident that the threshold question in such situations is whether the District Attorney of the appropriate jurisdiction has "entered the picture," or perhaps even had an opportunity to do so—a factor presumably to be assessed in the light of local practice and administrative arrangements, as well as time and place. If the prosecutor has in any way been involved with the case, then the statute ordinarily will not be applied to release the state from the double jeopardy bar to further prosecution, absent some sort of "procurement" involving an active misrepresentation by the defendant.[36] On the other hand, if the prosecutor has not actually entered the picture, then any manipulative behavior by the defense, particularly where it is aimed at advancing the case to avoid prosecutorial involvement, should be given greater weight. However, even if the prosecutor remains entirely ignorant of the proceedings on the lesser offense, it appears that a careful defendant who avoids affirmative manipulation and simply does not volunteer detrimental information may well be outside the reach of the statutory exception.

Library References:
West's Key No. Digests, Double Jeopardy ⟐52, 53, 165–168.

§ 2.4 Nullified Proceedings—Mistrials, Hung Juries, Vacated Pleas, and Appellate Reversals

Other statutory subdivisions, which do no more than repeat a basic constitutional principle, establish that a criminal proceeding that has advanced beyond the point where jeopardy has attached nevertheless does not constitute a bar to further proceedings if the original proceeding is nullified by a mistrial, the inability of a jury to reach a verdict, a trial order of dismissal, the vacation of a plea, the granting of a post-judgment motion to vacate a conviction, or appellate reversal. One subdivision speaks of retrial "under the same accusatory instrument," while another is applicable when the court that "nullifies" the former proceedings authorizes a new accusatory instrument.[37] Although these statutes lack any qualifying language and speak only of nullification in the blanket sense, constitutional precedent in this area is not so simple; accordingly, the rules governing these various situations are in reality established by the case law and not the bare language of the statute.

---

35. See, e.g., People v. Claud, 181 A.D.2d 830, 581 N.Y.S.2d 387 (2d Dep't 1992)(the prosecutor's "alleged ignorance of the Town Code prosecution was apparently caused by a lack of coordination between the District Attorney and the Town Attorney, and not by any affirmative act or misrepresentation on the part of the defendant"); People v. Snyder, 99 A.D.2d 83, 471 N.Y.S.2d 430 (4th Dep't 1984)("Arguably in this case the defendant chose to enter his plea at a time when he was aware [that he faced felony charges; however] the record does not establish that defendant made any misrepresentation to the arresting officer or did anything to induce that officer to charge him with the misdemeanor offense only.").

36. See, e.g., People v. Dishaw, 54 A.D.2d 1122, 388 N.Y.S.2d 795 (4th Dep't 1976)(where defense attorney made "affirmative representations to the Assistant District Attorney in Traffic Court that his [misdemeanor] plea had been specifically authorized by a senior assistant," statutory exception applies, and felony prosecution may proceed).

37. CPL § 40.30(3) and (4).

§ 2.4 DOUBLE JEOPARDY Ch. 2

Perhaps the most problematic and frequently encountered situation is the mistrial. This occurs when a criminal trial is terminated by the court, usually at a point following the attachment of jeopardy.[38] The application of double jeopardy to mistrials has generated a large, and complex, body of litigation. In broad outline, several basic rules have emerged. Initially, "if the defendant waives his double jeopardy protection ... by moving for a mistrial, retrial is generally not barred, regardless of whether there was manifest necessity for the mistrial."[39] The rule applies whether the defendant requests the motion or consents to a mistrial motion made by another party. However, a rarely applied exception to the rule exists, for double jeopardy will preclude further prosecution if judicial or prosecutorial conduct giving rise to the successful motion for a mistrial was intended to provoke the defendant into moving for a mistrial.[40] It should be noted that this exception requires a showing of specific intent on the part of the prosecutor or the court to provoke a defense mistrial motion, not merely intentional erroneous prosecutorial or judicial conduct that led the defendant to move for a mistrial. The standard is therefore very high, and findings that further proceedings are barred by double jeopardy are accordingly few and far between.[41]

38. This occurs after a jury has been sworn or, in a non-jury trial, after a witness is sworn. CPL § 40.30(1)(b). It is possible to have a mistrial before jeopardy has attached. In that situation, it has been held that "while the jury selection process is under way, and before double jeopardy attaches, the court should apply the alternative test ... and may declare a mistrial where, under all of the circumstances, the ends of public justice would otherwise be defeated." Brackley v. Donnelly, 53 A.D.2d 849, 850, 385 N.Y.S.2d 587, 588 (2d Dep't 1976); accord People v. Albarez, 209 A.D.2d 186, 618 N.Y.S.2d 528 (1st Dep't 1994); People v. Singh, 190 A.D.2d 640, 594 N.Y.S.2d 165 (1st Dep't 1993). However, because jeopardy has not attached, an erroneous grant of a mistrial at such a stage appears to have no consequences.

39. People v. Catten, 69 N.Y.2d 547, 554, 516 N.Y.S.2d 186, 190, 508 N.E.2d 920, 924 (1987)(citations omitted). CPL § 280.10(1) establishes the statutory standard for mistrials at the request of the defendant. Under that provision, the motion should be granted: "when there occurs during the trial an error or legal defect in the proceedings, or conduct inside or outside the courtroom, which is prejudicial to the defendant and deprives him of a fair trial. When such an error, defect or conduct occurs during a joint trial of two or more defendants and a mistrial motion is made by one or more but not all, the court must declare a mistrial only as to the defendant or defendants making or joining in the motion, and the trial of the other defendant or defendants must proceed." Improper denial of a defense mistrial motion may lead to appellate reversal and retrial, but will not bar further proceedings.

40. See Oregon v. Kennedy, 456 U.S. 667, 679, 102 S.Ct. 2083, 2091, 72 L.Ed.2d 416 (1982). However, in People v. Adames, 83 N.Y.2d 89, 90–91, 607 N.Y.S.2d 919, 920–21, 629 N.E.2d 391, 392–93 (1993), the Court of Appeals dealt with a case that had taken an "unusual procedural path." The trial court had reserved decision on a defense mistrial motion based on prosecutorial misconduct, accepted the jury's verdict of guilt, and then granted the mistrial motion. Rejecting a claim that further proceedings were barred by double jeopardy, the court noted that "[t]he corrective action for prosecutorial misconduct should ordinarily not vary whether the verdict is nullified by a trial or an appellate court. [The usual relief is a new trial]. Some prosecutorial error may be so egregious or provocative as to warrant the interposition of the double jeopardy bar, even when no mistrial is granted, but that is not this case." The court, which has not hesitated to depart from settled double jeopardy analysis in unusual cases (see note 72, infra, and accompanying text), may be suggesting something broader than the Oregon v. Kennedy rule.

41. See, e.g., People v. Copeland, 127 A.D.2d 846, 847, 511 N.Y.S.2d 949, 949 (2d Dep't, 1987)("However, while in acting contrary to the [trial] court's warnings, the prosecutor may well have been acting inten-

Several other aspects of the defense mistrial motion deserve a brief mention. The motion should be made on the record by the defense attorney—the defendant need not consent, or even be present—and the position of the parties should be clearly set forth,[42] although courts have occasionally been willing to construe ambiguous defense statements as sufficient in this regard.[43] In addition, a defense motion for a mistrial, once granted, may not be withdrawn as a matter of right, but the same motion, once denied, cannot thereafter be granted "on consent" so as to defeat a claim of double jeopardy.[44] Finally, it has been held that a mere declaration of a mistrial by the court, immediately rescinded and unaccompanied by the actual discharge of the jury or the entry of the mistrial order, is not effective.[45]

Absent consent by the defense, the granting of a mistrial motion made by the prosecutor, or the court's sua sponte ordering of a mistrial, involves both statutory and constitutional considerations. As to the former, CPL § 280.10 sets forth the standard for when such motions should be granted.[46]

As to the relation between non-consensual mistrials and double jeopardy, the standard is well-known: double jeopardy will not bar further proceedings when there is a "manifest necessity" for the mistrial or "the ends of public justice would otherwise be defeated."[47] However,

---

tionally, the evidence does not support the inference that his intent was to provoke a motion for a mistrial. Absent such a bad-faith intent, the misconduct does not constitute that type of prosecutorial overreaching contemplated by the United States Supreme Court as requiring the barring of reprosecution on the ground of double jeopardy."). See also People v. Medina, 208 A.D.2d 771, 617 N.Y.S.2d 491 (2d Dep't 1994); People v. Robinson, 199 A.D.2d 345, 606 N.Y.S.2d 998 (2d Dep't 1993) (rejecting double jeopardy claim).

42. See People v. Ferguson, 67 N.Y.2d 383, 502 N.Y.S.2d 972, 494 N.E.2d 77 (1986).

43. See, e.g., People v. Ferguson, supra (finding implied consent by defense counsel in an off-the-record conference); Harris v. Justices of Supreme Court, 44 N.Y.2d 874, 875, 407 N.Y.S.2d 478, 479, 378 N.E.2d 1048, 1048 (1978)(finding consent where, after making frequent mistrial requests, defense counsel, asked if he was joining in mistrial application of counsel for co-defendant, replied that "I stand on the record"); People v. Michallow, 201 A.D.2d 915, 916, 607 N.Y.S.2d 781, 783 (4th Dep't 1994)(finding consent due to defendant's "active participation" with the court and failure to object to the court's sua sponte mistrial).

44. People v. Catten, 69 N.Y.2d 547, 516 N.Y.S.2d 186, 508 N.E.2d 920 (1987).

45. People v. Rodriquez, 39 N.Y.2d 976, 387 N.Y.S.2d 110, 354 N.E.2d 850 (1976); see also People v. Dawkins, 82 N.Y.2d 226, 604 N.Y.S.2d 34, 624 N.E.2d 162 (1993)(mistrial declared because of deadlocked jury is not effective until discharge).

46. CPL § 280.10(2) requires a mistrial when:

Upon motion of the people ... there occurs during the trial, either inside or outside of the courtroom, gross misconduct by the defendant or some person acting on his behalf, or by a juror, resulting in substantial and irreparable prejudice to the people's case. When such misconduct occurs during a joint trial of two or more defendants, and when the court is satisfied that it did not result in substantial prejudice to the people's case as against a particular defendant and that such defendant was in no way responsible for the misconduct, it may not declare a mistrial with respect to such defendant but must proceed with the trial as to him.

CPL § 280.10(3) requires a mistrial when:

Upon motion of either party or upon the court's own motion ... it is physically impossible to proceed with the trial in conformity with law.

47. See, e.g., People v. Michael, 48 N.Y.2d 1, 9, 420 N.Y.S.2d 371, 375, 394 N.E.2d 1134, 1138 (1979).

§ 2.4　　　　　　　　DOUBLE JEOPARDY　　　　　　　　Ch. 2

the Court of Appeals has observed that "[t]hough well settled, the rules relating to manifest necessity are not always easy of application."[48] This is something of an understatement. Although there are many such cases, a few examples help to illustrate the variety of contexts in which the issue may arise. In the following situations, manifest necessity for the declaration of a mistrial was found to exist, defeating an argument that further proceedings were barred by double jeopardy: where, in the course of opening remarks, the prosecutor referred to a confession that was thereafter suppressed;[49] when an essential defense witness became unavailable, even though the defendant sought only a continuance, not a mistrial;[50] where one juror disappeared overnight and thereafter indicated that he could not be fair;[51] where a prosecution witness was unexpectedly hospitalized;[52] and where it was discovered that defense counsel had been suspended from the practice of law.[53]

By contrast, in the following examples, manifest necessity for a mistrial was held to be lacking, and therefore further proceedings were barred by double jeopardy: where a juror informed the court that defendant had spoken to her during jury selection but that she could still be fair, and the mistrial was granted without further inquiry;[54] where a relative of a prosecution witness died, allegedly causing the witness to become unavailable;[55] where a relative of the defense attorney died, but the court *sua sponte* declared a mistrial without the defendant's consent;[56] and where the trial judge, over objection in a non-jury trial, sought to recuse himself on the grounds of a tenuous potential conflict of interest.[57]

Special mention should be made of one frequently occurring mistrial scenario—the "hung" or "deadlocked" jury. Here, a separate statute[58]

---

48. Matter of Enright v. Siedlecki, 59 N.Y.2d 195, 201, 464 N.Y.S.2d 418, 422, 451 N.E.2d 176, 180 (1983).

49. Id.

50. Matter of Huntzinger v. Siedlecki, 59 N.Y.2d 195, 199, 464 N.Y.S.2d 418, 421, 451 N.E.2d 176, 179 (1983)(reported with Matter of Enright v. Siedlecki, supra.)

51. People v. Tinsley, 58 N.Y.2d 990, 461 N.Y.S.2d 1005, 448 N.E.2d 790 (1983).

52. Hall v. Potoker, 49 N.Y.2d 501, 427 N.Y.S.2d 211, 403 N.E.2d 1210 (1980). Witness illness is one of the more common mistrial scenarios. See, e.g., Atkinson v. Barone, 200 A.D.2d 438, 607 N.Y.S.2d 244 (1st Dep't 1994); Collins v. Quinones, 200 A.D.2d 569, 606 N.Y.S.2d 306 (2d Dep't 1994); People v. Allen, 204 A.D.2d 973, 614 N.Y.S.2d 949 (4th Dep't 1994).

53. People v. Anderson, 186 A.D.2d 140, 587 N.Y.S.2d 430 (2d Dep't).

54. Matter of Ziegler v. Morgenthau, 64 N.Y.2d 932, 488 N.Y.S.2d 633, 477 N.E.2d 1087 (1985).

55. Respeto v. McNab, 60 N.Y.2d 739, 469 N.Y.S.2d 695, 457 N.E.2d 802 (1983).

56. People v. Michael, 48 N.Y.2d 1, 420 N.Y.S.2d 371, 394 N.E.2d 1134 (1979).

57. Ferlito v. Judges of County Court, 31 N.Y.2d 416, 340 N.Y.S.2d 635, 292 N.E.2d 779 (1972).

58. As discussed, CPL § 280.10 is the primary statute governing mistrials in general (see also CPL § 270.35, governing the discharge of a sworn juror for illness or incapacity). However, in the case of deadlocked juries, CPL § 310.60 governs. The statute allows a deliberating jury to be discharged without reaching a verdict only when:

(a) The jury has deliberated for an excessive period of time without agreeing upon a verdict with respect to any of the charges submitted and the court is satisfied that any such agreement is unlikely within a reasonable time; or

(b) The court, the defendant and the people all consent to such discharge; or

(c) A mistrial is declared pursuant to section 280.10.

Although for double jeopardy purposes all of these statutes are subject to the constitu-

sets forth a standard that is also the subject of an extensive body of case law on the question of when "manifest necessity" exists to permit the discharge of a deliberating jury. There is no specific required minimum period of deliberations or other mechanical "bright line" test. Rather, the Court of Appeals has enumerated a number of "identifiable factors which are helpful." These include "the length and complexity of the trial, the length of the deliberations, the extent and nature of the communications between the court and the jury, and the potential effects of requiring further deliberation."[59] Generally, considerable deference is paid to the judgment of the trial court in this area. Manifest necessity has been found where the trial court discharged a jury that had declared itself, for the first time, hopelessly deadlocked after five hours of deliberation in a routine case;[60] where a jury repeatedly expressed an inability to reach a verdict after about six hours of deliberation in a vehicular homicide;[61] and where a juror had a psychiatric episode after several days of deliberations.[62] On the other hand, it has been held improper to discharge a jury that had intermittently deliberated for about twelve hours, in a case involving "serious discrepancies" among witnesses, without a proper indication from the jury that it was hopelessly deadlocked.[63]

A number of related problems should be noted. First, there are serious constitutional flaws in the statutes governing the status of an accusatory instrument at a retrial following the declaration of a mistrial. These statutes[64] purport to authorize a retrial of either the entire indictment, or the entire indictment less those counts that were deemed to have resulted in an acquittal or were dismissed pursuant to a motion for a trial order of dismissal.[65] As the Court of Appeals has recognized, this authorization does not comport with the Constitution. In *People v. Mayo*,[66] the defendant, at the close of trial, moved to dismiss the sole count of the indictment (robbery in the first degree) on the basis of insufficient evidence. The trial court agreed, but submitted lesser

tional requirement of "manifest necessity," the differences among them were accorded some significance by the Court of Appeals in People v. Dawson, 50 N.Y.2d 311, 428 N.Y.S.2d 914, 406 N.E.2d 771 (1980), on the question of when a court's declaration of mistrial becomes effective.

59. Matter of Plummer v. Rothwax, 63 N.Y.2d 243, 481 N.Y.S.2d 657, 471 N.E.2d 429 (1984).

60. Id.

61. Matter of Owen v. Stroebel, 65 N.Y.2d 658, 491 N.Y.S.2d 611, 481 N.E.2d 243 (1985).

62. Hameed v. Jones, 750 F.2d 154 (2d Cir.1984).

63. People v. Baptiste, 72 N.Y.2d 356, 533 N.Y.S.2d 853, 530 N.E.2d 377 (1988).

64. CPL §§ 280.20, 310.60. Section 280.20, entitled "Motion for mistrial; status of indictment upon new trial," provides:

Upon a new trial resulting from an order declaring a mistrial, the indictment is deemed to contain all the counts which it contained at the time the previous trial was commenced, regardless of whether any count was thereafter dismissed by the court prior to the mistrial order.

Section 310.60, governing discharge of jury before rendition of verdict and the effect thereof, essentially provides that when the jury is so discharged, the defendant may be retried upon an indictment that is deemed to contain all counts that it originally contained, except those that were dismissed pursuant to a motion for a trial order of dismissal or were deemed to have resulted in an acquittal.

65. See CPL § 290.10.

66. 48 N.Y.2d 245, 422 N.Y.S.2d 361, 397 N.E.2d 1166 (1979).

robbery charges to the jury, which then deadlocked. On the retrial, rather than obtaining a new indictment on the lesser charges, the prosecution, pursuant to CPL § 310.60(2), chose to proceed on the original indictment, which charged the dismissed count. The trial judge again submitted only the lesser charges, upon which the defendant was found guilty. The Court of Appeals reversed the conviction, however, holding that the retrial on the original indictment violated the prohibition against double jeopardy.[67]

A related problem involves the "partial verdict"—that is, a verdict on some, but not all, of the submitted offenses and a mistrial as to others. A partial verdict can occur when the jury announces agreement upon some of the submitted offenses but a deadlock as to others. Acceptance of partial verdicts is a relatively rare event in practice. Initially, the statute that governs the procedure[68] is confusing and a failure to follow it closely and to clearly establish the "manifest necessity" for the mistrial on the unresolved counts can lead to a jeopardy preclusion of further proceedings.[69] Beyond that, re-prosecution on the unresolved counts is precluded if a conviction on those counts would be inconsistent with a verdict actually rendered on a resolved count, or where conviction on the unresolved count would not increase the sentence.[70] Those determinations involve areas of law that are themselves complex, and accordingly re-prosecution after acceptance of a partial verdict frequently is more problematical than it first appears.[71]

Finally, with regard to mistrials, the extraordinary case of *Matter of Randall v. Rothwax*,[72] must be mentioned. The defendant was tried for attempted murder and related charges. After eight hours of deliberations, and after the jury had been sent back for further deliberations, the trial court informed defense counsel that the jury was divided 10–2 for conviction when, as it later turned out, the jury actually was deadlocked

---

67. The court did opine that the defendant could have been properly brought to trial on a new indictment charging only the lesser counts.

68. CPL § 310.70. The statute also allows a court to accept a "partial verdict" when the jury is deadlocked as between defendants.

69. Cf. Oliver v. Justices, 36 N.Y.2d 53, 364 N.Y.S.2d 874, 324 N.E.2d 348 (1974)(acceptance of partial verdict and declaration of mistrial under ambiguous circumstances does not create jeopardy bar) with Matter of Guido v. Berkman, 116 A.D.2d 439, 501 N.Y.S.2d 827 (1st Dep't 1986)(opposite result under other circumstances).

70. CPL § 310.70(2), which governs re-prosecution of the "deadlocked counts," provides that a defendant may be retried for any submitted offense upon which the jury was unable to agree unless:

(a) A verdict of conviction thereon would have been inconsistent with a verdict, of either conviction or acquittal, actually rendered with respect to some other offense, or

(b) The submitted offense which was the subject of the disagreement, and some other submitted offense of higher or equal grade which was the subject of a verdict of conviction, were so related that consecutive sentences thereon could not have been imposed upon a defendant convicted of both offenses.

71. See, e.g., People v. Walsh, 44 N.Y.2d 631, 635, 407 N.Y.S.2d 472, 473, 378 N.E.2d 1041, 1043 (1978)(no retrial where all of the counts of the indictment "relate to one inseparable event," and therefore, under prior statutory standard [amended L. 1974, c. 762], consecutive sentence could not be imposed on conviction for unresolved charge).

72. 78 N.Y.2d 494, 577 N.Y.S.2d 211, 583 N.E.2d 924 (1991).

10–2 for acquittal. The judge suggested a guilty plea, and ultimately accepted an *Alford* plea.[73] Later, when the error was discovered, the court allowed the defendant to withdraw the plea. The Court of Appeals, however, admitting that while "[t]he unusual developments in this case do not lend themselves to neat categorization within double jeopardy parlance or principles,"[74] found that the trial court's inducement of the guilty plea so completely deprived defendant of the option to take his chances with the particular jury that the termination of his trial while the jury was deliberating his fate was the legal equivalent of an acquittal. Although this case does support the notion that, even in an area as technical as double jeopardy, courts may sometimes be willing to defy principles of strict analysis to reach what is perceived as a just result, the decision is most likely *sui generis*.[75]

Another form of court order that nullifies part or all of a criminal proceeding at a point after jeopardy has attached is the trial order of dismissal. The governing statute allows the trial court to dismiss "any count of an indictment upon the ground that the trial evidence is not legally sufficient to establish the offense charged therein or any lesser offense."[76] If the dismissal occurs during the trial, it will be viewed as the functional equivalent of an acquittal for jeopardy purposes.[77] Thus, the statute, amended in the wake of a suggestion by the Court of Appeals, now allows the trial court to reserve decision on the trial order of dismissal until after the jury renders a verdict. This avoids a jeopardy bar to the prosecution's right to appeal.[78]

---

73. North Carolina v. Alford, 400 U.S. 25, 91 S.Ct. 160, 27 L.Ed.2d 162 (1970), allows a defendant to plead guilty without admitting guilt.

74. 78 N.Y.2d at 495, 577 N.Y.S.2d at 212.

75. Another, perhaps preferable, procedural route to the same result in such an extraordinary situation might have been a motion to dismiss the accusatory instrument on the basis of a deprivation of fundamental fairness and due process. See, e.g., People v. Isaacson, 44 N.Y.2d 511, 406 N.Y.S.2d 714, 378 N.E.2d 78 (1978).

76. CPL § 290.10(1).

77. People v. Fields, 45 N.Y.2d 986, 413 N.Y.S.2d 112, 385 N.E.2d 1040 (1978); People v. Brown, 40 N.Y.2d 381, 386 N.Y.S.2d 848, 353 N.E.2d 811 (1976); People v. Consolazio, 40 N.Y.2d 446, 387 N.Y.S.2d 62, 354 N.E.2d 801 (1976); People v. Baker, 39 N.Y.2d 923, 386 N.Y.S.2d 575, 352 N.E.2d 879 (1976). These decisions came in the wake of a series of United States Supreme Court decisions defining various forms of intra-trial determinations by the court, based upon the evidence presented at trial, as functionally equivalent to acquittal for jeopardy purposes. See People v. Key, 45 N.Y.2d 111, 117, 408 N.Y.S.2d 16, 20, 379 N.E.2d 1147, 1150 (1978); People v. Kurtz, 51 N.Y.2d 380, 434 N.Y.S.2d 200, 414 N.E.2d 699 (1980) for the history of this complex litigation. Parenthetically, since Key and Kurtz, the Supreme Court precedent has continued to evolve. See, e.g., Smalis v. Pennsylvania, 476 U.S. 140, 106 S.Ct. 1745, 90 L.Ed.2d 116 (1986)("demurrer" as functional acquittal).

78. The suggestion was made in People v. Key, 45 N.Y.2d 111, 120, 408 N.Y.S.2d 16, 22, 379 N.E.2d 1147, 1152 (1978). CPL § 450.20(2) allows the prosecution to appeal the trial court's order of dismissal if the order is entered after a guilty verdict. This procedure is not barred by double jeopardy. People v. Leach, 46 N.Y.2d 821, 414 N.Y.S.2d 121, 386 N.E.2d 1088 (1978). One commentator has noted the continued existence of one remaining unsettled—and esoteric—question, concerning the constitutional viability of a prosecutorial appeal from an intra-trial order of dismissal where the claim is made that the court improperly excluded evidence from the trial, rendering the remainder insufficient. Preiser, "Practice Commentary" to CPL § 450.20, McKinney's Cons. Laws of N.Y., Book 11A, at 702–03 (1994). Cf. Lockhart v. Nelson, 488 U.S. 33, 109 S.Ct. 285, 102 L.Ed.2d 265 (1988)(double jeopardy clause does not bar retrial where reviewing court determines that a defendant's conviction must be reversed, because absent erroneously admit-

Where a court, after initially granting a motion to dismiss, reconsiders that ruling, and, at a time when the proceeding was still pending, vacates its earlier decision, the court's original decision has been held not to be the equivalent of an acquittal for the purposes of double jeopardy.[79]

Although a trial order of dismissal, which is based on the court's view of the evidence presented at the trial, may be the functional equivalent of an acquittal for jeopardy purposes, the same is not true of other kinds of intra-trial dismissals. Thus, the granting of a defense motion to dismiss the accusatory instrument on the basis of facial insufficiency, made during the trial, is no bar to re-prosecution,[80] and neither is a dismissal based on a defense motion addressed to the insufficiency of the prosecutor's opening remarks.[81]

Of course, a withdrawn or vacated guilty plea cannot serve as a "previous prosecution" for double jeopardy purposes. However, if the plea is not voided at the instigation of the defendant, and the court lacks the power to vacate it, subsequent proceedings may be barred.[82] Moreover, when the initial proceeding is nullified by a court order that restores the case to its pre-pleading status, jeopardy does not bar further prosecution "under the same accusatory instrument."[83] In *People v. Maye*,[84] a case was presented to the grand jury on a murder theory, but the resulting indictment charged manslaughter. The defendant then pleaded guilty to the manslaughter charge, but successfully appealed the conviction. Thereafter, the prosecution, on the basis of newly discovered evidence, presented the case to another grand jury, which indicted for murder. The resulting trial under the new accusatory instrument led to a murder conviction, which, however, was held to be barred by double jeopardy. Of course, had the defendant originally been indicted for murder and then pleaded to manslaughter, he could have been tried for murder, on the original accusatory instrument, following the appellate nullification.

Certain permutations of the appellate review of convictions also implicate double jeopardy. To begin, the general rule is that the

---

ted evidence, remainder was insufficient to support charges).

79. In re Lionel F., 76 N.Y.2d 747, 559 N.Y.S.2d 228, 558 N.E.2d 30 (1990).

80. People v. Key, 45 N.Y.2d 111, 408 N.Y.S.2d 16, 379 N.E.2d 1147 (1978).

81. People v. Kurtz, 51 N.Y.2d 380, 387, 434 N.Y.S.2d 200, 204, 414 N.E.2d 699, 704 (1980)(court careful to note, however, that some types of prosecutorial opening remarks, such as concessions on key facts, might lead to the opposite result).

82. See Matter of Kisloff v. Covington, 73 N.Y.2d 445, 449, 541 N.Y.S.2d 737, 739, 539 N.E.2d 565, 567 (1989)("[W]here a court has the power to vacate the plea and restore the action to its pre-pleading status, further proceedings under the same accusatory instrument would not be barred.... Because Supreme Court had neither statutory nor inherent power to vacate the plea and sentence in the circumstances of this case, however ... further prosecution on this indictment is barred.") (citations omitted). Accord Matter of Campbell v. Pesce, 60 N.Y.2d 165, 468 N.Y.S.2d 865, 456 N.E.2d 806 (1983); People v. Moquin, 77 N.Y.2d 449, 568 N.Y.S.2d 710, 570 N.E.2d 1059 (1991); Cf. People v. Bartley, 47 N.Y.2d 965, 419 N.Y.S.2d 956, 393 N.E.2d 1029 (1979)(plea may be vacated by trial court before imposition of sentence).

83. CPL § 40.30(3).

84. 79 N.Y.2d 1041, 584 N.Y.S.2d 1011, 596 N.E.2d 409 (1992).

ordinary appellate reversal on the basis of non-harmless trial error does not bar a retrial on the same charges.[85] New York statutes generally reflect this principle.[86] However, where the appellate court reverses the judgment on the basis of evidentiary insufficiency—that is, where the court finds that there was legally insufficient evidence[87] adduced at trial to support the charged offenses—retrial is barred, both by statute[88] and constitutional interpretation.[89] The premise here is that the prosecution should be given only one fair opportunity to offer whatever proof of guilt that it can assemble. Additionally, New York statutes also require dismissal of the accusatory instrument, and not a retrial, when the basis of the appellate reversal is that the guilty verdict was against the weight of the evidence.[90] This is not constitutionally required.[91]

Although CPL § 470.55—which purports to regulate the status of the accusatory instrument upon retrial following appellate reversal of a judgment of conviction—literally allows a retrial of all the counts contained in the accusatory instrument at the commencement of the trial (except for those upon which the defendant was acquitted, deemed to have been acquitted, or which were dismissed on appeal), the statute is subject to the previously-discussed rule of *People v. Mayo*.[92] Thus, if a defendant is convicted of a lesser included offense, retrial on the original indictment containing the greater offense is precluded.

Library References:

West's Key No. Digests, Double Jeopardy ⇐86–99, 107–109.

§ 2.5 "Same Offense" Constitutional Double Jeopardy

Once there has been a "previous prosecution," the next question is whether that previous prosecution bars a second prosecution. The answer can be found in several places. First, the New York statutes essentially codify the federal constitutional standard.[93] Thereafter, those statutes also establish a separate statutory double jeopardy protection[94] and a rule of mandatory joinder[95] that, taken together, confer considerably broader protection than the federal Constitution requires. Finally,

---

85. See, e.g., United States v. Tateo, 377 U.S. 463, 84 S.Ct. 1587, 12 L.Ed.2d 448 (1964).

86. CPL § 470.20(1)(appellate court reversing for trial error must direct new trial).

87. See CPL § 70.10(1)(defining "legally sufficient evidence").

88. CPL § 470.20(2) and (3)(requiring dismissal of accusatory instrument or individual counts of accusatory instrument where appellate court finds insufficient trial evidence).

89. Burks v. United States, 437 U.S. 1, 98 S.Ct. 2141, 57 L.Ed.2d 1 (1978). Cf. Lockhart v. Nelson, 488 U.S. 33, 109 S.Ct. 285, 102 L.Ed.2d 265 (1988)(double jeopardy clause does not bar retrial where reviewing court determines that a defendant's conviction must be reversed because absent erroneously admitted evidence, remainder was insufficient to support charges).

90. CPL § 470.20(5). See People v. Bleakley, 69 N.Y.2d 490, 515 N.Y.S.2d 761, 508 N.E.2d 672 (1987)(difference between "weight" and "sufficiency" of evidence and history of provision discussed).

91. See Tibbs v. Florida, 457 U.S. 31, 102 S.Ct. 2211, 72 L.Ed.2d 652 (1982).

92. 48 N.Y.2d 245, 422 N.Y.S.2d 361, 397 N.E.2d 1166 (1979).

93. CPL §§ 40.10(1), 40.20(1).

94. CPL §§ 40.10(2), 40.20(2).

95. CPL § 40.40.

§ 2.5 DOUBLE JEOPARDY Ch. 2

returning to the constitutional arena, the double jeopardy-related doctrine of collateral estoppel must also be considered.

The "same offense" provisions[96] essentially subsume the federal constitutional rule, which is known colloquially as the "Blockburger"[97] test. The Supreme Court has restated the test as follows:

> In both the multiple punishment and multiple prosecution contexts, this Court has concluded that where the two offenses for which the defendant is punished or tried cannot survive the "same elements" test, the double jeopardy bar applies.... The same elements test, sometimes referred to as the "Blockburger" test, inquires whether each offense contains an element not contained in the other; if not, they are the "same offense" and double jeopardy bars additional punishment and successive prosecution.[98]

Some confusion seems to surround the exact phrasing of the test, and perhaps the boundaries of its application. In the above quoted language, the Supreme Court speaks only of comparing the elements of the offenses, as defined by the statutes in question. The New York Court of Appeals, however, has characterized the test as follows: "Under Blockburger, two distinct statutory provisions do not constitute the 'same offense' for double jeopardy purposes if each provision requires proof of a fact which the other does not."[99] And the United States Court of Appeals for the Second Circuit has held that while *Blockburger* is normally applied by examining the facts required to be proved for conviction under the statutes defining the offenses, "in certain circumstances, including where one of the statutes covers a broad range of conduct, it is appropriate under Blockburger to examine the allegations of the indictment rather than only the terms of the statutes."[100] In

---

96. Initially, CPL § 40.10(1) defines "offense" as any conduct
which violates a statutory provision defining an offense; and when the same conduct or criminal transaction violates two or more such statutory provisions each such violation constitutes a separate and distinct offense. The same conduct or criminal transaction also establishes separate and distinct offenses when, though violating only one statutory provision, it results in death, injury, loss or other consequences as to two or more victims, and such result is an element of the offense as defined. In such case, as many offenses are committed as there are victims.

Thereafter, CPL § 40.20(1) simply provides that "a person may not be twice prosecuted for the same offense."

97. See Blockburger v. United States, 284 U.S. 299, 52 S.Ct. 180, 76 L.Ed. 306 (1932).

98. United States v. Dixon, 525 U.S. 688, 113 S.Ct. 2849, 2856, 125 L.Ed.2d 556 (1993). For a brief period, it was thought that there was an additional constitutional test, known as the "Grady" rule, which was applicable when Blockburger was satisfied. Grady v. Corbin, 495 U.S. 508, 510, 110 S.Ct. 2084, 2087, 109 L.Ed.2d 548 (1990), held that "if, to establish an essential element of an offense charged in that prosecution, the government will prove conduct that constitutes an offense for which the defendant has already been prosecuted," the second prosecution is barred. Grady, however, was overruled in Dixon.

99. People v. Latham, 83 N.Y.2d 233, 238, 609 N.Y.S.2d 141, 143, 631 N.E.2d 83, 85 (1994). The Supreme Court has previously characterized the test in this fashion. See, e.g., Brown v. Ohio, 432 U.S. 161, 97 S.Ct. 2221, 53 L.Ed.2d 187 (1977).

100. United States v. Liller, 999 F.2d 61, 63 (2d Cir.1993).

many cases, a comparison of the elements should suffice to decide the question.

In practice, it is usually not difficult for the prosecution to meet the *Blockburger* test. For example, it has been held that the double jeopardy clause of the federal Constitution does not bar: prosecution of a defendant for possession of a firearm, despite a prior prosecution for transporting the same weapon in interstate commerce with knowledge that it was stolen;[101] prosecution of a defendant for involuntary vehicular manslaughter following prosecution for failing to reduce speed to avoid the accident;[102] and prosecution for robbery following a prosecution for criminal possession of stolen property.[103] On the other hand, *Blockburger* has been interpreted to bar the prosecution of a person for robbery, when he had been first convicted of a felony murder for which the robbery was the underlying felony.[104]

Analysis becomes more difficult when the offenses involved are of uncertain duration, such as possession of weapons, drugs or stolen property. Unlike crimes such as assault, robbery, or the sale of narcotics, these "continuing offenses" do not have an obvious and discrete consummation, and accordingly it can sometimes be difficult to ascertain for double jeopardy purposes whether a defendant's course of conduct involves a single continuing crime or a series of separate crimes. For example, the Supreme Court has held that an offense such as joyriding—taking or operating a vehicle without the owner's consent—can be viewed as a single continuing crime for double jeopardy purposes, even if committed over a lengthy period.[105] The New York Court of Appeals has applied this rule to two weapons possession statutes, with different results. Initially, in *Matter of Johnson v. Morgenthau*,[106] the court held that although the defendant had illegally possessed a handgun for six days and carried it from Bronx County to New York County, he could not be prosecuted in both counties for separate possession offenses. The underlying reasoning was that because the crime at issue, criminal possession of a weapon in the third degree,[107] was defined in terms of dominion and control over the weapon, it should be classified as a continuing offense for double jeopardy purposes. By contrast, in the

101. Id.

102. Illinois v. Vitale, 447 U.S. 410, 100 S.Ct. 2260, 65 L.Ed.2d 228 (1980).

103. People v. Prescott, 66 N.Y.2d 216, 495 N.Y.S.2d 955, 486 N.E.2d 813 (1985).

104. Harris v. Oklahoma, 433 U.S. 682, 97 S.Ct. 2912, 53 L.Ed.2d 1054 (1977); see also Payne v. Virginia, 468 U.S. 1062, 104 S.Ct. 3573, 82 L.Ed.2d 801 (1984)(conviction for capital murder during robbery bars prosecution for robbery itself.) Conversely, constitutional double jeopardy also applies "if every element of the lesser offense of which defendant has been convicted is included in the [subsequently prosecuted] greater offense." People v. Rivera, 60 N.Y.2d 110, 116, 468 N.Y.S.2d 601, 605, 456 N.E.2d 492, 496 (1983); see also People v. Prescott, 66 N.Y.2d 216, 495 N.Y.S.2d 955, 486 N.E.2d 813 (1985)(opining that under Blockburger, where one offense itself is a necessary element of the other, the two are the same, but holding that robbery and criminal possession of stolen property are different offenses for federal constitutional purposes).

105. Brown v. Ohio, 432 U.S. 161, 97 S.Ct. 2221, 53 L.Ed.2d 187 (1977).

106. 69 N.Y.2d 148, 512 N.Y.S.2d 797, 505 N.E.2d 240 (1987).

107. P.L. § 265.02(4).

§ 2.5 DOUBLE JEOPARDY Ch. 2

later case of *People v. Okafore*,[108] the court reached the opposite conclusion in a case involving a different weapon statute—criminal possession of a weapon in the second degree, which contains as an element the intentional use of the weapon unlawfully against another person.[109] This specific intent, the court reasoned, could have the effect of dividing the duration of the offense into periods during which the defendant harbors that intent. Thus, if there was a lapse in this intent, or in any other element of the crime, the offense itself then lapsed, and, if the intent was subsequently revived, a new crime was then committed, rather than a continuation of the old.

Conspiracy and RICO-type offenses present other problems. The Supreme Court has held that prosecution of a defendant for a conspiracy based upon overt acts that are substantive offenses upon which the defendant had been previously convicted does not violate the double jeopardy clause, essentially reasoning that the conspiracy and the overt act are not the same offense.[110] A New York appellate court has adopted similar reasoning with regard to RICO.[111]

Contempt presents another complex area. The Supreme Court has held that criminal contempt, at least in its non-summary form, is essentially a crime for double jeopardy purposes. Thus, if a defendant is first prosecuted for a contempt arising out of the commission of another crime, the separate prosecution for that crime, which did not include any element not contained in the prior contempt, fails the *Blockburger* test.[112]

Library References:
West's Key No. Digests, Double Jeopardy ⟐34, 132–137.

§ 2.6 "Same Criminal Transaction" Statutory Double Jeopardy

Under the constitutional double jeopardy rule, protection is limited to a bar against separate prosecutions for the same offense. Dissatisfied with only this protection, the New York Legislature chose to grant more comprehensive protection against separate prosecution for two offenses

---

108. 72 N.Y.2d 81, 531 N.Y.S.2d 762, 527 N.E.2d 245 (1988).

109. P.L. § 265.03. See generally Greenberg, Marcus, et al., New York Criminal Law § 35.20 (West 1996).

110. United States v. Felix, 503 U.S. 378, 112 S.Ct. 1377, 118 L.Ed.2d 25 (1992).

111. Application of Cooper v. Sheindlin, 154 A.D.2d 288, 289, 546 N.Y.S.2d 589, 589 (1st Dep't 1989)("The RICO statute does not charge the commission of the predicate crimes that comprise the pattern of racketeering activity but, rather, the furthering of a criminal enterprise by a pattern of racketeering activity.... Consequently a defendant may be punished both for a violation of the Federal RICO as well as for the predicate crimes that constitute the pattern of racketeering activity.")(citations omitted). It should be noted that there are special statutory rules in this area. See § 2.9, infra.

112. United States v. Dixon, 525 U.S. 688, 113 S.Ct. 2849, 125 L.Ed.2d 556 (1993). It should be noted that although Penal Law § 215.54 specifically provides that "[a]djudication for criminal contempt under subdivision A of section seven hundred fifty of the judiciary law shall not bar a prosecution for the crime of criminal contempt under [P.L.] section 215.50 based upon the same conduct," the constitutionality of this provision is dubious. See People v. Colombo, 31 N.Y.2d 947, 341 N.Y.S.2d 97, 293 N.E.2d 247 (1972). See generally Greenberg, Marcus, et al., New York Criminal Law § 27.14 (West 1996).

based upon the same act or criminal transaction.[113] Unlike the constitutional *Blockburger* rule, which is primarily a legal test based upon a comparison of the elements of the two offenses, whether two offenses arise out of the same act or criminal transaction is primarily a factual question, with resolution depending upon a case-by-case analysis of all of the facts and circumstances of the conduct underlying the charged offenses.[114]

A three-step analysis is required to decide whether a case is barred by "same criminal transaction" New York statutory double jeopardy. It is first necessary to examine the conduct involved in both the previously-prosecuted and the instant offense to see if it is all part of the same act or criminal transaction, as the statute defines the term. If this is the case, the next question is whether one of the eight statutory exceptions apply, and the final question is whether the mandatory joinder provision is relevant.

The statutory scheme begins with a broad definition of "criminal transaction," containing two alternative tests of whether two offenses can be considered to be part of the same criminal transaction for these purposes. The first[115] asks whether the two are "so closely related and connected in point of time and circumstance of commission as to constitute a single criminal incident."[116] This involves consideration of the nature, timing and circumstances of the offenses, and has been held to have been met where, for example, a seller of pornographic materials sells two pornographic items at the same time to a single purchaser.[117] On the other hand, two separate sales of drugs to the same person at the same place, but 48 hours apart, have been found to be separate transactions for this purpose.[118]

The second alternative test asks whether the two offenses are "so closely related in criminal purpose or objective as to constitute elements or integral parts of a single criminal venture."[119] This tends to be more applicable to crimes that involve planned, ongoing organized criminal activity, such as conspiracies, complex frauds or larcenies, or narcotics rings. Again, the test is primarily factual, and applied on a case-by-case

---

113. The Supreme Court, although occasionally seeming to veer in the direction of "same criminal transaction" double jeopardy for constitutional purposes, has never gone quite so far as to bar the separate prosecution of two "offenses" having separate elements—thereby meeting the Blockburger test—arising out of the same criminal transaction. See Grady v. Corbin, 495 U.S. 508, 110 S.Ct. 2084, 109 L.Ed.2d 548 (1990), overruled by United States v. Dixon, 525 U.S. 688, 113 S.Ct. 2849, 125 L.Ed.2d 556 (1993). However, in situations where two such offenses are serially prosecuted and the first prosecution ends in an acquittal, the doctrine of collateral estoppel may apply. This does not bar the second prosecution, but may severely impact upon the prosecution's ability to convict. See § 2.8, infra.

114. See Matter of Abraham v. Justices, 37 N.Y.2d 560, 376 N.Y.S.2d 79, 338 N.E.2d 597 (1975).

115. CPL § 40.10(2)(a). CPL § 40.20(2) contains the prohibition against multiple prosecutions for "two offenses based upon the same act or criminal transaction," while CPL § 40.20(2)(a)-(h) contains the exceptions to that prohibition.

116. CPL § 40.10(2)(a).

117. People v. North Street Book Shoppe, 139 A.D.2d 118, 530 N.Y.S.2d 869 (3d Dep't 1988).

118. People v. Robinson, 65 A.D.2d 896, 410 N.Y.S.2d 409 (3d Dep't 1978).

119. CPL § 40.10(2)(b).

basis. It has been held, for example, that under this test a single persisting criminal enterprise to sell dangerous drugs, which was previously prosecuted as a federal conspiracy, involved the same criminal transaction as a substantive drug possession offense that was an overt act of that conspiracy,[120] and that numerous frauds and tax offenses committed in the course of a scheme to renovate and decorate homes at taxpayer expense were all part of one criminal transaction.[121] On the other hand, where state crimes involving the use of stolen credit cards were prosecuted separately from federal crimes involving a conspiracy to obtain other stolen credit cards, the acts in question were found not to be part of the same criminal transaction.[122]

Fearful of the potential broad sweep of "same criminal transaction" double jeopardy combined with the abrogation of the "two sovereignties" rule,[123] the State Legislature also enacted a series of eight exceptions that limit the reach of "same criminal transaction" double jeopardy.[124] It should be emphasized that these exceptions are not mutually exclusive, and that in many cases courts have found more than one to be applicable. Thus, the entire list must be checked whenever a problem in this area is considered.

The first two exceptions are of general import, and are often considered together. The first[125] establishes an exception to the general rule that where two offenses are a part of the same act or criminal transaction, and jeopardy has attached on one, the other is barred, where the offenses as defined "have substantially different elements and the acts establishing one offense in the main are clearly distinguishable from those establishing the other." This is a mixed determination: whether the two offenses have substantially different elements is a legal question; and whether the acts establishing the offenses are in the main clearly distinguishable is a factual one. In practice, the factual part of the test is the more important component.[126] It should be remembered that this

---

120. Matter of Abraham v. Justices, 37 N.Y.2d 560, 376 N.Y.S.2d 79, 338 N.E.2d 597 (1975). The same result obtains where the facts underlying the substantive offense could have been alleged to support the earlier conspiracy. People v. Abbamonte, 43 N.Y.2d 74, 400 N.Y.S.2d 766, 371 N.E.2d 485 (1977). See also Matter of Schmidt v. Roberts, 74 N.Y.2d 513, 549 N.Y.S.2d 633, 548 N.E.2d 1284 (1989)(federal conspiracy and state larceny part of same criminal transaction). It should be noted that in 1984 subdivision (g) was added to CPL § 40.30(2), essentially allowing New York to prosecute certain offenses implicated in previous prosecutions for conspiracy and related crimes prosecuted in other states, but not by the federal government.

121. People v. Helmsley, 170 A.D.2d 209, 566 N.Y.S.2d 223 (1st Dep't 1991).

122. People v. Vesprey, 183 A.D.2d 212, 590 N.Y.S.2d 91 (1st Dep't 1992).

123. See Matter of Abraham v. Justices, 37 N.Y.2d at 565, 376 N.Y.S.2d at 83, 338 N.E.2d at 600("However, aware of the pitfalls in so broad a rule ... the Legislature followed, and wisely some of us think, the lead of the Model Penal Code ... and engrafted six [now eight] exceptions upon it."). As previously explained, New York affords statutory double jeopardy protection when there has been a previous prosecution in the courts of the federal government or another state. If "same criminal transaction" double jeopardy were not limited, the reach of that rule might cause unjust results, such as a statutory bar to a New York murder prosecution when the victim dies after a New Jersey prosecution for a minor offense.

124. CPL § 40.20(2)(a)-(h).

125. CPL § 40.20(2)(a).

126. Of course, if the two offenses do not have different elements, constitutional double jeopardy will bar the proposed prosecution. Although the requirement that the elements differ "substantially" is clearly in-

must be applied in the context of an assumption that the acts are sufficiently related to constitute part of the same criminal transaction as defined in the first part of the statute; if they are not, then there is no need to consider the exception.

A clear, albeit unusual, illustration is *Matter of Fuller v. Plumadore*,[127] where the defendant, initially prosecuted under the Environmental Conservation Law for illegally taking deer without a permit, was subsequently prosecuted for conspiracy and forgery charges arising out of a scheme to forge a party hunting permit. The court first ruled that all of these acts were a part of the same criminal transaction, thus meeting the statutory definition. It then found that the conspiracy charge was barred but the forgery was not, holding that the elements of and the acts establishing the forgery were clearly distinguishable from those involved in the offense of illegally taking deer without a permit.

By way of comparison, in *People v. Claud*,[128] the Court of Appeals refused to apply the exception, holding that although the relevant elements of a statute proscribing the failure to exercise due care in operating a boat were substantially different from the elements of a statute penalizing intoxicated operation of the vessel, the acts underlying those offenses were not distinguishable.[129]

The second exception[130] is applicable where each of the offenses contains an element that is not an element of the other, and the statutory provisions defining such offenses are designed to prevent very different kinds of harm or evil. This is more legal in nature. Once again, there are two parts to the exception. Whether each offense contains an element that is not an element of the other involves a fairly straightforward determination. Whether the statutes are designed to prevent different harms or evils is somewhat more esoteric.[131] At one time it was thought that if no geographic overlap existed between the prosecutions, different harm or evil could be made out on that basis; but this is no longer the law.[132]

---

tended to make the exception more difficult to apply, it does not seem to have added very much.

127. 88 A.D.2d 674, 450 N.Y.S.2d 918 (3d Dep't 1982).

128. 76 N.Y.2d 951, 563 N.Y.S.2d 720, 565 N.E.2d 469 (1990).

129. See also Matter of Schmidt v. Roberts, 74 N.Y.2d 513, 549 N.Y.S.2d 633, 548 N.E.2d 1284 (1989)(acts underlying federal crime of interstate transportation of stolen property and state larceny not clearly distinguishable); Matter of Abraham v. Justices, supra (acts underlying drug conspiracy and drug possession not clearly distinguishable).

130. CPL § 40.20(2)(b).

131. See, e.g., People v. Claud, 76 N.Y.2d 951, 563 N.Y.S.2d 720, 565 N.E.2d 469 (1990)(town ordinance penalizing careless operation of boat and state statute penalizing drunken operation of boat not aimed at different evils); Matter of Schmidt v. Roberts, 74 N.Y.2d 513, 549 N.Y.S.2d 633, 548 N.E.2d 1284 (1989)(federal interstate transportation of stolen property and state larceny not aimed at different evils); Matter of Wiley v. Altman, 52 N.Y.2d 410, 438 N.Y.S.2d 490, 420 N.E.2d 371 (1981)(Maryland conspiracy to murder and New York murder not aimed at different evils); Matter of Abraham v. Justices, supra (federal drug conspiracy and state drug possession not aimed at different evils). Cf. Matter of Kessler v. Sherman, 41 N.Y.2d 851, 393 N.Y.S.2d 703, 362 N.E.2d 254 (1977)(town wetlands ordinance and state Environmental Conservation Law are aimed at different evils; exception applies).

132. Matter of Wiley v. Altman, 52 N.Y.2d 410, 438 N.Y.S.2d 490, 420 N.E.2d 371 (1981). The result in this case was

§ 2.6 DOUBLE JEOPARDY Ch. 2

The remaining exceptions tend to be narrower in scope. The "contraband matter" exception[133] presumably would authorize separate prosecutions for, say, possession of a firearm and criminal use of that firearm, even if those offenses are committed within the same criminal transaction.[134] It should be noted that the exception itself contains an exception—"other than a sale thereof"—that excludes crimes involving sale of the contraband in question, thereby rendering them barred by statutory double jeopardy if prosecuted separately from a crime involving the possession of the contraband. Given the broad Penal Law definition of "sale" in the context of drug offenses,[135] many narcotics offenses of other jurisdictions may fall within the exception to the exception, thus bringing them within statutory double jeopardy protection.[136]

The important "delayed death" exception, which provides that an initial prosecution for assault or another offense resulting in physical injury does not bar a subsequent homicide prosecution if the victim dies after the initial prosecution,[137] was construed by the Court of Appeals in *People v. Latham*.[138] Weeks after the defendant pleaded guilty to attempted murder, his victim died, and the defendant was then indicted for the completed crime of murder. The court found that the exception applied and the indictment was not barred. The court noted that "[t]his delayed death exemption may be traced to ... sound policy reasons ... including the need for prompt adjudication. Particularly in an era where medical advances can prolong the life of a critically injured victim, a prosecution must proceed on the basis of the victim's present condition. Where death follows, however, it is also in society's interest that a homicide be redressed."[139] Note, however, that if the death of the victim occurs before jeopardy has attached upon the initial charges, the subdivision is inapplicable on its face, and statutory jeopardy will bar a subsequent prosecution.

effectively overruled by the later passage of CPL § 40.20(2)(g).

133. CPL § 40.20(2)(c). The statute does not define "contraband matter." Generally, "contraband is clearly defined by law as property whose simple possession is a crime, for example, counterfeit coins, narcotics, a machine gun, or an unlicensed pistol." Sullivan v. Grupposo, 77 Misc.2d 833, 835, 355 N.Y.S.2d 55, 57 (N.Y.C.Civ.Ct. 1974). Cf. P.L. § 205.00(3)(defining "contraband" for purposes of crime of promoting prison contraband as "any article or thing which a person confined in a detention facility is prohibited from obtaining or possessing by statute, rule, regulation or order"); People v. McDermott, 69 N.Y.2d 889, 515 N.Y.S.2d 225, 507 N.E.2d 1081 (1987) (construing that definition).

134. See P.L. §§ 265.01, 265.08.

135. See P.L. § 220.00(1): "Sell means to sell, exchange, give or dispose of to another, or to offer or agree to do the same." See generally Greenberg, Marcus, et al., New York Criminal Law § 28.31 (West 1996).

136. See Matter of Cirillo v. Justices, 43 A.D.2d 4, 349 N.Y.S.2d 129 (2d Dep't), aff'd 34 N.Y.2d 990, 360 N.Y.S.2d 416, 318 N.E.2d 607 (1974) (federal prosecution for attempted drug distribution bars New York prosecution for possession and possession with intent to sell).

137. CPL § 40.20(2)(d).

138. 83 N.Y.2d 233, 609 N.Y.S.2d 141, 631 N.E.2d 83 (1994).

139. 83 N.Y.2d at 237, 609 N.Y.S.2d at 143, 631 N.E.2d at 85 (citations omitted). The court also found that constitutional double jeopardy was not offended. See also People v. Rivera, 60 N.Y.2d 110, 468 N.Y.S.2d 601, 456 N.E.2d 492 (1983)(applying the exception, but leaving open the question of whether the exception applies where the initial prosecution was for attempted murder—which Latham answered in the affirmative).

The "different victim" exception[140] exempts separate offenses—each of which involve death, injury, loss or other consequence to a different victim—from the reach of statutory "same criminal transaction" double jeopardy. Perhaps the classic illustration is *People v. Luongo*,[141] in which the Court of Appeals held that a confidence man whose scheme involved numerous larcenies committed against residents of adjoining counties could be prosecuted separately in each county for the crimes against the appropriate victims. However, the court subsequently held that this exception is available only when each of the offenses in the separate prosecutions involves one or more specific, individually identifiable victims, and thus is inapplicable where crimes such as federal RICO and mail fraud have no specific victims, but only a general class of individuals such as citizens or taxpayers.[142] However, where such crimes do identify specific victims, the exception does apply.[143]

The rarely applied technical exception of the next subdivision[144] provides a jeopardy bar where there has been a prosecution for a crime in another jurisdiction that has been terminated by a court order expressly founded upon the insufficiency of an element of the foreign offense that is not an element of the New York offense upon which separate prosecution is sought. Illustrative is *Klein v. Murtagh*,[145] where a prior federal prosecution involving a bribery scheme committed over the telephone, which was dismissed in federal court because of the lack of a sufficient nexus to interstate commerce, was held not to bar a New York bribery prosecution.

The next exception[146] was added in 1984, and may negate prior case law. It applies where there has been a previous prosecution in "another state" for a conspiracy, facilitation or solicitation and New York seeks to prosecute for a "consummated result offense" that was the subject of the out-of-state prosecution. The Court of Appeals has held that the exception does not apply where the previous prosecution was federal; accordingly, in that situation, the basic underlying question of whether the New York crime was part of the "same criminal transaction" as the federal crime decides the issue.[147] The subsequent crime, upon which New York prosecution is sought, must be a "consummated result offense" that occurred in New York, and was the "result" of the offense prosecuted in another state. The concept of a result offense is borrowed from CPL Article 20, which deals with geographical jurisdiction[148] In that context, it has been interpreted fairly narrowly. For example, it has been held that because the crime of attempted larceny by extortion

---

140. CPL § 40.20(2)(e).
141. 47 N.Y.2d 418, 418 N.Y.S.2d 365, 391 N.E.2d 1341 (1979).
142. Matter of Kaplan v. Ritter, 71 N.Y.2d 222, 224, 525 N.Y.S.2d 1, 1, 519 N.E.2d 802, 802 (1987).
143. People v. Vesprey, 183 A.D.2d 212, 590 N.Y.S.2d 91 (1st Dep't 1992).
144. CPL § 40.20(2)(f).
145. 34 N.Y.2d 988, 360 N.Y.S.2d 416, 318 N.E.2d 606 (1974).
146. CPL § 40.20(2)(g).
147. Matter of Schmidt v. Roberts, 74 N.Y.2d 513, 549 N.Y.S.2d 633, 548 N.E.2d 1284 (1989).
148. See CPL §§ 20.10(3)(defining term), 20.20(2)(a)("result offense" interstate jurisdiction) and 20.40(2)(a)("result offense" intrastate jurisdiction). Geographical jurisdiction is discussed in Chapter 1.

is complete upon the making of an extortionate threat, the accomplishment of that threat was not the "result" of the attempted larceny for jurisdictional purposes.[149]

The final exception,[150] applicable only in prosecutions involving enterprise corruption or other RICO-type offenses, is addressed in § 2.9, *infra*.

It should also be noted that there is another exception, contained in a provision of the Vehicle and Traffic Law,[151] which purports to allow a prosecution for "assault or homicide" notwithstanding a previous conviction (*not* an acquittal) on VTL charges. As a special statute, this has been held to take precedence over the more general rules of CPL Article 40 for statutory jeopardy purposes, although the constitutionality of this provision is in serious doubt.[152]

Library References:

West's Key No. Digests, Double Jeopardy ⚖137, 150(3), 182, 183–187.

§ 2.7 Mandatory Joinder

The mandatory joinder provision of the CPL[153] bars "separate prosecution of jointly prosecutable offenses and deals with prosecutions for different and factually distinct offenses arising out of the same criminal transaction under circumstances wherein no violation of the double jeopardy principle can be maintained but the equities nevertheless seem to preclude separate prosecutions."[154] The section is based upon the same general concept as the "same criminal transaction" double jeopardy rule of CPL § 40.20(2), with which it meshes, effectuates, and in some instances supplants.

It should be noted that a violation of the rules set forth in this provision may bar a subsequent proceeding "even though such separate prosecutions are not otherwise barred by any other section of this article."[155] This is particularly applicable to the exceptions to "same criminal transaction" statutory double jeopardy, which this provision may sometimes circumvent. For example, assume that a defendant, as part of an overarching scheme to inherit property, kills a number of relatives, in a manner that makes the acts "separate offenses" constitutionally, but part of the "same criminal transaction" for statutory

---

149. People v. Zaccaro, 132 A.D.2d 589, 517 N.Y.S.2d 567 (2d Dep't 1987).

150. CPL § 40.20(2)(h).

151. Vehicle and Traffic Law § 1800(d) provides that "[a] conviction for a violation of any provision of this chapter shall not be a bar to a prosecution for an assault or for a homicide committed by any person in operating a motor vehicle or motorcycle."

152. Such a conflict was found in Matter of Corbin v. Hillery, 74 N.Y.2d 279, 545 N.Y.S.2d 71, 543 N.E.2d 714 (1989), aff'd 495 U.S. 508, 110 S.Ct. 2084, 109 L.Ed.2d 548 (1990). However, because the Supreme Court subsequently overruled that decision in United States v. Dixon, 509 U.S. 688, 113 S.Ct. 2849, 125 L.Ed.2d 556 (1993), the question is now in doubt.

153. CPL § 40.40.

154. People v. Dean, 56 A.D.2d 242, 246, 392 N.Y.S.2d 134, 138 (4th Dep't 1977), aff'd 45 N.Y.2d 651, 412 N.Y.S.2d 353, 384 N.E.2d 1277 (1978).

155. CPL § 40.40(1).

purposes.[156] However, because there are potential statutory exceptions applicable,[157] separate prosecutions for the killings may not be barred by the statutory double jeopardy prohibition itself. Nevertheless, if its terms are applicable and all of its tests are met, the mandatory joinder provision will bar separate prosecution of these crimes.

Two situations are covered by the statute. The first[158] protects against the separate (and presumably serial) prosecution of uncharged joinable offenses, while the other protects against piecemeal trials of joinable offenses that are charged in separate accusatory instruments. In the first situation, where an accusatory instrument is filed in a particular court, the statute bars a subsequent prosecution of (1) a joinable offense;[159] (2) that was not charged in any accusatory instrument filed in that court; (3) when the prosecution has legally sufficient evidence to convict for the uncharged offense; and (4) proceedings on the extant accusatory instrument progress to the commencement of trial or a guilty plea. In short, the prosecution is prevented from filing charges against a defendant for one crime arising out of a criminal transaction, and, if there is an acquittal, then separately charging another.

The elements of the statute contain a number of concepts. Generally, offenses are "joinable" when they arise out of the same criminal transaction and the court has subject matter and geographical jurisdiction over them.[160] The subsequent offense must not be charged in either the accusatory instrument containing the joinable offense or in any other accusatory instrument filed in the same court. If it is, then the subsequent subdivision of the statute may be applicable. If charges are simultaneously extant in separate courts, the question appears to turn on whether each of those courts possesses jurisdiction over all charges.[161]

---

156. That is, the killings may be either "a single criminal incident," or a "single criminal venture," thus meeting the definition of a single "criminal transaction" per CPL § 40.10(2).

157. An example is "different victims" exception of CPL § 40.20(2)(e).

158. CPL § 40.40(2).

159. CPL § 40.40(1) contains a cross-reference to CPL § 200.20(2)(a), which in turn provides that two offenses are "joinable" when "they are based upon the same act or upon the same criminal transaction, as that term is defined in subdivision two of section 40.10."

160. See, e.g., People v. Perkins, 161 Misc.2d 502, 506, 614 N.Y.S.2d 709, 711 (Sup.Ct., N.Y. County, 1994)("The principle of mandatory joinder is inapplicable here as the crimes at issue occurred in two different counties and could be tried only in the counties in which they occurred."). However, geographical jurisdiction may be based upon any of the provisions of CPL §§ 20.20, 20.40. Cf. People v. Ruzas, 54 A.D.2d 1083, 389 N.Y.S.2d 205 (4th Dep't 1976)(mandatory joinder bar where geographical jurisdiction over entire multi-county incident involving felony and felony murder existed in court in which first accusatory instrument, charging only part of incident, was filed) with Vega v. Rubin, 73 A.D.2d 658, 423 N.Y.S.2d 193 (2d Dep't 1979)(no "long arm" geographical jurisdiction over drug sale in separate county; hence that offense not joinable in another county).

161. See People v. Lindsly, 99 A.D.2d 99, 472 N.Y.S.2d 115 (2d Dep't 1984). The defendant in a village court was charged with leaving the scene of an accident, and then subsequently charged with driving while intoxicated—first in district court, and thereafter, following indictment, in County Court. The defendant pleaded guilty in the village court, which had no jurisdiction over the DWI charges. Although the Appellate Division held that the DWI offense could not have been "joinable" in the village court owing to this absence of jurisdiction, and thus CPL § 40.40(2) was inapplicable, the decision implies that the

However, where a simplified information and a felony complaint containing a joinable offense were both extant in a local criminal court at the time that court accepted a plea of guilty to the former, the statute did not bar a later superior court indictment that replaced the felony complaint and charged the same offense.[162] Next, the prosecution must have "legally sufficient evidence" *to convict* for the uncharged crime— *i.e.*, proof beyond a reasonable doubt.[163] For example, sufficient evidence to indict for the offense[164] is not enough.[165] Finally, the point at which this quasi-jeopardy attaches is when the charged crime contained in the accusatory instrument progresses to a guilty plea or to "the commencement of trial" that, by statutory definition, appears to be slightly different from the point at which jeopardy normally attaches.[166]

The second variety of mandatory joinder[167] is aimed at preventing multiple trials when separate accusatory instruments are in fact filed. This provision requires that the accusatory instruments charging the joinable offenses be filed in the same court, that the defendant move to consolidate those accusatory instruments for trial,[168] and that consolidation be improperly denied by the court. If all of these factors are present, the commencement of trial[169] on one such accusatory instrument bars a subsequent prosecution upon any of the other accusatory instruments with respect to any such offense.

Library References:

West's Key No. Digests, Double Jeopardy ⚖=138.

result might have been different if the DWI charges could have been filed therein.

162. People v. Easterling, 59 A.D.2d 537, 397 N.Y.S.2d 125 (2d Dep't 1977).

163. Although the statute speaks of "evidence legally sufficient to convict", it should be noted that "legally sufficient evidence" is defined as "competent evidence which, if accepted as true, would establish every element of an offense charged and the defendant's commission thereof; except that such evidence is not legally sufficient when corroboration required by law is absent." CPL § 70.10(1). The standard of proof required for conviction, of course, is proof beyond a reasonable doubt, which is defined as "evidence which is legally sufficient and which establishes beyond a reasonable doubt every element of such offense and the defendant's commission thereof." CPL § 70.20.

164. See CPL § 190.65(1).

165. For the most blatant example, see People v. Rivera, 60 N.Y.2d 110, 117, 468 N.Y.S.2d 601, 605, 456 N.E.2d 492, 496 (1983)("Manifestly, the joinder section is not applicable.... At the time the initial prosecution was brought, the People did not charge murder because the victim had not expired, the offense had thus not been consummated, and, consequently, legally sufficient evidence for the charge did not yet exist.").

166. CPL § 1.20(11) provides: "A jury trial commences with the selection of the jury.... A non jury trial commences with the first opening address, if there be any, and, if not, when the first witness is sworn." Cf. CPL § 40.20(1)(b)(jeopardy attaches when a case "proceeds to the trial stage and a jury has been impaneled and sworn or, in the case of a trial by the court without a jury, a witness is sworn").

167. CPL § 40.40(3).

168. Failure to so move is a waiver. Matter of Wiley v. Altman, 52 N.Y.2d 410, 438 N.Y.S.2d 490, 420 N.E.2d 371 (1981). However, it has been held that when the defendant is unaware that one of the accusatory instruments has been filed, a failure to move to consolidate is not a waiver. People v. Ballacchino, 126 Misc.2d 610, 484 N.Y.S.2d 765 (Buffalo City Ct.1984).

169. Notably, by its express terms, and unlike the preceding joinder provision, under this provision a guilty plea does not bar further proceedings on the separately filed accusatory instrument.

§ 2.8 Collateral Estoppel

In *Ashe v. Swenson*,[170] the defendant was tried and acquitted for the robbery of one of a group of six people who were playing cards when a group of intruders robbed them at gunpoint. Following the acquittal, he was tried again for the robbery of another participant in the game, based essentially on the testimony of the same witnesses, who at the second trial were more certain of his identity. Holding that in criminal cases the doctrine of collateral estoppel—which "means simply that when an issue of ultimate fact has once been determined by a valid and final judgment, that issue cannot again be litigated between the same parties in any future lawsuit"[171]—is embodied in the Fifth Amendment guarantee against double jeopardy, the Supreme Court reversed the conviction. The court parsed out the doctrine from other aspects of the double jeopardy clause,[172] and determined that under the circumstances presented, the first jury had found that the defendant was not one of the robbers, and that finding foreclosed another attempt by the State to prove the same thing.

The test to be applied under *Ashe* is as follows:

> Where a previous judgment of acquittal was based upon a general verdict, as is usually the case, this approach requires a court to "examine the record of a prior proceeding, taking into account the pleadings, evidence, charge, and other relevant matter, and conclude whether a rational jury could have grounded its verdict upon an issue other than that which the defendant seeks to foreclose from consideration." The inquiry "must be set in a practical frame and viewed with an eye to all the circumstances of the proceedings."[173]

In New York, the relationship between collateral estoppel and double jeopardy is more complex. In addition to the federal constitutional doctrine enunciated in *Ashe*, New York recognizes a common law, non-constitutional principle of collateral estoppel that is applicable in criminal as well as civil proceedings, and that is broader than the federal version.[174] There are three major requirements: (1) identity of the

---

170. 397 U.S. 436, 90 S.Ct. 1189, 25 L.Ed.2d 469 (1970).

171. 397 U.S. at 443, 90 S.Ct. at 1194.

172. "The question is not whether Missouri could validly charge the petitioner with six separate offenses for the robbery of the six poker players. It is not whether he could have received a total of six punishments if he had been convicted in a single trial of robbing the six victims. It is simply whether, after a jury has determined by its verdict that the petitioner was not one of the robbers, the State could constitutionally hale him before a new jury to litigate that issue again." 397 U.S. at 445, 90 S.Ct. at 1195.

173. 397 U.S. at 445, 90 S.Ct. at 1194 (citations omitted). The Supreme Court has returned to the doctrine on a number of occasions, perhaps most prominently in Dowling v. United States, 493 U.S. 342, 110 S.Ct. 668, 107 L.Ed.2d 708 (1990). In Dowling, the prosecution, at the defendant's bank robbery trial, introduced testimony of a witness concerning a similar alleged robbery by the defendant, for which he had been acquitted, for the purpose of buttressing the identification in the bank robbery. It was held that because this testimony did not establish an "ultimate fact" in the bank robbery, collateral estoppel did not apply.

174. See People v. Berkowitz, 50 N.Y.2d 333, 343–44, 428 N.Y.S.2d 927, 932–33, 406 N.E.2d 783, 788–89 (1980)("It is now well-settled that the doctrine of collateral estoppel is applicable to criminal as well as civil matters and exists independent of the pro-

§ 2.8 DOUBLE JEOPARDY Ch. 2

parties; (2) identity of the issues; and (3) a previous proceeding that resulted in a final judgment in which the party opposing estoppel was afforded a full and fair opportunity to litigate the issue in question. In addition, there is sometimes said to be a fairness or public policy limit to applying the doctrine under certain circumstances.

The first issue—identity of parties—is perhaps the simplest. It has been held that notwithstanding New York's abrogation of the "dual sovereignties" rule for purposes of statutory "same criminal transaction" double jeopardy protection,[175] because New York is not a party to a federal or other state prosecutions, such prosecutions have no collateral estoppel effect on subsequent New York prosecutions.[176] Further, other governmental entities within New York are usually deemed to be different parties from a criminal prosecutor for collateral estoppel purposes.[177] The parole board, however, has been held to be so closely related to the prosecution that a prior criminal acquittal based on an affirmative defense estops a revocation of parole based on commission of the criminal act.[178] Collateral estoppel also has no application where the initial prosecution did not involve the defendant himself, but only an accomplice.[179]

The "identity of issues" requirement is complex, and given that criminal trials usually involve multiple charges resulting in general verdicts, it is often quite difficult to decide what issues were necessarily decided in a prior proceeding. Illustrative is *People v. Acevedo*,[180] in which the Court of Appeals attempted to lay out some of the ground rules. Two indictments charged the defendant with robbery and weapons possession for two separate robberies, committed one after the other. He was initially tried for an attack on a person who, testifying for the prosecution at the trial, described a knife point attack occurring in a gas station. The defendant, however, testified that he had an encounter with the witness in a park, had rejected a sexual advance, and had left after the witness threatened him with retaliation. Both parties framed the issue for the jury as a credibility contest between the defendant and

hibition against double jeopardy."). It should also be noted that the underlying rationale of the constitutional doctrine is also to some extent subsumed in New York by the mandatory joinder rule of CPL 40.40(2), see § 2.8, supra, which also is directed at the evils of serial prosecutions. That provision is broader, for unlike the Ashe doctrine it actually precludes prosecution and also offers protection where the first proceeding resulted in a conviction. Given both mandatory joinder and "same criminal transaction" statutory double jeopardy, it is unlikely that the Ashe doctrine itself adds much protection for New York criminal defendants.

175. CPL § 40.30(1); see § 2.2, supra.

176. People v. Lo Cicero, 14 N.Y.2d 374, 251 N.Y.S.2d 953, 200 N.E.2d 622 (1964). See also People v. Phears, 53 N.Y.2d 1001, 441 N.Y.S.2d 666, 424 N.E.2d 553 (1981)(prior federal prosecution); People v. Reisman, 29 N.Y.2d 278, 327 N.Y.S.2d 342, 277 N.E.2d 396 (1971)(prior prosecution in another state).

177. See, e.g., Brown v. City of New York, 60 N.Y.2d 897, 470 N.Y.S.2d 573, 458 N.E.2d 1250 (1983)(City of New York and Queens County District Attorney are different parties); Matter of Saccoccio v. Lange, 194 A.D.2d 794, 599 N.Y.S.2d 306 (2d Dep't 1993)(district attorney and county attorney are different parties).

178. People ex rel. Dowdy v. Smith, 48 N.Y.2d 477, 423 N.Y.S.2d 862, 399 N.E.2d 894 (1979).

179. People v. Berkowitz, 50 N.Y.2d 333, 428 N.Y.S.2d 927, 406 N.E.2d 783 (1980).

180. 69 N.Y.2d 478, 515 N.Y.S.2d 753, 508 N.E.2d 665 (1987).

the prosecution's witness. The jury acquitted the defendant of all charges, including the weapons possession.

At the trial of the second robbery, another witness described a separate attack, committed at a point very near the gas station that was the situs of the encounter described by the witness at the first trial, at close to the same time. The prosecution then called the witness from the first trial, who testified, over the defendant's objection, that he had seen the defendant in that area at that time.

Initially, the court held that the defendant seeking the estoppel bears the burden of showing that the jury's verdict in a prior trial necessarily decided a particular factual issue raised in the second prosecution. Next, the court announced that, in New York, collateral estoppel is not, as the Supreme Court had held in *Ashe*, restricted to so-called "ultimate facts"—*i.e.*, facts essential to conviction in the second trial—but can apply to "evidentiary facts" as well, such as the defendant's presence in the area in question. Applying those principles, the court found that "the pleadings, evidence, charge and other relevant matter in the [first] robbery trial leave no doubt that the verdict of acquittal necessarily decided that the defendant and [the witness] encountered each other in the park (as related by defendant), not at the gas station (as related by [the witness])."[181] Thus, the doctrine of collateral estoppel foreclosed relitigation of the issues raised by the witness's testimony.

As is obvious from the above, the identity of issues component of collateral estoppel presents a difficult and complex question, which must be resolved on a case-by-case basis by examining the totality of the circumstances of the jury's verdict in the first proceeding—the pleadings, the evidence, the arguments of the attorneys, the court's charge to the jury, and the entirety of the verdict in terms of acquitted and convicted counts. If, taking in all of that, it cannot be said that the initial acquittal or other favorable resolution necessarily decided the fact in question, the doctrine will not apply.[182]

As for the "final determination" requirement, in the typical situation, it is the defendant who seeks to invoke the doctrine by virtue of a prior acquittal. It has been held that the pretrial dismissal of a criminal proceeding has no collateral estoppel effect on a subsequent criminal proceeding,[183] and that a determination in one court that a particular

---

181. 69 N.Y.2d at 487, 515 N.Y.S.2d at 760, 508 N.E.2d at 671. Cf. Dowling v. United States, 493 U.S. 342, 110 S.Ct. 668, 107 L.Ed.2d 708 (1990)(prior acquittal does not collaterally estop subsequent use of "similar act evidence" for identification purposes, because of "ultimate fact" limit).

182. See People v. Goodman, 69 N.Y.2d 32, 511 N.Y.S.2d 565, 503 N.E.2d 996 (1986)(no collateral estoppel where defendant, convicted of larceny but acquitted of other charges, was retried for larceny); People v. Dean, 45 N.Y.2d 651, 412 N.Y.S.2d 353, 384 N.E.2d 1277 (1978)(no collateral estoppel where defendant, tried for larceny, was previously acquitted of a series of similar larcenies).

183. McGrath v. Gold, 36 N.Y.2d 406, 369 N.Y.S.2d 62, 330 N.E.2d 35 (1975). It should be remembered that, in contrast to double jeopardy or mandatory joinder, which in a trial situation attach well before any determination by the jury as to guilt or innocence, collateral estoppel against the prosecution in a subsequent case requires a disposition favorable to the defendant, normally an acquittal, in the prior case.

offense did not qualify for recidivist sentencing enhancement, which was still subject to withdrawal or challenge on appeal, was not "final" and did not bar the use of the offense in question for such purposes in another prosecution.[184]

More rarified problems involve the relationship between criminal proceedings and civil proceedings. Generally speaking, a defendant is collaterally estopped in a subsequent civil proceeding from contesting the facts underlying a prior criminal conviction,[185] but because of the greater burden of proof in criminal proceedings, an acquittal does not have the same effect.[186]

Finally, collateral estoppel is not liberally or blindly applied in criminal actions, and there have been occasions when all of these tests have been met, but the courts have simply declined to apply the doctrine on grounds of fairness or public policy. Thus, announcing that collateral estoppel is a flexible doctrine, not to be applied automatically when its formal prerequisites are met, the Court of Appeals has held that the dismissal of parole revocation proceedings based on criminal charges does not bar a subsequent criminal prosecution for the same acts.[187] Further, a determination made in a prior Article 10 child protective proceeding in Family Court that a parent only negligently, rather than intentionally, caused a child's injury does not collaterally estop a subsequent criminal prosecution for an intentional crime based on the same incident,[188] although a prior criminal conviction may have such effect in a subsequent Family Court proceeding.[189] The Court of Appeals has also shown reluctance to apply the doctrine against criminal defendants, holding that under some circumstances the doctrine does not bar a defendant from relitigating issues involving the suppression of evidence sought to be introduced in separate proceedings.[190]

Library References:
West's Key No. Digests, Double Jeopardy ⬅3; Judgment ⬅713(1), 751.

§ 2.9 Enterprise Corruption Double Jeopardy

Special and elaborate statutory jeopardy rules govern the crime of enterprise corruption under the Organized Crime Control Act,[191] which is known as "OCCA" or State RICO. To understand these rules, it is

---

184. People v. Sanders, 71 N.Y.2d 946, 528 N.Y.S.2d 819, 524 N.E.2d 140 (1988). See also People v. Sailor, 65 N.Y.2d 224, 491 N.Y.S.2d 112, 480 N.E.2d 701 (1985)(also finding no collateral estoppel).

185. S.T. Grand, Inc. v. New York, 32 N.Y.2d 300, 344 N.Y.S.2d 938, 298 N.E.2d 105 (1973).

186. See, e.g., Johnson v. Oval Pharmacy, 165 A.D.2d 587, 569 N.Y.S.2d 49 (1st Dep't 1991).

187. People v. Fagan, 66 N.Y.2d 815, 498 N.Y.S.2d 335, 489 N.E.2d 222 (1985). Cf. People ex rel. Dowdy v. Smith, 48 N.Y.2d 477, 423 N.Y.S.2d 862, 399 N.E.2d 894 (1979)(criminal acquittal, based on affirmative defense, does bar parole revocation).

188. People v. Roselle, 84 N.Y.2d 350, 618 N.Y.S.2d 753, 643 N.E.2d 72 (1994).

189. Matter of Suffolk County DSS v. James M., 83 N.Y.2d 178, 608 N.Y.S.2d 940, 630 N.E.2d 636 (1994).

190. People v. Aguilera, 82 N.Y.2d 23, 603 N.Y.S.2d 392, 623 N.E.2d 519 (1993); People v. Plevy, 52 N.Y.2d 58, 436 N.Y.S.2d 224, 417 N.E.2d 518 (1980).

191. P.L. Article 460.

necessary to understand the nature of an OCCA prosecution. Although the OCCA statute is conceptually similar to its federal RICO counterpart, in the sense that both are broadly aimed at groups of individuals engaging in a series of illegal acts within the umbrella of an enterprise, there are some crucial differences. One of the most important differences is that the New York statute applies only to those who, as knowing members of a "criminal enterprise," intentionally "participate in a pattern of criminal activity" in a number of ways.[192] In other words, New York's version of RICO is limited to those who associate for specified kinds of shared criminal purposes in a structured criminal group. The terms "criminal enterprise," "pattern of criminal activity" and "criminal act" are all defined within the OCCA statute.[193] The underlying definition of "criminal act" is conduct constituting any of a lengthy list of specified felonies, conspiracy or attempt to commit any of those felonies.[194]

In practical terms, prosecutions for enterprise corruption are usually predicated upon the commission of a series of traditional individual crimes. To constitute a sufficient "pattern of criminal activity" to support a prosecution for enterprise corruption, there must be at least three of these "criminal acts" that are related to one another in a particular way.[195] When these individual criminal acts making up the pattern of criminal activity are set forth in the enterprise corruption count of an accusatory instrument, they are "specifically included" therein.[196]

Because OCCA prosecutions will be predicated in large part upon conduct that could also be prosecuted—and may well have been prosecuted—as separate crimes, and given that New York's general penchant for affording double jeopardy protection is broader than what the federal Constitution requires, the conceptual and practical problems of crafting double jeopardy rules in this context are obvious. The result is an overelaborate melange of statutes[197] that, in some instances, depart significantly from the settled double jeopardy rules applicable to other offenses. OCCA prosecutions have been relatively infrequent, and accordingly there has been little judicial interpretation of these rules.

192. P.L. § 460.20. There are essentially three ways to commit the crime. First, the defendant, knowing the existence and nature of a criminal enterprise, and being associated with the criminal enterprise, may intentionally participate in or conduct the affairs of any enterprise by participating in a pattern of criminal activity. P.L. § 460.20(1)(a). In this model, the enterprise is used as the focus of the criminal activity. Next, the defendant, again with knowledge of the existence of a criminal enterprise and associated with it, may intentionally acquire an interest in any enterprise by means of a pattern of criminal activity. P.L. § 460.20(1)(b). Here, the enterprise is the goal. Finally, the defendant, still acting with knowledge of and associated with a criminal enterprise, may participate in a pattern of criminal activity and invest the proceeds in an enterprise. P.L. § 460.20(1)(c). See generally Greenberg, Marcus, et al., New York Criminal Law, Chap. 38 (West 1996).

193. P.L. § 460.10(1), (3) and (4).

194. P.L. § 460.10(1).

195. P.L. § 460.10(4).

196. CPL § 40.50(1)(a). An indictment containing a count of enterprise corruption will often also contain counts charging those individual criminal acts that make up the pattern of criminal activity that were not previously prosecuted.

197. CPL §§ 40.20(2)(h), 40.50.

§ 2.9　　　　　　　　DOUBLE JEOPARDY　　　　　　　　Ch. 2

The OCCA double jeopardy provisions begin with a series of four definitions. Initially, a criminal act or offense is "specifically included" within an OCCA prosecution when a count of the indictment charging a person with enterprise corruption alleges a pattern of criminal activity and the act or offense is alleged to be a criminal act within such pattern.[198] Next, a criminal act is "a part of" a pattern of criminal activity alleged in a count of enterprise corruption when it is committed prior to the commencement of the criminal action in which enterprise corruption is charged, and was committed in furtherance of the "same common scheme or plan" with intent to participate in or further the affairs of the same criminal enterprise to which the crimes specifically included in the pattern are connected.[199] Third, a special and broad definition of when a person "is prosecuted" for an offense is provided for these purposes only; this occurs when the person either has "been prosecuted" in the traditional sense [i.e., pursuant to CPL § 40.30], or when a charge is dismissed without authorization to submit the charge to another grand jury, or the indictment is dismissed following the granting of a motion to suppress, unless an appeal from the order granting the motion to dismiss or suppress is pending.[200] Finally, an offense is said to be "not prosecutable" in an accusatory instrument charging enterprise corruption when there was no geographical jurisdiction of that offense in the county where the accusatory instrument was filed, or when the offense was prosecutable in the county and was not barred from such prosecution by double jeopardy or mandatory joinder, but the prosecutor filing the accusatory instrument was not empowered by law to prosecute the offense.[201]

In general, four situations are governed by the OCCA double jeopardy rules, with several variations in each case. The first situation involves an earlier prosecution for a criminal act—that is likely to be an individual crime such as extortion, forgery, or bribery—that then is either specifically included within the pattern of criminal activity alleged in a subsequent prosecution for enterprise corruption, or that is not so specifically included. The second situation is essentially the reverse, involving a person who has previously been prosecuted for enterprise corruption and is thereafter charged with an individual crime, again either specifically included or not specifically included in the enterprise corruption pattern of criminal activity. The third situation more broadly involves two separate prosecutions for enterprise corruption, or for enterprise corruption and an underlying criminal act. The last situation involves persons who have been previously prosecuted in other jurisdictions for federal RICO or other racketeering-type offenses.

As to the first situation, the provision in question[202] provides that a previous prosecution for a predicate offense bars a subsequent prosecution for enterprise corruption that is in part based either upon that

---

198. CPL § 40.50(1)(a).
199. CPL § 40.50(1)(b).
200. CPL § 40.50(1)(c).
201. CPL § 40.50(1)(d). Special OCCA provisions address both geographical jurisdiction, see P.L. § 460.40, and subject matter jurisdiction among prosecutors. See P.L. §§ 460.50, 460.60.

202. CPL § 40.50(2).

predicate offense, or upon another offense based upon the same act or criminal transaction, unless (1) the person was convicted of the prior offense, and (2) there is at least one felonious criminal act in the OCCA pattern for which the defendant was not previously prosecuted that occurred after the conviction on the prior offense. It should be recalled that the special definition of "is prosecuted" includes not only cases that have been "previously prosecuted" in the usual sense, but also cases where the charge has been dismissed or a motion to suppress has been granted. If the earlier criminal act was not specifically included in the enterprise corruption pattern of criminal activity, there is no bar, unless a crime based upon the same criminal act or criminal transaction was so included.

Next, as to the reverse situation, the statute[203] initially establishes that when the individual offense in question was either specifically included in the pattern of criminal activity of the earlier enterprise corruption or where that pattern specifically included another offense based on the same act or criminal transaction, the enterprise corruption prosecution bars the later prosecution for the individual offense unless (1) the offense is a Class A felony, and (2) it was not prosecutable in the enterprise corruption accusatory instrument. A separate provision[204] addresses a variation of this scenario. If the later individual offense was in fact a part of a pattern of criminal activity that was not specifically included in the earlier enterprise corruption, a person may be prosecuted only if the offense is a Class A or B felony and was either "not prosecutable" or there was then insufficient evidence to charge it.

Next, somewhat confusingly (and perhaps unnecessarily), in addition to provisions that speak of "previous" prosecutions, other provisions govern "separate" prosecutions. First,[205] there is a bar to two separate or subsequent prosecutions for enterprise corruption, unless no common criminal acts are specifically included in the pattern of criminal activity alleged in each. Next, there is a bar to "separate"[206] prosecutions for enterprise corruption and for another offense, where the offense was either specifically included within the enterprise corruption pattern of criminal activity or where that pattern specifically included another offense based on the same act or criminal transaction, unless it is a Class A felony and was not prosecutable. As a necessary corollary to that, a special rule allows separate prosecutions where a court orders a severance of enterprise corruption and specifically included offense counts originally charged in a single accusatory instrument.[207]

Finally, two separate, cross-referenced provisions[208] establish that a person previously prosecuted under federal RICO or another state's RICO statute may not be subsequently prosecuted in New York for the crime of enterprise corruption based upon a pattern of criminal activity

---

203. CPL § 40.50(3).
204. CPL § 40.50(5).
205. CPL §§ 450.60(6) and (7).
206. CPL § 40.50(4), mirroring CPL § 40.50(3). The prohibition is directed at prosecution in two separate accusatory instruments.
207. CPL § 40.50(8).
208. CPL §§ 40.20(2)(h), 40.50(9).

§ 2.9   DOUBLE JEOPARDY   Ch. 2

that specifically includes a criminal act that was also included within the racketeering activity in the other jurisdiction. If the New York enterprise corruption charge is based upon criminal acts that were not specifically included in the previous foreign racketeering prosecution, there is no bar; nor is there a bar to subsequent prosecution in New York for a criminal act that constitutes a crime other than enterprise corruption, whether specifically included or not.[209]

Library References:
West's Key No. Digests, Double Jeopardy ⟲151.

§ 2.10   Miscellaneous Issues—Multiple Punishment, Civil Proceedings and Juvenile Proceedings

Although the most common double jeopardy problem involves the prohibition against multiple criminal prosecutions for the same conduct, a number of other double jeopardy issues deserve mention. For example, a prohibition exists against multiple punishments for the same offense.[210] The most frequently encountered situation involves retrials. The Supreme Court has interpreted this aspect of the double jeopardy clause to require that punishment already exacted be fully credited where a defendant wins a retrial, but is then again convicted. The court held that neither the double jeopardy provision nor the equal protection clause imposes an absolute bar to a more severe sentence upon reconviction; however, to guard against the possibility of "vindictiveness," *i.e.*, retaliation against the defendant for bringing the appeal that led to the new trial, a judge's decision to impose a more severe sentence "must be based upon objective information concerning identifiable conduct on the part of the defendant occurring after the time of the original sentencing proceeding. And the factual data upon which the increased sentence is based must be made part of the record, so that the constitutional legitimacy of the increased sentence may be fully reviewed on appeal."[211]

In New York, this rule has been interpreted as creating a rebuttable presumption that a sentence upon re-conviction that is harsher than the originally imposed sentence is invalid.[212] For example, it has been held that imposing a heavier sentence after a trial conviction than that which

---

209. It should be noted that CPL § 40.20(2)(h), which cross-references CPL § 40.50, is an exception to the general rules of New York statutory "same criminal transaction" double jeopardy. The practical effect of that provision is to make the general rules of section 40.20 barring a subsequent prosecution inapplicable to a situation governed by section 40.50. However, these sections were effective on November 1, 1986 (see L. 1986, c. 516, § 15), and thus a different analysis is required if the criminal acts in question occurred before that date. See Mason v. Rothwax, 152 A.D.2d 272, 282–83, 548 N.Y.S.2d 926, 932–33 (1st Dep't 1989) ("However, CPL 40.20(2)(h) and 40.50(9) ... are applicable to a pattern of criminal activity beginning prior to its effective date only if a defendant's participation in the alleged pattern of criminal activity includes at least one felonious act committed on or after November 1, 1986.").

210. As the Supreme Court once put it, "[T]he Constitution was designed as much to prevent the criminal from being twice punished for the same offense as from being twice tried for it." Ex parte Lange, 85 U.S. (18 Wall.) 163, 173, 21 L.Ed. 872 (1874).

211. North Carolina v. Pearce, 395 U.S. 711, 727, 89 S.Ct. 2072, 2081, 23 L.Ed.2d 656 (1969).

212. People v. Van Pelt, 76 N.Y.2d 156, 556 N.Y.S.2d 984, 556 N.E.2d 423 (1990).

84

was imposed as the result of a plea bargain subsequently vacated on appeal is not constitutionally prohibited.[213] In addition, the rule has also been held to be entirely inapplicable where a defendant's sentence includes a period of probation that is subsequently violated.[214] However, the Court of Appeals has also held that the New York Constitution requires that the presumption apply even in those situations where a subsequent higher sentence is imposed by a different judge.[215]

Another multiple punishments problem, rarely encountered in ordinary practice, involves whether a defendant can be subjected to cumulative punishments under different statutes prescribing similar conduct. Generally, so long as it appears that the Legislature has authorized cumulative punishments, double jeopardy is not offended.[216]

The next multiple punishment area concerns recidivist sentencing. Generally, it has been held that "the protections embodied in the double jeopardy clauses of the Federal and State Constitutions do not apply to ... enhanced sentencing proceedings required under New York's second and persistent felony offender statutes."[217] The Supreme Court has also generally held that constitutional double jeopardy does not prevent the use of prior criminal conduct for enhanced sentencing.[218] Accordingly, for example, after the reversal of a defendant's recidivist sentence, which is found to have been improperly based upon a particular predicate offense, it is not improper for a prosecutor to utilize a different predicate offense at resentencing.[219] Moreover, the use of particular New York conduct to enhance a prior federal sentence does not preclude New York from subsequent prosecution for that conduct.[220]

The final multiple punishments area, which has generated substantial controversy, involves the relationship of criminal prosecutions and traditional criminal punishments such as imprisonment and fines to certain kinds of civil proceedings by the government, notably forfeiture proceedings. Civil forfeiture statutes[221] allow the state to bring an action

---

213. People v. Miller, 65 N.Y.2d 502, 493 N.Y.S.2d 96, 482 N.E.2d 892 (1985).

214. People v. Miles, 192 A.D.2d 781, 596 N.Y.S.2d 482 (3d Dep't 1993).

215. People v. Van Pelt, supra. Van Pelt concluded that the Supreme Court, in Texas v. McCullough, 475 U.S. 134, 106 S.Ct. 976, 89 L.Ed.2d 104 (1986), had held the presumption inapplicable where the sentencing judges were different.

216. See Missouri v. Hunter, 459 U.S. 359, 103 S.Ct. 673, 74 L.Ed.2d 535 (1983).

217. People v. Sailor, 65 N.Y.2d 224, 226–27, 491 N.Y.S.2d 112, 115, 480 N.E.2d 701, 703 (1985). P.L. §§ 70.06–70.10, in conjunction with CPL §§ 400.15–400.21, establish a procedure for recidivist sentencing that requires the prosecutor to file a statement specifying the proposed predicate offenses, following which a hearing is held to determine the matter.

218. See, e.g., Witte v. United States, ___ U.S. ___, 115 S.Ct. 2199, 132 L.Ed.2d 351 (1995)(convicting and sentencing a defendant for a crime when the conduct underlying that offense had previously been considered for enhancement purposes in determining the defendant's sentence on a prior conviction not barred).

219. People v. Hunt, 78 N.Y.2d 932, 574 N.Y.S.2d 178, 579 N.E.2d 208 (1991).

220. Matter of Cantave v. Supreme Court, 193 A.D.2d 277, 603 N.Y.S.2d 591 (3d Dep't 1993).

221. Forfeiture statutes may be civil or criminal. Criminal forfeiture is brought as an integral part of the same proceeding that decides the defendant's guilt or innocence for the crime upon which the forfeiture is based. New York has two criminal forfeiture statutes: Penal Law Article 480 (narcotics criminal forfeiture) and P.L. § 460.30 (OCCA—State RICO—forfeiture). Civil forfeiture is brought entirely apart from, and usually subsequent to, the criminal action, often before a different judge.

against a person who has benefited from criminal activity or against property that is linked to criminal activity in certain ways.[222] These statutes, as well as other crime-linked civil laws,[223] are often employed against people who have been criminally prosecuted for the crime that underlies the civil action, and typically require the state to prove that the property is the proceeds of criminal activity or is linked to criminal activity.[224] These laws have survived double jeopardy challenges because of their civil nature,[225] and courts have given great deference to the simple legislative assignment of the "civil" classification.[226] Accordingly, for the greater part of this century there have been crime-linked civil forfeiture statutes of one sort or another in most jurisdictions, and the use of such statutes has increased dramatically in recent years.

In recent years, however, the Supreme Court has twice voided, on double jeopardy grounds, civil actions that followed criminal prosecutions, both times under quite unusual circumstances. In the first case,[227] the defendant had been criminally convicted of a medicare fraud involving the theft of $585 from the federal government, and was sentenced to two years in prison and a $5000 fine. The subsequent civil action, brought under the federal False Claims Act, sought to recover some $130,000 in civil penalties, damages, and costs. The court stated that "under the Double Jeopardy Clause a defendant who already has been punished in a criminal prosecution may not be subjected to an additional civil sanction to the extent that the second sanction may not be fairly

---

222. Civil forfeiture proceedings may be either in personam or in rem. An in personam proceeding is against a person, much as an ordinary civil tort. An in rem proceeding is an action to settle the ownership of a particular piece of property. New York has both a comprehensive in personam civil forfeiture statute, CPLR Article 13–A, which is applicable to all felonies, and several narrower in rem civil forfeiture statues, such as Public Health Law § 3388 (forfeiture of vehicles used to transport illegal drugs), Penal Law § 415.00 (forfeiture of vehicles used to transport gambling records), Penal Law § 410.00 (forfeiture of pornography equipment), and Penal Law § 420.05 (forfeiture of equipment used in unauthorized recordings).

223. See, e.g., Real Property Actions and Proceedings Law § 711(5)(the "bawdy house" law, allowing for the eviction of tenants who use their premises for an illegal trade; now commonly used against drug sellers); New York City Admin. Code § 701 (the "nuisance abatement" law, aimed at illegal sex purveyors).

224. See, e.g., CPLR 1310(8)(defining a "criminal defendant" for forfeiture purposes as a person who has been criminally convicted of a felony or who can be proved, within the forfeiture action itself, to have committed a felony).

225. United States v. One Assortment of 89 Firearms, 465 U.S. 354, 104 S.Ct. 1099, 79 L.Ed.2d 361 (1984).

226. See, e.g., United States v. Ward, 448 U.S. 242, 248–49, 100 S.Ct. 2636, 2641, 65 L.Ed.2d 742 (1980)("First, we have set out to determine whether [the legislature] indicated either expressly or impliedly a preference for one label or the other.... Second, where [the legislature] has indicated an intention to establish a civil penalty, we have inquired further whether the statutory scheme was so punitive either in purpose or effect as to negate that intention.") See also Kennedy v. Mendoza–Martinez, 372 U.S. 144, 83 S.Ct. 554 9 L.Ed.2d 644 (1963) (providing criteria for that "further inquiry.") Some crime-linked civil statutes of recent vintage have accordingly included specific provisions declaring that they are civil in nature. See, e.g., CPLR 1311(1)(declaring that the statute is "civil, remedial and in personam in nature ... [not] a penalty ... and not a criminal proceeding and may not be deemed a previous prosecution under article forty of the criminal procedure law").

227. United States v. Halper, 490 U.S. 435, 109 S.Ct. 1892, 104 L.Ed.2d 487 (1989).

characterized as remedial, but only as a deterrent or retribution."[228] The opinion uneasily reviewed the extensive body of precedent giving great deference to a legislative characterization of "civil" for double jeopardy purposes, and took pains to specify that "[w]e cast no shadow on these time-honored judgments. What we announce now is a rule for the rare case."[229] The sense of unease permeated that opinion turned out to be quite prescient. Five years later, the court struck down a Montana statute that imposed a tax on the possession and storage of illegal drugs. The defendants, who had operated a marihuana farm, pleaded guilty to a criminal offense, were sentenced, and were also the subjects of a civil forfeiture proceeding. Thereafter, in a separate third proceeding, the state sought to collect almost $900,000 in "taxes" under a statutory scheme that, among other things, was conditioned upon commission of a crime, was due only after arrest, applied only to contraband goods that were in fact destroyed, and was assessed at eight times the market value of the goods. The court called the statute "a concoction of anomalies, too far removed in crucial respects from a standard tax assessment to escape characterization as punishment for the purpose of Double Jeopardy analysis."[230]

These two cases constitute something of a break with tradition, and reinforce the proposition that a legislature's characterization of a statute as "civil" in nature is not completely determinative. However, that proposition is not in itself startling, and given the court's cautionary language and the unique and extreme nature of the statutes at issue, one might conclude that the decisions have little practical impact beyond the restraint of what might be described as excessive creativity in the area of crime-linked civil statutes.

To the contrary, however, in highly controversial and potentially far-reaching decisions, at least two federal appellate courts have applied these holdings to invoke double jeopardy protection in the context of ordinary civil forfeiture statutes.[231] Obviously, the impact of these decisions may ultimately be determined by the Supreme Court. To date, however, the New York Court of Appeals has long recognized the distinction between civil and criminal proceedings for purposes of applying double jeopardy protection,[232] and the United States Court of Appeals for the Second Circuit has held that, at least where a criminal prosecu-

---

228. 490 U.S. at 448–49, 109 S.Ct. at 1902.

229. 490 U.S. at 449, 109 S.Ct. at 1902.

230. Montana Dept. of Revenue v. Kurth Ranch, 511 U.S. ___, 114 S.Ct. 1937, 1948, 128 L.Ed.2d 767 (1994).

231. See United States v. $405,089.23 U.S. Currency, 33 F.3d 1210, opinion amended, mot. for en banc review den., 56 F.3d 41 (9th Cir.1995); United States v. Ursery, 59 F.3d 568 (6th Cir.1995). See also United States v. Hudson, 14 F.3d 536 (10th Cir.1994)(expanding the Halper standard, if not the result). These decisions have "set off an avalanche of litigation over the double jeopardy implications of forfeiture." Casella, "Responding to Double Jeopardy Challenges," Financial Crimes Report (National Association of Attorneys General April/May 1995). They have also led to litigation in other areas, such as a nationwide flurry of claims that administrative suspension of a driver's license bars a subsequent criminal prosecution based on the same conduct.

232. Escobar v. Roberts, 29 N.Y.2d 594, 324 N.Y.S.2d 318, 272 N.E.2d 898 (1971)(prison disciplinary proceeding); See Barnes v. Tofany, 27 N.Y.2d 74, 313 N.Y.S.2d 690, 261 N.E.2d 617 (1970)(suspension of driver's license).

tion and civil forfeiture proceed essentially contemporaneously, they can be considered as one action for double jeopardy purposes.[233] Further, to date New York courts have refused to interpret the Supreme Court decisions as applying to ordinary civil forfeiture proceedings to bar an eviction based on illegal narcotics activity following a criminal conviction,[234] or to bar a criminal prosecution for driving while intoxicated following a suspension of the defendant's driver's license.[235] In sum, although logic and the force of some precedent mitigate against an expansive application of these Supreme Court cases, this area of law is currently unsettled. Thus, whenever the state brings both a criminal prosecution and a civil proceeding, involving the same conduct, the potential argument should be kept in mind.

Although at one time juvenile proceedings were thought to be noncriminal in nature, and constitutional guarantees therefore generally inapplicable, in 1975 the Supreme Court explicitly held that federal constitutional double jeopardy protection was applicable to such proceedings.[236] There, the court prohibited prosecution of a minor for a robbery after a delinquency proceeding in juvenile court. Moreover, the New York Family Court Act now provides that "the provisions of article forty of the criminal procedure law concerning double jeopardy shall apply to juvenile delinquency proceedings."[237] Thus, the whole panoply of statutory double jeopardy protection has at least theoretically been brought into juvenile delinquency proceedings by cross-reference.[238]

Library References:

West's Key No. Digests, Double Jeopardy ⚖ 23, 25, 28–30, 33.

§ 2.11 Procedure for Raising a Double Jeopardy Claim

A double jeopardy claim may be raised in several, non-mutually exclusive ways. First, if there is reason to believe that a current prosecution is barred by a previous prosecution under either a constitutional or a statutory theory, the defendant may move in the appropriate

---

233. United States v. Millan, 2 F.3d 17 (2d Cir.1993). Obviously, it is possible to argue about what is contemporaneous for these purposes. In CPLR Article 13–A forfeiture, it is routine to initiate the civil action contemporaneously with the criminal prosecution, in order to attach property. See CPLR 1311(1)(a)(staying forfeiture action during pendency of prosecution).

234. District Attorney of Kings County v. Iadarola, 164 Misc.2d 204, 623 N.Y.S.2d 999 (Sup.Ct., Kings County, 1995)(forfeiture proceeding); City of New York v. Wright, 162 Misc.2d 572, 618 N.Y.S.2d 938 (App. Term, 1st Dep't, 1994)(eviction proceeding).

235. People v. Frank, ___ Misc.2d ___, 631 N.Y.S.2d 1014 (N.Y.C.Crim.Ct.1995); People v. McLees, ___ Misc.2d ___, 631 N.Y.S.2d 990 (Dist.Ct., Suffolk County, 1995).

236. Breed v. Jones, 421 U.S. 519, 95 S.Ct. 1779, 44 L.Ed.2d 346 (1975).

237. Family Court Act § 303.2.

238. Accordingly, in the context of juvenile delinquency proceedings, courts have had to grapple with many of the same problems that occur in a criminal context. See, e.g., Matter of Jose R., 83 N.Y.2d 388, 610 N.Y.S.2d 937, 632 N.E.2d 1260 (1994)(deciding, inter alia, that a dismissal of a juvenile delinquency petition by the Appellate Division on the ground that the Family Court proceeding had been untimely was not the functional equivalent of a dismissal on the ground that the juvenile's guilt had not been established for double jeopardy purposes). Of course, some of the statutory rules of CPL Article 40 govern situations that are unlikely to arise in the context of juvenile delinquency proceedings.

trial court to dismiss the accusatory instrument.[239] If the motion is denied, the matter may then be raised in the appeal from any ensuing judgment of conviction. Constitutional double jeopardy claims may be raised on appeal even if they were not raised in the trial court,[240] but statutory double jeopardy claims "must be duly preserved if there is to be appellate review."[241] A constitutional double jeopardy claim is waivable, however, "in certain unusual cases, as where a defendant explicitly consents to retrial despite a double jeopardy defense."[242] Although a constitutional double jeopardy claim is not forfeited by a guilty plea,[243] such a plea does forfeit a statutory double jeopardy claim, even if it was expressly raised in the trial court before the plea was taken.[244]

Another method of raising either a statutory or constitutional double jeopardy claim is by a proceeding pursuant to CPLR Article 78.[245] It does not matter that the claim has been raised and denied in the trial court.[246] An Article 78 proceeding is a special proceeding, in this case in the nature of prohibition, brought against a government official on the theory that he or she is proceeding or about to proceed without or in excess of jurisdiction.[247] Normally, it is brought against the appropriate trial judge, or, in situations where no specific judge is yet assigned, against the entire panel of judges who would normally hear the prosecution that is sought to be prohibited. In felony cases, where the prosecution is before a Supreme Court justice, a County Court judge, or if no judge has been assigned, a panel of such judges, the Article 78 proceeding is brought directly in the appropriate Appellate Division. In other cases, it is brought in the civil term of the Supreme Court.[248]

Thus, in felony prosecutions it is possible to raise a double jeopardy claim by motion in the trial court, lose, and then proceed immediately to the Appellate Division rather than awaiting the usual direct appeal after conviction. Moreover, the claim can then be raised again on the direct appeal following a conviction. A claim based on the federal Constitution may also be raised in the federal courts by way of habeas corpus.

Library References:

West's Key No. Digests, Criminal Law ⇌289–297, 1030(3); Prohibition ⇌5(4), 10(3).

239. The appropriate motion should be made pursuant to CPL § 170.30(1)(c) (motion to dismiss non-felony local criminal court accusatory instrument), or CPL § 210.20(1)(e)(motion to dismiss indictment).

240. People v. Michael, 48 N.Y.2d 1, 420 N.Y.S.2d 371, 394 N.E.2d 1134 (1979).

241. People v. Dodson, 48 N.Y.2d 36, 38, 421 N.Y.S.2d 47, 48, 396 N.E.2d 194, 195 (1979).

242. People v. Michael, 48 N.Y.2d at 7, 420 N.Y.S.2d at 374, 394 N.E.2d at 1137.

243. Menna v. New York, 423 U.S. 61, 96 S.Ct. 241, 46 L.Ed.2d 195 (1975).

244. People v. Prescott, 66 N.Y.2d 216, 495 N.Y.S.2d 955, 486 N.E.2d 813 (1985), cert. den. 475 U.S. 1150, 106 S.Ct. 1804, 90 L.Ed.2d 349 (1986).

245. See, e.g., Forte v. Supreme Court, 48 N.Y.2d 179, 422 N.Y.S.2d 26, 397 N.E.2d 717 (1979); Matter of Abraham v. Justices, 37 N.Y.2d 560, 376 N.Y.S.2d 79, 338 N.E.2d 597 (1975).

246. Matter of Corbin v. Hillery, 74 N.Y.2d 279, 545 N.Y.S.2d 71, 543 N.E.2d 714, aff'd sub nom. Grady v. Corbin, 495 U.S. 508, 110 S.Ct. 2084, 109 L.Ed.2d 548 (1990).

247. CPLR 7803(2).

248. CPLR 506(b), 7804(b).

§ 2.12 Practice Summary

A. Attachment of Jeopardy

1. Before there can be double jeopardy, a prior proceeding must have progressed to a point where jeopardy has attached. There must have been a prosecution in New York, or in a federal court or a court of another state, in which:

   - a plea of guilty was entered;
   - there was a jury trial and a jury was sworn; or
   - in the case of a trial without a jury, a witness was sworn (*see* § 2.2).

2. However, even if there was such a prior proceeding, there will be no double jeopardy bar if:

   - the court in which the first proceeding took place lacked jurisdiction (*see* § 2.3);
   - the defendant deceitfully procured the prior prosecution, for a lesser offense, without the knowledge of the appropriate prosecutor (*see* § 2.3);
   - there was a mistrial, to which the defendant consented, unless the defendant was provoked into moving for, or consenting to, a mistrial by intentional judicial or prosecutorial conduct (*see* § 2.4);
   - there was manifest necessity for a non-consensual mistrial, or the ends of justice would otherwise have been defeated by continuance of the proceedings (*see* § 2.4);
   - there was a trial order of dismissal, unless it was made intra-trial and based upon evidence adduced at trial (*see* § 2.4); or
   - there was a withdrawn guilty plea or appellate reversal, unless the plea was vacated without consent by a court lacking power to do so or the reversal was based upon the weight or sufficiency of the trial evidence (*see* § 2.4).

B. Constitutional Double Jeopardy

1. It is important to remember that the United States and New York Constitutions on the one hand, and the CPL on the other, establish separate kinds of double jeopardy protection. In general, the CPL offers the greatest protection. Statutory "same criminal transaction" double jeopardy is broader than constitutional "same offense" double jeopardy. Also, constitutional double jeopardy does not prevent New York from prosecuting someone who has previously been prosecuted in another state or by the federal government; statutory double jeopardy does prevent such prosecutions (*see* § 2.1).

2. If the first prosecution involved the "same offense" as the second, then the Constitutions prohibit a second prosecution by the same authority. The elements of the two offenses must be examined, and if the statutes defining the offenses cover a broad range of conduct, the

allegations of the indictment or the facts of the two prosecutions should be examined as well (see § 2.5).

3. If the conduct in question was committed over a considerable period of time, the issue of whether there can be more than a single prosecution may depend on whether the offense can be classified as a "continuing offense," which depends on the nature of the elements of the offense and whether there were lapses or breaks in those elements over the period in question. In practice, this frequently arises in connection with criminal conduct which crosses the borders of several jurisdictions (see § 2.5).

C. Statutory Double Jeopardy

1. In determining whether New York statutory "same criminal transaction" double jeopardy bars a subsequent prosecution, it is first necessary to evaluate whether the conduct comprising the offense in the initial prosecution is part of the same criminal transaction as that which is involved in the instant prosecution. If the answer to that question is yes, it is then necessary to evaluate whether one of the statutory exemptions applies to defeat the claim of statutory jeopardy. Finally, the mandatory joinder prohibition must be considered (see § 2.7).

2. Two or more acts are part of the same criminal transaction if they are:

- so closely related and connected in point of time and circumstance of commission as to constitute a single criminal incident; or
- so closely related in criminal purpose or objective as to constitute elements or integral parts of a single criminal venture (see § 2.6).

3. Even if that definition is met, however, there is no statutory jeopardy bar to a New York prosecution if:

- the offense in the previous prosecution had substantially different elements and the acts underlying it are in the main clearly distinguishable from those establishing the instant offense;
- the previous offense and the instant offense each contain an element that is not an element of the other, and the statutes are designed to prevent very different kinds of evil or harm;
- one offense is possession of "contraband" and the other involves "use," not "sale," of that contraband;
- after an initial prosecution for an offense that involved physical injury, the victim dies, and the second prosecution is for homicide;
- each offense involved different individual victims;
- a previous prosecution in another jurisdiction was terminated by an order dismissing, on the basis of insufficient evidence, an element of that jurisdiction's offense that is not an element of the instant New York offense; or
- conspiracy, facilitation, or solicitation previously prosecuted in another state, but not in a federal court, results in a consummated result offense in New York (§§ 2.6, 2.9).

D. Mandatory Joinder (See § 2.7)

1. In addition to statutory double jeopardy, New York has another special rule, called "mandatory joinder", which is sometimes even broader than statutory double jeopardy. The rule will bar separate prosecution of "joinable offenses" in two instances:

- if one or more offenses are charged in an accusatory instrument, but another joinable offense is not charged in that instrument or in any other accusatory instrument filed in the same court, and the prosecution had legally sufficient evidence of that uncharged offense, commencement of a trial or a plea on the accusatory instrument precludes later prosecution for the uncharged offense; or

- if joinable offenses contained in two separate accusatory instruments are filed in the same court, and the defendant moves to consolidate them and that motion is improperly denied, the commencement of trial on one instrument bars prosecution on the other.

2. If separate accusatory instruments charging joinable offenses are filed in separate courts, and one of the accusatory instruments is disposed in a court with geographical and subject matter jurisdiction over the offenses charged in the other accusatory instrument, prosecution of joinable offenses charged in the other accusatory instrument is barred even if all other double jeopardy rules are not violated (*e.g.*, if one of the statutory exceptions to "same criminal transaction" statutory double jeopardy is applicable).

E. Collateral Estoppel (See § 2.8)

1. Assuming that all the foregoing protections are inapplicable, if a defendant has previously been prosecuted in a separate proceeding involving witnesses, evidence, or conduct similar to that involved in the instant proceeding, the doctrine of collateral estoppel should be considered. Although this doctrine, unlike double jeopardy or mandatory joinder, will not bar a subsequent prosecution, it may foreclose relitigation of issues previously decided in favor of a party—most often, a defendant who has previously been acquitted for a similar crime or for a crime close in time and space to the instant crime.

2. The New York doctrine of collateral estoppel is broader than the federal constitutional doctrine. The two proceedings must meet three requirements:

- identity of parties—in the typical case, the person who is currently being prosecuted must previously have been criminally prosecuted in New York, although the doctrine might apply if any governmental entity was involved in the prior proceeding;

- identity of issues—a difficult and complex question, which must be resolved on a case-by-case basis by examining all of the circumstances of the verdict in the first proceeding, such as the pleadings, the evidence, the arguments of the attorneys, the court's charge to the jury, and the totality of the verdict; and

- a final determination—typically a prior acquittal, but any final resolution of an issue may qualify.

F. Enterprise Corruption Cases (*See* § 2.9)

In cases involving a prosecution for the New York crime of enterprise corruption—State RICO—special statutory double jeopardy rules apply. These rules should be carefully checked if a defendant (1) is being prosecuted for enterprise corruption based upon prior criminal conduct that was the subject of a previous prosecution or dismissal or that was related thereto, or (2) was previously prosecuted for enterprise corruption and is currently being prosecuted for a criminal act that is related to the previous enterprise corruption.

G. Double Jeopardy Issues Relating to Multiple Punishment (*See* § 2.10)

1. If the defendant receives a greater sentence after an appellate reversal or other vacatur, the reasons for the increase must be unrelated to "vindictiveness," and based upon events subsequent to the original sentence.

2. If the defendant has been subjected to both a criminal prosecution and a governmental civil action involving the same conduct, the law currently is unsettled. Historically, the legislature's judgment that one of these actions was civil in nature was accorded great deference and avoided any potential double jeopardy claim. Recent federal precedent, however, including two Supreme Court decisions, has thrown the traditional rules into doubt. Accordingly, until the law is more settled, such a claim should always be considered.

H. Procedure for Raising Claim (*See* § 2.11)

1. Initially, if there is reason to believe that a current prosecution is barred by a previous proceeding, the defendant may move to dismiss in the trial court in which the instant prosecution is pending.

2. The matter can then be raised on appeal after conviction. Constitutional claims may be raised even if not raised below; statutory claims must be preserved. Constitutional claims are not forfeited by a guilty plea, but statutory claims are forfeited.

3. Another method of raising a constitutional or statutory double jeopardy claim is by a proceeding pursuant to CPLR Article 78, to prohibit the trial judge, or the panel of judges if no judge has yet been assigned, from proceeding with the prosecution. In felony cases, this proceeding is brought in the Appellate Division; otherwise, it is brought in the Supreme Court. An adverse decision can be further appealed.

§ 2.13 Forms

§ 2.13.1 Notice of Motion to Dismiss Accusatory Instrument on Ground That Prosecution Is Barred by Previous Prosecution

[Caption]

COUNSEL:

PLEASE TAKE NOTICE, that upon the annexed affirmation and upon all the prior papers and proceedings herein, the undersigned will move this Court, at Part ___ thereof, at the Courthouse at _____, New York, on the ___ day of _____, 19__, at ___ in the forenoon, or as soon thereafter as counsel can be heard, for an order pursuant to section [170.30(1)(c) or 210.20(1)(e)] of the Criminal Procedure Law dismissing the [specify accusatory instrument] on the ground that the prosecution herein is barred by a previous prosecution of the defendant, and for such other relief as the Court deems proper.

Dated: _____, 19__
_____, New York

                                                      [Name of defense attorney]
                                                      Attorney for Defendant
                                                      Address
                                                      Tel. No.

TO: HON. _____
     District Attorney
     _____ County

HON. _____
Clerk of the Court

§ 2.13.2 Affirmation in Support of Motion to Dismiss Accusatory Instrument on Ground That Prosecution Is Barred by Previous Prosecution

[Caption]

_____, an attorney duly admitted to practice in the Courts of this State, hereby affirms under penalty of perjury that the following statements are true, and as for this made upon information and belief he [she] believes them to be true:

1. I am the attorney for the defendant herein.

2. On _____, 19__, a [specify accusatory instrument] was filed with this Court charging defendant with the following offense(s): [specify offense(s) charged]. A copy of the [specify accusatory instrument] is attached hereto as Exhibit A.

3. No plea of guilty has been entered with respect to the [specify accusatory instrument], nor has a trial been commenced thereon.

4. The [specify accusatory instrument] should be dismissed because prosecution of defendant thereunder is barred by a previous prosecution. [Specify facts and circumstances of previous prosecution, and attach as exhibits all relevant records of the previous prosecution that support argument that previous prosecution bars instant prosecution].

5. No other application for the relief sought herein has been made.

WHEREFORE, defendant requests that the Court issue an order pursuant to section [170.30(1)(c) or 210.20(1)(e)] dismissing the [specify accusatory instrument].

Dated: _____, 19__
_____, New York

[Signature]
_____
[Name of defense attorney]

§ 2.13.3 Petition in Article 78 Proceeding to Prohibit Prosecution on Ground That it Is Barred by Previous Prosecution[249]

```
_____
In the Matter of the Application of )
_____,                  )
                                    )
                     Petitioner,    )
                                    )   VERIFIED PETITION
           -against-                )
                                    )   Index No. _____
Hon. _____,             )
[Specify title of judge], and       )
_____,                  )
District Attorney, _____ County,    )
                                    )
                     Respondents.   )
                                    )
_____         )
```

1. Petitioner is the named-defendant under a [specify accusatory instrument] filed in [specify trial court] on _____, 19__, charging petitioner with the following offense(s): [specify offense(s) charged]. A copy of the [specify accusatory instrument] is attached hereto as Exhibit A.

2. Respondent [name of trial judge] is a judge [justice] of the [specify court], and is currently presiding over the prosecution of the aforesaid [specify accusatory instrument].

3. Respondent [name of District Attorney], the District Attorney for _____ County, is prosecuting petitioner under the aforesaid [specify accusatory instrument].

4. The prosecution of petitioner under the aforesaid [specify accusatory instrument] is unlawful because it is barred by a previous prosecution.

5. [Specify facts and circumstances of previous prosecution, attaching as exhibits any relevant records and other information supporting argument that previous prosecution bars the instant prosecution].

---

249. Note that in felony cases, the petition is brought in the Appellate Division; in other cases, it is brought in the civil term of the Supreme Court. See § 2.11, supra.

§ 2.13   DOUBLE JEOPARDY   Ch. 2

6. No previous application for the relief sought herein has been made.

WHEREFORE, petitioner requests that this Court issue an order pursuant to Article 78 of the Civil Practice Law and Rules:

A. Prohibiting respondents from performing or taking any actions or proceedings with respect to the aforesaid [specify accusatory instrument] against petitioner;

B. Staying all further proceedings pursuant to the aforesaid [specify accusatory instrument] pending the hearing and determination of this petition; and

C. Directing any further relief that the Court deems proper.

Dated: _____, 19__
      _____, New York

                                                [Name of defense attorney]

[Verification]

Chapter 3

PRELIMINARY PROCEEDINGS IN LOCAL CRIMINAL COURTS

Table of Sections

3.1 Introduction.
3.2 Local Criminal Court Accusatory Instruments—Types.
3.3 ___ Form and Content.
3.4 ___ Supporting Depositions.
3.5 ___ Supporting Depositions Filed in Connection With Simplified Informations.
3.6 ___ Verification.
3.7 ___ Facial Sufficiency.
3.8 ___ Severance, Consolidation, Amendment and Bill of Particulars.
3.9 ___ Superseding Informations and Prosecutor's Informations.
3.10 Means of Compelling a Defendant's Appearance for Arraignment—In General.
3.11 The Arrest Warrant.
3.12 ___ Form and Content.
3.13 ___ Additional Procedural Requirements.
3.14 ___ Execution.
3.15 ___ Post-Arrest Procedure.
3.16 The Summons.
3.17 Warrantless Arrests—In General.
3.18 ___ Authorization and Execution.
3.19 ___ Post-Arrest Procedure.
3.20 Appearance Ticket—In General.
3.21 ___ Pre-arraignment Bail and Post-Issuance Procedures.
3.22 ___ Marihuana Violations.
3.23 Fingerprinting.
3.24 Arraignment on Non-felony Accusatory Instrument.
3.25 Conversion or Replacement of Misdemeanor Complaint to Information.
3.26 Motion to Dismiss—In General.
3.27 ___ Defective Accusatory Instrument.
3.28 ___ In Furtherance of Justice.
3.29 Adjournment in Contemplation of Dismissal.
3.30 Arraignment on Felony Complaints.
3.31 Return of Felony Complaint to Local Criminal Court.
3.32 Reduction of Felony Charges.
3.33 The Preliminary Hearing.
3.34 Release of Defendant in Custody.
3.35 Practice Summary.
3.36 Forms.
    3.36.1 Supporting Deposition.
    3.36.2 Defendant's Request for Supporting Deposition.
    3.36.3 Supporting Deposition for Simplified Information.
    3.36.4 Notice of Motion to Amend Prosecutor's Information.
    3.36.5 Affirmation in Support of Motion to Amend Prosecutor's Information.
    3.36.6 Notice of Motion to Amend Information.

Table of Sections

3.36 Forms (Cont'd)
- 3.36.7 Affirmation in Support of Motion to Amend Information.
- 3.36.8 Petition for Writ of *Habeas Corpus* on Behalf of Person Arrested Without Warrant Who Has Not Been Produced for Arraignment.
- 3.36.9 Notice of Motion to Dismiss Local Criminal Court Accusatory Instrument (or a count thereof).
- 3.36.10 Affirmation in Support of Motion to Dismiss Local Criminal Court Accusatory Instrument (or a count thereof).
- 3.36.11 Notice of Motion to Dismiss Local Criminal Court Accusatory Instrument in Furtherance of Justice.
- 3.36.12 Affirmation in Support of Motion to Dismiss Local Criminal Court Accusatory Instrument in Furtherance of Justice.
- 3.36.13 Notice of Motion to Restore Proceedings on Local Criminal Court Accusatory Instrument That Were Adjourned in Contemplation of Dismissal.
- 3.36.14 Affirmation in Support of Motion to Restore Proceedings on Local Criminal Court Accusatory Instrument That Were Adjourned in Contemplation of Dismissal.
- 3.36.15 Notice of Motion for Order Releasing Defendant From Custody for Failure to Replace Misdemeanor Complaint With Information.
- 3.36.16 Affirmation in Support of Motion for Order Releasing Defendant From Custody for Failure to Replace Misdemeanor Complaint With Information.
- 3.36.17 Notice of Motion for Order Releasing Defendant From Custody for Lack of Timely Disposition of Felony Complaint.
- 3.36.18 Affirmation in Support of Motion for Order Releasing Defendant From Custody for Lack of Timely Disposition of Felony Complaint.

WESTLAW Electronic Research

See WESTLAW Electronic Research Guide preceding the Summary of Contents.

§ 3.1 Introduction

Virtually all criminal actions in New York, whether they involve serious felony charges or the lowest level of offenses, are commenced in a local criminal court.[1] Although, unlike the superior courts, local criminal courts have only preliminary jurisdiction of cases involving felony charges, even that limited jurisdiction may involve these courts in significant proceedings in the action, such as bail determinations and preliminary hearings.[2]

A criminal action is formally commenced in local criminal court by the filing with the court of a local criminal court accusatory instrument—*i.e.*, an information, a simplified information, a prosecutor's infor-

---

1. A criminal action may be commenced directly in a superior court only if an indictment is filed in that court against a defendant who was never held for the action of the grand jury with regard to any of the charges set forth in the indictment. See CPL § 100.05. This occurs in an extremely small percentage of cases, which generally involve criminal actions that have resulted from extensive prosecutorial investigations, such as white collar or organized crime cases.

2. As is explained in § 3.30, however, preliminary hearings are conducted in relatively few criminal actions, particularly in New York City.

mation, a misdemeanor complaint or a felony complaint.[3] The filing of the accusatory instrument (and the consequent commencement of the criminal action) serves as the triggering event for other critical procedural benchmarks in the case. For example, the statutory speedy trial period is keyed to the filing of the accusatory instrument with the local criminal court,[4] as is the statute of limitations period.[5] In addition, important constitutional rights, such as the right to counsel, attach upon the filing of the accusatory instrument.[6]

Library References:
West's Key No. Digests, Criminal Law ⚖157, 207, 577.8(2), 641.3(3).

§ 3.2 Local Criminal Court Accusatory Instruments—Types

Five types of accusatory instruments may commence a criminal action in local criminal court. The most basic accusatory instrument is the complaint, which comes in two forms: the misdemeanor complaint and the felony complaint. A misdemeanor complaint must charge at least one misdemeanor offense; it may not charge a felony, but it may charge a petty offense.[7] Although a criminal action may be commenced by the filing of a misdemeanor complaint, the misdemeanor complaint may not serve as the basis for the trial of an action, unless the defendant, pursuant to CPL § 170.65(3), waives prosecution by information.[8]

The felony complaint must charge at least one felony offense; if it does, it may also charge non-felony offenses.[9] Unlike all other types of local criminal court accusatory instruments, it may never, under any circumstances, serve as the basis for trial of an action.[10]

Unlike misdemeanor and felony complaints, the three remaining local criminal court accusatory instruments—the information, the prosecutor's information and the simplified information—may serve as the basis for the trial of a criminal action. The information, which may charge any offense other than a felony,[11] is unique in that it must, either

---

3. CPL § 100.05.
4. See CPL §§ 1.20(17), 30.30(1).
5. See CPL § 30.10(1).
6. See People v. Settles, 46 N.Y.2d 154, 412 N.Y.S.2d 874, 385 N.E.2d 612 (1978).
7. CPL § 100.10(4). A "felony" is defined as "an offense for which a sentence to a term of imprisonment in excess of one year may be imposed." P.L. § 10.00(5). A "misdemeanor" is defined as "an offense, other than a 'traffic infraction,' for which a sentence to a term of imprisonment in excess of fifteen days may be imposed, but for which a sentence to a term of imprisonment in excess of one year cannot be imposed." P.L. § 10.00(4). A "violation" is defined as an "offense, other than a 'traffic infraction,' for which a sentence to a term of imprisonment in excess of fifteen days may not be imposed." P.L. § 10.00(3). A "traffic infraction" is any "offense defined as 'traffic infraction' by section one hundred fifty-five of the vehicle and traffic law." A "petty offense" includes a violation or a traffic infraction. CPL § 1.20(39).

8. CPL § 100.10(4). Waiver of prosecution by information is discussed in § 3.25, infra.

9. CPL § 100.10(5).

10. Id. Felony offenses may only be tried if charged in an indictment or a superior court information.

11. CPL § 100.10(1). An "offense" is defined as "conduct for which a sentence to a term of imprisonment or to a fine is provided by any law of this state or by any law, local law or ordinance of a political

alone or together with any supporting depositions filed in connection with it pursuant to CPL § 100.20, establish a *prima facie* case. This means that the information, together with any supporting depositions, must contain *non-hearsay* factual allegations providing reasonable cause to believe that the defendant committed every element of the offense or offenses that are charged.[12] This requirement promotes the purposes of an information, which are "to inform defendant of the nature of the charge and the acts constituting it so that he may prepare for trial" and to protect the defendant "from being tried again for the same offense."[13]

A prosecutor's information also may charge any offense other than a felony offense.[14] Its filing can result from one of several circumstances: (1) a grand jury may direct its filing pursuant to CPL § 190.70; (2) a local criminal court may direct its filing pursuant to CPL § 180.50 or CPL § 180.70; (3) the prosecutor may file it on his or her own initiative pursuant to CPL § 100.50(2); or (4) a superior court may direct its filing pursuant to CPL § 210.20(2–a). In all of these scenarios, which are more fully discussed in other sections of this Chapter and in Chapter 5, a *prima facie* case must have been established for the offense or offenses charged in the prosecutor's information prior to the actual filing of the prosecutor's information. For example, for a prosecutor's information to be filed at the direction of the grand jury or at the direction of a superior court, a *prima facie* case for the offense or offenses charged in the prosecutor's information must be established in the grand jury minutes.[15] If it is to be filed at the direction of a local criminal court, a *prima facie* case must be established in the felony complaint, and in any accompanying supporting depositions, that is being replaced by the prosecutor's information or in the evidence presented at the preliminary hearing.[16] And if it is to be filed on the prosecutor's own initiative, a *prima facie* case must be established in the original information that the prosecutor's information will supersede.[17]

A simplified information may take three forms: (1) a simplified traffic information (commonly known as a "traffic ticket"), in the form prescribed by the Commissioner of Motor Vehicles, charging non-felony offenses under the Vehicle and Traffic Law; (2) a simplified parks information, in the form prescribed by the Commissioner of Parks and Recreation, charging non-felony offenses under the Parks and Recreation Law and the Navigation Law; or (3) a simplified environmental conservation information, in the form prescribed by the Commissioner of Environmental Conservation, charging non-felony offenses under the Environmental Conservation Law.[18] A simplified information need set

subdivision of this state, or by any order, rule or regulation of any governmental instrumentality authorized by law to adopt the same." P.L. § 10.00(1).

12. See CPL § 100.40(1). See § 3.7, infra.

13. People v. Miles, 64 N.Y.2d 731, 732–33, 485 N.Y.S.2d 747, 748, 475 N.E.2d 118, 119 (1984).

14. CPL § 100.10(3).

15. See CPL §§ 190.70(1), 210.10(1–a).

16. See CPL §§ 180.50(3)(a), 180.70(2).

17. See CPL § 100.50(2).

18. CPL § 100.10(2).

forth no factual allegations, but only the offense or offenses charged.[19] The factual allegations, however, must be set forth in the supporting deposition, if one is requested pursuant to CPL § 100.25(2). A simplified information must be issued by a police officer or by another public servant authorized by law to do so; if not, it will be jurisdictionally defective.[20] Unlike the other local criminal court accusatory instruments, the filing of a simplified information may not serve as the basis for issuance of a warrant of arrest.[21]

Library References:

West's Key No. Digests, Automobiles ⟲351.1; Criminal Law ⟲205–246; Indictment and Information ⟲35–54.

§ 3.3 Local Criminal Court Accusatory Instruments—Form and Content

Local criminal court accusatory instruments must comply with certain form and content requirements. The requirements for informations, misdemeanor complaints and felony complaints are essentially the same. These accusatory instruments must specify the name of the court in which the accusatory instrument is filed and the title of the action.[22] The complainant, who must subscribe the document, may be anyone with knowledge of the offense or offenses charged, and that knowledge may be personal or based on information and belief.[23] For example, the complainant may be the actual victim of the alleged offense or the police officer to whom the offense was reported.

These three accusatory instruments also must contain the complainant's factual allegations in support of the charges.[24] The complainant's factual allegations must be verified, in accordance with CPL § 100.30.[25] If more than one offense is charged, the factual allegations should consist of a single factual account pertaining to all the counts in the accusatory instrument.[26] In addition, these accusatory instruments must designate the offense or offenses charged.[27] Whether two or more offenses may be charged in separate counts, and whether two or more defendants may be charged within the same accusatory instrument, are

19. Id.

20. People v. Shapiro, 61 N.Y.2d 880, 882, 474 N.Y.S.2d 470, 470, 462 N.E.2d 1188, 1188 (1984).

21. CPL § 120.20(1). See § 3.13, infra.

22. CPL § 100.15(1).

23. Id. However, as discussed in § 3.2, supra, and § 3.7, infra, an information may serve as the basis for the trial of a criminal action only if, along with any supporting depositions filed, it sets forth a prima facie case—i.e., non-hearsay factual allegations establishing reasonable cause to believe that the defendant committed every element of the offense or offenses charged.

24. CPL § 100.15(3).

25. CPL § 100.15(1). Verification of local criminal court accusatory instruments is discussed in § 3.6, infra.

26. CPL § 100.15(3).

27. CPL § 100.15(2). If a felony complaint charges an "armed felony offense" as defined in CPL § 1.20(41), the accusatory part of the complaint must expressly say so. CPL § 100.15(4)(a). The reason for this is to better ensure that a local criminal court does not reduce this felony offense to a misdemeanor, in violation of CPL §§ 180.50(2)(b) and 180.70(3). See §§ 3.32, 3.33, infra.

controlled by the joinder rules governing indictments.[28] Unlike with indictments, however, if two or more defendants are jointly charged in a single local criminal court accusatory instrument, they all must be jointly charged with every offense alleged in the accusatory instrument.[29]

A prosecutor's information must specify the court in which it is filed and the title of the action, and it must be subscribed by the prosecutor.[30] Like an indictment, it must allege in one or more counts each of the offenses charged along with a "plain and concise" statement of the conduct underlying each offense.[31] The rules regarding joinder of offenses and joinder of defendants that apply to indictments also apply to prosecutor's informations.[32]

A simplified information must be substantially in the form prescribed by the commissioner of the appropriate State executive agency—*i.e.*, Motor Vehicles, Parks and Recreation, and Environmental Conservation.[33] It is the most rudimentary of all the accusatory instruments, in that it must specify only the offense charged; no factual allegations need be included and no reasonable cause need be provided.[34] This is because it was "designed to provide an uncomplicated form for handling the large volume of traffic infractions and petty offenses for which it is principally used."[35]

Library References:

West's Key No. Digests, Automobiles ⇐351.1; Indictment and Information ⇐35–54.

§ 3.4 Local Criminal Court Accusatory Instruments—Supporting Depositions

CPL § 100.20 defines the supporting deposition, which is referred to in some local criminal courts as the "corroborating affidavit." The supporting deposition is a written statement, filed in connection with a local criminal court accusatory instrument (except for a prosecutor's information), that is subscribed and verified by a person other than the complainant of the accusatory instrument.[36] The purpose of the supporting deposition is to provide additional factual allegations that supplement the factual allegations contained in the accusatory instrument. The factual allegations contained in the supporting deposition may be

---

28. See CPL § 200.20 (joinder of counts in an indictment, which is discussed in Chapter 5, § 5.21); CPL § 200.40 (joinder of defendants in an indictment, discussed in Chapter 5, § 5.22).

29. CPL § 100.15(2).

30. CPL § 100.35.

31. Id. The rules governing the form and content of indictments are set forth in CPL § 200.50, and are discussed in Chapter 5, § 5.12

32. Id.

33. CPL § 100.25(1).

34. See People v. Key, 45 N.Y.2d 111, 115–16, 408 N.Y.S.2d 16, 18–19, 379 N.E.2d 1147, 1148–50 (1978).

35. People v. Nuccio, 78 N.Y.2d 102, 104, 571 N.Y.S.2d 693, 694, 575 N.E.2d 111, 112 (1991).

One commentator has argued that this lower standard for sufficiency, as compared to the sufficiency standard for an information, could be successfully challenged on equal protection grounds. Afsharnik, "Simplified Information v. Information: An Unconstitutional Standard?" New York State Bar Journal, p. 20 (December 1995).

36. CPL § 100.20.

based on personal knowledge or on information and belief.[37] Its primary function in non-felony cases that ultimately will be prosecuted on an information, however, is to provide the non-hearsay factual allegations that are necessary to convert a misdemeanor complaint to a facially sufficient information.[38] For example, if the complainant of a misdemeanor complaint is a police officer with no direct knowledge of the circumstances of the offense but to whom the circumstances of the offense were conveyed by a private citizen with direct knowledge of those circumstances, the private citizen's non-hearsay factual allegations could be set forth in a supporting deposition. Or, a lab report establishing that the substance seized from the defendant was a controlled substance, or a ballistics report establishing that the gun seized from the defendant was operable, could be filed in the form of a supporting deposition.

Library References:
West's Key No. Digests, Automobiles ⊱351.1; Indictment and Information ⊱41, 52.

§ 3.5 Local Criminal Court Accusatory Instruments— Supporting Depositions Filed in Connection With Simplified Informations

The supporting deposition filed in connection with a simplified information is defined in CPL § 100.25(2). A section 100.25 supporting deposition differs in significant respects from a section 100.20 supporting deposition. One important difference is that a section 100.25 supporting deposition must be filed by the complainant of the simplified information, who will always be a police officer or other public servant.[39] In addition, unlike a section 100.20 supporting deposition, a section 100.25 supporting deposition is necessary only to provide factual allegations establishing reasonable cause that the defendant committed the offense or offenses charged, and not to establish a *prima facie* case. Indeed, in contrast to an information, a simplified information may be facially sufficient, and thus may serve as the basis for trial of the charges contained therein, whether or not it (along with any accompanying supporting deposition) establishes a *prima facie* case against the defendant.[40]

A section 100.25 supporting deposition, moreover, need not be in the subscriber's own words. For example, the Court of Appeals has upheld the validity of a supporting deposition, filed in connection with a simplified information, that merely consisted of a pre-printed form on which the police officer designated factual allegations by checking appropriate boxes next to applicable conditions and observations.[41] Needless

37. Id.
38. See CPL § 100.45(1)(c).
39. CPL § 100.25(2).
40. Cf. CPL § 100.45(1)(requirements of a facially sufficient information) with CPL § 100.45(2)(requirements of a facially sufficient simplified information).

41. People v. Hohmeyer, 70 N.Y.2d 41, 517 N.Y.S.2d 448, 510 N.E.2d 317 (1987).

to say, a section 100.25 supporting deposition does not provide the defendant with particularly meaningful information about the allegations underlying the offenses charged.

In addition, unlike a section 100.20 supporting deposition, a section 100.25 supporting deposition need not be provided unless the defendant requests that the court order the police officer or appropriate public servant to do so.[42] Absent such a request, the case may proceed to trial on the cursory simplified information alone, which as noted only must provide notice of the offense or offenses charged.[43] And the defendant's request must be a timely one; it must be made before entry of a guilty plea or commencement of trial, and no later than 30 days after entry of: (1) a not guilty plea if the defendant is arraigned in person on the simplified information, or (2) the court's written notice to the defendant of the right to receive a supporting deposition when the defendant has pleaded not guilty by mail (as the Uniform Traffic Ticket promulgated by the Commissioner of Motor Vehicles permits the defendant to do).[44] Notably, the statute contains no provision authorizing the court to permit a defendant's tardy request for the supporting deposition, even upon a showing of good cause or in the interest of justice. Most courts, therefore, do not excuse a defendant's failure to request the supporting deposition in timely fashion. On the other hand, one court has recognized an apparent loophole in this statutory scheme that enables a defendant, in effect, to enlarge the time period for requesting the supporting deposition by simply failing to plead to the simplified information by mail or in person on the court return date that the police officer has designated on the ticket. The court's opinion, not surprisingly, recommends amendment of the statute to eliminate this undesirable result.[45]

If the defendant requests a section 100.25 supporting deposition in a timely manner, the court must order the police officer or other appropriate public servant to serve a copy of the supporting deposition on the defendant within 30 days of the date the court receives the defendant's request (or within five days of commencement of trial, if that is sooner).[46] The original must be filed with the court, along with proof of service.[47] If the defendant is represented by counsel who has made an appearance

---

42. CPL § 100.25(2). The statute also provides that only a defendant who has been "arraigned" may request a supporting deposition. Id. The Court of Appeals has held that the filing of an appearance letter by the defendant's attorney does not constitute, or obviate the need for, an arraignment. People v. Perry, ___ N.Y.2d ___, ___ N.Y.S.2d ___, ___ N.E.2d ___, 1996 WL 49014 (1996).

43. If, notwithstanding the absence of a timely request, a police officer serves a supporting deposition on his or her own initiative, the requirement that reasonable cause be established must still be met. People v. Key, 45 N.Y.2d 111, 116, 408 N.Y.S.2d 16, 19, 379 N.E.2d 1147, 1149 (1978).

44. CPL § 100.25(2).

45. People v. Lippman, 156 Misc.2d 333, 334, 601 N.Y.S.2d 365, 366 (App. Term, 9th & 10th Jud.Dists., 1993). Of course, a defendant who ignores a traffic ticket in this manner assumes the risk that an arrest warrant will be issued (see CPL § 130.50) or that his or her license will be suspended (see VTL § 510(4–a)).

46. CPL § 100.25(2).

47. Id.

in the action, service of the supporting deposition should be made on counsel.[48]

Confusion may arise when, as sometimes happens, a defendant requests a supporting deposition before the police officer actually files the simplified information with the court commencing the criminal action.[49] This occurs if the defendant makes the request immediately or shortly after receiving the ticket, and before the officer has had the opportunity to file the accusatory instrument with the court. Because the court has no jurisdiction of the action until the accusatory instrument is filed,[50] it may not order the officer to serve the supporting deposition until such filing occurs. The question thus arises whether the officer's 30-day period for serving the supporting deposition runs from the date of the court's receipt of the request, the date of the filing of the accusatory instrument or the date of the court's direction to the officer to serve the supporting deposition. Although several courts (in unpublished opinions) have held in this situation that the time period runs from the date of the court's direction to the officer, such a conclusion may conflict with the express language of the statute and, particularly when the filing of the accusatory instrument is unreasonably delayed by the police, may make for dubious policy. In any event, legislative clarification of this matter is needed.

Finally, it is important to note that the requirement of a section 100.25 supporting deposition is waivable. Thus, a guilty plea, or a failure to object prior to trial, waives an objection to the failure to file the supporting deposition or to any defect in a supporting deposition that was filed.[51]

Library References:

West's Key No. Digests, Automobiles ⚖351.1; Indictment and Information ⚖41, 52.

§ 3.6 Local Criminal Court Accusatory Instruments—Verification

All local criminal court accusatory instruments, as well as supporting depositions and proof of service of supporting depositions, must be verified. Verification serves several purposes. Although it is not a guarantee of truthfulness, the ritualistic quality of the verification reminds the witness of his or her obligation to be forthright. In

---

48. People v. Rossi, 154 Misc.2d 616, 587 N.Y.S.2d 511 (Muttontown Vill.Ct. 1992).

49. See CPL § 100.05.

50. CPL §§ 1.20(17), 100.05. See People v. Perry, ___ N.Y.2d ___, ___ N.Y.S.2d ___, ___ N.E.2d ___, 1996 WL 49014 (1996).

51. See People v. Beattie, 80 N.Y.2d 840, 587 N.Y.S.2d 585, 600 N.E.2d 216 (1992)(failure of supporting deposition to allege facts providing reasonable cause waived by defendant's guilty plea); People v. Key, 45 N.Y.2d 111, 116–17, 408 N.Y.S.2d 16, 19–20, 379 N.E.2d 1147, 1149–50 (1978)(court notes that a simplified information can proceed to trial without a supporting deposition if the defendant fails to request one).

§ 3.6   LOCAL CRIMINAL COURTS   Ch. 3

addition, if the witness has not been truthful, verification can serve as the foundation for a subsequent perjury prosecution.

Unless the court directs that verification be made in a particular way, a number of options are available.[52] Verification may be accomplished by having the instrument sworn to before the court with which it is filed,[53] before a police station desk officer or a desk officer's superior,[54] or before a notary public.[55] If an appearance ticket has been issued, the instrument also may be sworn to before any public servant with legal authority to administer the oath.[56] In addition, in lieu of swearing to the instrument before one of these officials or persons, verification may be accomplished if the deponent signs a form notice that is part of the instrument specifying that any false statement made is punishable as a Class A misdemeanor pursuant to section 210.45 of the Penal Law.[57] This latter procedure is the most commonly employed method of verification in many courts, including the New York City Criminal Court.

When the complainant is a child or a person with a mental disease or defect, questions may arise as to the complainant's capacity to swear to the instrument. Notably, CPL § 60.22 creates a rebuttable presumption that a child under 12 years of age is not competent to testify under oath.[58] This has led some courts to require that a child's supporting deposition may be verified only if the trial court itself conducts an inquiry of the child and determines that the child understands the nature of an oath and the consequences of not telling the truth.[59] Although this inquiry must be on the record, it is usually a brief, *ex parte* proceeding held *in camera*.[60] Other courts have not required a judicial inquiry of a child complainant; rather, they have required that the prosecutor conduct a stenographically or otherwise recorded inquiry of the child that the court subsequently may review to determine whether the child is of sufficient intelligence and ability to understand and appreciate the nature of an oath and the consequences of making a false statement and is aware of and understands the allegations being made

---

52. CPL § 100.30(2).
53. CPL § 100.30(1)(a).
54. CPL § 100.30(1)(b).
55. CPL § 100.30(1)(e).
56. CPL § 100.30(1)(c). An "oath" includes "an affirmation and every other mode authorized by law of attesting to the truth of that which is stated." CPL § 1.20(38). See also CPLR § 2309(a)(specifying persons authorized to administer oaths and affirmations).
57. CPL § 100.30(1)(d). P.L. § 210.45 provides that "[a] person is guilty of making a punishable false statement when he knowingly makes a false statement, which he does not believe to be true, in a written instrument bearing a legally authorized form notice to the effect that false statements made therein are punishable."
58. CPL § 60.20(2) provides as follows: Every witness more than twelve years old may testify only under oath unless the court is satisfied that such witness cannot, as a result of mental disease or defect, understand the nature of an oath. A child less than twelve years old may not testify under oath unless the court is satisfied that he understands the nature of an oath. If the court is not so satisfied, such child or such witness over twelve years old who cannot, as a result of mental disease or defect, understand the nature of an oath may nevertheless be permitted to give unsworn evidence if the court is satisfied that the witness possesses sufficient intelligence and capacity to justify the reception thereof.
59. See, e.g., People v. Pierre, 140 Misc.2d 623, 533 N.Y.S.2d 170 (N.Y.C.Crim. Ct.1988); People v. Cortez, 140 Misc.2d 267, 531 N.Y.S.2d 676 (N.Y.C.Crim.Ct. 1988).
60. Id.

against the defendant.[61] At least one court has held that the prosecutor has the authority to determine a child's capacity to verify a supporting deposition so long as the prosecutor files with the court an affidavit delineating the basis for concluding that the child is competent to do so.[62] And another court has held that the appropriate procedure for determining a child witness's capacity to verify a supporting deposition must be determined on a case-by-case basis.[63]

Library References:
West's Key No. Digests, Indictment and Information ⇔52; Infants ⇔197.

§ 3.7 Local Criminal Court Accusatory Instruments—Facial Sufficiency

Section 100.40 sets forth the requirements for facial sufficiency of accusatory instruments. Facial sufficiency is critical because its absence, particularly with respect to non-felony accusatory instruments, is a ground for dismissal of the accusatory instrument.[64] In addition, a local criminal court accusatory instrument must be facially sufficient to serve as the basis for issuance of an arrest warrant or a summons.[65]

Facial sufficiency requirements are the strictest for informations. An information must "substantially" adhere to the form and content requirements of section 100.15—*i.e.*, it must specify the court and the title of the action, be subscribed and verified by the complainant and contain an accusatory part designating the offenses charged and a factual part alleging facts in support of those charges.[66]

It is the specificity required of the factual portion of an information, however, that distinguishes it from the other local criminal court accusatory instruments. The factual portion (together with the factual allegations of any supporting depositions filed in connection with the information) must not only provide reasonable cause to believe that the defendant committed the offenses charged,[67] but it also must establish a

---

61. See, e.g., People v. Clarke, 160 Misc.2d 1018, 611 N.Y.S.2d 1006 (N.Y.C.Crim.Ct.1994); People v. Claxton, 160 Misc.2d 550, 610 N.Y.S.2d 735 (N.Y.C.Crim.Ct.1994); People v. Munnelly, 158 Misc.2d 340, 601 N.Y.S.2d 204 (Dist. Ct., Nassau County, 1993).

62. See People v. King, 137 Misc.2d 1087, 523 N.Y.S.2d 748 (N.Y.C.Crim.Ct. 1988).

63. People v. Wiggans, 140 Misc.2d 1011, 532 N.Y.S.2d 42 (N.Y.C.Crim.Ct. 1988). Cf. People v. Phillipe, 142 Misc.2d 574, 587–88, 538 N.Y.S.2d 400, 409–10 (N.Y.C.Crim.Ct.1989)(expressing preference for judicial inquiry of child, although emphasizing that such a procedure is not legally mandated). One factor that presumably would influence a court's determination as to the procedure to employ is whether there were any adult witnesses to the defendant's alleged criminal conduct. See People v. Clarke, 160 Misc.2d at 1024, 611 N.Y.S.2d at 1010.

64. See CPL §§ 170.35, 170.50. See § 3.26, infra.

65. See CPL §§ 120.20(1), 130.30. See §§ 3.13, 3.16, infra.

66. CPL § 100.40(1)(a). See § 3.3, supra.

67. CPL § 100.40(1)(b). The CPL defines reasonable cause to believe that a person has committed an offense as "when evidence or information which appears reliable discloses facts or circumstances which are collectively of such weight and persuasiveness as to convince a person of ordinary intelligence, judgment and experience that it is reasonably likely that such offense was committed and that such person committed it." CPL § 70.10(2). This standard applies in other procedural contexts that may

prima facie case. Thus, it must contain non-hearsay factual allegations that, if true, establish each and every element of the offense or offenses charged against the defendant.[68]

As the Court of Appeals has observed:

> [T]he reason for requiring the additional showing of a *prima facie* case for an information lies in the unique function that an information serves under the statutory scheme established by the Criminal Procedure Law. An information is often the instrument upon which the defendant is prosecuted for a misdemeanor or a petty offense. Unlike a felony complaint ... it is not followed by a preliminary hearing and a Grand Jury proceeding. Thus, the People need not, at any time prior to trial, present actual evidence demonstrating a prima facie case, as with an indictment following a felony complaint....[69]

The *prima facie* requirement, as one trial court has noted, "reduces the possibility that one could be unjustly forced to stand trial by an overzealous or negligent prosecutor based on an indirect, incomplete, or inadequately investigated accusation."[70] It also ensures that "a real person actually complained to the police and had an opportunity to review the accuracy of the factual allegations drafted by the prosecutor."[71]

An information's failure to allege every element of the offense or offenses charged is a jurisdictional defect, which is not waived even if the defendant fails to raise the issue in the trial court.[72] Thus, an information charging a defendant with the Penal Law misdemeanor offense of resisting arrest that set forth no factual allegations establishing an essential element of that offense—that the police officer "was effecting an authorized arrest"[73]—was jurisdictionally defective, requiring reversal of the conviction even though the defendant failed to raise any objection to the information until after completion of the trial.[74] The same was true for an information charging harassment in the first degree that lacked factual allegations that the defendant acted "with intent to

---

arise in a criminal action or investigation, such as the authority of an officer to make an arrest and the issuance of a search warrant. In these other contexts, "reasonable cause" is synonymous with "probable cause," the more commonly employed constitutional standard. See People v. Johnson, 66 N.Y.2d 398, 402 n. 2, 497 N.Y.S.2d 618, 621 n. 2, 488 N.E.2d 439, 442 n. 2 (1985).

68. CPL § 100.40(1)(c). The prima facie standard is somewhat less exacting than the "legally sufficient evidence" standard, which is applied in determinations such as a grand jury's authority to indict and the proof necessary for a conviction, and is defined as "competent evidence which, if accepted as true, would establish every element of an offense charged and the defendant's commission thereof." CPL § 70.10(1).

69. People v. Alejandro, 70 N.Y.2d 133, 137–38, 517 N.Y.S.2d 927, 929–30, 511 N.E.2d 71, 73–74 (1987)(citations omitted).

70. People v. Phillipe, 142 Misc.2d 574, 578, 538 N.Y.S.2d 400, 404 (N.Y.C.Crim.Ct. 1989).

71. Id.

72. Cf. CPL § 170.65(3)(a defendant may waive prosecution by information and consent to be prosecuted on a hearsay-based misdemeanor complaint). See § 3.25, infra.

73. P.L. § 205.30.

74. People v. Alejandro, 70 N.Y.2d 133, 517 N.Y.S.2d 927, 511 N.E.2d 71(1987).

harass, annoy or alarm,"[75] an essential element of that offense. Absent that allegation, "the acts complained of did not constitute criminal conduct," thereby creating a "fundamental and nonwaivable" jurisdictional defect.[76]

Because a challenge to a jurisdictionally defective information may be raised at any time, even after entry of a guilty plea, prosecutors must be particularly careful that the accusatory instruments on which they proceed allege evidentiary allegations for all elements of the offenses charged, or, when possible, to fill any evidentiary gaps in the accusatory instrument by filing appropriate supporting depositions. The failure to do so will enable a savvy defense counsel to move to dismiss after the statutory speedy trial period has elapsed, thereby effectively precluding the filing of a new accusatory instrument alleging the same wrongful acts.[77]

In general, courts have held that held that the non-hearsay requirement for informations can be satisfied by allegations that are technically hearsay but would be admissible evidence at trial as a recognized exception to the hearsay rule. For example, factual allegations contained in a "business record," within the meaning of CPLR § 4518, have been held to satisfy the non-hearsay requirement.[78] On a related issue, courts have split over whether a defendant's admission concerning an element of an offense charged is sufficient, by itself, to meet the non-hearsay requirement. The results of these cases turn on whether the court concludes that CPL § 60.50, which provides that "[a] person may not be convicted of an offense solely upon evidence of a confession or admission made by him without additional proof that the offense charged has been committed," has any application to the non-hearsay

---

75. P.L. § 240.25.

76. People v. Hall, 48 N.Y.2d 927, 425 N.Y.S.2d 56, 401 N.E.2d 179 (1979), reargument denied 49 N.Y.2d 918, 428 N.Y.S.2d 1028, 405 N.E.2d 712 (1980). Cf. People v. Iannone, 45 N.Y.2d 589, 600–01, 412 N.Y.S.2d 110, 118, 384 N.E.2d 656, 664 (1978)(citations omitted)("[I]n essence, an indictment is jurisdictionally defective only if it does not effectively charge the defendant with the commission of a particular crime. For example, an indictment will be jurisdictionally defective if the acts it accuses defendant of performing simply do not constitute a crime ... or if it fails to allege that a defendant committed acts constituting every material element of the crime charged. Insufficiency in the factual allegations alone, as opposed to a failure to allege every material element of the crime, does not constitute a nonwaivable jurisdictional defect.").

77. The Court of Appeals has held that, for speedy trial purposes, the prescribed time period within which the prosecution must be ready for trial runs from the filing of the original accusatory instrument, not the filing of a superseding accusatory instrument. See People v. Osgood, 52 N.Y.2d 37, 43, 436 N.Y.S.2d 213, 216, 417 N.E.2d 507, 510 (1980); People v. Lomax, 50 N.Y.2d 351, 356, 428 N.Y.S.2d 937, 939, 406 N.E.2d 793, 795 (1980). It should be noted, however, that when an original accusatory instrument is superseded by another one, all the periods deemed excludable under the first accusatory instrument remain excludable even after the superseding accusatory instrument is filed. See People v. Sinistaj, 67 N.Y.2d 236, 501 N.Y.S.2d 793, 492 N.E.2d 1209 (1986).

78. See, e.g., People v. Smith, 141 Misc.2d 568, 533 N.Y.S.2d 801 (N.Y.C.Crim.Ct.1988)(recognizing that a business record can be used to convert a misdemeanor complaint to an information, although holding that the record at issue did not qualify as a business record); People v. Haskins, 107 Misc.2d 480, 435 N.Y.S.2d 261 (N.Y.C.Crim.Ct.1981)(holding that one record constituted a business record but that another did not).

requirement for informations.[79] The courts that have held that such corroboration is not required have concluded, probably correctly, that the "legally sufficient evidence" standard,[80] which, for example, must be satisfied to indict an individual,[81] is a more exacting standard than the *prima facie* requirement applicable to informations.[82]

Facial sufficiency requirements are less demanding for the other local criminal court accusatory instruments. A simplified information must conform to the requirements of section 100.25(1)—*i.e.*, it must be substantially in the form prescribed by the appropriate State commissioner.[83] Moreover, if the defendant requests a supporting deposition and the court orders that one be filed, facial sufficiency requires that the relevant police officer or other public servant timely comply with such order.[84] Although, as noted, the simplified information itself need provide nothing more than the offense or offenses charged, the supporting deposition, when requested and ordered, must contain factual allegations providing reasonable cause to believe that the defendant committed the offense or offenses charged.[85] A dismissal of a simplified information on facial sufficiency grounds due to a police officer's failure to file a timely supporting deposition does not preclude renewal of the prosecution by the filing of a facially sufficient information following the dismissal.[86]

Facial sufficiency of misdemeanor and felony complaints also requires compliance with the form and content specifications of CPL § 100.15[87]—*i.e.*, they must contain the name of the court, the title of the action, they must be subscribed and verified by the complainant, and they must contain an accusatory part and a factual part.[88] In addition, the factual part, along with the factual allegations of any supporting depositions filed, must provide reasonable cause.[89]

---

79. Cf. People v. Mauro, 147 Misc.2d 381, 555 N.Y.S.2d 533 (N.Y.C.Crim.Ct. 1990); People v. Kaminiski, 143 Misc.2d 1089, 542 N.Y.S.2d 923 (N.Y.C.Crim.Ct. 1989); People v. Alvarez, 141 Misc.2d 686, 534 N.Y.S.2d 90 (N.Y.C.Crim.Ct.1988)(all holding that a defendant's admission, without more, is insufficient to meet requirement of non-hearsay factual allegations establishing every element of offense charged) with People v. McKinney, 145 Misc.2d 460, 546 N.Y.S.2d 927 (N.Y.C.Crim.Ct.1989); People v. Polito, 128 Misc.2d 71, 488 N.Y.S.2d 593 (Rochester City Ct.1985)(both holding that CPL § 60.50 has no application to facial sufficiency requirements for informations, and concluding that defendant's admission is sufficient in itself to meet non-hearsay requirement).

80. "Legally sufficient evidence" is defined as "competent evidence which, if accepted as true, would establish every element charged and the defendant's commission thereof; except that such evidence is not legally sufficient when corroboration required by law is absent." CPL § 70.10(1).

81. See CPL § 190.65(1).

82. See footnote 68, supra. For discussion of additional cases addressing the facial sufficiency of informations, see § 3.25, infra.

83. CPL § 100.40(2). See § 3.3, supra.

84. CPL § 100.40(2). See § 3.5, supra.

85. CPL § 100.25(2).

86. People v. Nuccio, 78 N.Y.2d 102, 571 N.Y.S.2d 693, 575 N.E.2d 111 (1991).

87. See CPL § 100.40(4)(a).

88. CPL § 100.15(1).

89. CPL § 100.40(4)(b). See, e.g., People v. Dumas, 68 N.Y.2d 729, 506 N.Y.S.2d 319, 497 N.E.2d 686 (1986)(misdemeanor complaint charging marihuana sale and possession offenses facially insufficient because it contained a conclusory statement that defendant sold and possessed marihuana without providing any factual basis, such as an allegation that the police officer was an expert in identifying marihuana, for concluding that the substance at issue was actually marihuana).

Facial sufficiency for a prosecutor's information merely requires compliance with the form and content requirements of CPL § 100.35.[90]

Library References:

West's Key No. Digests, Criminal Law ⟪208–214, 273.4(4); Indictment and Information ⟪41.

§ 3.8 Local Criminal Court Accusatory Instruments—Severance, Consolidation, Amendment and Bill of Particulars

A number of the procedures applicable to indictments also apply to the non-felony local criminal court accusatory instruments other than simplified informations. For example, the indictment procedures relating to severance and consolidation of counts and severance and consolidation of defendants apply to informations, prosecutor's informations and misdemeanor complaints.[91] The same is true for the indictment procedures relating to bills of particulars.[92]

The procedures governing amendment of indictments, however, apply only to prosecutor's informations;[93] as a result, a prosecutor's information may not be amended to charge or add an offense.[94] A separate and distinct provision regulates amendment of informations to charge or add an offense.[95] Under this provision, at any time before commencement of trial or entry of a guilty plea, the prosecution may apply to the court to amend an information to charge an offense that is supported by the factual allegations of the information and any supporting depositions accompanying it. The application must be on notice to the defendant, and if it is ultimately granted the defendant must be afforded any necessary adjournment.[96] The Court of Appeals has strictly construed this provision, holding that it is the exclusive means of amending an information. Thus, a prosecutor's failure to apply to the court to amend an information to add the two offenses for which the defendant was subsequently convicted required reversal of the conviction even though defense counsel stipulated during the trial to add those offenses to the information.[97]

---

90. CPL § 100.40(3). See § 3.3, supra.

91. CPL § 100.45(1). The indictment procedures, which are set forth in CPL § 200.20 (joinder of offenses and consolidation of indictments against a single defendant) and CPL § 200.40 (joinder of offenses and consolidation of indictments against different defendants) are discussed in Chapter 5, §§ 5.21, 5.22.

92. CPL § 100.45(4). Bills of particulars, which are addressed in CPL § 200.95, are discussed in Chapter 5, § 5.19. It should be noted here as well, however, that a defendant must request a bill of particulars in writing and generally within 30 days of arraignment. CPL § 200.95(3). The prosecution in turn generally must respond to a timely request for a bill of particulars within 15 days of service of the request. CPL § 200.95(2) and (4). Additional time requirements, including the time requirements for a motion for a bill of particulars, are discussed in Chapter 5, § 5.19 and generally in Chapter 8.

93. CPL § 100.45(2). Amendment of indictment procedures, set forth in CPL § 200.70, are discussed in Chapter 5, § 5.18.

94. CPL § 200.70(2)(a).

95. The CPL contains no provision authorizing amendment of a misdemeanor complaint or a simplified information.

96. CPL § 100.45(3).

97. People v. Harper, 37 N.Y.2d 96, 371 N.Y.S.2d 467, 332 N.E.2d 336 (1975).

§ 3.8

Although the prosecution may amend an information that is defective with respect to a matter of form that does not change the theory of the case, such as an amendment changing a name, time or place,[98] the courts have split over whether a jurisdictionally flawed information may be amended to add factual allegations establishing an omitted but essential element of the offense charged. Although a concurring opinion in a Court of Appeals case suggests that an information may be amended to cure a jurisdictional defect,[99] lower courts have held (or suggested) that such an amendment is impermissible, thereby requiring the prosecution to file a new accusatory instrument.[100] Given that the statute permits amendment of an information to add a *new* offense, so long as the new offense is "supported by the allegations of the factual part of such information and/or any supporting depositions which may accompany it,"[101] it would seem that amendment of an information to add factual allegations establishing an omitted element should be allowed.

Library References:
West's Key No. Digests, Indictment and Information ⟐121, 124–132, 144–144.2.

§ 3.9 Local Criminal Court Accusatory Instruments—Superseding Informations and Prosecutor's Informations

The CPL authorizes a prosecutor to file a superseding information or a prosecutor's information, charging one or more of the same offenses charged in the original accusatory instrument, so long as the prosecutor does so before commencement of trial on, or entry of a guilty plea to, the original information or prosecutor's information.[102] When the defendant is arraigned on the superseding instrument, the court must dismiss the count or counts in the original instrument charging offenses that are charged in the superseding instrument. The original instrument is not, however, superseded with respect to any count or counts charging offenses not charged in the superseding accusatory instrument; thus, those charges are not dismissed.[103] As is true for amendment of informations,[104] the courts have split over whether the prosecution may supersede a jurisdictionally defective information.[105] Notably, the statutory

---

98. See, e.g., People v. Smith, 141 Misc.2d 568, 571, 533 N.Y.S.2d 801, 803 (N.Y.C.Crim.Ct.1988); People v. Pacifico, 105 Misc.2d 396, 432 N.Y.S.2d 588 (N.Y.C.Crim.Ct.1980).

99. People v. Alejandro, 70 N.Y.2d 133, 140, 517 N.Y.S.2d 927, 931, 511 N.E.2d 71, 75 (1987)(Bellacosa, J., concurring).

100. See, e.g., People v. Smith, 141 Misc.2d at 571, 533 N.Y.S.2d at 803; People v. Parris, 113 Misc.2d 1066, 1069–70, 450 N.Y.S.2d 721, 723–24 (N.Y.C.Crim.Ct.1982).

101. CPL § 100.45(3). Cf. CPL § 100.50(2)(a prosecutor's information may only charge offenses supported by facially sufficient factual allegations contained in an existing information and/or supporting depositions accompanying the existing information).

102. CPL § 100.50(1).

103. Id.

104. See § 3.8, supra.

105. Cf. People v. Alejandro, 70 N.Y.2d 133, 140, 517 N.Y.S.2d 927, 931, 511 N.E.2d 71, 75 (1987)(Bellacosa, J., concurring); People v. Cibro Oceana Terminal Corp., 148 Misc.2d 149, 559 N.Y.S.2d 782 (N.Y.C.Crim.Ct.1990)(jurisdictionally defective informations may be superseded) with People v. Twine, 121 Misc.2d 762, 768, 468

Ch. 3   **COMPELLING APPEARANCE FOR ARRAIGNMENT § 3.10**

language does not preclude this.[106]

Prosecutors are also authorized, at any time before commencement of trial on, or entry of a guilty plea to, an information, to file a prosecutor's information charging any offense that is supported by facially sufficient factual allegations that are contained in the information to be replaced and any supporting depositions accompanying such information.[107] The filing of the prosecutor's information supersedes the original information, and when the defendant is arraigned on the latter instrument the former instrument is deemed dismissed.[108] The prosecutor's information can be a useful device for prosecutors, particularly in jurisdictions in which police officers draft accusatory instruments that, although containing facially sufficient factual allegations, may not always charge all offenses supported by those factual allegations. However, a prosecutor's information may be filed on the prosecution's own initiative to supersede only an information, not a felony or misdemeanor complaint.[109]

It is also worth noting here the general principle that, for speedy trial purposes, the prescribed time period within which the prosecution must be ready for trial runs from the filing of the original local criminal court accusatory instrument, not the filing of any amended or superseding instrument.[110]

Library References:

West's Key No. Digests, Criminal Law ⟐577.14; Indictment and Information ⟐45.

§ 3.10   Means of Compelling a Defendant's Appearance for Arraignment—In General

The CPL provides for a variety of methods for compelling a defendant's appearance in local criminal court for arraignment.[111] These methods fall into two categories: those that compel appearance when a criminal action against the defendant has already been commenced (*i.e.*, an accusatory instrument already has been filed with the court); and those that compel appearance when no criminal action has yet been commenced (*i.e.*, an accusatory instrument will be filed when the defendant is arraigned).

N.Y.S.2d 559, 564 (N.Y.C.Crim. Ct.1983)(jurisdictionally defective information may not be superseded).

106. Cf. CPL § 100.45(3)(information may be amended to add a new offense only if new offense is supported by the factual allegations contained in the existing information and/or any accompanying supporting depositions); CPL § 100.50(2)(prosecutor's information may only charge offense supported by facially sufficient factual allegations contained in information to be replaced and/or any supporting depositions accompanying such information).

107. CPL § 100.50(2).

108. Id.

109. See, e.g., People v. Young, 123 Misc.2d 486, 473 N.Y.S.2d 715 (N.Y.C.Crim. Ct.1984); People v. Thomas, 107 Misc.2d 947, 436 N.Y.S.2d 153 (Dist.Ct., Suffolk County, 1981). A prosecutor's information may supersede a felony complaint only upon the direction of a local criminal court. See CPL § 180.50(3)(a)(i).

110. See People v. Osgood, 52 N.Y.2d 37, 43, 436 N.Y.S.2d 213, 216, 417 N.E.2d 507, 510 (1980); People v. Lomax, 50 N.Y.2d 351, 356, 428 N.Y.S.2d 937, 939, 406 N.E.2d 793, 795 (1980).

111. See CPL § 110.10.

§ 3.10   LOCAL CRIMINAL COURTS   Ch. 3

The primary means of compelling appearance when a criminal action already has been commenced are the arrest warrant[112] and the summons.[113] If no criminal action has been commenced, the defendant's appearance for arraignment may be compelled as the result of a warrantless arrest[114] or by an appearance ticket.[115] These procedures are discussed in detail in the following sections.

Library References:

West's Key No. Digests, Automobiles ⟐351.1; Criminal Law ⟐215–220; Indictment and Information ⟐41.

§ 3.11   The Arrest Warrant

Unlike many other jurisdictions, New York authorizes issuance of an arrest warrant only if an accusatory instrument commencing a criminal action is first filed.[116] The commencement of the criminal action, however, carries with it significant consequences that may impede the investigation and prosecution of a criminal offense. For example, commencement of the criminal action triggers the time period within which the prosecution must be ready for trial;[117] and the defendant's right to counsel, which in New York may not be waived in the absence of counsel, attaches with the commencement of the criminal action.[118] An unintended result of the requirement that a criminal action first be commenced, therefore, may be that law enforcement has a disincentive to obtain an arrest warrant when a warrantless arrest is a viable alternative. Obviously, however, situations do arise when a warrantless arrest is not an alternative,[119] and when that is the case, a local criminal court accusatory instrument must be filed with the court commencing the criminal action.

The arrest warrant must be issued by a local criminal court.[120] The warrant directs a police officer (or a State University of New York peace officer) to arrest the defendant and bring him or her before the court.[121]

Library References:

West's Key No. Digests, Criminal Law ⟐215–220, 577.8(2), 641.3(4).

112. See CPL Article 120.

113. See CPL Article 130. If a defendant against whom a criminal action is commenced is not at liberty in the state, a number of procedures are available to compel his or her appearance for arraignment. See CPL Article 560 (defendant confined in an institution in New York); CPL Article 570 (defendant outside of New York but within the United States); CPL Article 580 (defendant imprisoned in another jurisdiction of the United States); CPL Article 590 (defendant outside of the United States). See also CPL Article 600 (securing appearance of corporate defendants). These procedures, which are rarely employed in day-to-day criminal practice, are not specifically discussed in this book.

114. See CPL Article 140.

115. See CPL Article 150.

116. CPL § 120.10(1).

117. See CPL § 30.30(1).

118. People v. Samuels, 49 N.Y.2d 218, 424 N.Y.S.2d 892, 400 N.E.2d 1344 (1980).

119. See, e.g., Payton v. New York, 445 U.S. 573, 100 S.Ct. 1371, 63 L.Ed.2d 639 (1980)(absent exigent circumstances, the police must obtain an arrest warrant before entering a suspect's home to make a routine arrest).

120. Cf. CPL § 210.10(3)(superior court warrant of arrest); CPL § 530.70(bench warrant).

121. CPL § 120.10(1).

§ 3.12 Arrest Warrant—Form and Content

The arrest warrant must contain rather specific information, the absence of which may render it invalid and potentially subject the arresting officer to liability for false arrest.[122] For example, the warrant must be subscribed by the issuing judge[123] and must specify the date it was issued, the name or title of an offense charged in the underlying accusatory instrument and the name of the issuing court.[124] The warrant must state the name of the defendant; but if the defendant's name is unknown, the warrant must specify any name or description by which the defendant "can be identified with reasonable certainty."[125] The latter type of warrant is known as a "John Doe" or a "Jane Doe" warrant.[126] If the police learn the identity of the "John Doe" or "Jane Doe" subsequent to the issuance of the warrant and, in the absence of exigent circumstances, fail to seek an amended warrant specifying the

---

122. Whether an arrest warrant's failure to comply with statutory form and content requirements can result in the suppression of evidence, such as physical evidence seized or statements made following the arrest, is an open question. The Court of Appeals has made clear, however, that a statutory violation does not require suppression of evidence unless the statute confers a "substantial" right that "operates directly to protect and preserve a constitutionally guaranteed right of a citizen," People v. Patterson, 78 N.Y.2d 711, 717–18, 579 N.Y.S.2d 617, 619–20, 587 N.E.2d 255, 257–58 (1991), or unless the statutory violation was intentional. People v. Sampson, 73 N.Y.2d 908, 910, 539 N.Y.S.2d 288, 289, 536 N.E.2d 617, 618 (1989). Thus, suppression was required when the requirements of CPL § 690.40(1), mandating that the court record or summarize on the record an examination made in determining an application for a search warrant, because fundamental Fourth Amendment rights were implicated. People v. Taylor, 73 N.Y.2d 683, 543 N.Y.S.2d 357, 541 N.E.2d 386 (1989). And suppression was required where wiretap evidence was obtained pursuant to a warrant, the issuance of which depended on information derived from a prior wiretap that was illegally obtained in violation of the extension and inactivation requirements of CPL Article 700. On the other hand, suppression was not required where a complainant identified the defendant from a photograph taken of the defendant in a prior and unrelated case, the record of which had been sealed pursuant to CPL § 160.50. People v. Patterson, 78 N.Y.2d 711, 579 N.Y.S.2d 617, 587 N.E.2d 255 (1991).

Presumably, therefore, suppression of evidence obtained as a result of an arrest pursuant to a warrant that, for example, did not contain the name of the issuing court would not be required. By contrast, suppression of evidence might be required if obtained following an arrest pursuant to a "John Doe" warrant containing an inadequate description of the defendant. Even in the latter situation, however, deficiencies in the arrest warrant could be overlooked if the police possessed an independent factual basis for concluding that reasonable cause existed to believe that the defendant had committed the charged offense. See, e.g., People v. Vasquez, 108 A.D.2d 701, 485 N.Y.S.2d 1008 (1st Dep't 1985).

123. Interestingly, no subscription requirement applies to bench warrants. See CPL § 530.70.

Although the term "subscribed" is not defined in the CPL, section 46 of the General Construction Law defines "signature" as including "any memorandum, mark or sign, written, printed, stamped, photographed, engraved or otherwise placed upon any instrument or writing with intent to execute or authenticate such instrument or writing." Assuming that this definition applies to the subscription requirement for arrest warrants—and nothing suggests that it does not apply—the issuing judge's actual handwritten signature on the warrant is not necessary to meet the requirement of the statute. In fact, for several years now, the New York City Criminal Court has issued computer-generated arrest warrants that contain merely a computer-printed version of the issuing judge's name.

124. CPL § 120.10(2). See Titus v. Hill, 134 A.D.2d 911, 912, 521 N.Y.S.2d 932, 933 (4th Dep't 1987)(arrest warrant invalid because it failed to specify name of issuing court).

125. CPL § 120.10(2).

126. See generally Boose v. City of Rochester, 71 A.D.2d 59, 421 N.Y.S.2d 740 (4th Dep't 1979).

§ 3.12 LOCAL CRIMINAL COURTS Ch. 3

defendant's name, the warrant is invalid.[127] Moreover, insufficient descriptive information in a "John Doe" warrant may not be remedied by descriptive information in supplemental documents, such as the underlying accusatory instrument; the requisite information must be contained in the warrant itself.[128]

Finally, the warrant must specify the officer or officers to whom it is addressed, and include a direction that such officer or officers must arrest the defendant and bring him or her before the issuing court.[129] The warrant may be addressed to an individual officer or to individual officers, or it may be addressed to a classification or classifications of officers.[130] The officer or department must be one whose geographical area of employment includes the situs of the offense charged or the locality of the court issuing the warrant.[131]

Library References:
West's Key No. Digests, Criminal Law ⟪218.

§ 3.13 Arrest Warrant—Additional Procedural Requirements

As discussed, a court may issue an arrest warrant only if a local criminal court accusatory instrument has been filed with the court, commencing the criminal action, and the defendant has yet to be arraigned on that accusatory instrument. The only exception is the simplified traffic information, the filing of which may never serve as the basis for issuance of an arrest warrant.[132] Further, the court may issue an arrest warrant only if the accusatory instrument is facially sufficient.[133] Because criminal actions charging a felony or a misdemeanor are almost always commenced by the filing of a felony complaint or a misdemeanor complaint, this means that issuance of an arrest warrant must be preceded by the court's determination that the factual allegations in the accusatory instrument provide reasonable cause to believe that the defendant committed the offense charged.[134] The statute,

127. Dabbs v. State, 59 N.Y.2d 213, 464 N.Y.S.2d 428, 451 N.E.2d 186 (1983)("John Doe" defendant named in arrest warrant subsequently identified by victim in photo array).

128. See, e.g., McIntyre v. State, 142 A.D.2d 856, 530 N.Y.S.2d 898 (3d Dep't 1988)(warrant merely described "John Doe" defendant as white male, approximately 17–18 years old, with slim build).

129. CPL § 120.10(2).

130. CPL § 120.10(3). Or, as is true for the form arrest warrants issued by the New York City Criminal Court, the warrant may be generally addressed to "any police officer whose geographical area of employment embraces either the place where the offense charged was allegedly committed or the locality of the Court by which this warrant is issued."

131. CPL § 120.50. CPL § 1.20(34–a) provides a general definition of the geographical area of employment of police officers.

132. CPL § 120.20(1). The statute's failure to include within this exception the simplified parks information and the simplified environmental conservation information was almost certainly a legislative oversight. See Preiser, "Practice Commentary," to CPL § 120.20, McKinney's Cons. Laws of N.Y., Book 11A, at 318 (1992).

133. CPL § 120.20(1).

134. See CPL § 100.40(4), and discussion in § 3.7, supra. If the criminal action has been commenced by the filing of an information—which may arise when no offense greater than a violation is being charged and that violation is not one that may be charged in a simplified informa-

moreover, authorizes the court, if it so chooses, to go beyond a facially sufficient accusatory instrument and inquire of witnesses, or formally examine them under oath, to satisfy itself reasonable cause exists.[135]

Even if a valid, facially sufficient local criminal court accusatory instrument has been filed against a defendant who has not yet been arraigned, the court may not issue an arrest warrant if it is satisfied that the defendant will appear for arraignment in response to the issuance of a summons.[136] In addition, as an alternative to issuing an arrest warrant or a summons, the court, when the prosecutor requests, may authorize the prosecutor to direct the defendant to appear for arraignment on a specified date so long as the court is satisfied that the defendant will do so.[137]

For purposes of issuance of an arrest warrant, the court in which the requisite local criminal court accusatory instrument must be filed is governed by the provisions of CPL § 100.55.[138] However, if the court specified in section 100.55 is a town or village court and such court is not available to receive the accusatory instrument and issue the arrest warrant, alternative courts may serve that function. In the case of a town court that is not available, the accusatory instrument may be filed with the town court of any adjoining town of the same county; if a village court is not available, filing may be accomplished with the town court of the town embracing that village or, if that town court is not available either, the town court of any adjoining town of the same county.[139]

Library References:
West's Key No. Digests, Criminal Law ⚖=215–220.

§ 3.14 Arrest Warrant—Execution

Generally, an arrest warrant may be executed only by the officer or officers to whom it is addressed. However, execution of the arrest warrant may be delegated to another officer whose geographical area of employment includes the area where the arrest is to be made if the officer to whom the warrant is addressed has reasonable cause to believe that the defendant is in a county other than the county in which the warrant is returnable.[140] If the warrant was issued by a city court, town court or village court, however, delegation is permissible only if the defendant is in an adjoining county.[141] The officer to whom the warrant is delegated need not receive a copy of the warrant as a requirement of

tion—section 120.20(2) would appear to require that the court, before issuing an arrest warrant, determine not only that reasonable cause has been provided but also that the information establishes a prima facie case. See CPL § 100.40(1), and discussion in § 3.7, supra.

135. CPL § 120.20(2).

136. CPL § 120.20(3). The procedures governing summonses are discussed in § 3.16, infra.

137. CPL § 120.20(3).

138. CPL § 120.30(2). CPL § 100.55 is discussed in Chapter 1, § 1.5.

139. CPL § 120.30(2).

140. CPL § 120.60(2).

141. CPL § 120.60(2)(b). See also CPL § 120.70(2).

§ 3.14   LOCAL CRIMINAL COURTS   Ch. 3

making the arrest so long as the relevant details are communicated, by telephone or otherwise.[142]

The officer to whom the warrant is addressed or to whom the warrant has been delegated may execute the warrant anywhere in the State if the warrant was issued by a district court, the New York City Criminal Court or a superior court judge sitting as a local criminal court.[143] If the warrant was issued by a city court, town court or village court, it may be executed in the county in which it was issued or in an adjoining county;[144] such a warrant may be executed in another county only if a local criminal court of the other county endorses on the warrant that it may be executed in that county.[145]

An arrest warrant may be executed on any day of the week and at any hour of the day.[146] This is in contrast to the procedure under the previous statute, which required express permission of the court to execute a non-felony warrant on a Sunday or at night.[147] Whether a court retains any discretion under the current statute to limit, at least with respect to non-felony warrants, the time of execution is not addressed in the case law. One commentator, however, is of the view that courts do have such discretion.[148]

Unless the defendant physically resists or flees, or unless other factors would render it impractical, the arresting officer must notify the defendant of the existence of the warrant and the charges made against him or her.[149] If the defendant asks to see the warrant, the officer must comply; but if the officer is not in possession of a copy of the warrant (the officer is not legally required to have a copy when making the arrest), a copy must be shown to the defendant as soon after the arrest as is possible.[150] In effectuating the arrest, the officer, in appropriate circumstances, may use physical force.[151]

The arrest warrant authorizes the officer to enter any premises, including the defendant's dwelling, to make the arrest, but only if the officer reasonably believes that the defendant is present therein.[152] If the defendant is in the dwelling of a third party, however, the officer must obtain a search warrant pursuant to CPL Article 690.[153] This is a

142. CPL § 120.60(3).
143. CPL § 120.70(1).
144. CPL § 120.70(2)(a).
145. CPL § 120.70(2)(b).
146. CPL § 120.80(1).
147. See Code of Criminal Procedure § 170.
148. See Preiser, "Practice Commentary," to CPL § 120.80, McKinney's Cons. Laws of N.Y., Book 11A, at 341(1992).
149. CPL § 120.80(2).
150. Id.
151. CPL § 120.80(3); P.L. § 35.30. For a discussion of the circumstances in which physical force, or even deadly physical force, may be used in effectuating an arrest, see Greenberg, Marcus, et al., New York Criminal Law § 3.16 (West 1996); Donnino, "Practice Commentary" to P.L. Article 35, McKinney's Cons. Laws of N.Y., Book 39, at 94–96 (1987).

152. CPL § 120.80(4). The Penal Law defines "dwelling," in the context of criminal trespass and burglary, as "a building which is usually occupied by a person lodging therein at night." P.L. § 140.00(3).

153. CPL § 120.80(4). A search warrant is not necessary if the third party consents to the search or if exigent circumstances exist. See Steagald v. United States, 451 U.S. 204, 216, 101 S.Ct. 1642, 1649, 68 L.Ed.2d 38 (1981). To obtain such a search warrant, the officer must allege facts providing reasonable cause to believe

constitutional requirement, that protects against the police having the "unfettered discretion" to decide which homes should be searched.[154]

Another constitutional requirement is that, before entering any premises to effectuate an arrest warrant, the officer must make a reasonable effort to provide notice of the reason and authority for the warrant.[155] The failure to provide such notice—commonly known as the "knock and announce" rule—requires that any evidence seized as a result of the arrest and search must be suppressed.[156] The officer may dispense with the knock and announce requirement if he or she has reasonable cause to believe that providing notice will result in the defendant's escape or attempted escape, endanger the life or safety of the officer or another person, or lead to the destruction, damage or secretion of material evidence.[157] If the officer has a lawful basis to dispense with the notice, or provides notice and is not admitted, he or she may enter the premises, by a breaking if necessary.[158]

Library References:
West's Key No. Digests, Arrest ⚖︎65, 68(12); Criminal Law ⚖︎218(2).

§ 3.15 Arrest Warrant—Post–Arrest Procedure

The procedures that apply following execution of an arrest warrant are exceedingly detailed and technical, and they turn on whether the warrant is a felony or non-felony warrant, whether the officer executing the warrant is an officer to whom the warrant is addressed or an officer to whom the warrant has been delegated, where the arrest is made and whether the court that issued the warrant is available to arraign the defendant at the time of arrest.

The most frequent situation involves execution of the warrant by the officer to whom the warrant is addressed. If the arrest is for a felony, or for a non-felony and the arrest is made in the county in which the warrant was issued or in an adjoining county, the officer must return the defendant to the issuing court "without unnecessary delay."[159] If the arrest is for a non-felony and is made in a county other than the issuing county or an adjoining county, the officer must advise the defendant of the right to appear before a local criminal court of the county in which the arrest is made for the purpose of being released on recognizance or having bail fixed. If the defendant declines this option, the officer must ask the defendant to so endorse the warrant, following

that the defendant may be found in the designated premises. CPL § 690.35 (3)(b).

154. Steagald v. United States, 451 U.S. at 220, 101 S.Ct. at 1652. Consequently, if the police fail to obtain a search warrant, and consent or exigent circumstances are lacking, the third party will have standing to suppress any evidence seized from the dwelling, see Steagald v. United States, supra, and may well have a cause of action against the officer under 42 U.S.C.A. § 1983.

155. See Wilson v. Arkansas, ___ U.S. ___, 115 S.Ct. 1914, 131 L.Ed.2d 976 (1995); People v. Frank, 35 N.Y.2d 874, 363 N.Y.S.2d 953, 323 N.E.2d 191 (1974).

156. Id.

157. CPL § 120.80(4).

158. CPL § 120.80(5).

159. CPL § 120.90(1). The "without unnecessary delay" standard is discussed below.

which the officer must bring the defendant without unnecessary delay to the issuing court. If the defendant accepts this option, or if the defendant declines the option but refuses to so endorse the warrant, the officer must bring the defendant without unnecessary delay to any local criminal court of the county in which the arrest was made.[160] That court then must either fix bail or release the defendant on his or her own recognizance, and it must also set a date for the defendant's appearance in the issuing court.[161]

On the other hand, if the arrest is made by an officer to whom the warrant has been delegated, that officer, "without unnecessary delay," must deliver the defendant to the officer to whom the warrant is addressed, who in turn must bring the defendant without unnecessary delay to the issuing court.[162] If, however, the officer to whom the warrant has been delegated arrests the defendant in a non-felony case in a county other than the county of issuance or an adjoining county, the officer may hold the defendant for up to two hours in the county of arrest for the purpose of delivering the defendant to the officer to whom the warrant is addressed, who in turn must bring the defendant without unnecessary delay to the issuing court. Alternatively, the officer to whom the warrant has been delegated may advise the defendant of the right to appear before a local criminal court in the county of arrest for the purpose of being released on recognizance or having bail fixed. If the defendant declines this option, the officer must request that the defendant sign a written statement to that effect,[163] and if the defendant does so, the officer must bring him or her without unnecessary delay to the officer to whom the warrant is addressed. If the defendant exercises this option, or refuses to sign the written statement,[164] the officer, without unnecessary delay, must bring the defendant before any local criminal court of the county of arrest and also submit to that court a written statement setting forth the material facts relating to the issuance of the warrant and the offense or offenses with which the defendant has been charged. Such court then must fix bail or release the defendant on his or her own recognizance, as well as set an appearance date before the issuing court.[165]

To make matters even more complicated, the CPL authorizes the arresting officer to bring the defendant to a variety of alternative courts when certain courts that issued the warrant are not available. Generally, an arrest warrant is returnable only in the court that issued the

---

160. If, however, a bench warrant has been issued against the defendant for defaulting on bail, the defendant does not have the option of appearing before a local criminal court in the county of arrest; instead, the officer must bring the defendant without unnecessary delay to the issuing court. CPL § 120.90(3).

161. CPL § 120.90(3).

162. CPL § 120.90(2).

163. The defendant's endorsement of the warrant is not required in this situation because the officer to whom the warrant has been delegated may not always have a copy of the warrant.

164. If a bench warrant has been issued against the defendant for default of bail, this option is not available, and the officer, without unnecessary delay, must bring the defendant to the officer to whom the warrant is addressed, who in turn, without unnecessary delay must bring the defendant to the issuing court. CPL § 120.90(4).

165. CPL § 120.80(4).

warrant.[166] However, if a city, town or village court attaches a copy of the accusatory instrument to a warrant it has issued, and that court is not available to arraign the defendant when the warrant is executed, the arresting officer must bring the defendant to another specifically designated court, which may conduct the arraignment.[167] If the issuing court that is not available is a town court, the defendant must be brought before any village court embraced in whole or in part by the town, or to any local criminal court of an adjoining town or city of the same county or any village court embraced in whole or in part by such adjoining town. If the issuing court is a village court, the officer must bring the defendant to the town court of the town embracing the village or to any other village court within the town; or if neither is available, to the local criminal court of any town or city of the same county adjoining such embracing town or to any village court embraced in whole or in part by such adjoining town. If the issuing court is a city court, the officer must bring the defendant to the local criminal court of any adjoining town of the same county or to the local criminal court of any village embraced in whole or in part by such adjoining town.[168]

Before returning a defendant arrested on a warrant to the issuing court, the arresting officer must without unnecessary delay perform any required fingerprinting, photographing and related preliminary police functions.[169] If the defendant has been arrested in another county and has been released by a local criminal court of that county on bail or recognizance, the court that issued the warrant must, when the defendant ultimately appears before it, direct the appropriate police agency to conduct any such required functions.[170]

The "without unnecessary delay" standard, which appears throughout the provisions governing the procedures following execution of an arrest warrant, also appears in the provisions governing the procedures following an arrest without a warrant.[171] The standard in the warrantless arrest provisions, unlike the standard in the arrest warrant provisions, has been subject to considerable judicial interpretation. For example, the Court of Appeals has upheld a trial court's determination

---

166. CPL § 120.30(1).

167. CPL § 120.40. This procedure is beneficial to defendants, who will receive a quicker arraignment (and thus a reduced period of pre-arraignment detention) than might otherwise be the case, and to police departments, which in many less populated areas lack facilities in which to detain persons prior to arraignment.

168. CPL § 120.90(5). Whether an alternative court can arraign the defendant if the court that issued the warrant did not attach the accusatory instrument to the warrant has not been addressed in the case law. One commentator has suggested that an alternative court may arraign in this situation. See Preiser, "Practice Commentary," to CPL § 120.40, McKinney's Cons. Laws of N.Y., Book 11A, at 331 (1992).

The arraignment and post-arraignment responsibilities and powers of the alternative court are addressed in CPL § 170.15 (for non-felony cases) and CPL § 180.20 (for felony cases).

169. CPL § 120.90(6).

170. Id.

171. See CPL § 140.20(1)(upon arresting a person without a warrant, the police must without unnecessary delay perform fingerprinting and other preliminary duties and, unless an appearance ticket is issued, must without unnecessary delay file a a local criminal accusatory instrument and bring the defendant to court for arraignment thereon).

that, in New York City, any delay beyond 24 hours in processing a defendant arrested without a warrant and bringing him or her to court for arraignment is presumptively "unnecessary."[172] Whether this presumption, or a similar presumption that may obtain elsewhere in the State, applies to the period following an arrest with a warrant has not been addressed by the courts. However, because the defendant's right to counsel, which may not be waived in New York in the absence of counsel,[173] will always have attached in a case in which an arrest warrant has been issued,[174] any incentive the police may have in delaying a defendant's arraignment following a warrantless arrest does not exist following an arrest pursuant to a warrant.

Library References:
West's Key No. Digests, Arrest ⊜65, 70.

§ 3.16 The Summons

The summons is an alternative, and in many cases, a preferred means of compelling a defendant's appearance in a local criminal court for arraignment after a criminal action has already been commenced. Indeed, the CPL provides that if the court is satisfied that the defendant will respond to a summons, it may not issue an arrest warrant.[175] Although historically the summons could be used only to compel a defendant's appearance for arraignment on a non-felony accusatory instrument, a 1993 amendment expanded the availability of the summons to felony complaints as well.[176]

Many of the procedural requirements for a summons are the same as those for an arrest warrant. A summons may be issued only after an accusatory instrument has been filed (thereby commencing a criminal action), and it is issued by the local criminal court itself.[177] In addition, a summons may not be issued to compel a defendant's appearance for arraignment on a simplified information.[178] As is true for an arrest warrant, a local criminal court may issue a summons only if the underlying accusatory instrument is facially sufficient.[179] Thus, the accusatory instrument must contain factual allegations providing reasonable cause to believe that the defendant committed an offense charged

---

172. People ex rel. Maxian (Roundtree) v. Brown, 77 N.Y.2d 422, 568 N.Y.S.2d 575, 570 N.E.2d 223 (1991).

173. See People v. Samuels, 49 N.Y.2d 218, 424 N.Y.S.2d 892, 400 N.E.2d 1344 (1980).

174. This is because, as discussed, an arrest warrant may not issue unless an accusatory instrument commencing a criminal action against the defendant has been filed. See CPL § 120.10(1).

175. CPL § 120.20(3). In addition, if the prosecutor requests, the court, as a further alternative, may authorize the prosecutor to direct the defendant to appear for arraignment on a specified date provided that the court is satisfied that the defendant will so appear. Id.

176. L.1993, c.446 (amending CPL § 130.10). The same amendment also authorized issuance of a summons, as an alternative to a superior court warrant of arrest, to compel a defendant's appearance for arraignment on an indictment or a superior court information. See CPL § 210.10(3).

177. CPL §§ 130.10(1), 130.20. Cf. CPL § 150.10 (an appearance ticket is issued by a police officer or other authorized public servant).

178. CPL § 130.10(1).

179. CPL § 130.30.

therein.[180] Unlike an arrest warrant, a summons is returnable only in the court that issued it; no alternative courts may arraign the defendant.[181]

A summons must be subscribed by the issuing judge,[182] and must contain specific information: the name of the court, the defendant, "an" offense charged in the accusatory instrument, the date of issuance, the date and time it is returnable and a direction that the defendant appear at such date and time.[183] It may be served on the defendant by a police officer, a complainant at least 18 years of age or any other person at least 18 years of age designated by the court.[184] It may only be served, however, in the county of issuance or in an adjoining county.[185] Although the statute does not require personal service, that would seem to be the overwhelmingly preferable method and, presumably, the issuing court may require it.

If a defendant does not appear on the date specified in a summons for arraignment, the court may issue an arrest warrant.[186] The failure of a defendant properly served with a summons to appear on the return date would subject him or her to a prosecution for, or a finding of, criminal contempt.[187]

Library References:
West's Key No. Digests, Criminal Law ⇔215–220.

§ 3.17 Warrantless Arrests—In General

If no criminal action has yet been commenced in a local criminal court, the defendant's appearance in court for arraignment on a yet to be filed accusatory instrument may be secured by a warrantless arrest or by an appearance ticket. Unlike the appearance ticket, which is discussed in §§ 3.20–3.22, *infra*, the legal rules governing warrantless arrests are set out, for the most part, in the case law. Most of these decisions, which number in the hundreds, if not the thousands, involve fact-specific determinations of whether the police had probable cause to arrest the defendant—a determination that cannot possibly be guided in any meaningful way by statutory standards.[188] Analysis of those decisions, there-

180. See § 3.7, supra.

181. CPL § 130.20. This is because the court, when issuing a summons, specifies the return date itself. When a court issues an arrest warrant, it does not know when it will be executed and, thus, when the arraignment will have to be conducted.

182. As is true for arrest warrants, "subscription" apparently does not mean an actual handwritten signature of the judge. See § 3.12, supra.

183. CPL § 130.10(2).

184. CPL § 130.40(1). Service by the complainant carries the potential for confrontation, and thus should be disfavored in many cases.

185. CPL § 130.40(2).

186. CPL § 130.50.

187. See P.L. § 215.50(3)(criminal contempt in the second degree, a Class A misdemeanor, includes the "[i]ntentional disobedience or resistance to the lawful process or other mandate of a court"); Judiciary Law § 750(A)(court of record has power to punish, as criminal contempt, willful disobedience of its lawful mandate). Cf. P.L. § 215.58 (separate Penal Law offense for "failing to respond to an appearance ticket").

188. The same can be said for the "stop and frisk" procedure which, although addressed in CPL § 140.50, is governed almost exclusively by the multitude of cases

fore, is beyond the scope of this book; indeed, it is a subject to which an entire book, or series of books, can be exclusively devoted.[189] Nevertheless, Article 140 of the CPL does prescribe a number of principles relating to warrantless arrests, and they are discussed in the following two sections of this chapter.

Library References:
West's Key No. Digests, Arrest ⟾63.

§ 3.18 Warrantless Arrests—Authorization and Execution

In general, a police officer may arrest a person without a warrant for any "offense"[190] if the officer has "reasonable cause"[191] to believe that the person has committed such offense in his or her presence.[192] If the offense is a "crime" (i.e., a felony or misdemeanor[193]) a police officer's authority is broader—if the officer has reasonable cause, the arrest may be committed whether or not the crime occurred within the officer's presence.[194] In addition, a police officer may make a warrantless arrest for a crime anywhere in the state, regardless of the geographical area of the officer's employment and regardless of where the crime occurred.[195] A police officer may make a warrantless arrest for any other offense, however, only if the offense occurred in the officer's geographical area of employment and only if the arrest is made in the county in which it was committed or an adjoining county.[196]

analyzing the myriad factual scenarios that arise in daily police-citizen encounters.

189. See, e.g., B. Kamins, New York Search and Seizure Law (Gould Publications 1994). See also W. LaFave, Search and Seizure: A Treatise on the Fourth Amendment (West Publishing Co.1987).

190. "Offense" is defined in the Penal Law as "conduct for which a sentence to a term of imprisonment or to a fine is provided by any law of this state or by an law, local law or ordinance of a political subdivision of this state, or by any order, rule or regulation of any governmental instrumentality authorized by law to adopt the same." P.L. § 10.00(1).

191. Although the statute uses the standard "reasonable cause," that term is identical to the more commonly used standard of "probable cause." See People v. Johnson, 66 N.Y.2d 398, 402 n. 2, 497 N.Y.S.2d 618, 621 n. 2, 488 N.E.2d 439, 442 n. 2 (1985). The Court of Appeals has defined this standard as "information which would lead a reasonable person who possesses the same expertise as the officer to conclude under the circumstances that [an offense] is being or was committed." People v. McRay, 51 N.Y.2d 594, 602, 435 N.Y.S.2d 679, 683, 416 N.E.2d 1015, 1019 (1980). See also Beck v. Ohio, 379 U.S. 89, 91, 85 S.Ct. 223, 225, 13 L.Ed.2d 142 (1964)(probable cause defined in terms of facts and circumstances "sufficient to warrant a prudent man in believing that the [suspect] had committed or was committing an offense"). See also CPL § 70.10(2)("reasonable cause" to believe a person has committed an offense exists "when evidence or information which appears reliable discloses facts or circumstances which are collectively of such weight and persuasiveness as to convince a person of ordinary intelligence, judgment and experience that it is reasonably likely that such offense was committed and that such person committed it").

192. CPL § 140.10(1)(a).

193. See P.L. § 10.00(6).

194. CPL § 140.10(1)(b).

195. CPL § 140.10(3). The officer may also pursue the person outside of New York and arrest him or her in another state if that state, like New York, has adopted the Uniform Close Pursuit Act. See CPL § 140.55.

196. CPL § 140.10(2). The only exception to this requirement is if the officer is in "continuous close pursuit" of the suspect, and such pursuit began in the county in which the offense was committed or an adjoining county. In that situation, the officer may make a warrantless arrest in

With one exception, the decision whether to make a warrantless arrest is left to the discretion of the individual police officer. The exception pertains to certain incidents of domestic violence.[197] Arrest is required if the police have reasonable cause to believe that a felony has been committed against a member of the defendant's household or family, as defined in CPL § 530.11(1).[198] Arrest is also required, unless the victim requests otherwise, if the police have reasonable cause to believe that a misdemeanor constituting a "family offense" has been committed.[199] Finally, arrest is required in certain situations if an order of protection has previously been issued against a person pursuant to CPL § 530.12,[200] Articles 4, 5, 6 or 8 of the Family Court Act or sections 240 or 252 of the Domestic Relations Law, and the order was duly served or was issued when the person was present in court. These situations include: (1) if the order contained a provision requiring the person to "stay away" from the individual whom the order was issued to protect, and the police have reasonable cause to believe that such provision has been violated;[201] or (2) the police have reasonable cause to believe that a "family offense" has been committed.[202]

any county in which the suspect is apprehended. CPL § 140.10(2)(b).

The more limited authority of a peace officer to make a warrantless arrest is set forth in CPL § 140.25; the even more limited authority of a private citizen to make a warrantless arrest is set forth in CPL § 140.30. See also CPL § 140.27 (warrantless arrest by a peace officer; when and how made and procedure after arrest); CPL § 140.35 (warrantless arrest by a private citizen; when and how made); CPL § 140.40 (warrantless arrest by a private citizen; procedure after arrest).

197. The mandatory arrest requirement applying to certain domestic violence incidents, which took effect on January 1, 1996, was created in the "Family Protection and Domestic Violence Intervention Act of 1994." L. 1994, C. 222, as amended by L. 1994, c. 224. This requirement was a legislative response to what was perceived to be a widespread disinclination among police agencies to make arrests in domestic violence situations. Unless extended by the Legislature, the mandatory arrest requirement will expire on January 1, 2000. L. 1995, c. 356.

198. CPL § 140.10(4)(a). Arrest is not required, however, if the Class E felony of grand larceny in the fourth degree is committed against a member of the defendant's household or family, under subdivisions three, four, nine or ten of that Penal Law offense. Id. See P.L. § 155.30. Interestingly, the statute requires arrest even though, with the exception of these specified grand larceny offenses, the crime against the family or household member does not involve violence or physical coercion.

199. CPL § 140.10(4)(c). In this situation, the statute forbids the police to inquire whether the victim seeks an arrest. Id. The misdemeanor family offenses are acts that would constitute harassment in the first degree (P.L. § 240.25), menacing in the second degree (P.L. § 120.14), menacing in the third degree (P.L. § 120.15), reckless endangerment in the second degree (P.L. § 120.20), assault in the third degree (P.L. § 120.00), attempt to commit assault in the second degree (P.L. §§ 110.00, 120.05) or attempt to commit assault in the second degree (P.L. §§ 110.00, 120.00), between spouses or between parent and child or between members of the same family or household. See CPL § 530.11(1).

200. CPL § 530.12 prescribes the procedures for issuance of an order of protection on behalf of a victim of a family offense.

201. CPL § 140.10(4)(b)(i). Apparently, the only offenses for which a person may be arrested in this situation are the Class A misdemeanor offense of criminal contempt in the second degree, see P.L. § 215.50(3)(intentional disobedience or resistance to the lawful process or other mandate of a court), and the Class E felony of criminal contempt in the first degree. See P.L. § 215.51 (commits the crime of criminal contempt in the second degree by violating a stay away provision of an order of protection and was previously convicted of criminal contempt in the second degree within the previous five years for violating an order of protection).

202. CPL § 140.10(4)(b)(ii).

§ 3.18　　　　　LOCAL CRIMINAL COURTS　　　　　Ch. 3

A warrantless arrest is executed in the same manner as an arrest warrant.[203] Thus, the arrest may be executed on any day of the week at any hour of day or night,[204] the officer must state his or her authority for the arrest and reason for making the arrest (unless the officer encounters physical resistance, flight or some other factor renders such statement impractical),[205] and the officer may use physical force if justified pursuant to P.L. § 35.30.[206] Absent consent or some exigency, the officer may not enter the dwelling of the target of the arrest to effectuate a warrantless arrest.[207] And, even if an arrest warrant has been issued, the officer, absent consent or some exigency, may not enter the dwelling of a third party in which the officer reasonably believes the target of the arrest is present without first obtaining a search warrant.[208] As is true for an arrest based upon a warrant, if, because of some exigency, the officer is authorized to enter premises without first stating the authority and reason for the arrest, or if such notice is provided and entry is denied, the officer may enter by a breaking if necessary.[209]

Library References:

West's Key No. Digests, Arrest ⟐63.4, 66–68.

§ 3.19　Warrantless Arrest—Post-Arrest Procedure

Upon making a warrantless arrest, the police officer, "without unnecessary delay," must perform all fingerprinting, photographing and other "booking"-related tasks and then, except in the situations discussed below, without unnecessary delay must bring the arrestee to the appropriate local criminal court and file with that court an accusatory instrument charging the offense or offenses upon which the arrest was based.[210] In *People ex rel. Maxian (Roundtree) v. Brown*,[211] the Court of Appeals interpreted this provision as requiring "that a prearraignment detention not be prolonged beyond a time reasonably necessary to accomplish the tasks required to bring an arrestee to arraignment."[212] The Court found no reason "to disturb the conclusion" of the lower courts in that case that, "in large urban centers such as New York County" [where the case arose], the "steps leading up to arraignment can generally be accomplished well within 24 hours after arrest."[213] Thus, the Court affirmed the lower courts' holdings that a delay of more than 24 hours is presumptively "unnecessary" and, if unexplained,

---

203. These procedures are discussed in greater detail in § 3.14, supra.

204. CPL § 140.15(1).

205. CPL § 140.15(2).

206. CPL § 140.15(3).

207. Payton v. New York, 445 U.S. 573, 100 S.Ct. 1371, 63 L.Ed.2d 639 (1980).

208. CPL § 140.15(4); CPL § 120.-80(4). See Steagald v. United States, 451 U.S. 204, 101 S.Ct. 1642, 68 L.Ed.2d 38 (1981).

209. CPL § 140.15(4); CPL § 120.-80(5).

210. CPL § 140.20(1).

211. 77 N.Y.2d 422, 568 N.Y.S.2d 575, 570 N.E.2d 223 (1991).

212. 77 N.Y.2d at 427, 568 N.Y.S.2d at 577, 570 N.E.2d at 225.

213. Id.

violates section 140.20(1) and requires the arrestee's release.[214]

Accordingly, at least in New York City, the failure of the police to deliver a detained arrestee to court for arraignment on the charges underlying the arrest within 24 hours of the arrest raises a presumptive violation of the statute, giving rise to a petition in Supreme Court for a writ of habeas corpus.[215] The courts have not addressed whether the 24-hour rule applies to arrests conducted outside of New York City or outside of the larger urban areas of the state. Given the extraordinarily high arrest levels in New York City and the resulting burdens on that City's police force, it would be surprising if such a rule, or even a rule specifying a shorter time requirement, did not apply to police agencies outside of New York City; in fact, with the possible exception of travel time to the police station and to the courthouse, most of the other post-arrest police functions are less time-consuming elsewhere in the State.

Whether the *Roundtree* decision actually requires an arraignment, rather than merely the completion of the police functions leading up to arraignment, within 24 hours of arrest is an interesting question, and of significant relevance to local criminal courts, such as many city courts, that do not hold court on weekends and holidays. Notably, the statute speaks only of the obligation of the police to carry out their functions and bring the arrestee to court "without unnecessary delay."[216] On the other hand, the trial court's opinion in *Roundtree* granted the arrestee's habeas corpus petition on the ground that the "delay in *arraigning* an arrestee who has been held in custody for more than 24 hours is presumptively 'unnecessary' and, failing an acceptable explanation, such arrestee is entitled to be released."[217] Although the precise holding of the Appellate Division's affirmance in that case is not as clear, it did affirm, without any modification, the trial court's order,[218] and the decision of the Court of Appeals, although also not entirely clear on this question, did affirm, without any modification, the Appellate Division's order. Thus, a strong argument can be made that the *Roundtree* decision, at least in cases arising in New York City, stands for the proposition, that the failure to arraign a detained arrestee within 24 hours of the arrest raises a presumptive violation of the statute.

214. 77 N.Y.2d at 426–27, 568 N.Y.S.2d at 577, 570 N.E.2d at 225.

215. See CPLR Article 70 (specifying the procedures for bringing a petition for a writ of habeas corpus).

In New York City, the police, upon arresting and fingerprinting an individual, fax a copy of the fingerprints to the Division of Criminal Justice Services (DCJS) in Albany for a criminal history search. Occasionally, the faxed copy will not be of sufficient quality to allow for the search, requiring that the police send an additional fax of the fingerprints or even retake the individual's fingerprints. See generally CPL § 160.30(2)(if fingerprints received by DCJS are not sufficiently legible to permit an accurate and complete search, they must be returned to police with an explanation of the problem and a request that the defendant be reprinted). Although no reported decisions address the issue, some judges have found that this may justify a failure to produce a person arrested without a warrant for arraignment within 24 hours of the arrest.

216. CPL § 140.10(1).

217. People ex rel. Maxian v. Brown, N.Y.L.J., 4/30/90, p. 26, col. 6 (Sup.Ct., N.Y. County)(emphasis supplied).

218. People ex rel. Maxian v. Brown, 164 A.D.2d 56, 67–68, 561 N.Y.S.2d 418, 424 (1st Dep't 1990).

§ 3.19   LOCAL CRIMINAL COURTS   Ch. 3

In any event, even if the CPL, as interpreted in the *Roundtree* case, does not require an arraignment within 24 hours of arrest, the Federal Constitution in effect requires that the arraignment be held within 48 hours of arrest. The Supreme Court has held that the Fourth Amendment requires a "judicial determination of probable cause as a prerequisite to extended restraint of liberty following arrest,"[219] and that this determination generally must be made within 48 hours of the arrest.[220] The judicial determination of probable cause can be accomplished without a formal hearing; a determination following a non-adversary proceeding based on hearsay and written testimony will suffice.[221] In New York, this constitutional requirement can be fulfilled at arraignment, at which the defendant may request the court's review of the accusatory instrument to determine whether, based on "the available facts or evidence," it would be "impossible" to draw an accusatory instrument that is sufficient on its face—*i.e.*, that demonstrated probable cause (in New York, "reasonable" cause) that the defendant committed an offense.[222] If the court determines that reasonable cause does not exist, it must dismiss the accusatory instrument and discharge the defendant.[223]

In general, the police must bring a defendant arrested without a warrant to the local criminal court that, pursuant to CPL § 100.55, is the appropriate court for commencement of the criminal action in question.[224] However, as is true when a defendant is apprehended on an arrest warrant, the police have other options when the appropriate court under section 100.55 is a city, town or village court that is not available to conduct the arraignment. If such court is a city court that is not available, the police may bring the arrestee to the local criminal court of

---

219. Gerstein v. Pugh, 420 U.S. 103, 95 S.Ct. 854, 43 L.Ed.2d 54 (1975).

220. County of Riverside v. McLaughlin, 500 U.S. 44, 111 S.Ct. 1661, 114 L.Ed.2d 49 (1991).

221. Gerstein v. Pugh, 420 U.S. at 120, 95 S.Ct. at 866.

222. CPL § 140.45. If the defendant's appearance for arraignment was obtained by an arrest warrant, the court, upon issuing the arrest warrant, will already have made this determination. See § 3.13, supra.

223. Id. In addition to giving rise to an application for a writ of habeas corpus resulting in a pre-arraignment detainee's release from custody, unreasonable delay in bringing a person to court for arraignment may give rise to the suppression of evidence obtained during the period of delay on the ground that the individual's constitutional right to counsel has been violated. See, e.g., People v. Cooper, 101 A.D.2d 1, 475 N.Y.S.2d 660 (4th Dep't 1984)(defendant's confession suppressed because police, in departure from usual procedure, delayed arraignment to interrogate defendant, negotiate a plea bargain and videotape the confession, all in the absence of counsel); People v. Klein, 130 Misc.2d 549, 554–55, 496 N.Y.S.2d 889, 893–94 (Westchester Co.Ct.1985)(four-day delay in producing defendant for arraignment provided alternative ground for suppressing confession). Cf. People v. Ortlieb, 84 N.Y.2d 989, 622 N.Y.S.2d 501, 646 N.E.2d 803 (1994)(record failed to establish that police postponed arraignment "for the sole purpose of depriving [defendant, who had waived his Miranda rights] of the right to counsel"); People v. Fisher, 199 A.D.2d 279, 604 N.Y.S.2d 223 (2d Dep't 1993)(although arraignment was "unduly" delayed to place defendant in a lineup, purpose of delay was not to deprive defendant of right to counsel); People v. Lopez, 185 A.D.2d 285, 585 N.Y.S.2d 797 (2d Dep't 1992)(delay in arraignment may be warranted while police investigate detainee's possible involvement in an unrelated crime of which they were unaware at time of arrest); People v. Coleman, 115 A.D.2d 488, 496 N.Y.S.2d 41 (2d Dep't 1985)(delay in arraignment was "normal result" of a weekend arrest and not intended to coerce a confession from defendant).

224. CPL § 140.20(1). Section 100.55 is discussed in Chapter 1, § 1.5.

any town or village adjoining the city that is within the same county, or to a village court embraced by an adjoining town within the same county.[225] If such court is a town court that is not available, the defendant has not been arrested for an offense more serious than a Class E felony,[226] and the offense has not been committed in a village that has a village court, the police may bring the arrestee to the local criminal court of any village within the town or to the local criminal court of any adjoining town, village embraced in whole or in part by such adjoining town, or city of the same county.[227] If such court is a village court that is not available and the defendant similarly has not been arrested for an offense more serious than a Class E felony,[228] the police may bring the arrestee to the town court of the town embracing the village or to any other village court within that town, or if none of those courts is available, to the local criminal court of any adjoining town, village embraced in whole or in part by such adjoining town, or city of the same county.[229] Finally, regardless of whether the appropriate local criminal court under section 100.55 is available to conduct the arraignment, the police may bring an individual arrested for a traffic infraction or a traffic misdemeanor to the local criminal court of the same county that is nearest (by highway travel) to the point of arrest.[230]

Not all persons arrested without a warrant must be detained pending their arraignment. If the arrest is for an offense no more serious than a Class E felony, the officer may issue an appearance ticket and release the person, or the police may fix pre-arraignment bail and, upon the posting of such bail, may issue an appearance ticket and release the person.[231] In addition, if the arrest was for such an offense and no local criminal court with authorization to arraign is available so that the arrestee cannot be arraigned "with reasonable promptness," and the arrestee does not appear to be under the influence of drugs or alcohol such that he or she could be dangerous, the police must either issue an appearance ticket and release the person or fix pre-arraignment bail.[232] If the police choose the latter option, and bail is not posted, the arrestee may be "temporarily" detained but then brought before a local criminal court "without unnecessary delay."[233]

Two other rules applying to warrantless arrests merit mention. One is obvious: if after the arrest the police, upon further investigation, conclude that reasonable cause is lacking that the person committed an

---

225. CPL § 140.20(1)(c).

226. With the exception of the following Class E felonies: rape in the third degree (P.L. § 130.25); sodomy in the third degree (P.L. § 130.40); escape in the second degree (P.L. § 205.10); absconding from temporary release in the first degree (P.L. § 205.17); absconding from a community treatment facility (P.L. § 205.19); and bail jumping in the second degree (P.L. § 215.56).

227. CPL § 140.20(1)(a).

228. With the same exceptions as specified in footnote 226, supra.

229. CPL § 140.20(1)(b).

230. CPL § 140.20(1)(d). The arraignment and post-arraignment responsibilities and powers of the alternate court are addressed in CPL § 170.15 (for non-felony cases) and CPL § 180.20 (for felony cases).

231. The procedures governing appearance tickets and pre-arraignment bail are discussed in §§ 3.20–3.22, infra.

232. CPL § 140.20(3). "Reasonable promptness" is not defined in the statute or in case law.

233. Id.

offense, the person must immediately be released from custody.[234] The second rule applies to an arrest of a "juvenile offender":[235] when a juvenile offender is arrested without a warrant, the officer must immediately notify the juvenile's parent or guardian (or the person with whom the juvenile is domiciled) that the juvenile has been arrested and of the location of the facility where he or she is being detained.[236]

Library References:
West's Key No. Digests, Arrest ⟪70; Criminal Law ⟪261–264.

§ 3.20 Appearance Ticket—In General

The other means of securing the appearance at arraignment of a person charged with an offense, but against whom an accusatory instrument has not yet been filed, is by issuance of an appearance ticket. An appearance ticket is a written notice issued by a public servant directing a person to appear in a particular local criminal court on a particular date in response to such person's alleged commission of a specified offense.[237] Traditionally, an appearance ticket could be issued only if the offense charged was a non-felony offense. However, in 1987 the eligible offenses were expanded to include most Class E felonies.[238] The appearance ticket is sometimes referred to as a desk appearance ticket (or DAT), and on occasion may even be mistakenly referred to as a summons. Unlike a summons or an arrest warrant, the appearance ticket is issued not by a court but by the officer charging the offense, and it is designed to save the officer the time and effort of detaining the person and bringing him or her to court for arraignment when the officer determines that the person can be trusted to submit to the jurisdiction of the court on his or her own. Indeed, in many situations, issuance of an appearance ticket is often the "preferred procedure,"[239] although the decision whether to issue one is left to the police's discretion.[240] In addition to police officers, other public servants may issue appearance tickets, but only if expressly authorized by state law[241] or a local law

---

234. CPL § 140.20(4).

235. The definition of a "juvenile offender" is set forth in CPL § 1.20(42). A "juvenile offender" should not be confused with a "youthful offender," which is defined in CPL § 720.10.

236. CPL § 140.20(6).

237. CPL § 150.10.

238. L.1987, c.549, 550. The ineligible Class E felonies are: P.L. § 130.25 (rape in the third degree); P.L. § 130.40 (sodomy in the third degree); P.L. § 205.10 (escape in the second degree); P.L. § 205.17 (absconding from temporary release in the first degree); P.L. § 205.19 (absconding from a community treatment facility); P.L. § 215.56 (bail jumping in the second degree). CPL § 150.20.

239. See People v. Howell, 49 N.Y.2d 778, 779, 426 N.Y.S.2d 477, 478, 403 N.E.2d 182, 183 (1980)(warrantless arrest for misdemeanor reckless driving offense was "neither called for nor the preferred procedure").

240. See People v. Stone, 128 Misc.2d 1009, 1011, 491 N.Y.S.2d 921, 923 (N.Y.C.Crim.Ct.1985). However, if the defendant was arrested without a warrant for an offense for which an appearance ticket may be issued, and no local criminal court with authorization to arraign is available so that the arrestee cannot be arraigned "with reasonable promptness," the officer generally must issue an appearance ticket and release the person or fix pre-arraignment bail. See CPL § 140.20(3).

241. Peace officers apparently may issue appearance tickets "when acting pursuant to their special duties." CPL § 2.20(1)(d). See also Op. Atty. Gen. 93–F2 (April 12, 1993).

enacted pursuant to the provisions of the Municipal Home Rule Law.[242] If the charged offense is only a petty offense, a public servant, other than a police officer, who is authorized to issue an appearance ticket may do so only if the offense was committed in such public servant's presence.[243]

An appearance ticket may be issued either in lieu of making a warrantless arrest or following a warrantless arrest.[244] In addition, if a peace officer who has arrested a person for an eligible offense is not authorized to issue an appearance ticket but requests a police officer to do so, the police officer may heed the peace officer's request.[245] Courts have split over whether a police policy of informing persons arrested for the offense of driving while intoxicated that an appearance ticket will not be issued if a breathalyzer test is refused is illegally coercive.[246] Except for a traffic infraction relating to parking, an appearance ticket must be served personally on the individual charged with the offense.[247] An appearance ticket may be served only in the county in which the offense allegedly occurred or in an adjoining county.[248] However, if a police officer begins a "continuous close pursuit" of a person in the county in which the offense allegedly occurred or in an adjoining county, the officer may serve an appearance ticket in any other county in which the person charged is ultimately overtaken.[249]

Library References:

West's Key No. Digests, Automobiles ⇒351.1; Criminal Law ⇒216; Indictment and Information ⇒4, 41.

§ 3.21 Appearance Ticket—Pre-arraignment Bail and Post-Issuance Procedures

The issuance of an appearance ticket by a police officer may be conditioned on the posting of pre-arraignment bail.[250] The amount of such bail may be fixed by the desk officer in charge at a police station, police headquarters or county jail, or by such desk officer's superior, but may not exceed a schedule of amounts specified in the CPL: $750 if the arrest is for a Class E felony; $500 if the arrest is for a Class A misdemeanor; $250 if the arrest is for a Class B misdemeanor; and $100 if the arrest is for a petty offense.[251] If pre-arraignment bail is posted, the person arrested must be issued an appearance ticket and released

---

242. CPL § 150.10. Section 10(4)(a) of the Municipal Home Rule Law authorizes local governments to designate peace officers and others to issue appearance tickets in connection with certain offenses.

243. CPL § 150.20(3).

244. CPL § 150.20(1) and (2).

245. CPL § 150.20(2)(b); CPL § 140.27(4)(b). The police officer also is authorized to do the same if the person has been arrested for an eligible offense by a civilian. CPL § 150.20(2)(c); CPL § 140.40(3)(a).

246. Cf. People v. Bracken, 129 Misc.2d 1048, 494 N.Y.S.2d 1021 (N.Y.C.Crim.Ct. 1985) and People v. Harrington, 111 Misc.2d 648, 444 N.Y.S.2d 848 (Monroe Co.Ct.1981)(policy reasonable and not unduly coercive) with People v. Stone, 128 Misc.2d 1009, 491 N.Y.S.2d 921 (N.Y.C.Crim.Ct.1985)(policy impermissibly coercive).

247. CPL § 150.40(2).

248. CPL § 150.40(3).

249. CPL § 150.40(4).

250. CPL § 150.30; CPL § 150.20(2).

251. CPL § 150.30(2).

from custody.[252] The person posting pre-arraignment bail must complete and sign a form containing the following: such person's name, residential address and occupation; the title of the action; the offense or offenses charged and the status of the action; the name of the principal (*i.e.*, the person who was arrested); the date of the next court appearance; an acknowledgment that the bail will be forfeited if the principal does not appear on such date; and the amount of bail posted.[253]

If a police officer who has arrested a motorist for a traffic infraction reasonably believes that the motorist has not been licensed to drive by the State of New York or by another state that has entered into a reciprocal agreement with New York guaranteeing its motorists' appearance to answer a traffic infraction charged in New York,[254] the officer may fix pre-arraignment bail in the amount of $50.[255] Interestingly, in an apparent effort to minimize an opportunity for police corruption, such bail may only be posted by credit card.[256]

After issuance of an appearance ticket, the issuing officer, on or before the return date specified in the ticket, must file with the appropriate local criminal court an accusatory instrument charging the offense or offenses specified in the appearance ticket.[257] A number of courts have addressed the appropriate remedy when an accusatory instrument is not filed by the return date. One court has held that the failure to file an accusatory instrument by the return date specified in the appearance ticket does not require dismissal of the action so long as a new return date is scheduled and an accusatory instrument is filed by that date.[258] Other courts have disagreed, holding that dismissal is required and thus an appearance ticket must be "re-served" on the defendant or a criminal action must be initiated in some other manner.[259]

---

252. Id.

253. CPL § 150.30(1). This form is essentially the same form that a person who posts bail that was fixed by a court must sign. See CPL § 520.15(2). Section 150.30(1), however, requires that a person posting pre-arraignment bail undertake only that the individual on whose behalf the bail is being posted will appear in court at arraignment, not for any additional court proceedings. This is because pre-arraignment bill serves a strictly limited purpose; any bail that the court fixes at arraignment will effectively supersede the pre-arraignment bail, and a person posting bail at that point will be required to sign another written statement undertaking that the defendant will appear in court "whenever required and will at all times render himself amenable to the orders and processes of the court." CPL § 520.20(2).

254. See Vehicle and Traffic Law § 517 (authorizing the Commissioner of Motor Vehicles to execute reciprocal agreements with other states providing, inter alia, that if a person licensed by either state is issued an appearance ticket for a moving traffic violation covered by the agreement, and he or she fails to appear in response thereto, the licensing state may suspend the license).

255. CPL § 150.30(3).

256. Id.

257. CPL § 150.50(1).

258. People v. Consolidated Edison Co., 153 Misc.2d 595, 582 N.Y.S.2d 614 (N.Y.C.Crim.Ct.1992). See also People v. D'Alessio, 134 Misc.2d 1005, 513 N.Y.S.2d 906 (N.Y.C.Crim.Ct.1986).

259. People v. Consolidated Edison Co., 161 Misc.2d 907, 615 N.Y.S.2d 978 (N.Y.C.Crim.Ct.1994)(continued prosecution on an appearance ticket for which an accusatory instrument has not been filed by the return date is impermissible); People v. Consolidated Edison Co., 159 Misc.2d 354, 604 N.Y.S.2d 482 (N.Y.C.Crim.Ct.1993)(noting that "[t]o hold any other way is to put the interests of enforcement agencies above the due process interests of defendants").

If an accusatory instrument is filed following issuance of an appearance ticket, and the defendant named in the accusatory instrument fails to appear in court on the date specified in the appearance ticket, the court may issue a summons or arrest warrant.[260] The defendant's appearance for arraignment in that situation also could be secured by a warrantless arrest. The failure to appear in court on the return date specified in an appearance ticket, or voluntarily within 30 days thereafter, is a violation offense under the Penal Law.[261]

As is true for an accusatory instrument that is filed following a warrantless arrest, the court, upon reviewing an accusatory instrument filed following issuance of an appearance ticket, must dismiss such accusatory instrument if it is not facially sufficient and it would be impossible, based on the available facts and evidence, to draw an accusatory instrument that is facially sufficient.[262]

Library References:

West's Key No. Digests, Bail ⚖︎40–43.

§ 3.22 Appearance Ticket—Marihuana Violations

If a person is arrested without a warrant for the Penal Law offense of unlawful possession of marihuana[263]—a violation offense—and no other offense is charged or alleged,[264] an appearance ticket must be issued.[265] Issuance of an appearance ticket may be conditioned on the posting of pre-arraignment bail, however, but only if the officer cannot ascertain the person's identity or residential address, reasonably suspects that the identification or address provided is false or reasonably suspects that the person is not a New York resident.[266] Such bail may not be fixed in an amount exceeding $100.[267]

Library References:

West's Key No. Digests, Bail ⚖︎51.

§ 3.23 Fingerprinting

Fingerprinting of persons charged with criminal offenses is useful, if not essential, in most cases for setting the terms of the securing order and for facilitating intelligent plea bargaining and sentencing. The

---

260. CPL § 150.60.

261. See P.L. § 215.58. Because this Penal Law statute expressly refers to the failure to respond to an appearance ticket that is based upon the alleged commission of a "crime," see P.L. § 215.58(1), the offense does not arise when a person fails to respond to an appearance ticket that is based on other than a felony or misdemeanor offense. See P.L. § 10.00(6) ("crime" defined as a misdemeanor or a felony).

262. CPL § 150.50(2). Cf. CPL § 140.45 (same standard for accusatory instrument filed following a warrantless arrest).

263. P.L. § 221.05.

264. Cf. People v. Terrero, 139 A.D.2d 830, 527 N.Y.S.2d 135 (3d Dep't 1988)(warrantless arrest could be made where police had probable cause that defendant was driving under influence of marihuana, a misdemeanor offense under the Vehicle and Traffic Law).

265. CPL § 150.75.

266. Id.

267. CPL § 150.30(2)(d).

police, however, are authorized to fingerprint persons only pursuant to statute.[268] The primary statute, CPL § 160.10, requires that the arresting or other appropriate police officer take the fingerprints of a person arrested for, or formally charged with, certain types of offenses.[269] These offenses include all felonies,[270] all misdemeanors defined in the Penal Law[271] and all misdemeanors defined outside the Penal Law that would constitute a felony if the offender had a prior criminal conviction.[272] Also included are two violations: loitering for the purpose of soliciting or engaging in deviate sexual behavior and loitering for the purpose of engaging in a prostitution offense.[273]

The statute also permits a police officer who arrests a person for any other offense to take the fingerprints of that person if certain factors are present. Thus, the officer may fingerprint if he or she is unable to ascertain the person's identity,[274] reasonably suspects that the person has provided a false identity[275] or reasonably suspects that the person is being sought for the commission of some other offense.[276]

The timing of the fingerprint taking is determined by whether the person charged with a fingerprintable offense is arrested or not. If the person is arrested, fingerprints must be taken before arraignment, even if the police do not further detain the person and instead issue an appearance ticket directing the person to appear in court at a specified date for arraignment.[277] The refusal of a person arrested for a fingerprintable offense to submit to fingerprinting authorizes the police to hold the person pending receipt of a court order compelling the person to submit to fingerprinting.[278]

268. See People v. Johnson, 88 Misc.2d 749, 753, 389 N.Y.S.2d 766, 769 (Onondaga Co.Ct.1976); see also Campbell v. Adams, 206 Misc. 673, 675, 133 N.Y.S.2d 876, 879 (Sup.Ct., Queens County, 1954); Fidler v. Murphy, 203 Misc. 51, 52–53, 113 N.Y.S.2d 388, 390 (Sup.Ct., Onondaga County, 1952)(both cases interpreting predecessor statute under the former Code of Criminal Procedure).

269. Whenever fingerprinting is authorized under section 160.10, the police may take photographs and palm prints as well. CPL § 160.10(3).

270. CPL § 160.10(1)(a).

271. CPL § 160.10(1)(b).

272. CPL § 160.10(1)(c). The most common example of such a misdemeanor is driving while intoxicated. See Vehicle and Traffic Law § 1193(1)(c).

273. CPL § 160.10(1)(d) and (e). The statute prohibiting loitering for the purpose of soliciting or engaging in deviate sexual behavior—P.L. § 240.35(3)—was declared unconstitutional in People v. Uplinger, 58 N.Y.2d 936, 460 N.Y.S.2d 514, 447 N.E.2d 62 (1983). Loitering for the purpose of engaging in a prostitution offense (P.L. § 240.37) apparently is included as a fingerprintable offense because a previous prostitution-related conviction raises this offense to a misdemeanor and because experience has shown that perpetrators of this offense frequently do not provide reliable identity when apprehended.

274. CPL § 160.10(2)(a).

275. CPL § 160.10(2)(b).

276. CPL § 160.10(2)(c).

277. CPL § 160.10(1); CPL § 140.-20(5). If the arrest has been made by a peace officer, the peace officer may take the fingerprints or may enlist the aid of a police officer to do so. CPL § 140.27(2). If the arrest has been made by a civilian, see CPL § 140.40, a police officer who would have been authorized to make the arrest himself or herself, upon concluding that the arrest was legally authorized, must conduct the fingerprinting if the arrest was for a felony. CPL § 140.40(1) and (4).

278. See People v. Batista, 128 Misc.2d 1054, 1056, 491 N.Y.S.2d 966, 967 (N.Y.C.Crim.Ct.1985).

If a person charged with a fingerprintable offense has not been arrested and has been served with an appearance ticket, the court must direct that fingerprints be taken at a designated time and place following the arraignment.[279] Or, if a person charged with a fingerprintable offense has been served with a summons that is based on an indictment or a prosecutor's information or on an accusatory instrument filed by a complainant who is a police officer, the court also most direct that fingerprints be so taken following arraignment.[280] If, however, the person has been served with a summons based on an accusatory instrument filed by a complainant who is not a police officer, the arraigning court, if it finds reasonable cause to believe that the defendant committed the offense charged, has the discretion to direct fingerprinting. If the court does not direct fingerprinting at that time, the court must do so if the defendant ultimately is convicted of a fingerprintable offense.[281]

After fingerprints are taken, the police must expeditiously transmit copies of the fingerprints to the State Division of Criminal Justice (DCJS), which maintains the state's fingerprint data base and also is connected to the Federal Bureau of Investigation's national fingerprint data base. Upon receiving the fingerprints, DCJS conducts a criminal history search and then transmits the results of its search back to the forwarding police agency.[282] The police agency must promptly provide the prosecution and the court with copies of the fingerprint report. The court then must provide the defense with a copy of the report.[283] Complaints periodically arise in some less populated areas of the state that courts are not providing the defense with a copy of the fingerprint report. When this occurs, it is important that the defense assert its clear statutory right to receive the report.

The CPL further requires that, before sentencing a defendant convicted of a fingerprintable offense, the court must receive the DCJS fingerprint report or a police department's report of the defendant's criminal history.[284] Although the court may rely on a report that was provided at the time of arrest or arraignment, it might be advisable in some cases for the court to order an updated report, particularly if a significant period of time has elapsed since the arrest or arraignment.

Library References:
West's Key No. Digests, Criminal Law ⚖=1224(3).

§ 3.24 Arraignment on Non–felony Accusatory Instrument

The procedures for arraignment on a non-felony accusatory instrument are set forth in CPL § 170.10.[285] At the arraignment, the court

279. CPL § 150.70.
280. CPL § 130.60(1).
281. CPL § 130.60(2).
282. CPL § 160.20, CPL § 160.30.
283. CPL § 160.40.
284. CPL § 390.10.

285. Cf. CPL § 180.10 (procedures for arraignment in local criminal court on a felony complaint, discussed in § 3.30, infra); CPL § 210.15 (procedures for arraignment in superior court on an indictment).

must inform the defendant of the charges filed against him or her, and provide the defendant with a copy of the accusatory instrument.[286] Although the statute does not require it, defendants charged in non-felony accusatory instruments routinely enter a plea at arraignment, at least when represented by counsel. Similarly, although the statute does not require the court to make a determination that there is reasonable cause to believe that the defendant committed the offense or offenses charged, Supreme Court case law requires that such a determination be made "as a prerequisite to extended restraint of liberty following arrest," at least when the defendant so requests.[287]

Generally, the defendant must personally appear at the arraignment. However, if the defendant has been charged in a simplified information, personal appearance may be waived in certain circumstances.[288] In addition, the court is authorized, "for good cause shown," to permit the defendant to appear by counsel whenever a summons or an appearance ticket has been issued.[289] "Good cause" is not defined or interpreted in the case law; presumably, it would apply if the defendant is ill or resides a great distance from the court.

The court must advise a defendant at arraignment of certain rights and information.[290] Most important, the court must advise the defendant of his or her right to counsel at the arraignment and at every other proceeding in the case.[291] If the defendant has appeared at the arraignment without counsel, the court must advise the defendant of his or her

---

286. CPL § 170.10(2). When defendants are represented at arraignment by counsel, it is common for counsel, who will receive a copy of the accusatory instrument, to waive the reading of the charges.

287. Gerstein v. Pugh, 420 U.S. 103, 95 S.Ct. 854, 43 L.Ed.2d 54 (1975); see also Riverside v. McLaughlin, 500 U.S. 44, 111 S.Ct. 1661, 114 L.Ed.2d 49 (1991); CPL § 140.45 (if local criminal court accusatory instrument filed with court following warrantless arrest is facially insufficient pursuant to CPL § 100.40, and court is satisfied that based on available facts or evidence it would be impossible to draw and file an accusatory instrument that is facially sufficient, court must dismiss accusatory instrument and discharge defendant). See discussion in § 3.19, supra. If the defendant's appearance at arraignment has resulted from an arrest warrant, a reasonable cause determination at arraignment will be unnecessary because the court will already have made such a determination. See § 3.13, supra.

288. CPL § 170.10(1)(a). For example, if the defendant is charged in a simplified information with a traffic infraction, he or she may plead not guilty by designating such a plea on the ticket, signing it and mailing it, by registered or certified mail (return receipt requested) or by first class mail, to the appropriate court within 48 hours of receiving the ticket. The court must then notify the defendant by first class mail of the trial date. Vehicle and Traffic Law § 1806. See also Vehicle and Traffic Law § 1805 (except when defendant is charged with a third speeding violation within an 18-month period, he or she may plead guilty by mail—registered or certified with return receipt requested or first class mail—or through a duly authorized agent, in accordance with certain prescribed procedures); Parks, Recreation and Historic Preservation Law § 27.07 (establishing procedure for plea of guilty by mail or duly authorized agent). Cf. CPL § 340.20(2)(except for traffic infraction cases, a plea to a non-felony local criminal court accusatory instrument must be entered orally by the defendant unless the court allows entry by counsel after the defendant has filed a signed statement waiving the right to plead personally and authorizing counsel to enter the plea).

289. CPL § 170.10(1)(b).

290. As is true for the reading of the charges, when defendants are represented by counsel at arraignment, the reading of these rights is commonly waived.

291. CPL § 170.10(3).

right to an adjournment for the purpose of obtaining counsel,[292] and to make a communication, without charge, by letter or telephone to attempt to obtain counsel or to inform a relative or friend that he or she has been charged with an offense.[293] The court also must advise the defendant of the right to assignment of counsel if he or she is financially unable to pay for an attorney.[294]

In addition to advising the defendant of the foregoing rights relating to the right to counsel, the court is obligated to take "such affirmative action as is necessary" to effectuate those rights.[295] The right to counsel in New York is a broad one, arising in all criminal actions, with the exception of cases in which the highest charge is only a traffic infraction;[296] whether a sentence of imprisonment is ultimately imposed upon conviction is irrelevant.[297] Although the right may be waived, the court may permit the defendant to proceed *pro se* only if it is satisfied that the defendant has made that decision with knowledge of its significance.[298] The Court of Appeals has held that, before accepting a waiver of the right to counsel at arraignment or at any other proceeding, a court must undertake a "sufficiently searching inquiry" for it to be "reasonably assured" that the defendant appreciates the "dangers and disadvantages" of waiving this fundamental right.[299] A trial court's declaration to the defendant that he is entitled to be represented by counsel, that he is facing a serious charge, and that if convicted he could receive a year in jail has been held to be inadequate.[300] Similarly, a declaration to the defendant that he is facing a "very serious charge," and that his own "best interests" would be better served if a lawyer represented him is also inadequate.[301] The court must go beyond these preliminary admonitions and advise the defendant of the risks inherent in representing himself or herself and of the value of counsel.[302] For example, one

---

292. CPL § 170.10(3)(a).

293. CPL § 170.10(3)(b).

294. CPL § 170.10(3)(c).

295. CPL § 170.10(4)(a).

296. CPL § 170.10(3)(c). In cases charging only a traffic infraction, the defendant is entitled to proceed with the aid of counsel; however, he or she is not entitled to assignment of counsel. Id. See also County Law § 722–a; People v. Letterio, 16 N.Y.2d 307, 266 N.Y.S.2d 368, 213 N.E.2d 670 (1965).

297. People v. Ross, 67 N.Y.2d 321, 326, 502 N.Y.S.2d 693, 695, 493 N.E.2d 917, 919 (1986). Cf. Scott v. Illinois, 440 U.S. 367, 99 S.Ct. 1158, 59 L.Ed.2d 383 (1979)(federal Constitution entitles defendant to assignment of counsel only if defendant ultimately sentenced to term of imprisonment).

298. CPL § 170.10(6). However, if the defendant is charged only with a traffic infraction, the court must grant his or her request to proceed without counsel. Id.

Waiver of the right to counsel at arraignment applies to the arraignment proceeding alone; it does not waive that right in any further proceedings in the case, no matter what the charge. Indeed, the court must so inform the defendant. Id.

299. See People v. Vivenzio, 62 N.Y.2d 775, 776, 477 N.Y.S.2d 318, 319, 465 N.E.2d 1254, 1255 (1984); People v. Kaltenbach, 60 N.Y.2d 797, 798–99, 469 N.Y.S.2d 685, 685–86, 457 N.E.2d 791, 791–92 (1983); People v. White, 56 N.Y.2d 110, 117, 451 N.Y.S.2d 57, 61, 436 N.E.2d 507, 511 (1982).

300. People v. Kaltenbach, 60 N.Y.2d 797, 469 N.Y.S.2d 685, 457 N.E.2d 791 (1983).

301. People v. Sawyer, 57 N.Y.2d 12, 21, 453 N.Y.S.2d 418, 423, 438 N.E.2d 1133, 1138 (1982).

302. See People v. Kaltenbach, 60 N.Y.2d 797, 469 N.Y.S.2d 685, 457 N.E.2d 791 (1983); People v. Harris, 85 A.D.2d 742, 744, 445 N.Y.S.2d 801, 803 (2d Dep't 1981), aff'd on opinion below 58 N.Y.2d 704, 458 N.Y.S.2d 544, 444 N.E.2d 1008 (1982).

§ 3.24

appellate court upheld a defendant's waiver where the trial court ensured that the defendant understood the perils of proceeding *pro se* by "forcefully" informing him that he had neither training nor knowledge to defend himself and that if he did represent himself he would be held to the same standards of procedure as counsel.[303] The court's inquiry must be on the record.[304]

In the New York City Criminal Court, the arraignment parts are always staffed by defense attorneys; thus, judges in that court do not have to take affirmative steps to ensure that defendants there are represented by counsel. However, in many other areas of the state, particularly less populated areas, local criminal courts are not routinely staffed by defense attorneys when arraignments are conducted. Thus, when defendants appear for arraignment in those courts, the courts must undertake affirmative steps to effectuate a defendant's right to counsel. If the defendant does not have an attorney or know of one but can afford to retain counsel, the court can provide him or her with the address and telephone of the county bar association, which generally will be able to locate an attorney to represent the defendant. If the defendant advises the court that he or she may be unable to pay for an attorney, the court can provide the defendant with the address and telephone number of the county's public defender office or legal aid society. If no such office exists in the county, the court can provide the defendant with the address and telephone number of the assigned counsel administrator, who can locate an attorney from an authorized roster to represent the defendant. And in some instances, the court may find it necessary to contact the assigned counsel administrator or take steps itself to locate an eligible attorney in the area whom the court can assign to represent the defendant.[305]

---

303. People v. Wright, 192 A.D.2d 875, 876, 596 N.Y.S.2d 896, 897 (3d Dep't 1993). See also People v. Williams, 143 A.D.2d 959, 533 N.Y.S.2d 742 (2d Dep't 1988)(waiver of counsel valid where court "forcefully" warned defendant that he lacked training or knowledge to adequately cross-examine the prosecution's key witnesses and that the court would not assist him in his defense and where defendant was given opportunity to reconsider his decision on a number of occasions); People v. Gaines, 136 A.D.2d 731, 524 N.Y.S.2d 70 (2d Dep't 1988)(waiver valid where court and prosecutor repeatedly warned defendant of the dangers of self-representation and that he would be subject to various evidentiary and other restraints, and defendant had extensive prior exposure to the criminal justice system).

304. People v. Sawyer, 57 N.Y.2d at 21, 453 N.Y.S.2d at 423, 438 N.E.2d at 1138.

305. Under Article 18–B of the County Law, every county in the state and New York City must adopt and finance a plan for providing counsel to persons charged with an offense (other than a traffic infraction). These plans may take a number of different forms. A county may create a public defender office, it may contract with a private legal aid society or bureau, it may establish an assigned counsel roster (referred to as an "18–B plan") of qualified private attorneys, or it may combine any of the foregoing options. County Law § 722. The larger jurisdictions in the state have created a public defender's officer or have contracted with a private legal aid society, although, because those offices at times may have a conflict of interest in representing certain defendants, these jurisdictions have also created assigned counsel plans. Most of the smaller jurisdictions have simply created assigned counsel plans. Generally, the public defender's office, legal aid society or assigned counsel administrator must ascertain whether the defendant qualifies financially for such representation. In many jurisdictions, this evaluation is a cursory one, at best.

A defendant eligible for assigned counsel is not entitled to his or her choice of assigned counsel.[306] Upon a showing of "good cause," however, a defendant desiring another counsel than the one assigned to him or her may be entitled to one. A defendant can demonstrate good cause for substitution of assigned counsel by showing a genuine conflict of interest, professional incompetence or a personal impediment that handicaps the attorney's professional performance.[307] When a defendant raises a serious possibility that such a situation exists, the court must conduct at least some inquiry to ascertain whether counsel should be substituted.[308]

If the criminal action has been commenced by the filing of a misdemeanor complaint, the arraignment court must advise that the defendant may not be tried on such accusatory instrument unless he or she consents, and that in the absence of consent the prosecution must replace the misdemeanor complaint with an information.[309]

In traffic offense cases, the court must advise the defendant of certain additional rights that are unique to such cases. The court must inform the defendant of his or her right to a supporting deposition.[310] In addition, the court must advise the defendant that a judgment of conviction may result in the suspension or revocation of his or her driver's license and vehicle registration, and that a guilty plea is as much a conviction as a verdict of guilty after trial.[311] If, however, the defendant's appearance for arraignment has been obtained by issuance of an appearance ticket, which is almost always the case, a printed statement of these rights on the ticket itself obviates the need for the court to recite them at the arraignment.[312]

A special provision of section 170.10 applies in cases in which the defendant is charged in a simplified traffic information with the offense of driving while intoxicated.[313] In these cases, if the accusatory instrument contains a notation that the case involved an accident in which a death or serious physical injury resulted, or if the court is otherwise aware of such a fact, the court may not accept a guilty plea at arraignment or within 30 days thereafter, unless the prosecutor consents in writing.[314] This provision was the Legislature's response to the Supreme Court's decision in *Grady v. Corbin*,[315] a New York case in which an intoxicated driver involved in an accident in which another person was killed pleaded guilty in local criminal court to the misdemeanor offense of driving while intoxicated and the traffic infraction of failing to keep to

---

306. People v. Sawyer, 57 N.Y.2d at 18–19, 453 N.Y.S.2d at 421–22, 438 N.E.2d at 1136–37.

307. 57 N.Y.2d at 19, 453 N.Y.S.2d at 422, 438 N.E.2d at 1137.

308. People v. Sides, 75 N.Y.2d 822, 552 N.Y.S.2d 555, 551 N.E.2d 1233 (1990).

309. CPL § 170.10(4)(d). For a discussion of the procedures for replacing a misdemeanor complaint with an information, see § 3.25, infra.

310. CPL § 170.10(4)(c). Apparently due to a legislative oversight, the statute does not require such an advisement for the two other types of simplified information: the simplified parks information and the simplified environmental conservation information.

311. CPL § 170.10(4)(b).

312. CPL § 170.10(6).

313. See Vehicle and Traffic Law § 1192(2), (3) and (4).

314. CPL § 170.10(8).

315. 495 U.S. 508, 110 S.Ct. 2084, 109 L.Ed.2d 548 (1990).

§ 3.24 LOCAL CRIMINAL COURTS Ch. 3

the right while, unbeknown to the the local criminal court judge who accepted the plea and the assistant district attorney who consented to the plea, he was about to be charged with a homicide arising out of the accident. The Court held, on double jeopardy grounds, that the guilty plea to the lesser charges insulated the defendant from prosecution on the homicide charges. This statutory amendment is designed to avoid recurrence of such a result.

If the court has received a copy of the defendant's criminal history record (or "rapsheet"), it must provide the defense with a copy at the arraignment.[316] In addition, although under CPL § 710.30 the prosecution has until 15 days after arraignment to serve notice of its intention to offer at trial evidence of the defendant's statements or evidence of an identification, many prosecutors, to avoid the draconian penalties that will result if they miss this deadline, serve such notice at the arraignment.[317] Similarly, although under CPL § 250.20, the prosecution has until 20 days after arraignment to serve a demand for notice of alibi, this demand, most particularly in cases in which identification of the perpetrator is an issue, is often served at arraignment.[318]

Two other points should be noted here. First, unlike in most other stages of a criminal action, audio-visual coverage of arraignments is permitted only if the parties consent.[319] Second, Article 182 of the CPL authorizes, upon the defendant's consent, certain court appearances, including arraignments in certain types of cases, to be conducted "electronically"—i.e., the defendant is not physically present in court but his or her image and voice are transmitted to the court from another location, such as a jail or police stationhouse, by electronic means. Although the CPL has authorized electronic court appearances since 1990, no program allowing for this procedure has yet to be implemented in any jurisdiction of the state.

Finally, a critical aspect of arraignment on a non-felony local criminal court accusatory instrument is the court's issuance of a securing order that either releases the defendant on his or her own recognizance or fixes bail.[320] The procedures relating to securing orders are discussed in Chapter 4.

Library References:
West's Key No. Digests, Criminal Law ⚖=261–264.

§ 3.25 Conversion or Replacement of Misdemeanor Complaint to Information

A defendant may not be prosecuted and tried on a misdemeanor complaint; unless the defendant waives this right, the prosecution must

---

316. See CPL § 160.40(2). See § 3.23, supra. In smaller jurisdictions, the rapsheet often is not available at the arraignment stage.

317. See Chapter 10, § 10.24.

318. See Chapter 7, § 7.27.

319. Judiciary Law § 218(5)(a).

320. CPL § 170.10(7). Issuance of a securing order is a precondition to the defendant's detention in a county jail. Correction Law § 500–a(2). In a non-felony case, however, pretrial detention is an option only if the court fixes bail and it is not posted. See CPL §§ 510.40(3), 530.20(1).

convert a misdemeanor complaint to, or replace it with, an information prior to commencement of trial.[321] Because the primary distinction between a misdemeanor complaint and an information is that the latter contains *non-hearsay* factual allegations establishing (if true) every element of the offense charged,[322] conversion requires that the prosecution proffer those non-hearsay allegations. Rather than necessitating the actual filing of a new accusatory instrument, this is typically accomplished by the prosecution's filing of supporting depositions that, together with the misdemeanor complaint, satisfy the requirements for a valid information.[323] In a typical situation, the factual allegations in the misdemeanor complaint may be those of a police officer to whom the victim conveyed the circumstances underlying the offense. Conversion of the hearsay complaint to an information will require the filing of a supporting deposition, subscribed and verified by the victim, recounting those underlying circumstances. In another common situation, a criminal action charging a drug possession offense is usually commenced by the filing of a misdemeanor complaint containing only the hearsay allegations of the arresting officer that the substance seized from the defendant was a controlled substance. In these cases, the prosecution can make the necessary conversion of the complaint to an information by filing a laboratory report establishing that the substance, in fact, was a controlled substance.[324] Similarly, in unlawful weapon possession cases, in which operability of the weapon is an essential element to be proved, the complaint can be converted to an information by the filing of a ballistics report.[325]

If the prosecution actually replaces the misdemeanor complaint with a new accusatory instrument, the new information need not charge the same offense or offenses as the complaint so long as it charges an offense that is based on the same conduct that was the subject of the misdemeanor complaint.[326] Subject to the rules of joinder,[327] the new information may charge any other offense, even if such offense is based on conduct different than that which was the subject of the misdemeanor complaint.[328]

---

321. CPL § 170.65(1).

322. See CPL § 100.40; see § 3.7, supra.

323. CPL § 170.65(1).

324. See generally People v. McGriff, 139 Misc.2d 361, 526 N.Y.S.2d 712 (N.Y.C.Crim.Ct.1988); People v. Paul, 133 Misc.2d 234, 238, 506 N.Y.S.2d 834, 837 (N.Y.C.Crim.Ct.1986); People v. Muniz, 129 Misc.2d 456, 493 N.Y.S.2d 241 (N.Y.C.Crim. Ct.1985); People v. Ranieri, 127 Misc.2d 132, 485 N.Y.S.2d 495 (N.Y.C.Crim.Ct. 1985). But see People v. McMillan, 125 Misc.2d 177, 180, 479 N.Y.S.2d 449, 452 (N.Y.C.Crim.Ct.1984)(suggesting that lab report not required in marihuana cases to convert misdemeanor complaint to information).

325. See, e.g., People v. Lynch, 145 Misc.2d 354, 546 N.Y.S.2d 538 (N.Y.C.Crim. Ct.1989); People v. Harvin, 126 Misc.2d 775, 778–79, 483 N.Y.S.2d 913, 917–18 (N.Y.C.Crim.Ct.1984). But see People v. Adorno, 128 Misc.2d 389, 489 N.Y.S.2d 441 (N.Y.C.Crim.Ct.1984)(ballistics report not required to convert misdemeanor complaint charging possession of a pellet gun to an information).

326. CPL § 170.65(2).

327. Joinder of offenses is discussed in Chapter 5, § 5.21.

328. CPL § 170.65(2).

§ 3.25   LOCAL CRIMINAL COURTS   Ch. 3

As noted, the defendant may waive the right to be tried on an information.[329] The defendant's failure to object to the absence of conversion or replacement does not in itself constitute a waiver of this right.[330] However, if a defendant represented by counsel generally waives the court's reading of the charges and rights at arraignment, including the right to be prosecuted on an information, and subsequently never objects in the trial court to the prosecution's failure to convert or replace the misdemeanor complaint, the defendant will have been deemed to have waived this right.[331]

If a defendant against whom a misdemeanor complaint has been filed has been committed to the custody of the sheriff pending disposition of the action, and the prosecution has failed to convert the complaint to an information within five days (not including a Sunday) of the commitment of the defendant to the custody of the sheriff, CPL § 170.70 provides that the court must order the defendant's release from commitment.[332] The only exceptions are if the defendant has waived prosecution by information,[333] or if the court finds "good cause," consisting of "some compelling fact or circumstance" that prevented replacement or conversion within the five-day time period.[334]

The obvious purpose of this provision is to protect against a defendant being held in custody for a lengthy period of time based solely on the hearsay allegations on which a misdemeanor complaint may be based. Ironically, however, unlike CPL § 180.80—the analogous protection for defendants against whom a felony complaint has been filed[335]— the time period commences from the first day the court commits the defendant to custody (which, by definition, cannot precede the arraignment), not the day of arrest.[336] Thus, in some cases a defendant charged with a misdemeanor may be kept in custody on hearsay allegations for a longer period than a defendant charged with a felony.[337] The courts have split over whether conversion of only one or some of the counts of a multi-count misdemeanor complaint satisfies section 170.70.[338]

---

329. CPL § 170.65(3). By contrast, an accusatory instrument that fails to allege facts establishing every element of the offense charged, and thus does not even meet the requirements of a misdemeanor complaint, is a non-waivable jurisdictional defect, that may even be challenged for the first time on appeal. See People v. Alejandro, 70 N.Y.2d 133, 517 N.Y.S.2d 927, 511 N.E.2d 71 (1987); People v. Hall, 48 N.Y.2d 927, 425 N.Y.S.2d 56, 401 N.E.2d 179 (1979). See § 3.7, supra.

330. People v. Weinberg, 34 N.Y.2d 429, 358 N.Y.S.2d 357, 315 N.E.2d 434 (1974).

331. People v. Connor, 63 N.Y.2d 11, 479 N.Y.S.2d 197, 468 N.E.2d 35 (1984).

332. Cf. CPL § 180.80 (analogous procedure in cases in which felony complaint has been filed against a defendant).

333. CPL § 170.70(1). See CPL § 170.65(3).

334. CPL § 170.70(2).

335. Section 180.80 is discussed in § 3.34, infra.

336. See People ex rel. Neufeld v. McMickens, 70 N.Y.2d 763, 520 N.Y.S.2d 744, 514 N.E.2d 1368 (1987).

337. For an illustrative factual scenario, see People v. Goodwine, 142 Misc.2d 1080, 539 N.Y.S.2d 273 (N.Y.C.Crim.Ct.1989).

338. Cf., e.g., People v. Hernandez, 145 Misc.2d 491, 546 N.Y.S.2d 958 (N.Y.C.Crim.Ct.1989)(statute requires that all counts of misdemeanor complaint be converted within five-day period) with People ex rel. Mack v. Warden, 145 Misc.2d 1016, 549 N.Y.S.2d 558 (N.Y.C.Crim.Ct.1989)(statute satisfied if only a single count of multi-count misdemeanor complaint is converted, reasoning that each count should be deemed a separate and distinct accusatory instrument).

For a discussion of the consequences of the prosecution's failure to convert or replace a misdemeanor complaint within the time period set forth in CPL § 30.30, see Chapter 9, § 9.23.

Library References:
West's Key No. Digests, Indictment and Information ⚖=41.

§ 3.26 Motion to Dismiss—In General

CPL § 170.30 lists the grounds upon which a local criminal court, after arraignment and upon the defendant's motion, may dismiss a non-felony accusatory instrument. Most of these grounds—e.g., speedy trial,[339] statute of limitations,[340] double jeopardy,[341] and immunity from prosecution[342]—are discussed in other chapters of this book. The additional grounds for dismissal—defective accusatory instrument,[343] furtherance of justice,[344] and any other jurisdictional or legal impediment to conviction[345]—are discussed in this chapter.

The Court of Appeals has held that the section 170.30 grounds are the exclusive grounds for dismissal of a non-felony accusatory instrument.[346] Thus, because no such ground is included in the statute, a trial court lacks authority to dismiss an accusatory instrument for failure to prosecute or to control its calendar where the prosecutor is not ready for trial and the statutory speedy trial time period has not yet elapsed.[347]

Except for a speedy trial motion, which must be made prior to commencement of trial or entry of a guilty plea, a motion to dismiss should be made within the time period specified in CPL § 255.20—i.e., within 45 days after arraignment and before commencement of trial.[348] All grounds for a motion to dismiss should be raised in a single motion (except, of course, a speedy trial motion, which is made later in the proceedings).[349] The court may summarily deny a subsequent motion,

---

339. CPL § 170.30(1)(e). See Chapter 9.

340. CPL § 170.30(1)(d). See Chapter 9.

341. CPL § 170.30(1)(c). See Chapter 2.

342. CPL § 170.30(1)(b). See generally Chapter 5, § 5.9 (compelled testimony).

343. CPL § 170.30(1)(a). See §§ 3.7, supra, and 3.27, infra.

344. CPL § 170.30(1)(g). See § 3.28, infra.

345. CPL § 170.30(1)(f).

346. People v. Douglass, 60 N.Y.2d 194, 201, 469 N.Y.S.2d 56, 59, 456 N.E.2d 1179, 1182 (1983).

347. Id. Interestingly, however, the Court of Appeals has also held that although a trial court has no authority to enter a non-appealable trial order of dismissal as a remedy for the prosecution's inability to produce the complaining witness after multiple adjournments, it noted in that case that a dismissal in furtherance of justice "may well be appropriate" to redress such a failure to prosecute. Holtzman v. Goldman, 71 N.Y.2d 564, 575, 528 N.Y.S.2d 21, 28, 523 N.E.2d 297, 304 (1988). See also Hynes v. George, 76 N.Y.2d 500, 561 N.Y.S.2d 538, 562 N.E.2d 863 (1990)(upholding trial court's authority to deny the request of a prosecutor, who previously had declared readiness for trial, for adjournment and instead order that jury selection begin; court rejected argument that ordering commencement of jury selection when prosecution was unable to proceed was tantamount to dismissal of the case).

348. See CPL § 170.30(2). Section 255.20 is discussed in Chapter 8.

349. CPL § 170.30(3). See also CPL § 255.20(2)(whenever practicable, all pretrial motions, with supporting documents, generally should be included within the

§ 3.26   LOCAL CRIMINAL COURTS   Ch. 3

although for good cause shown and in the interest of justice it may entertain such a motion.[350] The procedural rules governing motions to dismiss an indictment in superior court also govern motions to dismiss in local criminal court.[351] For example, a motion to dismiss in local criminal court must be made in writing and upon reasonable notice to the prosecution,[352] although the Court of Appeals has held that the prosecution may waive these requirements by failing to object.[353]

Library References:

West's Key No. Digests, Indictment and Information ⚖︎144–144.2.

§ 3.27 Motion to Dismiss—Defective Accusatory Instrument

A non-felony accusatory instrument, or any single count contained therein, may be dismissed as defective on a number of grounds. Such an accusatory instrument is defective if it is not facially sufficient,[354] if its allegations demonstrate that the court does not have jurisdiction of the offense charged,[355] or if the statute underlying the offense charged is unconstitutional.[356] In addition, an information replacing a misdemeanor complaint is defective if replacement is not accomplished in accordance with the requirements of CPL § 170.65.[357]

A prosecutor's information filed at the direction of a grand jury[358] is defective if the offense charged was not authorized by the grand jury,[359] if the evidence before the grand jury was not legally sufficient to support

same set of motion papers, returnable on the same date).

350. CPL § 170.30(3). A defendant, however, may raise a non-waivable jurisdictional defect at any point in the proceeding. Indeed, such an issue may even be raised for the first time on appeal. See People v. Alejandro, 70 N.Y.2d 133, 517 N.Y.S.2d 927, 511 N.E.2d 71 (1987).

351. CPL § 170.45. Section 210.45 is discussed in Chapter 5, § 5.26.

352. See CPL § 210.45(1).

353. See People v. Jennings, 69 N.Y.2d 103, 112–13, 512 N.Y.S.2d 652, 655–56, 504 N.E.2d 1079, 1082–83 (1986)(prosecution's silence in the face of an oral motion to dismiss constitutes waiver of the written motion requirement); see also People v. Mezon, 80 N.Y.2d 155, 589 N.Y.S.2d 838, 603 N.E.2d 943 (1992)(noting that a court, absent the prosecution's waiver of the written motion requirement for a suppression motion, lacks authority to waive the requirement). The courts also have permitted a defendant to orally join in the written motion to dismiss of a co-defendant. See, e.g., People v. Cruz, 161 A.D.2d 1182, 555 N.Y.S.2d 523 (4th Dep't 1990); People v. Johnson, 134 A.D.2d 284, 520 N.Y.S.2d 455 (2d Dep't 1987).

354. CPL § 170.30(1)(a). See CPL § 100.40 and discussion in § 3.7, supra. Of course, many facially insufficient accusatory instruments can be remedied by the filing of supporting depositions, or possibly by a superseding accusatory instrument or by amendment. See §§ 3.4, 3.8, 3.9, supra. And, if a non-felony accusatory instrument is dismissed on facial sufficiency grounds, the prosecution may file a new accusatory instrument without first obtaining authorization from the court. People v. Nuccio, 78 N.Y.2d 102, 571 N.Y.S.2d 693, 575 N.E.2d 111 (1991). Cf. CPL § 210.20(4)(following dismissal of an indictment, prosecution may re-submit charges to grand jury only upon authorization of the court). If the statutory speedy trial period has elapsed, however, filing of a new accusatory instrument will be barred. People v. Osgood, 52 N.Y.2d 37, 43, 436 N.Y.S.2d 213, 216, 417 N.E.2d 507, 510 (1980); People v. Lomax, 50 N.Y.2d 351, 356, 428 N.Y.S.2d 937, 939, 406 N.E.2d 793, 795 (1980).

355. CPL § 170.35(1)(b).

356. CPL § 170.35(1)(c).

357. CPL § 170.35(2). See § 3.25, supra.

358. See CPL § 190.70.

359. CPL § 170.35(3)(a).

the charge,[360] or if the grand jury proceeding was defective.[361] The procedures for moving to dismiss a prosecutor's information on the latter two grounds are the same as those for moving to dismiss an indictment.[362] As is true when an indictment is dismissed, if such a prosecutor's information is dismissed on these grounds, the prosecution must seek authorization from the court to resubmit the charges to a grand jury.[363] If authorization is denied and the defendant is in custody, the court must order his or her discharge, and any bail posted must be exonerated;[364] if the court authorizes resubmission, it must issue a new securing order.[365]

A prosecutor's information filed at the prosecution's own instance[366] is defective if the factual allegations of the original information underlying it and any supporting depositions are not "legally" sufficient[367] to support the charge in the prosecutor's information.[368]

Library References:
West's Key No. Digests, Indictment and Information ⚖=144.

§ 3.28 Motion to Dismiss—In Furtherance of Justice

The CPL authorizes the trial court to dismiss a non-felony local criminal court accusatory instrument "in furtherance of justice."[369] Commonly known as a "Clayton" motion, after a seminal appellate decision addressing a trial court's authority to dismiss on this ground,[370] the motion may be made by the defendant or the prosecution, or dismissal may be granted by the court on its own motion.[371] Dismissal is authorized if the court, in its discretion, determines that "the existence of some compelling factor, consideration or circumstance clearly demonstrat[es] that conviction or prosecution of the defendant ... would constitute or result in injustice."[372] In making its determination, the court must "examine and consider, individually and collectively," a series of statutorily-delineated factors. These factors are as follows: (a) the seriousness and circumstances of the offense; (b) the extent of harm caused; (c) the evidence of guilt, whether admissible or not; (d) the

---

360. CPL § 170.50(1)(a).

361. CPL § 170.50(1)(b).

362. CPL § 170.50(2). See CPL § 210.30 (motion to dismiss an indictment on the ground of insufficiency of grand jury evidence); CPL § 210.35 (motion to dismiss an indictment on the ground that the grand jury proceeding was defective). See also CPL § 210.45 (general procedures for motion to dismiss an indictment). These sections are discussed in Chapter 5, §§ 5.25–5.27.

363. CPL § 170.50(3). See CPL § 210.25(4), and discussion in Chapter 5, § 5.28.

364. See CPL § 210.45(8).

365. CPL § 210.45(9). See discussion in Chapter 5, § 5.28.

366. See CPL § 100.50(2).

367. Note that the statute refers to "legal" sufficiency, not "facial" sufficiency. For a discussion of the difference in these standards, see footnote 68 and accompanying text, supra.

368. CPL § 170.35(3)(b).

369. CPL § 170.40. Cf. CPL § 210.40 (motion to dismiss indictment in furtherance of justice, discussed in Chapter 5, § 5.27).

370. See People v. Clayton, 41 A.D.2d 204, 342 N.Y.S.2d 106 (2d Dep't 1973).

371. CPL § 170.40(2).

372. CPL § 170.40(1).

§ 3.28　　　　　LOCAL CRIMINAL COURTS　　　　　Ch. 3

defendant's history, character and condition; (e) any "exceptionally serious" misconduct by law enforcement in the investigation, arrest and prosecution; (f) the purpose and effect of imposing a sentence on the defendant; (g) the impact of dismissal on the safety or welfare of the community; (h) the impact of dismissal on the public's confidence in the criminal justice system; (i) the views of the complainant or victim regarding the motion (when the court deems it appropriate to consider them); and (j) any other factor indicating that a conviction "would serve no useful purpose."[373]

If the court dismisses in furtherance of justice, it must set forth its reasons in writing or orally on the record.[374] The Court of Appeals has held that the statute "does not compel catechistic on-the-record discussion" of the delineated factors.[375] On the other hand, vague and conclusory reasons, unsupported by a record giving them substance, are insufficient: "the need to show that the ultimate reasons given for the dismissal are both real and compelling almost inevitably will mean that one or more of the statutory criteria, even if only the catchall [factor], will yield to ready identification."[376]

Although reference to some of the reported decisions may be of guidance to a trial court in evaluating a Clayton motion, the ultimate determination is inevitably a discretionary, fact-specific one based on "a sensitive balancing of the interests of the individual and of the People."[377]

Library References:

West's Key No. Digests, Criminal Law ⚖ 303.30(2).

373. CPL § 170.40(1)(a)-(j).

374. CPL § 170.40(2). See People v. Rickert, 58 N.Y.2d 122, 128, 459 N.Y.S.2d 734, 736, 446 N.E.2d 419, 421 (1983).

375. People v. Rickert, 58 N.Y.2d at 128, 459 N.Y.S.2d at 736, 446 N.E.2d at 421.

376. Id.

377. People v. Rickert, 58 N.Y.2d at 127, 459 N.Y.S.2d at 735, 446 N.E.2d at 420. The following are a few examples of how courts have resolved Clayton motions: People v. Kelley, 141 A.D.2d 764, 529 N.Y.S.2d 855 (2d Dep't 1988)(court reverses dismissal of driving while intoxicated charge against police officer with no prior record and "exemplary" background, noting the seriousness of the charge and the absence of a compelling factor warranting dismissal); People v. Reyes, 148 Misc.2d 227, 564 N.Y.S.2d 954 (App. Term, 1st Dep't, 1990)(court reverses sua sponte dismissal of fare-beating charge, noting impact of offense on the transit system and absence of a compelling factor); People v. Doe, 158 Misc.2d 863, 602 N.Y.S.2d 507 (N.Y.C.Crim.Ct.1993)(assault charge dismissed where hearing impaired defendant had no prior record, was minimally involved in fight giving rise to charge and might have misperceived situation due to her disability); People v. Izsak, 99 Misc.2d 543, 416 N.Y.S.2d 1004 (N.Y.Crim.Ct.1979)(even though defendants charged with patronizing a prostitute had no prior criminal record, had been subjected to some incarceration as a result of the charges and also claimed other difficulties arising from their arrest, these factors did not constitute compelling circumstances). See also Holtzman v. Goldman, 71 N.Y.2d 564, 574, 528 N.Y.S.2d 21, 28, 523 N.E.2d 297, 303 (1988)(suggesting that prosecution's refusal to proceed with its case after trial court denied its motion for a further adjournment might give rise to a dismissal in the interest of justice); cf. People v. Duke, 158 Misc.2d 647, 606 N.Y.S.2d 516 (App. Term, 1st Dep't, 1993)(dismissal on ground that prosecution failed to proceed with preliminary and suppression hearings reversed where record did not reveal that court took into account any of the statutory factors).

§ 3.29 Adjournment in Contemplation of Dismissal

An adjournment in contemplation of dismissal—referred to as an "ACD" or an "ACOD"—is an adjournment of the action without a specified adjournment date with a view toward ultimate dismissal in the furtherance of justice.[378] Like a Clayton motion, an ACD may result from the motion of either party or from the court's own motion. Unlike a Clayton motion, an ACD is permissible only on the consent of both parties, and the statute sets forth no factors that the court must consider in evaluating an application.[379]

When issuing an ACD, the court must release the defendant on his or her own recognizance.[380] If the prosecution applies to the court during the six-month period following issuance of the ACD, the court may restore the action to the calendar and the prosecution will resume.[381] If the case involves a "family offense,"[382] however, the prosecution may apply for restoration to the calendar during the one-year period following issuance of the ACD. Speedy trial time is tolled during the period of adjournment.[383] If the case is not restored to the calendar during such period, the accusatory instrument will be deemed to have been dismissed, and the arrest and prosecution shall be a nullity.[384]

The statute provides for a number of conditions that may be imposed on the defendant during the period of adjournment. These include: compliance with the conditions of any temporary order of protection issued by the court;[385] in "family offense" cases, participation in an educational program addressing family violence issues;[386] participation in dispute resolution and compliance with any award or settlement resulting therefrom;[387] performance of community service (if the defendant consents);[388] and if the defendant is under the age of 21 and is charged with a misdemeanor (other than a driving-related misdemeanor) in which the record suggests that the defendant's consumption of alcohol may have been a contributing factor, participation in an alcohol awareness program.[389] Whether the court may impose conditions other than those specified in the statute is unclear. Notably, unlike the statute governing conditions that a court may impose in connection with a sentence of probation or a sentence of conditional discharge,[390] the ACD

---

378. CPL § 170.55. Cf. CPL Article 215 (setting forth the rarely used ACD procedure for referring selected felony charges to dispute resolution).

379. CPL § 170.55(1).

380. CPL § 170.55(2).

381. Although apparently not authorized by the statute, some courts occasionally shorten the period of adjournment.

382. "Family offenses" are defined in CPL § 530.11(1).

383. CPL § 30.30(4)(h).

384. Id.; CPL § 170.55(8). This results in the record of the action being sealed. See CPL § 160.50(3)(b).

385. CPL § 170.55(3). See CPL §§ 530.12, 530.13.

386. CPL § 170.55(4).

387. CPL § 170.55(5). See Judiciary Law § 849–a (establishing a community dispute resolution center program, administered by the Chief Administrator of the Courts).

388. CPL § 170.55(6).

389. CPL § 170.55(7). See Mental Hygiene Law § 19.07(a)(6–a).

390. See P.L. § 65.10(2)(*l*). See also CPL § 410.10(1)(requiring that the court provide the defendant at the time of sentencing with a written copy of the conditions of a sentence of probation or a sentence of conditional discharge).

statute does not include a catch-all condition clause. In addition, the Court of Appeals has held that the defendant's waiver, upon the prosecution's insistence, of any civil claims against the police or a municipality as a condition of receiving an ACD is void and unenforceable.[391]

One court has held that, in seeking to restore the case to the calendar, the prosecution must demonstrate the "existence of some compelling factor."[392] Obviously, a violation of an imposed condition would warrant restoration of the action, as would the revelation that the defendant procured the ACD through fraud by providing false documents to the prosecution.[393] On the other hand, the mistaken consent to an ACD by an inexperienced assistant district attorney would not warrant restoration.[394] Although a hearing apparently is not required when the prosecution seeks restoration of the action, the court should provide the defendant with an opportunity to be heard on the question.[395]

An ACD is not deemed a conviction or even an admission of guilt, and the statute provides that the defendant shall suffer no "disability or forfeiture" as a result.[396] One court has held, however, that an ACD only bars automatic forfeitures directly flowing from the order, and not a civil forfeiture based on the underlying facts leading to the defendant's arrest.[397] In addition, it has been held that a parole violation determination may be based on the underlying facts of a criminal charge that resulted in an ACD.[398]

A special ACD procedure is available in cases in which the only charge or charges are non-felony marihuana offenses.[399] On the defendant's motion, the court may ACD the case for a period of time not to exceed 12 months, or if the court explains on the record why an adjournment is unnecessary, it may immediately dismiss the action in furtherance of justice. The prosecution's consent is not required, unless the defendant has a prior criminal conviction or a prior youthful offender adjudication in a case involving a controlled substance. This procedure is not available, however, if the defendant previously has been granted such an ACD or dismissal or been convicted of a controlled substance

---

391. Cowles v. Brownell, 73 N.Y.2d 382, 540 N.Y.S.2d 973, 538 N.E.2d 325 (1989).

392. People v. Verardi, 158 Misc.2d 1039, 1042, 602 N.Y.S.2d 318, 320 (N.Y.C.Crim.Ct.1993).

393. See, e.g., People v. Clark, 120 Misc.2d 365, 466 N.Y.S.2d 211 (N.Y.C.Crim. Ct.1983).

394. People v. Verardi, supra.

395. See, e.g., People v. Clark, 120 Misc.2d 365, 466 N.Y.S.2d 211 (N.Y.C.Crim. Ct.1983); Matter of Richard C., 115 Misc.2d 314, 453 N.Y.S.2d 366 (Fam.Ct., Queens County, 1982).

396. CPL § 170.55(8).

397. Property Clerk of New York City Police Dept. v. Famiglietti, 160 A.D.2d 542, 554 N.Y.S.2d 519 (1st Dep't 1990)(permitting civil proceeding to forfeit automobile allegedly used in purchase of drugs, despite ACD of criminal charge).

398. People ex rel. Murray v. New York State Board of Parole, 70 A.D.2d 918, 417 N.Y.S.2d 286 (2d Dep't 1979), aff'd 50 N.Y.2d 943, 431 N.Y.S.2d 456, 409 N.E.2d 930 (1980).

399. See CPL § 170.56. These charges are: P.L. § 221.05 (unlawful possession of marihuana); P.L. § 221.10 (criminal possession of marihuana in the fifth degree); P.L. § 221.15 (criminal possession of marihuana in the fourth degree); P.L. § 221.35 (criminal sale of marihuana in the fifth degree); and P.L. § 221.40 (criminal sale of marihuana in the fourth degree).

offense.[400]

If the court issues an ACD in such a case, it must impose conditions it deems appropriate, including placing the defendant under the supervision of a public or private agency. At any time during the period of adjournment, the court may modify these conditions, and the court may enlarge or reduce the period of adjournment (although the total period may not exceed 12 months).[401] If a defendant violates a condition, the court can restore the case to the calendar and the prosecution shall proceed. If the case is not restored during the period of adjournment, the action is deemed dismissed in furtherance of justice.[402]

Library References:
West's Key No. Digests, Criminal Law ⇔303.30(4).

§ 3.30 Arraignment on Felony Complaints

Local criminal courts have only preliminary jurisdiction over felony complaints.[403] Their role in these cases essentially is limited to determining whether a reasonable basis exists for a grand jury to indict, and to issuing a securing order assuring that the defendant will appear for future proceedings in the superior court.

With a few important differences, an arraignment on a felony complaint proceeds much as does an arraignment on a non-felony local criminal court accusatory instrument.[404] The court must inform the defendant of the charges and provide him or her with a copy of the accusatory instrument.[405] The court also must inform the defendant of his or her right to counsel at arraignment and at every subsequent proceeding in the case; and if the defendant appears at arraignment without counsel, the court must advise him or her of the right to an adjournment to obtain counsel, to communicate (free of charge, by letter or telephone) to obtain counsel and inform a friend or relative of the criminal action, and to have counsel assigned if the defendant is indigent.[406] As is true in non-felony cases, the court, if necessary, must take "affirmative action" to effectuate the defendant's right to counsel.[407]

---

400. CPL § 170.56(1).

401. CPL § 170.56(2).

402. Id. Dismissal results in the sealing of the record of the action. CPL §§ 160.50(3)(b), 170.56(3). However, the record may be made available by court order in a subsequent action charging a non-felony marihuana offense to determine whether the defendant is eligible for an ACD or dismissal in furtherance of justice. CPL § 170.56(3).

403. CPL § 10.30(2).

404. Arraignment on non-felony local criminal court accusatory instruments is discussed in § 3.24, supra.

405. CPL § 180.10(1). The defense frequently waives the reading of the charges.

406. CPL § 180.10(3). Issues relating to these rights are discussed in § 3.24, supra.

407. CPL § 180.10(4). See discussion in § 3.24, supra.

In addition, in first degree murder cases (P.L. § 125.27) and in certain second degree murder cases (P.L. § 125.25) involving defendants who are financially unable to hire counsel, the state's Capital Defender Office (CDO) is authorized to provide temporary legal representation. The second degree murder cases are those in which the prosecution confirms, "upon inquiry by the court," that the prosecution is undertaking an investigation to determine whether the defendant can or should be charged with first degree murder and the court determines that there is a reasonable likelihood

§ 3.30

The court also must issue a securing order that, in appropriate cases, may involve committing the defendant to jail.[408]

In addition, as is true at arraignment on a non-felony accusatory instrument, the court, as a condition of any continued pretrial detention of the defendant, must ascertain whether the allegations in the felony complaint establish reasonable cause that the defendant committed an offense.[409] Although a local criminal court has no jurisdiction to accept a guilty plea to a felony charge,[410] and a plea on such a charge technically must await arraignment in the superior court on the superior court accusatory instrument,[411] it is not unusual for a defendant to enter a not guilty plea at arraignment on a felony complaint.

The court is also required to advise the defendant that the primary purpose of the arraignment is for the court to determine whether the defendant should be "held for the action of a grand jury,"[412] and that the defendant has the right to a "prompt hearing" on the question of whether sufficient evidence exists to do so.[413] Although the procedures governing this "preliminary hearing" are discussed in detail in § 3.33, *infra*, it should be noted here that, despite this express statutory language, preliminary hearings are conducted in only a small percentage of criminal actions in New York. The reason for this differs depending on the area of the state. In New York City, prosecutors generally proceed expeditiously in presenting evidence of felony charges to grand

that the defendant will be so charged. Judiciary Law § 35–b(1). If the court contacts the CDO, which has established a 24-hour hotline telephone number, the CDO will arrange to provide temporary counsel for the arraignment. Judiciary Law § 35–b(7).

Following the arraignment, the Capital Defender Office will begin the unique process for the trial court's appointment of permanent capital representation pursuant to Judiciary Law § 35–b(2). Permanent counsel may be one of four two-attorney teams of specially qualified attorneys assembled by the CDO, a public defender or legal aid society that has entered into an agreement with the CDO to handle capital cases, or the CDO itself. If the defendant is not ultimately indicted for first degree murder, or is indicted for first degree murder but the prosecution fails to file pursuant to CPL § 250.40 a notice of intent to seek the death penalty (which must be filed within 120 days of the defendant's arraignment on the indictment) or otherwise takes such action as to necessarily preclude imposition of the death penalty, capital representation must cease and successor counsel may be appointed pursuant to Article 18–B of the County Law.

408. See Chapter 4, § 4.6.

409. See Gerstein v. Pugh, 420 U.S. 103, 95 S.Ct. 854, 43 L.Ed.2d 54 (1975); see also County of Riverside v. McLaughlin, 500 U.S. 44, 111 S.Ct. 1661, 114 L.Ed.2d 49 (1991); cf. CPL § 140.45 (if local criminal court accusatory instrument filed with court following warrantless arrest is facially insufficient pursuant to CPL § 140.45, and court is satisfied that on basis of available facts and evidence it would be impossible to draw and file an accusatory instrument that is facially sufficient, court must dismiss accusatory instrument and discharge defendant). See discussion in §§ 3.19, 3.24, *supra*. If the defendant's appearance at arraignment has resulted from an arrest warrant, a reasonable cause determination at arraignment will be unnecessary because the court will already have made such a determination upon issuance of the warrant. See § 3.13, *supra*.

410. See, e.g., People v. Montanye, 95 A.D.2d 959, 960, 464 N.Y.S.2d 292, 294 (3d Dep't 1983).

411. See, e.g., CPL § 210.50 (requiring plea to an indictment).

412. CPL § 180.10(1). This is a statutory concept that constitutes the procedural step enabling the criminal action to move on to the superior court. It does not entail, as its language suggests, that the defendant must be held in custody as the case proceeds to the superior court.

413. CPL § 180.10(2).

juries; because a grand jury indictment voids the defendant's right to a preliminary hearing,[414] a preliminary hearing is conducted only in those relatively rare cases in which an indictment is not secured quickly. In many upstate communities, preliminary hearings, although more prevalent than in New York City, are still not conducted in the great percentage of cases, but for a separate reason: defendants frequently waive their right to the preliminary hearing. In this different legal culture, waivers are popular because they tend to facilitate plea bargaining; and although the defendant may lose the discovery benefits of the hearing,[415] waiver often facilitates significant voluntary pre-indictment disclosure by the prosecution.

Although the CPL recognizes that the defendant may waive the right to a preliminary hearing,[416] the courts have long recognized that such a waiver must be intelligently and knowingly made.[417] Thus, the arraignment court should expressly advise the defendant of the right to a preliminary hearing and not accept a waiver unless the defendant (or defense counsel) affirmatively waives the hearing in open court. Silence does not constitute a waiver of this right.[418]

If the defendant waives the right to a preliminary hearing, the court must order that he or she be held for the action of the grand jury, and it must promptly transmit the file papers to the superior court.[419] Until the superior court receives the papers, the case is still pending in the local criminal court.[420] Alternatively, the court may make inquiry, pursuant to CPL § 180.50, to determine whether the charge should be reduced to a non-felony charge.[421]

Although under CPL § 710.30 the prosecution in a felony case has until 15 days after arraignment in the superior court on the indictment to serve notice of its intention to offer at trial evidence of the defendant's statements or evidence of an identification,[422] many prosecutors, to avoid the draconian penalties that will result if they miss this deadline, serve such notice at the arraignment in local criminal court. In addition, in New York City, where the prosecution normally presents evidence to the grand jury immediately after arraignment, the prosecution serves notice (as required pursuant to CPL § 190.50(5)(a)) at arraignment of its intention to present the charges to the grand jury.[423] In this situation, a

---

414. People v. Hodge, 53 N.Y.2d 313, 319, 441 N.Y.S.2d 231, 234, 423 N.E.2d 1060, 1063 (1981).

415. See People v. Hodge, 53 N.Y.2d at 318–19, 441 N.Y.S.2d at 234, 423 N.E.2d at 1063.

416. CPL § 180.10(2).

417. See, e.g., Friess v. Morgenthau, 86 Misc.2d 852, 856, 383 N.Y.S.2d 784, 787 (Sup.Ct., N.Y. County, 1975); People ex rel. Pulver v. Pavlak, 71 Misc.2d 95, 97, 335 N.Y.S.2d 721, 724 (Greene Co.Ct.1972).

418. See, e.g., People v. Lupo, 74 Misc.2d 679, 345 N.Y.S.2d 348 (N.Y.C.Crim. Ct.1973).

419. CPL § 180.30(1).

420. Id. The failure of the local criminal court to transmit the file papers apparently does not, however, preclude a grand jury from indicting the defendant. See People v. Talham, 41 A.D.2d 354, 342 N.Y.S.2d 921 (3d Dep't 1973).

421. CPL § 180.50(2). See § 3.32, infra.

422. See Chapter 10, § 10.24.

423. In New York City, if the defendant is released at arraignment on his or her own recognizance, the prosecution's section 190.50 notice is usually served by mail subsequent to arraignment.

defendant who is considering testifying before the grand jury usually will serve the required cross-notice under section 190.50(5)(a) at arraignment.[424] Because the next court appearance date (for defendants whom the arraigning court commits to jail or for whom bail is fixed) following the arraignment is usually the last day of the CPL § 180.80 period, the defendant will be returned to court and have the opportunity to exercise the right to testify before the grand jury on that date.[425]

Finally, if the court has received the defendant's criminal history record (or "rapsheet"), it will provide the defense with a copy of that document at the arraignment.[426]

Library References:
West's Key No. Digests, Criminal Law ⟐261–264.

§ 3.31 Return of Felony Complaint to Local Criminal Court

After a local criminal court orders that the defendant be held for the action of a grand jury—thereby setting in motion the passage of jurisdiction of the case to the superior court—the prosecution may petition the superior court, *ex parte*, to return the action to the local criminal court.[427] The defendant is not authorized to bring this application. The superior court may grant the application only if evidence has not yet been presented to the grand jury, and only if it determines that the felony complaint is defective or that returning the action is "required" in the interest of justice.[428] This procedure is useful, for example, in cases in which, following the defendant's waiver of the preliminary hearing and the local criminal court's consequent loss of jurisdiction to the superior court, the parties agree on a disposition that allows the defendant to plead guilty to a misdemeanor offense.[429] Note, however, that upon revestiture in the local criminal court, that court must still be willing to reduce the felony charge to a non-felony charge, pursuant to CPL § 180.50, for the case to proceed to disposition there.[430]

---

424. Note, however, that the defendant's notice may be served at any time prior to the filing of an indictment or a grand jury's direction to file a prosecutor's information. CPL § 190.50(5)(a). See Chapter 5, § 5.8.

425. See generally Chapter 5, § 5.8.

426. See CPL § 160.40(2); see § 3.23, supra.

As was noted in the section discussing arraignments on non-felony local criminal court accusatory instruments, see § 3.24, supra, audio-visual coverage of arraignments is permitted only upon consent of the parties, Judiciary Law § 218(5)(a), and, although no such program has ever been implemented, the CPL authorizes "electronic court appearances" for certain arraignments, but only on the defendant's consent. CPL Article 182.

427. CPL § 180.40.

428. Id.

429. Conviction of only a non-felony offense may be critical for some defendants, such as those with a prior felony conviction, to avoid a mandatory state prison term. See, e.g., P.L. § 70.06 (prescribing mandatory sentences of imprisonment for second felony offenders). It should be noted, however, that the same result can be achieved if the defendant waives his or her right to indictment and pleads guilty in the superior court to a non-felony offense charged in a superior court information. See CPL §§ 195.40, 200.15.

430. See People v. Fulcher, 97 Misc.2d 239, 242, 411 N.Y.S.2d 167, 170 (N.Y.C.Crim.Ct.1978).

§ 3.32 Reduction of Felony Charges

Library References:
West's Key No. Digests, Criminal Law ⚖101.

§ 3.32 Reduction of Felony Charges

If the prosecution consents, and whether or not the defendant waives a preliminary hearing, the local criminal court may "make inquiry" to determine whether the available facts and circumstances merit reducing a felony charge to a non-felony charge.[431] In conducting this inquiry, the court is authorized to question anyone with relevant information about the case, including the defendant if he or she agrees.[432]

If this inquiry leads the court to conclude that there is reasonable cause to believe that the defendant committed a non-felony offense, the court may take one of two actions. First, if the court concludes that there is reasonable cause to believe that the defendant committed *only* a non-felony offense, the court may reduce the felony charge to that non-felony charge.[433] Second, if the court concludes that there is reasonable cause to believe that the defendant committed a felony in addition to a non-felony offense, the court may reduce the felony charge to that non-felony charge, but only if: (1) the prosecution consents; (2) such reduction would be in the interest of justice; and (3) there is no reasonable cause to believe that the defendant committed a non-drug Class A felony offense or an "armed felony offense."[434]

The actual reduction of the charge is accomplished by replacing the felony complaint with, or reducing it to, a non-felony accusatory instrument. For example, if the factual allegations in the felony complaint and any accompanying supporting depositions are "legally"[435] sufficient to make out a non-felony offense, the court may direct the prosecution to file a prosecutor's information, it may request that the complainant of the felony complaint (typically a police officer) file an information, or it may itself convert the felony complaint to an information by physically changing the title of the accusatory instrument and the names of the offense or offenses charged therein (or attaching to the accusatory instrument notes to that effect).[436] If the factual allegations in the felony complaint (and any accompanying supporting depositions) provide reasonable cause to believe that a misdemeanor was committed but such allegations are not legally sufficient, the court may request that the complainant of the felony complaint file a misdemeanor complaint or it may itself convert the felony complaint to a misdemeanor complaint by changing the title of the accusatory instrument and the names of the

---

431. CPL § 180.50.
432. CPL § 180.50(1).
433. CPL § 180.50(2)(a).

434. CPL § 180.50(2)(b). The non-drug Class A felony offenses are: P.L. § 125.25 (murder in the second degree) and P.L. § 125.27 (murder in the first degree); and P.L. § 135.25 (kidnapping in the first degree). An armed felony offense is defined in CPL § 1.20(41). The court should know that the felony charged is an armed felony offense because the prosecution is required to so designate on the felony complaint. See CPL § 100.15(4).

435. Notably, the statute refers to "legal" sufficiency, not "facial" sufficiency. For a discussion of the difference between these two standards, see footnote 68 and accompanying text, supra.

436. CPL § 180.50(3)(a).

offense or offenses (or attach to the accusatory instrument notes to that effect).[437]

If the reduction results in the filing of a new accusatory instrument (as opposed to a physical alteration of the felony complaint), the court must dismiss the felony complaint.[438] Subject to the rules of joinder,[439] the new accusatory instrument may charge two or more offenses or jointly charge two or more defendants.[440] Regardless of the method of conversion or replacement, the court must arraign the defendant on the new non-felony charge or charges, in accordance with the arraignment procedures set forth in CPL § 170.10.[441]

An interesting question arises if a local criminal court, in contravention of the statutory scheme, proceeds to make inquiry and reduce a felony charge to a non-felony offense without the prosecution's consent.[442] If the defendant is then permitted to plead guilty to the non-felony offense and is sentenced thereon, that judgment, absent fraud or misrepresentation on the part of the defendant, is a final one, notwithstanding the erroneous legal procedure that led to it.[443] As one commentator has suggested, the prosecution may be able to avoid this result by applying to the local criminal court, prior to the disposition in that court of the non-felony charge, for an adjournment of the proceedings pursuant to CPL § 170.20(2) to enable the prosecution to present the misdemeanor charge to a grand jury.[444]

Library References:

West's Key No. Digests, Criminal Law ⇒303.5–303.50.

§ 3.33 The Preliminary Hearing

The purpose of the preliminary hearing is for the court to determine whether reasonable cause exists to believe that the defendant committed a felony; legally sufficient evidence need not be shown. As discussed in § 3.30, *supra*, preliminary hearings are not held in the great majority of cases, either because the defendant waives the hearing[445] or the grand jury indicts the defendant before the hearing is conducted.[446]

At the hearing, the burden of proof is on the prosecution, which

---

437. CPL § 180.50(3)(b).

438. CPL § 180.50(3)(d).

439. See CPL §§ 200.20, 200.40, discussed in Chapter 5, §§ 5.21, 5.22.

440. CPL § 180.50(3)(c).

441. CPL § 180.50(3)(d). See § 3.24, supra.

442. See, e.g., People ex rel. Leventhal v. Warden of Rikers Island, 102 A.D.2d 317, 477 N.Y.S.2d 332 (1st Dep't 1984)(involving a case in which a local criminal court reduced a felony charge without the prosecution's consent).

443. See People v. Moquin, 77 N.Y.2d 449, 568 N.Y.S.2d 710, 570 N.E.2d 1059 (1991); Matter of Campbell v. Pesce, 60 N.Y.2d 165, 468 N.Y.S.2d 865, 456 N.E.2d 806 (1983).

444. See Preiser, "Practice Commentary," to CPL § 180.50, McKinney's Cons. Laws of N.Y., Book 11A, at 139 (1993).

445. See CPL § 180.10(2).

446. See People v. Hodge, 53 N.Y.2d 313, 319, 441 N.Y.S.2d 231, 234, 423 N.E.2d 1060, 1063 (1981)(right to preliminary hearing bypassed when grand jury indicts). See also Vega v. Bell, 47 N.Y.2d 543, 419 N.Y.S.2d 454, 393 N.E.2d 450 (1979).

must call and examine witnesses and offer other evidence.[447] In general, the prosecution must establish its burden by presenting non-hearsay evidence. An exception to this rule permits expert reports and sworn written statements of the type that are admissible in a grand jury proceeding pursuant to subdivisions two and three of CPL § 190.30.[448] These hearsay documents are not admissible at the preliminary hearing, however, if the defendant can demonstrate that they are unreliable.[449] In addition, the courts have split over whether evidence that, standing alone, would be insufficient to indict a defendant or convict a defendant at a trial—such as a confession—is sufficient to establish reasonable cause for purposes of holding the defendant for the action of a grand jury.[450]

Although the defense may cross-examine the prosecution's witnesses,[451] and the defendant may testify at the hearing as a matter of right,[452] the court has wide discretion in limiting the defendant's cross-examination and in determining whether the defense may call any other witnesses or present other evidence.[453] The court also has discretion to permit the defense to subpoena witnesses for the hearing.[454]

The defendant, of course, has the right to be present at a preliminary hearing.[455] The defendant may waive that right, however,[456] and should seriously consider doing so if identification is an issue in the case. The defendant also has the right to counsel at the hearing,[457] the denial of which may, at least theoretically, lead to appellate reversal of any

447. CPL § 180.60(5). All witnesses must testify under oath, unless they would be authorized to give unsworn testimony at a trial, pursuant to CPL § 60.20(2). CPL § 180.60(4). CPL § 60.20(2) permits children under 12 and persons suffering from a mental disease or defect to give unsworn testimony if they do not understand the oath but the court determines that they possess "sufficient intelligence and capacity" to justify receipt of their testimony.

448. These include not only scientific and other technical reports, but also sworn statements concerning a person's ownership or possessory interest in property, the value of such property and the defendant's lack of right to possession of such property. See CPL § 190.30(2) and (3). The purpose of this exception is to avoid the inconvenience to citizens of having to "make routine personal appearances at preliminary stages of a criminal proceeding where nothing more would be contributed other than the statements included" under CPL § 190.30(2) and (3). People v. Staton, 94 Misc.2d 1002, 1004, 406 N.Y.S.2d 242, 244 (N.Y.C.Crim.Ct.1978).

449. CPL § 180.60(8).

450. Cf. People v. Rice, 148 Misc.2d 204, 560 N.Y.S.2d 105 (Hornell City Ct.1990) and People v. Gurney, 129 Misc.2d 712, 493 N.Y.S.2d 957 (N.Y.C.Crim.Ct.1985)(both holding that a confession is enough) with People v. Searles, 135 Misc.2d 881, 517 N.Y.S.2d 370 (Rochester City Ct.1987) and People v. Barclift, 97 Misc.2d 994, 412 N.Y.S.2d 991 (N.Y.C.Crim.Ct.1979)(both taking the opposite position).

451. CPL § 180.60(4).

452. CPL § 180.60(6).

453. CPL § 180.60(7). See, e.g., People v. Staton, 94 Misc.2d at 1006, 406 N.Y.S.2d at 245 (court limits defense cross-examination relating to the complainant's animus toward defendant); People ex rel. Pierce v. Thomas, 70 Misc.2d 629, 334 N.Y.S.2d 666 (Sup.Ct., Bronx County, 1972)(cross-examination relating to matters that would be subject of a subsequent motion to suppress rarely permitted at preliminary hearing).

454. People v. Hodge, 53 N.Y.2d 313, 319, 441 N.Y.S.2d 231, 234, 423 N.E.2d 1060, 1063 (1981).

455. CPL § 180.60(2).

456. People v. Cummings, 109 A.D.2d 748, 749, 485 N.Y.S.2d 847, 849 (2d Dep't 1985).

457. People v. Hodge, 53 N.Y.2d 313, 441 N.Y.S.2d 231, 423 N.E.2d 1060 (1981).

resulting conviction.[458]

An unresolved question is whether the defense is entitled at a preliminary hearing to *Rosario* material—*i.e.*, the prior written or recorded statements of the witnesses who testify at the hearing.[459] CPL § 240.44 requires *Rosario* disclosure, upon request, at a "pre-trial hearing." Although a preliminary hearing may fit that description, this phrase, which is not defined in the CPL, is generally used in reference to a suppression hearing. In any event, the only reported decision addressing the issue since section 240.44 was adopted in 1982[460] holds that *Rosario* disclosure is required.[461] Whether the prosecution must also disclose the criminal histories of its witnesses, disclosure of which is also required under section 240.44,[462] has not been addressed. It would seem, however, that if a "pre-trial hearing" within the meaning of section 240.44 includes a preliminary hearing, then that section would require disclosure at a preliminary hearing not only of *Rosario* material but also of all information and material required to be disclosed thereunder.[463]

Although the statute provides the court, on the defendant's application, with discretion to close a preliminary hearing to the public and direct that a transcript of the proceeding not be disclosed,[464] that discretion is significantly limited by the First Amendment. In reviewing a trial court's decision to close a CPL Article 730 competency hearing, the Court of Appeals laid down specific rules that a trial court must follow in evaluating and granting an application for closure: the motion for closure must be made on the record in open court; the defendant, in support of the motion, must demonstrate "a strong likelihood that evidence relevant and admissible" at the hearing would prejudice his or her trial if it were disclosed; and if the court ultimately decides to close the courtroom, its reasons shall be given in open court.[465] Thus, a "hypothetical risk" of prejudice to the defendant is insufficient to justify

---

458. See People v. Wicks, 76 N.Y.2d 128, 556 N.Y.S.2d 970, 556 N.E.2d 409 (1990)(standard in determining whether reversal of conviction is required due to denial of defendant's right to counsel at preliminary hearing is whether error was harmless beyond a reasonable doubt).

459. For a discussion of Rosario material, see Chapter 7, §§ 7.16. 7.17.

460. L.1982, c.558.

461. People v. Diggs, 140 Misc.2d 794, 531 N.Y.S.2d 723 (Dist.Ct., Nassau County, 1988). See also Bellacosa, "Practice Commentary," to CPL § 180.60, McKinney's Cons. Laws of N.Y., Vol. 11A, at 138 (1981).

462. See CPL § 240.44(2) and (3).

463. Another unaddressed question is whether the prosecution must disclose Brady material (i.e., exculpatory evidence) at a preliminary hearing. Because a preliminary hearing is considered a "critical stage" in the criminal action, see Coleman v. Alabama, 399 U.S. 1, 9, 90 S.Ct. 1999, 2003, 26 L.Ed.2d 387 (1970); People v. Hodge, 53 N.Y.2d at 318, 441 N.Y.S.2d at 234, and exculpatory evidence may be directly relevant to the question of whether there is reasonable cause to believe that the defendant committed a felony, a credible argument can be made that Brady material should be disclosed. When the courts do address this question, however, the answer may turn on whether the prosecution would have been required to present the exculpatory evidence to the grand jury, a question not always easily resolved. See Chapter 5, § 5.7.

464. CPL § 180.60(9).

465. Matter of Westchester Rockland Newspapers, Inc. v. Leggett, 48 N.Y.2d 430, 442, 423 N.Y.S.2d 630, 637, 399 N.E.2d 518, 524 (1979). The Court noted that although the reasons for closure must be given in open court, the court must "be cautious in this pronouncement lest the expressed reasons create the prejudice or the disclosure sought to be avoided." Id.

disclosure.[466] Moreover, the court must afford the opponents of disclosure an adequate opportunity to argue against the motion. This may require a short adjournment of the hearing to enable the opponents' counsel to be heard on the motion, by telephone if necessary.[467]

In making its determination following the presentation of evidence at the hearing, the court must follow a procedure similar to that governing reduction of a felony charge under CPL § 180.50.[468] First, if the court concludes that the evidence establishes reasonable cause to believe that the defendant committed a felony, it must order that the defendant be held for the action of the grand jury, and send the file papers on to the superior court.[469] Second, if the court concludes that the evidence establishes reasonable cause to believe that the defendant committed a felony *and* a non-felony, it may reduce the charge to a non-felony offense, but only if the prosecution consents and such a reduction would be in the interest of justice.[470] As is true for reduction under section 180.50, however, reduction is not permitted if there is reasonable cause to believe that the defendant committed a non-drug Class A felony offense or an "armed felony offense." Third, if the court concludes that the evidence establishes reasonable cause to believe that the defendant committed only a non-felony offense, the court *may* reduce the felony charge to a non-felony offense.[471] And finally, if the court concludes that there is no reasonable cause to believe that the defendant committed any offense, it *must* dismiss the felony complaint, discharge the defendant if he or she is in custody, and exonerate any bail that has been posted.[472] Even if the court dismisses the complaint, however, the prosecution may still present the case to a grand jury and proceed to prosecute the defendant if the grand jury indicts.[473]

---

466. See Matter of Associated Press v. Bell, 70 N.Y.2d 32, 38, 517 N.Y.S.2d 444, 447, 510 N.E.2d 313, 316 (1987); Matter of Capital Newspapers Div. of the Hearst Corp. v. Lee, 139 A.D.2d 31, 35–36, 530 N.Y.S.2d 872, 875–76 (3d Dep't 1988). See also Press–Enterprise Co. v. Superior Ct. of California, 464 U.S. 501, 510, 104 S.Ct. 819, 824, 78 L.Ed.2d 629 (1984)("The presumption of openness may be overcome only by an overriding interest based on findings that closure is essential to preserve higher values and is narrowly tailored to serve that interest.").

467. See, e.g., Matter of Capital Newspapers Div. of the Hearst Corp. v. Lee, 139 A.D.2d at 36, 530 N.Y.S.2d at 876; Johnson Newspaper Corp. v. Parker, 101 A.D.2d 708, 475 N.Y.S.2d 951 (4th Dep't 1984).

468. See § 3.31, supra.

469. CPL § 180.70(1).

470. CPL § 180.70(3). Reduction is accomplished in accordance with the procedures set forth in CPL § 180.50(3). See § 3.31, supra.

471. CPL § 180.70(2). Again, reduction is accomplished in accordance with the CPL § 180.50(3) procedures.

The procedure in cases involving "juvenile offenders" is somewhat different. If the court concludes that the evidence presented at the preliminary hearing does not establish reasonable cause to believe that the juvenile committed one of the felony offenses that authorizes prosecution of the juvenile in a criminal court (see CPL § 1.20(42)), but does establish reasonable cause to believe that the defendant is a "juvenile delinquent" within the meaning of section 301.2(1) of the Family Court Act, the court must specify the acts for which such reasonable cause exists and then direct that the action be removed to Family Court pursuant to CPL Article 725. CPL § 180.75(3). Article 725, and related procedures for removing an action involving a juvenile offender, are discussed in Chapter 1, § 1.10.

472. CPL § 180.70(4).

473. See People v. Wicks, 76 N.Y.2d at 133, 556 N.Y.S.2d at 972, 556 N.E.2d at 411; People ex rel. Hirschberg v. Close, 1 N.Y.2d 258, 261, 152 N.Y.S.2d 1, 3, 134 N.E.2d 818, 819 (1956).

§ 3.34 Release of Defendant in Custody

Under CPL § 180.80, if a defendant has been held in custody on a felony complaint for more than 120 hours, or for more than 144 hours if a weekend day or holiday occurs during the period of custody (which almost always will occur), the court, on the defendant's application, must release the defendant on his or her own recognizance if a preliminary hearing has not been waived or commenced.[474] Unlike the analogous procedure for defendants held in custody on non-felony local criminal court accusatory instruments,[475] the time period applicable to felony complaints runs from the time of arrest, not the time of arraignment. And the statutory period, which must be applied literally, is 120 hours or 144 hours, not five days or six days.[476]

Note that a failure to comply with this statute requires only the defendant's release, not dismissal of the complaint. And the statute has no application to a case in which the defendant is not in custody.

The defendant's release is not required, however, if a statutorily-designated exception applies. Release is not required if the failure to commence a preliminary hearing was due to the defendant's "request, action or condition, or occurred with his consent."[477] In addition, release is not required if, prior to the defendant's application, the prosecution files a written certification that the grand jury has voted an indictment[478] or if, prior to the application, the grand jury actually has filed an indictment or has filed a direction that the prosecution file a prosecutor's information.[479] In practice, particularly in large, urban jurisdictions, indictments are not filed by the "180.80 day," and prosecutors do not file written certifications that an indictment has been voted. Instead, unless the defense specifically demands a written certification, the prosecution's oral, on-the-record, representation that the grand jury has voted an indictment is acceptable.[480]

Finally, release is not required if the prosecution can demonstrate "good cause," which must involve some "compelling" fact or circumstance that prevented disposition of the felony complaint within the statutory period or rendered such disposition against the interest of justice.[481] Examples of situations in which courts have found "good cause" include a grand jury's request to hear additional testimony

---

474. CPL § 180.80.
475. See CPL § 170.70, discussed in § 3.25, supra.
476. People ex rel. v. Koehler, 151 A.D.2d 309, 310, 542 N.Y.S.2d 578, 579 (1st Dep't 1989).
477. CPL § 180.10(1).
478. CPL § 180.80(2)(a).
479. CPL § 180.80(2)(b). The prosecution's written certification that the grand jury has directed it to file a prosecutor's information will not prevent the defendant's release under the statute. See People v. Gray, 146 Misc.2d 470, 551 N.Y.S.2d 154 (N.Y.C.Crim.Ct.1990).

480. See People v. Rivera, 132 Misc.2d 903, 505 N.Y.S.2d 798 (Sup.Ct., Bronx County, 1986)(discussing the accepted informal practice in that jurisdiction).

481. CPL § 180.80(3).

following its receipt of the defendant's testimony,[482] and the congested calendar of the court part in which the case is to be called on the 180.80 day.[483] A custodial authority's failure to deliver a detained defendant, who has served notice of intention to testify before the grand jury, to the courthouse so that the defendant may do so is not good cause to extend the section 180.80 period;[484] nor is a court-ordered examination of the defendant's fitness pursuant to CPL Article 730,[485] or the prosecution's representation that an indictment is "imminent."[486]

A defendant's challenge to his or her detention beyond the section 180.80 period can be made by a direct application under the statute to the local criminal court with jurisdiction over the action or by a habeas corpus application in a superior court.

Library References:
West's Key No. Digests, Bail ⚖40.

§ 3.35 Practice Summary

A. Accusatory Instruments/Supporting Depositions (See §§ 3.5, 3.6, 3.7, 3.9, 3.25)

1. A defendant charged in a simplified information must make a timely request for a supporting deposition: if the defendant pleads not guilty by mail, the request must be made within 30 days of receiving notice from the court of the right to a supporting deposition; if the defendant pleads not guilty in court, the request must be made within 30 days of such court appearance (*see* § 3.5).

2. If the complainant of an accusatory instrument or the affiant of a supporting deposition is a child under 12 years of age, the prosecution, at a minimum, should conduct a stenographically recorded inquiry of the child establishing that the child is of sufficient intelligence and ability to understand the nature of an oath and the allegations being made against the defendant (*see* § 3.6).

3. Unless a defendant charged in a misdemeanor complaint expressly waives prosecution by information, the prosecution must be sure that the accusatory instrument along with any accompanying supporting depositions establish reasonable cause to believe that the defendant committed the offense or offenses charged, and that non-hearsay facts are alleged establishing every element of the offense or offenses charged. The failure to allege facts establishing every element of the offense or offenses charged is a nonwaivable jurisdictional defect. If the defense moves to dismiss a jurisdictionally defective accusatory instrument after the statutory speedy trial period has elapsed, and such motion is granted, further prosecution will be barred (*see* § 3.7).

---

482. See, e.g., People v. Griffin, 163 Misc.2d 43, 48–49, 619 N.Y.S.2d 931, 935 (N.Y.C.Crim.Ct.1994).

483. See, e.g., People v. Sweeney, 143 Misc.2d 175, 539 N.Y.S.2d 677 (N.Y.C.Crim. Ct.1989).

484. People v. Evans, 79 N.Y.2d 407, 583 N.Y.S.2d 358, 592 N.E.2d 1362 (1992).

485. People v. Smith, 143 Misc.2d 100, 539 N.Y.S.2d 663 (N.Y.C.Crim.Ct.1989).

486. People ex rel. v. Koehler, 151 A.D.2d 309, 542 N.Y.S.2d 578 (1st Dep't 1989).

4. The court should not accept the waiver of a defendant charged in a misdemeanor complaint of prosecution by an information unless the defendant expressly waives this right and agrees to be prosecuted on the misdemeanor complaint (*see* § 3.25).

5. If an information fails to allege an offense or offenses that are supported by facially sufficient factual allegations contained in the information and any accompanying supporting depositions, the prosecution is authorized to file a prosecutor's information charging the additional offense or offenses and which will supersede the existing information (*see* § 3.9).

B. Arrest Warrants (*See* § 3.13)

1. A court may issue an arrest warrant only if a facially sufficient accusatory instrument (other than a simplified information) has been filed commencing a criminal action; thus, if a felony or misdemeanor complaint has been filed, the factual allegations contained therein must establish reasonable cause to believe that the defendant committed the offense charged. Before issuing an arrest warrant, however, the court must be satisfied that the defendant would not appear in court for arraignment if the court issued a summons instead. In addition, if the prosecution requests, the court, in lieu of issuing an arrest warrant or a summons, may authorize the prosecution to direct the defendant to appear in court on a specified date for arraignment (but only if the court is satisfied that the defendant will do so).

C. Arraignments (Non–Felonies) (*See* § 3.24)

1. At the arraignment of a defendant charged in a non-felony local criminal court accusatory instrument, the court must:

- inform the defendant of the charges and provide a copy of the accusatory instrument
- if the defendant has been arrested without a warrant, and the court intends to fix bail, the court must, if the defendant requests, review whether there is reasonable to believe that the defendant committed an offense
- advise the defendant of the right to counsel at arraignment and every other proceeding in the case and the right to assignment of counsel if the defendant cannot afford one
- if the defendant appears at arraignment without counsel, advise the defendant of the right to an adjournment to obtain counsel, and of the right to communicate free of charge to attempt to obtain counsel or speak with a friend or relative; when necessary, the court must take "affirmative action" to ensure that the defendant obtains counsel
- if the defendant is charged in a misdemeanor complaint, advise that the prosecution must convert the misdemeanor complaint to an information, unless the defendant consents to be prosecuted on the complaint

- issue a securing order either releasing the defendant on his or her own recognizance or fixing bail
- if the court has received a copy of the defendant's rapsheet, provide a copy to the defendant
- deny any application for audio-visual coverage of the arraignment, unless the parties consent

2. At the arraignment, the prosecution ordinarily should provide the defendant with any notice pursuant to CPL § 710.30 of its intention to offer evidence of the defendant's statements or evidence of an identification, as well as any demand pursuant to CPL § 250.20 for notice of alibi.

D. Release From Custody (Non–Felonies) (*See* § 3.25)

1. If a defendant against whom a misdemeanor complaint is pending is being held in custody, the court, on the defendant's application, must release the defendant on his or her own recognizance if the prosecution has failed to convert the complaint to an information within five days (not including a Sunday) of the arraignment. The only exceptions are if the defendant has waived prosecution by information, or if the court finds "good cause" (*i.e.*, some compelling fact or circumstance that prevented conversion within the required time period).

E. Motions to Dismiss (*See* § 3.26)

1. A defendant's motion to dismiss a non-felony local criminal court accusatory instrument must be made within 45 days of arraignment, unless the court extends such period for good cause shown. However, a motion to dismiss on speedy trial grounds may be made at any time prior to commencement of trial or entry of a guilty plea. A motion to dismiss must be in writing and made with reasonable notice to the prosecution, unless the prosecution fails to object to these requirements.

F. Arraignment (Felonies) (*See* § 3.29)

1. At the arraignment of a defendant charged in a felony complaint, the court must:

- inform the defendant of the charges and provide a copy of the accusatory instrument
- inform the defendant of the right to counsel at the arraignment and at every other proceeding in the case, and of the right to assignment of counsel if the defendant is unable to afford one
- if the defendant appears at arraignment without counsel, advise the defendant of the right to an adjournment to obtain counsel, and of the right to communicate free of charge to attempt to obtain counsel or to speak with a friend or relative; when necessary, the court must take "affirmative action" to secure the defendant's right to counsel
- issue a securing order releasing the defendant on his or her own recognizance, fixing bail or, when appropriate, committing the defendant to jail

- if the defendant was arrested without a warrant, and the court intends to fix bail or commit the defendant to jail, and the defendant so requests, the court must review whether there is reasonable cause to believe that the defendant committed an offense
- advise the defendant that he or she has the right to a prompt hearing to determine whether there is sufficient evidence to hold him or her for the action of the grand jury, but that the defendant may waive such hearing
- if the court has received a copy of the defendant's rapsheet, provide the defendant with a copy
- deny any application for audio-visual coverage of the arraignment, unless the parties consent

2. At the arraignment, the prosecution ordinarily should provide any notice pursuant to CPL § 710.30 of its intention to offer evidence of the defendant's statements or an identification, any demand pursuant to CPL § 250.20 for notice of alibi, and if it intends to present the case immediately to the grand jury, notice pursuant to CPL § 190.50(5)(a) of its intention to do so.

3. At the arraignment, if the prosecution serves notice pursuant to CPL § 190.50(5)(a) of its intention to present the case to the grand jury, and the defendant is contemplating testifying before the grand jury, the defense should serve cross-notice pursuant to that section.

G. Reduction of Felony Charges (*See* § 3.31)

1. If the prosecution consents, the court may make inquiry (which may include questioning persons with relevant information about the case) to determine whether a felony charge should be reduced to a non-felony charge. If, upon conducting this inquiry, the court concludes that there is reasonable cause to believe that the defendant committed only a non-felony, it may reduce the felony charge to the non-felony charge; if the court concludes that there is reasonable cause to believe that the defendant committed a felony and a non-felony, the court may reduce the felony charge to the non-felony charge only if the prosecution consents, reduction would be in the interest of justice, and there is no reasonable cause to believe that the defendant committed a non-drug Class A felony offense or an "armed felony offense."

H. Preliminary Hearings (*See* § 3.32)

1. At a preliminary hearing, the prosecution has the burden to establish that there is reasonable cause to believe that the defendant committed a felony offense. The prosecution's burden must be met with non-hearsay evidence, except for written statements admissible pursuant to CPL § 190.30(2) and (3) in a grand jury proceeding (although the defendant may challenge the admissibility of such statements as unreliable). Although the defendant may testify at the hearing as a matter of right, the court has broad discretion to limit cross-examination of

prosecution witnesses and to limit defense presentation of its own evidence. The defense should request all *Rosario* and *Brady* material.

2. Following the presentation of evidence, if the court concludes that there is reasonable cause to believe that the defendant committed a felony, it must order that the defendant be held for the action of the grand jury and send the file papers to the appropriate superior court; if the court concludes that there is reasonable cause to believe that the defendant committed a felony and a non-felony, it may reduce the felony charge to the non-felony charge, but only if the prosecution consents, reduction would be in the interest of justice, and there is no reasonable cause to believe that the defendant committed a non-drug Class A felony offense or an "armed felony offense;" if the court concludes that there is reasonable cause to believe that the defendant committed only a non-felony, it may reduce the felony charge to the non-felony charge; and if the court concludes that there is no reasonable cause to believe that the defendant committed any offense, it must dismiss the felony complaint, discharge the defendant if he or she is in custody, and exonerate any bail. Even if the court dismisses the felony complaint, however, the prosecution may still present evidence to the grand jury and proceed with the prosecution if the grand jury indicts.

I. Release From Custody (Non–Felonies) (*See* § 3.33)

1. If a defendant has been held in custody on a felony complaint for more than 120 hours or, more typically, for more than 144 hours if a weekend day or holiday occurs during this period, and a preliminary hearing has not been commenced or waived, the court, on the defendant's application, must release the defendant on his or her own recognizance. The only exceptions are if the failure to commence the preliminary hearing was due to the defendant's request or consent; if, prior to the defendant's application for release, the grand jury filed an indictment or the prosecution filed a written certificate that the grand jury has voted an indictment; or if the prosecution demonstrates "good cause" (*i.e.*, some compelling fact or circumstance that precluded disposition of the complaint within the required period).

§ 3.36 Forms

§ 3.36.1 Supporting Deposition

[Caption]

State of New York   )
) ss.:
County of _____   )

_____, deposes and says upon personal knowledge [or upon information and belief] that: [specify facts that supplement factual allegations of the accusatory instrument and support or tend to support the charge(s) therein].

Dated: _____, 19__

[Signature]
_____

NOTICE: False statements made herein are punishable as a Class A misdemeanor pursuant to section 210.45 of the Penal Law.

§ 3.36.2 Defendant's Request for Supporting Deposition

[Caption]

TO THE COURT:

Defendant, having been arraigned in the above-entitled action upon a [specify type of simplified information], hereby requests, pursuant to section 100.25(2) of the Criminal Procedure Law, that the complainant police officer [or specify other public servant] file with the court and serve upon defendant's attorney a supporting deposition containing factual allegations providing reasonable cause to believe that the defendant committed the offense(s) charged herein.

Dated: _____, 19__
_____, New York

[Name of defense attorney]
Attorney for Defendant
Address
Tel. No.

§ 3.36.3 Supporting Deposition for Simplified Information

[Caption]

State of New York   )
) ss.
County of _____   )

_____, deposes and says that he [she] is the complainant police officer [or specify other public servant] who issued the [specify simplified information] herein, and that he [she] makes this supporting deposition pursuant to section 100.25(2) of the Criminal Procedure Law:

[Specify facts establishing reasonable cause to believe that the defendant committed the offense(s)]

Dated: _____, 19__

[Signature]
_____
[Name]

NOTICE: False statements made herein are punishable as a Class A misdemeanor pursuant to section 210.45 of the Penal Law.

§ 3.36.4 Notice of Motion to Amend Prosecutor's Information

[Caption]

COUNSEL:

PLEASE TAKE NOTICE, that upon the annexed affirmation and upon all the prior papers and proceedings herein, the undersigned will move this Court, at Part _____ thereof, to be held at the Courthouse at _____, New York, on the ___ day of _____, 19__, at ___ in the forenoon, or as soon thereafter as counsel can be heard, for an order, pursuant to section 100.45(2) of the Criminal Procedure Law, directing an amendment of the prosecutor's information filed herein, and for such other and further relief as the Court deems proper.

Dated: _____, 19__
_____, New York

                                    HON. _____
                                    District Attorney
                                    _____ County
                                    Address
                                    Tel. No.

To: [Name of defense attorney]
    Attorney for Defendant

HON. _____
Clerk of the Court

§ 3.36.5 Affirmation in Support of Motion to Amend Prosecutor's Information

[Caption]

_____, an attorney duly admitted to practice in the Courts of this State, hereby affirms under penalty of perjury that the following statements are true, and as to those made upon information and belief, he [she] believes them to be true:

1. I am an assistant district attorney in the County of _____.

2. On _____, 19__, a prosecutor's information was filed charging the defendant with the following offense(s): [specify offense(s) charged]. A copy of the prosecutor's information is attached hereto as Exhibit A.

3. No plea of guilty has been entered herein, nor has trial been commenced.

4. This affirmation is made in support of the People's application pursuant to section 100.45(2) of the Criminal Procedure Law for an order directing the amendment of the aforesaid prosecutor's information as follows: [specify amendment sought].

5. The amendment sought herein does not change the theory or theories of the prosecution as reflected in the prosecutor's information nor, if it were granted, would it prejudice the defendant on the merits.

6. No previous application for the relief sought herein has been made.

WHEREFORE, the People request that the Court issue an order directing the aforesaid amendment of the prosecutor's information.

Dated: _____, 19__
_____, New York

                                    [Signature]
                                    _____
                                    [Name]

§ 3.36.6 Notice of Motion to Amend Information

[Caption]

COUNSEL:

PLEASE TAKE NOTICE, that upon the annexed affirmation and upon all the prior papers and proceedings herein, the undersigned will move this Court, at Part ___ thereof, at the Courthouse at _____, New York, on the __ day of _____, 19__, at __ in the forenoon, or as soon thereafter as counsel can be heard, for an order pursuant to section 100.45(3) of the Criminal Procedure Law directing amendment of the information filed herein, and for such other relief as the Court deems proper.

Dated: _____, 19__
_____, New York

                                  HON. _____
                                  District Attorney
                                  _____ County
                                  Address
                                  Tel. No.

TO: [Name of defense attorney]
     Attorney for Defendant

     HON. _____
     Clerk of the Court

§ 3.36.7 Affirmation in Support of Motion to Amend Information

[Caption]

_____, an attorney duly admitted to practice in the Courts of this State hereby affirms under penalty of perjury that the following statements are true, and as to those based upon information and belief he [she] believes them to be true:

1. I am an assistant district attorney in the County of _____.

2. On _____, 19__, an information was filed herein charging the defendant with the following offense(s): [specify offense(s) charged]. A copy of the information is attached hereto as Exhibit A.

3. No plea of guilty has been entered herein, nor has a trial been commenced.

4. This affirmation is made in support of the People's application pursuant to section 100.45(3) of the Criminal Procedure Law for an order directing the amendment of the aforesaid information to add the following count: [specify count sought to be added].

5. The count sought to be added is supported by the factual allegations contained in the information [and/or the factual allegations of the supporting deposition(s) of _____ filed in connection with the information].

6. No previous application for the relief sought herein has been made.

WHEREFORE, the People request that the Court issue an order directing the amendment of the information to add a new count as requested herein.

Dated: _____, 19__
_____, New York

[Signature]
_____
[Name]

§ 3.36.8 Petition for Writ of *Habeas Corpus* on Behalf of Person Arrested Without Warrant Who Has Not Been Produced for Arraignment

SUPREME COURT OF THE STATE OF NEW YORK
_____ COUNTY

People of the State of New York Ex Rel. [name of defense attorney] On Behalf of [name of defendant], Petitioners, -against- [Name of person(s) who has custody of arrestee—e.g., police commissioner, police chief, correction commissioner, sheriff], Respondent(s).	Petition for Writ of Habeas Corpus Index. No. _____

TO THE SUPREME COURT, _____ COUNTY:

1. Petitioner is the attorney for [name of arrestee](hereinafter referred to as "petitioner"), the person on whose behalf this petition is made.

2. Petitioner was arrested without a warrant on _____, 19__, at [specify time]. Since the arrest, petitioner has been continuously held in custody. He [she] is currently being detained at [specify stationhouse, precinct, central booking facility, or courthouse holding pen where arrestee is being detained].

3. Petitioner has now been held in custody for more than 24 hours, without being presented for arraignment.

4. This delay in producing petitioner for arraignment violates petitioner's right to a prompt arraignment under section 140.20(1) of the Criminal Procedure Law, *see People ex rel. Maxian v. Brown*, 77 N.Y.2d 422, 568 N.Y.S.2d 575, 570 N.E.2d 223 (1991), and petitioner's right to a prompt probable cause determination under the Fourth Amendment of the United States Constitution. *County of Riverside v. McLaughlin*, 500 U.S. 44, 111 S.Ct. 1661, 114 L.Ed.2d 49 (1991).

WHEREFORE, petitioner requests that the Court grant this petition for a writ of habeas corpus and order the issuance of an appearance ticket and petitioner's release from custody.

Dated: _____, 19__
_____, New York

[Name of defense attorney]

[Verification]

§ 3.36.9 Notice of Motion to Dismiss Local Criminal Court Accusatory Instrument (or a count thereof)

[Caption]

COUNSEL:

PLEASE TAKE NOTICE, that upon the annexed affirmation and upon all the prior papers and proceedings herein, the defendant will move this Court, at Part ___ thereof, to be held at the Courthouse at _____, New York, on the ___ day of _____, 19__, at ___ in the forenoon, or as soon thereafter as counsel can be heard, for an order pursuant to section 170.30 of the Criminal Procedure Law dismissing the [specify accusatory instrument] herein [or a count thereof] upon the ground that [specify ground for dismissal set forth in CPL § 170.30(1) upon which motion is based], and for such further relief as the Court deems proper.

Dated: _____, 19__
_____, New York

[Name of defense attorney]
Attorney for Defendant
Address
Tel. No.

Ch. 3   FORMS   § 3.36

TO: HON. _____
     District Attorney
     _____ County

HON. _____
Clerk of the Court

§ 3.36.10 Affirmation in Support of Motion to Dismiss Local Criminal Court Accusatory Instrument (or a count thereof)

[Caption]

_____, an attorney duly admitted to practice in the Courts of this State, hereby affirms under penalty of perjury that the following statements are true, and as to those made upon information and belief, he [she] believes them to be true:

1. I am the attorney for the defendant herein.

2. On _____, 19__, a [specify local criminal court accusatory instrument] was filed with this Court charging defendant with the commission of the following offense(s): [specify offense(s) charged]. A copy of the [specify accusatory instrument] is attached hereto as Exhibit A.

3. Defendant has not entered a plea of guilty nor has a trial been commenced as to the aforesaid charges.

4. This affirmation is made in support of defendant's motion, pursuant to section 170.30 of the Criminal Procedure Law, to dismiss the [specify accusatory instrument] [or a count thereof] on the ground that [specify ground of CPL § 170.30(1) upon which motion is based].

5. [discuss reasons why accusatory instrument is insufficient]

6. No previous application for the relief sought herein has been made.

WHEREFORE, defendant requests that this Court dismiss the [specify accusatory instrument] [or a count thereof].

Dated: _____, 19__
_____, New York

                         [Signature]
                         _____
                         [Name]

§ 3.36.11 Notice of Motion to Dismiss Local Criminal Court Accusatory Instrument in Furtherance of Justice

[Caption]

COUNSEL:

PLEASE TAKE NOTICE, that upon the annexed affirmation and all the prior papers and proceedings herein, the undersigned will move this

§ 3.36 LOCAL CRIMINAL COURTS Ch. 3

Court, at Part ____ thereof, at the Courthouse at _____, New York, on the ____ day of _____, 19__, at ____ in the forenoon, or as soon thereafter as counsel can be heard, for an order pursuant to sections 170.30(1)(g) and 170.40 of the Criminal Procedure Law dismissing the [specify accusatory instrument] herein, and for such other relief as this Court deems proper.

Dated: _____, 19__
_____, New York

[Name of defense attorney]
Attorney for Defendant
Address
Tel. No.

TO: HON. _____
District Attorney
_____, County

HON. _____
Clerk of the Court

§ 3.36.12 Affirmation in Support of Motion to Dismiss Local Criminal Court Accusatory Instrument in Furtherance of Justice

[Caption]

_____, an attorney duly admitted to practice in the Courts of this State, hereby affirms under penalty of perjury that the following statements are true, and as to those made upon information and belief, he [she] believes them to be true:

1. I am the attorney for the defendant herein.

2. On _____, 19__, a [specify accusatory instrument] was filed with this Court charging defendant with the following offense(s): [specify offense(s) charged]. A copy of the [specify accusatory instrument] is attached hereto as Exhibit A.

3. Defendant has not entered a plea of guilty, nor has a trial been commenced as to the aforesaid charge(s).

3. This affirmation is made in support of defendant's motion pursuant to sections 170.30(1)(g) and 170.40 of the Criminal Procedure Law to dismiss the [specify accusatory instrument] in furtherance of justice.

4. The [specify accusatory instrument] should be dismissed in furtherance of justice because [discuss grounds for motion in context of factors set forth in CPL § 170.40(1)].

5. No other application for the relief sought herein has been made.

WHEREFORE, defendant requests that this Court dismiss the [specify accusatory instrument] herein in furtherance of justice.

Dated: _____, 19__
_____, New York

                                [Signature]
                                _____
                                [Name]

§ 3.36.13 Notice of Motion to Restore Proceedings on Local Criminal Court Accusatory Instrument That Were Adjourned in Contemplation of Dismissal

[Caption]

COUNSEL:

PLEASE TAKE NOTICE, that upon the annexed affirmation and all the prior papers and proceedings herein, the undersigned will move this Court, at Part __ thereof, at the Courthouse at _____, New York, on the __ day of _____, 19__, at __ in the forenoon, or as soon thereafter as counsel can be heard, for an order pursuant to section 170.55(2) determining that dismissal of this action would not be in furtherance of justice and restoring the proceedings on the [specify local criminal court accusatory instrument] herein that were adjourned in contemplation of dismissal, and for such other relief as the Court deems proper.

Dated: _____, 19__
_____, New York

                                HON. _____
                                District Attorney
                                _____ County
                                Address
                                Tel. No.

TO: [Name of defense attorney]
      Attorney for Defendant

      HON. _____
      Clerk of the Court

§ 3.36.14 Affirmation in Support of Motion to Restore Proceedings on Local Criminal Court Accusatory Instrument That Were Adjourned in Contemplation of Dismissal

[Caption]

_____, an attorney duly admitted to practice in the Courts of this State, hereby affirms under penalty of perjury that the following statements are true, and as to those based upon affirmation and belief, he [she] believes them to be true:

    1. I am an assistant district attorney in _____ County.

2. On _____, 19__, a [specify accusatory instrument] was filed with this Court charging the defendant with the following offense(s): [specify offenses charged]. A copy of the [specify accusatory instrument] is attached hereto as Exhibit A.

3. On _____, 19__, this Court, pursuant to section 170.55 of the Criminal Procedure Law, ordered the adjournment of the proceedings in this action in contemplation of dismissal. A copy of the Court's order is attached hereto as Exhibit B.

4. Dismissal of this action would not be in the furtherance of justice because [specify reasons why action should be restored, including any facts, whether based upon information and belief or otherwise, that defendant violated a condition of the order adjourning the action in contemplation of dismissal].

5. Six months have not elapsed since the Court's issuance of the order adjourning the action in contemplation of dismissal.

WHEREFORE, the People request that the Court issue an order determining that dismissal of this action would not be in furtherance of justice and restoring the action to the calendar for further proceedings.

Dated: _____, 19__
_____, New York

[Signature]
_____
[Name]

§ 3.36.15 Notice of Motion for Order Releasing Defendant From Custody for Failure to Replace Misdemeanor Complaint With Information

[Caption]

COUNSEL:

PLEASE TAKE NOTICE, that upon the annexed affirmation and upon all the prior papers and proceedings herein, the undersigned will move this Court, at Part __ thereof, at the Courthouse at _____, New York, on the __ day of _____, 19__, at __ in the forenoon, or as soon thereafter as counsel can be heard, for an order pursuant to section 170.70 of the Criminal Procedure Law, releasing the defendant on his [her] own recognizance upon the ground that an information has not been filed, within the time period required by law, in replacement of the misdemeanor complaint pending herein against defendant, and for such other relief as the Court deems proper.

Dated: _____, 19__
_____, New York

[Name of defense attorney]
Attorney for Defendant
Address
Tel. No.

TO: HON. _____
District Attorney
_____ County

HON. _____
Clerk of the Court

§ 3.36.16 Affirmation in Support of Motion for Order Releasing Defendant From Custody for Failure to Replace Misdemeanor Complaint With Information

[Caption]

_____, an attorney duly admitted to practice in the Courts of this State, affirms under penalty of perjury that the following statements are true, except those made upon information and belief, which he [she] believes to be true:

1. I am the attorney for the defendant herein.

2. On _____, 19__, a misdemeanor complaint was filed with this Court charging defendant with the following offense(s): [specify offenses charged]. A copy of the misdemeanor complaint is attached hereto as Exhibit A.

3. On _____, 19__, defendant was arraigned in this Court on the aforesaid misdemeanor complaint, at which time he [she] was committed to the custody of [specify sheriff or other official who has custody of defendant].

4. Defendant now has been confined in such custody for a period of more than five days, not including Sunday, without any information having been filed in replacement of the aforesaid misdemeanor complaint.

5. Defendant has not waived prosecution by information or otherwise consented to prosecution on the aforesaid misdemeanor complaint. Upon information and belief, no compelling fact or circumstance has precluded replacement of the misdemeanor complaint with an information.

WHEREFORE, defendant requests that this Court issue an order pursuant to section 170.70 of the Criminal Procedure Law releasing him [her] on his [her] own recognizance.

Dated: _____, 19__
_____, New York

[Signature]
_____
[Name]

§ 3.36.17 Notice of Motion for Order Releasing Defendant From Custody for Lack of Timely Disposition of Felony Complaint

[Caption]

COUNSEL:

PLEASE TAKE NOTICE, that upon the annexed affirmation and all the prior papers and proceedings herein, the undersigned will move this Court, at Part ___ thereof, at the Courthouse at _____, New York, on the ___ day of _____, 19__, at ___ in the forenoon, or as soon thereafter as counsel can be heard, for an order pursuant to section 180.80 of the Criminal Procedure Law releasing the defendant from custody on his [her] own recognizance, and for any other relief that the Court deems proper.

Dated: _____, 19__
_____, New York

[Name of defense attorney]
Attorney for Defendant
Address
Tel. No.

TO: HON. _____
District Attorney
_____ County

HON. _____
Clerk of the Court

§ 3.36.18 Affirmation in Support of Motion for Order Releasing Defendant From Custody for Lack of Timely Disposition of Felony Complaint

[Caption]

_____, an attorney duly admitted to practice in the Courts of this State, hereby affirms under penalty of perjury that the following statements are true, and as to those based upon information and belief he [she] believes them to be true:

1. I am the attorney for the defendant herein.

2. On _____, 19__, a felony complaint was filed with this Court charging defendant with the following offense(s): [specify offense(s) charged]. Defendant was arraigned thereon on _____, 19__, at which time the Court committed him [her] to the custody of [specify sheriff or other official who has custody of defendant]. A copy of the felony complaint is attached hereto as Exhibit A.

3. Defendant has now been confined in such custody for a period of more than 144 hours [or 120 hours if a Saturday, Sunday or legal holiday has not occurred during such period of custody] without either a disposition of the felony complaint or the commencement of a preliminary hearing thereon.

4. The failure to dispose of the felony complaint or to commence a preliminary hearing thereon is not due to the defendant's request, action or condition and has not occurred with his [her] consent.

5. Prior to this application, no indictment or direction to file a prosecutor's information charging an offense based upon conduct alleged in the felony complaint has been filed by a grand jury, nor has the District Attorney filed a written certification that an indictment has been voted.

6. Upon information and belief, no compelling fact or circumstance has precluded disposition of the felony complaint.

WHEREFORE, defendant requests that this Court issue an order pursuant to section 180.80 of the Criminal Procedure Law releasing him [her] from custody on his [her] own recognizance.

Dated: _____, 19__
_____, New York

[Signature]
_____
[Name]

Chapter 4

BAIL AND RECOGNIZANCE

Table of Sections

4.1   Introduction.
4.2   Definitions.
4.3   Acceptable Varieties of Bail.
4.4   Fixing of Bail—In General.
4.5   Bail Applications and General Criteria.
4.6   Fixing of Bail by Local Criminal Courts.
4.7   Fixing of Bail by Superior Courts.
4.8   "Stationhouse" Pre-arraignment Bail.
4.9   Bail After Conviction and on Appeal.
4.10 Bail and Recognizance Conditions and Modification.
4.11 Examination of Sufficiency of Bail.
4.12 Forfeiture of Bail and Remission.
4.13 Procedure for Challenges to Excessive Bail.
4.14 Practice Summary.
4.15 Forms.
    4.15.1 Notice of Application for Recognizance or Bail in Superior Court When Action Pending in Local Criminal Court.
    4.15.2 Affirmation in Support of Application for Recognizance or Bail in Superior Court When Action Pending in Local Criminal Court.
    4.15.3 Petition for Writ of *Habeas Corpus* on Ground That Bail Fixed by Trial Court Is So Excessive as to Constitute an Abuse of Discretion.
    4.15.4 Notice of Application for Remission of Forfeiture of Bail.
    4.15.5 Affidavit in Support of Application for Remission of Forfeiture of Bail.

WESTLAW Electronic Research

See WESTLAW Electronic Research Guide preceding the Summary of Contents.

§ 4.1 Introduction

Bail is the method by which the criminal justice system seeks to reconcile the interest of a defendant in remaining at liberty prior to disposition of the action with society's interest in ensuring that the defendant will appear in court to face the charges. Essentially a corollary to the constitutional principle that an accused is innocent until proven guilty, the practice of posting monetary or other security with a court to ensure the defendant's appearance while he or she remains at liberty pending the adjudication of criminal charges is of ancient vintage and has been called a "fundamental principle of American criminal jurisprudence.'"[1]

Bail is not, however, a constitutional right. Although both the federal and New York Constitutions prohibit the imposition of "excessive" bail,[2] both the United States Supreme Court[3] and the New York Court of Appeals[4] have noted that these provisions do not establish a right to bail under all circumstances, but only a prohibition against the setting of excessive bail in cases where the right to bail is granted by the Legislature. Notwithstanding what appears to be the great weight of authority on this point, some commentators[5] and courts[6] continue to opine that there is a constitutional or "fundamental" right to bail in the absence of statutory entitlement.

In any event, the existence of the constitutional guarantee against excessive bail "certainly requires that legislative provisions must, to

1. For a historical overview, see Verelli, "The Eighth Amendment and the Right to Bail: Historical Perspectives," 82 Colum.L Rev. 328 (1982).

2. U.S. Const., Amend. XIV; N.Y. Const., Article 1, § 5. Both read as follows: "Excessive bail shall not be required nor excessive fines imposed, nor shall cruel and unusual punishments be inflicted." The New York Constitution adds a clause preventing the unreasonable detention of witnesses. As a technical matter, although the Supreme Court has never directly held that the "excessive bail" clause of the Eighth Amendment is applicable to the states via the due process clause of the Fourteenth Amendment, the court has held other parts of the Eighth Amendment applicable to the states, and many courts, both state and federal, have assumed that the federal clause binds the states as well as the federal government. See, e.g., People ex rel. Klein v. Krueger, 25 N.Y.2d 497, 307 N.Y.S.2d 207, 255 N.E.2d 552 (1969).

3. Carlson v. Landon, 342 U.S. 524, 72 S.Ct. 525, 96 L.Ed. 547 (1952). It should be noted that because Carlson dealt with a deportation proceeding, the statement in that case that the Eighth Amendment does not grant a constitutional right to bail in ordinary circumstances is dictum. In addition, in a case decided in the same term, Stack v. Boyle, 342 U.S. 1, 72 S.Ct. 1, 96 L.Ed. 3 (1951), the Court stressed the importance of bail as a fundamental protection of individual liberty, although that case itself dealt with a statutory right to bail. Subsequent discussion of the issue by the Supreme Court, however, strongly supports the Carlson dictum. See Browning–Ferris v. Kelco Disposal, 492 U.S. 257, 109 S.Ct. 2909, 106 L.Ed.2d 219 (1989)(holding that the "excessive fines" clause of the Eighth Amendment does not apply to civil litigation between private parties, and reiterating Carlson); United States v. Salerno, 481 U.S. 739, 107 S.Ct. 2095, 95 L.Ed.2d 697 (1987)(holding, inter alia, that the "preventive detention" provisions of the federal Bail Reform Act do not offend the Eighth Amendment, and discussing Carlson and Stack to the detriment of the latter). Although the collective weight of these opinions would seem to settle the matter, it remains technically possible to argue that the issue has not been determined by the Supreme Court.

4. People ex rel. Calloway v. Skinner, 33 N.Y.2d 23, 347 N.Y.S.2d 178, 300 N.E.2d 716 (1973); People ex rel. Klein v. Krueger, 25 N.Y.2d 497, 499, 307 N.Y.S.2d 207, 209, 255 N.E.2d 552, 554 (1969); People ex rel. Fraser v. Britt, 289 N.Y. 614, 43 N.E.2d 836 (1942); People ex rel. Shapiro v. Keeper of City Prison, 290 N.Y. 393, 49 N.E.2d 498 (1943). See also, Bellamy v. Judges, 41 A.D.2d 196, 342 N.Y.S.2d 137 (1st Dep't 1973), aff'd 32 N.Y.2d 886, 346 N.Y.S.2d 812, 300 N.E.2d 153 (1973)("no substance" to per se attack on bail system based on excessive bail clause of state and federal constitutions.)

5. Cf. Verelli, "The Eighth Amendment and the Right To Bail: Historical Perspectives," supra; Tribe, "An Ounce of Detention: Preventative Justice in the World of John Mitchell," 56 Va.L.Rev. 371 (1970)(arguing that there is some form of constitutional right to bail) with Duker, "Right to Bail: A Historical Inquiry," 42 Albany L.Rev. 33 (1977); Meyer, "Constitutionality of Pretrial Detention," 55 Va.L.Rev. 1223 (1969)(no constitutional right).

6. In Hunt v. Roth, 648 F.2d 1148 (8th Cir.1981), vacated as moot sub nom. Murphy v. Hunt, 455 U.S. 478, 102 S.Ct. 1181, 71 L.Ed.2d 353 (1982), the court held that there is a constitutional right to bail under certain circumstances, a view rejected in other circuits. Cf. United States v. Perry, 788 F.2d 100 (3d Cir.1986)(rejecting that view and collecting cases).

§ 4.1   BAIL & RECOGNIZANCE   Ch. 4

satisfy constitutional limitations, be related to the proper purposes for the detention of defendants before conviction, as must the judicial applications of discretion authorized by the Legislature."[7] As a practical matter, this means that even though the granting or denial of bail is discretionary, because of the constitutional guarantee the issue may be raised by *habeas corpus* and certain procedural safeguards are operative.[8]

Accordingly, both the substance and procedure of bail are governed largely by statute. The CPL treats the subject in five separate articles. Initially, Article 500 sets forth the basic definitions for the entire topic. Thereafter, Article 510 establishes the general rules as to when bail or other forms of court process are required and the basic criteria to be used in setting bail, Article 520 deals largely with the forms of bail, Article 530 determines which courts may issue bail and also sets forth the mechanism for the issuance of protective orders, and Article 540 deals with bail forfeiture and remission. Other relevant provisions appear elsewhere, both within the CPL and in other statutes.

Library References:
    West's Key No. Digests, Bail ⇒39, 42, 52.

§ 4.2   Definitions

Article 500 contains 20 definitions that establish the framework for all that follows. Many of these are self-evident, and have been the subject of little or no judicial interpretation. Initially, as used in later statutes, a "principal" is a person compelled to appear before a court that is authorized to exercise control over his or her person. In the overwhelming number of criminal cases, the "principal" is a criminal defendant.[9] Depending upon the authority granted by subsequent provisions, "court" can mean a judge as well as a sitting court.[10]

A court may take three fundamental actions with regard to a defendant or other "principal." "Release on own recognizance" occurs when the court simply allows the defendant to go free on condition that he or she return to court.[11] On the other hand, "commit to the custody of the sheriff"[12] means to order the defendant to be confined during the pendency of the criminal action or proceeding. Alternatively, the court can "fix bail," that is specify a sum of money that, if posted and approved, will permit the defendant to remain at liberty while awaiting

---

7. People ex rel. Klein v. Krueger, 25 N.Y.2d 497, 499–500, 307 N.Y.S.2d 207, 209–10, 255 N.E.2d 552, 554–55 (1969).

8. See § 4.13, infra. The CPL bail provisions have withstood general constitutional attack. Bellamy v. Judges, 41 A.D.2d 196, 342 N.Y.S.2d 137 (1st Dep't), aff'd 32 N.Y.2d 886, 346 N.Y.S.2d 812, 300 N.E.2d 153 (1973).

9. CPL § 500.10(1). A principal may also be a material witness, or any other person subject to court control.

10. CPL § 500.10(20). For example, after a defendant's conviction, bail can be granted by, among others, a single justice of the appropriate Appellate Division.

11. CPL § 500.10(2). The released principal must also "render himself amenable to the orders and processes of the court." Id.

12. In New York City, the Commissioner of Corrections replaces the sheriff. See CPL § 1.20(35); Corrections Law § 500–m.

adjudication.[13] A "securing order" is the order issued by the court choosing among these three alternatives,[14] and an "order of recognizance or bail" means a securing order that chooses release or bail, not commitment.[15] An "application for recognizance or bail" is the defendant's request for such relief.[16]

"Bail" itself is defined as to include both "cash bail" and the "bail bond."[17] The former is simply a sum of money, the amount of which is designated by the court, which is "posted"—*i.e.*, deposited[18]—with the appropriate court or agency, and which is forfeited if the defendant fails to appear or otherwise subject himself or herself to court process.[19]

The terminology of bail bonds is somewhat more elaborate. In addition to defining the concept, the statute further defines six varieties of bail bond, which are not in all cases mutually exclusive.[20] In general, a "bail bond" is

> a written undertaking, executed by one or more obligors, that the principal designated in such instrument will, while at liberty as the result of an order fixing bail and of the posting of the bail bond in satisfaction thereof, appear in a designated criminal action or proceeding when his attendance is required and otherwise render himself amenable to the orders and processes of the court, and that in the event that he fails to do so the obligor or obligors will pay to the people of the state of New York a specified sum of money, in the amount designated in the order fixing bail.[21]

---

13. CPL § 500.10(3).

14. CPL § 500.10(5).

15. CPL § 500.10(6). The separately defined term for the release or bail order is apparently intended to clarify other statutes, which require the issuance of this type of securing order—and thus essentially establish a statutory right to bail or release—in some circumstances. See, e.g., CPL §§ 530.20(1), 530.40(1)(requiring release on bail or recognizance for those charged with less than felony grade offenses). Cf., e.g., CPL §§ 530.20(2), 530.40(2)(allowing, at the court's discretion, release on bail or recognizance, but not mandating same, in felony cases).

16. CPL § 500.10(1).

17. CPL § 500.10(9). Interestingly, cash bail is a relatively modern statutory creation, while bail bonds are of ancient vintage and were known at common law. See Badolato v. Molinari, 106 Misc. 342, 174 N.Y.S. 512 (Sup.Ct., Kings County, 1919). Historically, the surety—essentially a person who puts up bail for another [see above definition]—had a personal obligation to deliver the principal to court, while the securing aspect of cash bail is the forfeiture of the deposited sum. Because of this, at one time the depositors of cash bail, if not the defendant, had significantly different obligations and liabilities than sureties. See People v. Castro, 119 Misc.2d 787, 464 N.Y.S.2d 650 (Sup.Ct., Kings County, 1983). In 1984, a series of amendments to the CPL helped to equalize the two. L. 1984, c. 384 (See CPL § 520.15(2)).

18. CPL § 500.10(8). The deposit need not be made by the defendant.

19. CPL § 500.10(10).

20. CPL § 520.10, which lists the acceptable forms of bail, uses these definitions, singly or in combination, to define the list.

21. CPL § 500.10(13). As the Court of Appeals has noted, "A bail bond is security which seeks to assure the defendant's appearance in court in a criminal proceeding. When bail is accepted by the state in lieu of the defendant's physical incarceration, the defendant is in effect remanded to the custody of the surety ... [who] pledges money against the possibility that the defendant will not appear at the court-appointed time." People v. Public Service Co., 37 N.Y.2d 606, 611, 376 N.Y.S.2d 421, 424, 339 N.E.2d 128, 130 (1975).

§ 4.2 BAIL & RECOGNIZANCE Ch. 4

In the parlance of bail, an "obligor" is the person (or persons) who executes the bail bond on behalf of the defendant "principal;" if the obligor is not the defendant, he or she is called a "surety."[22] The different forms of bail bonds include the "appearance bond," which is a bail bond in which the defendant "principal" is the only obligor, as opposed to the "surety bond," which is also undertaken by at least one surety.[23] A special form of the latter is the "insurance company bail bond," in which the surety is a corporation licensed to engage in the business of bail bonds.[24] This form of bail is perhaps the most familiar to the public, although insurance company bail bonds and bail bondsmen, once legendary figures in the state's criminal justice culture, seem less evident recently, perhaps due to changing statutory bail preferences and modern economic conditions. Finally, there are "unsecured bail bonds," "partially secured bail bonds," and "secured bail bonds." A secured bail bond is secured in one of two ways: either by "personal property which is not exempt from execution and which, over and above all liabilities and encumbrances, has a value equal to or greater than the total amount of the undertaking," or by "real property having a value of at least twice the total amount of the undertaking."[25] "Personal property" and "real property," while not specifically defined in the CPL for bail purposes, are defined elsewhere in the law[26] and appear to have their ordinary meanings. The reference to personal property that is "not exempt from execution" is an apparent reference to CPLR 5205, which generally exempts certain personal property from being seized to satisfy a money judgment.[27] Since exempt property cannot be forfeited, it cannot be used to secure the bail bond.

The statutory provision mandating that real property, unlike personal property, must be worth twice the total amount of the undertaking has been the subject of recent litigation. The provision's elaborate formula for computing the value of real property for bail purposes was revised[28] subsequent to the decisions of the court in *People v. Burton*,[29] which first found the posted real property insufficient and thereafter, in a separate decision, found the double value provision to be without a rational basis and therefore unconstitutional.[30] However, in a later case

22. CPL § 500.10(11) and (12). It should be noted that a person who posts cash bail on behalf of another does not technically become a "surety." People v. Castro, 119 Misc.2d 787, 464 N.Y.S.2d 650 (Sup.Ct., Kings County, 1983).

23. CPL § 500.10(14) and (15).

24. CPL § 500.10(16). The licensing and regulatory statutes are contained in sections 6801–6804 of the Insurance Law.

25. CPL § 500.10(17).

26. See General Construction Law §§ 39, 40 (defining "property, personal" and "property, real"); CPLR 105 ("real property"). Cf. CPLR 1310 ("property" for forfeiture purposes includes both real and personal property).

27. The list of exempt personal property includes, among other things, stoves, the family bible, wedding rings, wearing apparel, and household furniture. CPLR 5602, known as the "homestead exemption," also exempts up to ten thousand dollars worth of real property.

28. L.1992, c.316, § 26, eff. November 1, 1992, expanded the formula for property within a "special assessment unit."

29. 148 Misc.2d 716, 561 N.Y.S.2d 328 (Sup.Ct., Bronx County, 1990).

30. People v. Burton, 150 Misc.2d 214, 569 N.Y.S.2d 861 (Sup.Ct., Bronx County, 1990).

the Court of Appeals disagreed and upheld the provision.[31]

In contrast to the "secured bail bond," the "partially secured bail bond" is backed by the deposit of a sum of money not exceeding ten percent of the undertaking, while the "unsecured bail bond" is not backed by any lien or deposit.[32]

Library References:
West's Key No. Digests, Bail ⚖=39–97.

§ 4.3 Acceptable Varieties of Bail

When a court sets bail, it may, or may not, specify the form or forms in which it must be posted. The court also has the authority to designate alternative forms, and to vary the amount of bail depending upon which form is posted.[33] The court may choose from a statutory list of nine general forms, plus a tenth alternative applicable only to Vehicle and Traffic Law "violations." The general forms are: cash bail, an insurance company bail bond, a secured surety bond, a secured appearance bond, a partially secured surety bond, a partially secured appearance bond, an unsecured surety bond, and an unsecured appearance bond.

Obviously, some of these options are more onerous than others, ranging from the most stringent, cash bail, through the various forms of secured bail bonds, and down to the unsecured appearance bond, which is essentially a written promise by the defendant to appear or forfeit the amount in question.[34] An early amendment to the statute changed the "default" provision,[35] so that a court's failure to specify the form or forms of bail now allows the defendant to choose the least onerous alternative, such as the unsecured appearance bond.

The form of bail is important, because the actual amount of cash or other assets that the defendant will have to produce to remain at liberty may depend as much on the specified form as on the amount fixed by the court. For example, where a court fixes bail at $1,000, but specifies cash bail only, the defendant will have to produce $1,000, but where bail is fixed at $2,000 and a "partially secured" bond is allowed, $200 will suffice.[36] The number and variety of bail bond forms in the CPL is a deliberate attempt to liberalize bail decisions:

> [T]he theory of these innovations is that a judge who, despite an inclination to release a "good risk" defendant, feels impelled to fix bail in an amount which may be beyond the defendant's

---

31. People ex rel. Hardy v. Sielaff, 79 N.Y.2d 618, 584 N.Y.S.2d 742, 595 N.E.2d 817 (1992).

32. CPL § 500.10(18) and (19).

33. CPL § 520.10(2).

34. Of course, this is still more onerous than release on one's own recognizance. It should be noted that, despite the title, the crime of "bail jumping" is also committed by a failure to appear after release on recognizance. See P.L. §§ 215.55–215.57. See generally Greenberg, Marcus, et al., New York Criminal Law § 27.22 (West 1996).

35. CPL § 520.10(2) originally provided that when a court failed to specify the form of bail, only certain of the more onerous forms, such as cash bail, were acceptable. L.1972, c.784, replaced this with the present language.

36. See CPL § 500.10(18).

means under the former system, may achieve that release without reducing the bail sum. In short, by relaxing the *forms* of bail rather than the *amount* thereof, the unsecured and partially secured bonds should provide a method of release somewhere between bail as presently authorized [pre-CPL] and release on one's own recognizance.[37]

A tenth alternative form, applicable only "where the principal is charged with a violation under the Vehicle and Traffic Law,"[38] allows the use of a credit card to post bail. The restriction, which seems to evince a legislative judgment that the use of credit cards for non-VTL offenses is unwise, makes for questionable policy. Given the pervasiveness of credit cards in modern society and the possibility that expanding their use for bail purposes will allow both greater flexibility and, perhaps, more security, there appears to be no good reason to be so restrictive.[39]

The form and content of bail bonds are prescribed by statute.[40] Except in cases involving only traffic infractions, where the requirements are relaxed,[41] the bond must be subscribed and sworn to by each obligor, and contain the name, residence, and occupation of each obligor, the title and status of the criminal proceeding, the offenses involved, and the name of the defendant and the nature of his or her involvement with the proceeding. Further, the obligor(s) must undertake "that the principal will appear in such action ... whenever required and will at all times render himself amenable to the orders and processes of the court;" and "[t]hat in the event that the principal does not comply with any such requirement, order or process, such obligor or obligors will pay to the people of the state of New York a designated sum of money fixed by the court."[42] Similarly stringent requirements exist for the "justifying affidavit" accompanying the bail bond; these requirements vary depending upon the nature of the bail bond at issue.[43]

---

37. Bellamy v. Judges, 41 A.D.2d 196, 202, 342 N.Y.S.2d 137 (1st Dep't 1973), aff'd 32 N.Y.2d 886, 346 N.Y.S.2d 812, 300 N.E.2d 153 (1973)(quoting the original McKinney's Practice Commentary by Richard Denzer).

38. The reference to "violations" under the VTL is ambiguous, since the term is not defined in that statute while its Penal Law definition (see P.L. § 10.00(3)) excludes both crimes and traffic infractions.

39. Of course, it might be argued that forfeiture of a credit card debt is less onerous than, say, forfeiture of cash bail, and thus liberalizing the use of credit cards to post bail will provide less security. While this is certainly true in some cases, it is not a compelling objection to all forms of statutory revision. On the one hand, the current provision authorizing credit cards for VTL violations might be expanded to include only other minor offenses, where flight is less likely. Further, allowing the use of a credit card might provide a court with a means of requiring some security in cases where it presently feels constrained to release a defendant on recognizance or unsecured bond. And, of course, in any given case a court could disallow the option.

40. CPL § 520.20.

41. In such cases, CPL § 520.20(1)(b) permits an insurance company bail bond in a simplified form allowed by the State Superintendent of Insurance.

42. CPL § 520.20(2)(e) and (f).

43. See CPL § 520.20(4). The prescribed form varies depending upon whether the affidavit is for an insurance company bail bond, a secured bail bond, or a partially secured bail bond. For example, in the last instance, the obligor-affiant must state the place and nature of his or her business or employment, as well as his or her prior year's income and average income over the past five years. This is not required for the secured bail bond, where it would be irrelevant.

By operation of statute, a bail bond posted in a criminal action remains effective throughout the various stages of the case, regardless of whether the case has progressed from a local criminal court, through indictment, to a superior court for trial. It is terminated by the imposition of sentence or other disposition of the action—such as outright dismissal of the accusatory instrument—or by court order revoking or vacating the bail, or by surrender of the principal to the court. If the terms of the bond expressly limit its effectiveness to a lesser period, the obligor must provide notice to the court and the prosecutor at least 14 days before the bond's specified expiration date.[44]

Even though not provided for in the court's order, bail may always be posted in the form of cash bail, in whatever amount designated in the order fixing bail.[45] It may be deposited with the County Treasurer (or, in New York City, the Finance Commissioner), with the court that issued the order fixing bail, or with the Sheriff or other correctional official in whose custody the defendant has been placed. Upon deposit of the amount in question, the principal must "forthwith" be released from custody;[46] however, it has been held that the sheriff may not unilaterally do this without court direction or approval.[47]

A person posting cash bail must complete and sign a statutorily prescribed form that is similar to the forms used for bail bonds.[48] Money posted as cash bail remains the property of the person posting it, unless it is forfeited to the court.[49]

Library References:
West's Key No. Digests, Bail ⬦54–73.

§ 4.4 Fixing of Bail—In General

Two articles of the CPL generally establish the structure and authority for the fixing of bail by a court. Article 510 provides the general rules for when bail or other forms of court process are required and the basic criteria to be used in setting bail, while Article 530 establishes which courts may issue bail and limits the authority to do so under certain circumstances. In essence, when "a principal whose future court attendance at a criminal action or proceeding[50] is or may be

---

44. CPL § 520.20(3).
45. CPL § 520.15(1).
46. Id.
47. Matter of Ralys, 156 Misc.2d 268, 592 N.Y.S.2d 572 (Monroe Co.Ct.1992).
48. CPL § 520.10(2). The similarity is intentional, as this provision was part of the legislative attempt to equalize depositors of cash bail and sureties.
49. CPL § 520.10(3). The statutory declaration that cash bail remains the property of the depositor has implications for civil forfeiture. If cash bail posted by a third party were deemed to be the property of the criminal defendant, as was sometimes the case under prior law, the state could attach or otherwise restrain it for forfeiture purposes to satisfy a money judgment against the defendant. CPLR 1312. If it is deemed to be the property of the person who posts it, then it is subject to forfeiture only if that person can be shown to be a "non-criminal defendant." See CPLR 1310(10)(defining such a person as one who takes illicit money with knowledge of its character or under conditions where he or she should have had such knowledge).

50. "Criminal action," and "criminal proceeding" are defined terms, see CPL § 1.20(16) and (18), which, in this context, have been held to include prosecutions for

required, initially comes under the control of a court, such court must, by a securing order, either release the principal on his or her own recognizance, fix bail or commit him or her to the custody of the sheriff."[51] In the usual case, such control is normally first exerted at arraignment.[52] If a securing order is revoked or otherwise terminated, and the principal's attendance is still required, then a new securing order must be issued.[53]

A special rule governs commitment of persons under 16 years of age, who must be taken to and lodged in a facility certified by the State Division for Youth as a juvenile detention facility. The same rule normally precludes detention of such youths in the same place as adults, and also includes a measure designed to insure that absent good cause or consent, a juvenile principal, upon release, is delivered to a specified person or place, rather than simply being released, possibly away from home.[54]

Articles 510 and 520 are not, however, all-encompassing, as other statutes may govern in specific circumstances. For example, a person who has been taken into court for a violation of a condition of a sentence of probation or a sentence of conditional discharge must be brought forthwith to the court that imposed the sentence, which may commit the violator to the custody of the sheriff, or fix bail or release the violator on recognizance.[55] In addition, failure to pay a court-ordered fine may result in imprisonment without bail,[56] as may violation of a court order of protection.[57] It is unclear whether a person who is otherwise entitled to bail or recognizance may be committed without bail pending a psychiatric examination to determine his or her fitness to proceed.[58]

technically non-criminal "violations" (Penal Law § 10.00(3) and (6)), see People v. Ortiz, 75 Misc.2d 997, 349 N.Y.S.2d 944 (N.Y.C.Crim.Ct.1973), but exclude parole revocation hearings. People ex rel. Calloway v. Skinner, 33 N.Y.2d 23, 347 N.Y.S.2d 178, 300 N.E.2d 716 (1973).

51. CPL § 510.10. In Howell v. McGinity, 129 A.D.2d 60, 66, 516 N.Y.S.2d 694, 698 (2d Dep't 1987), a jail overcrowding case, the sheriff refused to take custody of defendants committed to his care by the courts, arguing that the jail was full and that to comply with the securing orders of the state courts would violate a federal consent decree capping prison population. The local courts responded by temporarily housing the prisoners in court detention cells. The Appellate Division held that "ordinarily a court's responsibility for the custody of a prisoner not eligible for release on his or her own recognizance and unable to raise bail ends at the point that the prisoner is remanded to the sheriff's custody and the time reasonably required to effectuate his transfer has passed. From that point on, the sheriff has exclusive responsibility for custody of the prisoner." However, the court also held the brief retention of the prisoners in court custody to have been justified by the extraordinary circumstances.

52. See, CPL §§ 170.10(7), 180.20(6), 210.15(6)(all requiring the court, at arraignment upon various accusatory instruments, to issue an appropriate securing order unless a final disposition of the proceeding is made then and there).

53. CPL § 510.10. When the court terminates a securing order that directs commitment, the court must give written notice to the appropriate correctional official. Id.

54. CPL § 510.15.

55. CPL § 410.60.

56. CPL § 420.10(3).

57. CPL § 530.13(8).

58. See CPL Article 730; see Matter of La Belle, 79 N.Y.2d 350, 360–61, 582 N.Y.S.2d 970, 974–76, 591 N.E.2d 1156, 1160–62 (1992)(issue raised, but not decided).

If circumstances such as these are present when a person is being arraigned on a new charge, as is frequently the case, the court's authority to release the defendant or set bail may be limited. For example, if a person is brought into court on a violation of probation as well as a new, non-felony charge, the latter charge entitles the defendant to bail or recognizance but the former authorizes commitment. Thus, it is important to know all of the circumstances involved when a defendant is brought into court, and the nature of the instant charges, while obviously important, is not necessarily determinative. Further, although recognizance or bail is usually advantageous to a defendant, in some of these situations this is not the case. For example, a defendant arrested upon a new charge and on a parole violation warrant might wish to eschew bail so as to receive maximum jail time credit.[59]

It should also be noted that in most jurisdictions of the state, pretrial service programs screen defendants for potential pretrial release. Typically, these programs will collect, verify, and submit to the court information about the defendant. They may also offer additional services such as phone notification of pending court appearances, and supervision and monitoring of court-ordered release conditions, all of which may induce a court to grant a release that would otherwise be denied. These programs perform a valuable service to both the defendant and the courts.

Library References:

West's Key No. Digests, Bail ⚖46–49; Infants ⚖134.

§ 4.5 Bail Applications and General Criteria

An application for recognizance or bail can be made "upon any occasion when a court is required to issue a securing order . . . or at any time when the principal is confined in the custody of the sheriff as a result of a previously issued securing order."[60] Usually, such applications are made at arraignment. However, it has been held that even without an application, at arraignment a court is required to issue the appropriate securing order, which, in non-felony cases, requires bail or recognizance.[61] Once the bail application is made, the court must afford the movant an opportunity to be heard, and an overly summary rejection of the application is improper.[62]

---

59. See P.L. §§ 70.30(3), 70.40(3)(c).

60. CPL § 510.20(1).

61. See Matter of La Belle, 79 N.Y.2d 350, 357–58, 582 N.Y.S.2d 970, 973–74, 591 N.E.2d 1156, 1159–60 (1992)("while an application may be required in some other procedural settings . . . in the usual case it is plainly the court's duty [per CPL § 170.10(7)] to order bail or recognizance in a nonfelony case at the time the defendant is arraigned").

62. See Becher v. Dunston, 142 Misc.2d 103, 536 N.Y.S.2d 396 (Sup.Ct., Rensselaer County, 1988)(improper to summarily reject bail application on grounds that defendant disobeyed a subpoena). See also Buthy v. Ward, 34 A.D.2d 884, 312 N.Y.S.2d 119 (4th Dep't 1970)(requiring that when issues of fact are raised by a contested application for bail or recognizance, an evidentiary hearing must be held).

It should be noted that, except in situations where new facts come to light and statutory review is authorized,[63] "a fundamental principle of the law governing securing orders is that a judge may not review a determination of bail or recognizance made by a judge of coordinate jurisdiction nunc pro tunc."[64]

The general criteria to be considered by a court in setting bail appear in CPL § 510.30(2)(a). Initially, the statute declares that bail is not always purely a matter of discretion, for other statutes limit the authority of a court to set bail, depending principally upon the level of the charges and the court in which the application is heard. These qualifications are discussed below. To the extent that a court has discretionary authority to grant or deny bail, a standard and a set of criteria are established. The court is directed to "consider the kind and degree of control or restriction that is necessary to secure [the principal's] court attendance when required."[65] In making that determination, the court is further directed to consider and take into account the following list of factors relating to the principal: (i) character, reputation, habits and mental condition; (ii) employment and financial resources; (iii) family ties and length of residence in the community; (iv) criminal record, if any; (v) record of previous adjudications as a juvenile delinquent or youthful offender, if any;[66] (vi) previous record in responding to court appearances or with respect to flight to avoid criminal prosecution; (vii) if the principal is a defendant, the weight of the evidence against him or her in the pending criminal action and any other factor indicating probability or improbability of conviction,[67] or, in the case of an application for bail pending appeal, the merit or lack of merit of the appeal; and (viii) if a defendant, the sentence which may be or has been imposed upon conviction.[68] In the appellate context, bail may be denied solely on the grounds that the appeal is "palpably without merit."[69]

Conspicuous by its absence from either the stated purpose of bail or the list of factors is any specific reference to a defendant's potential danger to the victim or the community—that is, "preventive detention."[70] This is a controversial subject that was settled, at least on the

---

63. See, e.g., CPL §§ 530.30, 530.60.

64. People v. Forman, 145 Misc.2d 115, 546 N.Y.S.2d 755 (N.Y.C.Crim.Ct.1989).

65. CPL § 510.30(2)(a).

66. This factor, CPL 510.30(2)(a)(v), requires that juvenile delinquency records or fingerprints be retained per the Family Court Act (§§ 306.1, 354.2) to qualify for such consideration.

67. It has been generally held that because the statute speaks of "available information," CPL § 530.10(2)(a), "the court is not limited to the consideration of admissible evidence. Indeed, except perhaps for sentencing, it is difficult to imagine a stage of the criminal process when it is more imperative for the court to obtain all relevant information, regardless of admissibility at trial, than at the time bail is set." Brunetti v. Scotti, 77 Misc.2d 388, 390–91, 353 N.Y.S.2d 630, 632–33 (Sup.Ct., N.Y. County, 1974). While there is force to that logic, it should be noted that in dealing with factor (vii), the statute speaks of the "weight of the evidence" against the defendant. This phrase seems to contemplate a weighing of "admissible" evidence.

68. CPL § 510.30(2)(a).

69. CPL § 510.30(2)(b).

70. Sometimes called "preventative" detention. See Application of Miller, 46 A.D.2d 177, 362 N.Y.S.2d 628 (4th Dep't 1974); People ex rel. Shaw v. Lombard, 95 Misc.2d 664, 408 N.Y.S.2d 664 (Monroe Co.

federal level, by the Bail Reform Act of 1984,[71] which allows a federal court to detain a defendant pending trial on the ground of the defendant's potential danger to any person or to the community at large. The Supreme Court has held the act constitutional.[72] In New York, however, the drafters of the CPL specifically excluded a recommended provision that would have allowed for preventive detention in the fixing of bail.[73] Thus, preventive detention as such does not exist in New York, and the denial or fixing of high bail[74] for this sole purpose is clearly improper.[75] What is less clear is whether a court is required entirely to ignore such considerations, at least when presented with a defendant who poses a very high level of risk—for example, a "clear and present danger"—to another person. Such a prohibition sits uneasily with many courts, some of which have held that it is indeed appropriate to take this factor into account, at least in "rare cases."[76] More practically, since a court is vested with wide discretion in setting bail, and "in the view of many, any bail which cannot be met leads to preventive detention,"[77] it is likely that such considerations frequently are accommodated without the court expressly saying so. It is also somewhat curious that the seriousness of the charged offense, a factor often given heavy weight in making bail determinations, is phrased in terms of "the sentence which may be ...

Ct.1978). "Preventive" detention seems to be the more common usage.

71. 18 U.S.C.A. § 3142.

72. United States v. Salerno, 481 U.S. 739, 107 S.Ct. 2095, 95 L.Ed.2d 697 (1987).

73. See Bellacosa, "Practice Commentary," to CPL § 510.30, McKinney's Cons. Laws of New York, Book 11A, at 22–23 (1984). See also People ex rel. Shaw v. Lombard, 95 Misc.2d 664, 408 N.Y.S.2d 664 (Monroe Co.Ct.1978); People ex rel. LaForce v. Skinner, 65 Misc.2d 884, 319 N.Y.S.2d 10 (Sup.Ct., Monroe County, 1971).

74. Under certain circumstances, previously set bail may be revoked for this reason. See § 4.10, supra.

75. People ex rel. Moquin v. Infante, 134 A.D.2d 764, 521 N.Y.S.2d 580 (3d Dep't 1987); People ex rel. Schweizer v. Welch, 40 A.D.2d 621, 336 N.Y.S.2d 556 (4th Dep't 1972); People ex rel. Bauer v. McGreevy, 147 Misc.2d 213, 555 N.Y.S.2d 581 (Sup.Ct., Rensselaer County, 1990). However, it should be noted that the Court of Appeals has held that the pretrial detention of a youth charged as a juvenile delinquent under an authorizing Family Court provision is not constitutionally offensive. People ex rel. Wayburn v. Schupf, 39 N.Y.2d 682, 385 N.Y.S.2d 518, 350 N.E.2d 906 (1976). Thus, the issue is purely statutory, and an adult preventive detention statute, if enacted, would stand a good chance of surviving constitutional attack.

76. See People ex rel. Fruchtman v. Ossakow, 30 N.Y.2d 867, 335 N.Y.S.2d 301, 286 N.E.2d 736 (1972) (affirming dismissal of habeas corpus writ in case involving witness threats); Matter of Wilson, 89 Misc.2d 1046, 393 N.Y.S.2d 275 (Fam.Ct., Onondaga County, 1977); People ex rel. LaForce v. Skinner, 65 Misc.2d 884, 319 N.Y.S.2d 10 (Sup.Ct., Monroe County, 1971); Brunetti v. Scotti, 77 Misc.2d 388, 353 N.Y.S.2d 630 (Sup.Ct., N.Y. County, 1974); People v. Melville, 62 Misc.2d 366, 308 N.Y.S.2d 671 (N.Y.C.Crim.Ct.1970)(all suggesting that it is proper to consider a defendant's potential danger in the rare case, on varying rationales). People v. Melville, supra, offers perhaps the most intriguing suggestion: "[L]ogic dictates that a defendant's potential danger to the community is not considered as a factor in the designation of bail because it is irrelevant to the question of the amount of bail. If a defendant would present a clear and present danger if freed then it would not matter whether he had posted $100,000 or been released on his own recognizance." 62 Misc.2d at 373, 308 N.Y.S.2d at 678. See also People v. Torres, 112 Misc.2d 145, 446 N.Y.S.2d 969 (Sup.Ct., N.Y. County, 1981)(same suggestion).

77. People v. Maldonado, 95 Misc.2d 113, 119, 407 N.Y.S.2d 393, 397 (N.Y.C.Crim.Ct.1978)($500 bail for low-lev-

imposed on conviction."[78]

The court is required by the statute to examine and balance all of the factors.[79] With two exceptions, no one factor is completely determinative. First, the statute itself permits, but does not require, a court considering an application for bail or recognizance on appeal to deny the application solely on the basis that the appeal "is palpably without merit."[80] Second, it has been held that likelihood of a defendant's flight alone is sufficient.[81] However, care should be taken to separate the process from the result. Although the factors must be weighed against one another, it seems reasonable to assume that in non-routine cases one exaggerated factor might suffice to determine the issue. For example, if a defendant's "character, reputation, habits and mental condition"[82] reveal him or her to be a psychopathic professional assassin, few would argue that the denial of bail is improper, even though other factors might weigh for release. Thus, although a court decision that announced such a denial purely for this reason, with no consideration of any other factor, might not survive review,[83] a decision that weighs this factor against the others and concludes that bail is inappropriate would likely be found a proper exercise of discretion.

In practice, particularly in busy jurisdictions, bail or recognizance decisions in routine cases fall into patterns, and local practitioners quickly learn what to expect under any given set of circumstances. These patterns can only become familiar through experience, but a few illustrations may be helpful. In the following cases, bail was held to be not excessive: $500 where the defendant was accused of assault and resisting arrest, although such was beyond the defendant's means;[84] $50,000 on a burglary charge, in a strong case, arising while the defendant was already on bail for another crime, had an extensive criminal record, and faced second felony offender sentencing;[85] and $500,000 where the defendant was shown to be involved in a large scale drug smuggling conspiracy, and his residency was dubious.[86] On the other hand, the following are examples of bail decisions held to be

el assault upheld against claim of preventive detention).

78. CPL § 510.30(2)(a)(viii).

79. CPL § 510.30(2). It should be remembered that these factors are applied in the context of the specific statutes establishing the authority of each court to fix bail under specific circumstances, and govern only those cases in which the court is vested with discretion. Thus, for example, regardless of what a balance of the factors would otherwise dictate, a court cannot release the defendant on bail or recognizance after a conviction for a class A felony (CPL § 530.45(1)).

80. CPL § 510.30(2)(b).

81. People ex rel. Weisenfeld v. Warden, 37 N.Y.2d 760, 374 N.Y.S.2d 631, 337 N.E.2d 140 (1975).

82. CPL § 510.30(2)(a)(i).

83. See, e.g., People ex rel. Yannarilli v. Draxler, 41 A.D.2d 684, 340 N.Y.S.2d 755 (3d Dep't 1973)(denial of application solely because the charge was murder improper). Cf. People ex rel. Benton v. Warden, 118 A.D.2d 443, 499 N.Y.S.2d 738 (1st Dep't 1986)(improper to fix high bail on the basis of length of potential imprisonment and defendant's prior record without consideration of court attendance, residence, and other factors).

84. People v. Maldonado, 95 Misc.2d 113, 407 N.Y.S.2d 393 (N.Y.C.Crim.Ct. 1978).

85. People ex rel. Robinson v. Campbell, 184 A.D.2d 988, 585 N.Y.S.2d 604 (3d Dep't 1992).

86. People ex rel. Washor v. Freckelton, 187 A.D.2d 406, 590 N.Y.S.2d 203 (1st Dep't 1992).

excessive: outright denial of bail for a subway motorman, indicted for multiple counts of murder, assault, and reckless endangerment, who had no prior criminal record and community ties (bail set at $100,000, and conditions imposed);[87] $150,000 for a defendant charged with two heroin sales, who was an employed local resident (remanded for reconsideration);[88] and $25,000 for a defendant charged with multiple counts of criminal possession of stolen property, who was 63, a local homeowner, employed and, although having a prior criminal record, had never missed a court appearance (reduced to $10,000).[89]

When releasing a principle or fixing bail, a court may impose one or more conditions. These are discussed below in connection with modification of bail.

Library References:

West's Key No. Digests, Bail ⚖=41–45, 49.

§ 4.6 Fixing of Bail by Local Criminal Courts

When a criminal action is pending in a local criminal court, that court, upon application of the defendant, *must* order recognizance or bail when the defendant is charged, by information, simplified information, prosecutor's information, or misdemeanor complaint, with an offense or offenses of less than felony grade.[90] A local criminal court *may* order recognizance or bail when the defendant is charged with a felony by felony complaint, except that a city, town, or village court has no authority to do so if the defendant is charged with a Class A felony or appears to have two previous felony convictions.[91] There are two preconditions to such action in felony cases. First, the prosecutor must either be heard, or, after having knowledge or notice and a reasonable opportunity to appear, fails to do so or otherwise waive his or her right to be heard.[92] Second, the court must have been furnished with the appropriate report concerning the defendant's criminal record.[93] This latter requirement may be waived by the prosecutor, or, in an emergency, by the court itself. The defendant is entitled to a copy of the criminal history report.[94]

Library References:

West's Key No. Digests, Bail ⚖=40–43.

§ 4.7 Fixing of Bail by Superior Courts

Bail may be also fixed by a superior court, either when the criminal

87. State ex rel. Ray v. Warden, 184 A.D.2d 477, 585 N.Y.S.2d 424 (1st Dep't 1992).
88. People ex rel. Mordkofsky v. Stancari, 93 A.D.2d 826, 460 N.Y.S.2d 830 (2d Dep't 1983)(case remanded because of a procedural error in the Supreme Court).
89. People ex rel. Benton v. Warden, 118 A.D.2d 443, 499 N.Y.S.2d 738 (1st Dep't 1986).

90. CPL § 530.20(1).
91. CPL § 530.20(2)(a).
92. CPL § 530.20(2)(b)(i).
93. CPL § 530.20(2)(b)(ii).
94. Id.

action is still pending in the local criminal court,[95] or when the criminal action is pending in the superior court itself. As to the former, the defendant may apply for recognizance or bail to a judge of a superior court when the local criminal court "lacks authority to issue the order."[96] Moreover, where recognizance or bail is denied in the local criminal court, or where "excessive" bail has been fixed, the defendant may apply—in effect, appeal—to a superior court judge for release or the fixing of bail "in a lesser amount or in a less burdensome form."[97] Not more than one such application can be made.[98] As with bail in the local criminal court, the prosecutor must be given an opportunity to appear, and the court must be furnished with a criminal history report.[99]

If the action is pending in the superior court—typically, when a defendant has been indicted by the grand jury—the court, after affording the prosecutor an opportunity to be heard and receiving a report of the defendant's criminal history, *must* order bail or recognizance when less than felony-grade offenses are involved, and *may* order recognizance or bail in felony cases.[100] If there is already an order from the local criminal court fixing bail or allowing recognizance, the superior court may direct that it be continued.[101]

Where a superior court orders bail and the defendant has previously posted cash bail pursuant to a local criminal court order, he or she may request that the cash bail be transferred from the local criminal court to the superior court.[102] Bail bonds originally posted when the case is in the local criminal court remain in effect in the superior court, unless expressly limited.[103]

Library References:
West's Key No. Digests, Bail ⟞40–43.

§ 4.8 "Stationhouse" Pre-arraignment Bail

Under certain conditions, the CPL permits, but does not require, a police or peace officer to issue an "appearance ticket" to a person whom the officer may arrest or has arrested for an offense that is either less than Class D felony grade or is not one of six listed Class E felony

---

95. An exception is when the local criminal court is a superior court judge sitting as a local criminal court. CPL § 530.30(1).

96. CPL §§ 530.30(1), 530.20(2)(a). This is applicable where the defendant appears before a city, town, or village court, and is either charged with a Class A felony or has two previous felony convictions. In such circumstances, the local criminal court lacks authority to order bail or recognizance, and accordingly the defendant is given the right to apply to the superior court.

97. CPL § 530.30(1).

98. CPL § 530.30(3).

99. CPL § 530.20(2).

100. CPL § 530.40(1) and (2). However, a defendant who is "convicted"—that is, who has entered a plea of guilty to or been the subject of a verdict of guilty (see CPL § 1.20(13))—upon a Class A felony must be committed or remanded to custody. CPL § 530.40(3).

101. This provision, CPL § 530.40(2), seems to require de novo review where a local criminal court securing order directs a defendant's commitment. If there is a lower court bail or recognizance order, the superior court is not obliged to continue it, but may require a new application. People ex. rel. Bauer on Behalf of Rhodes v. McGreevy, 147 Misc.2d 213, 555 N.Y.S.2d 581 (Sup.Ct., Rensselaer County, 1990).

102. CPL § 520.40.

103. CPL § 520.20(3).

offenses.[104] This is essentially a written notice requiring a person to appear before a local criminal court to answer the charge. The procedure serves as an alternative to arrest, or as an alternative to the requirement that an arrested person be brought before a local criminal court for arraignment.[105] Issuance of an appearance ticket by an officer can be made conditional upon the posting of a sum of money known as "pre-arraignment," or, in the vernacular, "stationhouse" bail.[106] The amount of bail is fixed by a desk officer or superior officer, within statutory maximums: no more than $750 for a class E felony; $500 for a class A misdemeanor; $250 for other misdemeanors; or $100 for petty offenses.[107] For unlicensed motorists charged with traffic infractions, any police officer may fix bail at $50.[108]

Stationhouse bail is posted in cash, except in the case of unlicensed motorists, who must pay by credit card.[109]

Library References:
West's Key No. Digests, Bail ⇒41–43, 48.

§ 4.9 Bail After Conviction and on Appeal

After a defendant is "convicted"—that is, after a plea of guilty or jury verdict, but before sentence[110]—he or she may apply for bail or recognizance pending the determination of an appeal[111] if: (a) the conviction was not for a Class A felony,[112] and (b), a prior order allowing bail or recognizance has been revoked and the defendant has either been remanded or bail has been increased in a more burdensome amount or form—that is, where the trial court has refused to continue previously-set bail or recognizance pending sentence. The application may be made to a justice of the Appellate Division, if the conviction was in Supreme or County Court,[113] or to a superior court if it was in a local criminal court.[114] Only one application can be made, upon reasonable notice to

104. CPL §§ 1.20(26), 140.20(2), 140.27(4) and CPL Article 150. The six listed Class E felonies that preclude the issuance of an appearance ticket are: rape or sodomy in the third degree (P.L. §§ 130.25, 130.40); escape in the second degree (P.L. § 205.10); absconding from temporary release in the first degree (P.L. § 205.17); absconding from a community treatment facility (P.L. § 205.19); and bail jumping in the second degree (P.L. § 215.56).

105. See Chapter 3, §§ 3.24, 3.30.

106. CPL § 150.30.

107. CPL § 150.30(2).

108. CPL § 150.30(3).

109. Id.

110. See CPL § 1.20(13).

111. CPL § 530.45. This section, enacted in 1974, remedied a previously-extant gap in CPL § 460.50, entitled "Stay of judgment pending appeal to intermediate appellate court," which is applicable only after sentence. Under prior law, a defendant remanded after verdict or guilty plea but before sentence had to wait in custody or seek habeas corpus relief. The statute now permits an application to the appellate court at this stage.

112. The restriction for Class A felonies was found constitutional in Matter of Gold v. Shapiro, 62 A.D.2d 62, 403 N.Y.S.2d 906 (2d Dep't), aff'd 45 N.Y.2d 849, 410 N.Y.S.2d 68, 382 N.E.2d 767 (1978), and has been held to apply to all Class A felonies. Rogers v. Leff, 45 A.D.2d 630, 360 N.Y.S.2d 652 (1st Dep't 1974). Cf. People v. Fikaris, 101 Misc.2d 460, 421 N.Y.S.2d 179 (Sup.Ct., N.Y. County, 1979)(bail allowed on resentence following reclassification of Class A–III felony).

113. CPL § 530.45(2)(a).

114. CPL § 530.45(2)(b).

the prosecution.[115] The defendant must allege in the application that he or she intends to appeal to the proper intermediate appellate court, and an appeal must be "taken"—essentially, a proper notice of appeal must be filed—within 30 days of the sentence, or else the court's order granting the application automatically terminates and the defendant must surrender.

Moreover, unless the appeal is "brought to argument or submitted"[116] within 120 days from the filing of the notice of appeal, the order also terminates automatically, unless the appellate court extends both the appeal and the order granting bail or recognizance.[117] If the defendant loses the appeal, the appellate court must remit the case to the sentencing court, which, upon at least two days notice to the defendant and the surety, direct the defendant to surrender.

It should be noted that, in the analogous context of CPL § 460.50, a defendant who has failed to perfect the appeal has an affirmative duty to surrender, and that a defendant receives no jail time credit for elapsed periods after the expiration of the time limit.[118] The same burden, however, does not fall on a defendant who has properly perfected the appeal if there is an affirmance.[119]

After sentence, bail or recognizance pending appeal[120] to the intermediate appellate court is governed by the aforementioned CPL § 460.50, which has similar provisions.[121] If the appeal is to the Appellate Division,[122] the application for a "stay" may be made either to a

---

115. Although only one application can be made at this stage, and a similar provision in CPL § 460.50, effective after sentence, allows only one application at that stage, a defendant is free to make one application under each statute. Accordingly, a defendant who is remanded or ordered to post more onerous bail after verdict or plea but before sentence should seek this relief immediately, and, if it is denied, seek it again under CPL § 460.50 after sentencing.

116. The phrase "brought to argument" also appears in CPL § 460.70, which grants power to the individual Appellate Divisions to set rules governing such matters. It appears to have been drawn from sections 759 and 760 of the former Code of Criminal Procedure, which governed procedure in an era when criminal appeals were rarer and much speedier. In practice, the defendant's obligation is deemed satisfied if he or she perfects the appeal within the prescribed period. See People v. Ridley, 65 Misc.2d 547, 318 N.Y.S.2d 331 (Tompkins Co.Ct.1971)(court delay in calendaring appeal does not affect defendant's status).

117. Under CPL § 530.45(5), although the original order granting bail or recognizance may be issued by a single justice of the Appellate Division, only the full court may extend it, and the applicant must expressly ask for, and receive, an extension of both the time to appeal and the stay. The grant of the former does not automatically grant the latter.

118. People ex rel. McCoy v. Higgins, 177 A.D.2d 1052, 578 N.Y.S.2d 70 (4th Dep't 1991); People v. Clapper, 131 Misc.2d 1079, 502 N.Y.S.2d 919 (Schoharie Co.Ct. 1986).

119. Hooray v. Cummings, 89 A.D.2d 790, 453 N.Y.S.2d 521 (4th Dep't 1982).

120. It should be noted that CPL § 460.50(1)(a), governing appeals to intermediate appellate courts, speaks generally of an appeal from a "judgment or sentence," while CPL § 460.60(1)(a), the statute governing appeals to the Court of Appeals, speaks generally of an appeal from "a judgment including a sentence of imprisonment [or] a sentence of imprisonment." This may well support an argument that the higher court lacks the authority to stay a non-incarceratory sentence, such as a fine.

121. CPL § 530.50 cross-references this statute and again bars the application in cases in which the conviction was for a Class A felony. In such cases, bail or recognizance is unobtainable.

122. See CPL § 460.50(2); see also CPL § 450.60, entitled "Appeal to intermediate appellate court; to what court taken."

justice of the appropriate Appellate Division, or to a justice of the Supreme Court, or, in the case of a conviction entered in County Court, to a judge of that court. There is no requirement that an application to the Supreme or County Court be made to the judge before whom the conviction was had, and forum shopping is therefore possible.[123] In this regard, however, it might be noted that although this statute, like CPL § 530.45, allows only one application,[124] a sometimes employed tactic is to informally sound out the trial judge concerning this relief, and if he or she appears unreceptive, follow up with a formal application in the Appellate Division, thus gaining in effect a second bite of the apple. Of course, counsel who chooses this course runs several risks. The trial judge may simply refuse to discuss the matter without a formal application, in which case the die must be cast, or if counsel receives a negative signal and proceeds in the Appellate Division, he or she may be met with an argument that a previous application has been made and denied, barring another. On a related note, the Court of Appeals has held that a trial court has no jurisdiction to consider an application made before the filing of a notice of appeal.[125]

Although applications for appellate bail are generally determined according to the same criteria governing other bail applications, it should be remembered that a special rule applicable only in the appellate context allows, but does not require, the denial of the application solely on the basis that the appeal is "palpably without merit."[126]

If the appeal is to the Appellate Term, the application is to a justice of the Supreme Court, while if the appeal is to the County Court, administrative rules determine the appropriate forum for the application.[127] The application must be on reasonable notice to the prosecution. As discussed above in connection with CPL § 530.45, the stay terminates automatically if the appeal is not perfected, and an affirmance of the appeal triggers notice and surrender procedures.

Generally speaking, appeals from convictions in the County or Supreme Court go to the Appellate Division, appeals from convictions in the New York City Criminal Court go to the Appellate Term of the Supreme Court (which has been established in both the First and Second Judicial Departments), and appeals from local criminal courts outside New York City go either to the County Court or to the Appellate Term, if one has been established.

123. See People v. Meredith, 152 Misc.2d 387, 578 N.Y.S.2d 79 (Sup.Ct., Kings County, 1991)(judge may not transfer application to trial judge). Note, however, that while a defendant convicted in the Supreme Court (primarily in New York City) has only two choices—the Appellate Division or the Supreme Court—a person convicted in County Court has three—the Appellate Division, Supreme Court or County court. The flexibility is probably designed to accommodate local conditions, and local practice as to such applications may vary.

124. As previously noted, this is not a bar where a previous application has been made under CPL § 530.45 after conviction but before sentence.

125. Matter of Morgenthau v. Rosenberger, 86 N.Y.2d 826, 633 N.Y.S.2d 473, 657 N.E.2d 494 (1995).

126. CPL § 510.30(2)(b).

127. 22 NYCRR § 200.31, that part of the Uniform Rules for State trial courts governing appeals to the County Court, provides that the stay "may be issued by a judge of the county court to which the appeal is taken or a justice of the supreme court in the judicial district in which the local court is located. In the case of an appeal as of right from a judgment or sentence of a city court, such order may also be issued by a judge of such city court."

After an affirmance of the judgment of conviction by the intermediate appellate court, normally the defendant's last resort is an appeal by permission to the Court of Appeals. In provisions that are substantially similar to those discussed above, CPL § 460.60 allows for a stay of the intermediate appellate court judgment and bail or recognizance pending appeal to the Court of Appeals. Only a judge empowered to grant leave to appeal to that court may grant the application.[128] The statute allows the judge considering the application for leave to appeal to grant what amounts to a temporary stay while he or she considers whether to grant leave to appeal and bail or recognizance until the Court of Appeals decides the case. This was the result of a statutory amendment designed to smooth over a rough spot in appellate practice—the gap between the intermediate appellate affirmance, which results in mandatory surrender in the trial court, and the time it normally takes to consider whether to grant leave to the Court of Appeals. In former practice, the granting of the stay and bail or recognizance was contingent upon granting leave to appeal, thus putting pressure on both the Court of Appeals judge who had the leave application and the trial judge who had the surrender, neither of whom was apparently authorized to act until the former granted leave. The amendment has helped, but may not have entirely eliminated the problem. Accordingly, at least in situations where the mandatory surrender is set for a date prior to or contemporaneous with the earliest point at which counsel can make application for leave to appeal, it may be wise to ask the trial court to postpone the surrender date. Moreover, this is best done before the actual surrender itself, as some trial judges may take the position that the statute gives them no discretion to do anything but commit the defendant once he or she is before them.[129]

Library References:
West's Key No. Digests, Bail ⚖=44.

§ 4.10 Bail and Recognizance Conditions and Modification

A court releasing a principal may attach certain conditions to that release. Curiously, the relevant statutes, with certain exceptions, are silent on the question of what conditions may be attached,[130] although it

---

128. CPL §§ 460.60(1), 460.20. Only a judge of the Court of Appeals itself, or, if the appeal is from an order of the Appellate Division, a justice of that court, may grant such permission. Routine practice is to make the application to a judge of the Court of Appeals unless there was a dissenter in the Appellate Division, in which case the odds favor the latter.

129. For example, CPL § 460.50(5) provides that upon affirmance, the intermediate appellate court must remit the case to the trial court, which "must, upon at least two days notice to the defendant, his surety and his attorney, promptly direct the defendant to surrender himself to the criminal court in order that execution of the judgment be commenced or resumed." Thus, although it remains possible to argue that the trial court, which has inherent power to control its own calendar, may nevertheless adjourn a surrender which is actually before it, postponing the original surrender date may seem more palatable.

130. CPL § 510.30 speaks only to the condition that the principal commit no additional felony while out on bail. Cf. CPL § 30.30(2)(requiring that a committed defendant be released "on bail or on his own recognizance, upon such conditions as may

has been held that there is inherent power in a court to set such conditions.[131] CPL § 510.30(3) requires a court to inform a defendant charged with the commission of a felony that the release is conditional and that if the defendant commits another felony while at liberty, the court's previous order may be revoked.

Another statutory bail condition is the "temporary order of protection" (commonly referred to as a TOP), which may be imposed in cases involving either family[132] or non-family[133] offenses. The former is defined as a criminal action involving "a complaint charging any crime or violation between spouses, parent and child, or between members of the same family or household."[134] In such cases, a court, as a condition of an order of bail or recognizance,[135] may issue a TOP that, in addition to any other conditions, may require the defendant to: (a) stay away from the home, school, business or place of employment of the family or household member; (b) permit a parent (or other person entitled to visitation) to visit the child at stated periods; (c) refrain from committing a "family offense"[136] against the child or family or household member or any person to whom custody of the child has been awarded, or from harassing, intimidating or threatening such person; or (d) refrain from acts of commission or omission that create an unreasonable risk to the health, safety and welfare of a child or family or household member.[137]

In making the determination to issue a "stay away" order, the court is directed, but not limited, to consider "whether the temporary order of protection is likely to achieve its purpose in the absence of such a condition, conduct subject to prior orders of protection, prior incidents of abuse, past or present injury, threats, drug or alcohol abuse, and access

be just and reasonable" if the prosecution is not ready for trial within certain periods). Interestingly, the comparable federal statute, 18 U.S.C.A. § 1342(c), is far more specific. In addition to the prohibition against the commission of another offense, the federal statute enumerates 14 conditions. These range from restrictions on a defendant's travel, associations, possession of firearms or use of alcohol or drugs, to requirements that he or she maintain employment, undergo medical or psychiatric treatment, commence an educational program, or report regularly to law enforcement. The last specified condition is a catch-all: a released defendant may be required to "satisfy any other condition that is reasonably necessary to assure the appearance of the person as required and to assure the safety of any other person and the community." 18 U.S.C.A. § 3142(c)(B)(xiv).

131. People v. Forman, 145 Misc.2d 115, 546 N.Y.S.2d 755 (N.Y.C.Crim.Ct. 1989); People ex rel. Shaw v. Lombard, 95 Misc.2d 664, 408 N.Y.S.2d 664 (Monroe Co. Ct.1978).

132. CPL § 530.12.

133. CPL § 530.13.

134. CPL § 530.12(1). The phrase "members of the same family or household" is further defined in CPL § 530.11(1) to mean persons: (a) related by consanguinity or affinity; (b) legally married to one another; (c) formerly married to one another; or (d) who have a child in common, regardless whether such persons have been married or have lived together at any time. In addition, CPL § 530.12(13) allows a protective order to issue "against a former spouse and persons who have a child in common, regardless whether such persons have been married or have lived together at any time."

135. Pursuant to the statute, orders of protection may also be issued as a condition of an adjournment in contemplation of dismissal or upon conviction. CPL §§ 170.55(3), 530.12(5), 530.13(4). They are "temporary" when issued during the pendency of the action. CPL §§ 530.12(1), 530.13(1).

136. "Family offenses" are defined in CPL § 530.11(1).

137. CPL § 530.12(1)(a)-(d).

§ 4.10 BAIL & RECOGNIZANCE Ch. 4

to weapons."[138] This determination should be on the record or in writing. In general, the court may issue the order *ex parte*, "for good cause shown,"[139] and, with the consent of the complainant, may modify such an order issued by the Family Court.[140] The defendant must receive notice of the contents of the order.[141] Violation of an order of protection, in addition to providing the basis for a contempt prosecution,[142] authorizes the court to revoke bail or recognizance and commit the defendant.[143]

In non-family offense cases, a separate statute, similarly structured, allows the court to issue a TOP requiring the defendant to (a) stay away from the home, school, business, or place of employment of the victim of, or designated witnesses to, the offense in question, or (b) refrain from harassing, intimidating, threatening or otherwise interfering with the victim of the offense in question, members of the victim's family or household, or designated witnesses named by the court.[144]

The absence of procedural guidance in the protective order statutes has caused the courts a good deal of concern. In *People v. Forman*,[145] the court addressed several constitutional challenges, the primary one being that due process requires an adversary hearing before a court can issue a TOP excluding the defendant from the home. The court, reading the order of protection statute in tandem with CPL § 510.20(2), which

138. CPL § 530.12(1)(a).

139. See People v. Hayday, 144 A.D.2d 207, 534 N.Y.S.2d 521 (3d Dep't 1988)("good cause" for issuance of order found based on evidence before the grand jury).

140. In general, pursuant to CPL § 530.11(1) and (2)(a), an action based on a family offense may be commenced and thereafter proceed in either the Family or a criminal court, primarily at the option of the complainant. Orders of protection can also be issued by the Family Court under its own applicable statutes.

141. CPL § 530.12(8) requires the clerk of the court to furnish a copy of the order to the defendant and defense counsel, as well as other affected parties, although notice on the record has been held sufficient. The Court of Appeals has held, however, that to support a contempt proceeding for violation of the order, there must be proof that the defendant received actual notice of the contents of the prohibitions contained in the order. People v. McCowan, 85 N.Y.2d 985, 629 N.Y.S.2d 163, 652 N.E.2d 909 (1995).

142. Such violations may be prosecuted as criminal contempt under the Penal Law or as so-called "criminal" contempt under Judiciary Law § 750(A). See, e.g., People v. Halper, 209 A.D.2d 637, 619 N.Y.S.2d 308 (2d Dep't 1994)(Penal Law prosecution permissible, although the court that issued the order does not lose jurisdiction). A recent amendment to the crime of criminal contempt under the Penal Law creates a specific class E felony for such violations, P.L. § 215.51(b). It has been held that each separate failure to obey the order may serve as the basis for a separate contempt. Camille A. v. David A, 162 Misc.2d 22, 615 N.Y.S.2d 584 (Fam.Ct., Queens County, 1994).

143. CPL § 530.12(11)(a). Commitment is authorized for a violation of an order of protection even in cases where the defendant would otherwise be entitled to bail or recognizance as a matter of right. Cf. CPL § 530.60(1)(defendant otherwise entitled to bail or recognizance as of right continues to enjoy that status even after revocation of original order). The court may also revoke a defendant's license to carry firearms under certain conditions. CPL § 530.12(11)(e).

144. CPL § 530.13(1). There are some differences between the two statutes, and because it is a precondition to the issuance of an order of protection under this statute that no such order be issued under section 530.12 (see CPL § 530.13(1)), situations may arise when a court is forced to choose between the two. However, both statutes permit imposition of "any other conditions" than those specified, and this may ameliorate any such problem.

145. 145 Misc.2d 115, 546 N.Y.S.2d 755 (N.Y.C.Crim.Ct.1989).

requires that a principal seeking recognizance or bail be accorded an opportunity to be heard, concluded that four procedural safeguards were necessary: (1) a probable cause determination must be made by a judicial officer, based on a verified complaint containing facts of an evidentiary character providing reasonable cause to believe that a crime has been committed; (2) the defendant is entitled to a presentation of reasons for the issuance of such a TOP by the prosecution and through counsel to be heard in opposition to its issuance; (3) before issuing the TOP as a condition of bail or release the court must be satisfied that there is a danger of injury or intimidation to the complainant; and (4) the defendant has a right to a prompt evidentiary hearing following the issuance of a TOP.[146]

Although the *Forman* conditions make good sense, and fill the void created by the regrettable absence of procedural guidance in the statute itself, they may go further than what is constitutionally necessary, particularly in cases involving orders that do not bar the defendant from his or her own home or property.[147] Post-*Forman*, at least one higher court has held that a Family Court TOP directing the respondent to refrain from harassing, menacing, and assaultive behavior and to stay away from portions of commercial property, that was entered *ex parte* and without a fact-finding hearing, was not constitutionally offensive.[148]

It has been held that a court may issue an order of protection directing a defendant to stay away from a domestic partner despite the existence of a superior court grant of visitation rights entered in civil proceedings,[149] and that TOP's issued in the lower courts survive despite the defendant's release pursuant to CPL § 180.80[150] or the referring of the case for action by the grand jury.[151]

Other more general bail conditions are not provided for by statute, but are said to be within the court's inherent power to impose. These include requiring the principal to surrender a passport, remain within the court's jurisdiction, waive extradition, periodically report to the local

---

146. Prior to Foreman, some courts had held that although a TOP could be issued without a hearing, a defendant was constitutionally entitled to a hearing on a post-arraignment application to vacate or modify a TOP barring him or her from the home. People v. Derisi, 110 Misc.2d 718, 442 N.Y.S.2d 908 (Dist.Ct., Suffolk County, 1981); People v. Faieta, 109 Misc.2d 841, 440 N.Y.S.2d 1007 (Dist.Ct., Nassau County, 1981).

147. Deprivation of property without a prior hearing has historically been of constitutional concern. See, e.g., Sniadach v. Family Finance Corp., 395 U.S. 337, 89 S.Ct. 1820, 23 L.Ed.2d 349 (1969)(garnishment of wages without hearing improper). Obviously, some forms of protective order, such as an order directing the defendant to stay away from his or her home, involve this consideration. Others, such as an order to refrain from visiting certain public places, may involve a lesser degree of intrusion into protected conduct, while still others, such as an order to refrain from assaulting a witness, may not involve this sort of constitutional concern.

148. Matter of Nadeau v. Sullivan, 204 A.D.2d 913, 612 N.Y.S.2d 501 (3d Dep't 1994); See also People v. Hayday, 144 A.D.2d 207, 208, 534 N.Y.S.2d 521, 522 (3d Dep't 1988).

149. People v. Duignan, 104 Misc.2d 351, 432 N.Y.S.2d 291 (N.Y.C.Crim.Ct. 1980).

150. Matter of Luster v. Howard, 123 Misc.2d 410, 473 N.Y.S.2d 750 (Tompkins Co.Ct.1984).

151. People v. Murphy, 154 Misc.2d 777, 586 N.Y.S.2d 716 (Monroe Co.Ct.1992).

police,[152] enroll in an alcohol rehabilitation program, surrender a driver's license or refrain from driving.[153] On the other hand, it has been held improper to require the principal to take and pass an AIDS test,[154] or to impose a curfew that, under the circumstances, was tantamount to preventive detention.[155]

The absence of specific statutory guidance in this area requires the courts to guess about the extent and limits of their so-called inherent power to set such conditions. To date, those guesses seem not to have produced any particularly unfortunate results. Ironically, however, one possible source of difficulty may be New York's statutory insistence that the sole purpose of bail is to insure the court appearance of the defendant,[156] as contrasted, for example, with the analogous federal statute's inclusion of the consideration that bail conditions also relate to whether release will "endanger the safety of any other person or the community."[157] Thus, while a curfew is a specifically authorized federal release condition,[158] it would not be, as noted above, a permissible condition in New York. Other conditions, such as requiring that the defendant refrain from possessing a firearm, are obviously relevant to the purposes of the federal statute, but, although few would contend that this is an undesirable or onerous condition, as a matter of theory it may be difficult to argue that it relates to insuring a court appearance.[159] Still other conditions, such as enrollment in a substance abuse program, while apparently authorized both federally and in New York,[160] present something of a mixed bag in terms of underlying purpose. Of course, it is not necessary to re-open the entire preventive detention debate to ameliorate this situation. Enacting a list of specified permissible conditions without broadening the general purposes of bail might raise a minor question of philosophical consistency, but added guidance and flexibility on the subject of bail conditions would be worth it.

Bail or recognizance, once fixed, can be modified or revoked, pursuant to CPL § 530.60. The structure of that statute, however, raises a problem. The statute is divided into two parts. Subdivision one generally provides that whenever a defendant is at liberty as a result of a court

152. People ex rel. Tannuzzo v. New York City, 174 A.D.2d 443, 571 N.Y.S.2d 230 (1st Dep't 1991); People ex rel. Lazer v. Warden, 173 A.D.2d 425, 571 N.Y.S.2d 441 (1st Dep't), rev'd on other grounds 79 N.Y.2d 839, 580 N.Y.S.2d 183, 588 N.E.2d 81 (1992).

153. Matter of Buckson v. Harris, 145 A.D.2d 883, 536 N.Y.S.2d 219 (3d Dep't 1988); People ex rel. Moquin v. Infante, 134 A.D.2d 764, 521 N.Y.S.2d 580 (3d Dep't 1987).

154. People ex rel. Glass v. McGreevy, 134 Misc.2d 1085, 514 N.Y.S.2d 622 (Sup. Ct., Rensselaer County, 1987).

155. People ex rel. Shaw v. Lombard, 95 Misc.2d 664, 408 N.Y.S.2d 664 (Monroe Co. Ct.1978).

156. CPL § 510.30(2)(a).

157. 18 U.S.C.A. § 1342(c).

158. 18 U.S.C.A. § 1342(c)(B)(vii).

159. Although possession of a firearm could facilitate a defendant's suicide or injury and thus literally prevent a court appearance, in People ex rel. Bryce v. Infante, 144 A.D.2d 898, 899, 535 N.Y.S.2d 215, 216 (3d Dep't 1988), the court stated: "It could be argued that suicide is the surest 'escape' from prosecution, but, in our view, a suicidal tendency cannot be equated with an intent to flee or abscond in the context of a bail application."

160. 18 U.S.C.A. § 1342(c)(B)(x)(medical, psychological, drug or alcohol treatment); People ex rel. Moquin v. Infante, supra (alcohol rehabilitation treatment).

order of bail or recognizance, "and the court considers it necessary to review such order, it may, and by a bench warrant[161] if necessary, require the defendant to appear before the court. Upon such appearance, the court, for good cause shown, may revoke the order of recognizance or bail."[162]

Subdivision two, added in 1981,[163] and thereafter expanded,[164] is a limited form of preventive detention. It provides that when a defendant charged with a felony is at liberty on bail or recognizance, "it shall be grounds for revoking such order that the court finds reasonable cause to believe the defendant *committed one or more specified class A or violent felony offenses or intimidated a victim or witness in violation of sections 215.15, 215.16, or 215.17 of the penal law while at liberty.*"[165] The subdivision goes on to detail the procedure that must be followed by a court in revoking bail on this basis. A hearing must be held, based on "relevant, admissible evidence, not legally privileged."[166] Grand jury testimony (presumably relating to the subsequent offense) is admissible.[167] Thereafter, revocation of the prior order and commitment is authorized only for a number of specified time periods, essentially until either the original or subsequent charges have been reduced to non-felonies or less than Class A or violent felonies, or 90 days, whichever comes first. A defendant may be committed for 72 hours pending the revocation hearing.[168]

The obvious question concerns the relationship of subdivision one to subdivision two: did the Legislature intend to restrict the power of a court to find "good cause" for bail revocation for commission of a subsequent crime only to those situations encompassed within the very limited conditions of the second subdivision—an original felony, followed by commission of a class A or violent felony? There is a split of opinion on the issue.[169] Analysis is not helped by the statute's failure to detail

161. A bench warrant is a form of court ordered process directing a police officer or other authorized official to take into custody a person who has previously been arraigned, for the purpose of achieving the court appearance of that person. CPL §§ 1.20(30), 530.70.

162. CPL § 530.60(1).

163. L.1981, c.788, § 2.

164. L.1986, c.794, § 3.

165. CPL § 530.60(2)(emphasis supplied).

166. Hearsay is inadmissible and simple prosecutorial allegations are insufficient. People v. Silvestri, 132 Misc.2d 1015, 506 N.Y.S.2d 251 (Sup.Ct., Kings County, 1986). Interestingly, general revocation applications under subdivision one of the statute do not contain this provision, and although courts will not revoke or modify bail under that provision without affording the defendant an opportunity to be heard, it is unclear whether these specific rules are meant to apply to such proceedings.

167. An in camera inspection of the grand jury presentation on the subsequent offense is not, however, a sufficient "hearing." People v. Warden, 113 A.D.2d 116, 495 N.Y.S.2d 373 (1st Dep't 1985).

168. If the defendant is in custody on the subsequent charge, the 72-hour period has been held inapplicable. People v. Bailey, 118 Misc.2d 860, 462 N.Y.S.2d 94 (Sup. Ct., Bronx County, 1983).

169. Cf. People v. Saulnier, 129 Misc.2d 151, 492 N.Y.S.2d 897 (Sup.Ct., N.Y. County, 1985)(subdivision two limits court) with People v. Torres, 112 Misc.2d 145, 446 N.Y.S.2d 969 (Sup.Ct., N.Y. County, 1981)(subdivision two inapplicable where original charge was misdemeanor, but no limit on court's power to revoke); People v. Silvestri, 132 Misc.2d 1015, 506 N.Y.S.2d 251 (Sup.Ct., Kings County, 1986)(subdivision two to be applied "cautiously" and in

§ 4.10   BAIL & RECOGNIZANCE   Ch. 4

the relationship between the two subdivisions and failure to specify whether the purpose of revocation under subdivision two is still to ensure the appearance of the defendant.[170] Moreover, the warning required by CPL § 510.30(3), which was added at the same time as and cross-references subdivision two, also fails to shed any light on the matter.[171]

Logic would seem to favor the argument for subsumption; in an area of law that is almost purely statutory, it would seem irrational to enact an extremely limited and cautious bail revocation mechanism, full of procedural safeguards,[172] if a court could entirely avoid the issue and order revocation for any new crime under subdivision one. On the other hand, if subdivision two provides the only basis for revocation upon commission of a new crime or witness threat, its limits seem excessive. In any event, as a practical matter a defendant who commits a second serious crime while on bail, particularly one that qualifies for revocation of bail under subdivision two, is unlikely to be at liberty pursuant to the securing order issued in the second offense,[173] so the question may be somewhat academic.

More generally, it has been held that "good cause" for revocation "is not synonymous with new information; rather, it is more broad, encompassing any substantial reason why bail should be revoked, or not have been granted."[174] Violation of an order of protection,[175] or, of course, flight, are common illustrations. The ultimate sanction for the former is a contempt prosecution, while the latter may lead to criminal prosecution for the offense of bail jumping.[176]

Even if the court revokes the original order, in cases where the defendant "is entitled to bail or recognizance as a matter of right, the court must issue another such order." Thus, for example, where the charged offense is a misdemeanor, a valid revocation of bail must

limited fashion, but does not limit subdivision one).

170. There is no specific reference to the purpose of revocation in either subdivision. Presumably, it is to ensure the defendant's court appearance, which is the stated purpose of all bail in New York. See CPL § 510.30(2)(a). The statement in subdivision two that the commission of the specified felonies "shall be grounds" for revocation is ambiguous. On the one hand, it is not the true "protection of any person" of preventive detention. On the other hand, there is no requirement that the court consider the other factors of CPL § 510.30. If the two subdivisions had clearly different purposes, this might support an argument that one does not subsume the other.

171. Notably, the warning, which advises a defendant of the possibility of revocation pursuant to subdivision two, refers only to the commission of a "subsequent felony."

172. Another question is whether the procedural safeguards are applicable to subdivision one, which apparently contemplates only a summary hearing of the ordinary sort applicable to all bail applications under CPL § 510.20. If subdivision one is independent of subdivision two, the anomaly could result that a defendant who commits a less egregious offense might lose his or her freedom pending trial more readily and with less procedural protection than would a Class A felon under subdivision two.

173. See, e.g., People v. Bailey, 118 Misc.2d 860, 462 N.Y.S.2d 94 (Sup.Ct., Bronx County, 1983).

174. People v. Torres, 112 Misc.2d 145, 446 N.Y.S.2d 969 (Sup.Ct., N.Y. County, 1981).

175. People v. Stevens, 113 Misc.2d 407, 506 N.Y.S.2d 995 (Oswego City Ct.1986).

176. P.L. §§ 215.55—215.57.

nevertheless be followed by another order of bail or recognizance, presumably with more stringent conditions.[177]

Library References:

West's Key No. Digests, Bail ⚛40, 42.5, 44, 73.1.

§ 4.11 Examination of Sufficiency of Bail

Following the posting of a bail bond or cash bail, the court is empowered to conduct an inquiry "for the purpose of determining the reliability of the obligors or person posting cash bail, the value and sufficiency of any security offered, and whether any feature of the undertaking contravenes public policy."[178] In cases involving cash bail, the court, before it may conduct such an inquiry, must have reasonable cause to believe that the person posting cash bail is not in rightful possession of the money or that the cash constitutes the fruits of criminal or unlawful conduct.[179]

The statute expressly permits, but does not limit, the court's inquiry. The inquiry may include an examination of the background, character, and reputation of any obligor, surety-obligor, or executing agent, any person who indemnifies any obligor or any person who posts cash bail; the inquiry may also explore the source of any deposited money or property, of any property delivered as indemnification on a bond, or of money posted as cash bail, to determine whether it is the fruit of criminal or unlawful conduct.[180] The court may examine persons under oath, and the prosecutor has the right to participate.[181] Following the inquiry, the court must issue an order approving or disapproving the bail.[182]

The court's authority under the statute has been characterized as one of "substantial discretion."[183] A good example is *People v. Esquivel*,[184] where the court rejected a bail bond supported by collateral of lawful origins on the ground that the providers of that collateral had been either threatened or bribed into providing it. The case involved a couple who had pledged their home with a bond company as collateral for the bail bond of the defendant, who had been charged with possession of a substantial quantity of narcotics, and whose bail was fixed at $125,000. The collateral providers were barely acquainted with the defendant. Questioned on the witness stand concerning this willingness to risk the family home, one of the providers, in the words of the court "did not appear overly concerned and responded that all he expected

---

177. See Matter of La Belle, 79 N.Y.2d 350, 582 N.Y.S.2d 970, 591 N.E.2d 1156 (1992)(criticizing trial court for, inter alia, not following statute).

178. CPL § 520.30(1).

179. In cases involving cash bail, an inquiry is authorized only if the prosecutor requests one.

180. CPL § 530.30(1).

181. CPL § 530.30(2).

182. CPL § 530.30(3).

183. Matter of Johnson v. Crane, 171 A.D.2d 537, 568 N.Y.S.2d 22 (1st Dep't 1991).

184. 158 Misc.2d 720, 601 N.Y.S.2d 541 (Sup.Ct., N.Y. County, 1993).

§ 4.11   BAIL & RECOGNIZANCE   Ch. 4

from the defendant was 'a thank you or something'."[185] After noting that the defendant bore the ultimate burden of persuasion by a preponderance of the evidence, the court held that although the collateral was lawfully the property of its providers, and there was no actual evidence of threats or improper collusion, public policy justified rejection of the bond: "Where a court believes that an indemnitor has been bribed or coerced to put up collateral, there is no assurance that the threat of forfeiture of that collateral will inhibit a defendant's flight."[186]

Esquivel, which has been criticized,[187] certainly represents an expansive application of the statute. Other illustrations include: disapproval of bail where a minister, in violation of corporate powers, pledged church funds as indemnification for the bond of a church member;[188] disapproval where the money pledged as collateral on a bail bond was the same as the cash bail previously rejected as fruit of criminal conduct;[189] and disapproval where there was a failure to provide sufficient property to meet the definition of a "fully secured bond."[190]

Library References:

West's Key No. Digests, Bail ⟺50–73.

§ 4.12 Forfeiture of Bail and Remission

"Forfeiture" of bail generally occurs "if, without sufficient excuse,"[191] a principal does not appear before the court when required[192] or otherwise does not render himself or herself amenable to the processes of the court. In such circumstances, the court in which bail was posted

---

185. 158 Misc.2d at 722, 568 N.Y.S.2d at 542.

186. 158 Misc.2d at 731, 568 N.Y.S.2d at 547.

187. See Note, 68 St. John's L.Rev. 297 (1994)(arguing that Esquivel improperly allocated the burden to defendant and may have extended the inquiry beyond what CPL § 520.30 permits).

188. In re CPL Inquiry, 78 Misc.2d 244, 356 N.Y.S.2d 749 (Sup.Ct., Bronx County, 1974).

189. Matter of Johnson v. Crane, 171 A.D.2d 537, 568 N.Y.S.2d 22 (1st Dep't 1991).

190. People v. Meredith, 152 Misc.2d 387, 578 N.Y.S.2d 79 (Sup.Ct., Kings County, 1991).

191. Some sufficient excuses are: hospitalization (although medical documentation must be sufficient), Matter of Indemnity Ins. Co. v. People, 133 A.D.2d 345, 519 N.Y.S.2d 244 (2d Dep't 1987); and deportation and exclusion from the country, People v. Alvarez, 94 Misc.2d 334, 404 N.Y.S.2d 509 (Sup.Ct., Queens County, 1978). Imprisonment in another state may or may not be an excuse. Cf. People v. Stuyvesant Ins. Co., 24 A.D.2d 989, 265 N.Y.S.2d 268 (2d Dep't 1965), aff'd 21 N.Y.2d 907, 289 N.Y.S.2d 624, 236 N.E.2d 857 (1968) with People v. Hernandez, 15 A.D.2d 798, 224 N.Y.S.2d 703 (2d Dep't 1962). Mistake or misunderstandings are ordinarily not an excuse. People v. Peerless Ins. Co., 21 A.D.2d 609. 253 N.Y.S.2d 91 (1st Dep't 1964).

192. If the person in question does not receive proper notice that his or her attendance is required, bail cannot be forfeited. See People v. Salabarria, 121 A.D.2d 438, 503 N.Y.S.2d 411 (2d Dep't 1986)(defendant's case placed on "appeals calendar" of trial court while prosecution successfully appealed suppression motion; bail improperly forfeited when case was restored to trial court calendar without notice to defendant). However, if the defendant contributes to the problem, this may not be a sufficient excuse. See People v. Scalise, 105 A.D.2d 869, 482 N.Y.S.2d 362 (3d Dep't 1984)(notice given to defendant's telephone answering machine found sufficient, in a case where defendant's whereabouts and actions were dubious).

"must enter such facts upon the minutes" and bail is thereupon forfeited.[193]

The procedure for bail forfeiture varies, depending upon the nature of the charges and the court in which the bail was posted. If bail was posted in a city court, town court or village court, and no felony is charged, CPL § 540.20 governs the procedure. Otherwise, CPL § 540.10 is applicable. The latter provides that once bail is forfeited—which occurs when the facts of the defendant's non-appearance are entered on the minutes[194]—the court may "discharge" (*i.e.*, overturn) the forfeiture, on "such terms as are just," if the principal appears at any time before the final adjournment of the court. If this does not happen, and the bail was posted as cash bail, then the procedure calls for the local treasurer to give written notice of the forfeiture to the person who posted the cash bail,[195] and, after the latter of the final adjournment of the court or 45 days, convert the money.[196] If the bail was posted in the form of a bond, the prosecution must take certain procedural steps to docket the forfeiture, obtain a judgment, and proceed against the obligors of the bond.[197] This must be done within 60 days of the court's adjournment.[198] It has been held that the failure of the prosecution to proceed within this period precludes the government's recovery on the bail bond.[199]

A separate statute, CPL § 540.20, governs in non-felony cases pending in city, town, or village courts, because of the need to allocate the resulting funds among competing governmental entities. Again, however, cash bail is simply forfeited, while forfeiture of bail bonds requires an action, brought in this context by local financial officers.

Once there has been a forfeiture of bail, CPL § 540.30 provides a mechanism for remission.[200] The application must be made to a superior

---

193. CPL § 540.10(1).

194. People v. Midland Ins. Co., 97 Misc.2d 341, 411 N.Y.S.2d 521 (Sup.Ct., Bronx County, 1978); People v. Brown, 96 Misc.2d 127, 408 N.Y.S.2d 927 (Sup.Ct., Queens County, 1978).

195. It has been held that if the person who posted the cash bail had actual notice of the forfeiture, failure to give written notice is of no moment. People v. Williams, 134 Misc.2d 860, 512 N.Y.S.2d 1007 (Schoharie Co.Ct.1987).

196. CPL § 540.10(2).

197. CPL § 540.10(2) and (3). The prosecutor must file a copy of the bond and the court's forfeiture order with the county clerk, who must docket the matter and enter a judgment, which may thereafter be executed.

198. CPL § 540.10(2).

199. People v. Schonfeld, 74 N.Y.2d 324, 547 N.Y.S.2d 266, 546 N.E.2d 395 (1989). In the words of a subsequent interpretation, "The *Schonfeld* Court has thus made the People's compliance with the statute's 60–day rule a condition precedent to the recovery of forfeiture judgments." Matter of International Fidelity Ins. Co. v. People, 208 A.D.2d 837, 618 N.Y.S.2d 566 (2d Dep't 1994). That case further held that the surety's failure to move to preclude enforcement of the forfeiture judgments for more than a year after they were entered was irrelevant.

200. In some jurisdictions, an additional remedy, known colloquially as "vacatur" of forfeiture, seems to have evolved. This is addressed to the bail-forfeiting court before a judgment of forfeiture is executed, and appears directed to the inherent power of the court to void its own previous order of forfeiture. It is not clear whether "vacatur" is an extension of an application to "discharge" the forfeiture under CPL § 540.10, which must be done before the court's "final adjournment," or whether it is an entirely court-created non-statutory mechanism. In People v. Varela, 124 Misc.2d 992, 479 N.Y.S.2d 116 (Sup.Ct.,

court—*i.e*, the Supreme or County Court—except in cases where the forfeiture was ordered by a District Court, in which case the application can be made to that court as well.[201] The application must be made within one year after the forfeiture was "declared"—again, this is the moment it was entered on the minutes. The Court of Appeals has held that this period is in effect a statute of limitations that cannot be waived or extended, and that a complete application must be filed within the prescribed period.[202] However, "[t]his statute of limitations is inapplicable where bail was illegally accepted[203] ... or where the forfeiture is claimed to be void or illegal."[204]

The applicant for remission must give five days notice to the prosecution. Once in receipt of a timely and proper application, "[t]he court may grant the application and remit the forfeiture or any part thereof, upon such terms as are just."[205] Litigation in this area has been lively. In terms of general principles, the Court of Appeals has indicated:

> [I]n order to prevent a defendant from evading justice by his escape from the jurisdiction of the court, the State offers an economic inducement to the surety. If the surety can successfully return the defendant to the court within a reasonable period of time, the forfeiture may be remitted. The strength of this inducement is weakened if remission is easily granted as a matter of course.[206]

In *People v. Peerless Ins. Co.*,[207] an appeal from 57 orders granting remission applications made by professional sureties, the court took a comprehensive look at the subject. Noting that there had been a "past

---

N.Y. County, 1984), it was held that this practice, which has certain tactical advantages over a bail remission application, was not precluded by the CPL provision.

201. CPL § 540.30(1).

202. People v. Public Service Mutual Ins. Co., 37 N.Y.2d 606, 376 N.Y.S.2d 421, 339 N.E.2d 128 (1975).

203. Presumably, bail is "illegally accepted" when it is taken in violation of a statute. See People v. Wirtschafter, 305 N.Y. 515, 114 N.E.2d 18 (1953)(recidivist admitted to bail in violation of then-extant statutory restriction). A modern example would be admitting to bail one convicted of a Class A felony, in violation of CPL § 530.40(3).

204. People v. Salabarria, 121 A.D.2d 438, 440, 503 N.Y.S.2d 411, 413 (2d Dep't 1986)(citations omitted). In that case, it was held that the failure to give the defendant proper notice that his appearance was required voided the forfeiture. See also People v. Montgomery, 205 A.D.2d 543, 614 N.Y.S.2d 277 (2d Dep't 1994)(where prior order had vacated forfeiture, one-year limit inapplicable); Matter of International Fidelity Ins. Co. v. People, 208 A.D.2d 838, 618 N.Y.S.2d 399 (2d Dep't 1994)(where prosecution failed to move for judgment of forfeiture on bond within 60-day period of CPL § 540.10, one-year limit inapplicable). It is interesting that the latter case was not brought by an application under CPL § 540.30; rather, the surety filed a special proceeding, pursuant to CPLR 5015 and 5240, to preclude enforcement of the judgment of forfeiture, a route also taken in People v. Schonfeld, 74 N.Y.2d 324, 547 N.Y.S.2d 266, 546 N.E.2d 395 (1989). This suggests an alternative path to relief.

205. CPL § 540.30(2). Similar language appears in CPL § 540.20(2), allowing the court that ordered the forfeiture to discharge it, and there seems to be no difference in the standard for relief.

206. People v. Public Service Mutual Ins. Co., 37 N.Y.2d 606, 611, 376 N.Y.S.2d 421, 424, 339 N.E.2d 128, 130 (1975).

207. 21 A.D.2d 609, 253 N.Y.S.2d 91 (1st Dep't 1964). Although this case was decided under the Code of Criminal Procedure, the statutory standard, "upon such terms as are just," was the same as provided in the current CPL.

looseness of practice," the court began by placing the initial burden of going forward on the surety. The court then discussed some specific commonly professed excuses: misunderstandings by defendants of when they had to appear ("this is the least reliable excuse and the least sufficient. It is too easily fabricated"); defendant's illness ("a medical certificate for a serious disabling illness may suffice, but for anything less a detailed explanatory medical affidavit should be required" as well as an explanation for failure to advise the court); or the illness of relatives (an "unreliable" excuse). In general, the court also noted that "whatever the excuse, if the defendant has contributed by careless, reckless, or willful act to the event offered as an excuse," this justifies denial.[208] Similarly, the surety's negligence weighs against the application.[209]

Although addressed in the CPL, remission applications are quasi-civil in nature, and appeal from an adverse determination is governed by the statutory and constitutional provisions applicable to civil appeals.[210]

It should be noted that where a sum of money is deposited in connection with a partially secured bail bond or as cash bail, there is a statutory administrative fee, usually totalling three percent, which is not returned to the depositor when the bail is exonerated or remitted.[211] Further, in cases involving cash bail posted by a defendant as principal, a court that imposes a fine, restitution, or reparation as part of the ultimate sentence may order that the bail be applied towards payment of the sanction.[212] Finally, under certain conditions, monies or property deposited in connection with bail may be subject to attachment by the prosecution and ultimate forfeiture under New York's comprehensive civil forfeiture statute.[213]

Library References:
West's Key No. Digests, Bail ⚖=75-80.

§ 4.13 Procedure for Challenges to Excessive Bail

Initially, a defendant who has been denied bail or whose bail has been fixed in an excessively burdensome form or amount is free to apply again, under CPL § 510.20, to the same court that fixed the terms of the securing order for release or reduction or modification of bail; however, in the absence of changed or unusual circumstances, such application is unlikely to succeed. There is no limit on the number of applications. In addition, in cases in which the action is pending in a local criminal court

---

208. 21 A.D.2d at 618-21, 253 N.Y.S.2d at 100-06. The court concluded that out-of-state criminal confinement, another common excuse, should suffice, but only if the defendant has surrendered. Other courts have disagreed. Cf. People v. Stuyvesant Ins. Co., 24 A.D.2d 989, 265 N.Y.S.2d 268 (2d Dep't 1965), aff'd 21 N.Y.2d 907, 289 N.Y.S.2d 624, 236 N.E.2d 857 (1968).

209. Other factors include hardship, prejudice to the people, timeliness of the surrender and whether it was voluntary, and many other considerations. See footnote 191, supra.

210. People v. Schonfeld, 74 N.Y.2d 324, 547 N.Y.S.2d 266, 546 N.E.2d 395 (1989); People v. Varela, 124 Misc.2d 992, 479 N.Y.S.2d 116 (Sup.Ct., N.Y. County, 1984).

211. See General Municipal Law § 99-m.

212. CPL § 420.10(1)(e).

213. See CPLR Article 13-A.

and the terms of the securing order were fixed by a judge of that court, and not by a superior court judge sitting as such, an application may be made, under CPL § 530.30(1), to a superior court judge of the county. Only one such application can be made. The statute permits review by the superior court judge in cases where the local criminal court either lacks authority to fix bail, denies bail or recognizance, or has fixed bail that is "excessive."[214] Such review is apparently *de novo*.[215]

Bail decisions cannot be directly appealed, but further review is available though *habeas corpus*. This is a special proceeding, brought civilly pursuant to CPLR Article 70. The statute permits a choice of courts under various conditions, although such writs are frequently brought in the Supreme Court.[216] CPLR 7010(b) provides the standard for the granting of the writ: "If the person detained has been admitted to bail but the amount fixed is so excessive as to constitute an abuse of discretion ... [or] if the person detained has been denied bail [and] ... if he is entitled to be admitted to bail as a matter of right, or it appears that the denial of bail constituted an abuse of discretion." This seems to echo the constitutional standard.[217]

Review by *habeas corpus* is collateral and not *de novo*. Accordingly, "[e]xcept perhaps in extraordinary circumstances, review on a writ of *habeas corpus* of the determination of a court at *nisi prius* denying or fixing the amount of bail before trial in a criminal action is limited to the record before the *nisi prius* court," and it is normally improper for the

---

214. CPL § 530.30(1)(a)-(c).

215. See Preiser, "Practice Commentary," to CPL §§ 510.20, McKinney's Cons. Laws of New York, Book 11A, at 21(1995)("prior [bail] decisions may be examined afresh and revised as a matter of discretion"). It should be noted, however, that at least in cases involving review under subdivision (c), the statutory use of the phrase "excessive bail" seems to imply some sort of standard other than a simple disagreement with the lower court about what bail is appropriate. It is interesting to compare this provision to former Code of Criminal Procedure § 22(8), which allowed the Supreme Court "to let to bail any person committed, before and after indictment ... with the power ... to reduce, increase or change the terms or amounts of bail as set by the committing magistrate." Of course, de novo review is clearly appropriate when the action progresses to the superior court, see CPL § 530.40, but is the local criminal court's judgment simply to be swept aside when the matter is still pending before that court? Perhaps there is an analogy to the power exercised by the Appellate Division under CPL § 470.15(2)(c) in reviewing an "unduly harsh or severe" sentence: "While this court will not normally disturb a sentence imposed by a trial court in the exercise of its sound discretion unless there is an abuse of discretion, we do have the power to reduce a sentence in an appropriate case." People v. Board, 97 A.D.2d 610, 468 N.Y.S.2d 209 (2d Dep't 1983). In truth, the superior court's standard of review, and what deference, if any, should be paid to the local criminal court's judgment under this statute, appear to be unsettled questions.

216. CPLR 7002 provides that the writ may be brought: in the Supreme Court of the judicial district or the Appellate Division of the judicial department where the person is detained; before any justice of the Supreme Court; before a County Court judge in the county where the person is detained—or, if none is available, or, if all such have refused, to a County Court judge in an adjoining county. If the defendant is being held in a New York City detention facility, the petition shall be brought or referred to the Supreme Court in the county where the defendant is detained, or to the Appellate Division in the department of detention. Note that although the writ may be brought in the Appellate Division in the first instance, and there may be tactical advantages to such a move, doing so deprives counsel of the opportunity to appeal a denial in the Supreme Court to that court.

217. See People ex rel. Klein v. Krueger, 25 N.Y.2d 497, 307 N.Y.S.2d 207, 255 N.E.2d 552 (1969).

habeas corpus court to receive new evidence.[218] This teaches two lessons. First, counsel should insure that a complete record of the bail application is made in the original court. Second, when there is a change of circumstances or new evidence, a new bail or recognizance application should be made to the original court, and *habeas corpus* should be sought only after a fresh denial by that court. Additionally, it should be noted that because the remedy afforded by the granting of an application for *habeas corpus* is release from custody,[219] the writ is not available to reduce bail if the defendant has in fact managed to post it and is at liberty.[220]

The procedure governing such applications, and the required format of the papers, are set forth in CPLR Article 70. Denial of the application is appealable.

Library References:

West's Key No. Digests, Bail ⚛︎50–53, 73.1; Habeas Corpus ⚛︎469, 800.

§ 4.14 Practice Summary

A. Release on Bail or Recognizance *(See §§ 4.5–4.7)*

1. In making this determination, in some circumstances the application for release must be granted, in others it must be denied, and in others the decision is discretionary. This depends on the severity of the charges, the existence of outstanding warrants, and the court that the defendant is before *(see §§ 4.5–4.7)*.

2. When the release decision is discretionary, the sole objective is to secure the defendant's court appearance. Preventive detention is not a legitimate factor in release decisions in New York *(see § 4.5)*.

3. The specific criteria that the court must consider are: the defendant's character, reputation, habits, and mental condition; his or her employment and financial resources; his or her family ties and length of community residence; his or her criminal record, including previous adjudications as a juvenile delinquent, or in some cases, youthful offender; his or her previous record of flight or responding to court appear-

---

218. People ex rel. Rosenthal v. Wolfson, 48 N.Y.2d 230, 231–32, 422 N.Y.S.2d 55, 55–56, 397 N.E.2d 745, 745–46 (1979). But see People ex rel. Moquin v. Infante, 134 A.D.2d 764, 765, 521 N.Y.S.2d 580, 581 (3d Dep't 1987): "The fact that the record of the [bail] proceeding in County Court was not before Supreme Court [on habeas corpus review] is irrelevant, since, after having vacated County Court's order as unlawful, Supreme Court was acting as the nisi prius court. We conclude that Supreme Court properly considered the bail application de novo." It appears that this decision was grounded upon a finding that the County Court's original denial of bail was based upon an *illegal* premise—preventive detention—and that accordingly once the Supreme Court vacated that order, that court, rather than remitting the matter to the County Court, could sit as an original superior court for bail purposes. If that is the case, while considerations of judicial economy may have been advanced, and this might even be said to constitute the "extraordinary case" excepted from the Rosenthal rule, it would have been better to specify that and circumscribe the holding more carefully.

219. See, e.g., People ex rel. McDonald v. Warden, 34 N.Y.2d 554, 354 N.Y.S.2d 939, 310 N.E.2d 537 (1974).

220. People ex rel. Modica v. Hoy, 51 Misc.2d 579, 273 N.Y.S.2d 634 (Sup.Ct., Westchester County, 1966).

ances; the weight of the evidence against the defendant; and the sentence that may be imposed on conviction. Additional criteria apply for post-conviction bail. All of the factors should be considered (*see* §§ 4.4, 4.5).

4. If bail is to be set, in addition to specifying an amount, the court may specify that it be posted in a particular form. The forms of bail are: cash bail, an insurance company bail bond, a secured surety bond, a secured appearance bond, a partially secured surety bond, a partially secured appearance bond, an unsecured surety bond, and an unsecured appearance bond. For VTL violations only, credit card payment is acceptable. A court's failure to specify a form allows a defendant to choose the least onerous alternative. Cash bail may always be substituted for any other form (§§ 4.2, 4.3).

5. If a pretrial services program exists in the local jurisdiction, it may be helpful in facilitating a defendant's release or in obtaining lower or less onerous bail (*see* § 4.4)

B. Release or Bail Conditions and Orders of Protection (*See* § 4.10)

1. With the exception of the order of protection and the general prohibition on commission of other offenses, bail and release conditions are not listed in any statute and are said to be within the inherent power of a court to impose. Some conditions found to be acceptable include requiring a defendant to surrender a passport, report periodically to the police, and enroll in a treatment program. Bail or release conditions should relate only to securing the defendant's court appearance.

2. A temporary order of protection (TOP) may issue in cases involving family or non-family offenses. In the former instance, the defendant may be required to stay away from the home, school, or place of business of a family or household member, permit a parent to visit a child, refrain from committing a family offense, or refrain from conduct that creates an unreasonable risk to the health, safety or welfare of a child or family or household member. In non-family offense cases, an order to stay away from a victim or witness or refrain from certain harassing or interfering conduct may be issued. The extent, if any, to which a hearing must be held before the issuance of certain of these orders is an unsettled question. Violation of the TOP justifies revocation of bail or release, and commitment of the defendant, as well as a potential contempt prosecution.

C. Examination of the Sufficiency of Bail (*See* § 4.11)

1. A court may conduct an inquiry to determine the reliability of the obligors or the person posting bail, the value and sufficiency of proffered security, and whether public policy is adversely affected by the undertaking. The inquiry is broad-based and the prosecutor may participate. Reasons for disapproval include insufficient security or findings that monies posted are the fruit of criminal activity. Disapproval may also result where the source of bail was intimidated or coerced.

D. Revocation of Bail (*See* § 4.10)

1. Once fixed or granted, bail or release can be modified or revoked. In general, whenever a court considers it necessary to review a release order, it may do so, by bench warrant if necessary, and "for good cause shown" may revoke the bail. Common reasons for such action are flight and violation of TOP, although revocation need not be based upon new information. A specific provision, which constitutes a limited form of preventive detention, allows for revocation where a defendant, having been charged with a felony and released, commits a Class A or violent felony or victim witness intimidation while at liberty. It is unclear whether this is the sole basis for revocation for commission of another crime.

E. Forfeiture of Bail and Remission (*See* § 4.12)

1. Forfeiture of bail occurs when, without sufficient excuse, a defendant fails to appear in court. Common sufficient excuses include hospitalization, deportation, and insufficient notice of the appearance. The procedure for forfeiture differs depending on the charges, the nature of the bail and the place where bail was posted. The court may discharge the forfeiture if the defendant appears before the court's final adjournment. In cases involving bail bonds, the prosecutor must take certain procedural steps within a 60-day period, and failure to do so may bar the forfeiture.

2. Forfeiture of bail may be remitted (*i.e.*, rescinded) by application to a superior court within one year from the time the forfeiture was declared. Remission applications are quasi-civil in nature and may be appealed. In some jurisdictions there may be an additional remedy of "vacatur," addressed to the bail-forfeiting court before a judgment of forfeiture has been executed. Another possible procedural remedy is a special proceeding to preclude enforcement of the judgment of forfeiture.

F. Challenging Excessive Bail (*See* § 4.13)

1. A defendant may challenge the denial of bail or excessive bail by: applying for a reduction to the court that set the bail; applying to a superior court judge when bail was fixed or denied by a local criminal court; filing a writ of *habeas corpus* in an appropriate superior or appellate court; and appealing the denial of such a writ.

§ 4.15 Forms

§ 4.15.1 Notice of Application for Recognizance or Bail in Superior Court When Action Pending in Local Criminal Court

[Add caption]

COUNSEL:

PLEASE TAKE NOTICE, that upon the annexed affirmation and all the prior papers and proceedings herein, the undersigned will move this Court, at Part ___ thereof, to be held at the Courthouse at _____, New

§ 4.15　　　　　BAIL & RECOGNIZANCE　　　　　Ch. 4

York, on the ___ day of _____, 19__, at ___ in the forenoon, or as soon thereafter as counsel can be heard, for an order pursuant to section 530.30 of the Criminal Procedure Law, vacating an order of the [specify local criminal court], entered _____, 19__, fixing bail herein in the amount of [specify amount], and releasing defendant on his [her] own recognizance pending disposition of the [specify accusatory instrument] herein or fixing bail in a lesser amount or in a less burdensome form than prescribed in the aforesaid order, on the ground that such amount is excessive, and for such other relief as this Court deems proper.

Dated: _____, 19__.
　　　　　_____, New York

　　　　　　　　　　　　　　　　[Name of attorney]
　　　　　　　　　　　　　　　　Attorney for Defendant
　　　　　　　　　　　　　　　　Address
　　　　　　　　　　　　　　　　Tel. No.

To: HON. _____
　　District Attorney
　　_____ County

　　HON. _____
　　Clerk of the Court

§ 4.15.2 Affirmation in Support of Application for Recognizance or Bail in Superior Court When Action Pending in Local Criminal Court

[Add caption]

STATE OF NEW YORK　）
　　　　　　　　　　　） ss.:
COUNTY OF _____　）

_____, an attorney duly admitted to practice in the Courts of this State, hereby affirms under the penalties of perjury that the following statements are true, except those made on information and belief, which he [she] believes to be true:

　　1. I am the attorney for the defendant herein. I make this affirmation in support of defendant's application, pursuant to section 530.30 of the Criminal Procedure Law, for an order of recognizance or bail pending disposition of the [specify accusatory instrument] herein, now pending in the [specify local criminal court].

　　2. Since _____, 19__, defendant has been detained in the [specify jail].

　　3. Defendant is charged in the [specify accusatory instrument] herein with the offense of [specify offense], which is classified as a [specify grade of offense] under the provisions of section ___ of the Penal Law. A copy of the accusatory instrument is attached hereto as Exhibit A.

4. On _____, 19__, the [specify local criminal court] entered an order granting defendant's application for recognizance or bail and fixing bail in the amount of $___. A copy of the court's order is attached hereto as Exhibit B.

5. Under the facts and circumstances of this case, the amount of bail fixed by the [specify local criminal court] is excessive for the following reasons: [explain why the amount that was fixed is excessive in light of the criteria set forth in CPL § 510.30(2)(a); attach any relevant supporting affidavits and information].

6. No previous application has been made for the relief sought herein.

WHEREFORE, defendant respectfully requests that an order be issued vacating the order of the [specify local criminal court] and releasing defendant on his [her] own recognizance pending disposition of the [specify accusatory instrument] herein or fixing bail for such release in a lesser amount or in a less burdensome form than specified in said order, and for such other and further relief as this Court deems just and proper.

[Signature]

───────────────────────────────
[Type Name]

Dated: _____, 19__.

§ 4.15.3 Petition for Writ of *Habeas Corpus* on Ground That Bail Fixed by Trial Court Is So Excessive as to Constitute an Abuse of Discretion

SUPREME COURT OF THE STATE OF NEW YORK
COUNTY OF _____

───────────────────────────────
)
People of the State of New York   )
Ex Rel. [name of defense attorney])
On Behalf of [name of defendant],)
)
         Petitioners,   )   Petition for Writ of
)   Habeas Corpus
     -against-   )
)
[name and title of person having   )   Index No. _____
custody of defendant],   )
)
         Respondent.   )
)
───────────────────────────────)

TO THE SUPREME COURT OF THE STATE OF NEW YORK,
_____ COUNTY:

1. Petitioner is the attorney for [name of defendant] (hereinafter referred to as "petitioner"), the person on whose behalf this petition is made.

2. On _____, 19__, petitioner was charged in a [specify accusatory instrument] filed in [specify court in which action pending] with the offense(s) of [specify offense(s)]. A copy of the accusatory instrument is attached hereto as Exhibit A.

3. Since _____, 19__, petitioner has been confined in the [specify jail] in the custody of [name and title of respondent].

4. On _____, 19__, the [specify court in which action pending] entered an order granting petitioner's application for recognizance or bail and fixing bail in the amount of $___.

5. Under the facts and circumstances of this case, the aforesaid amount of bail is so excessive as to constitute an abuse of discretion. [explain why the amount of bail fixed is grossly excessive in light of the criteria set forth in CPL § 510.30(2)(a); attach any relevant supporting affidavits and other information].

6. No previous application for the writ sought herein has been made.

WHEREFORE, to enforce petitioner's rights under Article 500 of the Criminal Procedure Law and under the New York and United States Constitutions, this Court should vacate the aforesaid order of the [specify court in which action pending] and release petitioner on his [her] own recognizance pending disposition of the accusatory instrument pending in such court or fix bail for such release in a lesser amount or in a less burdensome form than specified in the aforesaid order.

Dated: _____, 19__.
_____, New York

_____
[Name of Defense Attorney]

[Verification]

§ 4.15.4 Notice of Application for Remission of Forfeiture of Bail

[Add caption]

COUNSEL:

PLEASE TAKE NOTICE, that upon the annexed affidavit of _____, sworn to the ___ day of _____, 19__, and upon all the prior papers and proceedings herein, the undersigned will move this Court, at Part ___ thereof, to be held at the Courthouse at _____, New York, on the ___ day of _____, 19__, at ___ in the forenoon, or as soon thereafter as counsel can be heard, for an order, pursuant to section 540.30 of the Criminal Procedure Law, remitting the forfeiture of cash bail posted herein in the sum of $___, ordered by this Court on _____, 19__, and for such other and further relief as this Court deems just and proper.

Dated: _____, 19__.
_____, New York

          [Name of attorney]
          Attorney for _____
          Address
          Tel. No.

To: HON. _____
  District Attorney
  _____ County

  Hon. _____
  Clerk of the Court

§ 4.15.5 Affidavit in Support of Application for Remission of Forfeiture of Bail

[Add caption]

STATE OF NEW YORK)
) ss.:
COUNTY OF _____)

_____, being duly sworn, deposes and says:

1. On _____, 19__, an accusatory instrument was filed in this Court charging the defendant herein with the offense(s) of [specify offense(s)]. A copy of the accusatory instrument is attached hereto as Exhibit A.

2. On _____, 19__, I posted cash bail in the amount of $__ for defendant's release, upon the condition that such money would be forfeited to the People of the State of New York if defendant did not comply with the directions of the Court requiring his [her] attendance in this action or did not otherwise render himself [herself] amenable to the orders and processes of the Court.

3. I have since learned that defendant failed to appear in court, despite being directed to do so, on _____, 19__, and that this Court issued a bench warrant on such date ordering the defendant's arrest.

4. As a result of defendant's failure to appear in court, this Court, on _____, 19__, also ordered that the cash bail that I posted be forfeited. A copy of the Court's order of forfeiture is attached hereto as Exhibit B.

5. On _____, 19__, defendant ultimately returned to court [specify whether defendant returned to court voluntarily or pursuant to execution of bench warrant].

6. [explain reasons why forfeiture should be remitted: set forth why forfeiture would result in economic hardship to the deponent or

deponent's family, and if applicable any extenuating circumstances as to why defendant failed to appear in court]

7. One year has not elapsed since the Court ordered the forfeiture of the cash bail posted herein.

8. No previous application for remission of forfeiture of the aforesaid cash bail has been made.

WHEREFORE, deponent respectfully requests an order, pursuant to section 540.30 of the Criminal Procedure Law, remitting the forfeiture of bail herein, and for such other and further relief as the Court deems just and proper.

[Signature]
_____

[Type Name]

Sworn to before me this ___ day of _____, 19__.

_____
Notary Public

Chapter 5

GRAND JURY AND INDICTMENT

Table of Sections

5.1	Grand Jury—In General.
5.2	___ Formation and Organization.
5.3	___ Secrecy and Attendance.
5.4	___ Legal Advisors.
5.5	___ Legal Instructions.
5.6	___ Applicability of Rules of Evidence.
5.7	___ Exculpatory Evidence.
5.8	___ Appearance of Witnesses.
5.9	Compelled Testimony.
5.10	Waiver of Indictment and Superior Court Informations.
5.11	Indictment—In General.
5.12	___ Form and Content.
5.13	___ Purpose.
5.14	___ Adequate Notice.
5.15	___ Date of Offense.
5.16	___ Jurisdictional Defects.
5.17	___ Duplicitous Counts.
5.18	___ Curing Defects.
5.19	___ Bill of Particulars.
5.20	___ Lesser Offenses Prosecuted by Indictment.
5.21	___ Joinder of Offenses.
5.22	___ Joinder of Defendants.
5.23	___ Securing Defendant's Appearance.
5.24	___ Arraignment.
5.25	___ Motion to Dismiss—In General.
5.26	___ ___ Procedure.
5.27	___ ___ Grounds.
5.28	___ Disposition Following Dismissal.
5.29	___ Disposition Following Order Reducing Count.
5.30	Practice Summary—Grand Jury.
5.31	___ Waiver of Indictment.
5.32	___ Indictment.
5.33	Forms.
	5.33.1 Notice of Motion in Superior Court to Release Defendant Due to Failure of Timely Grand Jury Action.
	5.33.2 Affirmation in Support of Motion in Superior Court to Release Defendant Due to Failure of Timely Grand Jury Action.
	5.33.3 Notice of Motion to Dismiss Indictment Because Defendant Not Afforded Opportunity to Testify Before Grand Jury.
	5.33.4 Affirmation in Support of Motion to Dismiss Indictment Because Defendant Not Afforded Opportunity to Testify Before Grand Jury.
	5.33.5 Notice of Motion for Severance of Counts.
	5.33.6 Affirmation in Support of Motion for Severance of Counts.
	5.33.7 Notice of Motion to Consolidate Indictments Against the Same Defendant.

Table of Sections

5.33 Forms (Cont'd)
    5.33.8   Affirmation in Support of Motion to Consolidate Indictments Against the Same Defendant.
    5.33.9   Notice of Motion for Severance of Trials of Jointly Indicted Defendants.
    5.33.10   Affirmation in Support of Motion for Severance of Trials of Jointly Indicted Defendants.
    5.33.11   Notice of Motion to Consolidate Indictments Against Different Defendants.
    5.33.12   Affirmation in Support of Motion Consolidating Indictments Against Different Defendants.
    5.33.13   Notice of Motion to Amend Indictment.
    5.33.14   Affirmation in Support of Motion to Amend Indictment.
    5.33.15   Notice of Motion to Amend Bill of Particulars.
    5.33.16   Affirmation in Support of Motion to Amend Bill of Particulars.
    5.33.17   Notice of Motion to Dismiss Indictment (or Count(s) of Indictment) as Defective.
    5.33.18   Affirmation in Support of Motion to Dismiss Indictment (or Count(s) of Indictment) as Defective.
    5.33.19   Notice of Motion to Dismiss Indictment (Grand Jury Immunity).
    5.33.20   Affirmation in Support of Motion to Dismiss Indictment (Grand Jury Immunity).
    5.33.21   Notice of Motion to Dismiss Indictment in Furtherance of Justice.
    5.33.22   Affirmation in Support of Motion to Dismiss Indictment in Furtherance of Justice.
    5.33.23   Notice of Motion by Prosecutor to Submit Charge(s) to a New Grand Jury.
    5.33.24   Affirmation in Support of Prosecutor's Motion to Submit Charge(s) to a New Grand Jury.

WESTLAW Electronic Research Guide

See WESTLAW Electronic Research Guide preceding the Summary of Contents.

---

§ 5.1 Grand Jury—In General

While both the United States Constitution[1] and the New York Constitution[2] afford an accused the right to the protection of a grand jury,[3] neither document defines the form that such a body must take nor the procedures it should follow. In New York, while much of that is derived from common law,[4] "the Grand Jury's role and procedures are

---

1. U.S. Const., Amend. V. ("No person shall be held to answer for a capital, or otherwise infamous crime, unless on a presentment or indictment of a Grand Jury").

2. N.Y. Const., Art. 1, § 6 ("No person shall be held to answer for a capital or otherwise infamous crime ... unless on indictment of a grand jury").

3. However, a defendant may waive indictment by a New York grand jury, see § 5.10, infra, and the federal clause is not binding upon the states. Hurtado v. California, 110 U.S. 516, 4 S.Ct. 111, 28 L.Ed. 232 (1884).

4. For a discussion of the history of the grand jury as an institution, see People v. Doe, 151 Misc.2d 829, 835, 574 N.Y.S.2d 453, 457 (Sup.Ct., Kings County, 1991)(citations omitted):

Although little is known about the origins of the Grand Jury system, the institution did exist among the Saxons and was also recognized by the Constitution of Clarendon. It is believed that the first Grand Jury was composed of 12 knights, who stood as accusers or witnesses of suspected criminals. Its object was to secure to a subject the right of appeal to his peers under the immunity of secrecy before he

now defined by statute."[5]

CPL § 190.05 provides that a grand jury consist of "not less than sixteen nor more than twenty-three persons" whose function it is to "hear and examine evidence concerning offenses ... and to take action with respect to such evidence."[6] The grand jury has on frequent occasion been referred to as a "sword and a shield."[7] That is because the grand jury performs the "dual function of investigating criminal activity to determine whether sufficient evidence exists to accuse a citizen of a crime, and of protecting individuals from needless and unfounded prosecutions."[8]

It is said, on occasion, that the grand jury is an "arm of the court,"[9] and section 190.05 emphasizes this by not only directing that a superior court, not the prosecutor, impanel the jury, but, in addition, by explicitly

could be brought to public trial. It originally functioned as a trier of fact, as well an investigatory and accusatory body. This body also acted as a buffer between the Crown and a subject, protecting the latter against oppression and unfounded prosecutions. While it has retained its investigatory and accusatory functions, it no longer retains its power to act as a trier of fact as it was passed down through the common law.

5. People v. Pelchat, 62 N.Y.2d 97, 104, 476 N.Y.S.2d 79, 83, 464 N.E.2d 447, 451 (1984).

See Gershman, "Supervisory Power of the New York Courts," 14 Pace L.Rev. 41, 20–21 (Spring 1994)(citations omitted):

In New York State, the modern grand jury is hedged with broader constitutional and statutory restrictions than in the federal system. As a creature of the common law, the grand jury's pre-statutory powers in New York State have been described as "vague and unlimited." The first state constitution, ratified in 1777, made no reference to the grand jury. To provide "a clear and well understood definition of [the grand jury's] powers," New York's legislature in 1849 enacted several provisions dealing with grand jury practice. The state constitution subsequently was amended to add provisions empowering grand jury action. Moreover, to the extent that the state constitution explicitly declares that the common law is continued "subject to such alterations as the legislature shall make concerning the same," the detailed and comprehensive code subsequently enacted with respect to grand jury procedure "leaves no doubt that the Legislature manifested its intention to supplant the common law on the subject of grand jury practice." However, no code can cover every contingency. Aside from their interpretive responsibilities, courts are called upon to fill procedural gaps. Additionally, courts may be asked to oversee prosecutorial conduct inside the grand jury, even though the conduct is not claimed to violate specific constitutional or statutory guarantees.

6. The discussion of the grand jury in this chapter is confined to prosecution of criminal offenses in superior court. Grand jury functions related to investigation of neglect by public officials and related reports not leading to indictment are not discussed.

7. See, e.g., Matter of Healy, 161 Misc. 582, 599, 293 N.Y.S. 584, 602 (Queens Co. Ct.1937)("The history of our grand jury system is one of great nobility and of service, of protection to the humble from the unwarranted accusations of the great and mighty. For a thousand years it has been in the process of magnificent development—a shield to the innocent, a sword to the guilty."). See also People v. Doe, 151 Misc.2d 829, 574 N.Y.S.2d 453 (Sup.Ct., Kings County, 1991); People v. Nunez, 136 Misc.2d 1062, 1063, 519 N.Y.S.2d 623, 624 (Sup.Ct., N.Y.County, 1987); People v. Monroe, 125 Misc.2d 550, 552, 480 N.Y.S.2d 259, 262 (Sup.Ct., Bronx County, 1984).

8. People v. Lancaster, 69 N.Y.2d 20, 25, 511 N.Y.S.2d 559, 561, 503 N.E.2d 990, 992 (1986).

9. People v. Doe, 151 Misc.2d at 835, 574 N.Y.S.2d at 457 ("Since the Grand Jury is historically and statutorily an arm of the Court and not merely an extension of the prosecutor's office, courts are duty-bound to insure that presentations comply with the letter and spirit of the law.")(citations omitted).

providing that the jury "constitut[es] a part of such Court."[10] For that reason, in New York, it is within the discretion of the court to take affirmative steps to ensure that an ongoing grand jury proceeding be conducted fairly.[11]

It is rare, however, for a court to intervene in the presentation as it occurs, since the court has the authority to dismiss an indictment, once voted and filed, upon grounds that the proceeding in the grand jury was defective.[12] Thus, for example, when an alleged assault victim recants his story prior to grand jury action, where a "duty of good faith and fair dealing obligates the prosecutor to disclose ... [such] to the grand jury,"[13] the failure to do so requires dismissal. A failure to "see that justice is done" in the grand jury proceeding "may impair a defendant's due process rights and require reversal of a conviction" even after a guilty plea.[14]

At the same time, the grand jury is an autonomous constitutional body exercising authority independent of the court[15] and, likewise, not available to the prosecutor for his or her own purposes.[16]

Library References:
West's Key No. Digests, Grand Jury ⟶1.

§ 5.2 Grand Jury—Formation and Organization

CPL § 190.10 provides that the Appellate Division shall adopt rules governing the impaneling of grand juries by superior courts. However, that section, enacted in 1970,[17] was superseded by changes in the State Constitution regarding organization of the courts. Effective 1978, Article 6, § 28 of the State Constitution now provides that "[t]he chief administrator, on behalf of the chief judge, shall supervise the administration and operation of the unified court system." Accordingly, terms of court, including grand juries impaneled by them, are established by

---

10. Cf. United States v. Williams, 504 U.S. 36, 46, 112 S.Ct. 1735, 1741, 118 L.Ed.2d 352 (1992) ("It has not been textually assigned, therefore, to any of the branches described in the first three Articles. It 'is a constitutional fixture in its own right'.")(citation omitted).

11. Morgenthau v. Altman, 58 N.Y.2d 1057, 462 N.Y.S.2d 629, 449 N.E.2d 409 (1983)(denying a writ of prohibition against a judge who had directed the prosecution to present a prima facie case before the defendant testified); People v. Doe, supra (directing the prosecutor to interrupt a presentation and put the evidence before a new grand jury, untainted by prejudicial conduct occurring before the first grand jury).

12. See § 5.27, infra.

13. People v. Curry, 153 Misc.2d 61, 64, 579 N.Y.S.2d 1000, 1002 (Sup.Ct., Queens County, 1992).

14. People v. Pelchat, 62 N.Y.2d 97, 105–06, 476 N.Y.S.2d 79, 83–84, 464 N.E.2d 447, 451–52 (1984)("Indeed, courts have stated that indictments may be dismissed solely because they were obtained by the prosecutor for improper motives")(reversing a conviction where the witness informed the prosecution that his grand jury testimony wrongly named the defendant through a misunderstanding).

15. People ex rel. Hirschberg v. Close, 1 N.Y.2d 258, 152 N.Y.S.2d 1, 134 N.E.2d 818 (1956); cf. People v. Stern, 3 N.Y.2d 658, 171 N.Y.S.2d 265, 148 N.E.2d 400 (1958).

16. See, e.g., Hynes v. Lerner, 44 N.Y.2d 329, 405 N.Y.S.2d 649, 376 N.E.2d 1294 (1978)(calling it an "abuse" and a "misuse" of the grand jury process to issue a grand jury subpoena duces tecum for the sole or dominant purpose of preparing a pending indictment for trial).

17. L.1970, c.996.

rule of the Chief Administrator.[18] This is supplemented by the authority of the Governor to establish an extraordinary term of Supreme Court,[19] which may in turn impanel its own extraordinary special grand jury.[20]

Once a court has been authorized to impanel a grand jury for a specified term, the court may extend the term of that grand jury to complete certain business before it upon application of both the prosecutor and the grand jury itself.[21] The statute has been strictly construed. In *People v. Williams*,[22] the Court of Appeals looked behind a joint declaration of unfinished business by the prosecutor and the grand jury to dismiss an indictment based on matters that related to, but were not technically part of, an investigation undertaken during the grand jury's initial term. Rejecting a finding by the Appellate Division that dismissal was not required in the absence of prejudice, the court held that investigation into a new matter, even with court approval, rendered the proceedings defective, within the meaning of CPL § 210.20, because the grand jury was illegally constituted.

The mode of selecting grand jurors and of drawing and impaneling grand juries is governed by the Judiciary Law.[23] Section 500 provides

---

18. See 22 N.Y.C.R.R. § 128.17 ("The Chief Administrator of the Courts, in consultation and agreement with the presiding justice of the appropriate Appellate Division, shall designate: (a) the number of grand juries to be drawn and empaneled for each term of the Supreme Court or county court established within the judicial department and (b) such additional grand juries as may be required."); 22 N.Y.C.R.R. § 200.13 ("There shall be a grand jury drawn and impaneled for such terms of a superior court as may be provided on the annual schedule of terms established by the Chief Administrator of the Courts. Whenever the public interest requires, additional grand juries may be drawn and impaneled as authorized by the Chief Administrator.").

19. N.Y. Const., Art. 6, § 27 ("The governor may, when in his opinion the public interest requires, appoint extraordinary terms of the supreme court. He shall designate the time and place of holding the term and the justice who shall hold the term. The governor may terminate the assignment of the justice and may name another justice in his place to hold the term.").

20. Judiciary Law § 149 ("A justice named to preside at an extraordinary term appointed under this section shall have power to order the drawing of a grand jury or grand juries in place of or in addition to the grand jury originally drawn for such term. Such other grand jury or grand juries shall be summoned in the manner prescribed for grand juries in general and shall be subject to all the provisions of law applicable to a grand jury summoned pursuant to sections five hundred thirty-one, six hundred nine and six hundred eighty-four of this chapter.").

21. CPL § 190.15(1).

22. 73 N.Y.2d 84, 538 N.Y.S.2d 222, 535 N.E.2d 275 (1989).

23. CPL § 190.20(1). See generally Judiciary Law § 500, et. seq. In particular, Judiciary Law § 514 provides

The prospective grand jurors shall be drawn at random from the list, pool or reservoir of persons qualified as jurors in the county. The qualifications for service as a grand juror shall be the same as the qualifications for service as a petit juror. The commissioner of jurors may require the fingerprinting of all persons drawn for grand jury service. A record of the persons who are called for service as grand jurors and who are found not qualified or who are excused, and the reasons therefor, shall be maintained by the commissioner of jurors. The county jury board shall have the power to review any determination of the commissioner as to qualifications and excuses. The names of jurors drawn and qualified for service on a grand jury shall constitute the grand jury list, pool or reservoir for that county and shall be separated from the petit jury list, pool or reservoir. The duration of the grand jury list, pool or reservoir shall be prescribed by the appropriate appellate division.

§ 5.2   **GRAND JURY & INDICTMENT**   Ch. 5

that grand jurors must be drawn from a fair cross-section of the community. In *People v. Guzman*,[24] three claims against the fairness of the selection process were initially advanced: that grand jurors in Kings County were not drawn from a fair cross-section as required by Judiciary Law § 500; that systematic exclusion of Hispanics from the pool deprived the defendant of due process; and that intentional discrimination against Hispanics violated the equal protection clause. During the course of extensive litigation, the statutory claim was withdrawn. The due process claim was denied because, even though the defendants demonstrated underrepresentation of a substantial and identifiable segment of the community, they failed to show that it was the product of "systematic exclusion."[25] Finally, the equal protection claim was rejected because "the selection process in general is racially neutral" supporting the conclusion that "the People adequately established that the underrepresentation of Hispanics was not caused by intentional discrimination."[26]

CPL § 190.25 requires a quorum of 16 grand jurors to be "present," but allows any official action to be concluded upon the concurrence of only 12. It is not uncommon for a grand jury presentation to extend over a period of time. During that period, invariably, some jurors may not be in attendance at every occasion where evidence is presented. The question then arises whether a juror may vote or even participate in deliberations concerning a case where he or she did not hear all the evidence, and if not, what constitutes a proper quorum and a proper majority. In *People v. Collier*,[27] the Court of Appeals ruled that "[a] vote to indict by 12 jurors, each of whom has heard all the critical and essential evidence presented and the charge, satisfies statutory requirements for a valid indictment. The full 16-juror quorum need not deliberate and vote."[28] As a consequence of *Collier*, before a vote, the presenting prosecutor will commonly ask if all the jurors voting have heard all the evidence. When the issue presents itself to a reviewing court, attendance sheets may be examined.[29] Left open by *Collier* is the role to be played by non-voting members of the quorum. If 16 or more members are present—to constitute a quorum—but only some of them are eligible to vote because others did not hear all the "critical evidence," it is unclear whether the non-voting members may participate in discussions and deliberations concerning the vote. Without deciding the issue, the majority saw a potential advantage if non-voting members of

24. 60 N.Y.2d 403, 469 N.Y.S.2d 916, 457 N.E.2d 1143, cert. den. 466 U.S. 951, 104 S.Ct. 2155, 80 L.Ed.2d 541 (1984).

25. 60 N.Y.2d at 410–11, 469 N.Y.S.2d at 920, 457 N.E.2d at 1147 ("This has been interpreted to mean that the challenge to the jury selection process must show that the exclusion of a particular group is 'inherent in the particular jury-selection process utilized.' The record does not reflect that the underrepresentation of Hispanics was caused by any aspect of the selection process, so as to amount to 'systematic exclusion'.")(citation omitted).

26. 60 N.Y.2d at 414, 469 N.Y.S.2d at 922.

27. 72 N.Y.2d 298, 532 N.Y.S.2d 718, 528 N.E.2d 1191 (1988).

28. 72 N.Y.2d at 299, 532 N.Y.S.2d at 718.

29. See, e.g., People v. Perry, 199 A.D.2d 889, 605 N.Y.S.2d 790 (3d Dep't 1993).

the quorum were more than "four idle observers."[30] On the other hand, Judge Titone, in a concurring opinion, cautioned:

> Such participation, however, could lead to undesirable consequences. Jurors who have not heard all of the evidence could well have a substantial influence on the decision to indict, issue a report or take any other official action. At the very least, the result would be uninformed decision-making. Of even greater concern is the potential for manipulation. In the worst possible scenario, a "flying squad" of four especially persuasive grand jurors who heard only the most damaging evidence could influence the 12 jurors who, after having heard all the evidence, would not have returned an indictment but for the influence of those four.[31]

Library References:

West's Key No. Digests, Grand Jury ⚖2.5–20.

§ 5.3 Grand Jury—Secrecy and Attendance

CPL § 190.25 provides an exclusive list of who may be present during grand jury proceedings and provides for secrecy of those proceedings. The reasons for secrecy were enumerated *People v. Di Napoli*:

> (1) prevention of flight by a defendant who is about to be indicted; (2) protection of the grand jurors from interference from those under investigation; (3) prevention of subornation of perjury and tampering with prospective witnesses at the trial to be held as a result of any indictment the grand jury returns; (4) protection of an innocent accused from unfounded accusations if in fact no indictment is returned; and (5) assurance to prospective witnesses that their testimony will be kept secret so that they will be willing to testify freely.[32]

For those reasons, section 190.25 provides that the only persons who may be present during proceedings are the prosecutor, a clerk or other public servant assisting in the administrative conduct of the proceedings, a stenographer, an interpreter if needed, an appropriate public servant necessary to guard a witness in custody, an attorney representing a witness pursuant to section 190.52, a videotape operator as defined in section 190.32 and a support person for a child witness as provided in section 190.25(3)(h). While the above-listed persons may be present (as the occasion requires) during some of the proceedings, only the grand jurors themselves may be present during deliberations and voting.[33]

---

30. 72 N.Y.2d at 303, 532 N.Y.S.2d at 721 ("Even if they may be barred from participating in deliberations or voting, the nondeliberating members of the quorum may well contribute to the Grand Jury's traditional function of furnishing protection against malicious and unfounded prosecution, or being alert to 'fraud and improper practices' in the Grand Jury.")(citation omitted).

31. 72 N.Y.2d at 305, 532 N.Y.S.2d at 722 (Titone, J., concurring).

32. 27 N.Y.2d 229, 235, 316 N.Y.S.2d 622, 625, 265 N.E.2d 449, 452 (1970).

33. CPL § 190.25(3).

§ 5.3 GRAND JURY & INDICTMENT

Courts traditionally have been hostile to violations of the attendance rules, and have strictly construed the rule.[34] In *People v. DiFalco*,[35] an indictment was dismissed because the case was presented by a Special Prosecutor who exceeded the authority of the executive order creating his position.[36] Similarly, dismissal was required in *People v. Sayavong*,[37] where a police officer was present during the taping of the testimony of a child witness as a videotape operator " 'employed by the district attorney' (CPL 190.32[1][c])—one of the persons authorized to be present during Grand Jury proceedings under CPL 190.25."[38] The problem in *Sayavong*, however, was that the individual also testified as a "fact witness" before the grand jury, and "by now [it is] axiomatic that two witnesses are not authorized to be simultaneously present before the Grand Jury."[39]

Section 190.25 requires an oath of secrecy of every person authorized by subdivision three to be in the grand jury, except public servants, who otherwise are already required to take an oath of office.[40] The one exception is for an attorney who may be present to represent a witness. In effect, this means that all persons in the grand jury, including the jurors themselves,[41] vow to follow the rules compelling secrecy, either explicitly or implicitly, as part of their duties, except a witness and his or her attorney.[42] No witness before the grand jury is prohibited from repeating his or her own testimony outside the proceedings.[43]

---

34. See, e.g., People v. Gilbert, 149 Misc.2d 411, 565 N.Y.S.2d 690 (Sup.Ct., Bronx County, 1991)(dismissing an indictment where a videotaped statement of a witness in a hospital bed, later played in the grand jury, showed that another unidentified patient was present during the testimony of the witness in the hospital).

35. 44 N.Y.2d 482, 406 N.Y.S.2d 279, 377 N.E.2d 732 (1978).

36. 44 N.Y.2d at 485, 406 N.Y.S.2d at 281 ("The Special Prosecutor, lacking the necessary jurisdictional authority, was clearly an unauthorized person before the Grand Jury."). Cf. People v. Dunbar, 53 N.Y.2d 868, 440 N.Y.S.2d 613, 423 N.E.2d 36 (1981)(that district attorney was not a county resident and thereby was disqualified from office did not impair grand jury proceedings he attended); People v. Carter, 77 N.Y.2d 95, 564 N.Y.S.2d 992, 566 N.E.2d 119 (1990)(that assistant district attorney, who had held prosecuting position for more than 15 years, was unlicensed and therefore unqualified for office did not require dismissal of indictments where he had presented case to grand jury) with People v. Beauvais, 98 A.D.2d 897, 470 N.Y.S.2d 887 (3d Dep't 1983)(prosecuting attorney from State Department of Environmental Conservation should not have presented evidence of environmental misdemeanors to grand jury).

37. 83 N.Y.2d 702, 613 N.Y.S.2d 343, 635 N.E.2d 1213 (1994).

38. 83 N.Y.2d at 705, 613 N.Y.S.2d at 345. Note that the taping was not conducted in the presence of the grand jury, but since it was prepared as a substitute for testimony in the grand jury, it was deemed to constitute a part of the proceedings for purposes of limiting attendance of unauthorized persons.

39. 83 N.Y.2d at 707, 613 N.Y.S.2d at 346.

40. Public Officers Law § 10.

41. CPL § 190.20(4).

42. In People v. Karmye, 164 Misc.2d 746, 624 N.Y.S.2d 743 (Sup.Ct., Queens County, 1995) a prosecutor wrongly attempted to compel a witness's attorney to take an oath of secrecy. While the court condemned the prosecutor for doing so, it found the error did not impair the proceedings to such a degree as to require dismissal.

43. CPL § 190.25(4)("Nothing contained herein shall prohibit a witness from disclosing his own testimony"). See also P.L. § 215.70 (unlawful grand jury disclosure)("Nothing contained herein shall prohibit a witness from disclosing his own testimony."); People v. Doe, 47 Misc.2d 975, 263 N.Y.S.2d 607 (Suffolk Co.Ct.1965), aff'd 24 A.D.2d 843, 263 N.Y.S.2d 688 (2d Dep't 1965).

Section 190.25(4) provides that no person "specified in subdivision three" may "disclose the nature or substance of any grand jury testimony, evidence, or any decision, result or other matter attending a grand jury proceeding." That would seem to embrace everyone except a witness. Included in that list of persons who may not disclose is the attorney for the witness. However, the crime of unlawful grand jury disclosure[44] prohibits a specified list of persons from disclosing events in the grand jury and refers to all the same persons specified in CPL § 190.25(3), *except* attorneys for witnesses. In sum, the CPL prohibits the attorney from disclosing, but the Penal Law does not punish the attorney for disclosure.

Finally, while there is a strong public policy interest in grand jury secrecy,[45] disclosure is authorized upon court order.[46] The statute is silent regarding the parameters and conditions for court-ordered disclosure. The Court of Appeals has observed, however:

> [T]he rule of secrecy is not absolute and, in the discretion of the trial court, disclosure may be directed when, after a balancing of a public interest in disclosure against the one favoring secrecy, the former outweighs the latter. But since disclosure is "the exception rather than the rule," one seeking disclosure first must demonstrate a compelling and particularized need for access. However, just any demonstration will not suffice. For it and the countervailing policy ground it reflects must be strong enough to overcome the presumption of confidentiality. In short, without the initial showing of a compelling and particularized need, the question of discretion need not be reached, for then there simply would be no policies to balance.[47]

So, for example, a prosecutor may not obtain disclosure for the purpose of utilizing the grand jury information in preparation of an ancillary civil RICO suit.[48] Similarly, a prosecutor may not unseal grand jury minutes containing a defendant's testimony about his actions and whereabouts at approximately the same time as pertinent to a pending robbery complaint against him because "the People failed to demonstrate a current, compelling need for the minutes, since there is no evidence at this time that defendant will testify, and that he will interpose an alibi inconsistent with his prior grand jury testimony."[49]

In one unusual and highly publicized case, a grand juror petitioned for disclosure of what he thought were improprieties in the way the district attorney was handling the presentation. The court denied the

---

44. P.L. § 215.70. See generally Greenberg, Marcus, et al., New York Criminal Law § 27.27 (West 1996).

45. People v. DiNapoli, 27 N.Y.2d 229, 316 N.Y.S.2d 622, 265 N.E.2d 449 (1970).

46. CPL § 190.25(4)(a); P.L. § 215.70.

47. Matter of District Attorney of Suffolk County, 58 N.Y.2d 436, 444, 461 N.Y.S.2d 773, 776, 448 N.E.2d 440, 443 (1983)(citations omitted).

48. Id. (holding that targets and witnesses alike have standing to object to disclosure).

49. People v. Lester, 135 Misc.2d 205, 207, 514 N.Y.S.2d 861, 863 (Sup.Ct., Bronx County, 1987). However, this case involved a sealing order, pursuant to CPL § 160.50, as well as an application to disclose grand jury minutes.

application except to the extent that the juror could speak to a representative of the Governor, in private, on behalf of an application for removal of the district attorney.[50]

On the other hand, of course, grand jury testimony of a person who testifies at a subsequent hearing or trial in the case must be divulged to the opposing party through the discovery process.[51] This is true for civil proceedings as well.[52]

Library References:

West's Key No. Digests, Grand Jury ⟺13, 41.10–41.60.

§ 5.4 Grand Jury—Legal Advisors

CPL § 190.25(6) provides that both the district attorney and the court are legal advisors to the grand jury. It further provides:

> Where necessary or appropriate, the court or the district attorney, or both, must instruct the grand jury concerning the law with respect to its duties or any matter before it.

Similarly, CPL § 190.30(6) provides:

> Wherever it is provided in [CPL] article sixty that the court in a criminal proceeding must rule upon the competency of a witness to testify or upon the admissibility of evidence, such ruling may in an equivalent situation in a grand jury proceeding, be made by the district attorney.

And finally, CPL § 190.30(7) provides:

> Wherever it is provided in [CPL] article sixty that a court presiding at a jury trial must instruct the jury with respect to the significance, legal effect or evaluation of evidence, the district attorney, in an equivalent situation in a grand jury proceeding, may so instruct the grand jury.

Before discussing particular rules concerning the adequacy of instructions given to the grand jury or the propriety of evidentiary rulings made before that body, it is necessary to address the shared responsibility and authority conferred upon prosecutors and the courts by Article 190. As noted in Section 5.1, *supra*, the grand jury is an "arm of the court" and the courts have an obligation to maintain supervisory power over conduct in the grand jury.[53] It is to be expected, of course, that on

---

50. In the Matter of Grand Jury, New York County, 125 Misc.2d 918, 480 N.Y.S.2d 998 (Sup.Ct., N.Y. County, 1984).

51. People v. Rosario, 9 N.Y.2d 286, 213 N.Y.S.2d 448, 173 N.E.2d 881 (1961), cert. den. 368 U.S. 866, 82 S.Ct. 117, 7 L.Ed.2d 64 (1961). See CPL §§ 240.44, 240.45.

52. See, e.g., Martinez v. CPC Intern., Inc., 88 A.D.2d 656, 450 N.Y.S.2d 528 (2d Dep't 1982)(drawing a distinction between disclosure in advance of trial and disclosure of a witness's testimony when he does testify at a civil proceeding). See also Matter of Nelson v. Mollen, 175 A.D.2d 518, 573 N.Y.S.2d 99 (3d Dep't 1991).

53. See, e.g., People v. Glen, 173 N.Y. 395, 399, 66 N.E. 112, 114 (1903)("From time immemorial our common-law courts have exercised the power to set aside and quash indictments on motion, not only for defects in form, but for irregularities and errors that were proved by extrinsic evidence. Such matters are now regulated by the provisions of the Code of Criminal Procedure, and however inconvenient, or even oppressive, they may appear to be in specif-

occasion a prosecutor and a supervising court will disagree about a legal ruling. In this situation, two procedural issues arise: whether the court may insert itself into ongoing proceedings over objection of the prosecutor; and if the court awaits indictment before acting, what standard for review of the prosecutor's determination is applicable.

In *People v. DiFabio*,[54] a defendant complained that a judge should not have made a determination concerning the competency of a child witness before the grand jury on the grounds that the prosecutor has the obligation to make that determination.[55] The Court of Appeals rejected the claim, holding that section 190.30(6) does "not curtail the trial court's power to participate in Grand Jury proceedings."[56]

Thereafter, in *Morgenthau v. Altman*,[57] the Court of Appeals denied a writ of prohibition brought by a district attorney against a supervising judge who had directed the prosecution to present a *prima facie* case before the defendant appeared to testify. The court denied the writ, holding that "[t]he order in which witnesses are presented before the Grand Jury is a matter of procedure, within the supervisory jurisdiction of the court, who, together with the District Attorney, is a 'legal advisor' of the Grand Jury."[58]

Thus, it would appear to be a settled question, at this point, that an impaneling court may intervene, in its discretion, to supervise the conduct of ongoing grand jury proceedings.[59] However, in *People v. Thomas*,[60] a trial court was reversed when it dismissed an indictment and directed the parties to come before the court to settle a difference over a *Sandoval* ruling prior to re-presentation. The Appellate Divi-

---

ic cases, the courts must apply them as best they can, for they embody the commands of the lawmaking power in matters wherein its fiat is supreme and final. But our courts have also always asserted and exercised the power to set aside indictments whenever it has been made to appear that they have been found without evidence, or upon illegal and incompetent testimony. This power is based upon the inherent right and duty of the courts to protect the citizen in his constitutional prerogatives, and to prevent oppression or persecution. It is a power which the legislature can neither curtail nor abolish, and, to the extent that legislative enactments are designed to effect either of these ends, they are unconstitutional.")(citations omitted).

54. 79 N.Y.2d 836, 580 N.Y.S.2d 182, 588 N.E.2d 80 (1992).

55. See People v. Groff, 71 N.Y.2d 101, 524 N.Y.S.2d 13, 518 N.E.2d 908 (1987).

56. People v. DeFabio, 79 N.Y.2d at 838, 580 N.Y.S.2d at 183.

57. 58 N.Y.2d 1057, 462 N.Y.S.2d 629, 449 N.E.2d 409 (1983).

58. 58 N.Y.2d at 1059, 462 N.Y.S.2d at 629. Subsequently, in People v. Stepteau, 81 N.Y.2d 799, 595 N.Y.S.2d 371, 611 N.E.2d 272 (1993), the court reinforced this point by holding that the decision in Altman was not based upon a right of the defendant, but rather a proper exercise of discretion by the supervising judge.

59. See generally People v. Davis, 162 Misc.2d 662, 664, 618 N.Y.S.2d 194, 196 (Sup.Ct., Kings County, 1994)("When a dispute arises in the course of a grand jury proceeding, it is the proper course for the prosecutor 'to take the matter into open court for a ruling.' 'By requiring the matter to be taken to the presiding Justice, the proceeding is expedited and the danger of stalling tactics reduced. The judge can rule on issues of pertinency, after argument of counsel.' This practice avoids the disruptive effect of withholding such matters until after indictment, when a finding of a prejudicial defect would require dismissal and representation to another grand jury.")(citations omitted).

60. 160 Misc.2d 39, 607 N.Y.S.2d 871 (Sup.Ct., Queens County, 1994), rev'd 213 A.D.2d 73, 628 N.Y.S.2d 707 (2d Dep't 1995), lv. granted 86 N.Y.2d 803, 632 N.Y.S.2d 517, 656 N.E.2d 616 (1995).

§ 5.4   GRAND JURY & INDICTMENT   Ch. 5

sion's reversal may be explained, in part, by its determination that *Sandoval* was inapplicable to grand jury proceedings.[61] However, reaching beyond that as a basis for its decision, the Second Department also ruled that the prosecutor, not the court, should make any ruling on admissibility of prior record during the grand jury presentation, and the defendant's "sole remedy" would be a motion to dismiss after indictment.

Library References:
West's Key No. Digests, Grand Jury ⚖=34.

§ 5.5 Grand Jury—Legal Instructions

Upon administering the oath to a newly impaneled grand jury, the court "must deliver or cause to be delivered" all the provisions of Article 190.[62] In addition, thereafter the court may give further oral instructions.[63] In the usual case, further instruction comes from the prosecutor. It is common practice for the prosecutor to provide general instruction before a given presentation and not to repeat them at ensuing presentations when the same legal issue arises.[64] This means, in the typical case, that when a court reviews grand jury minutes upon a motion to inspect and dismiss it may not be supplied with all the pertinent instructions provided to the panel.

Both subdivisions six and seven of section 190.30 employ parallel sentence structure in providing that, in a situation where a court *must* rule or instruct, the district attorney *may* do so. This language could be interpreted in two ways. On the one hand, it could be argued that instructions must be given by either the court or the prosecutor, and that these provisions merely authorize the prosecutor to do so. On the other hand, it could be said that no instruction need be given—that the language merely consigns instruction to the prosecutor's discretion. The Second Department, in at least one case, has adopted the latter interpretation.[65]

Similarly, section 190.25(6) directs the court and the prosecutor to give legal instruction "where necessary and appropriate." In *People v. Calbud, Inc.*,[66] the court compared this language to the requirements of CPL § 300.10, regarding instructions at trial to a petit jury, and determined that

> [i]n view of the divergent functions of the two bodies, we hold that a Grand Jury need not be instructed with the same degree of precision that is required when a petit jury is instructed on

---

61. That ruling, in and of itself, appears contrary to the general principle that rules of evidence apply to grand jury proceedings. See § 5.6, infra.

62. CPL § 190.20(5).

63. Id. See generally New York Criminal Jury Instructions §§ 1.03, 1.04 (1983).

64. See, e.g., People v. McLaurin, 196 A.D.2d 511, 601 N.Y.S.2d 139 (2d Dep't 1993)(instructions on circumstantial evidence prior to presentation sufficient).

65. People v. McLaurin, 196 A.D.2d at 511, 601 N.Y.S.2d at 140. ("There is no legal requirement that the prosecutor deliver any particular charge to the Grand Jury," citing CPL § 190.30(7)).

66. 49 N.Y.2d 389, 426 N.Y.S.2d 238, 402 N.E.2d 1140 (1980).

the law. We deem it sufficient if the District Attorney provides the Grand Jury with enough information to enable it intelligently to decide whether a crime has been committed and to determine whether there exists legally sufficient evidence to establish the material elements of the crime.[67]

The court continued, in a footnote:

In the ordinary case, this standard may be met by reading to the Grand Jury from the appropriate sections of the Penal Law.[68]

Thus, in *Calbud*, it was sufficient for the prosecutor, in defining obscenity to a jury, to read the elements of the crime without further explaining the need for applying community standards.

In *People v. Valles*,[69] the holding in *Calbud* was extended. The defendant shot and killed a man who allegedly had raped his stepdaughter a year earlier, in order, the defendant asserted, to protect her from another attack. Thus, evidence of both an exculpatory defense, justification, and a mitigating defense, extreme emotional disturbance, were potentially presented. The prosecutor charged the grand jury on murder in the second degree, but refused a request to present a manslaughter option to the grand jury on the ground that more than two shots were fired. On appeal, the defendant contended the proceedings were defective because the grand jury was not instructed on the affirmative defense of extreme emotional disturbance. A four-judge majority opinion[70] stated:

[T]he question of whether a particular defense need be charged depends upon its potential for eliminating a needless or unfounded prosecution. The appropriate distinction for this purpose is between exculpatory and mitigating defenses. An exculpatory defense is one that would, if believed, result in a finding of no criminal liability. The Grand Jury's function being to protect citizens from having to defend against unfounded accusations, such complete defenses would ordinarily rest peculiarly within that body's proper domain. Thus, in the present case, had the Grand Jury believed that defendant's acts were justified, no indictment would have been returned and an unwarranted prosecution would have been avoided.[71]

---

67. 49 N.Y.2d at 394, 426 N.Y.S.2d at 24.

68. 49 N.Y.2d at 394 n.1, 426 N.Y.S.2d at 241 n.1.

69. 62 N.Y.2d 36, 476 N.Y.S.2d 50, 464 N.E.2d 418 (1984).

70. Judge Kaye and Chief Judge Cooke concurred on the grounds that it was not necessary under the facts of the case to charge the affirmative defense. They disagreed with the broad statement that defenses in mitigation need not be charged.

71. 69 N.Y.2d at 38–39, 476 N.Y.S.2d at 51. In dissent, Judge Meyer pointed out that the effect of the ruling was to take away from the grand jury one of its traditional functions—choosing an appropriate charge level. If the jury is not told of lesser included offenses and defenses in mitigation, it is deprived of its ability to use a community judgment in deciding not just whether to charge the defendant but in deciding what charge to bring. See § 5.7, infra.

Two years after *Valles*, the holding was extended in *People v. Lancaster*.[72] In that case, the defendant complained that, although the grand jury was instructed on the defense of not guilty by reason of mental disease or defect,[73] the prosecutor did not affirmatively present evidence of that defense. The court held that there was no duty to instruct the jury on the defense in the first place and, therefore, the prosecution had no concomitant duty to present evidence. In response to the defendant's contention that mental disease or defect is a "complete" defense, and under *Valles* complete defenses must be charged, the court ruled:

> Valles does not require that every complete defense suggested by the evidence be charged to the Grand Jury; rather "whether a particular defense need be charged depends upon its potential for eliminating a needless or unfounded prosecution".... Accordingly, where evidence establishes a potential defense of justification, prosecution may be needless and the Grand Jury should be charged on the law regarding that potential defense because its consideration is properly within that body's province.... On the other hand, although the defense of mental disease or defect also may be properly considered a complete defense in the sense that, if believed, it would relieve the defendant of responsibility for his otherwise criminal conduct, it is nevertheless a defense of a unique and specific nature—the defense of mental disease or defect does not have the potential for eliminating a "needless or unfounded prosecution."[74]

While *Lancaster* may appear to portend further retreat from a rule obligating a prosecutor to charge necessary instructions to the jury, that should not be assumed. For one thing, *Lancaster* presented an almost unique situation. A finding of mental disease or defect by the grand jury would have put the defendant in a better position than if he had prevailed upon the defense at trial, since there is no authority for, as there is upon a petit jury's verdict, for commitment of a defendant following a finding of mental defect by a grand jury.[75] Additionally, lack of mental responsibility is, under present law, an affirmative defense determined only after the jury has found the defendant guilty of the crime.[76] As such, it is more akin to a mitigation defense, as in *Valles*, than a defense of exculpation.

The majority in *Lancaster* reaffirmed the general principle that

> [t]he prosecutor's discretion in presenting the case to the Grand Jury ... is not unbounded, for it is settled that at a Grand Jury proceeding, the prosecutor performs the dual role of advocate and public officer, charged with the duty not only to secure indictments but also to see that justice is done; "as a public

---

72. 69 N.Y.2d 20, 511 N.Y.S.2d 559, 503 N.E.2d 990 (1986), cert. den. sub nom. Lancaster v. New York, 480 U.S. 922, 107 S.Ct. 1383, 94 L.Ed.2d 697 (1987).

73. See P.L. § 30.05.

74. 69 N.Y.2d at 27–28, 511 N.Y.S.2d at 563 (citations omitted).

75. See CPL Article 330.

76. P.L. § 30.05.

officer he owes a duty of fair dealing to the accused and candor to the courts." The prosecutor's duty of fair dealing extends not only to the submission of evidence, but also to instructions on the law.[77]

As if to underscore the point, *Lancaster* was decided on the same day[78] as *People v. Batashure*,[79] which affirmed the dismissal of an indictment because of the prosecutor's confusing instruction to the grand jury on the standard of legal sufficiency.[80] *Batashure* affirmed the principle that dismissal is required upon a showing of a potential for prejudice; actual prejudice need not be shown.[81]

In the wake of the *Lancaster-Batashure-Darby* trilogy, it is fair to say that the law concerning whether a charge need be given is still evolving. Subsequent cases have, for instance, set aside an indictment for failure to give proper instructions regarding an alibi,[82] failure to tell the grand jury that the burden does not shift when a defendant testifies,[83] and failure to explain what weight to give an inference after it has been rebutted.[84] Further guidance from the Court of Appeals would be welcome.[85]

Library References:
West's Key No. Digests, Grand Jury ⟹23.

§ 5.6 Grand Jury—Applicability of Rules of Evidence

CPL § 60.10 provides that the "rules of evidence applicable to civil cases are, where appropriate, also applicable to criminal proceedings." The term "criminal proceeding" includes grand jury presentations.[86] CPL § 190.65(1)(b) requires the "reasonable cause" determination by

77. 69 N.Y.2d at 26, 511 N.Y.S.2d at 562.

78. Also decided the same day was People v. Darby, 75 N.Y.2d 449, 554 N.Y.S.2d 426, 553 N.E.2d 974 (1990)(grand jury need not be instructed regarding voluntariness of confession).

79. 75 N.Y.2d 306, 552 N.Y.S.2d 896, 552 N.E.2d 144 (1990).

80. The prosecutor had instructed as follows: "The question of whether evidence is legally sufficient is a question of law, not fact. So it is a question that must be determined by me, legal advisor, whether evidence is legally sufficient, okay. This case, I'm your legal advisor."

81. See People v. Caracciola, 78 N.Y.2d 1021, 1022, 576 N.Y.S.2d 74, 74, 581 N.E.2d 1329, 1329 (1991)("While instructions to the Grand Jury need not be as precise as those given to a petit jury, they may not be so misleading or incomplete as to substantially undermine the integrity of the proceedings.").

82. People v. Hughes, 159 Misc.2d 663, 606 N.Y.S.2d 499 (Monroe Co.Ct.1992).

83. People v. Sutton, 149 Misc.2d 672, 564 N.Y.S.2d 646 (Sup.Ct., Bronx County, 1990).

84. People v. Rivera, 161 Misc.2d 237, 612 N.Y.S.2d 782 (Sup.Ct., N.Y. County, 1994).

85. It would be ironic, in light of the discussion concerning the joint responsibility of a court and the prosecutor to act as legal advisors, if the law were to develop two standards—holding prosecutors to a lesser standard when they instruct a grand jury than the standard to which a court would be held if it were to perform the same function.

86. In People v. Larry Smith, ___ N.Y.2d ___, ___ N.Y.S.2d ___, ___ N.E.2d ___, 1996 WL 49007 (1996), the prosecution argued that the trial court improperly intervened to issue an order prospectively precluding impeachment on pending criminal matters. The court stated that the "scope of cross-examination is not the exclusive province of the prosecutor, and the grand jury judge was empowered to issue the preliminary ruling." CPL § 1.20(18).

the grand jury to be based upon "competent and admissible evidence." In addition, CPL § 190.65(1)(a) provides that an indictment must be supported by "legally sufficient" evidence, and CPL § 70.10(1) requires "legally sufficient evidence" to be based only upon "competent evidence." Finally, CPL § 190.30(1) declares, "Except as otherwise provided in this section, the provisions of [CPL] article sixty, governing rules of evidence and related matters with respect to criminal proceedings in general, are, where appropriate, applicable to grand jury proceedings."

In sum, six separate provisions of the CPL conjoin to form one inescapable conclusion: that the rules of evidence that apply at trial also apply in the grand jury. Rarely has the Legislature spoken as unequivocally.

In keeping with that intent, the Court of Appeals has scrupulously enforced the rule, notwithstanding entreaties to ease the burden in the grand jury. Unlike the rule of *Calbud*,[87] tolerating less than precise instructions on the law in the grand jury, the court has not granted parallel flexibility in application of the rules of evidence.

So, for example, in *People v. Lopez*,[88] the court upheld a dismissal of an indictment for grand larceny, dependent upon the value of an automobile, where the proof of the value of the automobile was the opinion of the owner, without proper foundation having been established in the grand jury. Similarly, in *People v. Mitchell*,[89] the court agreed with the Appellate Division in reversing a lower court dismissal for failure to introduce an exculpatory statement by the defendant, and held that the statement was technically inadmissible. This was so, the court declared, because "the general criminal trial court evidentiary rules normally apply to grand jury proceedings ... [and these] standards were met in the grand jury proceedings here."[90]

CPL § 60.10(1), governing rules of evidence at trial, and CPL § 190.30(1), governing rules of evidence in the grand jury, both include the phrase "where appropriate" when requiring application of the rules of evidence. The origins and significance of that phrase were addressed at length by Justice Lazer, in dissent, in *People v. Brewster*.[91] In that case, by a 3–2 majority, the Second Department ruled that testimony of a photographic identification could be admitted in grand jury proceedings, notwithstanding its inadmissibility at trial, because a modification of the rule against its admission was "appropriate" under section 190.30(1). Justice Lazer countered that

> [t]he majority takes the Legislature's use of the words "where appropriate" to mean that while photographic identification evidence is not competent at a trial, it is "appropriate" for use

---

87. See People v. Calbud, Inc., 49 N.Y.2d 389, 426 N.Y.S.2d 238, 402 N.E.2d 1140 (1980). See § 5.5, supra.

88. 79 N.Y.2d 402, 583 N.Y.S.2d 356, 592 N.E.2d 1360 (1992).

89. 82 N.Y.2d 509, 605 N.Y.S.2d 655, 626 N.E.2d 630 (1993).

90. 82 N.Y.2d at 509, 605 N.Y.S.2d at 513.

91. 100 A.D.2d 134, 473 N.Y.S.2d 984 (2d Dep't 1984).

in the Grand Jury room. Analysis of the merits of this position leads first to the staff comments to the CPL which provide insight as to the meaning of "where appropriate". In the comment to CPL article 60, the drafters of the statute declare that "[u]pon the theory that the various types of criminal proceedings * * * are all subject to a basic evidentiary pattern, the proposed Criminal Procedure Law prescribes its rules of evidence in the 'General Provisions', thus according them across-the-board application, subject, of course, to qualification by the specialized provisions governing procedure in particular areas." In a further comment to CPL 190.30 (subd. 1), the section that contains the "where appropriate" language, the drafters remark that "[s]ubdivision 1 merely calls attention to the fact that the rules of evidence governing criminal proceedings in general * * * are applicable to grand jury proceedings except where a different rule is expressly predicated in this section." Thus, if there is a difference in the rules relating to the admissibility of evidence at a trial and in the Grand Jury room, it must be "expressly predicated" on a "specialized" provision of the CPL. The rules of evidence contained in CPL article 60 are therefore "appropriate" for Grand Jury proceedings unless a provision of article 190 specifically provides otherwise.[92]

Significantly, although the Court of Appeals sustained the indictment in *Brewster*,[93] it rejected the rationale of the majority and refused to bend the rules of evidence under the rubric that it was "appropriate" to do so:

> The Appellate Division ... reinstated the indictment (two Justices dissenting), holding it not "appropriate" within the meaning of CPL § 190.30 (subd. 1) to apply to Grand Jury proceedings the provisions of CPL § 60.30 which, as construed, prohibit the introduction of evidence of a prior photographic identification. *We affirm although on somewhat different reasoning....* Indeed, the identification testimony before the Grand Jury was not hearsay, for the Grand Jury which indicted defendants heard no evidence concerning how or when the identification was made. There was, therefore, no infringement of CPL 60.30.[94]

In light of Justice Lazer's careful research and the pointed conclusions of the Court of Appeals on this point, it is still safe to say that the rules of evidence at trial and in the grand jury are, except where the statute expressly provides otherwise, the same.[95]

92. 100 A.D.2d at 148–49, 473 N.Y.S.2d at 994 (Lazer, J., dissenting)(citations omitted).

93. 63 N.Y.2d 419, 482 N.Y.S.2d 724, 472 N.E.2d 686 (1984).

94. 63 N.Y.2d at 422–23, 482 N.Y.S.2d at 725 (emphasis supplied).

95. Cf. People v. Young, 163 Misc.2d 36, 620 N.Y.S.2d 223 (Sup.Ct., Queens County, 1994)(upholding admission of a laboratory report that would not otherwise be admissible under section 190.30) with People v. Calero, 163 Misc.2d 13, 618 N.Y.S.2d 996

§ 5.6   GRAND JURY & INDICTMENT   Ch. 5

Library References:

West's Key No. Digests, Grand Jury ⟲36.1–36.9.

§ 5.7 Grand Jury—Exculpatory Evidence

As discussed in Section 5.5, *supra*, "whether a particular defense need be *charged* depends upon its potential for eliminating a needless or unfounded prosecution."[96] The question arises whether the same standard applies to the prosecution's obligation to *present* exculpatory evidence in its possession.[97] The general rule, announced in *People v. Mitchell*,[98] is that

> the People maintain broad discretion in presenting their case to the Grand Jury and need not seek evidence favorable to the defendant or present all of their evidence tending to exculpate the accused.[99]

At the same time,

> [i]t is familiar doctrine that a prosecutor serves a dual role as advocate and public officer. He is charged with the duty not only to seek convictions but also to see that justice is done. In his position as a public officer he owes a duty of fair dealing to

(Sup.Ct., N.Y. County, 1994)(excluding a similar report).

One commentator has remarked:

> It would be an oversimplification, however, to conclude that New York grand jury rules of evidence are identical to those at trial save for the exceptions listed in subdivisions two through four of this section [CPL § 190.30]. In the absence of an explicit statutory restriction, evidence that would be excluded at trial under common law may be received in the grand jury, if the policy rationale for exclusion at trial does not apply to grand jury proceedings—e.g., evidence of identification from a photographic array.

Preiser, "Practice Commentary" to CPL § 190.30, McKinney's Cons. Laws of N.Y., Book 11A, at 242 (1993). As is evident from the discussion in this section, the accuracy of this statement would appear to be in doubt.

96. People v. Lancaster, 69 N.Y.2d 20, 27, 511 N.Y.S.2d 559, 563, 503 N.E.2d 990, 994 (1986), quoting People v. Valles, 62 N.Y.2d 36, 38, 476 N.Y.S.2d 50, 51, 464 N.E.2d 418, 419 (1984)(emphasis supplied).

97. The discussion herein applies to evidence known to have exculpatory potential at the time of the presentation. This is in contrast to the line of cases addressing weaknesses or problems with evidence uncovered after the presentation, where the usual rule is that evidence, which on its face was competent at the time of the presentation, can be used in gauging the sufficiency of the evidence in the grand jury. People v. Oakley, 28 N.Y.2d 309, 321 N.Y.S.2d 596, 270 N.E.2d 318 (1971); People v. Sian, 167 A.D.2d 435, 561 N.Y.S.2d 791 (2d Dep't 1990); People v. Vega, 80 A.D.2d 867, 436 N.Y.S.2d 748 (2d Dep't 1981); People v. Mauceri, 74 A.D.2d 833, 425 N.Y.S.2d 346 (2d Dep't 1980).

On the other hand, an infirmity in the evidence, first revealed after indictment, may present a legal impediment to conviction, requiring dismissal of the indictment before trial under CPL § 210.20(1)(h). See People v. Swamp, 84 N.Y.2d 725, 732, 622 N.Y.S.2d 472, 476, 646 N.E.2d 774 (1995).

98. 82 N.Y.2d 509, 605 N.Y.S.2d 655, 626 N.E.2d 630 (1993).

99. 82 N.Y.2d at 515, 605 N.Y.S.2d at 658. See also People v. Frazier, 200 A.D.2d 510, 606 N.Y.S.2d 682 (1st Dep't 1994)(complainant testified before grand jury that the defendant threw the first punch, and prosecutor, who was present during interview of complainant by fellow prosecutor who had presented the case to the grand jury, recalled that complainant had stated that he had thrown the first punch but had missed; court held prosecution was "not required to introduce the purported statement at issue to the Grand Jury"); People v. Zupan, 184 A.D.2d 888, 585 N.Y.S.2d 545 (3d Dep't 1992); People v. Townsend, 127 A.D.2d 505, 511 N.Y.S.2d 858 (1st Dep't 1987); People v. Isla, 96 A.D.2d 789, 466 N.Y.S.2d 16 (1st Dep't 1983).

the accused and candor to the courts, a duty which he violates when he obtains a conviction based upon evidence he knows to be false. Such misconduct may impair a defendant's due process rights and require a reversal of the conviction.[100]

There may be, then, "some circumstances in which the exculpatory evidence is so essential to a complete understanding of the case that the prosecution's failure to disclose it can actually prevent the Grand Jury from functioning as an intelligent and informed decision-making body."[101]

As a general proposition, courts are reluctant to overturn an indictment for failure to present exculpatory evidence. In the typical case, however, the supposedly exculpatory evidence merely raises a collateral issue, such as the credibility of the complainant, and is not therefore "essential" to the jury's determination.[102]

On the other hand, where exculpatory evidence is in the prosecution's possession and it directly implicates a potential defense, the obligation to present it to the jury may well exist. Just as *People v. Lancaster*[103] and *People v. Valles*[104] drew a distinction between defenses in exculpation and affirmative defenses in mitigation,[105] the same principle seems to be evolving with regard to exculpatory evidence in the grand jury. For example, in *People v. Falcon*,[106] the First Department held that an indictment was properly dismissed where the prosecution presented the defendant's written confession, admitting to a homicide, but withheld a videotaped confession that raised a justification defense. On the other hand, in *People v. Black*,[107] a videotaped confession need not have been presented to the grand jury merely because it suggested the affirmative defense of duress.[108]

100. People v. Pelchat, 62 N.Y.2d 97, 105, 476 N.Y.S.2d 79, 83, 464 N.E.2d 447, 451 (1984). Cf. United States v. Williams, 504 U.S. 36, 112 S.Ct. 1735, 118 L.Ed.2d 352 (1992)(no obligation to present "substantially exculpatory evidence" to federal grand jury).

101. People v. Mitchell, 82 N.Y.2d at 517, 605 N.Y.S.2d at 659 (Titone, J., dissenting).

102. See, e.g., People v. Dillard, 214 A.D.2d 1028, 627 N.Y.S.2d 184 (4th Dep't 1995)("The prosecutor's failure to present exculpatory evidence that the surviving victim had not identified defendant from a photographic array and that the witness had recanted his earlier statement that defendant was the perpetrator does not render the Grand Jury proceeding defective"); People v. Morris, 204 A.D.2d 973, 974, 613 N.Y.S.2d 66, 67 (4th Dep't 1994)(statement by defendant's companion that companion committed crime alone was collateral and "merely raised a question of fact"); People v. Perry, 187 A.D.2d 678, 590 N.Y.S.2d 251 (2d Dep't 1992)(failure to tell grand jury that boyfriend of defendant said he was the one who cut off complainant's fingers merely raised a question of fact).

103. 69 N.Y.2d 20, 511 N.Y.S.2d 559, 503 N.E.2d 990 (1986), cert. den. 480 U.S. 922, 107 S.Ct. 1383, 94 L.Ed.2d 697 (1987).

104. 62 N.Y.2d 36, 476 N.Y.S.2d 50, 464 N.E.2d 418 (1984).

105. See § 5.4, supra.

106. 204 A.D.2d 181, 612 N.Y.S.2d 130 (1st Dep't 1994).

107. ___ A.D.2d ___, 632 N.Y.S.2d 823 (2d Dep't 1995).

108. One unusual case, People v. Glenn, ___ A.D.2d ___, 632 N.Y.S.2d 188 (2d Dep't 1995), recently denied a request to inspect grand jury minutes for exculpatory evidence of a justification defense by asserting that the challenge was not jurisdictional, and thereby was forfeited by the defendant's guilty plea. However, since the issue raised went to a defect in the proceedings, that would seem to be clearly wrong under the current state of the law. See People v. Pelchat, 62 N.Y.2d 97, 476 N.Y.S.2d 79, 464 N.E.2d 447 (1984).

Paralleling the obligation to instruct a jury with regard to a defense, the obligation to present evidence of a defense rests upon "the potential of the defense in question to eliminate a 'needless or unfounded prosecution.'"[109] However, given that *Mitchell* was a narrowly decided, 4–3, opinion that rested in whole or in part upon the inadmissibility of the excluded evidence, not its potential for exculpation, it may be premature to conclude that the rule governing presentation of exculpatory evidence is precisely coextensive with the rule governing the duty to instruct a defense.[110]

Library References:
West's Key No. Digests, Grand Jury ⇔36.1–36.9.

§ 5.8 Grand Jury—Appearance of Witnesses

CPL § 190.50 regulates the appearance of witnesses before the grand jury.[111] Since a grand jury proceeding is, in effect, an "ex parte presentment of evidence by the prosecution,"[112] the prosecution is given wide latitude with regard to the presentation of testimonial evidence. As such, section 190.50 provides that a prosecutor may call as a witness any person whom he or she believes "possesses relevant information or knowledge."[113]

The prosecutor is granted broad discretion[114] in summoning witnesses to appear before the grand jury.[115] Absent a showing of bad faith, a prosecutor's subpoena seeking testimony for a grand jury is presumptively valid.[116] Accordingly, to quash a subpoena, the moving party must

---

109. People v. Ramjit, 203 A.D.2d 488, 489, 612 N.Y.S.2d 600, 601 (2d Dep't 1994)(quoting People v. Lancaster, 69 N.Y.2d 20, 511 N.Y.S.2d 559, 503 N.E.2d 990 (1986), cert. den. 480 U.S. 922, 107 S.Ct. 1383, 94 L.Ed.2d 697 (1987)). Accord People v. Erber, 210 A.D.2d 250, 619 N.Y.S.2d 344 (2d Dep't 1994)(evidence of the affirmative defense of duress need not have been presented because "the allegedly exculpatory evidence neither made out a complete legal defense nor was of such quality as to create the potential to eliminate a 'needless or unfounded prosecution'")(citing People v. Lancaster, 69 N.Y.2d at 27, 511 N.Y.S.2d at 563).

110. Cf. People v. Lancaster, 69 N.Y.2d at 26, 511 N.Y.S.2d at 562 ("In the ordinary case, it is the defendant who, through the exercise of his own right to testify and have others called to testify on his behalf before the Grand jury (CPL 190.50[5],[6]) brings exculpatory evidence [before] the Grand Jury.").

111. CPL § 190.50(1)(witnesses may be called in a grand jury proceeding only by the prosecutor, the grand jury, or a person who is the subject of a pending or ongoing grand jury investigation).

112. People v. Evans, 79 N.Y.2d 407, 414, 583 N.Y.S.2d 358, 361, 592 N.E.2d 1362, 1365 (1992). See also LaFave and Israel, Criminal Procedure, § 15.2 (1984)(criticizing grand jury procedure as being subject to the will of the prosecution).

113. CPL § 190.50(2).

114. This power may not be delegated by the district attorney. In re Kronberg, 95 A.D.2d 714, 464 N.Y.S.2d 466 (1st Dep't 1983), aff'd 62 N.Y.2d 853, 477 N.Y.S.2d 625, 466 N.E.2d 165 (1984)(district attorney may not delegate to the police power to call persons to testify before grand jury).

115. CPL § 190.50(2). See, e.g., People v. DiFalco, 44 N.Y.2d 482, 486, 406 N.Y.S.2d 279, 282, 377 N.E.2d 732, 735 (1978); Matter of Kuriansky v. Seewald, 148 A.D.2d 238, 544 N.Y.S.2d 336 (1st Dep't 1989); Matter of Rodriguez v. Morgenthau, 121 Misc.2d 694, 468 N.Y.S.2d 833 (Sup.Ct., N.Y. County, 1983).

116. See, e.g., People ex rel. Van Der Beek v. McCloskey, 18 A.D.2d 205, 238 N.Y.S.2d 676 (1st Dep't 1963); People v. Doe, 148 Misc.2d 286, 560 N.Y.S.2d 177 (St.Lawrence Co.Ct.1990)

demonstrate that the prosecution is seeking testimony unrelated to the legitimate objective of the grand jury's investigation.[117]

CPL § 190.50(3) provides that the grand jury's right to cause witnesses to be called is as extensive as the prosecutor's. Upon determining that it wishes to hear the testimony of a witness not called by the prosecutor, a grand jury may direct the prosecutor to issue a subpoena compelling a witness to appear before it.[118]

The grand jury's right to call witnesses is, however, subject to two limitations. First, the prosecutor may apply to the supervisory court to vacate the jury's direction, where issuance of the subpoena is not "in the public interest." A second limitation is that the prosecutor may demand that a witness called by the grand jury execute a waiver of immunity pursuant to CPL § 190.45 prior to being sworn.[119] This condition preserves the prosecution's control over who will receive "automatic" immunity. Indeed, "absent this provision, a lay body of grand jurors could immunize a suspect without consent of the People and without sufficient knowledge of, or even access to, all of the relevant facts."[120] However, the prosecution's right to demand such waiver must not be exercised capriciously, as it is held to the abuse of discretion standard in assessing the propriety of imposing a waiver.[121]

In the event that the prosecution is found to have improperly refused to call a witness whose testimony is requested by the grand jury, a defendant is entitled to dismissal of the indictment only upon the additional showing of the "possibility of prejudice."[122] The test to be applied is "whether such evidence might have materially influenced the grand jury's investigation."[123]

CPL § 190.50(5) guarantees an individual's right to appear[124] as a witness before a grand jury considering charges against him or her.

---

117. See, e.g., Virag v. Hynes, 54 N.Y.2d 437, 446 N.Y.S.2d 196, 430 N.E.2d 1249 (1981); People v. Doe, supra.

118. The jury's decision to direct the prosecutor to subpoena a witness is an "affirmative grand jury action" requiring the concurrence of at least 12 grand jurors. CPL § 190.25(1).

119. CPL § 190.50(4).

120. People v. Batista, 164 Misc.2d 632, 638, 625 N.Y.S.2d 1008, 1012 (Sup.Ct., Kings County, 1995), quoting Preiser, "Practice Commentary" to CPL § 190.50, McKinney's Cons. Laws of New York, Book 11A, at 284 (1993). See also People v. Hylton, 139 Misc.2d 645, 529 N.Y.S.2d 412 (Sup.Ct., Nassau County, 1988)(discretionary power of district attorney to demand that defendant's witnesses waive their immunity before giving evidence to the grand jury does not violate due process).

121. See, e.g., People v. Batista, supra (abuse of discretion for prosecution to demand that defendant's witness summoned by the grand jury testify under waiver of immunity, notwithstanding witness's refusal to "cooperate" and submit to interview by prosecutor outside presence of defense counsel; prosecution conceded witness was never a suspect). See also People v. Buszak, 185 A.D.2d 621, 587 N.Y.S.2d 52 (4th Dep't 1992)(no abuse of discretion to compel defendant's two alibi witnesses to waive immunity).

122. People v. Johnson, 155 Misc.2d 791, 590 N.Y.S.2d 153 (Sup.Ct., Monroe County, 1992). See also People v. McCullough, 141 A.D.2d 856, 530 N.Y.S.2d 198 (2d Dep't 1988). Cf. CPL § 190.50(5)(c)(indictment obtained in violation of defendant's statutory right to appear must be dismissed, notwithstanding lack of prejudice to defendant).

123. Johnson, 155 Misc.2d at 794, 590 N.Y.S.2d at 155–56.

124. The section requires live witness testimony, not simply the submission of written statements. People v. Smalls, 111 A.D.2d 38, 488 N.Y.S.2d 712 (1st Dep't

Where a defendant has served upon the prosecution timely written notice of his or her desire to testify, failure to provide him or her with an opportunity to appear mandates dismissal of the indictment. This right is absolute. Accordingly, where an indictment is obtained in violation of the statute, a court is not authorized to condition dismissal upon the defendant's certification that he or she will appear before the grand jury when the charges are re-presented. Rather, the indictment must be dismissed, and the defendant retains the *option* to appear when and if the charges are re-submitted.[125]

Before reviewing the substantive issues that routinely arise in motions to dismiss under section 190.50, one procedural point bears special mention: any defendant wishing to object to an indictment on the ground that it was obtained in violation of this section must do within *five days* of his or her arraignment upon the indictment.[126] This provision is strictly enforced,[127] and compliance is excused only where either the arraigning judge grants an extension,[128] or the defendant has been deprived of the right to assistance of counsel.[129]

As a practical matter, most defendants receive notice of the prosecution's intention to seek an indictment at their arraignment upon the felony complaint. An individual is not, however, automatically entitled to formal notice merely because a grand jury action is ongoing or about to occur.[130]

The prosecution is required to provide notice that a grand jury proceeding is in progress or about to occur *only* when a defendant is

1985)(defendant could not compel prosecutor to submit defendant's post-arrest statement to grand jury).

125. People v. Mason, 176 A.D.2d 356, 574 N.Y.S.2d 589 (2d Dep't 1991); People v. Bey–Allah, 132 A.D.2d 76, 521 N.Y.S.2d 422 (1st Dep't 1987); Matter of Borrello v. Balbach, 112 A.D.2d 1051, 492 N.Y.S.2d 822 (2d Dep't 1985).

126. CPL § 190.50(5)(c). See discussion concerning procedural aspects of motions to dismiss in § 5.25, infra.

127. See, e.g., People v. Wilkins, 188 A.D.2d 320, 591 N.Y.S.2d 18 (1st Dep't 1992); People v. Gonzalez, 176 A.D.2d 109, 573 N.Y.S.2d 689 (1st Dep't 1991).

128. See People v. Mason, 176 A.D.2d 356, 574 N.Y.S.2d 589 (2d Dep't 1991).

129. See, e.g., People v. McMoore, 203 A.D.2d 612, 614, 609 N.Y.S.2d 964, 966 (3d Dep't 1994)(failure to make timely motion to dismiss is deemed a waiver of defendant's right to appear, provided that such waiver was made after consultation with counsel); People v. Moskowicz, 192 A.D.2d 317, 595 N.Y.S.2d 464 (1st Dep't 1993)(trial court properly entertained new counsel's motion made beyond five-day mark after crediting defendant's sworn affidavit that prior counsel never consulted with him concerning his case or informed him of his right to appear before the grand jury); People v. Stevens, 151 A.D.2d 704, 542 N.Y.S.2d 754 (2d Dep't 1989) (strict application of five-day rule inappropriate where defendant was without counsel at time pro se dismissal motion was made); People v. Prest, 105 A.D.2d 1078, 482 N.Y.S.2d 172 (4th Dep't 1984).

130. People v. Munoz, 207 A.D.2d 418, 615 N.Y.S.2d 730 (2d Dep't 1994)(no error where prosecution failed to provide notice to defendant, whose case was submitted to grand jury to forestall his release under CPL § 180.80 following unsuccessful attempt to arraign him on felony complaint); People v. Simmons, 178 A.D.2d 972, 579 N.Y.S.2d 499 (4th Dep't 1991); People v. Roberson, 149 A.D.2d 926, 540 N.Y.S.2d 60 (4th Dep't 1989); People v. LaBounty, 127 A.D.2d 989, 512 N.Y.S.2d 950 (4th Dep't 1987). See also People v. Green, 110 A.D.2d 1035, 489 N.Y.S.2d 129 (4th Dep't 1985)(defendant originally charged with robbery in felony complaint not entitled to notice where preliminary hearing was conducted and matter was held for grand jury, as felony complaint was disposed of). Cf. People v. Tirado, 197 A.D.2d 927, 602 N.Y.S.2d 273 (4th Dep't 1993).

arraigned in local criminal court upon a "currently undisposed of felony complaint which is a subject of the prospective or pending grand jury proceeding."[131] While not all persons who are the subject of a pending or ongoing proceeding are entitled to formal grand jury notice, any individual who has reason to believe that he or she has been targeted by a grand jury may nevertheless exercise an option to appear as a witness, since this right is not contingent upon the prosecution's obligation to provide formal notice.[132]

The amount of information that must be included in the prosecution's grand jury notice is an issue that has been the subject of scant appellate review, and has never been fully considered by the Court of Appeals. Potential problems may arise when the defendant is arrested for a less serious charge and, after exercising his or her option, discovers that the prosecutor is seeking additional charges in the grand jury. The First Department has held, however, that the prosecution is not required to advise a defendant of the fact the it is seeking an indictment for more serious charges than those contained in the felony complaint.[133]

Similarly, where the prosecutor intends to submit *additional* charges arising from an incident which occurred on a date other than that contained in the complaint, there is appellate authority for the proposition that notice need only be provided as to those crimes that arise from the incident or incidents included in the complaint.[134] In other words, the scope of the grand jury notice may be limited to those crimes referenced in the felony complaint. On the other hand, the prosecution may not serve misleading notice that prevents a defendant from "appear[ing] meaningfully as a witness and ... secur[ing] the effective aid of counsel"[135]

Upon learning of a pending grand jury proceeding, an individual wishing to appear as a witness in his or her own behalf must serve upon the prosecution written notice—commonly referred to as "cross-grand jury notice"—of his or her unconditional[136] wish to do so.[137] Except in

---

131. CPL § 190.50(5)(a).

132. People v. Blackwell, 128 Misc.2d 584, 490 N.Y.S.2d 456 (Monroe Co.Ct.1985). See also People v. Luna, 127 Misc.2d 608, 486 N.Y.S.2d 839 (Sup.Ct., Queens County, 1985), aff'd 129 A.D.2d 816, 514 N.Y.S.2d 806 (2d Dep't 1987).

133. People v. Peter Hernandez, ___ A.D.2d ___, 636 N.Y.S.2d 45 (1st Dep't 1996). See also People v. Simmons, 178 A.D.2d 972, 579 N.Y.S.2d 499 (4th Dep't 1991); People v. Scott, 141 Misc.2d 623, 533 N.Y.S.2d 799 (Sup.Ct., Queens County, 1988); People v. Fletcher, 140 Misc.2d 389, 530 N.Y.S.2d 768 (Sup.Ct., Queens County, 1988). But see People v. Suarez, 103 Misc.2d 910, 427 N.Y.S.2d 187 (Sup.Ct., N.Y. County, 1980)(notice of more serious charge required).

134. See, e.g., People v. Choi, 210 A.D.2d 495, 620 N.Y.S.2d 131 (2d Dep't 1994); People v. Feliciano, 207 A.D.2d 803, 616 N.Y.S.2d 529 (2d Dep't 1994). But see People v. Smith, 155 Misc.2d 596, 589 N.Y.S.2d 254 (Orange Co.Ct.1992).

135. People v. Choi, supra, quoting People v. Martinez, 111 Misc.2d 67, 69, 443 N.Y.S.2d 576, 578 (Sup.Ct., Queens County, 1981).

136. See People v. Green, 187 A.D.2d 528, 589 N.Y.S.2d 916 (2d Dep't 1992); People v. Punter, 150 Misc.2d 136, 566 N.Y.S.2d 1005 (Sup.Ct., N.Y. County, 1991)(defense counsel's attempt to "reserve" defendant's right to appear did not constitute adequate notice). See also People v. Harris, 150 A.D.2d 723, 541 N.Y.S.2d 593 (2d Dep't 1989).

137. CPL § 190.50(5)(a).

§ 5.8   GRAND JURY & INDICTMENT   Ch. 5

extremely limited circumstances,[138] oral notice will not secure the right to testify.[139] An individual wishing to preserve this right should therefore do so in writing. Further, such notice must include an address to which communications are to be sent[140] and must be served "prior to the filing of any indictment or any direction to file a prosecutor's information in the matter."[141]

One point should be emphasized with regard to the timing of a defendant's cross-grand jury notice. The statute permits service prior to the *filing* of the indictment—thereby contemplating an appearance even after an indictment has been voted.[142] Notably, when an individual serves notice prior to the grand jury's vote, the prosecutor must provide him or her with a pre-vote opportunity to appear. In other words, re-opening the presentment for the defendant to make an appearance after the grand jury has already voted to indict will not suffice. In such a situation, the indictment must be dismissed and the charges re-presented. On the other hand, where service of cross-grand jury notice occurs after the indictment has been voted but prior to filing, the prosecutor is merely obligated to re-open the vote. And, as the Court of Appeals has observed:

> [T]he opportunity to testify prior to any Grand Jury vote is "qualitatively different" from and more advantageous than the opportunity to testify at a reopened presentment after the Grand Jury had committed itself to a vote based upon the prosecution's ex parte presentment of evidence.... [R]elegating defendants to an appearance before a reopened Grand Jury

---

138. Oral notice has been found sufficient in two categories of cases. The first is where the prosecutor is deemed to have waived the requirement. See, e.g., People v. Ocasio, 160 Misc.2d 422, 425, 609 N.Y.S.2d 523, 525 (Sup.Ct., Bronx County, 1994)(oral notice sufficient where "unequivocal demand of the defendant is met with an unequivocal response by the prosecutor" setting a specific date and time for defendant's appearance). See also People v. Bundy, 186 A.D.2d 357, 588 N.Y.S.2d 167 (1st Dep't 1992); People v. Young, 138 A.D.2d 764, 526 N.Y.S.2d 577 (2d Dep't 1988); People v. Dixon, 154 Misc.2d 454, 584 N.Y.S.2d 735 (Sup.Ct., Westchester County, 1992). The second category involves cases where the defendant was not afforded a "reasonable time to exercise his right to appear." People v. Gini, 72 A.D.2d 752, 421 N.Y.S.2d 269 (2d Dep't 1979); People v. Spence, 139 Misc.2d 77, 526 N.Y.S.2d 747 (Sup.Ct., Kings County, 1988). Finally, although no reported cases address this issue, it is conceivable that a court would deem oral notice sufficient upon a finding that defense counsel provided ineffective assistance.

139. See, e.g., People v. Robinson, 187 A.D.2d 296, 589 N.Y.S.2d 453 (1st Dep't 1992)(oral notification by defense counsel "communicated to an ADA other than the one assigned to the case minutes after being informed by the ADA assigned that she was immediately going to file the indictment, failed to comply with [the statute's] requirements"); People v. Green, 187 A.D.2d 528, 589 N.Y.S.2d 916 (2d Dep't 1992); People v. Saldana, 161 A.D.2d 441, 444, 556 N.Y.S.2d 534, 537 (1st Dep't 1990)(defendant's letter to Criminal Court judge and oral requests at two calendar calls insufficient to trigger prosecution's obligation to provide opportunity to appear). See also People v. Taylor, 165 A.D.2d 800, 564 N.Y.S.2d 60 (1st Dep't 1990); People v. Harris, 150 A.D.2d 723, 724, 541 N.Y.S.2d 593, 594 (2d Dep't 1989); People v. MacCall, 122 A.D.2d 79, 504 N.Y.S.2d 227 (2d Dep't 1986).

140. It is customary for the address provided to be that of defense counsel.

141. CPL § 190.50(5)(a).

142. People v. Evans, 79 N.Y.2d 407, 413, 583 N.Y.S.2d 358, 360, 592 N.E.2d 1362, 1364 (1992). See also People v. Kellman, 156 Misc.2d 179, 592 N.Y.S.2d 214 (Sup.Ct., Kings County, 1992).

that has already voted to indict them seems as dubious as listening to appellate counsel arguing only after an appeal has already been decided on the representation that the decision might be reexamined.[143]

Every effort should therefore be made to serve notice at the earliest possible juncture, since service prior to the vote ensures that the opportunity to appear is provided at the most meaningful time. Consequently, defense counsel ordinarily serve cross-notice immediately upon learning of the prosecutor's intention to seek an indictment, in order to protect this valuable right.

Courts have recognized that defendants seeking to enforce the right to appear are entitled to the effective assistance of counsel. Thus, notwithstanding the prosecution's compliance with the statute, an indictment must be dismissed where a defendant wishing to appear is "effectively precluded"[144] from doing so as a result of the ineffective assistance of defense counsel.[145]

Finally, an attorney, outside the presence of his or her client, may either waive the right to appear or withdraw a previously entered request to do so.[146] Such action cannot be unilaterally made by counsel, due to the personal nature of this right.[147] However, while an attorney cannot validly waive a client's section 190.50 rights merely because the attorney disagrees with the client's expressed intention to appear as a witness before the grand jury, one court has stated that counsel may

---

143. People v. Evans, 79 N.Y.2d at 414–415, 583 N.Y.S.2d at 361–62 (citation omitted).

144. People v. Lincoln, 80 A.D.2d 877, 436 N.Y.S.2d 782 (2d Dep't 1981).

145. See, e.g., People v. Wiggins, ___ A.D.2d ___, 634 N.Y.S.2d 747 (2d Dep't 1995)(defendant did not appear before grand jury due to late arrival of defense counsel, who had failed to note that the People's reciprocal notice stated exactly when the defendant was to appear and testify); People v. Moskowicz, 192 A.D.2d 317, 595 N.Y.S.2d 464 (1st Dep't 1993) (defendant could not have intelligently waived his right to testify where initial counsel repeatedly failed "to even appear on defendant's behalf when scheduled to do so" and trial court credited "defendant's sworn affidavit indicating that the attorney never consulted with him concerning his case or informed him of his right to testify before the grand jury"). But see People v. Bundy, 186 A.D.2d 357, 588 N.Y.S.2d 167 (1st Dep't 1992)(counsel's failure to submit written cross-grand jury notice does not, in and of itself, establish ineffective assistance, since such action may well have been deliberate).

On a related note, as a general rule, by pleading guilty a defendant forfeits appellate review of any claim of denial of the right to appear. People v. Ferrara, 99 A.D.2d 257, 472 N.Y.S.2d 407 (2d Dep't 1984). See also People v. Wheeler, 176 A.D.2d 1133, 575 N.Y.S.2d 951 (3d Dep't 1991). However, where a court determines that the defendant was deprived of the constitutional right to the assistance of counsel at the grand jury proceedings, "the forfeiture rule does not apply." People v. Stevens, 151 A.D.2d 704, 542 N.Y.S.2d 754 (2d Dep't 1989). See also People v. Lincoln, 80 A.D.2d 877, 436 N.Y.S.2d 782 (2d Dep't 1981); People v. Prest, 105 A.D.2d 1078, 482 N.Y.S.2d 172 (4th Dep't 1984).

146. See, e.g., People v. Helm, 69 A.D.2d 198, 419 N.Y.S.2d 287 (3d Dep't 1979), aff'd 51 N.Y.2d 853, 433 N.Y.S.2d 757, 413 N.E.2d 1172 (1980); People v. Jackson, 134 A.D.2d 521, 521 N.Y.S.2d 294 (2d Dep't 1987).

147. See, e.g., People v. Helm, supra; People v. Corona, 149 Misc.2d 581, 567 N.Y.S.2d 353 (Sup.Ct., Bronx County, 1991)(defendant entitled to dismissal of indictment where "original counsel's failure to consult with his client and then unilaterally waiving his client's [section 190.50] rights constitute[d] such a complete lack of meaningful representation as to be the equivalent of no representation at all").

nevertheless "execute a valid waiver when, after conferring with the defendant, he or she in good faith, albeit mistakenly, believes that by executing a waiver they are acting in accordance with the client's wishes."[148]

Once an individual serves notice of his or her intention to appear, the prosecutor must notify the foreperson of the grand jury of such request.[149] More importantly, the prosecutor must serve the applicant at the address specified in the request to appear with reciprocal written notice[150] of a specific time and place where he or she will be heard by the grand jury.

In the event that the prosecutor elects not to present the case on the scheduled date, the defendant is entitled, without making additional inquiries, to new notice specifying the subsequent date and time when the opportunity to appear will be provided.[151] Further, actual, rather than technical notice, "reasonably calculated to apprise the defendant of the Grand Jury proceeding," is contemplated by the statute.[152] Therefore, where the prosecution is aware that the defendant is no longer represented by the attorney whose address is specified in the defendant's cross-notice, it is obligated to serve "timely notice upon the defendant himself, or on an attorney subsequently entering the case if the People are aware of his appearance."[153] Although the prosecution is obliged to provide written reciprocal notice, the parties may dispense with this requirement and agree via telephone to arrange for a grand jury appearance.[154] In such a situation, an individual will be deemed to have waived the right to appear should either defense counsel fail to return the prosecutor's calls[155] or the defendant fail to remain in contact with defense counsel attempting to confirm his or her availability for a proposed opportunity to appear.[156] Several trial courts have held that the issuance of a bench warrant does not constitute a waiver such that the prosecution is relieved of its obligation to provide notice of a time

---

148. People v. Gaffney, N.Y.L.J., July 9, 1993, p. 23, col. 1 (Sup.Ct., N.Y. County). See also People v. Helm, supra (defense counsel's waiver valid where, despite discussing the matter with defendant, there was a misunderstanding between them regarding defendant's desire to appear).

149. CPL § 190.50(2).

150. See People v. Patterson, 189 A.D.2d 733, 593 N.Y.S.2d 8 (1st Dep't 1993). But see People v. Phillips, 88 A.D.2d 672, 450 N.Y.S.2d 925 (3d Dep't 1982)(oral notice a week in advance of scheduled presentment deemed adequate).

151. People v. Ocasio, 160 Misc.2d 422, 609 N.Y.S.2d 523 (Sup.Ct., Bronx County, 1994); People v. Martinez, 111 Misc.2d 67, 443 N.Y.S.2d 576 (Sup.Ct., Queens County, 1981). But see People v. Theard, 155 Misc.2d 475, 588 N.Y.S.2d 754 (Sup.Ct., Queens County, 1992)(defendant's failure to appear, in response to two prior notifications, or to contact prosecutor, constituted waiver such that prosecution not required to provide notice of date when case was actually presented).

152. People v. Abdullah, 189 A.D.2d 769, 592 N.Y.S.2d 406 (2d Dep't 1993).

153. People v. Jordan, 153 A.D.2d 263, 269, 550 N.Y.S.2d 917, 921 (2d Dep't 1990). See also People v. Davis, 133 Misc.2d 1031, 509 N.Y.S.2d 257 (Sup.Ct., Queens County, 1986).

154. See People v. Correa, 197 A.D.2d 430, 602 N.Y.S.2d 839 (1st Dep't 1993); People v. Patterson, 189 A.D.2d 733, 593 N.Y.S.2d 8 (1st Dep't 1993).

155. People v. Patterson, supra.

156. See People v. Perez, 158 Misc.2d 956, 602 N.Y.S.2d 307 (Sup.Ct., Queens County, 1993). See also People v. Correa, 197 A.D.2d 430, 431, 602 N.Y.S.2d 839, 840 (1st Dep't 1993); People v. Smith, 155 Misc.2d 596, 599, 589 N.Y.S.2d 254, 255 (Orange Co.Ct.1992).

when the defendant may appear.[157] One court has held, however, that a defendant will be deemed to have forfeited the right to appear where it is established, after a hearing, that the defendant's failure to appear on the date the warrant was issued was "willful."[158]

Reciprocal notice must be provided sufficiently in advance of the presentation so as to afford the defendant a "reasonable time to exercise his right to appear"[159] as a witness.[160] Not surprisingly, there is no clear-cut definition as to what constitutes a "reasonable time." While appellate courts have approved as little advance warning as four days,[161] one-day or same-day notice has consistently been found to be inadequate.[162] The guiding principle in such determinations appears to be that the reviewing court is satisfied that defense counsel had an adequate "opportunity to communicate with and advise his client" such that the defendant is not pressured into making a "spontaneous or even overnight decision regarding his appearance and testimony."[163]

In the event that a defendant is committed pursuant to a temporary order of observation in accordance with CPL Article 730, it is well-settled that the prosecution need not delay presentation.[164] However, it is unclear to what extent the prosecution is required to delay a presentation and vote so that an individual may appear before the grand jury with counsel of his or her choosing. Although there is little case law on point, the Second Department has held that a defendant is not entitled to an indefinite delay in presentment so that he or she may appear with retained counsel, particularly where an associate of counsel is available.[165] The court did not, however, state whether the fact that counsel

---

157. See, e.g., People v. Ocasio, 160 Misc.2d 422, 609 N.Y.S.2d 523 (Sup.Ct., Bronx County, 1994); People v. Gray, 158 Misc.2d 597, 601 N.Y.S.2d 526 (Sup.Ct., N.Y. County, 1993).

158. People v. Ocasio, supra.

159. CPL § 190.50(5)(a).

160. Notwithstanding this provision's placement in paragraph (a), cases have interpreted it as applying to the defendant's opportunity to serve "cross-grand jury notice", see, e.g., People v. Pugh, 207 A.D.2d 503, 615 N.Y.S.2d 912 (2d Dep't 1994); People v. Welsh, 124 A.D.2d 301, 508 N.Y.S.2d 278 (3d Dep't 1986); People v. Gini, 72 A.D.2d 752, 421 N.Y.S.2d 269 (2d Dep't 1979), as well as the full-blown preparations necessary between defense counsel and client for an effective appearance before the grand jury. People v. Taylor, 165 A.D.2d 800, 564 N.Y.S.2d 60 (1st Dep't 1990); People v. Eiffel, 139 Misc.2d 340, 527 N.Y.S.2d 347 (Sup.Ct., Queens County, 1988); People v. Singh, 131 Misc.2d 1094, 503 N.Y.S.2d 228 (Sup.Ct., Queens County, 1986).

161. People v. Pugh, supra. See also People v. Smith, 191 A.D.2d 598, 599, 594 N.Y.S.2d 799, 801 (2d Dep't 1993)(five days notice adequate).

162. See, e.g., People v. Gini, supra; People v. Singh, supra. At first blush, People v. Robinson, 187 A.D.2d 296, 589 N.Y.S.2d 453 (1st Dep't 1992) appears to sanction as little as one day notice. However, a careful reading of that decision makes clear that defendant's motion was denied for lack of written notice.

163. People v. Perez, 158 Misc.2d 956, 602 N.Y.S.2d 307 (Sup.Ct., Queens County, 1993). See also People v. Welsh, 124 A.D.2d 301, 508 N.Y.S.2d 278 (3d Dep't 1986).

164. CPL § 730.40(3). People v. Lancaster, 69 N.Y.2d 20, 31, 511 N.Y.S.2d 559, 565, 503 N.E.2d 990, 996 (1986).

165. People v. Ferrara, 99 A.D.2d 257, 472 N.Y.S.2d 407 (2d Dep't 1984). In Ferrara, the defendant, whose retained counsel had served notice on March 15, was afforded an opportunity to testify when he appeared in court on March 16 and March 24 with counsel's associate. After he declined to appear on both occasions upon the ground that the attorney actually representing him was engaged in federal court, the prosecutor telephoned defense counsel's office and advised a secretary that the case would be presented on March 30. Receiv-

§ 5.8 GRAND JURY & INDICTMENT Ch. 5

was assigned rather than retained would dictate a different result.[166] Given the limited authority on this point, a prosecutor would be ill-advised not to make all feasible efforts to accommodate reasonable scheduling requests by defense counsel.

Finally, in measuring the prosecutor's compliance with the statute, practical difficulties encountered by the prosecution are not legally cognizable. For example, where a defendant is not produced before the grand jury by the jailing authority on the date he or she is entitled to release pursuant to CPL § 180.80, the prosecution may not vote out the case and thereby ignore a request to appear in order to avoid such release.[167] Further, the prosecution may not condition a defendant's appearance upon his or her willingness to waive the defendant's right to section 180.80 release.[168] Therefore, a prosecutor scheduling a defendant's appearance on the "180.80 day" runs the risk that the defendant will be released in the event that "practical difficulties" make such appearance impossible.

Obviously, the most opportune time for a defendant to make an appearance before the grand jury is after that body has heard from all of the prosecution's witnesses. For, if the grand jury hears the defendant before the prosecutor's presentation, his or her testimony "will be out of context to the grand jurors who will not have heard any testimony as to the circumstances of the alleged offense and ... will not be in a position to raise questions with the defendant regarding the People's evidence."[169] It is therefore advisable for a defendant to apply to the supervisory court for an order that the prosecution's witnesses be presented before he or she testifies.[170] Although the court may, in its discretion, grant such request,[171] it is not required to do so.[172] It has therefore been suggested

ing no response from the defense, the prosecutor presented the case on that date and filed the indictment on March 31st. In denying defendant's motion to dismiss pursuant to section 190.50, the court held that the prosecution is not required to defer presentation "indefinitely or for an extended period of time because counsel chosen by a defendant is engaged in another case, particularly where ... the defendant has other counsel available to him." 99 A.D.2d at 410, 472 N.Y.S.2d at 410. But see People v. Young, 137 Misc.2d 400, 520 N.Y.S.2d 924 (Sup.Ct., Nassau County, 1987)(error for the prosecution to refuse a defendant's request for a three-week delay in presentment due to the unavailability of his retained counsel).

166. See People v. Bizzell, 144 Misc.2d 1000, 545 N.Y.S.2d 528, 530 (Sup.Ct., Queens County, 1989).

167. People v. Evans, 79 N.Y.2d 407, 583 N.Y.S.2d 358, 592 N.E.2d 1362 (1992).

168. People v. Wilson, 153 Misc.2d 784, 583 N.Y.S.2d 125 (Sup.Ct., Queens County, 1992).

169. Preiser, "Practice Commentary" to CPL § 190.50, McKinney's Cons. Laws of New York, Book 11A (Supp.).

170. On a related note, it has been held that where a defendant wishes to present evidence as to only one of two or more crimes that are properly joined pursuant to CPL § 200.20(2), he or she may not request an order from the supervisory court requiring the prosecutor to submit each charge to a separate grand jury. See, e.g., People v. Simon, 187 A.D.2d 740, 590 N.Y.S.2d 533 (2d Dep't 1992); Matter of Gold v. Booth, 79 A.D.2d 1013, 435 N.Y.S.2d 325 (2d Dep't 1981).

171. Matter of Morgenthau v. Altman, 58 N.Y.2d 1057, 462 N.Y.S.2d 629, 449 N.E.2d 409 (1983).

172. People v. Stepteau, 81 N.Y.2d 799, 800, 595 N.Y.S.2d 371, 372, 611 N.E.2d 272, 273 (1993)(a defendant is "not entitled to an order requiring the Grand Jury to call the prosecution's witnesses before hearing defendant's testimony.... The order in which witnesses are called is a matter for the discretion of the Grand Jury and the supervisory court").

that a defendant "can perhaps overcome the disadvantage of testifying in advance of the People's witnesses by making it clear to the jurors that he or she will be willing to return to answer questions after that body has received the People's evidence and that the jurors have the right to have the defendant returned for that purpose."[173]

Prior to giving testimony before the grand jury, a defendant must execute a waiver of immunity pursuant to CPL § 190.45.[174] Of course, such waiver must be made in the presence of counsel.[175] In the event that a defendant is permitted to testify after executing a waiver outside the presence of counsel, the indictment must be dismissed, with prejudice.[176]

Upon executing the waiver of immunity, the defendant "must be permitted to testify before the grand jury and to give any relevant and competent evidence concerning the case under consideration."[177] The defendant "must be given an opportunity to give [his or] her version of the events before being examined by the prosecutor."[178] Although it is permissible to interrupt the narrative briefly for purposes of "clarification,"[179] or to remind the defendant to confine his or her remarks to relevant matters,[180] an overly zealous prosecutor who interrupts the defendant at this time and commences cross-examination prior to the

---

173. Preiser, "Practice Commentary" to CPL § 190.50, McKinney's Cons. Laws of New York, Book 11A (Supp.).

174. The prosecution may properly refuse to allow a defendant to testify where he refuses to execute such a waiver. See People v. Devone, 163 Misc.2d 581, 620 N.Y.S.2d 927 (Sup.Ct., Queens County, 1994)(prosecution properly refused defendant's offer to sign waiver of immunity form under a name he claimed was his where fingerprints taken revealed a different name for defendant and fact that he had a lengthy criminal history). However, a defendant does not "generally and automatically waive the privilege against self-incrimination as to pending collateral criminal charges" unless he or she, "in taking the stand, makes assertions that open the door and render those charges relevant for contradiction and response." People v. Betts, 70 N.Y.2d 289, 295–96, 520 N.Y.S.2d 370, 372–73, 514 N.E.2d 865, 867–68 (1987). The rule in Betts was extended to grand jury presentations in People v. Smith, ___ N.Y.2d ___, ___ N.Y.S.2d ___, ___ N.E.2d ___, 1996 WL 49007 (1996).

175. See N.Y. Const., Art. 1, § 6; People v. Chapman, 69 N.Y.2d 497, 516 N.Y.S.2d 159, 508 N.E.2d 894 (1987).

176. People v. Valvano, 131 A.D.2d 615, 516 N.Y.S.2d 507 (2d Dep't 1987) (notwithstanding the fact that he "had been afforded every opportunity to have counsel present and chose not to exercise that option," defendant acquired transactional immunity which precluded further prosecution since waiver of immunity executed outside presence of counsel is invalid). Cf. People v. Caruso, 125 A.D.2d 403, 509 N.Y.S.2d 361 (2d Dep't 1986).

177. CPL § 190.50(5)(b).

178. People v. Smith, 84 N.Y.2d 998, 1000, 622 N.Y.S.2d 507, 508, 646 N.E.2d 809, 810 (1994). See also People v. Germosen, 86 N.Y.2d 822, 824, 633 N.Y.S.2d 472, 473, 657 N.E.2d 493, 494 (1995).

179. See, e.g., People v. Miller, 144 A.D.2d 94, 97, 537 N.Y.S.2d 318, 320 (3d Dep't 1989); People v. Millson, 93 A.D.2d 899, 461 N.Y.S.2d 586 (3d Dep't 1983).

180. People v. Smith, 84 N.Y.2d at 1001, 622 N.Y.S.2d at 508 (where defendant charged with criminal sale of a controlled substance spoke at length about her past and the consequences of her drug addiction, prosecutor permissibly interrupted her narrative to request that she confine her remarks to facts that were relevant to whether or not she sold drugs or was acting as an agent of the buyer). Cf. People v. Green, 80 A.D.2d 650, 436 N.Y.S.2d 420 (2d Dep't 1981)(defendant's remarks regarding her problem with communication since death of her deaf-mute child in a fire in her home two years earlier did not justify prosecutor's interruption and subsequent failure to permit her to complete her statement).

§ 5.8 GRAND JURY & INDICTMENT Ch. 5

completion of the statement runs the risk that the indictment will be dismissed.[181]

At the conclusion of the defendant's narrative, the prosecutor is entitled to conduct a thorough cross-examination. As the First Department has explained,

> By making a defendant "subject to examination by the people," the Legislature appreciated that if the prosecutor can do no more than passively inquire as to "what happened," "the grand jurors will not have any way of uncovering the true facts underlying the crime."[182]

Thus, a defendant may be impeached within the proper limits of cross-examination.[183] Notably, although a defendant's criminal record is a proper subject for cross-examination,[184] the Second Department has held that a defendant is not entitled to a *Sandoval* ruling from either the prosecutor or the supervisory court prior to appearing before the grand jury.[185]

Finally, subdivision six provides a means by which a defendant may attempt to cause exculpatory evidence to be presented to the grand jury. Since the grand jury proceeding is non-adversarial, the "People are not obligated to search for evidence favorable to the defense or to present all evidence in their possession that is favorable to the accused even though such information undeniably would allow the Grand Jury to make a more informed determination."[186] A defendant may therefore request, but may not require, the grand jury to call witnesses designated by him or her.[187] Such request may be made either orally or in writing.[188] Where the grand jury determines that it would like to hear a witness suggested by the defense, that witness is summoned pursuant to the procedures established in CPL § 190.50(3).[189] Thus, the limitations set

---

181. See, e.g., People v. Miller, supra; People v. Lerman, 116 A.D.2d 665, 497 N.Y.S.2d 733 (2d Dep't 1986); People v. Durante, 97 A.D.2d 851, 469 N.Y.S.2d 18 (2d Dep't 1983); People v. Green, 80 A.D.2d 650, 436 N.Y.S.2d 420 (3d Dep't 1981).

182. People v. Gonzalez, 201 A.D.2d 414, 415, 607 N.Y.S.2d 670, 671 (1st Dep't 1994), quoting People v. Karp, 158 A.D.2d 378, 389, 551 N.Y.S.2d 503, 510 (1st Dep't 1990)(Sullivan, J., dissenting), rev'd on dissenting opinion 76 N.Y.2d 1006, 565 N.Y.S.2d 751, 566 N.E.2d 1156 (1990). See also People v. Germosen, 86 N.Y.2d 822, 633 N.Y.S.2d 472, 657 N.E.2d 493 (1995); Gonzalez, 201 A.D.2d at 415, 607 N.Y.S.2d at 671–72; People v. Burton, 191 A.D.2d 451, 594 N.Y.S.2d 300 (2d Dep't 1993).

183. The Court of Appeals has cautioned that a prosecutor's possession of an immunized statement during a grand jury presentation, could, "where the defendant becomes aware of the statement's existence, be employed to compel the defendant to tailor the testimony to the statement or used in some other way to impair [the guarantee of immunity]." As such, the practice "should be avoided." People v. Corrigan, 80 N.Y.2d 326, 332, 590 N.Y.S.2d 174, 177, 604 N.E.2d 723, 726 (1992).

184. See People v. Burton, supra. See also People v. Gonzalez, 201 A.D.2d at 416, 607 N.Y.S.2d at 672; People v. Thompson, 116 A.D.2d 377, 381–82, 501 N.Y.S.2d 381, 383–84 (2d Dep't 1986).

185. People v. Thomas, 213 A.D.2d 73, 628 N.Y.S.2d 707 (2d Dep't 1995), lv. granted 86 N.Y.2d 803, 632 N.Y.S.2d 517, 656 N.E.2d 616 (1995).

186. People v. Lancaster, 69 N.Y.2d 20, 511 N.Y.S.2d 559, 503 N.E.2d 990 (1986). See § 5.7 supra.

187. CPL § 190.50(6).

188. Id.

189. See Matter of Relin v. Maloy, 182 A.D.2d 1142, 583 N.Y.S.2d 103 (4th Dep't 1992) (supervisory court does not have authority to deny prosecutor access to defen-

forth in that provision regarding witnesses summoned by the grand jury are applicable.[190]

Library References:
West's Key No. Digests, Grand Jury ⚖36.1–36.9.

§ 5.9 Compelled Testimony

Any person may be called upon to give evidence in the grand jury.[191] In addition, "Every witness in a grand jury proceeding must give any evidence legally requested of him regardless of any protest or belief on his part that it may tend to incriminate him."[192] This is true even where the witness is the target of the criminal investigation.[193]

At the same time, no person can be "compelled in any criminal case to be a witness against himself."[194] In New York, a witness who is called upon to testify in the grand jury receives assurance that he will not become a witness against himself by the combined operation of two separate and distinct principles. First, he receives "transactional immunity" from any subsequent prosecution related to his testimony in the grand jury.[195] Second, that immunity is "automatic", *i.e.*, he receives it whether or not he claims his privilege[196] by merely giving evidence in the grand jury.

Transactional Immunity. As to the first protection, transactional immunity, the scope of the protection provided is broader than that required by the Fifth Amendment.[197] It is provided by statute only;[198] it

dant's written request, exclude prosecutor from jury room when the jury receives and considers the request, or order that all questions the jury may have about such request be directed solely to the court).

190. See footnotes 119–121 and accompanying text, supra. See, e.g., People v. Buszak, 185 A.D.2d 621, 587 N.Y.S.2d 52 (4th Dep't 1992); People v. Batista, 164 Misc.2d 632, 625 N.Y.S.2d 1008 (Sup.Ct., Kings County, 1995); People v. Hylton, 139 Misc.2d 645, 529 N.Y.S.2d 412 (Sup.Ct., Nassau County, 1988).

191. Keenan v. Gigante, 47 N.Y.2d 160, 168, 417 N.Y.S.2d 226, 230, 390 N.E.2d 1151, 1155 (1979)("In furtherance of its essential function, the Grand Jury, as an arm of society, is entitled to the assistance of all members of the community in uncovering criminal acts. The enduring command that '(e)very man owes a duty to society to give evidence when called upon to do so' must be honored if the fundamental task of the Grand Jury is to be realized.")(citations omitted).

192. CPL § 190.40(1). See also P.L. § 215.51 (Class E felony to refuse to testify in grand jury).

193. Gold v. Menna, 25 N.Y.2d 475, 307 N.Y.S.2d 33, 255 N.E.2d 235 (1969).

194. N.Y. Const., Art. 1, § 6; U.S. Const., Amend. V. The phrase is said to derive from the Latin "Nemo tenetur prodere seipsum", pronounced by John Lambert in 1537 as he was burned at the stake for refusing to abjure heretical beliefs. Gray, "The Grand Jury in New York," New York State Bar Journal, p. 53 (1994).

195. CPL § 50.10(1)(a person who possesses immunity "cannot . . . be convicted of any offense or subjected to any penalty or forfeiture for or on account of any transaction, matter or thing concerning which he gave evidence therein.").

196. See generally CPL §§ 50.10, 190.40.

197. Kastigar v. United States, 406 U.S. 441, 453, 92 S.Ct. 1653, 1661, 32 L.Ed.2d 212 (1972)("We hold that . . . immunity from use and derivative use is coextensive with the scope of the privilege against self-incrimination, and therefore is sufficient to compel testimony over a claim of the privilege. While a grant of immunity must afford protection commensurate with that afforded by the privilege, it need not be broader. Transactional immunity, which accords full immunity from prosecution for the offense to which the compelled testimony relates, affords the witness considerably

198. See note 198 on p. 246.

§ 5.9   GRAND JURY & INDICTMENT   Ch. 5

is not, a federal or, apparently, a state constitutional right.[199]

In *Counselman v. Hitchcock*,[200] the Supreme Court held that any immunity statute that has the effect of compelling testimony must "supply a complete protection from all the perils against which the constitutional prohibition was designed to guard."[201] Subsequently, in *Kastigar v. United States*[202] and *Murphy v. Waterfront Comm'n of New York Harbor*,[203] the Supreme Court held that exclusion of "use" plus "fruits," *i.e.*, derivative evidence, adequately met that standard. Since then, a debate has continued in New York over the scope of immunity that should be provided by statute.[204]

broader protection than does the Fifth Amendment privilege. The privilege has never been construed to mean that one who invokes it cannot subsequently be prosecuted.").

198. Cf. 18 U.S.C.A. § 6002 ("[N]o testimony or other information compelled under [appropriate] order (or any information directly or indirectly derived from such testimony or other information) may be used against the witness in any criminal case, except a prosecution for perjury, giving a false statement, or otherwise failing to comply with the order.").

199. People v. Sobotker, 61 N.Y.2d 44, 471 N.Y.S.2d 78, 459 N.E.2d 187 (1984)(holding that the Fifth Amendment use immunity violation may survive a plea of guilty, while the statutory right of transactional immunity was forfeited by the plea). As such, Sobotker did not squarely decide the question of whether the New York Constitution itself requires transactional or use immunity. People v. LaBello, 24 N.Y.2d 598, 602, 301 N.Y.S.2d 544, 547, 249 N.E.2d 412, 414 (1969), cert. granted sub nom. Piccirillo v. New York, 397 U.S. 933, 90 S.Ct. 957, 25 L.Ed.2d 114 (1970), cert. dism. as improperly granted 400 U.S. 548, 91 S.Ct. 520, 27 L.Ed.2d 596 (1971), purported to decide the question as well, holding that neither the State Constitution nor existing statutes required transactional immunity. However, LaBello was overruled within eight short months as wrongly interpreting the statute, see Gold v. Menna, 25 N.Y.2d 475, 307 N.Y.S.2d 33, 255 N.E.2d 235 (1969), leaving unresolved the state constitutional issue. Nonetheless, two lower courts have subsequently held that the State Constitution is satisfied by a mere grant of use immunity, People v. Coles, 141 Misc.2d 965, 535 N.Y.S.2d 897 (Sup.Ct., Kings County, 1988); People v. Johnson, 133 Misc.2d 721, 723, 507 N.Y.S.2d 791, 792 (Sup.Ct., N.Y. County, 1986), and the Court of Appeals has suggested that transactional immunity is a child of statute. Matter of Anonymous Attorneys v. Bar Association of Erie County, 41 N.Y.2d 506, 509–10, 393 N.Y.S.2d 961, 962–63, 362 N.E.2d 592, 595–96 (1977). Cf. Doyle v. Hofstader, 257 N.Y. 244, 250, 177 N.E. 489, 490 (1931)(decided before Kastigar):

The Constitution of the state provides that no person shall "be compelled in any criminal case to be a witness against himself." Const. art. 1, § 6. The privilege may not be violated because in a particular case its restraints are inconvenient or because the supposed malefactor may be a subject of public execration or because the disclosure of his wrongdoing will promote the public weal. It is a barrier interposed between the individual and the power of the government, a barrier interposed by the sovereign people of the state; and neither legislators nor judges are free to overleap it. The appellant is therefore privileged to refuse to answer questions that may tend to implicate him in a crime, unless by some act of amnesty or indemnity, or some valid resolution equivalent thereto, he has been relieved from the risk of prosecution for any felony or misdemeanor that his testimony may reveal. The immunity is not adequate if it does no more than assure him that the testimony coming from his lips will not be read in evidence against him upon a criminal prosecution. The clues thereby developed may still supply the links whereby a chain of guilt can be forged from the testimony of others. To force disclosure from unwilling lips, the immunity must be so broad that the risk of prosecution is ended altogether.

200. 142 U.S. 547, 585, 12 S.Ct. 195, 206, 35 L.Ed. 1110 (1892).

201. 142 U.S. at 585, 12 S.Ct. at 206.

202. 406 U.S. 441, 92 S.Ct. 1653, 32 L.Ed.2d 212 (1972).

203. 378 U.S. 52, 84 S.Ct. 1594, 12 L.Ed.2d 678 (1964).

204. See, e.g., Preiser, "Practice Commentary" to CPL § 190.40, McKinney's Cons. Laws of N.Y., Book 11A, at 259

Although CPL §§ 50.10 and 190.40 require full transactional immunity, there are occasions when an immunized statement comes into the possession of the prosecution through means other than court-ordered or grand jury compulsion. For example, a public employee[205] or public contractor[206] may be required to answer questions related to his or her employment. In such a case, use immunity rather than transactional immunity results and, inevitably, the adequacy of the remedy is called into question.[207]

To assert a claim of immunity against a given prosecution, a defendant must move to dismiss the indictment.[208] Transactional immunity, afforded by statute, may be waived or forfeited by a plea of guilty.[209] In addition, a writ of prohibition is available to avert trial of a person who has immunity, even where the immunity is merely statutory and not constitutionally derived.[210]

Transactional immunity bars prosecution of "any transaction, matter or thing concerning which [the accused] gave evidence."[211] There is no statutory definition for the word "concerning," which requires some interpretation. In *People v. Williams*,[212] the prosecution appealed a dismissal of an indictment, claiming that the defendant, who had merely testified to some contact with the events in question without admitting any criminal involvement, was not entitled to immunity since his testimony did not establish a "substantial connection" to the crime under investigation.[213] In rejecting the argument, the court instead determined

(1993)(referring to New York's "unnecessary" adherence to transactional immunity).

205. See, e.g., Garrity v. New Jersey, 385 U.S. 493, 87 S.Ct. 616, 17 L.Ed.2d 562 (1967); Matter of Matt v. Larocca, 71 N.Y.2d 154, 159, 524 N.Y.S.2d 180, 518 N.E.2d 1172, 1174 (1987).

206. See, e.g., Lefkowitz v. Turley, 414 U.S. 70, 94 S.Ct. 316, 38 L.Ed.2d 274 (1973); People v. Avant, 33 N.Y.2d 265, 352 N.Y.S.2d 161, 307 N.E.2d 230 (1973).

207. See, e.g., People v. Corrigan, 80 N.Y.2d 326, 590 N.Y.S.2d 174, 604 N.E.2d 723 (1992)(prosecutor held immunized statement in his hand in front of grand jury while questioning the defendant-witness; majority held that the prosecutor did not "use" the statement and thus the defendant's privilege was not violated).

208. CPL § 210.20(1)(d).

209. People v. Flihan, 73 N.Y.2d 729, 535 N.Y.S.2d 590, 532 N.E.2d 96 (1988); People v. Sobotker, 61 N.Y.2d 44, 471 N.Y.S.2d 78, 459 N.E.2d 187 (1984).

210. Technically speaking, CPL § 50.10 bars "conviction, penalty or forfeiture" for one who possesses immunity, but does not, by its terms, prevent prosecution. However, the Court of Appeals has authorized a writ of prohibition, pursuant to CPLR Article 78, to avert a threatened prosecution.

See Rush v. Mordue, 68 N.Y.2d 348, 509 N.Y.S.2d 493, 502 N.E.2d 170 (1986)("Prohibition may lie, however, where the claim is substantial, implicates a fundamental constitutional right, and where the harm caused by the arrogation of power could not be adequately redressed through the ordinary channels of appeal .... Here, petitioner raises a claim of similar magnitude. Although his claim of immunity from prosecution arising out of compelled testimony before a Grand Jury is grounded in a statutory grant of immunity (CPL 190.40), the statute grants such immunity in recognition of the fundamental constitutional privilege against self-incrimination.").

211. CPL § 50.10(1).

212. 81 A.D.2d 418, 440 N.Y.S.2d 935 (2d Dep't 1981), aff'd 56 N.Y.2d 916, 453 N.Y.S.2d 430, 438 N.E.2d 1146 (1982).

213. 81 A.D.2d at 420, 440 N.Y.S.2d at 937 ("The test, argues the People, is not the mere relevance of the testimony; otherwise, unforeseen immunity would be bestowed on a witness who testifies only as to an aspect of the transaction; and consequently, the statutes should be interpreted to confer immunity on a witness before a Grand Jury solely where his testimony demonstrates a 'substantial connection' to the crime under inquiry.")(citations omitted).

§ 5.9 GRAND JURY & INDICTMENT Ch. 5

that the statute "must be interpreted liberally in order that the individual's rights are adequately guarded."[214] The "true test," adopted from an earlier opinion by Judge Cardozo, is whether "the testimony ... will prove some part or feature of [the crime], will tend to a conviction when combined with proof of other circumstances which others may supply."[215]

Thus, for example, in *People v. McFarlan*,[216] a witness in a grand jury investigating a homicide was asked how she supported herself. She said that she had been "busted" for selling drugs in the past. This resulted in immunizing her from prosecution upon a pending indictment for drug sale unrelated to the grand jury's investigation.[217]

Notwithstanding New York's decision to grant transactional rather than use immunity, the broader rule is not necessarily binding upon other jurisdictions. Thus, compelled testimony in a New York grand jury may only be exempted from use by other officials investigating the same subject matter, but will not, in and of itself, be a bar to federal prosecution[218] or sister state prosecution.[219]

Automatic Immunity. The second significant, and unusual, feature of the immunity provisions of Article 190 is that every witness who testifies in the grand jury receives immunity unless it is waived. Automatic immunity, provided by CPL § 190.40(2), was a response to *People v. Steuding*.[220] The statute in effect in 1959 when *Steuding* was decided required a witness in the grand jury to *claim* privilege as a prerequisite

214. 81 A.D.2d at 422, 440 N.Y.S.2d at 938.

215. 81 A.D.2d at 425–26, 440 N.Y.S.2d at 940. As the court stated (citations omitted):

We should not indulge in rarified refinements and overly subtle shades of difference between tests of incriminatory testimony resulting in immunity bottomed on whether the testimony elicited before the Grand Jury was "relevant" or "substantial" or "material." These linguistic aids are merely descriptive labels and not rigid models; the true test is ... whether "the testimony ... will prove some part or feature of it [the crime], will tend to a conviction when combined with proof of other circumstances which others may supply." The word "tends" thus is used in the light of "helps" or "contributes" to the witness' incrimination for the crime concerning which he testified. Here in that sense, the defendant's testimony, we think, tends to incriminate him of the crime concerning which he testified.

216. 89 Misc.2d 905, 396 N.Y.S.2d 559 (Sup.Ct., N.Y. County, 1975), rev'd 52 A.D.2d 112, 383 N.Y.S.2d 4 (1st Dep't 1976), rev'd 42 N.Y.2d 896, 397 N.Y.S.2d 1003, 366 N.E.2d 1357 (1977).

217. See also People v. Williams, 81 A.D.2d at 424, 440 N.Y.S.2d at 939 ("We are not without signposts from the past which point the direction for our decision. Chief Judge Cardozo wrote that '[i]t is enough, to wake the privilege into life, that there is a reasonable possibility of prosecution, and that the testimony, though falling short of proving the crime in its entirety, will prove some part or feature of it, will tend to a conviction when combined with proof of other circumstances which others may supply.' Earlier cases had alluded to the metaphor of the testimony constituting a 'link' in the 'chain of facts' against defendant.")(citations omitted).

218. See Murphy v. Waterfront Comm'n of New York Harbor, 378 U.S. 52, 84 S.Ct. 1594, 12 L.Ed.2d 678 (1964).

219. People v. Lev, 91 Misc.2d 241, 398 N.Y.S.2d 593 (Sup.Ct., Bronx County, 1977).

Regarding potential use at parole or probation revocation hearings, see People v. Moschelle, 96 Misc.2d 1030, 410 N.Y.S.2d 764 (Sup.Ct., Suffolk County, 1978); Matter of Mary Jane HH, 120 A.D.2d 906, 502 N.Y.S.2d 827 (3d Dep't 1986) (Family Court proceeding to demonstrate witness was person in need of supervision).

220. 6 N.Y.2d 214, 189 N.Y.S.2d 166, 160 N.E.2d 468, reargument den. 7 N.Y.2d 805, 194 N.Y.S.2d 1025, 163 N.E.2d 677 (1959).

to receiving immunity. Once alerted, the prosecutor could then decide whether to proceed, thereby conferring immunity, or to withdraw. However, in *Steuding* the court held that the New York Constitution did not allow the Legislature to shift the burden to the "target" of a criminal investigation to "assert" or "invoke" privilege in the grand jury in order to obtain immunity.[221] A target of the investigation automatically received immunity merely by giving evidence in the grand jury, regardless of whether he or she invoked the incriminatory privilege.[222] After the decision in *Steuding*, problems arose in determining who was a "target" and who was not.[223] The former received automatic immunity while the latter still needed to claim privilege to receive immunity under the statute.[224] With enactment of the CPL, the arbitrary distinction was eliminated.[225] As a consequence, on rare occasion a defendant may receive immunity that was unanticipated by the prosecutor who brought the witness to the grand jury.[226]

The automatic nature of immunity in the grand jury could lead to mischief if a witness were to enter the jury room and proceed to confess to crimes not foreseen by the prosecutor. As a check against the potential problem of "accidental immunity," section 190.40 confers immunity only if the evidence given is responsive to inquiry by the prosecutor or a grand juror and "it is not gratuitously given or volunteered by the witness with knowledge that it is not responsive."[227] Note that the language of the statute requires a showing that the answer was not responsive *and* that it was volunteered in bad faith, *i.e.*, gratuitously and with knowledge that it was unresponsive. Therefore, a witness who

---

221. People v. Steuding, 6 N.Y.2d at 216–217, 189 N.Y.S.2d at 167 ("[O]ne who is a target of an investigation may not be called and examined before a Grand Jury and, if he is, his constitutionally-conferred privilege against self incrimination is deemed violated even though he does not claim or assert the privilege."). Cf. CPL § 50.10(4)("A witness who without asserting his privilege against self-incrimination, gives evidence in a legal proceeding other than a grand jury proceeding does not receive immunity.").

222. In part, a rationale for the decision in Steuding was the fact that, at the time, a witness did not have a right to counsel in the grand jury. Steuding had asked to consult counsel but was denied the opportunity. Without advice of counsel, it seemed unfair, to the court, to find that he had forfeited immunity for want of timely assertion. Since then, the statute has been amended to permit counsel to accompany a witness to the grand jury. See CPL § 190.52 (added by L.1978, c.447).

223. See discussion in People v. LaBello, 24 N.Y.2d 598, 604, 301 N.Y.S.2d 544, 549, 249 N.E.2d 412, 415 (1969).

224. See, e.g., People v. Laino, 10 N.Y.2d 161, 218 N.Y.S.2d 647, 176 N.E.2d 571 (1961), cert. den. 374 U.S. 104, 83 S.Ct. 1687, 10 L.Ed.2d 1027 (1963).

225. CPL § 190.40.

226. See, e.g., Carey v. Kitson, 93 A.D.2d 50, 461 N.Y.S.2d 876 (2d Dep't 1983)(witness in Suffolk County grand jury was asked about volume of sales in his business; prosecution barred two years later in a case brought independently by Attorney General for sales tax avoidance); People v. McFarlan, 89 Misc.2d 905, 396 N.Y.S.2d 559 (Sup.Ct., N.Y. County, 1975), rev'd 52 A.D.2d 112, 383 N.Y.S.2d 4 (1st Dep't 1976), rev'd 42 N.Y.2d 896, 397 N.Y.S.2d 1003, 366 N.E.2d 1357 (1977)(witness in grand jury, when asked how she supported herself, said she was "busted" in the past for selling drugs; immunity obtained from pending indictment for drug sale); see also People v. Perri, 53 N.Y.2d 957, 441 N.Y.S.2d 444, 424 N.E.2d 278 (1981), aff'g 72 A.D.2d 106, 423 N.Y.S.2d 674 (2d Dep't 1980)(witness who provided handwriting exemplar in the grand jury receives immunity).

227. CPL § 190.40(2)(b).

provides an answer that might appear, objectively, to be unresponsive is nonetheless entitled to immunity unless the prosecution can also show that the answer was volunteered by a witness who knew the answer was not responsive.[228]

Non-testimonial Evidence. CPL § 190.40(2) provides that a witness who "gives evidence" in the grand jury receives immunity. CPL § 50.10(3) declares that the phrase "give evidence" means "to testify or *produce physical evidence*."[229] Federal jurisprudence has made clear that taking physical evidence from a defendant, such as a blood sample,[230] a handwriting sample,[231] or a voice exemplar[232] involves non-testimonial evidence and, as such, does not implicate the privilege against self-incrimination. However, by the plain terms of the statute, and notwithstanding a more narrow reading of the constitutional privilege by the federal courts, a person who produces physical evidence in the grand jury receives automatic transactional immunity.[233] That is not to say, of course, that non-testimonial evidence may not be obtained by lawful seizure[234] or court order.[235]

Production of Books and Records. CPL § 190.40(2)(c) provides that a witness does not receive immunity if the evidence given by the witness consists *only* of books, records or other physical evidence of an enterprise and the witness does not have a privilege against self-incrimination with respect to the production of the evidence.[236] The statute also provides that "[a]ny further evidence given by the witness entitles the witness to immunity."

When a subpoena *duces tecum* calls upon a named person to produce records, and assuming there is no independent privilege with regard to the records themselves,[237] the question arises whether the witness may oppose the subpoena on the ground that the very "act of production" would incriminate the defendant by permitting the inference that the defendant controlled the records or was aware of their nature and existence. The Supreme Court, in *United States v. Doe*, recognized this problem and held that in such a circumstance the privilege against self-

---

228. See, e.g., People v. Williams, supra, where the witness described drug busts in the past that had nothing to do with the witness's current means of supporting herself.

229. CPL § 50.10(3)(emphasis supplied).

230. Schmerber v. California, 384 U.S. 757, 86 S.Ct. 1826, 16 L.Ed.2d 908 (1966).

231. United States v. Mara, 410 U.S. 19, 93 S.Ct. 774, 35 L.Ed.2d 99 (1973).

232. United States v. Dionisio, 410 U.S. 1, 93 S.Ct. 764, 35 L.Ed.2d 67 (1973).

233. People v. Perri, 72 A.D.2d 106, 423 N.Y.S.2d 674 (2d Dep't 1980), aff'd 53 N.Y.2d 957, 441 N.Y.S.2d 444, 424 N.E.2d 278 (1981).

234. See Schmerber v. California, supra.

235. Matter of Abe A., 56 N.Y.2d 288, 452 N.Y.S.2d 6, 437 N.E.2d 265 (1982)(pre-arrest); People v. Middleton, 54 N.Y.2d 42, 444 N.Y.S.2d 581, 429 N.E.2d 100 (1981)(post-arrest).

236. CPL § 190.40(2)(c)(emphasis supplied).

237. Beyond the scope of discussion here are cases addressing personal privilege for "private papers", see Fisher v. United States, 425 U.S. 391, 96 S.Ct. 1569, 48 L.Ed.2d 39 (1976), the required records doctrine, see Braswell v. United States, 487 U.S. 99, 108 S.Ct. 2284, 101 L.Ed.2d 98 (1988), and the exception for corporate or "collective-entity" records, see Bellis v. United States, 417 U.S. 85, 94 S.Ct. 2179, 40 L.Ed.2d 678 (1974).

incrimination applies.[238] The New York statute, drafted before the *Doe* decision, does not recognize production as potentially incriminating, and thus does not confer statutory transactional immunity upon a mere act of production. However, the constitutional privilege still exists and demands remedy, presumably by conferring use immunity.[239]

Similarly, on occasion a prosecutor may want the witness to identify the records before the grand jury.[240] Once again, however, the plain language of the statute—"evidence given . . . consists only of books" and "any further evidence given by the witness entitles the witness to immunity"—would seem to grant transactional immunity to a witness who orally identifies records before the grand jury. Two Appellate Division cases have suggested that mere identification alone, as a necessary correlative right to production, would not confer immunity.[241] Both cases, however, were decided before *Doe* and thus are of dubious precedential authority. Further, in a subsequent and analogous situation, the Court of Appeals explicitly recognized that an act of production or authentication may well have testimonial attributes.[242]

Based on the language of the statute, the holding in *Doe*, the language in *Matter of Vanderbilt*, and the failure of the Legislature to amend the section over the years, the safest course for a prosecutor who seeks to avoid accidental conferral of immunity upon a witness is to avoid asking the witness to identify the documents produced in response to a subpoena.

Waiver of Immunity. CPL § 190.45 provides a mechanism for waiver of immunity. The waiver must be in writing and sworn to before the grand jury itself.[243] It must stipulate that the defendant "waives his privilege against self-incrimination and any possible or prospective immunity to which he would otherwise become entitled" by statute.[244] A witness who is asked to waive immunity must be advised that he has a right to confer with counsel before waiving and that he will be accorded a reasonable time to obtain or confer with counsel if he so desires.[245] If

238. 465 U.S. 605, 104 S.Ct. 1237, 79 L.Ed.2d 552 (1984).

239. Whether evidentiary use may be made of an act of production in special circumstances where a person has submitted to a regulatory regime and may be compelled to produce as part of that regime was left open in Baltimore City Dep't of Social Services v. Bouknight, 493 U.S. 549, 110 S.Ct. 900, 107 L.Ed.2d 992 (1990).

240. See, e.g., Altman v. Bradley, 184 A.D.2d 131, 591 N.Y.S.2d 403 (1st Dep't 1992).

241. People v. Doe, 90 A.D.2d 669, 455 N.Y.S.2d 866 (4th Dep't 1982), aff'd 59 N.Y.2d 655, 463 N.Y.S.2d 405, 450 N.E.2d 211 (1983); People v. MacLachlan, 58 A.D.2d 586, 395 N.Y.S.2d 106 (2d Dep't 1977).

242. Matter of Vanderbilt (Rosner-Hickey), 57 N.Y.2d 66, 79, 453 N.Y.S.2d 662, 670, 439 N.E.2d 378, 385 (1982)("[P]roduction of the tape by Dr. Rosen would be testimonial by virtue of his authentication, express or implied, of the tape. By producing Tape No. 2 in response to a subpoena, Dr. Rosen would not only express his belief that this is the tape sought by the Grand Jury, but would be vouching for the circumstances of its preparation, its accuracy, and the conclusions drawn from it. Thus, there is a testimonial element to the production of Tape No. 2.").

243. CPL § 190.45(2).

244. CPL § 190.45(1).

245. Id.

he cannot afford counsel, one will be provided by the court that impaneled the grand jury.[246]

The consequences to a prosecutor of allowing a witness to testify in the grand jury without securing an effective waiver are severe: transactional immunity is bestowed upon the witness.[247] In addition, "substantial compliance" with the provisions of section 190.45 is not good enough—the courts demand strict compliance.[248]

For example, where a witness signed the waiver before a notary instead of the grand jury, the waiver was ineffective and the indictment dismissed.[249] Similarly, where a criminal prosecution is commenced by the filing of a felony complaint, the right to counsel indelibly attaches,[250] and any subsequent waiver in the grand jury in the absence of counsel is ineffective, resulting in transactional immunity.[251] One court has taken the principle a step further and dismissed an indictment on the ground that lack of counsel rendered the waiver ineffective, even though the defendant did not have a pending felony complaint nor had he been arrested, but he was a "target" of the investigation.[252]

CPL § 190.45(4) permits "limited waivers" whereby the witness is interrogated on certain specified subjects and receives immunity as to those subjects only. The terms of the agreement must be in writing, and any testimony in response to a question that goes beyond the scope of the written agreement results in immunity for that subject area.[253]

Attorney in the Grand Jury. CPL § 190.52 affords any witness in the grand jury who has signed a waiver of immunity the right to have counsel, retained or assigned, present with him or her in the grand jury. "The attorney may advise the witness, but may not otherwise take any

---

246. CPL § 190.52. Since the right to counsel was not enacted until 1978, earlier statutory provisions did not include a reference to assigned counsel for indigents. Thus, section 190.45 refers only to a reasonable adjournment to "obtain and confer" with counsel, but does not specifically direct the prosecutor to advise the witness that counsel can be provided if needed. However, since a waiver is ineffective when a right to counsel is not adequately protected, the wiser course for prosecutors would be to advise a prospective witness that counsel can be provided by the court if the witness cannot afford a lawyer.

247. People v. Chapman, 69 N.Y.2d 497, 516 N.Y.S.2d 159, 508 N.E.2d 894 (1987).

248. People v. Higley, 70 N.Y.2d 624, 518 N.Y.S.2d 778, 512 N.E.2d 299 (1987).

249. People v. Higley, supra. But see People v. Cole, 196 A.D.2d 634, 601 N.Y.S.2d 352 (2d Dep't 1993)(waiver valid where defendant acknowledged before grand jury that signature on waiver form introduced into evidence was his).

250. See People v. Samuels, 49 N.Y.2d 218, 424 N.Y.S.2d 892, 400 N.E.2d 1344 (1980).

251. People v. Chapman, 69 N.Y.2d 497, 516 N.Y.S.2d 159, 508 N.E.2d 894 (1987); People v. Bartok, 209 A.D.2d 530, 619 N.Y.S.2d 626 (2d Dep't 1994). Chapman raised in a footnote, 69 N.Y.2d at 501 n.2, 516 N.Y.S.2d at 161 n. 2, but did not answer, the question of whether a searching inquiry by a court would render a waiver effective notwithstanding the "indelible" right to counsel.

252. People v. Cooper, 139 Misc.2d 44, 526 N.Y.S.2d 910 (Schoharie Co.Ct.1988).

253. See, e.g., People v. Baquadano, 164 Misc.2d 801, 626 N.Y.S.2d 691 (N.Y.C.Crim.Ct.1995)(defendant, police officer, who waived immunity as to excessive force in making arrest did not waive as to false reporting of the incident); People v. Coppola, 123 Misc.2d 31, 472 N.Y.S.2d 558 (Sup.Ct., Queens County, 1984)(defendant who signed blanket waiver to testify in grand jury about an assault charge could be asked about unrelated rape charge which was also pending against him).

part in the proceeding."[254] By right under the statute, a defendant may interrupt the questioning to consult with counsel.[255] On the other hand, the right to counsel is not impaired merely because counsel chooses to sit 20 feet away from the defendant instead of next to him.[256]

The statute authorizing counsel in the grand jury is relatively new,[257] and there is not much appellate authority regarding the role of counsel. One court reviewed the history of the statute and adopted a functional definition for the role of counsel in deciding that an attorney should be permitted, over the prosecutor's objection, to take notes in the grand jury. The court reasoned as follows:

> (1) Is the attorney's act normally performed in the course of his duties, that is, would note taking be deemed ordinary legal practice? (2) Does the act assist the witness or is it necessary for effective legal representation? (3) Does such act impede the deliberation of the Grand Jury? (4) Would the attorney's actions violate the secrecy of the Grand Jury?[258]

Another court suggested that the function of counsel in the grand jury is limited solely to giving advice upon matters

> critically affected before the grand jury, and as to which the witness should be entitled to consult with counsel: the decision whether to assert the privilege against self incrimination; the decision whether to answer a question that has no apparent bearing on the subject of the investigation; and the decision whether to invoke a testimonial privilege, such as the attorney-client privilege. These are legal matters that are likely to be raised by the questions the client will be called upon to answer during the grand jury proceeding.[259]

Similarly,

> There are other matters about which a witness before the grand jury may properly consult with the counsel prior to the client's testifying, such as the meaning of perjury or contempt, and the scope of an anticipated waiver or grant of immunity. And there are matters which counsel may resolve at the outset of the

---

254. CPL § 190.52(2).

255. Cf. People v. Branch, 83 N.Y.2d 663, 666, 612 N.Y.S.2d 365, 366, 634 N.E.2d 966, 967 (1994)(regarding consultation of a testifying defendant at trial, "[t]here can be no question that once a witness takes the stand the truth-seeking function of a trial will most often be best served by requiring that the witness undergo direct questioning and cross-examination without interruption for counseling").

256. People v. Diaz, 211 A.D.2d 402, 621 N.Y.S.2d 36 (1st Dep't 1995).

257. L.1978, c.447.

258. Grand Jury ex rel. Riley, 98 Misc.2d 454, 458, 414 N.Y.S.2d 441, 443 (Sup.Ct., Queens County, 1979).

259. People v. Smays, 156 Misc.2d 621, 626, 594 N.Y.S.2d 101, 105 (Sup.Ct., N.Y.County, 1993)(citations omitted)(dismissing an indictment for impaired proceedings where the prosecutor commented, more than once, that the attorney was feeding answers to the witness). The court went on to remark, "It is obvious that counsel is not present in the grand jury to give the witness strategic advice as to how to answer the prosecutor's questions." Id. It is difficult, however, to reconcile that observation with CPL § 190.52(2), which specifically provides that "[t]he attorney may advise the witness."

client's appearance before the grand jury, by instructing the client to inquire of the grand jury whether, for example, there exist any eavesdropping warrants from which the questions are derived.[260]

At least two lower courts have held that counsel in the grand jury may give advice but may not object to questions.[261] When an objectionable line of questioning is being pursued, the proper course is to ask for judicial intervention.[262]

Library References:
West's Key No. Digests, Criminal Law ⟐42; Grand Jury ⟐36.1–36.5.

§ 5.10 Waiver of Indictment and Superior Court Informations

Article 1, § 6 of the State Constitution provides (in relevant part):

No person shall be held to answer for a capital or otherwise infamous crime ... unless on indictment of a grand jury, except that a person held for the action of a grand jury upon a charge for such an offense, other than one punishable by death or life imprisonment, with the consent of the district attorney, may waive indictment by a grand jury and consent to be prosecuted on an information filed by the district attorney; such waiver shall be evidenced by written instrument signed by the defendant in open court in the presence of his counsel.

The allowance for waiver of indictment was enacted in 1974[263] in response to *Simonson v. Cahn*,[264] which had reaffirmed the long-standing rule in New York that the right of a grand jury to review and sift evidence was a "public fundamental right" that, without constitutional amendment, could not be waived.[265]

Article 195 of the CPL contains the implementing provisions for the constitutional amendment. The procedure for waiver is relatively straightforward and self-explanatory. The defendant signs a written waiver in open court in the presence of his or her attorney with the consent of the prosecutor endorsed thereon.[266] The form of the waiver instrument is described in section 195.20. The waiver is either before the local criminal court in which the defendant has been held for the action of the grand jury, at the time that he or she was so held, or in the

---

260. Id. (citations omitted). The last line is a reference to the holding in People v. Einhorn, 35 N.Y.2d 948, 365 N.Y.S.2d 171, 324 N.E.2d 551 (1974)(witness may refuse to answer questions based upon product of illegal wiretap).

261. People v. Davis, 119 Misc.2d 1013, 465 N.Y.S.2d 404 (Sup.Ct., Queens County, 1983); People v. Smays, supra.

262. People v. Ianniello, 21 N.Y.2d 418, 288 N.Y.S.2d 462, 235 N.E.2d 439 (1968).

263. By referendum November 6, 1973, effective January, 1, 1974.

264. 27 N.Y.2d 1, 313 N.Y.S.2d 97, 261 N.E.2d 246 (1970), reaffirming the holding in People ex rel. Battista v. Christian, 249 N.Y. 314, 164 N.E. 111 (1928).

265. See, e.g., Simonsohn v. Cahn, 27 N.Y.2d at 3, 313 N.Y.S.2d at 99 (the right is not "merely a personal right," nor are "we ... dealing with policy, expediency or convenience—as a district attorney or judges may see it").

266. CPL § 195.20.

appropriate superior court prior to the filing of an indictment.[267] If the court is satisfied that the provisions of sections 195.10 and 195.20 have been met, then it "shall" approve the waiver.[268] If the court approves the waiver, then the prosecutor files a superior court information ("SCI"),[269] which thereafter "has the same force and effect as an indictment and all procedures and provisions of law applicable to indictments are also applicable to superior court informations, except where otherwise expressly provided."[270]

A word of caution, however, is necessary. Failure to adhere to the statutory procedure, as well as the constitutional provision, is a jurisdictional defect that voids attempts to circumvent the statute by plea, waiver or agreement.[271]

Timing of Waiver. The first issue of concern in attempting to waive indictment is timing. The Constitution only allows a person "held for the action of a grand jury" to waive indictment. This occurs in one of two ways: a defendant may waive a hearing on a felony complaint in local criminal court, in which case he or she is held for the action of the grand jury with respect to the "charge or charges contained in the felony complaint,"[272] or at the conclusion of a preliminary hearing, upon a finding of reasonable cause to believe that the defendant committed a felony, the court must order that the defendant be held for the action of the grand jury. A plain reading of the constitutional provision alone would seem to permit a waiver anytime thereafter. However, the statute further provides that a waiver must occur either: (a) at the time the local criminal court issues the order holding the defendant; or (b) in superior court, any time prior to the filing of the indictment.[273] Thus, the statute, but not the Constitution, by its plain language prohibits waiver *after* an indictment has been filed.[274]

So, for example, in *People v. Boston*,[275] the defendant was indicted for intentional murder. He waived indictment to a new SCI containing a depraved indifference murder count. The SCI and the indictment were consolidated and he pleaded guilty to the added count. The Court of Appeals vacated the plea, holding that the failure to follow the statute, *i.e.*, a waiver employed after an indictment had already been filed, was a jurisdictional defect.[276]

---

267. See People v. Selby, 148 Misc.2d 447, 561 N.Y.S.2d 123 (N.Y.C.Crim.Ct. 1990), for a description of the process in "Part N" in New York City where preliminary jurisdiction resides for cases brought by the Special Narcotics Prosecutor and that also is as a "temporary" Supreme Court part for purposes of waivers and pleas.

268. CPL § 195.30.

269. See CPL § 200.15.

270. Id.

271. People v. Boston, 75 N.Y.2d 585, 555 N.Y.S.2d 27, 554 N.E.2d 64 (1990).

272. CPL § 180.30.

273. CPL § 195.10(2).

274. A waiver may still be accomplished after the grand jury has voted an indictment, but before the indictment has been formally filed. People v. Mills, 154 A.D.2d 405, 545 N.Y.S.2d 792 (2d Dep't 1989).

275. 75 N.Y.2d 585, 555 N.Y.S.2d 27, 554 N.E.2d 64.

276. Aside from the plain language of the statute, the court also pointed to the purpose of waiver: to expedite proceedings without the necessity of presentation to a grand jury. In a case where the grand jury has already acted there is no longer a need for a waiver, other than to avoid the conse-

Similarly, in *People v. Casdia*,[277] the parties sought to cure a defect in the indictment just before commencement of a bench trial.[278] The defendant agreed to be prosecuted upon an SCI that corrected the problem. After he was arraigned on the SCI, the indictment was dismissed and he was tried (and found guilty) on the SCI. As in *Boston*, the waiver was held to be ineffective because it occurred while a filed indictment was pending.

By contrast, in *People v. D'Amico*,[279] where the defendant was indicted for murder, the parties agreed, after extensive plea negotiations, to a procedure whereby a new felony complaint was filed charging the defendant with the Class B felony of criminal use of a firearm,[280] the defendant waived his right to a preliminary hearing and indictment, a new SCI was filed and the defendant pleaded guilty. The Court of Appeals distinguished *Boston* and approved the procedure because the SCI was based upon a felony complaint on which the defendant had been held for action of the grand jury and that contained a different charge than that of the previously voted indictment. Thus, the technical requirements of CPL § 195.10 were satisfied.[281]

Offenses that May be Charged in an SCI. As noted, Article 1, § 6 of the State Constitution provides that a defendant may waive indictment upon a charge only when he or she has been "held for the action of a grand jury upon a charge for such an offense."[282] Thereafter, the SCI may only contain charges that are listed in the waiver.[283]

The question arises whether the waiver and the SCI may only include offenses that were specifically charged in the felony complaint.

---

quences of the grand jury's determination—e.g., plea restrictions in CPL Article 220. The court rejected the prosecution's argument, however, that waiver was also enacted to provide "flexibility in the plea process generally." 75 N.Y.2d at 589, 555 N.Y.S.2d at 30. See also People v. Banville, 134 A.D.2d 116, 124, 523 N.Y.S.2d 844, 850 (2d Dep't 1988)(rejecting the "procedure commonly employed by prosecutors of the various counties within this Department" on the ground that to permit waiver after an indictment had been filed would "undermine" the plea-bargaining limitations of the CPL). The court in Banville was adamant, even denying the prosecution's request to re-present the charges to a new grand jury where the second grand jury presentation might result in a finding of lesser charges.

277. 78 N.Y.2d 1024, 576 N.Y.S.2d 75, 581 N.E.2d 1330 (1991).

278. The indictment's factual allegations in support of a count charging sexual abuse mistakenly repeated the allegations in support of another (sodomy) count. The trial court would not permit amendment of the indictment on the ground that doing so would impermissibly alter the theory of prosecution.

279. 76 N.Y.2d 877, 561 N.Y.S.2d 411, 562 N.E.2d 488 (1990).

280. P.L. § 265.09.

281. Left open for later resolution was the situation where an indictment is dismissed and a new felony complaint is drafted containing the same charge as the dismissed indictment.

282. This makes sense because it ensures that a defendant has an opportunity, which may be may waived, to satisfy himself or herself that the prosecution has evidence sufficient to satisfy a neutral factfinder at a probable cause hearing before he or she waives grand jury presentation. See, e.g., People v. Burke, 105 Misc.2d 722, 432 N.Y.S.2d 832 (Sup.Ct., Queens County, 1980)(a unique case holding that defendant had a right to move to dismiss an information, following waiver, unless the prosecution could demonstrate to the court, in camera, that the it had sufficient evidence to support the charges).

283. CPL § 200.15 ("A superior court information ... shall not include an offense not named in the written waiver of indictment executed pursuant to section 195.20.")

When a defendant waives a hearing on a felony complaint, it may be assumed that he or she was held for the action of the grand jury on every charge in the complaint.[284] However, upon a hearing, a local criminal court must hold the defendant for action of the grand jury "[i]f there is reasonable cause to believe that the defendant committed *a* felony."[285] Not every charge in the complaint need be established. And finally, the grand jury is not bound by the complaint or the action of the criminal court; it may indict for any offense where it finds reasonable cause to believe that the defendant committed such offense.[286]

It is not uncommon for an SCI to contain charges other than those listed in the felony complaint.[287] A waiver is usually the result of a bargaining process that will frequently call for adjustments in the charges. In *People v. Menchetti*,[288] the court held that a waiver and, as a consequence, an SCI may include any lesser included offense, notwithstanding the fact that the specific charge in the SCI was not charged in the felony complaint upon which the defendant was held for the grand jury. In *Menchetti*, the defendant was held over on a charge of criminal possession of a weapon in the third degree.[289] The waiver and SCI only charged him with the lesser included offense of criminal possession of a weapon in the fourth degree.[290] Thus, after *Menchetti*, it is now permissible to hold the defendant for one charge while drafting an SCI that charges the defendant with a lesser included offense.

In *Menchetti*, one of the arguments raised by the defendant in an attempt to overturn the plea was a policy argument that the practice of charging only lesser included offenses in an SCI would open the door to illegal plea arrangements. However, the court stated that "[w]e need not address this issue because here the plea to the information did not in

---

284. CPL § 180.30 reads in relevant part: "If the defendant waives a hearing upon the felony complaint, the court must ... [o]rder that the defendant be held for the action of a grand jury of the appropriate superior court with respect to the charge or charges contained in the felony complaint."

285. CPL § 180.70(1)(emphasis supplied).

286. CPL § 190.65(1).

287. In People v. Herne, 110 Misc.2d 152, 441 N.Y.S.2d 936 (Franklin Co.Ct. 1981), the court took the position that the felony complaint and the waiver must match. The court recounted the legislative history of Article 195, which had its origins in a legislative proposal that would have allowed a waiver to contain any charges that were factually supported by the allegations in the felony complaint or by the evidence at a hearing, regardless of whether the offense was actually charged in the felony complaint. The Legislature, however, did not adopt the proposal as written. The final draft requires inclusion of an offense for which the defendant was held, but does not authorize additional charges merely because they are supported by factual allegations in the complaint or evidence at a hearing.

In People v. Zanghi, 79 N.Y.2d 815, 580 N.Y.S.2d 179, 588 N.E.2d 77 (1991), the prosecution argued that factual allegations in the felony complaint were sufficient to support a charge in the SCI that had not been charged in the felony complaint. The court rejected the argument, holding that factual allegations tending to prove an element not charged were "mere surplusage." 79 N.Y.2d at 818, 580 N.Y.S.2d at 181.

288. 76 N.Y.2d 473, 560 N.Y.S.2d 760, 561 N.E.2d 536 (1990).

289. See P.L. § 265.02(4).

290. P.L. § 265.01(1). Interestingly, the court, without discussion, overruled People v. Ali, 36 N.Y.2d 880, 372 N.Y.S.2d 212, 334 N.E.2d 11 (1975), which had held that fourth degree possession was not a lesser included offense of third degree possession.

any way violate the restrictions of CPL 220.10."[291] It is unclear whether the court would void an SCI-plea arrangement on this basis.[292]

In *People v. Zanghi*,[293] the reverse situation arose. There, the defendant was charged in the SCI with a *greater* offense than that contained in the felony complaint upon which he had waived a preliminary hearing.[294] The court voided the plea and waiver, holding that the defendant had not been held for the action of the grand jury upon the greater offense and thus the waiver was unconstitutional. Of interest in *Zanghi* was language in CPL § 195.20 that permits inclusion in an SCI not only of an offense for which the defendant was held for action of the grand jury, but also for "any offense or offenses properly joinable therewith pursuant to sections 200.20 and 200.40." The court left open the question of the constitutionality of that provision.[295] Since the charge for which the defendant had been held, criminal possession of stolen property in the fourth degree, was *not* charged in the SCI, the court ruled that it was "unnecessary for us to decide in this case whether CPL § 195.20's provision for including joinable offenses along with the offense for which the defendant was held is consistent with the constitutional provisions for waiver of indictment."[296]

Finally, it is important to remember that an SCI may not charge a non-existent crime.[297] Because plea arrangements frequently may involve a plea to a lesser offense where the lesser crime is non-existent,[298] it is understandable that parties arranging an SCI as part of a plea agreement would draft an information charging a non-existent crime. The correct approach, however, is for the information to charge a crime, followed, if necessary, by a plea to the non-existent lesser offense.

Cases Involving Sentences of Life Imprisonment or Death. The State Constitution prohibits waiver in cases "punishable by death or life imprisonment."[299] The Third and Fourth Departments have voided waivers where a defendant was held for the action of the grand jury on a Class A felony, but waived indictment on a lesser included offense.[300]

291. 76 N.Y.2d at 477, 560 N.Y.S.2d at 763.

292. It would appear inconsistent, however, for the court to find that the defendant has a constitutional right to waive indictment for a lesser included offense, and thereafter hold that the right could be abnegated by a statutory restriction on plea bargaining.

293. 79 N.Y.2d 815, 580 N.Y.S.2d 179, 588 N.E.2d 77 (1991).

294. The felony complaint included a charge of criminal possession of stolen property in the fourth degree, P.L. § 165.45(1), while the SCI charged him with criminal possession of a weapon in the third degree, P.L. § 165.50.

295. The Constitution only permits waiver when the defendant has been held for "such offense." Under the broad provisions of Article 200, other offenses may be joinable therewith that bear little relationship to the offense charged in the felony complaint.

296. 79 N.Y.2d at 818, 580 N.Y.S.2d at 181.

297. People v. Roe, 191 A.D.2d 844, 595 N.Y.S.2d 121 (3d Dep't 1993)(SCI charging attempted reckless murder jurisdictionally defective).

298. Cf. People v. Ford, 62 N.Y.2d 275, 476 N.Y.S.2d 783, 465 N.E.2d 322 (1984); People v. Foster, 19 N.Y.2d 150, 278 N.Y.S.2d 603, 225 N.E.2d 200 (1967).

299. N.Y. Const., Art 1, § 6. See also CPL § 195.10(1)(b)(prohibiting waiver when the defendant is charged with a Class A felony).

300. People v. Woolson, 195 A.D.2d 949, 600 N.Y.S.2d 587 (4th Dep't 1993); People v. Sledge, 90 A.D.2d 588, 456 N.Y.S.2d 198 (3d Dep't 1982).

However, the Court of Appeals has specifically reserved decision on that issue.[301] Since there is no requirement that a grand jury vote an indictment for a Class A felony merely because one was charged in the felony complaint, it would seem that in the parallel situation of waiver, a reduced count could be charged in an SCI. On the other hand, CPL § 180.50(2)(b) prohibits reduction, in a local criminal court prior to grand jury presentation, of a Class A felony (or an armed felony) to a misdemeanor charge after there has been a showing of reasonable cause to support the greater charge. There is, of course, a vast difference between reduction in a local criminal court of a Class A felony or an armed felony to a misdemeanor in order to avoid grand jury presentation, and reduction from a Class A felony or an armed felony charged in a felony complaint to a lesser felony to be prosecuted in superior court by way of agreement between the parties. Nonetheless, at least one commentator has cautioned that a court may not allow reduction without grand jury action if it is viewed as an "end run" around "carefully crafted sentencing provision[s]."[302]

Library References:
West's Key No. Digests, Indictment and Information ⟠3–5.

§ 5.11 Indictment—In General

An indictment is a written accusation by a grand jury, filed with a superior court, that charges one or more defendants with the commission of one or more offenses and that serves as a basis for prosecution.[303] A filed indictment or a superior court information is necessary for a superior court to acquire trial jurisdiction.[304] An indictment is voted by a grand jury. Alternatively, a superior court information may be filed by a prosecutor upon waiver by the defendant in open court whereby he or she consents to prosecution without presentation to a grand jury.[305]

---

301. People v. D'Amico, 76 N.Y.2d 877, 879, 561 N.Y.S.2d 411, 412, 562 N.E.2d 488, 489 (1990)("It remains an open question whether the class A felony restriction of CPL 195.10(1)(b) would prohibit a waiver to lesser charges when the defendant is held for Grand Jury action for a class A felony ... or whether, instead, it prohibits only a waiver of indictment with respect to the class A felony.").

302. Preiser, "Practice Commentary" to CPL § 195.20, McKinney's Cons. Laws of N.Y., Book 11A, at 392–93 (1993).

303. See CPL § 1.20(3) for the definition of an "indictment." A "superior court" is either a Supreme Court or a County Court. CPL § 10.10(2).

304. CPL § 210.05 ("The only methods of prosecuting an offense in a superior court are by an indictment ... or by a superior court information ...").

"A valid and sufficient accusatory instrument is a nonwaivable jurisdictional prerequisite to a criminal prosecution." People v. Harper, 37 N.Y.2d 96, 99, 371 N.Y.S.2d 467, 469, 332 N.E.2d 336, 337 (1975). "Until the grand jury shall act, no court can acquire jurisdiction to try [a capital or infamous crime]." People ex rel. Battista v. Christian, 249 N.Y. 314, 319, 164 N.E. 111, 112 (1928).

"Trial jurisdiction" and "preliminary jurisdiction" are defined in CPL § 1.20(24) and (25). A local criminal court may acquire preliminary jurisdiction of a felony charge, but only a superior court has authority to accept a plea to, try or otherwise dispose of a felony count of an indictment or superior court information.

305. See generally CPL Article 195. See § 5.10, supra.

§ 5.11

When the CPL refers to an indictment, the term is meant to include a superior court information unless specifically provided otherwise.[306]

Grand jury review is required by the State Constitution[307] and statute.[308] The federal constitution does not require presentation to a grand jury in a state prosecution.[309]

On the other hand, a defendant in a state proceeding has a federal constitutional right, as a matter of due process, "to be informed of the nature and cause of the accusation."[310] This provision is contained in the New York Constitution as well.[311]

Library References:
West's Key No. Digests, Indictment and Information ⟨⇒⟩3, 6–16.

§ 5.12 Indictment—Form and Content

Section 200.50 details the requisite form and content of an indictment. At a minimum, the indictment should list the name of the court where filed,[312] the title of the action, a separate count for each offense charged,[313] a statement of accusation by the grand jury as to each count, a statement that the offense was committed in a designated county,[314] a

---

306. CPL § 200.10. Occasionally, the practitioner may hear an indictment referred to as a "presentment." A presentment and an indictment both are "accusations of crime [voted by a grand jury], the difference between them being that the former is made at the instance of the grand jury itself, while the latter is made at the instance of the public prosecutor." Matter of Wood v. Hughes, 9 N.Y.2d 144, 148 n. 1, 212 N.Y.S.2d 33, 34 n. 1, 173 N.E.2d 21, 22 n. 1 (1961). The revised CPL uses the term "indictment" to include both.

307. N.Y. Const., Art. 1, § 6.

308. CPL § 210.05.

309. The grand jury provision contained in the Fifth Amendment to the federal constitution is not applicable to the states. Hurtado v. California, 110 U.S. 516, 4 S.Ct. 292, 28 L.Ed. 232 (1885); People v. Iannone, 45 N.Y.2d 589, 593 n. 3, 412 N.Y.S.2d 110, 113 n. 3, 384 N.E.2d 656, 659 n. 3 (1978).

310. U.S. Const., Amend VI. See Cole v. Arkansas, 333 U.S. 196, 68 S.Ct. 514, 92 L.Ed. 644 (1948)(reversing a state conviction for variance—defendant was tried and convicted of promoting an unlawful assembly at a labor demonstration when he had been charged in an information with promoting use of force at the demonstration).

311. Art. 1, § 6. See People v. Morris, 61 N.Y.2d 290, 473 N.Y.S.2d 769, 461 N.E.2d 1256 (1984); People v. Iannone, 45 N.Y.2d 589, 594, 412 N.Y.S.2d 110, 113, 384 N.E.2d 656, 660 (1978).

312. See, e.g., People v. Riedd, 160 Misc.2d 733, 609 N.Y.S.2d 997 (Sup.Ct., Bronx County, 1993)(indictment not dismissed where caption of indictment incorrectly specified "The Bronx" as county of prosecution when proper name would have been "Bronx County").

313. See CPL § 200.30 and discussion concerning duplicitous counts, § 5.17, infra.

314. The statement is necessary to demonstrate geographic jurisdiction. Cf. Matter of Steingut v. Gold, 42 N.Y.2d 311, 397 N.Y.S.2d 765, 366 N.E.2d 854 (1977)(permitting extraordinary remedy of writ of prohibition against prosecution based upon review of grand jury minutes) with Matter of Sharpton v. Turner, 169 A.D.2d 947, 565 N.Y.S.2d 255 (3d Dep't 1991) (denying challenge to geographic jurisdiction by way of Article 78 proceeding). See generally, Chapter 1.

Regarding the need to allege venue properly, see People v. Puig, 85 Misc.2d 228, 378 N.Y.S.2d 925 (Sup.Ct., N.Y. County, 1976)(indictment fatally defective when it alleged commission of drug crime to be somewhere in New York City, without specifying county where crime committed); but see People v. Lowen, 100 A.D.2d 518, 473 N.Y.S.2d 22 (2d Dep't 1984) (defendant waived claim that he was wrongly prosecuted in Westchester County for drug sale that took place 500 yards over border, in Bronx County, by not objecting during trial).

specification of date or period of time of the offense,[315] the signature of the foreperson acknowledging the action of the grand jury,[316] and the signature of the district attorney.[317]

In the case of an armed felony charge, since certain limits are placed upon plea bargaining,[318] sentencing,[319] juvenile offender removal,[320] and youthful offender eligibility,[321] the indictment must also advise the parties that the offense is an armed felony, specifying the weapon used or displayed.[322]

Finally, section 200.50 provides that an indictment "must" contain in each count a plain and concise factual statement, without allegations of an evidentiary nature, that asserts facts supporting every element of the offense charged with sufficient precision to clearly apprise the defendant of the conduct that is the subject of the accusation.[323]

Library References:
West's Key No. Digests, Indictment and Information ⟐17–34.

§ 5.13 Indictment—Purpose

Generally speaking, a well-drafted indictment provides notice of the charges, guards against variance, avoids duplicitous charges within a count, and protects against double jeopardy.[324] Additionally, a facially sufficient indictment serves as "evidence that a panel of citizens has

---

315. See discussion concerning problems in allegations relating to date and time, § 5.15, infra.

316. But see People v. Miller, 75 Misc.2d 1, 346 N.Y.S.2d 144 (Sup.Ct., Dutchess County, 1973)(signature of foreperson on cover sheet of original indictment filed with court sufficient; indictment not dismissed for failure to sign copy provided defendant).

317. But see, People v. Rupp, 75 Misc.2d 683, 348 N.Y.S.2d 649 (Sullivan Co.Ct.1973)(signature requirement merely directory and clerical in nature; absence of signature not a ground for dismissal); see also People v. Sanchez, 144 Misc.2d 262, 543 N.Y.S.2d 878 (Sup.Ct., Bronx County, 1989)(typed name of district attorney on indictment satisfies requirement).

318. CPL § 220.10(5)(d)(i).

319. P.L. § 70.02(5).

320. CPL § 210.43(1)(b).

321. CPL § 720.10(2).

322. CPL § 200.50(7)(b). However, in one case, the Court of Appeals decided that this provision is satisfied if the indictment merely alleges use of a "handgun", a term not defined in the Penal Law, without further detail. People v. Singleton, 72 N.Y.2d 845, 531 N.Y.S.2d 798, 527 N.E.2d 281 (1988).

323. CPL § 200.50(7). Despite the clear language of the statute, requiring factual explication with precision, or what is known as a "long form" indictment, in practice and by case law this provision is honored in the breach. See People v. Fitzgerald, 45 N.Y.2d 574, 412 N.Y.S.2d 102, 384 N.E.2d 649 (1978).

324. The Court of Appeals has observed:

A criminal indictment serves three purposes. First, it provides "the defendant with fair notice of the accusations made against him, so that he will be able to prepare a defense." Second, the indictment provides "some means of ensuring that the crime for which the defendant is brought to trial is in fact one for which he was indicted by the Grand Jury, rather than some alternative seized upon by the prosecution." Finally, an indictment protects a criminal defendant from prosecution at another time for the same offense. Therefore, "an indictment must allege the crime charged with sufficient specificity to enable the defendant, once convicted, to raise the constitutional bar of double jeopardy against subsequent prosecutions for the same offense."

People v. Sanchez, 84 N.Y.2d 440, 445, 618 N.Y.S.2d 887, 889, 643 N.E.2d 509, 511 (1994)(citations omitted).

fulfilled the historic and statutorily mandated duties of a Grand Jury", *i.e.*, the panel concluded that there was legally sufficient evidence to establish all the essential elements of the crime charged.[325]

In part, these important goals are served by careful adherence to the formal requirements of an indictment.[326] However, not every deviation from the requirements of section 200.50 will result in dismissal of the indictment. Instead, litigation involving deficiencies in an indictment generally centers upon three issues: (1) whether shortcomings in the allegations can be met by supplying supplemental information in a bill of particulars or discovery; (2) whether an error or omission can be cured by amendment of the indictment itself;[327] and (3) whether any such defects are waived by failure to object or by a guilty plea. It is useful for the practitioner to keep these questions in mind as a tool for functional analysis when researching an alleged shortcoming in an indictment.

Library References:

West's Key No. Digests, Indictment and Information ⌸55, 71.2.

§ 5.14 Indictment—Adequate Notice

Since the constitutional imperative for an indictment is notice,[328] litigation involving the facial sufficiency of a charging instrument frequently involves the question of adequacy of notice. However, the Court of Appeals held in *People v. Iannone*[329] that the indictment should be read in conjunction with the bill of particulars in gauging whether the defendant is sufficiently informed of the nature and cause of the accusation and that no particular form of indictment is constitutionally man-

---

325. People v. Cohen, 52 N.Y.2d 584, 587, 439 N.Y.S.2d 321, 322, 421 N.E.2d 813, 814 (1981)(Gabrielli, J., concurring).

326. "Statutes governing the Grand Jury process should be strictly construed and compliance therewith meticulously observed." Matter of Grand Jury of Supreme Ct. of Rensselaer County [June 1982], 98 A.D.2d 284, 286, 471 N.Y.S.2d 378, 379 (3d Dep't 1983). As just one example, in People v. Perez, 83 N.Y.2d 269, 609 N.Y.S.2d 564, 631 N.E.2d 570 (1994), the Court of Appeals reversed a conviction upon a count that was added by amendment to an indictment notwithstanding the prosecution's demonstration that the failure to include the count was a clerical oversight and that, in fact, the grand jury had heard evidence upon and voted to indict for the omitted offense.

On the other hand, as one court has observed:

[I]t has been well stated that "state law, in this instance affording greater flexibility in the accusatory process, does not favor the dismissal of indictments for technical defects in the absence of a showing of fraud or prejudice to the defendant."

People v. Riedd, 160 Misc.2d 733, 737, 609 N.Y.S.2d 997, 1000 (Sup.Ct., Broome County, 1993) (citations omitted).

327. See discussion of CPL § 200.70, § 5.18, infra, which permits a court to order amendment of an indictment

with respect to defects, errors or variances from the proof relating to matters of form, time, place, names of persons and the like, when such an amendment does not change the theory or theories of the prosecution as reflected in the evidence before the grand jury ... or otherwise tend to prejudice the defendant on the merits.

The statute also provides that an indictment may not be amended for the purpose of curing a failure thereof to charge or state an offense, legal insufficiency of the factual allegations, or misjoinder.

328. U.S. Const., Amend. VI; N.Y. Const., Art. 1, § 6.

329. 45 N.Y.2d 589, 412 N.Y.S.2d 110, 384 N.E.2d 656 (1978).

dated.[330] As a result, the Legislature is free to alter the formal requisites for an indictment.[331] In *Iannone* and *People v. Jackson*,[332] the Court of Appeals approved indictments that did little more than recite the crime charged *in haec verba*. At the same time, *Iannone* and *Jackson* emphasized that the court did not condone a lack of notice to the defendant.[333]

330. In People v. Morris, 61 N.Y.2d 290, 295, 473 N.Y.S.2d 769, 772, 461 N.E.2d 1256, 1259 (1984), the court stated:

> The notice requirement of the Sixth Amendment is met if in addition to stating the elements of the offense, "the indictment contains such description of the offense charged as will enable [defendant] to make his defense and to plead the judgment in bar of any further prosecution for the same crime." In order for a defendant to make his defense "with all reasonable knowledge and ability" and to have "full notice of the charge", it is important that the indictment "charge the time and place and nature and circumstances of the offense with clearness and certainty." (citations omitted).

331. In Iannone, Judge Gabrielli recounted the historical development of the form of the indictment in New York. At common law, "the indictment was an arcane and intricate work of art which all too often served to mystify rather than to inform defendants." 45 N.Y.2d at 595, 412 N.Y.S.2d at 114. In 1881, with enactment of the Code of Criminal Procedure, "long-form" indictments were authorized. Very much like current CPL § 200.50, long-form indictments required "[a] plain and concise statement of the act constituting the crime." This was succeeded, in 1929, by authorization for a "simplified" indictment, which merely required "[a] statement of the specific crime with which the defendant is charged." Code Crim. Proc. § 295–b(2). The short-form indictment withstood constitutional challenge, on the grounds that necessary information could be obtained through a bill of particulars. People v. Bogdanoff, 254 N.Y. 16, 171 N.E. 890 (1930).

Significantly, the CPL, which took effect in 1971, eschewed short-form indictments and returned to the language of the 1881 code, requiring, once again, a long-form indictment, i.e., a plain and concise factual statement asserting facts supporting every element of the offense charged. A line of cases then ensued, applying the new statute, which dismissed indictments on jurisdictional grounds for failure to provide sufficient factual allegations in support of each crime charged. People v. Colloca, 57 A.D.2d 1039, 395 N.Y.S.2d 811 (4th Dep't 1977); People v. Guest, 53 A.D.2d 892, 385 N.Y.S.2d 376 (2d Dep't 1976); People v. Barnes, 44 A.D.2d 740, 354 N.Y.S.2d 459 (3d Dep't 1974).

Seemingly, in Iannone, the court ignored the revised statutory mandate in the new CPL. However, in Iannone, the defendant had failed to raise a timely objection. Therefore, the precise issue in that case was whether the defect was jurisdictional and, consequently, non-waivable. Since the history of the short-form indictment in New York made it clear that the form of an indictment was not constitutionally mandated, the literal holding in Iannone was merely that there was no fundamental jurisdictional defect in the notice provided by a short-form indictment, assuming that the indictment was supplemented by an adequate bill of particulars.

However, the court decided People v. Fitzgerald, 45 N.Y.2d 574, 412 N.Y.S.2d 102, 384 N.E.2d 649 (1978), the same day as Iannone. In that case, the Second Department had affirmed a dismissal of an indictment for criminally negligent homicide on the grounds that the indictment failed to itemize the negligent acts that supported the allegation of criminal negligence. The dismissal was based upon the revised CPL § 200.50. The Court of Appeals reinstated the indictment, holding that deficiencies in the factual allegations of an indictment that failed the notice requirement of section 200.50 could be cured by a bill of particulars, notwithstanding the Legislature's abolition of short-form indictments.

332. 46 N.Y.2d 721, 413 N.Y.S.2d 369, 385 N.E.2d 1296 (1978).

333. In Iannone, the court warned:

> A word of caution is in order. It is beyond cavil that a defendant has a basic and fundamental right to be informed of the charges against him so that he will be able to prepare a defense. Hence the courts must exercise careful surveillance to ensure that a defendant is not deprived of this right by an overzealous prosecutor attempting to protect his case or his witnesses. Any effort to leave a defendant in ignorance of the substance of the accusation until the time of trial must be firmly rebuffed. This is especially so where the indictment itself provides a paucity of information. In such cases, the court must be vigilant in safeguard-

The indictment must be read in conjunction with the bill of particulars in order to determine the specific criminal acts alleged and the theory of the prosecution as voted by the grand jury.

As a general proposition, in the wake of *Iannone* and *Jackson*, the constitutional and statutory notice requirements for an indictment are met if the accusatory instrument merely charges the commission of a specified offense in the language of the statute.[334] This assumes, of course, that any deficiencies in the adequacy of the notice are cured by a bill of particulars.[335]

Library References:

West's Key No. Digests, Indictment and Information ⇐56.

§ 5.15 Indictment—Date of Offense

One issue concerning adequacy of notice that has proven particularly troublesome is the requirement that an indictment contain a statement that "the offense charged therein was committed on, *or* on or about, a designated date, *or* during a designated period of time."[336]

This provision alludes to three different kinds of offenses. In some instances, a specific date is an essential element of the offense, in which case the indictment must state that the crime occurred "on" that date.[337] In other cases, where a single act is alleged but a specific date is not an essential element of the offense, it is sufficient to allege that an offense occurred "on or about" a designated date.[338] This means that the prosecution, either in the indictment or in a bill of particulars, should be as specific as it can under all the circumstances.[339] The test for adequacy

ing the defendant's rights to a bill of particulars and to effective discovery. 45 N.Y.2d at 599, 412 N.Y.S.2d at 117.

334. See, e.g., People v. Levin, 57 N.Y.2d 1008, 457 N.Y.S.2d 472, 443 N.E.2d 946 (1982)(indictment that charged larceny in the language of the statute was not insufficient on its face; see P.L. § 155.45, which specifically authorizes indictments in larceny cases "without designating the particular way or manner in which such property was stolen or the particular theory of larceny involved"); People v. Cohen, 52 N.Y.2d 584, 439 N.Y.S.2d 321, 421 N.E.2d 813 (1981)(failure to allege "willfulness" in prosecution for tax law violations, where it was argued the element had been added by judicial gloss to the language of the statute itself, does not render indictment facially deficient).

335. People v. Jackson, supra; People v. Iannone, supra; People v. Fitzgerald, supra.

336. CPL § 200.50(6)(emphasis added).

337. For example, the offense of bail-jumping is defined as a failure to appear on a given date. People v. Landy, 125 A.D.2d 703, 510 N.Y.S.2d 190 (2d Dep't 1986).

338. See, e.g., People v. Watt, 81 N.Y.2d 772, 774, 593 N.Y.S.2d 782, 783, 609 N.E.2d 135, 136 (1993)("When time is not an essential element of an offense, the indictment, as supplemented by a bill of particulars, may allege the time in approximate terms. The indictment must, however, set forth a time interval which reasonably 'serves the function of protecting defendant's constitutional right "to be informed of the nature and cause of the accusation"' so as to enable the defendant to prepare a defense and to use the judgment against further prosecution for the same crime.")(citation omitted).

339. Id. ("We have developed a set of criteria to be considered when making the necessary determinations pertinent to this distinct issue in cases in which the per se bar does not apply. The nonexclusive list of factors includes the length of the time span provided by the People and the knowledge the People possess or should acquire with reasonable diligence of the exact or approximate date or dates of the criminal conduct. Additionally, relevant factors include the age and intelligence of the victim and other witnesses; the nature of the of-

of notice "embraces good faith ... thereby requiring the prosecution to give necessary specifics to the best of its knowledge."[340] Litigation in this second category frequently involves charges of sex abuse committed over a period time.[341] However, difficulties in identifying the date of occurrence with precision are not limited to this kind of offense.[342]

Finally, some offenses, by the nature of their definition, are continuous crimes encompassing a designated period of time.[343] Defining an offense as a continuous one, however, does not mean that the prosecution is relieved of its obligation to be as precise as it can be with reasonable diligence.[344]

Library References:
West's Key No. Digests, Indictment and Information ⇒87.

§ 5.16 Indictment—Jurisdictional Defects

Aside from problems with adequate notice, an indictment can be jurisdictionally defective if "the acts it accuses [the] defendant of performing simply do not constitute a crime, or if it fails to allege that a defendant committed acts constituting every material element of the crime."[345] Similarly, if the indictment charges a nonexistent crime, it is

fense or offenses, including whether they are likely to be discovered immediately and whether there is a criminal pattern; and all other surrounding circumstances.").

340. Id.

341. People v. Watt, supra (on remand, 192 A.D.2d 65, 600 N.Y.S.2d 714 (2d Dep't 1993))(allegation that sex offense occurred within specified five-month period, under the circumstances, sufficiently precise); People v. Beauchamp, 74 N.Y.2d 639, 541 N.Y.S.2d 977, 539 N.E.2d 1105 (1989)(nine months excessive); People v. Keindl, 68 N.Y.2d 410, 509 N.Y.S.2d 790, 502 N.E.2d 577 (1986)(periods ranging from 10 to 16 months excessive); People v. Morris, 61 N.Y.2d 290, 473 N.Y.S.2d 769, 461 N.E.2d 1256 (1984)(24-day period sufficiently precise). See also People v. Miller, 197 A.D.2d 925, 602 N.Y.S.2d 272 (4th Dep't 1993)(indictment alleging 27 counts of rape that occurred approximately once per month over a 27-month period sustained as sufficiently precise).

342. See, e.g., People v. Sanchez, 84 N.Y.2d 440, 618 N.Y.S.2d 887, 643 N.E.2d 509 (1994)(larceny and fortune-telling are not continuous offenses; allegations covering a five-year period were too broad).

343. People v. Keindl, supra (rape and sodomy are not continuous offenses, but endangering the welfare of a child is); People v. Sanchez, supra (while larceny and fortune-telling are not continuous offenses, criminal impersonation and scheme to defraud are); People v. Okafore, 72 N.Y.2d 81, 531 N.Y.S.2d 762, 527 N.E.2d 245 (1988)(criminal possession of a weapon in the third degree is a continuous crime, but criminal possession in the second degree, involving a contemporaneous intent to use the gun unlawfully against another, is not).

344. See, e.g., People v. Sanchez, 84 N.Y.2d at 448, 618 N.Y.S.2d at 891-92 (dismissing count of criminal impersonation, a continuous crime, because allegation that the impersonation occurred over a five-year period was insufficiently precise).

345. People v. Iannone, 45 N.Y.2d 589, 412 N.Y.S.2d 110, 118, 384 N.E.2d 656 (1978) (citation omitted). Significantly, in both Iannone and People v. Fitzgerald, 45 N.Y.2d 574, 412 N.Y.S.2d 102, 384 N.E.2d 649 (1978), the indictments fully charged all the elements of each crime charged by reciting the statutory provisions in haec verba. The holdings in those cases dealt with the adequacy of notice, not a failure to charge a crime. In Fitzgerald, the court held that the new statutory "notice" requirement of section 200.50, i.e., the return to a "long form" indictment in the recodification of the CPL, could be met by reading the indictment and bill of particulars together. In Iannone, the court held that the constitutionally mandated notice function of an indictment could be met by reading it together with a bill of particulars and that a plea of guilty would waive any claim that the notice was insufficient. Neither case dealt with a claim that the indictment was jurisdictionally defective for failure to allege

§ 5.16   GRAND JURY & INDICTMENT   Ch. 5

jurisdictionally defective.[346]

Jurisdictional defects in an indictment are not waived by a plea of guilty or cured by a supplemental bill of particulars.[347] For the same reason, where an indictment fails to allege all the material elements of the crime charged, amendment to cure the problem is not permitted.[348] This, however, can be avoided by reference, in the indictment, to the specific statutory provision alleged to have been violated. Where a violation of a specific statutory provision is alleged, an omission in the specific factual allegations further detailing the particulars of the criminal conduct is not a jurisdictional defect "because the indictment incorporate[s] the statutory elements of the crime charged by reference."[349]

On the other hand, when an indictment cites to a statutory provision, presumably to incorporate by reference all the material elements of

a crime or a material element of a crime. "In essence, an indictment is jurisdictionally defective only if it does not effectively charge the defendant with the commission of a particular crime." People v. Iannone, 45 N.Y.2d at 600, 412 N.Y.S.2d at 118.

346. See, e.g., People v. Roe, 191 A.D.2d 844, 595 N.Y.S.2d 121 (3d Dep't 1993)(superior court information charging attempted murder in the second degree under a reckless conduct theory was jurisdictionally defective, requiring vacatur of subsequent plea).

347. People v. Iannone, supra. This elemental proposition may have been called into question by People v. Cohen, 52 N.Y.2d 584, 439 N.Y.S.2d 321, 421 N.E.2d 813 (1981). In Cohen, the court rejected a claim that the indictment should have alleged "willfulness" in a prosecution for tax evasion in addition to pleading the language of the statute, stating:

The incorporation by specific reference to the statute operates without more to constitute allegations of all the elements of the crime required by explicit provision of the statute itself or by judicial gloss overlaid thereon, if any, for conviction under that statute. The defendant's argument both before and since his plea that the indictment was jurisdictionally insufficient is therefore without merit.

52 N.Y.2d at 586–87, 439 N.Y.S.2d at 322. However, the opinion also noted that any issue concerning the proper interpretation of the statute in question was forfeited by a guilty plea. Id. In his concurring opinion, Judge Gabrielli, the author of Iannone, cautioned that this might be wrongly interpreted to imply that a guilty plea waived objection to a facially deficient indictment, i.e., one that failed to allege a material element of the crime charged. People v. Cohen, 52 N.Y.2d at 591, 439 N.Y.S.2d at 324–25 (Gabrielli, J., concurring). See also Preiser, "Practice Commentary" to CPL § 200.50, McKinney's Cons. Laws of N.Y., Book 11A, at 470 (1993)("[I]nsufficiency in the factual allegations is not a jurisdictional defect."). In light of Judge Gabrielli's caution, this statement should probably be understood to mean "insufficiency in the factual allegations—with regard to a claim of inadequate notice—is not a jurisdictional defect."

348. CPL § 200.70(2)(a). In some instances, in addition to alleging criminal conduct, the indictment must affirmatively allege that the defendant's conduct does not fall within a statutory exception contained within the statute defining the offense. See, e.g., People v. First Meridian Planning Corp., 201 A.D.2d 145, 614 N.Y.S.2d 811 (3d Dep't 1994), aff'd 86 N.Y.2d 608, 635 N.Y.S.2d 144, 658 N.E.2d 1017 (1995) (trial court's dismissal of counts charging failure to register as a commodities broker-dealer under the Martin Act upheld because indictment did not also allege that sale of coins was not excluded from definition of "commodity" by rules and regulations of Attorney General); People v. Best, 132 A.D.2d 773, 517 N.Y.S.2d 582 (3d Dep't 1987)(failure to allege gun possession was not in defendant's home or place of business, an exception contained within the statute defining the crime, requires dismissal).

349. People v. Ray, 71 N.Y.2d 849, 527 N.Y.S.2d 740, 522 N.E.2d 1037 (1988)(indictment omitted word "unlawfully" in charging criminal possession of a weapon in the second degree, but was not jurisdictionally defective because it specifically referred to P.L. § 265.03). But see People v. Chicas, 204 A.D.2d 476, 611 N.Y.S.2d 873 (2d Dep't 1994)(conviction reversed and count dismissed where indictment alleged criminal possession of a weapon, but failed to allege that dangerous instrument was possessed

a crime, unintended consequences may ensue. On occasion, the factual allegations may not match the crime that is statutorily referenced. Courts must then wrestle with options of dismissal or amendment. Any amendment, of course, must not alter the theory of prosecution adopted by the grand jury. But, if the indictment is to be amended, when the factual allegations in an indictment and the crime charged are not in accord, the appropriate amendment is not always clear. Should the statutory citation be changed to conform to the factual allegations, or should the reverse be done?[350] Because omissions in the factual allegations are generally cured by mere reference to the statutory citation, one might assume that courts would view the statutory reference as controlling and, therefore, presume it to reflect the grand jury vote. As a general rule, however, a conflict between the factual allegations and the statutory reference is resolved in favor of the factual allegations on the face of the indictment. This allows for amendment of the indictment, by conforming the statutory reference, to "correct" the error.[351] For example, in *People v. Oliver*,[352] the indictment charged the defendant with burglary in the first degree, but failed to allege that the unlawful entry occurred at night. The defendant was convicted, after trial, of the crime. The Court of Appeals ordered a new trial on the grounds that the indictment failed to allege a material element of burglary in the first degree and the omission could not be cured by amendment. Significantly, however, the court did not dismiss the indictment. Rather, it permitted retrial upon a charge of burglary in the second degree, which, while not charged in the indictment, was supported by the allegations because nighttime entry was not an element of the lesser crime. The court held that a conflict on the face of an indictment between factual allegations and the statutory reference may be resolved by an amendment that reduces the crime referenced to one that matches the factual allegations without the necessity of re-presenting the case to a new grand jury.[353]

Of course, such a conflict only arises where the indictment, on its face, references a statutory offense and, as well, recites factual allega-

---

"with intent to use unlawfully against another").

350. Distinguish the situation here, where the indictment is inconsistent on its face, from cases where the pleadings do not conform to the proof in the grand jury, discussed in § 5.18, infra.

351. People v. Weeks, 126 A.D.2d 857, 510 N.Y.S.2d 920 (3d Dep't 1987) ("technical" amendment permitted on eve of trial to charge sexual abuse in the first degree that was supported by factual allegations in the indictment, notwithstanding statutory reference in indictment to attempted sexual abuse in first degree); People v. Shannon, 129 Misc.2d 289, 488 N.Y.S.2d 348 (Sup.Ct., Queens County, 1985), aff'd 127 A.D.2d 863, 512 N.Y.S.2d 242 (2d Dep't 1987)(amendment ordered during trial where factual allegations supported charge of bail jumping in the first degree, but statutory reference in indictment was to bail jumping in the second degree; probable confusion and clerical error arising from recent amendments to Penal Law that renumbered the applicable sections).

352. 3 N.Y.2d 684, 171 N.Y.S.2d 811, 148 N.E.2d 874 (1958).

353. See also People v. Randall, 9 N.Y.2d 413, 214 N.Y.S.2d 417, 174 N.E.2d 507 (1961)(reduction in sodomy charge permitted to conform to allegations on face of indictment). Cf. People v. Shannon, 127 A.D.2d 863, 512 N.Y.S.2d 242 (2d Dep't 1987)(unusual case where court permitted amendment to increase charge from bail jumping in the second degree to bail jumping in the first degree, because "[t]he defendant was clearly aware of the erroneous designation and chose, as a matter of trial

tions that are disconsonant with the definition of the referenced offense. In light of *Iannone, Jackson* and *Levin*, a prosecutor runs little risk of creating such a conflict if he or she recites the elements of the referenced statute *in haec verba* and meets the notice requirements of CPL § 200.50 in the bill of particulars. Rules governing amendment of a bill of particulars are more liberal than those regarding amendment of an indictment.[354]

Library References:
West's Key No. Digests, Indictment and Information ⇐55–123.

§ 5.17 Indictment—Duplicitous Counts

Section 200.30 provides that "[e]ach count of an indictment may charge one offense only." The purpose of the section is to avoid duplicitous counts.[355] The prohibition against duplicitous counts exists for several reasons.[356] For one, a defendant is entitled to know the "exact nature" of the charges against him or her.[357] Obviously, if two charges are contained within one count, the nature of the charge becomes blurred. Second, if more than one criminal act is charged in a count or more than one crime is encompassed by one charge, there is no assurance that the jury unanimously agreed upon one criminal act or one particular crime.[358] Finally, the prohibition against duplicitous counts helps prevent potential double jeopardy problems that arise when, in retrospect, it becomes unclear which offenses were previously considered by the jury.

Counts are said to be "multiplicitous," as opposed to duplicitous, when two or more separate counts of an indictment are redundant, *i.e.*, they each charge commission of the same crime for the same conduct, merely differing in the proof that is offered to support the charge.[359] An indictment is not multiplicitous if each count requires proof of an additional fact that the other does not.[360] The principal objection to multiplicitous counts is the risk that a defendant will be punished twice

---

tactics, to rely thereon as the basis for his trial defense").

354. See § 5.19, infra.

355. "If a count charges more than one offense, it fails to meet these requirements and is void for duplicity." People v. Davis, 72 N.Y.2d 32, 38, 530 N.Y.S.2d 529, 532, 526 N.E.2d 20, 23 (1988).

356. See generally People v. Ribowsky, 77 N.Y.2d 284, 567 N.Y.S.2d 392, 568 N.E.2d 1197 (1991).

357. People v. Klipfel, 160 N.Y. 371, 54 N.E. 788 (1899).

358. People v. Beauchamp, 74 N.Y.2d 639, 541 N.Y.S.2d 977, 539 N.E.2d 1105 (1989); People v. Keindl, 68 N.Y.2d 410, 509 N.Y.S.2d 790, 502 N.E.2d 577 (1986).

359. See, e.g., People v. Senisi, 196 A.D.2d 376, 382, 610 N.Y.S.2d 542, 546 (2d Dep't 1994):

The People, in what was perhaps an unwarranted fear of committing the error of duplicity (one count charging what amounts to two separate crimes) lapsed into the converse error of multiplicity (two separate counts charging what amounts to one single crime). Both count one and count two of the present indictment were premised on the same subdivision of the same statute ... and, insofar as they applied to Senisi, they differed only in that they were each supported by a different specification of recklessness. They both related to the same mental state, the same act, the same course of conduct, and the same victim. As to the defendant Senisi, then, the second count is multiplicitous and subject to dismissal for this reason alone.

360. People v. Kindlon, ___ A.D.2d ___, 629 N.Y.S.2d 827, 829 (3d Dep't 1995).

for the same conduct. For that reason, it is permissible to allow proof at trial of both counts, but enter judgment upon only one conviction while dismissing the other.[361]

Duplicitous counts occur in one of two contexts: (1) the count may charge as one offense two separate and distinct criminal acts;[362] or (2) the count may specify one act but allege a violation of more than one crime.

In the first of these situations, while it is clear that two separate criminal acts may not be prosecuted under one count of an indictment, some crimes may involve multiple or repeated acts that combine in actuality to comprise just one offense.[363] For example, several larcenies may be charged in the aggregate if they are part of successive takings, all pursuant to a single, sustained, criminal impulse and in execution of a general fraudulent scheme, that together constitute a single larceny, regardless of the time that may elapse between each act.[364]

On the other hand, merely because a criminal act is done repeatedly does not mean that multiple acts can be included in one count.[365] A case illustrating the distinction between a duplicitous count charging two offenses and a non-duplicitous count combining several acts to prove one charge is *People v. Brannon*.[366] There, the defendant was charged with attempted sale of a controlled substance in the first degree, which

---

361. Ball v. United States, 470 U.S. 856, 105 S.Ct. 1668, 84 L.Ed.2d 740 (1985).

362. "[W]here a crime is made out by the commission of one act, that act must be the only offense alleged in the count." People v. Keindl, 68 N.Y.2d 410, 417, 509 N.Y.S.2d 790, 792, 502 N.E.2d 577, 579 (1986). On the other hand, "A count will not be found to be duplicitous ... if the crime charged may by its nature 'be committed either by one act or by multiple acts and readily permits characterization as a continuing offense over a period of time.'" People v. First Meridian Planning Corp., 201 A.D.2d 145, 149, 614 N.Y.S.2d 811, 814 (3d Dep't 1994), aff'd 86 N.Y.2d 608, 635 N.Y.S.2d 144, 658 N.E.2d 1017 (1995)(quoting People v. Keindl, supra).

363. See, e.g., People v. Ribowsky, 77 N.Y.2d 284, 567 N.Y.S.2d 392, 568 N.E.2d 1197 (1991)(allowing three alleged perjurious statements to prove one count of perjury where the statements were made at the same time and place towards one single purpose; to ensure against a potential lack of unanimity in the jury regarding the separate statements, the court submitted a special verdict sheet to the jurors, telling them they had to be unanimous as to at least one materially false statement). See also People v. First Meridian Planning, 86 N.Y.2d 608, 635 N.Y.S.2d 144, 658 N.E.2d 1017 (1995). In Meridian, a case involving potential multiple schemes to defraud charged within one count, the court reminded trial courts of their obligation to instruct the jurors that they must all agree upon the existence of the same single scheme to defraud and must also be unanimous as to each defendant found guilty that he or she participated in that same overall fraudulent scheme alleged in the indictment.

364. People v. Cox, 286 N.Y. 137, 36 N.E.2d 84 (1941). See also People v. Buckley, 75 N.Y.2d 843, 552 N.Y.S.2d 912, 552 N.E.2d 160 (1990) (simultaneous possession of stolen property from different owners may be aggregated); People v. Brown, 159 Misc.2d 11, 603 N.Y.S.2d 256 (Sup.Ct., Kings County, 1993)(multiple usurious loans at different times can be aggregated); but see People v. Roth, 129 Misc.2d 381, 492 N.Y.S.2d 971 (Suffolk Co.Ct.1985)(multiple incidents involving dumping of hazardous waste could not be aggregated; count dismissed as duplicitous).

365. See, e.g., People v. Keindl, 68 N.Y.2d at 417–18, 509 N.Y.S.2d at 793 ("each count of an indictment [may] charge only one offense" and "where one count alleges the commission of a particular offense occurring repeatedly during a designated period of time, that count encompasses more than one offense and is duplicitous"). See also People v. Beauchamp, 74 N.Y.2d 639, 541 N.Y.S.2d 977, 539 N.E.2d 1105 (1989).

366. 58 A.D.2d 34, 394 N.Y.S.2d 974 (4th Dep't 1977).

required a showing that he attempted to sell more than one ounce of a narcotic drug. The proof was that he negotiated a sale for one-half ounce of cocaine and, before that sale was consummated, he negotiated a sale for an additional one-half ounce, offering both quantities for an aggregate price. The Fourth Department held that there was an adequate basis for a jury to determine that the whole transaction was one, thereby permitting submission of one count of the indictment that combined the two offers as an attempt to sell one ounce of cocaine.[367] However, the court also determined that the trial court had erred in instructing the jury that it could consider either of the two offers to sell as a lesser included alternative, where both acts were submitted under one count. The *Brannon* court held that two separate and distinct criminal transactions could not be charged in one count as independent crimes descending from a single count in the indictment.[368] Rather, the two offers to sell a half-ounce should have been separately charged and submitted to the jury as independent counts.[369]

Another form of a duplicitous count in an indictment occurs where only one act is alleged, but the count charges, explicitly or implicitly, a violation of more than one statutory provision. Subdivision two of section 200.30 provides that one count of an indictment cannot reference two or more subdivisions or paragraphs of a statute defining a crime. That is because the Legislature intended each paragraph or subdivision to define a separate offense that, accordingly, should be distinctly pleaded.[370] Further, where a count of an indictment charges an offense that

---

367. Cf. People v. Butler, 161 Misc.2d 980, 615 N.Y.S.2d 843 (Sup.Ct., N.Y. County, 1994)(improper to join possession of heroin and cocaine in one count of indictment alleging illegal possession of a controlled substance).

368. "Under such an instruction, a verdict of guilty of the lesser crime would leave the defendants unaware as to which set of underlying facts or, indeed, which crime formed the basis of the verdict, and would also render impossible intelligent review by an appellate court." 58 A.D.2d at 43–44, 394 N.Y.S.2d at 981.

369. Where the commission of a greater crime necessarily includes the commission of lesser crimes, each of the lesser crimes may be submitted, in the alternative, to the jury. Where crimes are independently committed and are separate and distinct from one another, they must be charged in separate counts of the indictment. While it may be that on retrial the facts will justify the submission of a lesser included count, it may not be done in the style pursued here. 58 A.D.2d at 44, 394 N.Y.S.2d at 981 (citation omitted).

370. But see P.L. § 155.45(1), which creates an exception for larceny cases. In the prosecution's pleading and proof, it is sufficient to allege "that the defendant stole property of the nature or value required for the commission of the crime charged without designating the particular way or manner in which such property was stolen or the particular theory of larceny involved." It must be emphasized that this provision pertains to the sufficiency of pleading and proof at trial, but does not permit conviction without jury unanimity as to a particular statutory theory of larceny. For example, in People v. Cannon, 194 A.D.2d 496, 599 N.Y.S.2d 809 (1st Dep't 1993), the prosecution presented evidence of larceny by embezzlement and by false promise under one count. However, in an attempt to avoid problems with a potentially non-unanimous verdict or with double jeopardy, the trial court instructed the jury that it was to consider only the larceny by false promise first. If it was unanimous as to that theory, it was to so indicate and cease deliberations with regard to the alternate theory. The jury unanimously found the defendant guilty on the false promise theory, thereby avoiding potential problems of duplicitous pleading, i.e., the jury was unanimous on one theory sufficient to support a conviction. Cannon left unresolved a more troublesome problem. If the jury had not been unanimous on the first theory it was instructed to consider, could it then convict on the alternate crime of larceny by

may be committed in different ways defined by different subdivisions or paragraphs, and where the indictment fails to specify or clearly indicate which paragraph or subdivision is charged but alleges facts that would support a conviction under more than one such subdivision or paragraph, the count is duplicitous. Where a count is indefinitely drawn such that it would permit prosecution for more than one offense, the prosecution should be directed to specify with particularity the charge that the grand jury intended be filed.[371]

Application of the rule against duplicity is fairly straightforward when the indictment, directly or indirectly, permits prosecution under more than one subdivision or paragraph of a statute, each defining a distinct offense. More difficult, however, are the situations where the definition of a crime permits alternate theories of prosecution within one subdivision or paragraph. In that circumstance, the issue becomes one of legislative intent. Did the Legislature intend to describe mere alternative means of committing a single offense, or did it intend to define independent elements of the crime?

As to the former, the general rule is that "[w]here an offense may be committed by doing any one of several things, the indictment may, in a single count, group them together and charge the defendant with having committed them all, and a conviction may be had on proof of the commission of any one of the things, without proof of the commission of the others."[372] However, as to the latter, in order to preserve jury unanimity, the jury should not be forced to consider, in one count, alternate theories of prosecution that were intended by the Legislature to constitute separate elements of an offense.

For example, in *Schad v. Arizona*[373] the defendant was convicted of murder. One count of the indictment charged the alternate theories of felony murder and intentional murder in one sentence. The defendant argued that some jurors might find him guilty of felony murder while others might find him guilty of intentional murder. However, the trial court refused an instruction that all 12 jurors had to agree on one of the two theories before they could convict. The Supreme Court upheld the death sentence imposed, finding no due process violation in submission

---

embezzlement under the same count? As a practical matter, since it is relatively easy to charge each theory under a separate count, it is difficult to understand why a prosecutor would want to present alternate theories under one count of an indictment, risking problems with double jeopardy and non-unanimity.

371. See, e.g., People v. Mitchell S., 151 Misc.2d 208, 573 N.Y.S.2d 124 (N.Y.C.Crim.Ct.1991)(information that merely alleges lack of consent to sexual act without specifying whether lack of consent is by forcible compulsion or because of victim's age is inadequate); People v. Richlin, 74 Misc.2d 906, 346 N.Y.S.2d 698 (Schuyler Co.Ct.1973)(allegation of driving while intoxicated as a felony insufficient where count fails to specify which of two potential subdivisions of Vehicle and Traffic Law is charged).

372. People v. Charles, 61 N.Y.2d 321, 327–328, 473 N.Y.S.2d 941, 943–44, 462 N.E.2d 118, 120–21 (1984)(quoting Judge Cooke in People v. Nicholas, 35 A.D.2d 18, 20, 312 N.Y.S.2d 645, 647 (3d Dep't 1970)). See also McKoy v. North Carolina, 494 U.S. 433, 449, 110 S.Ct. 1227, 1237, 108 L.Ed.2d 369 (1990) ("Plainly there is no general requirement that the jury reach agreement on the preliminary factual issues which underlie the verdict.").

373. 501 U.S. 624, 111 S.Ct. 2491, 115 L.Ed.2d 555 (1991).

§ 5.17   GRAND JURY & INDICTMENT   Ch. 5

of a general verdict containing both theories.[374] In a plurality opinion, Justice Souter described the theories as merely alternative means of proving *mens rea*, *i.e.*, the defendant caused death intentionally by either intending to cause death or by intending to commit the felony that caused the death. Ultimately, in the view of the plurality, the question was one of statutory construction of Arizona law and, accordingly, the Supreme Court deferred to Arizona's courts that had decided the issue in favor of the state.[375] Since the Arizona legislature did not intend to define felony murder and intentional murder as two separate crimes or two separate elements of a crime, the count was not duplicitous.

The specific issue in *Schad* would not arise in a prosecution for murder in New York because intentional murder and felony murder are defined by two distinctly separate subdivisions of the Penal Law,[376] and CPL § 200.30 would require each subdivision to be separately charged. However, the Penal Law is replete with crimes whose definitions contain, within one paragraph or subdivision, alternate theories of prosecution, *i.e.*, the statute prescribes more than one way in which the offense can be committed.[377]

As just one example, a person is guilty of burglary in the third degree when "he knowingly enters *or* remains unlawfully in a building

---

374. The plurality opinion cautioned, however, as follows:

That is not to say, however, that the Due Process Clause places no limits on a State's capacity to define different courses of conduct, or states of mind, as merely alternative means of committing a single offense, thereby permitting a defendant's conviction without jury agreement as to which course or state actually occurred. The axiomatic requirement of due process that a statute may not forbid conduct in terms so vague that people of common intelligence would be relegated to differing guesses about its meaning ....

501 U.S. at 632, 111 S.Ct. at 2497.

375. But see United States v. Gipson, 553 F.2d 453 (5th Cir.1977), where the court held that a federal jury must agree on at least one of multiple alternative "conceptually" distinct acts that would constitute the actus reus of the crime. In a prosecution for possession and disposition of stolen property, the court found "two distinct conceptual groupings," receiving, concealing, and storing forming the first grouping (referred to by the court as "housing"), and bartering, selling, and disposing ("marketing") constituting the second. Jury unanimity was required as to at least one grouping. Writing for the plurality in Schad, Justice Souter criticized the Gipson formulation as "too conclusory to serve as a real test." Schad v. Arizona, 501 U.S. at 635, 111 S.Ct. at 2499.

To assure jury unanimity in a similar situation, the court in People v. Ribowsky, 77 N.Y.2d 284, 567 N.Y.S.2d 392, 568 N.E.2d 1197 (1991), submitted a special verdict sheet to the jury, requiring 12 jurors to agree on at least one set of material facts submitted in the alternative within one count of an indictment.

376. Cf. P.L. § 125.25(1)(intentional murder) with P.L. § 125.25(3) (felony murder). "[B]efore the Criminal Procedure Law, an indictment could properly charge in one count the same offense alleged to have occurred in different ways. An allegation of murder in a single count indictment could allege both common law murder and felony murder." People v. Richlin, 74 Misc.2d 906, 907, 346 N.Y.S.2d 698, 700 (Sup.Ct., N.Y. County, 1973).

377. A few examples include: P.L. § 120.10(1)(assault in the first degree by means of a deadly weapon or dangerous instrument); P.L. § 125.27(1)(a)(v)(murder in the first degree when victim was to testify as a witness in the future and purpose was to prevent his or her testimony or victim had testified in the past and murder was retribution for his past testimony); P.L. § 130.70 (aggravated sexual abuse to cause injury by insertion of foreign object in vagina, urethra, penis or rectum of victim); P.L. § 140.30 (burglary in the first degree requires prosecution to prove the defendant entered or remained unlawfully); P.L. § 150.20 (arson in the first degree requires

with intent to commit a crime therein."[378] An indictment may charge commission of the crime by reference to this language. However, depending upon the facts of the case, the prosecution may be compelled to elect one of the disjunctive theories, unlawful remaining or unlawful entry, before submission to the jury.[379]

One appellate case, *People v. Roberts*,[380] highlights the distinction between alternate allegations of criminal conduct and alternate means of proving that conduct. The defendant was charged, in one count, with burglary, in that he entered with the intent of committing a larceny, but then remained with the intent of committing an assault. The prosecution argued that the statute merely calls for proof that the defendant intended to commit a crime, and that it was not required to specify or prove an intent to commit any particular crime.[381] The Appellate Division agreed that *mens rea* could be proved by showing either an intent to commit assault or larceny. However, it reversed the conviction on other grounds, finding that, under the facts of the case, the trial court wrongly submitted to the jury in one count the alternate theories of unlawful remaining and unlawful entering.

A problem similar to that in *Schad* and *Roberts* can arise when the particular subdivisions or paragraphs defining separate crimes are not explicitly referenced by the indictment, but the allegations within the count contain language from distinctly separate provisions, thereby implicitly allowing for prosecution of two different offenses. For example, in *People v. Kaminski*,[382] the defendant was charged with rape in the first degree, which is accomplished by forcible compulsion. At the same time, "forcible compulsion" is defined by two separately numbered paragraphs that include either the use of physical force[383] or the threat of such force.[384] The indictment in *Kaminski* only alleged the use of physical force. However, the trial court instructed the jury that it could consider the threat of force as well. The Court of Appeals held that the trial court had constructively amended the indictment,[385] and thereby violated the rule against duplicitous counts since the jury considered two alternate definitions of forcible compulsion in its deliberations on the one count.[386]

proof of damage to a building or motor vehicle).

378. P.L. § 140.20 (emphasis supplied).

379. See, e.g., People v. Graves, 76 N.Y.2d 16, 22, 556 N.Y.S.2d 16, 18, 555 N.E.2d 268, 270 (1990)("appellant either entered or remained unlawfully, but not both," citing People v. Gaines, 74 N.Y.2d 358, 547 N.Y.S.2d 620, 546 N.E.2d 913 (1989)).

380. 162 A.D.2d 729, 557 N.Y.S.2d 127 (2d Dep't 1990).

381. See People v. Barnes, 50 N.Y.2d 375, 429 N.Y.S.2d 178, 406 N.E.2d 1071 (1980)(prosecution not required to plead any particular crime, as burglary statute merely proscribes trespass coupled with intent to commit a crime; however, where prosecution does elect to charge a particular crime, it may not vary proof at trial).

382. 58 N.Y.2d 886, 460 N.Y.S.2d 495, 447 N.E.2d 43 (1983).

383. P.L. § 130.00(8)(a).

384. P.L. § 130.00(8)(b). See generally Greenberg, Marcus, et al., New York Criminal Law §§ 8.4, 8.5 (West 1996).

385. See discussion on constructive amendments, § 5.18, infra.

386. Cf. People v. Grega, 72 N.Y.2d 489, 502, 534 N.Y.S.2d 647, 654, 531 N.E.2d 279, 286 (1988), a companion case to People v. Roberts, supra. In Grega, the indictment alleged forcible compulsion by physical force, and the trial court, as in Kaminski, charged both prongs of the definition, i.e., force and threat of force. However, in Grega, the only evidence at trial was that of

§ 5.17   GRAND JURY & INDICTMENT   Ch. 5

While it is permissible for one count of an indictment to refer to more than one way by which the prosecution intends to prove an offense, as opposed to charging multiple offenses, there are inherent risks in that approach. For example, difficulties can arise when, on appeal, the propriety of conviction upon one of the alternatives is challenged. Error as to the presentation of one theory can endanger the entire verdict, notwithstanding sufficient evidence to support the alternate theory. For example, in *People v. Martinez*,[387] a jury was told to consider a charge of drug possession under alternate theories of constructive possession and the "drug factory" presumption.[388] The Court of Appeals held that the trial court had erred in instructing the jury on the statutory presumption. The prosecution argued that the conviction should not be overturned because the evidence at trial was sufficient to support a conviction under the alternate theory of constructive possession, where no error was found. However, the court ruled it necessary to set aside the conviction because there was no way of knowing whether the jury had relied upon the erroneously charged presumption.[389] For that reason, the more prudent course may be to charge alternate theories under separate counts, assuming that could be done without running afoul of the rule against multiplicity.

Finally, an indictment may on occasion allege facts that are extraneous or immaterial to the charges or beyond what is necessary to support the charges. This surplusage is to be distinguished from a claim that counts are duplicitous. In such a case, the prosecution need not prove more than those factual allegations necessary to support a conviction.[390] A court has inherent authority to strike the surplusage when explaining the charges to a jury.[391]

Library References:

West's Key No. Digests, Indictment and Information ⚖125–131.

physical force without threat. Therefore, the Court of Appeals reasoned, the conviction need not be overturned since the defendant was placed on notice of the only theory of prosecution that could have convinced the jury to convict.

387. 83 N.Y.2d 26, 607 N.Y.S.2d 610, 628 N.E.2d 1320 (1993).

388. P.L. § 220.25(2).

389. "It is an established rule of Supreme Court jurisprudence that a general verdict of guilt must be set aside where the jurors in reaching their verdict may have relied on an illegal ground or on an alternative legal ground and there is no way of knowing which ground they chose.... Thus, the Supreme Court has consistently vacated general verdicts where one of the choices afforded to the jury was to find guilt on an unconstitutional theory. It has rejected the contention that the verdict should be upheld because the factfinder presumably based it on an alternative constitutional ground."

83 N.Y.2d at 32, 607 N.Y.S.2d at 613.

390. See People v. Charles, 61 N.Y.2d 321, 473 N.Y.S.2d 941, 462 N.E.2d 118 (1984)(indictment alleged that defendant solicited *and* accepted a bribe, while statute uses the disjunctive; prosecution did not have to prove solicitation and acceptance); People v. Rooney, 57 N.Y.2d 822, 455 N.Y.S.2d 595, 441 N.E.2d 1113 (1982)(in prosecution for criminally negligent homicide, allegations in indictment that defendant was driving while intoxicated were surplusage that did not have to be proved at trial).

391. People v. Adorno, ___ A.D.2d ___, 628 N.Y.S.2d 426 (3d Dep't 1995).

§ 5.18 Indictment—Curing Defects

Superseding Indictments. A prosecutor who discovers an error in an indictment may have several options available to cure the problem. He or she may elect to re-present the case to the same or a new grand jury and thereby supersede any counts in the first indictment that are overlapped by the second indictment.[392] This can be done before the same grand jury that voted the first indictment, without re-presenting the entire case or even recalling witnesses.[393] This procedure may be employed in any case where the grand jury has voted an indictment, whether or not the indictment has yet been filed.[394] The only limitation would be the statutory prohibition against re-presenting a case after a dismissal or following a rejection of the case by a grand jury, in which case leave of the supervising court becomes necessary.[395]

One commentator,[396] responding to *People v. Perez*,[397] goes even further by suggesting that a change correcting a "clerical error" in an indictment could be accomplished, in a case where the intention of the grand jury is clear from the minutes, by merely obtaining the signature of the foreperson and district attorney on a "superseding" indictment, presumably without any additional presentation to the grand jurors, without a new vote by the jurors themselves, and without application to the supervising court. Absent clear appellate authority for this course of action, a more cautious course would be to ask for a vote by the grand jury, a procedure already approved by the Court of Appeals in *People v. Cade*.[398]

---

392. CPL § 200.80 (permitting the filing of a superseding indictment "at any time before entry of a plea of guilty ... or commencement of trial thereof"). But for potential perils in this regard, see People v. Jones, 206 A.D.2d 82, 618 N.Y.S.2d 319 (1st Dep't 1994)(following indictment of defendant for felony murder, prosecutor re-presented the entire case for purpose of adding a burglary charge, but second grand jury voted no true bill; ensuing conviction on first indictment set aside on ground that the vote of the second grand jury superseded the indictment). Accord People v. Franco, 196 A.D.2d 357, 612 N.Y.S.2d 591 (2d Dep't 1994).

393. People v. Salerno, 3 N.Y.2d 175, 164 N.Y.S.2d 729, 143 N.E.2d 917 (1957)(grand jury may re-open case and reconsider vote without presentation of new evidence).

394. People v. Cade, 74 N.Y.2d 410, 548 N.Y.S.2d 137, 547 N.E.2d 339 (1989)(grand jury may re-open case, consider new evidence and reconsider vote, but at least 12 jurors who heard all the evidence needed to sustain vote).

395. CPL § 190.75(3). See also People v. Wilkins, 68 N.Y.2d 269, 508 N.Y.S.2d 893, 501 N.E.2d 542 (1986)(case cannot be "withdrawn" and presented to a new grand jury in anticipation of rejection).

396. Preiser, "Practice Commentary" to CPL § 200.70, McKinney's Cons. Laws of N.Y., Book 11A, at 36 (1994).

397. 83 N.Y.2d 269, 609 N.Y.S.2d 564, 631 N.E.2d 570 (1994)(disallowing an amendment, by the court and without further grand jury action, to specify a count that had been voted by the grand jury but omitted from the indictment as a result of a "clerical" error). See also People v. Jackson, 153 Misc.2d 270, 582 N.Y.S.2d 336 (Sup.Ct., Bronx County, 1991) (disallowing corrective amendment where grand jury voted one count of depraved mind murder and one count of intentional murder, but where, through administrative error, indictment alleged two counts of intentional murder).

398. 74 N.Y.2d 410, 548 N.Y.S.2d 137, 547 N.E.2d 339. Technically speaking, the result would be neither an "amended" indictment nor a "superseding" indictment, but instead is denominated a "replacement" indictment. Cf. People v. Livoti, N.Y.L.J., September 7, 1995, p. 26, col. 5 (Sup.Ct., Bronx County) (dismissing replacement indictment signed by foreperson after term of grand jury had ended) with

§ 5.18   GRAND JURY & INDICTMENT   Ch. 5

Amendment. Section 200.70 of the CPL authorizes amendment of an indictment upon application by the prosecution[399] to the court and with notice to the defendant. An amendment may only be made "with respect to defects, errors or variances from the proof relating to matters of form, time, place, names of persons and the like, when such an amendment does not change the theory or theories of the prosecution as reflected in the evidence before the grand jury."[400] In an apparent effort to limit the scope of subdivision one, the statute further provides a list of potentially material alterations that can not be accomplished by amendment. An indictment may not be amended for the purpose of curing a failure to charge or state an offense, legal insufficiency of the factual allegations, a misjoinder of an offense or a misjoinder of defendants.[401]

An application for amendment may be made "[a]t any time before or during trial."[402] With unfortunate frequency, defendants find themselves presented with testimony in the middle of trial that varies from the allegations in the indictment. In some cases, the prosecutor may formally ask the court to approve an amendment, which may be done as long as the amendment does not alter the theory of prosecution as found by the grand jury, does not tend to prejudice the defendant on the merits and the court grants the defendant any continuance or adjournment necessary to prepare his or her defense. On occasion a court will permit the prosecution to prove and argue material facts that depart from the allegations in the indictment and then submit for the jury's consideration a theory of prosecution differing from that previously alleged. When the newly presented allegations are submitted to a petit jury without formal revision of the indictment, the indictment is said to have undergone a "constructive amendment."[403] CPL § 200.70 applies with equal force to written and constructive amendments.

Section 200.70 reflects two concerns regarding amendments: any amendment must conform the indictment to the decision of the grand jury and a change should not work surprise.[404] The former concern is one of jurisdiction. For that reason, only amendments that conform the

---

People v. Patterson, 148 Misc.2d 528, 537, 561 N.Y.S.2d 502, 509 (N.Y.C.Crim. Ct.1990)(permitting foreperson to sign a prosecutor's information after the grand jury's term had expired because "[t]he foreperson's signature is not a jurisdictional prerequisite but rather a statutory method of authenticating the accusatory instrument").

399. While the statute requires an application of the prosecution, at least one court has reasoned that a court has the inherent power to grant a defendant's application to amend an indictment. People v. Cirillo, 100 Misc.2d 502, 419 N.Y.S.2d 820 (Sup.Ct., Bronx County, 1979)

400. CPL § 200.70(1).

401. CPL § 200.70(2).

402. CPL § 200.70(1).

403. See, e.g., People v. Spann, 56 N.Y.2d 469, 452 N.Y.S.2d 869, 438 N.E.2d 402 (1982), discussed infra, where the court was asked by the jury, during deliberations in a robbery trial, if it could consider the theft of property other than the jewelry or money alleged by the indictment to have been stolen. On appeal, the defendant complained that the court, by answering the jury question in the affirmative without application by either party, had constructively amended the indictment.

404. For a good discussion concerning the history of this section, see People v. Jackson, 153 Misc.2d 270, 582 N.Y.S.2d 336 (Sup.Ct., Bronx County, 1991).

face of an indictment to the evident vote of the grand jury can be made, even in the absence of surprise to the defendant.[405]

In addition, since the function of an indictment is to inform a defendant of "the nature and cause" of the action, an amendment may not be made where the defense has relied upon the information previously supplied and the change "tend[s] to prejudice the defendant on the merits." However, unlike an amendment that alters the theory of prosecution as voted by the grand jury, an amendment merely altering notice to the defendant, but consistent with the grand jury's action, can be made, in the absence of prejudice, as long as the defendant is granted "any adjournment of the proceedings which may, by reason of such amendment, be necessary to accord the defendant adequate opportunity to prepare his defense."[406]

Examples of amendments that have been permitted include changes in the date of the offense,[407] place of commission,[408] a designation of the weapon alleged to have been used,[409] a switch in the identity of the person to whom drugs were allegedly sold,[410] whether the defendant was acting as a principal or accessory,[411] or even a change in the identity of the victim.[412]

In *People v. Spann*,[413] the defendant was charged with stealing money and jewelry from the victim. He testified, denying that he stole money or jewelry, but instead claiming that the complainant had sold him drugs in the past, that he was addicted and in need of more drugs, and that he only took cocaine from the complainant's purse. The Court of Appeals reasoned that the statutory definition of larceny only refers to theft of "property" and, therefore, it was permissible for the trial court

---

405. Thus, it is inadvisable for a court to allow amendment of an indictment without first inspecting the grand jury minutes.

406. CPL § 200.70(1).

407. People v. Kroemer, 204 A.D.2d 1017, 613 N.Y.S.2d 304 (4th Dep't 1994); People v. Robinson, 119 A.D.2d 598, 500 N.Y.S.2d 768 (2d Dep't 1986).

408. People v. Parker, 186 A.D.2d 157, 587 N.Y.S.2d 718 (2d Dep't 1992).

409. People v. Sage, 204 A.D.2d 746, 612 N.Y.S.2d 648 (2d Dep't 1994)(midtrial amendment describing murder weapon as "deadly weapon" in place of "dangerous instrument" permitted); People v. Hood, 194 A.D.2d 556, 598 N.Y.S.2d 569 (2d Dep't 1993)(amendment describing deadly weapon used in assault as "shotgun" in place of "handgun" permitted); but see People v. Fata, 184 A.D.2d 206, 586 N.Y.S.2d 780 (1st Dep't 1992)(trial court erred in allowing constructive amendment designating dangerous instrument used in alleged robbery from knife to bottle since facts tended to show that defendant used both but grand jury specified knife as the dangerous instrument in the indictment).

410. People v. Feldman, 50 N.Y.2d 500, 504, 429 N.Y.S.2d 602, 604, 407 N.E.2d 448, 450 (1980).

411. People v. Rivera, 84 N.Y.2d 766, 622 N.Y.S.2d 671, 646 N.E.2d 1098 (1995)(since the crime charged is the same, in this case murder, whether or not the prosecution offers proof of conduct by another for which the defendant is culpable, the amendment merely altered the evidence used to support the charge, not the charge itself).

412. People v. Roberts, 204 A.D.2d 974, 613 N.Y.S.2d 67 (4th Dep't 1994)(court instructed jury that it "doesn't matter" who the owner is in case involving alleged larceny from gas station employee); People v. Ames, 115 A.D.2d 543, 496 N.Y.S.2d 65 (2d Dep't 1985)(indictment alleged theft from a particular employee of a restaurant, but court instructed jury it could consider any of five employees present to be the owner).

413. 56 N.Y.2d 469, 452 N.Y.S.2d 869, 438 N.E.2d 402 (1982).

§ 5.18 GRAND JURY & INDICTMENT Ch. 5

to charge the jury that it could convict upon a finding that *any* property, be it jewelry, money *or* drugs, was taken from the complainant.

Since the propriety of an amendment is measured by the alternate tests of surprise to the defendant and conformity with the intent of the grand jury, *Spann* is troubling. Regarding notice and prejudice, surely the defendant did not think he was convicting himself of the theft with which he was charged by denying the allegations in the indictment, *i.e.*, forcibly taking money and jewelry, while admitting that he took drugs from a seller to feed his habit.[414] Similarly, with regard to the theory of the indictment as voted by the grand jury, it is not altogether clear that the jurors intended to, or would, indict the defendant for taking drugs from the purse.[415]

Contrast *Spann* with *People v. Roberts*,[416] where a conviction for manslaughter was overturned because the indictment alleged the cause

---

414. Obviously, the issue here is not the truth of the claim. Rather, it is the defendant's right to rely upon the notice he was given. In any event, the jury must have credited at least a portion of his story since it spontaneously asked about the items to be considered in the robbery charge.

On the issue of notice, Judge Jones, dissenting, wrote, "[T]o permit such a critical change in the rationale of the prosecution ... after defendant had irretrievably committed himself and after the case had been submitted to the jury ... constituted ... a denial ... of due process." 56 N.Y.2d at 474, 452 N.Y.S.2d at 872 (Jones, J., dissenting). See also People v. Roberts, 72 N.Y.2d 489, 502, 534 N.Y.S.2d 647, 654, 531 N.E.2d 279, 286 (1988)(Bellacosa J., dissenting). In the words of Judge Bellacosa, comparing the results in Spann and Roberts, a case where the court reversed a conviction, "If surprise be the test, defendant Spann was surely more startled by the turn of events in his conviction than defendant Roberts could possibly be." In Roberts, the majority sought to distinguish Spann by the fact that Spann himself introduced the theory that the property stolen was drugs and not jewelry or money. Therefore, it was argued, he was not surprised to learn of the nature of the property stolen. As Judge Bellacosa's comment would indicate, however, this missed the point since the surprise to Spann was not that he took drugs from the complainant; the surprise was that, at the close of trial and after he had testified, "the nature and cause of the action" against him shifted from theft of jewelry and money to a theft of drugs.

415. Cf. People v. Geyer, 196 N.Y. 364, 368, 90 N.E. 48 (1909), which explained the distinction as follows:

Illustrations of the two classes of amendments which might be proposed readily occur to the mind. If the indictment charged the accused with stealing a horse, and alleged that the latter was of one color or of one age, when as a matter of fact it was of another, it is apparent that the court would be justified in allowing an amendment to cure this variation of evidence. The substance of the crime charged in either case would be the larceny of a horse; the latter's age or color would be an inconsequential detail. If, on the other hand, the indictment having charged the accused with stealing such a horse, the evidence should show that he had in fact stolen a wagon or some entirely different article of personal property than that specified in the indictment, it is quite clear that the court would not be justified in amending the indictment to fit such evidence. In such case the very substance of the crime would be involved in the variation, and to permit an amendment would quite change the identity of the crime.

See also People v. Jackson, 174 A.D.2d 444, 572 N.Y.S.2d 891 (1st Dep't 1991), appeal granted 79 N.Y.2d 858, 580 N.Y.S.2d 730, 588 N.E.2d 765 (1992), and appeal dismissed 80 N.Y.2d 112, 589 N.Y.S.2d 300, 602 N.E.2d 1116 (1992)(conviction for gun possession with intent to use unlawfully dismissed where jury was permitted to consider possession at time of robbery as well as later in the day when defendant was arrested).

416. 72 N.Y.2d 489, 534 N.Y.S.2d 647, 531 N.E.2d 279 (1988).

of death to be a blow to the neck[417] while proof at trial supported a strangulation theory. In *Roberts*, the conviction was reversed, *not* because the theory of prosecution was inconsistent with the vote of the grand jury, but rather for want of proper notice of the charges. The court ruled that the specific manner by which the death was caused is not an essential element of the crime, and therefore "the crime alleged in the indictment was technically the same one for which defendant was tried."[418] However, the conviction was upset on the alternate argument that the defendant was denied fair notice of the charges when the prosecution switched its medical theory of the cause of death from a blow to the neck to one of strangulation, in light of the defendant's testimony in the grand jury (and introduced at trial) that he accidentally caused the victim's death by striking her once during a struggle.[419] In the words of the majority:[420]

> Thus, though not an element of the crime, a description of the conduct that resulted in the victim's death cannot be said, under CPL 200.50(7)(a), to be extraneous to the material elements of the crime, and the People were bound to provide such factual allegations. Here, the People chose to include the cause of death in the indictment and to repeat that allegation in their answer to discovery. Having specified in the indictment, and later in their answer to discovery, that defendant struck the victim, thereby causing her death, the People were not then free to present proof at trial that virtually ruled out that theory as the cause of death and substituted another one.

As *Roberts* confirms, there are a number of instances where allegations in the indictment or the bill of particulars commit the prosecution to a particular theory although the particular theory is not, by itself, an essential element of the offense charged.[421] This applies, however, only to allegations particularizing the manner by which the crime was alleged to have been accomplished.[422] As one example, in a burglary charge,

---

417. Apparently causing asphyxia by traumatic compression of the neck resulting in a fracture of the hyoid bone.

418. 72 N.Y.2d at 499, 534 N.Y.S.2d at 652. The prosecution argued that the method whereby death was caused is not an essential element of the crime of manslaughter. As such, the factual allegations were extraneous to the material elements of the offense charged and could be varied. The court agreed that the method employed was not an essential element, but rejected the argument that it was extraneous.

419. Interestingly, on remand, the prosecution moved to amend the indictment to permit prosecution on a theory of strangulation. The trial court granted and the Appellate Division approved the change, holding that the amendment did not alter the theory of prosecution as voted by the grand jury and no longer, after appeal and retrial, could be said to be a surprise to the defendant. People v. Roberts, 163 A.D.2d 690, 558 N.Y.S.2d 296 (3d Dep't 1990).

420. 72 N.Y.2d at 498, 534 N.Y.S.2d at 652 (citations omitted).

421. Cf. People v. Kaminski, 58 N.Y.2d 886, 460 N.Y.S.2d 495, 447 N.E.2d 43 (1983), where alternate theories of force or threat of force were distinct and independent elements of forcible compulsion.

422. See, e.g., People v. Boyd, 59 A.D.2d 558, 397 N.Y.S.2d 150 (2d Dep't 1977)(in prosecution for sale of drugs, words in indictment alleging "each aiding the other and being actually present" concerned the theory of the case as presented to the grand jury; thus, error to delete them in submission to the petit jury). As previously noted, the prosecution need not specify in an indictment whether the defendant acted as a principal or an accessory since, in either event, the crime charged is the same. Peo-

defined as a trespass with the intent to commit a crime, the prosecution need not allege or prove any one particular crime was intended.[423] However, as in *Roberts*, once the prosecution has specified, in the indictment or in a bill of particulars, a crime that is the alleged object of the burglary, it "must prove that crime, not another one."[424]

Waiver of and Failure to Object to Amendment. As discussed in Section 5.16, *supra*, a jurisdictional defect cannot be waived, while inadequate notice can. This distinction can become important when an argument is made that a change in the prosecution's proof constructively amends or is at variance with the indictment. The former, constructive amendment, raises problems of jurisdiction while the latter, variance, can be waived, cured or found harmless.

When proof at trial permits a jury to consider an offense or theory of prosecution that was not voted by the grand jury, the indictment is said to have undergone a "constructive amendment." Since felony charges may only be brought by a grand jury, a constructive amendment raises problems of jurisdiction.[425]

"Variance" results when the proof at trial is at odds with material facts alleged in the indictment or bill of particulars, but consistent with the action of the grand jury. Since the proven facts are consistent with the charges and theory of prosecution voted by the grand jury, the necessary jurisdictional prerequisite has been met. Nevertheless, in the case of variance, due process issues arise, involving fairness and notice, because the proof varies from that previously reported to the defendant.

Simply put, variance occurs when the proof at trial is materially different from the description, in the indictment or bill of particulars, of the means by which the crime was committed. A constructive amendment of the indictment occurs when the jury is permitted to convict the defendant upon a factual basis that effectively modifies an essential element of the offense charged. The concern focuses upon whether the defendant has been convicted on a ground not charged in the indictment.[426] If the variation between proof and indictment does not alter an

ple v. Rivera, 84 N.Y.2d 766, 622 N.Y.S.2d 671, 646 N.E.2d 1098 (1995). However, in Boyd, it was impermissible to delete the theory of accessorial liability once it was specified by the grand jury.

423. People v. Mackey, 49 N.Y.2d 274, 425 N.Y.S.2d 288, 401 N.E.2d 398 (1980).

424. People v. Roberts, 74 N.Y.2d at 497, 534 N.Y.S.2d at 651, citing People v. Barnes, 50 N.Y.2d 375, 429 N.Y.S.2d 178, 406 N.E.2d 1071 (1980).

425. See, e.g., Stirone v. United States, 361 U.S. 212, 80 S.Ct. 270, 4 L.Ed.2d 252 (1960); Ex parte Bain, 121 U.S. 1, 7 S.Ct. 781, 30 L.Ed. 849 (1887). As the Court of Appeals has noted:

The State Constitution declares that no person shall be held to answer for an infamous crime unless upon indictment of the Grand Jury (N.Y. Const., art. I, § 6). The right to indictment by a Grand Jury has therefore been recognized as not merely a personal privilege of the defendant but a "public fundamental right," which is the basis of jurisdiction to try and punish an individual ..... Infringement of that right constitutes a defect that cannot be waived by a guilty plea.

People v. Boston, 75 N.Y.2d 585, 587, 555 N.Y.S.2d 27, 29, 554 N.E.2d 64, 66 (1990) (citations omitted).

426. "The right of an accused to be tried and convicted of only those crimes and upon only those theories charged in the indictment is fundamental and nonwaivable.... No exception is necessary to preserve for appellate review its deprivation." People v. Rubin, 101 A.D.2d 71, 77, 474 N.Y.S.2d 348, 352 (4th Dep't 1984).

essential element of the offense charged, "the trial court's refusal to restrict the jury charge to the words of the indictment is merely another of the flaws in [the] trial that mar its perfection but do not prejudice the defendant."[427] For that reason, variance, unlike a constructive amendment, may be waived, cured or subjected to a harmless error analysis.[428]

The line between amendments that merely vary the indictment's depiction of the means of commission, and those amendments that modify an essential element, is not an easy one to draw. In *People v. Powell*,[429] the defendant hit the complainant with a lamp and then, later, with a baseball bat. The defendant was charged with assault in the second degree, *i.e.*, causing physical injury with a dangerous instrument. While the baseball bat caused the injury, the indictment wrongly specified the lamp as the instrument used to cause the injury. Although the court conceded that "[i]t is not essential to its validity that an indictment charging assault in the second degree refer to the specific 'deadly weapon or ... dangerous instrument' used to cause physical injury," it analogized the situation to that of *Roberts*, holding that Powell was denied fair notice of the charges. As in *Roberts*, since the grand jury elected to specify the dangerous instrument in the indictment, the prosecution was not free to change the theory of prosecution. Once the court determined that variance had resulted because the defendant did not receive fair notice, or was misled, as to the means of commission, the next step, in the absence of a finding that the indictment had been constructively amended,[430] called for analysis under the prejudice or surprise test. In such cases, variance, under *Spann*, is waivable. In *Powell*, unlike *Roberts*, the defendant consented to the amendment. It would appear, therefore, that Powell waived the issue by consenting to the amendment. Nevertheless, the court ruled that the amendment was jurisdictional and non-waivable, resulting in a dismissal of the charge. Inescapably, in the court's view, the assault with a bat was not the same crime as assault with the lamp, and the amendment had modified an essential element of the crime as voted by the grand jury.[431]

Similarly, on occasion, the parties, with the concurrence of the court, will attempt to negotiate an agreement upon a plea or a submission to the jury of a lesser charge only to discover that they have run afoul of jurisdictional proscriptions. Until 1982 it was assumed that, by operation of law, a count in an indictment encompassed every lesser

---

427. United States v. Ylda, 653 F.2d 912, 914 (5th Cir.1981).

428. United States v. Carroll, 582 F.2d 942, 944 (5th Cir.1978)("the concept of harmless error is inapplicable to constructive amendment").

429. 153 A.D.2d 54, 549 N.Y.S.2d 276 (4th Dep't 1989).

430. The court found that "[p]roof of the relevant underlying facts was essentially the same before the grand jury and at trial." 153 A.D.2d at 55, 549 N.Y.S.2d at 277.

431. See also People v. Fata, 184 A.D.2d 206, 586 N.Y.S.2d 780 (1st Dep't 1992)(defendant, charged with robbery with knife, testified to hitting complainant with a champagne bottle; conviction reversed, notwithstanding an argument that (as in Spann) defendant could not claim lack of notice since she introduced the description of the instrument by her own testimony).

included offense as well.[432] However, in two memorandum opinions by the Court of Appeals, the prosecution was not permitted to proceed upon an amended indictment adding a lesser included offense after the greater offense had been dismissed.[433] Subsequently, in *People v. Lee*,[434] the First Department held this to be a jurisdictional requirement that could not be waived. In *Lee*, the defendant was indicted for murder. The jury convicted him of manslaughter as a lesser included offense. That conviction was reversed. Under the rule of *Beslanovics*, he could not be tried again for the murder and a new indictment should have been voted for the manslaughter charge. However, the defendant signed a written waiver in open court, purportedly allowing an amendment to the indictment to add the legal lesser included offense of manslaughter without representation to a new grand jury. Upon retrial, he was convicted again of manslaughter. The Appellate Division overturned the conviction, ruling that the signed waiver was ineffective since a new count, even if a legal lesser included offense, may not be added to an indictment by amendment once the greater count has been dismissed.

The problem in *Beslanovics* and *Lee* was that, after the greater count had been dismissed, technically speaking, no indictment remained. Therefore, it was impermissible to "add" the lesser count. This is an exception to the more usual occurrence where, in addition to crimes for which a defendant has been indicted, a court has authority to consider or submit to the jury lesser included offenses.[435] This general rule extends to include lesser offenses that are not even, by definition, lesser included offenses,[436] upon consent of the defendant. In *People v. Ford*,[437] the defendant permitted submission of grand larceny as a lesser to a robbery charge under circumstances where submission was not authorized.[438] The court held that the defendant could waive objection to addition of the non-lesser included offense as long as the new crime was "reasonably related" to the charge in the indictment. Similarly, the Court of Appeals has approved addition of, and a plea to, a non-existent crime to avoid a heavier penalty on a facially valid indictment.[439]

As these cases demonstrate, it is generally permissible for the parties to consent to the addition of a *lesser* count as long as the greater count is still viable, providing the necessary jurisdiction.[440] Compare

---

432. People ex rel. Colcloughley v. Montanye, 49 A.D.2d 1034, 1035, 374 N.Y.S.2d 504, 506 (4th Dep't 1975). See also People v. Gonzales, 96 A.D.2d 847, 465 N.Y.S.2d 694 (2d Dep't 1983), aff'd 61 N.Y.2d 633, 471 N.Y.S.2d 847, 459 N.E.2d 1285 (1983)(Titone, J., dissenting).

433. People v. Gonzalez, 61 N.Y.2d 633, 471 N.Y.S.2d 847, 459 N.E.2d 1285 (1983); People v. Beslanovics, 57 N.Y.2d 726, 454 N.Y.S.2d 976, 440 N.E.2d 1322 (1982).

434. 100 A.D.2d 357, 474 N.Y.S.2d 308 (1st Dep't 1984).

435. People v. Henderson, 41 N.Y.2d 233, 235, 391 N.Y.S.2d 563, 565, 359 N.E.2d 1357, 1359 (1976).

436. CPL § 1.20(37).

437. 62 N.Y.2d 275, 476 N.Y.S.2d 783, 465 N.E.2d 322 (1984).

438. See People v. Glover, 57 N.Y.2d 61, 453 N.Y.S.2d 660, 439 N.E.2d 376 (1982).

439. People v. Foster, 19 N.Y.2d 150, 278 N.Y.S.2d 603, 225 N.E.2d 200 (1967).

440. "The lesser still needs the greater 'to support' it. And so it remains, like the glue on the back of a stamp, its role strictly limited to one of invisible support." People v. McGee, 131 Misc.2d 770, 774, 501 N.Y.S.2d 1002, 1004 (Sup.Ct., Kings County, 1986), aff'd 147 A.D.2d 297, 543 N.Y.S.2d 686 (2d Dep't 1989) rev'd on other

this situation to one where the indictment, in the first instance, alleges a non-existent crime. In such a case, the charging instrument is jurisdictionally defective and any plea to the instrument is ineffective.[441]

Finally, on occasion parties will attempt to circumvent jurisdictional limitations upon amendments that add a count not voted by the grand jury by using a written waiver and consent to prosecution by a superior court information. However, this cannot be done once the indictment has been filed.[442]

Library References:

West's Key No. Digests, Indictment and Information ⊱15, 159, 170–184, 198.

§ 5.19 Indictment—Bill of Particulars

Contents. Section 200.95 defines a bill of particulars, in part, as a "written statement . . . specifying . . . items of factual information which are not recited in the indictment and which pertain to the offense charged and including the substance of each defendant's conduct encompassed by the charge." It continues, in the definition, to provide, "however, the prosecutor shall not be required to include . . . matters of evidence relating to how the people intend to prove the elements of the offense charged or how the people intend to prove any item of factual information included in the bill of particulars."

The two contrasting provisions create an inevitable tension: a defendant will frequently seek an item of factual information pertaining to the offense, only to hear the response that the information sought is "evidentiary" and, therefore, not required in a bill of particulars. However, the provisions are reconcilable: the prosecutor must detail *what* the defendant did by describing specific facts instead of conclusory allegations, but he or she need not explain *how*—i.e., by use of what evidence—he or she intends to prove those facts. The essential question in each case is whether the item sought specifies a description of the defendant's conduct demonstrating that he or she committed all the material elements of the offense charged, which information must be disclosed, or whether the material sought merely details testimony and exhibits that the prosecution hopes to introduce to prove the defendant's commission of the described conduct.

A good example of the distinction is *People v. Roberts*.[443] In that case, the defendant was alleged to have committed manslaughter. At

grounds 76 N.Y.2d 764, 559 N.Y.S.2d 953, 559 N.E.2d 647 (1990).

441. People v. Roe, 191 A.D.2d 844, 595 N.Y.S.2d 121 (3d Dep't 1993). The reverse situation occurred in People v. Martinez, 81 N.Y.2d 810, 595 N.Y.S.2d 376, 611 N.E.2d 277 (1993). The defendant was properly indicted for attempted murder in the second degree. He failed to object when the court submitted to the jury, as a lesser offense, attempted manslaughter in the first degree, which is a non-existent crime.

See People v. Campbell, 72 N.Y.2d 602, 535 N.Y.S.2d 580, 532 N.E.2d 86 (1988). The Court of Appeals held that the conviction represented a fundamental, non-waivable, error, i.e., it was without proper jurisdiction, since it was impossible for a jury to find that the defendant had committed a non-existent crime.

442. People v. Boston, 75 N.Y.2d 585, 555 N.Y.S.2d 27, 554 N.E.2d 64 (1990).

443. 72 N.Y.2d 489, 534 N.Y.S.2d 647, 531 N.E.2d 279 (1988).

§ 5.19   GRAND JURY & INDICTMENT   Ch. 5

issue was whether the cause of death was by a blow to the throat or by strangulation. It was not enough to merely allege that the defendant caused the victim's death with the appropriate mental culpability. Rather, the prosecution was required to specify the method employed to bring about her death.[444]

In *People v. Taylor*,[445] the prosecution argued that the theory of prosecution itself was evidentiary. The defendant was charged with acting in concert in commission of murder. He demanded to know if the prosecution's theory was that defendant directly caused the death of the victim or that he hired someone else to do it. The court held that it was error to deny the request.[446] A claim that something is "evidentiary," in the words of the court,

> can never operate to prevent disclosure of the facts ultimately to be established but only the manner in which the prosecutor intends to prove them. To hold otherwise would be to compromise the defendant's right to fair notice of the accusations against him—a right with firm constitutional as well as statutory underpinnings.[447]

It is a mistake to read section 200.95 in isolation. In light of *Iannone* and *Fitzgerald*, the bill of particulars frequently must assume the critical role that had been assigned to an indictment and as such they must be read together.[448] In permitting *in haec verba* indictments, notwithstanding the Legislature's decision to return to long-form accusatory instruments with the enactment of CPL § 200.50 in 1971, the Court of Appeals specifically held that the dual notice requirements of an indictment and a bill of particulars can and must be met by a combination of the two.[449]

---

444. "[T]hough not an element of the crime, a description of the conduct that resulted in 'the victim's death cannot be said, under CPL § 200.50(7)(a), to be extraneous to the material elements of the crime, and the prosecution was bound to provide such factual allegations." 72 N.Y.2d at 497, 534 N.Y.S.2d at 651. Query whether this is still good law after People v. Rivera, 84 N.Y.2d 766, 622 N.Y.S.2d 671, 646 N.E.2d 1098 (1995)(indictment need not specify if defendant acted as principal or accessory). Section 200.95 specifically requires the prosecution to specify "whether the people intend to prove that the defendant acted as a principal or accomplice or both."

445. 74 A.D.2d 177, 427 N.Y.S.2d 439 (2d Dep't 1980).

446. The court opined that the refusal to disclose the information would "ordinarily compel reversal," but not under the specific facts of that case. 74 N.Y.2d at 181, 427 N.Y.S.2d at 442.

447. 74 N.Y.2d at 181, 427 N.Y.S.2d at 442 (citations omitted). The case postdates Iannone and Fitzgerald and appears to be a logical consequence of those cases, i.e., if the theory of prosecution is gathered by reading the bill of particulars and indictment together, then it is inconsistent to assert that a bill of particulars should not contain the theory of prosecution, especially where the indictment by itself merely repeats or cites to a statute. For that reason, People v. Einhorn, 45 A.D.2d 75, 356 N.Y.S.2d 620 (1974) and People v. Smalley, 64 Misc.2d 363, 314 N.Y.S.2d 924 (1970), which pre-date Iannone, to the extent they could be read as holding that a defendant is not entitled to the prosecutor's theory of proof, are no longer useful precedent.

448. As previously noted, the purpose of an indictment is to provide the defendant with fair notice of the accusations made against him or her, to assure that the defendant only faces charges that have been found by a grand jury and to guard against double jeopardy. See § 5.13.

449. "There is no requirement that the information be contained in a single document, provided the defendant is adequately and timely informed of the precise nature of

§ 5.19 BILL OF PARTICULARS

In sum, the two provisions should be read together so that regardless of the label on the paper given to the defendant, be it "indictment" or "bill of particulars," the defendant must receive "a plain and concise factual statement ... which, without allegations of an evidentiary nature ... asserts facts supporting every element of the offense charged ... with sufficient precision to clearly apprise the defendant ... of the conduct which is the subject of the accusation"[450] and, as well, "items of factual information ... which pertain to the offense charge and including the substance of [the] defendant's conduct encompassed by the charge which the people intend to prove at trial on their direct case."[451]

One last caution. On occasion, *People v. Davis*[452] will be quoted, out of context, for the proposition that a bill of particulars "is not a discovery device."[453] However, in that case, the defendant sought information concerning practice and procedure in the grand jury "unrelated to the factual allegations of the charge [which] was, in truth, a trial gambit in the hope of finding evidence to rebut the regularity of the indictment."[454] In fact, *Davis* reaffirms that the very purpose of a bill of particulars is to enable a defendant to "discover" items of factual information specified in sections 200.50 and 200.95.[455]

Procedure. CPL § 200.95 provides for a "request for a bill of particulars," which is a written request served by the defendant upon the prosecution within 30 days of arraignment.[456] The statute then contemplates compliance or refusal by the prosecutor within 15 days of receipt of the request. Refusal can be based upon one of four grounds: (1) the information sought is not authorized to be included in a bill of particulars; (2) the information is not necessary to enable the defendant adequately to prepare or conduct his or her defense; (3) a protective order is warranted; or (4) the request is untimely.[457]

If the prosecutor refuses or fails to comply with all or any part of the request for a bill of particulars, the defendant may file a motion for a bill of particulars with the court seeking resolution of the issues.[458] The statute describes the motion as one "prescribed in section 255.20." Presumably, it is envisioned that the motion will become part of the

---

the charges he must prepare to meet. An indictment charging the defendant with [the offense charged] in the language of the statute, coupled with a bill of particulars setting forth the specific acts ... underlying the charge, has been held to satisfy the requirements of the long form indictment authorized under the Code of Criminal Procedure, and now mandated under the Criminal Procedure Law." People v. Fitzgerald, 45 N.Y.2d 574, 580, 412 N.Y.S.2d 102, 105, 384 N.E.2d 649, 652 (1978).

450. CPL § 200.50(7).

451. CPL § 200.95.

452. 41 N.Y.2d 678, 394 N.Y.S.2d 865, 363 N.E.2d 572 (1977).

453. 41 N.Y.2d at 679, 394 N.Y.S.2d at 867.

454. 41 N.Y.2d at 680, 394 N.Y.S.2d at 867.

455. The full quote is: "A bill of particulars serves to clarify the pleading; it is not a discovery device." 41 N.Y.2d at 680, 394 N.Y.S.2d at 867.

456. The period is extended when the defendant is without counsel, or for good cause shown. CPL § 200.95(3).

457. CPL § 200.95(4).

458. CPL § 200.95(6). See People v. Zvonik, 40 A.D.2d 840, 337 N.Y.S.2d 336 (2d Dep't 1972)(reversing conviction where prosecution failed to file a bill of particulars). Accord People v. Cobey, 184 A.D.2d 1002, 584 N.Y.S.2d 244 (4th Dep't 1992).

omnibus motion filed under that section for such other relief as discovery, inspection of grand jury minutes, etc.[459] It becomes readily apparent that the timing is, at best, a close fit. If the defense waits a full 30 days to serve a request and the prosecution waits a full 15 days to respond, even if one assumes actual receipt by each party of the other's papers on the day of service, *i.e.*, no mail service, it is unlikely that anything but boilerplate motions will be ready for the court on the forty-fifth day. For that reason, it is not uncommon for defense attorneys to serve a demand for discovery and a request for a bill of particulars in advance of the deadline. At the same time, the omnibus motion papers will frequently repeat a request for court intervention pertaining to these matters, in anticipation of some demands going unfulfilled. This is obviously not a desirable practice, nor one contemplated by the statute, since the CPL sought to have the parties engage in a meaningful dialogue with respect to these matters, followed by a call for court intervention and resolution only of particularized items about which genuine controversy existed.

Amendment. Note that a bill of particulars may be amended "without leave of court" at any time before commencement of trial.[460] Court approval is required to amend a bill of particulars during trial. Contrast this with CPL § 200.70, which requires a court order to amend an indictment at any time. Obviously, after *Iannone*, a prosecutor has more flexibility if he or she prepares a "bare-bones" indictment, that is, *in haec verba*, and later presents supporting facts and a theory of prosecution in the bill of particulars.

As with amendments to an indictment, a prosecutor must guard against constructively amending the indictment. The bill of particulars must be consistent with the proof before, and the findings of, the grand jury. To the extent that the prosecution relies upon the bill of particulars to satisfy the jurisdictional requirements surrounding an indictment, per *Iannone*, the bill of particulars becomes, in effect, part of the indictment. The bill must not alter the criminal acts alleged or the theory of prosecution voted by the grand jury. As discussed earlier, constructive amendment implicates the jurisdictional predicate for prosecution.[461] An amendment to a bill of particulars that constructively amends the indictment can deprive the court of jurisdiction even where the defendant consents, or fails to object, to the amendment.

Further, the statute provides that upon any amendment, the court must grant an adjournment requested by the defendant to prepare his or her defense. Aside from granting an adjournment, the court is empowered to order "any other action it deems appropriate, which may, by reason of the amendment be necessary to accord the defendant an adequate opportunity to defend."[462] It is unclear what remedies this might suggest, and the usual remedy is simply a continuance or adjourn-

---

459. See generally Chapter 8.
460. CPL § 200.95(5).
461. See § 5.18, supra.
462. CPL § 200.95(5).

ment.[463] However, as a practical matter, a late amendment might require re-examination of previously decided motions and rulings affected by the change. At the very least, the wisest course for a prosecutor and court would seem to allow discovery requests on an expedited basis concomitant with the amended bill.

Once trial commences, amendment of the bill of particulars requires court permission.[464]

Library References:

West's Key No. Digests, Indictment and Information ⇒121.1–121.6, 163.

§ 5.20 Indictment—Lesser Offenses Prosecuted by Indictment

In the ordinary course, an indictment will contain one or more felony counts.[465] However, the CPL authorizes an indictment in cases where lesser offenses are charged as long as at least one such offense is a crime, *i.e.*, at least a misdemeanor.[466] This may arise in a variety of circumstances.[467] Prior to grand jury presentation, the defendant may have been charged with a misdemeanor in a local criminal court. Then, upon application by the prosecutor,[468] or by the defendant and upon direction of a superior court,[469] the case may have been presented to a grand jury for removal, *i.e.*, for prosecution of the misdemeanor charge in a superior court. Alternatively, the prosecutor may have presented evidence to the grand jury after commencing the action in a local criminal court with the filing of a felony complaint, but the grand jury decided to charge only at the misdemeanor level. Finally, the prosecutor may have presented evidence directly to the grand jury without any accusatory instrument having been filed before the presentation and, once again, the grand jury voted to indict for one or more misdemeanors without charging a felony.

In three of the four situations described, the grand jury may choose the forum for prosecution—that is, it may direct the filing of a prosecutor's information in local criminal court or it may vote an indictment, in which case the action must proceed in superior court.[470] The exception

---

463. One court has threatened preclusion as an appropriate sanction for continued delay in filing a bill of particulars. People v. Thomas, 106 Misc.2d 64, 432 N.Y.S.2d 317 (N.Y.C.Crim.Ct. 1980).

464. CPL § 200.95(8).

465. Art. 1, § 6 of the State Constitution requires, with certain exceptions, that all "capital and infamous crimes" be prosecuted by indictment (except where a superior court information is authorized). "Infamous crimes" in this context has been defined as any offense where a term of imprisonment in excess of one year is authorized. People v. Bellinger, 269 N.Y. 265, 199 N.E. 213 (1935).

466. CPL § 200.10; CPL § 10.00(6). See, e.g., People v. Star Supermarkets, Inc., 40 A.D.2d 946, 339 N.Y.S.2d 262 (4th Dep't 1972).

467. The discussion here merely references the fact that a grand jury may vote an indictment requiring prosecution of one or more misdemeanors in superior court. Not discussed here are instances where a felony count voted by a grand jury may be reduced to a misdemeanor in superior court. See § 5.27. See also Chapter 1, § 1.8 (removal of a criminal case from local criminal court to superior court).

468. CPL § 170.20.

469. CPL § 170.25.

470. CPL § 190.70.

§ 5.20   GRAND JURY & INDICTMENT   Ch. 5

is a case in which a superior court has directed removal of a misdemeanor, upon application of the defendant, and where the grand jury has voted to indict for a misdemeanor. In such a case, the grand jury may not choose to return the case to local criminal court for prosecution upon an information. If it finds reasonable cause to charge either a misdemeanor or a felony, it may only vote an indictment to be prosecuted in superior court.[471]

At first blush, it might seem unusual for either party to seek prosecution by indictment of a misdemeanor. However, in some cases the defendant may seek removal to gain certain procedural advantages.[472] Similarly, on occasion, a prosecutor may wish to present a case to the grand jury after filing a misdemeanor complaint in the local criminal court. For example, the situation may arise where a superior court has issued an eavesdropping warrant[473] but only misdemeanor charges resulted against a particular defendant. The prosecutor in that case may prefer that the legality of the superior court authorization be tested in superior court.[474]

Library References:
West's Key No. Digests, Indictment and Information ⌐185–192.

§ 5.21   Indictment—Joinder of Offenses

Section 200.20 prescribes rules governing joinder of offenses. An indictment may contain more than one count, with each count charging the defendant with a separate offense, provided all such offenses are "joinable." Offenses are joinable under three sets of circumstances. Two offenses may be joined in the same indictment if: (a) they are based upon the same act or the same criminal transaction; (b) proof of one is material and admissible as evidence of the other; or (c) each offense is defined by the same or similar statutory provisions.[475] Thereafter, more offenses may be added, like links to a chain, if they are joinable with any one or more offenses already properly joined to the indictment.[476]

471. CPL § 190.70(1). Note that a grand jury is free to elect to indict the defendant upon a felony charge, even in a case where the prosecutor had merely charged a misdemeanor in a local criminal court and it was the defendant, not the prosecutor, who sought removal to superior court. People v. Ryback, 3 N.Y.2d 467, 168 N.Y.S.2d 945, 146 N.E.2d 680 (1957).

472. See, e.g., right to testify before the grand jury, CPL § 190.50; inspection of grand jury minutes by the court, CPL § 210.30; jury trial with twelve jurors as opposed to six jurors, People v. Dean, 80 A.D.2d 695, 436 N.Y.S.2d 455 (3d Dep't 1981); jury trial in the case of a mandatory youthful offender, People v. Robert Z., 134 Misc.2d 555, 511 N.Y.S.2d 473 (Dist.Ct., Nassau County, 1986); proceeding before a lawyer-judge where the defendant does not wish to proceed before a lay town or village justice, People v. Dean, supra; but see People v. Charles F., 60 N.Y.2d 474, 470 N.Y.S.2d 342, 458 N.E.2d 801 (1983), cert. den. 467 U.S. 1216, 104 S.Ct. 2660, 81 L.Ed.2d 367 (1984)(removal on this ground a matter of discretion, not right).

473. See CPL § 700.05(4)(only superior court justice may issue eavesdropping order).

474. See, e.g., People v. Kay, 125 Misc.2d 833, 480 N.Y.S.2d 171 (Amherst Town Ct.1984)(search warrant issued by Supreme Court justice acting as local criminal court can only be reviewed by a local criminal court judge when the local criminal court has trial jurisdiction of the matter, absent removal).

475. CPL § 200.20(2)(a), (b) and (c).

476. CPL § 200.20(2)(d).

§ 5.21 JOINDER OF OFFENSES

Same Act or Transaction. The first of the three situations is the most self-evident: one criminal transaction frequently involves multiple offenses—*e.g.*, gun possession and robbery—and the offenses should be tried at one time. This provision benefits the prosecution and defense alike. It provides one forum for presentation of witnesses of multiple acts or events and it protects against successive prosecutions for the same conduct.[477]

A "criminal transaction" is defined as

> conduct which establishes at least one offense, and which is comprised of two or more or a group of acts either (a) so closely related and connected in point of time and circumstance of commission as to constitute a single criminal incident, or (b) so closely related in criminal purpose or objective as to constitute elements or integral parts of a single criminal venture.[478]

When two or more indictments separately charge offenses that are part of a single criminal transaction, either party may apply for consolidation.[479] In that event, the court has discretion to grant or deny the prosecution's application. On the other hand, the court must order consolidation upon application of the defendant unless good cause to the contrary is shown. Since a defendant may compel joinder in this case, it is sometimes referred to as "mandatory" joinder.[480] If a court improperly denies a defense motion for consolidation of two accusatory instruments separately charging offenses that were part of one criminal transaction, then commencement of trial upon one indictment bars prosecution upon the other.[481] It is imperative that counsel consider

---

477. See CPL § 40.40(1):
Where two or more offenses are joinable in a single accusatory instrument against a person by reason of being based upon the same criminal transaction, pursuant to paragraph (a) of subdivision two of section 200.20, such person may not, under circumstances prescribed in this section, be separately prosecuted for such offenses even though such separate prosecutions are not otherwise barred by any other section of this article.

478. CPL § 40.10(2). See People v. Griffin, 137 A.D.2d 558, 524 N.Y.S.2d 298 (2d Dep't 1988)(upholding consolidation of two successive robberies of the same victim within seconds of each other); Meldish v. Braatz, 99 A.D.2d 316, 472 N.Y.S.2d 699 (2d Dep't 1984), app. den. 61 N.Y.2d 608, 475 N.Y.S.2d 1026, 464 N.E.2d 1004 (1984)(successive assaults by defendant against the same victim, the same evening, one occurring outside a barn followed by the other assault inside the barn, were parts of one lone transaction).

479. CPL § 200.20(4).

480. CPL § 200.20(5). See, e.g., People v. Sharpton, 141 Misc.2d 322, 325, 533 N.Y.S.2d 230, 232 (N.Y.C.Crim. Ct.1988)("Under CPL 200.20, determination of the application for consolidation is at the court's discretion but is mandatory if the defendants are seeking consolidation of offenses arising out of the same act or transaction.").

481. CPL § 40.40(3) provides:
When (a) two or more of such offenses are charged in separate accusatory instruments filed in the same court, and (b) an application by the defendant for consolidation thereof for trial purposes, pursuant to subdivision five of section 200.20 or section 100.45, is improperly denied, the commencement of a trial of one such accusatory instrument bars any subsequent prosecution upon any of the other accusatory instruments with respect to any such offense.

See, e.g., People v. Ruzas, 54 A.D.2d 1083, 1084, 389 N.Y.S.2d 205, 206 (4th Dep't 1976)("The enactment of CPL 40.40 is the legislative response to 'a problem that has proved highly perplexing to the United States Supreme Court and other tribunals. It deals with repeated prosecutions for different and factually distinct offenses arising out of the same criminal transaction under

§ 5.21   GRAND JURY & INDICTMENT   Ch. 5

carefully whether to move for consolidation of joinable indictments. On the one hand, notwithstanding that the crimes arose from the same transaction, a defendant may succeed in keeping certain evidence of uncharged crimes from the jury.[482] However, a failure to move to consolidate results in waiver of a claim against separate prosecutions under the statute.[483]

Offenses arising from the same transaction are joinable only when a court has geographical and subject matter jurisdiction of the offenses to be joined.[484] Similarly, if the prosecution does not possess legally sufficient evidence to support a charge, obviously it may not charge the defendant and there is nothing to be joined. This, however, can become a risky proposition since the prosecution forfeits its ability to prosecute separately if a court later determines it did possess sufficient evidence.[485]

Common Evidence. The second paragraph of CPL § 200.20 permits joinder when proof of one offense is "material and admissible as evidence in chief upon a trial" of the other.[486] As with joinder of offenses within one transaction, judicial and prosecutorial economy calls

circumstances wherein no violation of the double jeopardy principle can validly be maintained but the equities nevertheless seem to preclude separate prosecutions'.")(citations omitted).

482. The most orderly way to proceed would be a pre-trial motion in limine, seeking a ruling as to which crimes in the unconsolidated indictment would be admissible without consolidation. People v. Ventimiglia, 52 N.Y.2d 350, 438 N.Y.S.2d 261, 420 N.E.2d 59 (1981). See, e.g., People v. Yuk Bui Yee, 94 Misc.2d 628, 405 N.Y.S.2d 386 (Sup.Ct., N.Y.County, 1978)(calendar court should decide Molineux issues in context of a motion to sever, notwithstanding preference otherwise to defer such issues to the trial court).

483. People v. Dean, 56 A.D.2d 242, 392 N.Y.S.2d 134 (4th Dep't 1977), aff'd 45 N.Y.2d 651, 412 N.Y.S.2d 353, 384 N.E.2d 1277 (1978); Auer v. Smith, 77 A.D.2d 172, 432 N.Y.S.2d 926 (4th Dep't 1980), app. dismissed 52 N.Y.2d 1070, 438 N.Y.S.2d 1030, 420 N.E.2d 414 (1981).

484. People v. Lindsly, 99 A.D.2d 99, 472 N.Y.S.2d 115 (2d Dep't 1984)(plea to leaving the scene of an accident, a misdemeanor, in local criminal court does not bar subsequent prosecution in superior court upon indictment for driving while intoxicated as a felony since lower court did not have subject matter jurisdiction of felony counts). However, in Lindsly, the indictment was not pending at the time of the plea. If it had already been filed, then the defendant could have moved to join both offenses in superior court. See also Vega v. Rubin, 73 A.D.2d 658, 423 N.Y.S.2d 193 (2d Dep't 1979)(drug sale in Westchester County not joinable with subsequent arrest for drug possession in New York County, even though both crimes were part of one criminal transaction, because New York County lacked geographical jurisdiction of the drug sale). But see People v. Ruzas, 54 A.D.2d 1083, 389 N.Y.S.2d 205 (4th Dep't 1976)(robbery in Onondaga County joinable with ensuing felony murder in Madison County because robbery was one of the elements of the felony murder; therefore prosecution could be pursued in either county). Cf. People v. Perkins, 161 Misc.2d 502, 614 N.Y.S.2d 709 (Sup.Ct., N.Y. County, 1994)(prosecution for robbery in New York County not joinable with charge of possession of stolen property arising from same crime two days later in Kings County) with People v. Williams, 123 Misc.2d 165, 473 N.Y.S.2d 689 (Sup.Ct., N.Y. County, 1984)(charge of robbery in Bronx County joinable with charge of possession of the stolen property six days later in New York County).

485. CPL § 40.40(2)(a) forbids prosecution of an offense after commencement of trial or plea of guilty to another offense within the same criminal transaction when the prosecution had in its possession legally sufficient evidence to support a conviction of the uncharged crime. The rationale underlying this provision is that "[w]here the evidence against a person is in the prosecutor's hands, he may not—as a player in a game of chance—deal out indictments one at a time." Matter of Auer v. Smith, 77 A.D.2d 172, 189, 432 N.Y.S.2d 926, 937 (4th Dep't 1980), app. dismissed 52 N.Y.2d 1070, 438 N.Y.S.2d 1030, 420 N.E.2d 414 (1981).

486. CPL § 200.20(2)(b).

for combining proof of separate crimes in one proceeding when that proof depends upon one set of witnesses.

Unlike joinder of offenses within one transaction, a defendant may not compel joinder of separately prosecutable offenses that are not part of the same transaction, *i.e.*, joinder is "permissive" and the prosecution is not required to charge separate offenses in one instrument. Either party may move to consolidate indictments in this situation, and the court's determination is entirely discretionary.[487]

A court, as well, may sever counts that are joined under this provision. Since the basis for joinder under paragraph (b) is the evidentiary connection, the court must decide if, in fact, one offense is material and admissible evidence of the other. This is a two-pronged analysis. Admissibility is governed by *People v. Molineux*[488] and its progeny.[489] This means that the court must, in the first instance, exercise discretion in balancing prejudicial value against probative weight.[490] Thereafter, however, by the plain language of the statute, mere admissibility under *Molineux* will not defeat a motion to sever nor require consolidation unless and until the court also determines that the unrelated offenses are material to proof of the charges as part of the prosecution's direct case.[491]

Consistent with *Molineux*, joinder is permitted, pursuant to paragraph (b), when it is apparent that the crimes charged were parts of a common scheme or plan.[492] Joinder has been sustained where one count provided a motive for the commission of the other or demonstrated criminal intent.[493] Similarly, joinder is proper under paragraph (b) when

---

487. See People v. Lane, 56 N.Y.2d 1, 7, 451 N.Y.S.2d 6, 9, 436 N.E.2d 456, 459 (1982)("To obtain consolidation the applicant must demonstrate to the satisfaction of the court not only that the offenses charged in the separate indictments are joinable in accordance with the statutory criteria set forth in CPL 200.20 (subd. 2) but also that combination for a single trial is an appropriate exercise of discretion (CPL 200.20, subd. 4).").

488. 168 N.Y. 264, 61 N.E. 286 (1901).

489. People v. Alvino, 71 N.Y.2d 233, 525 N.Y.S.2d 7, 519 N.E.2d 808 (1987); see, e.g., People v. Allweiss, 48 N.Y.2d 40, 421 N.Y.S.2d 341, 396 N.E.2d 735 (1979).

490. See People v. Allweiss, 48 N.Y.2d at 47, 421 N.Y.S.2d at 344 ("If the evidence is actually of slight value when compared to the possible prejudice to the accused, it should not be admitted, even though it might technically relate to some fact to be proven.")(citations omitted).

491. It has been said that once a count has been properly joined pursuant to CPL § 200.20(2)(b), a court is without discretion to sever. People v. Bongarzone, 69 N.Y.2d 892, 515 N.Y.S.2d 227, 507 N.E.2d 1083 (1987). This, of course, is true only after the court has decided the counts are properly joined by reason of the materiality and admissibility of the proof of one charge as evidence of the other.

492. People v. Luciano, 277 N.Y. 348, 14 N.E.2d 433 (1938), reargument den. 278 N.Y. 624, 16 N.E.2d 129 (1938), cert. den. 305 U.S. 620, 59 S.Ct. 81, 83 L.Ed. 396 (1938). But see People v. Munger, 24 N.Y.2d 445, 301 N.Y.S.2d 39, 248 N.E.2d 882 (1969)(joinder not proper under theory of common scheme or plan where allegations of narcotics trafficking and bribery of police were combined; however, joinder was not error by dint of the alternate theory that a motive for the bribery was to cover-up narcotics activity).

493. People v. Bongarzone, supra (conspiracy to murder witness to leaving scene of an accident; counts properly joined); People v. Jackson, 144 A.D.2d 488, 534 N.Y.S.2d 203 (2d Dep't 1988)(kidnaping eyewitness to robbery day before he was to testify; counts properly joined); People v. Washpun, 134 A.D.2d 858, 521 N.Y.S.2d 915 (4th Dep't 1987)(subsequent assault upon burglary victim who was to testify against defendant; joinder proper).

evidence of one crime establishes the identity of the defendant as the perpetrator of another crime.[494]

Chief Judge Cardozo once observed that the " 'natural and inevitable tendency of the tribunal—whether judge or jury—is to give excessive weight to the vicious record of crime thus exhibited, and either to allow it to bear too strongly on the present charge, or to take the proof of it as justifying a condemnation irrespective of guilt of the present charge'."[495] For that reason, and in order to guard against introduction of unwarranted allegations in a non-joinder situation, evidence of uncharged crimes may only be introduced after a preliminary determination by the court that clear and convincing evidence supports the conclusion that the defendant did, in fact, commit the other crime.[496] However, a count adding a separate charge to an indictment need only be supported by a grand jury's determination that reasonable cause exists to believe the defendant committed the crime.[497] As a result, on occasion a jury may hear evidence of other crimes, supported by minimal proof, by way of joinder that would not otherwise be available to it under a *Molineux* theory.[498] When the added count, *i.e.*, the "other crime," is dismissed or results in acquittal, the integrity of the surviving count is then subject to re-examination.[499]

---

494. People v. West, 160 A.D.2d 301, 553 N.Y.S.2d 721 (1st Dep't 1990) (overall pattern of criminal conduct was of more than sufficient uniqueness to constitute a distinctive modus operandi); accord People v. West, 160 A.D.2d 301, 553 N.Y.S.2d 721(1st Dep't 1990); People v. Gallishaw, 143 A.D.2d 198, 531 N.Y.S.2d 816 (2d Dep't 1988)(identity of defendant as person who committed a series of burglaries and sexual abuse offenses established by his particularly rank body odor); People v. Tardbania, 130 A.D.2d 954, 515 N.Y.S.2d 936 (4th Dep't 1987) (evidence of one criminal incident just prior to other helps to disprove alibi).

495. People v. Zackowitz, 254 N.Y. 192, 198, 172 N.E. 466, 468 (1930)(quoting 1 Wigmore, Evidence § 194).

496. People v. Robinson, 68 N.Y.2d 541, 510 N.Y.S.2d 837, 503 N.E.2d 485 (1986); People v. Ventimiglia, 52 N.Y.2d 350, 359, 438 N.Y.S.2d 261, 264, 420 N.E.2d 59, 62 (1981).

497. CPL § 190.65.

498. For example, in People v. Castillo, 47 N.Y.2d 270, 417 N.Y.S.2d 915, 391 N.E.2d 997 (1979), the defendant was convicted on charges of sexual assault and burglary occurring at a household several days apart. As to the first count, the Appellate Division found that "under all the circumstances, there exists a substantial possibility of misidentification leading inevitably to the creation of a reasonable doubt." People v. Castillo, 62 A.D.2d 938, 939, 403 N.Y.S.2d 746, 747 (1st Dep't 1978). It sustained the burglary charge and remanded for resentencing on that count. The Court of Appeals, however, ordered a new trial as to the burglary, finding that the evidence as to the first charge had an "ineradicable" effect upon the burglary charge. As the court stated (47 N.Y.2d at 275, 417 N.Y.S.2d at 918):

> [T]he trial strategy blurred the separate features of each incident to a point where it cannot be said that the proofs relating to one episode did not supplement deficiencies in the proof on key elements of the other.

See also People v. Jenkins, 47 A.D.2d 832, 365 N.Y.S.2d 870 (1st Dep't 1975), aff'd 39 N.Y.2d 969, 387 N.Y.S.2d 107, 354 N.E.2d 848 (1976) (Murphy, P.J., dissenting)(defendant charged with two robberies, acquitted of one and convicted of the other where, in the eyes of the dissenter, the conviction rested upon weak identification evidence, was tainted by suggestiveness, and was a result of joinder with the first, unsupported, count).

499. People v. Castillo, supra; People v. Jenkins, supra. See also People v. Gadsden, 139 A.D.2d 925, 528 N.Y.S.2d 955 (4th Dep't 1988)(gun possession improperly joined with robbery charge; notwithstanding acquittal on possession charge, new trial ordered on robbery count).

Crimes That are the "Same or Similar." The third basis for joinder of offenses is when the offenses are "defined by the same or similar statutory provisions and consequently are the same or similar in law."[500] Unlike joinder prescribed in paragraphs (a) or (b), the benefits of judicial economy in this situation are minimal because the incidents are unrelated, and thereby presumably involve different witnesses.[501] Weighed in the balance is the concern that combining similar, but unrelated, charges in one indictment may confuse a jury or improperly suggest that the accused has a general propensity toward criminality.[502]

When the charges are the same—*i.e.*, identical—joinder under paragraph (c) is relatively straightforward. On the other hand, deciding whether offenses are "similar" can be more difficult. Joinder of possession of stolen property charges originating from theft with other possession of stolen property charges arising from stolen credit cards has been upheld.[503] The Second Department has upheld joinder of rape, sexual abuse and sodomy charges contained in three complaints on the ground that they were defined by the same or similar statutory provisions and consequently were the same or similar in law.[504] However, the same court has also held that consolidation of attempted rape and sexual abuse charges against two different child victims was, in the circumstances of the case before it, an abuse of discretion, notwithstanding the similarity of the crimes charged.[505]

The Third Department has rejected a claim that rape and kidnapping of one victim was similar to unrelated charges of coercion of a second female victim, notwithstanding an argument by the prosecution that the provisions were contained within the same article of the Penal Law and, consequently, should be considered to be similar.[506]

Severance and Consolidation—Procedure. Theoretically, motions for separate trials should be included within the omnibus motion filed pursuant to CPL § 255.10 within 45 days of arraignment.[507] However, more than one court has observed that a decision regarding severance or consolidation is better made after evidentiary issues have had an opportunity to develop and when trial strategies by both defense

---

500. CPL § 200.20(2)(c).

501. Some economy is achieved by reducing the number of juries that must be empaneled. Also, in some cases an investigating or arresting officer may have taken a confession, seized property or conducted a series of lineups, all of which relate to more than one crime. In that case, the officer can testify at one trial, rather than at a series of trials to explain his or her role in the investigation.

502. People v. Negron, 105 Misc.2d 492, 492–93, 432 N.Y.S.2d 348, 349 (Sup.Ct., N.Y. County, 1980)("Any consideration of the severance must begin with the proposition that the joinder of unrelated though similar crimes is inherently prejudicial to the defendant."). See also People v. Santarelli, 49 N.Y.2d 241, 425 N.Y.S.2d 77, 401 N.E.2d 199 (1980); People v. Shapiro, 50 N.Y.2d 747, 431 N.Y.S.2d 422, 409 N.E.2d 897 (1980); People v. Pinkas, 156 A.D.2d 485, 548 N.Y.S.2d 767 (2d Dep't 1989); People v. Sable, 138 A.D.2d 234, 525 N.Y.S.2d 45 (1st Dep't 1988).

503. People v. Blackwell, 156 A.D.2d 148, 548 N.Y.S.2d 197 (1st Dep't 1989).

504. People v. Berta, 213 A.D.2d 659, 624 N.Y.S.2d 211 (2d Dep't 1995).

505. People v. Pinkas, supra.

506. People v. Dabbs, 192 A.D.2d 932, 596 N.Y.S.2d 893 (3d Dep't 1993).

507. CPL § 255.10(1)(g).

§ 5.21 GRAND JURY & INDICTMENT Ch. 5

and prosecution have more clearly formulated.[508]

Upon a motion to sever, the court first looks to the basis for joinder to determine if the charges are properly joined. Thereafter, having determined that joinder was properly made, the court has no discretion to sever the counts unless the sole basis for joinder is paragraph (c).[509] By contrast, where a party seeks to *consolidate* separate indictments, the motion is left to the discretion of the court regardless of the basis for joinder.[510]

Subdivision three of section 200.20 provides that where the sole basis for joinability of offenses is the "same or similar" provisions of paragraph (c), the court "in the interest of justice and for good cause shown" may order severance upon application of either party.[511] While the decision to grant severance in this situation is left to the sound discretion of the trial court, misjoinder under this provision may, on occasion, become an abuse of discretion as a matter of law.[512] One court has observed that "[w]here joinder is based on subdivision 2(c), not only does the court have the discretion to grant a severance but the non-exercise of that discretion is most closely reviewed in light of subsequently developed events at trial."[513]

Section 200.20 was amended in 1984 to specify two examples of "good cause" for severance of similar charges.[514] The examples are merely illustrative and not all-inclusive.[515]

The first provision applies to instances where a jury would not be likely to follow an instruction to consider the charges separately, in part

---

508. See, e.g., People v. Negron, 105 Misc.2d 492, 493, 432 N.Y.S.2d 348, 349 (Sup.Ct., N.Y. County, 1980)("[T]his court feels that all motions for a severance or a motion for consolidation of offenses based on a Molineux theory should be referred to the trial court for decision immediately prior to trial."). See also People v. Yuk Bui Yee, 94 Misc.2d 628, 405 N.Y.S.2d 386 (Sup. Ct., N.Y. County, 1978); People v. Capitello, 139 Misc.2d 618, 528 N.Y.S.2d 263 (Suffolk Co.Ct.1988).

509. People v. Bongarzone, 69 N.Y.2d 892, 515 N.Y.S.2d 227, 507 N.E.2d 1083 (1987); People v. Lane, 56 N.Y.2d 1, 7, 451 N.Y.S.2d 6, 9, 436 N.E.2d 456, 459 (1982).

510. See People v. Lane, 56 N.Y.2d at 8, 451 N.Y.S.2d at 9:

Thus it is clear that the decision to consolidate separate indictments under CPL 200.20 (subd 4) is committed to the sound discretion of the Trial Judge in light of the circumstances of the individual case, and the decision is reviewable on appeal to this court only to the extent that there has been an abuse of that discretion as a matter of law. Trial courts should generally weigh the public interest in avoiding duplicative, lengthy and expensive trials against the defendant's interest in being protected from unfair disadvantage. While the trial courts must be afforded reasonable latitude in exercising discretion in these matters, we emphasize that compromise of a defendant's fundamental right to a fair trial free of undue prejudice as the quid pro quo for the mere expeditious disposition of criminal cases will not be tolerated.

511. CPL § 200.20(3). The application may be in writing or placed orally on the record. CPL § 200.20(3)(b).

512. See People v. Shapiro, 50 N.Y.2d 747, 431 N.Y.S.2d 422, 409 N.E.2d 897 (1980).

513. People v. Yuk Bui Yee, 94 Misc.2d at 630, 405 N.Y.S.2d at 387 (citing People v. Payne, 35 N.Y.2d 22, 358 N.Y.S.2d 701, 315 N.E.2d 762 (1974) and People v. Fisher, 249 N.Y. 419, 164 N.E. 336 (1928)).

514. L.1984, c.672.

515. CPL § 200.20(3)(a)("Good cause shall include, but not be limited to situations ... ").

because of a disparity in the quantum or nature of proof of the two charges.[516] An example of required severance in this category is *People v. Shapiro*.[517] In that case, a charge of promoting prostitution on one occasion was joined with multiple counts of sodomy occurring on numerous earlier occasions. The more serious charge, promoting prostitution, was evidenced in part by the testimony of arresting officers who raided the defendant's house. The lesser, unrelated, charges were based upon uncorroborated testimony of single witnesses to each incident. The Court of Appeals held that

> [s]ince prosecutions for sex crimes, particularly ones regarded as deviate, tend in any event to invoke prejudicial preconceptions among jurors, the joinder of the indictments created an impermissible risk.[518]

Similarly, reversible error has occurred when a defendant was tried upon all of seven separate robberies where there was substantially more proof on one or more such joinable offenses than on others, and there was a substantial likelihood that the jury would have been unable to consider separately the proof as it related to each offense.[519]

In *People v. Forest*,[520] the defendant was charged with three robberies. Identification evidence was weak or non-existent in each. He was acquitted of two and convicted of the third robbery. The First Department reversed, saying that severance should have been granted because of the "strong possibility, all three crimes being of a similar nature, of a conviction by reason of their cumulative effect rather than on the strength of the specific evidence regarding each crime."[521]

The second ground for severance suggested by CPL § 200.20(3) touches upon the not uncommon situation in which a defendant may wish to testify as to one charge but not the other. A typical example would be a case where the defendant is arrested at the scene of a crime in ambiguous circumstances and he wishes to explain his presence. At the same time, he may be charged with another, similar, offense where he claims misidentification. In such a circumstance, a court may entertain a motion for severance, but may also be uncertain of the sincerity of the asserted basis for the motion. In *People v. Lane*,[522] the Court of Appeals adopted the test employed in *Baker v. United States*,[523] which subsequently became engrafted, almost verbatim, in CPL

---

516. CPL § 200.20(3)(a) provides that good cause for severance includes where there is
> [s]ubstantially more proof on one or more such joinable offenses than on others and there is a substantial likelihood that the jury would be unable to consider separately the proof as it relates to each offense.

517. 50 N.Y.2d 747, 431 N.Y.S.2d 422, 409 N.E.2d 897 (1980).

518. People v. Shapiro, 50 N.Y.2d at 754, 431 N.Y.S.2d at 425.

519. People v. Sable, 138 A.D.2d 234, 525 N.Y.S.2d 45 (1st Dep't 1988).

520. 50 A.D.2d 260, 377 N.Y.S.2d 492 (1st Dep't 1975).

521. 50 A.D.2d at 261–262, 377 N.Y.S.2d at 495.

522. 56 N.Y.2d 1, 451 N.Y.S.2d 6, 436 N.E.2d 456 (1982).

523. 401 F.2d 958, 977 (D.C.Cir.1968), cert. den. 400 U.S. 965, 91 S.Ct. 367, 27 L.Ed.2d 384 (1970).

§ 200.20(3)(b).[524] It is worth noting that *Lane* was decided in the context of a motion to consolidate two indictments on a *Molineux* theory pursuant to paragraph (b). The Court of Appeals adopted the *Baker* "need to refrain" test as guidance to the trial court's exercise of discretion on the motion to consolidate. Shortly thereafter, the Legislature adopted the test as one of the grounds for severance in cases joined by paragraph (c), but not paragraph (b).

CPL § 200.20(3)(b)(ii) provides a mechanism by which a defendant may safely demonstrate his or her reluctance to testify in order to meet the "need to refrain" test. As a matter right, defense counsel may ask to be heard *ex parte* and *in camera* on the issue. The record is sealed for appellate review and representations by counsel, even if based upon information provided by the defendant, are not available for impeachment purposes.[525] This procedure is designed to afford a defendant the maximum opportunity to demonstrate cause for severance while preserving his or her right to remain silent throughout the proceedings. If a defendant wishes to make an *ex parte* and *in camera* application for severance on grounds other than the need to refrain from giving testimony, the court may, but is not required to, grant that relief as well.[526]

Finally, a question may arise concerning the appropriate remedy for misjoinder of offenses. CPL § 200.70 forbids amendment of an indictment to cure the defect of misjoinder of offenses. However, it is not uncommon for appellate courts to order, as relief for misjoinder, "separate trials" upon various counts of an indictment, apparently leaving the indictment itself intact and unamended.[527] One court, finding that

---

524. Id. ("[N]o need for a severance exists until the defendant makes a convincing showing that he has both important testimony to give concerning one count and strong need to refrain from testifying on the other.") Further guidance is provided in People v. Lane (56 N.Y.2d at 10, 451 N.Y.S.2d at 10):

The stated desire to take advantage of a perceived weakness in the People's case on the issue of identification is alone patently insufficient. Rather, it was incumbent upon defendants to articulate in concrete terms why they would be unduly prejudiced by giving testimony on the December 2 count either supporting misidentification or simply denying the charge. For example, the possibility of cross-examination regarding specific criminal convictions or prior sordid conduct and the attendant risk of serious impeachment may justify a desire to refrain from testifying on one count but not on another where testimony is essential regardless of the risk of impeachment. However, speculative fears of exposure to cross-examination regarding undocumented events and abstract claims of impeachment, like the "conclusory generalities" and "self-serving representations" identified in Shapiro, should never be considered dispositive absent the most obviously egregious circumstances.

525. Note that "good cause" for severance under either prong of section 200.20(3) may be established by counsel's representations alone, as long as the sources of the information or belief are provided. CPL § 200.20(3)(b)(i). The defendant is not obligated to provide the information personally. Cf. Simmons v. United States, 390 U.S. 377, 394, 88 S.Ct. 967, 976, 19 L.Ed.2d 1247 (1968)(statements made in support of a motion may be used to impeach contradictory testimony at trial).

526. People v. Smyers, 167 A.D.2d 773, 562 N.Y.S.2d 1017 (3d Dep't 1990). Cf. United States v. Zolin, 491 U.S. 554, 109 S.Ct. 2619, 105 L.Ed.2d 469 (1989).

527. See, e.g., People v. Communiello, 180 A.D.2d 809, 580 N.Y.S.2d 420 (2d Dep't 1992); People v. Gadsden, 139 A.D.2d 925, 528 N.Y.S.2d 955 (4th Dep't 1988); People v. Connors, 83 A.D.2d 640, 441 N.Y.S.2d 523 (2d Dep't 1981). Cf. CPL § 200.40(2)(specific statutory authorization for separated offenses to "remain in existence and ... be separately prosecuted" in the case of consolidation of indictments against different defendants).

misjoinder renders an indictment "defective" within the meaning of CPL § 210.25(1), has held that, in an appropriate case, misjoinder may be cured by dismissal, with leave to re-present, of one count in the indictment.[528]

Library References:
West's Key No. Digests, Criminal Law ⚖620; Indictment and Information ⚖124–132.

§ 5.22 Indictment—Joinder of Defendants

Section 200.40 prescribes rules governing joinder of charges against more than one defendant. Aside from special rules designed for enterprise corruption prosecutions, there are three basic grounds for joining two or more defendants in one accusatory instrument: (a) all the defendants are jointly charged with every offense; (b) all the offenses are joined by one common scheme or plan; or (c) all the offenses charged are based upon one criminal transaction.

Same Offense. Paragraph (1)(a) is straightforward: if each defendant is charged with committing the same offense, either by means of acting in concert[529] or as principals, they should, for the sake of judicial economy, be tried together.[530]

Each count of an indictment may only allege one criminal offense,[531] whether or not more than one defendant is alleged to have committed it. When two or more defendants are jointly charged with an offense, it is important to ensure that they are each charged with the same offense on any given count where they are so joined. So, for example, in a case charging a complex conspiracy involving multiple overt acts over a period of time, where it was possible to find that there were in fact multiple conspiracies included within the one conspiracy count, it was necessary to charge the jury that it could convict only if it found that the defendants had conspired together to commit one unitary conspiracy.[532]

Common Scheme or Plan. Paragraph (b) authorizes joinder where "all the offenses charged are based upon a common scheme or

---

528. People v. Porter, 157 Misc.2d 879, 599 N.Y.S.2d 436 (Sup.Ct., Queens County, 1993).

529. See P.L. § 20.00.

530. People v. Snyder, 246 N.Y. 491, 159 N.E. 408 (1927)(upholding statutory enactment—L.1926, c.461—that took away from a defendant the right to demand a separate trial). See People v. Mahboubian, 74 N.Y.2d 174, 183, 544 N.Y.S.2d 769, 773, 543 N.E.2d 34, 38 (1989)("The decision to grant or deny a separate trial is vested primarily in the sound judgment of the Trial Judge, and defendants' burden to demonstrate abuse of that discretion is a substantial one. Moreover '[w]here proof against the defendants is supplied by the same evidence, only the most cogent reasons warrant a severance.' While that is particularly true where the defendants are charged with acting in concert, in all cases a strong public policy favors joinder, because it expedites the judicial process, reduces court congestion, and avoids the necessity of recalling witnesses.")(citations omitted).

531. See discussion concerning duplicity and CPL § 200.30, § 5.17, supra.

532. People v. Leisner, 73 N.Y.2d 140, 150, 538 N.Y.S.2d 517, 522, 535 N.E.2d 647, 652 (1989)("[A] charge must be given explicitly recognizing the possibility of multiple conspiracies and directing an acquittal in the event that the jury concludes that something other than a single integrated conspiracy was proven. Such a charge is required whenever the possibility of more than one conspiracy is supported by a reasonable view of the evidence.").

plan."[533] As with joinder of offenses, the rules of evidence propounded by *Molineux* and its progeny apply here.[534] In essence, "[s]ome connection between the [acts] must be shown to have existed in fact and in the mind of the actor, uniting them for the accomplishment of a common purpose."[535] Also, "there must be such a clear concurrence of common features—i.e., time, place and character—that the various acts are naturally to be explained as caused by a general plan of which they are the individual manifestations."[536] And finally, there must exist "a single inseparable plan encompassing ... [all the] charged ... crimes."[537]

One court found that there was "no distinction between a single conspiracy and a 'common scheme or plan'" as defined by CPL § 200.40.[538] It is quite clear, however, that a conspiracy need not be charged in order to sustain a finding that counts are properly joined as part of a common scheme or plan.[539]

Note also that section 200.40 requires that "*all* the offenses charged are based upon a common scheme or plan."[540] Thus, counts charging other crimes that may have been committed by one of the defendants, but not as part of the universal scheme, may not be included in the indictment, notwithstanding the existence of a common scheme or plan among the defendants.

A good case illustrating this point is *People v. Kaatsiz*,[541] in which the defendant was charged with participating with seven co-defendants in a conspiracy to sell drugs from November 20, 1991 to December 10, 1991. Apparently this was a lesser conspiracy included within a more encompassing conspiracy shared by the seven co-defendants that lasted from September 17, 1991 to December 10, 1991. The seven co-defendants, but not Kaatsiz, were charged with the larger conspiracy as well. The court found joinder of the two conspiracies in one indictment to be improper as to Kaatsiz. That was because section 200.40 prohibited Kaatsiz from being charged in the same indictment with co-defendants who were facing other charges that were not part of the particular conspiracy or common scheme in which Kaatsiz participated.

---

533. CPL § 200.40(1)(b).

534. People v. Kaatsiz, 156 Misc.2d 898, 899, 595 N.Y.S.2d 648, 649 (Sup.Ct., Kings County, 1992)("No definition of 'common scheme or plan' is set forth in CPL 200.40 or the cases thereunder. The phrase is generally used in the context of the admissibility or inadmissibility of uncharged crimes or immoral acts.")(citing Molineux).

535. People v. Molineux, 18 N.Y. at 306, 61 N.E. at 299.

536. In re Estate of Brandon, 55 N.Y.2d 206, 212, 448 N.Y.S.2d 436, 439, 433 N.E.2d 501, 504 (1982).

537. People v. Fiore, 34 N.Y.2d 81, 85, 356 N.Y.S.2d 38, 42, 312 N.E.2d 174, 177 (1974).

538. People v. Ruiz, 130 Misc.2d 191, 496 N.Y.S.2d 612 (Sup.Ct., N.Y. County, 1985)(further defining the central element of a conspiracy, i.e., agreement, as "a concert of action, all parties working together understandingly, with a single design for the accomplishment of a common purpose"). But see People v. Alvarez, 88 Misc.2d 709, 389 N.Y.S.2d 980 (Sup.Ct., N.Y. County, 1976)(finding a common scheme or plan existed notwithstanding failure to make out a prima facie case of conspiracy).

539. People v. Luciano, 277 N.Y. 348, 14 N.E.2d 433 (1938), cert. den. 305 U.S. 620, 59 S.Ct. 81, 83 L.Ed. 396 (1938).

540. CPL § 200.40(1)(b)(emphasis supplied).

541. 156 Misc.2d 898, 595 N.Y.S.2d 648 (Sup.Ct., Kings County, 1992).

Each of Kaatsiz's co-defendants could have been charged individually with both conspiracies in one indictment (under either a theory of common scheme or plan[542] or a theory that the two conspiracies were the same or similar crimes).[543] Also, the co-defendants could have been joined together since they were jointly charged with all the offenses[544] and, in any event, had acted together throughout as part of a common scheme or plan.[545] However, Kaatsiz was only charged with entering the conspiracy late in the game; he did not participate in the larger conspiracy or participate in a larger common scheme or plan.[546] In sum, Kaatsiz's participation in one part of a common scheme or plan did not, by itself, permit joinder with other crimes committed by his co-defendants as part of a separate, larger, scheme.[547]

Prior to 1984, the only basis for joinder of defendants was the "same offense" provision of paragraph (a). In response to a call to expand the joinder provisions along the lines of Federal Rule of Criminal Procedure 8(b),[548] paragraphs (b) and (c) were enacted.[549] Rule 8(b) allows for joinder of defendants when they are charged with committing a "series of transactions." However, significantly, the 1984 amendment rejected this language in favor of joinder only when all offenses are part of one scheme or one transaction.[550]

A case illustrating the difference between federal and New York law is *People v. Ruiz*.[551] The theory of the prosecution's case was that seven separate conspiracies existed, each involving different landlords who hired a group of individuals to harass and intimidate tenants into vacating their apartments. The prosecution argued that the individual

542. CPL § 200.20(1)(b).
543. CPL § 200.20(1)(c).
544. CPL § 200.40(1)(a).
545. CPL § 200.40(1)(b).
546. "Without knowledge of or demonstrated participation by Kaatsiz in the broader conspiracy, Kaatsiz' alleged criminal activity cannot be considered part of a common scheme or plan vis-a-vis the [larger] conspiracy." 156 Misc.2d at 901, 595 N.Y.S.2d at 650–51.
547. "In essence, the theory upon which defendant was joined in the indictment ... is that the Kaatsiz conspiracy was part of what has been commonly denominated as a 'wheel conspiracy' with defendant Sevencan and others serving as the 'hub' and Kaatsiz as one of several 'spokes'." 156 Misc.2d at 900–01, 595 N.Y.S.2d at 650.

The result may have been the same under the more liberal provisions of Rule 8(b) of the Federal Rules of Criminal Procedure. "[T]he mere fact that two conspiracies have overlapping memberships will not authorize a single indictment if the conspiracies cannot be tied together into one conspiracy, one common plan or scheme." United States v. Velasquez, 772 F.2d 1348, 1353 (7th Cir.1985), cert. den. 475 U.S. 1021, 106 S.Ct. 1211, 89 L.Ed.2d 323 (1986). Cf. Kotteakos v. United States, 328 U.S. 750, 769, 66 S.Ct. 1239, 1250, 90 L.Ed. 1557 (1946).

548. That rule provides:

Two or more defendants may be charged in the same indictment or information if they are alleged to have participated in the same act or transaction or in the same series of acts or transactions constituting an offense or offenses. Such defendants may be charged in one or more counts together or separately and all of the defendants need not be charged in each count.

549. L.1984, c.672.

550. Although allowing joinder of offenses that are not part of one transaction or even one common scheme or plan, "Rule 8(b)'s language 'may not be read to embrace similar or even identical offenses, unless those offenses are related.... [T]here must be a logical relationship between the acts or transactions within the series'." United States v. Nicely, 922 F.2d 850, 853 (D.C.Cir.1991)(citing United States v. Perry, 731 F.2d 985, 990 (D.C.Cir.1984)).

551. 130 Misc.2d 191, 496 N.Y.S.2d 612 (Sup.Ct., N.Y. County, 1985).

§ 5.22   GRAND JURY & INDICTMENT   Ch. 5

conspiracies were related because they all shared the same objective, used similar means, and employed the same group of co-conspirators to terrorize the tenants. It was the prosecution's position that the conspiracies came together, like spokes in a wheel, to the common hub of thugs with whom they co-conspired. However, the court found that joinder, under the recent amendments to CPL § 200.40, required not just spokes and a hub but also a rim before the wheel was properly formed. That is, the separate conspiracies could not be joined because, although they were a "related series of transactions," they were not part of one overall common scheme or plan.

Same Transaction. Paragraph (c) permits joinder of defendants when all the offenses charged are based upon the same criminal transaction. As with the parallel provisions of CPL § 200.20(2)(a)(joinder of offenses), cross-reference is made to CPL § 40.10(2) for a definition of "criminal transaction."[552]

Note that one portion of the definition includes "a group of acts ... so closely related in criminal purpose or objective as to constitute elements or integral parts of a single criminal venture." As a practical matter, this may overlap with paragraph (b). In *People v. Ruiz*, the court, while analyzing the relationship of multiple conspiracies charged in the indictment, found "no distinction between a single conspiracy and a 'common scheme or plan' ... or ... 'a single criminal venture'."[553]

On the other hand, joinder has been allowed by some courts under the rubric of a criminal venture where there was no joint agreement (as required to establish a conspiracy)[554] or single purpose (necessary to establish a common scheme or plan).[555] For example, in *People v. Ramjit*,[556] the defendant was charged with rape and his two sons were charged with threatening the victim after their father was arrested. The trial court declared this to be misjoinder, but the Second Department found that the events were so closely related and connected in time and circumstance as to constitute one criminal transaction. Another trial court granted the prosecution's request to join eight defendants who were arrested during a "riot" where the defendants were not charged with acting together, but were charged with a variety of offenses occurring at separate locations in the vicinity of a public park.[557] Notwithstanding the absence of agreement, scheme or plan and notwithstanding the lack of simultaneity (the different defendants were charged

---

552. CPL § 40.10(2) provides: "Criminal transaction" means conduct which establishes at least one offense, and which is comprised of two or more or a group of acts either (a) so closely related and connected in point of time and circumstance of commission as to constitute a single criminal incident, or (b) so closely related in criminal purpose or objective as to constitute elements or integral parts of a single criminal venture.

553. People v. Ruiz, 130 Misc.2d at 195, 496 N.Y.S.2d at 615.

554. See generally Penal Law Article 105; People v. Schwimmer, 66 A.D.2d 91, 94, 411 N.Y.S.2d 922, 925 (2d Dep't 1978) aff'd 47 N.Y.2d 1004, 420 N.Y.S.2d 218, 394 N.E.2d 288 (1979).

555. People v. Fiore, 34 N.Y.2d 81, 356 N.Y.S.2d 38, 312 N.E.2d 174 (1974).

556. 203 A.D.2d 488, 612 N.Y.S.2d 600 (2d Dep't 1994).

557. People v. Biltsted, 151 Misc.2d 620, 574 N.Y.S.2d 256 (N.Y.City Crim.Ct.1991).

with committing separate offenses at different times over a four and one-half hour period), the court ruled that to fail to conclude that the incidents were components of single criminal transaction would be to "fancify reality."[558]

Consolidation. Unlike motions to consolidate offenses,[559] a motion to join separately charged defendants may only be brought by the prosecution.[560] The prosecution may have an interest in presenting the same evidence and the same witnesses at one proceeding, or in the alternative of prosecuting one defendant while reserving action upon another. On the other hand, a defendant suffers no inability to present evidence or assert a defense when he or she is tried separately. Unlike the issues relating to joinder of offenses, separation of defendants does not present the potential for successive prosecutions of related events against the same defendant.

Once the prosecution has moved to consolidate indictments against two defendants, the court has discretion to grant or deny the motion.[561]

CPL § 200.40(2) also addresses a common occurrence where, upon consolidation, some counts remain in one of the indictments that "are not properly the subject of a single indictment." For example, if X is charged with two separate and unrelated robberies in one indictment, and if Y is charged in a separate indictment with participating in one of the robberies, but is not chargeable with the other, then the two indictments may be consolidated as to the shared robbery, but the robbery count against X that is not common to them is not joinable with the indictment against Y.[562] In that event, the non-joinable count against X is not consolidated but remains in existence and may be separately prosecuted.[563]

---

558. 151 Misc.2d at 627, 574 N.Y.S.2d at 261.

559. CPL § 200.20(4) and (5).

560. One local criminal court has determined that joinder may be accomplished over the prosecution's objection where the offenses, if committed by one defendant, were joinable under section 200.20 as a part of one transaction or common scheme. People v. Sharpton, 141 Misc.2d 322, 533 N.Y.S.2d 230 (N.Y.C.Crim.Ct.1988). There appears to have been no appellate review of, or comment upon, what appears to be this strained reading of the interplay between sections 200.20 and 200.40.

561. CPL § 200.40(2). See, e.g., People v. Rowley, 119 Misc.2d 86, 462 N.Y.S.2d 366 (N.Y.C.Crim.Ct.1983)(motion to consolidate denied where two of three defendants were eligible youthful offenders, notwithstanding necessity to have 14-year-old victim testify at separate trials).

There is not much case law on this particular point, probably because the prosecution has the option, either in the first instance or by way of a superseding indictment, to join defendants without the necessity of obtaining permission from the court.

562. CPL § 200.40(1)(assuming that the two robberies were not part of one transaction or common scheme or plan). See, e.g., People v. Pepin, 6 A.D.2d 992, 176 N.Y.S.2d 15 (4th Dep't 1958) (finding consolidation in such a case an abuse of discretion under section 279 of the Code of Criminal Procedure).

563. CPL § 200.40(2). This happens more frequently than one might at first assume. It is not uncommon for a defendant to be arrested on one charge, only to have other similar charges brought against him after, for example, a confession or a series of lineups. At that point, evidence may point to a co-defendant who is later indicted for one or more, but not all, of the charges as well.

§ 5.22 GRAND JURY & INDICTMENT Ch. 5

Severance. Section 200.40(1) allows a court to sever an indictment joining two or more defendants for "good cause shown," which includes, but is not limited to, "a finding that a defendant or the People will be unduly prejudiced by a joint trial."[564] There is a rich tradition and body of case law permitting severance in a trial court's discretion, but grudgingly.[565]

Generally speaking, severance is granted for one of several reasons: (a) the prosecution intends to use an out-of-court statement made by one defendant that expressly or inferentially implicates the other; (b) the defendants have mutually antagonistic defenses; or (c) one defendant intends to call the other as a witness.[566]

Statements by Co-defendants. In *Bruton v. United States*,[567] the Supreme Court held that a defendant's right to confrontation[568] was violated by admission of a non-testifying co-defendant's out-of-court confession implicating the defendant as well, notwithstanding instructions by the trial judge to the jury that the statement could not be used as evidence against the defendant.[569] As a consequence, a court may be

---

564. Cf. Fed.R.Crim.Proc. 14 (permitting severance when "it appears that a defendant or the government is prejudiced by a joinder").

565. See generally People v. Mahboubian, 74 N.Y.2d 174, 183, 544 N.Y.S.2d 769, 773, 543 N.E.2d 34, 38 (1989)("The decision to grant or deny a separate trial is vested primarily in the sound judgment of the Trial Judge, and defendants' burden to demonstrate abuse of that discretion is a substantial one. Moreover '[w]here proof against the defendants is supplied by the same evidence, only the most cogent reasons warrant a severance.' While that is particularly true where the defendants are charged with acting in concert, in all cases a strong public policy favors joinder, because it expedites the judicial process, reduces court congestion, and avoids the necessity of recalling witnesses.")(citations omitted). Thus, the mere fact that a defendant does not enjoy all the privileges of a single trial when joined with co-defendants is not a ground for severance. For example, an argument that a joint trial illegally deprived a defendant of his right to make peremptory challenges on the selection of the jury is insufficient. People v. Lobel, 298 N.Y. 243, 257, 82 N.E.2d 145, 151 (1948); People v. Doran, 246 N.Y. 409, 159 N.E. 379 (1927).

566. This generalization, of course, does not include every possible basis for severance—only the most commonly asserted. Since the statute permits severance for good cause shown, on occasion a court will require separate trials where there is prejudicial spillover, difficulty in compartmentalization or impairment of a specific trial right. For example, in People v. Rodriguez, 148 A.D.2d 320, 538 N.Y.S.2d 535 (1st Dep't 1989), reversal was required because joinder prevented the defendant from presenting exculpatory testimony regarding a photographic array, which was inadmissible as to the co-defendant. See also People v. Papa, 47 A.D.2d 902, 366 N.Y.S.2d 205 (2d Dep't 1975)(defendant prejudiced by spillover effect of evidence of other crimes introduced to rebut entrapment defense asserted by co-defendants, but not by the defendant); People v. Pilon, 30 A.D.2d 365, 293 N.Y.S.2d 393 (3d Dep't 1968)(in close eyewitness identification case, defendant prejudiced by spillover effect of substantial corroborative evidence against co-defendants).

567. 391 U.S. 123, 88 S.Ct. 1620, 20 L.Ed.2d 476 (1968).

568. U.S. Const., Amend. VI; cf. N.Y. Const., Art. 1, § 6.

569. Lee v. Illinois, 476 U.S. 530, 545, 106 S.Ct. 2056, 2064, 90 L.Ed.2d 514 (1986)("As we have consistently recognized, a codefendant's confession is presumptively unreliable as to the passages detailing the defendant's conduct or culpability because those passages may well be the product of the codefendant's desire to shift or spread blame, curry favor, avenge himself, or divert attention to another."); see also People v. Payne, 35 N.Y.2d 22, 358 N.Y.S.2d 701, 315 N.E.2d 762 (1974)(plurality opinion declaring that principles of fairness may require severance where co-defendant's statement is to be introduced even in a case where the confrontation clause is not implicated).

required to sever charges against two or more defendants to avoid introduction of the co-defendant's statement.[570]

There are a number of exceptions to *Bruton*. For one, the confrontation clause does not require severance if the co-defendant testifies and is available for cross-examination.[571] However, as a matter of "minimum fair trial standards in cases involving multiple defendants," severance may be required to prevent introduction of an out-of-court statement of a co-defendant despite the fact that the co-defendant testifies at the trial.[572]

In the alternative, the court may redact the statement to eliminate reference to the defendant.[573] In such a case, the prosecution has the burden to establish that the statement "can be effectively redacted so that the jury would not interpret its admissions as incriminating the nonconfessing defendant."[574] For the moment, there appears to be a split among the Departments of the Appellate Division regarding redaction. The First Department, relying implicitly on language in *Richardson v. Marsh*,[575] has taken the position that a statement which is no longer "facially inculpatory" of the defendant is adequately redacted.[576] Under this theory, it is acceptable to allow into evidence an out-of-court statement of a non-testifying co-defendant that, combined with other evidence in the case, inferentially implicates the defendant but does not name him or her directly. This is so, *not* because the statement is admitted as evidence against the defendant—in fact it is inadmissible as to him or her. However, it is presumed that a jury will follow an instruction, which must be given, not to use the statement as evidence of the defendant's guilt.[577]

On the other hand, the Second Department, also citing language from *Richardson*, has concluded that substituting a neutral pronoun or a symbol for the name of a defendant in a co-defendant's statement is ineffective redaction if the statement "inferentially incriminated" the defendant by other evidence in the case or by the statement itself.[578] It

---

570. People v. Wheeler, 62 N.Y.2d 867, 478 N.Y.S.2d 254, 466 N.E.2d 846 (1984).

571. Nelson v. O'Neil, 402 U.S. 622, 91 S.Ct. 1723, 29 L.Ed.2d 222 (1971); People v. Jackson, 178 A.D.2d 438, 577 N.Y.S.2d 299 (2d Dep't 1991); People v. Velasquez, 147 A.D.2d 726, 538 N.Y.S.2d 949 (2d Dep't 1989).

572. People v. Payne, 35 N.Y.2d at 27, 358 N.Y.S.2d at 705.

573. Richardson v. Marsh, 481 U.S. 200, 209, 107 S.Ct. 1702, 1708, 95 L.Ed.2d 176 (1987).

574. People v. Wheeler, 62 N.Y.2d 867, 869, 478 N.Y.S.2d 254, 255, 466 N.E.2d 846, 847 (1984)(where pronoun "we" was substituted for names, but where two brothers were being tried for the crime together, the confession could only be read by the jury as inculpating defendant); accord People v. Charles, 78 N.Y.2d 1044, 576 N.Y.S.2d 81, 581 N.E.2d 1336 (1991).

575. 481 U.S. at 207, 107 S.Ct. at 1707.

576. People v. Arroyo, 209 A.D.2d 328, 618 N.Y.S.2d 783 (1st Dep't 1994); People v. Davis, 199 A.D.2d 61, 605 N.Y.S.2d 244 (1st Dep't 1993), cert. denied ___ U.S. ___, 115 S.Ct. 178, 130 L.Ed.2d 113 (1994).

577. 481 U.S. at 208 n. 3, 107 S.Ct. at 1707 n. 3. But see 481 U.S. at 213 n. 1, 107 S.Ct. at 1710 n. 1 (Stevens, J., dissenting)("Judge Hand addressed the subject several times. The limiting instruction, he said, is a 'recommendation to the jury of a mental gymnastic which is beyond, not only their powers, but anybody's else'.")(citing Nash v. United States, 54 F.2d 1006, 1007 (2d Cir.1932)).

578. People v. Ruiz, 207 A.D.2d 917, 616 N.Y.S.2d 658 (2d Dep't 1994); People v.

§ 5.22   GRAND JURY & INDICTMENT   Ch. 5

is uncertain how the Court of Appeals will resolve the issue, but prior to *Richardson*, in *People v. Wheeler*,[579] the court had ruled that inferentially incriminating statements were not cured by an instruction to the jury to disregard.[580] Since then, *Wheeler* has been cited with approval by the Court of Appeals for the same general proposition.[581]

On occasion, redaction may have the effect of denying the declarant an opportunity to put exculpatory information before the jury. In a joint trial, if defendant X has confessed to some participation in the offense but, in his statement sought to exculpate himself by shifting blame to the co-defendant, redaction of references to the co-defendant will have the effect of denying the defendant an opportunity to present his defense through introduction of his unredacted statement. In such a case, severance may become necessary.[582]

Another exception, created in the wake of *Bruton*, was the rule that if each defendant had confessed and their confessions matched or "interlocked," then admission with a caution was sufficient.[583] The Supreme Court rejected this "exception" in *Cruz v. New York*.[584] The doctrine survives to some extent, however, because shortly after the *Cruz* case was remanded to it the Court of Appeals decided that a *Bruton* violation could be harmless error if the defendant had also confessed.[585] As a result, the interlocking confession exception enjoyed an immediate and remarkable resurgence as numerous *Bruton* violations have been forgiven.[586]

No confrontation clause violation arises if the declarant, in this case the co-defendant, takes the witness stand and is available for cross-examination.[587] This is true even if the co-defendant's statement was

Khan, 200 A.D.2d 129, 613 N.Y.S.2d 198 (2d Dep't 1994); People v. Hussain, 165 A.D.2d 538, 568 N.Y.S.2d 966 (2d Dep't 1991).

579. 62 N.Y.2d 867, 478 N.Y.S.2d 254, 466 N.E.2d 846 (1984).

580. Redaction is ineffective if, after redaction, the confession "could only be read by the jury as inculpating [the] defendant." People v. Wheeler, 62 N.Y.2d at 869, 478 N.Y.S.2d at 255.

581. People v. Charles, 78 N.Y.2d 1044, 1046, 576 N.Y.S.2d 81, 83, 581 N.E.2d 1336, 1338 (1991).

582. People v. Mahboubian, 74 N.Y.2d 174, 544 N.Y.S.2d 769, 543 N.E.2d 34 (1989); People v. La Belle, 18 N.Y.2d 405, 276 N.Y.S.2d 105, 222 N.E.2d 727 (1966).

583. See, e.g., People v. Cruz, 66 N.Y.2d 61, 495 N.Y.S.2d 14, 485 N.E.2d 221 (1985); People v. Safian, 46 N.Y.2d 181, 413 N.Y.S.2d 118, 385 N.E.2d 1046 (1978); see also Parker v. Randolph, 442 U.S. 62, 99 S.Ct. 2132, 60 L.Ed.2d 713 (1979)(plurality opinion).

584. 481 U.S. 186, 107 S.Ct. 1714, 95 L.Ed.2d 162 (1987).

585. People v. Hamlin, 71 N.Y.2d 750, 530 N.Y.S.2d 74, 525 N.E.2d 719 (1988).

586. For just a tip of the iceberg, see People v. Faust, 73 N.Y.2d 828, 829, 537 N.Y.S.2d 118, 118, 534 N.E.2d 35, 35 (1988), reargument denied 73 N.Y.2d 995, 540 N.Y.S.2d 1006, 538 N.E.2d 358 (1989); People v. West, 72 N.Y.2d 941, 533 N.Y.S.2d 50, 529 N.E.2d 418 (1988); People v. Shelton, 209 A.D.2d 963, 619 N.Y.S.2d 436 (4th Dep't 1994); People v. Saddler, 166 A.D.2d 878, 879, 560 N.Y.S.2d 539, 540 (4th Dep't 1990), cert. denied 500 U.S. 955, 111 S.Ct. 2265, 114 L.Ed.2d 717 (1991); People v. Thompson, 161 A.D.2d 1203, 555 N.Y.S.2d 993 (4th Dep't 1990).

587. Nelson v. O'Neil, 402 U.S. 622, 91 S.Ct. 1723, 29 L.Ed.2d 222 (1971); People v. Griffin, 48 N.Y.2d 998, 425 N.Y.S.2d 547, 401 N.E.2d 905 (1980); People v. Payne, 35 N.Y.2d 22, 358 N.Y.S.2d 701, 315 N.E.2d 762 (1974).

introduced into evidence during the prosecution's direct case, prior to the co-defendant's testimony.[588]

Similarly, the confrontation clause and the rule against hearsay are not co-extensive. Hearsay exceptions that are "firmly rooted" provide sufficient indicia of reliability to justify reception into evidence without offending the Sixth Amendment.[589] Therefore, no *Bruton* violation arises when a co-defendant's statement is introduced, not as an admission of the co-defendant, but rather as evidence of the defendant's guilt by way of a reliable and accepted hearsay exception. For example, a co-defendant's statement may be admissible, without offending *Bruton*, if the statement qualifies as a declaration against penal interest[590] or a co-conspirator's statement in furtherance of the conspiracy,[591] or it may be admissible to impeach the defendant.[592]

On rare occasions, *Bruton* problems can be avoided by use of multiple juries. In *People v. Ricardo B.*,[593] a case where there were compelling reasons not to sever and where redaction was ineffective, the court empaneled a separate jury for each defendant. In that case, a "detailed procedure" was adopted as follows:

> The trial proceeded with the juries hearing evidence common to the charges against both defendants but with one jury excused from the courtroom during presentation of evidence which was admissible only before the other. Each defendant was given the option of withdrawing his jury during presentation of the other's defense.... Separate openings and summations were employed and, without objection, one charge was given to both juries omitting mention of defendant's statement. The juries were kept separated throughout the trial, they deliberated separately and neither was permitted to report a verdict until both

---

588. Nelson v. O'Neil, supra. If the statement is admitted against the codefendant as an admission, the rationale for allowing portions that accuse the defendant but are not necessarily part of the co-defendant's admission is unclear. One can easily envision a situation in which a co-defendant takes the stand to downplay his own role while shifting blame to the defendant. Could the co-defendant's mere availability for cross-examination justify use of his prior statement, further inculpating the defendant, by the prosecution?

589. White v. Illinois, 502 U.S. 346, 112 S.Ct. 736, 116 L.Ed.2d 848 (1992); Ohio v. Roberts, 448 U.S. 56, 63, 100 S.Ct. 2531, 2537, 65 L.Ed.2d 597 (1980).

590. People v. Brensic, 70 N.Y.2d 9, 517 N.Y.S.2d 120, 509 N.E.2d 1226 (1987)(recognizing the exception, but reversing a conviction where the co-defendant's statement did not properly qualify as a declaration against penal interest).

591. Bourjaily v. United States, 483 U.S. 171, 107 S.Ct. 2775, 97 L.Ed.2d 144 (1987); People v. Sanders, 56 N.Y.2d 51, 451 N.Y.S.2d 30, 436 N.E.2d 480 (1982).

592. In People v. Reid, 192 A.D.2d 1117, 596 N.Y.S.2d 282 (4th Dep't 1993), the court ruled that no Bruton violation occurred when a co-defendant's confession was used to impeach the co-defendant. This is understandable, assuming the co-defendant was available for cross-examination.

593. 73 N.Y.2d 228, 235, 538 N.Y.S.2d 796, 799, 535 N.E.2d 1336, 1339 (1989)("It should be clear, however, that multiple juries are the exception, not the rule.... Multiple juries are to be used sparingly and then only after a full consideration of the impact the procedure will have on the defendants' due process rights and after thorough precautions have been taken to protect those rights.").

had concluded deliberations.[594]

The procedures outlined by the Court of Appeals are recommended, but a failure to follow each procedure outlined does not, in and of itself, require reversal.[595]

A more common solution for *Bruton* problems, assuming waiver, is a joint bench and jury trial.[596] The judge and jury hear all the same evidence except for the admission of the co-defendant.[597]

Mutually Antagonistic Defenses. In *People v. Mahboubian*,[598] the Court of Appeals adopted a test requiring severance

> where the core of each defense is in irreconcilable conflict with the other and where there is a significant danger, as both defenses are portrayed to the trial court, that the conflict alone would lead the jury to infer defendant's guilt.[599]

In *Mahboubian*, two defendants were charged with arranging a burglary, attempting to steal a collection of artifacts from a storage vault as part of a conspiracy to defraud the insurer. One defendant, the owner of the collection, claimed that he knew nothing of the co-defendant's attempt to steal the items from the vault. The co-defendant, on the other hand, claimed that he was duped by the defendant into believing that the burglary was a publicity stunt. Neither defendant testified at trial. The court held that it was reversible error to have denied the motion to sever. It found that the defenses "were not only antagonistic but also mutually exclusive and irreconcilable."[600] This was because the jury could not have credited both defenses: to believe one, it necessarily had to disbelieve the other.[601] In this case "there was a significant possibility

---

594. 73 N.Y.2d at 232, 538 N.Y.S.2d at 797.

595. People v. Irizarry, 83 N.Y.2d 557, 611 N.Y.S.2d 807, 634 N.E.2d 179 (1994)(failure to seal first jury's verdict not prejudicial where no showing that second jury, which had been sequestered, was aware of the verdict).

596. See, e.g., People v. Cheswick, 166 A.D.2d 88, 570 N.Y.S.2d 318 (2d Dep't 1991), aff'd 78 N.Y.2d 1119, 578 N.Y.S.2d 873, 586 N.E.2d 56 (1991); People v. Lydon, 197 A.D.2d 640, 603 N.Y.S.2d 771 (2d Dep't 1993); People v. Amato, 173 A.D.2d 717, 570 N.Y.S.2d 1017 (2d Dep't 1991), cert. den. sub nom. Amato v. New York, 502 U.S. 1058, 112 S.Ct. 935, 117 L.Ed.2d 107 (1992); People v. Wallace, 153 A.D.2d 59, 549 N.Y.S.2d 515 (2d Dep't 1989).

597. In such cases, while the jury is deliberating, the judge should consider signing a verdict sheet, sealing it, and then handing it to the clerk in open court in an envelope. After the jury announces its verdict and is excused, the judge's verdict may be unsealed and announced as well. This procedure insulates each factfinder from the other's decision.

598. 74 N.Y.2d 174, 544 N.Y.S.2d 769, 543 N.E.2d 34 (1989).

599. 74 N.Y.2d at 184, 544 N.Y.S.2d at 774.

600. 74 N.Y.2d at 185, 544 N.Y.S.2d at 774.

601. At the time Mahboubian was decided, there was a conflict among the federal circuit courts on this issue. In United States v. Romanello, 726 F.2d 173 (5th Cir. 1984), the court held that Fed. Rule Crim. Proc. 14 requires severance when the two defenses are logically inconsistent: "The essence or core of the defenses must be in conflict, such that the jury, in order to believe the core of one defense, must necessarily disbelieve the core of the other." 726 F.2d at 177. However, in Rhone v. United States, 365 F.2d 980 (D.C.Cir.1966), the court held that there must exist "a danger that the jury will unjustifiably infer defendants' guilt simply from the conflicting and irreconcilable defenses; formal inconsistency in defenses would not necessarily compel severance." 365 F.2d at 981.

Mahboubian explicitly adopted "a standard that combines elements of both tests,

that the jury unjustifiably concluded by virtue of the conflict itself that both defenses were incredible and gave undue weight to the government's evidence."[602]

The *Mahboubian* Court emphasized that "some degree of prejudice is of course inherent in every joint trial ... [b]ut that alone does not outweigh the factors favoring joinder of defendants."[603] However, in this case there was "unfair prejudice to the moving party ... [which] substantially impair[ed] his defense."[604]

In sum, *Mahboubian* establishes a two-part test: irreconcilable conflict and prejudice. The second prong may be met in a variety of ways. For example, when defendants have defenses that are truly antagonistic, it follows naturally that they will attack each other's presentation at trial. A defendant may be prejudiced when one counsel takes an "aggressive adversarial stance against ... [a codefendant], in effect becoming a second prosecutor."[605] In such a situation, the harm flows not solely from the fact that counsel take competing positions. Rather, the potential for prejudice may be exacerbated by the fact that the "second prosecutor" frequently ventures into territories that would not, or could not, be explored by the prosecutor. The Supreme Court has highlighted the problem as follows:

> Defendants who accuse each other bring the effect of a second prosecutor into the case with respect to their codefendant. In order to zealously represent his client, each codefendant's counsel must do everything possible to convict the other defendant. The existence of this extra prosecutor is particularly troublesome because the defense counsel are not always held to the limitations and standards imposed on the government prosecutor.[606]

concluding that severance is compelled where the core of each defense is in irreconcilable conflict with the other and where there is a significant danger, as both defenses are portrayed to the trial court, that the conflict alone would lead the jury to infer defendant's guilt." 74 N.Y.2d at 184, 544 N.Y.S.2d at 774.

After Mahboubian was decided, the conflict in the federal courts was resolved by Zafiro v. United States, 506 U.S. 534, 113 S.Ct. 933, 122 L.Ed.2d 317 (1993), which held that mutually antagonistic defenses are not prejudicial per se. Instead, "a district court should grant a severance under Rule 14 only if there is a serious risk that a joint trial would compromise a specific trial right of one of the defendants, or prevent the jury from making a reliable judgment about guilt or innocence." 506 U.S. at 539, 113 S.Ct. at 938.

602. 74 N.Y.2d at 186, 544 N.Y.S.2d at 775. See also People v. Forbes, 203 A.D.2d 609, 609 N.Y.S.2d 961 (3d Dep't 1994).

603. 74 N.Y.2d at 183–84, 544 N.Y.S.2d at 773.

604. 74 N.Y.2d at 184, 544 N.Y.S.2d at 773 (quoting People v. Cruz, 66 N.Y.2d 61, 73–74, 495 N.Y.S.2d 14, 21–22, 485 N.E.2d 221, 228–29 (1985), rev'd on other grounds 481 U.S. 186, 107 S.Ct. 1714, 95 L.Ed.2d 162 (1987), on remand 70 N.Y.2d 733, 519 N.Y.S.2d 959, 514 N.E.2d 379 (1987)). See, e.g., People v. Reyes, 193 A.D.2d 452, 597 N.Y.S.2d 685 (1st Dep't 1993)(error to fail to sever rape charges where one defendant claimed no involvement while the other claimed he was manipulated by co-defendant who had intimidated the complainant without his knowledge).

605. People v. Cardwell, 78 N.Y.2d 996, 998, 575 N.Y.S.2d 267, 268, 580 N.E.2d 753, 754 (1991).

606. Zafiro v. United States, 506 U.S. at 543 n. 3, 113 S.Ct. at 940 n. 3 (Stevens, J., concurring), quoting United States v. Tootick, 952 F.2d 1078, 1082 (9th Cir.1991).

§ 5.22 GRAND JURY & INDICTMENT Ch. 5

This was exactly the problem, for example, in *People v. Gonzalez*,[607] where reversal resulted when counsel for the co-defendant repeatedly, and wrongly, suggested that the defendant had the burden of proving his innocence.[608] Improper conduct by co-counsel, however, is not a prerequisite to severance. It may be that co-counsel's questions are perfectly permissible, yet the defendant is unduly prejudiced. For example, in *People v. McGee*,[609] the court held that a co-defendant has a right to impeach a defendant with prior convictions, notwithstanding a *Sandoval* ruling prohibiting the prosecutor from asking the defendant about the very same acts. As a consequence, severance may be required to preserve the balance achieved in the *Sandoval* ruling.[610]

Calling a Co–Defendant as a Witness. In an appropriate case, severance may be required because one defendant intends to testify as a witness for a co-defendant.[611] Because a co-defendant cannot be compelled to take the stand, courts are reluctant to accept this as a basis for severance in the absence of a showing that the co-defendant will, in fact, testify on behalf of the defendant. In *People v. Bornholdt*,[612] the Court of Appeals announced the "governing principles" in such a situation:

> [U]pon a proper showing of need for a codefendant's testimony, it may be an abuse of discretion to deny severance. However, a proper showing of need imports that the movant clearly show what the codefendant would testify to and that such testimony would tend to exculpate the movant. Moreover, the court is not required to sever where the possibility of the codefendant's

---

607. 169 A.D.2d 646, 565 N.Y.S.2d 466 (1st Dep't 1991).

608. Gonzalez demonstrates the point well, since the court did not reverse on the basis of antagonistic defenses alone. In fact, that claim was rejected as to his co-defendant. See People v. Castro–Restrepo, 169 A.D.2d 454, 565 N.Y.S.2d 461 (1st Dep't 1991). See also De Luna v. United States, 308 F.2d 140 (5th Cir.1962)(comment by co-counsel on defendant's failure to testify).

609. 68 N.Y.2d 328, 508 N.Y.S.2d 927, 501 N.E.2d 576 (1986).

610. See, e.g., People v. McGee, 68 N.Y.2d at 333, 508 N.Y.S.2d at 930: "In a similar case, the court properly held that it 'could not limit the right of either defense attorney to examine his client's codefendant regarding prior criminal or immoral acts' [citing People v. Rodriguez, 91 A.D.2d 591, 592, 457 N.Y.S.2d 268, 269 (1st Dep't 1982)] and that severance should be granted where a significant possibility exists that each defense will prejudice the other." However, in People v. Williams, 142 A.D.2d 310, 536 N.Y.S.2d 814 (2d Dep't 1988), the court held that a defendant's right to impeach a co-defendant under McGee is not limitless. In the absence of a motion to sever, the court upheld a ruling by the trial court that restricted impeachment to use of prior convictions without allowing the defendant to examine as to the underlying facts on the ground that, under the circumstances of that particular case, there was a substantial risk that the jury would use the prior bad acts improperly to find a criminal propensity by the co-defendant. Thus, in the court's view, it became necessary to "limit ... such a cross-examination in order to achieve a balance between the often competing rights of a defendant and co-defendant to a fair trial when they are tried jointly." Although this ruling appears to be at odds with the clear language in McGee, an explanation may be that the defendants did not move for severance. Thus, in the absence of the best remedy—separate trials—the court was forced to "balance" the "competing rights."

611. See People v. Owens, 22 N.Y.2d 93, 291 N.Y.S.2d 313, 238 N.E.2d 715 (1968).

612. 33 N.Y.2d 75, 350 N.Y.S.2d 369, 305 N.E.2d 461 (1973), cert. den. sub nom. Victory v. New York, 416 U.S. 905, 94 S.Ct. 1609, 40 L.Ed.2d 109 (1974).

testifying is merely colorable or speculative.[613]

The proper procedure for a motion to sever on this basis begins with a timely motion.[614] There should be a showing that the codefendant will, in fact, waive any privilege and testify on the defendant's behalf.[615] A defendant may not, in the middle of trial, call to the witness stand a codefendant who has not indicated that he or she will waive the privilege against self-incrimination.[616]

Finally, on occasion a defendant may assert that his or her codefendant will offer exculpatory testimony if, and only if, after severance the co-defendant's case is tried first. In that event, the order of trials is left to the sound discretion of the court.[617]

Library References:

West's Key No. Digests, Criminal Law ⬅622; Indictment and Information ⬅124.

§ 5.23 Indictment—Securing Defendant's Appearance

After an indictment[618] has been filed, the defendant must appear personally for arraignment.[619] CPL § 210.10 provides three methods of securing that appearance.

If the defendant is in custody because he or she had previously been held by a local criminal court for the action of the grand jury, the court must direct the sheriff to produce him or her, with two days notice to counsel.[620] This is the court's obligation, not the prosecutor's. While the statute does not require the arraignment to be scheduled on any particular day,[621] for speedy trial purposes, the prosecution has the burden of

---

613. 33 N.Y.2d at 87, 350 N.Y.S.2d at 378–79 (citations omitted).

614. See, e.g., People v. Owens, 22 N.Y.2d 93, 98, 291 N.Y.S.2d 313, 317, 238 N.E.2d 715, 718 (1968)("[I]f a defendant knows or should have known in advance of trial of his intention to call a codefendant as a witness or that of a codefendant to call him as a witness the application for appropriate relief must be made in advance of trial, indeed, as early as it is reasonably feasible. If, however, the occasion or need for calling a codefendant as a witness does not arise until during the trial, then upon a proper showing as indicated above the trial court must consider the granting of a mistrial, if requested by one or the other of the codefendants.").

615. People v. Mayo, 201 A.D.2d 412, 607 N.Y.S.2d 654 (1st Dep't 1994).

616. People v. Rosenthal, 207 A.D.2d 364, 616 N.Y.S.2d 199 (2d Dep't 1994). Regarding potential witnesses for the defense who will assert a privilege, see generally People v. Thomas, 51 N.Y.2d 466, 434 N.Y.S.2d 941, 415 N.E.2d 931 (1980); see also Tague, "The Fifth Amendment: If an Aid to the Guilty Defendant, an Impediment to the Innocent One," 78 Geo. L.J. 1 (1989).

617. See, e.g., Matter of Santucci v. Di Tucci, 124 A.D.2d 850, 514 N.Y.S.2d 640 (2d Dep't 1986)(denying a writ of prohibition against an order); People v. Garnes, 134 Misc.2d 39, 510 N.Y.S.2d 409 (Sup.Ct., Queens County, 1986)(directing severance and trial upon co-defendant's case first in order to allow defendant to call co-defendant as witness at later trial).

618. Unless expressly provided otherwise, references herein to an "indictment" include a "superior court information." See CPL § 200.15.

619. CPL § 210.10.

620. Notice is provided to counsel, if any, who filed a notice of appearance in superior court, or in the absence of such notice, to counsel, if any, who filed a notice of appearance in local criminal court. Id.

621. See, e.g., People v. London, 164 Misc.2d 575, 579, 624 N.Y.S.2d 786, 789 (Sup.Ct., N.Y. County, 1995)("[T]he Clerk, without direction from the court, was in no position to require mutual consent by the

producing an incarcerated defendant who is in its custody.[622] Since the prosecution may not announce readiness until the defendant is arraigned, it has an incentive to arrange for a prompt arraignment.[623]

If the defendant is at liberty, the court must set a date for his appearance, giving at least two days notice to the defendant, his surety or any other person who posted cash bail, and his attorney.[624] If the defendant fails to appear, the court may issue a bench warrant, directing the executing police officer to bring the defendant to the court "without unnecessary delay."[625]

In some cases the filing of the indictment constitutes the commencement of the action, *i.e.*, the defendant has not previously been arrested or held in local criminal court.[626] In that event, the indictment must remain sealed until the defendant is produced or appears for arraignment.[627]

When there has been no arrest in the case and an indictment is filed, the defendant's appearance is accomplished by one of three meth-

parties as a prerequisite to scheduling a court date.").

622. People v. Jones, 66 N.Y.2d 529, 539–40, 498 N.Y.S.2d 119, 125–27, 488 N.E.2d 1231 (1985). See also People v. Middlemiss, 198 A.D.2d 755, 756, 604 N.Y.S.2d 308, 309 (3d Dep't 1993)(in measuring readiness, "[t]he People had the obligation of arranging for defendant's arraignment").

623. People v. England, 84 N.Y.2d 1, 613 N.Y.S.2d 854, 636 N.E.2d 1387 (1994). Cf. CPL § 190.80, which requires the release from custody of a defendant where there has been no grand jury action for more than 45 days after the defendant was held by a local criminal court. "Grand jury action" in that context has been interpreted to be a mere vote of the grand jury, not filing of the indictment or arraignment. People ex rel. Aponte [Gorfinkel] v. Warden, 146 Misc.2d 386, 550 N.Y.S.2d 792 (Sup.Ct., Kings County, 1990). See also People v. Jones, 56 Misc.2d 884, 290 N.Y.S.2d 771 (Sup.Ct., Queens County, 1968)(analyzing a comparable provision in the Code of Criminal Procedure and finding that, in the absence of prejudice to the defendant's case, a 13-day delay between filing and arraignment was not unreasonable).

624. Again, the statute does not specify when the arraignment should be scheduled. In one unusual case, the Supreme Court found a denial of due process, despite the absence of a finding of specific prejudice, where the government negligently failed to arrest the defendant until eight and one-half years after his indictment had been filed. Doggett v. United States, 505 U.S. 647, 112 S.Ct. 2686, 120 L.Ed.2d 520 (1992). Cf. People v. Zelkowitz, 84 Misc.2d 746, 375 N.Y.S.2d 1005 (Sup.Ct., N.Y.County, 1975)(permissible for prosecution to delay grand jury action for 18 months and to delay filing indictment for an additional two months while related investigations were still underway); People v. Ebbecke, 99 Misc.2d 1, 414 N.Y.S.2d 977 (Sup.Ct., N.Y.County, 1979)(seven-month delay between grand jury vote and filing of indictment justifiable where matters remained under investigation, rejecting the argument that, instead, the indictment should have been filed promptly then sealed).

625. "Unnecessary delay" is not defined. However, in a comparable situation—arrest without a warrant—the phrase was interpreted to require arraignment within 24 hours of arrest. People ex rel. Maxian v. Brown, 77 N.Y.2d 422, 568 N.Y.S.2d 575, 570 N.E.2d 223 (1991).

626. In the vernacular, this is called an "N/A" indictment, indicating that it was filed without an arrest.

627. CPL § 210.10(3). Cf. P.L. § 215.75 (unlawful disclosure of an indictment), which makes it a Class B misdemeanor for a public servant to disclose the fact that an indictment has been found or filed before the accused person is in custody. On occasion, law enforcement officials will make a public announcement concerning an arrest before the arraignment has occurred. This does not violate the Penal Law provision because the accused is in custody. Nonetheless, the indictment remains sealed until the arraignment itself. See generally Greenberg, Marcus et al., New York Criminal Law § 27.27 (West 1996).

ods: (a) a warrant of arrest is issued by the court; (b) a summons is issued upon application of the prosecutor; or (c) the court may direct that the defendant be informed of the date set for arraignment.

Until 1993, the only method for securing the appearance of a defendant who was charged with a felony in a sealed indictment was by arrest warrant. As a consequence, there was no alternative to a demeaning arrest process, including on occasion forcible seizure, incarceration pending arraignment and even public display in custody for the benefit of the media. Often, this was unnecessary since the defendant had been aware of, or even cooperating with, the grand jury investigation. Mostly in response to a case involving the Minority Leader of the State Senate, Manfred Ohrenstein, alternative means of surrender have been enacted.[628]

CPL § 210.10(3) now permits the court, upon application of the prosecutor, to issue a summons or authorize the district attorney to direct that the defendant appear for arraignment on a designated date.[629] The provisions regarding issuance of a summons are contained in CPL Article 130. Section 130.60 requires the court to order fingerprinting of the defendant upon the arraignment. However, as a practical matter, since the results of the fingerprinting process are necessary at the arraignment,[630] it makes little sense to bifurcate the process. Therefore, it is suggested that the defendant and prosecutor make arrangements for the fingerprinting to be done prior to the date set for arraignment.[631]

Library References:
West's Key No. Digests, Criminal Law ⚖︎261–264.

§ 5.24 Indictment—Arraignment

CPL § 210.15 outlines the requirements of an arraignment in supe-

---

628. Mr. Ohrenstein was publicly photographed as he was brought in custody to court with a trenchcoat thrown over handcuffs which had been placed upon him. The conspiracy charge against him was ultimately dismissed. People v. Ohrenstein, 77 N.Y.2d 38, 563 N.Y.S.2d 744, 565 N.E.2d 493 (1990).

629. In an apparent oversight, the 1993 amendment (L.1993, c.446) requires the consent of the prosecution in all cases where a warrant is not issued. The section previously allowed a court to issue a summons in the case of a misdemeanor without the prosecution's consent. It seems unlikely that the Legislature intended to reduce the authority of a court to avoid the necessity of an arrest warrant in a case where only a misdemeanor is charged while allowing a summons to be issued in the most serious of cases.

630. CPL § 530.40(4) requires, with limited exception, the court to obtain a report of the defendant's prior criminal record from the State Division of Criminal Justice Services (DCJS) or a report of prior arrests by a police department as a prerequisite to releasing the defendant on bail or recognizance.

631. Similarly, arrangements should be made to obtain a report from DCJS when a defendant appears by way of direction of the court without a summons. Again, a report from DCJS, or a police report of prior arrests, is a necessary prerequisite to the setting of bail. However, CPL §§ 130.60 and 160.10 require fingerprinting only when a person is arrested or responding to a summons. On the other hand, when a person appears in response to a direction of the court and prosecutor, pursuant to section 210.10(3), there is no statutory requirement of fingerprinting. It may be that the omission of a fingerprinting requirement by the Legislature was not an oversight, recognizing that a report from DCJS sufficient to satisfy the requirements of CPL § 530.40 may be obtainable on the basis of other available information, e.g., name, date of birth, social security number. Cf. CPL § 160.10(4).

§ 5.24   GRAND JURY & INDICTMENT   Ch. 5

rior court.[632] The provisions parallel those governing arraignment in local criminal court.[633] By statute, the defendant is informed of the charges and provided with a copy of the indictment.[634] At the conclusion of the arraignment, the court issues a securing order as provided in CPL § 530.40.

In the usual course, in superior court, counsel either appears or is assigned at the time of arraignment. In the event that the defendant is without counsel, the court must inform the defendant of his or her right to counsel, as well as ancillary rights spelled out in subdivision two. The right to counsel may be waived, but only where the court is satisfied that the decision was made "with knowledge of the significance thereof."[635] The defendant has a right to an adjournment of the proceeding for the purpose of obtaining counsel.[636]

It is worth noting that the statute requires the court not only to afford the defendant an opportunity to exercise the right to counsel, but must itself "take affirmative action as is necessary to effectuate" such right.[637]

Finally, although it is commonplace for the defendant to enter a plea of guilty or not guilty at the arraignment, it is permissible for the plea to be entered at a later time.[638] A defendant has a right to plead not guilty or guilty.[639] When the defendant refuses to enter a plea or stands mute, the court may enter a plea of not guilty on his or her behalf.[640] A defendant may, with the permission of the court and consent of the prosecution, enter a plea of not responsible by reason of mental disease or defect in the manner prescribed by CPL § 220.15.

632. See also CPL § 1.20(9)(" 'Arraignment' means the occasion upon which a defendant against whom an accusatory instrument has been filed appears before the court in which the criminal action is pending for the purpose of having such court acquire and exercise control over his person with respect to such accusatory instrument and of setting the course of further proceedings in the action.").

633. See Chapter 3, §§ 3.24, 3.30.

634. CPL § 210.15(1).

635. CPL § 210.15(5).

636. CPL § 210.15(2)(a). But see People v. Hughes, 24 A.D.2d 884, 264 N.Y.S.2d 874 (2d Dep't 1965), cert. den. sub nom. Hughes v. New York, 384 U.S. 980, 86 S.Ct. 1881, 16 L.Ed.2d 691 (1966)(in absence of showing of factual prejudice, fact that defendant was arraigned and pleaded not guilty at arraignment upon indictment without counsel, but was later represented by counsel, not a basis for setting aside judgment of conviction).

637. CPL § 210.15(3). See, e.g., Sardino v. State Com'n on Judicial Conduct, 58 N.Y.2d 286, 461 N.Y.S.2d 229, 448 N.E.2d 83 (1983)(judge removed from office where he acknowledged consistent failure to advise defendants of their right to counsel at arraignments because he considered it to be "counter-productive"); see also Matter of LaBelle, 79 N.Y.2d 350, 582 N.Y.S.2d 970, 591 N.E.2d 1156 (1992)(judge disciplined for failing to set bail in a number of cases where bail was required; court rejected his argument that the right was contingent upon a request, holding that it was the court's duty to act affirmatively in that regard even in the absence of a request for bail).

638. CPL § 210.50. See, e.g., People v. Updike, 125 A.D.2d 735, 509 N.Y.S.2d 158 (3d Dep't 1986)(court not denied jurisdiction over defendant where plea not entered until time of trial).

639. CPL § 220.10(1) and (2). However, a defendant may not plead guilty to the crime of murder in the first degree. CPL § 220.10(5)(e).

640. See, e.g., People v. Rogers, 27 N.Y.2d 749, 314 N.Y.S.2d 1000, 263 N.E.2d 396 (1970).

Library References:

West's Key No. Digests, Criminal Law ⟐261–264.

§ 5.25 Indictment—Motion to Dismiss—In General

CPL § 210.20 lists the available grounds upon which a defendant may move to dismiss an indictment or a count thereof. Grounds for dismissal are statutory; a court does not have an inherent authority to dismiss an indictment absent legislative authorization.[641] On the other hand, CPL § 210.40 (dismissal in furtherance of justice) accords courts some flexibility in that regard.[642]

Although section 210.20 lists the most common grounds for dismissal, it is not an exclusive list, as other statutory provisions may authorize dismissal as well.[643]

Library References:

West's Key No. Digests, Indictment and Information ⟐144–144.2.

§ 5.26 Indictment—Motion to Dismiss—Procedure

Before discussing the grounds for dismissal, a brief review of the procedures to be followed in making a motion to dismiss is in order.

Timing. CPL §§ 255.10 and 255.20 require that a motion to dismiss be made as part of the omnibus motion papers that must be served or filed within 45 days of arraignment.[644] However, there are two notable exceptions to this rule.

A motion to dismiss, pursuant to CPL § 210.35(4), on the ground that the defendant was not accorded an opportunity to appear and testify before the grand jury in accordance with the provisions of CPL § 190.50, must be made within five days of arraignment.[645]

---

641. Holtzman v. Goldman, 71 N.Y.2d 564, 528 N.Y.S.2d 21, 523 N.E.2d 297 (1988)(trial court could not dismiss case where prosecution not ready to proceed on trial date but speedy trial time had not elapsed); see also People v. Douglass, 60 N.Y.2d 194, 200, 469 N.Y.S.2d 56, 59, 456 N.E.2d 1179 (1983)(trial court could not dismiss cases for "calendar control" absent legislative authorization); but see Matter of Hynes v. George, 76 N.Y.2d 500, 561 N.Y.S.2d 538, 562 N.E.2d 863 (1990)(trial court has authority to order prosecution to trial notwithstanding prosecution's assertion that it does not have sufficient evidence to proceed).

642. See, e.g., People v. Singleton, 42 N.Y.2d 466, 398 N.Y.S.2d 871, 368 N.E.2d 1237 (1977)(dismissing an indictment "in the interest of justice" under the predecessor statutory provision upon the prosecution's failure to produce an informant for examination upon defense motion).

643. See, e.g., People v. Szychulda, 57 N.Y.2d 719, 454 N.Y.S.2d 705, 440 N.E.2d 790 (1982)(cited with approval in People v. Douglas, supra, for the proposition that a failure to comply with a discovery order authorizes dismissal under CPL § 240.70(1)).

644. Oddly enough, section 255.20(1) literally commands that motions are to be "served or filed" within 45 days of arraignment. Practically speaking, both should be done, since section 210.45(1) requires a motion to be made upon reasonable notice to the prosecution.

645. CPL § 190.50(5)(c)("If the contention is not so asserted in timely fashion, it is waived and the indictment or prosecutor's information may not thereafter be challenged on such ground.").

§ 5.26   GRAND JURY & INDICTMENT   Ch. 5

Second, for obvious reasons, a motion to dismiss on the ground that the defendant has been denied a speedy trial[646] cannot be brought, in the case of a felony, until at least six months have elapsed, but must be brought prior to commencement of trial or entry of a plea of guilty.[647]

As for other motions, the 45-day requirement is not absolute. CPL § 255.20(1) allows for three exceptions to the 45-day rule:

(1) the court may allow additional time upon application of the defendant made prior to entry of judgment.[648] However, the court may not shorten the period and must allow the defendant, if he or she insists, the full 45 days to file.[649]

(2) the court "*must* entertain and decide on its merits, at anytime before the end of the trial, any appropriate pre-trial motion based upon grounds of which the defendant could not, with due diligence, have been previously aware, or which for other good cause, could not reasonably have been raised ... [earlier]."[650] This exception applies to motions that had been made in a timely fashion, but were denied. When the defendant comes upon new information, the court must consider grounds for the motion that were not available to the defendant at the first application.[651]

(3) a court, "in the interest of justice, and for good cause shown, may, in its discretion, at any time before sentence, entertain and dispose of ... [any other pre-trial motion] on the merits."[652] This exception addresses the situation where the defendant had not made the motion previously.[653]

However, a word of caution is in order with regard to late motions under any of the three exceptions. Although the statutory scheme on its face appears fairly forgiving, the Court of Appeals, in *People v. Lawrence*[654] remarked upon the "strong public policy to further orderly trial

---

646. CPL §§ 210.20(1)(g).

647. CPL § 210.20(2); see People v. Lawrence, 64 N.Y.2d 200, 485 N.Y.S.2d 233, 474 N.E.2d 593 (1984)(speedy trial motion heard and decided after trial was untimely).

648. CPL § 255.20(1).

649. Matter of Veloz v. Rothwax, 65 N.Y.2d 902, 493 N.Y.S.2d 452, 483 N.E.2d 127 (1985).

650. CPL § 255.20(3)(emphasis supplied).

651. For example, a motion to dismiss a grand jury presentation as defective may be based upon grounds discovered at trial when the minutes are, in the ordinary course, shown to the defendant for the first time. The situation is comparable to one where a motion to suppress evidence is denied summarily for want of specificity in the allegations. See People v. Mendoza, 82 N.Y.2d 415, 422, 604 N.Y.S.2d 922, 924, 624 N.E.2d 1017 (1993); People v. Vasquez, 200 A.D.2d 344, 347, 613 N.Y.S.2d 595, 597 (1st Dep't 1994)("sufficiency of pleading is measured by the extent to which the defendant has been afforded access to such information as would enable him to set forth an optimally detailed factual predicate for suppression").

652. CPL § 255.20(3).

653. See People v. Taylor, 181 A.D.2d 408, 580 N.Y.S.2d 337 (1st Dep't 1992)(permissible for trial court to entertain motion, made for the first time after jury selection when minutes were disclosed to counsel, to dismiss indictment for defective grand jury presentation, despite earlier denial of insufficiency motion by calendar judge).

654. 64 N.Y.2d 200, 207, 485 N.Y.S.2d 233, 237, 474 N.E.2d 593 (1984)(defendant not permitted to pursue speedy trial claim after trial, where the prosecution did not object, despite the fact that he had raised the issue orally before trial, in a timely fashion, and had been directed by the court to wait until after trial to litigate the issue).

procedures and preserve scarce trial resources" as a reason to enforce the 45–day rule.[655] "Neither the court nor the parties may restructure the statute to adopt a procedure that is more convenient for them at the moment by waiving its clear provisions."[656] After *Lawrence*, given the clear preference expressed by the court for adherence to the time limits in the statute,[657] it would seem wise for counsel to alert the court and the prosecution at the earliest opportunity—*i.e.*, in the omnibus motion—of any anticipated motion to dismiss.[658] While it is not uncommon for omnibus motion papers to contain a "reservation of rights" clause asking for permission to make later motions, even the concurrence of the court and the prosecution may not be sufficient for a late filing.[659]

Motion in Writing and Containing Sworn Allegations. CPL § 210.45 also provides that a motion to dismiss an indictment must be made in writing, containing sworn allegations in support of the motion and made upon reasonable notice to the prosecution.[660] This requirement, unlike the obligation to file within time limits, is one that the Court of Appeals has allowed the parties to waive.[661] The reasoning here is that the rule is designed to protect the prosecution from unfair surprise. However, "[w]here the prosecution deems such protections unnecessary ... there is no sound reason why they should not be permitted to waive the rule's requirements."[662]

Thus, the statutory rule that a motion be in writing and contain sworn allegations may be explicitly waived or even implicitly waived by the prosecution's failure to complain or object in timely fashion.[663] This

---

655. Technically, at issue in Lawrence was the interplay between CPL § 210.20(2) and the 45–rule in CPL § 255.20. The defendant argued that section 210.20(2) was meant to enlarge the time within which a speedy trial motion could be brought, beyond 45 days. The majority, by a close reading of the section, also read it to limit speedy trial motions to the pre-trial phase of proceedings. In dissent, Judge Meyer argued that the majority opinion forged an anomalous result whereby motions other than speedy trial motions may now be heard, for good cause or in the interest of justice, up to the point of sentence, but speedy trial motions are now confined, even upon a showing of good cause, to pre-trial resolution only.

656. 64 N.Y.2d at 207, 485 N.Y.S.2d at 238.

657. See, e.g., People v. Dean, 74 N.Y.2d 643, 542 N.Y.S.2d 512, 540 N.E.2d 707 (1989)(motion made within 90 days untimely).

658. See also CPL § 210.20(3)(a defendant who is in a position adequately to raise more than one ground in support of a motion to dismiss should raise every such ground or risk summary denial of the motion).

659. The result in Lawrence may be explained, in part, by the fact that the court felt bound by the specific language of CPL § 210.20(1)(g), which explicitly limits the time within which a speedy trial motion may be made. In the future, the court may resolve cases not involving speedy trial motions in a different manner, with greater deference to a trial court's discretion as provided in section 250.20. Also, the claim in Lawrence was of a statutory speedy trial violation. The challenge was not to the validity of the proceeding or the jurisdiction of the court. The majority in Lawrence took pains to point out that jurisdictional claims are not waived by the failure to assert them in a timely fashion. 64 N.Y.2d at 205, 485 N.Y.S.2d at 236–37.

660. CPL § 210.45(1).

661. People v. Mezon, 80 N.Y.2d 155, 589 N.Y.S.2d 838, 603 N.E.2d 943 (1992); People v. Jennings, 69 N.Y.2d 103, 512 N.Y.S.2d 652, 504 N.E.2d 1079 (1986).

662. People v. Mezon, 80 N.Y.2d at 160, 589 N.Y.S.2d at 841.

663. People v. Jennings, 69 N.Y.2d at 113–14, 512 N.Y.S.2d at 656 ("Unlike the timing requirements of CPL 210.20(2) and 255.20, the written notice requirement of CPL 210.45(1) is not directly related to 'the

§ 5.26   GRAND JURY & INDICTMENT   Ch. 5

rule applies as well to speedy trial motions, notwithstanding *Lawrence*.[664]

Sufficiency of Motion Papers. After both parties have filed their papers and documentary evidence in support, the court must decide whether the motion is "determinable" without a hearing or if a hearing is necessary to resolve a factual issue.[665] A hearing is not necessary when the only issues in dispute are questions of law rather than questions of fact. Nor is a hearing required when the allegations are founded upon speculation or mere surmise.[666] On the other hand, the court must conduct a hearing when a ground constituting a legal basis for dismissal is asserted and all essential facts necessary to support the motion are alleged, but one or more such essential facts are in dispute.[667] Either side runs the risk of a summary grant or denial of the motion where the papers do not raise a legitimate dispute of an essential fact.[668] A motion may not be granted or denied without a hearing where the sworn allegations or papers raise a question of fact, regardless of the relative strength of the assertions.[669]

When a hearing is ordered, the defendant has the burden of proving by a preponderance of evidence every fact essential to support the

strong public policy to further orderly trial procedures and preserve scarce trial resources'.")(citations omitted). See also People v. Singleton, 42 N.Y.2d 466, 398 N.Y.S.2d 871, 368 N.E.2d 1237 (1977)(dismissal in interest of justice, mid-trial on oral application when prosecutor refused to produce informant for in camera inquiry, permissible where prosecutor did not object on that basis).

664. People v. Cook, 193 A.D.2d 366, 596 N.Y.S.2d 822 (1st Dep't 1993)(sua sponte speedy trial dismissal by calendar judge permitted in face of silence of prosecutor who did not object; prosecution may not object to lack of written notice for the first time on appeal). Cf. People v. Littles, 188 A.D.2d 255, 591 N.Y.S.2d 2 (1st Dep't 1992)(summary grant of motion reversed where prosecutor given insufficient opportunity to be apprised of, or contest, the issues being raised); accord People v. Hansel, 208 A.D.2d 1112, 617 N.Y.S.2d 542 (3d Dep't 1994).

665. CPL § 210.45(3).

666. People v. Rodriguez, 79 A.D.2d 539, 433 N.Y.S.2d 584 (1st Dep't 1980), aff'd 55 N.Y.2d 776, 447 N.Y.S.2d 246, 431 N.E.2d 972 (1981)(denying a hearing on a claim of selective prosecution for want of specific allegations in support of the claim).

667. CPL § 210.45(4) and (5).

668. A literal reading of CPL § 210.45(4)(c) would appear to require a hearing even in a case where the prosecution fails to put a material fact in dispute as long as it does not concede the defendant's factual allegations. However, in People v. Gruden, 42 N.Y.2d 214, 397 N.Y.S.2d 704, 366 N.E.2d 794 (1977), the court rejected this interpretation, holding that a defense motion may be summarily granted, even in the absence of an express concession by the prosecution, where the prosecution fails to submit allegations which put a material fact in dispute. See also People v. Cole, 73 N.Y.2d 957, 540 N.Y.S.2d 984, 538 N.E.2d 336 (1989)(speedy trial motion should have been summarily granted where defendant claimed readiness declaration was illusory because prosecution could not produce complainant, and where prosecution failed to submit papers containing factual allegations contesting that assertion). Cf. People v. Min Chi Ma, 161 Misc.2d 542, 615 N.Y.S.2d 222 (Sup.Ct., Queens County, 1994)(summarily granting motion to suppress where the prosecution failed to make specific factual allegations countering the defendant's claim of an illegal stop by the police).

669. See People v. Gruden, 42 N.Y.2d at 216, 397 N.Y.S.2d at 705 ("It should be noted that this statutory procedure is not peculiar to motions to dismiss. The same standard applies in those sections dealing with motions to suppress (CPL § 710.60, subd. 2, par. (b)), motions to set aside a verdict (CPL § 330.40, subd. 2, par.(d)) and motions to vacate a judgment or set aside a sentence (CPL § 440.30, subd. 3, par.(c)). In short it is the standard procedure to be followed in connection with nearly every pretrial and posttrial motion made in a criminal action.").

motion.[670] The burden of persuasion should not be confused with burdens of production or coming forward[671] or with a burden on a mixed question of fact and law.[672]

Library References:

West's Key No. Digests, Indictment and Information ⟜144, 144.2.

§ 5.27 Indictment—Motion to Dismiss or Reduce Indictment—Grounds

The nine grounds for dismissal of an indictment are listed in CPL § 210.20(1). They include dismissal on the ground that the defendant has immunity with respect to the offense charged,[673] that the prosecution is barred by reason of previous prosecution,[674] and that the prosecution is untimely or the defendant has been denied the right to a speedy trial.[675] These issues are discussed elsewhere in this book and the discussion is not repeated here. However, section 210.20 also authorizes dismissal on the ground that the indictment is defective,[676] that the evidence before the grand jury was legally insufficient,[677] that the grand jury proceeding was defective,[678] that a jurisdictional or legal impediment to conviction exists,[679] and that dismissal is required in the interest of justice.[680] A brief discussion of these grounds as a basis for dismissal follows.

Motion to Dismiss Defective Indictment. Section 210.25 provides a basis for dismissal when an indictment is defective. This occurs when the indictment does not substantially conform to the requirements of Article 200, the allegations demonstrate that the court does not have jurisdiction of the offense charged or the statute defining the offense charged is unconstitutional or otherwise invalid. This includes challenges based on facial sufficiency or validity of the indictment—*e.g.*, multiplicity, duplicity, insufficiency of the pleadings, and misjoinder of offenses or defendants.

As a general matter, all challenges to the form of the indictment made under this sections should be included in the omnibus motion. A failure to raise the issue at that stage is likely to be viewed as a waiver. The Second Department in particular has a history of rigorous applica-

670. CPL § 210.45(7).

671. See, e.g., People v. Drummond, 215 A.D.2d 579, 627 N.Y.S.2d 55, 57 (2d Dep't 1995)("A defendant satisfies his initial burden under CPL § 30.30 'by alleging only that the prosecution failed to declare readiness within the statutorily prescribed time period.' The burden then shifts to the People to identify the exclusions on which they intend to rely, commencing from the date on which the defendant was arraigned on the felony complaint.")(citations omitted).

672. See, e.g., People v. Pagnotta, 25 N.Y.2d 333, 305 N.Y.S.2d 484, 253 N.E.2d 202 (1969)(to declare a law unconstitutional, the invalidity of the law must be demonstrated beyond a reasonable doubt); People v. Shore Realty Corp., 127 Misc.2d 419, 486 N.Y.S.2d 124 (Dist.Ct., Nassau County, 1984)(defendant has "heavy burden" of demonstrating selective or discriminatory enforcement of the law).

673. CPL § 210.20(1)(d).
674. CPL § 210.20(1)(e).
675. CPL § 210.20(1)(f) and (g).
676. CPL § 210.20(1)(a).
677. CPL § 210.20(1)(b) and (1–a).
678. CPL § 210.20(1)(c).
679. CPL § 210.20(1)(h).
680. CPL § 210.20(1)(i).

§ 5.27 GRAND JURY & INDICTMENT Ch. 5

tion of the rule.[681] In one unusual case, the Second Department went as far as declaring that a claim "that the indictment was jurisdictionally defective because it charged the defendant with an act that did not constitute a crime" was not preserved for appellate review because it was not raised in the omnibus motion to dismiss,[682] notwithstanding the ordinary rule that jurisdictional issues are not so waived.[683]

Motion to Inspect, Reduce and Dismiss for Insufficiency. CPL §§ 210.20(1-a) and 210.30 should be read in conjunction with each other.[684] Section 210.30 provides for inspection of the minutes by the court for the purpose of determining whether the evidence presented supports the charges. Section 210.20(1-a) authorizes reduction, after inspection, of a count that is not supported by legally sufficient evidence to the most serious lesser included offense supported by the charges.[685] When the evidence neither supports the count charged nor any legal lesser included offense, CPL § 210.20(1)(b) requires dismissal of the count.

Inspection of Minutes. Sufficiency review is a two-step process. At the outset, a motion must be made by the defendant asking the court

---

681. People v. Danylocke, 150 A.D.2d 480, 541 N.Y.S.2d 84 (2d Dep't 1989); People v. Cassidy, 133 A.D.2d 374, 519 N.Y.S.2d 275 (2d Dep't 1987); People v. Byrdsong, 133 A.D.2d 164, 165, 518 N.Y.S.2d 828, 829 (2d Dep't 1987); People v. Smith, 113 A.D.2d 905, 493 N.Y.S.2d 623 (2d Dep't 1985); People v. Di Noia, 105 A.D.2d 799, 481 N.Y.S.2d 738 (2d Dep't 1984), cert. den. 471 U.S. 1022, 105 S.Ct. 2033, 85 L.Ed.2d 315 (1985).

682. People v. Warden, 170 A.D.2d 469, 565 N.Y.S.2d 828 (2d Dep't 1991).

683. See § 5.16, supra. See also People v. Taylor, 65 N.Y.2d 1, 5, 489 N.Y.S.2d 152, 154, 478 N.E.2d 755 (1985).

684. For a discussion of recent amendments regarding review of grand jury minutes for sufficiency, see People v. Santiago, N.Y.L.J., October 10, 1995, p. 27, col. 2 (Sup.Ct., N.Y.County) (citations omitted):

Courts have, on occasion, reminded us of the old claim that a grand jury could indict a "ham sandwich."

However, standing as a bulwark against the harm a wrongful indictment can wreak is the obligation of a reviewing court to weigh the evidence presented to the grand jury for legal sufficiency. Until recently, New York courts were not required to review grand jury evidence. Nor were they empowered to dismiss or reduce the charges in an indictment, even when they were unsupported, if any lesser offense were sustainable. These limits upon the power of a reviewing court had the unfortunate effect of requiring unnecessary trials at great expense and demand upon victims, witnesses, the public and the wrongly accused.

To correct these abuses, and in particular to answer the criticism that a "ham sandwich" could be indicted, the Legislature enacted two significant reforms. In 1980 (L. 1980, chs. 841, 842) it required inspection by a reviewing court, upon request, of all grand jury presentations, unless "good cause" exists to deny the motion. CPL§ 210.30(3). Thereafter, and more importantly, in 1990 (L. 1990, ch. 209) the standard by which sufficiency is measured was changed: Courts for the first time were instructed to dismiss or reduce a count which was not fully supported by evidence in the grand jury. CPL § 210.20(1-a). As a result of these two recent amendments, courts are now required to scrutinize grand jury evidence to ensure that it is sufficient to sustain each and every count.

Since 1990, the New York Court of Appeals has, on several occasions, observed that the standard for review of grand jury sufficiency is now the same as that to be applied by appellate courts in reviewing sufficiency of evidence upon conviction after trial. Thus, the test to be applied by a reviewing trial court is a simple one—"Would the evidence in the grand jury be sufficient to support a conviction after trial?"

685. Reduction to a lesser offense that is not a legal lesser included offense would implicate jurisdictional issues involving usurpation of the power of the grand jury. See § 5.16, supra.

to inspect the grand jury minutes for sufficiency. Until 1980, for the court to inspect grand jury minutes for sufficiency, a defendant was required to submit motion papers containing sworn allegations demonstrating reasonable cause to believe that the evidence may not have been legally sufficient.[686] This, of course, was exceedingly difficult when the defendant, denied access to the minutes, was forced to guess about what happened behind the closed doors of the grand jury.[687] On the other hand, as a compensating consideration, until adoption of the CPL in 1971, a defendant had a right to appellate review of grand jury sufficiency.[688] Eventually, therefore, the presentation would receive scrutiny, even if the trial court had refused a request to inspect. This would lead, on occasion, to anomalous results: if a lower court refused to inspect the minutes, the appellate panel was not authorized to review the refusal to inspect.[689] However, the appeals court could review the minutes *ab initio* and dismiss an indictment based upon an insufficient grand jury presentation, notwithstanding a conviction after trial.[690]

With enactment of the CPL, a defendant's right to appeal "an ensuing conviction based upon legally sufficient trial evidence"[691] was eliminated. This meant that appellate courts ceased reviewing grand jury minutes for sufficiency. Inspection was left entirely to the trial court. However, as noted, trial courts were not required to review the minutes. If the trial court refused to review the minutes, whether rightly or wrongly, the refusal was not appealable.[692] Nor could the defendant compel inspection or review by way of an Article 78 petition.[693] In sum, between 1971 and 1980, defendants were denied the right to demand inspection at either the trial or appellate level.

Additionally, with regard to *disclosure* to the defendant of the grand jury minutes, prior to enactment of the CPL,

> some judges, in granting the motion to inspect, [had] occasionally ordered the minutes given to the defendant and allowed

---

686. L.1980, c.842.

687. See, e.g., People v. Sexton, 187 N.Y. 495, 512, 80 N.E. 396, 402 (1907) (upholding denial of grand jury motion based on "vague and unsatisfactory" allegations that were the "broadest of generalizations").

688. People v. Nitzberg, 289 N.Y. 523, 47 N.E.2d 37 (1943).

689. See People v. Jackson, 18 N.Y.2d 516, 277 N.Y.S.2d 263, 223 N.E.2d 790 (1966).

690. Id. (reversing a murder conviction upon insufficiency of the evidence in the grand jury, notwithstanding a refusal to review the minutes by the trial court, and notwithstanding sufficient evidence at trial).

691. CPL § 210.30(6). One could question the constitutionality of this provision. Cf. Matter of Jaffe v. Scheinman, 47 N.Y.2d 188, 194, 417 N.Y.S.2d 241, 244, 390 N.E.2d 1165 (1979)("A defendant's procedural right to move for dismissal of an indictment founded upon inadequate or improper evidence is of constitutional dimension. Were this not so, the door would be opened to grave abuses and the safeguards against arbitrary and unwarranted exercise of the state prosecutorial power would be seriously jeopardized.")(citations omitted) with Miranda v. Isseks, 41 A.D.2d 176, 178, 341 N.Y.S.2d 541, 543 (2d Dep't 1973)("[T]here is no requirement in either the Federal or State constitutions that indictments must be based on 'legally sufficient evidence' "— rejecting an argument that a writ of mandamus would lie to compel review of sufficiency since the defendants had a right to review and no adequate remedy was available upon appeal after adoption of the CPL).

692. People v. Jackson, supra.

693. Miranda v. Isseks, supra.

§ 5.27 GRAND JURY & INDICTMENT Ch. 5

adversarial argument on the sufficiency issue for purposes of determining the dismissal motion.[694]

But in a 1979 opinion, *Jaffe v. Scheinman*,[695] the Court of Appeals held that trial courts could no longer disclose the minutes for purposes of hearing argument on the sufficiency of the grand jury presentation.[696]

Thus, for a one-year period, an intolerable situation existed that was promptly corrected by the Legislature in 1980. During that period, courts could not inspect minutes unless the defendant first alleged, with specificity, cause and need for inspection. Further, the denial of review was not appealable and the insufficiency of the presentation itself was no longer appealable—meaning that, in the normal course of events, neither trial nor appellate courts reviewed the minutes. And the defendant had no access to the minutes to argue the motion on his or her own behalf, even where a trial court felt inclined to disclose the minutes prior to trial.

Two changes were enacted in 1980.[697] First, CPL § 210.30(3) shifted the presumption in favor of inspection. Today, a trial court must inspect the minutes unless good cause exists to deny the motion to inspect. As a result, inspection by the court has become the rule rather than the exception.[698]

In addition, the 1980 amendments, overruling *Jaffe*, now permit disclosure to the parties where disclosure is "necessary to assist the court in making its determination on the motion."[699] Prior to release, the court must first give the prosecutor an opportunity to be heard as to why release would not be in the public interest. Since the Legislature acted quickly to overrule *Jaffe*, it may be fair to assume that it is not enough for the prosecutor to argue merely that public policy in general weighs in favor of grand jury secrecy. Rather, the prosecution should be required to make a particularized showing why disclosure in the case before the court would cause harm.[700]

Motion to Reduce or Dismiss. CPL § 210.20(1)(b) permits a court to *dismiss* a count of an indictment where the evidence before the grand jury was not legally sufficient to establish the offense charged or

694. Matter of Jaffe v. Scheinman, 47 N.Y.2d at 193, 417 N.Y.S.2d at 243 (quoting Denzer, "Practice Commentary" to CPL § 210.30, McKinney's Cons. Laws of N.Y., Book 11A, at 357 (1971)).

695. Id. Oddly enough, the court in Jaffe ruled that Article 78 relief was now available to prohibit trial judges from continuing to exercise any discretion at all in disclosing grand jury minutes as they had in the past—this despite the fact that no explicit statutory authorization had existed prior to enactment of the CPL and none was eliminated by its passage.

696. But see People v. Di Napoli, 27 N.Y.2d 229, 316 N.Y.S.2d 622, 265 N.E.2d 449 (1970)(CPL § 190.25(4) and Judiciary Law § 235 afford the court discretion and power to order the disclosure of grand jury materials if the public's interest for such disclosure outweighs its interest in maintaining secrecy and confidentiality).

697. L.1980, c.841; L.1980, c.842.

698. See, e.g., People v. Harris, 82 N.Y.2d 409, 413, 604 N.Y.S.2d 918, 921, 624 N.E.2d 1013 (1993).

699. CPL § 210.30(3).

700. In most instances, the testimony of grand jury witnesses will be disclosed to the defendant at trial, as Rosario material. Thus, the issue frequently is not whether the material will be disclosed, but when it will be disclosed.

any lesser included offense.[701] Alternatively, CPL § 210.20(1–a) permits a court to *reduce* a count in the same circumstance to the most serious lesser included offense.[702]

Prior to 1990, the CPL did not allow reduction, and prohibited dismissal even where the evidence in the grand jury was legally insufficient to support a charge if the evidence was sufficient to support any lesser included offense. Thus, for example, a murder indictment could stand despite the fact that only an assault was proven in the grand jury. This result, in the words of the Court of Appeals, was "contrary to reason and ... at variance with our fundamental concepts of criminal justice."[703]

In addition, a few short years after adoption of the CPL, significant restrictions upon available pleas and sentences for drug offenses[704] and violent felony offenses[705] altered the landscape with regard to plea and sentence negotiations. The "top count" in an indictment became of paramount significance in shaping those discussions. Judicial discretion was constrained to a large degree by charges in the indictment, even where the charges were not supportable by competent evidence or had not been supported in the grand jury presentation.[706] Because of these changes, complaints of "overcharging" by grand juries—*i.e.*, filing charges that were not justified by the evidence presented—took on added

---

701. Compare this to the federal system, as described in United States v. Williams, 504 U.S. 36, 53–54, 112 S.Ct. 1735, 1745–46, 118 L.Ed.2d 352 (1992)(citations omitted):

Motions to quash indictments based upon the sufficiency of the evidence relied upon by the grand jury were unheard of at common law in England. And the traditional American practice was described by Justice Nelson, riding circuit in 1852, as follows: "No case has been cited, nor have we been able to find any, furnishing an authority for looking into and revising the judgment of the grand jury upon the evidence, for the purpose of determining whether or not the finding was founded upon sufficient proof, or whether there was a deficiency in respect to any part of the complaint...." We accepted Justice Nelson's description in Costello v. United States, where we held that "it would run counter to the whole history of the grand jury institution" to permit an indictment to be challenged "on the ground that there was incompetent or inadequate evidence before the grand jury."

702. See CPL § 1.20(37)(defining "lesser included offense"). See also People v. Glover, 57 N.Y.2d 61, 453 N.Y.S.2d 660, 439 N.E.2d 376 (1982).

703. People v. Jackson, 18 N.Y.2d 516, 520, 277 N.Y.S.2d 263, 266, 223 N.E.2d 790 (1966)("It is alleged that if an accused is indicted for first degree murder, and is convicted for that crime, but the evidence presented to the Grand Jury was insufficient to sustain the indictment for that crime, nevertheless the indictment is sufficient if it would have sustained a conviction for a lesser included offense such as assault. Suffice it to say that this position is contrary to reason and is at variance with our fundamental concepts of criminal justice. The three cases cited in support thereof in no way advance this novel theory.").

704. See, e.g., "Drug and Repeat Offenders Law" (otherwise known as the "Rockefeller Drug Law"), L.1973, c.276 and c.277).

705. See, e.g. "Violent Felony Offender Law," L.1978, c.481.

706. Further aggravating the situation was the effect of the Court of Appeals ruling in People v. Valles, 62 N.Y.2d 36, 476 N.Y.S.2d 50, 464 N.E.2d 418 (1984). In Valles, the court held that the prosecutor, as legal advisor to the grand jury, need not instruct the jury on the availability of lesser offenses even when there was evidence in mitigation before the grand jury that would justify bringing a reduced charge. This meant, in effect, that a grand jury could have voted an indictment at a level that the grand jury itself would not have chosen had it been informed of the full panoply of justifiable choices.

§ 5.27　　　GRAND JURY & INDICTMENT　　　Ch. 5

significance. This led to calls for reform of the grand jury review process to permit reduction by a court when charges had been inflated.[707]

As a consequence, section 210.20 was amended to allow reduction by the court, after inspecting the grand jury minutes, to the most serious lesser included offense supported by legally sufficient evidence.[708] "Legally sufficient evidence" is defined in CPL § 70.10(1) as "competent evidence which, if accepted as true, would establish every element of an offense charged and the defendant's commission thereof." The same standard is used to measure sufficiency here as is employed in deciding whether a charge survives a mid-trial application for a trial order of dismissal[709] or a post-verdict appeal to overturn a conviction on the law.[710] At each of these three stages of the proceedings, after presentation to the grand jury, at completion of the prosecution's direct case at trial, and upon a review of the full trial record on appeal, the reviewing lower court or appellate court applies the same standard in deciding whether to dismiss or reduce a count.[711] That standard has been variously described as follows:

> The Grand Jury may not indict unless the People present evidence establishing a prima facie case of criminal conduct. The sufficiency of the People's presentation is properly determined by inquiring whether the evidence viewed in the light most favorable to the People, if unexplained or uncontradicted, would warrant conviction by a petit jury.[712]

Note the difference between the standard applied by reviewing courts on the question of law—legal sufficiency—as opposed to questions concerning the weight of the evidence, the burden that must be met to satisfy the factfinder. For example, an indictment may only be voted if there is legally sufficient evidence, as a matter of law, and, in addition, the grand jury finds reasonable cause to believe the defendant committed the crime.[713] Similarly, a conviction may be obtained only if there is

---

707. See "Determinate Sentencing Report and Recommendations," New York State Committee on Sentencing Guidelines (March 29, 1985); Report of the Advisory Committee on Criminal Law and Procedure to the Chief Administrator of the Courts of the State of New York (1990).

708. CPL § 210.20(1–a), enacted by L.1990, c.209.

709. CPL § 290.10(1).

710. CPL § 70.20 ("[N]o ... verdict is valid unless based upon trial evidence which is legally sufficient.").

711. People v. Swamp, 84 N.Y.2d 725, 622 N.Y.S.2d 472, 646 N.E.2d 774 (1995); People v. Jennings, 69 N.Y.2d 103, 512 N.Y.S.2d 652, 504 N.E.2d 1079 (1986).

712. People v. Jennings, 69 N.Y.2d at 114, 512 N.Y.S.2d at 657 (citations omitted).

713. Cf. CPL § 190.65(1)(a)(legally sufficient evidence) with CPL § 190.65(1)(b)(reasonable cause). Of course, the factfinder's determination must be based upon "competent and admissible evidence." CPL § 190.65(1)(b). For that reason, a reviewing court should satisfy itself not only that a prima facie case was made out, but in addition that the jury's reasonable cause determination was based upon competent and admissible evidence. See, e.g., People v. Edjardo Diaz, N.Y.L.J., December 29, 1995, p. 31, col. 1 (Sup.Ct., N.Y. County) (after reversal of trial court dismissal on grounds that integrity of presentation was impaired—i.e., defective, for inadmissible hearsay—trial court again dismissed on grounds that, without inadmissible hearsay, there was insufficient evidence before the jury).

legally sufficient evidence and, in addition, the factfinder, a petit jury, finds the defendant guilty beyond a reasonable doubt.[714]

Legal sufficiency for a reviewing court's determination and factual sufficiency are thereby separate and distinct inquiries.[715] The mere fact that one is satisfied does not necessarily mean that the other is also satisfied.[716]

At the same time, both prongs of CPL § 190.65 (legal sufficiency and reasonable cause) permit only "competent" evidence to meet the respective burdens. "Legally sufficient evidence," as defined in CPL § 70.10(1), "means *competent evidence* which, if accepted as true would establish every element of an offense charged."[717] Furthermore, a grand jury may only vote to indict if "*competent and admissible* evidence before it provides reasonable cause to believe that such person committed such offense."[718]

A court on occasion may confuse legal sufficiency with issues concerning a factfinder's determinations of reasonable cause (grand jury) or proof beyond a reasonable doubt (petit jury). A good study in this area is the interplay of two cases, *People v. Van Buren*[719] and *People v. Vollick*.[720] In *Vollick*, the defendant had been convicted of driving while intoxicated as a felony.[721] On appeal, the conviction was reduced to a

---

714. CPL § 70.10. See, e.g., People v. Galatro, 84 N.Y.2d 160, 163, 615 N.Y.S.2d 650, 651, 639 N.E.2d 7 (1994)("In the context of a motion to dismiss an indictment, the sufficiency of the People's presentation 'is properly determined by inquiring whether the evidence viewed in the light most favorable to the People, if unexplained and uncontradicted, would warrant conviction by a petit jury.' The People are required to make out a prima facie case that the accused committed the crime charged by presenting legally sufficient evidence establishing all of the elements of the crime.")(citations omitted).

715. See, e.g., People v. Galatro, 84 N.Y.2d at 163, 615 N.Y.S.2d at 651 ("On a motion to dismiss, the reviewing court's inquiry is confined to the legal sufficiency of the evidence and the court is not to weigh the proof or examine its adequacy. Indeed, 'all questions as to the quality or weight of the proof should be deferred'.").

716. People v. Batashure, 75 N.Y.2d 306, 308, 552 N.Y.S.2d 896, 897, 552 N.E.2d 144 (1990)("As is apparent from these definitions, legal sufficiency and reasonable cause are analytically distinct concepts. Evidence can satisfy either standard without necessarily satisfying the other.").

717. Note also that the section specifically requires corroboration, as a matter of legal sufficiency, in the grand jury when it is also required at trial, i.e., to support a confession (CPL § 60.50), accomplice testimony (CPL § 60.22), the testimony of an unsworn witness (CPL § 60.20(3)), or the testimony of a person suffering a mental incapacity or defect in certain prosecutions for sex offenses (P.L. § 130.16).

718. CPL § 190.65(1)(b)(emphasis supplied). See also People v. Swamp, 84 N.Y.2d 725, 730, 622 N.Y.S.2d 472, 474, 646 N.E.2d 774 (1995)("By contrast to the Federal Grand Jury system, where incompetent evidence may be considered, New York State indictments must be based on competent evidence, meaning evidence not subject to an exclusionary rule, such as the prohibition against hearsay.")(citations omitted). See also People v. Canty, 153 A.D.2d 640, 544 N.Y.S.2d 857 (2d Dep't 1989)(prosecution failed to present at trial legally sufficient evidence of auto theft when police officer testified that he determined that car was stolen from a computerized printout rather than from first-hand knowledge); People v. Calero, 163 Misc.2d 13, 618 N.Y.S.2d 996 (Sup.Ct., N.Y. County, 1994)(indictment dismissed where based upon improper, hearsay certification of drug analysis).

719. 187 A.D.2d 925, 590 N.Y.S.2d 362 (4th Dep't 1992), rev'd 82 N.Y.2d 878, 609 N.Y.S.2d 170, 631 N.E.2d 112 (1993).

720. 148 A.D.2d 950, 539 N.Y.S.2d 187 (4th Dep't 1989), aff'd 75 N.Y.2d 877, 554 N.Y.S.2d 473, 553 N.E.2d 1021 (1990).

721. Vehicle and Traffic Law § 1192(5).

§ 5.27　　　　GRAND JURY & INDICTMENT　　　　Ch. 5

misdemeanor,[722] on the ground that the felony could only be sustained upon proof that the defendant had been previously convicted of driving while intoxicated and the prosecution had failed to prove the defendant's identity as the person named in the certificate of prior conviction. In effect, the Appellate Division had reversed the conviction upon the ground that the evidence before the petit jury was insufficient as a matter of law in the absence of evidence to connect the defendant to the certificate. This finding was affirmed by the Court of Appeals. Thereafter, a trial court, in *Van Buren*, was confronted with the identical failure of proof in reviewing the grand jury minutes before it. For the reasons stated in *Vollick*, the trial court in *Van Buren* was required, as a matter of law, to reduce the felony to a misdemeanor charge. The Appellate Division, however, reversed that determination, declaring:

> The court's reliance on Vollick is misplaced. Vollick addressed whether the People's proof at trial established beyond a reasonable doubt that defendant was the person previously convicted. The issue now before us, however, relates to the sufficiency of the evidence before the Grand Jury, and Vollick is not controlling.[723]

Thereafter, appropriately enough, the Court of Appeals reversed the Appellate Division, on the ground that the evidence before the grand jury was legally insufficient, citing *Vollick*. Since the standard of measurement for sufficiency is identical at trial and in the grand jury, the reversal after trial in *Vollick* required dismissal of the indictment in *Van Buren* as well. The Appellate Division had erred when it attempted to justify reinstatement of the indictment by contrasting reasonable doubt to reasonable cause. Those are standards used to measure the weight of the evidence but are irrelevant to legal sufficiency.

On the other hand, since the nature of a grand jury presentation is significantly different from that of a trial, the requirement that both meet the same standard of legal sufficiency does, on occasion create tension. For example, in *People v. Swamp*,[724] the Court of Appeals struggled to find "field test" evidence[725] in the grand jury to be sufficient to warrant a drug charge, while recognizing that a field test determination alone was not an adequate basis upon which to rest a conviction after trial. The dissent complained that "[t]he evidence which is legally sufficient to indict must be legally sufficient to convict unless there is some explanation,"[726] and that existing case law would not permit a conviction to rest upon a field test.[727] The majority avoided the issue by pointing to the unique circumstances of the case, whereby another provision of law, CPL § 715.50, required further testing of the drug. Therefore, the majority felt assured that, if further tests tended to

---

722. Vehicle and Traffic Law § 1192(3).
723. 187 A.D.2d at 926, 590 N.Y.S.2d at 362–63.
724. 84 N.Y.2d 725, 622 N.Y.S.2d 472, 646 N.E.2d 774 (1995).
725. The test was the Scott–Reagent (NIK) field test for cocaine.
726. People v. Swamp, 84 N.Y.2d at 736, 622 N.Y.S.2d at 478 (Smith, J., dissenting).
727. See People v. Dumas, 68 N.Y.2d 729, 506 N.Y.S.2d 319, 497 N.E.2d 686 (1986).

exonerate the defendant, a dismissal on the basis of CPL § 210.20(1)(h), legal impediment to conviction, would result.

This last argument as a rationale for the result in *Swamp* touches upon another concern: whether subsequent determinations affecting evidence can be applied retrospectively in assessing sufficiency of the presentation to the grand jury. The general rule is that the evidence is to be evaluated by the competency of the evidence at the time of the presentation.[728] Thus, for example, a determination at a *Wade* hearing that the identification is unreliable does not affect the sufficiency determination, although it may reflect an impediment to further prosecution requiring dismissal.[729]

Theoretically, in the alternative, a defendant who is confident that the evidence about to be submitted to a grand jury was illegally acquired may move in superior court for an order of suppression *prior* to the presentation.[730] If successful, an indictment would be averted. However, the court has discretion to grant a hearing in advance of the presentation or to delay it, and may not be compelled to decide a motion to suppress in advance of the grand jury presentation.[731] Notwithstanding the availability of the procedure, pre-submission hearings are rare, if not non-existent.[732]

Because the right to inspection, review and reduction at the trial level are relatively recent innovations, the case law in this area is still evolving. Appellate courts, unaccustomed to this shift to the trial courts of authority to review sufficiency, are hostile to lower court dismissals or reductions. As a consequence, reversals in this area are common.[733]

---

728. People v. Swamp, 84 N.Y.2d at 732, 622 N.Y.S.2d at 475 ("evidence deemed inadmissible at trial after extrinsic proof reveals some infirmity may nevertheless have supported a prima facie case at the Grand Jury stage"). See also People v. Oakley, 28 N.Y.2d 309, 321 N.Y.S.2d 596, 270 N.E.2d 318 (1971).

729. Cf. People v. Gordon, 214 A.D.2d 1029, 626 N.Y.S.2d 601 (4th Dep't 1995), lv. granted 86 N.Y.2d 781, 631 N.Y.S.2d 627, 655 N.E.2d 724 (1995)(holding that a weakness in an identification would not be a ground to dismiss the indictment on the basis of insufficiency or CPL § 210.20(1)(h)(legal impediment to conviction)) with People v. Swamp, supra (subsequent laboratory test would justify dismissal under CPL § 210.20(1)(h)). Interestingly, Judge Smith, the dissenter in Swamp, granted leave in Gordon. A question for the court in Gordon should be whether subsequently exposed defects in the evidence submitted to the grand jury should be considered in determining a motion to dismiss under CPL § 210.20(1)(h). If the court determines that this is not the case, then the result in Swamp becomes more difficult to explain.

730. CPL § 710.50.

731. Matter of Burse v. Bristol, 203 A.D.2d 962, 612 N.Y.S.2d 990 (4th Dep't 1994), appeal dism. 83 N.Y.2d 960, 616 N.Y.S.2d 12, 639 N.E.2d 751 (1994).

732. See generally People v. Darby, 75 N.Y.2d 449, 554 N.Y.S.2d 426, 553 N.E.2d 974 (1990)(holding that a prosecutor need not instruct a grand jury that it must first find a confession to have been voluntarily given before it may consider the confession as evidence).

733. See, e.g., People v. Wilson, 210 A.D.2d 666, 619 N.Y.S.2d 884 (3d Dep't 1994); People v. Brown, 204 A.D.2d 789, 611 N.Y.S.2d 707 (3d Dep't 1994); People v. Jensen, 203 A.D.2d 820, 611 N.Y.S.2d 363 (3d Dep't 1994); People v. Diaz, 201 A.D.2d 580, 607 N.Y.S.2d 959 (2d Dep't 1994); People v. Matos, 195 A.D.2d 287, 599 N.Y.S.2d 598 (1st Dep't 1993); People v. Guzman, 180 A.D.2d 469, 579 N.Y.S.2d 386 (1st Dep't 1992); People v. Oreckinto, 178 A.D.2d 562, 577 N.Y.S.2d 470 (2d Dep't 1991); People v. Marini, 173 A.D.2d 742, 570 N.Y.S.2d 360 (2d Dep't 1991).

However, over time, as they come to realize that proclamations restricting lower court grand jury sufficiency determinations will, by necessary implication, bind and confine their own power to review for legal sufficiency after conviction at trial, it is likely that the promise of the 1990 reform legislation will be fulfilled.[734]

Motion to Dismiss for Defective Grand Jury Proceedings. CPL § 210.35 enumerates five grounds for dismissal of an indictment where the grand jury proceeding was defective. The first four require a dismissal when the grand jury was illegally constituted, the proceeding was conducted before fewer than 16 jurors, the indictment was voted by fewer than 12 jurors or the defendant was not accorded an opportunity to appear and testify in accordance with the provisions of section 190.50. These grounds call for dismissal *per se*, without regard to prejudice to the defendant or the proceedings.[735] The requirements of a proper grand jury presentation, and in particular the requirements outlined in section 210.35, subdivisions one through four, are discussed in Sections 5.2—5.9, *supra*.[736]

More generally, however, a proceeding is also "defective" within the meaning of the statute when it "fails to conform to the requirements of article one hundred ninety to such degree that the integrity thereof is impaired and prejudice to the defendant *may* result."[737] Note that the definition contains two prongs: impairment and possible prejudice. The former, a finding of impairment, has been described as "a very high hurdle" that must be met before the "exceptional remedy" of dismissal results.[738] On the other hand, once impairment is shown, a defendant need not claim or demonstrate actual prejudice. A potential for prejudice is sufficient to require dismissal.[739] The Court of Appeals has declared that the "mere possibility of prejudice" justifies dismissal.[740]

---

734. See, e.g., People v. Swamp, 84 N.Y.2d at 736, 622 N.Y.S.2d at 478 (Smith, J., dissenting).

735. People v. Williams, 73 N.Y.2d 84, 538 N.Y.S.2d 222, 535 N.E.2d 275 (1989).

736. See generally People v. Williams, supra, regarding the "de facto grand jury doctrine" that predated the current statutory scheme. Under that doctrine, a defect in grand jury proceedings did not require dismissal if it did not prejudice or affect a substantial right of the accused. However, in Williams, in rejecting the Appellate Division's application of that doctrine, the court pointed out that under the revised CPL the statutorily enumerated defects call for dismissal even in the absence of any prejudice.

737. CPL § 210.35(5)(emphasis supplied).

738. People v. Darby, 75 N.Y.2d 449, 455, 554 N.Y.S.2d 426, 428, 553 N.E.2d 974 (1990).

739. See, e.g., People v. Sayavong, 83 N.Y.2d 702, 711, 613 N.Y.S.2d 343, 348, 635 N.E.2d 1213 (1994)("The dissent contends that an affirmance is warranted because 'a conclusive lack of actual prejudice is demonstrable.' However, it is precisely because of the problem recognized by the dissent— that '[n]ot a shred of evidence is discernible or deducible from the record' that the governing inquiry focuses not on whether a defendant was actually prejudiced, but on whether some conduct during Grand Jury proceedings created the possibility of prejudice to a defendant. That a defendant need only demonstrate that a defect in Grand Jury proceedings created a risk of prejudice is not a rule invented by the majority in this case, but one with strong jurisprudential roots, and supported by the plain language of CPL 210.35(5). Indeed, an actual prejudice test, included in two earlier drafts of that section, was changed in the final draft enacted by the Legislature to read 'prejudice to the defendant may result'.")(citations omitted).

740. People v. Wilkins, 68 N.Y.2d 269, 277 n. 7, 508 N.Y.S.2d 893, 897 n. 7, 501 N.E.2d 542 (1986)(the "de facto doctrine"

Claims that grand jury proceedings were impaired and thereby defective, unlike challenges to sufficiency of the evidence, are jurisdictional. They raise concerns involving the integrity of the accusatory process itself.[741] For that reason, they may be heard upon appeal, notwithstanding CPL § 210.30(6), and are not waived by a plea of guilty,[742] or cured by a subsequent conviction after trial.[743]

Challenges to grand jury proceedings are myriad and varied, with each case turning largely upon the individual facts. A few broad principles, however, may be gleaned and deserve comment. First, except as provided in section 190.30, the rules of evidence at a trial apply with equal force in the grand jury.[744] At the same time, the proceeding is not a "mini-trial."[745] Minor errors in evidentiary determinations by the prosecutor that could not possibly have affected the outcome do not require dismissal.[746]

In addition, a proceeding may be defective because the grand jurors received faulty legal instructions. The prosecutor, along with the court, is a legal advisor to the grand jury.[747] In that capacity, he or she instructs the grand jury on principles of law "(w)here necessary or appropriate."[748] A grand jury need not be instructed, however, with the same degree of precision as a petit jury. Instructions are sufficient if they provide the grand jury with enough information to enable it intelligently to decide whether a crime has been committed and to determine whether there exists legally sufficient evidence to establish the material elements of the crime.[749] Nonetheless, an indictment is defective when the instructions are "so misleading or incomplete as to substantially undermine the integrity of the [grand jury] proceeding."[750] Similarly, instructions to the grand jury that the prosecutor has determined that the evidence is legally sufficient impairs the integrity of the

survived in the CPL only in "modified form" in the catchall provision).

741. Id.

742. People v. Pelchat, 62 N.Y.2d 97, 476 N.Y.S.2d 79, 464 N.E.2d 447 (1984).

743. People v. Sayavong, 83 N.Y.2d 702, 613 N.Y.S.2d 343, 635 N.E.2d 1213 (1994).

744. People v. Mitchell, 82 N.Y.2d 509, 605 N.Y.S.2d 655, 626 N.E.2d 630 (1993). See § 5.6, supra.

745. People v. Lancaster, 69 N.Y.2d 20, 30, 511 N.Y.S.2d 559, 565, 503 N.E.2d 990, 996 (1986), cert. den. 480 U.S. 922, 107 S.Ct. 1383, 94 L.Ed.2d 697 (1987) (quoting People v. Brewster, 63 N.Y.2d 419, 422, 482 N.Y.S.2d 724, 472 N.E.2d 686 (1984)).

746. See People v. Calero, 163 Misc.2d 13, 18, 618 N.Y.S.2d 996, 999 (Sup.Ct., N.Y. County, 1994)("Of course, relatively minor errors, such as admitting hearsay which is neither material nor critical to the Grand Jury's determination, do not require dismissal of an indictment, since Grand Jury presentations are not subject to the same level of scrutiny as trials. However, where, as here, the inadmissible hearsay is the only evidence supporting a critical element of the offense, re-presentation is required."). See also People v. Avant, 33 N.Y.2d 265, 271, 352 N.Y.S.2d 161, 165, 307 N.E.2d 230, 233 (1973)("the submission of some inadmissible evidence during the [grand jury presentation] is held to be fatal only when the remaining legal evidence is insufficient to sustain the indictment").

747. CPL § 190.25(6). See § 5.4, supra.

748. CPL § 190.25(6).

749. People v. Calbud, Inc., 49 N.Y.2d 389, 395 n. 1, 426 N.Y.S.2d 238, 241 n. 1, 402 N.E.2d 1140, 1143 n. 1 (1980)("In the ordinary case, this standard may be met by reading to the Grand Jury from the appropriate sections of the Penal Law.").

750. People v. Caracciola, 78 N.Y.2d 1021, 1022, 576 N.Y.S.2d 74, 74, 581 N.E.2d 1329, 1329 (1991).

§ 5.27 GRAND JURY & INDICTMENT Ch. 5

proceeding.[751]

Motion to Dismiss in Interest of Justice. CPL § 210.40 permits a court, on its own motion or on application of either party,[752] to dismiss an indictment in the interest of justice "even though there may be no basis for dismissal as a matter of law."[753] Popularly referred to as "*Clayton* motions,"[754] such motions are directed toward that rare class of cases that "cr[y] out for fundamental justice beyond the confines of conventional considerations."[755]

At the outset, it should be emphasized that *Clayton* motions are granted only in exceptional circumstances.[756] Trial courts granting such relief are frequently reversed.[757] Although the power to dismiss in furtherance of justice is, in theory, committed to the discretion of trial courts, trial courts granting such motions are routinely reversed and reminded by appellate tribunals that their discretion is "not absolute" and is to be exercised "sparingly."[758] Notably, however, trial courts

---

751. People v. Batashure, 75 N.Y.2d 306, 552 N.Y.S.2d 896, 552 N.E.2d 144 (1990).

752. CPL § 210.40(2).

753. See CPL § 210.20(1)(a)-(h).

754. This term refers to the Second Department's decision in People v. Clayton, 41 A.D.2d 204, 342 N.Y.S.2d 106 (2d Dep't 1973). In that case, the court enumerated seven criteria to be considered by trial courts entertaining motions to dismiss in the interest of justice. Although Clayton was decided prior to the enactment of section 210.40, the principles enunciated in that case are nevertheless embodied in the statute.

755. People v. Belge, 41 N.Y.2d 60, 62–63, 390 N.Y.S.2d 867, 868–69, 359 N.E.2d 377, 378–79 (1976)(Fuchsberg, J., concurring).

756. The power to dismiss in the interest of justice is wholly statutory. Trial courts do not possess an "inherent" power to dismiss an indictment. People v. Guzman, 168 A.D.2d 154, 570 N.Y.S.2d 827 (2d Dep't 1991). See also Matter of Holtzman v. Goldman, 71 N.Y.2d 564, 528 N.Y.S.2d 21, 523 N.E.2d 297 (1988); People v. Douglass, 60 N.Y.2d 194, 469 N.Y.S.2d 56, 456 N.E.2d 1179 (1983).

757. In retrospect, it is perhaps ironic that the very case that prompted the passage of the chapter (L.1979, c.996) enacting CPL § 210.40 in its present form, People v. Belge, supra, was an affirmance of a dismissal that, under today's standards, likely would result in denial of the motion. In Belge, an attorney was indicted for failing to report, in timely fashion and in violation of Public Health Law § 4143, a body he uncovered in the woods while investigating and preparing a defense for an accused murderer. His delay in reporting the body was held to be proper in light of his ethical obligation of confidentiality. At the time, Section 210.40 read precisely as it does today, but without an enumeration of illustrative factors that should be considered. Upon appeal of the dismissal, the Court of Appeals ruled that "insofar as the dismissal of this indictment was granted in the interest of justice it is outside the scope of our review, unless it could be said that there was an abuse of discretion as a matter of law." People v. Belge, 41 N.Y.2d at 62, 390 N.Y.S.2d at 868. However, the court proceeded to ask the Legislature to "to prescribe specific criteria for the responsible exercise of the discretion granted by the section." Id. Shortly thereafter, the Legislature adopted factors, listed in Clayton, that should be considered, without changing the standard or restricting the discretionary provisions of the section. Nonetheless, history has shown that the statute's enumeration of factors to be examined and considered has resulted in a body of appellate reversals of the exercise of that discretion.

758. See, e.g., People v. Hudson, 217 A.D.2d 53, 634 N.Y.S.2d 752 (2d Dep't 1995); People v. Dunlap, ___ A.D.2d ___, 629 N.Y.S.2d 407 (1st Dep't 1995); People v. Brown, 194 A.D.2d 548, 598 N.Y.S.2d 88 (2d Dep't 1993); People v. Harmon, 181 A.D.2d 34, 586 N.Y.S.2d 922 (1st Dep't 1992); People v. Serrano, 163 A.D.2d 497, 558 N.Y.S.2d 593 (2d Dep't 1990); People v. Natarelli, 154 A.D.2d 769, 546 N.Y.S.2d 219 (3d Dep't 1989); People v. Howard, 151 A.D.2d 253, 542 N.Y.S.2d 172 (1st Dep't 1989); People v. Riccelli, 149 A.D.2d 941, 540 N.Y.S.2d 74 (4th Dep't 1989); People v. Insignares, 109 A.D.2d 221, 491 N.Y.S.2d

denying such relief are, almost without exception,[759] never reversed.

To ensure that trial courts do not "act on purely subjective considerations"[760] when considering the merits of *Clayton* motions, the Legislature enumerated ten criteria that must be examined "individually and collectively."[761] They are:

(a) the seriousness and circumstances of the offense;

(b) the extent of harm caused by the offense;

(c) the evidence of guilt, whether admissible or inadmissible at trial;

(d) the history, character and condition of the defendant;

(e) any exceptionally serious misconduct of law enforcement personnel in the investigation, arrest and prosecution of the defendant;

(f) the purpose and effect of imposing upon the defendant a sentence authorized for the offense;

(g) the impact of a dismissal upon the confidence of the public in the criminal justice system;

(h) the impact of a dismissal on the safety or welfare of the community;

(i) where the court deems it appropriate, the attitude of the complainant or victim with respect to the motion;

(j) any other relevant fact indicating that a judgment of conviction would serve no useful purpose.[762]

Although "the statute does not compel catechistic on-the-record discussion" of all ten factors,[763] the record must reflect that the court made a "value judgment 'based upon a sensitive balancing of the interests of the individual and the state'."[764]

Clayton motions are, by necessity, particularly fact-driven. As such, there are no absolute "rules" that militate for or against dismissal. For example, while the fact that a defendant has a criminal record generally results in denial of the motion,[765] the presence of other countervailing

---

166 (1st Dep't 1985); People v. Varela, 106 A.D.2d 339, 483 N.Y.S.2d 13 (1st Dep't 1984).

759. See People v. Hirsch, 85 A.D.2d 902, 447 N.Y.S.2d 80 (4th Dep't 1981). See also People v. Mitchell, 99 A.D.2d 609, 472 N.Y.S.2d 166 (3d Dep't 1984).

760. People v. Rickert, 58 N.Y.2d 122, 126, 446 N.E.2d 419, 420, 459 N.Y.S.2d 734, 735 (1983).

761. See CPL § 210.20(1)(a)–(h).

762. Id.

763. People v. Rickert, 58 N.Y.2d at 128, 459 N.Y.S.2d at 736.

764. People v. Benevento, 59 A.D.2d 1029, 399 N.Y.S.2d 770 (4th Dep't 1977), quoting People v. Belkota, 50 A.D.2d 118, 377 N.Y.S.2d 321 (4th Dep't 1975).

765. See, e.g., People v. Bebee, 175 A.D.2d 250, 572 N.Y.S.2d 715 (2d Dep't 1991); People v. McGraw, 158 A.D.2d 719, 552 N.Y.S.2d 166 (2d Dep't 1990); People v. Natarelli, 154 A.D.2d 769, 546 N.Y.S.2d 219 (3d Dep't 1989); People v. Foster, 127 A.D.2d 684, 511 N.Y.S.2d 677 (2d Dept. 1987). Similarly, the fact that a defendant is re-arrested during the pendency of the case strongly militates toward dismissal. See e.g., People v. Smith, ___ A.D.2d ___, 630 N.Y.S.2d 84 (2d Dep't 1995); People v. Harmon, 181 A.D.2d 34, 38, 586 N.Y.S.2d 922, 925 (1st Dep't 1992); People v. Howard, 151 A.D.2d 253, 256, 542 N.Y.S.2d 172, 174 (1st Dep't 1989).

§ 5.27

factors has, on occasion, resulted in the dismissal of charges pending against a defendant with prior felony convictions.[766] Notwithstanding the fact-specific nature of *Clayton* jurisprudence, a number of general principles may be gleaned from the decisional law in this area.

Of course, the nature of the crime charged and the resultant harm[767] are factors which weigh heavily upon the determination of such motions. As such, the motion of a defendant charged with a violent felony is unlikely to meet with much success.[768] Again, however, the fact that a defendant is charged with such an offense does not automatically preclude the granting of a *Clayton* motion, provided that extraordinary factors favoring dismissal are present.[769]

Defendants charged with drug offenses have fared only a little better than those charged with violent felonies. In *People v. Harmon*,[770] the First Department rejected the argument that drug possession is a "victimless" crime. However, where it is established that the defendant engaged in drug activity to support a drug habit rather than to turn a profit, the likelihood of success may be somewhat greater.[771]

---

766. See People v. Colon, 209 A.D.2d 254, 620 N.Y.S.2d 935 (1st Dep't 1994), aff'd 86 N.Y.2d 861, 635 N.Y.S.2d 165, 658 N.E.2d 1038 (1995).

767. CPL § 210.40(1)(a) and (b).

768. See, e.g., People v. Figueroa, 203 A.D.2d 72, 610 N.Y.S.2d 25 (1st Dep't 1994)(firing gunshots into residential street is a serious crime that left unpunished would undermine public confidence in the criminal justice system); People v. Bebee, supra (assault); People v. Serrano, supra (kidnapping); People v. McGraw, supra (assault in the second degree); People v. Foster, supra (gun); People v. Doe, 159 Misc.2d 799, 801, 606 N.Y.S.2d 862, 863 (Sup.Ct., N.Y. County, 1993)("While there is no evidence before the court that the defendant intended to use the gun to facilitate another crime or to perform an act of violence, the court is mindful that a gun, even if possessed defensively, has no purpose other than to threaten, wound or kill human beings and is always a dangerous object.").

769. See, e.g., People v. Sales, 169 A.D.2d 411, 412, 563 N.Y.S.2d 825, 825 (1st Dep't 1991)(motion of 19-year-old defendant charged with second degree robbery of fast-food delivery man granted, in light of defendant's lack of prior convictions, that "the property stolen was a relatively small amount of food, that no weapon was displayed during the incident, in which no one was injured, and that defendant's prospects for future schooling and employment are good, [and] that any number of resolutions other than a conviction for a violent felony would have held this defendant responsible for his acts"). See also People v. Taibi, 174 A.D.2d 585, 571 N.Y.S.2d 88 (2d Dep't 1991)(quadriplegic defendant's motion granted, notwithstanding fact that he was charged with conspiracy to commit murder).

770. 181 A.D.2d 34, 37, 586 N.Y.S.2d 922, 924 (1st Dep't 1992)("narcotics trafficking could not flourish without the demand created by drug users ... [and] the desperate drug user will often resort to crime for the wherewithal to support his habit"). See also People v. Howard, 151 A.D.2d 253, 255, 542 N.Y.S.2d 172, 173 (1st Dep't 1989). But see People v. Colon, 209 A.D.2d 254, 256, 620 N.Y.S.2d 935, 936 (1st Dep't 1994), aff'd 86 N.Y.2d 861, 635 N.Y.S.2d 165, 658 N.E.2d 1038 (1995)(noting that although crime of criminal sale of a controlled substance in fifth degree is harmful, "the immediate harm is not visited upon unwilling persons.... [i]f defendant sells methadone again, she will have inflicted a wound upon society, but not a great wound. Society is strong enough to take that risk.").

771. See, e.g., People v. Lawson, 198 A.D.2d 71, 72, 603 N.Y.S.2d 311, 312 (1st Dep't 1993), aff'd sub nom. People v. Herman L., 83 N.Y.2d 958, 615 N.Y.S.2d 865, 639 N.E.2d 404 (1994)(defendant sold drugs "to feed his own addiction rather than the very much more sinister wish to reap an economic windfall from the suffering of others"). See also People v. Varela, 106 A.D.2d 339, 340, 483 N.Y.S.2d 13, 14 (1st Dep't 1984).

Clayton motions are often brought by defendants who are either mentally or physically challenged.[772] As a practical matter, defense counsel seeking dismissal due to a client's illness would be well-advised to supply the court with medical documentation.[773] Not surprisingly, a fair amount of recent litigation in this area has focused upon defendants infected with the HIV virus. Reasoning that granting dismissal merely because an individual has contracted AIDS "would rise to the level of a blanket excuse for criminal activity and may well encourage commission of crimes,"[774] courts generally deny such motions unless it is evident that defendants are in the "advanced stages of their illness and [are] ... 'literally at death's door'."[775] Moreover, courts have been particularly unreceptive to *Clayton* motions filed by defendants who were aware of their illness at the time of the charged crime.[776]

A number of issues arise with respect to defendants who are mentally ill or mentally retarded. The Court of Appeals held in *People v. Schaffer*[777] that a defendant who is found to be incompetent pursuant to CPL Article 730 is precluded from seeking dismissal under section 210.40. Thus, a defendant deemed "not fit" to stand trial may only seek dismissal pursuant to the four methods contained within Article 730.[778]

With regard to defendants who are found "fit" to stand trial, courts tend to look more favorably upon *Clayton* motions brought by defendants suffering from mental retardation[779] as opposed to mental illness.[780] In *People v. Colon*, the First Department drew such a distinction and affirmed a trial court's order dismissing an indictment against a mildly retarded defendant with an IQ of 64, finding her to be "horrendously handicapped."[781]

---

772. See CPL § 210.40(1)(d). See also People v. Hudson, supra (schizophrenia); People v. Colon, supra (mental retardation); People v. Anderson, 204 A.D.2d 168, 612 N.Y.S.2d 21 (1st Dep't 1994)(lengthy history of substance and alcohol abuse); People v. Lawson, supra (AIDS); People v. Harmon, supra (dyslexia); People v. Taibi, supra (quadriplegic); People v. Natarelli (old age); People v. Doe, 158 Misc.2d 863, 602 N.Y.S.2d 507 (N.Y.C.Crim.Ct.1993)(hearing impairment and learning disability); People v. Reets, 157 Misc.2d 515, 597 N.Y.S.2d 577 (Sup.Ct., Kings County, 1993)(deaf-mute).

773. People v. Lawson, 198 A.D.2d at 74, 603 N.Y.S.2d at 313 (although a court may grant a Clayton motion for medical reasons without reviewing medical records, "it is generally desirable that the defendant's condition be well-documented").

774. People v. Pender, 156 Misc.2d 325, 593 N.Y.S.2d 447 (Sup.Ct., Queens County, 1992).

775. People v. Murray, 166 Misc.2d 828, 634 N.Y.S.2d 985 (Sup.Ct., Kings County, 1995), quoting People v. Camargo, 135 Misc.2d 987, 516 N.Y.S.2d 1004 (Sup.Ct., Bronx County, 1986).

776. See, e.g., People v. Sierra, 149 Misc.2d 588, 566 N.Y.S.2d 818 (Sup.Ct., Kings County, 1990); People v. Pender, supra. See also People v. Anderson, supra (motion properly denied where defendant, who had "a history of substance and alcohol abuse, was aware of her illness for seven years but nevertheless continued to commit crimes").

777. 86 N.Y.2d 460, 634 N.Y.S.2d 22, 657 N.E.2d 1305 (1995).

778. CPL §§ 730.50(1), 730.50(4) and (5), 730.60(4), 730.60(5).

779. See, e.g., People v. Colon, supra.

780. See, e.g., People v. Hudson, supra (trial court's dismissal of indictment against schizophrenic defendant frustrated the goals embodied in CPL § 330.20, which requires that an acquittee who is found to suffer from a dangerous mental disorder or defect must be confined to a secure facility until adjudicated no longer dangerous).

781. 209 A.D.2d 254, 256, 620 N.Y.S.2d 935, 936 (1st Dep't 1994), aff'd 86 N.Y.2d 861, 635 N.Y.S.2d 165, 658 N.E.2d 1038 (1995). Noting that the "circumstance upon which the motion court heavily relied and which the majority [found] most compelling [was] the defendant's mental retardation," the dissent argued that dismissal

Juvenile offenders comprise another class of defendants who frequently file *Clayton* motions. In *Matter of Vega v. Bell*,[782] the Court of Appeals interpreted section 210.40 as granting superior courts the authority to remove juvenile offender cases to the Family Court over the prosecution's objection, thereby, as the Second Department later remarked, "filling a void in and preserving the integrity of the statutory scheme governing such removals."[783] On a related note, however, the Second Department has held that although a superior court may *remove* a juvenile's case to Family Court, it may not *dismiss* an indictment pursuant to section 210.40 merely because a minor is subsequently adjudicated a juvenile offender and placed in a State Division for Youth facility.[784]

Finally, the following grounds have been held not to constitute a compelling circumstance warranting dismissal: (1) absence of prior convictions[785]; (2) adverse impact on defendant's family[786]; (3) immigration consequences of conviction[787]; (4) the trial court's dissatisfaction with the plea agreement offered by the prosecution[788]; (5) defendant's belief that the conduct forming the basis of the charge was lawful;[789] and (7) the prosecution's perceived failure to prosecute.[790]

Several procedural points should be mentioned. First, motions to dismiss pursuant to section 210.40 are, technically speaking, "pretrial motions."[791] As a general rule, they should therefore be filed within 45 days of arraignment.[792] Accordingly, although trial courts frequently consider *Clayton* motions made well after the 45-day deadline,[793] counsel wishing to make such a motion nevertheless would be well-advised to do so at the earliest opportunity. Second, the motion must be made in

---

was not proper since Clayton relief is only available in exceptional circumstances and all too many criminal defendants suffer from this handicap. 209 A.D.2d at 257, 620 N.Y.S.2d at 937 (Sullivan, J., dissenting). Perhaps in response to the dissenting judge's criticism, the Court of Appeals affirmed the First Department's ruling but noted that although a court may consider a defendant's mental retardation in determining a Clayton motion, it may not summarily dismiss the indictment solely because of the defendant's mental handicap.

782. 47 N.Y.2d 543, 419 N.Y.S.2d 454, 393 N.E.2d 450 (1979).

783. People v. Hipp, 197 A.D.2d 590, 591, 602 N.Y.S.2d 428, 429 (2d Dep't 1993).

784. People v. Brown, 194 A.D.2d 548, 598 N.Y.S.2d 88 (2d Dep't 1993).

785. People v. Harmon, supra. See also People v. Perez, 156 A.D.2d 7, 10, 553 N.Y.S.2d 659, 661 (1st Dep't 1990); People v. Varela, supra.

786. People v. Reyes, 174 A.D.2d 87, 579 N.Y.S.2d 34 (1st Dep't 1992).

787. People v. Doe, 159 Misc.2d 799, 606 N.Y.S.2d 862 (Sup.Ct., N.Y. County, 1993).

788. See, e.g., People v. Molfino, 178 A.D.2d 238, 577 N.Y.S.2d 787 (1st Dep't 1991); People v. Harmon, supra. But see People v. Sales, supra (compelling factor supporting dismissal "is that any number of resolutions other than a conviction for a violent felony [the plea offered by the prosecution] would have held this defendant responsible for his acts").

789. People v. Riccelli, supra.

790. People v. Roesch, 163 A.D.2d 429, 430, 558 N.Y.S.2d 144, 145 (2d Dep't 1990). Although a trial court may not dismiss an indictment for purposes of "calendar control" it may, under certain circumstances, deny further adjournments. Id.

791. See CPL § 255.10(1)(a).

792. See, e.g., People v. Figueroa, supra; People v. Field, 161 A.D.2d 660, 555 N.Y.S.2d 437 (2d Dep't 1990); People v. Longwood, 116 A.D.2d 590, 497 N.Y.S.2d 450 (2d Dep't 1986).

793. See, e.g., People v. Dolan, 184 A.D.2d 892, 585 N.Y.S.2d 549 (3d Dep't 1992); People v. Weaver, 112 A.D.2d 782, 492 N.Y.S.2d 280 (4th Dep't 1985).

writing upon reasonable notice to the prosecution, which must be provided an adequate opportunity to respond.[794] Third, while a court is empowered to *dismiss* a charge in the interest of justice, it may not *reduce* a charge on this ground.[795] Similarly, the statute does not authorize trial courts to fashion a less drastic alternative to dismissal by imposing a sentence that is not authorized by law.[796] Finally, a defendant forfeits the right to challenge the denial of his or her *Clayton* motion by pleading guilty.[797]

Library References:
West's Key No. Digests, Indictment and Information ⚷144.1.

§ 5.28 Indictment—Disposition Following Dismissal

The consequences of an order dismissing an indictment may vary depending upon the basis for the dismissal. In all cases, the prosecution may appeal a dismissal as a matter of right.[798] However, except as provided in CPL § 210.20(6),[799] the taking of an appeal will not stay the proceedings.[800] In the absence of a stay, in a case where one or more counts are dismissed but other counts survive, there is always the possibility that the court will permit the defendant to plead to the remaining counts of the indictment, in which case the plea and commencement of sentence may act as a bar to further prosecution of the dismissed count, despite a later reversal and reinstatement by an appellate court.[801]

Resubmission Following Dismissal. When the court orders a dismissal on the ground that: (1) the indictment is defective within the meaning of CPL § 210.25; (2) the evidence before the grand jury was legally insufficient; (3) the grand jury proceeding was defective, within the meaning of CPL § 210.35; or (4) in the interest of justice, it may authorize resubmission to the same or another grand jury.[802] In that event, a new indictment may be voted after presentation of evidence anew to the grand jury.[803]

794. People v. Dunlap, ___ A.D.2d ___, 629 N.Y.S.2d 407, 409 (1st Dep't 1995); People v. Loria, 214 A.D.2d 1043, 626 N.Y.S.2d 941 (4th Dep't 1995); People v. Smith, 191 A.D.2d 598, 594 N.Y.S.2d 799 (2d Dep't 1993). See also People v. Dolan, supra (trial "is not an adequate substitute for a Clayton hearing, as evidence bearing directly on defendant's guilt or innocence is dispositive of only a few of the 10 factors to be considered by the court").

795. People v. Panibianci, 134 Misc.2d 274, 510 N.Y.S.2d 801 (Sup.Ct., Monroe County, 1986).

796. People v. Hipp, supra. See generally People v. Thompson, 83 N.Y.2d 477, 496, 611 N.Y.S.2d 470, 481, 633 N.E.2d 1074, 1085 (1994)(Bellacosa, J., dissenting)(urging legislative reform to permit an interest of justice exception from mandatory sentences).

797. People v. Merlo, 195 A.D.2d 576, 600 N.Y.S.2d 494 (2d Dep't 1993); People v. Mitchell, 189 A.D.2d 900, 592 N.Y.S.2d 988 (2d Dep't 1993); People v. Purcell, 161 A.D.2d 812, 556 N.Y.S.2d 375 (2d Dep't 1990).

798. CPL § 450.20(1).

799. See discussion, infra.

800. CPL § 460.40(2).

801. See People v. Moquin, 77 N.Y.2d 449, 568 N.Y.S.2d 710, 570 N.E.2d 1059 (1991).

802. CPL § 210.20(4).

803. See CPL § 190.75 (where evidence before grand jury was legally insufficient court may only approve resubmission one time).

§ 5.28   GRAND JURY & INDICTMENT   Ch. 5

When an entire indictment is dismissed, but authorization for resubmission is granted, the dismissal order is deemed to constitute an order holding the defendant for the action of a grand jury.[804] The court then issues a securing order pending action of the grand jury. This securing order remains in effect for at least 45 days and may be extended by the court.[805] However, the securing order expires if, and when, the prosecution files a statement that it does not intend to resubmit the case to a grand jury, or the grand jury dismisses, or the defendant is arraigned upon the superseding indictment following resubmission.[806]

Resubmission Not Authorized. Where an indictment is dismissed on grounds of immunity from prosecution, previous prosecution, speedy trial, statute of limitations or some other jurisdictional or legal impediment, authorization for resubmission is not authorized.[807] If the court dismisses the indictment and there is no authorization for resubmission, the defendant must be discharged from custody, or if he or she was at liberty, bail must be exonerated. This is so even where the prosecution has appealed the dismissal.[808]

Library References:
West's Key No. Digests, Indictment and Information ⟐15, 144–144.2.

§ 5.29 Indictment—Disposition Following Order Reducing Count

CPL § 210.20(6) establishes an intermediate level of disposition in two unique situations: (1) where a count charging murder in the first degree is dismissed; or (2) where a count, be it a charge of murder or otherwise, is reduced to a lesser offense pursuant to CPL § 210.20(1-a). In either event, the prosecutor must choose among three options: (1) accept the court's decision; (2) resubmit the count to the same or a different grand jury; or (3) appeal the order. The effectiveness of the order is automatically stayed for 30 days, unless waived by the prosecution, to give the prosecution an opportunity to exercise one of the three options.[809] Once an option has been made, there is no explicit authorization for abandoning the option and pursuing another.

On occasion, the prosecutor fails to exercise an option within the 30 days provided in subdivision six. In that event, one court has determined that the court itself has the authority to impose the first of the three options upon the prosecution, *i.e.*, deem the indictment to have

---

804. CPL § 210.45(9).
805. CPL § 210.45(9)(d).
806. Id.
807. CPL § 210.20(4).
808. CPL § 210.45(8).
809. Oddly, there is no provision for a stay when a non-murder count is dismissed, but a stay automatically ensues when a non-murder count is reduced. This leaves open the possibility of inconsistent treatment, for example, if a lower court dismisses one count of an indictment for legal sufficiency while reducing another. Similarly, an indictment containing a murder count and another count, such as robbery, might suffer the same inconsistent fate where both counts are dismissed.

been filed and amended as directed by the court's order.[810] Another court has ruled that the 30-day rule is merely "directory" to the prosecution and that the prosecution is free to present the case to the grand jury at a later time.[811] The Second Department has twice rejected that position, holding that resubmission after the 30-day period, without court permission, is unlawful.[812] The Second Department has also vacated a plea based upon an indictment submitted after the 30-day period, holding that a late presentation renders the indictment jurisdictionally invalid.[813]

Option One: Prosecutor Accepts Court's Order. CPL § 210.20(6)(a) allows the prosecutor to accept the court's order of reduction of a felony count (or dismissal of a murder count) by "filing a reduced indictment ... [or] by dismissing the indictment and filing a prosecutor's information."[814] The new indictment may be filed without the necessity of obtaining a vote by the grand jury or the foreperson's signature.[815] There is no provision for a stay of the proceedings for the purpose of exercising this option.

Option Two: Resubmit Count to Grand Jury. CPL § 210.20(6)(b) permits the prosecution to resubmit the reduced felony count (or a dismissed first degree murder charge) to the same or a different grand jury within 30 days.[816] There are several differences between this option and the usual pattern for resubmission of dismissed counts. First, the prosecution may opt to resubmit as of right, as opposed to other dismissals, including dismissals for legal insufficiency where murder is not charged, where leave of the court is required.[817] Second, a comparison of the language in subdivisions four and six might lead one to conclude that the choice between re-presentation to the same or a different grand jury is, in the latter subdivision, the prosecutor's.[818]

---

810. People v. Nunez, 157 Misc.2d 793, 598 N.Y.S.2d 917 (Sup.Ct., Queens County, 1993).

811. People v. Powell, 148 Misc.2d 966, 564 N.Y.S.2d 663 (Sup.Ct., Monroe County, 1990). Cf. People v. Nunez, supra, holding that the prosecution is barred, not only from exercising this option after 30 days, but, in addition, it may not supersede the indictment pursuant to CPL § 200.80.

812. People v. Rios, 203 A.D.2d 491, 610 N.Y.S.2d 871 (2d Dep't 1994); People v. Jackson, 212 A.D.2d 732, 622 N.Y.S.2d 808 (2d Dep't 1995), lv. granted 85 N.Y.2d 974, 629 N.Y.S.2d 734, 653 N.E.2d 630 (1995).

813. People v. Jackson, supra.

814. A prosecutor's information would be filed, in a local criminal court, when the court orders a felony count reduced to a petty offense and no crime remains to be charged. CPL § 210.20(1–a).

815. CPL § 200.50(8). Perhaps as the result of an oversight, the 1995 amendments enacting the death penalty (L.1995, c.1) failed to cross-reference this section. It seems unlikely that the drafters intended to require the concurrence of the foreperson to amend the indictment in this situation.

816. In determining whether the prosecutor has successfully exercised one of the three options in a timely manner, the term "resubmit" is not defined. It could be interpreted to mean introduction of all the evidence the prosecutor intends to present, within 30 days, followed by a request for grand jury action. Alternatively, it could mean merely commencement of the presentation. Since the statute provides that the stay continues beyond 30 days "pending determination by the grand jury," CPL § 210.20(6)(b), a fair reading of the section would require complete presentation within 30 days unless the court permits additional time as provided within the same section.

817. CPL § 210.20(4), discussed in § 5.28, supra.

818. In some cases, for example, where the integrity of the proceedings was impaired, it would seem imperative that the presentation be before a new grand jury.

§ 5.29   **GRAND JURY & INDICTMENT**   Ch. 5

Finally, although the prosecution has 30 days to resubmit, the court may permit additional time for good cause shown.[819] Compare this to other dismissals, including dismissals of non-murder charges for legal insufficiency, where the prosecution has 45 days to resubmit, which period may also be extended if necessary.[820]

Option Three: Prosecutor Appeals Order. Within 30 days of the entry of order reducing a count (or dismissing a first degree murder charge), the prosecution may take an interlocutory appeal.[821] The taking of an appeal automatically stays the proceedings.[822]

§ 5.30   Practice Summary—Grand Jury

A. Form and Function (*See* §§ 5.1, 5.2, 5.3)

1. A grand jury consists of 23 persons drawn at random from the existing jury pool, representing a fair cross-section of the community, in accordance with the Judiciary Law. It is impaneled pursuant to rules of the Chief Administrator of the Courts. The grand jury is impaneled for a specified term or, in the case of an extraordinary grand jury, to conduct a specified investigation. A grand jury that strays beyond its authorized term, even with consent of the prosecutor and the supervising judge, is illegally constituted and acts without jurisdiction.

2. A challenge to the composition of the grand jury must be made as part of the omnibus motion papers. A challenge on due process grounds must demonstrate "systematic exclusion" of a segment of the community. A challenge on equal protection grounds must demonstrate discrimination.

3. A quorum of 16 members must be present for the grand jury to take any official action. However, a vote of 12 jurors, a majority of the entire grand jury, is sufficient to achieve any official action, as long as each voting juror heard "all the critical and essential evidence presented." If this becomes an issue, the court may examine attendance sheets for the jurors.

Cf. People v. Lane, 143 Misc.2d 385, 540 N.Y.S.2d 664 (Sup.Ct., Bronx County, 1989)(permitting a "resubmission," while dismissal motion pending, whereby the same grand jury votes again without considering any new evidence, but relying upon the prior presentation). See also People v. Cade, 74 N.Y.2d 410, 548 N.Y.S.2d 137, 547 N.E.2d 339 (1989); People v. Puig, 85 Misc.2d 228, 378 N.Y.S.2d 925 (Sup.Ct., N.Y. County, 1976).

819. CPL § 210.20(6)(b). Note that where the court grants additional time for the resubmission, the automatic stay of the proceedings is extended until the filing of the indictment.

820. CPL § 210.45(9). There may be some logic to the different treatment here. In the case of a reduction, the proceedings are stayed so the time to act is short; in the case of a dismissal, the proceedings are not stayed, but a securing order remains in effect.

821. CPL § 450.20.

822. CPL § 460.40. In light of People v. Moquin, 77 N.Y.2d 449, 568 N.Y.S.2d 710, 570 N.E.2d 1059 (1991), this is probably necessary, in a case involving a first degree murder charge, to avoid a deliberate bypass of the death penalty without the prosecution's consent. See Preiser, "Practice Commentary" to CPL § 210.20, McKinney's Cons. Laws of N.Y., Book 11A (Supp.).

B. Grand Jury Secrecy (*See* § 5.3)

1. Grand jury secrecy is required by the CPL, and a violation of the secrecy requirement is punishable under the Penal Law as a Class E felony. The secrecy provisions do not apply, however, to a witness who wishes to discuss his or her testimony publicly or otherwise. The Penal Law proscription does not apply to an attorney who accompanies a witness-client into the grand jury, and the attorney may not be compelled to take an oath of secrecy.

2. A court may disclose minutes of a grand jury proceeding upon a demonstration of "compelling and particularized need" for access, or to a defendant when necessary to assist in the court's determination of legal sufficiency of the evidence.

3. The CPL provides an exclusive list of persons who may be present in the grand jury. Courts are hostile to violations of this rule and the presence of an unauthorized person is considered to be a defect in the proceedings, warranting dismissal notwithstanding a validly obtained conviction. The district attorney is not authorized to be present during deliberations and voting.

C. Legal Instructions and Rulings on Evidence (*See* §§ 5.4, 5.5, 5.6)

1. The supervising court and the prosecutor are both "legal advisors" to the grand jury. In the ordinary course, the presenting prosecutor will make evidentiary rulings and give legal instructions to the grand jury in the same fashion as a court presiding at trial. However, a person affected by the outcome may apply to the supervising judge for a ruling, which then becomes binding upon the presenting prosecutor.

2. The Court of Appeals has been tolerant in reviewing instructions to a grand jury, holding that the grand jury need not be instructed "with the same degree of precision" as a trial jury, and that, in the ordinary course, merely reading from the appropriate sections of the Penal Law is sufficient.

3. As a general rule, however, the prosecutor must instruct the grand jury on a defense if it carries the "potential for eliminating a needless or unfounded prosecution." In practice, this means that an exculpatory defense, such as justification, should be charged where the evidence raises the issue. On the other hand, affirmative defenses in mitigation need not be charged unless a lack of clarity in the instruction would tend to confuse the grand jury.

4. Similarly, where the prosecutor is aware of exculpatory evidence, the general rule, once again, is that he or she has an obligation to present it only where it raises an exculpatory defense or carries the potential for eliminating a needless or unfounded prosecution. For example, there is no obligation to present collateral exculpatory information, such as matters that might generally impeach a witness's credibility. On the other hand, where a prosecutor learns, during the presentation, that a

§ 5.30   GRAND JURY & INDICTMENT   Ch. 5

witness gave misinformation to the grand jury, he or she has an obligation to so inform the jury.

5. In sharp contrast to the rule governing legal instructions, and in contrast to federal law, the Court of Appeals has consistently held that the rules of evidence in the grand jury are the same as those at trial, rejecting a claim that the prosecutor may employ inadmissible evidence when he or she deems it to be "appropriate" for grand jury purposes.

D. Witnesses in the Grand Jury (*See* § 5.8)

1. The prosecutor may call any person to testify if the prosecutor believes the witness possesses relevant information or knowledge. The grand jury may, on its own initiative, call witnesses subject to two limitations: (a) the prosecutor may ask the supervising court to deny the request "in the public interest"; and (b) the prosecutor may refuse to allow a witness to testify where the witness does not sign a waiver of immunity.

2. A defendant or "target" does not have the right to call witnesses, but may request, orally or in writing, the grand jury to call specified witnesses.

3. A person against whom a criminal charge is being submitted to a grand jury has a statutory right to appear before the grand jury. To exercise that right, he or she must serve written notice on the prosecutor, specifying a contact address, usually an attorney's office. Oral notice is insufficient, although it has been allowed in two limited situations: (a) where the prosecutor accepts oral notice; and (b) where the prosecutor otherwise failed to provide an adequate opportunity to serve notice.

4. The prosecutor is not required to advise a defendant in advance of a pending grand jury investigation. However, a defendant who is named in a "currently undisposed of felony complaint" must be notified of potential grand jury action and afforded a reasonable opportunity to appear and testify. Where a defendant is incarcerated and has served "cross grand jury notice," the prosecution has an obligation to produce the defendant before the grand jury. The prosecution has no obligation to produce a defendant who is being held pursuant to an order adjudging him incompetent under CPL Article 730. Similarly, a defendant who intentionally absents himself from the proceeding waives his right to testify.

5. The prosecutor is not required to complete a presentation of all other witnesses before calling the defendant to testify. However, a defendant or target who has an interest in the order of presentation may apply to the supervising judge for relief. Additionally, he may always inform the grand jury that he requests an opportunity to be heard again at the conclusion of the presentation.

E. Immunity in the Grand Jury (*See* § 5.9)

1. Any person may be called to testify in the grand jury and no one may refuse to give evidence demanded of him. This includes witnesses,

defendants and targets. However, no person may be compelled to incriminate himself. The privilege against self-incrimination is protected, in New York, by conferring "automatic" and "transactional" immunity upon every witness who gives evidence in response to a demand, unless that witness waives immunity.

2. "Automatic" immunity means that a witness receives immunity by merely giving evidence. As opposed to the general rule in other proceedings (where a witness does not receive immunity unless he or she "invokes" or "asserts" the privilege), a witness in the grand jury receives immunity despite a failure to request immunity. This is true, however, only where the evidence provided is responsive, *i.e.*, not gratuitously given or volunteered by the witness with knowledge that it is not responsive.

3. In New York, immunity, by statute, is transactional. This means that no further conviction, penalty or forfeiture may thereafter be sought for "any transaction, matter or thing concerning which [the witness] gave evidence." A motion to dismiss on the basis of immunity should be made as part of the omnibus motion or by way of a writ of prohibition. Failure to raise the issue will result in a forfeiture of the claim.

4. Grand jury immunity conferred by statute in New York will not protect the witness from prosecution in federal court or in another state. However, use of a compelled statement and its "fruits" is barred by the federal Constitution.

5. Immunity is conferred when a person "gives evidence" as defined by CPL § 50.10. This extends beyond testimonial compulsion, protected by the Fifth Amendment, to include the production of physical evidence. For example, a witness who gives a handwriting exemplar or is otherwise compelled to appear is granted transactional immunity.

6. On the other hand, the statute exempts from the immunity provisions compelled production of books and records of an enterprise where the records are not otherwise privileged. For example, a corporate officer may be compelled to produce business records of a "collective entity" without receiving immunity. If, however, the act of production, in and of itself, carries testimonial value—*i.e.*, the act in response to a subpoena tends to implicate the defendant as someone who had knowledge of the existence, or control, of a particular document, then a constitutional privilege exists, and the scope of immunity conferred is uncertain. Similarly, although not addressed by the appellate courts, it is probable that a witness who is compelled to identify documents by testimony receives immunity.

F. Waiver of Immunity (*See* § 5.9)

1. A witness may waive immunity when testifying in the grand jury. The procedural requirements of CPL § 190.45 should be closely observed or else the waiver will be deemed ineffective and immunity will result. The statute requires the witness to swear to a written statement, before

the grand jury, stipulating that he or she waives his privilege against self-incrimination and any possible or prospective immunity.

2. The defendant has a right to obtain and confer with counsel prior to signing the waiver. If the right to counsel has "attached," for example by virtue of a pending felony complaint, a waiver signed in the absence of counsel is ineffective. The Court of Appeals has explicitly reserved decision on the issue of whether a "searching inquiry" by the supervising judge could render a waiver effective in the absence of counsel.

3. A "limited waiver" may be signed by the parties, allowing testimony on specified subjects.

G. Attorney in the Grand Jury (*See* § 5.9)

1. A witness who testifies without immunity has a right to be accompanied into the grand jury by counsel, who may advise the witness but not otherwise participate in the proceeding. This means, in effect, that counsel may not personally address the grand jury or object to questions put by the prosecutor. If there is an objection to a line of questioning, the proper procedure is to seek the supervising court's intervention.

2. Some lower courts have stated that the scope of advice is limited in nature, but the statute does not imply any limits on the advice that may be given and appellate approval for limitations on the nature of advice to be rendered seems unlikely.

§ 5.31 Practice Summary—Waiver of Indictment (*See* § 5.10)

1. Article 1, § 6 of the New York Constitution permits a person held for the action of a grand jury to waive indictment for such offense by signing a written instrument in open court in the presence of counsel. It is a two-step process: a written and signed waiver is presented, followed by the filing of a superior court information (SCI) conforming to the waiver.

2. CPL Article 195 defines the procedure to be followed. Waiver may be accomplished either in local criminal court at the time the defendant has been held for action of the grand jury or in superior court prior to the filing of the indictment. Timing is of critical importance here. A defendant may not waive indictment prior to the point in time where he has been held for the action of the grand jury, nor may he or she waive indictment after an indictment has already been filed. This is a jurisdictional, non-waivable, requirement.

3. A waiver and SCI may only include offenses for which the defendant had been held. However, the Court of Appeals has allowed a plea to stand where the SCI only charged a lesser included offense of a greater offense that had been charged in the felony complaint. On the other hand, the court voided a plea where the SCI charged a greater offense than that contained in the felony complaint, but did not charge an offense for which the defendant had been held. The case has cast doubt upon the constitutionality of CPL § 195.20, which permits inclusion in

an SCI of any "joinable" offense to the offense for which the defendant had been held.

4. An SCI may not charge a non-existent crime. However, as with indictments, it may charge a cognizable crime, that then may be disposed of by a plea to a non-existent lesser offense.

5. Finally, the Constitution does not permit waiver in cases punishable by death or life imprisonment. The Court of Appeals has specifically reserved decision on the question of whether a defendant may be held for the action of the grand jury on a Class A felony, only to waive indictment and permit prosecution upon a lesser offense not so punishable.

§ 5.32 Practice Summary—Indictment

A. In General (*See* §§ 5.11, 5.12, 5.13, 5.14, 5.15, 5.16)

1. As a matter of state constitutional law, a valid indictment, voted by a grand jury, is a jurisdictional prerequisite to prosecution for a felony. CPL § 200.50 provides that an indictment must contain a plain and concise statement, without allegations of an evidentiary nature, that asserts facts supporting every element of the offense charged with sufficient precision to clearly apprise the defendant of the conduct that is the subject of the accusation. Notwithstanding the explicit language of the statute, the Court of Appeals has held that the statute, and the concomitant constitutional right to be "informed of the nature and the cause of the accusation," is satisfied in most cases by *in haec verba* recitation of the elements of the crime charged—as long as the bill of particulars meets the prescribed notice requirements.

2. The purpose of an indictment is to provide notice of the charges, guard against variance, avoid duplicitous charges within one count and protect against double jeopardy.

3. With regard to the notice requirement, one particularly troublesome area has been in specifying the date or time of commission. In that regard, the Court of Appeals recognizes three categories of offenses: (a) crimes, such as bail jumping, where the exact date is an element of the offense and must be contained in the indictment with specificity; (b) "continuous" crimes that by definition encompass a period of time (*e.g.*, engaging in a scheme to defraud), in which case the prosecution has an obligation to designate the period included in the charge with reasonable diligence; and (c) other offenses that are neither continuous nor time-specific, in which case the test "embraces good faith ... thereby requiring the prosecution to give necessary specifics to the best of its knowledge."

4. An indictment that accuses a defendant of engaging in conduct that does not constitute a crime, fails to allege that the defendant committed acts constituting every material element of the crime or charges a defendant with a non-existent crime is jurisdictionally defective and may not be cured by amendment. Nor is the claim waived by plea or forfeited by later conviction or a failure to preserve the issue. This is

§ 5.32   GRAND JURY & INDICTMENT   Ch. 5

true not because the indictment failed to adequately inform the defendant (defects in notice may be cured by a bill of particulars and waived or forfeited by a defendant), but because proper indictment by a grand jury is jurisdictionally necessary under the state Constitution.

B. Duplicitous and Multiplicitous Counts (*See* § 5.17)

1. A count of an indictment is duplicitous if it charges two criminal acts or if it alleges a violation of two separately defined crimes in one count. The CPL provides that each count of an indictment may charge one offense only. The prohibition against duplicitous counts serves three purposes: (a) the defendant is entitled to notice of the charge(s); (b) the proscription ensures jury unanimity; and (c) the risk of being twice prosecuted for the same offense is reduced.

2. A count is not duplicitous merely because it alleges more than one means of commission of an offense. For example, an intentional murder count may allege that the defendant killed the victim with a knife and baseball bat. On the other hand, a count charging assault with a dangerous instrument, to wit, a knife and a baseball bat, is duplicitous. Because proof of an assault by a particular dangerous instrument is an element of the crime of assault with a dangerous instrument, the indictment in the latter example charges two separate criminal acts in one count.

3. Multiplicity is also forbidden. An indictment is said to be multiplicitous when the same crime is charged in two separate counts. For example, an indictment that charged a defendant in one count with robbery by forcible taking in that the accused punched the complainant and took his wallet, while in a second count charged him with the same offense in that he pushed the complainant and took his wallet, would be multiplicitous. On the other hand, counts are not multiplicitous if each count requires proof of an additional fact that the other does not. The proscription against multiplicitous counts is designed to prevent multiple punishment. As such, it is permissible to allow proof at trial of both counts, but enter judgment upon only one conviction while dismissing the other.

C. Curing Defects in an Indictment (*See* § 5.18)

1. At any time before entry of a plea of guilty or commencement of trial, the prosecution may supersede one or more counts of an indictment by asking the grand jury to vote again or by presenting new evidence to the same or a different grand jury. However, a case may not be re-submitted without court approval if it has been dismissed or the grand jury had refused to indict. Court approval is also necessary where a prosecutor has "withdrawn" a case from the grand jury, prior to a vote, in anticipation of a "no bill." If the grand jury rejects a count upon resubmission, the prosecutor may not rely upon the pre-existing indictment; in effect, the grand jury has superseded the prior count with a no bill.

2. An indictment may be amended by application to the court, but only with respect to defects, errors or variances from the proof relating to matters of form, time, place, names of persons and the like, when such an amendment does not change the theory or theories of the prosecution as reflected in the evidence before the grand jury. An indictment may not be amended for the purpose of curing a failure to charge or state an offense, legal insufficiency of the factual allegations, a misjoinder of an offense or a misjoinder of defendants.

3. The limitations on amendment serve two purposes: an amendment in an indictment carries the potential for prejudice to a defendant who has relied upon the indictment to his or her detriment in preparation for trial, and an amendment that changes the crime charged or the theory of prosecution results in a prosecution for a felony that was not voted by the grand jury and is, therefore, jurisdictionally defective.

4. An amendment may occur formally, by application to the court, prior to trial. Sometimes an indictment is said to have undergone "constructive" amendment when the proof at trial or the submission to the jury is of a crime or theory not voted by the grand jury and contained in the indictment.

5. When an indictment, or an indictment read together with the bill of particulars, delineates the manner in which a crime was alleged to have been committed, but thereafter the proof at trial is different, even though the same crime is charged, "variance" may have occurred. As long as the crime charged and theory of prosecution are the same as that voted by the grand jury, there is no jurisdictional problem; instead, the issue is whether the variance has prejudiced the defendant by surprise.

6. A claim of surprise or lack of notice may be waived or forfeited. A constructive amendment altering the theory voted upon by the grand jury raises jurisdictional concerns and may not be forfeited or waived.

7. An amendment to add a lesser included offense for purposes of disposition may be made upon consent of the parties. Presumably, by voting for the greater offense, the grand jury was satisfied that the lesser was committed as well. In addition, the Court of Appeals has sanctioned an amendment, upon consent, to add a lesser included offense that, technically speaking, was not a "legal lesser included" under the test of *People v. Glover*, as long as the added lesser count is "reasonably related" to the charges in the indictment. Similarly, a count may be added by amendment charging a non-existent crime, for purposes of plea, but not for submission to a jury.

8. The Court of Appeals has determined that the parties may not replace an indictment with a superior court information, even upon a written waiver in open court, for the purpose of circumventing the rules limiting amendment of an indictment.

D. Bill of Particulars (*See* § 5.19)

1. A bill of particulars is a written statement specifying items of factual information that are not recited in the indictment and that pertain to

the offense charged, including the substance of each defendant's conduct encompassed by the charge. The prosecution is not required to include matters of evidence relating to how it intends to prove its case. In sum, the prosecution must detail what the defendant did by describing specific facts instead of conclusory allegations, but need not explain how it will prove those facts.

2. In light of case law approving *in haec verba* indictments, the bill of particulars assumes an added burden. In addition to the above definition, the bill of particulars and indictment must be read together, and thereby provide a plain and concise factual statement asserting facts supporting every element of the offense charged with sufficient precision to clearly apprise the defendant of the conduct that is the subject of the accusation.

3. Where the indictment, read together with the bill of particulars, alleges commission of the crime in a particular way, amendment on a late occasion will raise problems of variance, as described above.

4. On occasion, *People v. Davis* will be quoted out of context for the proposition that a bill of particulars is not a discovery device. That case involved a request for information regarding practice and procedure in the grand jury, unrelated to an explication of the nature of the accusation. To the contrary, a bill of particulars is a discovery device to the extent that it affords a defendant a right to demand items of factual information relating to the offense in the possession of the prosecutor.

5. The statute requires service upon the prosecution of a written request for a bill of particulars within 30 days of arraignment; the prosecutor has 15 days to respond. Thereafter, the defendant, if not satisfied with the response, may move the court for an order. However, that motion should be made as part of the omnibus motion, required to be made within 45 days of arraignment. Obviously, the timing is too close a fit. For that reason, it is not uncommon for defense motion papers to repeat a demand for court intervention in the omnibus motion papers, before a response has been served by the prosecution. In many counties, prior to receipt of a demand for a bill of particulars, the prosecutor serves a "voluntary disclosure form," frequently denominated "bill of particulars," containing a description of the offense. Thereafter, rather than responding to the demand for a bill by the defendant, the prosecution awaits service of the omnibus motion papers and supplements the voluntary disclosure form with allegations in its response to the omnibus motion. The practice that has evolved is not the one prescribed by statute, but since the statutory framework is awkward, it has been accepted by both sides until the statute is revised.

6. Unlike an indictment, a bill of particulars may be amended, at any time before commencement of trial, without leave of court. For that reason, it is easier for a prosecutor to draft a bare bones indictment and flesh out the facts in the bill of particulars. Once again, prosecutors should guard against an amendment that either constructively amends the indictment or that, by variance, prejudices the defendant.

E. Joinder of Offenses (*See* § 5.21)

1. Two offenses, charged in separate counts, may be joined in one indictment if: (a) they are based upon the same act or the same criminal transaction; (b) proof of one is material and admissible as evidence of the other; or (c) each offense is defined by the same or similar statutory provisions. Thereafter, more offenses may be added, like links to a chain, if they are properly joinable to an offense already contained in the indictment.

2. A criminal transaction is defined as a group of acts either (a) so closely related and connected in point of time and circumstances of commission as to constitute a single criminal incident; or (b) so closely related in criminal purpose or objective as to constitute elements or integral parts of a single criminal venture.

3. A defendant has a right to compel joinder, *i.e.*, "mandatory joinder," when two indictments charge offenses arising from one transaction. The defendant's application must be granted unless good cause is shown in opposition to the motion. An improper denial of a motion to consolidate bars a separate prosecution of an offense once trial is commenced upon the other. A failure to move to consolidate pending charges in the same court forfeits a later claim of separate prosecution under CPL Article 40.

4. Since the decision, for a defendant, to move to join offenses arising from one transaction depends, in part, upon the admissibility of evidence of the other crime if it is not joined, a prudent course is to seek a preliminary *Molineux* determination while asking permission to defer the application to consolidate until the evidentiary issue is resolved.

5. The prosecutor may, as well, move for consolidation of separate indictments charging offenses arising from a single transaction. Consolidation in this situation is permissive, *i.e.*, it rests in the sound discretion of the court. However, the prosecutor still has the option of obtaining consolidation by submission of a superseding indictment to the grand jury.

6. A second ground for joining separate offenses is where proof of one offense is material and admissible as evidence-in-chief upon a trial of the other. In effect, the propriety of joinder here rests upon a *Molineux* determination by the court. Either party may move to consolidate charges in this situation, and the determination is left to the discretion of the court.

7. If the counts are already joined, by dint of the grand jury's vote, a motion to sever is in order. It has been said that once a count has been properly joined pursuant to this provision a court is without discretion to sever. This, of course, is true only after the court had determined that the counts are properly joined by reason of the materiality and admissibility of the proof of one charge as evidence-in-chief of the other.

8. Common grounds for consolidation under this provision are instances where the offenses are part of a common scheme or plan or where commission of one offense provides a motive for commission of the other.

However, mere repetition of a crime is not, in and of itself, demonstration of a common scheme or plan.

9. Where evidence of an uncharged crime is material proof of a charged crime, it may only be introduced after a showing, by clear and convincing evidence, that the defendant, in fact, committed the uncharged crime. On the other hand, a grand jury may indict upon a mere showing of reasonable cause. For that reason, on occasion, charges are joined and a jury convicts on the stronger count while acquitting on the weaker. In such a case, the integrity of the conviction is subject to attack if it can be demonstrated that the jury was improperly influenced by the joinder.

10. A third basis for joinder of offenses lies when the offenses are defined by the same or similar statutory provisions and consequently are the same or similar in law. This ground for joinder poses the greatest risk of prejudice to a defendant in that it is not unlikely that a jury will consider that multiple charges of the same, albeit unrelated, criminal conduct tend to prove a propensity to commit the crime. For that reason, the statute provides that a court may sever such counts in the interest of justice and for good cause shown. Good cause includes, but is not limited to, a disparity in the evidence ("substantially more proof on one ... than on the others ... and ... a substantial likelihood that the jury would be unable to consider separately the proof as it relates to each offense"). Another example of a basis for severance in this situation arises where the defendant makes a convincing showing that he or she has both important testimony to give concerning one count and a strong need to refrain from testifying on the other. This ground may be met by demonstrating the need to refrain *ex parte* and *in camera*.

F. Joinder of Defendants (*See* § 5.22)

1. Multiple defendants may be charged in one indictment only if: (a) all the defendants are jointly charged with every offense; (b) all the offenses are joined by one common scheme or plan; or (c) all the offenses charged are based upon one criminal transaction. Each of these grounds requires *all* the offenses to be so joinable. Defendants may not be joined together merely because they are mutually associated with a third defendant. For example, where one or more defendants act as a hub of a wheel entering into separate conspiracies or criminal ventures with separate defendants, the "spokes" of the wheel may not be joined unless they are mutually charged with one all-embracing common scheme or plan or one transaction.

2. Assuming the predicate bases for joinder are satisfied, severance is left to the sound discretion of the court. However, "[w]here proof against the defendant is supplied by the same evidence, only the most cogent reasons warrant a severance." Grounds for severance include the potential use of statements by one defendant implicating another, prejudicial spillover, and mutually antagonistic defenses.

3. Where the prosecution intends to introduce a statement of a defendant, the court must be careful to consider whether redaction of references to the co-defendant will adequately protect the co-defendant's

right of confrontation. If not, severance becomes necessary. The First and Second Departments are divided on the question of whether use of a neutral pronoun suffices.

4. Where the declarant takes the stand and is available for cross-examination, the threat to the right of confrontation is substantially reduced.

5. Although the United States Supreme Court has rejected the so-called exception for "inter-locking" confessions, appellate courts frequently find introduction of such statements to be harmless error.

6. In the rare case where multiple trials are impractical but the prosecution has a strong need to introduce a confession, multiple juries may be utilized—hearing all the same evidence, save for the confession.

7. On occasion, the evidence against one defendant will preclude a fair trial for another defendant. For example, where a defendant wishes to introduce exculpatory evidence that is inadmissible as to his or her co-defendant, separate trials may be necessary. Similarly, where evidence of other crimes is introduced to rebut a co-defendant's entrapment defense, there is a risk of spillover prejudice to the defendant. Even a substantial disparity in the proof against separate defendants has been held to require severance in a case involving a close eyewitness identification.

8. Where a defendant demonstrates, convincingly, that a co-defendant will testify and exculpate him or her at a trial, once severed, a motion to sever is in order.

9. Where the core of each defense is in irreconcilable conflict with the other and where there is a significant danger that the conflict alone would lead the jury to infer a defendant's guilt, severance is required. It is not uncommon for co-defendants to assert defenses that are at some variance with each other. To meet the "*Mahboubian*" test, however, the defenses must be mutually exclusive and irreconcilable, *i.e.*, the jury could not credit both defenses: to believe one it necessarily must disbelieve the other.

10. In addition, there must be a demonstration of prejudice—a substantial impairment of the defendant's ability to present a defense. A common example of such prejudice arises when one defense lawyer becomes a "second prosecutor" by seeking to destroy the co-defendant's defense in order to bolster his or her client's position.

11. A *Sandoval* ruling limiting cross-examination by the prosecutor of prior bad acts does not restrict a co-defendant's ability to inquire as to the very same acts.

G. Arraignment (*See* §§ 5.23, 5.24)

1. After an indictment is filed, the defendant must appear personally for arraignment. If the defendant is in custody, the court must direct the sheriff to produce him, with two days notice to counsel. (The prosecution has an incentive to facilitate the process since the speedy trial clock commences when the indictment is filed.) If the defendant is

at liberty, the court must set a date for his appearance, with at least two days notice to the defendant, his surety and his attorney. If he fails to appear, the court may issue a bench warrant directing him to be brought before the court "without unnecessary delay."

2. If the defendant has not previously been arrested or held in local criminal court, the indictment remains sealed until the defendant is arraigned. In such a case, the court may either: (a) issue a warrant of arrest; (b) issue a summons, upon application of the prosecutor; or (c) set a date for the defendant to appear. The latter two situations require the prosecution's consent.

3. At the arraignment, the court sets bail or releases the defendant on his own recognizance. This cannot be done without a criminal history report. For that reason, although it is not explicitly required by statute, where arrangements for surrender on a given date are made by the parties, a fingerprint report should be obtained.

4. In addition, the court must take steps at the arraignment to ensure that the defendant is aware of the right either to assigned counsel or to be given an opportunity to obtain one, depending upon his eligibility for assigned counsel.

5. It is the usual course, but not required, that the defendant enter a plea of guilty or not guilty at the arraignment. Where the defendant stands mute, the court may enter a plea of not guilty on his behalf. With the consent of the court and the prosecution, the defendant may also enter a plea of not responsible by reason of mental disease or defect.

H. Motions to Dismiss an Indictment (*See* §§ 5.26, 5.27)

1. CPL Article 210 prescribes the manner in which a motion to dismiss an indictment may be made. Courts do not have inherent power to dismiss an indictment; a dismissal must be based upon statutory authority.

2. With limited exception, a motion to dismiss should be made as part of the omnibus motion. Notably, a motion to dismiss on the ground that the defendant was not accorded an opportunity to appear and testify before the grand jury in accordance with CPL § 190.50 *must* be made within five days of arraignment. Another exception is a speedy trial motion; for obvious reasons, this may be made at a later time, when it is appropriate to so move, but even then the motion must be made prior to commencement of trial or entry of a plea of guilty.

3. The statute authorizes a court, upon application of the defendant, to allow additional time; however, the court may not shorten the 45-day period without consent. Additionally, a motion may be heard after the 45-day period when new grounds come to the attention of the parties, or in the interest of justice and for good cause shown.

4. A motion must be in writing and contain sworn allegations in support thereof. The prosecution may waive this requirement, either explicitly or implicitly, by responding to the oral motion on the merits.

5. After exchange of the motion papers, the court must conduct a hearing if a ground constituting a legal basis for dismissal is asserted and all essential facts necessary to support the motion are alleged but one or more such essential facts are in dispute. To put an essential fact in dispute, the prosecution must assert facts that tend to negate the allegation; merely denying the truth of allegations without countering them will not forestall summary disposition of the motion.

6. When a hearing is ordered, the defendant has the burden of persuasion (not production or coming forward) by a preponderance of evidence with regard to every fact essential to support the motion.

7. CPL § 210.20 lists nine grounds for dismissal of an indictment: immunity, previous prosecution, untimeliness, speedy trial, insufficiency of evidence in the grand jury, defective indictment, defective grand jury proceeding, interest of justice, or some other legal impediment to conviction.

8. A defendant, within the omnibus motion papers, may request the court to inspect the grand jury minutes for legal sufficiency. This is granted in the ordinary course. In addition, the court may disclose all or portions of the minutes to the defendant where disclosure is necessary to assist the court in arriving at its determination regarding sufficiency. Disclosure in a difficult case can facilitate exposition of the legal and underlying factual issues involved in the case. Since the material is made available, in the usual course, at a later date as part of the *Rosario* material, there is little harm in advancing disclosure unless there is a risk of harassment or intimidation of a witness or interference with an ongoing investigation. On the other hand, the prosecution has a right to be heard, prior to disclosure, as to whether disclosure is against the public interest.

9. A reviewing court is not authorized to second guess the grand jury's determination that reasonable cause exists to charge the defendant with a given crime. However, the court is required to decide if a *prima facie* case has been demonstrated. A charge either will be dismissed or reduced to the most serious lesser included offense supported by legally sufficient evidence, which is defined as "competent evidence" that, if accepted as true, would establish every element of an offense charged and the defendant's commission thereof. This is the same standard employed in deciding whether a charge should survive a mid-trial application for a trial order of dismissal or a post-verdict appeal to overturn a conviction on the law.

10. In deciding whether a legally sufficient case has been presented, the court looks only at the *competent and admissible* evidence; unlike federal law, an indictment may not be based upon inadmissible hearsay.

11. The examination for legal sufficiency is based upon the competence of the evidence at the time of the presentation. If subsequent events render evidence inadmissible, that determination is not applied retroactively to void an indictment.

12. Legal insufficiency in the grand jury is not jurisdictional. A validly obtained conviction cures any insufficiency of evidence in the grand jury and an appeal may not be based upon such ground.

13. A grand jury proceeding is defective and a dismissal is required when the grand jury was illegally constituted, the proceeding was conducted by a quorum of fewer than 16 jurors, the indictment was voted by fewer than a majority of 12 jurors or the defendant was not afforded an opportunity to appear and testify before the grand jury.

14. More generally, a grand jury proceeding is also defective when it fails to conform to the requirements of CPL Article 190 to such a degree that the integrity thereof is impaired and prejudice to the defendant may result. This is a two-prong test: impairment and prejudice. The former is described as a "high hurdle"; not every error in the proceedings requires dismissal. On the other hand, where impairment has occurred, the second standard is relatively low: the mere potential for prejudice is sufficient to require dismissal.

15. Typical examples of impaired proceedings are claims of faulty instructions, use of inadmissible evidence or the presence of unauthorized personnel.

16. Instructions are sufficient if they provide the grand jury with enough information to enable it intelligently to decide whether a crime has been committed and to determine whether there exists legally sufficient evidence to establish the material elements of the crime. Nonetheless, an indictment is defective when the instructions are "so misleading or incomplete as to substantially undermine the integrity of the grand jury proceeding."

17. The submission of some inadmissible evidence in the grand jury is fatal only when the remaining evidence is insufficient to sustain the indictment.

18. Claims of defective grand jury proceedings are jurisdictional in nature and are not waived or forfeited by plea or subsequent conviction.

19. CPL § 210.40 permits a court, on its own motion or on application of either party, to dismiss an indictment in the interest of justice "even though there may be no basis for dismissal as a matter of law." Popularly referred to as "*Clayton* motions," such motions are directed toward that rare class of cases that "cr[y] out for fundamental justice beyond the confines of conventional considerations."

20. The statute lists ten factors that must be considered by the court in granting a motion. By nature, *Clayton* dismissals are rare and are carefully scrutinized on appeal. Use of an interest of justice dismissal to circumvent other restrictions, such as plea bargaining limitations or constraints upon removal to Family Court, are disfavored. *Clayton* motions are not available as alternative dispositions for persons suffering mental incapacity.

I. Options Following Dismissal (*See* §§ 5.28, 5.29)

1. The prosecution may appeal any dismissal or reduction of a count as a matter of right. The taking of an appeal does not stay the proceed-

ings, with the exception of a dismissal of a count charging murder in the first degree or a reduction of a count for legal insufficiency. In the absence of a stay, a plea may be entered to the remaining charges, which may act as a bar to further proceedings.

2. Resubmission may be allowed by the court only for a dismissal on the grounds that: (1) the indictment was defective; (2) the evidence was insufficient; (3) the grand jury proceeding was defective; or (4) a *Clayton* motion was granted. In the event of resubmission, the prosecutor may return to the same grand jury or a new grand jury. The dismissal is deemed to constitute an order holding the defendant for the action of a grand jury, which permits a securing order to remain in effect for at least 45 days, and may be extended by the court.

3. Where an indictment is dismissed on grounds of immunity, previous prosecution, speedy trial, statute of limitations or some other legal impediment, resubmission is not authorized.

4. Where a count is reduced for legal insufficiency, the prosecutor has a third option, apart from resubmission or appeal: he or she may accept the court's reduction by filing an information and proceeding upon it.

§ 5.33 Forms

§ 5.33.1 Notice of Motion in Superior Court to Release Defendant Due to Failure of Timely Grand Jury Action

[Caption]

COUNSEL:

PLEASE TAKE NOTICE, that upon the annexed affirmation and upon all the prior papers and proceedings herein, the undersigned will move this Court, at Part ___ thereof, at the Courthouse at _____, New York, on the ___ day of _____, 19__, at ___ in the forenoon, or as soon thereafter as counsel can be heard, for an order pursuant to section 190.80 of the Criminal Procedure Law releasing defendant due to failure of timely grand jury action, and for such other relief as the Court deems proper.

Dated: _____, 19__
_____, New York

[Name of defense attorney]
Attorney for Defendant
Address
Tel. No.

TO: HON. _____
District Attorney
_____ County

HON. _____
Clerk of the Court

§ 5.33.2 Affirmation in Support of Motion in Superior Court to Release Defendant Due to Failure of Timely Grand Jury Action

[Caption]

_____, an attorney duly admitted to practice in the courts of this State, hereby affirms under penalty of perjury that the following statements are true, and as for those statements made upon information and belief he [she] believes them to be true:

1. I am the attorney for the defendant herein.

2. On _____, 19__, a felony complaint was filed with the [specify local criminal court] charging defendant with the following offense(s): [specify offense(s) charged]. A copy of the felony complaint is attached hereto as Exhibit A.

3. On _____, 19__, following [a preliminary hearing; or defendant's waiver of a preliminary hearing], the [specify local criminal court] held defendant for the action of the grand jury. Since that date, defendant has been held in the custody of [specify sheriff or other official having custody of defendant].

4. Defendant has now been confined in custody for a period of more than 45 days [or more than 30 days if defendant is a juvenile offender] without the grand jury taking any action pursuant to section 190.60 of the Criminal Procedure Law.

5. The grand jury's failure to take such action is not due to defendant's request, action or condition and is not based on defendant's consent. Upon information and belief, no compelling fact or circumstance has precluded the grand jury from so acting.

6. No prior application for the relief sought herein has been made.

WHEREFORE, defendant requests that the Court issue an order pursuant to section 190.80 of the Criminal Procedure Law releasing defendant from custody.

Dated: _____, 19__
_____, New York

[Signature]
_____
[Name of defense attorney]

§ 5.33.3 Notice of Motion to Dismiss Indictment Because Defendant Not Afforded Opportunity to Testify Before Grand Jury

[Caption]

COUNSEL:

PLEASE TAKE NOTICE, that upon the annexed affirmation and upon all the prior papers and proceedings herein, the undersigned will move this Court, at Part __ thereof, at the Courthouse at _____, New

York, on the ___ day of _____, at ___ in the forenoon, or as soon thereafter as counsel can be heard, for an order pursuant to sections 190.50 and 210.35(4) of the Criminal Procedure Law dismissing the indictment on the ground that defendant was not afforded an opportunity to testify before the grand jury, and for such other relief as the Court deems proper.

Dated: _____, 19__
_____, New York

[Name of defense attorney]
Attorney for Defendant
Address
Tel. No.

TO: HON. _____
District Attorney
_____ County

HON. _____
Clerk of the Court

§ 5.33.4 Affirmation in Support of Motion to Dismiss Indictment Because Defendant Not Afforded Opportunity to Testify Before Grand Jury

[Caption]

_____, an attorney duly admitted to practice in the Courts of this State, hereby affirms under penalty of perjury that the following statements are true, and as for those statements made upon information and belief he [she] believes them to be true:

1. I am the attorney for the defendant herein.

2. On _____, 19__, defendant was arraigned in [specify local criminal court] on a felony complaint charging the following offense(s): [specify offense(s)]. At the arraignment [or specify subsequent date], defendant served notice upon the Hon. _____, District Attorney, _____ County, pursuant to section 190.50(5) of the Criminal Procedure Law requesting an opportunity to testify before the grand jury.

3. On _____, 19__, the grand jury voted an indictment against defendant based on the conduct charged in the felony complaint. A copy of the indictment is attached hereto as Exhibit A.

4. Although defendant's request to testify before the grand jury was never withdrawn, [specify why defendant not afforded opportunity to testify before grand jury—e.g., never notified that charges were to be presented to grand jury, never produced to present testimony, etc.].

5. No prior application for the relief sought herein has been made.

WHEREFORE, defendant requests that this Court issue an order pursuant to sections 190.50(5) and 210.35(4) dismissing the indictment.

§ 5.33   GRAND JURY & INDICTMENT   Ch. 5

Dated: _____, 19__
      _____, New York

                         [Signature]
                         _____
                         [Name of defense attorney]

§ 5.33.5 Notice of Motion for Severance of Counts

[Caption]

PLEASE TAKE NOTICE, that upon the annexed affirmation and upon all the prior papers and proceedings herein, the undersigned will move this Court, at Part ___ thereof, at the Courthouse at _____, New York, on the ___ day of _____, 19__, at ___ in the forenoon, or as soon thereafter as counsel can be heard, for an order pursuant to section 200.20(3) of the Criminal Procedure Law severing count(s) ___ from the remaining count(s) of the indictment filed against the defendant, and for such other relief as the Court deems proper.

Dated: _____, 19__
      _____, New York

                         [Name of defense attorney]
                         Attorney for Defendant
                         Address
                         Tel. No.

TO: HON. _____
     District Attorney
     _____ County

HON. _____
Clerk of the Court

§ 5.33.6 Affirmation in Support of Motion for Severance of Counts

[Caption]

_____, an attorney duly admitted to practice in the Courts of this State, hereby affirms under penalty of perjury that the following statements are true, and as for those statements made upon information and belief he [she] believes them to be true:

1. I am the attorney for the defendant herein.

2. On _____, 19__, an indictment was filed with this Court charging defendant with the following offenses: [specify charges in indictment]. A copy of the indictment is attached hereto as Exhibit A.

3. No plea of guilty has been entered with respect to the indictment, nor as a trial been commenced thereon.

4. [Specify why defendant would be prejudiced if the counts sought to be severed are not severed]

5. No previous application for the relief sought herein has been made.

WHEREFORE, defendant requests that this Court issue an order pursuant to section 200.20(3) of the Criminal Procedure Law severing count(s) ___ from the remaining count(s) of the indictment.

Dated: _____, 19__
_____, New York

[Signature]
_____
[Name of defense attorney]

§ 5.33.7 Notice of Motion to Consolidate Indictments Against the Same Defendant

[Caption]

COUNSEL:

PLEASE TAKE NOTICE, that upon the annexed affirmation and upon all the prior papers and proceedings herein, the undersigned will move this Court, at Part ___ thereof, at the Courthouse at _____, New York, on the ___ day of _____, 19__, at ___ in the forenoon, or as soon thereafter as counsel can be heard, for an order pursuant to section 200.20(4) of the Criminal Procedure Law consolidating indictments [specify indictment numbers] filed against the defendant, and for such other relief as the Court deems proper.

Dated: _____, 19__
_____, New York

[Name of District Attorney]
District Attorney
_____ County
Address
Tel. No.

TO: [Name of defense attorney]
Attorney for Defendant

HON. _____
Clerk of the Court

§ 5.33.8 Affirmation in Support of Motion to Consolidate Indictments Against the Same Defendant

[Caption]

_____, an attorney duly admitted to practice in the Courts of this State, hereby affirms under penalty of perjury that the following statements are true, and as to those statements made upon information and belief he [she] believes them to be true:

1. I am an assistant district attorney in _____ County.

§ 5.33 GRAND JURY & INDICTMENT Ch. 5

2. On _____, 19__, an indictment was filed with this Court [specify indictment number] charging defendant with the following offense(s): [specify charge(s)]. A copy of [specify indictment number] is attached hereto as Exhibit A.

3. On _____, 19__, a separate indictment was filed with this Court [specify indictment number] charging defendant with the following offense(s): [specify charge(s)]. A copy of [specify indictment number] is attached hereto as Exhibit B.

4. No plea of guilty has been entered with respect to the aforesaid indictments, nor has a trial been commenced thereon.

5. [Explain why the offenses in the two indictments are joinable, based on the criteria set forth in section 200.20(2) of the Criminal Procedure Law, so that all the charges may be adjudicated in a single trial]

6. No prior application for the relief sought herein has been made.

WHEREFORE, the undersigned requests that the Court issue an order consolidating [specify indictment numbers].

Dated: _____, 19__
_____, New York

[Signature]
_____
[Name of assistant district attorney]

§ 5.33.9 Notice of Motion for Severance of Trials of Jointly Indicted Defendants

[Caption]

COUNSEL:

PLEASE TAKE NOTICE, that upon the annexed affirmation and upon all the prior papers and proceedings herein, the undersigned will move this Court, at Part __ thereof, at the Courthouse at _____, New York, on the __ day of _____, 19__, at __ in the forenoon, or as soon thereafter as counsel can be heard, for an order pursuant to section 200.40(1) of the Criminal Procedure Law granting defendant [specify defendant's name] a separate trial from his [her] co-defendant(s), and for such other relief as the Court deems proper.

Dated: _____, 19__
_____, New York

[Name of defense attorney]
Attorney for Defendant
Address
Tel. No.

TO: HON. _____
District Attorney
_____ County

HON. _____
Clerk of the Court

§ 5.33.10 Affirmation in Support of Motion for Severance of Trials of Jointly Indicted Defendants

[Caption]

_____, an attorney duly admitted to practice in the Courts of this State, hereby affirms under penalty of perjury that the following statements are true, and as to those statements made upon information and belief he [she] believes them to be true:

1. I am the attorney for defendant [specify defendant's name].

2. On _____, 19__, an indictment was filed with this Court against defendant and his [her] co-defendant(s). A copy of the indictment is attached hereto as Exhibit A.

3. No plea of guilty has been entered with respect to the indictment, nor has a trial been commenced thereon.

4. [Explain why defendant would be prejudiced if jointly tried with the co-defendant(s)]

5. No prior application for the relief sought herein has been made.

WHEREFORE, defendant [specify name] requests that the Court issue an order pursuant to section 200.40(1) of the Criminal Procedure Law granting him [her] a separate trial.

Dated: _____, 19__
_____, New York

[Signature]

_____
[Name of defense attorney]

§ 5.33.11 Notice of Motion to Consolidate Indictments Against Different Defendants

[Caption]

COUNSEL:

PLEASE TAKE NOTICE, that upon the annexed affirmation and upon all the prior papers and proceedings herein, the undersigned will move this Court, at Part __ thereof, at the Courthouse at _____, New York, on the __ day of _____, 19__, at __ in the forenoon, or as soon thereafter as counsel can be heard, for an order pursuant to section 200.40(2) of the Criminal Procedure Law consolidating indictments [specify indictment numbers], and for such other relief as the Court deems proper.

Dated: _____, 19__
_____, New York

[Name of District Attorney]
District Attorney
_____ County
Address
Tel. No.

TO: [Name of defense attorney]
Attorney for Defendant

HON. _____
Clerk of the Court

§ 5.33.12 Affirmation in Support of Motion Consolidating Indictments Against Different Defendants

_____, an attorney duly admitted to practice in the Courts of this State, hereby affirms under penalty of perjury that the following statements are true, and as to those statements made upon information and belief he [she] believes them to be true:

1. I am an assistant district attorney in _____ County.

2. On _____, 19__, [specify indictment number] was filed with this Court against [specify defendant]. A copy of [specify indictment number] is attached hereto as Exhibit A.

3. On _____, 19__, [specify indictment number] was filed with this Court against [specify defendant]. A copy of that indictment is attached hereto as Exhibit B.

4. No plea of guilty has been entered with respect to the aforesaid indictments, nor has a trial been commenced thereon.

5. [Explain why the counts in these indictments could have been jointly charged in a single indictment, based on the criteria set forth in section 200.40(1) of the Criminal Procedure Law, so that the charges in both indictments can be adjudicated in a single trial]

6. No prior application for the relief sought herein has been made.

WHEREFORE, the undersigned requests that the Court issue an order pursuant to section 200.40(2) of the Criminal Procedure Law consolidating [specify indictment numbers].

Dated: _____, 19__
_____, New York

[Signature]
_____
[Name of assistant district attorney]

§ 5.33.13 Notice of Motion to Amend Indictment

[Caption]

COUNSEL:

PLEASE TAKE NOTICE, that upon the annexed affirmation and upon all the prior papers and proceedings herein, the undersigned will move this Court, at Part ___ thereof, at the Courthouse at _____, New York, on the ___ day of _____, 19__, at ___ in the forenoon, or as soon thereafter as counsel can be heard, for an order pursuant to section 200.70 of the Criminal Procedure Law amending the indictment herein, and for such other relief as the Court deems proper.

Dated: _____, 19__
_____, New York

[Name of District Attorney]
District Attorney
_____ County
Address
Tel. No.

TO: [Name of defense attorney]
Attorney for Defendant

HON. _____
Clerk of the Court

§ 5.33.14 Affirmation in Support of Motion to Amend Indictment

[Caption]

_____, an attorney duly admitted to practice in the Courts of this State, hereby affirms under penalty of perjury that the following statements are true, and as to those statements made upon information and belief he [she] believes them to be true:

1. I am an assistant district attorney in _____ County.

2. On _____, 19__, an indictment was filed with this Court charging defendant with the following offense(s): [specify charge(s)]. A copy of the indictment is attached hereto as Exhibit A.

3. This affirmation is made in support of the People's application to amend the indictment as follows: [specify amendment sought].

4. Such amendment would not change the theory or theories of the prosecution as reflected in the evidence that was presented to the grand jury, nor would it otherwise tend to prejudice the defendant on the merits.

5. No prior application for the relief sought herein has been made.

WHEREFORE, the undersigned requests that the Court order the aforesaid amendment of the indictment.

§ 5.33 GRAND JURY & INDICTMENT Ch. 5

Dated: _____, 19__
       _____, New York

                              [Signature]
                              _____
                              [Name of assistant district
                              attorney]

§ 5.33.15 Notice of Motion to Amend Bill of Particulars

[Caption]

COUNSEL:

PLEASE TAKE NOTICE, that upon the annexed affirmation and upon all the prior papers and proceedings herein, the undersigned will move this Court, at Part ___ thereof, at the Courthouse at _____, New York, on the ___ day of _____, 19__, at ___ in the forenoon, or as soon thereafter as counsel can be heard, for an order pursuant to section 200.95(8) of the Criminal Procedure Law authorizing the People to amend the bill of particulars previously served herein, and for such other relief as the Court deems proper.

Dated: _____, 19__
       _____, New York

                              [Name of District Attorney]
                              District Attorney
                              _____ County
                              Address
                              Tel. No.

TO: [Name of defense attorney]
    Attorney for Defendant

    HON. _____
    Clerk of the Court

§ 5.33.16 Affirmation in Support of Motion to Amend Bill of Particulars

_____, an attorney duly admitted to practice in the Courts of this State, hereby affirms under penalty of perjury that the following statements are true, and as to those statements made upon information and belief he [she] believes them to be true:

1. I am an assistant district attorney in _____ County.

2. On _____, 19__, an indictment was filed with this Court charging defendant with the following offense(s): [specify offense(s)]. A copy of the indictment is attached hereto as Exhibit A.

2. On _____, 19__, the People served a bill of particulars on the defendant. A copy of the bill of particulars is attached hereto as Exhibit B.

3. Trial on the indictment commenced in this Court on _____, 19__, and [specify current status of trial].

4. The People now seek authorization from the Court to amend the previously served bill of particulars in the following manner: [specify amendment sought].

5. [Explain reasons why amendment is sought]

6. No undue prejudice will result to defendant if the amendment sought herein is granted.

7. No prior application for the relief sought herein has been made.

WHEREFORE, the undersigned requests that the Court issue an order authorizing the People to amend the bill of particulars.

Dated: _____, 19__
_____, New York

[Signature]
_____
[Name of assistant district attorney]

§ 5.33.17 Notice of Motion to Dismiss Indictment (or Count(s) of Indictment) as Defective

[Caption]

COUNSEL:

PLEASE TAKE NOTICE, that upon the annexed affirmation and upon all the prior papers and proceedings herein, the undersigned will move this Court, at Part ___ thereof, at the Courthouse at _____, New York, on the ___ day of _____, 19__, at ___ in the forenoon, or as soon thereafter as counsel can be heard, for an order pursuant to sections 210.20(1)(a) and 210.25(1) of the Criminal Procedure Law on the ground that the indictment [or count(s) ___ of the indictment] herein is defective, and for such other relief as the Court deems proper.

Dated: _____, 19__
_____, New York

[Name of defense attorney]
Attorney for Defendant
Address
Tel. No.

TO: HON. _____
    District Attorney
    _____ County

    HON. _____
    Clerk of the Court

§ 5.33.18 Affirmation in Support of Motion to Dismiss Indictment (or Count(s) of Indictment) as Defective

[Caption]

_____, an attorney duly admitted to practice in the Courts of this State, hereby affirms under penalty of perjury that the following statements are true, and as to those statements made upon information and belief he [she] believes them to be true:

1. I am the attorney for the defendant herein.

2. On _____, 19__, an indictment was filed with this Court charging defendant with the following offense(s): [specify charge(s)]. A copy of the indictment is attached hereto as Exhibit A.

3. No plea of guilty has been entered with respect to the indictment, nor has a trial been commenced thereon.

4. The indictment [or count(s) __ of the indictment] is defective because it fails to conform with the requirements set forth in Article 200 of the Criminal Procedure Law. [Explain]

5. Such defects cannot be cured by an amendment of the indictment pursuant to section 200.70 of the Criminal Procedure Law.

6. No prior application for the relief sought herein has been made.

WHEREFORE, defendant requests that the Court dismiss the indictment [or count(s) __ of the indictment] pursuant to sections 210.20(1)(a) and 210.25(1) of the Criminal Procedure Law on the ground that the indictment [or count(s) __ of the indictment] is defective.

Dated: _____, 19__
_____, New York

[Signature]
_____
[Name of defense attorney]

§ 5.33.19 Notice of Motion to Dismiss Indictment (Grand Jury Immunity)

[Caption]

COUNSEL:

PLEASE TAKE NOTICE, that upon the annexed affirmation and upon all the prior papers and proceedings herein, the undersigned will move this Court, at Part __ thereof, at the Courthouse at _____, New York, on the __ day of _____, 19__, at __ in the forenoon, or as soon thereafter as counsel can be heard, for an order pursuant to section 210.20(1)(d) of the Criminal Procedure Law dismissing the indictment on the ground that defendant has immunity with respect to the offense(s) charged therein, and for such other relief as the Court deems proper.

Dated: _____, 19__
_____, New York

[Name of defense attorney]
Attorney for Defendant
Address
Tel. No.

TO: HON. _____
District Attorney
_____ County

HON. _____
Clerk of the Court

§ 5.33.20 Affirmation in Support of Motion to Dismiss Indictment (Grand Jury Immunity)

[Caption]

_____, an attorney duly admitted to practice in the Courts of this State, hereby affirms under penalty of perjury that the following statements are true, and as to those statements made upon information and belief he [she] believes them to be true:

1. I am the attorney for the defendant herein.

2. On _____, 19__, an indictment was filed with this Court charging defendant with the following offense(s): [specify charge(s)]. A copy of the indictment is attached hereto as Exhibit A.

3. No plea of guilty has been entered with respect to the indictment, nor has a trial been commenced thereon.

4. On _____, 19__, defendant appeared and testified before the grand jury that returned the indictment against him [her]. Defendant never executed a waiver of immunity regarding such appearance and testimony before the grand jury.

5. No prior application for the relief sought herein has been made.

WHEREFORE, defendant requests that the Court issue an order pursuant to section 210.20(1)(d) of the Criminal Procedure Law dismissing the indictment on the ground that he [she] has immunity with respect to the offense(s) charged therein.

Dated: _____, 19__
_____, New York

[Signature]

_____
[Name of defense attorney]

§ 5.33.21 Notice of Motion to Dismiss Indictment in Furtherance of Justice

[Caption]

COUNSEL:

PLEASE TAKE NOTICE, that upon the annexed affirmation and upon all the prior papers and proceedings herein, the undersigned will move this Court, at Part ___ thereof, at the Courthouse at _____, New York, on the ___ day of _____, 19__, at ___ in the forenoon, or as soon thereafter as counsel can be heard, for an order pursuant to sections 210.20(1)(i) and 210.40 of the Criminal Procedure Law dismissing the indictment in furtherance of justice, and for such other relief as the Court deems proper.

Dated: _____, 19__
_____, New York

[Name of defense attorney]
Attorney for Defendant
Address
Tel. No.

TO: HON. _____
District Attorney
_____ County

HON. _____
Clerk of the Court

§ 5.33.22 Affirmation in Support of Motion to Dismiss Indictment in Furtherance of Justice

[Caption]

_____, an attorney duly admitted to practice in the Courts of this State, hereby affirms under penalty of perjury that the following statements are true, and as to those statements made upon information and belief he [she] believes them to be true:

1. I am the attorney for the defendant herein.

2. On _____, 19__, an indictment was filed with this Court charging defendant with the following offense(s): [specify charge(s)]. A copy of the indictment is attached hereto as Exhibit A.

3. No plea of guilty has been entered with respect to the indictment, nor has a trial been commenced thereon.

4. Compelling circumstances exist in this case supporting dismissal of the indictment in furtherance of justice. [Explain reasons supporting dismissal, with reference to the factors set forth in section 210.40(1)(a)-(j) of the Criminal Procedure Law]

5. No prior application for the relief sought herein has been made.

WHEREFORE, defendant requests that the Court issue an order pursuant to sections 210.20(1)(i) and 210.40 of the Criminal Procedure Law dismissing the indictment in furtherance of justice.

Dated: _____, 19__
_____, New York

[Signature]
_____
[Name of defense attorney]

§ 5.33.23 Notice of Motion by Prosecutor to Submit Charge(s) to a New Grand Jury

[Caption]

COUNSEL:

PLEASE TAKE NOTICE, that upon the annexed affirmation and upon all the prior papers and proceedings herein, the undersigned will move this Court, at Part __ thereof, at the Courthouse at _____, New York, on the __ day of _____, 19__, at __ in the forenoon, or as soon thereafter as counsel can be heard, for an order pursuant to section 210.20(4) of the Criminal Procedure Law authorizing the People to submit the charge(s), previously dismissed by this Court, to a Grand Jury of _____ County, and for such other relief as the Court deems proper.

Dated: _____, 19__
_____, New York

[Name of District Attorney]
District Attorney
_____ County
Address
Tel. No.

TO: [Name of defense attorney]
   Attorney for Defendant

   HON. _____
   Clerk of the Court

§ 5.33.24 Affirmation in Support of Prosecutor's Motion to Submit Charge(s) to a New Grand Jury

[Caption]

_____, an attorney duly admitted to practice in the Courts of this State, hereby affirms under penalty of perjury that the following statements are true, and as to those statements made upon information and belief he [she] believes them to be true:

1. I am an assistant district attorney in _____ County.

2. On _____, 19__, an indictment was filed with this Court charging defendant with the following offense(s): [specify charge(s)]. A copy of said indictment is attached hereto as Exhibit A.

3. On _____, 19__, the Court granted defendant's motion pursuant to section __ of the Criminal Procedure Law to dismiss the indict-

ment on the ground that [specify ground of dismissal]. A copy of the Court's order of dismissal is attached hereto as Exhibit B.

4. It is the People's view that the offense(s) charged against defendant in the dismissed indictment are well founded, and that if such offense(s) are submitted to a new grand jury a second indictment will be returned against defendant.

5. Accordingly, justice will be furthered if the People are permitted to submit the dismissed charge(s) against defendant to a new grand jury.

6. No prior application for the relief sought herein has been made.

WHEREFORE, the undersigned requests that the Court issue an order authorizing the People to submit the charge(s), previously dismissed by the Court, to a Grand Jury of _____ County.

Dated: _____, 19__
_____, New York

[Signature]

_____

[Name of assistant district attorney]

Chapter 6

COMPETENCY PROCEEDINGS

Table of Sections

6.1   In General.
6.2   Order of Examination.
6.3   Effect on Case of Order of Examination.
6.4   Initial Examination—By Whom Conducted.
6.5   Initial Examination—How and When Conducted.
6.6   Post–Examination Procedure in Superior Court.
6.7   Post–Examination Procedure in Local Criminal Court.
6.8   The 1980 Amendments.
6.9   Hearing Procedure.
6.10 Additional Considerations.
6.11 Practice Summary.
6.12 Forms.
    6.12.1 Notice of Motion for Order of Examination.
    6.12.2 Affirmation in Support of Motion for Order of Examination.

WESTLAW Electronic Research

See WESTLAW Electronic Research Guide preceding the Summary of Contents.

§ 6.1 In General

No defendant can be tried or sentenced for a crime if he or she is not mentally competent. That is of course the law not only in New York, but in every state,[1] for the right not to be adjudged a criminal while incompetent is a fundamental principle of due process.[2] That principle is rooted in the early common law[3] and has been recognized throughout New York's history.

The Supreme Court has stated that a defendant is competent if he has

> sufficient present ability to consult with his lawyer with a reasonable degree of rational understanding—and . . . a rational

---

1. Medina v. California, 505 U.S. 437, 447, 112 S.Ct. 2572, 2578, 120 L.Ed.2d 353 (1992).

2. Medina v. California, 505 U.S. at 449, 112 S.Ct. at 2579; Drope v. Missouri, 420 U.S. 162, 172–73, 95 S.Ct. 896, 904–05, 43 L.Ed.2d 103 (1975); Pate v. Robinson, 383 U.S. 375, 386, 86 S.Ct. 836, 842, 15 L.Ed.2d 815 (1966).

3. See Medina v. California, 505 U.S. at 446–47, 112 S.Ct. at 2577–78 (1992); Freeman v. People, 4 Denio 1, 19–21, 25–27 (N.Y. Sup.Ct.1847); People ex rel. Schildhaus v. Warden, 37 Misc.2d 660, 235 N.Y.S.2d 531 (Sup.Ct., N.Y. County, 1962).

as well as factual understanding of the proceedings against him.[4]

The CPL definition is no different in substance: an "incapacitated person" is a defendant who "as a result of mental disease or defect lacks capacity to understand the proceedings against him or to assist in his own defense."[5] A claim of incompetence thus turns on the defendant's mental state at the time of the criminal proceedings.

In that regard, incompetence differs from "insanity." The insanity defense applies to a defendant who, at the time of the crime, was unable to know or appreciate the nature and consequences of his or her conduct, or that such conduct was wrong.[6] Moreover, insanity is an affirmative defense, which negates substantive responsibility for a crime.[7] A defendant's incompetence is not a defense; as a general matter, a finding that a defendant is incompetent merely suspends a criminal proceeding until the defendant becomes competent.[8]

Article 730 of the CPL sets out how the courts should ensure that no incompetent person is convicted or sentenced for a crime. This chapter will address that Article and the cases decided under its provisions. First, Section 6.2 and Section 6.3 will address when a judge should order an examination into a defendant's competence, and the effects on a prosecution of the judge's decision to do so.

Second, Section 6.4 and Section 6.5 will discuss the examination process. Those sections will consider who should evaluate the defendant, and who can be present at interviews with the defendant. In addition, those sections will consider where examinations can be held, and whether the defendant can be detained during the examination process. Finally, those sections will address the nature of the reports that must be produced by the examiners.

Third, in Sections 6.6 to 6.9, this chapter will discuss the aftermath of an examination in a superior court case, and in a case in a local criminal court. Notably, relatively swift procedures are applicable in the local criminal courts, in correlation with the lesser punishments available to defendants who face charges in those courts. Discussion is warranted in particular concerning how the court is to evaluate the reports of the examiners, and concerning the consequences of a finding of incompetence.

Finally, in Section 6.10 and Section 6.11, this chapter will take note of the case law concerning some specific mental disorders, and concerning other, miscellaneous competence issues.

4. Dusky v. United States, 362 U.S. 402, 403, 80 S.Ct. 788, 789, 4 L.Ed.2d 824 (1960).

5. CPL § 730.10(1); see People v. Francabandera, 33 N.Y.2d 429, 435–36, 354 N.Y.S.2d 609, 613–14, 310 N.E.2d 292, 295 (1974). Despite the statute's reference to a defendant's "incapacity," this chapter will refer to "competence" and "incompetence" in accord with common usage.

6. P.L. § 40.15. See generally Greenberg, Marcus, et al., New York Criminal Law § 3.21 (West 1996).

7. Id.

8. See §§ 6.6, 6.7, infra.

§ 6.2 Order of Examination

The procedures set forth in Article 730 are initiated by an "order of examination," which is

> an order issued ... by a criminal court wherein a criminal action is pending against a defendant, directing that such defendant be examined for the purpose of determining if he is an incapacitated person.[9]

Such an order may be issued at any time after arraignment and before sentence by the court in which a criminal action is pending.[10]

Of course, an order of examination will not issue, and the procedures set forth in Article 730 will not be followed, in every case. In the words of the statute,

> the court must issue an order of examination when it is of the opinion that the defendant may be an incapacitated person.[11]

In that regard, a defendant is presumed competent,[12] and

> is not entitled, as a matter of right, to have the question of his capacity to stand trial passed upon before the commencement of the trial, if the court is satisfied from the available information that there is no proper basis for questioning the defendant's sanity.[13]

Thus, defense counsel's insistence that his or her client is in need of examination is, by itself, not necessarily a basis for the issuance of an order of examination.[14] Indeed, even an affirmation by a psychiatrist

---

9. CPL § 730.10(2).

10. CPL § 730.30(1). One exception is made in the statute: when the defendant has been arraigned on a felony complaint in a local criminal court, that court loses the power to issue an order of examination when it orders the defendant held for the action of the grand jury.

Orders of examination may also be issued by Family Court judges in juvenile delinquency proceedings pursuant to section 322.1 of the Family Court Act. CPL § 730.10(2). Description of the effects of an order of examination in a Family Court proceeding is beyond the scope of this book.

The case law has also recognized a right to competency determinations, conducted along the lines set out in Article 730, during extradition proceedings. Welkes v. Brennan, 79 A.D.2d 644, 433 N.Y.S.2d 817 (2d Dep't 1980); People ex rel. Fusco v. Sera, 123 Misc.2d 19, 472 N.Y.S.2d 564 (Sup.Ct., Bronx County, 1984). At least one case has held that Article 730 applies in a probation violation proceeding, Matter of Tompkins, 146 Misc.2d 754, 553 N.Y.S.2d 69 (Montgomery Co.Ct.1990), but that is inconsistent with the understanding of the drafters. See Staff Comment, Proposed New York Criminal Procedure Law, CPL § 405.30, p. 464 (Edward Thompson Co. 1967).

11. CPL § 730.30(1).

12. People v. Gelikkaya, 84 N.Y.2d 456, 459, 618 N.Y.S.2d 895, 897, 643 N.E.2d 517, 519 (1994); see People v. Silver, 33 N.Y.2d 475, 354 N.Y.S.2d 915, 310 N.E.2d 520 (1974).

13. People v. Armlin, 37 N.Y.2d 167, 171, 371 N.Y.S.2d 691, 695, 332 N.E.2d 870, 873 (1975); accord People v. Morgan, 87 N.Y.2d 878, 638 N.Y.S.2d 942, 662 N.E.2d 260 (1995); United States ex rel. Roth v. Zelker, 455 F.2d 1105, 1108 (2d Cir.1972); see also People v. McElvaine, 125 N.Y. 596, 609, 26 N.E. 929, 933 (1891).

14. People v. Morgan, 87 N.Y.2d 878, 638 N.Y.S.2d 942, 662 N.E.2d 260 (1995);

expressing doubt about the defendant's competence will not automatically entitle the defendant to an order of examination.[15]

On the other hand, if the facts of the particular case fairly suggest to the court that the defendant "may" be incompetent, the court "must" order an examination even in the absence of a request by a party for such an examination.[16] In the words of a leading opinion of the Court of Appeals, issued even before the enactment of Article 730,

> If at any time before final judgment ... it shall appear to the court that there is reasonable ground for believing that a defendant is in such a state of idiocy, imbecility or insanity that he is incapable of understanding the charge, indictment or proceedings or of making his defense, it is the duty of the court to direct him to be examined in these respects.[17]

As these opposing principles suggest, the decision whether to order an examination is often a very difficult one, "in which a wide range of manifestations and subtle nuances are implicated."[18] Among the relevant considerations are the defendant's history, if any, of irrational behavior; the defendant's demeanor in the trial court; any prior medical opinion on his or her competence to stand trial;[19] and, with respect to post-conviction examinations, the contents of the presentence report.[20] Further, in considering the propriety of an order of examination, the court should take into account the closely related questions of whether the defendant:

- is oriented as to time and place
- is able to perceive, recall and relate
- has an understanding of the process of the trial and the roles of judge, jury, prosecutor and defense attorney
- can establish a working relationship with defense counsel
- has sufficient intelligence and judgment to listen to the advice of counsel and, based on that advice, appreciate the fact that one course of conduct may be more beneficial to him or her than another; and

People v. Seidman, 206 A.D.2d 257, 613 N.Y.S.2d 875 (1st Dep't 1994); People v. Rogers, 32 A.D.2d 756, 756–57, 300 N.Y.S.2d 868, 868–69 (1st Dep't 1969), aff'd 27 N.Y.2d 711, 314 N.Y.S.2d 177, 262 N.E.2d 413 (1970); but see People v. Arnold, 113 A.D.2d 101, 103, 495 N.Y.S.2d 537, 539 (4th Dep't 1985).

15. People v. Gronachan, 162 A.D.2d 852, 557 N.Y.S.2d 753 (3d Dep't 1990).

16. People v. Armlin, 37 N.Y.2d 167, 171, 371 N.Y.S.2d 691, 695, 332 N.E.2d 870, 873 (1975); see People v. Rogers, 32 A.D.2d 756, 757, 300 N.Y.S.2d 868, 869 (1st Dep't 1969), aff'd 27 N.Y.2d 711, 314 N.Y.S.2d 177, 262 N.E.2d 413 (1970)(defense counsel's view that defendant is competent is not controlling).

17. People v. Smyth, 3 N.Y.2d 184, 187, 164 N.Y.S.2d 737, 739, 143 N.E.2d 922, 923 (1957).

18. Drope v. Missouri, 420 U.S. 162, 180, 95 S.Ct. 896, 908, 43 L.Ed.2d 103, 118 (1975).

19. People v. Arnold, 113 A.D.2d at 103, 495 N.Y.S.2d at 539.

20. People v. Clickner, 128 A.D.2d 917, 918, 512 N.Y.S.2d 572, 572 (3d Dep't 1987); see People v. Bangert, 22 N.Y.2d 799, 292 N.Y.S.2d 900, 239 N.E.2d 644 (1968).

- is sufficiently stable to withstand the stresses of the trial without suffering a serious prolonged or permanent breakdown.[21]

In light of the court's need to weigh many facts derived from many sources, it is not surprising that the decision whether to order an examination into the defendant's competence is entrusted to the discretion of the trial judge.[22] And it follows that the court's determination not to order an examination will be upheld on appeal, absent an abuse of discretion.[23] In that regard, the factor that appears to be most influential during review of a trial judge's determination not to order an examination is the judge's opportunity personally to observe the defendant,[24] and in particular while the defendant is pleading guilty[25] or on the witness stand.[26] Important as well is the trial judge's advantage over an appellate court in recognizing whether a motion for an order of examination is a dilatory tactic.[27]

Of course, defense counsel will also have personal knowledge about the defendant's mental condition. As noted above, the opinion of defense counsel that the defendant might be incompetent does not mandate an examination; it is the trial court's opinion that is controlling.[28] On the other hand, defense counsel's statement that he or she believes that the defendant is competent, or even counsel's failure to suggest that he or she has had difficulties communicating with the defendant, can provide strong support for a decision not to order an examination.[29]

21. People v. Picozzi, 106 A.D.2d 413, 482 N.Y.S.2d 335 (2d Dep't 1984).

22. People v. Morgan, 87 N.Y.2d 878, 638 N.Y.S.2d 942, 662 N.E.2d 260, (1995); People v. Arnold, 113 A.D.2d at 102, 495 N.Y.S.2d at 539; People v. Charon, 113 A.D.2d 950, 493 N.Y.S.2d 847 (2d Dep't 1985); see People v. McElvaine, 125 N.Y. 596, 605–09, 26 N.E. 929, 932–33 (1891); United States v. Nichols, 56 F.3d 403, 414 (2d Cir.1995).

23. People v. Rodriguez, 56 N.Y.2d 557, 449 N.Y.S.2d 962, 434 N.E.2d 1340 (1982); People v. Delgado, 202 A.D.2d 299, 610 N.Y.S.2d 770 (1st Dep't 1994); People v. Jones, 134 A.D.2d 701, 702, 521 N.Y.S.2d 194, 196 (3d Dep't 1987).

24. People v. Morgan, supra; People v. Russell, 74 N.Y.2d 901, 902, 549 N.Y.S.2d 646, 647, 548 N.E.2d 1297, 1298 (1989); People v. Clickner, 128 A.D.2d 917, 918–19, 512 N.Y.S.2d 572, 572–73 (3d Dep't 1987); People v. Rios, 126 A.D.2d 860, 862, 510 N.Y.S.2d 923, 925 (3d Dep't 1987); People v. Salladeen, 50 A.D.2d 765, 766, 377 N.Y.S.2d 63, 65 (1st Dep't 1975), aff'd 42 N.Y.2d 914, 397 N.Y.S.2d 994, 366 N.E.2d 1348 (1977); see also People v. Klein, 30 Misc.2d 334, 217 N.Y.S.2d 885 (Sup.Ct., Bronx County, 1961)(denying writ of habeas corpus).

25. People v. Thomas, 188 A.D.2d 431, 592 N.Y.S.2d 586 (1st Dep't 1992); People v. Claudio, 183 A.D.2d 945, 583 N.Y.S.2d 563 (3d Dep't 1992); People v. Helm, 178 A.D.2d 656, 577 N.Y.S.2d 889 (2d Dep't 1991).

26. People v. Seidman, 206 A.D.2d 257, 613 N.Y.S.2d 875 (1st Dep't 1994); People v. Chisolm, 162 A.D.2d 267, 556 N.Y.S.2d 625 (1st Dep't 1990); People v. Jones, 134 A.D.2d 701, 702, 521 N.Y.S.2d 194, 196 (3d Dep't 1987).

27. People v. Gonzalez, 168 A.D.2d 568, 562 N.Y.S.2d 785 (2d Dep't 1990); People v. Rios, 126 A.D.2d 860, 862, 510 N.Y.S.2d 923, 925 (3d Dep't 1987); People v. Salladeen, 50 A.D.2d 765, 377 N.Y.S.2d 63 (1st Dep't 1975), aff'd 42 N.Y.2d 914, 397 N.Y.S.2d 994, 366 N.E.2d 1348 (1977); People v. Rogers, 32 A.D.2d 756, 756–57, 300 N.Y.S.2d 868, 869–70 (1st Dep't 1969), aff'd 27 N.Y.2d 711, 314 N.Y.S.2d 177, 262 N.E.2d 413 (1970); see also People v. Klein, 30 Misc.2d 334, 217 N.Y.S.2d 885 (Sup.Ct., Bronx County, 1961).

28. See footnote 14, supra.

29. United States ex rel. Roth v. Zelker, 455 F.2d 1105, 1108 (2d Cir.1972), cert. den. 408 U.S. 927, 92 S.Ct. 2512, 33 L.Ed.2d 340 (1972); People v. Gelikkaya, 84 N.Y.2d 456, 460, 618 N.Y.S.2d 895, 897, 643

§ 6.2   COMPETENCY PROCEEDINGS   Ch. 6

In keeping with the deference accorded to trial judges, many appellate decisions have rejected arguments that individual facts should necessarily have caused a trial judge to order an examination into the defendant's competence. For example, a history of psychiatric problems will not, without more, require that an examination be ordered.[30] The defendant's use of medication will not mandate examination.[31] Attempts at suicide or other self-inflicted injuries, which of course may be more or less serious, do not necessarily suggest that the defendant might be incompetent.[32] Disruptive conduct in court does not prove that the defendant should be examined,[33] nor does defendant's disagreement with the judgment of his or her attorney.[34] Low intelligence is not a clear indicator of incompetence.[35] And, as one trial judge noted in a *habeas corpus* proceeding, a defendant is not necessarily a fit candidate for examination merely because his crime is incomprehensible or cruel.[36]

Of course, in a particular case such facts may well persuade the judge that the defendant should be examined. Indeed, an order of examination is mandatory if the trial judge has reason to believe that the defendant "may" be incompetent,[37] and thus a trial judge's failure to issue an order of examination will not always be affirmed. In that regard, once the order of examination has been issued, there is no shortcut that avoids the complex procedural mechanisms of Article 730.[38]

N.E.2d 517, 519 (1994); People v. Shapard, 199 A.D.2d 888, 606 N.Y.S.2d 103 (3d Dep't 1993); People v. Ross, 185 A.D.2d 661, 586 N.Y.S.2d 75 (4th Dep't 1992); People v. Swan, 158 A.D.2d 158, 161, 557 N.Y.S.2d 791, 793 (4th Dep't 1990); People v. Rogers, 32 A.D.2d 756, 757, 300 N.Y.S.2d 868, 869 (1st Dep't 1969), aff'd 27 N.Y.2d 711, 314 N.Y.S.2d 177, 262 N.E.2d 413 (1970).

30. People v. Morgan, 87 N.Y.2d 878, 638 N.Y.S.2d 942, 662 N.E.2d 260 (1995); People v. Parker, 191 A.D.2d 717, 595 N.Y.S.2d 519 (2d Dep't 1993); People v. Ross, 185 A.D.2d 661, 586 N.Y.S.2d 75 (4th Dep't 1992); People v. Helm, 178 A.D.2d 656, 577 N.Y.S.2d 889 (2d Dep't 1991); People v. Abdul–Malik, 156 A.D.2d 1023, 549 N.Y.S.2d 304 (4th Dep't 1989); People v. Jones, 134 A.D.2d 701, 702, 521 N.Y.S.2d 194, 195 (3d Dep't 1987); People v. Clickner, 128 A.D.2d 917, 918–19, 512 N.Y.S.2d 572, 572–73 (3d Dep't 1987).

31. People v. Grant, 188 A.D.2d 1052, 592 N.Y.S.2d 206 (4th Dep't 1992) (epilepsy medication); People v. Thomas, 188 A.D.2d 431, 592 N.Y.S.2d 586 (1st Dep't 1992)(psychiatric medication); cf. People v. Pringle, 186 A.D.2d 413, 589 N.Y.S.2d 8 (1st Dep't 1992).

32. People v. Rogha, 213 A.D.2d 266, 624 N.Y.S.2d 125 (1st Dep't 1995); People v. Delgado, 202 A.D.2d 299, 610 N.Y.S.2d 770 (1st Dep't 1994)(genital mutilation); People v. Bacic, 202 A.D.2d 234, 608 N.Y.S.2d 452 (1st Dep't 1994); People v. Clickner, 128 A.D.2d 917, 918–19, 512 N.Y.S.2d 572, 572–73 (3d Dep't 1987); see People v. Rogers, 163 A.D.2d 337, 557 N.Y.S.2d 168 (2d Dep't 1990)("suicidal tendencies").

33. People v. Johnson, 204 A.D.2d 188, 612 N.Y.S.2d 26 (1st Dep't 1994); People v. Bancroft, 110 A.D.2d 773, 488 N.Y.S.2d 215 (2d Dep't 1985); People v. Salladeen, 50 A.D.2d 765, 377 N.Y.S.2d 63 (1st Dep't 1975), aff'd 42 N.Y.2d 914, 397 N.Y.S.2d 994, 366 N.E.2d 1348 (1977).

34. People v. Vasquez, 172 A.D.2d 435, 569 N.Y.S.2d 11 (1st Dep't 1991); People v. Soto, 189 A.D.2d 712, 592 N.Y.S.2d 721 (1st Dep't 1993); People v. Rios, 126 A.D.2d 860, 510 N.Y.S.2d 923 (3d Dep't 1987); People v. Picozzi, 106 A.D.2d 413, 414, 482 N.Y.S.2d 335, 337 (2d Dep't 1984).

35. People v. Charlton, 192 A.D.2d 757, 758–59, 596 N.Y.S.2d 210, 212 (3d Dep't 1993).

36. People ex rel. Schildhaus v. Warden, 37 Misc.2d 660, 673–76, 235 N.Y.S.2d 531, 547–50 (Sup.Ct., N.Y. County, 1962).

37. CPL § 730.30(1).

38. People v. Armlin, 37 N.Y.2d 167, 172, 371 N.Y.S.2d 691, 696, 332 N.E.2d 870, 873 (1975); People v. Mullins, 137 A.D.2d 227, 528 N.Y.S.2d 698 (3d Dep't 1988); People v. Lowe, 109 A.D.2d 300, 304, 491 N.Y.S.2d 529, 533 (4th Dep't 1985); People v. McCabe, 87 A.D.2d 852, 449 N.Y.S.2d 245 (2d Dep't 1982); People v. Ross, 50 A.D.2d 1064, 375 N.Y.S.2d 714 (4th Dep't 1975).

Nonetheless, the trial court may not surrender to the temptation to adjudicate a viable competency issue, in the guise of determining whether to order an examination. Thus, where the court ignores plain signs that the defendant lacks the ability to understand the proceedings or assist in his or her defense, remand for a competency hearing and perhaps a new trial[39] will be in order.[40]

Finally, when the court does resolve to order an examination, and the defendant ultimately is found competent to proceed, the competence issue does not inevitably disappear from the case. Competence is a variable state, and at any subsequent time in the criminal action the court may have renewed grounds to doubt the defendant's ability to understand the proceedings and assist his or her defense. The test set out in CPL § 730.30(1) is again applicable in these instances: if the court has reason to think that the defendant "may" be incompetent, it "must" once more issue an order of examination. But of course the court will be aided in its evaluation of whether the defendant may be incompetent by the inquiries conducted in the wake of the initial order of examination.[41]

Library References:
West's Key No. Digests, Criminal Law ⚖981(2); Mental Health ⚖434.

§ 6.3 Effect on Case of Order of Examination

The premise for an order of examination is a concern that the defendant may not be competent to participate in the criminal action. Not surprisingly, therefore, Article 730 provides generally that the order suspends the action until the defendant's competence is established, unless the case is earlier dismissed. In particular, if the examination does not establish the defendant's competence, he or she will be committed for care and treatment.[42] At that point, depending on the charges against the defendant, the case will either end[43] or be

> suspended until the superintendent of the institution in which the defendant is confined determines that he is no longer an incapacitated person.[44]

The court may not consider the defendant competent to understand and assist in pretrial proceedings or at a bench trial if he or she is not competent to be tried by jury.[45] Nor may the defendant plead guilty, for

39. See § 6.10, infra.

40. People v. Peterson, 40 N.Y.2d 1014, 391 N.Y.S.2d 530, 359 N.E.2d 1325 (1976); People v. Frazier, 114 A.D.2d 1038, 495 N.Y.S.2d 478 (2d Dep't 1985); People v. Arnold, 113 A.D.2d 101, 495 N.Y.S.2d 537 (4th Dep't 1985); People v. Cartagena, 92 A.D.2d 901, 459 N.Y.S.2d 896 (2d Dep't 1983).

41. People v. Morgan, 87 N.Y.2d 878, 638 N.Y.S.2d 942, 662 N.E.2d 260 (1995); People v. Vasquez, 172 A.D.2d 435, 569 N.Y.S.2d 11 (1st Dep't 1991); People v. Rogers, 163 A.D.2d 337, 557 N.Y.S.2d 168 (2d Dep't 1990); People v. Konits, 159 A.D.2d 590, 552 N.Y.S.2d 448 (2d Dep't 1990); People v. Picozzi, 106 A.D.2d 413, 482 N.Y.S.2d 335 (2d Dep't 1984).

42. See §§ 6.6, 6.7, infra.

43. CPL §§ 730.40(2), 730.50(1).

44. CPL § 730.60(2).

45. People v. Vallen, 128 Misc.2d 397, 488 N.Y.S.2d 994 (Orange Co.Ct.1985).

the standard for competence to waive important constitutional rights is identical to the standard for competence to stand trial.[46]

Exceptions are expressly made in section 730.60 to the general rule that the order of examination suspends the prosecution. A defendant held in custody by virtue of an order of commitment[47] or an order of retention[48] may make any motion authorized by the CPL "which is susceptible of fair determination without his personal participation"; if such a motion is denied, the defendant may renew it after he or she becomes competent.[49] In particular, if the accusatory instrument is subject to dismissal on legal grounds, there is no reason why counsel for an incompetent defendant should not be as free as in any other case to obtain an order dismissing that instrument.[50] But presumably motions that would require hearings would not fall within the exception.[51]

In addition, defendants who have been held in custody by virtue of an order of commitment or an order of retention for at least two years, or who are residents or citizens of another state or country and will be removed there upon a dismissal, may move for dismissal of the indictment. The court may grant such a motion if the prosecution consents, if dismissal is in the interest of justice, if the public will not be endangered, and if continued custody is not necessary for effective care and treatment of the defendant.[52]

Five other consequences of an order of examination and of commitment for care and treatment should be discussed. First, under CPL § 30.30(4)(a), periods of examination and periods in which the defendant is incompetent are excluded for statutory speedy trial purposes.[53] Notably, the exclusion is not made contingent on efforts by the prosecution to monitor the defendant's progress during commitment, so as to ensure that the prosecution is resumed at the earliest possible date.[54] And the Court of Appeals has held that a determination of incompetence in one case can under some circumstances be the occasion for the exclusion in another case of the period of incompetence.[55]

---

46. Godinez v. Moran, 509 U.S. 389, 113 S.Ct. 2680, 125 L.Ed.2d 321 (1993); People v. Gensler, 72 N.Y.2d 239, 247, 532 N.Y.S.2d 72, 77, 527 N.E.2d 1209 (1988), cert. den. 488 U.S. 932, 109 S.Ct. 323, 102 L.Ed.2d 341 (1998); see People v. Reason, 37 N.Y.2d 351, 372 N.Y.S.2d 614, 334 N.E.2d 572 (1975)(ability to waive counsel).

47. See § 6.6, infra.

48. Id.

49. CPL § 730.60(4).

50. Mead v. Walker, 839 F.Supp. 1030, 1033 (S.D.N.Y.1993); People v. Schaffer, 86 N.Y.2d 460, 634 N.Y.S.2d 22, 657 N.E.2d 1305 (1995); Neely v. Hogan, 62 Misc.2d 1056, 310 N.Y.S.2d 63 (Sup.Ct., N.Y. County, 1970); see Jackson v. Indiana, 406 U.S. 715, 740–41, 92 S.Ct. 1845, 1859, 32 L.Ed.2d 435 (1972).

51. See People v. Matthews, 154 Misc.2d 848, 585 N.Y.S.2d 948 (Sup.Ct., Bronx County, 1992)(motion to suppress physical evidence).

52. CPL § 730.60(5); see People v. Von Wolfersdorf, 69 Misc.2d 896, 330 N.Y.S.2d 813 (Dutchess Co.Ct.1972)(denying motion despite prosecution's consent).

53. People v. Santana, 80 N.Y.2d 92, 101–02, 587 N.Y.S.2d 570, 574–75, 600 N.E.2d 201, 205–06 (1992).

54. People v. Lebron, 211 A.D.2d 208, 628 N.Y.S.2d 54 (1st Dep't 1995) (lv. granted).

55. People v. Santana, 80 N.Y.2d at 102–03, 587 N.Y.S.2d at 575.

Second, under section 730.40, when a local criminal court has issued an order of examination or a temporary order of observation,[56] the defendant's right to testify in the grand jury pursuant to CPL § 190.50 is voided.[57] Section 730.40 also provides that the right to testify is reinstated if the defendant can persuade the superior court that impaneled the grand jury to rule that he or she is not incompetent. At least one appellate court has upheld a dismissal of an indictment in the interest of justice, with permission to re-present, when the "unique facts" of the case left the defendant with too little time to make an application to the superior court before the indictment was filed.[58]

Third, the defendant's incompetence is not a proper basis for dismissing an accusatory instrument in the interest of justice under CPL § 210.40, where the conditions for dismissal under Article 730 are not present.[59]

Fourth, a declaration that the defendant is incompetent does not invalidate prior proceedings, including a decision by the defendant to waive his or her rights, if there is no additional reason to conclude that the defendant was incompetent at the time of those proceedings.[60]

Finally, the examination process and any course of treatment will almost inevitably produce statements by the defendant that bear on potential issues in the case other than the defendant's competence. As a general matter, the prosecution cannot use that evidence in presenting its case against the defendant, once the defendant has been found competent. The Fifth Amendment so requires,[61] and the CPL so provides.[62] But that rule does not apply if the defendant decides to place his or her mental condition in issue at trial. A defendant who makes an issue of mental condition must cooperate in examinations into his or her mental state.[63] Further, the results of those examinations, including the defendant's statements, are admissible at trial on the issue of the defendant's mental condition.[64] The CPL quite practically provides that the available evidence on these issues includes evidence obtained as a result of the examination and treatment of a defendant for incom-

---

56. See § 6.7, infra.

57. CPL § 730.40(3); People v. Lancaster, 69 N.Y.2d 20, 31, 511 N.Y.S.2d 559, 565, 503 N.E.2d 990, 996 (1986), cert. den. 480 U.S. 922, 107 S.Ct. 1383, 94 L.Ed.2d 697 (1987).

58. People v. Balukas, 95 A.D.2d 813, 463 N.Y.S.2d 534 (2d Dep't 1983); see also People v. Baxley, 140 Misc.2d 516, 531 N.Y.S.2d 491 (Sup.Ct., Queens County, 1988); People v. Searles, 79 Misc.2d 850, 361 N.Y.S.2d 568 (Sup.Ct., N.Y. County, 1974).

59. People v. Schaffer, 86 N.Y.2d 460, 634 N.Y.S.2d 22, 657 N.E.2d 1305 (1995); People v. Hudson, 217 A.D.2d 53, 634 N.Y.S.2d 752 (2d Dep't 1995).

60. People v. Gelikkaya, 84 N.Y.2d 456, 618 N.Y.S.2d 895, 643 N.E.2d 517 (1994).

61. Estelle v. Smith, 451 U.S. 454, 101 S.Ct. 1866, 68 L.Ed.2d 359 (1981); see People v. Grisset, 118 Misc.2d 450, 460 N.Y.S.2d 987 (Sup.Ct., Queens County, 1983); People v. Angelillo, 105 Misc.2d 338, 432 N.Y.S.2d 127 (Suffolk Co.Ct.1980)(barring use of defendant's hearing testimony except for impeachment).

62. CPL § 730.20(6).

63. CPL § 250.10.

64. People v. McNamee, 145 Misc.2d 187, 191, 547 N.Y.S.2d 519, 522 (Sup.Ct., N.Y. County, 1989); People v. Grisset, 118 Misc.2d 450, 460 N.Y.S.2d 987 (Sup.Ct., Queens County, 1983).

petence.[65]

Library References:

West's Key No. Digests, Criminal Law ⚖=273(2), 303.30(2), 393, 412, 641.6(2); Mental Health ⚖=434–438.

§ 6.4 Initial Examination—By Whom Conducted

A court's order to examine a defendant's competence is issued to the appropriate "director."[66] Under the terms of the statute, the "director" must be the director of a state hospital operated by the Office of Mental Health; the director of a developmental center operated by the Office of Mental Retardation and Developmental Disabilities; the director of a local government hospital certified by the State Commissioner of Mental Health or the State Commissioner of Mental Retardation and Developmental Disabilities as having adequate facilities for a competence examination; or the director of community mental health services.[67]

The court rules for designating a "director" provide that, in New York City, an order of examination should be addressed to the City's Commissioner of Mental Health, Mental Retardation and Alcoholism Services, who is the director of community mental health services.[68] Outside New York City, the order should be addressed to the county's director of community mental health services.[69] If there is no county director of community mental health services, the order should be addressed to the director of a local government hospital within the county that has been certified for this purpose by the State Commissioner of Mental Health.[70] If there is no such hospital, the order should be addressed to the director of the state hospital operated by the Department of Mental Health that serves the county in which the criminal action is pending.[71]

The director to whom the order is addressed is obliged to designate two "qualified psychiatric examiners," of whom he or she may be one, to examine the defendant.[72] The designation of only one examiner is reversible error.[73] As originally enacted, the CPL provided that both examiners had to be "qualified psychiatrists," except that, when the director believed the defendant might be mentally "defective" rather than mentally ill, one examiner could be a "certified psychologist."[74] In

---

65. CPL § 730.20(6); People v. McNamee, 145 Misc.2d at 190–96, 547 N.Y.S.2d at 519–25. Some cases decided under the Code of Criminal Procedure disapproved or discouraged the use of evidence derived from competency proceedings on trial issues. See, e.g., People v. Draper, 278 App. Div. 298, 104 N.Y.S.2d 703 (4th Dep't 1951), aff'd 303 N.Y. 653, 101 N.E.2d 763 (1951); People v. Butchino, 13 A.D.2d 183, 215 N.Y.S.2d 321 (3d Dep't 1961).

66. CPL § 730.10(2).

67. CPL § 730.10(4).

68. 22 NYCRR § 111.2(a); New York City Charter, §§ 591, 593.

69. 22 NYCRR § 111.2(a).

70. Id.

71. Id.

72. CPL § 730.20(1).

73. People v. Armlin, 37 N.Y.2d 167, 371 N.Y.S.2d 691, 332 N.E.2d 870 (1975); People v. Mullins, 137 A.D.2d 227, 528 N.Y.S.2d 698 (3d Dep't 1988); People v. Ross, 50 A.D.2d 1064, 375 N.Y.S.2d 714 (4th Dep't 1975).

74. Former CPL § 730.20(1)(1970); see People v. Gans, 119 Misc.2d 843, 845, 465 N.Y.S.2d 147, 148 (Sup.Ct., N.Y. County, 1983). The director's decision to designate

1989, the Legislature resolved that certified psychologists could be designated in all circumstances.[75] "Qualified psychiatrists" are physicians who are diplomates of the American Board of Psychiatry and Neurology, physicians who are certified by the American Osteopathic Board of Neurology and Psychiatry, and physicians who are "eligible" to be certified by either board.[76] "Certified psychologists" are those individuals who are registered as such under Article 153 of the Education Law.[77]

If the two psychiatric examiners disagree as to the defendant's competence, the director must appoint a third examiner to conduct additional inquiry.[78] The CPL permits the court to allow a psychiatrist or psychologist hired by the defendant to attend an examination of the defendant.[79]

The case law recognizes the defendant's right to have counsel present to observe an examination by a prosecution expert concerning the insanity defense.[80] It has sometimes been assumed that this right extends to competence examinations.[81] However, competence examinations by court-appointed experts are not like insanity examinations by the prosecution's experts. At least one court has concluded that only the latter are the equivalent of "interrogation" designed to produce inculpatory evidence, and therefore that only the latter implicate the right to counsel.[82] However, the fact that competence examinations can produce evidence on trial issues[83] undercuts the rationale for distinguishing them from insanity examinations. Ultimately, there seems little reason to forbid counsel for the prosecution or the defense to attend competence examinations as observers. At the same time, if no timely request to attend is made, the absence of counsel should not cause the trial court to exclude any relevant testimonial insights by the examiners. The unhappy result would be that the jury would hear only about examinations more distant from the time of the crime.

Library References:

West's Key No. Digests, Mental Health ⇔434.

a psychologist was presumed correct absent proof to the contrary. People v. Phelps, 74 N.Y.2d 919, 550 N.Y.S.2d 259, 549 N.E.2d 461 (1989); People v. Miller, 167 A.D.2d 958, 562 N.Y.S.2d 300 (4th Dep't 1990).

75. L.1989, c.693, § 2; see Preiser, "Practice Commentary" to CPL § 730.20, McKinney's Cons. Laws of N.Y., Book 11A, at 449–50 (1995).

76. CPL § 730.10(5). One is "eligible" for certification when he or she has the specialized training required for taking the examination for certification. People v. Lopez, 126 Misc.2d 1072, 484 N.Y.S.2d 974 (Sup.Ct., Kings County, 1985).

77. CPL § 730.10(6).

78. CPL § 730.20(5).

79. CPL § 730.20(1).

80. Lee v. County Court, 27 N.Y.2d 432, 443–45, 318 N.Y.S.2d 705, 714–16, 267 N.E.2d 452, 458–60 (1971), cert. den. 404 U.S. 823, 92 S.Ct. 46, 30 L.Ed.2d 50 (1971); CPL § 250.10(3). The prosecutor has no corresponding right to attend an examination of the defendant by the defendant's own expert. People v. Thomas, 77 Misc.2d 1095, 355 N.Y.S.2d 909 (Sup.Ct., N.Y. County, 1974).

81. See, e.g., People v. Perkins, 166 A.D.2d 737, 562 N.Y.S.2d 244 (3d Dep't 1990); People v. Wood, 64 A.D.2d 767, 407 N.Y.S.2d 271 (3d Dep't 1978); People v. Rice, 76 Misc.2d 632, 351 N.Y.S.2d 888 (Suffolk Co.Ct.1974).

82. People v. McNamee, 145 Misc.2d 187, 190–96, 547 N.Y.S.2d 519, 522–24 (Sup.Ct., N.Y. County, 1989).

83. See § 6.3, supra.

§ 6.5 Initial Examination—How and When Conducted

If the defendant has been released on bail or recognizance before the issuance of the order of examination, the court may direct that the examination be conducted on an "out-patient basis," at such time and place as the director shall specify.[84] But if the director believes that hospital confinement is necessary for a successful examination, the court "may" direct that the defendant be confined in a hospital designated by the director for the period of the examination.[85]

If the defendant is in custody when the order of examination is issued, the examination will presumptively be conducted where he or she is confined.[86] However, if the director believes that hospital confinement is necessary for a successful examination, the defendant "must" be held at a hospital designated by the director for the period of the examination.[87]

In either instance, the period of hospital confinement is not to exceed 30 days, subject to a single extension of up to 30 days if, upon application of the director, the court finds an additional period necessary to complete the examination.[88] Notably, the court, rather than the director, bears the responsibility to determine the appropriate length of confinement.[89] During the period of hospital confinement, the physician in charge of the hospital may provide for such emergency psychiatric, medical or other therapeutic treatment of the defendant as he or she believes appropriate.[90]

The examiners may examine the defendant together or separately.[91] To determine whether the defendant is competent, the examiners are authorized to employ "any method which is accepted by the medical profession for the examination of persons alleged to be mentally ill or mentally defective."[92] Thereafter, each examiner must "promptly" prepare an examination report and submit it to the director. The director submits the reports to the court, which in turn provides copies to the parties.[93]

Pursuant to statutory directive,[94] a standardized form for the reports has been promulgated. The form obliges the examiner to declare that he

---

84. CPL § 730.20(2).

85. Id. See Staff Comment, Proposed New York Criminal Procedure Law, CPL § 405.30, p. 463 (Edward Thompson Co.1967), citing People ex rel. Schildhaus v. Warden, 37 Misc.2d 660, 235 N.Y.S.2d 531 (Sup.Ct., N.Y. County, 1962).

86. CPL § 730.20(3).

87. Id. If, during a period of commitment, the defendant takes the position that there are no grounds for confinement, the defendant's proper course is to seek a writ of habeas corpus. See Staff Comment, Proposed New York Criminal Procedure Law, CPL § 405.30, p. 463 (Edward Thompson Co.1967), citing People ex rel. Schildhaus v. Warden, 37 Misc.2d 660, 235 N.Y.S.2d 531 (Sup.Ct., N.Y. County, 1962).

88. CPL § 730.20(4). The drafters of the CPL had suggested that hospital confinement be permitted for 60 days, subject to one extension of no more than 30 days. Proposed New York Criminal Procedure Law, CPL § 405.20(4), p. 421 (Edward Thompson Co.1967).

89. People v. Robustelli, 189 A.D.2d 668, 671, 592 N.Y.S.2d 704, 707 (1st Dep't 1993).

90. CPL § 730.20(4).

91. 22 NYCRR § 111.3.

92. CPL § 730.20(1).

93. CPL § 730.20(5).

94. CPL § 730.10(8).

or she is a qualified psychiatrist or certified psychologist; to explain the nature and extent of the examination; and to state whether, in the examiner's opinion, the defendant is competent. If the examiner concludes that the defendant is not competent, he or she must provide a "History and Clinical Summary, including Mental Status," along with a diagnosis, a prognosis, and the "reasons for [his or her] opinion, specifying those aspects of the proceedings wherein the defendant lacks capacity."[95] The failure to submit

> the examination report upon a proper form is not merely a technical defect since the forms are prescribed so that certain information considered to be essential will be communicated to the court to enable it to make a proper determination of defendant's mental capacity.[96]

Library References:
West's Key No. Digests, Mental Health ⟶434.

§ 6.6 Post–Examination Procedure in Superior Court

The events that follow the receipt of the examiners' reports vary, depending on whether the order of examination was issued by a superior court or a local criminal court. This section addresses the procedures that apply when a superior court issued the order of examination.[97]

At least two examiners will submit reports to a superior court that has issued an order of examination. In a case in which the examiners agree that the defendant is competent, and neither the court nor a party believes that a hearing should be held on the issue, the case simply proceeds.[98] If the court or one of the parties believes a hearing should be held, a hearing must be held.[99] A request for a hearing need not be made immediately, if it is not unnecessarily delayed.[100] If the court finds at the conclusion of the hearing that the defendant is competent, again,

---

95. 22 NYCRR Subtitle D, Chapter I, pp. 2522–23.

96. People v. Lowe, 109 A.D.2d 300, 303, 491 N.Y.S.2d 529, 533 (4th Dep't 1985). See also People v. Meurer, 184 A.D.2d 1067, 1068, 584 N.Y.S.2d 370, 371 (4th Dep't 1992); People v. Whysong, 175 A.D.2d 576, 572 N.Y.S.2d 243 (4th Dep't 1991). At least one court has sanctioned the use of reports that are not on official forms, so long as they contain all the required information. People v. Carkner, 213 A.D.2d 735, 739, 623 N.Y.S.2d 350, 355 (3d Dep't 1995).

97. The procedures that apply when a local criminal court issued the order of examination are described in § 6.7, infra. Separately discussed, in § 6.8, are certain 1980 amendments to Section 730.60, affecting whether the routine procedures governing the termination of confinement under superior court orders and local criminal court orders will apply to a particular defendant's case. Finally, set out in § 6.9 are the rules that govern competency hearings both in a superior court and in a local criminal court.

98. CPL § 730.30(2). See, e.g., People v. Gensler, 72 N.Y.2d 239, 532 N.Y.S.2d 72, 527 N.E.2d 1209 (1988), cert. den. 488 U.S. 932, 109 S.Ct. 323, 102 L.Ed.2d 341 (1988); People v. Basir, 141 A.D.2d 745, 529 N.Y.S.2d 841 (2d Dep't 1988); People v. Paxhia, 140 A.D.2d 962, 529 N.Y.S.2d 638 (4th Dep't 1988); People v. Bronson, 115 A.D.2d 484, 495 N.Y.S.2d 716 (2d Dep't 1985); People v. Griffin, 100 A.D.2d 659, 473 N.Y.S.2d 851 (3d Dep't 1984). See also People v. Williams, 85 N.Y.2d 945, 626 N.Y.S.2d 1002, 650 N.E.2d 849 (1995).

99. CPL § 730.30(2).

100. People v. Maddicks, 118 A.D.2d 437, 499 N.Y.S.2d 93 (1st Dep't 1986).

the case simply proceeds.[101] If instead the court is not able to conclude that the defendant is competent, it must issue a new order of examination, and the director must assign different examiners to the case.[102] Following the second round of examinations and reports, the court presumably must follow the procedures that apply after an initial round of examinations.

In a case in which the examiners agree that the defendant is incompetent, the court must hold a hearing if the court or one of the parties believes that the examiners' conclusion should be tested.[103] If the hearing results in a finding that the defendant is competent, the case proceeds.[104] If the hearing results in a finding that the defendant is not competent, or if the court and the parties accepted the examiners' conclusion and no hearing was held, the defendant must be committed to the custody of the State Commissioner of Mental Health or the State Commissioner of Mental Retardation and Developmental Disabilities. In a case in which the defendant is charged with a felony or has been convicted of a felony, the order assigning custody is denominated an "order of commitment."[105] Such an order commits the defendant for care and treatment for a period not to exceed one year.[106]

In cases in which the examiners disagree, the court must hold a hearing.[107] A finding after the hearing that the defendant is competent results in a resumption of the criminal action. A finding that the defendant is not competent, in a case in which the defendant is charged with a felony or has been convicted of a felony, results in the issuance of an order of commitment.[108]

Not every superior court case involves a felony charge. In cases in which the indictment does not charge a felony, or in which the defendant has already been convicted of an offense other than a felony, if the court finds the defendant incompetent it must issue a "final order of observation" rather than an order of commitment. The effects of such an order are discussed in Section 6.7, *infra*. In particular, however, the issuance of a final order of observation results in the dismissal of the accusatory instrument, with prejudice to any further prosecution of the charge or charges contained in it.[109]

Of course, in most superior court cases, the defendant is charged with or convicted of a felony. As described above, in such cases an order

---

101. CPL § 730.30(2).
102. Id.
103. CPL § 730.30(3).
104. CPL § 730.50(1).
105. CPL § 730.50(1). If the indictment does not charge the defendant with a felony, or if at the time of the examination the defendant has already been convicted of an offense other than a felony, the court must instead issue a "final order of observation." Id.
106. CPL § 730.50(1). An escape tolls the period of the order, and of any ensuing order of retention. CPL § 730.60(2).

107. CPL § 730.30(4). As a result of a drafting error, subdivision four refers to a possible finding that a defendant is a "dangerous incapacitated person." That status was abolished in 1974. See Preiser, "Practice Commentary" to CPL § 730.30, McKinney's Cons. Laws of N.Y., Book 11A, at 462 (1995); People v. Arendes, 92 Misc.2d 372, 379, 400 N.Y.S.2d 273, 277 (Sup.Ct., Queens County, 1977).
108. CPL § 730.50(1).
109. Id.

of examination will ultimately result either in a finding of competence and the resumption of normal procedures, or an order of commitment. The remainder of this section will therefore address what follows the issuance of an order of commitment.

The order of commitment suspends the criminal action.[110] If, when the order is about to expire, the superintendent of the institution in which the defendant is confined believes that the defendant remains incompetent, the superintendent must apply to the court for an order of retention.[111] The application must be made on a standardized form at least 60 days before the expiration of the order of commitment, on notice to the defendant and the Mental Hygiene Legal Service. While the statute does not provide for notice to the prosecution, the form that has been promulgated does so.[112] The form also requires the superintendent to indicate the defendant's maximum potential prison term and the length of his or her commitment to date,[113] and thus helps the court ensure that further retention is permissible.

If the court, the defendant, and the Mental Hygiene Legal Service all accept the superintendent's conclusion that the defendant remains incompetent, the court must issue an order of retention authorizing further custody for a period of up to a year.[114] If instead the court, the defendant, or the Mental Hygiene Legal Service wishes to test the superintendent's conclusion, a hearing must be held. At the end of the hearing, the court must either find the defendant competent and order that the case resume its normal course, or issue an order of retention. Notably, the statute does not accord the prosecution standing to insist that a hearing be held.[115]

At the end of a period of retention, the superintendent may continue to believe that the defendant is incompetent. If so, the superintendent must apply to the court for another order of retention.[116] The procedures just outlined govern such applications, except that later orders of retention can be for periods of up to two years.[117]

During the period of the order of commitment or of any subsequent retention order, the superintendent of the institution in which the defendant is confined may determine that the defendant is no longer incompetent. In that event, he or she must so notify the court and the District Attorney in writing.[118] The court must then follow the procedures, set out in CPL § 730.30(2), which apply when the examiners appointed pursuant to an initial order of examination unanimously agree that the defendant is competent.[119]

110. CPL § 730.60(2). The exceptions to that general rule are noted in § 6.3, supra.
111. CPL § 730.50(2).
112. Id.; 22 NYCRR Subtitle D, Chapter I, p. 2525.
113. CPL § 730.50(2); 22 NYCRR Subtitle D, Chapter I, p. 2524.
114. CPL § 730.50(2).
115. Id.
116. CPL § 730.50(3).
117. Id.
118. CPL § 730.60(2); 22 NYCRR Subtitle D, Chapter I, p. 2529.
119. CPL § 730.60(2).

Under those procedures, described above, the case proceeds in a normal manner if neither the court nor a party believes that a hearing should be held as to the defendant's competence.[120] If, instead, the court or a party concludes that a hearing is in order, a hearing must be held. A finding after the hearing that the defendant is competent causes the case to resume its normal course. If the hearing does not satisfy the court that the defendant is competent, a new order of examination must issue, and new examiners will examine the defendant.[121] The court also has the option, if the parties consent, to reinstate the order of commitment or order of retention and thus renew the defendant's commitment at the institution where he or she was being treated.[122]

The periods of commitment cannot last forever. In *Jackson v. Indiana*,[123] the Supreme Court held that an incompetent defendant cannot, consistent with constitutional due process guarantees, be confined for longer than reasonably necessary to establish whether there is a "substantial probability that he will attain [competence] in the foreseeable future."[124] In 1995, the Court of Appeals had occasion to consider the import of *Jackson*.[125] The court noted that *Jackson* does not mandate dismissal of the accusatory instrument against a defendant, even when the defendant's chances of becoming competent are "minimal" or "non-existent." Rather, the rule of *Jackson* is that, once it is clear that a defendant will not become competent, any further confinement must be pursuant to civil commitment rules.[126] Accordingly, a defendant who persuades the court that his or her chances of ever becoming competent are "minimal" or "non-existent" is entitled to be judged under civil commitment rules—but not to a dismissal.

The *Jackson* rule is complemented by a provision of CPL § 730.50 applicable in felony cases. A defendant who has not yet been convicted may be confined, by virtue of an order of commitment and orders of retention, for only two-thirds of the maximum term of imprisonment available for the highest class of felony charged in the indictment[127]— which is to say, for as long as his or her likely maximum prison

---

120. CPL § 730.30(2); People v. Gensler, 72 N.Y.2d 239, 532 N.Y.S.2d 72, 527 N.E.2d 1209, cert. den. 488 U.S. 932, 109 S.Ct. 323, 102 L.Ed.2d 341 (1988); People v. Heasley, 133 A.D.2d 977, 521 N.Y.S.2d 128 (3d Dep't 1987).

121. CPL § 730.30(2).

122. CPL § 730.60(2).

123. 406 U.S. 715, 92 S.Ct. 1845, 32 L.Ed.2d 435 (1972).

124. 406 U.S. at 738, 92 S.Ct. at 1858.

125. People v. Schaffer, 86 N.Y.2d 460, 634 N.Y.S.2d 22, 657 N.E.2d 1305 (1995).

126. People v. Schaffer, 86 N.Y.2d at 468, 634 N.Y.S.2d at 27. Accord People v. Arendes, 92 Misc.2d 372, 400 N.Y.S.2d 273 (Sup.Ct., Queens County, 1977); People ex rel. Anonymous v. Waugh, 76 Misc.2d 879, 351 N.Y.S.2d 594 (Sup.Ct., N.Y. County, 1974); Kesselbrenner v. Anonymous, 75 Misc.2d 289, 347 N.Y.S.2d 369 (Sup.Ct., N.Y. County, 1973).

Notably, a defendant is normally entitled to dismissal of the indictment under section 730.50(4) at the expiration of the last order of retention. But that rule obviously envisions that orders of retention will continue during the defendant's incompetence until the end of his effective prison exposure, as provided in section 730.50(3) and discussed immediately below. Section 730.50(4) can logically be treated as inapplicable when a *Jackson* finding truncates the period of confinement in a manner not anticipated in Article 730.

127. CPL § 730.50(3).

exposure.[128] If the defendant has already been convicted, he or she may not be confined, by virtue of the order of commitment and orders of retention, for more than two-thirds of the maximum term for the highest class of felony for which he or she was convicted.[129] At the end of the permissible period of retention, the superintendent of the facility in which the defendant is confined can keep the defendant confined for an additional 30 days while the superintendent initiates civil commitment procedures under the Mental Hygiene Law.[130] If the defendant has remained committed pursuant to orders of retention until the end of the permissible period, the indictment must be dismissed with prejudice.[131]

Finally, the rules concerning the possible periods of the defendant's confinement pursuant to an order of commitment may be affected by the provisions of section 730.60(6), which was added to the CPL in 1980. Those provisions are discussed in § 6.8, *infra*.

Library References:

West's Key No. Digests, Criminal Law ⚖︎623–625; Mental Health ⚖︎435–438.

§ 6.7 Post–Examination Procedure in Local Criminal Court

A local criminal court that issues an order of examination will, like a superior court, find itself faced with one of three possible scenarios: either the examiners will agree that the defendant is competent, the examiners will agree that the defendant is incompetent, or the examiners will disagree.

When the examiners agree that the defendant is competent, the court's options are identical to those of a superior court: the case will proceed in its normal course, unless the court or one of the parties believes that the examiners' conclusions should be tested at a hearing.[132] In that event, a finding after the hearing that the defendant is competent will restore the case to its normal path. If the court is not persuaded that the defendant is competent, a new order of examination must issue, and new experts must examine the defendant.[133]

When the examiners agree that the defendant is not competent, a hearing must be held if the court or a party believes that a hearing is

---

128. When this "two-thirds of the maximum" limitation was promulgated, the most severe possible sentence for any convicted felon was an indeterminate state prison sentence with a specified minimum and maximum term. The two-thirds figure assumed that the defendant would receive the greatest possible "good time" reduction of the greatest possible maximum term. No amendment has been made to accommodate the possibility of determinate sentences under the Sentencing Reform Act of 1995, under which the greatest possible "good time" reduction is one-sixth of the term. L.1995, c.3. Thus, in a case in which the defendant now faces a determinate sentence, application of the language of section 730.50 will result in an end to confinement somewhat before the end of the defendant's effective prison exposure. See Correction Law § 803(1); P.L. §§ 70.30(4), 70.40(1)(b)(as amended by L.1995, c.3).

129. CPL § 730.50(3).

130. CPL § 730.70.

131. CPL § 730.50(4).

132. CPL § 730.30(2).

133. Id.

§ 6.7 COMPETENCY PROCEEDINGS Ch. 6

appropriate.[134] If the result of the hearing is a finding that the defendant is competent, the case proceeds normally.[135] If the court finds after the hearing that the defendant is incompetent, or if the conclusion of the examiners to that effect was accepted without a hearing, an "order of observation" must issue.[136]

When the examiners disagree as to whether the defendant is competent, a hearing must be held.[137] If the result of the hearing is a finding that the defendant is competent, the prosecution resumes. If the court finds that the defendant is incompetent, an "order of observation" must issue.[138]

In a case in which the accusatory instrument is not a felony complaint, the order of observation is "final." A final order of observation commits the defendant for care and treatment at a facility operated by the Department of Mental Health for a period of up to 90 days.[139] The issuance of a final order of observation does not, like an order of commitment in a superior court case, suspend the prosecution; it instead brings the prosecution to an end. The court must dismiss the accusatory instrument, and that dismissal bars further prosecution of the charges in the instrument.[140] The defendant may be discharged at any time, and may otherwise be treated by the Department of Mental Health as if he or she were not confined pursuant to the order of a criminal court.[141] When the order expires, the superintendent of the facility in which the defendant is confined has the option of maintaining custody of the defendant for up to 30 days to initiate civil commitment proceedings.[142]

When the accusatory instrument is a felony complaint, the order of observation must be "temporary," unless the prosecution consents to a final order of observation that will terminate the prosecution.[143] A temporary order of observation, like a final order of observation, commits the defendant for care and treatment at a facility operated by the Department of Mental Health for a period of up to 90 days.[144] But during the duration of a temporary order of observation, as in a superior court case, the prosecution is merely suspended until the superintendent determines that the defendant is no longer incompetent. At that point

---

134. CPL § 730.30(3).
135. CPL § 730.40(1).
136. Id.
137. CPL § 730.30(4).
138. CPL § 730.40(1).
139. CPL §§ 730.40(1), 730.60(1). The running of the 90 days is tolled during the period of an escape. CPL § 730.60(2).
140. CPL § 730.40(2); 22 NYCRR Subtitle D, Chapter I, pp. 2534–35. See People v. Paulides, 88 Misc.2d 1061, 389 N.Y.S.2d 1018 (Nassau Co.Ct.1976) (local criminal court had no power to recall order two days later).

141. CPL § 730.60(3). At least one court has held that it violates equal protection even to commit such a defendant initially under rules different from those applicable to individuals committed civilly. Ritter v. Surles, 144 Misc.2d 945, 545 N.Y.S.2d 962 (Sup.Ct., Westchester County, 1988).
142. CPL § 730.70. See People v. Helfman, 91 A.D.2d 1034, 458 N.Y.S.2d 628 (2d Dep't 1983).
143. CPL § 730.40(1) and (2).
144. CPL §§ 730.40(1), 730.60(1). The running of the 90 days is tolled during the period of an escape. CPL § 730.60(2).

the court and the District Attorney must be notified in writing of that determination.[145]

The court must then follow the procedures, set out in section 730.30(2), applicable when the examiners appointed pursuant to an initial order of examination unanimously agree that the defendant is competent.[146] As noted above, under section 730.30(2) the case proceeds in a normal manner if neither the court nor a party believes that a hearing should be held as to the defendant's competence. If instead the court or a party believes a hearing is in order, a hearing must be held. A finding after the hearing that the defendant is competent causes the case to resume its normal course. If the hearing does not satisfy the court that the defendant is competent, a new order of examination must issue, and new examiners will examine the defendant.[147]

After a finding of incompetence in a superior court case, and if the parties consent, the court has the option to reinstate the order of commitment or order of retention and thereby renew the defendant's commitment at the institution in which he or she was being treated.[148] The CPL does not expressly provide the option of reinstating the temporary order of observation in a case in which the accusatory instrument is a felony complaint. Thus, if the statute is read literally, upon finding that the defendant is not competent, the court's only option would be to issue a new order of examination.[149]

If, at the expiration of the temporary order of observation, the defendant is still confined, the court and the prosecution must be so notified.[150] At that point, proceedings in the local criminal court terminate and the felony complaint is dismissed.[151]

At any time during the pendency of the felony complaint, an indictment may be filed divesting the local criminal court of jurisdiction.[152] As noted above, the defendant's right to testify in the grand jury pursuant to section 190.50 is voided by the issuance of an order of examination or a temporary order of observation, subject to reinstatement if the defendant can persuade the superior court that impaneled the grand jury to rule that he or she is competent.[153] If an indictment is filed after the issuance of an order of examination, and before the issuance of a temporary or final order of observation, the defendant must be promptly arraigned in superior court. The proceedings in the local criminal court terminate, and the examination reports are forwarded to the superior court.[154] At least one case has made the eminently practical assumption that the superior court should not then consider whether it

---

145. CPL § 730.60(2).
146. Id.
147. CPL § 730.30(2).
148. CPL § 730.60(2).
149. CPL § 730.30(2).
150. CPL § 730.40(2); NYCRR Subtitle D, Chapter I, pp. 2528.
151. CPL § 730.40(2).
152. CPL § 10.30(2).
153. CPL § 730.40(3); see § 6.3, supra.
154. CPL § 730.40(4). The same procedure would apply in a case in which the accusatory instrument was not a felony complaint, and in which an indictment was filed after the issuance of an order of examination and before the issuance of a final order of observation.

should issue an order of examination, but can instead continue the process begun in the local criminal court.[155]

If an indictment is filed during or after the period of a temporary order of observation, the defendant must be promptly arraigned in superior court.[156] The indictment nullifies the temporary order of observation, if it is still pending, or any civil order issued after its expiration pursuant to the Mental Hygiene Law.[157] However, the indictment is timely only if it was filed within six months of the expiration of the period of the temporary order of observation, or there was "good cause" for additional delay. If the indictment is untimely, it must be dismissed.[158]

Finally, all of the rules concerning the possible periods of a defendant's confinement pursuant to a final order of observation are subject to limitation by the provisions of section 730.60(6), which was added to the CPL in 1980. Those provisions are discussed in Section 6.8, *infra*.

Library References:
West's Key No. Digests, Criminal Law ⊕623–625; Mental Health ⊕435–438.

§ 6.8 The 1980 Amendments

CPL § 730.60 invested broad discretion in mental health officials over the custody and treatment of individuals who have been adjudged incompetent.[159] Indeed, a defendant committed pursuant to a final order of observation could be treated like a civil patient, and discharged at any time.[160] In 1980, however, the Legislature amended section 730.60 in ways that impact on that discretion, and especially on the nature and potential length of a defendant's confinement pursuant to a final order of observation or an order of commitment.[161] Those provisions are sufficiently out of line with the otherwise integrated scheme created by Article 730 to require independent discussion.

Since 1980, section 730.60(6) has provided that no one committed pursuant to Article 730 or retained in custody after such a commitment may be

> discharged, released on condition or placed in any less secure facility or on any less restrictive status, including, but not limited to vacations, furloughs and temporary passes

unless four days written notice, exclusive of weekends and holidays, is first provided. That notice is to be given to the District Attorney whose case resulted in the commitment, various other law enforcement agencies, anyone "who may reasonably be expected to be the victim of any

---

155. People v. Gonzalez, 132 Misc.2d 1004, 506 N.Y.S.2d 276 (Sup.,Ct., Richmond County, 1986).

156. CPL § 730.40(5). Notably, if the prosecution consented to the issuance of a final order of observation in a case initiated by a felony complaint, it may not thereafter obtain an indictment. CPL § 730.40(1) and (2).

157. CPL § 730.40(5).

158. CPL § 730.40(5).

159. CPL § 730.60(1), (2), (3) and (4).

160. CPL § 730.60(3).

161. L.1980, c.549, §§ 2, 3.

assault or any violent felony offense" that would be carried out by the committed person, and any other person the court designates.[162]

On receipt of such notice, the District Attorney may within three days apply to a superior court for an order directing that a hearing be held as to whether the defendant is a danger to himself or others, but only if the defendant is in custody pursuant to a final order of observation or an order of commitment.[163] If the order is signed, the hearing must be held within the next 10 days. The order may provide that, in the interim, the defendant's confinement status shall not be changed.[164] Further, if the order is signed, the District Attorney and the defendant's attorney are entitled to receive the clinical records created during the defendant's confinement.[165] After the hearing, if the court finds that the defendant is a danger to himself or others, it shall issue an order authorizing retention of the defendant in his prior status for up to six months.[166]

These provisions were a response to a perception on the part of some observers that the state's mental institutions were discharging or furloughing individuals likely to commit violent crimes, and that a check on discretionary releases should therefore be provided.[167] Other observers have viewed certain of the new provisions as unconstitutional, or at least quite arguably so, on equal protection and due process grounds.[168] To evaluate their arguments, the notice provision and the retention provision should be considered separately.

As to notice, if all that subdivision (6)(a) did was provide that the authorities should be given notice before any alteration of the conditions of confinement of a defendant in a pending criminal case, there could be no constitutional objection. The pendency of the case would create ample reason for a special rule for the defendants.[169] Moreover, it hardly

---

162. CPL § 730.60(6)(a). Presumably the court would designate private parties who should be notified, if any, as a part of a prior commitment or retention proceeding. There would be no procedural vehicle through which the court could make such designations on the actual occasion of a change in the defendant's commitment status.

Similar notice must be provided if a committed person makes an unauthorized "departure" from custody. CPL § 730.60(6)(b).

163. CPL § 730.60(3)(c). No provision is expressly made for a defendant in custody pursuant to an order of retention, rather than the initial order of commitment. Given the purpose of the 1980 amendments, as discussed infra, it is difficult to explain that omission except as an oversight.

164. Id.
165. Id.
166. Id.
167. See, e.g., Letter of Assemblyman Paul E. Harenberg, dated June 18, 1980, and Letter of Assemblyman Arthur J. Kramer, dated June 13, 1980, both in Bill Jacket for L.1980, c.549. Indeed, some did not believe that the amendments went far enough to achieve their purpose. See People v. Anonymous A, 118 Misc.2d 427, 460 N.Y.S.2d 864 (Sup.Ct., Queens County, 1983).

168. See, e.g., Memorandum of Attorney General Robert Abrams, dated June 23, 1980, and Letters of Paul Litwak, Deputy Counsel of the Office of Mental Health, dated June 19, 1980 and May 20, 1980, all in Bill Jacket for L.1980, c.549.

169. See Heller v. Doe By Doe, 509 U.S. 312, 113 S.Ct. 2637, 2642–43, 125 L.Ed.2d 257 (1993)(discussing equal protection principles in the context of commitment); see also Jones v. United States, 463 U.S. 354, 366–68, 103 S.Ct. 3043, 3050–51, 77 L.Ed.2d 694 (1983)(due process permits distinctions in treatment of those committed after an acquittal by reason of insanity, and those committed civilly).

violates due process for prosecutors and police to be kept aware of a defendant's conditions of confinement.[170] Those conclusions would remain valid even if the notice requirement delayed the change in the conditions of confinement, but in fact a scheduled change need not be delayed at all if the mental health authorities can anticipate it by a mere four days. And the provision of notice to identifiable civilians who could be affected by a defendant's release or potential escape would likewise seem to be rationally related to the pendency of the case, and to involve no unfair impairment of the defendant's liberty.

In fact, however, subdivision (6)(a) reaches farther than the individuals committed pursuant to Article 730 whose criminal cases are pending. The notice provisions apply to all defendants who were committed pursuant to Article 730. Thus, subdivision (6)(a) applies in the case of a defendant committed under a final order of observation, even though the criminal action against such a defendant will have been dismissed when that order was issued.[171] And, no matter what type of order is involved, subdivision (6)(a) applies if civil commitment follows the end of commitment under Article 730.[172] But the criminal charges against the civilly committed defendants will have been dismissed, at the latest, at the end of custody pursuant to Article 730.[173] With respect to these individuals—former defendants who have never been convicted and no longer face a criminal charge—the equal protection clause might well invalidate subdivision (6)(a), for it applies only to them and not to others committed civilly.[174] On the other hand, one might argue that there are rational bases for a notice rule applicable whenever the commitment arose out of a criminal charge: for example, the notice rule permits knowledgeable individuals to contribute information about the defendant's dangerousness that could impact on the decision to change the conditions of confinement.

A different analysis pertains to the retention provisions. Subdivision (6)(c) applies to defendants who are committed pursuant to orders of commitment.[175] The subdivision must have been meant to apply as well to defendants committed pursuant to orders of retention; the absence of a reference to those defendants is inexplicable except as an accident, for an order of retention is simply a continuation of an order of commitment upon a finding that the defendant's mental condition has not materially changed.[176] The remainder of this discussion will assume that defen-

170. See Jones v. United States, supra.

171. CPL §§ 730.40(2), 730.50(1).

172. That is the only possible interpretation of the language requiring notice about individuals

committed to the custody of the commissioner pursuant to this article, or continuously thereafter retained in such custody.

CPL § 730.60(6)(a). The quoted language differs slightly from that enacted in 1980, as a result of a stylistic amendment in 1987. L.1987, c.440, § 2.

173. CPL §§ 730.40(2), 730.50(4), 730.60(4) and (5).

174. See Jackson v. Indiana, 406 U.S. 715, 729–30, 738, 92 S.Ct. 1845, 1853–54, 1858, 32 L.Ed.2d 435, 445–46, 451 (1972).

175. The situation of defendants committed pursuant to final orders of observation is discussed below.

176. CPL § 730.50(2).

dants subject to orders of retention fall within the reach of subdivision (6)(c).

During the duration of an order of commitment or an order of retention, the criminal case is merely suspended. It therefore does no violence to equal protection principles that subdivision (6)(c) provides rules with no analogue in civil commitment cases.[177] In particular, these defendants are not subject to discharge from confinement by mental health authorities, and it is not irrational for the subdivision to permit a change in the nature of confinement only when the defendants' "dangerousness" is considered. And once the final order of retention expires, and these defendants are subject only to civil commitment, subdivision (6)(c) no longer applies.[178] They can therefore be discharged, or the conditions of their confinement can otherwise be changed, without regard to subdivision (6)(c).

Due process analysis is more convoluted, but yields a comparable result. First, if the defendant becomes competent before the expiration of the orders of commitment and retention, the criminal case will resume and the commitment will end. A defendant remains incompetent only if he continues to suffer from a mental disease or defect, and it is therefore not possible that a defendant could be confined pursuant to subdivision (6)(c) merely because he is "dangerous" to himself or others, and not mentally ill. If the defendant is both dangerous and mentally ill, he will be confined until he becomes competent, without regard to subdivision (6)(c), and that confinement will accord with due process.[179] *A fortiori*, due process would not be offended by the less severe impositions on changing the defendant's status that might follow from subdivision (6)(c) procedures.

Subdivision (6)(c) should not be read to authorize continuing commitment of a defendant beyond the permissible limits on orders of commitment and retention. Subdivision (6)(c) of course could not authorize commitment beyond a term permissible under *Jackson v. Indiana*.[180] And it would be difficult as well to persuade a court that the "two-thirds" limits on confinement and on the life of the criminal case provided in section 730.50 could be ignored, simply because subdivision (6)(c) contains no reference to that section.

---

177. See Heller v. Doe By Doe, supra.

178. In that regard, subdivision (6)(c) contains no language paralleling that of subdivision (6)(a) that would make it applicable to an individual confined civilly after the expiration of commitment pursuant to Article 730. See People v. Helfman, 91 A.D.2d 1034, 458 N.Y.S.2d 628 (2d Dep't 1983)(concerning the expiration of a final order of observation); People v. Anonymous A, 118 Misc.2d 427, 460 N.Y.S.2d 864 (Sup. Ct., Queens County, 1983)(same); see also People v. Merrill, 123 Misc.2d 498, 474 N.Y.S.2d 198 (Sup.Ct., Bronx County, 1984)(concerning defendant in felony case who had been afforded Jackson relief); People v. McArthur, 118 Misc.2d 665, 461 N.Y.S.2d 173 (Sup.Ct., Queens County, 1983)(same).

179. Foucha v. Louisiana, 504 U.S. 71, 112 S.Ct. 1780, 118 L.Ed.2d 437 (1992); Matter of Francis S., ___ N.Y.2d ___, ___ N.Y.S.2d ___, 663 N.E.2d 881 (1995). Needless to say, if a defendant did become competent, any order committing him or her on account of dangerousness could not survive review. Foucha v. Louisiana, supra.

180. See § 6.6, supra.

§ 6.8 COMPETENCY PROCEEDINGS Ch. 6

The preceding discussion applies only to a defendant who is committed pursuant to an order of commitment or an order of retention. Subdivision 6(c) also purports to authorize retention of individuals committed pursuant to a final order of observation. But the criminal case against such a defendant will not have survived the issuance of the final order of observation.[181] The application of subdivision (6)(c) to former defendants who have never been convicted, individuals who initially were committed civilly, would seem to be inconsistent with *Jackson*. Equal protection would therefore appear to bar application of subdivision 6(c) in such cases.[182] Indeed, at least one court has held that such defendants cannot in any regard be treated differently from those committed civilly.[183]

In short, in many situations the 1980 amendments can constitutionally be enforced. Still, those amendments represent an unwieldy answer to the perceived problem of the discharge or furlough of dangerous mental patients. The 1980 amendments cannot prevent the release of dangerous individuals against whom criminal charges were never brought. Presumably, the amendments cannot constitutionally block the release of dangerous individuals who once were charged, but whose cases were dismissed. Release may be prevented in pending cases, but the method selected turns mental health officials into partisans in criminal litigation over the future conduct of their patients.

In that regard, even if the 1980 amendments could all be enforced, they skew the purpose of Article 730. The procedures set out in the original article were designed to determine whether an individual can be prosecuted for a past crime, and not to confine him or her on a prediction of future misconduct. For example, under the original Article 730, the case against an incompetent individual charged in a felony complaint could be dismissed with the prosecution's consent at the beginning of a 90 day commitment, and the defendant would in short order be treated as a civil patient or released. Under the 1980 amendments, the same individual could instead be confined for years under the rudimentary procedures of subdivision 6(c), on account of a criminal charge that had long been dismissed. No doubt, in some cases, the 1980 procedures will produce a good result. Nonetheless, a more precisely targeted response to the release problem that depended less on litigators would be preferable.

Library References:
West's Key No. Digests, Constitutional Law ⚖=255(5); Mental Health ⚖=437.

§ 6.9 Hearing Procedure

As is evident from the foregoing discussion, a hearing may be held either after a defendant has been examined pursuant to an order of

---

181. See CPL § 730.40(1) and (2).
182. Jackson v. Indiana, 406 U.S. 715, 92 S.Ct. 1845, 32 L.Ed.2d 435 (1972); but see People v. Jones, 114 Misc.2d 31, 449 N.Y.S.2d 409 (Sup.Ct., Queens County, 1982).
183. Ritter v. Surles, 144 Misc.2d 945, 545 N.Y.S.2d 962 (Sup.Ct., Westchester County, 1988).

examination, or after a defendant has been in custody pursuant to an order of commitment, an order of retention, or a temporary order of observation.[184] This section will address the rules governing such hearings, and the evolution of those rules.

Competence issues are fact-specific, and therefore it was inevitable that New York law would recognize the need for competency hearings. A court making the basic decision of whether to order that a defendant be examined will likely have to assess conflicting information from diverse sources, and on numerous topics.[185] After a defendant has been examined, perhaps by many psychiatrists and psychologists, the newly available facts and opinions only complicate the issues. If the CPL did not provide for competency hearings, one judge or another would quite reasonably have declared them necessary anyway.[186]

But it was not inevitable that hearing procedures would be complicated. As initially enacted, Article 730 made provision for hearings after the issuance of an order of examination,[187] but arguably envisioned a procedure in which the court might simply ask the two or three examiners appointed by the director to explain their reports.[188] Similarly, when the institution with custody of the defendant applied for an order of retention, any ensuing hearing might have involved simple inquiries of the experts from that institution. No provision was made for additional examinations of the defendant by experts hired by the parties.[189] And no provision was made for hearings once a defendant, having been committed as incompetent, was certified as competent by the superintendent of the facility in which he or she was confined.[190] Instead, the statute provided that upon a defendant's return the criminal action "must" resume,[191] and the only recourse for a party dissatisfied with the assessment of the defendant's competence was to ask the court to re-initiate the entire process with a new order of examination.[192]

Almost immediately, judicial resistance emerged to the provision that the superintendent's certification of competence would be controlling.[193] Then, in 1981, the Legislature made plain that it did not intend that the certification bind the court. An amendment to section 730.60(2) struck the language mandating that the case resume when the

---

184. §§ 6.6, 6.7, supra.

185. See § 6.2, supra.

186. Indeed, even after the CPL went into effect, one judge felt it pertinent to note that

where a statute does not provide procedures and where essential due process rights must be protected in the sense that the defendant should be able to understand the proceedings against him or to assist in his own defense, the court has the inherent power to order a hearing to safeguard the rights of the accused.

People v. Acevedo, 84 Misc.2d 563, 564, 377 N.Y.S.2d 932, 934 (Dutchess Co.Ct.1975).

187. CPL § 730.30 (2), (3) and (4).

188. See People v. Christopher, 65 N.Y.2d 417, 433–35, 492 N.Y.S.2d 566, 575–77, 482 N.E.2d 45, 54–56 (1985)(Simons, J., dissenting).

189. Section 730.20(1) did give the court discretion to authorize an expert retained by the defense to observe the examinations by the court-appointed experts.

190. CPL § 730.60(2).

191. Id.

192. People v. Rodriguez, 79 A.D.2d 576, 434 N.Y.S.2d 347 (1st Dep't 1980).

193. People v. Acevedo, 84 Misc.2d 563, 377 N.Y.S.2d 932 (Dutchess Co.Ct.1975); People v. Kurtz, 71 Misc.2d 493, 336 N.Y.S.2d 322 (Orange Co.Ct.1972).

§ 6.9 COMPETENCY PROCEEDINGS Ch. 6

defendant was returned to court, and substituted a provision that the court should follow the procedures applicable after the initial competence examination.[194] That ensured that the court or either party could insist on a hearing.[195]

It was in that context that the Court of Appeals decided *People v. Christopher*[196] in 1985. Christopher initially had been found incompetent and committed, but was later certified as competent. His attorneys requested a hearing, and then asked the court to authorize the hiring of psychiatrists to assist the defense and testify at the hearing. The court refused to hear any experts other than those who had certified the defendant's competence, and persisted in that position even when the defense attorneys offered to pay the additional experts themselves.[197] The Court of Appeals held that this had denied Christopher his rights under Article 730. After the 1981 amendment a defendant was entitled to challenge expert competency findings at a "hearing," both after the initial examination and after any period of commitment for treatment. And

> [t]o say that [a] defendant is ensured the right to a hearing and to contest a psychiatric determination but may not present psychiatric testimony is a contradiction in terms.[198]

Since *Christopher*, a report on the defendant's competence by neutral examiners, whether made after an order of examination or after a period of commitment, may be only the starting point for a series of examinations by the parties. While the number of experts who can be called at a hearing in addition to the neutral examiners is subject to the court's discretion,[199] both the defense and the prosecution are entitled to adjournments reasonably necessary to obtain at least some expert testimony.[200]

When the competency hearing is held, the defendant has a right to be present.[201] At first blush that might seem ironic, at least where the defendant's position is that he or she is not competent, *i.e.*, not able to understand the proceedings or assist his or her attorney. But incompetence takes many forms, and a defendant may well be able to assist at a short hearing even if he or she could not remain competent under the

---

194. L.1981, c.791.

195. CPL § 730.30(2).

196. 65 N.Y.2d 417, 492 N.Y.S.2d 566, 482 N.E.2d 45 (1985).

197. 65 N.Y.2d at 421–23, 492 N.Y.S.2d at 567–69.

198. 65 N.Y.2d at 424, 492 N.Y.S.2d at 569.

199. 65 N.Y.2d at 425, 492 N.Y.S.2d at 570; People v. McMillan, 212 A.D.2d 445, 622 N.Y.S.2d 935 (1st Dep't 1995).

200. See People v. McMillan, supra; People v. West, 171 A.D.2d 1026, 569 N.Y.S.2d 33 (4th Dep't 1991); People v. Perkins, 166 A.D.2d 737, 562 N.Y.S.2d 244 (3d Dep't 1990); People v. Dobbs, 156 A.D.2d 990, 549 N.Y.S.2d 283 (4th Dep't 1989); People v. Gonzalez, 132 Misc.2d 1004, 506 N.Y.S.2d 276 (Sup.Ct., Richmond County, 1986); People v. Broccolo, 130 Misc.2d 606, 497 N.Y.S.2d 816 (Suffolk Co. Ct.1985).

201. See People v. Williams, 85 N.Y.2d 945, 626 N.Y.S.2d 1002, 650 N.E.2d 849 (1995)(distinguishing a hearing from a proceeding at which defense counsel withdraws a prior motion for a hearing).

pressures of a lengthy trial. Moreover, observing the defendant may assist the court in reaching its decision at the hearing.[202] Accordingly, where there is a factual issue to be resolved about the defendant's competence, he or she should not be permitted to waive the right to be present.[203]

At the hearing, both sides have the right to call witnesses[204] and confront witnesses.[205] The *Rosario* rule is applicable to pre-trial hearings like competency hearings,[206] but the disclosure obligation is triggered only by the opposing party's request for a witness's statements, and disclosure need not be made before the conclusion of the witness's direct examination.[207] The courtroom should be open to the public, absent unusual and compelling circumstances.[208] It has been held that, at the hearing, the defendant can be required personally to give an unsworn statement to help the court resolve the competency issue,[209] subject to a complete bar on use of the statement at trial.[210] Should the defendant testify, his or her testimony is inadmissible at trial except to impeach.[211] Defense experts may be impeached with their hearing testimony if they testify in support of an insanity defense at trial.[212]

The court must be satisfied by a preponderance of the evidence that a defendant is competent,[213] but its determination will be informed by the presumption of competence.[214] In making its decision the court will again rely on the types of facts that are considered when issuing an order of examination.[215] The court will therefore weigh many consider-

202. See People v. Williams, 204 A.D.2d 77, 611 N.Y.S.2d 849 (1st Dep't 1994), rev'd on other grounds 85 N.Y.2d 945, 626 N.Y.S.2d 1002, 650 N.E.2d 849 (1995).

203. See People v. Gensler, 72 N.Y.2d 239, 247, 532 N.Y.S.2d 72, 77, 527 N.E.2d 1209 (1988), cert. den. 488 U.S. 932, 109 S.Ct. 323, 102 L.Ed.2d 341 (1988); People v. Christopher, 65 N.Y.2d at 421, 492 N.Y.S.2d at 567.

204. People v. Christopher, 65 N.Y.2d at 425, 492 N.Y.S.2d at 567. Expert witnesses need not possess the statutory qualifications of "psychiatric examiners" provided in section 730.10. People v. Gans, 119 Misc.2d 843, 465 N.Y.S.2d 147 (Sup.Ct., N.Y. County, 1983).

205. "A 'hearing' or 'trial' of ... an issue of fact is an empty form unless it takes place ... with the right, on each side, to examine and cross-examine." People v. Christopher, 65 N.Y.2d at 425, 492 N.Y.S.2d at 570 quoting People v. Richetti, 302 N.Y. 290, 297, 97 N.E.2d 908, 911 (1951).

206. See CPL § 240.44(1); People v. McPhee, 161 Misc.2d 660, 614 N.Y.S.2d 884 (Sup.Ct., Queens County, 1994).

207. CPL § 240.44.

208. Matter of Westchester Rockland Newspapers v. Leggett, 48 N.Y.2d 430, 423 N.Y.S.2d 630, 399 N.E.2d 518 (1979); People v. Berkowitz, 93 Misc.2d 873, 403 N.Y.S.2d 699 (Sup.Ct., Kings County, 1978); see also Associated Press v. Bell, 70 N.Y.2d 32, 517 N.Y.S.2d 444, 510 N.E.2d 313 (1987).

209. People v. Grisset, 118 Misc.2d 450, 460 N.Y.S.2d 987 (Sup.Ct., Queens County, 1983).

210. See New Jersey v. Portash, 440 U.S. 450, 99 S.Ct. 1292, 59 L.Ed.2d 501 (1979).

211. People v. Angelillo, 105 Misc.2d 338, 432 N.Y.S.2d 127 (Suffolk Co.Ct.1980).

212. People v. Swan, 158 A.D.2d 158, 557 N.Y.S.2d 791 (4th Dep't 1990).

213. People v. Christopher, 65 N.Y.2d at 424–25, 492 N.Y.S.2d at 570; People v. Cox, 196 A.D.2d 596, 601 N.Y.S.2d 175 (2d Dep't 1993); People v. Vega, 73 Misc.2d 857, 342 N.Y.S.2d 693 (N.Y.C.Crim.Ct. 1973). The cases often suggest that the prosecution bears the burden of proving the defendant's competence, but the prosecution will not necessarily always take the position that the defendant is competent.

214. People v. Gelikkaya, 84 N.Y.2d 456, 618 N.Y.S.2d 895, 643 N.E.2d 517 (1994).

215. See § 6.2, supra.

ations, and substantial deference will be accorded to its findings.[216] Critically, while the court will consider the testimony and reports of the experts, the ultimate conclusion about competence is a legal conclusion for the court; it need not accept the opinions of the experts.[217]

Library References:

West's Key No. Digests, Criminal Law ⟳623–625.

§ 6.10 Additional Considerations

As noted, a defendant is considered incompetent under New York law if, as a result of "mental disease or defect," he "lacks capacity to understand the proceedings against him or to assist in his own defense."[218] As that definition indicates, a defendant can be mentally ill and still be competent to stand trial. For example, depression does not inevitably incapacitate a defendant.[219] An individual with schizophrenia may be able to understand the criminal process and aid in his or her own defense[220]—or he may not be able to do so.[221] And paranoia is not incompatible with competence,[222] even when complicated by schizophrenia.[223]

The case law under Article 730 addresses other conditions that might be placed on the borderline between mental defects and physical defects. First, low intelligence or "mild" retardation, even when accompanied by psychiatric disorders or "developmental disabilities," will not inevitably render a defendant incompetent to stand trial.[224] In addition, as indicated in Section 6.2, *supra*, a defendant is not incompetent simply because he is on medication, albeit medication that affects his mental awareness.[225] Indeed, "synthetic" competence—competence maintained

---

216. See, e.g., People v. Delgado, 202 A.D.2d 299, 610 N.Y.S.2d 770 (1st Dep't 1994); People v. Gordon, 125 A.D.2d 587, 509 N.Y.S.2d 651 (2d Dep't 1986).

217. See, e.g., People v. Phipps, ___ A.D.2d ___, 631 N.Y.S.2d 853 (1st Dep't 1995); People v. Claron, 103 Misc.2d 841, 427 N.Y.S.2d 146 (Sup.Ct., N.Y. County, 1980); People v. Greene, 203 Misc. 191, 116 N.Y.S.2d 561 (Sup.Ct., Kings County, 1952); see also People v. Christopher, 65 N.Y.2d at 434, 492 N.Y.S.2d at 576 (Simons, J., dissenting).

218. CPL § 730.10(1).

219. People v. Alexander, 161 A.D.2d 1035, 558 N.Y.S.2d 200 (3d Dep't 1990); People v. Collins, 154 A.D.2d 901, 545 N.Y.S.2d 959 (4th Dep't 1989); People v. Dudasik, 112 A.D.2d 20, 490 N.Y.S.2d 385 (4th Dep't 1985).

220. People v. Lacher, 59 A.D.2d 725, 398 N.Y.S.2d 363 (2d Dep't 1977); People v. Miller, 84 Misc.2d 310, 376 N.Y.S.2d 393 (Sup.Ct., Bronx County, 1975).

221. People ex rel. Fazio v. McNeill, 4 A.D.2d 686, 164 N.Y.S.2d 156 (2d Dep't 1957), cert. den. 356 U.S. 943, 78 S.Ct. 787, 2 L.Ed.2d 817 (1958).

222. People v. Hinsman, 182 Misc. 61, 43 N.Y.S.2d 89 (Schenectady Co.Ct.1943).

223. People v. Morgan, 87 N.Y.2d 878, 638 N.Y.S.2d 942, 662 N.E.2d 260 (1995).

224. People v. Hart, 205 A.D.2d 943, 613 N.Y.S.2d 762 (3d Dep't 1994); People v. Charlton, 192 A.D.2d 757, 758–59, 596 N.Y.S.2d 210, 212 (3d Dep't 1993); People v. Bronson, 115 A.D.2d 484, 495 N.Y.S.2d 716 (2d Dep't 1985); People v. Claron, 103 Misc.2d 841, 427 N.Y.S.2d 146 (Sup.Ct., N.Y. County, 1980).

225. People v. Grant, 188 A.D.2d 1052, 592 N.Y.S.2d 206 (4th Dep't 1992)(epilepsy medication); People v. Thomas, 188 A.D.2d 431, 592 N.Y.S.2d 586 (1st Dep't 1992) (psychiatric medication); People v. Wolf, 176 A.D.2d 1070, 1072, 575 N.Y.S.2d 726, 729 (3d Dep't 1991)("psychoactive" drugs); People v. Lopez, 160 A.D.2d 335, 554 N.Y.S.2d 98 (1st Dep't 1990)(medication that slowed defendant's reaction to questions); cf. People v. Pringle, 186 A.D.2d 413, 589 N.Y.S.2d 8 (1st Dep't 1992).

only as a result of medication—is sufficient to defeat a defendant's assertions that he was not competent to be tried.[226]

Amnesia straddles the line between mental illness and physical illness—and indeed may fall on the "physical" side of that line. Yet a defendant's alleged amnesia is likely to be evaluated under Article 730 principles. In *People v. Francabandera*,[227] for example, witnesses to the crimes committed by the defendant related that, while intoxicated, he had fired a shotgun and a rifle at civilians and the police. Return fire from the police struck the defendant in the head, leaving him with no recollection of the shootings. He nonetheless was able to understand the proceedings subsequently initiated against him.[228]

The Court of Appeals determined that, "for lack of a better procedural device," a trial court should evaluate the amnesia claims of a defendant like Francabandera pursuant to an Article 730 motion.[229] The court further concluded that a defendant is not inevitably unable to assist his or her counsel by virtue of an inability to remember a crime.[230] The controlling issue is whether, on the facts of the case, a defendant with amnesia can receive a fair trial.[231] In Francabandera's case, had the defendant not pleaded guilty he would have been able, with his own testimony, to advance the only colorable defense, an intoxication defense. The court found, under those circumstances, that Francabandera's amnesia had not made it impossible for him to receive a fair trial.[232]

A profound hearing impairment may also have an impact on a defendant's competence comparable to that of mental illness. One appellate court has held that deafness, rendering a defendant incapable of understanding the proceedings, should be evaluated under Article 730.[233] Another appellate court, perhaps more appropriately, has stated that a deaf defendant who may be unable to understand the proceedings or assist in his or her own defense must be examined by a qualified otolaryngologist.[234] Under either view, if the defendant cannot understand the proceedings or assist in the defense, he or she cannot be tried.

Apart from claims concerning amnesia or deafness, defendants' efforts to have physical ailments evaluated under Article 730 have not found much favor. For example, sleep apnea, a breathing disorder,

226. People v. Williams, 144 A.D.2d 402, 533 N.Y.S.2d 963 (2d Dep't 1988); People v. Parsons, 82 Misc.2d 1090, 371 N.Y.S.2d 840 (Nassau Co.Ct.1975)(defendant was competent, despite need to be alert for his "fugue" states).

227. 33 N.Y.2d 429, 354 N.Y.S.2d 609, 310 N.E.2d 292 (1974).

228. 33 N.Y.2d at 432–33, 354 N.Y.S.2d at 610–11.

229. 33 N.Y.2d at 438, 354 N.Y.S.2d at 616.

230. 33 N.Y.2d at 435–38, 354 N.Y.S.2d at 613.

231. 33 N.Y.2d at 438, 354 N.Y.S.2d at 615.

232. See also People v. Goodell, 164 A.D.2d 321, 565 N.Y.S.2d 929 (4th Dep't 1990), aff'd 79 N.Y.2d 869, 581 N.Y.S.2d 157, 589 N.E.2d 380 (1992); People v. Pisco, 69 Misc.2d 675, 330 N.Y.S.2d 542 (Dutchess Co.Ct.1972); People v. Soto, 68 Misc.2d 629, 327 N.Y.S.2d 669 (Nassau Co. Ct.1972); see also People ex rel. Fazio v. McNeill, 4 A.D.2d 686, 164 N.Y.S.2d 156 (2d Dep't 1957), cert. den. 356 U.S. 943, 78 S.Ct. 787, 2 L.Ed.2d 817 (1958).

233. New York City Human Resources Administration v. Carey, 107 A.D.2d 625, 484 N.Y.S.2d 10 (1st Dep't 1985).

234. People v. Jackson, 88 A.D.2d 604, 449 N.Y.S.2d 759 (2d Dep't 1982).

renders its victims unable to sleep for more than brief periods. A court is obliged to examine the effects of such a physical disorder on a defendant, but Article 730 procedures need not be followed.[235] Similarly, serious physical complications alleged to follow from AIDS do not trigger a requirement for special proceedings akin to Article 730 proceedings.[236] Nor are special procedures required by the claims of a defendant on trial that he or she has received insufficient food, poor medical attention, and inadequate sleep.[237] That is not to suggest that a defendant, unable to understand the proceedings or assist in his or her defense for reasons unrelated to mental disease or defect, deserves no remedy. But such a defendant will be able to invoke Article 730, if at all, only by analogy.

Several miscellaneous principles affecting competence determinations should be noted. First, Article 730 applies to defendants, and only to defendants. There is no basis in New York law to order an examination of victims or witnesses on account of a defendant's assertion that such persons might not be competent.[238]

Second, while examinations of the defendant are at the heart of any Article 730 determination, sometimes defendants do not make such evaluations easy. At least one appellate court has held that a defendant forfeits the right to a hearing on competence if he or she repeatedly refuses to cooperate with Article 730 examiners.[239] That conclusion is troubling, however, in that a defendant's refusal to cooperate with examinations could be a by-product of mental illness.

Third, the appellate courts have consistently refused to recognize waivers of competence claims, even by virtue of a guilty plea,[240] or to require that such claims be "preserved" for appellate review by objection.[241] As the Court of Appeals noted in one case:

> [T]here is an inherent contradiction in arguing that a defendant may be incompetent, and yet knowingly or intelligently waive his right to have a court determine his capacity to stand trial.[242]

But even the willingness to consider a competence claim presented for the first time on appeal cannot help a defendant if the appellate record does not contain facts sufficient to permit intelligent evaluation of his or her claim.[243]

---

235. People v. Bisnett, 144 A.D.2d 567, 534 N.Y.S.2d 424 (2d Dep't 1988).

236. People v. Parker, 132 A.D.2d 629, 517 N.Y.S.2d 783 (2d Dep't 1987).

237. People v. Garcia, 161 A.D.2d 796, 556 N.Y.S.2d 667 (2d Dep't 1990).

238. People v. Earl, ___ A.D.2d ___, 632 N.Y.S.2d 689 (3d Dep't 1995); People v. Souvenir, 83 Misc.2d 1038, 373 N.Y.S.2d 824 (N.Y.C.Crim.Ct.1975).

239. People v. Torres, 194 A.D.2d 488, 599 N.Y.S.2d 561 (1st Dep't 1993).

240. See, e.g., People v. Armlin, 37 N.Y.2d 167, 172, 371 N.Y.S.2d 691, 696, 332 N.E.2d 870 (1975).

241. See, e.g., People v. Bangert, 22 N.Y.2d 799, 292 N.Y.S.2d 900, 239 N.E.2d 644 (1968).

242. People v. Armlin, 37 N.Y.2d at 172, 371 N.Y.S.2d at 697; see Pate v. Robinson, 383 U.S. 375, 384, 86 S.Ct. 836, 841, 15 L.Ed.2d 815 (1966).

243. People v. Phelps, 74 N.Y.2d 919, 550 N.Y.S.2d 259, 549 N.E.2d 461 (1989); see People v. Kinchen, 60 N.Y.2d 772, 469 N.Y.S.2d 680, 457 N.E.2d 786 (1983).

Finally, there remains the issue of the appropriate remedy if a defendant does persuade an appellate court that proper Article 730 procedures were not followed in his or her case. In *Pate v. Robinson*,[244] the United States Supreme Court ordered that the defendant receive a new trial, and not simply a retrospective hearing into whether he was competent during his trial. The court noted that it is preferable for the finder of fact as to competence to have had the opportunity to observe the defendant at the time of trial, and noted the undesirability of having experts opine about competence based solely on a cold record. And, critically, in *Pate* the hearing would have been held a full six years after trial.[245]

The first application of *Pate* by the New York Court of Appeals came in *People v. Hudson*.[246] In that case, the court held that a retrospective examination could succeed three years after trial, when expert examinations of the defendant's mental condition had been conducted at the time of trial in furtherance of an insanity defense. The court provided that the hearing would be conducted before a judge other than the trial judge, so that the testimony of that judge about his observations of the defendant could be objectively evaluated.[247]

Many cases have since followed *Hudson* and ordered retrospective competence hearings instead of new trials.[248] One court, uncertain whether there had been expert examinations of the defendant before trial, ordered that the trial judge first explore that issue, and hold a retrospective competency hearing if such examinations had been conducted.[249] In at least some cases, hearings were able to produce a satisfactory conclusion that the defendant had been competent at the time of the conviction.[250]

The Court of Appeals reached a different result, one apparently inconsistent with *Hudson*, in *People v. Peterson*.[251] In that case, the court's brief memorandum opinion simply noted,

> A new trial must be ordered because with the passage of time, it has been held, it is too difficult to make a retrospective determination of trial competence.[252]

244. 383 U.S. 375, 86 S.Ct. 836, 15 L.Ed.2d 815 (1966).

245. 383 U.S. at 387, 86 S.Ct. at 843.

246. 19 N.Y.2d 137, 278 N.Y.S.2d 593, 225 N.E.2d 193 (1967), cert. den. 398 U.S. 944, 90 S.Ct. 1852, 26 L.Ed.2d 281 (1970).

247. 19 N.Y.2d at 140, 278 N.Y.S.2d at 595, 225 N.E.2d at 194.

248. See, e.g., People v. Armlin, 37 N.Y.2d 167, 371 N.Y.S.2d 691, 332 N.E.2d 870 (1975); People v. Gonzalez, 20 N.Y.2d 289, 282 N.Y.S.2d 538, 229 N.E.2d 220 (1967), cert. den. 390 U.S. 971, 88 S.Ct. 1093, 19 L.Ed.2d 1182 (1968); People v. Bey, 144 A.D.2d 972, 534 N.Y.S.2d 275 (4th Dep't 1988); People v. Whysong, 175 A.D.2d 576, 572 N.Y.S.2d 243 (4th Dep't 1991); People v. Wright, 105 A.D.2d 1088, 482 N.Y.S.2d 591 (4th Dep't 1984).

249. People v. Arnold, 113 A.D.2d 101, 495 N.Y.S.2d 537 (4th Dep't 1985).

250. See, e.g., People v. Bey, 167 A.D.2d 868, 562 N.Y.S.2d 896 (4th Dep't 1990); People v. Whysong, 187 A.D.2d 1037, 591 N.Y.S.2d 103 (4th Dep't 1992); People v. Wright, 124 A.D.2d 1015, 508 N.Y.S.2d 1017 (4th Dep't 1986).

251. 40 N.Y.2d 1014, 391 N.Y.S.2d 530, 359 N.E.2d 1325 (1976).

252. 40 N.Y.2d at 1015, 391 N.Y.S.2d at 530, 359 N.E.2d at 1325.

§ 6.10 COMPETENCY PROCEEDINGS Ch. 6

In dissent, three judges noted that only two years had passed since the defendant's trial, and that he had been examined by psychiatrists during and immediately after trial.[253] Other cases have found retrospective proceedings to be inadequate after longer periods of time,[254] because contemporaneous examinations had not been conducted,[255] or because of the length of time since trial and the fact that the defendant had not been present at trial.[256] The Fourth Department, joining these factors into a three-pronged test, has concluded that a court determining whether a retrospective competence hearing is practicable should consider:

1. the extent to which there were contemporaneous psychiatric examinations, particularly for competency, but also those performed in conjunction with the preparation of an insanity defense;

2. the length of time since trial so as to determine whether witnesses at the reconstruction hearing can testify from memory rather than from records made at the time; and

3. the opportunity to observe defendant's behavior at trial to gauge the extent to which he was able to cooperate with his counsel and to understand the nature of the proceedings.[257]

Whether such a hearing can be conducted may also turn on the nature of the error in the original competence proceedings. In particular, in *People v. Christopher*,[258] the trial court had erred by refusing to permit defense experts to provide assistance to the defendant. The Court of Appeals concluded:

Because the psychiatric assistance that can be provided at a new hearing will relate to defendant's present condition, rather than his capacity at the time of the ... hearing held without such assistance, a new hearing will not provide him with the safeguards he was entitled to at the time of [that] hearing....
There must, therefore, be a reversal and a remand for a new hearing as to defendant's present capacity, followed, if he is found capable to proceed, by a new trial....[259]

Perhaps inconsistently, however, retrospective hearings have repeatedly been permitted when the original error was in having only one qualified examiner, rather than two, examine the defendant.[260] And in *People v.*

253. 40 N.Y.2d at 1016–17, 391 N.Y.S.2d at 531–32 (Jasen, J., dissenting).

254. See, e.g., People v. Williams, 204 A.D.2d 77, 611 N.Y.S.2d 849 (1st Dep't 1994), rev'd on other grounds 85 N.Y.2d 945, 626 N.Y.S.2d 1002, 650 N.E.2d 849 (1995)(almost five years); but see People v. Mullooly, 37 A.D.2d 6, 322 N.Y.S.2d 7 (1st Dep't 1971)(hearing after seven years might be adequate if experts testified).

255. See, e.g., People v. Cartagena, 92 A.D.2d 901, 459 N.Y.S.2d 896 (2d Dep't 1983).

256. People v. Lowe, 109 A.D.2d 300, 305–06, 491 N.Y.S.2d 529, 534–35 (4th Dep't 1985).

257. People v. Arnold, 113 A.D.2d 101, 107, 495 N.Y.S.2d 537, 541 (4th Dep't 1985); People v. Lowe, supra.

258. 65 N.Y.2d 417, 492 N.Y.S.2d 566, 482 N.E.2d 45 (1985).

259. 65 N.Y.2d at 426, 492 N.Y.S.2d at 570–71 (citations omitted).

260. People v. Armlin, 37 N.Y.2d 167, 371 N.Y.S.2d 691, 332 N.E.2d 870 (1975); People v. Gray, 190 A.D.2d 1057, 593 N.Y.S.2d 681 (4th Dep't 1993); People v. Kennedy, 151 A.D.2d 831, 542 N.Y.S.2d 806 (3d Dep't 1989); People v. Mulholland, 129 A.D.2d 857, 514 N.Y.S.2d 135 (3d Dep't 1987); People v. Wright, 105 A.D.2d 1088, 482 N.Y.S.2d 591 (4th Dep't 1984).

Weech,[261] the court noted that, in determining whether the defendant had originally been competent, the hearing court could rely on the testimony of experts who were not qualified examiners under the provisions of Article 730.

Library References:
West's Key No. Digests, Criminal Law ⟜625.25; Mental Health ⟜432.

§ 6.11 Practice Summary

A. The Order of Examination (*See* §§ 6.1, 6.2)

1. A defendant may not be tried if he is not competent. In New York, a defendant is considered incompetent to stand trial if as a result of mental disease or defect he lacks capacity to understand the proceedings against him or assist in his own defense. If at any point in a criminal action the court believes that the defendant "may" be incompetent, the court "must" initiate competency proceedings under Article 730.

2. In making such a determination, the court should take into account, for example, whether the defendant is oriented as to time and place; whether he is able to perceive, recall, and relate; whether he understands the trial process and the roles of the judge, jury, and attorneys; whether he can work with the defense attorney and appreciate his advice; and whether he is sufficiently stable to withstand the pressures of a trial.

3. Whether Article 730 proceedings must be initiated is a matter entrusted to the discretion of the court. Important to the determination will be the court's opportunities to observe the defendant, the views of defense counsel, and the defendant's psychiatric history. If, after consideration of all relevant circumstances, the court has cause to doubt the defendant's competence, the court will issue an "order of examination."

B. Impact on the Case (*See* § 6.3)

1. If the examination process results in a conclusion that the defendant is competent, the criminal action resumes its regular course. On the other hand, a finding of incompetence will result in suspension of the case until the defendant becomes competent, if not a dismissal of the case. Until the defendant is competent, he cannot plead guilty or otherwise waive his rights. In a superior court case his attorney may in the meantime make certain motions on his behalf as to which his presence is not important, such as a motion to dismiss, but the defendant is entitled to have any unsuccessful motion reconsidered when he becomes competent. If the prosecution consents and other prerequisites are satisfied, the court may dismiss a case in the interest of justice.

2. Periods in which the defendant is being examined or treated for incompetence are excludable for statutory speedy trial purposes. The defendant's right to testify in the grand jury is voided by an order of

---

261. 105 A.D.2d 1085, 482 N.Y.S.2d 174 (4th Dep't 1984).

examination, subject to a motion for relief in the court that has impaneled the grand jury.

3. Statements made by the defendant during a period of examination or subsequent treatment cannot be used against the defendant on the prosecution's direct case at trial unless the defendant places his mental state in issue. Even then, the statements are admissible only on that issue.

C. The Examination Process (*See* §§ 6.4, 6.5)

1. Upon the issuance of the order of examination, a "director"—a mental health official or hospital director—will be placed in charge of the examination of the defendant. The director will designate two psychiatrists or psychologists to determine, in accordance with standard medical procedure, whether the defendant is competent. If the two designated individuals disagree, a third expert is named to conduct a further examination. Upon the completion of the examinations, the experts submit their findings to the court on standardized forms.

2. The court may authorize a defense expert to observe the examinations. It remains unsettled whether defense counsel is entitled to attend, but there seems little reason to exclude counsel or the prosecutor.

3. If the defendant is not in custody, the court may, upon the director's recommendation, commit him to a hospital for purposes of examination. If the defendant is in custody, the court must order his transfer to a hospital if the director so requests. The examination of a defendant confined in a hospital should be completed by a date set by the court that is within 30 days of the date of the order of examination. One extension of up to 30 days may be authorized by the court if necessary.

D. Subsequent Proceedings in Superior Court (*See* § 6.6)

1. If the examiners agree that the defendant is competent, or if they agree that he is incompetent, the court may confirm their finding without a hearing if neither the court nor a party believes a hearing should be held. If the court or any party believes that a hearing should be held, or if the examiners disagree, a hearing must be held.

2. If the examiners believed defendant to be competent, but after a hearing the court is not satisfied on that score, the court must issue another order of examination. Otherwise, a confirmation or finding that the defendant is competent causes the case against him to resume. A confirmation or finding that the defendant is incompetent results in the issuance of an order of commitment, if the defendant is charged with or convicted of a felony. If the defendant is charged with or convicted of a lesser offense, a final order of examination will issue and the case will be dismissed.

3. An order of commitment commits the defendant for treatment at a mental health facility for up to a year and suspends the criminal case. If the superintendent of the facility believes that the defendant remains incompetent, the court may issue orders of retention, although the

defendant is entitled to a hearing before such orders are issued. Under *Jackson v. Indiana*, commitment on account of criminal proceedings cannot continue once it is clear that the defendant will not become competent. Moreover, the commitment must end after a period equal to two-thirds of the defendant's maximum prison term, and at that point the accusatory instrument must be dismissed. In either event, the defendant may thereafter be retained pursuant to civil commitment procedures.

4. If, during a period of commitment or retention, the superintendent concludes that the defendant is competent, he or she shall so certify. On motion of the court or either party, a hearing must be held to test that conclusion. If no hearing is held, or if the defendant is found competent, the case resumes. If, after a hearing, the court is not satisfied that the defendant is competent, a new order of examination will issue, or the defendant will be returned to the same facility for further treatment.

E. Subsequent Proceedings in Local Criminal Court (*See* § 6.7)

1. Following the examination process, a local criminal court resolves the competence issue in the same way as a superior court. If the defendant is found competent, the case resumes. If the defendant is found incompetent, and if the accusatory instrument is not a felony complaint, a final order of observation will issue. Such an order commits the defendant for treatment for up to 90 days, during which he is treated like a civil patient and can be released. Such an order also results in dismissal of the case with prejudice.

2. If the accusatory instrument is a felony complaint, the prosecution may consent to the issuance of a final order of observation. If not, a temporary order of observation will issue. Such an order likewise commits the defendant for treatment for up to 90 days, but the case is only suspended, and not dismissed. If the defendant is certified as competent within the period of the order, the local criminal court follows the same procedure as would a superior court. If the defendant remains incompetent at the end of the period of the order, the case is dismissed and any further custody could only be pursuant to civil proceedings.

3. If an indictment is filed during the period of an order of examination, the local criminal court is divested of jurisdiction. The examiners' reports are thereafter forwarded to the superior court. If an indictment is filed after the issuance of a temporary order of observation, that order or any successor civil orders of commitment are nullified. However, an indictment may not be filed more than six months after the date of the temporary order of observation absent a showing of good cause.

F. The 1980 Amendments (*See* § 6.8)

1. Pursuant to provisions added to Article 730 in 1980, law enforcement officials and others must be notified of certain changes in status of individuals who remain committed after competence examinations in criminal cases, even if the individuals have been transferred to civil status. In addition, the prosecution is authorized to contest the reason-

ableness of changes in status in cases in which orders of commitment, final orders of observation, and perhaps orders of retention have been issued, on the ground that the defendant is dangerous to himself or others.

2. These provisions are subject to attack on equal protection and due process theories. They are particularly problematic to the extent that they treat a class of civilly committed individuals, those originally charged in a criminal case but never convicted, differently from other civilly committed individuals.

G. Hearing Procedure (*See* § 6.9)

1. Since amendments to Article 730 passed in 1981, and in particular since *People v. Christopher*, a hearing to determine a defendant's competence at any of the pertinent stages of competence proceedings is one in which both parties are entitled to aid from and testimony from experts that will permit challenges to the conclusions of neutral examiners.

2. Such hearings also possess attributes typical of other types of hearings in criminal actions. For example, the defendant is entitled to be present, to present evidence, and to confront witnesses. If the defendant testifies, his testimony is admissible at trial only for purposes of impeachment.

3. At the conclusion of the hearing the court will resolve whether the defendant can understand the proceedings and assist in his own defense by considering the same types of facts it did in ordering an examination. The court can find the defendant competent, and order the case to resume, only if satisfied of his competence by a preponderance of the evidence. However, a presumption of competence applies in a criminal action.

H. Additional Considerations (*See* § 6.10)

1. A number of cases roughly define the applicability of Article 730 proceedings to ailments that may be more physical than mental. In particular, the cases have treated amnesia and profound deafness as raising issues to which Article 730 proceedings are at least analogous.

2. If an appellate court finds that the trial court wrongly ignored or applied the procedures of Article 730, whether the defendant is entitled to a retrospective competence hearing, or instead to a vacatur of the conviction, will turn on whether a retrospective hearing is practicable. A court considering whether such a hearing is practicable should consider the available expert information about the defendant's mental state contemporaneous with the conviction, the length of time since the conviction, and the court's ability to observe the defendant at the time of the conviction.

3. In some circumstances, erroneous curtailment of the defendant's ability to participate in an Article 730 hearing may mandate that the appellate court vacate the conviction.

§ 6.12 Forms

§ 6.12.1 Notice of Motion for Order of Examination

[Caption]

COUNSEL:

PLEASE TAKE NOTICE, that upon the annexed affirmation and upon all the prior papers and proceedings herein, the undersigned will move this Court, at Part ___ thereof, at the Courthouse at _____, New York, on the ___ day of _____, 19__, at ___ in the forenoon, or as soon thereafter as counsel can be heard, for an order pursuant to section 730.30 of the Criminal Procedure Law directing that defendant be examined to determine whether he [she] is an incapacitated person, and for such other relief as the Court deems proper.

Dated: _____, 19__
_____, New York

[Name of defense attorney]
Attorney for Defendant
Address
Tel. No.

TO: HON. _____
District Attorney
_____ County

HON. _____
Clerk of the Court

§ 6.12.2 Affirmation in Support of Motion for Order of Examination

[Caption]

_____, an attorney duly admitted to practice in the Courts of this State, hereby affirms under penalty of perjury that the following statements are true, and as to those statements made upon information and belief he [she] believes them to be true:

1. I am the attorney for the defendant herein.

2. On _____, 19__, a [specify accusatory instrument] was filed with this Court charging defendant with the following offense(s): [specify charge(s)]. A copy of the [specify accusatory instrument] is attached hereto as Exhibit A.

3. No plea of guilty has been entered with respect to the [specify accusatory instrument], nor has a trial been commenced thereon.

4. [Specify reasons why undersigned has concluded that defendant may be incapacitated—e.g., conversations with defendant revealing that defendant does not understand the charges, the process of the trial and the role of the participants in the trial process; other difficulties defense counsel has had in communicating with defendant; defendant's behavior

in court; defendant's psychiatric history. Attach any relevant documents].

5. For the reasons discussed above, defendant may be an incapacitated person who as a result of a mental disease or defect lacks capacity to understand the proceedings against him [her] or to assist in his [her] own defense.

WHEREFORE, the undersigned requests that the Court issue an order pursuant to section 730.30 of the Criminal Procedure Law directing that defendant be examined to determine whether he [she] is an incapacitated person.

Dated: _____, 19__
_____, New York

[Signature]

_____
[Name of defense attorney]

Chapter 7

DISCOVERY

Table of Sections

7.1 Introduction.
7.2 Criminal Discovery in New York.
7.3 Demand Disclosure—In General.
7.4 ____ By Defendant.
7.5 ____ By Prosecution.
7.6 ____ Refusal of Demand.
7.7 Defense Motion for Discovery—Statutory Basis.
7.8 ____ Subpoenas.
7.9 ____ Identity of Prosecution Witnesses.
7.10 ____ Identity of Informant.
7.11 Prosecution Motion for Discovery.
7.12 *Brady*—In General.
7.13 ____ Materiality.
7.14 ____ Other Issues.
7.15 Disclosure of Uncharged Prior Bad Acts.
7.16 *Rosario*—In General.
7.17 ____ Specific Issues.
7.18 Witness Criminal History Information.
7.19 Protective Orders.
7.20 Sanctions—In General.
7.21 ____ Belated Disclosure.
7.22 ____ Complete Failure to Disclose.
7.23 ____ Loss or Destruction of Discoverable Material.
7.24 ____ Against the Defense.
7.25 Pretrial Notices of Defenses—In General.
7.26 ____ Psychiatric Evidence.
7.27 ____ Alibi.
7.28 ____ Computer-Related Offenses.
7.29 Prosecution's Notice of Intent to Seek Death Penalty.
7.30 Discovery of Privileged and Confidential Material.
7.31 The Work Product Exemption.
7.32 Defendant's Right to Test of Physical Evidence.
7.33 Miscellaneous Issues.
7.34 Practice Summary—Defense.
7.35 ____ Prosecution.
7.36 ____ Court.
7.37 Forms.
    7.37.1 Demand to Produce (Made by Defendant).
    7.37.2 Demand to Produce (Made by Prosecutor).
    7.37.3 Refusal of Demand to Produce (Either Party).
    7.37.4 Notice of Motion by Defendant for Disclosure in Response to Refusal of Prosecution to Comply With Demand to Produce.
    7.37.5 Affirmation in Support of Defendant's Motion for Disclosure After Refusal of Prosecutor to Comply With Demand to Produce.
    7.37.6 Notice of Motion by Defendant for Discovery Beyond That Required Under Demand to Produce.

Table of Sections

7.37 Forms (Cont'd)
    7.37.7   Affirmation in Support of Defendant's Motion for Discovery Beyond That Required Under Demand to Produce.
    7.37.8   Notice of Motion by Prosecutor for Discovery of Non-testimonial Evidence.
    7.37.9   Affirmation of Prosecutor in Support of Motion for Discovery of Non-testimonial Evidence.
    7.37.10   Notice of Motion for Protective Order.
    7.37.11   Affirmation in Support of Motion for Protective Order.
    7.37.12   Demand for Notice of Alibi.
    7.37.13   Notice of Alibi.

WESTLAW Electronic Research

See WESTLAW Electronic Research Guide preceding the Summary of Contents.

§ 7.1 Introduction

Criminal discovery serves a number of important goals. Discovery promotes the parties' ability to prepare for trial, thereby minimizing surprises, interruptions and complications during the trial. In addition, it provides the accused with critical information with which to make a more informed plea, and thus avoids the necessity of conducting a trial in a significant number of cases. Discovery also helps to eliminate differences in pretrial investigative capacities between indigent and wealthy defendants.[1]

Despite these substantial benefits, few, if any, jurisdictions have criminal discovery rules that even remotely resemble the extensive disclosure procedures that are authorized in civil cases. The primary arguments against criminal discovery, and particularly broad criminal discovery, are that the defendant's constitutional rights (mainly, the privilege against self-incrimination) limit reciprocal discovery from the defense, that discovery of the prosecution's evidence will promote perjury by the defendant at trial and that discovery will engender increased intimidation of victims and witnesses.[2]

These concerns, however, do not appear to outweigh the benefits of broad criminal discovery. The United States Supreme Court has made clear that the privilege against self-incrimination does not "entitle[] a defendant as a matter of constitutional right to await the end of the State's case before announcing the nature of his defense."[3] Thus,

---

1. See, e.g., Brennan, "The Criminal Prosecution: Sporting Event or Quest for Truth?" 1963 Wash.U.L.Q. 279 (1963); American Bar Association Standards for Criminal Justice § 11.1 (1986); National Advisory Commission on Criminal Justice Standards and Goals, Courts § 4.9; Report of the Advisory Committee on Criminal Law and Procedure to the Chief Administrative Judge of the Courts of the State of New York, p. 2 (1995). See also People v. Copicotto, 50 N.Y.2d 222, 226, 428 N.Y.S.2d 649, 652, 406 N.E.2d 465, 468 (1980).

2. For an excellent analysis of the arguments of the proponents and opponents of broad criminal discovery, see W. Lafave & J. Israel, Criminal Procedure, § 20.1 (2d ed.1992).

3. Williams v. Florida, 399 U.S. 78, 90 S.Ct. 1893, 26 L.Ed.2d 446 (1970). See CPL §§ 240.30, 250.10, 250.20, 250.30 (all of which require pretrial disclosure by the defense of specified material and information). Indeed, the Supreme Court has upheld the constitutionality of precluding defense evidence as a sanction in appropriate

although some of the more extensive civil discovery procedures, such as depositions, obviously could not be used to take discovery of criminal defendants, considerable legal latitude exists to couple defense discovery with comparable prosecution discovery.

The contention that extensive discovery will promote defendant perjury at trial ignores the presumption of innocence by assuming that a criminal defendant is guilty and thus is unable to provide a truthful version of the events when testifying.[4] In any event, because the prosecution always must present its case at trial first, even guilty defendants who are inclined to testify untruthfully will be able to do so, with or without the benefit of extensive pretrial discovery.

Probably the most serious argument against liberalized criminal discovery is that it will lead to increased intimidation of victims and witnesses. Although this concern has little or no application to law enforcement and most other government witnesses, pretrial identification of civilian witnesses and disclosure of the substance of their knowledge of the case could enhance the capacity and inclination of some defendants to threaten or even injure those witnesses. Although one recent study, which surveyed practitioners in a number of states that require pretrial disclosure of the identity of prosecution witnesses, suggests that this concern is exaggerated,[5] unfortunately little if any empirical evidence on this question is available. The use of protective orders in appropriate cases could help to minimize this problem, although prosecutors in many cases might have difficulty justifying the issuance of such an order.

Library References:
West's Key No. Digests, Criminal Law ⚖627.5–631, 700.

§ 7.2 Criminal Discovery in New York

New York is a jurisdiction in which the arguments against broad criminal discovery have, to a significant extent, held sway. Indeed, many other sizeable states with one or more large urban centers—*e.g.*, California, Florida, Illinois, Michigan, New Jersey and Pennsylvania—have broader criminal discovery rules, particularly with regard to disclosure of prosecution witness lists.[6] Proposals developed by the New York State Unified Court System and others to bring New York more in line with the discovery procedures of these other jurisdictions have yet to

---

cases for the defense's failure to comply with pretrial discovery and notice requirements. See Michigan v. Lucas, 500 U.S. 145, 111 S.Ct. 1743, 114 L.Ed.2d 205 (1991); Taylor v. Illinois, 484 U.S. 400, 108 S.Ct. 646, 98 L.Ed.2d 798 (1988). See also People v. Copicotto, 50 N.Y.2d 222, 428 N.Y.S.2d 649, 406 N.E.2d 465 (1980).

4. Moreover, as Wigmore noted: "The possibility that a dishonest accused will misuse such an opportunity [for pretrial discovery] is no reason for committing the injustice of refusing the honest accused a fair means of clearing himself. That argument is outworn; it was the basis (and with equal logic) for the one-time refusal of the criminal law ... to allow the accused to produce any witnesses at all." 6 J. Wigmore, Evidence § 1863, p. 488 (3d ed.1940).

5. See "Criminal Discovery in New York State," A Report to the New York State Assembly Codes Committee (1992).

6. Id., pp. 68–82.

advance in the State Legislature.[7] Criminal discovery in New York is largely a creature of statute, the primary statute being Article 240 of the Criminal Procedure Law. However, although New York courts lack inherent authority to compel general pretrial discovery,[8] and defendants have no general constitutional right to pretrial discovery,[9] the courts have recognized a criminal defendant's constitutional or fundamental right to discovery of certain information. First, the prosecution must disclose to the defendant *Brady* evidence—*i.e.*, exculpatory and material evidence of which the prosecution knows or should know.[10] Second, the prosecution must disclose its witnesses' prior recorded statements—known in New York as *Rosario* material—even if the prior statements are consistent with the witness's hearing or trial testimony.[11] Third, a defendant is generally entitled to discovery of information that is "relevant and helpful" to the preparation of the defense.[12] This rather vague standard has been applied, for example, to require disclosure, in certain cases, of the identity of a police informant.[13]

These broad constitutionally-mandated areas of discovery are reflected in both general[14] and specific[15] provisions of Article 240. They are more fully discussed in many of the remaining sections of this chapter.

Library References:

West's Key No. Digests, Criminal Law ⟸627.5–629.5, 700(2)–700(9).

§ 7.3 Demand Disclosure—In General

Prior to the enactment of the current Article 240, which took effect in 1980, discovery of any information from an opposing party required a motion.[16] The primary disclosure provision in the current statute, though not requiring a motion, requires disclosure of specified property

---

7. See S.2791 (introduced in 1993 at the request of the Judiciary); S.4791 (introduced in 1993 at the request of the Governor).

8. People ex rel. Lemon v. Supreme Court, 245 N.Y. 24, 156 N.E. 84 (1927). See also People v. Ronald Colavito, 87 N.Y.2d 423, 639 N.Y.S.2d 996, 663 N.E.2d 308 (1996).

9. Miller v. Schwartz, 72 N.Y.2d 869, 532 N.Y.S.2d 354, 528 N.E.2d 507 (1988); Mulvaney v. Dubin, 80 A.D.2d 566, 435 N.Y.S.2d 761 (2d Dept.1981).

10. See Brady v. Maryland, 373 U.S. 83, 83 S.Ct. 1194, 10 L.Ed.2d 215 (1963); People v. Vilardi, 76 N.Y.2d 67, 556 N.Y.S.2d 518, 555 N.E.2d 915 (1990). See §§ 7.12–7.14, infra.

11. See Jencks v. United States, 353 U.S. 657, 77 S.Ct. 1007, 1 L.Ed.2d 1103 (1957); People v. Rosario, 9 N.Y.2d 286, 213 N.Y.S.2d 448, 173 N.E.2d 881 (1961), reargument den. 9 N.Y.2d 908, 216 N.Y.S.2d 1025, 176 N.E.2d 111 (1961), cert. den. 368 U.S. 866, 82 S.Ct. 117, 7 L.Ed.2d 64 (1961). See §§ 7.16, 7.17, infra.

12. See Roviaro v. United States, 353 U.S. 53, 60–61, 77 S.Ct. 623, 628, 1 L.Ed.2d 639 (1957).

13. See, e.g., People v. Goggins, 34 N.Y.2d 163, 356 N.Y.S.2d 571, 313 N.E.2d 41 (1974), cert. den. 419 U.S. 1012, 95 S.Ct. 332, 42 L.Ed.2d 286 (1974). See § 7.10, infra.

14. See CPL § 240.20(1)(h)(upon demand, prosecution must disclose prior to trial anything required to be disclosed under the constitution); CPL § 240.40(1)(c)(upon a reasonable request demonstrating materiality to the preparation of the defense, the court may order discovery of any property the prosecutor intends to introduce at trial).

15. See CPL §§ 240.44, 240.45 (the Rosario statutes).

16. See former CPL § 240.20.

upon service of a written demand to produce.[17] The demand, whether by the defendant or the prosecution, must be made within 30 days of arraignment.[18] If a defendant is not yet represented by counsel and desires one, the 30-day period for serving the demand commences on the date that counsel initially appears on the defendant's behalf.[19] The court has discretion to allow late service of a demand that, for good cause shown, could not have been made within the 30-day period.[20]

Service of the demand requires the party from whom discovery is sought to disclose statutorily prescribed property[21] within 15 days or as soon thereafter as is practicable.[22] "Property" is a generic term that is intended to cover a broad range of tangible materials and information.[23]

Library References:
West's Key No. Digests, Criminal Law ⇌627.8.

§ 7.4   Demand Disclosure—By Defendant

CPL § 240.20, the primary disclosure provision of Article 240, requires the prosecution, upon receipt of a demand, to disclose a wide array of items. The prosecution must disclose any statement, whether written, recorded or oral, that the defendant or a jointly tried co-defendant made to a law enforcement official or to a person acting at the direction of a law enforcement official.[24] The statement must bear some connection to the pending action; for example, a confession to a wholly unrelated crime need not be disclosed.[25] A statement made during the course of the criminal transaction that gave rise to the prosecution need not be disclosed,[26] however, unless it is contained within a tape, which

---

17. CPL §§ 240.10(1), 240.20(1), 240.30(1).

18. CPL § 240.80(1). In a felony case, arraignment as used in this context means arraignment in superior court on an indictment or superior court information, not arraignment in local criminal court on a felony complaint. See CPL § 240.20(1). Indeed, Article 240 generally precludes discovery when only a felony complaint or a misdemeanor complaint is pending against a defendant. See CPL §§ 240.20(1), 240.30(1), 240.40(1) and (2). As one trial court has explained, this is because property and information sought may no longer be relevant if, as is often the case, the charges after indictment or conversion to an information are different than the charges in the complaint. See People v. Webb, 105 Misc.2d 660, 432 N.Y.S.2d 826 (N.Y.C.Crim.Ct.1980). See also People v. Russo, 128 Misc.2d 876, 879, 491 N.Y.S.2d 951, 954 (Suffolk Co.Ct.1985); People v. Arturo, 122 Misc.2d 1058, 472 N.Y.S.2d 998 (N.Y.C.Crim.Ct.1984); People v. Zisis, 113 Misc.2d 998, 1004, 450 N.Y.S.2d 655 (N.Y.C.Crim.Ct.1982).

19. CPL § 240.80(1).

20. Id.

21. CPL §§ 240.20(1), 240.30(1).

22. CPL § 240.80(3).

23. CPL § 240.10(3).

24. CPL § 240.20(1)(a). Except in the relatively few instances when the prosecutor does not intend to offer the defendant's statement as evidence at trial, the prosecutor already will have disclosed the defendant's statement pursuant to CPL § 710.30 (see Chapter 10, § 10.23). Thus, with respect to the defendant's own statements, this provision is largely superfluous in most cases.

25. See People v. D'Amico, 136 Misc.2d 16, 517 N.Y.S.2d 881 (Oneida Co.Ct.1987), aff'd 148 A.D.2d 982, 538 N.Y.S.2d 965 (4th Dep't 1989).

26. Id.; see also People v. Sherman, 156 A.D.2d 889, 550 N.Y.S.2d 109 (3d Dep't 1989); People v. Wells, 133 A.D.2d 385, 519 N.Y.S.2d 553 (2d Dep't 1987).

§ 7.4 DISCOVERY Ch. 7

must be disclosed under a separate provision of section 240.20 if the prosecution intends to introduce it at trial.[27] A related provision of section 240.20 requires that the prosecution disclose the transcript of any grand jury testimony given in the case by the defendant or a jointly tried co-defendant.[28]

In addition, the prosecution must disclose all reports prepared by or at the direction of a law enforcement official that relate to a physical or mental examination or a scientific test or experiment.[29] Even if such reports were not prepared by or at the direction of a law enforcement official, they must be disclosed if prepared by a prosecution trial witness or if the prosecution intends to introduce the report at trial.[30] For example, a hospital record ordinarily would not have been prepared at the direction of a law enforcement official, but it would have to be disclosed if the prosecution intended to introduce it at trial or intended to call as a witness the physician who prepared it. Among the types of scientific reports that typically must be disclosed under this provision are reports of autopsies, ballistics tests, laboratory drug tests, blood tests and DNA tests. A report of the results of a polygraph test of a possible witness must also be disclosed.[31] One court has held that formal notes or checklists made as part of a laboratory routine or protocol, although technically not a report, must be disclosed to the defendant.[32] In some instances, a scientific test—e.g., a DNA test—may not be conducted until after the expiration of the time period for complying with a defendant's demand to produce. In that situation, the general continuing obligation to disclose would require disclosure promptly after the prosecution receives the report.[33] Although nothing requires that the results of a physical or mental examination or a scientific test or experiment be recorded in a report, one trial court has held that the failure of a critical prosecution expert witness to do so compelled pretrial disclosure to the defense of the expert's grand jury testimony.[34]

The prosecution must further disclose any relevant photographs or drawings made or prepared by a law enforcement official. Again, even if not prepared by law enforcement, these items must be disclosed if the prosecution intends to call the person who prepared them or intends to introduce the items at trial.[35] Probably the most common items dis-

27. See CPL § 240.20(1)(g).

28. CPL § 240.20(1)(b).

29. See People v. Dagata, 86 N.Y.2d 40, 629 N.Y.S.2d 186, 652 N.E.2d 932 (1995)(failure to disclose notes underlying written summary prepared by FBI lab that conducted DNA test of defendant's and complainant's blood sample erroneous, even though trial court concluded that notes did not constitute Brady material).

30. CPL § 240.20(1)(c).

31. See, e.g., People v. Mondon, 129 Misc.2d 13, 492 N.Y.S.2d 344 (Sup.Ct., N.Y. County, 1985).

32. People v. Slowe, 125 Misc.2d 591, 479 N.Y.S.2d 962 (Tompkins Co.Ct.1984). The court held, however, that informal scratch notes need not be disclosed. See also People v. Dagata, 86 N.Y.2d 40, 629 N.Y.S.2d 186, 652 N.E.2d 932 (1995).

33. See CPL § 240.60.

34. People v. Delaney, 125 Misc.2d 928, 481 N.Y.S.2d 229 (Suffolk Co.Ct.1984). Given the carefully circumscribed rule authorizing pretrial release of grand jury testimony, see CPL § 210.30, this is a questionable ruling.

35. CPL § 240.20(1)(d).

closed under this provision are mug shots and photographs of a lineup. Although a photo "array" technically may not fall within the language of this provision, the Court of Appeals has held that the prosecution has a pretrial obligation to disclose the array as well.[36]

A 1984 amendment to CPL § 240.20 requires disclosure of a law enforcement official's photograph, copy or other reproduction of non-contraband stolen property that is returned to its owner pursuant to the procedure set forth in section 450.10 of the Penal Law. Disclosure is mandated regardless of whether the prosecution intends to introduce the reproduction or the stolen property itself at trial.[37]

Any property that the police recovered from the defendant or a jointly tried co-defendant must be disclosed.[38] This includes any property that was in the defendant's possession, even if such possession was unlawful.[39] The prosecution's failure to disclose property on the ground that the defendant had abandoned it immediately before being apprehended by the police was held to be improper where the defendant was charged in the case with unlawfully possessing the property.[40] The property, however, must have been possessed by the defendant. For example, the prosecution need not disclose a defendant's bank signature card and a deposit slip completed by the defendant if the items were recovered from the defendant's bank and not from the defendant himself.[41]

The prosecution also must disclose tapes or other electronic recordings that will be introduced at trial.[42] To the extent that a tape may contain the defendant's or a jointly tried co-defendant's statements, this provision is both broader than the general requirement that the prosecutor disclose a defendant's (or jointly tried co-defendant's) statements to law enforcement,[43] in that it includes recorded statements made during the course of the criminal transaction, and narrower, in that it applies only to recordings that the prosecutor intends to introduce at trial.

In addition, the approximate date, time and place of the crime charged and of the defendant's arrest must be disclosed.[44] Some of this

---

36. People v. Brown, 67 N.Y.2d 555, 505 N.Y.S.2d 574, 496 N.E.2d 663 (1986), cert. den. 479 U.S. 1093, 107 S.Ct. 1307, 94 L.Ed.2d 161 (1987).

37. CPL § 240.20(1)(e). P.L. § 450.10 itself contains a discovery-type provision, in that it provides the defense with notice and an opportunity to examine, test and photograph or otherwise reproduce stolen property before it is returned to the owner. See P.L. § 450.10(2). Evidentiary photographs of a stolen motor vehicle, which under this statute may be returned to its owner more expeditiously than other stolen property, must be furnished to the defense within 15 days of arraignment. See P.L. § 450.10(4)(c).

38. CPL § 240.20(1)(f).

39. See, e.g., People v. Kelly, 62 N.Y.2d 516, 478 N.Y.S.2d 834, 467 N.E.2d 498 (1984).

40. People v. Brown, 104 Misc.2d 157, 427 N.Y.S.2d 722 (N.Y.C.Crim.Ct.1980). Cf. People v. McKay, 101 A.D.2d 960, 479 N.Y.S.2d 87 (3d Dep't 1984)(prosecution not required to disclose jacket, identified by witness as belonging to defendant, that was found at scene several hours after defendant had left).

41. People v. Ordine, 177 A.D.2d 734, 575 N.Y.S.2d 977 (3d Dep't 1991).

42. CPL § 240.20(1)(g).

43. See CPL § 240.20(1)(a).

44. CPL § 240.20(1)(i).

§ 7.4

information, particularly the date and place of the crime charged, is usually contained in the accusatory instrument.

Finally, section 240.20 requires disclosure of specified information in cases involving two types of crimes. First, in cases involving charges of unauthorized use of a computer[45] and computer trespass,[46] the time, place and manner of the notice element of those offenses must be disclosed.[47] Second, in cases involving violations of the Vehicle and Traffic Law, the prosecution must disclose any reports relating to the most recent record of inspection, calibration or repair of machines or instruments, such as breathalyzer testing equipment, as well as any certification of the operator of the equipment, if the test was conducted by or at the request of law enforcement or if the prosecution intends to call the operator as a witness or intends to introduce the test results at trial.[48] Although this disclosure presumably would be required under the general section 240.20 provision requiring disclosure of reports of scientific tests,[49] and a number of courts had held precisely that,[50] the Legislature added this provision in 1989 to remove any doubt as to the requirement that this material be disclosed.[51]

Section 240.20 generally requires that the prosecution, when demanded property is not within its custody or control, make a diligent and good faith effort to ascertain the existence of the property.[52] "Control" is not defined in the statute. Presumably, the line of cases that has held that *Rosario* material in the possession of the police is deemed to be in the control of the prosecution would apply equally to property discoverable under section 240.20.[53] "Diligence" is not defined in the statute either. The statute, however, provides that the prosecutor need not subpoena demanded property that the defendant may subpoena.[54] Further, a number of trial courts have held that if demanded property is not within the prosecution's exclusive control and is accessible to the defen-

---

45. P.L. § 156.05.

46. P.L. § 156.10.

47. CPL § 240.20(1)(j). P.L. § 156.00(6) includes within the definition of unauthorized use of a computer or computer service a requirement that the owner or lessor provide notice as to the permissible use of the computer. See generally Greenberg, Marcus, et al., New York Criminal Law, Chap. 15 (West 1996).

48. CPL § 240.20(1)(k).

49. See CPL § 240.20(1)(c).

50. See, e.g., People v. Corley, 124 A.D.2d 390, 507 N.Y.S.2d 491 (3d Dep't 1986); People v. English, 103 A.D.2d 979, 480 N.Y.S.2d 56 (3d Dep't 1984); People v. Briggs, 136 Misc.2d 687, 519 Misc.2d 294 (Brighton Town Ct.1987).

51. Because section 240.20 does not apply to cases involving Vehicle and Traffic Law offenses of less than misdemeanor level, see CPL § 240.20(1), this provision does not require disclosure in speeding cases (VTL § 1180(d)) of such records and reports relating to radar equipment. See generally Matter of Miller v. Schwartz, 72 N.Y.2d 869, 532 N.Y.S.2d 354, 528 N.E.2d 507 (1988).

52. CPL § 240.20(2). Cf. People v. Ronald Colavito, 87 N.Y.2d 423, 639 N.Y.S.2d 996, 663 N.E.2d 308 (1996) (prosecution under no obligation to seek out and obtain trial evidence not in its possession or control where evidence was not otherwise subject to discovery under Article 240).

53. See, e.g., People v. Ranghelle, 69 N.Y.2d 56, 511 N.Y.S.2d 580, 503 N.E.2d 1011 (1986). By contrast, property in the possession of a state agency such as the Department of Motor Vehicles presumably would not be deemed to be within the control of the prosecutor. See People v. Flynn, 79 N.Y.2d 879, 581 N.Y.S.2d 160, 589 N.E.2d 383 (1992)(so holding for Rosario material). For further discussion of when Rosario material is deemed to be within the control of the prosecutor, see § 7.17, infra.

54. Id.

dant, the prosecution is under no obligation to produce it.[55] However, given the limited subpoena authority that many courts have prescribed for the defense,[56] the prosecution ordinarily should not be excused for failing to exert a good faith effort to obtain and disclose properly demanded material not within its actual possession or custody.

Library References:
West's Key No. Digests, Criminal Law ⚖627.6–627.9.

§ 7.5 Demand Disclosure—By Prosecution

CPL § 240.35, although far more limited than section 240.20, requires the defendant, when served with a demand to produce, to disclose certain property to the prosecution. First, the defendant must disclose any report made at his or her direction relating to a physical or mental examination or scientific test, if the defendant intends to introduce the report at trial or if it was made by a person the defendant intends to call as a witness at trial.[57] If the defendant has filed a notice of intent to present psychiatric evidence,[58] any report relating to that evidence that was made at the defendant's direction must also be disclosed.[59] Second, the defendant must disclose any photographs, drawings and tapes or other recordings that he or she intends to introduce at the trial.[60]

The defense must make the same effort as the prosecution to obtain properly demanded materials not within its possession, custody or control—*i.e.*, a good faith, diligent effort.[61] As is true for the prosecution, that effort does not require the defense to subpoena property that the prosecution could subpoena itself.[62]

Library References:
West's Key No. Digests, Criminal Law ⚖627.5–629.5.

§ 7.6 Demand Disclosure—Refusal of Demand

A refusal to comply with a demand to produce must be in writing, and served on the party seeking disclosure and filed with the court within 15 days of service of the demand.[63] The court may permit later service of the refusal for good cause shown.[64] The refusal must set forth the reasons why the party reasonably believes the property sought in the demand is not discoverable under Article 240, or the reasons why the court should issue a protective order pursuant to section 240.50.[65] When specification of the grounds for a protective order would reveal the very

---

55. See, e.g., People v. Grissom, 128 Misc.2d 246, 490 N.Y.S.2d 110 (N.Y.C.Crim. Ct.1985); People v. Caban, 123 Misc.2d 943, 475 N.Y.S.2d 330 (Sup.Ct., Kings County, 1984); People v. Grosunor, 108 Misc.2d 932, 439 N.Y.S.2d 243 (N.Y.C.Crim. Ct.1981).

56. See § 7.8, infra.

57. CPL § 240.35(1)(a).

58. See CPL § 250.10. For a discussion of section 250.10, see § 7.26, infra.

59. CPL § 240.30(1)(a).

60. CPL § 240.30(1)(b).

61. CPL § 240.30(2).

62. Id.

63. CPL §§ 240.35, 240.80(2).

64. CPL § 240.80(2).

65. CPL § 240.35. For further discussion of section 240.50, see § 7.19, infra.

§ 7.6   DISCOVERY   Ch. 7

information that a party is seeking not to reveal, those grounds may be submitted to the court *ex parte* or argued to the court *in camera*.[66]

Library References:

West's Key No. Digests, Criminal Law ⇐627.8.

§ 7.7   Defense Motion for Discovery—Statutory Basis

CPL § 240.40 authorizes the defense to move for additional discovery beyond the property that the prosecution has disclosed upon demand pursuant to section 240.20.[67] First, and most basic, when the prosecution has served a refusal to disclose any property that the defendant has demanded pursuant to section 240.20, the defense may move for an order requiring the prosecution to disclose such property.[68] If the court finds that the prosecution's refusal to disclose is unjustified, the court *must* order disclosure.[69] Similarly, if the prosecution has failed to serve a timely refusal to disclose properly demanded property and is unable to show good cause why the property should not be disclosed, the court, upon the defendant's motion, *must* order disclosure;[70] or, presumably, if the prosecution is unable to disclose such property because it is lost or has been destroyed and the defendant is prejudiced thereby, the court must impose a sanction pursuant to section 240.70, which may include preclusion of evidence.[71]

In addition, the court *may* order the disclosure of any property that the prosecutor "intends to introduce at trial," but only upon the defendant's showing that disclosure of the property is material to the preparation of the defense and that the request is a reasonable one.[72] Several points should be made regarding this provision. Although it would seem to afford the defendant an opportunity to seek discovery of a wide range of property and information not expressly delineated in Article 240, it is not widely invoked and, as a result, has received virtually no attention in the case law. One reason for this is that the provision requires the court to condition its order against the prosecution on the defendant's disclosure of the property that he or she intends to introduce at trial. Indeed, before the trial begins, the defense often has not decided, or does not even know, if it will present any evidence, whether testimonial or physical, at the trial; or, even if it does know that it will present certain evidence, it often will be reluctant to reveal that to the prosecution. Although the determination of whether or not disclosure is appropriate under this provision is left to the discretion of the trial court, no

---

66. See CPL § 240.90(3). In such a case, any papers submitted and the transcript of any such argument are sealed. Id.

67. The timing of a defense motion for discovery is set forth in sections 240.90 and 255.20, which are discussed in Chapter 8.

68. CPL § 240.40(1)(a).

69. Id.

70. CPL § 240.40(1)(b).

71. Id. Even if the prosecution is able to disclose the property, an unjustified failure to serve a timely refusal of demand probably would require the court to order disclosure and possibly impose an appropriate sanction as well, particularly if the defendant has been prejudiced as a result. Section 240.70 sanctions are more fully discussed in § 7.20–7.24, infra.

72. CPL § 240.40(1)(c).

reported decision provides any meaningful guidance as to how that discretion should be exercised.[73]

Library References:
West's Key No. Digests, Criminal Law ⛬627.8.

§ 7.8 Defense Motion for Discovery—Subpoenas

In general, the courts have imposed fairly narrow limits on the use of subpoenas duces tecum for criminal discovery purposes.[74] Although CPL § 610.25 was amended in 1979 to allow the defendant (or the prosecution) to subpoena documentary and other physical evidence prior to trial,[75] the Court of Appeals has consistently held that a subpoena duces tecum may not be used for the purposes of general discovery. Rather, the purpose of a subpoena duces tecum is " 'to compel the production of specific documents that are relevant and material to facts at issue in a pending judicial proceeding.' "[76] Operating within this limitation, most courts have upheld the issuance of subpoenas duces tecum only upon a showing that the materials sought (1) would be admissible as evidence at the trial, or (2) will yield exculpatory evidence.

If a defense subpoena seeks documents from a governmental agency such as a district attorney or a police department, section 610.20(3) requires that the subpoena be a "so ordered" subpoena—*i.e.*, issued on the defendant's behalf by the court—with one day's notice to the agency.[77] Unless the subpoenaed agency successfully moves to quash the subpoena, the subpoenaed evidence must be submitted to the court, which will afford the party that issued the subpoena the opportunity to inspect the evidence prior to trial.[78] Many courts, however, will permit the prosecution, prior to the inspection, to redact from subpoenaed documents any information that identifies potentially endangered wit-

---

73. For example, one trial court decision suggests that the materials upon which an expert witness for the prosecution bases his or her opinion is discoverable under this provision. The decision does not, however, explain why, nor does it discuss whether in that case the materials would be material to preparation of the defense. See People v. Leon, 134 Misc.2d 757, 758, 512 N.Y.S.2d 991, 992 (Westchester Co.Ct.1987). Cf. People v. Ronald Colavito, 87 N.Y.2d 423, 639 N.Y.S.2d 996, 663 N.E.2d 308 (1996) (prosecution's voluntary disclosure of selected trial exhibits prior to trial not improper where remaining exhibits not disclosed were not in prosecution's possession or control, prosecution did not act in bad faith, and court never ordered disclosure under section 240.40(1)(c)).

74. A subpoena duces tecum is defined as a "subpoena requiring [a] witness to bring with him and produce specified physical evidence." CPL § 610.10(3).

75. L.1979, c.413, § 3.

76. Matter of Terry D., 81 N.Y.2d 1042, 1044, 601 N.Y.S.2d 452, 619 N.E.2d 389 (1993)(citing Matter of Constantine v. Leto, 157 A.D.2d 376, 378, 557 N.Y.S.2d 611, 612 (3d Dep't 1990), aff'd for reasons stated in opinion below 77 N.Y.2d 975, 571 N.Y.S.2d 906, 575 N.E.2d 392 (1991)). See also People v. Gissendanner, 48 N.Y.2d 543, 551, 423 N.Y.S.2d 893, 399 N.E.2d 924 (1979).

77. Section 610.20(3) incorporates the one-day notice rule set forth in CPLR § 2307.

78. CPL § 610.25(2). Although the prosecution need not obtain the court's authorization prior to issuing a subpoena duces tecum, the Court of Appeals has held that the evidence must be made returnable to the trial court. See People v. Natal, 75 N.Y.2d 379, 384–85, 553 N.Y.S.2d 650, 652–653, 553 N.E.2d 239 (1990), cert. den. 498 U.S. 862, 111 S.Ct. 169, 112 L.Ed.2d 134 (1990).

nesses or that would compromise the integrity of ongoing investigations.[79]

The 1979 amendment permitting the pretrial subpoenaing of evidence was intended to minimize trial disruption and delay, particularly in more complex trials involving numerous exhibits.[80] Most courts have interpreted the amendment, however, as addressing only the timing of the production of evidence, and as not altering the statute's pre-existing requirement that the documents or physical items be evidentiary in nature.[81] A few courts, however, have interpreted the amendment more broadly, holding that defendants may, pursuant to section 610.25, subpoena the police reports that are routinely prepared in criminal cases.[82] This disagreement hinges on the definition of the statute's use of the term "evidence." The majority view defines the term literally, *i.e.*, as competent evidence that would be admissible at trial.[83] The minority view defines the term to include "potential evidence" and information that might "lead to" evidence that could exculpate the defendant.[84] No appellate court has addressed this issue, and unless the narrow interpretation is ultimately adopted, defense counsel ordinarily should seek to subpoena all police reports well in advance of the trial.

Aside from the statutory subpoena provision set forth in CPL § 610.25, defendants have a general right to subpoena materials containing exculpatory evidence. Although the prosecution is constitutionally and statutorily required on its own to disclose exculpatory evidence within its possession or control,[85] the defendant need not wait for the prosecution to do so. Additionally, exculpatory evidence may not always be in the possession or control of the prosecution.

The mere potential that material may contain exculpatory evidence, however, will not necessarily support issuance of a subpoena duces tecum. As the Court of Appeals has held, the defendant must assert as a "factual predicate" that it is "reasonably likely" that the materials sought will bear relevant and exculpatory evidence.[86] Under this stan-

---

79. See, e.g., People v. Miranda, 115 Misc.2d 533, 537–38, 455 N.Y.S.2d 247, 248–249 (Sup.Ct., Bronx County, 1982).

80. See Bellacosa, "Practice Commentary" to CPL § 610.25, McKinney's Cons. Laws of N.Y., Book 11A, at 270 (1984).

81. See, e.g., People v. Cammilleri, 123 Misc.2d 851, 852, 475 N.Y.S.2d 228, 229 (Sup.Ct., Richmond County, 1984); People v. Crean, 115 Misc.2d 526, 454 N.Y.S.2d 231 (Sup.Ct., Westchester County, 1982); People v. Edgar Cruz, N.Y.L.J., October 1, 1990, p. 25, col. 5 (N.Y.C.Crim.Ct.); People v. Morrison, 148 Misc.2d 61, 67, 559 N.Y.S.2d 1013, 1017 (N.Y.C.Crim.Ct.1990). Cf. People v. Miranda, 115 Misc.2d at 535–36, 455 N.Y.S.2d at 248 (subpoena duces tecum may be employed to obtain evidence or "potential evidence," and trial court will review documents in camera to determine if they meet that definition).

82. See, e.g., People v. Burnette, 160 Misc.2d 1005, 612 N.Y.S.2d 774 (Sup.Ct., N.Y. County, 1994); People v. Cabon, 148 Misc.2d 260, 560 N.Y.S.2d 370 (N.Y.C.Crim. Ct.1990), appeal dism. 150 Misc.2d 1028, 579 N.Y.S.2d 312 (App.Term 1991).

83. See, e.g., People v. Morrison, 148 Misc.2d 61, 64, 559 N.Y.S.2d 1013, 1016 (N.Y.C.Crim.Ct.1990).

84. See, e.g., People v. Cabon, 148 Misc.2d at 270, 560 N.Y.S.2d at 378.

85. For a discussion of the Brady rule, see §§ 7.12–7.14, infra.

86. People v. Gissendanner, 48 N.Y.2d 543, 550, 423 N.Y.S.2d 893, 897, 399 N.E.2d 924 (1979); Matter of Terry D., 81 N.Y.2d 1042, 1044, 601 N.Y.S.2d 452, 452, 619 N.E.2d 389 (1993); Matter of Constantine v. Leto, 157 A.D.2d 376, 378, 557 N.Y.S.2d 611, 612 (1990), aff'd for reasons stated in

dard, an application for a subpoena duces tecum must assert more than simply that the documents sought may contain exculpatory evidence. A few trial courts, however, have interpreted the 1990 Court of Appeals decision in *People v. Vilardi*,[87] which emphasized the importance of devising sanctions for *Brady* violations that encourage prosecutors to search their files for exculpatory material,[88] as authorizing issuance of a subpoena duces tecum for the routine police reports that are prepared in criminal cases.[89] These courts have reasoned that authorizing subpoenas for this purpose is an effective guarantee that exculpatory evidence that the prosecution may overlook will be disclosed to the defense.[90]

Library References:

West's Key No. Digests, Criminal Law ⛉627.5(4); Witnesses ⛉16.

§ 7.9 Defense Motion for Discovery—Identity of Prosecution Witnesses

Another somewhat unsettled area of defense discovery is pretrial disclosure of the identity of prosecution witnesses. Although the Court of Appeals, in *People v. Andre W.*,[91] remarked that it is an open question whether the CPL authorizes general pretrial discovery of the names and addresses of prosecution witnesses, three of the four Appellate Divisions have held that a trial court has the discretion to order such disclosure. The First Department has held that, absent compelling circumstances such as the danger of witness intimidation, trial courts should order pretrial disclosure of material witnesses (*e.g.*, the sole identification witness).[92] In another case, the Second Department held that, although trial courts have the discretion to order disclosure of the names and addresses of prosecution witnesses, the trial court's refusal to do so in that case was not an abuse of discretion, particularly in that the defendant had admitted on several occasions that he had shot the victim because the victim was an informant.[93] And the Third Department has held that trial courts have discretion to order pretrial disclosure of the

opinion below 77 N.Y.2d 975, 571 N.Y.S.2d 906, 575 N.E.2d 392 (1991).

87. 76 N.Y.2d 67, 556 N.Y.S.2d 518, 555 N.E.2d 915 (1990).

88. Id. at 77, 556 N.Y.S.2d at 523.

89. See People v. Burnette, 160 Misc.2d 1005, 612 N.Y.S.2d 774, 778 (Sup.Ct., N.Y. County, 1994); People v. Cabon, 148 Misc.2d 260, 265–66, 560 N.Y.S.2d 370, 373–74 (N.Y.C.Crim.Ct.1990).

90. Defendants seeking to subpoena relevant documents, without specific knowledge that the documents may contain exculpatory evidence, may also want to assert their rights under the compulsory process and confrontation clauses of the Sixth Amendment. See generally Pennsylvania v. Ritchie, 480 U.S. 39, 107 S.Ct. 989, 94 L.Ed.2d 40 (1987); United States v. Nixon, 418 U.S. 683, 94 S.Ct. 3090, 41 L.Ed.2d 1039 (1974). But see People v. Chipp, 75 N.Y.2d 327, 336, 553 N.Y.S.2d 72, 77, 552 N.E.2d 608 (1990), cert. den. 498 U.S. 833, 111 S.Ct. 99, 112 L.Ed.2d 70 (1990)("the right to compulsory process is essentially a trial right, enabling an accused to present his own version of the facts to the trial jury"). Although no appellate decision directly supports a defendant's Sixth Amendment right to subpoena documents absent a specific showing that the documents contain exculpatory evidence, one trial court decision seems to support this proposition. See People v. Cabon, 148 Misc.2d at 262, 560 N.Y.S.2d at 372–73.

91. 44 N.Y.2d 179, 184–85, 404 N.Y.S.2d 578, 581, 375 N.E.2d 758 (1978).

92. People v. Rivera, 119 A.D.2d 517, 501 N.Y.S.2d 38 (1st Dep't 1986).

93. People v. Torres, 164 A.D.2d 923, 559 N.Y.S.2d 584 (2d Dep't 1990).

§ 7.9

names of prosecution witnesses, but only upon a showing of material need, not simply a bare allegation that disclosure is necessary to prepare for trial.[94]

The Court of Appeals decision in *Matter of Terry D.*,[95] may cast some doubt on the defendant's capacity to discover the identity of prosecution witnesses. In that case—a juvenile delinquency proceeding in Family Court—the court held that a subpoena duces tecum issued to a high school principal could not be used to discover the names, addresses and telephone numbers of all the students who were present at the scene of the incident. The court's reluctance to uphold the subpoena may, at least in part, be explained by the confidential nature under federal and New York law of information that identifies students.[96] Moreover, the subpoena did not seek the identity of prosecution witnesses but of all potential witnesses who were present at the scene. On the other hand, the court reiterated the general principle that the procedural mechanism of a subpoena duces tecum may not be used "to expand the discovery available under existing law."[97] In any event, given the questionable applicability of this decision to a motion in a criminal case seeking the identity of prosecution witnesses, defense counsel, relying on the considerable Appellate Division authority, should exhibit no reluctance in making such a motion.

Library References:
West's Key No. Digests, Criminal Law ⚖=629.

§ 7.10 Defense Motion for Discovery—Identity of Informant

A separate line of cases addresses the defendant's right to disclosure of the identity of a police informant. Because of the need to protect a police informant from physical and other harm as well as from the social stigma that can result from providing information to the police, an informant's identity is privileged and generally protected from disclosure.[98] The defense may attempt to seek discovery of an informant's identity, and the information that an informant provided to law enforcement, in connection with a probable cause determination at a pretrial suppression hearing or in connection with the ultimate question of the

---

94. People v. Miller, 106 A.D.2d 787, 484 N.Y.S.2d 183 (3d Dep't 1984). The Third Department has also held that, in a case in which the prosecution did provide a list of its witnesses to the defendant prior to trial, the defendant's right to a fair trial was not denied by the trial court's refusal to preclude the testimony of two prosecution witnesses who were not included in that list. People v. Coleman, 178 A.D.2d 842, 844–45, 577 N.Y.S.2d 900, 903 (3d Dep't 1991), rev'd on other grounds 81 N.Y.2d 826, 595 N.Y.S.2d 384, 611 N.E.2d 285 (1993).

95. 81 N.Y.2d 1042, 601 N.Y.S.2d 452, 619 N.E.2d 389 (1993).

96. See 20 U.S.C.A. § 1232g(b)(2)(B); New York Education Law § 3212–a(1).

97. 81 N.Y.2d at 1045, 601 N.Y.S.2d at 453 (citing People v. Gissendanner, 48 N.Y.2d 543, 423 N.Y.S.2d 893, 399 N.E.2d 924 (1979)).

98. See People v. Liberatore, 79 N.Y.2d 208, 214, 581 N.Y.S.2d 634, 637, 590 N.E.2d 219 (1992); People v. Pena, 37 N.Y.2d 642, 644, 376 N.Y.S.2d 452, 453, 339 N.E.2d 149 (1975). See also Roviaro v. United States, 353 U.S. 53, 77 S.Ct. 623, 1 L.Ed.2d 639 (1957). For a discussion of other legal privileges that often protect against disclosure of information in criminal cases, see § 7.30, infra.

defendant's guilt or innocence at trial. The Court of Appeals has established separate standards and procedures for each of these situations.

The Court of Appeals first addressed the question of disclosure of the identity of an informant in the context of a suppression hearing in *People v. Darden*.[99] In that case, the court held that when the defense seeks disclosure of the identity of an informant in connection with a suppression hearing, and the hearing testimony of the arresting officer as to communications received from the informant is insufficient to establish probable cause, the identity of the informant need not be disclosed to the defense. Instead, the prosecution must make the informant available for an *in camera* inquiry, at which the prosecutor may be present but the defendant and defense counsel may not. The court must take the testimony of the informant, with opportunity to the defense to submit written questions for the court to ask of the informant. The court then must make a summary report as to the existence of the informant and the communications made by the informant to the police. The report must be made available to the defense and the prosecution, and the informant's testimony must be sealed and made available to the appellate courts if the case is ultimately appealed.[100] The *Darden* decision and related issues are more fully discussed in Chapter 10.[101]

The Court of Appeals has established a different standard when the defense seeks disclosure of the identity of an informant at trial. In *People v. Goggins*,[102] the court held that when the defendant's guilt or innocence is the issue, the informant's privilege must yield if the defendant demonstrates that the informant's testimony is relevant to the defendant's guilt or innocence. The court emphasized, however, that "[b]are assertions or conclusory allegations by a defendant that a witness is needed to establish his innocence will not suffice."[103] Thus, if the informant performed only a minor role in the case, such as merely providing a tip or other minimal information to the police, the privilege ordinarily should prevail. On the other hand, if the informant was an eyewitness or participated in the alleged crime or was an "active participant in setting the stage," or if the question of the defendant's guilt is closely contested, disclosure of the informant's identity may be required.[104]

In *Goggins*, the defendant, who had no criminal record and was gainfully employed, was charged with selling drugs to an undercover

99. 34 N.Y.2d 177, 356 N.Y.S.2d 582, 313 N.E.2d 49 (1974).

100. 34 N.Y.2d at 181, 356 N.Y.S.2d at 586.

101. See Chapter 10, § 10.13. Also discussed in Chapter 10 § 10.13 are issues relating to the prosecution's obligation to disclose materials identifying an informant that are submitted in connection with a warrant application. See, e.g., People v. Castillo, 80 N.Y.2d 578, 592 N.Y.S.2d 945, 607 N.E.2d 1050 (1992), cert. den. 507 U.S. 1033, 113 S.Ct. 1854, 123 L.Ed.2d 477 (1993); People v. Liberatore, 79 N.Y.2d 208, 581 N.Y.S.2d 634, 590 N.E.2d 219 (1992).

102. 34 N.Y.2d 163, 356 N.Y.S.2d 571, 313 N.E.2d 41, cert. den. 419 U.S. 1012, 95 S.Ct. 332, 42 L.Ed.2d 286 (1974).

103. 34 N.Y.2d at 169, 356 N.Y.S.2d at 575.

104. 34 N.Y.2d at 169–70, 356 N.Y.S.2d at 576.

police officer. Because he had a credible explanation for his presence in the bar where the alleged drug sales occurred and where he was arrested and because the undercover officer had provided a "sketchy" description of the seller to the arresting officers, the court held that the identity of the informant, who had introduced the undercover to the drug seller, should have been disclosed.[105] By contrast, in the companion case to *Goggins*, which also involved drug sales to an undercover officer, the two sales were made in the apartment in which the defendant was found when arrested and the undercover officer subsequently identified the defendant at the station house as the seller. Accordingly, the court held that, unlike *Goggins*, the risk of misidentification was minimal and thus disclosure of the identity of the informant, who had taken the undercover officer to the apartment but had left before the first sale, was not required.[106] Subsequent Court of Appeals cases provide further examples of how the *Goggins* standard has been applied. In one case, the court held that the trial court had correctly ordered disclosure of the informant's identity where the undercover officers' testimony created a close question as to whether the defendant's actions during a drug sale amounted to active participation in the sale, particularly in that the police reports made no mention of the defendant's alleged overt involvement.[107] Similarly, in another case, the court held that disclosure should have been ordered where the defendant and six other defense witnesses testified that the defendant was elsewhere at the time of the alleged crime and, significantly, the prosecution had conceded at the trial that the informants had not been active for the past two and one-half years.[108] By contrast, the court held in another case that denial of disclosure was appropriate where the informant introduced the undercover officer to the defendant but was not present during the ensuing crimes, other undercover officers observed one of the illegal transactions from a short distance and the primary undercover officer observed the back-up team arrest the defendant and had no difficulty in identifying him.[109] The *Goggins* standard has been applied in numerous other appellate decisions.[110]

Once the defense establishes its right to disclosure of the identity of a police informant, it may subpoena the informant to testify at trial. If

---

105. 34 N.Y.2d at 170–72, 356 N.Y.S.2d at 576–77.

106. People v. Brown, 34 N.Y.2d 163, 172–73, 356 N.Y.S.2d 571, 577–78, 313 N.E.2d 41 (1974), cert. den. 419 U.S. 1012, 95 S.Ct. 332, 42 L.Ed.2d 286 (1974).

107. People v. Singleton, 42 N.Y.2d 466, 398 N.Y.S.2d 871, 368 N.E.2d 1237 (1977). This decision also notes that the Goggins standard does not apply only to cases in which the identity of the perpetrator is at issue. 42 at 468–69, 398 N.Y.S.2d at 873.

108. People v. Peltak, 45 N.Y.2d 905, 411 N.Y.S.2d 4, 383 N.E.2d 556 (1978). Given the informants' lack of recent activity, the court held that the prosecution should have been required to provide reasons why their identity should not have been disclosed. 45 N.Y.2d at 906, 411 N.Y.S.2d at 5.

109. People v. Pena, 37 N.Y.2d 642, 376 N.Y.S.2d 452, 339 N.E.2d 149 (1975).

110. Cf. People v. Rios, 60 N.Y.2d 764, 469 N.Y.S.2d 670, 457 N.E.2d 776 (1983)(disclosure not required in light of "marginal" nature of information provided by informant); People v. Leyva, 38 N.Y.2d 160, 379 N.Y.S.2d 30, 341 N.E.2d 546 (1975)(disclosure not required where informant did not set up drug sale, did not participate at all in the main events relating to the crime and was not present at the arrest); People v. Jefferson, 181 A.D.2d 1007, 581 N.Y.S.2d 501 (4th Dep't

the defense is unable to locate the informant, the prosecution must make a diligent effort to produce the informant for the defense.[111] If the prosecution fails to do so or is responsible for the informant's unavailability knowing that the informant's testimony would be material and relevant to the defense, dismissal of the case is an appropriate sanction.[112] However, even if the prosecution exerts a good faith, albeit unsuccessful, effort to make the informant available, dismissal may be required if the defendant demonstrates that the informant's testimony would have been exculpatory.[113]

Finally, it should be noted that, because the determination of whether an informant's identity should be disclosed to the defense generally hinges on the evidence that is presented at the trial, pretrial disclosure of the informant's identity is relatively rare. An exception would arise when the defendant is able to show prior to trial that the informant has exculpatory testimony to offer.

Library References:
West's Key No. Digests, Criminal Law ⇔627.10.

§ 7.11 Prosecution Motion for Discovery

CPL § 240.40 also permits the prosecution to move for discovery beyond that which the defense has disclosed upon demand pursuant to

1992)(disclosure not required where informant not present during transaction, identification evidence was overwhelming and defendant's testimony that he was elsewhere at time of crime was weak); People v. Chavis, 113 A.D.2d 896, 493 N.Y.S.2d 613 (2d Dep't 1985)(no right to disclosure where undercover spent 20 minutes with defendant, had conversed with her on previous occasions and had identified her at confirmatory showup after arrest); People v. Yattaw, 106 A.D.2d 679, 484 N.Y.S.2d 140 (3d Dep't 1984)(disclosure not required where undercover expressly disputed that she had purchased the drugs from person defendant claimed he had been confused with and another officer identified defendant as the person who met the undercover outside the building and accompanied her into building) with People v. Estrada, 142 A.D.2d 512, 514, 530 N.Y.S.2d 148, 149 (1st Dep't 1988)(error to refuse to order disclosure of identity of informant who told police that acquaintance of defendant had worked for murder victim as a drug runner and was dismissed by murder victim after attempting to rob and threatening murder victim with a gun); People v. Lamar, 86 A.D.2d 751, 447 N.Y.S.2d 772 (4th Dep't 1982)(error to refuse to order disclosure where undercover was present during entire transaction and had seen defendant on numerous previous occasions, defendant testified he did not participate in transaction and prosecution made no attempt to show informant was in any danger or could not be located); People v. Taylor, 83 A.D.2d 595, 441 N.Y.S.2d 116 (2d Dep't 1981)(error to deny disclosure where informant was present during transaction and alibi defense raised significant issues of credibility and identification); People v. Martin, 54 A.D.2d 624, 387 N.Y.S.2d 434 (1st Dep't 1976)(error to refuse to order disclosure where informant was present immediately before and after transaction, undercover's original description of perpetrator was general and defendant was not arrested until seven and one-half months after alleged crime); People v. Canales, 75 A.D.2d 875, 427 N.Y.S.2d 879 (2d Dep't 1980)(error to refuse to order disclosure where informant was present during most of transaction, defendant was not arrested until nine months after alleged crime and testified at trial that he had never seen undercover officer before).

111. People v. Jenkins, 41 N.Y.2d 307, 392 N.Y.S.2d 587, 360 N.E.2d 1288 (1977).

112. 41 N.Y.2d at 311, 392 N.Y.S.2d at 590.

113. 41 N.Y.2d at 311–12, 392 N.Y.S.2d at 590. Cf. People v. Maneiro, 49 N.Y.2d 769, 426 N.Y.S.2d 471, 403 N.E.2d 176 (1980)(prosecution had not contributed to unavailability of informant and made reasonably diligent effort to locate him, and defendant failed to demonstrate that informant's testimony would be exculpatory).

§ 7.11   DISCOVERY   Ch. 7

section 240.30. Initially, if the court has granted a defense motion pursuant to section 240.40(1)(c) for discovery of property that the prosecution intends to introduce at trial,[114] the court must, if the prosecution so requests, condition such order upon disclosure by the defense of the property that it intends to introduce at trial. As is required of the defense when it moves for disclosure of this evidence, the prosecution must demonstrate that disclosure is material to the preparation of its case and that the request is reasonable.[115] As previously noted, this reciprocity requirement casts a chilling effect on the defense's inclination to move for discovery of the property that the prosecution intends to introduce at trial.[116]

The prosecution also may move for an order directing the defense to disclose any material that it has refused to disclose upon the prosecution's demand under section 240.30. The court must order such disclosure if it finds that the defense's refusal to disclose is unjustified.[117]

In addition, section 240.40 authorizes the prosecution to move for an order directing the defendant to provide various types of "non-testimonial" physical evidence.[118] This qualification is critical because a defendant may not be compelled to provide evidence that will infringe upon his or her Fifth Amendment privilege against self-incrimination.[119] The list of physical evidence that the prosecution may obtain is a nonexclusive one. The court may order the defendant to appear in a line-up.[120] Such an order may even go so far as to require a defendant to remove his beard before appearing in the line-up.[121] The court may also require the defendant to speak for identification by a witness or potential witness,[122] to be fingerprinted,[123] to pose for photographs that do not involve a

---

114. See § 7.7, supra.

115. CPL § 240.40(1)(c).

116. See § 7.7, supra.

117. CPL § 240.40(2)(a).

118. CPL § 240.40(2)(b).

119. The Supreme Court has held that the constitutional privilege against self-incrimination "protects an accused only from being compelled to testify against himself, or otherwise provide the State with evidence of a testimonial or communicative nature." Schmerber v. California, 384 U.S. 757, 86 S.Ct. 1826, 16 L.Ed.2d 908 (1966). See also People v. Copicotto, 50 N.Y.2d 222, 228–29, 428 N.Y.S.2d 649, 653–54, 406 N.E.2d 465 (1980)(the Fifth Amendment privilege "proscribes only testimonial compulsion, not that which merely makes a person the source of real of physical evidence"). For example, in appropriate cases, a defendant may be ordered to provide blood samples, Schmerber v. California, supra, handwriting and voice exemplars, Gilbert v. California, 388 U.S. 263, 87 S.Ct. 1951, 18 L.Ed.2d 1178 (1967); United States v. Dionisio, 410 U.S. 1, 93 S.Ct. 764, 35 L.Ed.2d 67 (1973), fingernail scrapings, Cupp v. Murphy, 412 U.S. 291, 93 S.Ct. 2000, 36 L.Ed.2d 900 (1973), or be compelled to appear in a lineup. United States v. Wade, 388 U.S. 218, 87 S.Ct. 1926, 18 L.Ed.2d 1149 (1967).

120. CPL § 240.40(2)(b)(i). Unlike most prearraignment line-ups, the defendant is entitled to have counsel present at a court-ordered lineup. See Kirby v. Illinois, 406 U.S. 682, 92 S.Ct. 1877, 32 L.Ed.2d 411 (1972); United States v. Wade, 388 U.S. 218, 87 S.Ct. 1926, 18 L.Ed.2d 1149 (1967); Gilbert v. California, 388 U.S. 263, 87 S.Ct. 1951, 18 L.Ed.2d 1178 (1967).

121. See Little v. Savarese, 156 A.D.2d 564, 565–66, 550 N.Y.S.2d 715, 716–17 (2d Dep't 1989); People v. La Placa, 127 A.D.2d 610, 511 N.Y.S.2d 410 (2d Dep't 1987). See also Ford v. Kreindler, 206 A.D.2d 425, 614 N.Y.S.2d 439 (2d Dep't 1994)(court rejected defendant's contention that being required to shave beard for lineup would violate his religious beliefs).

122. CPL § 240.40(2)(b)(ii).

123. CPL § 240.40(2)(b)(iii). For a discussion of fingerprinting under the CPL, see Chapter 3, § 3.23.

reenactment of an event[124] and to provide handwriting samples.[125] In addition, the court may order the defendant to provide blood, hair or other bodily evidence, provided that the taking of such samples will not involve an unreasonable intrusion of the defendant's body or subject the defendant to a risk of serious physical injury.[126]

Although the provision in section 240.40 that authorizes the prosecution to obtain non-testimonial evidence from the defendant does not require the prosecution to make any specific showing in support of an order directing disclosure, the provision states that the court "may" order such disclosure.[127] This has led several trial courts to conclude that the prosecution, in seeking non-testimonial evidence from the defendant under this provision, must demonstrate probable cause for the necessity of the evidence sought.[128] Applying this standard, one court held that the prosecution had established probable cause for the necessity of directing the defendant to appear in a lineup upon a showing that several eyewitnesses to the crime had identified the defendant in a photo array but had not had the opportunity to identify her in a showup or lineup.[129] Not surprisingly, another court held that the prosecution's mere contention that blood, saliva and hair samples it was seeking would be needed for "comparison purposes" was insufficient, without more, to justify an order directing disclosure.[130]

Library References:

West's Key No. Digests, Criminal Law ⚖=393, 627.5(3), 1224(3).

124. CPL § 240.40(2)(b)(iv). Requiring the defendant to pose for a photograph involving reenactment of the alleged crime undoubtedly would violate the defendant's constitutional privilege against self-incrimination.

125. CPL § 240.40(2)(b)(vi).

126. CPL § 240.40(2)(b)(v).

127. CPL § 240.40(2).

128. See, e.g., People v. Boudin, 114 Misc.2d 523, 452 N.Y.S.2d 496 (Sup.Ct., Rockland County, 1982); People v. Handley, 105 Misc.2d 215, 431 N.Y.S.2d 982 (Sup.Ct., Monroe County, 1980). See also Bellacosa, "Practice Commentary" to CPL § 240.40, McKinney's Cons. Laws of N.Y., Book 11A, at 383–84 (1982)(in seeking such an order, the prosecution should be required to show "special need or justification").

The Court of Appeals has established a more rigorous standard that the prosecution must meet when seeking bodily evidence from a person merely suspected of committing a crime, as opposed to a defendant who has formally been charged with a crime. In Matter of Abe A., 56 N.Y.2d 288, 452 N.Y.S.2d 6, 437 N.E.2d 265 (1982), the court held that the prosecution, in seeking bodily samples from a suspect, must establish probable cause that the suspect has committed the crime suspected, a clear indication that relevant evidence will be found and that the method used to secure the evidence is safe and reliable. In addition, in making its determination, the trial court must weigh the seriousness of the crime suspected, the importance of the evidence and the unavailability of less obtrusive means of obtaining it, all against the suspect's general right to be free from bodily intrusion. 56 N.Y.2d at 291, 452 N.Y.S.2d at 7. See also Matter of David M. v. Dwyer, 107 A.D.2d 884, 484 N.Y.S.2d 323 (3d Dep't 1985).

A suspect may challenge a trial court order directing that he or she furnish bodily samples by way of a CPLR Article 78 proceeding. See Matter of Abe A., 56 N.Y.2d at 296, 452 N.Y.S.2d at 11.

129. People v. Boudin, 114 Misc.2d at 527, 452 N.Y.S.2d at 499.

130. People v. Handley, 105 Misc.2d 215, 431 N.Y.S.2d 982 (Sup.Ct., Monroe County, 1980).

§ 7.12   Brady—In General

In *Brady v. Maryland*,[131] the Supreme Court held that due process requires the prosecution to disclose to the defense material evidence in its possession that "would tend to exculpate" the accused. Unlike *Rosario* material, which is limited to written or recorded statements of prosecution witnesses, *Brady* material may encompass a broad range of written or unwritten information or physical evidence that originated from any person or any thing. For example, even information provided by a missing witness that would contradict the testimony of a prosecution trial witness was held to be *Brady* material.[132]

Moreover, the Supreme Court has held that *Brady* material includes not only evidence that relates to substantive questions of guilt or innocence but also evidence involving the credibility of prosecution witnesses.[133] Thus, prosecutors may be required to disclose information that reveals a witness's bias against the defendant,[134] that raises questions about an identifying witness's powers of perception,[135] and that suggests a complainant's possible motivation to fabricate.[136]

Prosecutors also must disclose any promises they make, or agreements they enter into, in exchange for their witnesses' testimony. As the Court of Appeals has explained, this obligation to disclose "arises from the fact that the prosecutor and the witness have reached an understanding in which the witness's cooperation has been exchanged for some *quid pro quo* on the part of the prosecutor."[137] An express agreement is not necessary; a "tacit understanding between the witness

---

131. 373 U.S. 83, 83 S.Ct. 1194, 10 L.Ed.2d 215 (1963).

132. People v. Barreras, 92 A.D.2d 871, 459 N.Y.S.2d 828 (2d Dep't 1983). See also People v. Smith, 127 A.D.2d 864, 512 N.Y.S.2d 243 (2d Dep't 1987)(prosecution improperly withheld information regarding possible conspiracy against defendant, pre-dating instant offense, involving police officer and two others). But see People v. Jones, 44 N.Y.2d 76, 404 N.Y.S.2d 85, 375 N.E.2d 41, cert. den. 439 U.S. 846, 99 S.Ct. 145, 58 L.Ed.2d 148 (1978)(prosecutor's failure to notify defendant, who ultimately pleaded guilty, that the complaining witness had died did not violate Brady rule because fact of the complainant's death was not exculpatory in that it did not suggest that defendant did not commit the crime charged).

133. See United States v. Bagley, 473 U.S. 667, 676, 105 S.Ct. 3375, 3380, 87 L.Ed.2d 481 (1985); Giglio v. United States, 405 U.S. 150, 154, 92 S.Ct. 763, 766, 31 L.Ed.2d 104 (1972).

134. See, e.g., People v. Baxley, 84 N.Y.2d 208, 616 N.Y.S.2d 7, 639 N.E.2d 746 (1994)(although recantation of allegations against defendant on part of person who never testified at trial or hearing was not Brady material, that person's statement to prosecution that a critical prosecution trial witness had falsely accused defendant to gain leniency in that witness's pending criminal case was Brady material); People v. Velez, 118 A.D.2d 116, 504 N.Y.S.2d 404 (1st Dep't 1986)(prosecution required to disclose that burglary complainant believed that defendant had robbed his wife two months before complainant testified at trial).

135. See, e.g., People v. Davis, 81 N.Y.2d 281, 598 N.Y.S.2d 156, 614 N.E.2d 719 (1993)(prosecutor required to disclose information demonstrating that crime victim had misidentified one suspect).

136. See, e.g., People v. Wallert, 98 A.D.2d 47, 469 N.Y.S.2d 722 (1st Dep't 1983)(prosecution required to disclose that complainant intended to file civil lawsuit against defendant).

137. People v. Novoa, 70 N.Y.2d 490, 497, 522 N.Y.S.2d 504, 508, 517 N.E.2d 219 (1987). See generally People v. LaDolce, 196 A.D.2d 49, 55–56, 607 N.Y.S.2d 523, 526–27 (4th Dep't 1994)("package deal" in which one prosecution witness's testimony was conditioned on a favorable plea arrangement for his father, who was also a prosecution witness, required to be disclosed).

and the prosecution" may create an obligation to disclose.[138] Thus, the Court of Appeals has held that the prosecution was required to disclose that it had written to the Parole Board on behalf of its witness advising of the witness's significant cooperation and expressing the hope that the cooperation be taken into account when the witness was considered for parole.[139] Similarly, the prosecution was required to disclose its promise to a witness to make the witness's cooperation known to another prosecutor who was prosecuting the witness in an unrelated case.[140]

Notably, a failure to disclose material exculpatory evidence violates due process regardless of the good faith or bad faith of the prosecution.[141] Thus, a good faith but negligent prosecutorial effort to disclose *Brady* evidence may still require reversal of a conviction.[142]

Library References:
West's Key No. Digests, Constitutional Law ⚖=268(5); Criminal Law ⚖=700(2)–700(9).

§ 7.13 Brady—Materiality

In *United States v. Agurs*,[143] the court developed a two-tiered standard for determining whether exculpatory evidence is material. Under the *Agurs* standard, if the defense had made a specific request for exculpatory evidence, the evidence is material if, had it been disclosed, it "might have affected the outcome of the trial."[144] If the defense had made no request or only a general request for exculpatory evidence, the evidence is material if, had it been disclosed, it would have created "a

---

138. People v. Cwikla, 46 N.Y.2d 434, 441, 414 N.Y.S.2d 102, 105, 386 N.E.2d 1070 (1979).

139. Id.

140. People v. Novoa, 70 N.Y.2d 490, 522 N.Y.S.2d 504, 517 N.E.2d 219 (1987). See also People v. Conlan, 146 A.D.2d 319, 541 N.Y.S.2d 347 (1st Dep't 1989)(prosecution obligated to disclose that another prosecutor had tacitly advised a witness that the witness's testimony would somehow be rewarded).

The Supreme Court has held that the *Brady* rule requires disclosure of a promise made to a witness by another prosecutor in the same office as the prosecutor who actually tries the case. Giglio v. United States, 405 U.S. 150, 92 S.Ct. 763, 31 L.Ed.2d 104 (1972). Although recognizing that this may place a significant burden on prosecutors' offices, the court noted that "procedures and regulations can be established to carry that burden and to insure communication of all relevant information on each case to every lawyer who deals with it." See also People v. Steadman, 82 N.Y.2d 1, 8, 603 N.Y.S.2d 382, 385, 623 N.E.2d 509 (1993) (promises made to a witness by a supervising prosecutor are "certainly" binding on subordinates in the same office); People v. Gaines, 199 A.D.2d 335, 604 N.Y.S.2d 272 (2d Dep't 1993)(same). The Court of Appeals has never squarely addressed the extent to which knowledge of a promise made to a witness by one prosecutor's office may be imputed to another prosecutor's office. In the Novoa case, however, the court held that an agreement entered into by a second prosecutor's office relating to a witness's cooperation in a separate case should have been disclosed because the prosecutor in the office that tried the case knew that her witness had been indicted in that separate case and thus should have inquired whether there was any agreement. People v. Novoa, 70 N.Y.2d at 498, 522 N.Y.S.2d at 509. See also People v. Steadman, 82 N.Y.2d at 8, 603 N.Y.S.2d at 385 (promises made to a witness by one prosecutor are "generally binding on others in the law enforcement system").

141. Brady v. Maryland, 373 U.S. at 87, 83 S.Ct. at 1197.

142. See People v. Simmons, 36 N.Y.2d 126, 365 N.Y.S.2d 812, 325 N.E.2d 139 (1975).

143. 427 U.S. 97, 96 S.Ct. 2392, 49 L.Ed.2d 342 (1976).

144. 427 U.S. at 104, 96 S.Ct. at 2398.

reasonable doubt which did not otherwise exist."[145] Nine years later, in *United States v. Bagley*,[146] a divided Supreme Court reconsidered the *Agurs* two-tier standard and replaced it with a single standard: regardless of the nature of the defense request or whether a request is made at all, exculpatory evidence is material only if there is a "reasonable probability" that it "would" affect the outcome of the trial.[147]

In New York, the Court of Appeals, as a matter of state constitutional law, has rejected the *Bagley* standard and reaffirmed the *Agurs* two-tier approach.[148] In rejecting *Bagley*, the Court of Appeals noted the New York courts' long-standing adherence to the two-tier approach, and suggested that such approach provides the prosecution with a greater incentive to thoroughly review its files for exculpatory evidence and to err on the side of disclosure when exculpatory value is debatable.[149] Accordingly, in New York, undisclosed exculpatory evidence specifically requested by the defense is deemed material, and thus will require reversal of a conviction, if the defendant demonstrates a "reasonable possibility" that the failure to disclose the material "contributed to the verdict."[150] If the defense made only a general request for exculpatory evidence, or no request at all, undisclosed exculpatory evidence is deemed material only if the defendant demonstrates that the evidence creates a reasonable doubt that did not otherwise exist.[151] Obviously, the "specific request" standard is a considerably easier one for the defendant to meet; indeed, the Court of Appeals has noted that a failure to disclose specifically requested exculpatory evidence is "seldom, if ever, excusable."[152]

Library References:

West's Key No. Digests, Criminal Law ⚍627.8(3), 700(2)–700(9).

§ 7.14 *Brady*—Other Issues

Unlike in the *Rosario* context, in which an extensive line of cases explores the question of when *Rosario* material that is not in the actual

---

145. 427 U.S. at 112, 96 S.Ct. at 2402.

146. 473 U.S. 667, 105 S.Ct. 3375, 87 L.Ed.2d 481 (1985).

147. 473 U.S. at 682, 105 S.Ct. at 3383.

148. People v. Vilardi, 76 N.Y.2d 67, 556 N.Y.S.2d 518, 555 N.E.2d 915 (1990).

149. 76 N.Y.2d at 77, 556 N.Y.S.2d at 523.

150. Id.

151. 76 N.Y.2d at 73, 556 N.Y.S.2d at 521; People v. Smith, 63 N.Y.2d 41, 67, 479 N.Y.S.2d 706, 718, 468 N.E.2d 879 (1984), cert. den. 469 U.S. 1227, 105 S.Ct. 1226, 84 L.Ed.2d 364 (1985).

152. See People v. Vilardi, 76 N.Y.2d at 74, 556 N.Y.S.2d at 521; People v. Brown, 67 N.Y.2d 555, 559, 505 N.Y.S.2d 574, 575, 496 N.E.2d 663 (1986), cert. den. 479 U.S. 1093, 107 S.Ct. 1307, 94 L.Ed.2d 161 (1987); People v. Cwikla, 46 N.Y.2d 434, 441–42, 414 N.Y.S.2d 102, 105–06, 386 N.E.2d 1070 (1979). See also United States v. Agurs, 427 U.S. at 106, 96 S.Ct. at 2399.

Whether a discovery request for exculpatory evidence is specific or general is not always easily discernible. See, e.g., People v. Vicki–Crystal Wright, 86 N.Y.2d 591, 635 N.Y.S.2d 136, 658 N.E.2d 1009 (1995)(court does not resolve whether defendant's pretrial request for "any deals, promises or agreements entered into by the People or any agent thereof and any prosecution witness" included agreements with a prosecution witness that were unrelated to defendant's case). For an example of an extensive pretrial Brady request, see Chapter 8, § 8.2.2.

possession of the prosecution will be deemed within the control of the prosecution,[153] very few cases analyze this question with respect to *Brady* evidence.[154] *Brady* evidence is typically defined as material exculpatory evidence that is "in the possession of the prosecution."[155] Because it is now settled, however, that *Rosario* material (which may not necessarily be exculpatory and frequently is inculpatory) that is in the actual possession of the police is considered to be within the prosecution's control or constructive possession, it would seem to follow that the same must be true for *Brady* evidence; and at least one appellate court has so noted.[156] In fact, the Court of Appeals has held that the prosecution's lack of knowledge that a prosecution witness had acted as a police informant in unrelated cases was unavailing; accordingly, the prosecution was "not relieved of [its] obligation to turn over *Brady* materials by [its] failure to discover that the police were in possession of [this] exculpatory information."[157]

As is true for *Rosario* material, the courts have emphasized that, if the prosecution is not sure whether a document or information qualifies as *Brady* evidence, it should make disclosure to the trial judge for a determination.[158] In appropriate cases, the prosecution may avail itself of the *in camera* procedure set forth in CPL § 240.90(3).

Although the prosecution technically should disclose *Brady* evidence to the defense as soon as it becomes aware of it,[159] the courts often overlook belated disclosure so long as the defense is afforded a "meaningful opportunity" to use the evidence.[160] The Court of Appeals has

---

153. See § 7.17, supra.

154. See, e.g., People v. Gissendanner, 48 N.Y.2d 543, 551, 423 N.Y.S.2d 893, 898, 399 N.E.2d 924 (1979)(court raised, but did not resolve, question of whether police personnel files are within constructive possession of prosecution for Brady purposes).

155. See, e.g., People v. Vilardi, 76 N.Y.2d at 73, 556 N.Y.S.2d at 520; People v. Cwikla, 46 N.Y.2d at 441, 414 N.Y.S.2d at 105.

156. See People v. Russo, 109 A.D.2d 855, 856, 486 N.Y.S.2d 769, 771 (2d Dep't 1985). Cf. County of Nassau v. Sullivan, 194 A.D.2d 236, 239, 606 N.Y.S.2d 249, 251 (2d Dep't 1993)(although it is "reasonable to conclude" that material prepared by law enforcement agencies in connection with criminal investigations is within the prosecution's control for Brady and Rosario purposes, a report in the possession of a county attorney was not within control of the prosecution).

157. People v. Vicki-Crystal Wright, 86 N.Y.2d 591, 635 N.Y.S.2d 136, 658 N.E.2d 1009 (1995). See also Kyles v. Whitley, ___ U.S. ___, 115 S.Ct. 1555, 1567, 131 L.Ed.2d 490 (1995)("the individual prosecutor has a duty to learn of any favorable evidence known to the others acting on the government's behalf in the case, including the police"). People v. Jackson, 154 Misc.2d 718, 728–30, 593 N.Y.S.2d 410, 417–18 (Sup.Ct., Kings County, 1992)(fire department required to disclose exculpatory evidence gathered in connection with its investigation of alleged arson).

158. See, e.g., People v. Jones, 85 A.D.2d 50, 448 N.Y.S.2d 543 (3d Dep't 1982); People v. Davis, 105 Misc.2d 409, 432 N.Y.S.2d 350 (Syracuse City Ct.1980), aff'd 109 Misc.2d 230, 439 N.Y.S.2d 798 (Onondaga Co.Ct.1981). See also United States v. Agurs, 427 U.S. at 108, 96 S.Ct. at 2399–2400 (because the "significance of an item of evidence can seldom be predicted accurately until the record is complete," the "prudent" prosecutor should "resolve doubtful questions in favor of disclosure").

159. Cf. CPL § 240.20(1)(h)(in response to defendant's demand, prosecution must disclose anything that it is required to disclose "pursuant to the constitution of this state or of the United States").

160. People v. Steadman, 82 N.Y.2d 1, 8, 603 N.Y.S.2d 382, 385, 623 N.E.2d 509 (1993); People v. Cortijo, 70 N.Y.2d 868, 870, 523 N.Y.S.2d 463, 464, 517 N.E.2d 1349 (1987).

§ 7.14   DISCOVERY   Ch. 7

failed to condemn disclosure as late as during the trial itself.[161] Indeed, in one case, the defendant did not receive *Brady* evidence until during the prosecutor's summation. Yet, because the trial court in that case interrupted the prosecutor's summation, allowed defense counsel to recall the relevant witness and place the evidence before the jury, and permitted counsel to address the jury on the issue before the prosecutor resumed his summation, the Court of Appeals found no reversible error.[162]

Several courts have held that the prosecution's failure to disclose *Brady* evidence was not error because the defense was already aware of the evidence. For example, appellate courts have held that the failure to disclose the grand jury testimony of a witness who supported the defendant's defense is not error because the defendant knew the witness and was aware of his or her testimony.[163] Similarly, no *Brady* violation was found where the prosecution did not disclose a report containing a defense witness's statement exculpating the defendant because the defendant knew of the statement and it conformed to the witness's trial testimony.[164] In addition, several courts, in failing to condemn a prosecutor's belated disclosure of *Brady* evidence, have emphasized the defendant's prior knowledge of the evidence.[165]

Finally, it should be noted that the prosecution's failure to perform a scientific test on physical evidence is not a *Brady* violation. Although such a test might itself yield exculpatory evidence, the *Brady* doctrine does not extend to that speculative potential.[166]

Library References:

West's Key No. Digests, Criminal Law ⚖700(6)–700(9).

§ 7.15   Disclosure of Uncharged Prior Bad Acts

At the defendant's request, the prosecution must notify the defendant of any instances of the defendant's uncharged prior criminal, vicious or immoral conduct that the prosecution intends to use to

---

161. See People v. Cortijo, 70 N.Y.2d 868, 523 N.Y.S.2d 463, 517 N.E.2d 1349 (1987). See also People v. Jemmott, 144 A.D.2d 694, 535 N.Y.S.2d 84 (2d Dep't 1988); People v. Clark, 89 A.D.2d 820, 453 N.Y.S.2d 525 (4th Dep't 1982), cert. den. 459 U.S. 1090, 103 S.Ct. 577, 74 L.Ed.2d 937 (1982).

162. People v. Smith, 63 N.Y.2d 41, 67–68, 479 N.Y.S.2d 706, 718, 468 N.E.2d 879 (1984), cert. den. 469 U.S. 1227, 105 S.Ct. 1226, 84 L.Ed.2d 364 (1985).

163. People v. Cramer, 166 A.D.2d 316, 560 N.Y.S.2d 777 (1st Dep't 1990); People v. Gardner, 162 A.D.2d 466, 556 N.Y.S.2d 163 (2d Dep't 1990); People v. Johnson, 157 A.D.2d 855, 550 N.Y.S.2d 430 (2d Dep't 1990); People v. Dukes, 156 A.D.2d 203, 548 N.Y.S.2d 462 (1st Dep't 1989).

164. People v. Murray, 140 A.D.2d 949, 529 N.Y.S.2d 628 (4th Dep't 1988). See also People v. LaRocca, 172 A.D.2d 628, 568 N.Y.S.2d 431 (2d Dep't 1991)(defendant aware and in possession of alleged Brady material).

165. See, e.g., People v. Brown, 167 A.D.2d 847, 562 N.Y.S.2d 254 (4th Dep't 1990); People v. Thornton, 130 A.D.2d 78, 517 N.Y.S.2d 807 (3d Dep't 1987).

166. See, e.g., People v. Buxton, 189 A.D.2d 996, 593 N.Y.S.2d 87 (3d Dep't 1993); People v. Yourdon, 142 A.D.2d 998, 530 N.Y.S.2d 419 (4th Dep't 1988). Also supporting this conclusion is the fact that the defense generally has the right to perform its own scientific test of physical evidence. See § 7.32, infra.

impeach the defendant's credibility if he or she testifies at trial.[167] Disclosure must be made no later than the commencement of jury selection, although the court has the discretion to order disclosure, and to make its determination as to the admissibility of the prior bad acts, three days prior to the commencement of jury selection (excluding weekends and holidays).[168]

The rationale for this 1987 addition to Article 240 is that the defendant, before deciding whether to testify at trial, should know whether the prosecution will seek, and be permitted, to impeach his or her testimony with what ordinarily will be highly prejudicial evidence of uncharged prior bad conduct. Thus, this disclosure, in conjunction with the court's *Sandoval* determination as to which, if any, of the defendant's prior criminal convictions will be admissible to impeach his or her testimony,[169] will enable the defendant to make a more fully informed decision regarding whether to testify.[170] Unlike the *Sandoval* motion, however, which requires that the defendant inform the court of which prior convictions should not be admitted, this provision requires that the prosecution specify to the defendant (and the court) which prior uncharged acts it will seek to introduce. This distinction is necessary because the defendant, who receives a copy of his or her criminal history record,[171] and thus will be aware of the existence of any prior convictions, will not necessarily be readily aware of his or her specific acts of prior uncharged conduct. Moreover, as one appellate court has observed, a procedure that required the defendant to divulge to the court and the prosecutor uncharged prior behavior would be based on the untenable assumption that the defendant in fact committed a crime for which he or she was never arrested.[172]

A subsequent decision of the Court of Appeals, however, may have largely eliminated the prosecution's ability to impeach a testifying defendant with uncharged prior bad acts. In *People v. Betts*,[173] the court held that cross-examination of a defendant regarding an unrelated pending criminal charge, solely for the purpose of impeaching the defendant's credibility, is impermissible. This is because allowing such cross-examination would "unduly compromise[] the defendant's right to testify with respect to the case on trial, while simultaneously jeopardizing the

---

167. CPL § 240.43.

168. Id.

169. See People v. Sandoval, 34 N.Y.2d 371, 357 N.Y.S.2d 849, 314 N.E.2d 413 (1974).

170. But see People v. Brown, 202 A.D.2d 266, 609 N.Y.S.2d 2 (1st Dep't 1994)(trial court did not abuse discretion in allowing prosecution to seek ruling on admissibility of any prior bad acts of which the prosecution had knowledge at the time of the Sandoval hearing, thereby allowing for the possibility that the prosecution could seek the admission of additional prior bad acts of which it subsequently learned).

171. See CPL § 160.40(2).

172. See People v. Simpson, 109 A.D.2d 461, 465–66, 492 N.Y.S.2d 609, 612–13 (1st Dep't 1985), appeal dism. 67 N.Y.2d 1026, 503 N.Y.S.2d 325, 494 N.E.2d 456 (1986). The Court of Appeals has held, with respect to evidence of the defendant's prior uncharged criminal conduct that the prosecution seeks to introduce as evidence-in-chief (see generally People v. Molineux, 168 N.Y. 264, 61 N.E. 286 (1901)), that the prosecution must request a ruling out of the presence of the jury before attempting to introduce the evidence. People v. Ventimiglia, 52 N.Y.2d 350, 362, 438 N.Y.S.2d 261, 265, 420 N.E.2d 59 (1981).

173. 70 N.Y.2d 289, 520 N.Y.S.2d 370, 514 N.E.2d 865 (1987).

§ 7.15

correspondingly important right not to incriminate oneself as to the pending matter."[174] Although the *Betts* decision involved cross-examination regarding an actual and pending charge, similar concerns would arise from cross-examination regarding uncharged conduct that could result in a criminal charge, particularly if the defendant were forced under oath to make incriminating admissions relating to that conduct. Thus, the *Betts* ruling may foreclose the prosecution's impeachment of a testifying defendant as to any prior criminal conduct that has not resulted in a conviction.[175]

Library References:
West's Key No. Digests, Witnesses ⚖︎337.

§ 7.16 *Rosario*—In General

A major area of discovery involves the prior statements of witnesses who testify at pretrial hearings and at trial. Known as *Rosario* material, after the 1961 Court of Appeals decision that first required that prior recorded statements of prosecution witnesses be disclosed to the defense,[176] disclosure by both the prosecution and the defense is now required under sections 240.44 and 240.45 of the CPL. Under both sections, each party must disclose to the other any written or recorded statements made by its witnesses that relate to the subject matter of the witnesses' testimony.[177] Disclosure is not required of witness statements that are not written or recorded, and neither party is obligated to record or reduce to writing the statements of its witnesses.[178] Prior statements that must be disclosed include a prosecution witness's grand jury testimony (including a videotaped examination pursuant to CPL § 190.32).

Disclosure of the prior statements of a prosecution or defense hearing witness must be disclosed no later than the direct examination of the witness. Disclosure of the prior statements of a prosecution trial witness must be disclosed before the prosecutor's opening statement, although disclosure, either in the prosecution's discretion or at the court's direction, is frequently made at the commencement of jury selection.[179] One appellate court, however, has held that a trial court may not direct the prosecution to disclose *Rosario* material before the

---

174. 70 N.Y.2d at 295, 520 N.Y.S.2d at 373. See also People v. Bennett, 79 N.Y.2d 464, 583 N.Y.S.2d 825, 593 N.E.2d 279 (1992).

175. The one exception probably is uncharged prior criminal conduct that could not be prosecuted because the statute of limitations had run out.

176. People v. Rosario, 9 N.Y.2d 286, 213 N.Y.S.2d 448, 173 N.E.2d 881 (1961), reargument den. 9 N.Y.2d 908, 216 N.Y.S.2d 1025, 176 N.E.2d 111, cert. den. 368 U.S. 866, 82 S.Ct. 117, 7 L.Ed.2d 64 (1961).

177. CPL §§ 240.44(1), 240.45(1)(a). Although section 240.44, unlike section 240.45, requires that the party receiving disclosure "request" the materials, in practice disclosure of *Rosario* material at a pretrial hearing is as automatic as it is at trial.

178. See Matter of Catterson v. Rohl, 202 A.D.2d 420, 423, 608 N.Y.S.2d 696, 699 (2d Dep't 1994); People v. Littles, 192 A.D.2d 314, 595 N.Y.S.2d 463 (1st Dep't 1993); People v. Steinberg, 170 A.D.2d 50, 76, 573 N.Y.S.2d 965, 981 (1st Dep't 1991), aff'd 79 N.Y.2d 673, 584 N.Y.S.2d 770, 595 N.E.2d 845 (1992).

179. In bench trials, the prosecution must disclose Rosario material before the submission of evidence. CPL § 240.45(1).

trial commences.[180] The defense must disclose the prior statements of its trial witnesses before it presents its direct case.[181]

The prosecution's failure to disclose *Rosario* material is treated extremely harshly under New York case law: in most cases, a failure to disclose at trial will require automatic reversal of a conviction, without regard to whether the nondisclosure contributed to the conviction or otherwise prejudiced the defendant. The automatic reversal rule for *Rosario* violations is discussed more fully in § 7.22, *infra*. Moreover, the prosecution's good faith effort "to locate, identify, and discover" all *Rosario* material does not excuse a failure to produce material within its possession or control.[182] Needless to say, a prosecutor runs a grave risk in failing to disclose *Rosario* material, and as the Court of Appeals has cautioned, "the better practice is to turn over the statements immediately without further analysis as to whether the defendant is technically entitled to disclosure."[183] Certainly, if any doubt exists, the prosecution should always disclose the materials to the court, which must examine them and determine whether they constitute *Rosario* material.[184] And if the prosecution fails to do so, the defendant's assertion of a factual basis that the prosecution is improperly denying the existence of *Rosario* material requires that the court, *in camera*, inspect the document in question, or the prosecution's file if need be, to resolve the dispute.[185]

Library References:
West's Key No. Digests, Criminal Law ⚖627.7, 700(2)–700(8).

§ 7.17 *Rosario*—Specific Issues

The *Rosario* rule has engendered extensive litigation, with a significant number of the cases reaching the Court of Appeals. For example, the Court of Appeals has made clear that the prosecution must disclose

---

180. See Matter of Catterson v. Rohl, 202 A.D.2d at 423, 608 N.Y.S.2d at 698–99.

181. CPL § 240.45(2). Unlike prosecution witnesses, whose statements are usually contained in routinely prepared police reports and, in felony cases, in their testimony to the grand jury, the prior statements of defense witnesses are infrequently recorded. This is because defense counsel, in reaction to this disclosure requirement, are loathe to memorialize or record statements of witnesses that they intend to call at trial. See Bellacosa, "Practice Commentary" to CPL § 240.45, McKinney's Cons. Laws of N.Y., Book 11A, at 409 (1982).

Because of the defendant's Fifth Amendment privilege against self-incrimination, the CPL does not, and could not, require the defense to disclose a testifying defendant's prior written or recorded statements. See CPL §§ 240.44(1), 240.45(2)(a).

182. People v. Ranghelle, 69 N.Y.2d 56, 63, 511 N.Y.S.2d 580, 584, 503 N.E.2d 1011 (1986).

183. People v. Ranghelle, 69 N.Y.2d at 63, 511 N.Y.S.2d at 584 (citing People v. Consolazio, 40 N.Y.2d 446, 387 N.Y.S.2d 62, 354 N.E.2d 801 (1976)).

184. See People v. Adger, 75 N.Y.2d 723, 725–26, 551 N.Y.S.2d 190, 191, 550 N.E.2d 443 (1989); People v. Poole, 48 N.Y.2d 144, 149–50, 422 N.Y.S.2d 5, 8, 397 N.E.2d 697 (1979).

185. People v. Poole, 48 N.Y.2d at 149–50, 422 N.Y.S.2d at 8; People v. Ellis, 188 A.D.2d 1043, 592 N.Y.S.2d 200 (4th Dep't 1992); People v. Gallardo, 173 A.D.2d 636, 570 N.Y.S.2d 222 (2d Dep't 1991). See also People v. Shaw, 196 A.D.2d 558, 601 N.Y.S.2d 151 (2d Dep't 1993)(trial court improperly relied on prosecutor's assertion that document was not Rosario); People v. James, 193 A.D.2d 694, 598 N.Y.S.2d 38 (2d Dep't 1993)(trial court erred in failing to inspect undercover officer's buy report where trial prosecutor admitted existence of report but maintained it was irrelevant to undercover's testimony).

§ 7.17 DISCOVERY Ch. 7

not only prior statements that its witnesses made to law enforcement, but also statements that its witnesses made to private citizens.[186] However, a series of cases has established that prior statements of witnesses do not constitute *Rosario* material unless the statements are within the prosecution's possession or control. And the Court of Appeals has made clear that statements not within the prosecution's actual possession will be deemed within the prosecution's control (or constructive possession) only if they are in the possession of a police agency.[187] Thus, witness statements recorded by private security guards,[188] statements recorded by a social worker employed by an independent agency,[189] statements in the possession of the State Department of Motor Vehicles,[190] an audiotape in the possession of a medical examiner,[191] and the private notes of the complainant[192] are not *Rosario* material if not within the actual possession of the prosecution.[193] Statements not in the actual possession of the prosecution or a law enforcement agency, however, may be deemed *Rosario* material if made at the direction of the prosecution or a

---

186. People v. Perez, 65 N.Y.2d 154, 490 N.Y.S.2d 747, 480 N.E.2d 361 (1985).

187. The court has also held that the prosecution must disclose Rosario material within its control even if the documents could be subpoenaed directly by the defense. See People v. Ranghelle, 69 N.Y.2d 56, 64, 511 N.Y.S.2d 580, 585, 503 N.E.2d 1011 (1986)("[S]ociety's interest in maintaining criminal trials as truth-finding processes requires that the burden of locating and producing prior statements of complaining witnesses, filed with police agencies, remain solely with the People.").

Several appellate courts have held, however, that statements in the possession of law enforcement agencies other than the police are not within the control of the prosecution. See People v. Astacio, 173 A.D.2d 834, 571 N.Y.S.2d 60 (2d Dep't 1991)(Kings County grand jury testimony not in control of Queens County prosecutor); People v. Rodriguez, 155 A.D.2d 257, 546 N.Y.S.2d 861 (1st Dep't 1989)(statement in federal Drug Enforcement Administration file not in prosecution's control). Cf. People v. Testa, 48 A.D.2d 691, 367 N.Y.S.2d 838 (2d Dep't 1975), aff'd 40 N.Y.2d 1018, 391 N.Y.S.2d 573, 359 N.E.2d 1367 (1976), cert. den. 431 U.S. 925, 97 S.Ct. 2199, 53 L.Ed.2d 239 (1977)(statement made to FBI agent should have been disclosed because prosecution had actual possession of FBI file).

188. People v. Bailey, 73 N.Y.2d 812, 537 N.Y.S.2d 111, 534 N.E.2d 28 (1988).

189. People v. Tissois, 72 N.Y.2d 75, 531 N.Y.S.2d 228, 526 N.E.2d 1086 (1988).

190. People v. Flynn, 79 N.Y.2d 879, 882, 581 N.Y.S.2d 160, 161, 589 N.E.2d 383 (1992).

191. People v. Washington, 86 N.Y.2d 189, 630 N.Y.S.2d 693, 654 N.E.2d 967 (1995).

192. People v. Reedy, 70 N.Y.2d 826, 523 N.Y.S.2d 438, 517 N.E.2d 1324 (1987).

193. See also People v. Howard, 87 N.Y.2d 940, 663 N.E.2d 1252 (1996) (witnesses' statements made at defendant's prison disciplinary proceedings not Rosario); County of Nassau v. Sullivan, 194 A.D.2d 236, 606 N.Y.S.2d 249 (2d Dep't 1993)(internal police report in possession of county attorney defending against lawsuit brought by complainant in criminal case not Rosario); People v. Letizia, 159 A.D.2d 1010, 552 N.Y.S.2d 732 (4th Dep't 1990)(victim's statement to Crime Victims Compensation Board not Rosario); People v. Berkley, 157 A.D.2d 463, 549 N.Y.S.2d 392 (1st Dep't 1990)(victim's statement to Victim Services Agency not Rosario); People v. Morris, 153 A.D.2d 984, 545 N.Y.S.2d 427 (3d Dep't 1989)(co-offender's presentence report not Rosario); In Matter of Gina C., 138 A.D.2d 77, 531 N.Y.S.2d 86 (1st Dep't 1988)(witness's statement to a newspaper reporter not Rosario). Cf. People v. Kelly, 209 A.D.2d 439, 618 N.Y.S.2d 821 (2d Dep't 1994)(police officer's statement to parole officer not Rosario) with People v. Fields, 146 A.D.2d 505, 537 N.Y.S.2d 157 (1st Dep't 1989)(police officer's statement to parole officer was Rosario because Division of Parole is a law enforcement agency and preparation of parole violation charges is a prosecutorial function).

law enforcement agency.[194] On the other hand, statements to which the prosecution does not have its "own immediate access," such as untranscribed plea minutes of a co-defendant, are not *Rosario* material.[195]

The prosecution need not disclose a witness's prior statements that are the "duplicative equivalent" of the witness's statements that it has already disclosed.[196] This is a strictly applied doctrine; statements are not duplicative equivalents merely because they are "harmonious" or "consistent," and even "minor inconsistencies" between two documents will disqualify them as duplicative equivalents.[197] Or, as one appellate court has noted, documents are not duplicative equivalents if "even the slightest of differences" exists between them.[198] For example, a report that the prosecution had failed to produce was held to be the duplicative equivalent of a document that was produced only because it contained a statement that was an "exact word-for-word transcription" of the statement contained in the disclosed document.[199] By contrast, it was held that a videotaped examination of the victim was not the duplicative equivalent of a previously disclosed transcript of the examination, because transcripts do not convey a witness's demeanor.[200] Moreover, an undisclosed report containing information also contained in a disclosed report was found not to be a duplicative equivalent because the reports attributed this information to different witnesses.[201] And a document that has been destroyed can never be deemed the duplicative equivalent of one that exists and remains available for inspection.[202]

In sum, the duplicative equivalent standard is a difficult one to meet. Given that prosecutors have nothing to lose by disclosing a document that contains identical, or virtually identical, information as a document that has already been disclosed to the defense, they would be foolish to deliberately fail to disclose a record on the ground that it is a duplicative equivalent.[203] Nevertheless, when prosecutors do seek to avail themselves of this exception to the *Rosario* rule, they must make an appropriate record in the trial court as to which documents they

---

194. See Matter of Gina C., 138 A.D.2d 77, 531 N.Y.S.2d 86 (1st Dep't 1988); People v. Anonymous, 154 Misc.2d 963, 587 N.Y.S.2d 103 (N.Y.C.Crim.Ct.1992); People v. Argudin, 151 Misc.2d 507, 573 N.Y.S.2d 572 (N.Y.C.Crim.Ct.1991).

195. People v. Fishman, 72 N.Y.2d 884, 532 N.Y.S.2d 739, 528 N.E.2d 1212 (1988). See also People v. Thomas, 147 A.D.2d 725, 538 N.Y.S.2d 330 (2d Dep't 1989), aff'd 75 N.Y.2d 888, 554 N.Y.S.2d 474, 553 N.E.2d 1022 (1990)(issue not preserved); People v. Bradley, 119 A.D.2d 993, 500 N.Y.S.2d 892 (4th Dep't 1986).

196. See People v. Consolazio, 40 N.Y.2d 446, 454–55, 387 N.Y.S.2d 62, 66, 354 N.E.2d 801 (1976), cert. den. 433 U.S. 914, 97 S.Ct. 2986, 53 L.Ed.2d 1100 (1977).

197. People v. Ranghelle, 69 N.Y.2d 56, 63, 65, 511 N.Y.S.2d 580, 584, 586, 503 N.E.2d 1011 (1986).

198. People v. Quinones, 139 A.D.2d 404, 406, 527 N.Y.S.2d 5, 6 (1st Dep't 1988), aff'd 73 N.Y.2d 988, 540 N.Y.S.2d 993, 538 N.E.2d 345 (1989).

199. People v. Mahones, 136 A.D.2d 745, 524 N.Y.S.2d 84 (2d Dep't 1988).

200. People v. Gaskins, 171 A.D.2d 272, 575 N.Y.S.2d 564 (2d Dep't 1991).

201. People v. Young, 79 N.Y.2d 365, 370, 582 N.Y.S.2d 977, 980, 591 N.E.2d 1163 (1992)(duplicative equivalent exception cannot be invoked unless the two statements in question come from the same source).

202. People v. Joseph, 86 N.Y.2d 565, 635 N.Y.S.2d 123, 658 N.E.2d 996 (1995).

203. See People v. Consolazio, 40 N.Y.2d 446, 455, 387 N.Y.S.2d 62, 66, 354 N.E.2d 801 (1976), cert. den. 433 U.S. 914, 97 S.Ct. 2986, 53 L.Ed.2d 1100 (1977).

§ 7.17　　　　　　　　　DISCOVERY　　　　　　　　　Ch. 7

claim are the duplicative equivalents of documents that they have disclosed to the defense; absent such a record, they will be barred from invoking the duplicative equivalent doctrine on any ensuing appeal.[204]

Although a police officer's or prosecutor's synopsis of a witness's statements does constitute *Rosario* material,[205] a prosecutor's synopsis of the events leading to the charges that attributes no information to prosecution witnesses does not.[206] One court has succinctly defined *Rosario* material as "a prior recorded statement which was made by the witness himself or by an individual who directly heard the statement."[207] Under this definition, a police officer's record of an interview with a witness to the crime would be *Rosario* material, but a second officer's record of the first officer's account of the interview would not.[208]

As noted, the actual language of sections 240.44 and 240.45 define *Rosario* material as prior statements that concern the subject matter of the witness's testimony.[209] This definition is broad enough to include prior statements that relate solely to the witness's credibility, but only if the statements are "directly related" to the witness's trial testimony.[210] Thus, a prosecution witness's taped conversation with a relative of the defendant, in which the possibility of the witness becoming unavailable in exchange for a sum of money was discussed, was held to be related to the witness's subsequent trial testimony because it was the trial testimony that the bribe discussions were intended to influence.[211] In another

204. See People v. Quinones, 73 N.Y.2d 988, 540 N.Y.S.2d 993, 538 N.E.2d 345 (1989).

205. People v. Ranghelle, 69 N.Y.2d 56, 63–64, 511 N.Y.S.2d 580, 584–85, 503 N.E.2d 1011 (1986). See also People v. Consolazio, 40 N.Y.2d 446, 387 N.Y.S.2d 62, 354 N.E.2d 801 (1976), cert. den. 433 U.S. 914, 97 S.Ct. 2986, 53 L.Ed.2d 1100 (1977).

206. People v. Chavis, 190 A.D.2d 683, 593 N.Y.S.2d 271 (2d Dep't 1993). See also People v. Roberts, 178 A.D.2d 622, 577 N.Y.S.2d 672 (2d Dep't 1991)(prosecutor's notes consisting of "catch words" designed to jog the prosecutor's memory not Rosario). If a prosecutor's memorandum contains only theories, opinions or conclusions concerning the case, the record would be exempt from disclosure under the work product privilege. See generally CPL § 240.10(2). If a record contains both work product material and also a synopsis of witness statements, the prosecution may seek a protective order under section 240.50 to redact the work product portions of the record. See generally People v. Essner, 125 Misc.2d 908, 480 N.Y.S.2d 857 (Sup.Ct., N.Y. County, 1984)(prosecutor's internal memorandum was protected under work product privilege except as to statements made to prosecutor by defendant and by prosecution witnesses).

207. People v. Williams, 165 A.D.2d 839, 841, 560 N.Y.S.2d 220, 221 (2d Dep't 1990), aff'd on other grounds 78 N.Y.2d 1087, 578 N.Y.S.2d 870, 586 N.E.2d 53 (1991)(issue not preserved for review). See also People v. Miller, 183 A.D.2d 790, 791, 583 N.Y.S.2d 517, 518 (2d Dep't 1992); People v. Mills, 142 A.D.2d 653, 654, 530 N.Y.S.2d 593, 594 (2d Dep't 1988).

208. Cf. People v. Williams, supra (police department "sprint" 911 tape containing description of robbery perpetrator was not Rosario material because record was based on second-hand report of robbery, not first-hand report of eyewitness to incident).

209. CPL §§ 240.44(1), 240.45(1)(a). See, e.g., People v. Mobley, 190 A.D.2d 821, 593 N.Y.S.2d 839 (2d Dep't 1993)(receipt that complainant signed upon retrieving property from property clerk's office not Rosario because it contained no information related to subject matter of complainant's testimony); People v. Velez, 161 A.D.2d 823, 556 N.Y.S.2d 147 (2d Dep't 1990)(notes that merely described color of hosiery worn by decedent not Rosario); People v. Watkins, 157 A.D.2d 301, 556 N.Y.S.2d 541 (1st Dep't 1990)(police officer's overtime voucher not Rosario).

210. People v. Perez, 65 N.Y.2d 154, 159, 490 N.Y.S.2d 747, 750, 480 N.E.2d 361 (1985).

211. Id.

case, a prosecution witness's written waiver of immunity prior to testifying before the grand jury was not *Rosario* material because it concerned only the witness's credibility and not the subject matter of the witness's testimony.[212]

Finally, courts have held that the defense can waive its right to receive, or at least waive its right to later object to not receiving, *Rosario* material. For example, in *People v. Rogelio*,[213] the prosecutor, although telling the defense counsel prior to the start of trial that he would provide a copy of a report containing a witness's statements, forgot to disclose the report. Defense counsel also apparently forgot about the report until after the court's jury charge, at which point he raised the issue with the court for the first time. In affirming the conviction, the First Department stated that, although the prosecutor was "willing and able to comply," it was "defense counsel's own inattention that ultimately resulted in his not obtaining the material."[214] The court's reasoning in *Rogelio* is somewhat questionable, given that CPL § 240.45 does not even require that the defense make a request for disclosure of *Rosario* material and that the Court of Appeals has held that good faith does not excuse a prosecutor's failure to disclose.[215] Nevertheless, other appellate rulings have also deemed *Rosario* violations to be waived, particularly if the defense missed an opportunity to complain to the trial court at a time when the trial court could have acted to rectify the violation.[216] Accordingly, when the defense is aware of a document that may contain *Rosario* material, it should aggressively assert its right to access to the document, not assume that a single request at the commencement of trial will preserve its right to object to the prosecution's failure to disclose and, if unsuccessful in obtaining disclosure, request appropriate sanctions from the court.

---

212. People v. Coker, 134 A.D.2d 507, 521 N.Y.S.2d 96 (2d Dep't 1987), appeal dism. 73 N.Y.2d 819, 537 N.Y.S.2d 479, 534 N.E.2d 317 (1988).

213. 160 A.D.2d 359, 553 N.Y.S.2d 743 (1st Dep't 1990), aff'd 79 N.Y.2d 843, 580 N.Y.S.2d 185, 588 N.E.2d 83 (1992)(issue not preserved for review).

214. 160 A.D.2d at 361, 553 N.Y.S.2d at 745.

215. See People v. Ranghelle, 69 N.Y.2d 56, 63, 511 N.Y.S.2d 580, 584, 503 N.E.2d 1011 (1986).

216. See, e.g., People v. Graves, 85 N.Y.2d 1024, 630 N.Y.S.2d 972, 654 N.E.2d 1024 (1995)(defense counsel's failure to mention again non-disclosure of police report after court deferred discussion of issue deemed abandonment of claim); People v. West, 184 A.D.2d 743, 585 N.Y.S.2d 467 (2d Dep't 1992)(failure to raise Rosario objection or request any type of remedy deprived trial court of opportunity to explore issue of prejudice and determine an appropriate sanction); People v. Valentine, 182 A.D.2d 655, 583 N.Y.S.2d 168 (2d Dep't 1992)(failure to object to nondisclosure or seek sanction waived Rosario claim); People v. Cierra, 178 A.D.2d 303, 577 N.Y.S.2d 607 (1st Dep't 1991)(defense counsel never developed adequate record concerning details of statements that purportedly were memorialized but destroyed); People v. Mathews, 173 A.D.2d 565, 570 N.Y.S.2d 814 (2d Dep't 1991)(failure to object to nondisclosure of complaint report waived Rosario claim); People v. Torres, 173 A.D.2d 284, 569 N.Y.S.2d 676 (1st Dep't 1991)(failure to request sanction regarding destruction of police notes waived Rosario claim); People v. Diaz, 170 A.D.2d 395, 566 N.Y.S.2d 283 (1st Dep't 1991)(failure to object to nondisclosure of chemist's laboratory report waived Rosario claim); People v. Best, 145 A.D.2d 499, 535 N.Y.S.2d 108 (2d Dep't 1988)(court did not err in failing, sua sponte, to impose sanction for Rosario violation where defense made no objection to nondisclosure).

§ 7.18 Witness Criminal History Information

In addition to requiring disclosure of *Rosario* material, CPL §§ 240.44 and 240.45 require both the prosecution and the defense to disclose the criminal histories of their pretrial hearing and trial witnesses. At the conclusion of the direct examination of each of their pretrial hearing witnesses, the prosecution and the defense, upon request, must disclose any known prior convictions of the witnesses as well as any known pending criminal actions against the witnesses.[217] Disclosure is automatic for trial witnesses, and must be made, for prosecution witnesses, before the prosecutor's opening statement,[218] and for defense witnesses, before the defendant's direct case.[219] Section 240.45 also provides that the prosecution need not fingerprint its witnesses or otherwise request a rapsheet for its witnesses.[220]

Library References:
West's Key No. Digests, Criminal Law ⟲700(4).

§ 7.19 Protective Orders

Section 240.50 permits the prosecution, the defense or any "affected person" to move for a protective order "denying, limiting, conditioning, delaying or regulating" discovery. A court also may issue a protective order *sua sponte*.[221] A protective order may be issued for "good cause," and the statute lists a number of nonexclusive circumstances that qualify. The primary circumstance supporting issuance of an order is a "substantial" risk of physical harm, intimidation, economic reprisal, bribery or unjustified annoyance or embarrassment to any person.[222] For example, a protective order limiting disclosure of prosecution witnesses' names until just prior to their testimony was upheld in light of evidence of the defendants' past involvement in witness intimidation.[223] On the other hand, a witness's unsubstantiated apprehension about

---

217. CPL § 240.44(2) and (3). Courts have held that, until the period of adjournment expires, an "adjournment in contemplation of dismissal," see CPL §§ 170.55, 170.56, 210.46, 215.30, is deemed a pending charge, not a conviction, for purposes of the disclosure requirements of sections 240.44 and 240.45. See People v. Clark, 194 A.D.2d 868, 598 N.Y.S.2d 847 (3d Dep't 1993); People v. Benjamin, 147 Misc.2d 617, 558 N.Y.S.2d 825, 827 (N.Y.C.Crim.Ct. 1990).

218. CPL § 240.45(1)(b) and (c).

219. CPL § 240.45(2)(b) and (c). Of course, neither statute requires the defense to disclose a testifying defendant's criminal history.

220. CPL § 240.45(1).

221. CPL § 240.50(1).

222. Id.

223. See People v. Boyd, 164 A.D.2d 800, 560 N.Y.S.2d 15 (1st Dep't 1990). See also People v. Robinson, 200 A.D.2d 693, 694–95, 606 N.Y.S.2d 906 (2d Dep't 1994); People v. Boone, 194 A.D.2d 407, 599 N.Y.S.2d 540 (1st Dep't 1993); People v. Torres, 164 A.D.2d 923, 559 N.Y.S.2d 584 (2d Dep't 1990); People v. Mobley, 162 A.D.2d 305, 558 N.Y.S.2d 1 (1st Dep't 1990). A protective order may be based on a prosecutor's in camera representations concerning a defendant's history of threatening witnesses. See People v. Robinson, 200 A.D.2d 693, 606 N.Y.S.2d 908 (2d Dep't 1994); People v. Boyd, 164 A.D.2d at 802–03, 560 N.Y.S.2d at 18.

disclosing his or her identity would not justify an order permitting the redaction of the witness's identity from documents that the prosecution is required to disclose.[224] Indeed, the statute requires a "substantial" risk, because the mere possibility of a risk is present in virtually every criminal case.

Good cause for issuance of a protective order also includes a danger to the integrity of physical evidence,[225] the compromising of an ongoing investigation by, among other things, divulging the confidentiality of informants,[226] and any other factor or concern that outweighs the benefits of disclosure.[227] In addition, good cause includes the existence of a constitutional limitation on disclosure.[228] A common example of this is when disclosure would violate an individual's privilege against self-incrimination. The prosecution need not seek a protective order to support a refusal to disclose the personal residence of a police officer or a correction officer; disclosure of that information is required only upon an order of the court based on a finding of good cause.[229]

In appropriate cases, the court may receive a motion for a protective order *ex parte* and *in camera* and seal any papers in support of the motion.[230] In addition, a protective order may require that any materials disclosed be kept in the exclusive possession of the receiving attorney and not be used for any purpose other than preparation for the case.[231]

Library References:
West's Key No. Digests, Criminal Law ⊜627.8, 629.

§ 7.20 Sanctions—In General

Issues relating to sanctions for prosecutorial discovery violations are addressed in an extensive body of case law. In general, the severity of the sanction is determined by two factors: (1) the nature of the material or information that the prosecution is required to disclose; and (2) whether such material or information was belatedly disclosed or was not disclosed at all during the trial court proceedings. CPL § 240.70 lists an array of sanctions that the trial court, "during the course of discovery proceedings," may impose upon finding that a party has failed to comply with any of the provisions of Article 240. These sanctions include ordering a party to permit discovery of property, granting a continuance, issuing a protective order, precluding evidence or witness testimony, or "any other appropriate action."[232] The statute, however, provides no guidance as to which of these sanctions are appropriate in particular situations. The details regarding a court's obligations and authority to

224. See, e.g., People v. Leon, 134 Misc.2d 757, 760–61, 512 N.Y.S.2d 991, 993–94 (Westchester Co.Ct.1987).

225. Cf. People v. White, 40 N.Y.2d 797, 390 N.Y.S.2d 405, 358 N.E.2d 1031 (1976)(defense entitled to make its own scientific test of controlled substance but under supervision of court and in accordance with safeguards designed to protect against contamination or destruction of evidence).

226. The "informant's" privilege is discussed in § 7.10, supra.

227. CPL § 240.50(1).

228. Id.

229. CPL § 240.50(4).

230. See CPL § 240.90(3).

231. CPL § 240.50(2).

232. CPL § 240.70(1).

impose sanctions for discovery violations are delineated in the case law, as is the ultimate sanction that may be imposed following the trial itself—reversal of a conviction.

Library References:

West's Key No. Digests, Criminal Law ⇔627.8(6), 700(8).

§ 7.21 Sanctions—Belated Disclosure

Although the prosecution should always make a good faith effort to disclose discoverable material in a timely manner, its belated disclosure of discoverable material ordinarily will not result in a sanction more serious than a continuance, so long as the defendant may make "meaningful" use of the material.[233] As a number of appellate courts have held, an adjournment of the proceedings ordinarily will be sufficient to eliminate any prejudice to the defense arising from a delay in disclosure.[234] Indeed, even a prosecutor's failure to disclose exculpatory evidence until his summation did not, held the Court of Appeals, warrant reversal of the resulting conviction, because the trial court had interrupted the summation and permitted the defense to recall a witness, place the exculpatory evidence before the jury and address the jury as to the evidence, all before allowing the prosecutor to resume his summation.[235] On the other hand, a trial court's refusal to grant even a continuance in response to the prosecution's delayed disclosure of autopsy photographs led to a reversal of the conviction in that case,[236] as did

---

233. See, e.g., People v. Cortijo, 70 N.Y.2d 868, 870, 523 N.Y.S.2d 463, 464, 517 N.E.2d 1349 (1987); People v. Perez, 65 N.Y.2d 154, 159, 490 N.Y.S.2d 747, 750, 480 N.E.2d 361 (1985).

234. See, e.g., People v. Cunningham, 189 A.D.2d 821, 592 N.Y.S.2d 447 (2d Dep't 1993)(belated disclosure of ballistic test results); People v. Hall, 181 A.D.2d 1008, 581 N.Y.S.2d 951 (4th Dep't 1992)(defendant's spontaneous statements not disclosed upon demand); People v. Bonet, 176 A.D.2d 641, 643, 575 N.Y.S.2d 294, 295 (1st Dep't 1991)(correct arrest photo not disclosed until during trial); People v. Beam, 161 A.D.2d 1153, 556 N.Y.S.2d 181 (4th Dep't 1990)(Brady evidence not disclosed until commencement of trial); People v. Emery, 159 A.D.2d 992, 552 N.Y.S.2d 746 (4th Dep't 1990)(laboratory test results not disclosed until fifth day of trial); People v. Hess, 140 A.D.2d 895, 528 N.Y.S.2d 921 (3d Dep't 1988)(accident reconstruction report not disclosed until eve of trial); People v. Eleby, 137 A.D.2d 708, 525 N.Y.S.2d 51 (2d Dep't 1988)(ballistics report not disclosed upon demand). See generally People v. Goodell, 164 A.D.2d 321, 565 N.Y.S.2d 929 (4th Dep't 1990), aff'd 79 N.Y.2d 869, 581 N.Y.S.2d 157, 589 N.E.2d 380 (1992)(delay in disclosing allegedly exculpatory evidence until trial did not violate defendant's due process rights where defendant had meaningful opportunity to use evidence).

235. People v. Smith, 63 N.Y.2d 41, 67, 479 N.Y.S.2d 706, 718, 468 N.E.2d 879 (1984), cert. den. 469 U.S. 1227, 105 S.Ct. 1226, 84 L.Ed.2d 364 (1985). See generally People v. Cortijo, 70 N.Y.2d 868, 870, 523 N.Y.S.2d 463, 464, 517 N.E.2d 1349 (1987); People v. Brown, 67 N.Y.2d 555, 559, 505 N.Y.S.2d 574, 575, 496 N.E.2d 663 (1986), cert. den. 479 U.S. 1093, 107 S.Ct. 1307, 94 L.Ed.2d 161 (1987); People v. Turcios–Umana, 153 A.D.2d 707, 544 N.Y.S.2d 682 (2d Dep't 1989); People v. Keppler, 92 A.D.2d 1032, 461 N.Y.S.2d 513 (3d Dep't 1983); People v. Clark, 89 A.D.2d 820, 453 N.Y.S.2d 525 (4th Dep't), cert. den. 459 U.S. 1090, 103 S.Ct. 577, 74 L.Ed.2d 937 (1982).

236. People v. Zlochevsky, 196 A.D.2d 701, 603 N.Y.S.2d 433 (1st Dep't 1993). People v. Corley, 124 A.D.2d 390, 507 N.Y.S.2d 491 (3d Dep't 1986)(trial court erred in refusing to grant continuance in response to prosecution's delayed disclosure of breathalyzer documents until minutes before commencement of trial).

the prosecution's deliberate failure in another case to disclose exculpatory medical records until the eve of trial.[237]

A delay in the disclosure of *Rosario* material occasionally will engender the "substantial" prejudice[238] that warrants reversal of a conviction. For example, when the mid-trial disclosure of a witness's prior statement seriously undercut the strategy that the defense had already revealed to the jury, the delay led to a reversal of the conviction.[239] Or, a trial court's refusal to allow the defendant to recall the complainant for further cross-examination or impose any sanction after belated disclosure of a document containing an arguably inconsistent statement of the complainant warranted a reversal.[240]

Library References:
West's Key No. Digests, Criminal Law ⚖627.8(2, 6), 700(5).

§ 7.22 Sanctions—Complete Failure to Disclose

In a series of cases, the Court of Appeals has established and reaffirmed an extraordinarily severe sanction for the prosecution's complete failure to disclose *Rosario* material during the trial court proceedings. The court has held that a complete failure to disclose mandates a reversal of the conviction, without regard to whether the defendant was harmed by the failure to disclose. The court has justified this "per se" rule by emphasizing that "[t]he essence of the *Rosario* requirement, that the prosecutor supply all of a witness' statement or statements relating to his testimony, is that a judge's impartial determination as to what portions may be useful to the defense, is no substitute for the single-minded devotion of counsel for the accused."[241] The court has also rejected a good faith exception to its *per se* rule that would have excused the prosecution's failure to disclose *Rosario* material.[242] And it reaffirmed the *per se* rule in response to a prosecutor's contention that the consequences of the rule would wreak havoc on the state's criminal justice system, noting again that when *Rosario* material is not disclosed at all "there is no way, short of speculation, of determining how it might

237. People v. Baba-Ali, 179 A.D.2d 725, 578 N.Y.S.2d 633 (2d Dep't 1992).

238. See People v. Martinez, 71 N.Y.2d 937, 940, 528 N.Y.S.2d 813, 815, 524 N.E.2d 134 (1988); People v. Ranghelle, 69 N.Y.2d 56, 63, 511 N.Y.S.2d 580, 584, 503 N.E.2d 1011 (1986).

239. See People v. Goins, 73 N.Y.2d 989, 540 N.Y.S.2d 994, 538 N.E.2d 346 (1989). See also People v. Thompson, 71 N.Y.2d 918, 528 N.Y.S.2d 532, 523 N.E.2d 819 (1988); People v. Jarrells, 190 A.D.2d 120, 122–24, 597 N.Y.S.2d 305, 306 (1st Dep't 1993).

240. People v. Khadaidi, 201 A.D.2d 585, 608 N.Y.S.2d 471 (2d Dep't 1994). Cf. People v. Forrest, 78 N.Y.2d 886, 888, 573 N.Y.S.2d 458, 458, 577 N.E.2d 1050 (1991), aff'g 163 A.D.2d 213, 558 N.Y.S.2d 60 (1st Dep't 1990)(following delayed Rosario disclosure, defense counsel able to continue cross-examination of complainant and establish inconsistencies); People v. Polanco, 174 A.D.2d 468, 571 N.Y.S.2d 710 (1st Dep't 1991)(although disclosure was during trial, it was before both sides had rested and when material was still useful to defense); People v. Harris, 130 A.D.2d 939, 516 N.Y.S.2d 554 (4th Dep't 1987)(late disclosure did not impair defense counsel's cross-examination of witness).

241. People v. Perez, 65 N.Y.2d 154, 160, 490 N.Y.S.2d 747, 750, 480 N.E.2d 361 (1985).

242. People v. Ranghelle, 69 N.Y.2d 56, 63, 511 N.Y.S.2d 580, 584, 503 N.E.2d 1011 (1986).

§ 7.22   DISCOVERY   Ch. 7

have been used or how its denial to counsel might have damaged defendant's case."[243] The court has also held that the prosecution's failure to disclose prior statements of its suppression hearing witnesses requires that a new hearing be held; however, a retrial is necessary only if the court, after the new hearing, grants the motion to suppress.[244]

In a significant retraction from this line of cases, however, the Court of Appeals subsequently cut back on its *per se* rule. In a 1991 decision, the court, although reaffirming the *per se* rule when a *Rosario* violation is challenged on a direct appeal of a conviction, devised a harmless error test for a violation that is challenged in a motion to vacate a conviction brought after a defendant's direct appeals have been exhausted.[245] Noting that the statute upon which a motion to vacate a conviction on this ground must be brought—CPL § 440.10(1)(f)—requires a showing of "prejudicial" conduct on the part of the prosecutor, and emphasizing society's interest in the finality of judgments and the difficulty of retrying cases years after the direct appeals have been decided, the court held that a post-direct appeal motion to vacate a conviction that alleges a *Rosario* violation must demonstrate a "reasonable possibility" that the failure to disclose contributed to the verdict.[246] The *per se* rule still applies, however, when a *Rosario* claim is the subject of both a direct appeal and a motion to vacate.[247]

The Court of Appeals has also held that the prosecution's failure to disclose *Rosario* material relating to a prosecution witness who testified only to some, but not all, of the offenses charged against the defendant does not always require a reversal of the conviction of all of the offenses charged.[248] The court suggested, however, that in cases in which the offenses charged are "factually related" in a "meaningful way," a failure to disclose the prior statements of a witness who testified only as to some of the offenses might cause a "spillover" effect that could require reversal of the conviction of all the offenses.[249]

Unlike *Rosario* violations, a complete failure to disclose *Brady* evidence does not automatically require a reversal of a conviction. As discussed in § 7.13, supra, the Court of Appeals has adhered to the two-tier *Agurs* standard for determining whether undisclosed exculpatory evidence is material, which in turn provides the standard for determining whether the failure to disclose necessitates the reversal of a conviction. Under this approach, if the defendant specifically requested excul-

---

243. People v. Jones, 70 N.Y.2d 547, 552, 523 N.Y.S.2d 53, 56, 517 N.E.2d 865 (1987).

244. People v. Banch, 80 N.Y.2d 610, 593 N.Y.S.2d 491, 608 N.E.2d 1069 (1992).

245. People v. Jackson, 78 N.Y.2d 638, 578 N.Y.S.2d 483, 585 N.E.2d 795 (1991).

246. 78 N.Y.2d at 648–49, 578 N.Y.S. at 490.

247. 78 N.Y.2d at 649, 578 N.Y.S.2d at 490. See also People v. Novoa, 70 N.Y.2d 490, 522 N.Y.S.2d 504, 517 N.E.2d 219 (1987).

248. People v. Baghai–Kermani, 84 N.Y.2d 525, 620 N.Y.S.2d 313, 644 N.E.2d 1004 (1994).

249. 84 N.Y.2d at 533, 620 N.Y.S.2d at 317. In Baghai–Kermani, the court found no such spillover effect, because each of the charged illegal drug sale counts "involved a discrete and separate sale conducted in the presence of a single buyer-witness and each buyer-witness gave evidence that directly related only to the sales made to him or her." 84 N.Y.2d at 532, 620 N.Y.S.2d at 317.

patory evidence that was not disclosed, reversal is required if the defendant establishes a "reasonable possibility" that the nondisclosure contributed to the verdict.[250] If, however, the defendant made only a general request for exculpatory evidence, reversal is required if the defendant establishes that the undisclosed evidence "creates a reasonable doubt that did not otherwise exist."[251]

The differences in the standards established by the Court of Appeals for the prosecution's failure to disclose *Rosario* material and its failure to disclose *Brady* material are not easily reconcilable. It is difficult to understand why a failure to disclose *Rosario* material, which may not necessarily be exculpatory and frequently is inculpatory, requires automatic reversal of a conviction (at least if raised on a direct appeal), but a failure to disclose *Brady* evidence, which by definition supports the defendant's innocence, requires reversal only upon a showing of harm. Moreover, it does not seem logical that a failure to disclose *Brady* evidence that happens to be contained in a prior written or recorded statement of a prosecution witness compels an automatic reversal (if raised on direct appeal), but that a failure to disclose *Brady* evidence contained in some other form compels a reversal only upon a showing of harm. Several proposals, in fact, have been introduced in the Legislature to rectify this seeming inconsistency.[252]

Library References:

West's Key No. Digests, Criminal Law ⚖︎629.5, 700(2)–700(8), 919(1), 998(6.1), 1166(10.10).

§ 7.23 Sanctions—Loss or Destruction of Discoverable Material

In *People v. Kelly*,[253] the Court of Appeals held that the prosecution is obligated to exercise diligence and care in preserving discoverable evidence, and its failure to do so compels the trial court to impose a sanction that will eliminate the prejudice to the defendant.[254] In developing an appropriate sanction, the trial court must consider the proof available at trial, the significance of the lost or destroyed evidence and whether the loss or destruction was intentional or inadvertent.[255] The trial court's "overriding" consideration, however, must be curing the

---

250. People v. Vilardi, 76 N.Y.2d at 77, 556 N.Y.S.2d at 523.

251. 76 N.Y.2d at 73, 556 N.Y.S.2d at 523 (citing United States v. Agurs, 427 U.S. 97, 112, 96 S.Ct. 2392, 2401, 49 L.Ed.2d 342 (1976)).

252. See, e.g., S.7574; S.4791/A.6048; S.2791 (all introduced in 1993–94 Legislative Session).

253. 62 N.Y.2d 516, 478 N.Y.S.2d 834, 467 N.E.2d 498 (1984).

254. See also People v. Martinez, 71 N.Y.2d 937, 940, 528 N.Y.S.2d 813, 815, 524 N.E.2d 134 (1988); People v. Boyne, 174 A.D.2d 103, 579 N.Y.S.2d 338 (1st Dep't 1992). Cf. California v. Trombetta, 467 U.S. 479, 104 S.Ct. 2528, 81 L.Ed.2d 413 (1984)(due process not violated by destruction of evidence unless defendant demonstrates that evidence was exculpatory and that he or she would be unable to obtain comparable evidence by other reasonably available means); Arizona v. Youngblood, 488 U.S. 51, 109 S.Ct. 333, 102 L.Ed.2d 281 (1988)(due process not violated by destruction of evidence that potentially might have been exculpatory unless defendant demonstrates government's bad faith in destroying evidence).

255. People v. Haupt, 71 N.Y.2d 929, 528 N.Y.S.2d 808, 524 N.E.2d 129 (1988).

§ 7.23   DISCOVERY   Ch. 7

harm.[256] Although the nature of the sanction is left to the sound discretion of the trial court, the "drastic" remedy of dismissal of the charges may not be invoked if less severe measures will rectify the prejudice caused by the loss of the evidence.[257] The *Kelly* decision cited several examples of the types of sanctions that trial courts have imposed in response to the loss or destruction of discoverable material:[258] reducing a conviction of criminal sale of a controlled substance to criminal possession where tape recordings of an alleged drug sale were erased, thereby hindering the defendant's agency defense;[259] precluding a witness from testifying where minutes of the witness's prior testimony were lost;[260] ordering a reconstruction hearing where minutes of prior testimony were lost;[261] and directing the disclosure of all grand jury testimony concerning a forcible entry, and reserving the right to impose additional sanctions, including an adverse inference instruction, where the failure to preserve a door allegedly undermined a defendant's justification defense.[262]

The sanction for the loss or destruction of *Rosario* material, therefore, will almost always be considerably less severe than the sanction for the failure to disclose existing *Rosario* material. For example, the Court of Appeals has held that a trial court properly exercised its discretion by providing an adverse inference instruction to the jury as a sanction for the loss of *Rosario* material, rather than precluding the testimony of the prosecution's primary witness, where the lost statement apparently was of little relevance and the prosecution was unable to locate the statement despite the exercise of due diligence.[263] However, if the material was not destroyed in bad faith and its destruction has resulted in no prejudice to the defense, then no sanction is required. Thus, destruction of a piece of paper on which the arresting officer noted the defendant's name and address and the time and place of the arrest required no sanction because the defendant was unable to demonstrate any harm.[264]

The burden of establishing that *Rosario* material was lost or destroyed, which will avoid the *per se* reversal rule for the nondisclosure of existing *Rosario* material, is on the prosecution. That burden is not satisfied merely upon a showing that the report is absent from the prosecutor's file and that the prosecutor could not locate it during a brief

---

256. People v. Kelly, 62 N.Y.2d at 520, 478 N.Y.S.2d at 836.

257. 62 N.Y.2d at 521, 478 N.Y.S.2d at 837. See also People v. Wallace, 76 N.Y.2d 953, 563 N.Y.S.2d 722, 565 N.E.2d 471 (1990).

258. 62 N.Y.2d at 521, 478 N.Y.S.2d at 836–37.

259. See People v. Saddy, 84 A.D.2d 175, 445 N.Y.S.2d 601 (2d Dep't 1981).

260. See People v. Lunney, 84 Misc.2d 1090, 378 N.Y.S.2d 559 (Sup.Ct., N.Y. County, 1975).

261. See People v. Hicks, 85 Misc.2d 649, 381 N.Y.S.2d 794 (N.Y.C.Crim.Ct. 1976).

262. See People v. Emmons, 99 Misc.2d 941, 417 N.Y.S.2d 432 (Monroe Co.Ct.1979).

263. People v. Martinez, 71 N.Y.2d 937, 528 N.Y.S.2d 813, 524 N.E.2d 134 (1988).

264. People v. Rivera, 185 A.D.2d 152, 586 N.Y.S.2d 114 (1st Dep't 1992). See also People v. McIntosh, 184 A.D.2d 662, 587 N.Y.S.2d 165 (2d Dep't 1992)(destruction of arresting officer's application for commendation was not deliberate and did not prejudice defendant); People v. Hyde, 172 A.D.2d 305, 568 N.Y.S.2d 388 (1st Dep't 1991)(destruction of handwritten copy of complaint report was routine and defense counsel able to adequately cross-examine on matter).

recess.[265] In addition, when the prosecution claims that *Rosario* material has been lost or destroyed, the trial court must make an appropriate inquiry to attempt to determine the contents of the material and the circumstances of its loss or destruction.[266] The defendant, however, has the burden of establishing prejudice resulting from the loss or destruction of the material.[267]

It should be noted that the defense's actions or omissions during the trial court proceedings may waive its right to a sanction or to a more severe sanction than the one that the trial court chooses to impose. For example, a defense request for a mistrial (which was denied) or preclusion of any testimony as to the "reconstruction" of a destroyed police memo book (which was granted) barred the defense from arguing on appeal that a stricter sanction, such as an adverse inference instruction, would have been more appropriate.[268] And the inadvertent destruction of a "rape kit" did not necessitate a sanction where the defense knew of its existence some eight months before it was destroyed yet never sought its production or expressed an interest in performing any independent tests.[269]

The loss or destruction of discoverable material, whether *Rosario* or otherwise, may occasionally require dismissal of the charges or a reversal of the conviction if exceptional prejudice results therefrom. In one case, a conviction was reversed due to the deliberate, although not necessarily bad faith, destruction of the audiotape of a critical conversation between an undercover officer and one of the defendants; reversal was required even though the trial court had precluded the testimony of two officers who had monitored the conversation as to what they had heard.[270] In another case, a conviction was reversed because the police department had destroyed an envelope on which the undercover officer, who was unable to identify the defendant at trial, had written information relating to the arrest.[271] And in another case, the "blatantly careless" manner in which the police unsuccessfully attempted to preserve a television set compelled the trial court to dismiss the charges because the defense would have been greatly disadvantaged in attempting to demonstrate that the repairs for which the defendant billed the owners were actually done.[272] In addition, a court's failure to impose any sanction at all on the prosecution when the defense is prejudiced by even an

---

265. People v. Banch, 80 N.Y.2d 610, 620–21, 593 N.Y.S.2d 491, 497, 608 N.E.2d 1069 (1992).

266. Id.

267. People v. Albelo, 166 A.D.2d 313, 560 N.Y.S.2d 1014 (1st Dep't 1990).

268. People v. Spivey, 81 N.Y.2d 356, 599 N.Y.S.2d 477, 615 N.E.2d 961 (1993). See also People v. Ciola, 136 A.D.2d 557, 523 N.Y.S.2d 553 (2d Dep't 1988)(defense counsel expressly declined to seek adjournment and instead agreed to review material during recess in trial). Cf. People v. Roberts, 178 A.D.2d 622, 577 N.Y.S.2d 672 (2d Dep't 1991)(trial court did not abuse its discretion in denying defendant's request for a mistrial or a dismissal of the indictment as a sanction for destruction of notes taken during police interview with victim; dismissal too drastic a remedy, and mistrial would be futile gesture since notes would not be available at any retrial).

269. People v. Allgood, 70 N.Y.2d 812, 523 N.Y.S.2d 431, 517 N.E.2d 1316 (1987).

270. People v. Torres, 190 A.D.2d 52, 597 N.Y.S.2d 492 (3d Dep't 1993).

271. People v. Watkins, 189 A.D.2d 623, 592 N.Y.S.2d 347 (1st Dep't 1993).

272. People v. Churba, 76 Misc.2d 1028, 353 N.Y.S.2d 130 (N.Y.C.Crim.Ct.1974).

inadvertent destruction of evidence may lead to reversal of the conviction.[273]

Library References:

West's Key No. Digests, Criminal Law ⬉700(9).

§ 7.24 Sanctions—Against the Defense

Although at one time serious questions existed about the legality of imposing sanctions on the defendant for failure to comply with discovery requirements, these concerns in large part have been laid to rest by several Supreme Court decisions. In one case, the trial court had precluded the testimony of two defense witnesses because of the defense counsel's willful failure to comply with a state rule requiring pretrial disclosure of the identity of defense witnesses upon the prosecution's request. The Supreme Court held that, because the failure to disclose was motivated by a willful attempt to gain a tactical advantage, the defendant's Sixth Amendment right to present material evidence was not violated by the preclusion of the defense witness's testimony, even though less drastic sanctions were available.[274] And in a second case, a defendant charged with rape failed to comply with a statutory requirement to provide notice of his intent to present evidence of the complainant's past sexual conduct. The court held that the preclusion of that evidence as a sanction for the failure to comply with the statute did not violate the defendant's rights to confrontation and to present a defense.[275]

In addition, the Court of Appeals has held that a defendant who seeks to offer psychiatric evidence but refuses to submit to a mental examination by a psychiatrist designated by the prosecution may be precluded from introducing expert testimony as to his or her mental state.[276]

Thus, trial courts may make use of the various sanctions specified in section 240.70 for discovery violations by the defense as well as for those by the prosecution. Yet, in selecting an appropriate sanction for a defense discovery violation, courts should be mindful of the defendant's potentially affected constitutional rights, including the rights to confrontation and compulsory process and the right to present a defense. The strictest sanctions, therefore, such as preclusion of testimony or other evidence in support of a defense, should be limited to cases in which the

---

273. See People v. Scalzo, 176 A.D.2d 363, 574 N.Y.S.2d 782 (2d Dep't 1991), app. withdrawn 79 N.Y.2d 1045, 584 N.Y.S.2d 1012, 596 N.E.2d 410 (1992) (trial court's failure to impose any sanction in vehicular homicide case in response to destruction of defendant's blood sample warranted reversal of conviction).

274. Taylor v. Illinois, 484 U.S. 400, 108 S.Ct. 646, 98 L.Ed.2d 798 (1988). See also Escalera v. Coombe, 852 F.2d 45 (2d Cir.1988)(defendant's right to compulsory process not violated by trial court's preclusion of alibi witness's testimony where defense counsel, motivated by desire to gain tactical advantage, willfully failed to list that witness in notice of alibi).

275. Michigan v. Lucas, 500 U.S. 145, 111 S.Ct. 1743, 114 L.Ed.2d 205 (1991).

276. See People v. Segal, 54 N.Y.2d 58, 444 N.Y.S.2d 588, 429 N.E.2d 107 (1981); Lee v. County Court of Erie County, 27 N.Y.2d 432, 318 N.Y.S.2d 705, 267 N.E.2d 452 (1971), cert. den. 404 U.S. 823, 92 S.Ct. 46, 30 L.Ed.2d 50 (1971).

discovery violation was willful and motivated by a desire to obtain a tactical advantage.

Library References:

West's Key No. Digests, Criminal Law ⟐627.8(6), 629.5, 662.4.

§ 7.25 Pretrial Notices of Defenses—In General

The CPL requires that the defendant, prior to trial, provide the prosecution with specified information whenever he or she intends to allege certain defenses at trial.[277] The rationale for these notice requirements is to avoid unfair surprise to the prosecution, which would usually be prejudiced if unable to investigate the defense and develop its response thereto until the trial itself. This in turn would cause substantial disruption and delay of trials.

Library References:

West's Key No. Digests, Criminal Law ⟐629.

§ 7.26 Pretrial Notice of Defenses—Psychiatric Evidence

CPL § 250.10 requires the defendant to provide pretrial notice of intent to offer "psychiatric" evidence. Psychiatric evidence includes evidence of mental disease or defect that the defendant intends to offer in support of any statutory or common law defense, including the affirmative defense of lack of responsibility by reason of mental disease or defect and the affirmative defense of extreme emotional disturbance.[278] The statute has been interpreted as applying not only to the testimony of psychiatrists and psychologists but also to the testimony of certified social workers.[279]

Within 30 days of arraignment of an indictment,[280] the defendant must serve on the prosecution (and file with the court) written notice of his or her intent to offer psychiatric evidence. The statute authorizes the court in the interest of justice to permit late notice—as late as the close of the evidence at trial—if the defendant can demonstrate good

---

277. CPL Article 250.

278. CPL § 250.10(1). The affirmative defense of extreme emotional disturbance is set forth in sections 125.25(1)(a) and 125.27(2)(a) of the Penal Law. The affirmative defense of lack of responsibility by reason of mental disease or defect is set forth in section 40.15 of the Penal Law. Other defenses which may involve evidence of mental disease or defect include justification, entrapment and diminished capacity.

279. See People v. Scala, 128 Misc.2d 831, 491 N.Y.S.2d 555 (Sup.Ct., N.Y. County, 1985).

280. The statute requires service of notice within 30 days of arraignment on "the indictment," CPL § 250.10(2), and thus makes no reference to the time of service in a nonfelony case, even though it is not unheard of, albeit rare, for a defendant to offer evidence of mental disease or defect in such a case. Although it is possible that the statute's notice requirement is not intended to apply in nonfelony cases, the defense runs a serious risk in making that assumption and not providing notice. The more prudent course of action in a nonfelony case in which the defendant expects to offer this evidence is to seek a ruling from the local criminal court shortly after arraignment as to whether notice is required.

§ 7.26   DISCOVERY   Ch. 7

cause for doing so. Psychiatric evidence is inadmissible at trial unless the defendant serves this notice.[281]

Upon receiving notice, the prosecution may apply to the court, with notice to the defendant, for an order directing that the defendant be examined by a psychiatrist or licensed psychologist designated by the prosecution. The prosecutor and the defense attorney, who must be notified of the time and place of the examination, may attend the examination, although only to observe and not to take an active role.[282] The examining psychiatrist or psychologist must promptly prepare a written report containing his or her findings and evaluation, and the report must be made available to the prosecutor and the defense attorney. Whether a transcript or recording of the examination is required is left to the discretion of the trial court,[283] but if one is made, it must be provided to both parties prior to trial.[284]

If the defendant willfully refuses to cooperate fully in an examination ordered by the court, the court may preclude the trial testimony of the defendant's own expert witness on the question of the defendant's mental disease or defect.[285] Competent evidence offered by the defendant, other than expert testimony, on the question of his or her mental disease or defect is admissible even if the defendant refused to cooperate in the court-ordered examination.[286] In that situation, however, the court must advise the jury of the defendant's failure to cooperate and instruct that such failure may be considered by the jury in evaluating the defendant's affirmative defense.[287]

The defendant's failure to provide timely notice under this provision may, in some cases, substantially prejudice the prosecution's ability to challenge the defendant's evidence. For example, if the defendant was examined by his or her own expert shortly after the events giving rise to the criminal action but the prosecution's expert, because of untimely notice, is unable to examine the defendant until long after that time, preclusion of the defendant's evidence may be appropriate, particularly if the delay in providing notice was designed to gain a tactical advantage. On the other hand, absent bad faith or actual prejudice to the prosecution, courts should strongly consider exercising their considerable discretion to permit late notice in the interest of justice.[288]

281. CPL § 250.10(2).
282. CPL § 250.10(3).
283. See People v. Santana, 80 N.Y.2d 92, 98–99, 587 N.Y.S.2d 570, 572–73, 600 N.E.2d 201 (1992).
284. CPL § 250.10(4).
285. CPL § 250.10(5).
286. Id.
287. Id.
288. See CPL § 250.10(2). See People v. Oakes, 168 A.D.2d 893, 565 N.Y.S.2d 648 (4th Dep't 1990)(trial court's refusal to permit late notice of intent to proffer psychiatric evidence was abuse of discretion where failure to provide timely notice was result of defendant's mistaken position that evidence was not subject to notice requirement and there was no showing that any prejudice to prosecution could not have been cured by short adjournment). Cf. People v. Mai, 175 A.D.2d 692, 573 N.Y.S.2d 90 (1st Dep't 1991)(trial court did not abuse discretion in precluding psychiatric evidence where defendant inexcusably failed to comply with notice requirement even though evidence was in counsel's possession over two months prior to trial and prosecution would have been prejudiced by delay that admission of evidence would have caused in trial).

A separate statute governs notice of intent to offer psychiatric evidence in a first

Library References:

West's Key No. Digests, Criminal Law ⚖=629(9.5, 11).

§ 7.27 Pretrial Notices of Defenses—Alibi

CPL § 250.20 permits the prosecution, within 20 days of arraignment, to serve on the defendant (and file with the court) a demand that the defendant file a notice of alibi with the court specifying the details of any defense that he or she was elsewhere at the time of the alleged crime.[289] If the defendant intends to assert such a defense, he or she must serve the notice of alibi on the prosecution (and file the notice with the court) within eight days of receiving the demand. The notice must specify the place or places that the defendant claims to have been at the time of the alleged crime, as well as the name and residential and business addresses of each alibi witness that the defendant intends to call as a witness.[290]

Within a "reasonable" time of receiving the defendant's notice of alibi, but no later than ten days before trial, the prosecution must serve on the defendant (and file with the court) a list of any witnesses that the prosecution will call at trial to rebut the defendant's claim of being elsewhere at the time of the alleged crime. The list must provide the same information as the defendant's alibi notice—i.e., the name and residential and business addresses of each witness.[291] A prosecution witness who will testify that the defendant was at the crime scene need not be included in the prosecution's list.[292]

For good cause shown, the court may extend the period for service of the defendant's notice of alibi or service of the prosecution's list of rebuttal witnesses.[293] The statute provides no authorization, however, for the court to extend the time period for service of the prosecution's demand for a notice of alibi.

If the defendant seeks to call at trial an alibi witness without previously having served a demanded notice of alibi or without having identified the alibi witness in a notice that was served, the court may

degree murder case. See CPL § 400.27(13). The provision applies to psychiatric evidence offered in connection with a mitigating factor at the sentencing phase of such a case or in connection with a mental retardation hearing. The notice provisions are similar to those of section 250.10, but with some important differences, including: the party that intends to offer psychiatric evidence must provide notice, and must do so "within a reasonable time prior to trial"; the notice must specify the witness, nature and type of psychiatric evidence sought to be introduced; the court may not preclude admission of the evidence for failure to serve timely notice, although it may impose a reasonable monetary sanction on the offending counsel; the court may not preclude admission of the defendant's psychiatric evidence for the defendant's failure to comply fully with an examination by the prosecution's expert, although it must (if the prosecution requests) instruct the jury on the defendants failure to cooperate; and the prosecution's expert's examination of the defendant must be transcribed and disclosed.

289. CPL § 250.20(1). Prosecutors frequently serve the demand at arraignment, to eliminate any risk that they may miss the statutory deadline for service.

290. Id.

291. CPL § 250.20(2).

292. Id.

293. CPL § 250.20(1) and (2).

§ 7.27

preclude any alibi aspects of the witness's testimony.[294] Similarly, if the prosecution seeks to call at trial an alibi rebuttal witness without having served an alibi rebuttal list or without having identified the witness in a list that was served, the court may preclude the witness.[295] In either situation, however, if the court in its discretion decides to permit the testimony of a previously nondisclosed alibi witness or alibi rebuttal witness, it must grant the opposing party an adjournment of up to three days.[296]

Again, the primary purpose of this statute is to avoid unfair surprise to the prosecution and the burdensome delay that inevitably would result if the prosecution had to wait until the presentation of the defense case at trial before it could investigate the defendant's alibi defense. Thus, the defendant must offer a reasonable explanation for the court to overlook the requirements of the statute, particularly when the defense first discloses its intention to call an alibi witness on the eve of, or even during, the trial.[297] Of course, if the defendant did not learn of the existence of an alibi witness until an advanced stage in the proceedings, that generally should be a valid explanation. In that regard, it should be noted that the statute imposes a continuing duty on both parties to disclose promptly the names and addresses of witnesses who come to their attention after a notice of alibi or an alibi rebuttal witness list has been served.[298]

One court has held that, when it is "arguable" that a witness not specified in a notice of alibi is not an alibi witness, the trial court should not preclude the witness's testimony, even though the "better practice" is to include such a witness in the notice.[299] On the other hand, if the failure to provide timely notice was motivated by a desire to obtain a tactical advantage,[300] or if the prosecution's ability to locate witnesses to refute the alibi will be unduly hampered,[301] a trial court has broad discretion to deny an application for late service.[302]

---

294. CPL § 250.20(3).
295. CPL § 250.20(4).
296. CPL § 250.20(3) and (4).
297. See, e.g., People v. Toro, 198 A.D.2d 532, 604 N.Y.S.2d 189 (2d Dep't 1993); People v. Davis, 193 A.D.2d 885, 597 N.Y.S.2d 780 (3d Dep't 1993); People v. Caputo, 175 A.D.2d 290, 572 N.Y.S.2d 922 (2d Dep't 1991); People v. Marshall, 170 A.D.2d 463, 565 N.Y.S.2d 551 (2d Dep't 1991); People v. Peralta, 127 A.D.2d 803, 512 N.Y.S.2d 201 (2d Dep't 1987). Cf. People v. Peterson, 96 A.D.2d 871, 872, 465 N.Y.S.2d 743, 745 (2d Dep't 1983)(even though defendant failed to provide any explanation for failure to serve notice of alibi until two weeks before tentative scheduling of trial, preclusion of alibi witnesses was not warranted given that prosecution was not unduly prejudiced).
298. CPL § 250.20(5).

299. People v. Cuevas, 67 A.D.2d 219, 226, 414 N.Y.S.2d 520, 525 (1st Dep't 1979)(witness not included in notice of alibi would have testified that defendant was elsewhere 15 minutes after alleged crime).
300. Cf. People v. Rosado, 153 Misc.2d 477, 583 N.Y.S.2d 130 (Sup.Ct., Bronx County, 1992)(late notice permitted where no suggestion that defense acted in bad faith).
301. See, e.g., People v. Caputo, 175 A.D.2d at 290, 572 N.Y.S.2d at 922.
302. Cf. People v. Gonzalez, 201 A.D.2d 667, 609 N.Y.S.2d 824 (2d Dep't 1994)(trial court's refusal to allow defendant to substitute an alibi witness on his list after the court had already allowed him to present three alibi witnesses for whom late notice was served was not error).

Although a trial court may preclude the testimony of a defendant's alibi witnesses for failure to comply with the statute's notice requirements, one appellate court has held that a defendant may not be barred from testifying that, at the time of the alleged crime, he was with certain persons, even though the defendant never identified those persons in a notice of alibi.[303] In addition, another appellate court has held that a prosecutor may not comment on a defendant's failure to corroborate an alibi defense where the trial court had excluded alibi testimony because of a failure to comply with statutory notice requirements.[304] A prosecutor may, however, cross-examine an alibi witness with regard to the witness's failure to come forward before the trial with the substance of the witness's exculpatory testimony.[305]

The question of whether a defendant who takes the stand and testifies that he or she was elsewhere at the time of the alleged crime qualifies as an alibi witness, and thus should be included in a notice of alibi, apparently has been addressed in only a single reported decision. In that case, the court ruled that CPL § 250.20 does require that a defendant who testifies to being elsewhere at the time of the alleged crime be included in a notice of alibi. The court held, however, that if the failure to list the defendant was not willful and not designed to obtain a tactical advantage or conceal a plan to present fabricated testimony, the defendant, who has a general constitutional right to testify, should not be precluded from testifying.[306]

The Supreme Court has rejected a constitutional challenge to statutorily mandated pretrial disclosure of an alibi defense. In *Williams v. Florida*,[307] the court held that requiring such disclosure does not violate a defendant's privilege against self-incrimination, stating that "[n]othing in the Fifth Amendment privilege entitles a defendant as a matter of constitutional right to await the end of the State's case before announcing the nature of his defense."[308] The court subsequently held, however, that a statute mandating pretrial disclosure of an alibi defense must (as does section 250.20) require reciprocal disclosure by the prosecution of the names and addresses of its alibi rebuttal witnesses.[309]

Library References:

West's Key No. Digests, Criminal Law ⟸629(9), 629.5(6).

§ 7.28 Pretrial Notice of Defenses—Computer-Related Offenses

The final type of pretrial notice of a defense, added to the CPL in 1986, arises in cases involving computer-related offenses set forth in

---

303. People v. Cuevas, 67 A.D.2d 219, 414 N.Y.S.2d 520 (1st Dep't 1979).

304. See People v. Peterson, 96 A.D.2d 871, 465 N.Y.S.2d 743 (2d Dep't 1983).

305. See People v. Williams, 51 N.Y.2d 803, 433 N.Y.S.2d 94, 412 N.E.2d 1320 (1980).

306. People v. Rosado, 153 Misc.2d 477, 583 N.Y.S.2d 130 (Sup.Ct., Bronx County, 1992).

307. 399 U.S. 78, 90 S.Ct. 1893, 26 L.Ed.2d 446 (1970).

308. 399 U.S. at 85, 90 S.Ct. at 1898.

309. Wardius v. Oregon, 412 U.S. 470, 93 S.Ct. 2208, 37 L.Ed.2d 82 (1973).

§ 7.28 DISCOVERY Ch. 7

Article 156 of the Penal Law. These offenses include unauthorized use of a computer,[310] computer trespass,[311] computer tampering[312] and unlawful duplication of computer-related material.[313] Article 156 creates various defenses to these crimes. These defenses arise when the defendant had reasonable grounds to believe that he or she had authorization to use the computer or to alter, destroy or duplicate the computer related material.[314] Whenever the defendant seeks to invoke one of these defenses, CPL § 250.30 requires that he or she serve written notice of such intent, including specification of the particular defense and the basis for it. The notice must be served within 45 days after arraignment (and no later than 20 days before commencement of trial), although the court may permit late service for good cause shown.[315] If the defendant fails to provide notice, the court may preclude any evidence in support of the defense; if the court chooses to permit such evidence despite a lack of notice, it must grant the prosecution's application for an adjournment.[316]

The statute's lack of a reciprocal disclosure requirement compelling the prosecution to provide the defendant with notice of the evidence it intends to offer to rebut the defense may render it unconstitutional. In *Wardius v. Oregon*,[317] the Supreme Court invalidated a state statute that required pretrial disclosure of the basis for, and the evidence in support of, an alibi defense, because the statute did not also require pretrial disclosure of the evidence with which the prosecution intended to rebut the defendant's alibi. The comparable shortcoming in section 250.30 may well make it vulnerable to constitutional challenge.[318]

Library References:
West's Key No. Digests, Criminal Law ⚖️629.

§ 7.29 Prosecution's Notice of Intent to Seek Death Penalty

In cases in which the defendant has been indicted for murder in the first degree,[319] conviction of which carries the potential for imposition of the death penalty, the prosecution, if it intends to seek the death penalty, must provide notice expressing that intention. The death penalty may not be imposed if this notice is not filed.[320] Written notice must be served on the defendant and filed with the court within 120 days of the arraignment on the indictment, although for good cause shown the court may extend this period.[321] When such notice is filed, the defendant is entitled to an additional 60 days to file new pretrial

310. P.L. § 156.05.
311. P.L. § 156.10.
312. P.L. §§ 156.20, 156.25, 156.26 and 156.27.
313. P.L. § 156.30.
314. P.L. § 156.50.
315. CPL § 250.30(1).
316. CPL § 250.30(3).
317. 412 U.S. 470, 93 S.Ct. 2208, 37 L.Ed.2d 82.
318. See Preiser, "Practice Commentary" to CPL § 250.30, McKinney's Cons. Laws of New York, Book 11A, at 345 (1993).
319. See P.L. § 125.27.
320. CPL § 250.40(1).
321. CPL § 250.40(2).

motions or to supplement pending motions.[322] The prosecution may withdraw its notice of intent to seek the death penalty at any time; if notice is withdrawn, it may not be re-filed.[323]

Library References:
West's Key No. Digests, Criminal Law ⇐1208.1(6); Homicide ⇐358(1).

§ 7.30 Discovery of Privileged and Confidential Material

A third party (or occasionally a party in the litigation) may object to disclosure of information in its possession on the ground that it is confidential and protected from disclosure by a legal privilege. Included among the types of information that is protected by a privilege are: psychiatric records;[324] certain law enforcement personnel records;[325] sealed court records;[326] medical records;[327] social worker records;[328] substance abuse treatment records;[329] information that a reporter obtains in the course of news gathering;[330] information contained in the state register of child abuse and maltreatment;[331] records of a rape crisis counselor;[332] and education records.[333]

Unlike other types of proceedings, in a criminal case a defendant's constitutional rights may supersede any privilege that otherwise would protect against the disclosure of confidential material and information. These rights include not only a defendant's right to receive exculpatory evidence,[334] but also the right to information that is helpful and relevant to preparation of the defense.[335] Thus, as the Court of Appeals has recognized, a privilege must yield to the "overriding consideration of avoiding the risk of convicting the innocent."[336]

Notwithstanding these constitutional rights, a defendant may not obtain access to privileged information simply for the asking. Indeed, if highly personal and confidential information concerning prosecution witnesses were so readily available to criminal defendants, many people would be unwilling to cooperate in criminal prosecutions. In *People v.*

322. CPL § 250.40(3).
323. CPL § 250.40(4).
324. Mental Hygiene Law § 33.13(c).
325. Civil Rights Law § 50–a.
326. See, e.g., CPL § 160.50 (court records in criminal actions that terminate favorably to the accused); CPL § 160.55 (law enforcement records in criminal actions that result in conviction of a noncriminal offense); CPL § 720.25 (court records in youthful offender adjudications); CPL § 725.15 (court records in cases removed from Criminal Court to Family Court); Family Court Act § 166 (Family Court records).
327. CPLR § 4504.
328. CPLR § 4508.
329. 42 U.S.C.A. § 290dd–2.
330. Civil Rights Law § 79–h.
331. New York Soc. Serv. Law §§ 422 (12), 424–a.
332. CPLR § 4510.
333. 20 U.S.C.A. § 1232g(b)(2)(B).
334. See Brady v. Maryland, 373 U.S. 83, 83 S.Ct. 1194, 10 L.Ed.2d 215 (1963); People v. Vilardi, 76 N.Y.2d 67, 556 N.Y.S.2d 518, 555 N.E.2d 915 (1990). See §§ 7.12–7.14, supra.
335. See Pennsylvania v. Ritchie, 480 U.S. 39, 57, 107 S.Ct. 989, 1001, 94 L.Ed.2d 40 (1987); Roviaro v. United States, 353 U.S. 53, 77 S.Ct. 623, 1 L.Ed.2d 639 (1957).
336. People v. Goggins, 34 N.Y.2d 163, 169, 356 N.Y.S.2d 571, 313 N.E.2d 41, cert. den. 419 U.S. 1012, 95 S.Ct. 332, 42 L.Ed.2d 286 (1974).

§ 7.30

Gissendanner,[337] a case involving a defendant's efforts to subpoena the personnel files of two police officers who were to testify against her at trial, the court established a standard for determining a defendant's access to privileged information that has been generally applied in cases involving other types of privileges: *i.e.*, the defendant must demonstrate some factual predicate that makes it reasonably likely that the information sought contains relevant and exculpatory material.[338] Because the defendant in that case had offered nothing in support of her request for the records suggesting why they might yield such material—"nothing better than conjecture" was presented to the trial court—the Court of Appeals held that the trial court had acted well within its discretion in denying disclosure.[339] Since *Gissendanner*, a number of courts have remarked on the difficulty that most defendants, who will not know precisely what is contained in a privileged document, will have in establishing a reasonable likelihood that the document contains relevant and exculpatory material. Thus, these courts, in liberally construing the *Gissendanner* standard, have ordered that privileged documents sought by the defendant be provided initially to the court for an *in camera* review. Only if the court then determines that the documents contain relevant and exculpatory information will they then be disclosed to the defense.[340]

In reviewing claims for access to privileged documents, the courts have weighed the competing interests in a variety of situations. A significant number of cases have addressed issues relating to the defendant's right of access to a prosecution witness's psychiatric records. Several appellate courts, upon reviewing the psychiatric records in question, have upheld the trial courts' exercise of discretion in denying access to the records, finding that the records raised no serious questions about the veracity of the witness's testimony.[341] Other courts have upheld the trial court's denial of unrestricted access to psychiatric records because the defendant had ample opportunity to cross-examine the witnesses regarding their psychiatric histories.[342] Appellate courts

---

337. 48 N.Y.2d 543, 423 N.Y.S.2d 893, 399 N.E.2d 924 (1979).

338. 48 N.Y.2d at 550, 423 N.Y.S.2d at 897.

339. Id.

340. See, e.g., People v. Herrera, 131 Misc.2d 96, 499 N.Y.S.2d 311 (Sup.Ct., Queens County, 1985), aff'd 135 A.D.2d 830, 522 N.Y.S.2d 934 (2d Dep't 1987); People v. Morales, 97 Misc.2d 733, 412 N.Y.S.2d 310 (N.Y.C.Crim.Ct.1979); see also Cox v. New York City Hous. Auth., 105 A.D.2d 663, 482 N.Y.S.2d 5 (1st Dep't 1984). This two-step procedure, in fact, has been codified with respect to two categories of privileged materials. See CPL § 60.76 (records of rape crisis counselors); Civil Rights Law § 50–a (personnel records of police officers, firefighters and correction officers).

341. See, e.g., People v. Murphy, 188 A.D.2d 742, 591 N.Y.S.2d 860 (3d Dep't 1992)(records not probative of rape victim's veracity or any tendency to falsely report sex crimes); People v. Serrando, 184 A.D.2d 1094, 583 N.Y.S.2d 245 (1st Dep't 1992)(nothing in records suggested that robbery complainant suffered at the relevant time periods from any impairment of perception or memory, or any psychotic delusions); People v. Graham, 117 A.D.2d 832, 498 N.Y.S.2d 730 (3d Dep't 1986)(nothing in records suggested that rape victim suffered from hallucinations or fantasies, or that she had ever made false claims about sexual attacks).

342. People v. Brooks, 199 A.D.2d 275, 604 N.Y.S.2d 219 (2d Dep't 1993); People v. Serrando, 184 N.Y.2d at 1095, 583 N.Y.S.2d at 246; People v. Arnold, 177 A.D.2d 633, 576 N.Y.S.2d 339 (2d Dep't 1991). Cf. Peo-

have made clear, however, that when the defendant demonstrates a reasonable likelihood that psychiatric records contain material bearing on the reliability and accuracy of a witness's testimony, the trial court must conduct an *in camera* review of the records, and if it is then apparent that the records raise serious questions about the witness's judgment and perception, then the records must be disclosed to the defendant.[343] Another category of privileged materials that has generated extensive litigation is police and correction officer personnel files. The courts have emphasized that a general request for access to such files that fails to advance any information suggesting that probative evidence would be revealed will not justify production of the files even for an *in camera* review by the trial court.[344] A few decisions, however, provide examples of the types of showings that will justify a trial court's ordering the production of files for its own review.[345]

Although the "shield law" provides an absolute privilege with respect to information that a news reporter obtains in confidence,[346] it is likely that this absolute privilege would not protect against disclosure to a defendant who made a credible showing that the reporter was in possession of information that was exculpatory. Indeed, one trial court has applied the same three-pronged standard in determining whether to order a news reporter to disclose confidential information as is applied with regard to nonconfidential information[347]—*i.e.*, the defendant must make a clear and specific showing that the information is: (1) highly relevant and material; (2) critical or necessary to the defense; and (3) not obtainable from other sources.[348]

ple v. Bugayong, 182 A.D.2d 450, 582 N.Y.S.2d 175 (1st Dep't 1992)(court erred in refusing to disclose additional portions of witness's medical records, which contained information that "arguably could have provided some assistance to the defense").

343. See People v. Knowell, 127 A.D.2d 794, 512 N.Y.S.2d 190 (2d Dep't 1987)(court erred in refusing to order production of witness's psychiatric records for in camera review upon defendant's showing that witness had lengthy psychiatric history, had been confined to mental hospitals on several occasions and had been diagnosed as paranoiac); People v. Rivera, 138 A.D.2d 169, 530 N.Y.S.2d 802 (1st Dep't 1988)(court erred in failing to order disclosure of deceased's psychiatric records to defendant, who had asserted justification defense, where records revealed a 20-year psychological history of impaired judgment, violent and assaultive behavior and a person who "clearly represents a potential danger to others").

344. See, e.g., People v. Gissendanner, 48 N.Y.2d at 550, 423 N.Y.S.2d at 897–98; People v. Stubbs, 183 A.D.2d 178, 590 N.Y.S.2d 539 (3d Dep't 1992); People v. Harris, 121 A.D.2d 788, 504 N.Y.S.2d 552 (3d Dep't 1986).

345. See, e.g., People v. Palumbo, N.Y.L.J., December 29, 1994, p. 25, col. 6 (Sup.Ct., Bronx County)(trial court ordered production for in camera review where defendant, charged with assaulting police officer and causing back injury, alleged that officer had previously suffered back injury in course of employment and also had committed prior acts of assaultive behavior while on the job); People v. Francis, 149 Misc.2d 693, 566 N.Y.S.2d 486 (Sup.Ct., Monroe County, 1991)(trial court ordered production for in camera review where defendant, charged with assaulting police officer and resisting arrest, alleged that officer had committed unprovoked assault and filed false charge against another individual); People v. Herrera, 131 Misc.2d 96, 499 N.Y.S.2d 311 (Sup.Ct., Queens County, 1985)(trial court ordered production for in camera review where defendant, charged with bribery, alleged that officers whose files were sought were themselves under investigation for alleged bribe-taking).

346. Civil Rights Law § 79–h(b).

347. See Civil Rights Law § 79–h(c).

348. See People v. Troiano, 127 Misc.2d 738, 486 N.Y.S.2d 991 (Suffolk Co.Ct.1985). The memorandum in support of the Legis-

§ 7.31 **The Work Product Exemption**

Information that meets the definition of attorneys' "work product" is also generally exempt from disclosure. The CPL defines attorneys' work product as property "that contains the opinions, theories, or conclusions of the prosecutor, defense counsel or members of their legal staff."[350] Thus, a synopsis of a witness's statements and other "factual" information do not fall within this definition.[351] A prosecutor's evaluation of the quality of factual information, however, does meet the definition. This distinction may not always be apparent, and when a party contends that material is exempted work product, the trial court must review the material *in camera* and make the determination.[352] A document that contained both work product and factual information should be redacted so that the nonexempt material is disclosed.

The voluntary disclosure of work product to a third party can serve to waive the confidentiality of the material with respect to a party in a

---

lature's 1990 amendments of the shield law also notes that, in some cases, a reporter's privilege under the shield law may yield to a criminal defendant's constitutional rights. See McKinney's 1990 Session Laws, Vol. 2, p. 2332.

349. See, e.g., Pennsylvania v. Ritchie, 480 U.S. 39, 107 S.Ct. 989, 94 L.Ed.2d 40 (1987)(due process required that trial court review file of state agency charged with investigating child abuse and neglect to determine whether file contained exculpatory evidence material to child sex abuse allegations against defendant); People v. Castillo, 80 N.Y.2d 578, 592 N.Y.S.2d 945, 607 N.E.2d 1050 (1992), cert. den. 507 U.S. 1033, 113 S.Ct. 1854, 123 L.Ed.2d 477 (1993)(trial court properly denied defendant access to search warrant and supporting documents on ground that disclosure would reveal identity of potentially endangered confidential informant); People v. Tissois, 72 N.Y.2d 75, 531 N.Y.S.2d 228, 526 N.E.2d 1086 (1988)(disclosure of child witness's statements to social worker properly denied by trial court, although defendant sought discovery of statements only on Rosario grounds and did not make any constitutional claim to access); Sabol v. People, 203 A.D.2d 369, 610 N.Y.S.2d 93 (2d Dep't 1994)(defendant's subpoena of confidential social service agency records properly quashed where no showing was made that records were relevant); People v. Simon, 180 A.D.2d 866, 580 N.Y.S.2d 493 (3d Dep't 1992)(defendant's access to witness's drug rehabilitation records properly denied where information was sought only for impeachment purposes and was cumulative of other evidence); People v. Harder, 146 A.D.2d 286, 540 N.Y.S.2d 557 (3d Dep't 1989)(trial court erred in refusing to conduct in camera review of court records relating to prosecution witness's Family Court case); People v. Davis, 86 A.D.2d 956, 448 N.Y.S.2d 315 (4th Dep't 1982)(trial court erred in refusing to disclose court records relating to prosecution witness's pending criminal case that were sealed because witness was eligible for youthful offender adjudication); People v. Manzanillo, 145 Misc.2d 504, 546 N.Y.S.2d 954 (N.Y.C.Crim.Ct.1989)(court ordered production, for in camera review, of special education records of complainant, even though defendant made no specific showing that records were reasonably likely to contain relevant and material information).

350. CPL § 240.10(2).

351. See generally People v. Banch, 80 N.Y.2d 610, 620, 593 N.Y.S.2d 491, 497, 608 N.E.2d 1069 (1992).

352. See, e.g., People v. Nielson, 115 A.D.2d 972, 497 N.Y.S.2d 537 (4th Dep't 1985); People v. Jones, 91 A.D.2d 1175, 459 N.Y.S.2d 144 (4th Dep't 1983).

criminal case.[353] And as is true for other types of privileges, a defendant's constitutional rights would probably require that work product that included exculpatory evidence be disclosed to the defense.[354]

Library References:

West's Key No. Digests, Criminal Law ⊜627.5(6).

§ 7.32 Defendant's Right to Test of Physical Evidence

The Court of Appeals has recognized that the defense has a general right, prior to trial, to conduct its own scientific test of physical evidence that is in the possession of law enforcement authorities.[355] In authorizing such testing, however, the trial court should impose reasonable safeguards, similar to those that the prosecution must adhere to in its own testing, to protect against contamination or destruction of the evidence.[356] In addition, if a legitimate risk exists that a test may significantly alter the nature of the evidence, the trial court is authorized to postpone the defendant's test until after the evidence has been introduced at the trial.[357]

For several reasons, it is important that the defense not delay in seeking authorization to conduct its own test of physical evidence. Some types of physical evidence, such as blood, may change over time as a result of evaporation, physical decomposition, oxidation or other natural processes. In these situations, the probative value of the test may diminish with the passage of time.[358] Also, when the defense does not assert its right to test the evidence at an early stage in the proceedings, the authorities may destroy the evidence. Particularly if the destruction was inadvertent and not in bad faith, the defense may be deemed to have forfeited its right to test the evidence.[359]

Library References:

West's Key No. Digests, Criminal Law ⊜627.6.

§ 7.33 Miscellaneous Issues

The courts have addressed a variety of other discovery issues that do not easily fall within the other sections of this chapter. For example, the Court of Appeals has stated that, when a personal version of the crime written by the victim is not in the possession of the prosecution and does not contain *Brady* material, a trial court has no authority to

---

353. See People v. Calandra, 120 Misc.2d 1059, 1060–61, 467 N.Y.S.2d 141, 142 (Sup.Ct., N.Y. County, 1983).

354. 120 Misc.2d at 1061, 467 N.Y.S.2d at 143.

355. People v. White, 40 N.Y.2d 797, 390 N.Y.S.2d 405, 358 N.E.2d 1031 (1976).

356. 40 N.Y.2d at 799, 390 N.Y.S.2d at 407.

357. Id.

358. See generally People v. Karpeles, 146 Misc.2d 53, 58–60, 549 N.Y.S.2d 903, 906–08 (Sup.Ct., Richmond County, 1989).

359. See People v. Allgood, 70 N.Y.2d 812, 523 N.Y.S.2d 431, 517 N.E.2d 1316 (1987)(defense forfeited its right to production of inadvertently destroyed rape kit where it was aware of kit's existence some eight months before the destruction but never expressed interest in performing its own test during that time).

order the disclosure of the document to the defendant.[360] One trial court, however, ordered an *in camera* inspection of the deceased victim's personal diary on the grounds that the diary previously had been in the possession of the prosecution, it contained references to the defendant, the deceased (obviously) would not be available to testify at the trial, and sharply conflicting accounts had been given regarding the contents of the diary.[361] Upon reviewing the diary, though, the court found nothing relevant or material and thus refused to disclose it to the defendant.[362]

Two lower courts have split over whether a trial court is authorized to order the complainant to provide blood or saliva samples to the defendant for testing.[363] Another trial court denied the defendant's request to inspect the complainant's residence, holding that the defendant had made no showing that an inspection of the residence, where the defendant himself had once lived, would reveal anything more than the photographs of the residence that the prosecution had provided to the defense.[364] And an appellate court held that, absent a showing that inspection of the deceased victim's corpse would yield exculpatory evidence, a trial court has no authority to permit the defendant such an inspection.[365]

Finally, limited opportunities may exist under the New York Freedom of Information Law (FOIL)[366] to obtain pretrial disclosure of law enforcement records. Although most of the FOIL cases relating to disclosure of law enforcement records involve post-conviction attempts to obtain records, the courts have stated that, even if records were discoverable pursuant to Article 240 or some other legal authority during the pendency of the criminal proceeding, access to those records under FOIL is not precluded.[367] The FOIL statute expressly exempts certain law

---

360. People v. Reedy, 70 N.Y.2d 826, 523 N.Y.S.2d 438, 517 N.E.2d 1324 (1987).

361. People v. Chambers, 134 Misc.2d 688, 691, 512 N.Y.S.2d 631, 633–34 (Sup. Ct., N.Y. County, 1987).

362. 134 Misc.2d at 691–92, 512 N.Y.S.2d at 634.

363. Cf. People v. Nelson, 151 Misc.2d 951, 574 N.Y.S.2d 144 (Sup.Ct., Kings County, 1991)(holding that a court has no authority to order the complainant to provide a blood or saliva sample) with People v. Trocchio, 107 Misc.2d 610, 435 N.Y.S.2d 639 (Suffolk Co.Ct.1980)(since court had ordered defendant to provide blood and saliva samples to the prosecution, court also granted defendant's request to such samples from the complainant so that defendant would be given "every reasonable opportunity" to challenge the testimony of the prosecution's expert). See also People v. Harley H. Earl, ___ A.D.2d ___, 632 N.Y.S.2d 689 (3d Dep't 1995)(trial court lacks inherent authority to order victim of sex offense to submit to psychiatric examination); People v. Gutkaiss, 206 A.D.2d 628, 614 N.Y.S.2d 599 (3d Dep't 1994)(neither CPL nor interest of justice supported defendant's request for an independent psychiatric examination of alleged victim in child sex abuse prosecution); but see People v. Griffin, 138 Misc.2d 279, 524 N.Y.S.2d 153 (Sup. Ct., Kings County, 1988)(trial court authorized to order complainant to submit to psychiatric examination, but only if a compelling reason exists to do so; no such reason demonstrated in case).

364. People v. Nicholas, 157 Misc.2d 947, 599 N.Y.S.2d 779 (Sup.Ct., Bronx County, 1993).

365. People v. Rose, 122 A.D.2d 484, 505 N.Y.S.2d 244 (3d Dep't 1986).

366. Pub. Off. Law § 84 et seq.

367. See, e.g., Moore v. Santucci, 151 A.D.2d 677, 678, 543 N.Y.S.2d 103, 105 (2d Dep't 1989); Billups v. Santucci, 151 A.D.2d 663, 664, 542 N.Y.S.2d 726, 727 (2d Dep't 1989). Of course, if the agency in possession of the records can show that the records sought were previously disclosed to the person seeking them, denial of access is appropriate. Moore v. Santucci, 151 A.D.2d

enforcement records from disclosure—*i.e.*, if their disclosure would interfere with law enforcement investigations or judicial proceedings; deprive a person of a right to a fair trial or impartial adjudication; identify a confidential source or disclose confidential information relating to a criminal investigation; or reveal nonroutine investigative techniques or procedures.[368] Applying the FOIL exemption provisions, courts have held that grand jury testimony,[369] undercover drug operation reports[370] and the names, addresses and statements of confidential witnesses[371] may not be obtained under FOIL.[372] On the other hand, reports relating to ballistic and fingerprinting tests[373] and the criminal convictions and any pending criminal actions of prosecution witnesses[374] have been held to be obtainable under FOIL.

Library References:

West's Key No. Digests, Criminal Law ⚙︎627.5–627.8, 1226; Records ⚙︎30–68; Witnesses ⚙︎216.

§ 7.34 Practice Summary—Defense

A. Demand to Produce (*See* §§ 7.3–7.4)

1. Within 30 days of arraignment, serve on prosecution a written demand to produce the following property and information:

- statements of the defendant and jointly tried co-defendants made to law enforcement or a person acting at the direction of or in cooperation with law enforcement

- transcript of grand jury testimony of the defendant and jointly tried co-defendants

- written reports of scientific tests and experiments and physical or mental examinations that the prosecution intends to introduce at trial or made by or at the request of law enforcement or by a person the prosecution intends to call at trial

- photographs or drawings that the prosecution intends to introduce at trial or made by or at the request of law enforcement or by a person the prosecution intends to call at trial

---

at 678, 543 N.Y.S.2d at 106; Billups v. Santucci, 151 A.D.2d at 664, 542 N.Y.S.2d at 727.

368. Pub. Off. Law § 87(2)(e). FOIL also exempts from disclosure records that, if disclosed, would endanger the life or safety of any person. Pub. Off. Law § 87(2)(f).

369. Thompson v. Weinstein, 150 A.D.2d 782, 783, 542 N.Y.S.2d 33, 33 (2d Dep't 1989).

370. Ennis v. Slade, 179 A.D.2d 558, 559, 579 N.Y.S.2d 59, 59 (1st Dep't 1992).

371. Allen v. Strojnowski, 129 A.D.2d 700, 701, 514 N.Y.S.2d 463, 465 (2d Dep't 1987), appeal dism. 70 N.Y.2d 871, 523 N.Y.S.2d 493, 518 N.E.2d 5 (1987).

372. See also Fink v. Lefkowitz, 47 N.Y.2d 567, 419 N.Y.S.2d 467, 393 N.E.2d 463 (1979)(special prosecutor's manual revealing techniques used in investigating and successfully prosecuting nursing home fraud exempt from disclosure).

373. Moore v. Santucci, 151 A.D.2d at 679, 543 N.Y.S.2d at 106.

374. Thompson v. Weinstein, 150 A.D.2d at 783, 542 N.Y.S.2d at 33.

§ 7.34 DISCOVERY Ch. 7

- photographs or copies made by or at the direction of law enforcement of stolen property released to its owner pursuant to P.L. § 450.10
- property obtained from the defendant or jointly tried co-defendants
- tapes or other recordings that the prosecution intends to introduce at trial
- *Brady* material (the demand should be as specific as possible)
- the approximate date, time and place of the offense charged and of the defendant's arrest
- in computer offense cases, information relating to the notice set forth in Article 156 of the Penal Law; and in Vehicle and Traffic Law cases, specified information concerning scientific tests and experiments

B. Refusal of Demand (*See* § 7.6)

1. Refusal to disclose any property that the prosecution has demanded must be served on prosecution within 15 days of service of the prosecution's demand.

C. Motion for Discovery (*See* §§ 7.7, 7.9, 7.10)

1. Within 45 days of arraignment, move for disclosure, when appropriate, of the following property and information:

- property previously demanded pursuant to CPL § 240.20 that the prosecution has refused to disclose; explain why the prosecution's refusal is not warranted
- property that the prosecution intends to introduce at trial; explain why the property will facilitate preparation for trial and why disclosure will impose no undue burden on the prosecution
- police reports within the prosecution's possession or control; explain why disclosure will facilitate preparation for trial and, if possible, show that the reports contain relevant and material information
- the names and addresses of the witnesses that the prosecution intends to call at trial; explain why disclosure will facilitate preparation for trial and, if possible, show that the witnesses have relevant and material information
- the identity of any confidential informants and the information that they provided to law enforcement; show that the informant performed a significant role in the criminal transaction and that the question of the defendant's guilt is a close one
- prior convictions or prior uncharged bad acts of the defendant that the prosecution intends to introduce at trial, whether as direct or as collateral evidence (ordinarily, however, the prosecution need not disclose this information until shortly before, or at the commencement of, trial)

Ch. 7   PRACTICE SUMMARY—PROSECUTION   § 7.35

- prior statements and criminal histories of witnesses that the prosecution intends to call at a pretrial hearing or at trial (again, the prosecution need not disclose this property and information until the commencement of the hearing or trial, as the case may be)
- any additional property or information that is relevant and material to the case and that, if disclosed, will facilitate preparation of the defense

D. Scientific Test

1. At as early a stage in the proceedings as is possible, move for leave to conduct an independent scientific test of physical evidence that is in the possession of law enforcement.

E. Subpoena Duces Tecum (*See* § 7.8)

1. After the prosecution makes disclosure of property demanded pursuant to CPL § 240.20, serve a subpoena duces tecum, signed by the trial court, on appropriate governmental agencies (with one day's notice) for relevant police and other law enforcement reports that the prosecution has not disclosed; many courts, prior to authorizing issuance of the subpoena, will require the defense to demonstrate that the documents sought contain highly relevant and material, or even exculpatory, evidence.

F. Notice of Defenses (*See* §§ 7.25, 7.26, 7.27)

1. Within 30 days of arraignment, serve on the prosecution and file with the court notice of intention to offer psychiatric evidence.

2. Within eight days of receiving demand by prosecution, serve on the prosecution and file with the court notice of alibi, specifying details of alibi and names and addresses of alibi witnesses.

3. Within 45 days of arraignment, serve on prosecution and file with the court notice of intent to rely on statutorily defined defense to computer-related offenses.

G. Objection and Request for Sanction (*See* §§ 7.20, 7.21, 7.22, 7.23)

1. If defense is aware or suspects that prosecution has failed to disclose property or information that defense believes it is entitled to, make objection known to court and request appropriate sanction if prosecution persists in failure to disclose.

§ 7.35 Practice Summary—Prosecution

A. Demand to Produce (*See* § 7.5)

1. Within 30 days of arraignment, serve on defense a written demand to produce the following property and information:

- written reports of scientific tests or experiments and physical or mental examinations made by or at request of defense if defense

§ 7.35   DISCOVERY   Ch. 7

intends to introduce report at trial or if report was made by person defense intends to call at trial

- if defense has served notice of intention to present psychiatric evidence, any reports relating to that evidence made at defense's direction

- photographs, drawings and tapes or other recordings that defense intends to introduce at trial

B. Refusal of Demand (*See* § 7.6)

1. Refusal to disclose any property that the defense has demanded must be served on defense within 15 days of service of the defense's demand.

C. Motion for Discovery (*See* § 7.11)

1. Within 45 days of arraignment, move for disclosure, when appropriate, of the following property and information:

- property previously demanded pursuant to section 240.30 that the defense has refused to disclose; explain why refusal to disclose is not warranted

- if ordered to disclose to defense property that prosecution intends to introduce at trial, reciprocal disclosure of similar property from defense; explain why disclosure will facilitate preparation of prosecution case, will impose no undue burden on defense and will be consistent with fairness given court's order that prosecution disclose similar property to defense

- non-testimonial evidence from defendant, such as requiring defendant to appear in line-up, speak for identification, be fingerprinted, pose for photograph, provide blood, hair or other physical samples, provide handwriting specimen, and submit to physical or medical inspection; if court requires, demonstrate probable cause for the necessity of the evidence sought; or, when seeking blood or other physical examples, emphasize that the procedure to be used is safe and reliable and, if court requires, show clear indication that relevant evidence will be found

D. Request for Disclosure of Statements of Defense Witnesses (*See* § 7.16)

1. Request disclosure of prior statements and criminal histories of the defense's pretrial hearing witnesses (disclosure of this material and information for the defense's *trial* witnesses is automatic).

E. Notice of Defenses (*See* §§ 7.26, 7.27)

1. Upon receipt of defense's notice of intention to offer psychiatric evidence, apply to court for order directing that defendant be examined by psychiatrist or licensed psychologist designated by prosecution.

2. Within 20 days of arraignment, serve on defense and file with court demand that defense file a notice of alibi; within reasonable time of

receiving notice of alibi, but not later than ten days before commencement of trial, serve on defense list of any alibi rebuttal witnesses.

F. Obligation to Disclose Regardless of Defense Request or Demand (*See* §§ 7.20, 7.21. 7.22, 7.23)

1. To avoid possible draconian post-conviction sanction for failure to disclose, make concerted effort to disclose all *Rosario* and *Brady* material in prosecution's possession and custody or in possession or custody of police department; *Brady* material includes not only exculpatory evidence relating directly to guilt or innocence of defendant but also exculpatory evidence relating to credibility of prosecution witnesses, such as promises or agreements with witnesses.

2. If any doubt exists about whether property or information constitutes *Rosario* or *Brady* material, seek ruling from court, *ex parte* and *in camera* when appropriate.

G. Obligation to Obtain Demanded Property (*See* § 7.4)

1. If property specified in defense's demand to produce is not in prosecution's possession, custody or control, exercise diligent, good faith effort to ascertain existence of property and to cause it to be made available to defense.

H. Continuing Duty to Disclose

1. If property or information subject to disclosure subsequently comes into prosecution's possession or custody, make disclosure to defense as soon as possible.

I. Protective Order (*See* § 7.19)

1. If disclosure to the defense of any property or information that defense is entitled to will create substantial risk of harm to witness or other person, compromise an ongoing investigation, pose danger to integrity of physical evidence or will raise some other concern that outweighs the usefulness of disclosure, seek protective order from court; if possible, support request with examples of defendant's prior attempts to intimidate; when appropriate, application may be made to court *ex parte* and *in camera*.

§ 7.36 Practice Summary—Court

A. In General

1. If both parties fully comply with their disclosure obligations, the court generally will perform a minimal role in discovery proceedings. However, when the parties do not comply with, or seek an exemption from, those obligations, the court will be called upon to intervene.

B. Motions for Discovery (*See* §§ 7.7, 7.11)

1. When one party moves for discovery of property or information that the other party has refused to produce in response to a demand, the court generally must decide whether the property at issue is discoverable

under CPL §§ 240.20 or 240.30, as the case may be, or whether issuance of a protective order is warranted.

C. Protective Orders (*See* § 7.19)

1. If the prosecution seeks a protective order against disclosure of property or information sought by defense and claims that such order is necessary to protect against risk of harm to a witness or other person (the most commonly alleged ground), note that the statute requires showing of "substantial" risk; this is because a potential risk probably exists in almost every case; issuance of order on this ground, therefore, is generally not justified absent showing of defendant's past involvement in witness intimidation.

D. Sanctions (*See* §§ 7.20, 7.21, 7.22, 7.23, 7.24)

1. If discoverable material is belatedly disclosed, a continuance is usually the appropriate sanction so long as the receiving party may still make meaningful use of the material; if discoverable material that is relevant to the testimony of a particular witness is not disclosed until after the witness has testified, the court ordinarily should order return of witness to stand for further cross-examination by receiving party.

2. If discoverable material has been lost or destroyed, the court *must* impose sanction that eliminates prejudice to injured party; in devising sanction, which is left to court's discretion, the court should consider the evidence that has been offered at trial, the significance of the lost or destroyed material and whether the loss or destruction was intentional or inadvertent; dismissal of the charges in response to the loss or destruction of material discoverable by the defense is always a last resort that may be invoked only if no other, less severe sanction will rectify the harm to the defense.

E. Sanctions on Defense for Failure to Comply with Notice Requirements (*See* §§ 7.26, 7.27)

1. The court is authorized to preclude psychiatric evidence or alibi evidence when the defense has failed to provide timely notice of such evidence to the prosecution, but given the defendant's constitutional right to present evidence, the court should strongly consider exercising its discretion to permit late notice if the delay was not designed to gain a tactical advantage and the prosecution is not prejudiced by the delay.

2. If the defendant refuses to cooperate fully with a court-ordered psychiatric examination by a prosecution-designated expert, the court has broad authority to preclude testimony of a defense expert with respect to the defendant's alleged mental disease or defect.

§ 7.37 Forms 💾

§ 7.37.1 Demand to Produce (Made by Defendant)[375]

[Caption]

---

[375]. An extensive recitation of the property and information discoverable in a defendant's demand to produce is contained in the sample omnibus motion included at the end of Chapter 8.

COUNSEL:

PLEASE TAKE NOTICE that, pursuant to section 240.20 of the Criminal Procedure Law, demand is made upon you to produce and permit inspection by the defendant of the following property at _____, New York, on the ___ day of _____, 19__, at ___ in the forenoon of that day: [specify property prosecutor required to produce under CPL § 240.20].

Dated: _____, 19__
_____, New York

> [Name of defense attorney]
> Attorney for Defendant
> Address
> Tel. No.

TO: HON. _____
District Attorney
_____ County

§ 7.37.2 Demand to Produce (Made by Prosecutor)

[Caption]

COUNSEL:

PLEASE TAKE NOTICE that, pursuant to section 240.30 of the Criminal Procedure Law, demand is made upon you to produce and permit inspection by the District Attorney of _____ County of the following property at _____, New York, on the ___ day of _____, 19__, at ___ in the forenoon of that day: [specify property defense required to disclose under CPL § 240.30].

Dated: _____, 19__
_____, New York

> [Name of District Attorney]
> Address
> Tel. No.

TO: [Name of defense attorney]
Attorney for Defendant

§ 7.37.3 Refusal of Demand to Produce (Either Party)

[Caption]

COUNSEL:

PLEASE TAKE NOTICE, that the District Attorney of _____ County [or the defendant], pursuant to section 240.35 of the Criminal Procedure Law, refuses to disclose the following information sought in

§ 7.37   DISCOVERY   Ch. 7

your Demand to Produce dated _____, 19__: [specify information that party refuses to disclose]. Refusal is made because the District Attorney [or the defendant] reasonably believes that such information is not discoverable by a Demand to Produce pursuant to section 240.20 [or 240.30] of the Criminal Procedure Law [or reasonably believes that a protective order would be warranted for such information] in that: [specify reasons].

Dated: _____, 19__
       _____, New York

                                      [Name of District Attorney]
                                      or [Name of defense attorney]
                                        Address
                                        Tel. No.

To: [Name of defense attorney]
    or [Name of District
    Attorney]

       HON. _____
       Clerk of the Court

§ 7.37.4 Notice of Motion by Defendant for Disclosure in Response to Refusal of Prosecution to Comply With Demand to Produce

[Caption]

COUNSEL:

PLEASE TAKE NOTICE, that upon the annexed affirmation and all the prior papers and proceedings herein, the undersigned will move this Court, at Part ___ thereof, to be held at the Courthouse at _____, New York, on the ___ day of _____, 19__, at ___ in the forenoon, or as soon thereafter as counsel can be heard, for an order, pursuant to section 240.40 of the Criminal Procedure Law, directing the District Attorney to permit discovery and inspection by the defendant of the following property, upon the ground that the District Attorney's refusal to disclose such property in response to defendant's Demand to Produce is not justified: [specify property sought to be disclosed]; and for such other and further relief as the Court deems just and proper.

Dated: _____, 19__
       _____, New York

                                        [Name of defense attorney]
                                        Attorney for Defendant
                                        Address
                                        Tel. No.

TO: HON. _____
     District Attorney
     _____ County

HON. _____
Clerk of the Court

§ 7.37.5 Affirmation in Support of Defendant's Motion for Disclosure After Refusal of Prosecutor to Comply With Demand to Produce

[Caption]

_____, an attorney duly admitted to practice in the Courts of this State, hereby affirms under the penalties of perjury that the following statements are true, except those made on information and belief, which he [she] believes to be true:

1. I am the attorney for the defendant herein.

2. In a [an] [specify accusatory instrument] filed on _____, 19__, defendant is charged with committing the offense(s) of [specify offenses]. A copy of the accusatory instrument is attached hereto as Exhibit A. Defendant entered a plea of not guilty on _____, 19__. No trial has commenced on the aforesaid charges.

3. On _____, 19__, I served on the District Attorney a demand to produce pursuant to section 240.20 of the Criminal Procedure Law. A copy of the demand to produce is attached hereto as Exhibit B.

4. On _____, 19__, the District Attorney served on me a refusal to comply with the aforesaid demand to produce with regard to the following material: [specify material prosecutor refuses to produce]. A copy of the District Attorney's refusal is attached hereto as Exhibit C.

5. The refusal of the District Attorney to comply with the demand to produce is not justified because [specify reasons why the refusal is not justified].

6. No previous application for the relief sought herein has been made.

WHEREFORE, defendant respectfully requests that an order be issued directing the District Attorney to produce for discovery and inspection by defendant the material specified above.

[Signature]

_____
[Name of defense attorney]

Dated: _____, 19__

§ 7.37.6 Notice of Motion by Defendant for Discovery Beyond That Required Under Demand to Produce

[Caption]

COUNSEL:

PLEASE TAKE NOTICE, that upon the annexed affirmation and all the prior papers and proceedings herein, the undersigned will move this Court, at Part ___ thereof, to be held at the Courthouse at _____, New

York, on the ___ day of _____, 19__, at ___ in the forenoon, or as soon thereafter as counsel may be heard, for an order pursuant to section 240.40 of the Criminal Procedure Law directing the District Attorney to permit defendant herein discovery and inspection of the following property, upon the ground that discovery of such property is material to the preparation of the defense: [specify property sought]; and for such other and further relief as the Court deems just and proper.

Dated: _____, 19__
_____, New York

[Name of defense attorney]
Attorney for Defendant
Address
Tel. No.

TO: HON. _____
District Attorney
_____ County

HON. _____
Clerk of the Court

§ 7.37.7 Affirmation in Support of Defendant's Motion for Discovery Beyond That Required Under Demand to Produce

[Caption]

_____, an attorney duly admitted to practice in the Courts of this State, hereby affirms under the penalties of perjury that the following statements are true, except those made on information and belief, which he [she] believes to be true:

1. I am the attorney for the defendant herein.

2. In a [specify accusatory instrument] filed with this Court on _____, 19__, defendant was charged with committing the following offenses: [specify offenses]. A copy of the [specify accusatory instrument] is attached hereto as Exhibit A.

3. On _____, 19__, defendant entered a plea of not guilty. No trial has been commenced on the aforesaid accusatory instrument.

4. Upon information and belief, the District Attorney is in possession of the following property that he [she] intends to introduce at trial: [specify property]. Such property is not discoverable under section 240.20 of the Criminal Procedure Law pursuant to a demand to produce.

5. On _____, 19__, I asked the District Attorney's Office if I could inspect such property, but that request was refused.

6. Discovery of such property is material to the preparation of the defense in this case because [specify reasons why discovery of the property will facilitate preparation of the defense].

7. No previous application for the relief requested herein has been made.

WHEREFORE, defendant requests that an order be issued directing the District Attorney to produce for discovery and inspection by the defendant the property specified above.

[Signature]
_____
[Name of defense attorney]

Dated: _____, 19__

§ 7.37.8 Notice of Motion by Prosecutor for Discovery of Non-testimonial Evidence

[Caption]

COUNSEL:

PLEASE TAKE NOTICE, that upon the annexed affirmation and all the prior papers and proceedings herein, the undersigned will move this Court, at Part ___ thereof, to be held at the Courthouse at _____, New York, on the ___ day of _____, 19__, at ___ in the forenoon, or as soon thereafter as counsel may be heard, for an order pursuant to section 240.40 of the Criminal Procedure Law directing the defendant herein to [specify the non-testimonial evidence sought of defendant], and for such other and further relief as this Court deems just and proper.

Dated: _____, 19__
_____, New York

HON. _____
District Attorney
_____ County
Address
Tel. No.

TO: [Name of defense attorney]
    Attorney for Defendant

HON. _____
Clerk of the Court

§ 7.37.9 Affirmation of Prosecutor in Support of Motion for Discovery of Non-testimonial Evidence

[Caption]

_____, an attorney duly admitted to practice in the Courts of this State, hereby affirms under the penalties of perjury that the following statements are true, except those made on information and belief, which he [she] believes to be true:

1. I am an assistant district attorney of _____ County.

2. In a [specify accusatory instrument] filed in this Court on _____, 19__, defendant herein was charged with committing the offense[s] of [specify offense(s)].

3. Defendant has entered a plea of not guilty to the charges. No trial in this case has been commenced.

4. It is material to the preparation of the prosecution's case in this action that defendant be required to provide the following non-testimonial evidence: [specify non-testimonial evidence sought]. [specify reasons why receipt of such non-testimonial evidence will facilitate the prosecution's preparation of its case].

5. No previous application for the relief requested herein has been made.

WHEREFORE, affirmant respectfully requests that an order be issued, pursuant to section 240.40 of the Criminal Procedure Law, directing the defendant to provide [specify non-testimonial evidence sought].

[Signature]

[Name of assistant district attorney]

Dated: _____, 19__

§ 7.37.10 Notice of Motion for Protective Order

[Caption]

COUNSEL:

PLEASE TAKE NOTICE, that upon the annexed affirmation and all the prior papers and proceedings herein, the undersigned will move this Court, at Part ___ thereof, to be held at the Courthouse at _____, New York, on the ___ day of _____, 19__, at ___ in the forenoon, or as soon thereafter as counsel can be heard, for a protective order pursuant to section 240.50 of the Criminal Procedure Law [denying, limiting, conditioning, delaying or regulating] the disclosure to defendant herein of [specify property concerning which protective order is sought], and for such other and further relief as this Court deems just and proper.

Dated: _____, 19__
_____, New York

[Name of District Attorney]
District Attorney
_____ County
Address
Tel. No.

TO: [Name of defense attorney]
Attorney for Defendant

HON. _____
Clerk of the Court

§ 7.37.11 Affirmation in Support of Motion for Protective Order

[Caption]

_____, an attorney duly admitted to practice in the Courts of this State, hereby affirms under the penalties of perjury that the following statements are true, except those made on information and belief, which he [she] believes to be true:

1. I am an assistant district attorney in _____ County.

2. In an order dated _____, 19__, this Court directed the District Attorney to produce for discovery and inspection by defendant the following property: [specify property].

3. Affirmant believes that good cause exists for a protective order pursuant to section 240.50 of the Criminal Procedure Law [denying, limiting, conditioning, delaying or regulating] the disclosure and inspection of such property because [specify facts establishing such good cause].

4. No previous application for the relief sought herein has been made.

WHEREFORE, affirmant respectfully requests that a protective order be issued [denying, limiting, conditioning, delaying or regulating] the discovery granted defendant in the order of this Court dated _____, 19__, and for such other and further relief as this Court deems just and proper.

[Signature]

_____
[Name of assistant district attorney]

Dated: _____, 19__

§ 7.37.12 Demand for Notice of Alibi

[Caption]

COUNSEL:

PLEASE TAKE NOTICE, that if defendant intends to offer a defense at the trial in this action that, at the time of the commission of the offense[s] charged, defendant was at some place or places other than the scene of the crime and to call witnesses in support of such defense, you are hereby required, within eight days of service of this demand, to serve a notice of alibi upon the undersigned and to file a copy thereof with the Court, specifying the place or places defendant claims to have been at the time of the offense[s] charged and the names, residential addresses, places of employment and addresses thereof of every such alleged alibi witness upon whom defendant intends to rely.

Dated: _____, 19__

[Name of District Attorney]
District Attorney
_____ County
Address
Tel. No.

TO: [Name of defense attorney]
    Attorney for Defendant

§ 7.37.13 Notice of Alibi

[Caption]

COUNSEL:

PLEASE TAKE NOTICE, that defendant intends to offer a defense at the trial in this action that at the time of the commission of the offense[s] charged herein he [she] was at the following place[s] other than the scene of the crime: [specify location[s]].

PLEASE TAKE FURTHER NOTICE, that defendant intends to call as witnesses at the trial in this action the following persons in support of the defense that he [she] was not at the scene of the crime: [specify name, residential address, place of employment and employment address of such witness[es]].

Dated: _____, 19__

[Name of defense attorney]
Attorney for Defendant
Address
Tel. No.

TO: HON. _____
    District Attorney
    _____ County

    HON. _____
    Clerk of the Court

Chapter 8

THE OMNIBUS MOTION

Table of Sections

8.1 The Omnibus Motion.
8.2 Forms.
    8.2.1 Notice of Omnibus Motion in Felony Case.
    8.2.2 Affirmation in Support of Omnibus Motion in Felony Case.

WESTLAW Electronic Research
See WESTLAW Electronic Research Guide preceding the Summary of Contents.

§ 8.1 The Omnibus Motion

Criminal actions can proceed more expeditiously to disposition if most, if not all, pretrial motions are combined in a single set of motion papers and heard by a single judge at an early stage in the proceedings. The CPL seeks to accomplish this goal in Article 255, which lays out the general requirement of the pretrial omnibus motion and the specific rules underlying that requirement. The Court of Appeals has described the purpose of Article 255 as follows:

> [T]o regulate pretrial proceedings by requiring a single omnibus motion to be made promptly after arraignment and thus to avoid the proliferation experienced under prior procedure in which a defendant could bombard the courts and Judges with dilatory tactics continuing right up to the eve of trial.[1]

Article 255 requires that all "pretrial" motions be served or filed[2] within 45 days after arraignment.[3] This rule applies whether the defendant is represented by counsel or is proceeding *pro se*.[4] However, if the defendant has received an adjournment to obtain counsel or have counsel assigned, the 45-day period commences from the date of counsel's initial appearance in court.[5] In addition, if the prosecution has

---

1. People v. Lawrence, 64 N.Y.2d 200, 204–05, 485 N.Y.S.2d 233, 235–36, 474 N.E.2d 593 (1984).

2. Although the statute's use of the disjunctive suggests, oddly enough, that either filing or serving will suffice, as a practical matter both should be done because other statutes require notice to the moving party's adversary, see, e.g., CPL § 210.45(1)(motion to dismiss indictment),

and, in any event, the trial court will expect and require such notice.

3. For criminal actions pending in superior courts, this means 45 days after arraignment on the indictment.

Interestingly, the statute provides no time period for the prosecution's response to the omnibus motion.

4. CPL § 255.20(1).

5. Id.

served notice pursuant to CPL § 710.30 of its intention to introduce evidence of the defendant's statements or evidence of an identification, or has served the materials constituting notice pursuant to CPL § 700.70 of an eavesdropping warrant, the 45–day period commences from the date of such service.[6]

The trial court, upon the defendant's application, has discretion to extend the 45–day period.[7] The Court of Appeals has stated, however, that a trial court has no authority to shorten the 45–day period over a defendant's objection.[8]

Article 255 further requires that, whenever practicable, all pretrial motions must be included in the same set of motion papers and made returnable on the same date. An example of when this may not be practicable is where one motion seeks to provide the basis for another motion.[9] In addition, if the defendant was not previously aware of the grounds for a motion, and could not have become aware of such grounds through the exercise of due diligence, or if the defendant otherwise demonstrates good cause why the motion could not have been made within the statutory time period, the court *must* entertain the motion at any time before the end of trial.[10] If not, the court *may* summarily deny the motion, although it may always, in the interest of justice, entertain a late motion at any time before the imposition of sentence.[11] Examples of cases in which courts found good cause to entertain late pretrial motions include where difficulties arose early in the proceedings concerning the defendant's efforts to obtain counsel and the underlying scientific basis for the late motion was not apparent until later on,[12] and where voluminous materials were disclosed to the defense during discovery and it took the court an unusually long time to determine preliminary pretrial motions in the case.[13] A trial court is entirely within its discretion, however, in summarily denying a tardy pretrial motion if the defendant offers no excuse at all for the delay.[14]

Notably, not all pretrial motions fall within the requirements of Article 255. The statute expressly defines "pretrial motion as used in this article" as including motions to: dismiss or reduce an indictment pursuant to Article 210 or dismiss a nonfelony local criminal court accusatory instrument pursuant to Article 170; grant discovery pursuant to Article 240 or grant a bill of particulars pursuant to sections

---

6. Id. In practice, section 710.30 notice is frequently served at arraignment.

7. CPL § 255.20(1).

8. Matter of Veloz v. Rothwax, 65 N.Y.2d 902, 493 N.Y.S.2d 452, 483 N.E.2d 127 (1985).

9. CPL § 255.20(2).

10. CPL § 255.20(3). See also CPL § 710.40(2)(pretrial motion to suppress evidence pursuant to CPL Article 710 must be made within the time period prescribed in Article 255, unless "owing to unawareness of facts constituting the basis thereof or to other factors, the defendant did not have reasonable opportunity to make the motion previously").

11. CPL § 255.20(3).

12. People v. Colon, 180 A.D.2d 876, 580 N.Y.S.2d 95 (3d Dep't 1992).

13. People v. Melillo, 112 Misc.2d 1004, 1005, 448 N.Y.S.2d 108, 109 (Sup.Ct., N.Y. County, 1982).

14. See, e.g., People v. Stafford, 79 A.D.2d 435, 440, 437 N.Y.S.2d 195, 198 (4th Dep't 1981).

100.45 or 200.90[15]; suppress evidence pursuant to Article 710; grant separate trials pursuant to Article 100 or 200; or remove the action pursuant to sections 170.15, 210.43, 230.20 or 230.30.[16] The pretrial motion most conspicuously absent from this list is the motion to dismiss on speedy trial grounds, which obviously could never, or virtually never, be made at this early stage in the proceedings.[17] Other pretrial motions not included within this list are prosecution motions to amend an accusatory instrument and to consolidate accusatory instruments,[18] and defense motions to dismiss on the ground that the defendant was not afforded an opportunity to appear and testify before the grand jury (which must be made within five days of the arraignment in the local criminal court).[19] Also not included are what are characterized as the various *in limine* motions, such as the *Sandoval* motion,[20] which technically may be pretrial motions but usually are made, often orally, on the eve of trial.

Several other points should be made here. First, notwithstanding the requirements of Article 255, a motion to dismiss based on a nonwaivable jurisdictional defect may be raised at any time during the proceedings, even in some instances for the first time on appeal following conviction.[21] Also, even though Article 255 expressly includes within its definition of "pretrial motion" a removal application pursuant to CPL

15. The inclusion of motions for discovery and motions for a bill of particulars within the 45-day period required for the filing of an omnibus motion creates somewhat of an awkward situation. This is because the CPL allows the defendant to demand certain disclosure and to request a bill of particulars without the necessity of obtaining a court order. This is accomplished by service on the prosecution of a written demand to produce, see CPL § 240.20, and a written request for a bill of particulars, see CPL § 200.95(1)(b), within 30 days after arraignment. CPL §§ 200.95(3), 240.80(1). The prosecution must respond within 15 days of service. CPL §§ 200.95(2) and (4), 240.80(2). See generally Chapter 5, § 5.19; Chapter 7, § 7.5. If the defense waits the full, or most of the 30 days to serve the demand and request, and the prosecution waits the full 15 days to respond, no time is left for timely service and filing of a pretrial motion seeking disclosure of information that the prosecution fails to disclose in response to the demand and the request. As a result, it is not unusual for defense counsel to serve a demand to produce and a request for a bill of particulars in advance of the 30-day deadline, and also to include within the omnibus motion an application for a court order disclosing the same information sought in the previously served demand to produce and request for a bill of particulars. This patently wasteful practice is often necessary to comply with the statutory timetables.

16. CPL § 255.10(1).

17. See CPL §§ 170.30(2) and 210.20(2)(excepting motions to dismiss on speedy trial grounds from the requirements of Article 255).

18. See, e.g., People v. Johnson, 112 Misc.2d 578, 447 N.Y.S.2d 380 (Jefferson Co.Ct.1982)(motion for consolidation not subject to Article 255 requirements); see also People v. Negron, 105 Misc.2d 492, 493, 432 N.Y.S.2d 348, 349 (Sup.Ct., N.Y. County, 1980)(motion for consolidation should be referred to trial court for decision immediately prior to trial).

19. See CPL § 190.50(5)(c).

20. The Sandoval motion is the defendant's application for a ruling on the permissible scope of the prosecution's cross-examination, should he or she take the stand at trial, as to the defendant's prior convictions. See People v. Sandoval, 34 N.Y.2d 371, 357 N.Y.S.2d 849, 314 N.E.2d 413 (1974).

21. For example, the failure of a nonfelony local criminal accusatory instrument to allege facts establishing every element of the offense charged is a jurisdictional defect that may be raised at any time in the proceedings. See People v. Alejandro, 70 N.Y.2d 133, 517 N.Y.S.2d 927, 511 N.E.2d 71 (1987); see also Chapter 3, § 3.7.

§ 8.1 THE OMNIBUS MOTION Ch. 8

§ 230.20(2)[22]—which pertains to applications to the Appellate Division to remove an action from the superior court of one county to the superior court of another—appellate courts have consistently held that, except in unusual circumstances, this application is premature if made before jury selection.[23] Some trial courts have articulated a similar exception for motions for severance.[24] Finally, although pretrial motions generally must be made in writing and on notice, the Court of Appeals has recognized that the prosecution may waive these requirements by failing to object to an oral or unnoticed motion.[25] The prudent defense attorney, however, should rarely, if ever, consider making an oral omnibus motion, because of the increased danger in the context of this multiple issue application that a particular motion might be inadvertently omitted.[26]

Library References:

West's Key No. Digests, Criminal Law ⚿627.8, 632(3.1).

§ 8.2 Forms[27]

§ 8.2.1 Notice of Omnibus Motion in Felony Case

[Caption]

PLEASE TAKE NOTICE, that upon the annexed affirmation and all the prior papers and proceedings herein, the undersigned will move this Court, at Part ___ thereof, at the Courthouse at _____, New York, on the ___ day of _____, 19__, at ___ in the forenoon, or as soon thereafter as counsel can be heard, for an order granting the following relief:

1. Inspection of the grand jury minutes and dismissal or, in the alternative, reduction of the indictment on the ground that the evidence before the grand jury was legally insufficient to establish defendant's commission of the offense(s) charged in the indictment;

---

22. See CPL § 255.10(1)(e).

23. See, e.g., People v. Brensic, 136 A.D.2d 169, 172, 526 N.Y.S.2d 968, 970 (2d Dep't 1988); People v. Shedrick, 83 A.D.2d 988, 443 N.Y.S.2d 716 (4th Dep't 1981); see People v. Boudin, 90 A.D.2d 253, 457 N.Y.S.2d 302 (2d Dep't 1982)(finding exceptional circumstances to entertain, and grant, application prior to jury selection). See Chapter 1, § 1.9.

24. See, e.g., People v. Negron, supra.

25. See People v. Mezon, 80 N.Y.2d 155, 160, 589 N.Y.S.2d 838, 841, 603 N.E.2d 943 (1992); People v. Jennings, 69 N.Y.2d 103, 512 N.Y.S.2d 652, 504 N.E.2d 1079 (1986); People v. Singleton, 42 N.Y.2d 466, 470–71, 398 N.Y.S.2d 871, 874, 368 N.E.2d 1237 (1977).

26. Moreover, the written omnibus motion is by far the best vehicle through which the defendant may "specifically" request that the prosecution disclose exculpatory evidence. This is critical because, if the prosecutor ultimately fails to disclose exculpatory evidence, the success of a post-conviction claim raising that issue may turn on whether a specific request had been made for the undisclosed evidence. See Chapter 7, § 7.13.

27. Examples of individual motions that should, when applicable, be included in the omnibus motion are provided in the "Forms" sections of the other chapters of this book. The forms contained in this chapter merely provide an example of an omnibus motion that might be made in a routine felony case. Because each case is different, this particular omnibus motion does not purport to incorporate all possible motions that might be included in an omnibus motion in every case.

2. Release to defendant of the grand jury testimony of [specify key prosecution witness(es)] so that defendant may assist the Court in determining the legal sufficiency of the evidence before the grand jury;

3. Dismissal of the indictment on the ground that the grand jury proceeding failed to conform to Article 190 of the Criminal Procedure Law to such degree that the integrity of such proceeding was impaired;

4. Discovery and inspection;

5. A bill of particulars;

6. Suppression of any and all statements made by defendant on the ground that they were obtained in violation of defendant's constitutional rights; and

7. Any further relief that the Court deems proper.

[Name of defense attorney]
Attorney for Defendant
Address
Tel. No.

TO: HON. _____
District Attorney
_____ County

HON. _____
Clerk of the Court

§ 8.2.2 Affirmation in Support of Omnibus Motion in Felony Case

[Caption]

_____, an attorney duly admitted to practice in the Courts of this State, hereby affirms under penalty of perjury that the following statements are true, and as to those made upon information and belief he [she] believes them to be true:

1. I am the attorney for the defendant herein.

2. In an indictment filed with this Court on _____, 19__, defendant is charged with commission of the following offenses: [specify charges against defendant].

3. This affirmation is made in support of a motion requesting several different forms of relief.

Inspection of Grand Jury Minutes and Dismissal of Indictment

4. Under section 190.65(1)(a) of the Criminal Procedure Law, a grand jury is authorized to indict a person for an offense when the evidence presented to it is legally sufficient to establish the defendant's commission of that offense. "Legally sufficient evidence" is defined in section 70.10(2) of the Criminal Procedure Law as "competent evidence which, if accepted as true, would establish every element of an offense charged and the defendant's commission thereof; except that such

evidence is not legally sufficient when corroboration required by law is absent." Upon information and belief, the evidence presented to the grand jury was legally insufficient to establish that defendant committed the offense(s) charged in the indictment.

5. [Here, if possible, allege facts supporting argument that evidence before grand jury was not legally sufficient to establish defendant's commission of the charged offense(s)].

6. Under section 210.30(3) of the Criminal Procedure Law, the Court is authorized to release to the defendant the grand jury minutes, or portions thereof, if such release is necessary to assist the court in making its determination of whether the evidence before the grand jury was legally sufficient. [Here, if possible, allege reasons why the release of specified portions of the grand jury minutes to the defense would enable the defense to assist the court's determination of the legal sufficiency of the evidence—*e.g.*, where the evidence is of a highly technical nature].

Integrity of the Grand Jury Proceeding

7. When inspecting the grand jury minutes, defendant respectfully requests that the Court, at a minimum, make the following determinations:

a. Was a quorum of grand jurors present prior to hearing evidence and prior to voting? CPL § 190.25(1); *People v. Collier*, 72 N.Y.2d 298, 532 N.Y.S.2d 718, 528 N.E.2d 1191 (1988);

b. Was the indictment voted by an extended term of the grand jury? *People v. Williams*, 73 N.Y.2d 84, 538 N.Y.S.2d 222, 535 N.E.2d 275 (1989)(extended term may not consider new matters that were not pending during original term);

c. Was the presentation of evidence withdrawn prior to a vote being taken and then re-submitted? *People v. Wilkins*, 68 N.Y.2d 269, 508 N.Y.S.2d 893, 501 N.E.2d 542 (1986)(withdrawal tantamount to a dismissal; leave of court is required to re-submit);

d. Was the grand jury properly instructed with regard to who decides the legal sufficiency of the evidence? *People v. Batashure*, 75 N.Y.2d 306, 552 N.Y.S.2d 896, 552 N.E.2d 144 (1990)(grand jurors, not prosecutor, decide sufficiency of evidence; improper for prosecutor to inform grand jurors that prosecutor has already determined that enough evidence exists to warrant an indictment);

e. Did the prosecutor properly answer any questions raised by the grand jurors? CPL § 190.25(6);

f. Were the prosecutor's legal instructions too confusing to be understood by the grand jury in considering the charges? *People v. Caracciola*, 164 A.D.2d 755, 560 N.Y.S.2d 133 (1st Dep't 1990), aff'd 78 N.Y.2d 1021, 576 N.Y.S.2d 74, 581 N.E.2d 1329 (1991);

g. Did the prosecutor inject his [her] personal opinions or beliefs or vouch for the credibility of prosecution witnesses? *People v. Bartolomeo*, 126 A.D.2d 375, 513 N.Y.S.2d 981 (2d Dep't 1987); and

h. Was there excessive delay between the instructions at the beginning of the term and the legal instructions in defendant's case made at the close of the presentation of the evidence? *People v. Augustine*, 172 A.D.2d 843, 569 N.Y.S.2d 207 (2d Dep't 1991).

Discovery and Inspection

8. Pursuant to section 240.20 of the Criminal Procedure Law, defendant seeks discovery and inspection of the following property and information:

a. Any written, recorded or oral statements of defendant or an alleged co-conspirator or accomplice, except as previously provided to defendant, made other than in the course of the criminal transaction, to a public servant engaged in law enforcement activity or to a person acting under such public servant's direction or in cooperation with him or her, regardless of whether the prosecution intends to offer such statement at trial and regardless of whether such statement was made under a promise of full or partial immunity;

b. [If applicable: Any transcript of testimony relating to the criminal action herein, given by defendant, or by a co-defendant to be tried jointly, before any grand jury;]

c. Any written report or document, or portion thereof, concerning a physical or mental examination or scientific test or experiment, relating to the criminal action or proceeding that was made by, or at the request or direction of a public servant engaged in law enforcement activity, or that was made by a person whom the prosecution intends to call as a witness at trial, or that the prosecution intends to introduce at trial;

d. Any photographs, drawings, diagram, chart or other reproduction made by or at the direction of a police officer, peace officer or prosecutor of any property prior to the release pursuant to the provisions of section 450.10 of the Penal Law, irrespective of whether the prosecution intends to introduce at trial the photograph, photocopy, drawing, diagram, chart or other reproduction;

f. A list of any property obtained from defendant;

g. Any tapes or electronic recordings made in the investigation of the charges herein, irrespective of whether such recording was made during the course of the alleged criminal transaction; and

h. Anything required to be disclosed to defendant, prior to trial, by the prosecution pursuant to the Constitution of this State or of the United States.

9. Because this property and information are material to the preparation of the defense, defendant also seeks discovery and inspection of the following:

a. A list of all tangible objects, including books, records, photographs and contraband, that the prosecution intends to offer at any pretrial hearing or at trial, and copies thereof;

b. The names and addresses of any uncharged individuals who allegedly participated in the offense(s) charged against defendant;

c. The names, shield numbers, and commands of all law enforcement personnel who participated in the investigation, arrest and any interrogation of defendant;

d. All police reports, complaint reports, follow-up reports, arrest reports and other reports maintained by law enforcement personnel in this case;

e. A written list of the names, addresses and qualifications of all experts the prosecution intends to call as witnesses at trial, together with all reports prepared by such experts or, if reports have not been prepared, a brief description of the opinion and subject matter of the opinion to which each will testify; and

f. Pursuant to sections 240.44 and 240.45 of the Criminal Procedure Law, all statements made by persons the prosecution intends to call as witnesses at any pretrial hearing or at trial that relate to the subject matter of their testimony.

10. Pursuant to the prosecution's obligation under the federal and New York Constitutions, *see Brady v. Maryland*, 373 U.S. 83, 83 S.Ct. 1194, 10 L.Ed.2d 215 (1963); *People v. Vilardi*, 76 N.Y.2d 67, 556 N.Y.S.2d 518, 555 N.E.2d 915 (1990), defendant also seeks disclosure of all exculpatory evidence in the prosecution's possession, custody or control that may be used to impeach any person the prosecution intends to call as a witness at any pretrial hearing or at trial (hereinafter a "prospective witness"), including, without limitation:

a. All records and information revealing prior criminal convictions or guilty verdicts or juvenile adjudications, including but not limited to relevant "rap sheets," of any prospective witness;

b. Whether any prospective witness has been incarcerated in a federal, state or local correctional facility, and if so the prison records of such witness;

c. A full and complete statement of any and all criminal cases currently known by the prosecution to be pending against any prospective witness, regardless of whether such cases are the subject of promise, regard or inducement;

d. A full and complete statement of any and all regulatory, licensing or other governmental or quasi-governmental proceedings now pending, closed, discontinued, settled or completed against any prospective witness;

e. A full and complete statement as to any and all considerations or promises of consideration given during the course of the investigation and preparation of this action by any law enforcement officials, including prosecutors or agents, police or informers, to or on behalf of any prospective witness, or any such consideration or promises expected or hoped for by any such witness. Such "considerations" refer to anything that arguably could be of value or use to the witness, including but not limited to—formal or informal, direct or indirect—leniency, favorable treatment or recommendations or other assistance with respect to any past, pending or potential criminal, parole, probation, pardon, clemency, civil, administrative, forfeiture, licensing or other matter involving any local, state or federal government or any other authority or parties; relief from forfeiture, payments of money, rewards or fees, witness fees and special witness fees; provisions of food, clothing, transportation, legal services or other benefits; placement in a "witness protection" program; letters to anyone informing the recipient of the witness's cooperation; recommendations concerning federal or state aid or benefits; recommendations concerning licensing, certification or registration; promises to take affirmative action to help the status of the witness in a profession, business or employment situation or promises not to jeopardize such status; aid or efforts in securing or maintaining the business or employment of a witness; and anything else that arguably could reveal an interest, motive or bias in the witness in favor of the prosecution or against the defendant or act as an inducement to testify or color the witness's testimony;

f. A full and complete statement of any and all criminal conduct of which the prosecution has knowledge that has been committed by any prospective witness concerning which there has been no conviction, regardless of whether these crimes are the subject of a promise, reward or inducement and regardless of whether these crimes are the subject of a pending criminal charge;

g. A statement as to the existence of any and all statements—formal or informal, oral or written—by the prosecution, its agents and representatives to a prospective witness (including counsel for witness) pertaining in any way to the possibility, likelihood, course or outcome of any government or quasi-government action—state or federal, civil or criminal—or anyone related by blood or marriage to the witness;

h. A statement as to the existence of any and all threats—expressed or implied, direct or indirect—or other coercion directed against any prospective witness; criminal prosecutions, forfeiture actions, investigations, or potential prosecutions pending or that could be brought or re-instituted against any such witness; any probationary, parole, deferred prosecution or custodial status of any such witness; and any civil, tax court, court of claims, administrative, or other pending or potential legal disputes or transactions involving any such witness and the state or federal government or over which the state or federal government has real, apparent or perceived influence;

i. A statement as to whether the prosecution has requested or authorized payment of any sums of money to any informant, cooperating witness or potential co-defendants who have agreed to testify for the prosecution or who participated in the investigation that led to the instant action, or to any other prospective witness;

j. Any logs, records or other documents relating to the payment of sums of money to any individual described in subparagraph (i) and the source of any such payments;

k. A list of any and all requests, demands or complaints made to the government by a prospective witness that defendant arguably could develop on cross-examination to demonstrate any hope or expectation on the witness's part for favorable governmental action in his or her behalf, regardless of whether the government has agreed to provide any favorable action;

l. Any material not otherwise listed herein that reflects or evidences the motivation of a prospective witness either to cooperate with the government or of any bias or hostility against defendant;

m. The existence and identification of each occasion on which a prospective witness has testified before any court, grand jury or other tribunal or body, or otherwise officially narrated in connection with the investigation of the facts of this case;

n. Any statement or documents, including but not limited to grand jury testimony and federal, state and local tax returns, made or executed by any prospective witness that the prosecution knows, or through reasonable diligence, should have reason to know is false;

o. The existence and identification of each occasion on which a prospective witness who is an informant, accomplice, co-conspirator or expert has testified before any court, grand jury or other tribunal or body;

p. A copy of all medical and psychiatric reports or information known to the prosecution or that can reasonably become known to the prosecution concerning any prospective witness that may arguably affect the witness's credibility, ability to perceive or relate or recall events;

q. Whether or not any prospective witness has been hospitalized or treated for psychiatric or emotional disorders or alcoholism or drug abuse, and if so the names of any institutions involved and the dates of any hospitalizations, and any and all reports relating to any treatment for such conditions;

r. Any written or oral statements, whether or not reduced to writing, made by any prospective witness, that in any way contradicts or is inconsistent with or different from other oral or written statements he or she has made, and any such statements made by any person, whether a prospective witness or not, that in any way contradicts or is inconsistent with or different from statements made by a prospective witness;

s. Any evidence that may be used to impeach or discredit any prospective witness—particularly, but not exclusively, inconsistent statements of bias or prejudice against defendant—by a prospective witness, or admissions of poor memory by a prospective witness;

t. Any requests prepared by the prosecution for permission to grant immunity or leniency for any prospective witness, whether or not such request was granted, and the identities of any and all such witnesses who have been offered immunity;

u. Any and all other records or information that arguably could be helpful or useful to the defense in impeaching or otherwise detracting from the probative force of the prosecution's evidence;

v. The same records and information specified in subparagraphs (a) through (u) with respect to each non-witness declarant whose statements will be offered in evidence at any pretrial hearing or at trial;

w. The names and addresses of all persons whom the prosecution, its agents and representatives believe to have relevant knowledge or information concerning the charges herein but whom the prosecution does not expect to call as witnesses at any pretrial hearing or at trial;

x. Copies of any and all records of law enforcement or other governmental agencies reflecting intra-departmental disciplinary action taken against any law enforcement or agency official who will testify in this action, including all such records from any governmental agency for which the witness previously worked; and

y. Copies of any and all records of law enforcement or other governmental agencies reflecting any commendations, awards or other recognition of any kind received by, or requests for any commendations, awards or recognition of any kind made by, any of the agents or law enforcement officers involved in this case with respect to this case.

Bill of Particulars

11. Pursuant to section 200.95 of the Criminal Procedure Law, defendant hereby seeks the following information, disclosure of which is necessary for defendant to adequately prepare and conduct a defense:

a. [Request disclosure of any the factual information relating to the offense(s) charged against defendant, *e.g.*, the exact date(s), time(s) and place(s) where the offense(s) allegedly occurred; the identity of any persons referred to but not identified in the indictment; the names of any unindicted accomplices or co-conspirators; how defendant acted in concert with another; the facts and circumstances tending to prove that defendant acted with the intent to commit the charged offense(s); and whether any of the information leading to defendant's arrest was supplied by a confidential informant].

12. All of the items specified in paragraphs 8–11 are requested with respect to property and information within the possession and control of the prosecution. Defendant also demands that the prosecution, pursuant to section 240.20(2) of the Criminal Procedure Law, make a diligent, good faith effort to ascertain the existence of demanded property and information and to cause such property and information to be made available for discovery and inspection if it exists but is not within the prosecution's possession, custody or control. To the extent that any item is known by the prosecution to exist but is not within the prosecution's possession or is claimed not to be within its control but is available to defendant by subpoena, defendant respectfully requests

disclosure of such information necessary to form the basis for a subpoena directed to the custodian or person possessed of such item.

13. Pursuant to section 240.60 of the Criminal Procedure Law, defendant hereby demands that the prosecution abide by the continuing duty to disclose all additional property and information sought herein that the prosecution learns or comes into possession of subsequent to this demand.

Suppression of Statements

14. Pursuant to section 710.20(3) of the Criminal Procedure Law, defendant hereby moves to suppress any and all statements he [she] allegedly made to any public servant or servants engaged in law enforcement; in the alternative, defendant moves for a hearing to determine whether such statements should be suppressed. Upon information and belief, such statements were involuntarily made and obtained from defendant in violation of defendant's rights under the State and federal Constitutions.

* * *

15. Defendant requests the right to make further motions that may be appropriate based upon material that the prosecution discloses in response to the motions made herein.

WHEREFORE, defendant requests that the Court issue an order granting the relief sought herein.

Dated: _____, 19__
_____, New York

[Signature]
_____
[Name of defense attorney]

Chapter 9

TIMELINESS OF PROSECUTION AND SPEEDY TRIAL

Table of Sections

9.1 CPL Article 30—Introduction.
9.2 Statute of Limitations—Introduction.
9.3 ____ Relevant Time Periods.
9.4 ____ Extensions.
9.5 ____ Tolling.
9.6 ____ How and When to Raise; Burden of Proof.
9.7 ____ Waiver of Defense by Guilty Plea.
9.8 Federal Constitutional Speedy Trial.
9.9 State Speedy Trial and Due Process Guarantees—In General.
9.10 ____ *Taranovich* Factors.
9.11 Preference of Criminal Over Civil Cases.
9.12 Constitutional Speedy Trial/Due Process Claims—Procedural Requirements.
9.13 Prosecutorial Readiness Rule—In General.
9.14 Nonapplicability to Some Criminal Actions.
9.15 "Commencement" of the Criminal Action Starts the Clock Ticking.
9.16 Special Recommencement Rule—Plea Withdrawal, Mistrial, or Order for New Trial.
9.17 Desk Appearance Tickets.
9.18 Reduction of Original Charges—Reduction of Felony Complaint.
9.19 ____ Inspection and Reduction of Indicted Felony.
9.20 ____ Other Reductions.
9.21 Prosecutor's "Readiness" Stops the Clock—"Readiness" Defined.
9.22 ____ Genuine "Readiness" Defined.
9.23 ____ Valid Communication of "Present" Readiness Defined.
9.24 Time Within Which Prosecution Must Be Ready to Avoid Dismissal.
9.25 Time Within Which Prosecution Must Be Ready to Avoid Release of Jailed Defendant on Bail or Recognizance.
9.26 Excludable Periods—In General.
9.27 ____ Other Proceedings Concerning the Defendant.
9.28 ____ ____ Competency.
9.29 ____ ____ Discovery.
9.30 ____ ____ Pretrial Motions.
9.31 ____ ____ Appeals.
9.32 ____ ____ Trial of Other Charges.
9.33 ____ ____ The Period During Which Such Matters Are Under Consideration by the Court.
9.34 ____ Continuances.
9.35 ____ Absence or Unavailability of the Defendant.
9.36 ____ ____ Cause of Prosecution's Unreadiness.
9.37 ____ ____ Bench Warrants.
9.38 ____ ____ Absent.
9.39 ____ ____ Unavailable.
9.40 ____ Co-defendant Joinder.
9.41 ____ Incarcerated Defendants.

Table of Sections

9.42 ___ Defendant Without Counsel.
9.43 ___ Exceptional Circumstances.
9.44 ___ Adjournments in Contemplation of Dismissal.
9.45 ___ Prosecutor's Direction to Appear at Arraignment.
9.46 ___ Family Offenses.
9.47 Post–Readiness Delay.
9.48 Procedural Considerations—Calculating Time.
9.49 ___ Motion Practice Requirements.
9.50 ___ Sufficiency of Motion Papers and Burden of Proof.
9.51 ___ Sufficiency of Motion Papers.
9.52 ___ Burden of Proof.
9.53 Interstate Agreement on Detainers (CPL § 580.20).
9.54 Interstate Agreement on Detainers—The Prisoner's Request (Article III).
9.55 ___ The Receiving State's Request (Article IV).
9.56 Practice Summary—Defense.
9.57 ___ Prosecution.
9.58 Forms.
    9.58.1 Notice of Motion to Dismiss for Statute of Limitations Violation.
    9.58.2 Affirmation in Support of Motion to Dismiss for Statute of Limitations Violation.
    9.58.3 Notice of Motion to Dismiss Indictment for Violation of Right to Speedy Trial (Constitutional/CPL § 30.20).
    9.58.4 Affirmation in Support of Motion to Dismiss Indictment for Violation of Right to Speedy Trial (Constitutional/CPL § 30.20).
    9.58.5 Notice of Motion to Dismiss Indictment for Failure of the Prosecution to Timely Announce Readiness for Trial (CPL § 30.30(1) Only).
    9.58.6 Affirmation in Support of Motion to Dismiss Indictment for Failure of the Prosecution to Timely Announce Readiness for Trial (CPL § 30.30(1) Only).
    9.58.7 Notice of Motion For Bail/Recognizance for Failure of the Prosecution to Timely Announce Readiness for Trial (CPL § 30.30(2) Only).
    9.58.8 Affirmation in Support of Motion for Bail/Recognizance for Failure of the Prosecution to Timely Announce Readiness for Trial (CPL § 30.30(2) Only).

WESTLAW Electronic Research

See WESTLAW Electronic Research Guide preceding the Summary of Contents.

§ 9.1 CPL Article 30—Introduction

CPL Article 30 contains the various provisions governing timeliness of prosecution and speedy trial.

The statute of limitations, codified in CPL § 30.10, bars prosecutions following specified periods of pre-accusatory delay. This section applies neither to post-accusatory delay, nor to class A felonies.

Section 30.20(1) contains New York State's speedy trial guarantee, which incorporates the federal constitutional Sixth Amendment speedy trial guarantee as well as the right to a speedy trial contained in New York Civil Rights Law § 12. As this chapter will show, however, the most fruitful vehicle for raising a speedy trial claim is under the due process clause (Art. 1, § 6) of the New York State Constitution.

By invoking the state due process clause, a defendant raising a claim of untimely prosecution (1) may aggregate pre- and post-accusatory delay, (2) need not make a specific showing of prejudice, (3) and need not have insisted throughout the delay on a speedy trial. Moreover, the prosecution has the burden of showing good cause where the delay is protracted. Any defense practitioner raising a constitutional speedy trial claim, but not relying in part on the state due process clause, is doing the client a disservice.

Constitutional speedy trial claims, unlike statute of limitation (CPL § 30.10) or CPL § 30.30 claims, are applicable to homicide prosecutions; accordingly, that is the arena in which they are the most useful for the defense. Constitutional claims also have the advantage, not shared by section 30.10 and 30.30 claims, of clearly surviving a plea of guilty.

CPL § 30.30 contains New York's prosecutorial readiness rule. Section 30.30 is applicable only to non-homicide prosecutions, and covers only post-accusatory delay. No showing of prejudice is required to prevail on such a claim. This statute does not actually mandate a speedy trial, only that the prosecution declare readiness within designated deadlines.

While section 30.30 has engendered many dismissals of criminal actions, it generally has not promoted speedier trials, nor has it altered the culture of "unreadiness" pervasive to busy criminal courtrooms, especially those in New York City. On any given day in such courtrooms, many criminal cases are on "for trial," yet in few of those cases do the parties expect to actually start a trial, and in fewer still do trials actually occur. Notably, in no way does section 30.30 encourage defense lawyers to move cases along.

Section 30.30 is also a procedural quagmire and, since the burden of proof is often on the prosecution in the litigation of such claims, the section is often a deathtrap for unwary prosecutors. Nor is the statute user-friendly for defense lawyers. While this chapter makes every effort to render section 30.30's exacting language and interpretive caselaw comprehensible, that effort is, at best, a difficult one. Practitioners should make their peace with section 30.30, but not aspire to master its unfathomable nuances.

Finally, neither the defense nor the prosecution should overlook the Interstate Agreement on Detainers, codified in CPL § 580.20. It not only allows for the production of out-of-state or federal prisoners to resolve outstanding New York charges, but sets stringent deadlines for resolution of those charges. Failure to meet these deadlines results in dismissal of the outstanding charges, with prejudice.

Library References:
> West's Key No. Digests, Constitutional Law ⟜268(4); Criminal Law ⟜106–145, 577.1–577.16.

§ 9.2 Statute of Limitations—Introduction

Statutes of limitation, such as those embodied in CPL § 30.10, are creatures of public policy that "limit exposure to criminal prosecution to

§ 9.2 TIMELINESS OF PROSECUTION & SPEEDY TRIAL Ch. 9

a certain fixed period of time following the occurrence of those acts the legislature has decided to punish by criminal sanctions."[1] Such statutes provide protection against prosecution once the passage of time has rendered proof of innocence difficult to obtain, as well as encourage the prompt investigation and prosecution of criminal acts.[2] It has often been stated that because such limitations are meant, in part, to protect individuals against the loss of proof of innocence, they are to be liberally construed in favor of the defendant.[3]

Nonetheless, it has been held, convincingly, that a defendant has no "vested right" in the statute of limitations as it reads at the time of the commission of the criminal act, as opposed to the way it reads at the time the statute has run; at any time up to the point it has run for a particular defendant, the Legislature may alter the statute without offending the defendant's rights.[4]

Library References:
West's Key No. Digests, Criminal Law ⚖145.5.

§ 9.3 Statute of Limitations—Relevant Time Periods

The relevant CPL § 30.10 time period within which a prosecution must be brought is measured from the date the crime is committed to the date the criminal action is commenced.[5] There is no statute of limitation for any Class A felony.[6] For all other offenses (except those specified in CPL § 30.10[3][7]), the time periods are: five years for a non-Class A felony,[8] two years for a misdemeanor,[9] and one year for a petty offense.[10]

The time period commences on the date the crime is committed; for "continuous" offenses, the relevant date is the termination date of the offense, not its starting date.[11] For conspiracy prosecutions, the crime is

---

1. Toussie v. United States, 397 U.S. 112, 114, 90 S.Ct. 858, 859, 25 L.E.2d 156 (1970).

2. 397 U.S. at 114–115, 90 S.Ct. at 860.

3. United States v. Scharton, 285 U.S. 518, 522, 52 S.Ct. 416, 417, 76 L.Ed. 917 (1932); People ex rel. Reibman v. Warden, 242 A.D. 282, 275 N.Y.S. 59 (3d Dep't 1934); People v. McAllister, 77 Misc.2d 142, 352 N.Y.S.2d 360 (N.Y.C.Crim.Ct.1974).

4. See People v. Glowa, 87 Misc.2d 471, 384 N.Y.S.2d 673 (Sup.Ct., Kings County, 1976) and cases cited therein.

5. CPL § 30.10(1) and (2).

6. CPL § 30.10(2)(a).

7. See § 9.4, infra. These are prosecutions for larceny by a person violating a fiduciary duty, offenses by public servants while in office, certain violations of the environmental conservation law, and certain misdemeanor tax offenses.

8. CPL § 30.10(2)(b).

9. CPL § 30.10(2)(c).

10. CPL § 30.10(2)(d).

11. People v. Rosich, 170 A.D.2d 703, 567 N.Y.S.2d 749 (2d Dep't 1991); People v. Eastern Ambulance Service, Inc., 106 A.D.2d 867, 483 N.Y.S.2d 508 (4th Dep't 1984).

Examples of crimes which have been held to be "continuous" are: usury (People v. Brown, 159 Misc.2d 11, 603 N.Y.S.2d 256 (Sup.Ct., Kings County, 1993)); endangering the welfare of a child (People v. DeLong, 206 A.D.2d 914, 615 N.Y.S.2d 168 (4th Dep't 1994)); some larcenies (People v. Rosich, supra); and restraint of trade (People v. Eastern Ambulance Service, Inc., supra). Others have been held noncontinuous, e.g., bookmaking (People v. Erickson, 302 N.Y. 461, 99 N.E.2d 240 (1951)); and most sex crimes (People v. Keindl, 68 N.Y.2d 410, 509 N.Y.S.2d 790, 502 N.E.2d 577 (1986)).

The weight of authority is that bail jumping is not a continuous offense. See People

Ch. 9   **EXTENSIONS**   § 9.4

considered complete when the overt act—or the last of more than one overt acts—has occurred.[12]

The criminal action is commenced with the filing of a jurisdictionally valid accusatory instrument; an invalid accusatory instrument that fails to confer jurisdiction will not toll the running of the statute.[13]

Library References:

West's Key No. Digests, Criminal Law ☞148–160.

§ 9.4   Statute of Limitations—Extensions

Notwithstanding the time periods specified in CPL § 30.10(2), for certain offenses (listed in subdivision three) those periods may be extended. These extensions reflect the difficulty of uncovering the specified crimes.

Under subdivision (3)(a), a prosecution for larceny committed by someone with a fiduciary duty may be commenced within one year after the discovery of the facts underlying the offense, or within one year after those facts reasonably should have been discovered by the "aggrieved party," or that party's legal representative who is not him or herself implicated.

Pursuant to subdivision (3)(b), a prosecution for any offense involving misconduct in "public office" by a "public servant"[14] may be commenced at any time during the defendant's service in that office, or within five years after the termination of that service. This extension, however, cannot be for a period greater than five years beyond what it would have been under subdivision two.

As per subdivision (3)(c), the prosecution of any crime set forth in Title 27 of Article 71 of the Environmental Conservation Law[15] may be commenced within four years after the facts underlying such an offense either have been discovered, or reasonably should have been discovered by the public official responsible for enforcing those provisions.[16]

Finally, pursuant to subdivision (3)(d), a prosecution for any misdemeanor set forth in the Tax Law or Chapter 46 of the New York City

---

v. Landy, 125 A.D.2d 703, 510 N.Y.S.2d 190 (2d Dep't 1986); People v. Barnes, 130 Misc.2d 1058, 499 N.Y.S.2d 343 (Sup.Ct., N.Y. County, 1986); People v. McAllister, 77 Misc.2d 142, 352 N.Y.S.2d 360 (N.Y.C.Crim.Ct.1974). But see People v. Ingram, 74 Misc.2d 635, 345 N.Y.S.2d 441 (N.Y.C.Crim.Ct.1973)(holding to the contrary).

12. People v. Leisner, 73 N.Y.2d 140, 146, 538 N.Y.S.2d 517, 519, 535 N.E.2d 647 (1989); People v. Hines, 284 N.Y. 93, 113, 29 N.E.2d 483, 493 (1940).

13. People v. Kase, 76 A.D.2d 532, 431 N.Y.S.2d 531 (1st Dep't 1980) aff'd 53 N.Y.2d 989, 441 N.Y.S.2d 671, 424 N.E.2d 558 (1981).

14. A former police officer, prosecuted for perjury committed before a grand jury, was deemed a "public servant" under this section, since the incident about which he lied occurred while he was on duty, in uniform, and on police business. People v. Vogler, 92 Misc.2d 462, 400 N.Y.S.2d 315 (Sup.Ct., Westchester County, 1977).

15. See ECL §§ 71–2707 to 2717, regarding the unlawful possession of, disposal of, or dealing in hazardous wastes or substances.

16. This extension has been held not to deprive public officials of equal protection under the law. People v. Glowa, 87 Misc.2d 471, 384 N.Y.S.2d 673 (Sup.Ct., Kings County, 1976).

§ 9.4 TIMELINESS OF PROSECUTION & SPEEDY TRIAL Ch. 9

Administrative Code may be commenced within three years of commission.

Library References:
West's Key No. Digests, Criminal Law ⚖151–154.

§ 9.5 Statute of Limitations—Tolling

In calculating the time limitations contained in subdivisions two and three, certain periods are excluded under subdivision four: tolling the running of the statute are any periods following the commission of the offense during which either the defendant was "continuously outside" New York State,[17] or the defendant's whereabouts were continuously "unknown" or "unascertainable by the exercise of reasonable diligence."[18]

Pursuant to subdivision (4)(b), the running of the statute also may be tolled, under certain circumstances, during the life of a jurisdictionally valid accusatory instrument that is nonetheless dismissed. That subdivision provides that when a criminal action is "lawfully"[19] commenced prior to the running of the statute, and the accusatory instrument is subsequently dismissed by an "authorized court" that gives leave to reprosecute for the same offense, the statute is tolled by "the period extending from the commencement of the thus defeated prosecution to the dismissal of the accusatory instrument."

An open question is whether the statute is thus tolled when a dismissed accusatory instrument contains a felony for which the statutory period of five years had not run as of the time of the filing of the accusatory instrument, and that felony is then subject to reduction by the court to a misdemeanor for which the statutory period had run. In *People v. Norman*,[20] a lower court held that the filing of the felony complaint in such circumstances commenced the action for all purposes, and subsequent reduction to a misdemeanor pursuant to CPL § 180.50 did not constitute the commencement of a new criminal action so as to time-bar prosecution of the misdemeanor. Other lower courts, however, have held the misdemeanor time-barred under similar circumstances.[21]

---

17. CPL § 30.10(4)(a)(i). There is no statutory minimum duration of time for an absence to toll the statute. People v. Ferrari, 155 Misc.2d 749, 589 N.Y.S.2d 983 (Ulster Co.Ct.1992). Cf. CPLR 207 (providing that an absence must be four months or more in duration to toll the civil statute of limitations). Even so, vacations or other brief excursions from the state have been deemed not to toll the statute. See People v. Ferrari, supra; People v. Yanez, 128 Misc.2d 716, 723, 490 N.Y.S.2d 971 (Sup. Ct., N.Y. County, 1985).

18. CPL § 30.10(4)(a)(ii). Good faith efforts by a civilian complainant to locate a defendant have been held not to toll the statute. People v. Lennertz, 156 Misc.2d 88, 591 N.Y.S.2d 955 (N.Y.C.Crim.Ct.1992).

19. The filing of an accusatory instrument that is jurisdictionally defective is not a "lawful" commencement and would not toll the running of the statute. See § 9.3, supra.

20. 150 Misc.2d 583, 569 N.Y.S.2d 573 (N.Y.C.Crim.Ct.1991).

21. People v. Tomassetti, 159 Misc.2d 969, 607 N.Y.S.2d 588 (Sup.Ct., Kings County, 1993); People v. Crosby, 140 Misc.2d 904, 531 N.Y.S.2d 753 (Dist.Ct., Suffolk County, 1988); People v. Soto, 76 Misc.2d 491, 352 N.Y.S.2d 144 (N.Y.C.Crim. Ct.1974).

If certain criminal charges would otherwise be time-barred, of course, the bar cannot be avoided simply by including them in an accusatory instrument along with counts that are not time-barred.[22]

Library References:
West's Key No. Digests, Criminal Law ⚖151–160.

§ 9.6 Statute of Limitations—How and When to Raise; Burden of Proof

A defendant seeking to raise a statute of limitations defense may make a pretrial motion for dismissal of the accusatory instrument.[23] The burden of proof on such a motion has been the subject of an as yet unresolved debate. Some courts have adhered to the historical view—conceived at a time when the statute of limitations defense could only be raised at trial—that the prosecution must disprove the defense beyond a reasonable doubt.[24] Other courts have noted, correctly, that CPL § 210.45(7) places the burden on the defendant, by a preponderance of the evidence, of establishing his or her right to a pretrial dismissal of an accusatory instrument.[25] Definitive resolution of this issue must await legislative revision or Court of Appeals clarification.

Although a statute of limitations violation is a valid defense, the accusatory instrument need not appear timely on its face, nor need it allege any facts tolling or extending the CPL § 30.10 time limitations.[26]

If not raised in a timely fashion in a pretrial motion to dismiss, the statute of limitations defense is foreclosed to the defendant, unless the court, for good cause shown, extends the time for raising it.[27]

Another unresolved question is whether the defendant, assuming he or she has raised the statute of limitations issue pretrial and has failed to prevail, may again raise the issue as a defense at trial. Prior to the

---

22. See, e.g., People v. Monaco, 121 Misc.2d 976, 469 N.Y.S.2d 863 (Sup.Ct., N.Y. County, 1983); People v. Lohnes, 76 Misc.2d 507, 351 N.Y.S.2d 279 (Sup.Ct., N.Y. County, 1973). At least two intermediate appellate courts have held that an uncharged offense that would have been time-barred under the statute of limitations cannot be submitted to the fact-finder at trial as a lesser included offense of a timely charged higher count. People v. Hughes, ___ A.D.2d ___, 632 N.Y.S.2d 585 (2d Dep't 1995); People v. DiPasquale, 161 App.Div. 196, 146 N.Y.S. 523 (3d Dep't 1914). The Court of Appeals has yet to rule on this issue.

23. CPL §§ 170.30(1)(d), 210.20(1)(f). Prior to the enactment of the CPL, a statute of limitations defense could only be raised at trial, not by pretrial motion. See People v. Kohut, 30 N.Y.2d 183, 192, 331 N.Y.S.2d 416, 423, 282 N.E.2d 312 (1972).

24. See People v. Kohut, 30 N.Y.2d at 191, 331 N.Y.S.2d at 423; People v. Dickson, 133 A.D.2d 492, 519 N.Y.S.2d 419 (3d Dep't 1987); People ex. rel. Barnes v. N.Y.C. Penitentiary, 75 Misc.2d 291, 347 N.Y.S.2d 383 (Sup.Ct., Bronx County, 1973).

25. See People v. Ferrari, 155 Misc.2d 749, 589 N.Y.S.2d 983 (Ulster Co.Ct.1992); People v. Yanez, 128 Misc.2d 716, 721, 490 N.Y.S.2d 971, 975 (Sup.Ct., N.Y. County, 1985).

26. People v. Kohut, 30 N.Y.2d at 191, 331 N.Y.S.2d at 423.

27. CPL §§ 210.20(2) and (3), 255.10(1)(a), 255.20; People v. Blake, 193 N.Y. 616, 86 N.E. 1129 (1908); People v. DePillo, 168 A.D.2d 899, 565 N.Y.S.2d 650 (4th Dep't 1990); People v. Gross, 148 Misc.2d 232, 560 N.Y.S.2d 227 (N.Y.C.Crim. Ct.1990). Cf. People v. Perico, 143 Misc.2d 961, 542 N.Y.S.2d 911 (Dist.Ct., Nassau County, 1989)(defense may be raised even if 45-day limit has run).

§ 9.6 TIMELINESS OF PROSECUTION & SPEEDY TRIAL Ch. 9

enactment of the CPL such a defense could only be raised at trial, and the People had the burden of disproving it, once raised, beyond a reasonable doubt.[28] No case has determined whether the right of the defendant to raise this defense at trial, and to require the prosecution to disprove it beyond a reasonable doubt, survived the enactment of the CPL, and its creation of the right to move to dismiss pretrial pursuant to CPL § 210.20(1)(f).[29]

In *People v. Leisner*,[30] the Court of Appeals held that it was error, in a conspiracy prosecution, for the court to refuse to charge the jury that the prosecution bore the burden of proving, beyond a reasonable doubt, that at least one overt act took place within the statute of limitations period. The Court noted that such proof was required both by CPL § 30.10(2) and by Penal Law § 105.20 (requiring the proof of an overt act in a conspiracy prosecution).[31] Although the *Leisner* rationale could conceivably be limited to conspiracy prosecutions, it would be an analytical strain to distinguish the requirement of proof of an overt act from the requirement of proof that the underlying offense occurred. Hence, *Leisner* foreshadows, at the very least, a holding that the prosecution must disprove beyond a reasonable doubt any statute of limitations defense raised at trial.[32]

Library References:
West's Key No. Digests, Criminal Law ⟐288, 330, 335, 565.

§ 9.7 Statute of Limitations—Waiver of Defense by Guilty Plea

Courts have held that a plea of guilty waives any statute of limitations defense, at least where the issue was not litigated by timely motion.[33] Less clear is whether the defense is waived by a guilty plea where it has been fully litigated and decided prior to the plea. Like constitutional speedy trial claims—which are not waived by a guilty plea—the statute of limitations claim may implicate the loss to the defendant of the means to prove him or herself innocent.[34] On the other

---

28. People v. Kohut, 30 N.Y.2d at 191–92, 331 N.Y.S.2d at 423–24.

29. See Preiser, "Practice Commentary" to CPL § 30.10, McKinney's Cons. Laws of New York, Book 11A, at 137–138 (1992). See also People v. Schwenk, 92 Misc.2d 331, 400 N.Y.S.2d 291 (Suffolk Co.Ct.1977)(pretrial motion to dismiss for CPL § 30.10 violation denied, with right to re-raise at trial).

30. 73 N.Y.2d 140, 538 N.Y.S.2d 517, 535 N.E.2d 647 (1989).

31. 73 N.Y.2d at 146, 538 N.Y.S.2d at 520.

32. Note also that the Court of Appeals has held that lack of geographical jurisdiction (CPL § 20.40), if raised as a trial defense, must be disproved beyond a reason-able doubt. People v. McLaughlin, 80 N.Y.2d 466, 591 N.Y.S.2d 966, 606 N.E.2d 1357 (1992).

33. People v. Verkey, 185 A.D.2d 622, 585 N.Y.S.2d 897 (4th Dep't 1992); People v. Dickson, 133 A.D.2d 492, 519 N.Y.S.2d 419 (3d Dep't 1987); People v. Soto, 76 Misc.2d 491, 352 N.Y.S.2d 144 (N.Y.C.Crim. Ct.1974). But see People v. Walsh, 123 Misc.2d 1042, 1055, 476 N.Y.S.2d 408, 416 (Sup.Ct., Richmond County, 1984), rev'd on other grounds 108 A.D.2d 464, 489 N.Y.S.2d 933 (2d Dep't 1985)(statute of limitations violation held to be "jurisdictional defect" not waived by guilty plea).

34. People v. Blakley, 34 N.Y.2d 311, 314–15, 357 N.Y.S.2d 459, 462, 313 N.E.2d 763 (1974).

hand, since a statute of limitations defense is solely a creature of statute and is generally considered nonjurisdictional,[35] the answer, when it comes, may well be that it is always waived by operation of the guilty plea.

Library References:
West's Key No. Digests, Criminal Law ⬅273.4(1).

§ 9.8 Federal Constitutional Speedy Trial

The federal constitutional right to a speedy trial is contained in the Sixth Amendment to the United States Constitution, and is applicable to the states via the due process clause of the Fourteenth Amendment.[36] The only appropriate relief for a deprivation of this right is dismissal of the accusatory instrument, with prejudice.[37]

The Supreme Court has identified three interests that the defendant might have in a speedy trial: to "prevent oppressive pretrial incarceration," to "minimize [the defendant's] anxiety and concern," and to "limit the possibility that the defense will be impaired."[38] That court has also noted, however, the "societal interest" in swift justice "which exists separate from, and at times in opposition to, the interests of the accused."[39]

In *Barker v. Wingo*, the Supreme Court recognized that it is "impossible to determine with precision when the right has been denied,"[40] and that the right cannot "be quantified into a specified number of days or months."[41] Thus, the court enunciated a four-pronged "balancing test," under which each set of facts must be evaluated on an *"ad hoc"* basis.[42]

The substance of this *Barker* test is best articulated in the subsequent case of *Doggett v. United States*,[43] in which the Supreme Court listed the "four separate enquiries" as follows:

> [W]hether delay before trial was uncommonly long, whether the government or the criminal defendant is more to blame for that delay, whether, in due course, the defendant asserted his right to a speedy trial, and whether he suffered prejudice as the

---

35. See People v. Kohut, 30 N.Y.2d 183, 331 N.Y.S.2d 416, 282 N.E.2d 312 (1972); People v. DePillo, 168 A.D.2d 899, 565 N.Y.S.2d 650 (4th Dep't 1990); People v. Dickson, 133 A.D.2d 492, 519 N.Y.S.2d 419 (3d Dep't 1987).

36. Klopfer v. North Carolina, 386 U.S. 213, 87 S.Ct. 988, 18 L.Ed.2d 1 (1967).

37. Strunk v. United States, 412 U.S. 434, 439–440, 93 S.Ct. 2260, 2263, 37 L.Ed.2d 56 (1973); Barker v. Wingo, 407 U.S. 514, 522, 92 S.Ct. 2182, 2187, 33 L.Ed.2d 101 (1972); People v. Taranovich, 37 N.Y.2d 442, 444, 373 N.Y.S.2d 79, 80, 335 N.E.2d 303 (1975).

38. Barker v. Wingo, 407 U.S. at 532, 92 S.Ct. at 2193. See also United States v. Marion, 404 U.S. 307, 320, 92 S.Ct. 455, 463, 30 L.Ed.2d 468 (1971); United States v. Ewell, 383 U.S. 116, 120, 86 S.Ct. 773, 776, 15 L.Ed.2d 627 (1966).

39. Barker v. Wingo, 407 U.S. at 519, 92 S.Ct. at 2186.

40. 407 U.S. at 521, 92 S.Ct. at 2187.

41. 407 U.S. at 523, 92 S.Ct. at 2188.

42. 407 U.S. at 530, 92 S.Ct. at 2191–2192.

43. 505 U.S. 647, 112 S.Ct. 2686, 120 L.Ed.2d 520 (1992).

§ 9.8 TIMELINESS OF PROSECUTION & SPEEDY TRIAL   Ch. 9

delay's result.[44]

The four *Barker* factors are considered "guidelines" only, not "rigid tests."[45] No one factor is "either a necessary or sufficient condition of the deprivation of a right to a speedy trial."[46] For example, in *Doggett*, the defendant, despite his inability to prove either particularized prejudice, prosecutorial bad faith, or persistent assertions of his right to a speedy trial, prevailed in light of the 8½-year delay, prosecutorial negligence, and defendant's unawareness of the pendency of the indictment.[47]

The federal right to a speedy trial protects not only those criminally accused, but those prosecuted as juveniles as well.[48] Additionally, even those criminal defendants lawfully incarcerated on an unrelated matter are covered by the federal speedy trial clause.[49] Not covered are defendants in such non-criminal matters as police departmental disciplinary proceedings,[50] international extradition proceedings,[51] and parole or probation revocation proceedings.[52]

Moreover, the New York Court of Appeals has squarely held that the Sixth Amendment right to a speedy trial—as opposed to the state and federal due process clauses—covers a defendant only until the accused is brought to trial.[53] It thus does not provide protection against delay in the appellate process.[54]

The Court of Appeals has also held that unreasonable delays in bench trial verdicts, or in imposing sentence, are prohibited by the CPL.[55] Federal courts have held that the federal speedy trial clause

---

44. 112 S.Ct. at 2690. The need for a court to engage in the balancing test however, is not even triggered unless the length of the delay crosses the threshold separating "ordinary" from "presumptively prejudicial" delay. Barker v. Wingo, 407 U.S. at 530–31, 92 S.Ct. at 2192. In Doggett, the Supreme Court accepted the collective wisdom of lower courts and legal commentators that a delay of one year meets this minimal threshold. Once this minimal threshold is met, the court must weigh the length of the delay against, or with, the three other Barker factors.

45. Perez v. Sullivan, 793 F.2d 249, 254 (10th Cir.1986), cert. den. 479 U.S. 936, 107 S.Ct. 413, 93 L.Ed.2d 364 (1986).

46. Barker v. Wingo, 407 U.S. at 533, 92 S.Ct. at 2193.

47. Doggett v. United States, supra.

48. See In re Gault, 387 U.S. 1, 13, 87 S.Ct. 1428, 1436, 18 L.Ed.2d 527 (1967); Matter of Dora P., 68 A.D.2d 719, 726, 418 N.Y.S.2d 597, 600 (1st Dep't 1979).

49. Smith v. Hooey, 393 U.S. 374, 89 S.Ct. 575, 21 L.Ed.2d 607 (1969).

50. Fitzgerald v. Cawley, 368 F.Supp. 677 (S.D.N.Y.1973).

51. McDonald v. Burrows, 731 F.2d 294, 297 (5th Cir.1984), cert. den. 469 U.S. 852, 105 S.Ct. 173, 83 L.Ed.2d 108 (1984); Sabatier v. Dabrowski, 586 F.2d 866, 869 (1st Cir.1978); Jhirad v. Ferrandina, 536 F.2d 478, 485 n. 9 (2d Cir.), cert. den. 429 U.S. 833, 97 S.Ct. 97, 50 L.Ed.2d 98, rehearing den. 429 U.S. 988, 97 S.Ct. 511, 50 L.Ed.2d 600 (1976).

52. Gagnon v. Scarpelli, 411 U.S. 778, 93 S.Ct. 1756, 36 L.Ed.2d 656 (1973). See also People v. Johnson, 159 A.D.2d 725, 553 N.Y.S.2d 206 (2d Dep't 1990)(speedy trial clause is not applicable to probation revocation proceedings, although a delay in lodging charges might, in special circumstances, constitute a due process violation).

53. People v. Cousart, 58 N.Y.2d 62, 458 N.Y.S.2d 507, 444 N.E.2d 971 (1982).

54. Id. An unjustifiable and prejudicial delay in a defendant's criminal appeal may violate the federal and state due process clauses, however. Muwwakkil v. Hoke, 968 F.2d 284 (2d Cir.1992)(federal due process); People v. Cousart, 58 N.Y.2d at 68–69, 458 N.Y.S.2d at 510 (state due process).

55. In People v. South, 41 N.Y.2d 451, 454, 393 N.Y.S.2d 695, 696, 362 N.E.2d 246 (1977), the court held that CPL § 350.10(3)(d) prohibited bench trial verdicts that are not rendered within a "reasonable time." In People v. Drake, 61

protects defendants up through the sentencing phase of the proceedings.[56]

The protections afforded by the Sixth Amendment's speedy trial clause are not triggered unless there has been "either a formal indictment or information or else the actual restraints imposed by arrest and holding to answer a criminal charge."[57] Lengthy pre-accusatory delay, even if resulting in actual prejudice to the defendant, is not covered by the Sixth Amendment's speedy trial clause.[58] Similarly not covered is any post-accusatory period during which the accusatory instrument stands dismissed, even if the instrument is later reinstated or superseded.[59]

In the rare circumstance in which the defendant can show that the pre-accusatory delay caused "substantial prejudice to [the defendant's] rights to a fair trial," the prosecution might run afoul of federal due process—as opposed to speedy trial—protections.[60] Proof of prejudice to the defense, however, is a "necessary but not sufficient element" of a federal due process claim. Rather, the due process inquiry must consider not only the prejudice to the defendant but the reason for the delay.[61] "[I]nvestigative delay," even if causing some prejudice to the defense, would not violate due process,[62] whereas prejudicial delay, as "an intentional device to gain tactical advantage over the accused," might very well do so.[63]

For the purpose of federal constitutional analysis, the pre-accusatory delay covered by the due process clause and the post-accusatory delay covered by the Sixth Amendment's speedy trial clause are not aggregated to assess a claim of untimely prosecution; rather, the pre- and post-accusatory portions of delay are evaluated separately.[64] This is in contrast to the more liberal state constitutional analysis, in which pre- and post-accusatory delay are aggregated and evaluated in their totality.[65] This fact, plus the lack of a strict requirement under state

N.Y.2d 359, 364, 474 N.Y.S.2d 276, 278, 462 N.E.2d 376 (1984), it held that the failure to impose sentence within a reasonable time, as required by CPL § 380.30(1), may result in the court's loss of jurisdiction over the defendant.

56. Burkett v. Cunningham, 826 F.2d 1208, 1220 (3d Cir.1987); Perez v. Sullivan, 793 F.2d 249, 252–253 (10th Cir.), cert. den. 479 U.S. 936, 107 S.Ct. 413, 93 L.Ed.2d 364 (1986). See Pollard v. United States, 352 U.S. 354, 361, 77 S.Ct. 481, 485, 1 L.Ed.2d 393 (1957)(assuming "arguendo" that sentencing is part of the trial for the purposes of speedy trial protections).

57. United States v. Marion, 404 U.S. 307, 320, 92 S.Ct. 455, 463, 30 L.Ed.2d 468 (1971).

58. United States v. Lovasco, 431 U.S. 783, 97 S.Ct. 2044, 52 L.Ed.2d 752 (1977), rehearing den. 434 U.S. 881, 98 S.Ct. 242, 54 L.Ed.2d 164 (1977); United States v. Marion, supra.

59. United States v. Loud Hawk, 474 U.S. 302, 106 S.Ct. 648, 88 L.Ed.2d 640 (1986); United States v. MacDonald, 456 U.S. 1, 102 S.Ct. 1497, 71 L.Ed.2d 696 (1982).

60. United States v. Marion, 404 U.S. at 324, 92 S.Ct. at 465.

61. United States v. Lovasco, supra.

62. 431 U.S. at 795–96, 97 S.Ct. at 2051–52.

63. Id. See also United States v. Marion, 404 U.S. at 324, 92 S.Ct. at 465.

64. United States v. Loud Hawk, supra; United States v. McDonald, supra.

65. See § 9.9, infra.

constitutional due process analysis that actual prejudice be shown,[66] almost guarantees that a speedy trial/due process claim will receive more favorable treatment under state analysis than under federal analysis.

Therefore, defense practitioners are well-advised not to rely exclusively on the Sixth Amendment speedy trial and Fourteenth Amendment due process clauses in framing their motions to dismiss for want of a speedy trial. Instead, primary reliance should be on state constitutional and statutory authority. The notices of motion to dismiss on such grounds should by all means incorporate the federal speedy trial and due process clauses—if for no other reason than to preserve the defendant's right later to seek relief in federal court. But both the notice of motion and the body of the motion should rely principally on state constitutional and statutory authority.[67]

Library References:
West's Key No. Digests, Constitutional Law ⚖268(4); Criminal Law ⚖577.4, 577.6.

§ 9.9 State Speedy Trial and Due Process Guarantees— In General

CPL § 30.20(1) contains New York's speedy trial guarantee.[68] There is no speedy trial clause in the New York State Constitution. However, Article 1, § 6 of the State Constitution provides that "[n]o person shall be deprived of life, liberty or property without due process of law." An "unreasonable delay" in prosecuting a defendant constitutes a violation of state due process.[69] New York courts, additionally, have never "drawn a fine distinction between due process and speedy trial standards,"[70] and "the State due process requirement of a prompt prosecution is broader than the right to a speedy trial" guaranteed by CPL § 30.20.[71]

Additionally, New York's constitutional due process requirement of a prompt prosecution is broader and more flexible than federal speedy trial/due process protections. Under state due process analysis, in contrast to the federal provisions, unjustifiable pre- and post-accusatory delay are aggregated to determine whether an accused has been deprived of a prompt prosecution;[72] dismissal may be required even where the

---

66. Cf. United States v. Lovasco, supra (showing of prejudice necessary to federal due process claim) with People v. Singer, 44 N.Y.2d 241, 253–54, 405 N.Y.S.2d 17, 24–25, 376 N.E.2d 179 (1978)("lengthy and unjustifiable period of delay" may require dismissal even absent a showing of specific prejudice).

67. For the appropriate state authority which the motion papers should incorporate, see § 9.12, infra.

68. This guarantee is also contained in New York Civil Rights Law § 12.

69. People v. Singer, 44 N.Y.2d 241, 253, 405 N.Y.S.2d 17, 24, 376 N.E.2d 179 (1978); People v. Staley, 41 N.Y.2d 789, 791, 396 N.Y.S.2d 339, 341, 364 N.E.2d 1111 (1977).

70. People v. Singer, 44 N.Y.2d at 253, 405 N.Y.S.2d at 25.

71. Id.

72. People v. Singer, 44 N.Y.2d at 253, 405 N.Y.S.2d at 25; People v. Staley, 41 N.Y.2d 789, 791–92, 396 N.Y.S.2d 339, 341–42, 364 N.E.2d 1111 (1977). Under the federal constitution, periods of pre-accusatory delay are covered solely by the due process clause, whereas periods of post-accusatory delay are covered solely by the

defendant cannot show prejudice;[73] and no assertion by the defendant of his or her right to a speedy trial is necessary or considered.[74] Furthermore, it is the prosecutor's burden, under state due process analysis, to establish good cause excusing "a protracted delay."[75] Hence, New York defense practitioners are well advised to frame their motions to dismiss primarily, although not exclusively, in terms of state rather than federal analysis.[76]

New York cases make no distinction between the interpretation of the state's due process prompt prosecution guarantee and CPL § 30.20; accordingly, criminal practitioners need not draw such a distinction in analyzing the facts of their cases. However, both the statutory and the constitutional authority should be cited in defense motion papers, so as to preserve both—and especially the constitutional authority—for subsequent appellate consideration.[77]

Library References:

West's Key No. Digests, Constitutional Law ⚖=268(4); Criminal Law ⚖=577.5.

§ 9.10 State Speedy Trial and Due Process Guarantees—*Taranovich* Factors

In *People v. Taranovich*,[78] the Court of Appeals set forth five factors to weigh in determining whether the defendant has been denied his or her state due process right to a prompt prosecution: (1) the extent of the delay, (2) the reason for the delay, (3) the nature of the underlying charge, (4) whether there has been an extended period of pretrial incarceration, and (5) whether there is any indication that the defense has been prejudiced by reason of the delay.[79] No one factor or any combination of factors is decisive; rather, "the trial court must engage in a sensitive weighing process of the diversified factors present in the

speedy trial clause; each period of delay is separately considered in determining a claim of untimely prosecution. United States v. Loud Hawk, 474 U.S. 302, 106 S.Ct. 648, 88 L.Ed.2d 640 (1986).

73. People v. Staley, 41 N.Y.2d at 792, 396 N.Y.S.2d at 342. Under federal due process analysis, relating to pre-accusatory delay, a showing of prejudice is a prerequisite to obtaining relief. United States v. Lovasco, 431 U.S. 783, 97 S.Ct. 2044, 52 L.Ed.2d 752, rehearing den. 434 U.S. 881, 98 S.Ct. 242, 54 L.Ed.2d 164 (1977). Under federal speedy trial analysis, however, which covers post-accusatory delay, neither prejudice nor any other factor is an absolute prerequisite to relief. Barker v. Wingo, 407 U.S. 514, 533, 92 S.Ct. 2182, 2193, 33 L.Ed.2d 101 (1972).

74. People v. Staley, 41 N.Y.2d at 793, 396 N.Y.S.2d at 343; People v. Prosser, 309 N.Y. 353, 358–359, 130 N.E.2d 891, 894–95 (1955). In contrast, under federal speedy trial analysis, whether and how often the defendant has demanded a speedy trial is a factor in evaluating the claim, albeit not necessarily a controlling one. Barker v. Wingo, supra.

75. People v. Lesiuk, 81 N.Y.2d 485, 490, 600 N.Y.S.2d 931, 933, 617 N.E.2d 1047 (1993); People v. Singer, 44 N.Y.2d at 254; People v. Prosser, 309 N.Y. 353, 130 N.E.2d 891 (1955); People v. Santiago, 209 A.D.2d 885, 618 N.Y.S.2d 925 (3d Dep't 1994).

76. See § 9.12, infra.

77. See Preiser, "Practice Commentary" to CPL § 30.20, McKinney's Cons. Laws of N.Y., Book 11A, at 152 (1992).

78. 37 N.Y.2d 442, 373 N.Y.S.2d 79, 335 N.E.2d 303 (1975).

79. 37 N.Y.2d at 445, 373 N.Y.S.2d at 81–82.

§ 9.10   TIMELINESS OF PROSECUTION & SPEEDY TRIAL   Ch. 9

particular case."[80]

Since each CPL § 30.20/due process claim rises or falls on its own set of facts, it is unlikely that any one case citation will be controlling. In applying the *Taranovich* test to the facts of any particular case, however, the following case law is instructive:

The Extent of the Delay. The Court of Appeals has "steadfastly refused to set forth a per se period beyond which a criminal prosecution may not be pursued."[81] Thus, while in one case a seven-month pre-accusatory delay was found to be unreasonable and violative of due process,[82] a twenty-five year pre-accusatory delay in another case was found to be reasonable and consistent with due process.[83] The greater the period of delay, "the more probable it is that the accused will be harmed thereby."[84] Still, it is likely that the other *Taranovich* factors, especially the reason—or lack of reason—for the delay, will be more controlling than the length of the period in question.

The Reason for the Delay. A good faith prearrest investigative delay, even if resulting in some prejudice to the defendant, does not offend the due process clause. The police have no duty to arrest a suspect as soon as probable cause exists; rather, they may hold off until satisfied that there is sufficient evidence to prove the defendant's guilt beyond a reasonable doubt, or until the investigation of the entire criminal transaction is complete.[85] By the same token, delays are excusable if they are due to genuine difficulties in locating a suspect,[86] locating prosecution witnesses,[87] or in obtaining sufficient evidence to arrest or indict.[88] Moreover, the prosecution may properly hold off if a

---

80. 37 N.Y.2d at 445; 373 N.Y.S.2d at 81. See also People v. Johnson, 38 N.Y.2d 271, 276, 379 N.Y.S.2d 735, 740, 342 N.E.2d 525 (1975).

81. People v. Taranovich, 37 N.Y.2d at 445, 373 N.Y.S.2d at 82.

82. People v. Ilardo, 103 Misc.2d 454, 426 N.Y.S.2d 212 (Buffalo City Ct.1980)(prosecution offered invalid reason for delay). See also People v. Wallace, 26 N.Y.2d 371, 310 N.Y.S.2d 484, 258 N.E.2d 904 (1970)(eleven-month delay found to be inexcusable).

83. People v. Hoff, 110 A.D.2d 782, 487 N.Y.S.2d 851 (2d Dep't 1985)(police lacked strong case against the defendant until end of period); see also People v. LaRocca, 172 A.D.2d 628, 568 N.Y.S.2d 431 (2d Dep't 1991)(seventeen-year pre-accusatory delay justified by lack of sufficient evidence to prosecute during that period).

84. People v. Taranovich, 37 N.Y.2d at 445, 373 N.Y.S.2d at 82.

85. United States v. Lovasco, 431 U.S. 783, 791–92, 97 S.Ct. 2044, 2049, 52 L.Ed.2d 752, reh'g den. 434 U.S. 881, 98 S.Ct. 242, 54 L.Ed.2d 164 (1977); People v. Lesiuk, 81 N.Y.2d 485, 490–91, 600 N.Y.S.2d 931, 933–34, 617 N.E.2d 1047 (1993); People v. Singer, 44 N.Y.2d at 254, 405 N.Y.S.2d at 25; People v. Connor, 137 A.D.2d 701, 524 N.Y.S.2d 791 (2d Dep't 1988); People v. Hoff, 110 A.D.2d 782, 487 N.Y.S.2d 851 (2d Dep't 1985); People v. Bryant, 79 A.D.2d 867, 869, 434 N.Y.S.2d 558, 560 (4th Dep't 1980).

86. People v. Staley, 41 N.Y.2d 789, 792, 396 N.Y.S.2d 339, 342, 364 N.E.2d 1111 (1977). See also People v. Johnston, 111 A.D.2d 262, 489 N.Y.S.2d 99 (2d Dep't 1985)(delay excused where caused by defendant's flight to Florida and settlement there under an assumed name). But cf. People v. Jordan, 141 A.D.2d 886, 887–88, 528 N.Y.S.2d 951, 951–52 (3d Dep't 1988)(inability to locate defendant not excused where defendant lived "openly and notoriously" throughout the period of delay and made no efforts to conceal his whereabouts).

87. People v. Clemente, 150 A.D.2d 709, 541 N.Y.S.2d 583 (2d Dep't 1989); People v. Rodriguez, 81 A.D.2d 840, 841, 438 N.Y.S.2d 845, 845 (2d Dep't 1981).

88. People v. Staley, 41 N.Y.2d at 792, 396 N.Y.S.2d at 342. Such delays will not ordinarily extend the time limitations contained in the statute of limitations, however. Id.

premature arrest would hamper the investigation of new charges.[89]

Even so, the prosecution cannot justify delay simply by uttering the talismanic words "continuing investigation"; instead, there must be significant, substantial activity behind the delay.[90]

Absolutely unacceptable are delays caused by the prosecution's desire to obtain a "tactical advantage" over the accused, or to hinder the defense.[91] Delays due to the prosecution's "[s]heer neglect and trifling" are also inherently unreasonable.[92]

Weighing against the prosecution, albeit less heavily, are delays due to inadvertence, inattention, or clerical errors on the part of the prosecution or correctional authorities;[93] similarly weighing less are delays caused by the shortage of court facilities or personnel, or calendar congestion.[94]

A reasonable priority system on the part of the prosecutor—*e.g.*, the trial of jail cases first—will justify some delay.[95] On the other hand, an "unrefined" and inflexible priority system, which takes into account *only* the date of indictment and the jail status of the accused, without reference to the nature of the crime, the weight of the evidence, or the delay's potential for prejudice, has been disapproved.[96]

The defendant's service of a sentence on another crime is not considered a reasonable ground for delay, since such delay might foreclose the possibility of concurrent time and deprive the defendant of opportunities for rehabilitation.[97]

The prosecution's unreasonable delay in perfecting an interlocutory appeal, resulting in the belated reinstatement of the accusatory instru-

---

89. People v. Nocerino, 159 A.D.2d 358, 553 N.Y.S.2d 2 (1st Dep't 1990); People v. Bryant, 65 A.D.2d 333, 338, 411 N.Y.S.2d 932, 936 (2d Dep't 1978).

90. See, e.g., People v. Rodriguez, 205 A.D.2d 417, 613 N.Y.S.2d 398 (1st Dep't 1994)(prosecutor's allegations that arrest was delayed due to obtaining leads to defendant's cohorts in drug trade found to be undercut by fact that prosecution knew that the defendant was a paraplegic for most of the delay); People v. Townsend, 38 A.D.2d 569, 328 N.Y.S.2d 333 (2d Dep't 1971)("mere claim" of continuing narcotics investigation insufficient to justify pre-indictment delay).

91. United States v. Marion, 404 U.S. 307, 324, 92 S.Ct. 455, 465, 30 L.Ed.2d 468 (1971). See also Barker v. Wingo, 407 U.S. 514, 531, 92 S.Ct. 2182, 2192, 33 L.Ed.2d 101 (1972); People v. Johnson, 38 N.Y.2d at 279, 379 N.Y.S.2d at 743.

92. People v. Staley, 41 N.Y.2d at 792, 396 N.Y.S.2d at 342.

93. People v. Taranovich, 37 N.Y.2d at 446–47, 373 N.Y.S.2d at 82; People v. King, 114 A.D.2d 650, 494 N.Y.S.2d 484 (3d Dep't 1985).

94. People v. Watts, 57 N.Y.2d 299, 456 N.Y.S.2d 677, 442 N.E.2d 1188 (1982); People v. Johnson, 38 N.Y.2d at 278–79, 399 N.Y.S.2d at 742–43; People v. McCummings, 203 A.D.2d 656, 610 N.Y.S.2d 634 (3d Dep't 1994); People v. Charles, 180 A.D.2d 868, 580 N.Y.S.2d 99 (3d Dep't 1992)(delay in transcription of pretrial hearing transcript because of court reporter's backlog weighs against the prosecution, albeit less heavily than deliberate prosecution delay).

95. People v. Imbesi, 38 N.Y.2d 629, 632, 381 N.Y.S.2d 862, 863, 345 N.E.2d 333 (1976).

96. People v. Johnson, 38 N.Y.2d at 277–78, 379 N.Y.S.2d at 742. See also People v. Mason, 125 A.D.2d 595, 509 N.Y.S.2d 842 (2d Dep't 1986)(prosecutor's decision to try the codefendant first was unreasonable where the decision had no legitimate strategic benefit to prosecution).

97. People v. Singer, 44 N.Y.2d at 252–53, 405 N.Y.S.2d at 24; People v. Staley, 41 N.Y.2d at 791, 396 N.Y.S.2d at 342; People v. Santiago, 209 A.D.2d 885, 618 N.Y.S.2d 925 (3d Dep't 1994).

§ 9.10   TIMELINESS OF PROSECUTION & SPEEDY TRIAL   Ch. 9

ment, may also amount to a due process deprivation.[98]

Certain reasons for delay, on the other hand, weigh against the defendant, such as the defendant's own motion practice or discovery efforts.[99]

The Nature of the Charges. A valid ground for delay might be the serious or complex nature of the crimes charged, as the prosecution is expected to proceed more slowly and cautiously in such cases.[100] Serious crimes or complex cases may require more careful preparation than relatively minor or simple ones.[101]

However, the seriousness of the crime weighs in the prosecution's favor only if it has *contributed* to the delay.[102] Appellate courts have not hesitated to reject prosecution claims that delays were justified by the serious nature of the charges where those claims were belied by the particular facts of the case.[103]

Whether There Has Been an Extended Period of Pretrial Incarceration. A lengthy period of pretrial incarceration weighs heavily against the prosecution, whereas the defendant's liberty while awaiting trial weighs against the defendant.[104] The defendant's incarceration during pretrial delay only weighs in his or her favor—under this *Taranovich* factor—if it was solely due to the belated prosecution in question. If the defendant was incarcerated on another matter, or would have been incarcerated on another matter in any event, then the incarceration does not weigh in the defendant's favor.[105] Note, however, that the defen-

---

98. People v. Green, 139 A.D.2d 760, 527 N.Y.S.2d 509 (2d Dep't 1988). See also People v. Anderson, 201 A.D.2d 432, 609 N.Y.S.2d 773 (1st Dep't 1994); People v. McIntosh, 173 A.D.2d 490, 570 N.Y.S.2d 298 (2d Dep't 1991).

99. People v. McCummings, 203 A.D.2d 656, 610 N.Y.S.2d 634 (3d Dep't 1994)(defendant's own request to locate witnesses); People v. Allen, 203 A.D.2d 97, 610 N.Y.S.2d 40 (1st Dep't 1994)(defendant's own motion practice or discovery efforts). See also People v. Graham, 135 A.D.2d 563, 521 N.Y.S.2d 783 (2d Dep't 1987)(defendant's motion practice leads to excludable time pursuant to CPL § 30.30).

100. People v. Lomax, 50 N.Y.2d 351, 428 N.Y.S.2d 937, 406 N.E.2d 793 (1980); People v. Johnson, 38 N.Y.2d at 277, 379 N.Y.S.2d at 741; People v. Taranovich, 37 N.Y.2d at 446, 373 N.Y.S.2d at 82.

101. People v. Taranovich, 37 N.Y.2d at 446, 373 N.Y.S.2d at 82; People v. Graham, 135 A.D.2d 563, 521 N.Y.S.2d 783 (2d Dep't 1987); People v. Rodriguez, 81 A.D.2d 840, 841, 438 N.Y.S.2d 845, 845 (2d Dep't 1981)(first-degree manslaughter charge, by its very nature, required careful preparation).

102. People v. Watts, 57 N.Y.2d at 303, 456 N.Y.S.2d at 680; People v. Johnson, 38 N.Y.2d at 277, 379 N.Y.S.2d at 741.

103. See, e.g., People v. Charles, 180 A.D.2d 868, 580 N.Y.S.2d 99 (3d Dep't 1992)(prosecution claim that delay justified by seriousness of charges, consolidation of indictments and joinder of defendants was undercut by prosecution's early declaration of readiness and swiftness of trial's completion); People v. Brown, 117 A.D.2d 978, 499 N.Y.S.2d 529 (4th Dep't 1986)(prosecution's early declaration of readiness for trial belied claim that trial was delayed due to the complexity of the case); People v. Bradley, 74 A.D.2d 850, 425 N.Y.S.2d 382 (2d Dep't 1980) (prosecution's claim that it needed more time to prepare because of seriousness of charges was undercut by its demonstrated inattention to the case, and the simplicity of the crime's fact pattern).

104. Cf. People v. Imbesi, 38 N.Y.2d at 632, 381 N.Y.S.2d at 864 (defendant's liberty for all but three days between arrest and trial weighed against the defense speedy trial claim) with People v. Charles, 180 A.D.2d 868, 871, 580 N.Y.S.2d 99, 102 (3d Dep't 1992)(defendant's pretrial incarceration for 41 of 43 months weighed heavily against the prosecution).

105. See People v. McCummings, 203 A.D.2d 656, 610 N.Y.S.2d 634 (3d Dep't 1994)(pretrial incarceration due to another sentence defendant was serving did not

dant's imprisonment on another crime does not excuse an otherwise unwarranted period of delay.[106]

Whether There Is Any Indication that the Defense Has Been Prejudiced by the Delay. A delay is deemed to have resulted in prejudice to the defendant if it affects "the likelihood of the defendant's acquittal."[107] Thus, delay is prejudicial if it results in loss of defense witnesses, faded memories, or other demonstrable inability to present a viable defense due to the passage of time.[108]

Pro forma, or "routine-like," claims of prejudice on the part of the defense, however, are deemed unpersuasive.[109]

Where the period of delay is sufficiently lengthy, prejudice is presumed without the necessity of any particularized showing.[110]

Library References:
West's Key No. Digests, Criminal Law ⛔577.10–577.15.

§ 9.11 Preference of Criminal Over Civil Cases

Subdivision two of CPL § 30.20 provides that criminal trials should receive priority over civil trials "[i]nsofar as is practicable." Additionally, in criminal cases, jail cases should receive priority over bail cases.[111]

This subdivision's advisory is hardly absolute, however. That a defendant's trial occurs out of sequence does not, in itself, support a determination that he or she has been deprived of a speedy trial.[112]

---

weigh in defendant's favor); People v. Allen, 203 A.D.2d 97, 610 N.Y.S.2d 40 (1st Dep't 1994)(25–month incarceration on conviction for unrelated crime); People v. Cardwell, 194 A.D.2d 550, 598 N.Y.S.2d 319 (2d Dep't 1993)(pretrial incarceration attributable to separate murder conviction); People v. Jackson, 178 A.D.2d 305, 577 N.Y.S.2d 609 (1st Dep't 1991)(defendant would have been incarcerated in any event on other charges). See also People v. Hernandez, 190 A.D.2d 752, 593 N.Y.S.2d 335 (2d Dep't 1993)(incarceration necessitated by defendant's having fled the jurisdiction after the crime).

106. People v. Prosser, 309 N.Y. 353, 358–59, 130 N.E.2d 891, 894–95 (1955).

107. People v. Taranovich, 37 N.Y.2d at 447, 373 N.Y.S.2d at 83.

108. People v. Johnson, 38 N.Y.2d at 276–77, 379 N.Y.S.2d at 740–41; People v. Taranovich, 37 N.Y.2d at 447, 373 N.Y.S.2d at 83; People v. Jordan, 141 A.D.2d 886, 528 N.Y.S.2d 951 (3d Dep't 1988)(loss of alibi defense due to 13-year delay); People v. Mason, 125 A.D.2d 595, 509 N.Y.S.2d 842 (2d Dep't 1986)(loss of alibi witness); People v. Liberatore, 96 A.D.2d 1047, 466 N.Y.S.2d 683 (2d Dep't 1983)(delay led to defendant's inability to recall events of the day of the crime).

109. People v. Fuller, 57 N.Y.2d 152, 160, 455 N.Y.S.2d 253, 257, 441 N.E.2d 563 (1982); People v. Quiroz, 192 A.D.2d 730, 597 N.Y.S.2d 106 (2d Dep't 1993); People v. Hoskins, 95 A.D.2d 899, 464 N.Y.S.2d 55 (3d Dep't 1983). See also People v. Clemente, 150 A.D.2d 709, 541 N.Y.S.2d 583 (2d Dep't 1989)(general claim that defense witness left the state unconvincing where there was no indication witness left state prior to time speedy trial issue arose).

110. People v. Lesiuk, 81 N.Y.2d at 490, 600 N.Y.S.2d at 934; People v. Singer, 44 N.Y.2d at 253–54, 405 N.Y.S.2d at 25; People v. Taranovich, 37 N.Y.2d at 447, 373 N.Y.S.2d at 83; People v. Charles, 180 A.D.2d 868, 580 N.Y.S.2d 99 (3d Dep't 1992).

111. CPL § 30.20(2). See also People v. Kelly, 38 N.Y.2d 633, 636, 382 N.Y.S.2d 1, 2, 345 N.E.2d 544 (1976)("[s]ome sort of priority should go to jail cases"); People v. Imbesi, 38 N.Y.2d 629, 381 N.Y.S.2d 862, 345 N.E.2d 333 (1976).

112. People v. Murphy, 99 A.D.2d 613, 472 N.Y.S.2d 202 (3d Dep't 1984)(language in CPL § 30.20(2) is not absolute; trial court has discretion in applying it). People v. Kornegay, 55 A.D.2d 462, 390 N.Y.S.2d 666 (3d Dep't 1977)(fact that defendant's

Rather, the rationality of the priority system employed in a particular case is but one factor to consider in assessing a speedy trial claim.[113] Even so, the mere fact that a defendant's case is tried in logical sequence will not excuse a delay for an otherwise unconscionable period.[114]

Library References:

West's Key No. Digests, Criminal Law ⟸577.10(7), 632(2).

§ 9.12 Constitutional Speedy Trial/Due Process Claims—Procedural Requirements

A motion to dismiss based upon the denial of the right to a speedy trial, and/or the due process right to a timely prosecution, must be made prior to the commencement of trial or the entry of a guilty plea.[115] The motion must be made in writing—an oral application is not sufficient—and upon reasonable notice to the prosecution.[116] Failure to follow these procedures constitutes a waiver of the claim.[117]

A fortiori, a speedy trial/due process claim cannot be raised for the first time on appeal. It must be raised in the first instance in the trial court.[118]

Unlike the other grounds listed in CPL §§ 170.30(1) or 210.20(1), a motion to dismiss based upon speedy trial/due process grounds pursuant to §§ 170.30(1)(e) or 210.20(1)(g) need not be made within 45 days after arraignment on the accusatory instrument. Rather, the motion may be made any time up to the commencement trial or the entry of a guilty plea.[119]

Furthermore, unlike claims raised upon the other grounds contained in CPL §§ 170.30(1) and 210.20(1), the court has no discretion to entertain, or defer decision on, a speedy trial motion up to the end of

trial did not occur in perfect calendar sequence did not, standing alone, constitute speedy trial violation).

113. People v. Imbesi, 38 N.Y.2d 629, 381 N.Y.S.2d 862, 345 N.E.2d 333 (1976)(prosecutor's system of giving priority to incarcerated defendants was reasonable, at least where the defendant could not show prejudice); People v. Bellach, 58 A.D.2d 613, 395 N.Y.S.2d 673 (2d Dep't 1977)(trial of civil cases before defendant's criminal trial was one factor in appellate determination that defendant had been deprived of constitutional right to a speedy trial).

114. People v. Walston, 60 Misc.2d 531, 303 N.Y.S.2d 239 (Sup.Ct., Nassau County, 1969), aff'd sub nom. People ex rel. Walston v. Krueger, 35 A.D.2d 813, 316 N.Y.S.2d 990 (2d Dep't 1970).

115. CPL §§ 170.30(1)(e) and (2), 210.20(1)(g), (2); People v. Lawrence, 64 N.Y.2d 200, 485 N.Y.S.2d 233, 474 N.E.2d 593 (1984).

116. CPL § 210.45(1); People v. Lawrence, supra; People v. Key, 45 N.Y.2d 111, 116, 408 N.Y.S.2d 16, 379 N.E.2d 1147 (1978); see People v. DeRosa, 42 N.Y.2d 872, 873, 397 N.Y.S.2d 780, 780, 366 N.E.2d 868 (1977).

117. People v. Lawrence, supra; People v. Key, 45 N.Y.2d at 116, 408 N.Y.S.2d at 19; People v. DeRosa, 42 N.Y.2d at 873, 397 N.Y.S.2d at 780–81.

118. People v. Jordan, 62 N.Y.2d 825, 477 N.Y.S.2d 605, 466 N.E.2d 145 (1984), aff'g 96 A.D.2d 1060, 466 N.Y.S.2d 486 (2d Dep't 1983); People v. Martinez, 126 A.D.2d 942, 511 N.Y.S.2d 988 (4th Dep't 1987); People v. Ruiz, 107 A.D.2d 770, 484 N.Y.S.2d 136 (2d Dep't 1985); People v. Walton, 98 A.D.2d 842, 470 N.Y.S.2d 831 (3d Dep't 1983).

119. CPL §§ 170.30(2), 210.20(2).

trial. A speedy trial motion not made prior to trial or entry of the guilty plea is untimely and the issue is thus waived.[120]

Conversely, once properly raised and decided, a speedy trial/due process claim cannot be waived by a guilty plea, not even with a purported bargained-for waiver of the right to appeal that issue.[121]

A speedy trial claim may also incorporate a CPL § 30.30 prosecutorial readiness claim, in which case section 30.30 should also be cited in the notice of motion. A note of caution, however: a claim noticed *solely* as a CPL § 30.30 motion will not later be construed as a speedy trial/due process claim;[122] likewise, a traditional speedy trial/due process claim will not subsequently be construed as a section 30.30 claim.[123]

Library References:

West's Key No. Digests, Criminal Law ⚖577.16, 1035(1).

§ 9.13 Prosecutorial Readiness Rule—In General

CPL § 30.30 is not meant to guarantee a defendant's right to a speedy trial; that guarantee is contained in section 30.20. Rather, section 30.30 is meant to encourage speedy trials by requiring that prosecutors be *ready* for trial within a reasonable amount of time after the criminal action is commenced.[124]

Thus, CPL § 30.30 is properly characterized as a prosecutorial readiness rule. Circumstances beyond the prosecutor's control, such as delays occasioned by the defense or by calendar congestion, may serve to delay the trial even after the prosecutor is ready to proceed. Delays beyond the prosecutor's announcement of readiness for trial—assuming that the readiness is maintained—are not covered by section 30.30.

Conversely, since section 30.30 focuses on the *prosecutor's* readiness, the defendant may claim relief under this statute despite his or her own

120. People v. Lawrence, supra.

121. People v. Callahan, 80 N.Y.2d 273, 590 N.Y.S.2d 46, 604 N.E.2d 108 (1992); People v. Blakley, 34 N.Y.2d 311, 357 N.Y.S.2d 459, 313 N.E.2d 763 (1974). See also People v. Fuller, 57 N.Y.2d 152, 159 n. 7, 455 N.Y.S.2d 253, 441 N.E.2d 563 (1982)(state due process untimely prosecution claim not waived by guilty plea).

The speedy trial claim, once raised, may be abandoned prior to decision, however, provided the record reflects an "intentional relinquishment or abandonment" of the claim by the defense. People v. Rodriguez, 50 N.Y.2d 553, 557, 429 N.Y.S.2d 631, 632, 407 N.E.2d 475 (1980), citing Johnson v. Zerbst, 304 U.S. 458, 464, 58 S.Ct. 1019, 1023, 82 L.Ed. 1461 (1938); People v. Harris, 103 A.D.2d 891, 478 N.Y.S.2d 188 (3d Dep't 1984).

The nonforfeiture of a constitutional or section 30.20 speedy trial/due process claim by virtue of a guilty plea does not extend to a purely statutory CPL § 30.30 claim of prosecutorial unreadiness. A section 30.30 claim is always forfeited by operation of a guilty plea. People v. O'Brien, 56 N.Y.2d 1009, 453 N.Y.S.2d 638, 439 N.E.2d 354 (1982); People v. Friscia, 51 N.Y.2d 845, 433 N.Y.S.2d 754, 413 N.E.2d 1168 (1980).

122. See People v. Cedeno, 52 N.Y.2d 847, 437 N.Y.S.2d 72, 418 N.E.2d 665 (1981); People v. Pleban, 108 A.D.2d 880, 485 N.Y.S.2d 377 (2d Dep't 1985); People v. Jones, 103 A.D.2d 973, 479 N.Y.S.2d 819 (3d Dep't 1984).

123. People v. Price, 145 A.D.2d 445, 535 N.Y.S.2d 398 (2d Dep't 1988).

124. Section 30.30 does not address delay occurring prior to the initial commencement of the criminal action.

§ 9.13 TIMELINESS OF PROSECUTION & SPEEDY TRIAL Ch. 9

unreadiness, and without any showing of prejudice.[125]

Section 30.30 provides for two distinct sanctions for the failure of the prosecution to be ready within the time periods specified. The most well known, contained in section 30.30(1), is dismissal.[126] The other, contained in section 30.30(2), is often overlooked: the lesser sanction of release on bail or recognizance of a jailed defendant.[127]

The Court of Appeals has interpreted the language of CPL § 30.30 strictly and, where possible, according to its plain terms.[128] Hence, the statute's clear terms, not any contravening policy considerations, govern.[129]

A special note of caution to defense practitioners and prosecutors alike: section 30.30 motion practice is a procedural minefield. As set forth below,[130] special care must be taken in formulating your own arguments and responding to your adversary's. Note also that a section 30.30 claim is always forfeited by a guilty plea.[131]

Library References:
West's Key No. Digests, Criminal Law ⇔577.7.

§ 9.14 Nonapplicability to Some Criminal Actions

CPL § 30.30 is applicable to all criminal offenses except certain homicide offenses specified in subdivision three, to wit: P.L. §§ 125.10 (criminally negligent homicide), 125.15 (second-degree manslaughter), 125.20 (first-degree manslaughter), 125.25 (second-degree murder), and 125.27 (first-degree murder). If the indictment includes any of these homicide counts, it is not subject to section 30.30 relief.[132] *Attempted* homicide counts *are* subject to section 30.30 relief, however.[133]

Non-criminal offenses that are classified as "violations"[134] are subject to section 30.30.[135] "Traffic infractions,"[136] which are not classified

---

125. See, e.g., People v. Hamilton, 46 N.Y.2d 932, 933–34, 415 N.Y.S.2d 208, 209, 388 N.E.2d 345 (1979)(defendant's entitlement to relief under section 30.30 "is not dependent in any way on whether the defendant has expressed his readiness for trial or whether the defendant can demonstrate prejudice resulting from the delay.")

126. See § 9.17, infra.

127. See § 9.18, infra.

128. See, e.g., People v. Tychanski, 78 N.Y.2d 909, 911–912, 573 N.Y.S.2d 454, 455–56, 577 N.E.2d 1046 (1991)(court refused to remedy an apparent oversight in legislative crafting of section 30.30(5)(c), since statute must be given effect as written not as the court may think it should have been written).

129. See, e.g., People v. Bolden, 81 N.Y.2d 146, 154, 597 N.Y.S.2d 270, 274, 613 N.E.2d 145 (1993)(court rejected prosecution's "policy arguments" as to interpretation of section 30.30(4)(c), since those arguments went "beyond the question of statutory construction" to be resolved on appeal).

130. See §§ 9.35, 9.36, infra.

131. See § 9.12, supra.

132. People v. Ortiz, 209 A.D.2d 332, 619 N.Y.S.2d 12 (1st Dep't 1994); People v. O'Sullivan, 121 A.D.2d 658, 504 N.Y.S.2d 49 (2d Dep't 1986); People v. Smith, 53 A.D.2d 652, 384 N.Y.S.2d 488 (2d Dep't 1976).

133. People v. Williams, 130 A.D.2d 697, 515 N.Y.S.2d 622 (2d Dep't 1987)(attempted first-degree murder); People v. Gordon, 125 A.D.2d 257, 509 N.Y.S.2d 543 (1st Dep't 1986)(attempted second-degree murder).

134. See PL § 10.00(3)

135. CPL § 30.30(1)(d).

136. PL § 10.00(2).

as "violations," are not covered by section 30.30.[137]

Library References:
West's Key No. Digests, Criminal Law ⚍577.6.

§ 9.15 "Commencement" of the Criminal Action Starts the Clock Ticking

CPL § 30.30 requires the prosecution to announce readiness for trial within certain specified times from the "commencement" of the action. An action is commenced—and thus the section 30.30 clock starts ticking—with the *filing* of the accusatory instrument.[138] If more than one accusatory instrument is filed in a given case, the action commences with the filing of the *first* of those instruments.[139] Successive accusatory instruments "directly derived" from the initial one do not commence a new criminal action; rather, for section 30.30 purposes, all subsequent instruments are deemed to relate back to the first one.[140]

In the seminal case of *People v. Lomax*,[141] for example, the filing of a felony complaint was followed by an indictment, which was in turn dismissed with leave to re-present. A second indictment ensued. The court held that the action commenced for 30.30 purposes with the filing of the original felony complaint, not the filing of the second indictment. In so holding, the court noted that "if there can only be one criminal action for any given set of charges, there also can be only one date which marks the 'commencement' of the action, the date on which the first accusatory paper is filed."[142]

In the subsequent case of *People v. Osgood*,[143] a felony complaint was dismissed for "failure to prosecute," and the defendant was not held for further proceedings. The prosecutor then procured an indictment. As in *Lomax*, the Court of Appeals held that the commencement of the action related back to the filing of the felony complaint.[144]

Although the *Osgood/Lomax* relation-back doctrine is advantageous to defendants, it has a corollary benefit to the prosecution. Where an original accusatory instrument is superseded by another one, all the

---

137. See People v. Matute, 141 Misc.2d 988, 535 N.Y.S.2d 524 (N.Y.C.Crim.Ct. 1988); see also Preiser, "Practice Commentary" to CPL § 30.30, McKinney's Cons. Laws of New York, Book 11A, at 168–169 (1992).

138. CPL § 1.20(17).

139. People v. Osgood, 52 N.Y.2d 37, 436 N.Y.S.2d 213, 417 N.E.2d 507 (1980); People v. Lomax, 50 N.Y.2d 351, 428 N.Y.S.2d 937, 406 N.E.2d 793 (1980); CPL § 1.20(17).

140. CPL § 1.20(16); People v. Lomax, 50 N.Y.2d at 356, 428 N.Y.S.2d at 939.

141. 50 N.Y.2d 351, 428 N.Y.S.2d 937, 406 N.E.2d 793 (1980).

142. 50 N.Y.2d at 356, 428 N.Y.S.2d at 939.

143. 52 N.Y.2d 37, 436 N.Y.S.2d 213, 417 N.E.2d 507 (1980).

144. 52 N.Y.2d at 45, 436 N.Y.S.2d at 217. See also People v. Hamilton, 187 A.D.2d 451, 590 N.Y.S.2d 731 (2d Dep't 1992)(felony complaint followed by indictment, which was then dismissed and replaced by second indictment; action commenced with the initial filing of the felony complaint). Cf. People v. Rodriguez, 150 A.D.2d 265, 541 N.Y.S.2d 423 (1st Dep't 1989) (commencement of action relates back as to original charges but not as to additional charges contained in superseding accusatory instrument); People v. Murray, 127 A.D.2d 704, 512 N.Y.S.2d 111 (2d Dep't 1987)(same).

§ 9.15 TIMELINESS OF PROSECUTION & SPEEDY TRIAL Ch. 9

periods deemed excludable pursuant to CPL § 30.30(4) under the first accusatory instrument remain excludable even after the superseding accusatory instrument is filed.[145]

Library References:
West's Key No. Digests, Criminal Law ⬩577.8(2), 577.14.

§ 9.16 Special Recommencement Rule—Plea Withdrawal, Mistrial, or Order for New Trial

Ordinarily, for CPL § 30.30 purposes, a criminal action commences only once, with the filing of the first accusatory instrument in a criminal action.[146] Subdivision five contains an exhaustive list of exceptions to this general rule.[147]

Subdivision (5)(a) provides that, "where the defendant is to be tried following the withdrawal of the plea of guilty or is to be retried following a mistrial, an order for a new trial or an appeal or collateral attack," the criminal action (or any commitment to the sheriff's custody for subdivision two purposes[148]) is deemed to commence on the date the guilty plea withdrawal, or the retrial order, becomes final.

Thus, the section 30.30 clock starts ticking afresh—with no inclusion of any delay previously chargeable to the prosecution—where the defendant is to be tried following the withdrawal or vacatur of a guilty plea, or the reinstatement of a not guilty plea;[149] a mistrial declaration;[150] or a new trial brought about by appellate reversal, collateral attack, or any other judicial order.[151]

In *People v. Davis*,[152] the First Department, held that the withdrawal of a plea of not responsible by reason of mental disease or defect[153]

---

145. People v. Sinistaj, 67 N.Y.2d 236, 501 N.Y.S.2d 793, 492 N.E.2d 1209 (1986).

146. People v. Osgood, 52 N.Y.2d 37, 436 N.Y.S.2d 213, 417 N.E.2d 507 (1980). See § 9.15, supra.

147. See People v. Tychanski, 78 N.Y.2d 909, 573 N.Y.S.2d 454, 577 N.E.2d 1046 (1991)(subdivision's list of applicable reduced instruments held exhaustive).

148. See § 9.25, infra.

149. People v. Hutchenson, 136 A.D.2d 737, 524 N.Y.S.2d 76 (2d Dep't 1988); People v. Williams, 72 A.D.2d 950, 422 N.Y.S.2d 237 (4th Dep't 1979); People v. Amendolara, 135 Misc.2d 170, 514 N.Y.S.2d 598 (Sup.Ct., N.Y. County, 1987)(even where guilty plea never formally entered, its vacatur recommenced the action); People v. Juhans, 126 Misc.2d 868, 484 N.Y.S.2d 432 (Sup.Ct., Queens County, 1984)(action recommenced with reinstatement of not guilty plea).

150. People v. Weaver, 162 A.D.2d 486, 556 N.Y.S.2d 173 (2d Dep't 1990); People v. Carswell, 120 Misc.2d 274, 465 N.Y.S.2d 687 (Sup.Ct., Kings County, 1983)(mistrial following hung jury).

151. People v. Wilson, 188 A.D.2d 671, 591 N.Y.S.2d 513 (2d Dep't 1992)(appellate reversal); People v. Holmes, 105 A.D.2d 803, 481 N.Y.S.2d 741 (2d Dep't 1984)(action deemed recommenced on date of Court of Appeals affirmance of Appellate Division's new trial order); People v. Greenwaldt, 103 A.D.2d 933, 479 N.Y.S.2d 781 (3d Dep't 1984); People v. Passero, 96 A.D.2d 721, 465 N.Y.S.2d 360 (4th Dep't 1983)(where Appellate Division ordered a new trial, action deemed recommenced on date prosecution was denied leave to appeal to the Court of Appeals). But see People v. Colas, 206 A.D.2d 183, 191, 619 N.Y.S.2d 702, 707 (1st Dep't 1994)(upon reversing a conviction for unrelated error, Appellate Division granted leave to file section 30.30 motion in interest of justice, where defense counsel had unjustifiably failed to make such a motion).

152. 195 A.D.2d 1, 606 N.Y.S.2d 899 (1st Dep't 1994).

153. See CPL § 220.15.

started the section 30.30 clock running afresh pursuant to subdivision (5)(a). Although such a plea is not specifically enumerated in subdivision (5)(a) as one for which withdrawal starts the clock ticking afresh, the court analogized it to a guilty plea, the withdrawal of which is specifically mentioned in the subdivision.[154] While the holding's analogy is apt, its reasoning is inconsistent with the preference of the Court of Appeals for strict construction of the language of section 30.30.[155]

Library References:
West's Key No. Digests, Criminal Law ⚖=577.8(2), 577.14.

§ 9.17 Desk Appearance Tickets

Another exception to the rule that the CPL § 30.30 clock starts ticking with the filing of the first accusatory instrument is contained in subdivision (5)(b). That paragraph provides that where a defendant has been served with an appearance ticket (commonly referred to as a desk appearance ticket, or "DAT"), the action commences for section 30.30 purposes "on the date the defendant first appears in a local criminal court in response to the ticket."

This 1982 addition to subdivision five eliminated the effect of the holding in *People v. Sturgis*,[156] in cases in which the defendant was served with a DAT in lieu of arrest or in lieu of an arrested defendant's being transported to court for arraignment. Prior to the amendment, the action commenced on the return date of the appearance ticket with the filing of the complaint and, pursuant to the *Sturgis* case, the defendant's mere failure to appear in court on that date did not render the ensuing period excludable.[157]

In *People v. Parris*,[158] the defendant had been unable to appear in court on the DAT because he had, subsequent to its issuance, been incarcerated on another charge. The Court of Appeals rejected the

154. 195 A.D.2d at 6, 606 N.Y.S.2d at 901.

155. See § 9.13, supra.

156. 38 N.Y.2d 625, 381 N.Y.S.2d 860, 345 N.E.2d 331 (1976). See also People v. Colon, 59 N.Y.2d 921, 466 N.Y.S.2d 319, 453 N.E.2d 548 (1983).

157. See also § 9.35, infra, regarding the Legislature's responses to the Sturgis holding.

158. 79 N.Y.2d 69, 580 N.Y.S.2d 167, 588 N.E.2d 65 (1992).

An unresolved question is the consequence under subdivision (5)(b) when the defendant arrives at the courthouse in response to a DAT, but does not actually appear before a judge because the accusatory instrument has not yet been filed, and the matter is adjourned to a subsequent date. This is an increasingly common scenario. See "Tactics Vary on Attacking Desk Appearance Tickets," N.Y.L.J., December 6, 1995, p. 1, col. 5. No appellate decisions address whether such an adjournment is chargeable to the prosecution under section 30.30. Since section 30.30 time does not begin to run under subdivision (5)(b) until the defendant "appears in a local criminal court," and mere presence in the courthouse might not legally constitute such an appearance, a defendant may have no recourse under section 30.30 regarding such a delay. See People v. Fysekis, 164 Misc.2d 627, 625 N.Y.S.2d 861 (N.Y.C.Crim. Ct.1995)(mere issuance of a DAT does not commence criminal action); but see People v. Vescur, 134 Misc.2d 574, 511 N.Y.S.2d 997 (N.Y.C.Crim.Ct.1987) (criminal action "commenced" for section 30.30 purposes on date defendant "appeared" in court in response to DAT, even though accusatory instrument not filed); accord People v. Brisotti, N.Y.L.J., December 15, 1995, p. 27, col. 3 (N.Y.C.Crim.Ct.).

defense suggestion that the action be deemed to have commenced on the date the prosecution "learned or should have learned of their obligation to produce the defendant in court." Construing the statute strictly, it held that "when a defendant who has received a DAT fails to appear in court on the return date, the speedy trial clock does not begin to run until the defendant actually appears in court, regardless of the reason for a defendant's failure to appear."[159]

Library References:

West's Key No. Digests, Criminal Law ⟐577.8(2).

§ 9.18 Reduction of Original Charges—Reduction of Felony Complaint

CPL § 30.30(5) provides for the resetting of the section 30.30 clock where a felony complaint is "replaced with or converted to an information, prosecutor's information or misdemeanor complaint."

Subdivision (5)(c) covers such reductions for the purposes of dismissal motions pursuant to subdivision one. Where a felony complaint is reduced via information, prosecutor's information or misdemeanor complaint, the section 30.30 clock is reset at zero as of the date of the filing of the new accusatory instrument. The time period within which the prosecution must be ready is the one applicable to the charges in the new instrument.

There is an exception designed to eliminate any prosecutorial temptation to misuse the reduction: if the pre-reduction time chargeable to the prosecution plus the time applicable to the reduced charge is greater than six months, then the original period applicable to the felony charge remains applicable, as if the reduction had not occurred.

Subdivision (5)(d) is the parallel provision applicable to bail or ROR motions pursuant to subdivision two. It reads the same, except that the proviso designed to eliminate prosecutorial misuse contains the 90-day period applicable to subdivision (2)(a), rather than the six-month period applicable to subdivision (1)(a).

In *People v. Tychanski*,[160] the Court of Appeals held that neither subdivision (5)(c) nor (5)(d) is applicable where a felony complaint is replaced by a misdemeanor indictment voted by a grand jury, as such instrument is not one of those listed in either subparagraph. Thus, in such circumstance, the section 30.30 clock is not reset.[161]

Library References:

West's Key No. Digests, Criminal Law ⟐577.5, 577.14.

159. 79 N.Y.2d at 71–72, 580 N.Y.S.2d at 168.
160. 78 N.Y.2d 909, 573 N.Y.S.2d 454, 577 N.E.2d 1046 (1991).
161. Id.

§ 9.19 Reduction of Original Charges—Inspection and Reduction of Indicted Felony

Paragraphs (e) and (f) of CPL § 30.30(5) provide the same benefits and protections as paragraphs (c) and (d), but concern indicted felonies reduced to misdemeanors or petty offenses upon a motion to inspect and reduce pursuant to CPL § 210.20. Again, paragraph (e) covers section 30.30 motions to dismiss under subdivision one and paragraph (f) covers bail or ROR motions under subdivision two.[162]

Library References:

West's Key No. Digests, Criminal Law ⬤⇒577.5.

§ 9.20 Reduction of Original Charges—Other Reductions

Section 30.30 makes no provision for resetting the clock when a Class A misdemeanor is reduced to a B misdemeanor, and courts wrestling with this situation have come to disparate results.[163] The same is true where a misdemeanor charge is replaced by a felony prosecution,[164] or where a misdemeanor is reduced to a traffic infraction,[165] to which § 30.30 is ordinarily inapplicable.[166]

Given the tendency of the Court of Appeals to construe the language of section 30.30 strictly,[167] it would likely hold the absence of these reduction scenarios from subdivision five to mean that the section 30.30 clock is not reset when they occur; rather, the initially applicable commencement time and readiness period upon the filing of the initial charges would continue to control.[168]

---

162. One important difference in the wording of paragraphs (e) and (f) from that of paragraphs (c) and (d) is in the proviso designed to deter prosecutorial abuse. Paragraphs (e) and (f) provide that when the aggregate of the newly applicable readiness period and the non-excludable time already elapsed between indictment and reduction exceeds six months, the period applicable to the original indicted charges remains in effect. In paragraphs (c) and (d), one adds the newly applicable period to the non-excludable time already elapsed between felony complaint and reduction. The effect is to deprive the defendant covered by paragraphs (e) and (f) of the benefit of all non-excludable time prior to the filing of the indictment.

163. Cf. People v. Matute, 141 Misc.2d 988, 535 N.Y.S.2d 524 (N.Y.C.Crim.Ct.1988)(reduced misdemeanor charges do not affect section 30.30 time calculations) with People v. Bernard, 129 Misc.2d 1083, 495 N.Y.S.2d 634 (N.Y.C.Crim.Ct.1985)(period applicable to reduced charge operative, calculated from date of initial accusatory instrument).

164. See People v. Williams, 141 A.D.2d 402, 529 N.Y.S.2d 991 (1st Dep't 1988)(felony complaint reduced to misdemeanor replaced by felony indictment; 90-day period apparently controlling); People v. Perez, 145 Misc.2d 446, 551 N.Y.S.2d 1021 (Sup. Ct., Bronx County, 1990)(felony period applicable); People v. Matute, supra (court states, in dictum, misdemeanor period applicable).

165. Cf. People v. Matute, supra (section 30.30 applicable to traffic infractions where action commenced as misdemeanor) with People v. Wise, 141 Misc.2d 409, 532 N.Y.S.2d 833 (Dist.Ct., Nassau County, 1988)(reaching contrary result).

166. See § 9.14, supra.

167. See, e.g. People v. Tychanski, 78 N.Y.2d 909, 573 N.Y.S.2d 454, 577 N.E.2d 1046 (1991).

168. Id. See also People v. Sommersell, 166 Misc.2d 774, 638 N.Y.S.2d 272 (App. Term., 2d & 11th Jud.Dists., 1995); People v. Stateikin, 163 Misc.2d 517, 620 N.Y.S.2d 903 (N.Y.C.Crim.Ct.1994); People v. Ma-

§ 9.20 TIMELINESS OF PROSECUTION & SPEEDY TRIAL Ch. 9

Library References:
West's Key No. Digests, Criminal Law ⚖577.8(2).

§ 9.21 Prosecutor's "Readiness" Stops the Clock—"Readiness" Defined

The prosecution meets its obligation under CPL § 30.30 by making a valid communication of present readiness for trial. The present readiness must be (a) genuine, not illusory, and (b) validly communicated to the court and defense counsel.[169]

Library References:
West's Key No. Digests, Criminal Law ⚖577.8(1).

§ 9.22 Prosecutor's "Readiness" Stops the Clock—Genuine "Readiness" Defined

The prosecution is genuinely ready for trial when it has "done everything [it] could up to that point to move the case to trial."[170] While that test may at first blush be overly subjective and susceptible to prosecutorial abuse, certain objective facts may support or undermine the validity of a declaration of readiness.

First of all, to be ready, the prosecution must have obtained the filing of a valid accusatory instrument sufficient to confer the court's jurisdiction to try the defendant. Thus, the prosecution cannot be ready to try a defendant based upon a felony complaint or a misdemeanor complaint, as neither confers jurisdiction to try the defendant.[171] Similarly, since arraignment on the jurisdiction-conferring accusatory instrument is a prerequisite to bringing a defendant to trial, the prosecution cannot validly declare readiness "where, wholly as a result of their own conduct defendant could not be arraigned, and thus trial could not commence, within the statutory time period."[172]

---

tute, 141 Misc.2d at 989–90, 535 N.Y.S.2d at 525.

169. People v. England, 84 N.Y.2d 1, 4–5, 613 N.Y.S.2d 854, 856, 636 N.E.2d 1387 (1994).

170. People v. Cortes, 80 N.Y.2d 201, 210, 590 N.Y.S.2d 9, 14, 604 N.E.2d 71 (1992).

171. People v. Colon, 59 N.Y.2d 921, 466 N.Y.S.2d 319, 453 N.E.2d 548 (1983), rev'g for the reasons stated at 110 Misc.2d 917, 919–20, 443 N.Y.S.2d 305, 306–07 (N.Y.C.Crim.Ct.1981); People v. Delgado, 209 A.D.2d 218, 618 N.Y.S.2d 311 (1st Dep't 1994)(readiness declaration prior to filing of indictment was invalid); People v. Caussade, 162 A.D.2d 4, 8, 560 N.Y.S.2d 648, 650 (2d Dep't 1990).

172. People v. England, 84 N.Y.2d at 5–6, 613 N.Y.S.2d at 857. See also People v. Fields, 214 A.D.2d 332, 625 N.Y.S.2d 483 (1st Dep't 1995)(basic form attached to a prosecution's voluntary disclosure form purporting to declare readiness insufficient to convey indication of present readiness for trial).

Although England might be read broadly to preclude any valid declaration of readiness prior to arraignment, see, e.g., People v. Avery, 214 A.D.2d 1018, 626 N.Y.S.2d 904 (4th Dep't 1995) lv. granted June 26, 1995 (Wesley, J.), its holding may in fact be much narrower. England might be limited to "the unusual circumstances presented" in that case, 84 N.Y.2d at 3, 613 N.Y.S.2d at 855, where it was only the prosecutor's "unexplained laxity in obtaining an indictment" that prevented an arraignment within the statutory period. 84 N.Y.2d at 3, 613 N.Y.S.2d at 856. Where the prosecutor is not to blame for the delay in arraignment, an argument could be made that England does not require that such arraignment occur before a genuine declaration of readiness might be made. See People v. Avery, 214 A.D.2d at 1019, 626 N.Y.S.2d at 905 (Wesley, J., and Davis, J., dissenting).

A genuine declaration of readiness also assumes that the prosecution's witnesses are available.[173] Post-readiness unavailability of prosecution witnesses, however, does not necessarily invalidate an earlier, genuine, readiness declaration; moreover, the prosecution is not required to re-contact its witnesses prior to every adjourned date.[174]

Furthermore, the prosecution cannot be deemed ready for trial if it has failed to produce an incarcerated defendant in court.[175]

The final objective indicium of readiness is the prosecution's compliance in the resolution of all outcome-dispositive motions.[176] Thus, for example, the prosecution cannot be presently ready for trial when it has failed to provide to the court the grand jury minutes necessary to the resolution of the defendant's motion to inspect and dismiss.[177]

Library References:
West's Key No. Digests, Criminal Law ⚖577.8(1).

§ 9.23 Prosecutor's "Readiness" Stops the Clock—Valid Communication of "Present" Readiness Defined

To pass muster under under CPL § 30.30, a communication of readiness must meet two procedural requirements: (1) it must appear on the record, and (2) it must declare *present* readiness, not past or anticipated readiness.[178]

In the lead case of *People v. Kendzia*,[179] the Court of Appeals summarized the various means of communicating readiness. The court stated that such communication

> requires either a statement of readiness by the prosecutor in open court, transcribed by a stenographer, or recorded by the clerk or a written notice of readiness sent by the prosecutor to both defense counsel and the appropriate Court Clerk, to be placed in the original record....[180]

The *Kendzia* court also noted that, if the prosecutor's open-court declaration of readiness takes place in defense counsel's absence, the prosecutor must promptly notify counsel of the readiness declaration.[181]

---

173. People v. Cole, 73 N.Y.2d 957, 540 N.Y.S.2d 984, 538 N.E.2d 336 (1989)(defense properly challenged prosecution's assertion of readiness as illusory when the complainant was not available).

174. People v. Robinson, 171 A.D.2d 475, 477, 567 N.Y.S.2d 401, 403 (1st Dep't 1991).

175. People v. England, 84 N.Y.2d at 4, 613 N.Y.S.2d at 856.

176. Id.

177. Id. See also People v. McKenna, 76 N.Y.2d 59, 556 N.Y.S.2d 514, 555 N.E.2d 911 (1990).

178. People v. England, 84 N.Y.2d at 4, 613 N.Y.S.2d at 856; People v. Kendzia, 64 N.Y.2d 331, 486 N.Y.S.2d 888, 476 N.E.2d 287 (1985).

179. 64 N.Y.2d 331, 486 N.Y.S.2d 888, 476 N.E.2d 287 (1985).

180. 64 N.Y.2d at 337, 486 N.Y.S.2d at 890.

181. 64 N.Y.2d at 337 n. *, 486 N.Y.S.2d at 890 n. *. Cf. People v. Holmes, 206 A.D.2d 542, 615 N.Y.S.2d 52 (2d Dep't 1994)(readiness declaration in defense counsel's absence ineffective since counsel was not promptly notified).

§ 9.23 TIMELINESS OF PROSECUTION & SPEEDY TRIAL Ch. 9

The representation of readiness must be an "affirmative" one. Moreover, readiness is not conveyed merely by acquiescing to placing the case on a "trial calendar" or to the setting of a trial date.[182]

The communication must not only be one of readiness, but of "present readiness." Predictions of future readiness do not stop the section 30.30 clock.[183] No more effective are assertions of past readiness, such as *post hoc* allegations in response to a defense section 30.30 motion that the prosecution was, in fact, ready on a certain date, without any contemporaneous record notation to support the allegation.[184]

In *People v. Wilson*,[185] the issue was whether the prosecution validly re-declared its readiness to proceed with a second trial after the first one had been reversed on appeal. The Court of Appeals held that the prosecutor's on-the-record statement, "We have been in contact with the victim. Our intentions are to go forward," constituted a valid restatement of present readiness.[186]

Once the prosecution has declared readiness for trial, it has satisfied its burden under section 30.30. Repeated declarations of readiness during the pendency of the case are not generally necessary.[187] One exception is where an indictment is dismissed and a new one filed. In that circumstance, there is a "substantial break in the proceeding" so as to require the prosecution to re-declare readiness when it is ready to proceed on the new indictment.[188]

Library References:

West's Key No. Digests, Criminal Law ⚖577.8(1).

§ 9.24 Time Within Which Prosecution Must Be Ready to Avoid Dismissal

In determining which of the time periods set forth below is applicable to a particular case, one looks to the highest count contained in the accusatory instrument.[189] Thus, if an indictment charges a number of misdemeanors and only one felony, the applicable CPL § 30.30 time period is the one for a felony.

---

182. People v. Kendzia, 64 N.Y.2d at 337, 486 N.Y.S.2d at 890.

183. People v. England, 84 N.Y.2d at 4, 613 N.Y.S.2d at 856; People v. Kendzia, 64 N.Y.2d at 336–37, 486 N.Y.S.2d at 890.

184. See People v. Hamilton, 46 N.Y.2d 932, 933, 415 N.Y.S.2d 208, 209, 388 N.E.2d 345 (1979)(claim of past readiness in prosecution's response to section 30.30 motion insufficient as a matter of law). See also People v. Brothers, 50 N.Y.2d 413, 416, 429 N.Y.S.2d 558, 559, 407 N.E.2d 405 (1980)(prosecutor's assurance of past readiness at oral argument on the section 30.30 motion insufficient).

185. 86 N.Y.2d 753, 631 N.Y.S.2d 127, 655 N.E.2d 168 (1995).

186. Id.

187. People v. Cortes, 80 N.Y.2d at 214–15, 590 N.Y.S.2d at 17.

188. Id. See also People v. Johnson, 112 A.D.2d 1, 490 N.Y.S.2d 399(4th Dep't 1985)(declaration of readiness on initial indictment did not cover count first charged in superseding indictment).

189. CPL § 30.30(1)(a)-(d).

The applicable time period to avoid dismissal in felony cases—except for certain homicide felonies[190]—is six months from the commencement of the criminal action.[191] Six months means six *calendar* months, not 180 days.[192] The applicable period is thus calculated by adding six calendar months to the date of the commencement of the criminal action, and then by counting all the days in between. That sum, whether it be 180 days or 184 days, is then the numbers of days within which the prosecution must be ready in that particular case.[193] "Day one" of the six-month period, for calculation purposes, is the day *following* the filing of the first accusatory instrument.[194]

The applicable time period in misdemeanor cases depends upon the amount of jail time to which the defendant is exposed if convicted after trial. Where the potential sentence is greater than three months (for example, Class A misdemeanors), the time limit is 90 days from commencement.[195] Where the potential sentence is three months or less (for example, Class B misdemeanors), the time limit is 60 days.[196] For a fuller explication of how to calculate section 30.30 time periods, *see* § 9.48, *infra*.

With respect to violations, the prosecution must be ready within 30 days of commencement to avoid dismissal.[197]

Library References:
West's Key No. Digests, Criminal Law ⚖577.5, 577.8, 577.15.

§ 9.25 Time Within Which Prosecution Must Be Ready to Avoid Release of Jailed Defendant on Bail or Recognizance

Pursuant to the underutilized subdivision two of section 30.30, if the prosecution is not ready for trial within certain prescribed periods from the time of the defendant's commitment to the sheriff's custody, the defendant must be released on bail or recognizance "upon such conditions as may be just and reasonable."[198]

The statutory time periods are 90 days where one of the counts is a felony—other than the homicide felonies specified in subdivision (3)(a);[199] 30 days where the top count is a misdemeanor punishable by a jail sentence of more than three months;[200] 15 days where the top count is a

---

190. See § 9.14, supra.
191. CPL § 30.30(1)(a).
192. People v. Cortes, 80 N.Y.2d 201, 207–08 n. 3, 590 N.Y.S.2d 9, 12–13 n. 3, 604 N.E.2d 71 (1992); People v. Rhee, 111 A.D.2d 655, 656, 490 N.Y.S.2d 215, 216 (1st Dep't 1985); People v. Horney, 99 A.D.2d 886, 472 N.Y.S.2d 477 (3d Dep't 1984); People v. Smith, 97 A.D.2d 485, 468 N.Y.S.2d 129 (2d Dep't 1983); People v. Battles, 77 A.D.2d 405, 407, 433 N.Y.S.2d 936, 937 (4th Dep't 1980).
193. People v. Jones, 105 A.D.2d 179, 188, 483 N.Y.S.2d 345, 352 (2d Dep't 1984), aff'd sub nom. People v. Anderson, 66 N.Y.2d 529, 498 N.Y.S.2d 119, 488 N.E.2d 1231 (1985); People v. Smith, 97 A.D.2d 485, 468 N.Y.S.2d 129 (2d Dep't 1983).
194. People v. Stiles, 70 N.Y.2d 765, 520 N.Y.S.2d 745, 514 N.E.2d 1368 (1987).
195. CPL § 30.30(1)(b).
196. CPL § 30.30(1)(c).
197. CPL § 30.30(1)(d).
198. CPL § 30.30(2).
199. CPL § 30.30(2)(a).
200. CPL § 30.30(2)(b).

§ 9.25 TIMELINESS OF PROSECUTION & SPEEDY TRIAL Ch. 9

misdemeanor punishable by a jail sentence of three months or less;[201] and five days where the top count is a violation.[202]

Note that, for the purposes of time calculations under subdivision two, the clock starts to run from the commencement of the defendant's "commitment to the custody of the sheriff," not from the commencement of the action itself.[203]

The denial of a motion for release of the defendant pursuant to subdivision two is not, in itself, effectively appealable. The commencement of the trial will render moot the issue whether subdivision two has been violated.[204] The Court of Appeals has held, however, that a state *habeas corpus* petition does lie to seek release for a violation of section 30.30(2).[205] Indeed, a defendant may bring a *habeas corpus* petition to challenge a denial of a pretrial section 30.30(2) motion for release in the same way he or she might bring such a petition to challenge an adverse bail determination.[206]

Where the time limits set forth in subdivision two have been violated, the court must set bail in an amount the defendant can post or else release the defendant on recognizance.[207] Merely lowering the bail to an amount the defendant cannot meet does not satisfy the statutory mandate.[208]

Subdivision two relief is not available to defendants who are serving a term of imprisonment on another offense,[209] or who are also being held in custody on another charge as to which the subdivision two period has not yet lapsed.[210] Subdivision two relief is also not available to a defendant who, having already been released on bail or recognizance pursuant to subdivision two "or otherwise," violates the conditions of release.[211]

Library References:
West's Key No. Digests, Criminal Law ⚖=577.11(1).

§ 9.26 Excludable Periods—In General

In computing the time within which the prosecution must declare readiness to avoid dismissal (CPL § 30.30(1)) or the defendant's release

---

201. CPL § 30.30(2)(c).

202. CPL § 30.30(2)(d).

203. CPL § 30.30(2). Since the commitment to custody often precedes the filing of the first accusatory instrument, the clock may start to run under this subdivision prior to the commencement of the criminal action. This possibility was noted, but not definitively resolved, in a footnote in the Court of Appeals decision in People ex rel. Chakwin v. Warden, 63 N.Y.2d 120, 126, 480 N.Y.S.2d 719, 721, 470 N.E.2d 146 (1984).

204. People ex rel. Chakwin v. Warden, 63 N.Y.2d 120, 125–126, 480 N.Y.S.2d 719, 721, 470 N.E.2d 146 (1984); People ex rel. Meurer v. Bentley, 202 A.D.2d 1042, 609 N.Y.S.2d 466 (4th Dep't 1994).

205. People ex rel. Chakwin v. Warden, 63 N.Y.2d at 125, 480 N.Y.S.2d at 721.

206. People ex rel. Chakwin v. Warden, 63 N.Y.2d at 125–126, 480 N.Y.S.2d at 721; People v. Fredericks, 157 Misc.2d 822, 598 N.Y.S.2d 682 (Sup.Ct., Bronx County, 1993). See also People ex rel. Sykes v. Mitchell, 184 A.D.2d 466, 586 N.Y.S.2d 937 (1st Dep't 1992).

207. People ex rel. Chakwin v. Warden, 63 N.Y.2d at 125, 480 N.Y.S.2d at 731.

208. See People ex rel. Ellis v. Koehler, 165 A.D.2d 848, 560 N.Y.S.2d 226 (2d Dep't 1990).

209. CPL § 30.30(3)(c)(i).

210. CPL § 30.30(3)(c)(ii).

211. CPL § 30.30(3)(c)(iii).

on bail or recognizance (§ 30.30(2)), certain periods of time are statutorily excludable pursuant to CPL § 30.30(4). This subdivision "recognizes that certain delays are inherent in any criminal justice system and must be tolerated, and that other delays are caused by the defendant and should not prejudice the People's right to bring him to trial."[212]

The ten basic types of pre-readiness excludable delay are set forth in paragraphs (a) through (j) of subdivision four, and are discussed separately in §§ 9.27–9.46, *infra*. This statutory list of acceptable pre-readiness excludable delays is *exhaustive*; only those delays specifically recognized under subdivision four will be excludable from the time in which the prosecution must declare readiness.[213] For example, court congestion is not one of the statutorily cognizable excludable grounds for delay, as the inability of the court to proceed does not excuse the prosecution's lack of readiness.[214]

Once the defendant's moving papers have shown a pre-readiness delay of greater than six months, the burden is squarely on the prosecution of proving that periods of delay are excludable pursuant to subdivision four.[215]

Moreover, in pleading a subdivision four exclusion, the prosecution must point to a delaying event that actually occurred, not an event that might have occurred but did not. For example, in *People v. Collins*,[216] the prosecution argued that a particular adjournment was excludable under subdivision (4)(a), as caused by defense motion practice. The adjournment was for the transfer of the case to an Individual Assignment Part. The prosecution argued that, since such transfer was a condition precedent to the filing of any defense motions, the adjournment was excludable under (4)(a), even though no motions had yet been filed. The court rejected the prosecution's reasoning, holding that the fact that a defense motion might later be made did not render the pre-motion delay excludable under (4)(a).[217]

Another example is found in the case of *People v. McIntosh*,[218] where the prosecution filed an interlocutory appeal from an order suppressing evidence, but then withdrew it. The Court held that a withdrawn

---

212. People v. Dean, 45 N.Y.2d 651, 656–57, 412 N.Y.S.2d 353, 355–56, 384 N.E.2d 1277 (1978).

213. See People v. Cortes, 80 N.Y.2d 201, 208, 590 N.Y.S.2d 9, 13, 604 N.E.2d 71 (1992)(one computes time within which prosecution must be ready by "subtracting any periods of delay that are excludable under the terms of the statute"); People v. Santos, 68 N.Y.2d 859, 861, 508 N.Y.S.2d 411, 413, 501 N.E.2d 19 (1986)(prosecution must allege the "factual and statutory basis for each exclusion"); People v. Bolden, 81 N.Y.2d 146, 156, 597 N.Y.S.2d 270, 275, 613 N.E.2d 145 (1993)(only "statutorily cognizable" periods of delay may be excluded).

214. People v. Brothers, 50 N.Y.2d 413, 429 N.Y.S.2d 558, 407 N.E.2d 405 (1980).

215. People v. Luperon, 85 N.Y.2d 71, 623 N.Y.S.2d 735, 647 N.E.2d 1243 (1995); People v. Cortes, 80 N.Y.2d at 213, 590 N.Y.S.2d at 17; People v. Zirpola, 57 N.Y.2d 706, 708, 454 N.Y.S.2d 702, 703, 440 N.E.2d 787 (1982); People v. Berkowitz, 50 N.Y.2d 333, 349, 428 N.Y.S.2d 927, 936, 406 N.E.2d 783 (1980).

216. 82 N.Y.2d 177, 604 N.Y.S.2d 11, 624 N.E.2d 139 (1993).

217. 82 N.Y.2d at 181, 604 N.Y.S.2d at 13.

218. 80 N.Y.2d 87, 587 N.Y.S.2d 568, 600 N.E.2d 199 (1992).

§ 9.26 TIMELINESS OF PROSECUTION & SPEEDY TRIAL Ch. 9

appeal could not serve as a basis for an exclusion based on a People's appeal pursuant to subdivision (4)(a).[219]

The exclusions set forth in subdivision four are, by the very terms of the statute, not applicable once the prosecution has declared itself ready. Post-readiness delays are governed by a separate subdivision—(3)(b).[220]

Library References:

West's Key No. Digests, Criminal Law ⚖=577.8–577.12.

§ 9.27 Excludable Periods—Other Proceedings Concerning the Defendant

CPL § 30.30(4)(a) excludes from the time within which the prosecution must be ready

> a *reasonable* period of delay resulting from other proceedings concerning the defendant, including but not limited to: proceedings for the determination of competency and the period during which defendant is incompetent to stand trial; demand to produce; request for a bill of particulars; pre-trial motions; appeals; trial of other charges; and the period during which such matters are under consideration by the court ... (emphasis added).

Library References:

West's Key No. Digests, Criminal Law ⚖=577.10.

§ 9.28 Excludable Periods—Other Proceedings Concerning the Defendant—Competency

A delay between a party's application for a competency determination pursuant to CPL Article 730 and the determination itself is excludable.[221] Likewise, a period during which the defendant is incompetent, together with the subsequent delay caused by proceedings necessary to determine that the defendant is competent, are excludable.[222]

Less clear is the excludability of delay due to a defendant's simply becoming lost in the system once a commitment order expires. In *People*

---

219. 80 N.Y.2d at 90, 587 N.Y.S.2d at 569. See also People v. Cortes, 80 N.Y.2d at 211–12, 590 N.Y.S.2d at 15 (prosecution's re-presentation to new grand jury of dismissed charges was not the "functional equivalent of a successful People's appeal" of the dismissal, so as to justify exclusion under subdivision 4(a)); People v. Correa, 77 N.Y.2d 930, 569 N.Y.S.2d 601, 572 N.E.2d 42 (1991)(pre-arraignment delay not excludable on ground that defendant might plead guilty at arraignment); People v. O'Connell, 133 A.D.2d 970, 521 N.Y.S.2d 121 (3d Dep't 1987)(fact that defense chose not to make pretrial motions did not extend the six-month period an additional 45 days).

220. See People v. Cortes, 80 N.Y.2d at 210, 590 N.Y.S.2d at 14 (pre-readiness analysis inapplicable to delays once prosecution has announced readiness); People v. Myers, 171 A.D.2d 148, 151, 575 N.Y.S.2d 152, 154 (2d Dep't 1991); People v. Woods, 150 Misc.2d 1070, 572 N.Y.S.2d 279 (N.Y.C.Crim.Ct.1991).

For a discussion of post-readiness exclusions, see § 9.47, infra.

221. People v. Miller, 78 A.D.2d 817, 433 N.Y.S.2d 130 (1st Dep't 1980).

222. People v. Rivera, 151 A.D.2d 789, 543 N.Y.S.2d 120 (2d Dep't 1989).

v. Santana,[223] a Queens County prosecution, the Queens County Supreme Court found the defendant to be incompetent and ordered him committed for six months. Although that order expired in October 1985, and the Queens prosecutor did not declare readiness for trial until October 1986, the Court of Appeals held essentially all of the post-expiration, pre-readiness period to be excludable. The court expressly declined to address the effect of the Queens prosecutor's failure to monitor the defendant's post-commitment status, since the defendant fortuitously had been deemed legally incompetent pursuant to a New York County Supreme Court order on a separate case throughout all but one month of that period.[224]

The question left open in *Santana* was decided by the First Department in *People v. Lebron*.[225] There, because of an administrative mix-up, a commitment order lapsed while the defendant was serving a prison term on another charge. The prosecutor was not aware of the expiration of the order and was not ready for trial until well after its expiration. The defense argued that the prosecution should be charged with the post-expiration period during which the defendant was lost in the system. Rejecting this contention, the appellate court held that the CPL imposes no duty on the prosecutor to monitor a commitment order, and that once such an order is issued, the prosecution of the case "ceases," just as if a guilty plea had been entered.[226]

Library References:

West's Key No. Digests, Criminal Law ⟶577.11(6).

§ 9.29 Excludable Periods—Other Proceedings Concerning the Defendant—Discovery

A reasonable period of delay caused by the prosecution's compliance with discovery requests or demands is excludable.[227] Unreasonable delay, or any portion of the total delay beyond that which is reasonable, is not excludable.[228]

---

223. 80 N.Y.2d 92, 587 N.Y.S.2d 570, 600 N.E.2d 201 (1992).

224. 80 N.Y.2d at 101–03, 587 N.Y.S.2d at 574–75.

225. 211 A.D.2d 208, 628 N.Y.S.2d 54 (1st Dep't 1995), lv. granted 86 N.Y.2d 797, 632 N.Y.S.2d 510, 656 N.E.2d 609 (1995).

226. 211 A.D.2d at 210, 628 N.Y.S.2d at 55.

227. People v. Celestino, 201 A.D.2d 91, 615 N.Y.S.2d 346 (1st Dep't 1994)(22-day adjournment to allow prosecutor's compliance with discovery held excludable); People v. Coker, 131 A.D.2d 585, 516 N.Y.S.2d 293 (2d Dep't 1987)(26-day delay for prosecutor's response to discovery demand held excludable).

228. People v. Holmes, 206 A.D.2d 542, 615 N.Y.S.2d 52 (2d Dep't 1994)(66 days held includable since they were in excess of the statutory 15 days in which the prosecutor was to respond to demand to produce); People v. Jones, 105 A.D.2d 179, 185–86, 483 N.Y.S.2d 345, 349–50 (2d Dep't 1984), aff'd sub nom. People v. Anderson, 66 N.Y.2d 529, 498 N.Y.S.2d 119, 488 N.E.2d 1231 (1985)(prosecutor's pre-readiness delay in providing discovery and responding to motions, beyond that which was reasonable, would be includable); People v. Cole, 90 A.D.2d 27, 30, 457 N.Y.S.2d 589, 589 (3d Dep't 1982)(same); People v. Rivera, 72 A.D.2d 922, 422 N.Y.S.2d 211 (4th Dep't 1979)(unreasonable delay in discovery compliance includable).

§ 9.30 Excludable Periods—Other Proceedings Concerning the Defendant—Pretrial Motions

Reasonable delay caused by a prosecutor's response to defense pretrial motion practice,[229] or by the prosecution's own pretrial motion practice,[230] is excludable. Conversely, delay in excess of that which is reasonable is includable.[231]

A reasonable period of delay between the court's ordering a hearing on the defense motion and the holding of the hearing itself is excludable.[232] There is even some case law for the proposition that the first adjournment after the hearing is held and decided—or after the motion is decided without a hearing—should be excluded on the theory that the prosecution should not be expected to be ready immediately once the motion is decided.[233] The statutory basis for automatically excluding the first adjournment after motion practice is completed, however, is not clear.

Library References:

West's Key No. Digests, Criminal Law ☞577.10(8), 577.12.

§ 9.31 Excludable Periods—Other Proceedings Concerning the Defendant—Appeals

Any *reasonable* delay attributable to the prosecution's taking an appeal, pursuant to CPL Article 450, of an adverse order in the case at

---

229. People v. Weirich, 49 N.Y.2d 1020, 429 N.Y.S.2d 635, 407 N.E.2d 479 (1980), aff'g for the reasons stated at 65 A.D.2d 932, 410 N.Y.S.2d 439 (4th Dep't 1978)(two week adjournment for prosecutor's response to defense pretrial motions excludable); People v. Dean, 45 N.Y.2d 651, 657, 412 N.Y.S.2d 353, 356, 384 N.E.2d 1277, 1279 (1978)(period during which defense pretrial motion prepared, argued, and considered, excludable).

230. People v. Rodriguez, 214 A.D.2d 347, 625 N.Y.S.2d 20 (1st Dep't 1995)(time spent litigating prosecution motion to compel defendant to undergo AIDS test excludable); People v. Chapman, 185 A.D.2d 892, 587 N.Y.S.2d 379 (2d Dep't 1992)(prosecution motion to reargue dismissal of indictment); People v. Vidal, 180 A.D.2d 447, 580 N.Y.S.2d 13 (1st Dep't 1992)(prosecution motion to amend indictment).

231. People v. Collins, 82 N.Y.2d 177, 181, 604 N.Y.S.2d 11, 13, 624 N.E.2d 139 (1993)(adjournment to IAS Part, where motion practice normally ensues, not excluded because no motion practice in fact took place); People v. Vidal, 180 A.D.2d 447, 580 N.Y.S.2d 13 (1st Dep't 1992)(only delay beyond that which was reasonable in responding to omnibus motion found includable); People v. Collado, 125 A.D.2d 584, 509 N.Y.S.2d 839 (2d Dep't 1986)(delay found includable where caused by prosecution's failure to order and obtain necessary minutes).

232. People v. Carpenito, 199 A.D.2d 522, 606 N.Y.S.2d 24 (2d Dep't 1993)(pre-Darden hearing adjournment excludable); People v. Green, 90 A.D.2d 705, 455 N.Y.S.2d 368 (1st Dep't 1982)(adjournment for hearing on defendant's motion, to give prosecution time to prepare, held excludable).

233. People v. Ali, 195 A.D.2d 368, 600 N.Y.S.2d 55 (1st Dep't 1993)(39-day adjournment after denial of section 30.30 motion, so prosecution could prepare for trial, excluded); People v. Douglas, 156 A.D.2d 173, 548 N.Y.S.2d 217 (1st Dep't 1989)(seven-day adjournment after denial of section 30.30 motion excludable).

bar is excludable.[234] Periods of *unreasonable* delay in the taking of such an appeal are includable.[235] Even delay attributable to an appeal in a related case may be excludable, if the outcome of that appeal would directly affect the case at bar.[236]

Library References:
West's Key No. Digests, Criminal Law ⟐577.12.

§ 9.32 Excludable Periods—Other Proceedings Concerning the Defendant—Trial of Other Charges

A period of delay while the defendant is actually undergoing a trial on other charges is excludable,[237] but the same is not true for time spent by the prosecution merely preparing for trial on the other case,[238] or time spent engaged in motion practice on the other case.[239]

Library References:
West's Key No. Digests, Criminal Law ⟐577.11.

§ 9.33 Excludable Periods—Other Proceedings Concerning the Defendant—The Period During Which Such Matters Are Under Consideration by the Court

This CPL § 30.30 subdivision (4)(a) exclusionary language is self-explanatory. The time during which competency issues, discovery requests/demands, pre-trial motions and appeals are under consideration by the court for decision are excludable. The key distinction between this period of delay and the others contained in subdivision (4)(a) is that

---

234. People v. Grafton, 73 N.Y.2d 779, 536 N.Y.S.2d 738, 533 N.E.2d 668 (1988), aff'g 136 A.D.2d 960, 524 N.Y.S.2d 947 (4th Dep't 1988)(four-month delay due to prosecution's successful request for an extension of time to perfect appeal held reasonable and thus excludable); People v. Aaron, 201 A.D.2d 574, 607 N.Y.S.2d 950 (2d Dep't 1994)(prosecution's taking nine months to perfect its appeal, as allowed by court rules, excludable as reasonable delay). But see People v. McIntosh, 80 N.Y.2d 87, 90, 587 N.Y.S.2d 568, 569, 600 N.E.2d 199 (1992)(delay caused by prosecution appeal which was withdrawn prior to decision is includable).

235. People v. Holmes, 206 A.D.2d 542, 615 N.Y.S.2d 52 (2d Dep't 1994)(93 days of delay caused by prosecution's failure to obtain a copy of dismissal order deemed includable); People v. Green, 139 A.D.2d 760, 527 N.Y.S.2d 509 (2d Dep't 1988)(18-month delay in perfection of appeal charged to prosecution where it failed to diligently prosecute appeal).

236. See People v. Dean, 45 N.Y.2d 651, 658, 412 N.Y.S.2d 353, 357, 384 N.E.2d 1277 (1978)(delay in appeal of related case excludable since that appeal could have been outcome-determinative of the case at bar).

237. People v. Hardy, 199 A.D.2d 49, 605 N.Y.S.2d 23 (1st Dep't 1993)(excluding period during which defendant tried on another case); People v. Boyd, 189 A.D.2d 433, 436–437, 596 N.Y.S.2d 760, 762 (1st Dep't 1993)(excluding adjournment between verdict and sentence in other case). See also People v. Johnson, 191 A.D.2d 709, 595 N.Y.S.2d 515 (2d Dep't 1993)(excluding week-long adjournment for defendant's parole hearing).

238. People v. Dean, 45 N.Y.2d at 657, 412 N.Y.S.2d at 356; People v. Boyd, 123 A.D.2d 638, 639, 506 N.Y.S.2d 904, 905 (2d Dep't 1986).

239. People v. Boyd, 189 A.D.2d 433, 436–37, 596 N.Y.S.2d 760, 762 (1st Dep't 1993).

the adjective "reasonable" does not modify this clause. Section 30.30 is, after all, a *prosecutorial* readiness rule, not a court readiness rule. Hence, even unreasonable delay by the court in considering the above matters is excludable.[240]

Not excludable under subdivision (4)(a) are delays between the filing of the felony complaint and the filing of an indictment,[241] or between the filing of an indictment and the arraignment thereon.[242] Similarly, delays occasioned by the presentment of a misdemeanor case to the grand jury to obtain a felony indictment,[243] and by the conversion of a misdemeanor complaint to an information,[244] are not excludable. Nor does the mere fact that plea negotiations are taking place result in exclusion of time under subdivision (4)(a).[245] Such periods are excludable only if the adjournment is at the defense's request or with explicit defense consent, in which case the time would be excludable pursuant to subdivision (4)(b).[246]

Note that, in establishing that delays are excludable under subdivision (4)(a), the prosecution is "not required to causally trace [its] lack of readiness to defendant's actions before the court is warranted in excluding the periods resulting from adjournments" authorized by this subdivision.[247] That is because the Court of Appeals has decided to treat time

240. People v. Conrad, 44 N.Y.2d 863, 407 N.Y.S.2d 694, 379 N.E.2d 220 (1978), aff'g for the reasons stated at 93 Misc.2d 655, 405 N.Y.S.2d 559 (Monroe Co.Ct.1976); People v. Douglas, 209 A.D.2d 161, 617 N.Y.S.2d 765 (1st Dep't 1994).

Note, however, that delays caused by court congestion alone are not excludable if the prosecution is not ready for trial. People v. Brothers, 50 N.Y.2d 413, 429 N.Y.S.2d 558, 407 N.E.2d 405 (1980).

241. People v. England, 84 N.Y.2d 1, 613 N.Y.S.2d 854, 636 N.E.2d 1387 (1994); People v. Cortes, 80 N.Y.2d 201, 213, 216, 590 N.Y.S.2d 9, 16, 18, 604 N.E.2d 71 (1992); People v. Brown, 207 A.D.2d 556, 616 N.Y.S.2d 389 (2d Dep't 1994).

242. People v. Correa, 77 N.Y.2d 930, 931, 569 N.Y.S.2d 601, 601, 572 N.E.2d 42 (1991); People v. Cortes, 80 N.Y.2d at 213, 590 N.Y.S.2d at 16–17; People v. Palacios, 79 N.Y.2d 897, 581 N.Y.S.2d 661, 590 N.E.2d 246 (1992), rev'g 173 A.D.2d 745, 570 N.Y.S.2d 246 (2d Dep't 1991).

243. People v. Jacquin, 127 Misc.2d 241, 485 N.Y.S.2d 477 (Nassau Co.Ct.1985), aff'd 124 A.D.2d 594, 507 N.Y.S.2d 736 (2d Dep't 1986), aff'd on other grounds 71 N.Y.2d 825, 527 N.Y.S.2d 728, 522 N.E.2d 1026 (1988).

244. People v. Colon, 59 N.Y.2d 921, 466 N.Y.S.2d 319, 453 N.E.2d 548 (1983), rev'g for the reasons stated at 112 Misc.2d 790, 450 N.Y.S.2d 136 (N.Y.C.Crim.Ct. 1981).

245. People v. Brown, 206 A.D.2d 326, 615 N.Y.S.2d 16 (1st Dep't 1994); People v. Chapman, 185 A.D.2d 892, 587 N.Y.S.2d 379 (2d Dep't 1992); People v. Moulton, 172 A.D.2d 1001, 569 N.Y.S.2d 220 (3d Dep't 1991); People v. McCaffery, 78 A.D.2d 1003, 433 N.Y.S.2d 909 (4th Dep't 1980).

246. People v. Urraea, 214 A.D.2d 378, 625 N.Y.S.2d 163 (1st Dep't 1995); People v. LoPizzo, 151 A.D.2d 614, 543 N.Y.S.2d 88 (2d Dep't 1989). See People v. Friscia, 73 A.D.2d 702, 422 N.Y.S.2d 538 (3d Dep't 1979), aff'd on other grounds 51 N.Y.2d 845, 433 N.Y.S.2d 754, 413 N.E.2d 1168 (1980)(excluding period during which defendant attempted to cooperate pursuant to written agreement); People v. Weirich, 49 N.Y.2d 1020, 429 N.Y.S.2d 635, 407 N.E.2d 479 (1980), aff'g for the reasons stated at 65 A.D.2d 932, 410 N.Y.S.2d 439 (4th Dep't 1978)(excluded under 4(b) period during which defendant cooperating with police pursuant to agreement).

247. People v. Worley, 66 N.Y.2d 523, 527, 498 N.Y.S.2d 116, 118, 488 N.E.2d 1228 (1985). See also People v. Douglas, 209 A.D.2d 161, 617 N.Y.S.2d 765 (1st Dep't 1994); People v. Heller, 120 A.D.2d 612, 502 N.Y.S.2d 498 (2d Dep't 1986).

The same is true for exclusions under subdivision 4(b), but not necessarily for exclusions under subdivision 4(c). See §§ 9.34–9.39, infra.

periods covered by subdivision (4)(a) as delays for which there is an "express waiver" by the defense.[248]

Library References:

West's Key No. Digests, Criminal Law ⚖577.10.

§ 9.34 Excludable Periods—Continuances

Subdivision (4)(b) excludes from CPL § 30.30 time calculations any period of delay "resulting from a continuance granted by the court at the request of, or with the consent of, the defendant or his counsel." An uncounseled defendant, under this subdivision, will "not be deemed to have consented to a continuance unless he has been advised by the court of his rights under these rules and the effect of his consent." The subdivision also explicitly gives the court the power to refuse to grant even a consent adjournment if it is not in the "interest of justice, taking into account the public interest in the prompt dispositions of criminal charges."

In *People v. Liotta*,[249] the Court of Appeals squarely held that, for an adjournment to be excludable, any defense consent to it had to be explicit. Tacit consent, consent by silence, or the failure to object were not sufficient to render the adjournment excludable. Rather, such "consent to an adjournment must be clearly expressed by the defendant or defense counsel to relieve the People of the responsibility for that portion of the delay."[250]

The Court of Appeals went one step further in *People v. Smith*,[251] which dealt with the common situation of a pre-readiness adjournment by the prosecution to a date beyond that which was originally requested. The court held that, absent express defense consent, the entire adjournment was includable time.[252] The court explained:

> The adjournments at issue here were, in the first instance, precipitated by the People's failure to be ready for trial. Other than stating that certain dates were inconvenient, defense counsel never formally consented to the adjournments and did not

---

248. People v. Worley, 66 N.Y.2d at 527, 498 N.Y.S.2d at 118–19.

249. 79 N.Y.2d 841, 580 N.Y.S.2d 184, 588 N.E.2d 82 (1992).

250. 79 N.Y.2d at 843, 580 N.Y.S.2d at 185. See also People v. Cortes, 80 N.Y.2d 201, 214, 216, 590 N.Y.S.2d 9, 17, 18, 604 N.E.2d 71 (1992). The Liotta holding effectively overruled a long line of cases which held that the defense "consented to [delays by the prosecutor] by failing to object." People v. Gaggi, 104 A.D.2d 422, 423, 478 N.Y.S.2d 732, 733 (2d Dep't 1984), appeal dism. 65 N.Y.2d 636, 491 N.Y.S.2d 159, 480 N.E.2d 748 (1985). See also People v. Pappas, 128 A.D.2d 556, 512 N.Y.S.2d 493 (2d Dep't 1987); People v. Brown, 113 A.D.2d 812, 493 N.Y.S.2d 568 (2d Dep't 1985);

People v. Garfinkel, 112 A.D.2d 949, 492 N.Y.S.2d 630 (2d Dep't 1985).

251. 82 N.Y.2d 676, 601 N.Y.S.2d 466, 619 N.E.2d 403 (1993).

252. 82 N.Y.2d at 678, 601 N.Y.S.2d at 467. A different rule obtains where the prosecution's request is for a post-readiness adjournment. In that situation, the additional period beyond the date requested will be excluded. That is because the prosecution is presumed to revert to its ready status after the requested delay. People v. Cortes, 80 N.Y.2d at 217 n. 11, 590 N.Y.S.2d at 19; People v. Urraea, 214 A.D.2d 378, 625 N.Y.S.2d 163 (1st Dep't 1995); People v. Lourens, 208 A.D.2d 768, 617 N.Y.S.2d 779 (2d Dep't 1994).

§ 9.34 TIMELINESS OF PROSECUTION & SPEEDY TRIAL Ch. 9

participate in setting the adjourned dates. Because the actual dates were set either by the court or prosecution, no justification exists for excluding the additional adjournment time required to accommodate defense counsel's schedule.[253]

The *Smith* court suggested that the prosecution could file a certificate of readiness, if it were ready prior to the next court date, in order to stop the clock during the adjournment period.[254]

Adjournments granted at defense request or with its express consent are excludable, whether or not the adjournment has any causal relationship to the prosecution's unreadiness. In this situation, the defense request or consent operates as a waiver of the delay regardless of whether the prosecutorial unreadiness "resulted from" defendant's actions.[255]

If the defendant is proceeding *pro se*, is absent, or is without his or her attorney on this particular date, the delay ordinarily is not charged to the defense as a consent adjournment.[256]

Adjournments to delay grand jury action, if the delay is for the express purpose of accommodating the defendant's desire to testify, are ordinarily excludable under this subdivision.[257]

Library References:
West's Key No. Digests, Criminal Law ⇐577.10, 577.13.

---

253. 82 N.Y.2d at 678, 601 N.Y.S.2d at 467.

254. Id.

255. People v. Worley, 66 N.Y.2d 523, 527, 498 N.Y.S.2d 116, 118, 488 N.E.2d 1228 (1985). See also People v. Kopciowski, 68 N.Y.2d 615, 616–617, 505 N.Y.S.2d 52, 53, 496 N.E.2d 211 (1986)(defense adjournments to file motions and prepare for trial excludable); People v. Meierdiercks, 68 N.Y.2d 613, 505 N.Y.S.2d 51, 496 N.E.2d 210 (1986)(adjournments of preliminary hearings excluded where requested or consented to by defense); People v. Torres, 214 A.D.2d 401, 625 N.Y.S.2d 166 (1st Dep't 1995)(by requesting new counsel, defendant implicitly consented to adjournment and rendered delay excludable).

256. See, e.g., People v. Holley, 191 A.D.2d 401, 595 N.Y.S.2d 206 (1st Dep't 1993)(adjournment granted to defendant in absence of counsel, where court did not explain defendant's section 30.30 rights, not excludable); People v. Knight, 163 A.D.2d 583, 558 N.Y.S.2d 967 (2d Dep't 1990)(defense counsel's consent did not render adjournment excludable since defendant, pro se, urged prompt resolution of charges); People v. Bernier, 141 A.D.2d 750, 529 N.Y.S.2d 847 (2d Dep't 1988), aff'd on other grounds 73 N.Y.2d 1006, 541 N.Y.S.2d 760, 539 N.E.2d 588 (1989) (incarcerated defendant not deemed to consent to delay); People v. Greene, 134 A.D.2d 612, 521 N.Y.S.2d 507 (2d Dep't 1987)(uncounseled defendant may not consent to delay unless advised of section 30.30 rights). But see People v. Brown, 195 A.D.2d 310, 600 N.Y.S.2d 53 (1st Dep't 1993)(adjournment excluded pursuant to subdivision 4(f) as caused by defense counsel's failure to appear).

257. People v. Johnson, 191 A.D.2d 709, 595 N.Y.S.2d 515 (2d Dep't 1993)(12–day adjournment, during which prosecution put off grand jury vote to accommodate defendant's request to testify, held excludable); People v. Muhanimac, 181 A.D.2d 464, 581 N.Y.S.2d 301 (1st Dep't 1992)(defense adjournment to determine whether defendant would testify held excludable). Cf. People v. Smith, 211 A.D.2d 586, 622 N.Y.S.2d 19 (1st Dep't 1995)(delay between presentment and voting of indictment not excludable since defendants did not request an opportunity to testify before the grand jury); People v. Waring, 206 A.D.2d 329, 615 N.Y.S.2d 21 (1st Dep't 1994)(adjournment not excludable where it was preceded merely by defense stating that defendant would testify before grand jury); People v. Marte, 177 A.D.2d 347, 576 N.Y.S.2d 122 (1st Dep't 1991)(adjournment not excludable despite defendant's request to testify before grand jury, where defendant did not consent and was not notified of the presentment date).

§ 9.35 Excludable Periods—Absence or Unavailability of the Defendant

CPL § 30.30(4)(c), which deals with absent or unavailable defendants, must be closely scanned to divine its meaning. It excludes

> the period of delay resulting from the absence or unavailability of the defendant or, where the defendant is absent or unavailable and has either escaped from custody or has previously been released on bail or on his own recognizance, the period extending from the day the court issues a bench warrant pursuant to section 530.70 because of the defendant's failure to appear in court when required, to the day defendant subsequently appears in the court pursuant to a bench warrant or voluntarily or otherwise.

The subdivision goes on to define the terms "absent" and "unavailable":

> A defendant must be considered absent whenever his location is unknown and he is attempting to avoid apprehension or prosecution, or his location cannot be determined by due diligence. A defendant must be considered unavailable whenever his location is known but his presence for trial cannot be obtained by due diligence....

If the defendant is established to be "absent" or "unavailable" as defined by the subdivision, then the prosecution may exclude periods of delay under either of two related circumstances.

Library References:

West's Key No. Digests, Criminal Law ⚖577.11.

§ 9.36 Excludable Periods—Absence or Unavailability of the Defendant—Cause of Prosecution's Unreadiness

First, the prosecution is entitled to exclude any pre-readiness period during which the defendant is absent/unavailable provided that it can also establish a causal relationship between the defendant's absence and the prosecution's lack of readiness. In other words, unless the delay literally "results from" the defendant's absence/unavailability, under this provision it does not stop the CPL § 30.30 clock.[258]

This doctrine of causal relationship was first set forth in *People v. Sturgis*,[259] where the defendant was "absent" during a period of delay between the filing of the felony complaint and the filing of an indictment. The Court of Appeals held the period includable, since the

---

258. People v. Colon, 59 N.Y.2d 921, 466 N.Y.S.2d 319, 453 N.E.2d 548 (1983), rev'g for the reasons stated at 112 Misc.2d 790, 450 N.Y.S.2d 136 (N.Y.C.Crim.Ct. 1981); People v. Williams, 56 N.Y.2d 824, 452 N.Y.S.2d 571, 438 N.E.2d 104 (1982); People v. Sturgis, 38 N.Y.2d 625, 381 N.Y.S.2d 860, 345 N.E.2d 331 (1976).

259. 38 N.Y.2d 625, 381 N.Y.S.2d 860, 345 N.E.2d 331.

§ 9.36 TIMELINESS OF PROSECUTION & SPEEDY TRIAL Ch. 9

defendant's absence "in no way impeded or prevented" the procuring of an indictment.[260]

The impact of *Sturgis* was lessened by three subsequent events. One of these was the Court of Appeals decision in *People v. Bratton*.[261] In that case, the prosecution had proven that it had a systematic policy of not indicting absent/unavailable defendants. Where such a policy exists, the court held, the prosecution's lack of readiness "results from" the defendant's absence, and the delay is excludable.[262]

Another event was the Legislature's 1982 addition of section 30.30 (5)(b), which excludes the period between the commencement of the action and the defendant's first appearance in court in response to a desk appearance ticket.[263]

A third event was the Legislature's 1984 amendment to subdivision (4)(c), which created the second circumstance under which pre-readiness delay is excludable with respect to absent/unavailable defendants.

§ 9.37 Excludable Periods—Absence or Unavailability of the Defendant—Bench Warrants

In 1984, the Legislature amended subdivision (4)(c) by adding the following italicized language to the first sentence:

> the period of delay resulting from the absence or unavailability of the defendant *or, where the defendant is absent or unavailable and has either escaped from custody or has previously been released on bail or on his own recognizance, the period extending from the day the court issues a bench warrant pursuant to section 530.70 because of the defendant's failure to appear in court when required, to the day the defendant subsequently appears in the court pursuant to a bench warrant or voluntarily or otherwise.*

The intent and effect of this amendment was to relieve the prosecution of the *Sturgis/Colon* requirement of establishing a causal nexus between the defendant's absence/unavailability and its own lack of readiness, provided a bench warrant has been issued against the defendant. Notably, as the Court of Appeals made clear in *People v. Bolden*,[264] the amendment did not relieve the prosecution of the independent burden of establishing that the defendant was "absent" or "unavailable" within the meaning of the rest of subdivision (4)(c), including the burden of showing "due diligence" in locating or producing the defendant.[265]

---

260. 38 N.Y.2d at 628, 381 N.Y.S.2d at 861.

261. 65 N.Y.2d 675, 491 N.Y.S.2d 623, 481 N.E.2d 255 (1985), aff'g for the reasons stated at 103 A.D.2d 368, 374, 480 N.Y.S.2d 324, 328 (2d Dep't 1984).

262. Id. Cf. People v. Smolen, 186 A.D.2d 292, 588 N.Y.S.2d 312 (2d Dep't 1992)(Bratton exclusion did not apply where prosecution did not allege general policy of not indicting absent defendants).

263. See § 9.17, supra.

264. 81 N.Y.2d 146, 597 N.Y.S.2d 270, 613 N.E.2d 145 (1993).

265. 81 N.Y.2d at 153, 597 N.Y.S.2d at 273–74. See also People v. Mace, 206 A.D.2d 296, 614 N.Y.S.2d 416 (1st Dep't 1994); People v. Wiggins, 194 A.D.2d 840, 598 N.Y.S.2d 391 (3d Dep't 1993); People v. Brunskill, 192 A.D.2d 666, 597 N.Y.S.2d 89 (2d Dep't 1993); People v. Delacruz, 189

By its terms, the statute speaks of "bench warrants," *i.e.*, warrants issued after the defendant has already been arraigned and has failed to appear,[266] not arrest warrants.[267]

In *People v. Luperon*,[268] the Court of Appeals confronted the issue of the excludability of an unreasonable period of delay in executing a bench warrant. In that case, the prosecution made no effort to have the warrant executed for 69 days. The court rejected the prosecution's argument that its eventual diligent efforts in seeking to execute the warrant were sufficient to require exclusion of the entire post-issuance period. Instead, the court held, only those post-issuance periods during which the prosecution exercised due diligence in attempting to locate or apprehend the defendant were excludable.[269]

Where the court stays execution of the warrant at defendant's request, however, that period of delay is excludable.[270]

Courts have excluded not only the period the defendant is absent or unavailable, but also the first adjournment after the defendant's return, as a reasonable period for the prosecution to re-commence its case.[271]

Of course, no delay is excludable under subdivision (4)(c) unless the defendant is first established to have been "absent" or "unavailable," as those terms are defined in the statute.[272]

Library References:

West's Key No. Digests, Criminal Law ⛙577.11.

A.D.2d 717, 592 N.Y.S.2d 732 (1st Dep't 1993). The Bolden holding, that the prosecution must show "due diligence" even with a warranting defendant might not be applicable to post-readiness exclusions under subdivision (3)(b). See § 9.47, infra.

266. See CPL § 1.20(3)(defining "bench warrant"). In People v. Luperon, 85 N.Y.2d 71, 623 N.Y.S.2d 735, 647 N.E.2d 1243 (1995), the defendant argued that the bench warrant issued in his particular case was not of the type defined in subdivision (4)(c), since he had never been advised of when he was required to appear. The court did not consider that contention because it was unpreserved in that particular case. Thus, the issue whether the language of subdivision (4)(c) covers every bench warrant is still open.

267. See CPL § 1.20(28) and (29) for the definitions of warrants of arrest.

268. 85 N.Y.2d 71, 623 N.Y.S.2d 735, 647 N.E.2d 1243 (1995).

269. 85 N.Y.2d at 79–80, 623 N.Y.S.2d at 739. See also People v. Drummond, 215 A.D.2d 579, 627 N.Y.S.2d 55 (2d Dep't 1995)(54-day delay in assigning warrant officer not excludable). Some administrative delay in the processing of a bench warrant, however, has been deemed reasonable and thus excludable. See People v. Reid, 214 A.D.2d 396, 625 N.Y.S.2d 171 (1st Dep't 1995)(35-day period prior to warrant squad officer's assignment to the case excludable as a reasonable period of administrative processing).

270. People v. Medina, 198 A.D.2d 146, 603 N.Y.S.2d 858 (1st Dep't 1993); People v. Parker, 186 A.D.2d 593, 588 N.Y.S.2d 390 (2d Dep't 1992); People v. Toro, 151 A.D.2d 142, 546 N.Y.S.2d 842 (1st Dep't 1989), appeal dism. 75 N.Y.2d 818, 552 N.Y.S.2d 568, 551 N.E.2d 1246 (1990).

271. See People v. Muhanimac, 181 A.D.2d 464, 581 N.Y.S.2d 301 (1st Dep't 1992); People v. Lewis, 150 Misc.2d 886, 578 N.Y.S.2d 393 (N.Y.C.Crim.Ct.1992); People v. Degro, 141 Misc.2d 810, 535 N.Y.S.2d 330 (N.Y.C.Crim.Ct.1988).

272. In Bolden, the court left open the question whether "there may be circumstances other than those enumerated in the statute when a defendant may be considered 'absent' or 'unavailable'" for the purpose of determining a subdivision 4(c) exclusion. 81 N.Y.2d at 153 n.3, 597 N.Y.S.2d at 274 n. 3.

§ 9.38 Excludable Periods—Absence or Unavailability of the Defendant—Absent

A defendant is considered "absent" under one of two circumstances: (1) "his location is unknown and he is attempting to avoid apprehension or prosecution," or (2) "his location cannot be determined by due diligence."[273]

In the first situation ("his location is unknown and he is attempting to avoid apprehension or prosecution"), there is no literal requirement that the prosecution show "due diligence."[274] The prosecution must still show, however, not only that the defendant's location was unknown but also that he or she was attempting to avoid apprehension or prosecution.[275] An attempt to avoid apprehension or prosecution may be shown by such factors as the defendant's use of aliases,[276] flight from the jurisdiction,[277] or the failure to show up in court.[278]

The defendant is also "absent" if "his location cannot be determined by due diligence." The determination whether prosecution efforts to locate the defendant constitute due diligence is heavily factbound and depends upon a large number of variables. Two cases reaching different results are instructive, however.

In *People v. Bratton*,[279] the police attempted to locate the defendant by entering the warrant for his arrest into a national computer system, speaking with relatives and neighbors at his last known address, and

---

273. CPL § 30.30(4)(c).

274. See People v. Luperon, 85 N.Y.2d at 80 n.3, 623 N.Y.S.2d at 739; People v. Bolden, 81 N.Y.2d at 152 n.3, 155, 597 N.Y.S.2d at 273 n.1; People v. Rogers, 195 A.D.2d 977, 601 N.Y.S.2d 755 (4th Dep't 1993); People v. Banham, 175 A.D.2d 166, 573 N.Y.S.2d 899 (2d Dep't 1991).

275. People v. Davis, 205 A.D.2d 697, 613 N.Y.S.2d 668 (2d Dep't 1994).

276. See People v. Colon, 59 N.Y.2d 921, 466 N.Y.S.2d 319, 453 N.E.2d 548 (1983); People v. Sturgis, supra; People v. Davis, supra; People v. Johnson, 191 A.D.2d 709, 595 N.Y.S.2d 515 (2d Dep't 1993); People v. Rodriguez, 180 A.D.2d 517, 580 N.Y.S.2d 24 (1st Dep't 1992); People v. Brazeau, 162 A.D.2d 979, 557 N.Y.S.2d 205 (4th Dep't 1990). Where the uses of aliases or false pedigree has prevented the location of even an incarcerated defendant, the courts have sometimes deemed the defendant "absent." See People v. Ladson, 202 A.D.2d 212, 608 N.Y.S.2d 966 (1st Dep't 1994), aff'd on other grounds 85 N.Y.2d 926, 626 N.Y.S.2d 999, 650 N.E.2d 846 (1995); People v. Johnson, 191 A.D.2d 709, 595 N.Y.S.2d 515 (2d Dep't 1993); People v. Neal, 160 Misc.2d 173, 607 N.Y.S.2d 866 (Sup.Ct., N.Y. County, 1994). Cf. People v. Davis, 184 A.D.2d 575, 584 N.Y.S.2d 638 (prosecution ordinarily deemed to know incarcerated defendant's whereabouts).

277. See People v. Davis, 205 A.D.2d 697, 613 N.Y.S.2d 668 (1994); People v. Delacruz, 189 A.D.2d 717, 592 N.Y.S.2d 732 (1st Dep't 1993); People v. James, 187 A.D.2d 672, 591 N.Y.S.2d 784 (2d Dep't 1992); People v. Rodriguez, 180 A.D.2d 517, 580 N.Y.S.2d 24 (1992); People v. Brazeau, 162 A.D.2d 979, 557 N.Y.S.2d 205 (4th Dep't 1990).

278. See People v. Colon, 59 N.Y.2d 921, 466 N.Y.S.2d 319, 453 N.E.2d 548 (1983) (defendant "absent" where, inter alia, he failed to respond to three desk appearance tickets); People v. Sturgis, 38 N.Y.2d 625, 381 N.Y.S.2d 860, 345 N.E.2d 331 (1976) (defendant "absent" where, inter alia, other courts had issued bench warrants on other charges); People v. Jackson, 150 A.D.2d 609, 541 N.Y.S.2d 478 (2d Dep't 1989)(failure to appear for scheduled court appearance); People v. Walker, 133 A.D.2d 2, 518 N.Y.S.2d 392 (failure to report to parole officer). Cf. People v. Peterson, 115 A.D.2d 497, 496 N.Y.S.2d 231 (2d Dep't 1985)(where defendant unaware of indictment until arrest, no attempt to avoid apprehension).

279. 65 N.Y.2d 675, 491 N.Y.S.2d 623, 481 N.E.2d 255 (1985).

watching that residence an hour per day for the next six weeks. Ultimately, the defendant was apprehended after being arrested in another town under an assumed name. The court found due diligence on the part of the police.[280] In *People v. Fuggazzatto*,[281] on the other hand, the prosecution failed to deliver the bench warrants to the central warrant squad for over five months, and that squad failed to take any action for an additional month. The six-month period was not excludable because no due diligence was shown.[282]

Library References:

West's Key No. Digests, Criminal Law ⚖577.11.

§ 9.39 Excludable Periods—Absence or Unavailability of the Defendant—Unavailable

A defendant is unavailable when "his location is known but his presence for trial cannot be obtained by due diligence." If a defendant is incarcerated, the prosecution must exercise due diligence to procure his or her presence.[283] A hospitalized defendant has been held to be unavailable,[284] as is a defendant who had agreed to surrender on an arrest warrant, but has not yet done so.[285]

Library References:

West's Key No. Digests, Criminal Law ⚖577.11.

280. Id. See also People v. Maldonado, 210 A.D.2d 259, 619 N.Y.S.2d 730 (2d Dep't 1994)(due diligence found where warrant squad went to defendant's last known address, contacted his sister, and checked with the Department of Motor Vehicles and the Human Resources Administration); People v. Marrin, 187 A.D.2d 284, 589 N.Y.S.2d 874 (1st Dep't 1992)(due diligence found where police reviewed defendant's rap sheet, interviewed defendant's relatives and the complainant, visited defendant's last known address, surveilled his "known haunts," reviewed phone company records, and checked with the post office, corrections and motor vehicles; four days of actual effort over two-year period sufficient); People v. Hudson, 167 A.D.2d 950, 561 N.Y.S.2d 1014 (4th Dep't 1990)(police exercised due diligence by checking at defendant's place of employment, going to his sister's house, and interviewing his relatives and acquaintances).

281. 62 N.Y.2d 862, 477 N.Y.S.2d 619, 466 N.E.2d 159 (1984), modifying 96 A.D.2d 538, 464 N.Y.S.2d 847 (2d Dep't 1983).

282. Id. See also People v. Davis, 205 A.D.2d 697, 613 N.Y.S.2d 668 (2d Dep't 1994)(no due diligence where police conducted only sporadic computer checks and failed to visit last known address); People v. Alston, 191 A.D.2d 176, 594 N.Y.S.2d 37 (1st Dep't 1993)(no due diligence for delay in executing warrant where defendant incarcerated under his own name in New York on an unrelated charge); People v. Wittmann, 73 A.D.2d 1053, 1055, 425 N.Y.S.2d 416, 418 (4th Dep't 1980)(no due diligence where police failed to contact defendant through attorney of record).

283. People v. Davis, 184 A.D.2d 575, 584 N.Y.S.2d 638 (2d Dep't 1992); People v. Knight, 163 A.D.2d 583, 558 N.Y.S.2d 967 (2d Dep't 1990); People v. Traficante, 147 A.D.2d 843, 538 N.Y.S.2d 331 (3d Dep't 1989). Cf. People v. Goode, ___ A.D.2d ___, 628 N.Y.S.2d 727 (2d Dep't 1995), lv. granted 86 N.Y.2d 842, 634 N.Y.S.2d 451, 658 N.E.2d 229 (1995)(incarcerated defendant unavailable while under medical quarantine); People v. Mitchell, 106 A.D.2d 478, 482 N.Y.S.2d 574 (2d Dep't 1984)(excluding delay while defendant incarcerated in another county under an assumed name).

284. People v. Toro, 151 A.D.2d 142, 546 N.Y.S.2d 842 (1st Dep't 1989), appeal dism. 75 N.Y.2d 818, 552 N.Y.S.2d 568, 551 N.E.2d 1246 (1990); People v. Walters, 127 A.D.2d 870, 511 N.Y.S.2d 957 (2d Dep't 1987).

285. People v. Pappas, 128 A.D.2d 556, 512 N.Y.S.2d 493 (2d Dep't 1987).

§ 9.40 Excludable Periods—Co-defendant Joinder

CPL § 30.30(4)(d) provides for the excludability of "a reasonable period of delay when the defendant is joined for trial with a co-defendant as to whom the time for trial pursuant to this section has not run and good cause is not shown for granting a severance."

Under this provision, where a defendant is properly joined with a co-defendant, and the section 30.30 time for the co-defendant has not yet run, any reasonable period of delay properly excludable with respect to the co-defendant is also excludable as to the defendant.[286] Thus, for example, delay legitimately excludable as to the co-defendant because the co-defendant is considering a plea offer,[287] making pretrial motions,[288] asking to testify before the grand jury,[289] or requesting adjournments,[290] is excluded as to the defendant as well.

To avoid the effects of this statutory exclusion, one must obtain a severance based upon good cause. The eventual severance, however, does not divest the prosecution of the benefit of the earlier exclusions.[291]

Library References:
West's Key No. Digests, Criminal Law ⇔577.10(5).

§ 9.41 Excludable Periods—Incarcerated Defendants

CPL § 30.30(4)(e) renders excludable "the period of delay resulting from the detention of the defendant in another jurisdiction provided the district attorney is aware of such detention and has been diligent and has made reasonable efforts to obtain the presence of the defendant for trial."

Notwithstanding its seeming application only to incarcerations outside of New York, this subdivision, and its due diligence requirement, have been held to apply to defendants incarcerated both in and outside the state.[292] Consequently, the prosecution is chargeable with any unreasonable delay in producing an incarcerated defendant, including such delay on the part of correction officials.[293] Merely lodging a

---

286. People v. Cortes, 80 N.Y.2d 201, 207 n.2, 590 N.Y.S.2d 9, 13 n.2, 604 N.E.2d 71 (1992).

287. People v. Ali, 195 A.D.2d 368, 600 N.Y.S.2d 55 (1st Dep't 1993); People v. Rodriguez, 184 A.D.2d 317, 584 N.Y.S.2d 831 (1st Dep't 1992).

288. People v. Bissereth, 194 A.D.2d 317, 598 N.Y.S.2d 781 (1st Dep't 1993); People v. Dery, 115 A.D.2d 996, 497 N.Y.S.2d 560 (4th Dep't 1985).

289. People v. Khan, 172 A.D.2d 231, 568 N.Y.S.2d 367 (1st Dep't 1991); People v. Fluellen, 160 A.D.2d 219, 553 N.Y.S.2d 670 (1st Dep't 1990).

290. People v. Vidal, 180 A.D.2d 447, 580 N.Y.S.2d 13 (1st Dep't 1992).

291. Id.

292. People v. Anderson, 66 N.Y.2d 529, 538, 540, 498 N.Y.S.2d 119, 124, 126, 488 N.E.2d 1231 (1985), aff'g 105 A.D.2d 38, 482 N.Y.S.2d 745 (1st Dep't 1984). See also People v. Davis, 205 A.D.2d 697, 613 N.Y.S.2d 668 (2d Dep't 1994)(where no due diligence in executing warrant lodged against New York State prisoner, time held not excludable); People v. Knight, 163 A.D.2d 583, 558 N.Y.S.2d 967 (2d Dep't 1990); People v. Traficante, 147 A.D.2d 843, 538 N.Y.S.2d 331 (3d Dep't 1989).

293. People v. Ali, 209 A.D.2d 227, 618 N.Y.S.2d 640 (1st Dep't 1994)(prosecution charged with delay in producing defendant in its custody); People v. Worley, 201 A.D.2d 520, 607 N.Y.S.2d 408 (2d Dep't 1994)(where prosecution failed to produce defendant for Wade hearing, delay not ex-

detainer against a defendant incarcerated in another county has been held not to constitute, by itself, due diligence.[294]

As to defendants incarcerated in non-New York jurisdictions, CPL § 30.30(4)(e) has been held to operate independently of the Interstate Agreement on Detainers (CPL Article 580) and the Uniform Criminal Extradition Act (CPL Article 570).[295] Compliance with those CPL provisions is a factor in determining whether due diligence has been established, but is not in itself sufficient to establish it.[296]

Library References:
West's Key No. Digests, Criminal Law ⚖︎577.11.

§ 9.42 Excludable Periods—Defendant Without Counsel

CPL § 30.30(4)(f) excludes "the period during which the defendant is without counsel through no fault of the court; except when the defendant is proceeding as his own attorney with the permission of the court."

This subdivision is applicable where the defendant has no attorney at all representing him or her, not where the defendant is represented but the attorney has simply failed to appear on a particular date.[297] In

---

cludable); Cf. People v. Lloyd, 141 A.D.2d 669, 529 N.Y.S.2d 801 (2d Dep't 1988)(where prosecution diligently sought to obtain defendant's production from another county pursuant to CPL Article 560, delay excludable); People v. Taylor, 124 A.D.2d 843, 509 N.Y.S.2d 46 (2d Dep't 1986)(where nonproduction of incarcerated defendant resulted from false pedigree information, delay excludable).

294. People v. Orse, 118 A.D.2d 816, 500 N.Y.S.2d 173 (2d Dep't 1986)(merely lodging detainer, without seeking judicial order pursuant to CPL Article 560, does not satisfy due diligence standard); People v. Billups, 105 A.D.2d 795, 481 N.Y.S.2d 430 (2d Dep't 1984).

A "detainer" is "a request filed by a criminal justice agency with the institution in which a prisoner is incarcerated asking either to hold the prisoner for the agency or to notify the agency when the release of the prisoner is imminent." Reed v. Farley, ___ U.S. ___, n. 1, 114 S.Ct. 2291, 2294 n. 1, 129 L.Ed.2d 277 (1994).

295. People v. Santos, 68 N.Y.2d 859, 861–62, 508 N.Y.S.2d 411, 413, 501 N.E.2d 19 (1986).

296. Id. See also People v. Smith, 73 N.Y.2d 961, 540 N.Y.S.2d 987, 538 N.E.2d 339 (1989), aff'g for the reasons stated at 138 A.D.2d 972, 526 N.Y.S.2d 303 (4th Dep't 1988)(where prosecution sought defendant's production from federal facility pursuant to IAD, did necessary paperwork and maintained contact with federal authorities, delay excludable); People v. Hinton, 181 A.D.2d 696, 581 N.Y.S.2d 65 (2d Dep't 1992), appeal dism. 81 N.Y.2d 867, 597 N.Y.S.2d 926, 613 N.E.2d 958 (1993) (prosecution's initial compliance with IAD insufficient, by itself, to establish due diligence, where prosecution failed to also monitor progress of extradition proceedings); People v. Wills, 201 A.D.2d 519, 607 N.Y.S.2d 409 (2d Dep't 1994)(excluding delay where prosecution acted diligently in seeking defendant's production from sister state); People v. Johnson, 115 A.D.2d 794, 496 N.Y.S.2d 306 (3d Dep't 1985)(excluding delay where prosecution diligently sought extradition, but sister state refused to release defendant); People v. Melendez, 92 A.D.2d 904, 459 N.Y.S.2d 900 (2d Dep't 1983)(merely lodging detainer did not constitute due diligence); People v. Cook, 71 A.D.2d 801, 419 N.Y.S.2d 350 (4th Dep't 1979)(diligent efforts to obtain defendant from federal custody permit exclusion of delay).

297. See People v. Holley, 191 A.D.2d 401, 595 N.Y.S.2d 206 (1st Dep't 1993); People v. Smith, 91 A.D.2d 928, 457 N.Y.S.2d 822 (1st Dep't 1983); People v. Gatling, 160 Misc.2d 886, 611 N.Y.S.2d 762 (Sup.Ct., N.Y. County, 1994). But see People v. Brown, 195 A.D.2d 310, 600 N.Y.S.2d 53 (1st Dep't 1993)(adjournment at which defense counsel failed to appear excluded pursuant to subdivision 4(f)).

§ 9.42 TIMELINESS OF PROSECUTION & SPEEDY TRIAL Ch. 9

the latter circumstances, the excludability of the delay based on counsel's absence would be governed by subdivision (4)(b).[298]

In *People v. Cortes*,[299] the Court of Appeals interpreted "the court" under this subdivision to include the assigned counsel plan under Article 18–B of the County Law. The court held it "both fair and reasonable to hold the courts accountable for deficiencies in the [assigned counsel] system such as occurred in this case, where the 18–B Panel failed to perform its basic mission of furnishing counsel to a defendant who could not afford to retain an attorney on his own."[300] Thus, *Cortes* deemed lengthy and unreasonable delay in the assignment of counsel to be the "fault of the court."[301]

Shorter, more reasonable delays in the assignment of counsel to indigent defendants, however, have been held to be excludable.[302]

Adjournments to allow the defendant to retain counsel are excludable under this subdivision.[303]

It has been held that there is no requirement, under this subdivision, that the defendant's lack of representation have impacted on the prosecutor's ability to be ready in order to render the delay excludable.[304]

Library References:

West's Key No. Digests, Criminal Law ⚖=577.10(4).

§ 9.43 Excludable Periods—Exceptional Circumstances

Pursuant to CPL § 30.30(4)(g), the prosecution may exclude

other periods of delay occasioned by exceptional circumstances, including but not limited to, the period of delay resulting from a continuance granted at the request of a district attorney if (i) the continuance is granted because of the unavailability of evidence material to the people's case, when the district attorney has exercised due diligence to obtain such evidence and there are reasonable grounds to believe that such evidence will become available in a reasonable period; or (ii) the continuance is granted to allow the district attorney additional time to

---

298. See § 9.34, supra.

299. 80 N.Y.2d 201, 590 N.Y.S.2d 9, 604 N.E.2d 71 (1992).

300. 80 N.Y.2d at 208–09, 590 N.Y.S.2d at 14.

301. Id.

302. See People v. Rodriguez, 212 A.D.2d 368, 622 N.Y.S.2d 243 (1st Dep't 1995)(seven-day delay for appointment of counsel excluded); People v. Parker, 186 A.D.2d 593, 588 N.Y.S.2d 390 (2d Dep't 1992)(five-day delay); People v. Robinson, 171 A.D.2d 475, 567 N.Y.S.2d 401 (1st Dep't 1991)(four-day delay); People v. Greene, 134 A.D.2d 612, 521 N.Y.S.2d 507 (2d Dep't 1987)(35-day delay held reasonable).

303. People v. Stefano, 159 A.D.2d 1016, 552 N.Y.S.2d 727 (4th Dep't 1990)(excluding 14-day period during which defendant attempted to obtain counsel after being told he was not eligible for assigned counsel); People v. Boyd, 116 A.D.2d 978, 498 N.Y.S.2d 932 (4th Dep't 1986)(32-day adjournment for defendant to retain counsel excluded); People v. Roberson, 99 A.D.2d 619, 472 N.Y.S.2d 157 (3d Dep't 1984)(two-month delay to obtain private counsel excluded).

304. People v. Drake, 205 A.D.2d 996, 613 N.Y.S.2d 961 (3d Dep't 1994).

prepare the people's case and additional time is justified by the exceptional circumstances of the case.

By its own terms, the examples listed in subdivision (4)(g) of what is an "exceptional circumstance" are not exhaustive. For example, the prosecution is "not limited to" excluding periods of delay occasioned by "continuances" it has requested.[305]

At the same time, the prosecution may not invoke subdivision 4(g) if the type of delay involved is governed by another of the exclusions in subdivision four. By its terms, subdivision (4)(g) covers only *other periods of delay* beyond those contemplated in subdivision (4)(a-f) and subdivision (4)(h-j).[306] For example, an adjournment requested by the prosecutor that is not excludable under subdivision (4)(b), because defense counsel did not expressly consent,[307] could not, without more, be excludable under subdivision (4)(g) as an "exceptional circumstance."

A prime example of an "exceptional circumstance" justifying exclusion is the unavailability of a material prosecution witness because of either medical reasons,[308] the witness's absence from the country,[309] or any other circumstance beyond the prosecutor's control.[310]

---

305. People v. Zirpola, 57 N.Y.2d 706, 454 N.Y.S.2d 702, 440 N.E.2d 787 (1982); People v. Goodman, 41 N.Y.2d 888, 393 N.Y.S.2d 985, 362 N.E.2d 615 (1977).

306. See People v. Goodman, 41 N.Y.2d at 889, 393 N.Y.S.2d at 985 (subdivision (4)(g) "allows exceptional circumstances to justify periods of delay not expressly covered by the statute").

307. See § 9.34, supra.

308. People v. Goodman, 41 N.Y.2d 888, 393 N.Y.S.2d 985, 362 N.E.2d 615 (1977) (unavailability of complainant for medical reasons is a sufficient exceptional circumstance to warrant exclusion); People v. Rodriguez, 212 A.D.2d 368, 622 N.Y.S.2d 243 (1st Dep't 1995)(illness of complainant's father); People v. Celestino, 201 A.D.2d 91, 615 N.Y.S.2d 346 (1st Dep't 1994)(police witness's broken leg, even without hospitalization); People v. DeJesus, 190 A.D.2d 1012, 593 N.Y.S.2d 633 (4th Dep't 1993)(police officer's illness led to excludable delay); People v. Johnson, 191 A.D.2d 709, 595 N.Y.S.2d 515 (2d Dep't 1993)(excluded 20-day adjournment due to unavailability of police officer injured in accident); People v. Pressley, 115 A.D.2d 228, 496 N.Y.S.2d 147 (4th Dep't 1985)(where complainant medically unavailable and due diligence would have been to no avail, prosecution not required to prove actual due diligence); People v. Hall, 61 A.D.2d 1050, 403 N.Y.S.2d 112 (2d Dep't 1978)(nervous breakdown of grand jury stenographer, necessitating superseding indictment, constituted an exceptional circumstance); People v. Familia–Morel, 151 Misc.2d 55, 570 N.Y.S.2d 895 (N.Y.C.Crim.Ct.1991)(serious illness of police witness's daughter deemed exceptional circumstance, but only for period that witness was unable to work).

309. People v. Rodriguez, 212 A.D.2d 368, 622 N.Y.S.2d 243 (1st Dep't 1995) (complainant's inability to return to country because of hurricane deemed an exceptional circumstance); People v. Kato, 178 A.D.2d 381, 578 N.Y.S.2d 143 (1st Dep't 1991)(delay due to prosecution witness leaving New York to attend brother's funeral is exceptional circumstance). Cf. People v. Boyd, 189 A.D.2d 433, 437–438, 596 N.Y.S.2d 760, 762–63 (1st Dep't 1993)(adjournment due to prosecution witness's unexplained absence from country not excludable where there was no showing of due diligence).

310. See, e.g., People v. Zirpola, 57 N.Y.2d 706, 454 N.Y.S.2d 702, 440 N.E.2d 787, modifying 88 A.D.2d 758, 451 N.Y.S.2d 483 (4th Dep't 1982)(co-defendant's unavailability as a prosecution witness between his indictment and cooperation agreement would constitute exceptional circumstance); People v. Lashway, 187 A.D.2d 747, 589 N.Y.S.2d 687 (3d Dep't 1992)(nearly two-year delay in grand jury presentation, due to young rape victim's refusal to testify despite diligent efforts of prosecutor, excludable as the product of an exceptional circumstance); People v. Weeks, 126 A.D.2d 857, 510 N.Y.S.2d 920 (3d Dep't 1987)(delay in grand jury presentation due to victim's emotional upset excludable as exceptional circumstance). Cf. People v. Thomas, 210 A.D.2d 736, 620 N.Y.S.2d 555 (3d Dep't

§ 9.43 TIMELINESS OF PROSECUTION & SPEEDY TRIAL Ch. 9

To constitute an exceptional circumstance, the unavailability would have to be of a *necessary* witness.[311] Moreover, the prosecution would need to establish a reasonable belief that the witness would ultimately become available in a reasonable time.[312]

A delay due to an ongoing investigation that otherwise would be compromised,[313] or that must be resolved before the prosecution of the defendant can continue,[314] may be excludable as due to an exceptional circumstance. The prosecution would have to demonstrate, however, that the investigation was pursued with "credible, vigorous activity."[315]

Not constituting "exceptional circumstances" are inadequate staffing, overwork, or disorganization in the prosecutor's office;[316] nor is court congestion an "exceptional circumstance" excusing the prosecution's own lack of trial readiness.[317]

1994)(delay in trial to accommodate prosecution witness's vacation schedule not due to an exceptional circumstance); People v. Meyers, 114 A.D.2d 861, 494 N.Y.S.2d 897 (2d Dep't 1985)(seven-month delay due to witnesses' purported fear of testifying not excludable where prosecution took no affirmative steps to secure their testimony); People v. Holmes, 105 A.D.2d 803, 481 N.Y.S.2d 741 (2d Dep't 1984)(delay in locating witness for retrial after appellate reversal not excludable where prosecution failed to exercise due diligence); People v. Williams, 132 Misc.2d 549, 504 N.Y.S.2d 364 (Sup.Ct., N.Y. County, 1986)(delay to protect identity of undercover officer, by allowing him to testify first in another case, not excludable as due to an exceptional circumstance).

311. See People v. Lowman, 102 A.D.2d 896, 476 N.Y.S.2d 937 (2d Dep't 1984)(delay in indictment due to witness's reluctance to testify not excludable where, inter alia, witness not vital to prosecution's case in the grand jury); People v. Stanton, 71 A.D.2d 932, 419 N.Y.S.2d 717 (2d Dep't 1979)(preindictment delay due to witness's absence, where witness's testimony not necessary to procure indictment, not excludable).

312. Cf. People v. Pomales, 159 A.D.2d 451, 553 N.Y.S.2d 131 (1st Dep't 1990)(delay due to complainant's medical unavailability excludable since prosecution expected complainant would ultimately be available) with People v. Spadafora, 131 A.D.2d 40, 519 N.Y.S.2d 979 (1st Dep't 1987)(seven-month absence of witness not excludable, despite due diligence, since prosecution had no grounds to believe witness would become available).

313. See People v. Hinson, 203 A.D.2d 480, 610 N.Y.S.2d 578 (2d Dep't 1994)(delay to allow remaining indictments in large-scale narcotics investigation to be handed down was properly excludable). Cf. People v. Lopez, 77 A.D.2d 287, 433 N.Y.S.2d 569 (1st Dep't 1980)(13–month delay in arresting defendant not excludable, since prosecution failed to establish sufficient nexus between defendant and the subject of the large-scale narcotics investigation).

314. See People v. Azcona, 180 A.D.2d 690, 580 N.Y.S.2d 52 (2d Dep't 1992)(preindictment delay due to prosecution's investigation into defendant's allegations of police brutality, excludable as due to exceptional circumstances); People v. Johnson, 167 A.D.2d 422, 561 N.Y.S.2d 830 (2d Dep't 1990)(delay excluded as due to prosecution's attempt to verify defendant's alibi); People v. Rodriguez, 214 A.D.2d 347, 625 N.Y.S.2d 20 (1st Dep't 1995)(delay caused by defendant's opposition to prosecution request for HIV blood test, to determine whether to seek attempted murder charge, is excludable).

315. People v. Washington, 43 N.Y.2d 772, 773–74, 401 N.Y.S.2d 1007, 1007–08, 372 N.E.2d 795 (1977)(proof of ongoing narcotics investigation was insufficient to exclude delay). See also People v. O'Neal, 99 A.D.2d 844, 845, 472 N.Y.S.2d 449, 451 (2d Dep't 1984)("general claim" of need to conduct further investigation insufficient); People v. Papa, 96 A.D.2d 601, 465 N.Y.S.2d 295 (2d Dep't 1983)(where prosecution claimed five-month delay for on-going investigation, but substantiated its activities for only the first three months, the remaining two months were not excludable).

316. People v. Sturgis, 38 N.Y.2d 625, 628–29, 381 N.Y.S.2d 860, 861, 345 N.E.2d 331 (1976); People v. Warren, 85 A.D.2d 747, 445 N.Y.S.2d 797 (2d Dep't 1981); People v. Bonterre, 87 Misc.2d 243, 384 N.Y.S.2d 351 (N.Y.C.Crim.Ct.1976).

317. People v. Brothers, 50 N.Y.2d 413, 417, 429 N.Y.S.2d 558, 560, 407 N.E.2d 405

In *People v. Cortes*,[318] the Court of Appeals held that the erroneous dismissal of the first indictment was not an exceptional circumstance even though it necessitated the prosecutor's motion to re-present, and then the obtaining of a second indictment. The court noted that, had the prosecution sought to appeal the erroneous dismissal, the delay between the dismissal and the reinstatement of the indictment could have been excludable under subdivision (4)(a), as a reasonable time in which to take an appeal.[319]

Library References:
West's Key No. Digests, Criminal Law ⚖577.10.

§ 9.44 Excludable Periods—Adjournments in Contemplation of Dismissal

CPL § 30.30(4)(h) excludes "the period during which an action has been adjourned in contemplation of dismissal pursuant to sections 170.55, 170.56 and 215.10" of the CPL. This section was added in 1986, by amendment.[320] The necessity for the amendment is unclear, since an adjournment in contemplation of dismissal is by definition one at defense request for or by defense consent,[321] and thus would have been clearly excludable pursuant to subdivision (4)(b).[322] In any event, the proposition that such adjournments should be excludable is unexceptional.

Library References:
West's Key No. Digests, Criminal Law ⚖577.10(8).

§ 9.45 Excludable Periods—Prosecutor's Direction to Appear at Arraignment

CPL § 30.30(4)(i), added in 1993,[323] excludes the "period prior to the defendant's actual appearance for arraignment in a situation in which the defendant has been directed to appear by the district attorney pursuant to subdivision three of [CPL] section 120.20 or subdivision three of [CPL] section 210.10."

Ordinarily, the period between the filing of an accusatory instrument and the arraignment thereon is includable time, even where the defendant's attendance must be secured by an arrest warrant or summons issued pursuant to CPL §§ 120.20 or 210.10.[324] That is because the fact that the defendant has not yet been arraigned does not impede the prosecution's readiness.[325]

(1980); People v. Perez, 189 A.D.2d 625, 592 N.Y.S.2d 349 (1st Dep't 1993). Once the prosecution has declared readiness, however, delay due to court congestion is excludable. People v. Moorhead, 61 N.Y.2d 851, 473 N.Y.S.2d 967, 462 N.E.2d 144 (1984).

318. 80 N.Y.2d 201, 590 N.Y.S.2d 9, 604 N.E.2d 71 (1992).

319. 80 N.Y.2d at 211–12, 590 N.Y.S.2d at 15–16.

320. L.1986, c.837, § 2, eff. Nov. 1, 1986.

321. See CPL §§ 170.55, 170.56, 215.10.

322. People v. Clark, 120 Misc.2d 365, 466 N.Y.S.2d 211 (N.Y.C.Crim.Ct.1983).

323. L.1993, c.446, § 2, eff. Nov. 1, 1993.

324. People v. Correa, 77 N.Y.2d 930, 569 N.Y.S.2d 601, 572 N.E.2d 42 (1991).

325. Id.

§ 9.45 TIMELINESS OF PROSECUTION & SPEEDY TRIAL Ch. 9

Sections 120.20(3) and 210.10(3) of the CPL, as amended in 1993 as part of the same legislation that created subdivision (4)(i),[326] allow the court—in lieu of the issuance of an arrest warrant or summons—to authorize "the district attorney to direct the defendant to appear for arraignment on a designated date if [the court] is satisfied that the defendant will so appear."[327]

The effect of this amendment is to encourage the use of this new device as the least intrusive method for procuring the defendant's appearance, and to allow the prosecutor to be generous in giving advance notice of the arraignment date to the defendant. Only by use of this alternative to the arrest warrant or summons will the prosecutor be assured of avoiding being charged with post-accusatory, pre-arraignment delay.

Library References:

West's Key No. Digests, Criminal Law ⚖=577.12.

§ 9.46 Excludable Periods—Family Offenses

The most recently enacted[328] CPL § 30.30 subdivision four exclusion is paragraph (j), which excludes "the period during which a family offense is before a family court until such time as an accusatory instrument or indictment is filed against the defendant alleging a crime constituting a family offense, as such term is defined in section 530.11"[329] of the CPL.

This amendment is a component of the Family Protection and Domestic Violence Intervention Act of 1994, which eliminated the requirement that the complainant choose between proceeding in Family Court or a criminal court on a designated "family offense," and now allows proceeding in either court or both courts concurrently.[330] The amendment is apparently unnecessary because no period of time prior to the filing of an accusatory instrument in a criminal court (including an indictment) would be chargeable to the prosecution under section 30.30 in any event, as the section 30.30 clock only starts ticking with the filing of such instrument in criminal court.[331] A Family Court petition is not an accusatory instrument that commences a criminal action for section 30.30 purposes.

Library References:

West's Key No. Digests, Criminal Law ⚖=577.8.

326. L.1993, c.446, §§ 3, 9, eff. Nov. 1, 1993.

327. CPL §§ 120.20(3), 210.10(3).

328. L.1994, c.222 § 29, eff. Jan. 1, 1995.

329. CPL § 530.11 designates as "family offenses" those acts that would constitute "disorderly conduct, harassment in the first degree, harassment in the second degree, menacing in the third degree, reckless endangerment, an assault in the second degree or assault in the third degree or an attempted assault," if those acts are between spouses, parent and child, or members of the same family/household.

330. See CPL §§ 100.07, 530.11(2), (2)(h),(2)(i) and (2-a).

331. See CPL §§ 1.20(1)(16)and (17), 30.30(1). See also Preiser, "Practice Commentary" to CPL § 30.30, McKinney's Cons. Laws of New York, Book 11A (Supp.).

§ 9.47 Post-Readiness Delay

CPL § 30.30(3)(b) provides that a section 30.30 motion to dismiss or motion for bail/ROR release made

> upon the expiration of the specified period may be denied where the people are not ready for trial if the people were ready for trial prior to the expiration of the specified period and their present unreadiness is due to some exceptional fact or circumstance, including, but not limited to, the sudden unavailability of evidence material to the people's case, when the district attorney has exercised due diligence to obtain such evidence and there are reasonable grounds to believe that such evidence will become available in a reasonable period.

Simply put, the court may deny a section 30.30 motion despite the prosecution's present lack of readiness if the prosecution previously had made a timely declaration of readiness and the present unreadiness is due to an exceptional circumstance. In practical terms, this subdivision means that the prosecution may be charged with periods of delay when, after having made a valid declaration of readiness, it then inexcusably becomes unready for trial.[332]

In even more practical terms, it means that both pre-readiness and post-readiness nonexcludable periods of delay are aggregated to determine whether the prosecution has exceeded the applicable periods set forth in subdivisions one and two. Thus, when the prosecution first announces readiness, the section 30.30 clock stops ticking. If the prosecution inexcusably becomes unready thereafter, the clock starts ticking again, and keeps ticking until the prosecution again announces readiness. The latter post-readiness delay is "tacked" onto the chargeable pre-readiness delay. If both periods, added together, exceed the applicable statutory period within which the prosecution must be ready, then the section 30.30 motion must be granted.[333]

Post-readiness delay is excusable, and thus not chargeable to the prosecution for section 30.30 purposes, if it is due to some exceptional circumstance bearing on prosecutorial readiness for trial.[334] To establish that a circumstance is "exceptional," the prosecution must do more than show "good faith" on its part: "The necessary implication of the use of 'sudden unavailability' and 'due diligence' in [subdivision (3)(b)] . . . is

---

332. People v. Anderson, 66 N.Y.2d 529, 498 N.Y.S.2d 119, 488 N.E.2d 1231 (1985). Prior to the Anderson decision, some courts had interpreted People v. Giordano, 56 N.Y.2d 524, 449 N.Y.S.2d 955, 434 N.E.2d 1333 (1982), as meaning that the prosecution's duty under section 30.30 was satisfied with its announcement of readiness and it was not chargeable with any period of delay thereafter. See, e.g., People v. Mastrangelo, 100 A.D.2d 914, 474 N.Y.S.2d 572 (2d Dep't 1984); People v. Collins, 98 A.D.2d 947, 472 N.Y.S.2d 796 (4th Dep't 1983); People v. Morrell, 97 A.D.2d 703, 468 N.Y.S.2d 127 (1st Dep't 1983); People v. Campbell, 91 A.D.2d 1075, 458 N.Y.S.2d 322 (3d Dep't 1983). Anderson made clear that Giordano should not be read so broadly. 66 N.Y.2d at 535-36, 498 N.Y.S.2d at 123.

333. People v. Anderson, 66 N.Y.2d at 534, 536–37, 498 N.Y.S.2d at 122–24. See also § 9.48, infra, on calculating time.

334. People v. Anderson, 66 N.Y.2d at 534, 498 N.Y.S.2d at 122.

§ 9.47 TIMELINESS OF PROSECUTION & SPEEDY TRIAL   Ch. 9

that postreadiness delay is not excused because inadvertent, no matter how pure the intention."[335]

Post-readiness delay is also excusable when the prosecution's lack of readiness "directly 'results from' action taken by defendant within the meaning of subdivisions 4(a), 4(b), 4(c) or 4(e)."[336]

Additionally, post-readiness delay is excludable when it does not relate to the prosecution's *own* state of readiness to go to trial.[337] Thus, once the prosecution has announced readiness, delays due to court congestion are excludable,[338] as is any portion of an adjournment period beyond a date actually requested by the prosecution.[339]

In *People v. Anderson*,[340] the Court of Appeals first addressed the situation where the prosecution, having announced readiness, acts in a manner that obstructs the defendant's, but not its own, ability to proceed to trial. The court held that the prosecution could be charged with such delay—and thus be subject to section 30.30 relief—only if no lesser alternative "corrective action" was available to the court under CPL Article 240, "such as preclusion or a continuance."[341] In *Anderson*, the defense claimed that the post-readiness delay due to the prosecution's failure to turn over discovery material and to provide timely CPL § 710.30 notice should be nonexcludable. The court disagreed, noting that the prosecution's failure did not affect its own readiness, and the impact of those failures on defense readiness could be obviated by lesser remedies, such as preclusion.[342]

The court revisited this question in *People v. McKenna*,[343] where the prosecution, after having announced readiness, negligently delayed five months in providing the grand jury transcripts necessary to decide the

---

335. People v. Anderson, 66 N.Y.2d at 536, 498 N.Y.S.2d at 123–24. For a full discussion of what does and does not constitute an "exceptional circumstance," see § 9.43, supra, which concerns the similarly-worded subdivision (4)(g).

336. People v. Anderson, 66 N.Y.2d at 536, 498 N.Y.S.2d at 124. See also People v. Acevedo, 176 A.D.2d 1007, 575 N.Y.S.2d 174 (3d Dep't 1991)(post-readiness delay at defense request excludable); People v. Roberts, 176 A.D.2d 1200, 576 N.Y.S.2d 698 (4th Dep't 1991)(post-readiness delay due to defendant's absconding excludable).

In pre-readiness analysis, there is no requirement that the prosecution establish a causal nexus between the defense action and the prosecution's unreadiness in order to render a subdivision (4)(a) or (4)(b) delay excludable. People v. Worley, 66 N.Y.2d 523, 498 N.Y.S.2d 116, 488 N.E.2d 1228 (1985). See §§ 9.27–9.33, 9.34, supra. The language from Anderson quoted above, however, suggests that the prosecution must establish such a nexus in seeking to exclude post-readiness delay caused by defense motions, for example, or defense-requested adjournments. In other words, this language in Anderson suggests that the Worley holding does not apply to post-readiness analysis. No court has expressly so held, however.

337. People v. Anderson, 66 N.Y.2d at 534, 498 N.Y.S.2d at 122.

338. People v. Cortes, 80 N.Y.2d 201, 210, 590 N.Y.S.2d 9, 14, 604 N.E.2d 71 (1992); People v. McKenna, 76 N.Y.2d 59, 63, 556 N.Y.S.2d 514, 515, 555 N.E.2d 911 (1990); People v. Johnson, 209 A.D.2d 986, 619 N.Y.S.2d 452 (4th Dep't 1994); People ex rel. Ferguson v. Campbell, 175 A.D.2d 959, 573 N.Y.S.2d 539 (3d Dep't 1991).

339. People v. Urraea, 214 A.D.2d 378, 625 N.Y.S.2d 163 (1st Dep't 1995); People ex rel. Sykes v. Mitchell, 184 A.D.2d 466, 586 N.Y.S.2d 937 (1st Dep't 1992).

340. 66 N.Y.2d 529, 498 N.Y.S.2d 119, 488 N.E.2d 1231 (1985).

341. 66 N.Y.2d at 534, 537–38, 498 N.Y.S.2d at 122, 124.

342. Id.

343. 76 N.Y.2d 59, 556 N.Y.S.2d 514, 555 N.E.2d 911 (1990).

defense motion to inspect and dismiss pursuant to CPL § 210.30. Distinguishing the case from *Anderson*, the court charged this delay to the prosecution:

> In contrast to the discovery delays considered in *Anderson*, the People's omission did not merely impair defendant's ability to proceed to trial. Rather, because the trial could simply not go forward until the CPL 210.30 motion was decided, the People's dilatory conduct in failing to provide the minutes necessary to that decision was a direct, and virtually insurmountable, impediment to the trial's very commencement. As such, the prosecutorial failure here must be deemed to be one having a direct bearing on the People's readiness, since the People can hardly claim to be "ready" when they have not done all that is required of them to bring the case to the point where it may be tried.[344]

Thus, *McKenna* essentially holds that unexcused post-readiness prosecutorial delay in responding to any outcome-determinative motion is not excludable.[345]

Not an exceptional circumstance is the prosecution's failure to produce for trial a defendant in its custody, and delay caused by such failure is not excludable.[346] Nor are a prosecutor's vacation[347] or misplaced file[348] considered exceptional circumstances. Also not excludable, by the very terms of subdivision (3)(b), are delays caused by the sudden unavailability of material prosecution evidence despite due diligence on the prosecution's part, where there is no reason to believe that the evidence will become available within a reasonable period.[349]

Library References:

West's Key No. Digests, Criminal Law ⟾577.8, 577.12.

§ 9.48 Procedural Considerations—Calculating Time

In calculating CPL § 30.30 time limits, the day *after* the commence-

---

344. 76 N.Y.2d at 64, 556 N.Y.S.2d at 516 (citation omitted).

345. See People v. Commack, 194 A.D.2d 619, 599 N.Y.S.2d 56 (2d Dep't 1993)(unreasonable prosecution delay in responding to section 30.30 motion charged to prosecution).

346. People v. McKenna, 76 N.Y.2d at 64, 65 n.1, 556 N.Y.S.2d at 516–17 n.1; People v. Anderson, 66 N.Y.2d at 538, 498 N.Y.S.2d at 125; People v. Cropper, 202 A.D.2d 603, 609 N.Y.S.2d 288 (2d Dep't 1994); People v. Hilton, 151 A.D.2d 364, 542 N.Y.S.2d 990 (1st Dep't 1989); People v. Traficante, 147 A.D.2d 843, 538 N.Y.S.2d 331 (3d Dep't 1989). The Second Department has held, however, that with respect to post-readiness, as opposed to pre-readiness delay, the prosecution need not establish due diligence in producing an absent nonincarcerated defendant in order to exclude delay. See People v. Cephas, 207 A.D.2d 903, 616 N.Y.S.2d 668 (2d Dep't 1994). See also People v. Woods, 150 Misc.2d 1070, 572 N.Y.S.2d 279 (N.Y.C.Crim.Ct.1991)(subdivision (4)(c) analysis not applicable to post-readiness delay).

347. People v. Jones, 68 N.Y.2d 717, 506 N.Y.S.2d 315, 497 N.E.2d 682 (1986).

348. People v. Cortes, 80 N.Y.2d at 217, 590 N.Y.S.2d at 19.

349. People v. Anderson, 66 N.Y.2d at 538, 498 N.Y.S.2d at 125.

§ 9.48 TIMELINESS OF PROSECUTION & SPEEDY TRIAL Ch. 9

ment of the action is the first day to be counted.[350] The last day is also counted. Thus, if the action commences on January 10th, and the prosecution declares readiness on January 25th, the total pre-readiness delay is 15 days. January 11th is the first, and January 25th the last, day counted. The same is true in counting adjournment periods, or other periods of delay. An adjournment from February 10th to February 25th would add up to a 15-day period of delay, with February 11th being the first day counted and February 25th the last.[351]

To calculate whether the prosecution has exceeded the six-month limit for felonies, one must first determine the number of days in those six months. The six-month limit means six *calendar* months, not 180 days.[352] To find the number of days in any six-month period, first fix the date of the commencement of the action, then add six months to it, and finally count all the days in between. For example, if the action commenced on March 15th, six months from that date is September 15th. Since there happen to be 184 days between those dates, 184 days is the applicable period in which the prosecution has to be ready in that particular case.[353] Depending upon the month in which the action is commenced, six months might translate into as much as 184 days.

To determine whether the prosecutor has met the section 30.30 time limit applicable to the particular felony—up to 184 days—one must compute the number of days elapsed between the action's declaration of readiness, subtracting the amount of delay that is excludable under subdivision four. To that sum one adds the amount of post-readiness delay, if any, that is chargeable to the prosecution pursuant to subdivision (3)(b). If the end sum of pre- and post-readiness delay exceeds the time limit applicable to the case, the section 30.30 motion must be granted.[354]

For example, if the action commenced on March 15th, the applicable felony time limit is 184 days. If the nonexcludable pre-readiness delay, added to the post-readiness delay chargeable to the prosecution, is 185 days or more, the section 30.30 dismissal motion must be granted; if it is 184 days or less, the motion fails.[355]

Library References:

West's Key No. Digests, Criminal Law ⚖577.8.

350. People v. Stiles, 70 N.Y.2d 765, 520 N.Y.S.2d 745, 514 N.E.2d 1368 (1987).

351. Id.

352. People v. Cortes, 80 N.Y.2d 201, 207–08 n.3, 590 N.Y.S.2d 9, 604 N.E.2d 71 (1992).

353. See, e.g., People v. Jones, 105 A.D.2d 179, 188, 483 N.Y.S.2d 345 (2d Dep't 1984), aff'd sub nom. People v. Anderson, 66 N.Y.2d 529, 498 N.Y.S.2d 119, 488 N.E.2d 1231 (1985); People v. Smith, 97 A.D.2d 485, 468 N.Y.S.2d 129 (2d Dep't 1983).

354. People v. Cortes, 80 N.Y.2d at 208, 590 N.Y.S.2d at 13.

355. See, e.g., People v. Johnson, 191 A.D.2d 709, 595 N.Y.S.2d 515 (2d Dep't 1993)(where both the six-month period and the includable delay equalled 184 days, no dismissal); People v. Battles, 77 A.D.2d 405, 407, 433 N.Y.S.2d 936, 937 (4th Dep't 1980)(where applicable period was 182 days and prosecutor declared readiness on the 182nd day, no dismissal).

§ 9.49 Procedural Considerations—Motion Practice Requirements

Subdivision one of CPL § 30.30 requires that a section 30.30 motion to dismiss be brought pursuant to CPL §§ 170.30(1)(e) or 210.20(2)(g).[356] A section 30.30 motion to dismiss, as opposed to a motion for bail or recognizance under section 30.30(2),[357] cannot be brought via a *habeas corpus* petition.[358]

The section 30.30 motion must be made in writing and on reasonable notice to the prosecution; "[f]ailure to follow the statutory procedure results in a waiver of the claim."[359] Since the notice and writing requirements are for the prosecution's benefit, it may waive them by failing to object to an oral or unnoticed motion.[360] The smart defense practitioner, however, should not count on this happening.

Unlike other motions brought pursuant to CPL § 210.20, a motion brought on speedy trial grounds (including a section 30.30 motion) need not be made within 45 days of arraignment on the indictment; rather, pursuant to section 210.20(2), it simply must be made "prior to the commencement of trial."[361] This requirement may not be waived—neither by the prosecutor nor the court. Thus, even if the court so directs, without prosecutorial objection, the section 30.30 motion cannot validly be filed once trial has commenced.[362] As long as the motion is *filed* prior to trial, however, it properly may be decided afterwards.[363]

---

356. CPL § 170.30(1)(e) covers speedy trial motions to dismiss an information, simplified information, prosecutor's information, or misdemeanor complaint. Section 210.20(2)(g) covers speedy trial motions to dismiss indictments. There is no procedural mechanism to bring a motion to dismiss a felony complaint on section 30.30 grounds. See Morgenthau v. Roberts, 65 N.Y.2d 749, 492 N.Y.S.2d 21, 481 N.E.2d 561 (1985)(CPL § 210.20 provides solely for dismissal of indictments, not felony complaints). See also People v. Leonardo, 141 Misc.2d 526, 533 N.Y.S.2d 660 (Greene Co. Ct.1988)(court cannot dismiss felony complaint on section 30.30 grounds).

357. For the procedural mechanisms for bringing a bail or recognizance motion pursuant to section 30.30(2), see § 9.21, supra.

358. People ex rel. Chakwin v. Warden, 63 N.Y.2d 120, 124–25, 480 N.Y.S.2d 719, 720–21, 470 N.E.2d 146 (1984).

359. People v. Lawrence, 64 N.Y.2d 200, 203–04, 485 N.Y.S.2d 233, 235, 474 N.E.2d 593 (1984); People v. Baxter, __ A.D.2d __, 629 N.Y.S.2d 347 (4th Dep't 1995); People v. Harvall, 196 A.D.2d 553, 601 N.Y.S.2d 146 (2d Dep't 1993); People v. Rodriguez, 193 A.D.2d 363, 596 N.Y.S.2d 824 (1st Dep't 1993); People v. O'Connell, 133 A.D.2d 970, 521 N.Y.S.2d 121 (3d Dep't 1987). See also CPL § 210.45(1).

360. People v. Mezon, 80 N.Y.2d 155, 160, 589 N.Y.S.2d 838, 841, 603 N.E.2d 943 (1992); People v. Jennings, 69 N.Y.2d 103, 512 N.Y.S.2d 652, 504 N.E.2d 1079 (1986); People v. Singleton, 42 N.Y.2d 466, 470–471, 398 N.Y.S.2d 871, 874, 368 N.E.2d 1237 (1977); People v. Brown, 207 A.D.2d 556, 616 N.Y.S.2d 389 (2d Dep't 1994); People v. Cook, 193 A.D.2d 366, 596 N.Y.S.2d 822 (1st Dep't 1993); People v. Smith, 91 A.D.2d 928, 457 N.Y.S.2d 822 (1st Dep't 1983).

361. Section 210.20(2) also provides that a speedy trial motion may be made prior to the "entry of a plea of guilty." A plea of guilty, however, always operates as a forfeiture of a section 30.30 claim. See, e.g., People v. O'Brien, 56 N.Y.2d 1009, 453 N.Y.S.2d 638, 439 N.E.2d 354 (1982).

362. People v. Lawrence, supra; People v. Hudson, 205 A.D.2d 367, 613 N.Y.S.2d 374 (1st Dep't 1994).

363. People v. Waring, 206 A.D.2d 329, 615 N.Y.S.2d 21 (1st Dep't 1994); People v. Johnson, 184 A.D.2d 862, 585 N.Y.S.2d 111 (3d Dep't 1992). See People v. Harris, 82 N.Y.2d 409, 411, 604 N.Y.S.2d 918, 919, 624 N.E.2d 1013 (1993)(motion filed before trial commenced but decided after; Court of Appeals affirms section 30.30 dismissal); People v. Papa, 96 A.D.2d 601, 465 N.Y.S.2d 295 (2d Dep't 1983)(Second Department

§ 9.49 TIMELINESS OF PROSECUTION & SPEEDY TRIAL Ch. 9

If a section 30.30 dismissal motion is denied, and then additional nonexcludable delay accrues prior to the commencement of trial, the defense must renew the section 30.30 claim by filing an additional motion; otherwise, the defense does not get the benefit of the additional accrued delay.[364]

Library References:
West's Key No. Digests, Criminal Law ⚖577.16.

§ 9.50 Procedural Considerations—Sufficiency of Motion Papers and Burden of Proof

The case law regarding both the sufficiency of motion papers and the burdens of proof in section 30.30 claims is both evolving and murky. Particular care should be paid to the form of such papers, lest the merits of the claim fall victim to procedural default.

Library References:
West's Key No. Digests, Criminal Law ⚖577.16.

§ 9.51 Procedural Considerations—Sufficiency of Motion Papers

Any defense speedy trial motion based on CPL § 30.30, either in whole or in part, should cite to that statute in the notice of motion. Otherwise, the section 30.30 claim is not preserved and cannot be raised on appeal.[365]

The Court of Appeals has repeatedly held that the defense, in its section 30.30 affirmation, may satisfy its initial burden as movant under CPL § 210.45(1)[366] "by alleging only that the prosecution failed to declare readiness within the statutorily prescribed time period."[367]

---

dismissed on section 30.30 grounds where motion filed before trial but decided midtrial).

364. People v. Schiavo, B & S Salvage, Inc., 212 A.D.2d 816, 623 N.Y.S.2d 273 (2d Dep't 1995); People v. Gomez, 210 A.D.2d 14, 619 N.Y.S.2d 561 (1st Dep't 1994); People v. Robles, 139 A.D.2d 781, 527 N.Y.S.2d 527 (2d Dep't 1988).

365. People v. Simon, 202 A.D.2d 302, 610 N.Y.S.2d 769 (1st Dep't 1994); People v. Zambito, 153 A.D.2d 975, 545 N.Y.S.2d 414 (3d Dep't 1989); People v. Brooks, 105 A.D.2d 977, 481 N.Y.S.2d 914 (3d Dep't 1984); People v. Pasquino, 65 A.D.2d 629, 409 N.Y.S.2d 518 (2d Dep't 1978). By the same token, a written motion that only mentions section 30.30 cannot be converted into a section 30.20 or constitutional speedy trial claim on appeal. People v. Cedeno, 52 N.Y.2d 847, 437 N.Y.S.2d 72, 418 N.E.2d 665 (1981); People v. Lieberman, 47 N.Y.2d 931, 419 N.Y.S.2d 946, 393 N.E.2d 1019 (1979).

A defense practitioner filing a motion relying on both CPL § 30.30 and the constitutional speedy trial claim should cite not only to section 30.30 but to: section 30.20 (embodying the state speedy trial guarantee); the Sixth Amendment to the federal constitution (embodying the federal speedy trial guarantee); the Fourteenth Amendment to the federal constitution (containing the federal due process guarantee); and Article 1, § 6 of the state constitution (containing the state due process guarantee). See § 9.12, supra.

366. The procedures set forth in CPL § 210.45 are also applicable to motions to dismiss pursuant to CPL § 170.30 in the local criminal court. CPL § 170.45.

367. People v. Luperon, 85 N.Y.2d 71, 623 N.Y.S.2d 735, 647 N.E.2d 1243 (1995); People v. Cortes, 80 N.Y.2d 201, 590 N.Y.S.2d 9, 604 N.E.2d 71 (1992); People v. Santos, 68 N.Y.2d 859, 508 N.Y.S.2d 411, 501 N.E.2d 19 (1986); People v. Berkowitz,

Thus, the defense need not refer specifically to every pre-readiness adjournment period to sustain this initial burden;[368] rather, the initial affirmation need only include "sworn allegations that there has been unexcused delay in excess of the statutory minimum."[369] If the affirmation indicates the existence of facially excludable periods, however, the defense must further show that the remaining, non-excludable, time exceeds six months.[370]

Once the defense satisfies its initial burden, the burden shifts to the prosecution to identify the statutory exclusions on which it is relying to bring it within the statutory time limit for declaring readiness.[371] Thus, if the prosecution wishes to rely on subdivision (3)(b) or a particular subdivision four exclusion, or on a particular legal or factual theory within subdivision (3)(b) or within a subdivision four paragraph, it should do so in this response, or such claim later will not be cognizable on any subsequent appeal.[372] Moreover, any claim the prosecution might have about deficiencies in the defense moving papers—e.g., lack of notice or failure to adequately set forth specific allegations of fact—should be raised at this point, or any such claim will be considered waived.[373]

50 N.Y.2d 333, 428 N.Y.S.2d 927, 406 N.E.2d 783 (1980); People v. Betancourt, __ A.D.2d __, 629 N.Y.S.2d 423 (1st Dep't 1995); People v. Drummond, 215 A.D.2d 579, 627 N.Y.S.2d 55 (2d Dep't 1995); People v. Lashway, 187 A.D.2d 747, 589 N.Y.S.2d 687 (3d Dep't 1992); People v. Gushlaw, 112 A.D.2d 792, 492 N.Y.S.2d 292 (4th Dep't 1985).

368. People v. Luperon, supra.

369. People v. Santos, 68 N.Y.2d at 861, 508 N.Y.S.2d at 412. See also People v. Daniels, __ A.D.2d __, 630 N.Y.S.2d 5 (1st Dep't 1995), lv. granted September 8, 1995.

370. People v. Lomax, 50 N.Y.2d 351, 357, 428 N.Y.S.2d 937, 939, 406 N.E.2d 793 (1980)(where defense papers indicated that some delays were due to defense motion practice, it was incumbent on the defense to set forth the applicable adjournment dates relevant to these motions). A number of "pre-Luperon" Appellate Division decisions have suggested that the defense, to satisfy its initial burden under Berkowitz, must go so far as to allege that particular periods of pre-readiness delay are not excludable. See, e.g. People v. Stukes, 211 A.D.2d 565, 621 N.Y.S.2d 79 (1st Dep't 1995); People v. Thomas, 200 A.D.2d 419, 606 N.Y.S.2d 217 (1st Dep't 1994). These cases are inconsistent with the Luperon holding. Nonetheless, even "post-Luperon," some judges may seek to shoulder the defense with this initial burden. See, e.g., People v. Daniels, __ A.D.2d at __, 630 N.Y.S.2d at 13 (Nardelli, J., dissenting) (suggesting that Luperon requires the initial defense motion papers to identify specific pre-readiness nonexcludable periods).

Thus, it may well be only the most intrepid of defense practitioners who seek to frame their initial motion papers in the spare, minimalist fashion suggested by Luperon and its Court of Appeals antecedents. At the very least, it may be wise for the initial defense affirmation to allege the relevant dates—e.g., the date the action commenced, and the date (if any) that the prosecution declared readiness—and to allege further that the total unexcused delay exceeds the allowable statutory time period. If this recitation indicates the existence of facially excludable periods, however, the defense must further show either why those periods are not in fact excludable or that the total delay without those excluded periods still exceeds the statutory time limit. People v. Lomax, 50 N.Y.2d 351, 357, 428 N.Y.S.2d 937, 939, 406 N.E.2d 793 (1980).

371. People v. Berkowitz, 50 N.Y.2d at 349, 428 N.Y.S.2d at 936.

372. People v. Cortes, 80 N.Y.2d at 213, 213 n.6, 214 n.7, 216 n.10, 217 n.12, 590 N.Y.S.2d at 16–19; People v. Bolden, 81 N.Y.2d 146, 155–56, 597 N.Y.S.2d 270, 274–75, 613 N.E.2d 145 (1993); People v. Mace, 206 A.D.2d 296, 614 N.Y.S.2d 416 (1st Dep't 1994); People v. Wiggins, 197 A.D.2d 802, 603 N.Y.S.2d 81 (3d Dep't 1993); People v. Bryant, 153 A.D.2d 636, 544 N.Y.S.2d 661 (2d Dep't 1989).

373. People v. Betancourt, __ A.D.2d __, 629 N.Y.S.2d 423 (1st Dep't 1995); People v. Fields, 214 A.D.2d 332, 625 N.Y.S.2d 483 (1st Dep't 1995); People v. Brown, 207 A.D.2d 556, 616 N.Y.S.2d 389 (2d Dep't 1994). See § 9.49, supra.

§ 9.51 TIMELINESS OF PROSECUTION & SPEEDY TRIAL Ch. 9

Similarly, omissions or deficiencies in the defense moving papers may be cured by statements the prosecution makes in its response.[374] Should the prosecution fail to respond at all to sufficient defense motion papers, the defense is entitled to summary dismissal.[375]

Once the prosecution has responded to the defense motion by "identify[ing] the exclusions on which [it] intend[s] to rely," the defense must then "identify any legal or factual impediments to the use of these exclusions."[376] In practical terms, this means that the defense should file a reply affirmation setting forth any objections it has to the legal or factual assertions in the prosecutor's response. Any "impediment to the use of these exclusions" not so identified by the defense will be forfeited and thus not later be cognizable on appeal.[377]

In *People v. Ladson*,[378] the prosecutor had asserted in response to the defense section 30.30 motion that the defendant was "absent" during a period of time, within the meaning of subdivision (4)(c), in that the defendant's location was unknown and also that he was attempting to avoid apprehension. The Court of Appeals held that, since the defense did not reply and did not identify any legal or factual impediment to the use of the (4)(c) exclusion, the defense could rely on no such legal or factual theory on appeal.[379]

Where the prosecutor's claimed exclusions do not, as a matter of law, excuse a sufficient amount of delay so as to bring them within the statutory period, the defense motion should be summarily granted.[380] On the other hand, where the claimed exclusions are legally cognizable and, if factually correct, would bring the prosecution within the statutory limit, the court should order a hearing on the motion.[381] In the event that the opposing papers conclusively establish, by documentary proof or otherwise, the excludability of sufficient delay so as to bring the prosecution into compliance, the court may deny the motion without a hear-

---

374. People v. Santos, 68 N.Y.2d 859, 508 N.Y.S.2d 411, 501 N.E.2d 19 (1986).

375. People v. Cole, 73 N.Y.2d 957, 540 N.Y.S.2d 984, 538 N.E.2d 336 (1989); People v. Gruden, 42 N.Y.2d 214, 397 N.Y.S.2d 704, 366 N.E.2d 794 (1977); People v. Channer, 209 A.D.2d 1056, 619 N.Y.S.2d 1013 (4th Dep't 1994); People v. Gonzalez, 116 A.D.2d 735, 497 N.Y.S.2d 778 (2d Dep't 1986); People v. Jackson, 103 A.D.2d 858, 477 N.Y.S.2d 1011 (3d Dep't 1984).

376. People v. Luperon, 85 N.Y.2d at 78, 623 N.Y.S.2d at 739.

377. People v. Ladson, 85 N.Y.2d 926, 928, 626 N.Y.S.2d 999, 1000, 650 N.E.2d 846 (1995); People v. Luperon, 85 N.Y.2d at 78, 623 N.Y.S.2d at 739; People v. Padilla, ___ A.D.2d ___, 627 N.Y.S.2d 914 (1st Dep't 1995); People v. Pagano, 207 A.D.2d 685, 616 N.Y.S.2d 366 (1st Dep't 1994).

378. 85 N.Y.2d 926, 626 N.Y.S.2d 999, 650 N.E.2d 846 (1995).

379. 85 N.Y.2d at 928, 626 N.Y.S.2d at 1000.

380. People v. Cortes, 80 N.Y.2d at 213, 590 N.Y.S.2d at 17 (prosecution, having alleged an exclusion not recognized by section 30.30, is fully chargeable with the delay); People v. Allen, 203 A.D.2d 582, 611 N.Y.S.2d 221 (2d Dep't 1994); People v. Auslander, 168 A.D.2d 759, 563 N.Y.S.2d 912 (3d Dep't 1990); People v. Bryant, 153 A.D.2d 636, 544 N.Y.S.2d 661 (2d Dep't 1989). See CPL § 210.45(4)(c).

381. People v. Santos, 68 N.Y.2d at 861, 508 N.Y.S.2d at 413; People v. Gruden, 42 N.Y.2d at 217, 397 N.Y.S.2d at 706; People v. Staton, 209 A.D.2d 652, 619 N.Y.S.2d 667 (2d Dep't 1994); People v. Wiggins, 194 A.D.2d 840, 598 N.Y.S.2d 391 (3d Dep't 1993); People v. Vidal, 161 A.D.2d 313, 555 N.Y.S.2d 233 (1st Dep't 1990); People v. Grant, 127 A.D.2d 965, 512 N.Y.S.2d 747 (4th Dep't 1987). See CPL § 210.45(6).

ing.[382]

Library References:
West's Key No. Digests, Criminal Law ⚖577.16(6).

§ 9.52 Procedural Considerations—Burden of Proof

At a hearing held pursuant to CPL § 210.45(6) on a section 30.30 motion, once the defendant has shown the existence of a delay greater than the applicable statutory time limit,[383] the burden shifts to the prosecution to show the existence of pre-readiness excludable periods of delay.[384] In this regard, the court's calendar notations are, in themselves, insufficient to meet the prosecution's burden.[385]

As to post-readiness periods of delay, the burden is stated somewhat differently. The "defendant ordinarily has the burden of showing that any postreadiness adjournments occurred under circumstances that should be charged to the People," but "it is the People's burden to ensure, in the first instance, that the record of the proceedings at which the adjournment was actually granted is sufficiently clear to enable the court considering the subsequent CPL 30.30 motion to make an informed decision as to whether the People should be charged."[386] Simply put, with respect to post-readiness delay, the prosecution has the burden of providing a record of the facts underlying the delay, but the defense has the burden of showing that those facts require the delay to be charged to the prosecution.[387]

---

382. People v. Davis, 184 A.D.2d 575, 577–78, 584 N.Y.S.2d 638, 640–41 (2d Dep't 1992); People v. Hammpud, 161 A.D.2d 179, 554 N.Y.S.2d 567 (1st Dep't 1990)(summary denial of motion upheld where opposing papers agreed about reason for adjournment in question); People v. Santiago, 127 A.D.2d 619, 511 N.Y.S.2d 415 (2d Dep't 1987). See CPL § 210.45(5)(c).

383. Pursuant to CPL § 210.45(7), the defense has the burden of showing the existence of such a delay "by a preponderance of the evidence." See People v. Anderson, 66 N.Y.2d at 541, 498 N.Y.S.2d at 126 (it is defendant's burden under CPL § 210.45(7) to establish his or her right to a dismissal by reason of delay).

384. People v. Cortes, 80 N.Y.2d at 213, 590 N.Y.S.2d at 17; People v. Zirpola, 57 N.Y.2d 706, 708, 454 N.Y.S.2d 702, 703, 440 N.E.2d 787 (1982); People v. Berkowitz, 50 N.Y.2d at 348–49, 428 N.Y.S.2d at 935.

385. People v. Berkowitz, 50 N.Y.2d at 349, 428 N.Y.S.2d at 936. People v. Klaus, 104 A.D.2d 566, 568–69, 479 N.Y.S.2d 273, 275 (2d Dep't 1984). But see People v. Russo, 99 A.D.2d 498, 470 N.Y.S.2d 447 (2d Dep't 1984)(calendar notations met prosecution's burden of proof at section 30.30 hearing where the minutes of the adjournments were unavailable and the notations set forth the reasons for those adjournments).

It is unclear whether the prosecution is required, in its response, to meet its burden by appending the transcripts to the various pre-readiness adjourned dates. Such transcripts would be the best proof of the excludability of such adjournments; procuring them, however, may significantly delay the prosecution's response to the § 30.30 motion.

386. People v. Cortes, 80 N.Y.2d at 215–16, 590 N.Y.S.2d at 18. See also People v. Collins, 82 N.Y.2d 177, 181–82, 604 N.Y.S.2d 11, 13, 624 N.E.2d 139 (1993); People v. Daniels, __ A.D.2d __, 630 N.Y.S.2d 5 (1st Dep't 1995) lv. granted September 8, 1995; People v. Fields, 214 A.D.2d 332, 625 N.Y.S.2d 483 (1st Dep't 1995); People v. Hall, 213 A.D.2d 558, 624 N.Y.S.2d 58 (2d Dep't 1995).

387. It is unclear whether, under this post-readiness standard, the prosecution must make a "contemporaneous" record of the reason for the adjournment, or whether it is sufficient for the prosecution to re-create the record after the fact, as in its affirmation in response to the defense section 30.30 motion. Cf. People v. Cortes, 80 N.Y.2d at 215–16, 590 N.Y.S.2d at 18 ("no contemporaneous record" made of the rea-

§ 9.52 TIMELINESS OF PROSECUTION & SPEEDY TRIAL Ch. 9

Library References:
West's Key No. Digests, Criminal Law ⇐577.16(8).

§ 9.53 Interstate Agreement on Detainers (CPL § 580.20)

The Interstate Agreement on Detainers ("IAD"), codified in CPL § 580.20, is a compact among 48 states, the federal government, and the District of Columbia. Through its procedural mechanisms, a participating state, such as New York, may gain custody of a prisoner serving a sentence in another state or in a federal facility, so as to try him or her on pending criminal charges.

The IAD provides two ways for a prisoner in a "sending state" (the state with custody of the prisoner) to be brought to trial in the "receiving state" (the state seeking custody) once a detainer has been filed.[388] Article III contains the procedures that the *prisoner* might initiate to request the resolution of charges against him or her in the receiving state; Article IV sets forth the procedures that a *receiving state* might initiate to obtain the defendant's presence for trial. Each article carries with it a different stipulated time limit for bringing the defendant to trial. Failure to meet those time limits requires dismissal of the criminal action, with prejudice.

Library References:
West's Key No. Digests, Extradition and Detainers ⇐50–60.

§ 9.54 Interstate Agreement on Detainers—The Prisoner's Request (Article III)

Under Article III of the IAD, a prisoner against whom a detainer[389] has been lodged by a receiving state may request that the outstanding charges be resolved.[390] Such a request constitutes a waiver of extradition and consent to both his or her production in the receiving state and ultimate return to the sending state.[391] The receiving state must bring the prisoner to trial within 180 days of its receipt of the prisoner's request,[392] or within such additional time as the court may grant "for

---

son for the adjournment) with People v. Collins, 82 N.Y.2d at 181–82, 604 N.Y.S.2d at 13–14 (bemoaning lack of "unequivocal statement by someone with firsthand knowledge," in prosecution's response to motion, as to circumstances of adjournment). This question is still open. See Preiser, "Practice Commentary" to CPL § 30.30, McKinney's Cons. Laws of New York, Book 11A (Supp.). An absolute requirement that the record be contemporaneously made at the time of adjournment would likely be too onerous for the prosecution to meet.

388. CPL § 580.20, Art. II.

389. The United States Supreme Court, the ultimate arbiter of the correct interpretation of the IAD, see Cuyler v. Adams, 449 U.S. 433, 438–42, 101 S.Ct. 703, 706–08, 66 L.Ed.2d 641 (1981), has defined a "detainer" as "a request filed by a criminal justice agency with the institution in which a prisoner is incarcerated asking either to hold the prisoner for the agency or to notify the agency when the release of the prisoner is imminent." Reed v. Farley, ___ U.S. ___, ___ n.1, 114 S.Ct. 2291, 2294 n.1, 129 L.Ed.2d 277 (1994).

390. CPL § 580.20, Art. III(a)—(d).

391. CPL § 580.20, Art. III(e).

392. The 180 days start to run from the date the request is delivered to the court and prosecutor of the receiving state, not from the date the prisoner gives the request

good cause shown in open court, the prisoner or his counsel being present."[393]

If the prisoner is not actually brought to trial within this time limit, the criminal charges must be dismissed, with prejudice.[394]

Library References:

West's Key No. Digests, Extradition and Detainers ⟲57.

§ 9.55 Interstate Agreement on Detainers—The Receiving State's Request (Article IV)

The receiving state may initiate a request for the prisoner's removal to that state. This request triggers the Uniform Criminal Extradition Act.[395] The prisoner must actually be brought to trial within 120 days of the prisoner's arrival in the receiving state, or within such additional time as the court may grant, "for good cause shown in open court, the prisoner or his counsel being present."[396] If this time limit is not met, the charges must be dismissed, with prejudice.[397]

With respect to both Articles III and IV, the time limits "shall be tolled whenever and for as long as the prisoner is unable to stand trial, as determined by the court having jurisdiction of the matter."[398]

Both Articles III and IV have "anti-shuttling" provisions providing that once the prisoner arrives in the receiving state, he or she must be brought to trial prior to being returned to the sending state, or else the charges must be dismissed.[399]

A motion to dismiss based upon a violation of the IAD, like any speedy trial dismissal motion, must be made prior to trial in conformity

to the prison authorities of the sending state for forwarding. Fex v. Michigan, 507 U.S. 43, 113 S.Ct. 1085, 122 L.Ed.2d 406 (1993).

393. CPL § 580.20, Art. III(a).

394. CPL § 580.20, Art. V(c).

395. CPL Art. 570; Cuyler v. Adams, 449 U.S. 433, 101 S.Ct. 703, 66 L.Ed.2d 641 (1981).

396. CPL § 580.20, Art. IV(c).

397. CPL § 580.20, Art. V(c).

398. CPL § 580.20, Art. IV(a). The periods to be tolled include those reasonably necessary for motion practice, People v. Torres, 60 N.Y.2d 119, 127–28, 468 N.Y.S.2d 606, 610, 456 N.E.2d 497 (1983), and those caused by the defendant's unavailability due to competing law enforcement interests in separate states. People v. Vrlaku, 73 N.Y.2d 800, 537 N.Y.S.2d 24, 533 N.E.2d 1053 (1988); People v. Allen, 178 A.D.2d 994, 579 N.Y.S.2d 262 (4th Dep't 1991).

399. CPL § 580.20, Arts. III(d) and IV(e). See People v. Fargher, 112 A.D.2d 599, 492 N.Y.S.2d 123 (3d Dep't 1985)(premature return to sending state required dismissal pursuant to III(d)). It is unclear whether the IAD anti-shuttling provision is triggered by same-day round-trip transfers of a prisoner to state courts from federal facilities that happen to be within the state where the prisoner is confined. The federal circuits are split on this question. See Taylor v. United States, 504 U.S. 991, 112 S.Ct. 2982, 119 L.Ed.2d 599 (1992)(White, J., dissenting from certiorari denial). The Second Department has held that the anti-shuttling provision is not invoked by this sort of transfer. People v. Reilly, 136 A.D.2d 355, 527 N.Y.S.2d 234 (2d Dep't 1988), denial of writ of habeas corpus aff'd sub nom. Reilly v. Warden, 947 F.2d 43 (2d Cir.1991)(IAD claim by state prisoner not cognizable under habeas corpus statutes, 28 U.S.C.A. §§ 2254, 2255), cert. den. 502 U.S. 1115, 112 S.Ct. 1227, 117 L.Ed.2d 462 (1992).

with the provisions CPL §§ 210.20, 210.45.[400] The Appellate Divisions have generally held that the denial of an IAD dismissal motion does not survive a guilty plea.[401] The Court of Appeals has not yet definitely ruled on this question.[402]

The denial of a state prisoner's IAD claim cannot later be raised in federal court via a petition for a writ of *habeas corpus*.[403]

Library References:

West's Key No. Digests, Extradition and Detainers ⚖=55.

§ 9.56 Practice Summary—Defense

A. Pre-accusatory Delay

1. Check for a statute of limitations violation, especially in conspiracy cases and where the crime is claimed to be a "continuing offense" (*see* §§ 9.2–9.6).

    - The statute of limitation periods are generally as follows:

Class A Felonies	— none
Other Felonies	— 5 years
Misdemeanors	— 2 years
Petty Offenses	— 1 year

2. Consider a motion to dismiss based, in part, on the due process clause of the New York State Constitution (Art. 1, § 6) (*see* §§ 9.9–9.10).

B. Post-accusatory Delay

1. Look into motion for bail/recognizance under CPL § 30.30(2) (*see* § 9.25).

    - The time periods relevant to such a motion are (starting from the defendant's commitment to custody):

Felonies	— 90 days
Class A Misdemeanors	— 30 days

---

400. See People v. Zambito, 153 A.D.2d 975, 545 N.Y.S.2d 414 (3d Dep't 1989); People v. Harden, 151 A.D.2d 777, 543 N.Y.S.2d 947 (2d Dep't 1989); People v. Fargher, 112 A.D.2d 599, 492 N.Y.S.2d 123 (3d Dep't 1985)(IAD issue preserved by pre-plea motion); People v. Primmer, 59 A.D.2d 221, 399 N.Y.S.2d 478 (3d Dep't 1977), aff'd 46 N.Y.2d 1048, 416 N.Y.S.2d 548, 389 N.E.2d 1070 (1979)(IAD violation waived by failure to raise it prior to guilty plea).

401. People v. Bundy, 186 A.D.2d 1042, 590 N.Y.S.2d 829 (4th Dep't 1992); People v. Woodson, 176 A.D.2d 186, 574 N.Y.S.2d 310 (1st Dep't 1991); People v. Gooden, 151 A.D.2d 773, 542 N.Y.S.2d 757 (2d Dep't 1989). But see People v. Fargher, 112 A.D.2d 599, 492 N.Y.S.2d 123 (3d Dep't 1985)(IAD issue reached in the interest of justice, despite guilty plea, where trial court had assured defense counsel issue would survive).

402. See People v. Primmer, 59 A.D.2d 221, 399 N.Y.S.2d 478 (3d Dep't 1977), aff'd 46 N.Y.2d 1048, 416 N.Y.S.2d 548, 389 N.E.2d 1070 (1979)(ruling that IAD violation waived by failure to litigate it prior to guilty plea).

The interpretation of the IAD is governed by federal law, however (Cuyler v. Adams, 449 U.S. 433, 101 S.Ct. 703, 66 L.Ed.2d 641 (1981)), and the weight of both federal and out-of-state authority is that an IAD claim is waived by a guilty plea. See, e.g., Mohler v. State, 84 Md.App. 431, 579 A.2d 1208 (1990), and the cases collected therein.

403. Reilly v. Warden, 947 F.2d 43 (2d Cir.1991), cert. den. 502 U.S. 1115, 112 S.Ct. 1227, 117 L.Ed.2d 462 (1992).

Ch. 9　　　　　　　　　　　FORMS　　　　　　　　　　　§ 9.58

    Class B Misdemeanors　—　15 days
    Violations　—　5 days

2. Look into motion to dismiss under CPL § 30.30(1) (*see* § 9.24).
   - The time periods relevant to such a motion are (starting from the filing of the 1st accusatory instrument):

     Homicide　—　not applicable
     Other Felonies　—　6 months
     Class A Felonies　—　90 days
     Class B Misdemeanor　—　60 days
     Violations　—　30 days

C. Speedy Trial Motions

1. All speedy trial/untimeliness-of-prosecution motions must be in writing, upon notice to the prosecution, and filed prior to the commencement of trial or the entry of the guilty plea (*see* §§ 9.12, 9.49).
2. If the prosecution responds to the CPL § 30.30 motion by specifying the exclusions on which it intends to rely, submit a reply identifying the legal and factual impediments to their use (*see* § 9.50).
3. Note that a plea of guilty always forfeits a CPL § 30.30 claim, but cannot forfeit a fully litigated constitutional speedy trial claim (*see* §§ 9.12, 9.13).
4. If the defendant has been brought in from an out-of-state or federal prison pursuant to the Interstate Agreement on Detainers (CPL § 580.20), check into motion to dismiss for failure to meet deadlines for bringing the defendant to trial (*see* § 9.53).
   - Where the request that the outstanding charges be resolved comes from the prisoner, the receiving state has 180 days from the receipt of the request to bring the prisoner to trial, unless the period is extended for good cause shown in open court.

§ 9.57　Practice Summary—Prosecution

1. It is your burden under CPL § 30.30 to ensure that the record indicates the reasons for all adjournments (*see* § 9.50).
2. Make sure that your readiness declaration pursuant to CPL § 30.30 is either contemporaneously recorded in open court or else sent in writing both to defense counsel and to the court clerk for placement in the court file (*see* § 9.21).
3. In responding to a defense CPL § 30.30 motion, raise all deficiencies in the defense papers, and identify all exclusion theories on which you intend to rely (*see* §§ 9.49–9.50).
4. If the defendant has been produced from an out-of-state or federal prison pursuant to the Interstate Agreement on Detainers (CPL § 580.20), make sure that you meet the statutory deadlines for bringing the defendant to trial (*see* § 9.53).

§ 9.58　Forms 💾

§ 9.58.1　Notice of Motion to Dismiss for Statute of Limitations Violation

[Caption]

§ 9.58 TIMELINESS OF PROSECUTION & SPEEDY TRIAL Ch. 9

COUNSEL:

PLEASE TAKE NOTICE, that upon the annexed affirmation and all the prior papers and proceedings herein, the undersigned will move this Court, at Part ___ thereof, to be held at the Courthouse at _____, New York, on the ___ day of _____, 19__, at ___ in the forenoon, or as soon thereafter as counsel can be heard, for an order dismissing the indictment pursuant to section 210.20(1)(f) of the Criminal Procedure Law, on the ground that the prosecution of this action is untimely in violation of defendant's rights under section 30.10 of the Criminal Procedure Law, and for such other and further relief as this Court deems just and proper.

Dated: _____, 19__
 _____, New York

[Name of defense attorney]
Attorney for Defendant
Address
Tel. No.

TO: HON. _____
District Attorney
_____ County

HON. _____
Clerk of the Court

§ 9.58.2 Affirmation in Support of Motion to Dismiss for Statute of Limitations Violation

[Caption]

_____, an attorney duly admitted to practice in the Courts of this State, hereby affirms under the penalties of perjury that the following statements are true, except those made on information and belief, which he [she] believes to be true:

1. I am the attorney for the defendant herein.

2. The criminal action herein commenced on _____, 199__, with the filing of the [specify first accusatory instrument filed] against defendant. A copy of the [specify first accusatory instrument] is annexed hereto as "Exhibit A."

3. An indictment against the defendant was filed with this Court on _____, 199__. On _____, 19__, defendant entered a "not guilty" plea to the indictment. To date, no plea of guilty has been entered, nor has trial commenced.

4. The [specify first accusatory instrument filed] charges defendant with the offense(s) of _____. It alleges that defendant committed these offenses in the County of _____ "on or about the ___ day of _____, 199__." That date is more than ___ years prior to the filing of the [specify first accusatory instrument] herein.

5. The period of limitations applicable to the commencement of a criminal action charging a violation of PL § ___, as set forth in CPL § 30.10(2)(___), is ___ years. This period has not been extended as provided in CPL § 30.10(3).

6. On the date on which the [specify first accusatory instrument filed] alleges defendant committed the offense(s), and at all times since then, defendant was continuously in this State. Additionally, his [her] whereabouts were continuously known, or ascertainable, by the exercise of reasonable diligence.

7. No other prosecution for this offense, or for an offense based upon the same conduct, has been commenced against defendant.

WHEREFORE, defendant requests that an order be issued dismissing the [specify pending accusatory instrument], and for such further relief as this Court deems just and proper.

[Signature]

[Name of defense attorney]

Dated: _____, 199__.

§ 9.58.3 Notice of Motion to Dismiss Indictment for Violation of Right to Speedy Trial (Constitutional/CPL § 30.20)

[Caption]

COUNSEL:

PLEASE TAKE NOTICE, that upon the annexed affirmation and all the prior papers and proceedings herein, the undersigned will move this Court, at Part ___ thereof, to be held at the Courthouse at _____, New York, on the ___ day of _____, 199__, at ___ in the forenoon, or as soon thereafter as counsel can be heard, for an order dismissing the indictment herein, pursuant to section 210.20(1)(g) of the Criminal Procedure Law, upon the ground that the defendant has been denied his right to a timely prosecution and a speedy trial as guaranteed by the Sixth Amendment of the United States Constitution, section 30.20 of the Criminal Procedure Law, and the Due Process Clauses of the United States and New York State Constitutions (U.S. Const., Amend. XIV; N.Y. Const., Art. 1, § 6), and for such other and further relief as this Court may deems just and proper.

Dated: _____, 199__.
_____, New York

[Name of defense attorney]
Attorney for Defendant
Address
Tel. No.

§ 9.58 TIMELINESS OF PROSECUTION & SPEEDY TRIAL Ch. 9

TO: HON. _____
District Attorney
_____ County

HON. _____
Clerk of the Court

§ 9.58.4 Affirmation in Support of Motion to Dismiss Indictment for Violation of Right to Speedy Trial (Constitutional/CPL § 30.20)

[Caption]

_____, an attorney duly admitted to practice in the Courts of this State, hereby affirms under the penalties of perjury that the following statements are true, except those made on information and belief, which he [she] believes to be true:

1. I am the attorney for the defendant herein and am personally familiar with the facts stated herein.

2. On _____, 199__, a felony complaint was filed in the _____ Court of _____ County charging defendant with the offenses of _____ in violation of section(s) _____ of the Penal Law.

3. On _____, 199__, an indictment was filed charging defendant with the offense(s) of _____ in violation of section(s) _____ of the Penal Law.

4. Arraignment on that indictment took place on _____, 199__, in Part ____. Defendant entered a "not guilty" plea at that time. To date, no plea of guilty has been entered, and trial has not commenced.

5. This affirmation is made in support of defendant's motion to dismiss the indictment on the ground that defendant has been denied his right to a timely prosecution and a speedy trial as guaranteed by the Sixth Amendment to the United States Constitution, section 30.20 of the Criminal Procedure Law, and the Due Process Clauses of the United States and New York State Constitutions (U.S. Const., Amend. XIV; N.Y. Const., Art. 1, § 6).

6. This motion is predicated, in part, upon the ___ month delay between the time that the subject matter of the indictment came to the prosecutor's attention on or about _____, 199__, and the date this action was commenced with the filing of the felony complaint on _____, 199__. [Set forth the facts underlying claim of pre-accusatory delay]. Defendant is not responsible for this pre-accusatory delay.

7. Additionally, it has been ___ months and ___ days since the commencement of the action by the filing of the felony complaint, and the defendant has not yet been brought to trial upon the ensuing indictment. The defendant has not caused this delay. [If defendant is responsible for any portion of the delay, set out the facts concerning the portion for which defendant is responsible.]

8. [In a paragraph or paragraphs, set forth facts establishing the reason for the pre and post-accusatory delay; the nature of the underly-

ing charges (asserting that it did not justify the extensive delay); the length of pretrial incarceration undergone by defendant as a result of the delay; and any *specific* prejudice that the defendant suffered as a result of the delay. If the defendant asserted his or her right to a speedy trial during the delay, allege those facts as well.]

9. The total pre and post-accusatory delay of ___ years and ___ months has in the aggregate resulted in a denial of defendant's right to a timely prosecution and a speedy trial, in violation of the Sixth Amendment to the United States Constitution, section 30.20 of the Criminal Procedure Law, and the Due Process Clauses of the Federal and State Constitutions.

10. No previous motion has been made for the relief requested herein.

WHEREFORE, defendant requests that an order be issued dismissing the indictment herein, and for such other and further relief on this Court deems just and proper.

[Signature]

_____

[Name of defense attorney]

Dated: _____, 199__.

§ 9.58.5 Notice of Motion to Dismiss Indictment for Failure of the Prosecution to Timely Announce Readiness for Trial (CPL § 30.30(1) Only)

[Caption]

COUNSEL:

PLEASE TAKE NOTICE, that upon the annexed affirmation and all the prior papers and proceedings herein, the undersigned will move this Court, at Part ___ thereof, to be held at the Courthouse at _____, New York, on the ___ day of _____. 199__, at ___ in the forenoon, or as soon thereafter as counsel can be heard, for an order dismissing the indictment herein, pursuant to sections 30.30(1) and 210.20(g) of the Criminal Procedure Law, for failure of the prosecution to be ready for trial within six months of the commencement of this criminal action, and for such other and further relief as this Court deems just and proper.

Dated: _____, 199__.
_____, New York

[Name of defense attorney]
Attorney for Defendant
Address
Tel. No.

TO: HON. _____
District Attorney
_____ County

§ 9.58 TIMELINESS OF PROSECUTION & SPEEDY TRIAL Ch. 9

HON. _____
Clerk of the Court

§ 9.58.6 Affirmation in Support of Motion to Dismiss Indictment for Failure of the Prosecution to Timely Announce Readiness for Trial (CPL § 30.30(1) Only)

[Caption]

_____, an attorney duly admitted to practice in the Courts of this State, hereby affirms under the penalties of perjury that the following statements are true, except those made on information and belief which he [she] believes to be true:

1. I am the attorney for the defendant herein and am personally familiar with the facts stated herein.

2. This action commenced on _____, 199__, with the filing of a felony complaint in the _____ Court of _____ County charging defendant with the offenses of _____ in violation of section(s) _____ of the Penal Law.

3. On _____, 199__, an indictment was filed charging defendant with the offense(s) of _____ in violation of section(s) of the Penal Law.

4. Arraignment on that indictment took place on _____, 199__, in Part ___. Defendant entered a "not guilty" plea at that time. To date, no plea of guilty has been entered, and trial has not commenced.

5. This affirmation is made in support of defendant's motion to dismiss the indictment on the ground that the prosecutor has failed to timely announce readiness for trial in violation of CPL § 30.30(1). No previous motion has been made for the relief requested herein.

6. Under CPL § 30.30(1)(a), the prosecution was required to announce readiness for trial within six months of the commencement of this criminal action on _____, 199__. Six months from that date is _____, 199__. Since the period between those dates consists of 18__ days, the prosecution had that number of days, minus excludable time, in which to announce readiness for trial.

7. The prosecution did not announce readiness until _____, 199__, ___ days from the date of the commencement of the action, and well in excess of the 18__ days within which it was statutorily required to announce readiness.

8. [Where your affirmation indicates the existence of facially excludable periods, you must further establish why those periods are not in fact excludable, or that the total delay without those excluded periods still exceeds the statutory time limit.]

9. [Note: The burden is on the prosecution to identify any pre-readiness excludable periods that bring it within the statutory time limit for declaring readiness. However, for strategic reasons, you may wish to include in this initial affirmation the specific pre-readiness nonexcludable periods on which you are relying in your claim that the prosecution

has exceeded the time limit for declaring readiness. If you do so, you must also allege that these periods are not subject to any statutory exclusion. Moreover, if your recitation indicates that any of these periods are facially excludable, you must also allege either that the periods are not in fact excludable, or that the statutory time period is exceeded even if that time is excluded.]

10. [Note: The defense has the burden of showing that *post-readiness* adjournments occurred under circumstances that should be charged to the prosecution. Hence, your initial affirmation should allege any post-readiness periods that should be tacked onto the pre-readiness delay.]

11. Since the pre-readiness period of delay [along with the periods of post-readiness delay chargeable to the prosecution] is well in excess of six months, defendant is entitled to dismissal of the indictment pursuant to CPL § 30.30(1).

WHEREFORE, defendant requests that an order be issued dismissing the indictment herein, and granting such other an further relief that this Court deems just.

[Signature]

_____
[Name of defense attorney]

Dated: _____, 199__.

§ 9.58.7 Notice of Motion for Bail/Recognizance for Failure of the Prosecution to Timely Announce Readiness for Trial (CPL § 30.30(2) Only)

[Caption]

COUNSEL:

PLEASE TAKE NOTICE, that upon the annexed papers and all the prior papers and proceedings herein, the undersigned will move this Court, at Part ___ thereof, to be held at the Courthouse at _____, New York, on the ___ day of _____, 199__, at ___ in the forenoon, or as soon thereafter as counsel can be heard, for an order pursuant to CPL § 30.30(2), releasing the defendant on bail/recognizance, for want of the prosecution to announce readiness within 90 days of the date of his commitment to the custody of the sheriff, and for such other and further relief as this Court deems just and proper.

Dated: _____, 199__.
_____, New York

[Name of defense attorney]
Attorney for Defendant
Address
Tel. No.

§ 9.58 TIMELINESS OF PROSECUTION & SPEEDY TRIAL Ch. 9

TO: HON. _____
    District Attorney
    _____ County

HON. _____
Clerk of the Court

§ 9.58.8 Affirmation in Support of Motion for Bail/Recognizance for Failure of the Prosecution to Timely Announce Readiness for Trial (CPL § 30.30(2) Only)

[Caption]

_____, an attorney duly admitted to practice in the Courts of this State, hereby affirms under the penalties of perjury that the following statements are true, except those made on information and belief which he [she] believes to be true:

1. I am the attorney for the defendant herein and am personally familiar with the facts stated herein.

2. This action commenced on _____, 199__, with the filing of a felony complaint in the _____ Court of _____ County charging defendant with the offenses of _____ in violation of section(s) _____ of the Penal Law. On that date, bail was set at $___. Defendant was unable to make such bail.

3. On _____, 199__, an indictment was filed charging defendant with the offense(s) of _____ in violation of section(s) of the Penal Law.

4. Arraignment on the indictment took place on _____, 199__, in Part ___. Defendant entered a "not guilty" plea at that time. Bail was [re-set] [continued] at $___, which sum defendant was unable to post. To date, no plea of guilty has been entered, and trial has not commenced.

5. This affirmation is made in support of defendant's motion for the release of the defendant on bail or recognizance on the ground that the prosecutor has failed to timely announce readiness for trial in violation of CPL § 30.30(2). No previous motion has been made for the relief requested herein.

6. Defendant was first committed to custody on _____, 199__, the date of his arrest. He has been held in custody in lieu of bail continuously since that date.

7. Under CPL § 30.30(2)(a), the prosecution was required to announce readiness for trial within 90 days from the date of defendant's first commitment to custody.

8. [The prosecution has yet to announce readiness for trial, even though more than 90 days have passed since the date defendant was first committed to custody.] [The prosecution did not announce readiness for trial until _____, 199__, ___ days from the date defendant was first committed to custody, and in excess of 90 days from the date defendant was so committed.]

9. Defendant is not serving a term of imprisonment for another offense, or being held in custody on another charge as to which the period specified in CPL § 30.30(2) has not yet lapsed.

10. Defendant has not previously been released on bail or recognizance in this action, pursuant to CPL § 30.30(2) or otherwise.

11. [If the affirmation indicates the existence of facially excludable periods, further establish why those periods are not in fact excludable, or that the total delay without those excluded periods still exceeds the statutory time limit.]

12. [Note: The burden is on the prosecution to identify any pre-readiness excludable periods that bring it within the statutory time limit for declaring readiness. However, for strategic reasons, you may wish to include in this initial affirmation the specific pre-readiness nonexcludable periods on which you are relying in your claim that the prosecution has exceeded to time limit for declaring readiness. If you do so, you must also allege that these periods are not subject to any statutory exclusion. Moreover, if your recitation indicates that any of these periods are facially excludable, you must also allege either that the periods are not in fact excludable, or that the statutory time period is exceeded even if that time is excluded.]

12. [Note: The defense has the burden of showing that *post*-readiness adjournments occurred under circumstances that should be charged to the prosecution. Hence, the initial affirmation should allege any post-readiness periods which should be tacked onto the pre-readiness delay.]

13. Since the pre-readiness period of delay [along with the periods of post-readiness delay chargeable to the prosecution] is in excess of 90 days, defendant is entitled to release on bail or recognizance, pursuant to CPL § 30.30(2), upon such conditions as may be just and reasonable.

WHEREFORE, defendant requests that an order be issued releasing defendant on his own recognizance, or setting reasonable bail, and granting such other and further relief that this Court deems just.

[Signature]

_____
[Name of defense attorney]

Dated: _____, 199__.

Chapter 10

SEARCH WARRANTS AND SUPPRESSION PROCEEDINGS

Table of Sections

10.1   Search Warrants—In General.
10.2   ___ Application for and Issuance of Search Warrant.
10.3   ___ Facial Sufficiency of Warrant and Warrant Application.
10.4   ___ Controverting the Warrant.
10.5   ___ Execution of Warrant.
10.6   ___ Extent of Search Allowed Under Proper Warrant.
10.7   Suppression Proceedings—Introduction.
10.8   Suppressible Evidence—In General.
10.9   ___ Indirect Fruits.
10.10 ___ Attenuation.
10.11 Standing.
10.12 Motion to Suppress—Court.
10.13 ___ Time of Motion.
10.14 ___ Time of Decision.
10.15 ___ Renewal.
10.16 The Defendant's Motion Papers—In General.
10.17 ___ Factual Allegations.
10.18 The Prosecution's Motion Papers.
10.19 Suppression Hearings—In General.
10.20 ___ Burden of Proof.
10.21 ___ Decision.
10.22 Implications for Subsequent Proceedings.
10.23 Notice—In General.
10.24 ___ Timing and Content of Notice.
10.25 ___ Statements Within and Without the Rule.
10.26 ___ Identifications Within and Without the Rule.
10.27 ___ Good Cause for Lateness.
10.28 ___ Scope of Preclusion.
10.29 ___ Waiver and Appeal.
10.30 Practice Summary.
10.31 Forms. 💾
    10.31.1 Notice of Motion to Suppress Statements.
    10.31.2 Affirmation in Support of Motion to Suppress Statements.
    10.31.3 Notice of Motion to Suppress Identification Evidence.
    10.31.4 Affirmation in Support of Motion to Suppress Identification.
    10.31.5 Notice of Motion to Suppress Physical Evidence.
    10.31.6 Affirmation in Support of Motion to Suppress Physical Evidence.

WESTLAW Electronic Research
See WESTLAW Electronic Research Guide preceding the Summary of Contents.

§ 10.1 Search Warrants—In General

If an experienced prosecutor or criminal defense attorney involved in a case in which the police recovered incriminating evidence pursuant to a search warrant was asked the most likely strategy to suppress the evidence, he or she would undoubtedly answer that the attack would allege that there was no probable cause supporting the issuance of the warrant. While that is the typical concern in one of these cases, the following sections will illustrate that a substantial number of other requirements must be fulfilled not only in the application and issuance process, but also during the execution of the warrant. Prosecutors, defense attorneys, issuing judges, the police, and reviewing courts should familiarize themselves with these statutory obligations.

Designed to protect privacy in the home, office, personal or business vehicle and any other place where someone would enjoy a reasonable expectation of privacy,[1] a search warrant "is a court order and process" directing a police officer (or a State University peace officer) to search a specific place or premises,[2] a particular vehicle,[3] or a "designated or described" person[4] for designated property and to deliver the property to the court that issued the warrant.[5] A search warrant may also be used to search any dwelling to search and arrest a suspect wanted pursuant to an arrest warrant, a felony bench warrant, or a felony arrest warrant from another state or from federal court.[6] The use of a search warrant is limited to these situations.[7]

Since the purpose of a search warrant is to aid in the detection and punishment of crime,[8] it may only be issued and used to seize personal property if there is reasonable or probable cause to believe that the property: (1) is stolen;[9] (2) is contraband;[10] (3) has been used, or is being used to commit or to conceal a crime;[11] or (4) constitutes evidence of a crime, or tends to demonstrate that a crime was committed or that a particular person committed a crime.[12] A search warrant for property in

---

1. People v. Perel, 34 N.Y.2d 462, 358 N.Y.S.2d 383, 315 N.E.2d 452 (1974).

2. CPL §§ 690.05(2)(a), 690.15(1)(a).

3. CPL §§ 690.05(2)(a), 690.15(1)(b). "Vehicle" is defined in P.L. § 10.00(14) as a motor vehicle, trailer or semi-trailer, as defined in the Vehicle and Traffic Law, a snowmobile as defined in the Parks and Recreation Law, an aircraft, or "any vessel equipped for propulsion by mechanical means or by sail."

4. CPL §§ 690.05(2)(a), 690.15(1)(c).

5. CPL §§ 690.05(2) and (2)(a).

6. CPL §§ 690.05(2)(b) and (2)(b)(ii), 690.40(2); see also Steagald v. United States, 451 U.S. 204, 101 S.Ct. 1642, 68 L.Ed.2d 38 (1981)(an arrest warrant for a person in a third party's home does not authorize a search of that home for property); Barr v. Albany County, 50 N.Y.2d 247, 253, 428 N.Y.S.2d 665, 667, 406 N.E.2d 481 (1980)(warrant authorizing a search of premises does not authorize the arrest of everyone found there).

7. B.T. Productions, Inc. v. Barr, 44 N.Y.2d 226, 405 N.Y.S.2d 9, 376 N.E.2d 171 (1978).

8. B.T. Productions, Inc. v. Barr, 44 N.Y.2d at 236, 406 N.Y.S.2d at 14; but see Zurcher v. Stanford Daily, 436 U.S. 547, 98 S.Ct. 1970, 56 L.Ed.2d 525 (1978) (approving search warrant for premises even though occupant was not suspected of a crime).

9. CPL §§ 690.10(1), 690.40(2).

10. CPL §§ 690.10(2), 690.40(2).

11. CPL §§ 690.10(3), 690.40(2).

12. CPL §§ 690.10(4), 690.40(2); People v. Robinson, 68 N.Y.2d 541, 551–52, 510 N.Y.S.2d 837, 842–43, 503 N.E.2d 485 (1986). Evidence of a crime is not limited to tangible property; a search warrant may be issued to seize intangible property such

the third and fourth categories may also be issued for a crime committed in another state if the crime constitutes a felony in New York.[13]

Library References:

West's Key No. Digests, Searches and Seizures ⇨101–140.

§ 10.2 Search Warrants—Application for and Issuance of Search Warrant

A police officer, district attorney, or "other public servant acting in the course of his official duties" may apply for a search warrant.[14] The warrant application may be oral or in writing.[15] As a procedural safeguard against perjury,[16] a written application must be made, subscribed and sworn to by a police officer, district attorney, or other public servant acting in the course of his or her official duties.[17] Substantial, not literal, compliance is enough to satisfy these written application requirements.[18]

In contrast to a written application, an "oral" application is communicated to a judge by telephone, radio, or other means of electronic communication.[19] The oral applicant must identify himself or herself to the court and state the purpose of the communication.[20] The judge must put under oath the applicant and anyone else providing information in support of the application, which must be memorialized by a tape recording, stenographer, or verbatim longhand notes.[21]

as the visual images secured by a video recording. People v. Teicher, 52 N.Y.2d 638, 651, 439 N.Y.S.2d 846, 852, 422 N.E.2d 506 (1981).

13. CPL §§ 690.10(3) and (4).

14. CPL § 690.05(1). A police officer acting solely as an agent for the New York State Organized Crime Task Force was not a "public servant acting in the course of his official duties" because the Task Force did not have the statutory authority to apply for a search warrant. B.T. Productions, Inc. v. Barr, 44 N.Y.2d 226, 405 N.Y.S.2d 9, 376 N.E.2d 171 (1978). But a warrant was validly issued to a police officer acting in his role as a local town police officer even though he was working for a county drug task force that came into existence after the warrant was issued. People v. Martin, 163 A.D.2d 536, 537, 558 N.Y.S.2d 192, 193 (2d Dep't 1990); accord People v. Pearson, 179 A.D.2d 786, 579 N.Y.S.2d 150 (2d Dep't 1992).

When the warrant is issued to the police, it must be addressed to an officer who works in the geographical area covering or partially covering the county of issuance. C.P.L. § 690.25 (1); see Matter of B.T. Productions, Inc. v. Barr, supra; People v. Martin, 163 A.D.2d 536, 558 N.Y.S.2d 192 (2d Dept. 1990).

15. CPL § 690.35(1).

16. People v. Zimmer, 112 A.D.2d 500, 490 N.Y.S.2d 912 (3d Dep't 1985).

17. CPL §§ 690.35(1), 690.05(1). The issuing judge's failure to sign the jurat is a defect curable by subsequent affidavits or testimony and does not invalidate the warrant. People v. Zimmer, supra; People v. Rodriguez, 150 A.D.2d 622, 541 N.Y.S.2d 491 (2d Dep't 1989).

18. People v. Taylor, 73 N.Y.2d 683, 688–89, 543 N.Y.S.2d 357, 358–59, 541 N.E.2d 386 (1989); People v. Brown, 40 N.Y.2d 183, 186–88, 386 N.Y.S.2d 359, 360–61, 352 N.E.2d 545 (1976); People v. Zimmer, 112 A.D.2d 500, 490 N.Y.S.2d 912, 913 (3d Dep't 1985).

19. CPL § 690.36(1). A written application supported by oral testimony is not an "oral" application. People v. Taylor, supra (even though supported by oral testimony, the application was written because it involved a formal document, sworn and subscribed by a police officer, with a supporting deposition).

20. CPL § 690.36(2).

21. CPL § 690.36(1) and (3).

If the oral application is memorialized by a tape recorder or by a stenographer, the court must have the application transcribed, certify its accuracy, then file the transcription and the original application with the court not later than 24 hours after the warrant is issued.[22] A delay beyond the 24-hour limitation, however, is not fatal if the audiotape is filed within 24 hours of issuance.[23] Similarly, if the application is recorded by "longhand," the judge must "subscribe" a copy and file it within 24 hours of the issuance of the warrant.[24]

When the court issues a warrant based on an oral application, the applicant must prepare the warrant then read it "verbatim" to the court.[25] Because this read-back requirement ensures the regularity of the application process and requires the issuing judge to focus on the particular description of the place to be searched and the property or persons to be seized, the applicant's failure to read the warrant back to the court requires suppression of the recovered property.[26] The warrant should also state the judge's name, the time and the date when it was issued, and that it was based on an oral application.[27]

A district court, the New York City Criminal Court, or a superior court judge sitting as a local criminal court may issue a search warrant to be executed anywhere in the state.[28] A search warrant issued by a city court, town court, or village court may be executed only in the county where it is issued or in an adjoining county.[29] A town or village court, however, cannot issue a search warrant to be executed outside the town absent proof that the offense was committed within the town.[30] This limitation applies even if the justice of the town where the offense was committed is unavailable when the police apply for the warrant.[31] CPL § 690.35 provides alternative courts for a search warrant applicant when the court of obvious jurisdiction is unavailable. If a village court having jurisdiction to issue a warrant is not available, another village court within the town encompassing the village, or the town court itself,

---

22. CPL § 690.36(3).

23. People v. Brinson, 177 A.D.2d 1019, 578 N.Y.S.2d 38 (4th Dep't 1991); see also People v. Camarre, 171 A.D.2d 1003, 569 N.Y.S.2d 224 (4th Dep't 1991)(filing after 24-hour period condoned because audiotape filed on next business day following the search).

24. CPL § 690.36(3); People v. McGriff, 142 A.D.2d 934, 530 N.Y.S.2d 360 (4th Dep't 1988).

25. CPL § 690.40(3); People v. Price, 204 A.D.2d 753, 611 N.Y.S.2d 675 (3d Dep't 1994).

26. People v. Price, 204 A.D.2d at 755, 611 N.Y.S.2d at 676.

27. CPL § 690.45(2).

28. CPL §§ 690.35(2), 690.20(1). If the applicant wants the search warrant to search for, and to arrest, the subject of an arrest warrant, superior court warrant, or felony bench warrant, see CPL § 690.05(2)(b), then only a local criminal court may issue the warrant. CPL § 690.35(2)(b).

29. CPL §§ 690.35(2), 690.20(2).

30. People v. Hickey, 40 N.Y.2d 761, 390 N.Y.S.2d 42, 358 N.E.2d 868 (1976); People v. Herrara, 112 A.D.2d 315, 491 N.Y.S.2d 763 (2d Dep't 1985); People v. Garrow, 91 A.D.2d 699, 457 N.Y.S.2d 611 (3d Dep't 1982); see People v. Fishman, 40 N.Y.2d 858, 387 N.Y.S.2d 1003, 356 N.E.2d 475 (1976); People v. Johnson, 44 A.D.2d 451, 355 N.Y.S.2d 601 (1st Dep't 1974), aff'd 36 N.Y.2d 864, 370 N.Y.S.2d 923, 331 N.E.2d 698 (1975)(Suffolk County District Court could issue search warrant for stolen property in Bronx apartment since robbery occurred in Suffolk County).

31. People v. Garrow, 91 A.D.2d 700, 457 N.Y.S.2d at 612.

§ 10.2   SEARCH WARRANTS & SUPPRESSION   Ch. 10

may issue the warrant.[32] If those courts are unavailable, the local criminal court of any adjoining town or village, which is a part of that town or city of the same county, may issue the warrant.[33] When a city court judge is unreachable, the warrant may be issued by the local criminal or village court of any adjoining town or village within the county encompassing the city.[34]

Before issuing the warrant, the court must examine the affidavits in support of the warrant application to determine if the crime occurred within its jurisdiction.[35] Nevertheless, when a warrant application did not expressly state that any crimes had been committed in the issuing county, the warrant was still valid, because the court had reason to believe that the crimes referred to occurred in the county since a county detective and a county prosecutor applied for the warrant.[36]

The Fourth Amendment and Article 1, § 12 of the New York Constitution require an oath or affirmation in support of the warrant.[37] While a conference with an informant, who provides information supporting the warrant application, should be taken under oath, the absence of an informant's sworn statement will not vitiate a warrant when the police officer's sworn affidavit established probable cause to issue the warrant.[38] An unsworn statement will also be sufficient if it contains notice that false statements are punishable as misdemeanor perjury.[39] An examination under oath must be recorded or summarized by the court on the record.[40] While substantial compliance with this memorialization requirement is sufficient, substantial compliance only occurs when the regularity of the application process is assured and when the grounds upon which the warrant was issued are preserved for appellate review.[41] Specifically, if there has been "a conscientious effort to comply with constitutional and statutory requirements applicable to search warrants," then a lack of literal compliance will be condoned.[42] Other-

32. CPL § 690.35(2)(ii).
33. Id.
34. CPL § 690.35(2)(iii).
35. People v. Garrow, 91 A.D.2d at 700, 457 N.Y.S.2d at 612; see People v. Fishman, supra.
36. People v. Herrara, 112 A.D.2d at 316, 491 N.Y.S.2d at 764.
37. The wording of these rights is identical: "and no warrants shall issue, but upon probable cause, supported by oath or affirmation...."
38. People v. Fici, 114 A.D.2d 468, 494 N.Y.S.2d 377 (2d Dep't 1985); see also People v. Hetrick, 80 N.Y.2d 344, 348, 590 N.Y.S.2d 183, 185, 604 N.E.2d 732 (1992) (magistrate need not question 9-year-old child to determine her ability to understand nature of the oath because as a presumptively reliable citizen informant her information constituted probable cause).
39. People v. Sullivan, 56 N.Y.2d 378, 452 N.Y.S.2d 373, 437 N.E.2d 1130 (1982);

accord People v. Brown, 40 N.Y.2d 183, 386 N.Y.S.2d 359, 352 N.E.2d 545 (1976)(informant's statement need not be under oath if it "tallies" with sworn statement of officer). See Penal Law § 210.45.

40. CPL § 690.40(1); People v. Taylor, 73 N.Y.2d 683, 543 N.Y.S.2d 357, 541 N.E.2d 386 (1989); People v. McGriff, 142 A.D.2d 934, 530 N.Y.S.2d 360 (4th Dep't 1988).

41. People v. Taylor, 73 N.Y.2d at 689, 543 N.Y.S.2d at 359.

42. People v. Lopez, 134 A.D.2d 456, 521 N.Y.S.2d 78 (2d Dep't 1987) (issuing court's failure to record examination of police informant not fatal because warrant application provided sufficient facts for issuance of warrant, informant was reliable, his identity was known, he had personally seen criminal activity, and the court questioned him under oath).

wise, failure to comply with this recording requirement warrants suppression.[43]

The issued warrant must contain the name of the issuing court, its subscription if the warrant was based on a written application, a description of the targeted property or of the person who is the subject of the search, and a designation of the place or premises to be searched.[44] The warrant must also include a direction that it and any property recovered be returned and delivered to the issuing court "without unnecessary delay."[45]

The warrant must state the name, department, or classification of the police officer to whom it is addressed, and must be addressed to a police officer who works in the county where the warrant was issued or to an officer who works in the geographical area "partially embraced" by the issuing county.[46] The warrant need not be addressed to a named officer; it may be addressed to an officer of a "designated classification," or to an officer of any classification who works in the county or who has "general jurisdiction to act as a police officer in the county."[47]

Library References:

West's Key No. Digests, Searches and Seizures ⟐101–140.

§ 10.3 Search Warrants—Facial Sufficiency of Warrant and Warrant Application

To ascertain the validity of a search warrant, the reviewing court must examine the warrant application and the warrant itself for the substance of the information supporting the warrant and for the propriety of the process that led to the issuance of the warrant. Because search warrants are preferred over the police acting on their own, warrants are presumed to be valid.[48] This presumption means that courts will not analyze warrant applications "in a grudging or hypertechnical manner when determining whether they meet constitutional standards"[49] so as not to discourage the police from submitting their evidence

---

43. People v. Taylor, 73 N.Y.2d 683, 543 N.Y.S.2d 357, 541 N.E.2d 386 (1989); People v. Blair, 155 A.D.2d 676, 547 N.Y.S.2d 897 (2d Dep't 1989).

44. CPL § 690.45(1),(4) and (5). Substantial compliance with these requirements is sufficient. People v. Pizzuto, 101 A.D.2d 1024, 476 N.Y.S.2d 696 (4th Dep't 1984)(leaving space at top of warrant and supporting affidavit for name of issuing court blank condoned because both documents bore judge's signature).

45. CPL § 690.45(8).

46. CPL §§ 690.25(1), 690.45(3). If the warrant is addressed to a State University peace officer, it must likewise state his or her name, department or classification. CPL § 690.45(3).

47. CPL § 690.25(1); see CPL § 690.45(3). Even when the issuing court failed to address the warrant to a specific police department, the warrant was valid because it was obvious that the judge contemplated it would be executed by the police department conducting the investigation, one of whose officers had applied for the warrant. People v. Davis, 93 A.D.2d 970, 463 N.Y.S.2d 67 (3d Dep't 1983).

48. Franks v. Delaware, 438 U.S. 154, 98 S.Ct. 2674, 57 L.Ed.2d 667 (1978).

49. People v. Edwards, 69 N.Y.2d 814, 816, 513 N.Y.S.2d 960, 960, 506 N.E.2d 530 (1987); People v. Hanlon, 36 N.Y.2d 549, 558, 369 N.Y.S.2d 677, 683, 330 N.E.2d 631 (1975).

to a court before acting.[50] The validity of the warrant is determined by examining the information known to the court at the time it issues the warrant.[51]

When promulgating the requirements of the warrant application, the Legislature apparently wanted the court considering the application to take nothing for granted. Accordingly, the application must include the name of the court where the application is being made, the applicant's name and title, and a request that the court issue a search warrant directing a search and seizure of the designated property or person.[52] The warrant application must also provide the judge with "reasonable cause" to believe[53] that evidence of illegal activity will be present at the specific time and place of the search[54] and specify that the property sought constitutes evidence of a specific offense.[55] To satisfy the "reasonable cause" requirement, the application only has to demonstrate that there is a "substantial probability that the seizable property will be on the premises searched."[56] A search warrant may be issued before the targeted property will be possessed by the suspect,[57] or if the owner or possessor of the place to be searched is not then reasonably suspected of criminal involvement.[58]

The warrant application must also include "allegations of fact" supporting the "reasonable cause" requirement.[59] These factual allega-

50. See United States v. Ventresca, 380 U.S. 102, 108, 85 S.Ct. 741, 745, 13 L.Ed.2d 684 (1965); People v. Grimes, 51 A.D.2d 625, 378 N.Y.S.2d 978 (3d Dep't 1976).

51. People v. Hendricks, 25 N.Y.2d 129, 303 N.Y.S.2d 33, 250 N.E.2d 323 (1969); People v. DeLago, 16 N.Y.2d 289, 266 N.Y.S.2d 353, 213 N.E.2d 659 (1965).

52. CPL §§ 690.35(3)(a) and (d).

53. The "reasonable cause" requirement restates the federal and state constitutional requirements that "no Warrants shall issue but upon probable cause." U.S. Const., Amend. IV; N.Y. Const., Art 1, § 12.

54. CPL § 690.35(3)(b); People v. Pinchback, 82 N.Y.2d 857, 858, 609 N.Y.S.2d 158, 159, 631 N.E.2d 100 (1993); People v. Edwards, 69 N.Y.2d 814, 816, 513 N.Y.S.2d 960, 960, 506 N.E.2d 530 (1987); People v. Bigelow, 66 N.Y.2d 417, 423, 497 N.Y.S.2d 630, 634, 488 N.E.2d 451 (1985); see also People v. Aaron, 172 A.D.2d 842, 843, 569 N.Y.S.2d 206, 207 (2d Dep't 1991)(reasonable to infer that additional marihuana would be in apartment because it was apparently being used as dealers' base of operations); People v. Schiavo, 162 A.D.2d 639, 556 N.Y.S.2d 954 (2d Dep't 1990)(affidavit contained details of tape recorded conversation in which appellant said "don't forget my gun because I want to put it in my house"); People v. Smith, 145 A.D.2d 517, 518–19, 535 N.Y.S.2d 110, 111–12 (2d Dep't 1988)(accomplice's confession included statement that he had given murder weapon to defendant in his apartment).

If the warrant is to search for the subject of an arrest warrant, see CPL § 690.05(2), then the application must contain a statement that there is reasonable cause to believe that the wanted person may be found in the designated premises. CPL § 690.35(3)(b).

55. CPL §§ 690.10(4), 690.35(2)(b); People v. Robinson, 68 N.Y.2d 541, 551–52, 510 N.Y.S.2d 837, 842–43, 503 N.E.2d 485 (1986). If the warrant is to search for the subject of an arrest warrant, see CPL § 690.05(2), then the application, and the warrant ultimately issued, must contain a copy of the arrest warrant and of the underlying accusatory instrument. CPL §§ 690.45(9), 690.35(3)(e).

56. People v. Glen, 30 N.Y.2d 252, 259, 331 N.Y.S.2d 656, 661, 282 N.E.2d 614 (1972).

57. People v. Glen, supra; People v. Wyatt, 60 A.D.2d 958, 401 N.Y.S.2d 890 (3d Dep't 1978), aff'd 46 N.Y.2d 926, 415 N.Y.S.2d 211, 388 N.E.2d 348 (1979).

58. Zurcher v. Stanford Daily, 436 U.S. 547, 98 S.Ct. 1970, 56 L.Ed.2d 525 (1978).

59. CPL § 690.35(3)(c). A warrant application that failed to include a specific statement of "reasonable cause" was nevertheless valid because the "obvious purport" of the police officer's affidavit was that con-

tions may be predicated on the applicant's personal knowledge or upon "information and belief," provided that the applicant states the sources of the information and the grounds for the belief.[60] Alternatively, the applicant may include someone else's deposition containing factual allegations "supporting or tending to support" the factual allegations of the application or have witnesses give sworn testimony supporting the application.[61] The factual allegation requirement does not require lawyerly precision draftsmanship.[62] An "imprecisely drafted" application containing "factual statements intermingled with conclusory statements" was enough to issue a warrant.[63] Generally, the court may rely upon reasonable inferences that may be drawn from the allegations of fact and "mere doubts" as to the veracity of the allegations supporting the application "should be resolved in favor of the warrant."[64]

Before issuing a search warrant, the court "must conduct a full and searching inquiry" into the facts on which the application is based and "may not delegate in whole or in part" the inquiry to another person.[65] The judge may incorporate by reference previously submitted material if it was given under oath, the information is either available to the court or sufficiently fresh in the judge's memory so that he or she can accurately assess it, and the information is available in a form that can be reviewed at a later date.[66]

A warrant based on hearsay may be issued if there is "a substantial basis for crediting the hearsay statement."[67] The hearsay may be unsworn if the applicant provides facts demonstrating the informant's reliability and basis of knowledge.[68] Accordingly, when an affidavit is

traband would be at the defendant's residence or on his person. People v. Bowers, 92 A.D.2d 669, 670, 461 N.Y.S.2d 900, 901 (3d Dep't 1983).

60. CPL § 690.35(3)(c); see People v. Fromen, 125 A.D.2d 987, 510 N.Y.S.2d 384 (4th Dep't 1986)(police officer's affidavit was insufficient and "misleading" because he did not have "first hand knowledge" of events he said he saw).

61. CPL §§ 690.35(3)(c), 690.40(1). The court may also review tape recordings of telephone conversations between the informant and the defendant, which were submitted with the sworn warrant application. People v. Seager, 147 A.D.2d 932, 537 N.Y.S.2d 392 (4th Dep't 1989).

62. United States v. Ventresca, 380 U.S. 102, 108, 85 S.Ct. 741, 745, 13 L.Ed.2d 684 (1965).

63. People v. Finch, 57 A.D.2d 641, 642, 393 N.Y.S.2d 222, 223 (3d Dep't 1977).

64. People v. Williams, 119 A.D.2d 606, 607, 500 N.Y.S.2d 778, 779 (2d Dep't 1986).

65. Monserrate v. Upper Court Street Book Store, 49 N.Y.2d 306, 425 N.Y.S.2d 304, 401 N.E.2d 414 (1980); People v. Potwora, 48 N.Y.2d 91, 95, 421 N.Y.S.2d 850, 852, 397 N.E.2d 361 (1979)(as basis for search warrant, issuing magistrate cannot rely on determination of three other judges that recovered magazines were obscene); see People v. P.J. Video, Inc., 68 N.Y.2d 296, 508 N.Y.S.2d 907, 501 N.E.2d 556 (1986).

66. People v. Tambe, 71 N.Y.2d 492, 502, 527 N.Y.S.2d 372, 376, 522 N.E.2d 448 (1988); cf. People v. Lalli, 43 N.Y.2d 729, 401 N.Y.S.2d 489, 372 N.E.2d 330 (1977)(insufficient showing of probable cause cannot be overcome by unsworn, unwritten, and unrecorded details of investigation related by detective to issuing magistrate) with People v. Seager, 147 A.D.2d 932, 537 N.Y.S.2d 392 (4th Dep't 1989)(issuing judge could consider unsworn tape recordings of telephone conversations between informant and defendant because officer's warrant application independently demonstrated probable cause).

67. United States v. Ventresca, 380 U.S. 102, 108, 85 S.Ct. 741, 745, 13 L.Ed.2d 684 (1965); People v. Hanlon, 36 N.Y.2d 549, 557, 369 N.Y.S.2d 677, 682, 330 N.E.2d 631 (1975); People v. Whelan, 165 A.D.2d 313, 567 N.Y.S.2d 817 (2d Dep't 1991).

68. People v. Hetrick, 80 N.Y.2d 344, 348, 590 N.Y.S.2d 183, 185, 604 N.E.2d 732 (1992). A discussion of the probable cause

§ 10.3 SEARCH WARRANTS & SUPPRESSION Ch. 10

signed only by a confidential informant, who does not reveal his name, and the officer's affidavit does not contain any information concerning the informant's reliability, the application is insufficient.[69]

The information contained in the warrant application must allege that the property sought to be recovered was in the premises in the recent past. A warrant based on stale information—factual allegations that do not reasonably lead to the conclusion that the property sought will be in the premises when the warrant will be executed—is invalid.[70] If the crime is an isolated event, then delay between it and issuance of the warrant will generally not be condoned.[71] More often than not, the warrant application is not stale.[72] Indeed, stale information in an initial warrant application may be used to apply for a second warrant if there is additional information in the second application supporting issuance of

necessary for the issuance of a search warrant is beyond the scope of this book. See generally, People v. Griminger, 71 N.Y.2d 635, 529 N.Y.S.2d 55, 524 N.E.2d 409 (1988). To illustrate very briefly the information necessary to constitute probable cause, the following cases are provided: People v. Wirchansky, 41 N.Y.2d 130, 391 N.Y.S.2d 70, 359 N.E.2d 666 (1976)(affidavit insufficient because it failed to disclose how informant came to know information he provided to the police); People v. Correa, 188 A.D.2d 542, 591 N.Y.S.2d 447 (2d Dep't 1992)(application sufficient because it recited that the source of informant's knowledge was his personal observations); People v. Whelan 165 A.D.2d 313, 567 N.Y.S.2d 817 (2d Dep't 1991)(application defective since it neglected to disclose sources of hearsay statements); People v. O'Donnell, 146 A.D.2d 923, 536 N.Y.S.2d 889 (3d Dep't 1989)(application insufficient because hearsay contained no facts concerning informant's "track record" for reliability).

69. People v. Martinez, 80 N.Y.2d 549, 592 N.Y.S.2d 628, 607 N.E.2d 775 (1992).

70. Sgro v. United States, 287 U.S. 206, 210–11, 53 S.Ct. 138, 140, 77 L.Ed. 260 (1932) ("the proof must be of facts so closely related to the time of the issue of the warrant as to justify a finding of probable cause at that time"). Whether the proof meets this test is determined by the circumstances of each case. Id.

The police must execute the warrant not later than ten days after it is issued. CPL § 690.30(1).

71. People v. Glen, 30 N.Y.2d 252, 331 N.Y.S.2d 656, 282 N.E.2d 614 (1972); cf. People v. Acevedo, 175 A.D.2d 323, 572 N.Y.S.2d 101 (3d Dep't 1991)(warrant stale since application indicated a solitary drug sale two months prior to the application and failed to allege ongoing or continuing criminal activity) with People v. Telesco,

207 A.D.2d 920, 616 N.Y.S.2d 773 (2d Dep't 1994) (three-week gap between date of last crime mentioned in the warrant application and issuance of warrant did not make information stale because drug dealing was "ongoing and continuing"); see also People v. McCants, 59 A.D.2d 999, 399 N.Y.S.2d 715 (3d Dep't 1977)(judge properly issued second warrant based on the same information used for the first, which was not executed within ten days, because initial application indicated "frequent" drug activity and excessive delay was caused by defendant's absence from place to be searched).

72. See, e.g., People v. Munoz, 205 A.D.2d 452, 613 N.Y.S.2d 892 (1st Dep't 1994)(observations over a five-month period, the last one four days before warrant application, sufficient for warrant); People v. Hawley, 192 A.D.2d 742, 596 N.Y.S.2d 205 (3d Dep't 1993)(information not stale because "the circumstances" existing 13 days before warrant was issued "were indicated to be continuing"); People v. Bryan, 191 A.D.2d 1029, 1030, 595 N.Y.S.2d 150, 151 (4th Dep't 1993)(information acquired 11 days before warrant issued not stale because probable cause "continued to exist" at the time the warrant application was made); People v. Clarke, 173 A.D.2d 550, 570 N.Y.S.2d 305 (2d Dep't 1991)(warrant not stale where application described drug transactions eight days and 48 days before issuance of warrant); People v. Villanueva, 161 A.D.2d 552, 556 N.Y.S.2d 293 (1st Dep't 1990)("the continuing nature of the crime justified a search warrant issued just six days after the last drug transaction"); People v. Freitag, 148 A.D.2d 544, 538 N.Y.S.2d 872 (2d Dep't 1989) (critical fingerprint results disclosed eight days before the warrant was issued rendered it valid although six months had passed between the incident and the issuance of the warrant).

the second warrant.[73]

Library References:
West's Key No. Digests, Searches and Seizures ⊜101–140.

§ 10.4 Search Warrants—Controverting the Warrant

The defendant bears the burden of proof in attacking the sufficiency of the information underlying the issuance of a search warrant.[74] Recent rulings have made this burden particularly difficult to meet. A court reviewing the propriety of a search warrant may seal the warrant affidavit to protect the anonymity of the confidential informant and to protect him from danger "given the defendant's 'prior record and the nature of his present activities'."[75] The reviewing court may even deny the defendant access to the warrant and the supporting documents when "the reliability of the evidence of probable cause and the necessity for confidentiality are clearly demonstrated."[76] The court may not, however, redact the warrant application to protect the identity of the informant without first holding an *in camera* inquiry to determine whether the informant's life or ongoing investigations will be jeopardized if identity is disclosed.[77]

A defendant may challenge the truthfulness of the allegations in an affidavit supporting a search warrant, but only where the veracity of the police officer is in issue; the credibility of the informant is irrelevant.[78] The defendant bears the burden of proving that the officer "knowingly made false statements or did so with reckless disregard for their truth."[79]

---

73. People v. Davis, 93 A.D.2d 970, 463 N.Y.S.2d 67 (3d Dep't 1983).

74. People v. Glen, 30 N.Y.2d 252, 262, 331 N.Y.S.2d 656, 663, 282 N.E.2d 614 (1972).

75. People v. Woolnough, 180 A.D.2d 837, 580 N.Y.S.2d 776 (2d Dep't 1992).

76. People v. Castillo, 80 N.Y.2d 578, 587, 592 N.Y.S.2d 945, 950, 607 N.E.2d 1050 (1992). In Castillo, the Court of Appeals endorsed a four-step procedure to guide the reviewing court in determining whether revelation of the warrant and its supporting documents, and therefore the informant's identity, is necessary. The reviewing court should: (1) review the search warrant to determine whether it alleged probable cause under Aguilar–Spinelli standards (see footnote 68 supra); People v. Griminger, 71 N.Y.2d 635, 529 N.Y.S.2d 55, 524 N.E.2d 409 (1988); (2) conduct an in camera ex parte inquiry of the informant and examine the prosecution's exhibits to determine whether the informant's life or future investigations will be jeopardized by disclosure; (3) try to redact portions of the affidavit to conceal the informant's identity while giving the defense a description of the information resulting in his arrest; (4) if this is impossible, the prosecution should produce the informant for an in camera inquiry to determine his or her credibility (see People v. Darden, 34 N.Y.2d 177, 356 N.Y.S.2d 582, 313 N.E.2d 49 (1974)). People v. Castillo, 80 N.Y.2d at 586, 592 N.Y.S.2d at 949.

77. People v. Pimental, 182 A.D.2d 80, 587 N.Y.S.2d 365 (2d Dep't 1992).

78. Franks v. Delaware, 438 U.S. 154, 98 S.Ct. 2674, 57 L.Ed.2d 667 (1978); People v. Slaughter, 37 N.Y.2d 596, 376 N.Y.S.2d 114, 338 N.E.2d 622 (1975); People v. Solimine, 18 N.Y.2d 477, 276 N.Y.S.2d 882, 223 N.E.2d 341 (1966). The informant's credibility is relevant only if the police knew the informant to be lying when they applied for the warrant. Otherwise, the informant's perjury will not invalidate the warrant if the falsity is discovered after the police execute the warrant. People v. Bashian, 190 A.D.2d 681, 593 N.Y.S.2d 526 (2d Dep't 1993); People v. Bradley, 181 A.D.2d 316, 586 N.Y.S.2d 119 (1st Dep't 1992).

79. Franks v. Delaware, 438 U.S. at 155–56, 171, 98 S.Ct. at 2675, 2684; People v. Tambe, 71 N.Y.2d 492, 527 N.Y.S.2d 372, 522 N.E.2d 448 (1988); People v. Hawley, 192 A.D.2d 742, 596 N.Y.S.2d 205 (3d Dep't

§ 10.4   SEARCH WARRANTS & SUPPRESSION   Ch. 10

"Mere doubts" as to the veracity of the warrant application allegations should be resolved in favor of upholding the warrant.[80] Conclusory allegations and/or allegations that the police were negligent or innocently mistaken are not enough even to obtain a hearing on the propriety of the warrant.[81]

Library References:

West's Key No. Digests, Searches and Seizures ⇔191–202.

§ 10.5   Search Warrants—Execution of Warrant

The Fourth Amendment and Article 1, § 12 of the New York Constitution prohibit general warrants authorizing blanket searches and indiscriminate rummaging through a citizen's personal effects.[82] The warrant must enable the officer executing it to ascertain and identify with reasonable certainty those items that the court has authorized be seized.[83] "[N]othing should be left to the discretion of the searcher in executing the warrant."[84] Accordingly, CPL § 690.15(1) provides that a search warrant "must" direct the search of a "described or designated" place, vehicle or person. "The degree of precision ... necessarily must vary with the type of items, the nature of the operation, and the circumstances of the case."[85]

A general warrant clause will be acceptable only when it limits the scope of the search to a specific crime[86] or when the designated property is contraband, which may be described generally as to its character.[87]

1993); People v. Jenkins, 184 A.D.2d 585, 586, 584 N.Y.S.2d 643, 644 (2d Dep't 1992).

80. People v. Williams, 119 A.D.2d 606, 607, 500 N.Y.S.2d 778, 779 (2d Dep't 1986).

81. Franks v. Delaware, 438 U.S. at 171, 98 S.Ct. at 2675.

82. "[N]o warrants shall issue, but upon probable cause supported by Oath or affirmation, and particularly describing the place to be searched, and the ... things to be seized." See Lo-Ji Sales, Inc. v. New York, 442 U.S. 319, 325, 99 S.Ct. 2319, 2323, 60 L.Ed.2d 920 (1979); Andresen v. Maryland, 427 U.S. 463, 96 S.Ct. 2737, 49 L.Ed.2d 627 (1976); Coolidge v. New Hampshire, 403 U.S. 443, 467, 91 S.Ct. 2022, 2038, 29 L.Ed.2d 564 (1971); People v. Rainey, 14 N.Y.2d 35, 36, 248 N.Y.S.2d 33, 35, 197 N.E.2d 527 (1964); People v. Masters, 33 A.D.2d 637, 305 N.Y.S.2d 132 (4th Dep't 1969).

83. See Steele v. United States, 267 U.S. 498, 503, 45 S.Ct. 414, 416, 69 L.Ed. 757 (1925). Thus, a warrant authorizing a search for "any other evidence relating to the commission of a crime" is too general. United States v. George, 975 F.2d 72 (2d Cir.1992); People v. Giordano, 72 A.D.2d 550, 420 N.Y.S.2d 719 (2d Dep't 1979)(authorization to search for any other contraband too broad).

84. People v. Nieves, 36 N.Y.2d 396, 401, 369 N.Y.S.2d 50, 56, 330 N.E.2d 26 (1975); People v. Caruso, 174 A.D.2d 1051, 572 N.Y.S.2d 216 (4th Dep't 1991).

85. People v. Hulsen, 178 A.D.2d 189, 577 N.Y.S.2d 48 (1st Dep't 1991). When a search warrant authorizes the seizure of materials that may be protected by the First Amendment, the warrant must contain "particular exactitude" to protect the First Amendment interests that would be endangered by the search. Zurcher v. Stanford Daily, 436 U.S. 547, 98 S.Ct. 1970, 56 L.Ed.2d 525 (1978).

86. Andreson v. Maryland, 427 U.S. at 480–482, 96 S.Ct. at 2747–49 (1976); People v. Niemczycki, 67 A.D.2d 442, 415 N.Y.S.2d 258 (2d Dep't 1979) (authorization to search for "any other contraband which is unlawfully possessed" violated particularity requirement).

87. People v. Sinatra, 102 A.D.2d 189, 191, 476 N.Y.S.2d 913, 915 (2d Dep't 1984); People v. DeMeo, 123 A.D.2d 879, 507 N.Y.S.2d 658 (2d Dep't 1986) (authorization to search for "drugs" not overbroad). An authorization to search for "drugs" may be overbroad, however, if the warrant is based solely on the observation of a single item, or of a small quantity, of a specific drug. See

§ 10.5 EXECUTION OF WARRANT

An overbroad warrant clause concerning the property to be seized may be cured by referring to the documents supporting the warrant.[88]

A warrant authorizing the search of a place is sufficiently specific if the description provides a reasonable means of identifying the premises to be searched.[89] Applying a "common-sense test," the warrant must be specific enough so that there will be no confusion about the identity of the place to be searched.[90] The authority to search is limited to the place described in the warrant and does not include additional or different places.[91] For example, a warrant to search a building does not allow the search of vehicles at the premises and vice-versa.[92]

Similarly, a warrant to search a unit of a multiple occupancy building must describe the sub-unit to be searched; it is void if it describes only the larger structure.[93] The sub-unit may be identified by number or by naming the occupant.[94] As with an overbroad warrant clause pertaining to the property sought, a warrant overbroad on its face concerning the place to be searched may be cured by referring to the heading or to the supporting documents, such as the warrant application, including affidavits.[95]

If the police make a factual mistake in the warrant application and describe the targeted premises in too broad terms, the validity of the warrant turns on the information available to them when they acted.[96]

People v. Reeves, 44 N.Y.2d 761, 762, 406 N.Y.S.2d 36, 36, 377 N.E.2d 480 (1978); People v. Germaine, 87 A.D.2d 848, 449 N.Y.S.2d 508 (2d Dep't 1982).

88. People v. Telesco, 207 A.D.2d 920, 616 N.Y.S.2d 773 (2d Dep't 1994); People v. Brooks, 54 A.D.2d 333, 335, 388 N.Y.S.2d 450, 451 (4th Dep't 1976); see also People v. Taggart, 51 A.D.2d 863, 380 N.Y.S.2d 168 (4th Dep't 1976)(although body of accompanying affidavit erroneously requested a search of downstairs apartment, the caption of that document and the warrant itself properly designated upstairs flat).

89. Steele v. United States, 267 U.S. 498, 45 S.Ct. 414, 69 L.Ed. 757 (1925); People v. Edwards, 69 N.Y.2d 814, 816, 513 N.Y.S.2d 960, 960, 506 N.E.2d 530 (1987); People v. Rainey, 14 N.Y.2d 35, 248 N.Y.S.2d 33, 197 N.E.2d 527 (1964); People v. Fahrenkopf, 191 A.D.2d 903, 595 N.Y.S.2d 139 (3d Dep't 1993).

90. People v. Nieves, 36 N.Y.2d 396, 369 N.Y.S.2d 50, 330 N.E.2d 26 (1975); People v. Rainey, 14 N.Y.2d 35, 248 N.Y.S.2d 33, 197 N.E.2d 527 (1964); People v. Sprague, 47 A.D.2d 510, 367 N.Y.S.2d 598 (3d Dep't 1975).

91. People v. Caruso, 174 A.D.2d 1051, 572 N.Y.S.2d 216 (4th Dep't 1991)(search of shed at defendant's residence not authorized by warrant that specified search of "two story flat roof dwelling"); People v. Nibur, 113 A.D.2d 957, 493 N.Y.S.2d 855 (2d Dep't 1985)(warrant authorizing search of "Bug Motors" did not authorize search of "Mount Vernon West Automotive Repair Services" in the same building and next to Bug Motors).

92. People v. Sciacca, 45 N.Y.2d 122, 127, 408 N.Y.S.2d 22, 25, 379 N.E.2d 1153 (1978).

93. People v. Rainey, 14 N.Y.2d 35, 248 N.Y.S.2d 33, 197 N.E.2d 527 (1964); People v. Brooks, 54 A.D.2d 333, 388 N.Y.S.2d 450 (4th Dep't 1976); see also People v. Arnau, 58 N.Y.2d 27, 457 N.Y.S.2d 763, 444 N.E.2d 13 (1982)("top floor" at specific address was adequate description of designated premises).

94. People v. De Lago, 16 N.Y.2d 289, 266 N.Y.S.2d 353, 213 N.E.2d 659 (1965); People v. Fahrenkopf, 191 A.D.2d 903, 595 N.Y.S.2d 139 (3d Dep't 1993); People v. Brooks, 54 A.D.2d 333, 388 N.Y.S.2d 450 (4th Dep't 1976). But an error in discovering the occupant's true name will not void an otherwise valid warrant. People v. Brooks, supra.

95. People v. De Lago, 16 N.Y.2d 289, 266 N.Y.S.2d 353, 213 N.E.2d 659 (1965); People v. Brooks, supra; People v. Taggart, 51 A.D.2d 863, 380 N.Y.S.2d 168 (4th Dep't 1976).

96. Maryland v. Garrison, 480 U.S. 79, 85, 107 S.Ct. 1013, 1017, 94 L.Ed.2d 72 (1987)(when police applied for, and execut-

A discrepancy concerning the place to be searched may be immaterial if the warrant is amended before its execution to state the correct designation of the apartment to be searched, the informant accompanied the police to the apartment, and he was admitted by the person named as the occupant and confirmed to the police that the occupant was the person referred to in the warrant.[97]

In contrast to a warrant designating a place to be searched, a search warrant targeting a person to be searched permits the police to search that person wherever he or she might be unless the focus of the warrant application is that the person is at a particular place.[98]

An invalid warrant clause will not necessarily render the warrant invalid. Under the concept of "severability," the invalid clause may be severed from the warrant, which remains valid if there is probable cause to support the surviving part of the warrant.[99] Therefore, an overbroad warrant clause will not mandate suppression of all the evidence recovered if there was probable cause to search for the particularly described property and if there is no evidence that the overbreadth caused the executing officers to expand the scope of their search beyond permissible limits.[100]

A search warrant must be executed not more than ten days after the date it is issued, and then it must be returned to the court "without

---

ed, the search warrant they reasonably believed there was only one apartment on premises described in warrant; therefore contraband discovered from an apartment not designated in the warrant was not suppressed); People v. Rodriguez, 188 A.D.2d 565, 591 N.Y.S.2d 461 (2d Dep't 1992)(warrant sufficient because officer unaware of circumstances giving rise to the overbreadth and made diligent attempt to ascertain the number of the targeted apartment); People v. Otero, 177 A.D.2d 284, 285–86, 575 N.Y.S.2d 862, 863–64 (1st Dep't 1991)(warrant not overbroad since applications for warrants and evidence at hearing failed to show that police knew or should have known that second floor was divided into separate living spaces); People v. Davis, 146 A.D.2d 942, 537 N.Y.S.2d 93 (3d Dep't 1989)(since police made responsible attempt to obtain an accurate location and could not further pinpoint it without jeopardizing secrecy of surveillance of defendant, warrant not overbroad); People v. Nibur, 113 A.D.2d 957, 493 N.Y.S.2d 855 (2d Dep't 1985) (warrant overbroad because no reasonable person would be directed to defendant's business by warrant issued for business next door); People v. Germaine, 87 A.D.2d 848, 449 N.Y.S.2d 508 (2d Dep't 1982)(search warrant sufficiently specific where outward appearance of building conformed with description of premises).

97. People v. Salgado, 57 N.Y.2d 662, 454 N.Y.S.2d 69, 439 N.E.2d 878 (1982).

98. People v. Sanin, 60 N.Y.2d 575, 467 N.Y.S.2d 38, 454 N.E.2d 119 (1983)(warrant authorizing search of defendant's person and of his apartment allowed the police to search him in his driveway); People v. Carter, 56 A.D.2d 948, 392 N.Y.S.2d 712 (3d Dep't 1977)(warrant authorizing search of defendant for drugs permitted police to search him outside methadone clinic); cf. People v. Green, 33 N.Y.2d 496, 354 N.Y.S.2d 933, 310 N.E.2d 533 (1974)(warrant authorizing search of defendant, his apartment, and anyone else who might be there, did not permit search of defendant 19 blocks from the apartment).

99. Franks v. Delaware, 438 U.S. 154, 156, 98 S.Ct. 2674, 2676, 57 L.Ed.2d 667 (1978); People v. Arnau, 58 N.Y.2d 27, 33 n. 1, 457 N.Y.S.2d 763, 766 n. 1, 444 N.E.2d 13 (1982); People v. Hansen, 38 N.Y.2d 17, 21, 377 N.Y.S.2d 461, 464, 339 N.E.2d 873 (1975); People v. Conte, 159 A.D.2d 993, 552 N.Y.S.2d 743 (4th Dep't 1990); People v. Pizzichillo, 144 A.D.2d 589, 590, 534 N.Y.S.2d 432, 433 (2d Dep't 1988); see also People v. Niemczycki, 67 A.D.2d 442, 415 N.Y.S.2d 258 (2d Dep't 1979)(overbroad authorization to search for "any other contraband which is unlawfully possessed" severable from rest of warrant because there was probable cause to search for narcotics).

100. People v. Niemczycki, 67 A.D.2d 442, 444, 415 N.Y.S.2d 258, 259 (2d Dep't 1979).

unnecessary delay."[101] If execution occurs after ten days, the property recovered must be suppressed.[102] This time limitation only affects execution after the tenth day; a warrant authorizing an "immediate search" may be executed anytime within the ten-day period.[103] The officer to whom the warrant is addressed may execute it anywhere in the issuing, or in an adjoining, county or in any other county in the state if "his geographical area of employment embraces the entire county of issuance" or if he works for the police in a city located in the county of issuance.[104] Therefore, a town or village officer cannot execute a warrant beyond the county of issuance or an adjoining county.

The police must provide notice before executing a search warrant. They must "make a reasonable effort" to give notice of their authority and of their purpose to the occupants before entering unless the designated premises or vehicle is unoccupied at that time or the police "reasonably" believe that no one is present.[105] The warrant must be displayed only if the occupants request to see it.[106] Substantial compliance with this statutory notice requirement is sufficient.[107] If after giving notice, the occupant or someone else refuses to allow the police to enter the premises or vehicle, or "resists or refuses" to allow the search, the police may use "physical force" to execute the warrant.[108] They can use "deadly physical force" only when it is necessary to defend themselves or another against such force.[109]

The police cannot search the targeted premises before the warrant

101. CPL § 690.30(1).

102. People v. Jacobowitz, 89 A.D.2d 625, 452 N.Y.S.2d 679 (2d Dep't 1982). Warrants not executed within the ten-day period may be reissued based upon the initial application and executed after the ten-day period. People v. Davis, 93 A.D.2d 970, 463 N.Y.S.2d 67 (3d Dep't 1983); People v. McCants, 59 A.D.2d 999, 399 N.Y.S.2d 715 (3d Dep't 1977); People v. DeJesus, 125 Misc.2d 963, 480 N.Y.S.2d 807 (Sup.Ct., Kings County, 1984).

103. People v. Cordero 124 Misc.2d 43, 475 N.Y.S.2d 973 (Sup.Ct., Kings County, 1984); see People v. Glen, 30 N.Y.2d 252, 261, 331 N.Y.S.2d 656, 662, 282 N.E.2d 614 (1972).

104. CPL § 690.25(2). A warrant addressed to a State University peace officer may be executed on the university campus or other university property including any public highway on, or adjoining, the property. CPL § 690.25(3). Similarly, such a peace officer may execute a warrant for any vehicle on the campus or university property even if it is on a public highway crossing or adjoining the property. Id.

105. CPL § 690.50(1) and (2)(a); People v. Tarallo, 48 A.D.2d 611, 367 N.Y.S.2d 286 (1st Dep't 1975).

106. People v. Cotroneo, 199 A.D.2d 670, 604 N.Y.S.2d 979 (3d Dep't 1993); People v. Rhoades, 126 A.D.2d 774, 510 N.Y.S.2d 718 (3d Dep't 1987); People v. Pischetola, 63 A.D.2d 687, 404 N.Y.S.2d 658 (2d Dep't 1978); People v. Tarallo, 48 A.D.2d 611, 367 N.Y.S.2d 286 (1st Dep't 1975).

107. People v. Drapala, 93 A.D.2d 956, 463 N.Y.S.2d 70 (3d Dep't 1983) (police officers knocked on door and then waited 30 seconds before using passkey to enter dormitory room); People v. Clinton, 65 A.D.2d 692, 409 N.Y.S.2d 739 (1st Dep't 1978)(no substantial compliance where officer knocked on door, announced he wanted to speak to occupant and then put his foot in the door preventing occupant from closing it before pushing his way into apartment).

108. CPL § 690.50 (1) and (3); see People v. Gomez, 193 A.D.2d 882, 597 N.Y.S.2d 815 (3d Dep't 1993)(police could forcibly open door after identifying themselves and announcing they had search warrant because defendant said he had lost his key).

109. CPL § 690.50(1) and (3).

§ 10.5 SEARCH WARRANTS & SUPPRESSION Ch. 10

arrives even if the occupant consents to their entry.[110] Once a court issues a warrant, however, the police may enter the premises without possessing the warrant.[111]

The Legislature has established a protocol enabling the police to enter, unannounced, the place designated in the warrant. Under this "no-knock" provision, the police need not give notice when the premises are unoccupied or the police "reasonably believe" them to be unoccupied, or if the judge expressly authorizes unnoticed entry.[112] To obtain a "no-knock" warrant, the applicant must demonstrate "reasonable cause to believe" that the property sought may be easily and quickly destroyed or disposed of, or that by giving notice the life or safety of the executing officer or another person may be endangered.[113] Since the issuance of a valid "no-knock" warrant means that the police have made a sufficient showing that danger may await them during execution of the warrant, when they execute a valid "no-knock" warrant in premises used to sell drugs, they may frisk the renter of the premises for weapons to protect themselves from harm "in this violence-prone environment."[114]

A warrant authorizing unannounced entry must contain that authorization.[115] A "no-knock" warrant is valid, despite failure to comply with these statutory requirements, if the police did not use the "no-knock" procedure.[116] But failure to comply with these constraints will result in suppression when the police enter unannounced.[117]

Besides being obligated to give notice, the police are also limited as to when they can execute the warrant. A search warrant may be executed on any day of the week but only between the hours of 6:00 a.m. and 9:00 p.m.[118] The typical warrant to be executed between these hours must still contain "a direction" stating this.[119] A search begun before 9 o'clock at night may be continued after that time.[120]

By alleging facts supporting a nighttime or "all hours" search, the police may request that the warrant authorize execution at any time if there is "reasonable cause to believe" that it cannot be executed between

---

110. People v. Okun, 135 A.D.2d 1064, 522 N.Y.S.2d 991 (3d Dep't 1987); People v. Carson, 99 A.D.2d 664, 472 N.Y.S.2d 68 (4th Dep't 1984); see People v. Mahoney, 58 N.Y.2d 475, 462 N.Y.S.2d 410, 448 N.E.2d 1321 (1983)(execution proper because police, after entering, waited for the warrant before searching).

111. People v. Mahoney, supra; People v. Mikolasko, 144 A.D.2d 760, 535 N.Y.S.2d 167 (3d Dep't 1988).

112. CPL § 690.50(2)(a) and (b); People v. Mahoney, 58 N.Y.2d 475, 462 N.Y.S.2d 410, 448 N.E.2d 1321 (1983).

113. CPL § 690.35(4)(b); see also CPL § 690.40(2). A State University peace officer may also apply for a no-knock warrant. CPL § 690.35(4)(b).

Cf. People v. Clinton, 59 A.D.2d 854, 399 N.Y.S.2d 131 (1st Dep't 1977) (more than 100 pounds of narcotics did not justify "no-knock" warrant because it was not easily disposable) with People v. Brown, 46 A.D.2d 590, 364 N.Y.S.2d 512 (1st Dep't 1975)(guns in the apartment demonstrated necessity for no-knock warrant).

114. People v. Soler, 92 A.D.2d 280, 285, 460 N.Y.S.2d 537, 540 (1st Dep't 1983).

115. CPL § 690.45(7). This stated authorization requirement also applies to no-knock warrants issued to State University peace officers. Id.

116. People v. Parliman, 56 A.D.2d 966, 393 N.Y.S.2d 94 (3d Dep't 1977).

117. People v. Izzo, 50 A.D.2d 905, 377 N.Y.S.2d 558 (2d Dep't 1975).

118. CPL § 690.30(2).

119. CPL § 690.45(6).

120. People v. Vara, 117 A.D.2d 1013, 499 N.Y.S.2d 296 (4th Dep't 1986).

6:00 a.m. and 9:00 p.m. or if the property sought will be removed or destroyed if not seized "forthwith."[121] If the judge grants the request, the warrant must contain "a direction" that it be executed at any time of the day or night.[122] The absence of an "all hours" application request, however, does not invalidate the warrant if it authorized an "all hours" search and an immediate search was reasonably necessary.[123] But if there is no basis for the any-time search and the warrant application does not allege a need for an any-time search, then the warrant is invalid.[124]

Library References:
West's Key No. Digests, Searches and Seizures ⚖141-160.

§ 10.6 Search Warrants—Extent of Search Allowed Under Proper Warrant

The search and its scope authorized by a proper warrant are limited by the terms of its authorization and do not include additional or different places, or places that are unlikely to contain the property sought.[125] For example, a warrant to search for stolen air conditioners

---

121. CPL §§ 690.30(2), 690.35(4)(a); see People v. Arnau, 58 N.Y.2d 27, 457 N.Y.S.2d 763, 444 N.E.2d 13 (1982)(reasonable cause to believe that a 24-hour warrant was necessary since the warrant was signed at 8:30 p.m. and the defendant's apartment was a 30-minute drive from the courthouse); People v. Israel, 161 A.D.2d 730, 555 N.Y.S.2d 865 (2d Dep't 1990)("no knock" and "nighttime" entry reasonable because items sought—rods, staffs, a wooden statue, and containers of hot sauce—could be readily destroyed or disposed of); People v. Harrison, 122 A.D.2d 223, 505 N.Y.S.2d 3 (2d Dep't 1986)(issuance of extended hours search warrant was justified because the targeted property, drugs, could be easily removed or destroyed); People v. Crispell, 110 A.D.2d 926, 927, 487 N.Y.S.2d 174, 175 (3d Dep't 1985)(informant's tip that drugs would be imminently removed from apartment justified all-hours warrant); People v. Brown, 46 A.D.2d 590, 591, 364 N.Y.S.2d 512, 512 (1st Dep't 1975)(warrant application describing narcotics "mill" operation sufficient for issuance of all-hours warrant).

The all-hours warrant may also be requested when the search warrant is being used to search for the subject of an arrest warrant, see CPL § 690.05(2), and the person sought is likely to flee, commit another crime, or endanger the safety of the police executing the warrant or someone else "if not seized forthwith or between 9:00 p.m. and 6:00 a.m." CPL § 690.35(4)(a).

122. CPL §§ 690.45(6), 690.40(2); see People v. Eldridge, 173 A.D.2d 975, 569 N.Y.S.2d 482 (3d Dep't 1991)(warrant valid because transcript of warrant application indicated that judge authorized nighttime execution but officer inadvertently neglected to delete 6 a.m. to 9 p.m. restriction). Apparently, the last notation determines the validity of a nighttime warrant. Even though the "all hours" provision of a warrant was crossed out, it was still a valid nighttime warrant since the provision was subsequently circled, evincing the court's intention to make it an extended hours warrant. People v. Crispell, supra.

123. People v. Silverstein, 74 N.Y.2d 768, 545 N.Y.S.2d 86, 543 N.E.2d 729 (1989).

124. People v. Acevedo, 179 A.D.2d 813, 814, 579 N.Y.S.2d 156, 157 (2d Dep't 1992).

125. Walter v. United States, 447 U.S. 649, 656, 100 S.Ct. 2395, 2401, 65 L.Ed.2d 410 (1980); People v. Green, 33 N.Y.2d 496, 354 N.Y.S.2d 933, 310 N.E.2d 533 (1974); People v. Holley, 56 A.D.2d 684, 391 N.Y.S.2d 482 (3d Dep't 1977); see also People v. Marshall, 13 N.Y.2d 28, 241 N.Y.S.2d 417, 191 N.E.2d 798 (1963)(warrant authorizing search of persons in "rear room and on premises" permitted search of basement storeroom because warrant elsewhere thrice recited that probable cause existed for the "premises").

Of course, the occupants of the premises to be searched can consent to a search broader than that authorized by the warrant. See People v. Reichbach, 131 A.D.2d 515, 515 N.Y.S.2d 891 (2d Dep't 1987)(after defendant voluntarily consented to police examining ledger book, they could seize it even though it was not designated in the warrant); People v. Horton, 32 A.D.2d 707,

§ 10.6 SEARCH WARRANTS & SUPPRESSION Ch. 10

would not authorize the opening of dresser drawers,[126] but a warrant to search for cocaine, drug paraphernalia, and currency did allow the search of a safe in a bedroom closet.[127] The police may seize items not specified in the warrant if it authorizes seizure of that type of property.[128] A warrant naming a specific place and persons to be searched does not confer authority to frisk, or to arrest, other people not named in the warrant who happen to be present when it is executed.[129]

---

300 N.Y.S.2d 15 (3d Dep't 1969)(police could search room "immediately adjacent" to defendant's apartment when warrant used terms "room" and "apartment" interchangeably and defendant took police to the room and never claimed that it was a separate apartment).

126. Walter v. United States, 447 U.S. at 657, 100 S.Ct. at 2401; see People v. Haas, 55 A.D.2d 683, 390 N.Y.S.2d 202 (2d Dep't 1976)(warrant authorizing search for "marijuana plants" did permit seizure of passport, an envelope containing coins, and documents, items which would not contain the plants); cf. People v. Sciacca, 45 N.Y.2d 122, 408 N.Y.S.2d 22, 379 N.E.2d 1153 (1978)(warrant to search a car did not authorize entry into garage, where the car was parked, to effectuate the search) with People v. Powers, 173 A.D.2d 886, 887–88, 570 N.Y.S.2d 362, 363–64 (3d Dep't 1991)(warrant authorizing search of garage permitted search of car, in the garage, as a container that might hold items sought in warrant).

Previously, the police could not seize items of potential evidentiary value beyond those authorized in the warrant itself. Marron v. United States, 275 U.S. 192, 48 S.Ct. 74, 72 L.Ed. 231 (1927); People v. Baker, 23 N.Y.2d 307, 296 N.Y.S.2d 745, 244 N.E.2d 232 (1968); People v. Dwork, 116 Misc.2d 411, 453 N.Y.S.2d 319 (Nassau Co.Ct.1982). The validity of Baker's prohibition against seizure of "mere evidence" is doubtful after Coolidge v. New Hampshire, 403 U.S. 443, 91 S.Ct. 2022, 29 L.Ed.2d 564 (1971) and Chimel v. California, 395 U.S. 752, 89 S.Ct. 2034, 23 L.Ed.2d 685 (1969), which permitted the seizure of "mere evidence" in plain view. See People v. Neulist, 43 A.D.2d 150, 350 N.Y.S.2d 178 (2d Dep't 1973). Nevertheless, one appellate court recently cited Baker in concluding that the seizure of "buy money" while executing a warrant authorizing a search for drugs was improper. People v. Farmer, 198 A.D.2d 805, 604 N.Y.S.2d 391 (4th Dep't 1993).

127. People v. Padilla, 132 A.D.2d 578, 517 N.Y.S.2d 299 (2d Dep't 1987).

128. See People v. Lawrence, 166 A.D.2d 164, 563 N.Y.S.2d 794 (1st Dep't 1990)(while defendant's pants were not specified in the warrant, it was clear from other items specified and from the affidavit in support of the warrant that it authorized seizure of defendant's clothing worn on day of homicide); People v. Sargeant, 128 A.D.2d 914, 512 N.Y.S.2d 570 (3d Dep't 1987)(warrant authorizing seizure of "bailing twine" permitted the recovery of a shoelace because complainant's supporting affidavit described the item as "rope like" baling twine); People v. Rhoades, 126 A.D.2d 774, 510 N.Y.S.2d 718 (3d Dep't 1987)(police could obtain fingernail scrapings from defendant pursuant to executing warrant for "scratches, cuts, bruises, blood and hair to be found on [the defendant]"); cf. People v. Smith, 138 A.D.2d 932, 526 N.Y.S.2d 682 (4th Dep't 1988)(police could not seize defendant's clothing because warrant authorized, inter alia, "soiled men's clothing" without further specifying type, color, size, or ownership and warrant application did not establish that clothing sought was connected with criminal activity).

129. Ybarra v. Illinois, 444 U.S. 85, 100 S.Ct. 338, 62 L.Ed.2d 238 (1979)(cannot frisk others); Barr v. Albany County, 50 N.Y.2d 247, 253, 428 N.Y.S.2d 665, 668, 406 N.E.2d 481 (1980)(cannot arrest others); see People v. Nieves, 36 N.Y.2d 396, 369 N.Y.S.2d 50, 330 N.E.2d 26 (1975). Therefore, CPL § 690.15(2), which provides that a search warrant for a place or vehicle also allows a search of "any" person "present thereat or therein," may be unconstitutional. Despite this provision, the warrant must also specifically describe the person to be searched, see Ybarra v. Illinois, supra, and the application underlying the warrant must demonstrate probable cause for the search of that person. People v. Nieves, supra; but see People v. Abernathy, 175 A.D.2d 407, 572 N.Y.S.2d 478 (3d Dep't 1991)(warrant to search defendant's girlfriend's apartment authorized search of girlfriend and "anyone found in the apartment during execution" of the warrant permitted search of defendant even though he was not named in the warrant).

Ybarra and Nieves, however, may only apply to premises designated open to the public. A search authorized under CPL

After the property is seized, the police (or State University peace officer) must "write and subscribe a receipt itemizing the property taken," and give it to the person who possessed the property or leave it with the owner, tenant, or other possessor of the premises or vehicle searched.[130] Then the warrant, the seized property, and a written inventory of the property must be returned to the issuing court "without unnecessary delay." [131] Again, these are considered "ministerial" duties and the failure to comply with them will not invalidate the warrant.[132]

When the police return the recovered property to the issuing court, that court must retain the property until the court where the case is being prosecuted requests the property.[133] Alternatively, the court may direct that the warrant applicant, the officer who executed the warrant, or the governmental body employing the executing officer hold it until the issuing court, or the court where the prosecution resides, requests it.[134] The rightful owner of seized property that is not contraband may regain possession of it pursuant to the procedure set forth in Penal Law § 450.10 before the prosecution is terminated or through the common law action of replevin after the prosecution is completed.[135]

Library References:
West's Key No. Digests, Searches and Seizures ⚖147–149.

§ 10.7 Suppression Proceedings—Introduction

The Warren Court precipitated a revolution in criminal procedure when it determined that evidence obtained through a violation of a criminal defendant's constitutional rights is inadmissible in a state court prosecution.[136] Because of that rule, a typical prosecution no longer

---

§ 690.15(2) was sanctioned because the issuing magistrate could reasonably infer that a basement apartment was the scene of ongoing illegal activity, unlikely to contain innocent bystanders, and that there was a substantial likelihood that anyone present was a participant. People v. Betts, 90 A.D.2d 641, 642, 456 N.Y.S.2d 278, 279 (3d Dep't 1982); see People v. Miner, 126 A.D.2d 798, 800, 510 N.Y.S.2d 300, 302 (3d Dep't 1987)(warrant authorizing search of "persons" was validly issued because the targeted place was residential premises being used for drug sales).

130. CPL § 690.50(4).

131. CPL § 690.50(5). If the search warrant is used to arrest the subject of an arrest warrant pursuant to CPL § 690.05(2)(b), the officer must file a subscribed and sworn statement that the person has been arrested and has been brought to the court that issued the arrest warrant, then return the search warrant, any property recovered, and a subscribed and sworn inventory of the recovered property to the issuing court. CPL § 690.50(6).

132. People v. Camarre, 171 A.D.2d 1003, 569 N.Y.S.2d 224, 225 (4th Dep't 1991)(return requirement is "ministerial" and "even relatively lengthy delays" will not invalidate a properly executed warrant); People v. Earl, 138 A.D.2d 839, 525 N.Y.S.2d 952 (3d Dep't 1988)(same); People v. Morgan, 162 A.D.2d 723, 558 N.Y.S.2d 88 (2d Dep't 1990)(failure to provide a receipt does not invalidate warrant); People v. Hernandez, 131 A.D.2d 509, 516 N.Y.S.2d 254 (2d Dep't 1987)(warrant survives failure to return it in a timely manner); People v. Davis, 93 A.D.2d 970, 971, 463 N.Y.S.2d 67, 69 (3d Dep't 1983)(failure to return a written inventory does not invalidate the warrant).

133. CPL § 690.55(1) and (2).

134. Id.

135. See Boyle v. Kelley, 42 N.Y.2d 88, 396 N.Y.S.2d 834, 365 N.E.2d 866 (1977).

136. See, e.g., Mapp v. Ohio, 367 U.S. 643, 81 S.Ct. 1684, 6 L.Ed.2d 1081 (1961); Jackson v. Denno, 378 U.S. 368, 84 S.Ct. 1774, 12 L.Ed.2d 908 (1964); United States v. Wade, 388 U.S. 218, 87 S.Ct. 1926, 18 L.Ed.2d 1149 (1967).

§ 10.7 SEARCH WARRANTS & SUPPRESSION Ch. 10

proceeds from the filing of an accusatory instrument directly to a determination of guilt or innocence. Rather, a suppression motion will quickly be made, alleging that evidence was improperly obtained. Thereafter, a preliminary "trial" will be held on the propriety of the methods used to gather the evidence, and improperly obtained evidence will be suppressed. The decision on the suppression motion will often determine the outcome of the entire prosecution, and indeed in many cases the suppression "defense" is the only viable one available to the defendant. As a result, no criminal law practitioner can afford to be unfamiliar with the rules governing suppression proceedings.

But those rules cannot be found in the decisions of the Supreme Court that inaugurated the revolution; for the most part those decisions did not address procedural issues.[137] Nor was the New York Legislature quick to define the procedures through which motions were to be made. In the 1960's, the Legislature did add sections to the Code of Criminal Procedure authorizing motions to suppress unlawfully seized physical evidence and illegally obtained confessions.[138] However, those provisions were fairly general. Until the adoption of the CPL, it was left to the Court of Appeals to prescribe procedures from time to time through which the lower courts should resolve defendants' motions to suppress evidence.[139]

Article 710 of the CPL was the Legislature's comprehensive response to the Warren Court's expansion of the exclusionary rule. The seven sections in Article 710 address (1) what evidence should be suppressed; (2) when and where suppression motions should be brought; (3) how suppression motions should be made; (4) how suppression motions should be resolved; and (5) how a suppression decision impacts on subsequent proceedings in the case.

The next 15 sections of this chapter will address, in the order just delineated, the rules set out in Article 710. In addition, the Legislature has required that notice be provided to the defense, early in a criminal proceeding, specifying what statement and identification evidence the prosecution intends to introduce at trial. The last seven sections of this chapter will separately discuss the special, and extremely important,

---

137. But see Jackson v. Denno, supra.

138. Before 1962, the Code authorized only one type of suppression hearing: a hearing to controvert a search warrant and require the return of seized property. Code Crim. Proc. §§ 807, 809. Section 395 provided that confessions would be inadmissible if coerced by threats or obtained on a promise of immunity, but no procedural mechanism for exploring the facts was provided. In 1962, provisions were added to govern motions to suppress evidence obtained in any type of unlawful search. Code Crim.Proc. §§ 813–c, 813–d, 813–e. In 1965, the Legislature provided for hearings on motions to suppress defendants' confessions and admissions. Code Crim. Proc. §§ 813–f, 813–g, 813–h, 813–i. In 1969, amendments authorized motions to suppress the fruits of illegal wiretapping. Code Crim.Proc. §§ 813–l, 813–m.

139. See, e.g., People v. Berrios, 28 N.Y.2d 361, 321 N.Y.S.2d 884, 270 N.E.2d 709 (1971)(motions to suppress physical evidence); People v. Whitehurst, 25 N.Y.2d 389, 306 N.Y.S.2d 673, 254 N.E.2d 905 (1969) (same); People v. Huntley, 15 N.Y.2d 72, 255 N.Y.S.2d 838, 204 N.E.2d 179 (1965)(motions to suppress statements); People v. Rahming, 26 N.Y.2d 411, 311 N.Y.S.2d 292, 259 N.E.2d 727 (1970)(motions to suppress identification testimony); People v. Ballott, 20 N.Y.2d 600, 286 N.Y.S.2d 1, 233 N.E.2d 103 (1967) (same).

rules that now attend the notice requirement. Notably, Article 710 is a quarter century old, and its provisions have been developed extensively in the many cases decided since the Article was adopted. The holdings of those decisions will be an integral part of the discussion of the statutory suppression procedures.

Finally, the proceeding sections of this chapter will not seek to explain the "substantive" law that governs suppression decisions. Of course, it will occasionally be necessary, in explaining suppression procedures, to make general references to substantive legal principles. However, thorough exploration of substantive rules is beyond the scope of this book.

Library References:
West's Key No. Digests, Criminal Law ⚖394.1–394.6.

§ 10.8 Suppressible Evidence—In General

CPL § 710.20 authorizes a court to suppress evidence upon motion of a "defendant" who is "aggrieved" by the improper acquisition of that evidence. Suppression motions are often based on supposed violations of statutory or common-law principles,[140] and motions made on such theories presumably can be granted only if the defendant's theory is recognized in section 710.20. But, of course, if the federal or New York Constitution requires that evidence be suppressed on a theory not recognized in section 710.20, the Legislature's failure to recognize that theory would not prevent the defendant from obtaining relief. Accordingly, the statute must be considered to state only approximately the reach of the suppression sanction.

Section 710.20 provides for the suppression of these types of evidence:

1. tangible property obtained through an unlawful search;[141]

2. a record of, or testimony about, illegally intercepted conversations or illegal video surveillance;[142]

3. a record of, or testimony about, statements "involuntarily made" by a defendant, *i.e.* statements obtained through coercion, or otherwise in violation of the defendant's constitutional rights;[143]

4. chemical tests of a defendant's blood obtained in violation of section 1194(3) of the Vehicle and Traffic Law, section 49–a(8) of the Navigation Law, "or any other applicable law";[144]

5. a witness's identification evidence if that evidence is derived from a prior "improperly made" identification;[145]

---

140. See, e.g., People v. Hollman, 79 N.Y.2d 181, 195–96, 581 N.Y.S.2d 619, 627, 590 N.E.2d 204 (1992).

141. CPL § 710.20(1).

142. CPL § 710.20(2).

143. CPL § 710.20(3). The section incorporates the detailed definition of "involuntarily made" set out in CPL § 60.45.

144. CPL § 710.20(5).

145. CPL § 710.20(6).

§ 10.8   SEARCH WARRANTS & SUPPRESSION   Ch. 10

6. information obtained from a pen register, or a trap and trace device, in violation of CPL Article 705.[146]

The *"Mapp,"*[147] *"Huntley,"*[148] and *"Wade"*[149] motions familiar to every New York criminal law practitioner—motions intended to obtain the suppression of physical evidence acquired in illegal searches, of illegally obtained admissions, and of improper identification evidence—have been resolved on authority of section 710.20 since the CPL took effect in 1971. And since 1971, section 710.20(2) has authorized as well the suppression of evidence of conversations obtained through illegal "eavesdropping." Article 710 defines eavesdropping as "wiretapping" or the "mechanical overhearing of a conversation" within the meaning of section 250.00(1) and (2) of the Penal Law.

Some of the more interesting, if unheralded, developments in section 710.20 since 1971 have come with respect to subsection five. That provision, first added in 1983, authorizes suppression of the results of a chemical test of a defendant's blood if the test was made in violation of any rule set out in section 1194-a of the Vehicle and Traffic Law.[150] Five years later, when the VTL provisions were re-drafted and re-numbered, section 710.20 was amended to authorize suppression in much narrower circumstances than before.[151] The statute now authorizes suppression only when a test is made pursuant to VTL § 1194(3), the subdivision allowing courts to issue orders for the testing of blood. As a result, the tests that have been the most likely to engender litigation—those administered after the defendant gave express consent, or on a theory of implied consent within two hours of arrest[152]—apparently can no longer be challenged in CPL suppression proceedings.[153]

In 1988, the Legislature also showed its awareness of recent developments in investigative technology. In that year, CPL § 710.20(2) was amended to authorize the suppression, not only of conversations, but also of "other communications" intercepted electronically, such as communications to beepers.[154] At the same time, the Legislature provided

146. CPL § 710.20(7).

147. Mapp v. Ohio, 367 U.S. 643, 81 S.Ct. 1684, 6 L.Ed.2d 1081 (1961).

148. People v. Huntley, 15 N.Y.2d 72, 255 N.Y.S.2d 838, 204 N.E.2d 179 (1965).

149. United States v. Wade, 388 U.S. 218, 87 S.Ct. 1926, 18 L.Ed.2d 1149 (1967).

150. L.1983, c.481, §§ 2, 5.

151. L.1988, c.47, § 18.

152. See VTL § 1194(2).

153. This limitation seems not to be an accident. In CPL § 710.20(5), the limiting reference to VTL 1194(3) is express. The same limitation was placed in the parallel reference in section 710.20(5) to the Navigation Law, added in 1992. And the same limitation appears in the complementary exclusionary provision of VTL § 1195(3), first added in 1988. To date, the 1988 amendment has received scant attention in the case law, and its full effects are therefore still to be determined. But too much should not be made of it. A defendant who articulates a colorable constitutional objection to any chemical test presumably is entitled to litigate the issue. Further, in VTL cases some judges permit defendants to litigate their challenges under VTL § 1195(1), which renders admissible only the results of chemical tests "administered pursuant" to VTL § 1194. Still, such defendants lose certain advantages that inhere in suppression procedures, such as the right to appeal an unfavorable ruling after a guilty plea.

154. L.1988, c.744, § 24.

for the suppression of evidence obtained by means of video surveillance[155] and, in a new section 710.20(7), of evidence obtained either from illegally employed pen registers or illegally employed "trap and trace" devices.[156] This 1988 amendment was designed in part to address the ability of law enforcement officials (and others) to seek information through methods not foreseen when the CPL was passed in 1970.[157]

Three final notes should be made on the scope of section 710.20. First, under the section only a "defendant" can move to suppress, and a "defendant" is a person who has been charged in an accusatory instrument.[158] An individual who has not been charged with a crime, but seeks the return of property or some other relief on account of illegal action by the authorities, must pursue a civil remedy. Second, in general, only a defendant "aggrieved" by the unlawful acquisition of evidence can obtain suppression of that evidence;[159] the relevant standing principles are discussed in § 10.11, *infra*. Third, a motion to suppress evidence pursuant to section 710.20 cannot properly be brought or granted on the theory that evidence has been fabricated, or that the defendant is not guilty. With respect to a confession, for example, the court cannot suppress because it does not believe that the confession was made. The court must assume that the confession was made, and suppress only if it believes that the confession was illegally obtained.[160]

In short, subdivisions one through three and subdivisions five through seven of section 710.20 provide a helpful approximation of what evidence a defendant can move to suppress in New York. Also significant, though not yet discussed, is subdivision four of section 710.20. That subdivision provides for the exclusion of certain "fruits evidence," *i.e.*, evidence that was derived from other, improperly obtained evidence. The implications of the limited provisions concerning derivative evidence are discussed in the next section.

Library References:

West's Key No. Digests, Criminal Law ⇐339.5–339.11, 394.1–394.6, 412–414.

§ 10.9 Suppressible Evidence—Indirect Fruits

Since its enactment, section 710.20 has effectively been split in two by its subdivision four. Subdivision four provides that evidence may be suppressed if it "[w]as obtained as a result of other evidence obtained in a manner described in subdivisions one, two and three." A court may suppress evidence indirectly derived from (1) an illegal search and

---

155. L.1988, c.744, § 24; cf. People v. Teicher, 52 N.Y.2d 638, 439 N.Y.S.2d 846, 422 N.E.2d 506 (1981).

156. L.1988, c.744, § 25.

157. See generally L.1988, c.744; see also Marcus, "The New State Law on Eavesdropping and Other Forms of Surveillance," N.Y.L.J, 12/23/88, p. 1.

158. CPL § 710.10(1). See also Rakas v. Illinois, 439 U.S. 128, 132–33, n.2, 99 S.Ct. 421, 424, n.2, 58 L.Ed.2d 387 (1978).

159. CPL § 710.20.

160. People v. Washington, 51 N.Y.2d 214, 433 N.Y.S.2d 745, 413 N.E.2d 1159 (1980); see also People v. Johnson, 83 N.Y.2d 831, 611 N.Y.S.2d 496, 633 N.E.2d 1100 (1994)(Mapp motion).

§ 10.9 SEARCH WARRANTS & SUPPRESSION Ch. 10

seizure; (2) illegal eavesdropping or video surveillance; or (3) illegal interrogation of the defendant.

Defendants obtain very limited benefits from subdivision four. The indirect fruits of a "subconstitutional" infringement on a defendant's liberty,[161] or of a statement that was illegally obtained solely by virtue of a statute and not the constitution,[162] might be suppressible only because of subdivision four. Generally, however, a defendant who seeks suppression under subdivision one, two or three complains of a violation of constitutional rights, and even without subdivision four that defendant would be constitutionally entitled to the suppression of evidence indirectly derived from the violation.[163] That constitutional entitlement is not absolute, for the taint of the illegality can be attenuated.[164] However, subdivision four has not been interpreted to authorize suppression without consideration of these same attenuation principles.[165]

Arguably, therefore, the true significance of section 710.20(4) lies in its plain indication that the Legislature did not intend traditional "derivative fruits" analysis to apply when one of the final three subdivisions of section 710.20 is violated. In that regard, section 710.20(4) makes no provision for suppressing the derivative fruits with respect to subdivision five (concerning illegal court-ordered blood tests), subdivision six (concerning improper identifications), or subdivision seven (concerning pen registers and trap and trace devices used in violation of CPL Article 705).

At the same time, nothing significant attends the failure of subdivision four to mention subdivision six, and thereby deal with the indirect fruits of illegally obtained identification evidence. When the CPL was adopted, subdivision six (then subdivision five) was the only part of section 710.20 that was not made subject to the derivative fruits principles of subdivision four. The drafters must have believed it significant that identification testimony receive separate treatment, but they included in subdivision six itself a similar principle. Under subdivision six, potential testimony from a witness about an observation of the defendant is suppressible if it would not be admissible at trial owing to an improperly made identification of the defendant by that witness. When that somewhat circular provision is parsed, the result is, as the constitution requires, that identification testimony will be suppressed if it is either the direct or the indirect fruit of an improper identification.[166] True, there is no statutory authority for the suppression of non-identification evidence obtained as a direct or indirect result of an improper identification procedure. But it is rare for a defendant to complain that

---

161. People v. Hollman, 79 N.Y.2d 181, 195, 581 N.Y.S.2d 619, 627, 590 N.E.2d 204 (1992).

162. See, e.g., Family Court Act § 305.2 (interrogation of juveniles).

163. See, e.g., Wong Sun v. United States, 371 U.S. 471, 83 S.Ct. 407, 9 L.Ed.2d 441 (1963).

164. See, e.g., United States v. Ceccolini, 435 U.S. 268, 98 S.Ct. 1054, 55 L.Ed.2d 268 (1978).

165. See, e.g., People v. Arnau, 58 N.Y.2d 27, 457 N.Y.S.2d 763, 444 N.E.2d 13 (1982).

166. See United States v. Wade, 388 U.S. 218, 239–41, 87 S.Ct. 1926, 1938–39, 18 L.Ed.2d 1149 (1967).

non-identification evidence was derived from an improper identification procedure. In any event, if non-identification evidence should be obtained as a result of a constitutionally improper identification procedure, the defendant would, subject to attenuation principles, presumably be constitutionally entitled to the suppression of that derivative evidence even in the absence of relevant language in subdivision four or six.

With respect to section 710.20(5), which deals with the suppression of the results of illegal court-ordered blood tests, the analysis is different. Unlike subdivision six, subdivision five contains no language extending its reach beyond the direct fruits of illegal conduct. Court-ordered chemical tests of a defendant's blood conducted pursuant to VTL § 1194(3) may of course be challenged on Fourth Amendment grounds, such as the absence of probable cause.[167] Should there be indirect fruits of a Fourth Amendment violation, they will be suppressible with or without statutory provisions to that effect. But other attacks on court-ordered blood tests will be based on purely statutory grounds, and as to such attacks the Legislature may limit the suppression sanction as it sees fit. Section 710.20 provides a defendant with no remedy for the acquisition of evidence as the indirect result of a court-ordered blood test when that test is conducted in violation of VTL § 1194(3), but not of any constitutional provision.

Of course, once again, it is a rare case in which a court-ordered blood test yields any but direct fruit. Perhaps more importantly, therefore, no remedy is provided by section 710.20 to a defendant who is aggrieved by the indirect acquisition of evidence as a consequence of the use of a pen register, or a trap and trace device, in violation of CPL Article 705. Article 705 was enacted in the wake of court decisions holding that the use of a device like a pen register that reveals only which telephone makes calls to another telephone does not intrude on any legitimate expectation of privacy, and therefore is not a search within the meaning of the Fourth Amendment that would require court authorization.[168] In the Article, the Legislature imposed restrictions on the use of pen registers and trap and trace devices, including a requirement that they be authorized by court order, but made those restrictions less stringent that those that apply to eavesdropping.

Because these restrictions on the use of pen registers and trap and trace devices are purely statutory in origin, the scope of the suppression sanction will likewise be solely that provided by statute. The addition of subdivision seven to section 710.20 makes plain that a court may suppress evidence directly obtained from a pen register or trap and trace device that was not installed in accordance with Article 705. But subdivision four was not amended to authorize the suppression of the indirect fruits of a violation of Article 705, and therefore the defendant

---

167. See People v. Moselle, 57 N.Y.2d 97, 454 N.Y.S.2d 292, 439 N.E.2d 1235 (1982); Matter of Abe A., 56 N.Y.2d 288, 452 N.Y.S.2d 6, 437 N.E.2d 265 (1982).

168. Smith v. Maryland, 442 U.S. 735, 99 S.Ct. 2577, 61 L.Ed.2d 220 (1979); People v. Guerra, 65 N.Y.2d 60, 489 N.Y.S.2d 718, 478 N.E.2d 1319 (1985); see also People v. Bialostok, 80 N.Y.2d 738, 594 N.Y.S.2d 701, 610 N.E.2d 374 (1993).

§ 10.9   SEARCH WARRANTS & SUPPRESSION   Ch. 10

aggrieved by the acquisition of such evidence is left without a remedy. As indicated by the Governor's approval memorandum, the decision to authorize suppression only of evidence directly produced by a violation of Article 705 was purposeful.[169]

In this instance, the Legislature's choice is most significant. While a pen register or trap and trace device can yield relevant and admissible evidence, investigators frequently use the information obtained from such devices to take other investigative steps that produce far more damning evidence.[170] It will do a defendant little good to obtain suppression of a pen register record showing that he spoke to an accomplice, if eavesdropping tapes of the defendant's subsequent incriminating conversations with that accomplice will be admissible even though the eavesdropping order was obtained with the aid of the tainted pen register results.

At the same time, one key attack on the use of pen registers will likely be unaffected by the failure to provide in section 710.20(4) and (7) for the suppression of indirect fruits. In *People v. Bialostok*, the Court of Appeals determined that some supposedly advanced types of pen registers are eavesdropping devices subject to the restrictions of CPL Article 700, even if they are not used to overhear conversations, simply because they are capable of intercepting conversations.[171] In *Bialostok*, the police did not comply with Article 700 before using such a pen register, and the court found that this failure tainted the evidence obtained from the pen register. More importantly for purposes of this discussion, the court also concluded that the taint extended to evidence obtained through court-ordered eavesdropping based in part on the pen register information.[172] The *Bialostok* investigation had been conducted before 1988, and the court therefore had no reason to analyze the failure to provide in 1988 for the suppression of the indirect fruits of the unlawful use of a pen register. But the court's analysis would in any event seem to make section 710.20(2), rather than section 710.20(7), the controlling statute if a pen register is capable of intercepting conversations, and of course the indirect fruits of a violation of subdivision two are suppressible.

Library References:
West's Key No. Digests, Criminal Law ⚍394.1(3), 412(4), 537.

§ 10.10   Suppressible Evidence—Attenuation

Attenuation principles limit the reach of suppression sanctions, whether those sanctions are constitutionally or statutorily based. In

---

[169]. L.1988, c.744, Governor's Approval Memorandum, 1988 New York State Legislative Annual, p. 299.

[170]. See, e.g., People v. Bialostok, 80 N.Y.2d at 745, 594 N.Y.S.2d at 705.

[171]. The prosecution questioned on technical grounds the court's assumption that the pen register at issue was more advanced than other pen registers, but did so too late to affect the decision of the Bialostok case itself. People v. Bialostok, 81 N.Y.2d 995, 599 N.Y.S.2d 532, 615 N.E.2d 1016 (1993).

[172]. At the same time, the court found that the untainted evidence in the eavesdropping application was by itself sufficient to sustain the application, and that the inclusion of the information derived from the pen register was harmless. 80 N.Y.2d at 745–46, 594 N.Y.S.2d at 705.

general, the attenuation doctrine recognizes that the exclusion of evidence not directly related to police illegality may be too high a price to impose on society in response to such illegality; only if the evidence is realistically the product of "exploitation" of the illegality should it be suppressed.[173]

Thus, evidence will not be suppressed on account of illegal investigative conduct if circumstances preceding the discovery of the evidence have effectively "dissipated" the illegality. For example, in *People v. Dentine*,[174] the police discovered the identity of a witness as a result of an illegal search; that witness's subsequent live testimony was held not to be sufficiently the product of the search to justify its suppression.[175] In *People v. Townes*,[176] after the police unlawfully ordered the defendant to stop, the defendant drew a handgun and attempted to fire it at the police. The defendant's improper actions attenuated the taint of the illegal seizure, and the gun was not suppressed. In *Johnson v. Louisiana*,[177] the Supreme Court concluded that arraignment served to attenuate the taint of an illegal arrest. And a defendant whose identity is discovered because of illegal police action cannot obtain suppression of his or her identity, and effective immunity from prosecution.[178]

Two important variants on these typical attenuation scenarios should be noted. In its original formulation, the independent source doctrine permitted the use of information that was illegally obtained when the same information is in fact located in a second and legal way that is independent of the illegal action.[179] The concept has more recently been applied by the New York Court of Appeals in a more problematic context—when specific objects of physical evidence like contraband, rather than information, are at issue. In *People v. Arnau*,[180] for example, a police officer purchased cocaine in the defendant's apartment, and an application for a search warrant was prepared. Before the warrant was obtained, however, other officers entered the apartment, arrested the defendant, and "froze" the scene. The Court of Appeals

---

173. United States v. Ceccolini, 435 U.S. 268, 98 S.Ct. 1054, 55 L.Ed.2d 268 (1978); Wong Sun v. United States, 371 U.S. 471, 488, 83 S.Ct. 407, 417, 9 L.Ed.2d 441 (1963); Nardone v. United States, 308 U.S. 338, 60 S.Ct. 266, 84 L.Ed. 307 (1939); People v. Arnau, 58 N.Y.2d 27, 32, 457 N.Y.S.2d 763, 765, 444 N.E.2d 13 (1982).

174. 27 A.D.2d 139, 276 N.Y.S.2d 963 (1st Dep't), aff'd without opinion 21 N.Y.2d 700, 287 N.Y.S.2d 427, 234 N.E.2d 462 (1967). In subsequently granting a motion to amend the remittitur, the Court of Appeals expressly stated that it had agreed that the taint of the illegality had been attenuated. 21 N.Y.2d 971, 971–72, 290 N.Y.S.2d 199, 237 N.E.2d 361 (1968). See also People v. Mendez, 28 N.Y.2d 94, 320 N.Y.S.2d 39, 268 N.E.2d 778 (1971); People v. Pleasant, 54 N.Y.2d 972, 446 N.Y.S.2d 29, 430 N.E.2d 905 (1981), cert. den. 455 U.S. 924, 102 S.Ct. 1285, 71 L.Ed.2d 466 (1982).

175. See also United States v. Ceccolini, 435 U.S. 268, 98 S.Ct. 1054, 55 L.Ed.2d 268 (1978); Michigan v. Tucker, 417 U.S. 433, 450–51, 94 S.Ct. 2357, 2367, 41 L.Ed.2d 182 (1974).

176. 41 N.Y.2d 97, 390 N.Y.S.2d 893, 359 N.E.2d 402 (1976).

177. 406 U.S. 356, 365, 92 S.Ct. 1620, 1626, 32 L.Ed.2d 152 (1972). See also People v. Pleasant, 54 N.Y.2d at 973–74, 466 N.Y.S.2d at 30–31.

178. United States v. Crews, 445 U.S. 463, 474, 100 S.Ct. 1244, 1251, 63 L.Ed.2d 537 (1980). See People v. Pleasant, 54 N.Y.2d at 974, 446 N.Y.S.2d at 31.

179. Silverthorne Lumber Co. v. United States, 251 U.S. 385, 40 S.Ct. 182, 64 L.Ed. 319 (1920).

180. 58 N.Y.2d 27, 457 N.Y.S.2d 763, 444 N.E.2d 13 (1982).

§ 10.10   SEARCH WARRANTS & SUPPRESSION   Ch. 10

assumed that this entry was unlawful, but held that, because no search was conducted until the warrant arrived, the evidence was discovered through a source independent of the illegality. In reality, of course, there was but one "source" of the evidence, the search that uncovered it.[181]

The original understanding of the independent source doctrine still applies with respect to identification testimony. A witness whose testimony about an unduly suggestive identification proceeding is suppressed may nevertheless identify the defendant at trial, if that witness plainly can base his trial identification on independently obtained "information"—observations of the defendant that were made prior to, and thus independent of, the suggestive proceeding.[182] The original understanding of the doctrine applies as well when a defendant claims that the fruits of immunized testimony have been used against him.[183]

Closely related to the independent source rule is the inevitable discovery doctrine. That doctrine applies when illegal police conduct provides a link in a chain of circumstances culminating in the discovery of evidence, but a distinct path to that evidence could have been located, and but for the illegal step likely would have been located. More precisely, evidence located as the indirect result of illegal conduct will not be suppressed if there is a "very high degree of probability" that it would have been found in another way had the illegal conduct never occurred.[184] Thus, in *People v. Payton*,[185] a gun dealer who sold the murder weapon to the defendant was located because a receipt from the sale was discovered during an illegal intrusion into the defendant's apartment. The gun dealer's testimony was not subject to suppression despite the illegal source of the information, because it was highly probable that the police would have located the gun dealer in the normal course of the investigation.[186] In *Nix v. Williams*,[187] the victim's body was in fact located because of a statement by the defendant that was taken in violation of his right to counsel. However, the evidence was not suppressed because a search for the body had been underway, and the body would soon have been located.

---

181. The situation in Arnau could perhaps more helpfully have been analyzed as one in which an illegal entry uncovered no evidence until after the illegality was attenuated by the independent arrival of a warrant, rather than as one in which there were two "independent sources" for evidence. See Murray v. United States, 487 U.S. 533, 537–39, 108 S.Ct. 2529, 2533–34, 101 L.Ed.2d 472 (1988).

182. Gilbert v. California, 388 U.S. 263, 87 S.Ct. 1951, 18 L.Ed.2d 1178 (1967); People v. Ballott, 20 N.Y.S.2d 600, 606–07, 286 N.Y.S.2d 1, 5–6, 233 N.E.2d 103 (1967).

183. Kastigar v. United States, 406 U.S. 441, 460–61, 92 S.Ct. 1653, 1664–65, 32 L.Ed.2d 212 (1972); Murphy v. Waterfront Commission of New York Harbor, 378 U.S. 52, 79, 84 S.Ct. 1594, 1609, 12 L.Ed.2d 678 (1964).

184. People v. Payton, 45 N.Y.2d 300, 313–14, 408 N.Y.S.2d 395, 401–02, 380 N.E.2d 224 (1978), rev'd on other grounds 445 U.S. 573, 100 S.Ct. 1371, 63 L.Ed.2d 639 (1980).

185. Id.

186. The court noted the possibility that the testimony would have been admissible as well under the "live witness" attenuation theory. 45 N.Y.2d at 314 n.6, 408 N.Y.S.2d at 402 n.6.

187. 467 U.S. 431, 104 S.Ct. 2501, 81 L.Ed.2d 377 (1984).

Notably, in New York the inevitable discovery doctrine can save only "secondary," or derivative, evidence, and not the "primary" evidence that is directly produced by the illegal conduct.[188] Thus, in *Payton* the inevitable discovery principle could render admissible the testimony of the gun dealer, but not the receipt discovered in Payton's apartment. The same distinction between primary and secondary evidence exists with respect to New York's application of the independent source doctrine.[189]

As to statement evidence, traditional attenuation analysis is employed to determine whether a defendant's admissions are tainted by an illegal arrest.[190] But a special variant of that analysis applies when the defendant makes a statement that must be suppressed on any theory, and the court must determine whether to suppress as well a subsequent statement not directly tainted by the same illegality. If as a matter of fact the defendant made the second admission because of the first—because "the cat was out of the bag"—then the second statement is too much the product of the first to be admissible.[191] However, at least where the defendant has testified at the suppression hearing, he cannot rely on a "cat out of the bag" theory if his own testimony does not establish that he made the second statement because he had made the first.[192] And the theory is unavailable as well where the differing content of the two statements itself establishes that the second was not made under influence of the first.[193]

Another variant of attenuation principles relevant to statements is the "continuous interrogation" principle enunciated in *People v. Chapple*.[194] *Chapple* holds that an illegal interrogation process is not suddenly cured as soon as the interrogators begin to follow proper procedures, such as the giving of *Miranda* warnings. If, however, "there is such a definite, pronounced break in the interrogation that the defendant may be said to have returned, in effect, to the status of one who is not under

---

188. Compare People v. Stith, 69 N.Y.2d 313, 514 N.Y.S.2d 201, 506 N.E.2d 911 (1987) with Murray v. United States, 487 U.S. 533, 540–41, 108 S.Ct. 2529, 2534–35, 101 L.Ed.2d 472 (1988); see also People v. Knapp, 52 N.Y.2d 689, 697–98, 439 N.Y.S.2d 871, 875–76, 422 N.E.2d 531 (1981).

189. See People v. Burr, 70 N.Y.2d 354, 361–63, 520 N.Y.S.2d 739, 742–43, 514 N.E.2d 1363 (1987). This analysis is somewhat artificial, for if there were in the original sense an independent source for information, then the "primary" and "secondary" distinction applicable in inevitable discovery analysis would not be relevant. But that distinction is necessary in light of the application of the independent source rubric to cases, like Arnau and Burr, in which the recovery of specific items of evidence rather than information is at issue. See footnote 181, supra. And the distinction is consistent with the rule, traditionally applied in New York identification cases, that an independent source for identification testimony will not the save the "primary" evidence obtained in a tainted identification proceeding, but will save subsequent identification testimony.

The United States Supreme Court has rejected New York's view that the independent source doctrine will not save "primary" evidence. Murray v. United States, 487 U.S. at 540–41, 108 S.Ct. at 2529.

190. See, e.g., Brown v. Illinois, 422 U.S. 590, 95 S.Ct. 2254, 45 L.Ed.2d 416 (1975).

191. People v. Tanner, 30 N.Y.2d 102, 105–06, 331 N.Y.S.2d 1, 3, 282 N.E.2d 98 (1972).

192. Id.

193. See, e.g., People v. Marino, 135 A.D.2d 573, 521 N.Y.S.2d 791 (2d Dep't 1987).

194. 38 N.Y.2d 112, 378 N.Y.S.2d 682, 341 N.E.2d 243 (1975).

§ 10.10 SEARCH WARRANTS & SUPPRESSION Ch. 10

the influence of questioning," the subsequent statements may be admissible.[195] The federal courts no longer follow the underlying rule that late *Miranda* warnings are insufficient by themselves to undo the effect of prior interrogation, but that rule remains the law in New York.[196] Nonetheless, the "pronounced break" test has not proved an impossible one for the prosecution to meet.[197]

Finally, it has long been the rule that suppression of evidence after it was used to obtain an indictment does not entitle the defendant to dismissal of the indictment.[198] Similarly, a defendant is not constitutionally entitled to make a suppression motion so as to prevent a grand jury from learning information that was wrongfully acquired.[199] Nor may a defendant who commits perjury or evasive contempt in the grand jury obtain a dismissal by complaining that the questions put to him or her in the grand jury were based on information that was illegally obtained.[200]

Library References:
West's Key No. Digests, Criminal Law ⚍394.1(3).

§ 10.11 Standing

As noted in the previous section, not every defendant can prevent illegally seized evidence from being introduced against him or her. However, the text of Article 710 contains little information about who may move to suppress the various types of evidence described in the seven subdivisions of section 710.20. The statute provides that a "defendant," one who has been charged in an accusatory instrument, may file a suppression motion.[201] The statute further provides that, except with respect to identification evidence, a defendant must have been "aggrieved" by the acquisition of the evidence to have standing to suppress that evidence.[202] But the CPL's definition of an "aggrieved person" is very much open-ended:

> An "aggrieved person" includes, but is in no wise limited to, an "aggrieved person" as defined in subdivision two of section forty-five hundred six of the civil practice law and rules.[203]

Accordingly, by far the better part of standing law is derived from the case law.

195. 30 N.Y.2d at 115, 378 N.Y.S.2d at 685–86.

196. Compare People v. Bethea, 67 N.Y.2d 364, 502 N.Y.S.2d 713, 493 N.E.2d 937 (1986) with Oregon v. Elstad, 470 U.S. 298, 105 S.Ct. 1285, 84 L.Ed.2d 222 (1985).

197. See, e.g., People v. Dunkley, 200 A.D.2d 499, 606 N.Y.S.2d 638 (1st Dep't 1994); People v. Nova, 198 A.D.2d 193, 603 N.Y.S.2d 863 (1st Dep't 1993); People v. Vientos, 164 A.D.2d 122, 127, 561 N.Y.S.2d 443, 446 (1st Dep't 1990), aff'd 79 N.Y.2d 771, 579 N.Y.S.2d 633, 587 N.E.2d 271 (1991); People v. Kern, 149 A.D.2d 187, 222, 545 N.Y.S.2d 4, 26 (2d Dep't 1989), aff'd 75 N.Y.2d 638, 555 N.Y.S.2d 647, 554 N.E.2d 1235 (1990).

198. People v. Oakley, 28 N.Y.2d 309, 321 N.Y.S.2d 596, 270 N.E.2d 318 (1971); People v. Kersch, 135 A.D.2d 570, 521 N.Y.S.2d 788 (2d Dep't 1987).

199. United States v. Calandra, 414 U.S. 338, 94 S.Ct. 613, 38 L.Ed.2d 561 (1974).

200. People v. McGrath, 46 N.Y.2d 12, 412 N.Y.S.2d 801, 385 N.E.2d 541 (1978).

201. CPL §§ 710.10(1), 710.20.

202. CPL § 710.20.

203. CPL § 710.10(5).

The statute incorporated by reference, CPLR 4506(2), is part of a rule that governs the admissibility of eavesdropping evidence in civil and criminal proceedings. It defines an "aggrieved person" as:

a. A person who was a sender or receiver of a telephonic or telegraphic communication that was intercepted without consent of any party through use of any device;

b. A party to a conversation which was overheard without consent of any party by means of any device;

c. A person against whom eavesdropping "was directed."

That definition of standing approximates the rule that is constitutionally required in the eavesdropping area. *Alderman v. United States*[204] recognizes that the parties to conversations that were overheard have standing, and the CPLR definition thus expressly extends standing to the parties of intercepted conversations. The constitutional rule goes further, however, for it accords standing as well to the owners of homes in which conversations were intercepted[205] and the owners of telephones that were wiretapped.[206] Only in granting protection to those at whom eavesdropping "was directed," rather than to these owners, is the statute not on its face coextensive with the constitutional rule.

And in fact even the statutory "was directed" terminology seems not to create a statutory standing rule that is broader than the constitutional rule. In that regard, this language was included in the CPLR when a new section 4506 was added in 1969,[207] as part of an effort to conform New York's eavesdropping law to federal law.[208] The "was directed" language had appeared in *Jones v. United States*,[209] a case involving a physical search. The language had been quoted with approval in *Alderman* earlier in 1969 when that case limited standing in eavesdropping cases to those who were overheard, or who owned the home in which the conversations took place.[210] The use of the identical language in the CPLR can only be read as an attempt to conform the CPLR provisions on standing to federal constitutional norms, and not as an effort to diverge from those norms. Further, the holdings of *Jones* and *Alderman*, and in particular of the subsequently-decided *Rakas v. Illinois*,[211] make plain that standing is not available as a matter of constitutional law to one at whom police investigation literally "was directed," but whose personal and legitimate expectations of privacy

---

204. 394 U.S. 165, 89 S.Ct. 961, 22 L.Ed.2d 176 (1969).

205. 394 U.S. at 176, 89 S.Ct. at 968.

206. People v. McDonnell, 18 N.Y.2d 509, 277 N.Y.S.2d 257, 223 N.E.2d 785 (1966).

207. L.1969, c.1147, § 8.

208. See Governor's Approval Memorandum, 90 New York State Legislative Annual, p. 586.

209. 362 U.S. 257, 80 S.Ct. 725, 4 L.Ed.2d 697 (1960). In Jones, the court stated (362 U.S. at 261, 80 S.Ct. at 731): In order to qualify as a "person aggrieved by an unlawful search and seizure," one must have been a victim of a search and seizure, *one against whom the search was directed*, as distinguished from one who claims prejudice only through the use of evidence gathered as a consequence of a search or seizure directed at someone else. (emphasis supplied).

210. Alderman v. United States, 394 U.S. at 173, 89 S.Ct. at 966.

211. 439 U.S. 128, 99 S.Ct. 421, 58 L.Ed.2d 387 (1978).

§ 10.11   SEARCH WARRANTS & SUPPRESSION   Ch. 10

were not violated. Accordingly, although the language of the CPLR accords standing to one at whom eavesdropping "was directed," that cannot be taken to mean that an individual has standing to complain of eavesdropping simply because he or she was a target of the investigation.

Outside the eavesdropping area, the language of Article 710 provides no guidance at all as to the identity of the "aggrieved person" who can move to suppress evidence, except in its broad statement that the scope of the CPL term is not "limited to" the definition in CPLR section 4506.[212] Presumably, however, defendants complaining of video surveillance, pen registers, and trap and trace devices will find their claims subjected by analogy to the standing principles applicable in eavesdropping cases.

As to other suppression claims, the case law makes plain, if the statute does not, that constitutional rights are personal and may not be "vicariously" asserted.[213] Thus, as a general matter only a defendant who was himself or herself the victim of unconstitutional action can successfully move to suppress evidence. That principle is sufficiently clear in its application to statement evidence as to have left little need for discussion in the case law. Only the defendant who makes a statement can move to suppress that statement.[214] Further, the case law does not suggest that a defendant has ever moved to suppress the results of a chemical blood test except one administered to him—or that a defendant has ever had reason to do so.

Similarly, in practice only those identified in improper identification proceedings are heard to move to suppress identification testimony. However, note must be made that, for whatever reason, identification evidence and identification evidence alone is not expressly made subject to standing rules in the introductory language of section 710.20. Under section 710.20, a defendant who "claims that improper identification testimony may be offered against him or her in a criminal action" may move to suppress it, whether or not that defendant is an "aggrieved" person.

That leaves for discussion the area in which standing principles are litigated most frequently, the Fourth Amendment area. Before the Supreme Court's decision in *Jones*, whether the defendant had property rights in the area searched was central to standing analysis. *Jones* and subsequent decisions shifted the focus, so that now the governing principle is that a defendant has standing to contest a search if the police action impinged on his or her legitimate expectations of privacy. In *Jones* itself, for example, the defendant was a guest in the apartment of another, and despite the lack of any property interest in the premises he was held to be entitled to contest the propriety of a police intrusion onto

212. CPL § 710.10(5).
213. See, e.g., Alderman v. United States, 394 U.S. at 174, 89 S.Ct. at 966–67; People v. Wesley, 73 N.Y.2d 351, 355, 540 N.Y.S.2d 757, 759, 538 N.E.2d 76 (1989).
214. People v. Portelli, 15 N.Y.2d 235, 257 N.Y.S.2d 931, 205 N.E.2d 857, cert.

the premises. Similarly, in *Katz v. United States*[215] a defendant was permitted to dispute the legality of the placement of an eavesdropping device on a public telephone booth, despite his obvious lack of a property interest in that phone booth.

Of course, whether an individual's legitimate expectations of privacy have been violated often determines not only standing, but also whether his or her Fourth Amendment rights were violated. *Katz* was in fact written as an analysis, not of standing principles, but of the reach of the Fourth Amendment.[216] Thus, in many cases resolution of the standing issue merges into resolution of the merits of a suppression claim. In recognition of that fact, in *Rakas v. Illinois*[217] the Supreme Court suggested that the concept of standing was superfluous, and that standing inquiries could be subsumed in substantive Fourth Amendment analysis. In particular, where, as in *Rakas*, the issue before a court is whether the defendant possessed a legitimate expectation of privacy that was offended by an official intrusion, a duplicative resolution of a standing issue will not advance the discussion. However, in many cases the courts have found it helpful to retain the concept of standing in their analysis.

As noted above, in *Jones* the Supreme Court abandoned the notion that standing was purely a product of property rights, and accorded standing to a guest in an apartment. The court provided two rationales for doing so. First, Jones was charged with possessing contraband found in the apartment; the court believed it would not be appropriate to require a defendant who sought to be heard on a constitutional issue to prove that he owned contraband and thus was guilty of the substantive offense.[218] Second, the court believed it unjust to make standing contingent on property concepts, and that an illegal intrusion should be subject to challenge by anyone legitimately on the premises.[219] Those two rationales for granting standing have in large part been the focus of debate in subsequent standing decisions.

The concept that those charged with the possession of contraband should have "automatic standing" to protest a search was disavowed by the Supreme Court in 1980.[220] After *Jones*, the court had held that the factual allegations submitted by a defendant in a motion to suppress could not be used against the defendant on his or her case-in-chief,[221] and that had eliminated the primary rationale for according standing to every defendant accused of a possessory offense.[222] Ironically, the court noted as well that, since standing had been divorced from property

den. 382 U.S. 1009, 86 S.Ct. 612, 15 L.Ed.2d 1009 (1966).

215. 389 U.S. 347, 88 S.Ct. 507, 19 L.Ed.2d 576 (1967).

216. 389 U.S. at 351–53, 88 S.Ct. at 511–12.

217. 439 U.S. 128, 99 S.Ct. 421, 58 L.Ed.2d 387 (1978).

218. Jones v. United States, 362 U.S. at 263–65, 80 S.Ct. at 732–33.

219. 362 U.S. at 265–67, 80 S.Ct. at 733–34.

220. United States v. Salvucci, 448 U.S. 83, 100 S.Ct. 2547, 65 L.Ed.2d 619 (1980).

221. Simmons v. United States, 390 U.S. 377, 88 S.Ct. 967, 19 L.Ed.2d 1247 (1968).

222. United States v. Salvucci, 448 U.S. at 88–90, 100 S.Ct. at 2551–52.

concepts, it was no longer self-contradictory for the government both to assert that a defendant possessed property, and that he or she lacked standing to contest a search.[223] New York followed suit in 1981 in *People v. Ponder*,[224] abandoning the "automatic standing" doctrine as a matter of state law.

However, a subsequent decision, *People v. Millan*,[225] on its face was inconsistent with *Ponder*, and brought the holding of that case into doubt. Accordingly, the Court of Appeals re-visited the automatic standing debate in *People v. Wesley*,[226] leaving us with that court's most comprehensive treatment of the subject to date. In *Wesley*, the court reaffirmed that a defendant charged with a possessory offense, like any other defendant, would generally be obliged to establish standing before he could challenge a search. But the court created a major exception to that general rule. In cases in which the defendant's possession of contraband was established by use of the statutory presumption that one possesses a weapon found in an automobile in which he or she is riding,[227] the defendant will be accorded automatic standing to protest the recovery of the weapon.[228]

The announcement of the exception did serve, however artificially, to harmonize the holdings of *Ponder* and *Wesley* with that of *Millan*. However, there would seem to be little if any connection between reliance on a statutory presumption in a jury charge and a grant of standing, and no clear rationale for the exception is stated in *Wesley*.[229] The lack of a clear rationale left the scope of the exception open to debate—for example, as to which statutory presumptions give rise to the exception,[230] the extent of the standing accorded to defendants when more than the contraband addressed in the presumption is recovered,[231] and how much reliance the prosecution must place on the presumption to trigger the exception.[232] At least for now, the cautious prosecutor will avoid reliance on statutory presumptions whenever possible where a lack of standing may be the only obstacle to a defendant's ability to suppress the contraband that is the basis for a prosecution.

Controversy has also followed in the wake of the second rationale of the Supreme Court in *Jones*—that guests legitimately on the premises

---

223. United States v. Salvucci, 448 U.S. at 90, 100 S.Ct. at 2552; see also Rawlings v. Kentucky, 448 U.S. 98, 100 S.Ct. 2556, 65 L.Ed.2d 633 (1980).

224. 54 N.Y.2d 160, 445 N.Y.S.2d 57, 429 N.E.2d 735 (1981).

225. 69 N.Y.2d 514, 516 N.Y.S.2d 168, 508 N.E.2d 903 (1987); see also People v. Mosley, 68 N.Y.2d 881, 508 N.Y.S.2d 931, 501 N.E.2d 580 (1986).

226. 73 N.Y.2d 351, 540 N.Y.S.2d 757, 538 N.E.2d 76 (1989).

227. See Penal Law § 265.15(3).

228. 73 N.Y.2d at 360–62, 540 N.Y.S.2d at 762–64.

229. Essentially all that the court states in Wesley is that "fundamental tenets of fairness require that a defendant charged with possession under the statutory presumption be given an opportunity to contest the search." 73 N.Y.2d at 360, 540 N.Y.S.2d at 762.

230. People v. Mato, 160 A.D.2d 435, 554 N.Y.S.2d 121 (1st Dep't 1990).

231. People v. Tejada, 81 N.Y.2d 861, 597 N.Y.S.2d 626, 613 N.E.2d 532 (1993).

232. People v. Andrews, 176 A.D.2d 530, 574 N.Y.S.2d 719 (1st Dep't 1991).

have standing to contest an intrusion into those premises.[233] The Supreme Court determined in *Rakas v. Illinois* that this formulation was too generous to defendants, and that the true test for standing was simply whether a defendant had a legitimate expectation of privacy in the premises.[234] Consistent with that test, the New York Court of Appeals announced a rule of standing that called for analysis of all the circumstances surrounding the defendant's connection with the searched premises, and under which a defendant discovered sleeping in an apartment that supposedly belonged to his drug supplier was held to lack standing to contest the entry into that apartment.[235]

Shortly thereafter, however, the Supreme Court complicated the analysis with its decision in *Minnesota v. Olson*.[236] The court had earlier held that the police may not generally enter a defendant's house to arrest him without a warrant,[237] and the question for the court in *Olson* was whether a warrant was required to enter a home to arrest a visitor therein. Relying on the facts if not the language of *Jones*, the court held that a defendant does have an expectation of privacy in a house by virtue of being an overnight guest there.[238] And the court's rationale was sufficiently broad as to have apparent application beyond cases in which an entry is made to effect an arrest. While the New York Court of Appeals has since tersely acknowledged *Olsen* in another arrest case,[239] it has not addressed its impact in search cases and on the test set out in *People v. Rodriguez*.

Library References:

West's Key No. Digests, Criminal Law ⇨394.5(2); Searches and Seizures ⇨161–170.

§ 10.12 Motion to Suppress—Court

In most cases, CPL § 710.50 resolves all questions about where a defendant should file a suppression motion, and does so in unsurprising fashion. After indictment in a felony case, a suppression motion must be made in the superior court in which the indictment is pending.[240] In a non-felony case, when a misdemeanor complaint, an information, a simplified information, or a prosecutor's information is pending in a local criminal court, a suppression motion must be made in that local criminal court.[241] In most cases a defendant will have no reason, or practical

---

233. 362 U.S. at 265–67, 80 S.Ct. at 733–34.

234. 439 U.S. at 142–43, 99 S.Ct. at 429–30.

235. People v. Rodriguez, 69 N.Y.2d 159, 513 N.Y.S.2d 75, 505 N.E.2d 586 (1987).

236. 495 U.S. 91, 110 S.Ct. 1684, 109 L.Ed.2d 85 (1990).

237. Payton v. New York, 445 U.S. 573, 100 S.Ct. 1371, 63 L.Ed.2d 639 (1980).

238. 495 U.S. at 96–100, 110 S.Ct. at 1687–90.

239. People v. Ortiz, 83 N.Y.2d 840, 611 N.Y.S.2d 500, 633 N.E.2d 1104 (1994). Judge Smith's dissent in Ortiz expressed the view that even an occasional relationship to premises at which relatives resided was sufficient to provide standing to contest an entry into those premises. 83 N.Y.2d at 844–45, 611 N.Y.S.2d at 502–03 (Smith, J., dissenting).

240. CPL § 710.50(1)(a).

241. CPL § 710.50(1)(c).

§ 10.12   SEARCH WARRANTS & SUPPRESSION   Ch. 10

opportunity, to initiate suppression proceedings until an indictment is pending in superior court or until a misdemeanor complaint or an information is pending before a local criminal court. Accordingly, a defendant generally will have no difficulty deciding in which court to file his suppression motion.

Note should nonetheless be made of two rules that apply when a defendant facing a felony charge wishes to make a suppression motion before he or she is indicted. First, if a felony complaint has been filed in a local criminal court, but that court has not yet determined whether the defendant should be held for the action of a grand jury, a suppression motion may be made in the superior court that would have trial jurisdiction of the offense should an indictment ultimately be filed.[242] Where only the Supreme Court has trial jurisdiction of felonies, that court will of course be the Supreme Court. In counties in which a County Court sits, whether the County Court or the Supreme Court has trial jurisdiction of the offense varies from county to county.

Similarly, when a local criminal court has ordered that a defendant be held for the action of a grand jury, but the grand jury has not yet made its determination, the defendant may make a suppression motion in the superior court that has impanelled, or will impanel, the grand jury.[243] If the county is one in which a County Court sits, and if the grand jury is not yet impanelled, the defendant may choose to file a suppression motion in the County Court even if the grand jury will be impanelled in the Supreme Court.[244]

Presumably, the CPL authorizes motions at early stages of a felony prosecution to enable a defendant who faces charges solely by virtue of illegally obtained evidence to avoid an indictment and its consequences.[245] In that regard, once an indictment is voted, it will not be dismissed simply because evidence presented to the grand jury was illegally obtained.[246] A defendant may therefore have a strong motive to move, before indictment, to suppress critical evidence and thereby prevent the prosecution from obtaining an indictment. Nevertheless, pre-indictment motions to suppress remain a rarity.

Section 710.50 expressly addresses other unusual procedural circumstances as well. First, if a suppression motion is made and decided in a superior court, but a local criminal court ultimately obtains trial jurisdiction of the case by virtue of the filing of an information, the decision of

---

242. CPL § 710.50(1)(b).
243. CPL § 710.50(1)(a).
244. CPL § 710.50(1)(a).
245. Indeed, the original draft of section 710.50 would have permitted a potential defendant to make a suppression motion even before the initiation of a criminal action, if the defendant knew "that a grand jury proceeding against him involving the evidence in question [was] in progress or about to be commenced." See Staff Comment, Proposed New York Criminal Procedure Law, § 375.40(1), p. 418 (Edward Thompson Co.1967). See § 10.13, infra. That was in fact the rule under the Code of Criminal Procedure. See Code Crim. Proc. § 813–e; People v. Pagano, 40 Misc.2d 930, 244 N.Y.S.2d 214 (Sup.Ct., Dutchess County, 1963); Preiser, "Practice Commentary" to CPL § 710.40, McKinney's Cons. Laws of New York, Book 11A at 266 (1995).

246. People v. Oakley, 28 N.Y.2d 309, 321 N.Y.S.2d 596, 270 N.E.2d 318 (1971); People v. Kersch, 135 A.D.2d 570, 521 N.Y.S.2d 788 (2d Dep't 1987).

the superior court is binding on the local criminal court.[247] Notably, the statute does not state that a local criminal court ruling would bind a superior court, should a superior court obtain jurisdiction in a misdemeanor case after a suppression ruling has been made in the local criminal court, and that omission appears deliberate.[248]

Second, if the motion is made in the superior court, but is not decided at the time an information is filed, the superior court may not decide the motion, but must instead refer the motion to the local criminal court.[249] In that regard, section 710.50 generally speaks to whether motions can be "made" in a court, and only in this circumstance does the statute recognize that a motion properly "made" in a court might nonetheless not properly be decided by that court. And in this instance, the same rule would presumably govern in all circumstances: a court in which a motion is pending should not proceed to resolve the motion once it is clear that the trial of the case will occur in a different court.[250] That conclusion is in fact obvious with respect to a motion that is pending in a local criminal court, for once grand jury action creates trial jurisdiction for a superior court, the local criminal court loses all jurisdiction of the case.[251] Of course, should a court that lacks jurisdiction to decide a motion nonetheless decide it, the decision will not bind the court that should decide the motion.[252]

The CPL addresses which court may entertain a suppression motion, but not which judge of the court should hear a motion. However, issues concerning which judge may decide a suppression motion seem to arise only when a particular judge has signed a search warrant, and then in the normal course that judge or another judge receives a motion to suppress evidence obtained by virtue of that warrant. The Court of Appeals has resolved that a judge may properly hear an attack on a warrant that he or she signed, both because the judge presumptively will give the motion impartial consideration, and because his or her decision will be examined on appeal by an intermediate appellate court with plenary review power.[253] Furthermore, when one judge reviews a warrant signed by a different judge of coordinate jurisdiction, the reviewing judge is not bound by the first judge's conclusions.[254] Finally, pursuant to CPL § 255.20(4), a motion can be referred to a judicial hearing officer.

247. CPL § 710.50(2).

248. Under a provision added to the Code of Criminal Procedure in 1962, any court's decision, made when that court had jurisdiction to consider the defendant's motion, was binding on any other court that came to have trial jurisdiction of the case. But the statute did not seem to anticipate that a local criminal court's order might bind a superior court. See Code Crim. Proc. § 813–e.

249. CPL § 710.50(2).

250. That principle was expressly stated in the Code of Criminal Procedure. See Code Crim. Proc. § 813–e.

251. CPL § 170.20.

252. People v. Kelly, 40 A.D.2d 624, 336 N.Y.S.2d 514 (4th Dep't 1972); see also People v. Kellog, 53 Misc.2d 560, 279 N.Y.S.2d 104 (Onondaga Co.Ct.1967).

253. People v. Tambe, 71 N.Y.2d 492, 506, 527 N.Y.S.2d 372, 379, 522 N.E.2d 448 (1988).

254. People v. Guerra, 65 N.Y.2d 60, 63, 489 N.Y.S.2d 718, 719, 478 N.E.2d 1319 (1985)("[T]he law of the case doctrine does not prevent the defendant from challenging a determination which he had no opportunity to litigate at the time it was made.").

§ 10.12   SEARCH WARRANTS & SUPPRESSION   Ch. 10

The judicial hearing officer can conduct proceedings on the motion, but the motion must ultimately be decided by a judge.[255]

Library References:

West's Key No. Digests, Criminal Law ⚖=394.5, 394.6.

§ 10.13 Motion to Suppress—Time of Motion

CPL § 710.40 specifies when suppression motions must be made. Section 710.40 incorporates by reference,[256] and must be read in conjunction with, the provisions of CPL § 255.20(1) dealing generally with the timing of pretrial motions. And under section 255.20(1), a defendant is generally obliged to make an "omnibus" motion, including a motion to suppress evidence, within 45 days of arraignment.[257] In the typical case, that is the only rule that comes into play.

That 45-day period is extended by operation of law in three different circumstances. First, and most simply, where the defendant is not represented by counsel at arraignment but wishes to be represented by counsel, the 45-day period begins to run from the date counsel appears for the defendant.[258]

Second, in cases in which eavesdropping notice[259] or identification or statement notice[260] is served after arraignment, the 45-day period does not begin to run until the last service date.[261] Those types of notice must be given within 15 days of arraignment unless good cause is shown for later notice,[262] and so generally this rule will add no more than 15 days to the period in which the omnibus motion must be filed. In the unusual case in which there is good cause for late notice, the particular circumstances of the case determine when notice can be served,[263] and thus the 45-day motion period could theoretically be extended indefinitely.

Until the notice is forthcoming, the defendant presumably will be in the dark as to the fact that late notice will be served. Thus, the defense

---

255. CPL § 255.20(4); see generally People v. Scalza, 76 N.Y.2d 604, 562 N.Y.S.2d 14, 563 N.E.2d 705 (1990).

256. CPL § 710.40(1).

257. CPL § 255.20(1); see CPL § 255.10(1)(f). See generally Chapter 8. For this purpose, "arraignment" means the arraignment on the accusatory instrument that conveys trial jurisdiction. Thus, in a felony case, the defendant should make the motion within 45 days of the arraignment on the indictment. See Matter of Veloz v. Rothwax, 103 A.D.2d 715, 478 N.Y.S.2d 14 (1st Dep't 1984), rev'd on other grounds 65 N.Y.2d 902, 493 N.Y.S.2d 452, 483 N.E.2d 127 (1985); cf. People v. Penasso, 142 A.D.2d 691, 531 N.Y.S.2d 291 (2d Dep't 1988); People v. Alcindor, 157 Misc.2d 725, 598 N.Y.S.2d 449 (N.Y.C.Crim.Ct.1993).

258. CPL § 255.20(1).

259. CPL § 700.70.

260. CPL § 710.30. See §§ 10.23–10.29, infra.

261. CPL § 255.20(1). In light of this specific provision, more general language earlier enacted in CPL §§ 710.30(2) and 710.40(2), requiring that a defendant be given a "reasonable opportunity" to make a motion after late notice, would seem to be a dead letter.

262. See §§ 10.24, 10.27, infra.

263. CPL § 710.30(2).

attorney must make an omnibus motion, with any available suppression component addressing other evidence, within the regularly applicable motion period, unless the late notice is actually served within that period. Where late notice is provided, either before or after the filing of the omnibus motion, the defense attorney's first instinct should be to move to "preclude" the newly noticed evidence for late notice, rather than to "suppress" it.[264] There is no statutory limit on how late a preclusion motion can be made.[265] But where the prosecution may conceivably show good cause, caution dictates that any viable suppression motion also be filed, and such a motion presumably will be due within 45 days of the late notice. And, as to statement and identification evidence, the filing of a motion to suppress before the determination of a preclusion motion may endanger a valid preclusion claim.[266] Where late notice is given of statement or identification evidence, therefore, an attorney should file a preclusion motion as soon as possible, and if necessary seek permission to reserve a suppression motion until after the preclusion motion is resolved. If the suppression component of this joint motion is to be timely, the motion must be filed within 45 days of the late notice.

Third, section 710.40(2) provides that the 45-day motion period is inapplicable when, owing to a lack of knowledge of pertinent facts or to "other factors," the defendant has not had a reasonable opportunity to make his motion. Section 710.40(2) does not clearly state how quickly, after the defendant belatedly becomes able to make a motion, the motion must be filed. But the language of the section suggests that the defendant must make a belated suppression motion with reasonable dispatch.

Section 255.20(3) includes similar language obliging the court to entertain an untimely pretrial motion at any time before sentence if the defendant could not previously have been aware of the grounds for the motion, or otherwise can show "good cause" for the delay.[267] If section 710.40(1) is read literally, this provision of section 255.20 is not applicable to suppression motions. At the time section 255.20 was adopted, section 710.40 was amended, but to incorporate by reference only subdivision one of the new section.[268] The "good cause" provision is contained in subdivision three. That reading may be *too* literal.[269] In any event, section 710.40(2) covers the same ground, and does so without the loaded "good cause" language of section 255.20(3).

---

264. See generally People v. Laing, 79 N.Y.2d 166, 581 N.Y.S.2d 149, 589 N.E.2d 372 (1992).

265. CPL §§ 700.70, 710.30(3).

266. See § 10.29, infra; CPL § 710.30(3); compare People v. Merrill, 87 N.Y.2d 948, ___ N.E.2d ___ (1996) with People v. Bernier, 73 N.Y.2d 1006, 541 N.Y.S.2d 760, 539 N.E.2d 588 (1989).

267. It is unclear whether the "good cause" test in this grace provision is as stringent as the "good cause" test that the prosecution must meet before it can give late notice of its intent to offer identification or statement evidence. See § 10.27, infra; see also People v. O'Doherty, 70 N.Y.2d 479, 522 N.Y.S.2d 498, 517 N.E.2d 213 (1987).

268. L.1974, c.763, § 8.

269. See, e.g., People v. Reid, 190 A.D.2d 575, 593 N.Y.S.2d 521 (1st Dep't 1993).

The 45-day period for making a suppression motion is shortened by operation of law in only one circumstance. In a case in which the trial commences within the applicable 45-day period, the motion must be made before trial commences.[270] That limitation is unlikely to affect a typical prosecution. Moreover, when a defendant's 45 days to file has been extended by operation of law on account of late notice or an unawareness of pertinent facts, the requirement that the motion be made before trial is inapplicable, at least when the defendant makes the motion with reasonable dispatch.[271]

The court has no discretion to shorten the time allowed to a defendant to move to suppress.[272] However, under section 255.20(1), the court has unlimited discretion to "fix" a later time for motions if the defendant moves for an extension before judgment is entered.[273] Section 255.20(3) also grants the court discretion to decide a pretrial motion on the merits "in the interest of justice, and for good cause shown," if it is made at any point before sentence. As noted, subdivision three may not apply to suppression motions, but in light of subdivision one its language is redundant.[274]

The existence of judicial discretion to entertain a late motion on the merits does not mean that defense counsel can be casual about compliance with the relevant deadlines. As the Court of Appeals has emphasized, the Legislature meant to impose "order and speed" on pretrial motion practice by requiring that motions be filed timely, and in a single set of papers.[275] Consistent with that policy, judges may well exercise their discretion by denying late motions.[276]

Finally, the CPL speaks not only to the last date on which a defendant can make a suppression motion, but also to the first. Under the Code of Criminal Procedure, a person could move to suppress evidence even before any charge was brought against him or her.[277] While the early drafts of the CPL would have continued that policy,[278] the CPL as enacted authorizes a suppression motion only when a criminal action is pending against the defendant.[279] And a "criminal

---

270. CPL § 255.20(1).

271. CPL § 710.40(1) and (2).

272. Matter of Veloz v. Rothwax, 65 N.Y.2d 902, 493 N.Y.S.2d 452, 483 N.E.2d 127 (1985).

273. CPL § 255.20(1).

274. Even after sentence is imposed, challenges to the judgment of conviction, including challenges implicating suppression principles, may be made pursuant to CPL § 440.10(h). But of course a defendant could hope to succeed with such a claim only if he or she could not have presented it earlier. See CPL § 710.70(3).

275. People v. O'Doherty, 70 N.Y.2d 479, 488–89, 522 N.Y.S.2d 498, 503–04, 517 N.E.2d 213, 218–19 (1987).

276. See, e.g., People v. Gibbs, 210 A.D.2d 4, 618 N.Y.S.2d 813 (1st Dep't 1994); People v. Reid, 190 A.D.2d 575, 593 N.Y.S.2d 521 (1st Dep't 1993); People v. Dunn, 155 A.D.2d 75, 81, 553 N.Y.S.2d 257, 260 (4th Dep't 1990), aff'd 77 N.Y.2d 19, 563 N.Y.S.2d 388, 564 N.E.2d 1054 (1990); see also People v. Hults, 76 N.Y.2d 190, 196, 557 N.Y.S.2d 270, 273, 556 N.E.2d 1077 (1990)(belated motion for hearing on admissibility of hypnotically refreshed testimony).

277. Code Crim. Proc. § 813–e.

278. See Proposed New York Criminal Procedure Law, § 375.40(1), p. 418 (Edward Thompson Co.1967).

279. CPL § 710.40(1); see §§ 10.8, 10.11, supra.

action" commences only when charges are filed against the defendant.[280]

Library References:
West's Key No. Digests, Criminal Law ⚖394.6(3).

§ 10.14 Motion to Suppress—Time of Decision

When a suppression motion is made before trial, the motion must be decided before trial commences.[281] A timely decision plainly helps a defendant know what evidence he or she must be prepared to face at trial, and helps both sides to know what evidence to discuss with the trier of fact during the preliminary phases of the trial. In addition, the prosecution may be unable to exercise its right to appeal an unfavorable ruling if the decision does not precede trial.[282]

A jury trial commences with jury selection.[283] Accordingly, if the trial court puts off the decision of a suppression motion until after *voir dire* or opening statements without the defendant's express consent, it does so at risk of reversal.[284] On the other hand, such a practice is sometimes upheld on a finding that the defendant did not protest the trial court's procedure, or was not prejudiced by the late decision.[285]

In one particular context, judges commonly defer a suppression decision until well into trial. A defendant's pretrial statements are sometimes of little value as part of the prosecution's case-in-chief, but would be highly valuable as impeachment material should the defendant offer inconsistent testimony. The prosecution may therefore state that it intends to use a statement only as impeachment material. Such an announcement may well render moot any suppression motion as to that statement, for statements can generally be used to impeach the defendant even if they were illegally obtained.[286]

The complication arises from the exception to the general rule permitting impeachment. An illegally obtained statement may not be used for any purpose, even to impeach, if it was obtained through coercive methods that render the statement "classically" involuntary.[287] A defendant who asserts in good faith that statements were obtained through coercion may insist on a pretrial decision on whether impeach-

---

280. CPL § 1.20(16) and (17).

281. CPL § 710.40(3).

282. See CPL § 450.20(8).

283. CPL § 1.20(11). Under the terms of that section, a non-jury trial commences with the first opening statement or, if there is none, when the first witness is sworn.

284. See People v. Hibbler, 111 A.D.2d 67, 489 N.Y.S.2d 191 (1st Dep't 1985); People v. Blowe, 130 A.D.2d 668, 515 N.Y.S.2d 812 (2d Dep't 1987); People v. La Congo, 30 A.D.2d 757, 292 N.Y.S.2d 214 (4th Dep't 1968)(decided under Code Crim. Proc. § 813–h).

285. People v. Correa, 200 A.D.2d 415, 608 N.Y.S.2d 802 (1st Dep't 1994)(defendant was not "compelled" to conduct jury selection before *Wade* hearing); People v. Gonzalez, 214 A.D.2d 451, 625 N.Y.S.2d 203 (1st Dep't 1995)(harmless error); People v. Melendez, 141 A.D.2d 860, 530 N.Y.S.2d 202 (2d Dep't 1988).

286. See, e.g., People v. Harris, 25 N.Y.2d 175, 303 N.Y.S.2d 71, 250 N.E.2d 349 (1969), aff'd 401 U.S. 222, 91 S.Ct. 643, 28 L.Ed.2d 1 (1971). Cf. People v. Dawson, 101 A.D.2d 816, 475 N.Y.S.2d 454 (2d Dep't 1984) (identification testimony).

287. Mincey v. Arizona, 437 U.S. 385, 398, 98 S.Ct. 2408, 2416, 57 L.Ed.2d 290 (1978); People v. Hults, 76 N.Y.2d 190, 198, 557 N.Y.S.2d 270, 274, 556 N.E.2d 1077 (1990).

ment will be permitted. Such a defendant may assert that his decision whether to testify will turn on whether he can be impeached with his statements, and that he is entitled to shape his trial strategy knowing whether he can take the stand.

But even defendants who have no valid coercion claim, and defendants who are unlikely to testify no matter what the outcome of a coercion claim, can make the same assertion. By doing so they may be rewarded with a pretrial hearing that would otherwise not have been necessary, with the attendant preview of part of the prosecution's trial case and waste of the court's time. When prosecutors have announced that statements will not be employed on their case-in-chief, some judges have declined to take the time to hold hearings on whether statements were "classically" involuntary before it is resolved, after the close of the prosecution's case, that the defendant actually intends to testify. The First Department has approved that practice.[288]

Note should be made of an experiment conducted in misdemeanor cases in the 1970's. As originally enacted, section 710.40 provided that in local criminal courts a suppression motion had to be determined during trial if the prosecution so requested.[289] A majority of the Court of Appeals in fact suggested that judicial economy would properly be promoted if the Legislature would allow judges to resolve suppression motions during trials, on the basis of the trial testimony, even in felony cases.[290] That suggestion was not adopted, and indeed the misdemeanor provision was eliminated in 1977.[291]

Library References:

West's Key No. Digests, Criminal Law ⚖394.6(5).

§ 10.15 Motion to Suppress—Renewal

Presumably, any court has inherent discretion to grant a motion for reconsideration of its own suppression decision, made by any party, if the motion for reconsideration is made expeditiously and before trial.[292] Article 710 makes the power to reconsider a suppression decision express in two circumstances. Before trial, a suppression motion that has been denied may be reconsidered if the defendant shows that he or she has discovered additional pertinent facts that could not have been discovered with due diligence before the decision.[293] During trial, a defendant whose suppression motion has been denied may obtain reconsideration if he or she makes that same showing, and the timing of the discovery of

288. People v. Whitney, 167 A.D.2d 254, 561 N.Y.S.2d 754 (1st Dep't 1990).

289. CPL § 710.40(3).

290. People v. Ganci, 27 N.Y.2d 418, 424–29, 318 N.Y.S.2d 484, 488–92, 267 N.E.2d 263, cert. den. 402 U.S. 924, 91 S.Ct. 1398, 28 L.Ed.2d 663 (1971).

291. L.1977, c.273, § 1. The legislative memorandum suggests that the amendment was required because suppression motions were too complex to be decided "on the spot," in mid-trial. 1977 New York State Legislative Annual, p. 139.

292. But see People v. Havelka, 45 N.Y.2d 636, 412 N.Y.S.2d 345, 384 N.E.2d 1269 (1978).

293. CPL § 710.40(4).

the new facts was such that the motion for reconsideration could not have been made before trial.[294]

Those statutory principles are unremarkable. One very important and related principle is less obvious, and not evident from the provisions of Article 710. Since *People v. Giles*,[295] it has been clear that evidence introduced into the case after the suppression decision cannot be considered during appellate review of the suppression decision unless the defendant moved for reargument of the suppression decision after the evidence became known to the court.

In *Giles* itself, no suppression hearing was held as a result of an incorrect ruling that the defendant lacked standing to contest a search. The Appellate Division identified the error, but instead of remanding for a hearing the court granted the suppression motion outright. In doing so, the court, over the prosecution's objection, considered the evidence presented at trial to determine that the actions of the police had been improper.[296] The Court of Appeals reversed, noting that the focus of a trial is different from that of a hearing and that it was unfair to the prosecution not to permit it an opportunity to prove at a hearing that the police conduct was legal.[297]

Giles was not a case in which a suppression hearing was held, and the defendant on appeal based his suppression argument on both the trial evidence and the hearing evidence. But *Giles* has since routinely been cited for the proposition that the defendant may not rely on trial evidence in making his or her appellate suppression arguments.[298] And the *Giles* principle logically does preclude such reliance, for in some cases the prosecution would be motivated to supplement its trial evidence with additional, explanatory evidence if it was clear that suppression arguments might be based upon it. The cases in which the prosecution might do so cannot be identified simply from a review of the trial evidence, and therefore as a general matter it makes sense not to consider the trial evidence on appeal.[299]

But that is where the defendant's ability to make a reargument motion is critical. Defendants often learn of evidence at trial that they could not reasonably have learned earlier—for example, in testimony of police witnesses that is inconsistent with the testimony adduced at the hearing. The defendant who believes that such new evidence might help undermine the suppression decision on appeal should cite that evidence

---

294. Id.; People v. Kuberka, 215 A.D.2d 592, 626 N.Y.S.2d 855 (2d Dep't 1995).

295. 73 N.Y.2d 666, 543 N.Y.S.2d 37, 541 N.E.2d 37 (1989).

296. People v. Giles, 137 A.D.2d 1, 527 N.Y.S.2d 409 (1st Dep't 1988).

297. 73 N.Y.2d at 671–72, 543 N.Y.S.2d at 39–40.

298. See, e.g., People v. Church, ___ A.D.2d ___, 630 N.Y.S.2d 16 (1st Dep't 1995); People v. Wise, 204 A.D.2d 133, 612 N.Y.S.2d 117 (1st Dep't 1994).

299. Notably, that same principle can work to the benefit of the defense. The prosecution cannot successfully cite trial evidence to argue that the trial court's failure to accord the defendant a proper hearing should be overlooked, People v. Davis, 169 A.D.2d 379, 564 N.Y.S.2d 320 (1st Dep't 1991), or that the trial evidence supports affirmance of the denial of a suppression motion after a hearing. People v. Gonzalez, 55 N.Y.2d 720, 447 N.Y.S.2d 145, 431 N.E.2d 630 (1981).

§ 10.15   SEARCH WARRANTS & SUPPRESSION   Ch. 10

and ask to reargue the suppression ruling.[300] At that point the prosecution presumably will have motive and fair opportunity to identify any additional explanatory evidence that would put the trial evidence into context. Even if the court, after granting reconsideration, adheres to its initial suppression decision, the new evidence will be part of the suppression record for appellate review.[301]

Of course, the defendant who moves to reargue based on the trial evidence still bears the burden of demonstrating that the evidence was not reasonably available to him or her before trial.[302] The defendant may not be able to satisfy that burden if he or she could have called the trial witness at the hearing.[303] Whether a witness was available to the defendant at the time of the suppression proceedings may be a complicated issue, particularly where the defendant never asked that the witness be called.[304]

Brief note should be made of the holdings of three additional cases. First, *People v. Miller*[305] rejected a defendant's claim that an appellate reversal automatically entitled him on remand to reconsideration of suppression proceedings unrelated to the reversal. As *Miller* notes, however, after a remand the trial court has discretion to reopen suppression proceedings on grounds previously unavailable to the defendant.[306]

Second, the Third Department has suggested that trial courts should permit defendants to advance new suppression theories at late stages of the trial court proceedings, even where those theories were not articulated in the defense motion papers, particularly where the prosecution will not be prejudiced by the tardiness of a new argument.[307]

Third, the First Department has ruled that independent source can be demonstrated at a mid-trial, re-opened *Wade* hearing, necessitated by new evidence that a prior identification proceeding was improperly conducted, even though the witness had already made an in-court identification.[308] That holding limits, and arguably is inconsistent with,

---

300. The trial court has the discretion to grant reconsideration sua sponte. People v. Corso, 135 A.D.2d 551, 553, 521 N.Y.S.2d 773, 775 (2d Dep't 1987).

301. See People v. Figliolo, 207 A.D.2d 679, 616 N.Y.S.2d 367 (1st Dep't 1994)(remanding for further suppression proceedings based on trial evidence); People v. Brigante, 115 A.D.2d 547, 496 N.Y.S.2d 70 (2d Dep't 1985) (same); People v. Perez, 104 A.D.2d 454, 478 N.Y.S.2d 968 (2d Dep't 1984)(same); see People v. Horonzy, 81 N.Y.2d 853, 597 N.Y.S.2d 622, 613 N.E.2d 528 (1993)(refusing to consider claim that trial evidence entitled defendant to a new Wade hearing for which defendant did not ask below); People v. Stafford, 215 A.D.2d 212, 626 N.Y.S.2d 763 (1st Dep't 1995)(affirming trial court's holding that defendant's new evidence did not justify re-opening Wade hearing).

302. CPL § 710.40(4).

303. Cf. People v. Fuentes, 74 A.D.2d 753, 425 N.Y.S.2d 589 (1st Dep't), aff'd 53 N.Y.2d 892, 440 N.Y.S.2d 625, 423 N.E.2d 48 (1981) with People v. Andriani, 67 A.D.2d 20, 23–24, 414 N.Y.S.2d 159 (1st Dep't), cert. den. 444 U.S. 866, 100 S.Ct. 139, 62 L.Ed.2d 90 (1979).

304. People v. Chipp, 75 N.Y.2d 327, 553 N.Y.S.2d 72, 552 N.E.2d 608 (1990). See § 10.19, infra.

305. 65 N.Y.2d 502, 511–12, 493 N.Y.S.2d 96, 101, 482 N.E.2d 892 (1985), cert. den. 474 U.S. 951, 106 S.Ct. 317, 88 L.Ed.2d 300 (1985).

306. 65 N.Y.2d at 511, 493 N.Y.S.2d at 101.

307. People v. Okun, 135 A.D.2d 1064, 522 N.Y.S.2d 991 (3d Dep't 1987).

308. People v. Rosales, ___ A.D.2d ___, 628 N.Y.S.2d 656 (1st Dep't 1995).

the determination of the Court of Appeals in *People v. Burts*,[309] concerning whether independent source hearings held after an appellate reversal can retroactively validate in-court identifications. But because *Burts* is itself considerably difficult to explain, a narrow interpretation of its reach is not surprising.

Library References:

West's Key No. Digests, Criminal Law ⚎394.6(5).

§ 10.16 The Defendant's Motion Papers—In General

In a typical case defense counsel will have no difficulty determining what evidence the defendant would like to have suppressed, where the motion should be filed, and when it should be filed. What is problematic is what the defendant must put in the motion papers to obtain a hearing and, perhaps, the suppression order he or she seeks. From the prosecution's perspective, the issue is what the prosecutor must articulate in his or her motion papers to reduce the likelihood that the defendant can succeed. Substantive suppression rules are, as noted above, beyond the scope of this chapter. Once the defendant identifies a substantive suppression theory, however, he and the prosecutor still need to know what type of pleadings are necessary to promote or defeat that theory.

In that regard, the papers that initiate and define a motion resemble the pleadings that traditionally shape the issues in civil proceedings— and determine whether there is to be a trial. In particular, if material factual issues are framed in the motion papers, those issues must be resolved at a hearing. This section and the next discuss the rules governing the form and content of the defendant's papers, the "complaint" of motion practice, as those rules are set forth in CPL § 710.60(1) and (5).[310]

Most fundamentally, and as this discussion of motion "papers" would suggest, the defendant's motion generally must be made in writing.[311] The writing requirement helps ensure that the prosecution is protected from unfair surprise, and also helps frame and narrow the suppression issues so that the prosecution may prepare an appropriate response.[312] Because the writing requirement exists to aid the prosecution, the prosecutor can waive that requirement. Indeed, the prosecutor does so by simply failing to object to the court's consideration of a defendant's oral suppression motion.[313] But such a waiver will not be inferred where the prosecutor has at least requested that the defendant be required to put the motion in writing.[314]

309. 78 N.Y.2d 20, 571 N.Y.S.2d 418, 574 N.E.2d 1024 (1991).

310. The rules governing the prosecutor's papers are discussed in § 10.18, infra.

311. CPL § 710.60(1).

312. People v. Mezon, 80 N.Y.2d 155, 160, 589 N.Y.S.2d 838, 841, 603 N.E.2d 943 (1992).

313. Id.

314. 80 N.Y.2d at 160–61, 589 N.Y.S.2d at 841.

§ 10.16   SEARCH WARRANTS & SUPPRESSION   Ch. 10

The only exception to the writing requirement applies to mid-trial suppression motions.[315] When exigent circumstances require that a motion be made during trial, the court may in its discretion absolve the defendant of the writing requirement, for obvious reasons. But the defendant's oral motion must be made "in open court."[316] And, given that necessity is the only reason for ignoring the prosecution's statutory right to receive a written motion, the court presumably should require that an oral motion conform, to the extent practicable, with the rules that govern written motions.

In addition, the defendant's suppression motion must be made on reasonable notice to the prosecution.[317] What is reasonable will obviously vary with the circumstances of the case. But, to take note of a reversal in extreme circumstances, a court errs when, at the conclusion of a suppression hearing, it *sua sponte* suppresses evidence that was not put in issue by the defendant's motion papers, on a legal theory not raised by the defendant.[318] Further, the Second Department has upheld a trial court's refusal to take notice of a belated allegation that false factual statements were included in an eavesdropping application.[319] And a decision by a court to suppress evidence, including breathalyzer results, on account of a delay in the prosecution's response to the defendant's motion, has been reversed based on an analogy to the time frame created for the service of motion papers in the CPLR.[320]

As to content, a defendant's motion papers must state the legal grounds on which the motion is based.[321] The failure to state a legal basis for a motion "may" result in summary denial of the motion.[322] But it is in fact quite unusual for a defendant's suppression motion to be denied because counsel has not stated a legal theory for suppression.[323] In that regard, this pleading requirement should be an extremely easy one to satisfy. To state a legal basis for a suppression motion it should suffice to allege, in rough conformity with the terms of section 710.20, that a statement was "involuntarily made," that property was taken in violation of the defendant's rights under the Fourth Amendment, or that an identification procedure was unduly suggestive.[324] Nor is the defendant likely to be bound by and limited to whatever grounds he or she initially recites. For example, one Third Department precedent states that a court should liberally allow the presentation of grounds in

315. See § 10.13, supra.
316. CPL § 710.60(5).
317. CPL § 710.60(1).
318. People v. Pimentel, 140 A.D.2d 270, 272, 528 N.Y.S.2d 568, 570 (1st Dep't 1988).
319. People v. Manuli, 104 A.D.2d 386, 388, 478 N.Y.S.2d 712, 714 (2d Dep't 1984).
320. People v. Zimmerman, 157 Misc.2d 293, 596 N.Y.S.2d 307 (Monroe Co.Ct.1993).
321. CPL § 710.60(1).
322. CPL § 710.60(3). As the use of the permissive word "may" would suggest, the court has discretion to consider the motion in spite of the pleading deficiency. See People v. Mendoza, 82 N.Y.2d 415, 429, 604 N.Y.S.2d 922, 928, 624 N.E.2d 1017, 1023–24 (1993).

323. See, e.g., People v. Murray, 172 A.D.2d 437, 569 N.Y.S.2d 12 (1st Dep't 1991), app. withdrawn 79 N.Y.2d 942, 583 N.Y.S.2d 196, 592 N.E.2d 804 (1992)(Huntley and Wade motions).

324. See, e.g., People v. Cooper, 162 Misc.2d 192, 194–95, 616 N.Y.S.2d 442, 444–45 (Town of Perinton Ct.1994).

addition to those specified in the motion papers—at least where the prosecution will not be prejudiced.[325]

In addition to the legal basis for the motion, the motion papers must "contain sworn allegations of fact, whether of the defendant or of another person or persons, supporting" the legal grounds alleged.[326] That obligation to make sworn allegations of fact applies to every type of suppression motion, including *Huntley* and *Wade* motions. As to every motion, therefore, the trial court can oblige the defendant to state what facts he or she believes justify the relief sought in the motion. The ultimate sanction for the failure to make such allegations—denial of the motion—is not available as to *Huntley* motions or, since 1986, *Wade* motions.[327] But the failure to allege facts sufficient to support the specified legal basis for the motion is a frequent basis for denial of other types of motions, and in particular of *Mapp* motions.[328] The rules governing the sufficiency of factual allegations are discussed at length in § 10.17, *infra*.

The defendant's sworn factual allegations may be based either on "personal knowledge of the deponent" or on "information and belief."[329] When facts are stated on information and belief, the "sources of such information and the grounds of such belief" must be provided.[330] That obligation to state the sources of the defense allegations is straightforward. And of course the prosecution may not introduce on its direct case admissions made by a defendant in support of suppression motions—for example, an admission that the defendant was in possession of contraband.[331] Nonetheless, many defense attorneys choose to be vague about the sources of the information in the motions they file, and in particular hesitate to attribute particular factual allegations to their clients. The reason may be that some defendants are unable or unwilling to make critical admissions even to their attorneys. Or counsel may wish to forestall the possibility that identifying the defendant as a source of information may result in the defendant's impeachment if he or she offers inconsistent testimony at trial.[332]

Whatever the motive for obfuscation by defense counsel, judges should require explicit statements of the sources of critical factual allegations.[333] After all, hearings are not available "merely for the asking,"[334] and if the defendant is unable or unwilling to comply with the

---

325. People v. Okun, 135 A.D.2d 1064, 522 N.Y.S.2d 991 (3d Dep't 1987). But see cases noted at footnotes 318–320, supra.

326. CPL § 710.60(1).

327. CPL § 710.60(3).

328. See People v. Mendoza, 82 N.Y.2d 415, 421–22, 604 N.Y.S.2d 922, 923–24, 624 N.E.2d 1017 (1993). Again, the court has the discretion to overlook the deficiency. 82 N.Y.2d at 429, 604 N.Y.S.2d at 928.

329. CPL § 710.60(1).

330. Id.

331. Simmons v. United States, 390 U.S. 377, 389–94, 88 S.Ct. 967, 973–76, 19 L.Ed.2d 1247 (1968).

332. See People v. Rivera, 58 A.D.2d 147, 396 N.Y.S.2d 26 (1st Dep't 1977), aff'd 45 N.Y.2d 989, 413 N.Y.S.2d 146, 385 N.E.2d 1073 (1978).

333. See, e.g., People v. McCoy, 71 Misc.2d 381, 337 N.Y.S.2d 49 (Sup.Ct., Bronx County, 1972).

334. People v. Gruden, 42 N.Y.2d 214, 217, 397 N.Y.S.2d 704, 706, 366 N.E.2d 794 (1977). See also People v. Mendoza, 82

statute by identifying a source of information on a critical fact, he or she has not shown that a true issue of fact exists that must be resolved at a hearing. In particular, a court should hardly give weight to a defendant's desire to hold open the possibility of giving inconsistent testimony without fear of impeachment. Nonetheless, while an occasional opinion does hold that a defendant's motion should be denied on account of a failure adequately to identify his or her sources of information,[335] the courts often seem reluctant to require express attribution of individual factual allegations to particular sources.

For example, in *People v. Foster*,[336] the defendant's motion papers disguised the sources of specific facts by attributing his allegations to a group of sources: "conversations with the defendant, the court records and information provided by" the prosecutor.[337] Only one fact was attributed to a specific source—that the police recovered property either from Foster or his co-defendant. The source given for that allegation was the prosecutor's voluntary disclosure form.[338] Needless to say, defendant should have been able to tell his attorney whether property was recovered from him, but the motion papers gave no hint that he did so. The Appellate Division concluded nonetheless that defendant's allegations were adequate, and in particular that counsel had adequately stated the sources of her statements.[339] Moreover, even a court that will insist on definite attribution of facts should afford a defendant an opportunity to cure deficiencies in the papers before denying a motion,[340] and thus defense counsel has little incentive to make specific attributions until directed to do so.

If the court does not resolve the motion summarily on account of a defect in the defendant's papers or after review of the prosecution's answer,[341] the defendant's factual allegations will be tested in a suppression hearing.[342]

Library References:
West's Key No. Digests, Criminal Law ⚖394.6.

§ 10.17 The Defendant's Motion Papers—Factual Allegations

As noted, in making a suppression motion a defendant is obliged to allege facts that, if true, would justify an order of suppression, and also to identify the sources of information on which the allegations are based.

N.Y.2d 415, 422, 604 N.Y.S.2d 922, 924, 624 N.E.2d 1017 (1993).

335. See, e.g., People v. Bonilla, 193 A.D.2d 362, 597 N.Y.S.2d 46 (1st Dep't 1993), rev'd on other grounds 82 N.Y.2d 825, 604 N.Y.S.2d 937, 624 N.E.2d 1032 (1993); People v. Alexander, 88 A.D.2d 749, 451 N.Y.S.2d 473 (4th Dep't 1982).

336. 197 A.D.2d 411, 602 N.Y.S.2d 395 (1st Dep't 1993).

337. People v. Foster, Brief for Respondent at 32.

338. Id.

339. People v. Foster, 197 A.D.2d 411, 602 N.Y.S.2d 395. See also, People v. Tyrell B., 177 A.D.2d 375, 375–76, 576 N.Y.S.2d 127, 127–28 (1st Dept.1991).

340. See People v. Bonilla, 82 N.Y.2d 825, 827, 604 N.Y.S.2d 937, 938, 624 N.E.2d 1032 (1993).

341. See § 10.18, infra.

342. See §§ 10.19–10.20, infra.

Huntley and *Wade* motions may not be denied simply because the defendant's factual pleadings are inadequate.[343] *Mapp* motions, however, are frequently denied on account of the defendant's failure to allege facts that would require suppression,[344] and the rules that have developed with respect to *Mapp* papers are instructive on the requirements for motions of the remaining types brought under Article 710. But how much is required of a defendant's factual allegations in a *Mapp* motion, in terms of the defendant's standing to protest a search or arrest, of whether the defendant possessed contraband, and of the circumstances that could justify a conclusion that the police actions were illegal, has proved surprisingly difficult to define.

On the most fundamental level, one must distinguish *"Wade"* and *"Huntley"* motions, as to which the court must entertain the motion despite any deficiency in the factual allegations, from *"Mapp"* motions. The CPL does not use these informal terms; the statute instead provides that a motion brought pursuant to section 710.20(3) or section 710.20(6) cannot be denied on account of insufficient factual allegations.[345] Included in the exempt category, therefore, are motions to suppress a defendant's statements as "involuntarily made" and motions to suppress identification testimony on account of a prior, "improperly made" identification.[346] Among the motions that can be denied on account of insufficient factual allegations are motions to suppress "tangible" property taken in an unlawful search or seizure.[347] Arguably, then, the statute places in the exempt category any motion to suppress statements or identifications, even if based on a violation of the Fourth Amendment—for example, a motion to suppress statements and identification testimony on account of an illegal arrest.[348]

Unfortunately for defendants, that interpretation has not found favor in the courts. The prevailing view is that any Fourth Amendment motion, even one to suppress statements or identification testimony rather than tangible property, may be denied summarily if the defendant's factual allegations are insufficient.[349] In that regard, a defendant

---

343. CPL § 710.60(3).

344. See People v. Mendoza, 82 N.Y.2d 415, 421–22, 604 N.Y.S.2d 922, 923–24, 624 N.E.2d 1017 (1993).

345. CPL § 710.60(3)(b).

346. CPL § 710.20(3) and (6).

347. CPL § 710.20(1).

348. Important in this regard is the broad definition of an "involuntarily made" statement contained in CPL § 60.45 and incorporated by express reference in CPL § 710.20(3).

349. The leading case is People v. Covington, 144 A.D.2d 238, 533 N.Y.S.2d 433 (1st Dep't 1988), but Covington decided the issue without discussing the contrary statutory language set out above. See also People v. Henderson, ___ A.D.2d ___, 629 N.Y.S.2d 239 (1st Dep't 1995). In People v. Mendoza, 82 N.Y.2d 415, 421–22, 604 N.Y.S.2d 922, 923–24, 624 N.E.2d 1017 (1993), the Court of Appeals drew distinctions in dictum that assume that Covington was correctly decided:

The two exceptions to the court's authority to summarily deny suppression motions for lack of adequate factual allegations relate to motions to suppress statements as involuntarily made (Huntley motions) or an identification stemming from an improper procedure (Wade)(CPL 710.60[3][b]). Accordingly, the sufficiency of the movant's factual allegations most often arises on motions to suppress tangible evidence (Mapp) or other evidence as the fruit of an unlawful seizure (Dunaway).

On this view, it naturally follows that a court can refuse to permit a defendant to

§ 10.17   SEARCH WARRANTS & SUPPRESSION   Ch. 10

will likely know the facts about virtually any violation of his or her Fourth Amendment rights, no matter what type of evidence might have been derived from it. But a defendant will not necessarily be aware of facts that would render statements or identifications inadmissible on other grounds.[350] That circumstance bolsters the position that all Fourth Amendment motions should be treated consistently for pleading purposes, even if the evidence at issue includes statements or identifications rather than just "tangible" evidence.

As to what must be alleged to obtain a *Mapp* hearing, the evolution of the pleading rules is well reflected in a series of First Department cases that stretches from 1982 to 1993. In *People v. Sutton*,[351] a weapons case, the defendant's motion papers alleged "on information and belief" that the defendant was seized by the police while walking down the street, and alleged further that the defendant was arrested before the gun was seized. The prosecutor answered that officers responding to a radio run had spotted the defendant, that upon observing the officers the defendant had thrown down his gun and fled, and that the arrest had followed the recovery of the gun. The trial court then denied the defendant a hearing for lack of standing, because he did not allege that he had ever possessed the gun. The Appellate Division remanded for a hearing, finding that "the police officer's version of the occurrence confirms the fact that defendant was, at one point, in possession of the gun," that the defendant therefore had standing. As to the defendant's allegations about the police, while defense counsel's affirmation "could have been more specific," it was "adequate to place in question the lawfulness of the police conduct."

After *Sutton*, in cases involving the possession of contraband, defense counsel might well have felt it necessary to include little more in their motion papers about "the lawfulness of the police conduct" than conclusory assertions that their clients were unlawfully arrested. But *People v. Taylor*,[352] another gun case, soon made clear that the defense had some obligation to specify facts showing that the police acted improperly. In *Taylor*, the defendant's motion papers cited the prosecutor's voluntary disclosure form and the Criminal Court complaint for the proposition that a gun had been recovered from the defendant's pocket. The trial court denied the defendant's motion on the theory that his own allegations did not make out standing, but the Appellate Division disagreed. The appellate court cited *Sutton* for the proposition that "a defendant from whose person it is alleged by the prosecution that contraband was seized has standing to move to suppress," thus reaffirming that a defendant's motion papers need not include an admission that

expand the scope of a Huntley or Wade hearing to include a Fourth Amendment challenge to statement or identification evidence if the factual allegations did not entitle him or her to a Mapp hearing. See People v. Fuller, 200 A.D.2d 498, 606 N.Y.S.2d 640 (1st Dep't 1994).

350. See Preiser, "Practice Commentary" to CPL § 710.60, McKinney's Cons.

Laws of New York, Book 11A, at 279 (1995); see also People v. Rodriguez, 79 N.Y.2d 445, 453, 583 N.Y.S.2d 814, 819, 593 N.E.2d 268 (1992).

351. 91 A.D.2d 522, 456 N.Y.S.2d 771 (1st Dep't 1982).

352. 97 A.D.2d 381, 467 N.Y.S.2d 590 (1st Dep't 1983).

he possessed contraband. But, the court noted, *Sutton* "did not eliminate the requirement that facts be alleged to demonstrate that the property ... was procured under circumstances precluding admissibility." The defendant in *Taylor* had not made such allegations.[353]

In 1991, *People v. Murray*[354] lent additional support to the view that specific facts demonstrating illegality must be pleaded by the defendant. The *Murray* panel not only believed that the defendant's initial motion papers had to articulate a basis for finding that police action was illegal, but also concluded that in some circumstances the defendant must reply to prosecution papers that explained away the defense allegations. In *Murray* the defendant's only pertinent factual allegation had been that he was acting innocently at the time he was seized by the police; the prosecution had responded that the arrest was based on a complaint by a civilian that the defendant had robbed him. When that response "was not controverted" by the defendant, his motion was denied. The Appellate Division affirmed, finding that if "[i]n other circumstances an accused's protest that he was acting innocently at the time of his seizure might raise viable issues," in this case the prosecution's uncontroverted response made plain that the arrest was proper.

Finally, in *People v. Coleman*,[355] the defense papers alleged, based on a conversation with the defendant, that at the time of the defendant's arrest he "was not engaged in any criminal activity" and had not given the police probable cause to believe that he was. The defendant then noted that the police claimed that he threw down a gun when they approached him; the defendant denied that he had done so, but, citing *Sutton*, asserted that the allegations of the police were sufficient to establish standing. The defendant suggested in the alternative that if he threw down the gun, he did so in response to an unlawful detention. The trial court denied the motion without a hearing, and the Appellate Division affirmed. That court concluded that defendant's papers contained only "legal conclusions and conclusory allegations" about his conduct, and that the absence of specific factual allegations, coupled with defendant's equivocation about whether he was searched, justified summary denial of the motion.[356]

After *Coleman* there was little left of *Sutton*. In cases involving the possession of contraband, defense counsel were obliged to include much more in their motion papers than conclusory assertions that their clients were unlawfully arrested. In particular, counsel had to include a specific

---

353. The court nonetheless remanded for a hearing because the prosecutor, misreading Sutton, had conceded that the defendant should receive a hearing if he had standing. Id.

354. 172 A.D.2d 437, 569 N.Y.S.2d 12 (1st Dep't 1991), app. withdrawn 79 N.Y.2d 942, 583 N.Y.S.2d 196, 592 N.E.2d 804 (1992).

355. 191 A.D.2d 390, 595 N.Y.S.2d 431 (1st Dep't), aff'd sub nom. People v. Mendoza, 82 N.Y.2d 415, 604 N.Y.S.2d 922, 624 N.E.2d 1017 (1993).

356. The court noted that affirmance was also required "because at his plea allocution the defendant stated unequivocally that he had thrown the pistol away" before being stopped by the police, contrary to his statement to his attorney, and that it was therefore apparent that there was no factual basis for suppression. 191 A.D.2d at 392–93, 595 N.Y.S.2d at 433.

§ 10.17 SEARCH WARRANTS & SUPPRESSION Ch. 10

statement—based on whatever source—that the defendant possessed the contraband, at least until the illegal police conduct commenced.

In the meantime, the Court of Appeals had also begun to put teeth into the requirement that defendants make specific factual allegations to earn *Mapp* hearings. In *People v. Reynolds*,[357] the court upheld the summary denial of a motion based on the defendant's failure to make sufficient factual allegations. In *Reynolds*, the defense alleged that a search warrant was based on illegal observations of marijuana in the "curtilage" of the defendant's house, "hidden in enclosed areas" rather than visible in an "open field." The court noted that these were "conclusory assertions" and that no sworn allegations of fact were offered to support them. In particular, the defendant did not address averments in the warrant application that the marijuana had been observed in open areas and in an open-frame "greenhouse" structure some 150 feet from the defendant's house.

Then, in *People v. Mendoza*[358] the court, deciding four separate appeals including a further appeal in *People v. Coleman*, sought to set out a general framework for determining whether defendants were entitled to *Mapp* hearings. In all four cases, the defense papers had effectively said nothing about the defendant's conduct other than that the defendant was not visibly doing anything illegal at the time he was seized.[359] The court found that these allegations, like the "curtilage" allegation in *Reynolds*, stated legal conclusions that were impossible to assess in the absence of factual particulars.[360]

But, the court noted, the lack of specificity in the defendants' allegations was not necessarily dispositive. Specific allegations might not entitle one defendant to a hearing, and the "barebones" allegations of another might be sufficient, depending on the context in which their motions were made. Of particular importance are the documents that define the prosecution's position on the facts of the case, including documents submitted in advance of the defendant's motion papers. The court cited, by way of example, the search warrant papers in *Reynolds*, and noted that a defendant's failure to dispute assertions by the prosecution about a search or arrest might make a hearing unnecessary.[361]

Similarly, in "buy and bust" drug cases, in which probable cause is typically created by incidents occurring a few minutes before an arrest, it will not be enough for a defendant's papers to allege only that the defendant was not visibly committing a crime at the moment of the arrest. To create a material issue of fact, the defendant must deny that

---

357. 71 N.Y.2d 552, 558, 528 N.Y.S.2d 15, 523 N.E.2d 291 (1988).

358. 82 N.Y.2d 415, 604 N.Y.S.2d 922, 624 N.E.2d 1017 (1993).

359. 82 N.Y.2d at 422–25, 604 N.Y.S.2d at 924–26.

360. 82 N.Y.2d at 426–27, 604 N.Y.S.2d at 926–27. The court supplied an example of an indisputably proper, "plainly factual" allegation: "On June 19, 1993, at 3:00 p.m., I was waiting for a bus on the corner of Broadway and 42nd St. when a uniformed police officer approached me stating 'people like you don't belong in this neighborhood.' She reached into my jacket pocket and removed a one-inch vial of cocaine." 82 N.Y.2d at 426, 604 N.Y.S.2d at 926.

361. 82 N.Y.2d at 428, 604 N.Y.S.2d at 927–28.

he or she was a party to the drug transaction. On the other hand, in a case in which a frisk or search of the defendant is alleged to have been justified by the defendant's furtive conduct, it may well suffice for a defendant to say only that he or she was doing nothing suspicious at the time the police approached.[362]

Finally, on some critical questions it will be impossible for the defendant to make specific allegations, and in such a case the court should not expect the defendant to do so. In particular, a defendant may well not be able to determine whether the security guard who apprehended him or her was a peace officer, or under the supervision of a peace officer, and thus may not be able to say much in support of a claim that a "state actor" conducted the search. In such a circumstance, a general allegation that the guard was a peace officer, or was supervised by one, will suffice.[363] On the other hand, a defendant is presumptively able to allege facts demonstrating standing, for he must know his own connection to the area of a search.[364]

Having stated these principles, and having also emphasized that a trial court might elect to grant a hearing to which the defendant was not legally entitled,[365] the court ruled that in three of the cases before it the defendant had not been entitled to a suppression hearing. In two cases it was evident at the time of the motion that the arrest was based on prior drug sales, and the defendants' assertions that they were acting lawfully when arrested were not only conclusory, but beside the point.[366] In *Coleman*, the defendant's allegations did not "lay out a scenario which, if credited, would have warranted suppression." Even Coleman's alternative argument, that if he threw down the gun as alleged by the police it was in response to an unlawful detention, made no sense, in that the detention occurred only after the gun had been thrown. And the court rejected as an appellate afterthought a defense claim that he might have thrown the gun while being unlawfully pursued by the police. Had that occurred, the defendant should have been able to say so in his motion papers.[367] In the fourth case, the court remanded for a hearing, having found a factual issue as to whether a store security guard was acting as a state agent.[368]

The sufficiency of the factual allegations in a defendant's motion papers can now be determined only by reference to the framework

---

362. 82 N.Y.2d at 428–29, 604 N.Y.S.2d at 928.

363. 82 N.Y.2d at 429, 433–34, 604 N.Y.S.2d at 928, 931. The First Department had taken the position that bald assertions about a store guard's status were insufficient to make out state action and a Fourth Amendment violation. People v. Lovejoy, 197 A.D.2d 353, 602 N.Y.S.2d 126 (1st Dep't 1993); People v. Mendoza, 186 A.D.2d 458, 589 N.Y.S.2d 35 (1st Dep't 1992).

364. People v. Mendoza, 82 N.Y.2d at 429, 604 N.Y.S.2d at 928. If unusual circumstances would prevent the defendant from making such expected allegations, he or she should notify the court of those circumstances in the motion papers. People v. Gomez, 67 N.Y.2d 843, 501 N.Y.S.2d 650, 492 N.E.2d 778 (1986).

365. 82 N.Y.2d at 429–30, 604 N.Y.S.2d at 928; see CPL § 710.60(3).

366. 82 N.Y.2d at 430–31, 604 N.Y.S.2d at 929–30.

367. 82 N.Y.2d at 432–33, 604 N.Y.S.2d at 930.

368. 82 N.Y.2d at 433–34, 604 N.Y.S.2d at 931–32.

created by *Mendoza*. For example, in *People v. Vasquez*,[369] the defendant was arrested for a murder that had occurred 11 days before, and had no idea what grounds the police had for believing him to be the killer. The First Department found that a defendant in that position could be forgiven for alleging very generally that he was arrested without probable cause. But the same court denied relief to a defendant whose knowledge of the facts would have permitted him to make specific allegations:

> Since the People were obviously justifying the search on an abandonment theory, it was incumbent upon defendant to set forth a specific alternate scenario which, if credited, would have warranted suppression.[370]

And, after *Mendoza* the First Department concluded that a defendant in a buy-and-bust case would properly be denied a hearing when he alleged only that he committed no crime and that the police had no probable cause to arrest him. In the court's view, the defendant was at fault both because his allegations were conclusory and because he did not deny the earlier drug transaction.[371] Surprisingly, however, in *People v. Hightower*[372] the Court of Appeals appeared to relax the *Mendoza* pleading rules in the case of a defendant who allegedly was observed selling drugs with two accomplices. The court found that this defendant had done enough to earn a hearing when he denied having possessed or sold narcotics, or having helped those arrested with him to do so. As the court saw it, the "meager information" available to the defendant would not have permitted him to allege more.[373]

One case does not necessarily create a trend, but after *Hightower* it will be much more difficult for a trial court to deny a *Mapp* motion on the pleadings, in a buy-and-bust or observation sale case, where the defendant alleges that he or she did not sell or possess drugs at the time of the crime. And indeed, hard on the heels of *Hightower*, the First Department found that a defendant had been entitled to a hearing in an observation sale case after he alleged that he was legitimately in a restaurant, that he was not acting suspiciously, and that "no illegal

---

369. 200 A.D.2d 344, 613 N.Y.S.2d 595 (1st Dep't 1994).

370. People v. Omaro, 201 A.D.2d 324, 607 N.Y.S.2d 44 (1st Dep't 1994).

371. People v. Marte, 207 A.D.2d 314, 615 N.Y.S.2d 678 (1st Dep't 1994). See also People v. Henderson, ___ A.D.2d ___, 629 N.Y.S.2d 239 (1st Dep't 1995); People v. Moore, 213 A.D.2d 352, 624 N.Y.S.2d 412 (1st Dep't 1995). Notably, a Mapp hearing in a buy-and-bust or observation sale case in which the defendant cannot allege particulars of innocent conduct will generally not be much more than a rehearsal of the trial, no doubt helpful to the defense for its preview of the prosecution case, but serving little jurisprudential purpose.

372. 85 N.Y.2d 988, 629 N.Y.S.2d 164, 652 N.E.2d 910 (1995).

373. The court did not explain why the defendant could not have, in the words of the First Department, "refute[d] the People's detailed statements relating the officers' observation of defendant and co-defendants selling narcotics," People v. Hightower, 206 A.D.2d 253, 614 N.Y.S.2d 407 (1st Dep't 1994). In that regard, the defendant certainly had personal knowledge of his relationship with those arrested with him, how he came to be with them, what he had seen them do, and whether he had, as alleged, handled money on the scene.

contraband was in such a position so as to be seen by a police officer."[374] The court read in *Hightower* a rejection of the proposition that the defendant must "offer an innocent explanation for his conduct or at least respond to the People's papers."[375]

Separate treatment is due to the pleading requirements concerning standing. Except under special circumstances involving the prosecution's reliance on a statutory presumption,[376] a defendant's pleadings cannot make out a violation of the Fourth Amendment if they do not contain allegations establishing his or her standing to protest the illegality.[377] In those cases in which evidence is recovered from the defendant's person, the defendant need allege no more than that[378]—and some judges may permit the defendant to do so without a personal admission that the evidence was on his person.[379] But where the evidence is not taken from the defendant's person, the defendant will be obliged to set out the particulars of his or her connection either to the evidence, or to the area in which it was seized.[380] Or, at least, the defendant will be required to do so if the prosecution has not already done it for him.[381]

Finally, whatever the subject area of a motion, defense counsel should be alert on receipt of the prosecution's answer to the potential need to submit a reply. As noted above, a defendant may find the motion summarily denied if he or she does not address pertinent facts in the prosecution's answer. And if the answer introduces new legal concepts into the case, a pertinent factual dispute may have to be created to prevent those concepts from being dispositive of the motion.[382]

Library References:
West's Key No. Digests, Criminal Law ⚖394.6.

374. People v. Bailey, ___ A.D.2d ___, 630 N.Y.S.2d 499 (1st Dep't 1995). But see People v. Henderson, ___ A.D.2d ___, 629 N.Y.S.2d 239 (1st Dep't 1995).

375. People v. Bailey, ___ A.D.2d ___, ___, 630 N.Y.S.2d 499, 501 (1st Dep't 1995).

376. See People v. Wesley, 73 N.Y.2d 351, 540 N.Y.S.2d 757, 538 N.E.2d 76 (1989).

377. People v. Carter, 86 N.Y.2d 721, 631 N.Y.S.2d 116, 655 N.E.2d 157 (1995).

378. People v. Zarate, 160 A.D.2d 466, 554 N.Y.S.2d 137 (1st Dep't 1990).

379. But see People v. Mendoza (Coleman), 82 N.Y.2d at 424–25, 432–33, 604 N.Y.S.2d at 925–26, 930.

380. People v. Mendoza, 82 N.Y.2d at 429, 604 N.Y.S.2d at 928; People v. Gomez, 67 N.Y.2d 843, 501 N.Y.S.2d 650, 492 N.E.2d 778 (1986); People v. Lovejoy, 197 A.D.2d 353, 602 N.Y.S.2d 126 (1st Dep't 1993)(defendant's inadequate allegation was that robbery evidence in a bag was "seized from a nearby location"); see also People v. Wesley, 73 N.Y.2d 351, 358–59, 540 N.Y.S.2d 757, 760–61, 538 N.E.2d 76 (1989).

381. In a First Department case decided before Mendoza but well after Gomez, People v. Fuentes–Borda, 186 A.D.2d 405, 589 N.Y.S.2d 5 (1st Dep't 1992), cocaine was discovered both in an apartment and in a gym bag outside the apartment. Although the defendant asked for a Mapp hearing, he denied having been inside the apartment or that he had any proprietary interest in the gym bag. But the police officers alleged that the bag was taken from defendant and his co-defendant, and that the two of them had been seen leaving and locking the apartment. The court concluded that the police allegations sufficiently connected defendant to the bag and the apartment to require a hearing.

382. See generally § 10.18, infra. Of particular note is the lesson of People v. Rodriguez, 79 N.Y.2d 445, 583 N.Y.S.2d 814, 593 N.E.2d 268 (1992), in which successive factual arguments and averments by the defense kept alive an issue about the propriety of an allegedly "confirmatory" civilian identification.

§ 10.18 The Prosecution's Motion Papers

In civil cases, the answer is as critical as the complaint to the framing of the factual issues. Similarly, the prosecution's response to a defendant's suppression motion is critical to the determination of whether a hearing must be conducted.

The text of Article 710 says comparatively little about the nature of the prosecution's response to the defendant's motion. Under section 710.60(1),

> The people may file with the court, and in such cases must serve a copy thereof upon the defendant or his counsel, an answer denying or admitting any or all of the allegations of the motion papers.

While the section is permissive, there is no rational alternative to filing an answer for a prosecutor who intends to contest the defendant's motion; failure to respond can result in a waiver of meritorious responses.[383]

If the answer concedes the truth of the defendant's factual allegations, the court must summarily grant the suppression motion—assuming, of course, that the defendant's papers stated both a legal basis for suppression and proper factual allegations in support of that basis.[384] The Court of Appeals has plainly indicated that silence in response to an opponent's factual allegation can be read as a concession.[385] The wise choice for the prosecutor therefore is to employ a civil practice tactic and deny any fact alleged by the defendant that may not be true—perhaps in a catch-all statement that facts not expressly admitted in the answer should be deemed denied. And common sense should lead the prosecutor to indicate which of the defendant's legal theories he or she disputes.

Other contents of the prosecutor's answer are suggested by the case law. For example, under the rules set out in *People v. Mendoza*,[386] it may well be advisable to respond to a *Mapp* motion by spelling out the

---

[383]. A literal reading of the statute might suggest that the consequence of a failure to answer should be a hearing, not a summary grant of the motion. See People v. Butor, 75 Misc.2d 558, 560–61, 348 N.Y.S.2d 89 (Dutchess Co.Ct.1973). Nonetheless, failing to answer is far too risky a course to contemplate. See, e.g., People v. Paul, 139 A.D.2d 916, 527 N.Y.S.2d 905 (4th Dep't 1988). See also People v. Gruden, 42 N.Y.2d 214, 397 N.Y.S.2d 704, 366 N.E.2d 794 (1977)(rejecting "literal" reading of similar statute).

[384]. CPL § 710.60(2)(a). The court must also grant the motion if the prosecution stipulates that the evidence at issue will not be offered against the defendant in any criminal action or proceeding. CPL § 710.60(2)(b). There is no ready explanation for why the Legislature chose to state that such a stipulation would bar the use of the evidence against the defendant in "any" action or proceeding, rather than merely in the action in which the stipulation was entered. In any event, the fact that the required stipulation extends to all proceedings should put a prosecutor on guard about the potential of a stipulation to prevent use of the disputed evidence in other cases—although it is far from certain that independent prosecutorial offices could be bound by such a stipulation. As noted in § 10.8, supra, such a stipulation does not prevent use of the evidence to impeach the defendant if he or she offers inconsistent testimony.

[385]. People v. Gruden, 42 N.Y.2d 214, 397 N.Y.S.2d 704, 366 N.E.2d 794 (1977)(interpreting similar language in CPL § 210.45(4)).

[386]. 82 N.Y.2d 415, 604 N.Y.S.2d 922, 624 N.E.2d 1017 (1993).

prosecution's theory of the facts, or at least by incorporating by reference other documents already in the case that outline the facts. Detailed allegations may result in the summary denial of the defendant's motion if the defendant maintains a conclusory position on the facts—particularly if the defendant makes general allegations that he or she was doing nothing illegal when confronted by the police, and the police action was based on an event that occurred at a time prior to that confrontation.[387] The prosecution should also note any patent deficiencies in the defendant's factual presentation—for example, a failure to allege standing.[388]

A detailed factual response may, however, simply underline the need for a hearing if the defendant has effectively placed the prosecution's facts in dispute.[389] What can therefore be more effective is to introduce a new issue into the equation, along the lines of a defense of "confession and avoidance." Thus, a defendant's factual allegation that the police entered his apartment without a warrant, whether true or false, would become irrelevant upon a response that his wife consented to the entry, or that the police entered in "hot pursuit" of a fleeing felon. Under *Mendoza*, the defendant's motion would presumably be denied summarily unless he replied with new factual allegations going to the "avoidance" defense.

Indeed, the prosecutor may be able to avoid an unjustified plenary hearing on a frivolous motion even in the *Huntley* and *Wade* areas. Certain types of statement and identification evidence are so unlikely to be suppressed that the law permits denial of suppression motions on a summary basis, in derogation of routine suppression procedure.[390] For example, a "confirmatory" identification by a long-standing acquaintance will not be suppressed, even if obtained through what might otherwise be questionable procedures.[391] Likewise, "pedigree" statements obtained from the defendant after the arrest will not be suppressed, even if not preceded by *Miranda* warnings.[392] Accordingly, there is no need for *Huntley* or *Wade* hearings on such evidence. Should the prosecutor accurately interpose in the answer the "defense" that statement or identification evidence falls into one of these categories, or a similar category, the need for a hearing may be eliminated. If the defendant creates a factual dispute as to the applicability of the doctrine cited by the prosecution, the hearing that will ensue can be limited to that issue if the prosecution prevails on it.[393]

---

387. See, e.g., People v. Murray, 172 A.D.2d 437, 569 N.Y.S.2d 12 (1st Dep't 1991), app. withdrawn 79 N.Y.2d 942, 583 N.Y.S.2d 196, 592 N.E.2d 804 (1992).

388. See, e.g., People v. Gomez, 67 N.Y.2d 843, 501 N.Y.S.2d 650, 492 N.E.2d 778 (1986).

389. See, e.g., People v. Zarate, 160 A.D.2d 466, 554 N.Y.S.2d 137 (1st Dep't 1990).

390. See §§ 10.25–10.26, infra.

391. People v. Rodriguez, 79 N.Y.2d 445, 583 N.Y.S.2d 814, 593 N.E.2d 268 (1992).

392. People v. Rodney, 85 N.Y.2d 289, 624 N.Y.S.2d 95, 648 N.E.2d 471 (1995).

393. People v. Rodriguez, 79 N.Y.2d at 453, 583 N.Y.S.2d at 820.

§ 10.18 SEARCH WARRANTS & SUPPRESSION Ch. 10

Library References:

West's Key No. Digests, Criminal Law ⚖ 394.6.

§ 10.19 Suppression Hearings—In General

As noted in the preceding sections, a suppression motion must be summarily granted if the defendant's papers satisfy the requirements of section 710.60(1) and the prosecution concedes the facts alleged, or if the prosecution agrees not to use the evidence against the defendant. And a suppression motion may be summarily denied if the defendant does not state a legal basis for the motion, or—except in *Huntley* and *Wade* motions—does not make sworn allegations of fact sufficient to support the proffered legal basis for the motion.[394] In other circumstances, the court "must conduct a hearing and make findings of fact essential to the determination thereof."[395]

In other contexts, New York law permits informal "hearings," in which it suffices that the parties have a fair opportunity to state their positions on an issue.[396] Even in the suppression context, "due process requirements for a hearing may be less elaborate and demanding than those at the trial proper."[397] But it has always been held that a suppression "hearing" must be a relatively formal proceeding, closely akin to a trial.[398] The CPL and the case law recognize that:

1. The defendant has a right to be present at a suppression hearing.[399]

2. The defendant can waive the right to be present.[400] Typically, waivers are made in *Wade* proceedings, in which the defendant may fear that his or her presence in the courtroom will permit an identification witness to refresh—or form—a recollection of the defendant's appearance in a way that will harm the defendant at trial.[401]

3. The public is entitled to be present. The defendant may successfully move to exclude the public only by showing a substantial probability that his or her right to a fair trial would otherwise be

---

394. See §§ 10.16–10.18, supra.

395. CPL § 710.60(4).

396. See, e.g., People v. Ventimiglia, 52 N.Y.2d 350, 362, 438 N.Y.S.2d 261, 265, 420 N.E.2d 59 (1981)(evidence of uncharged crimes); People v. Friedman, 39 N.Y.2d 463, 384 N.Y.S.2d 408, 348 N.E.2d 883 (1976)(withdrawal of guilty plea); People v. Sandoval, 34 N.Y.2d 371, 357 N.Y.S.2d 849, 314 N.E.2d 413 (1974)(scope of impeachment of defendant).

397. People v. Castillo, 80 N.Y.2d 578, 582, 592 N.Y.S.2d 945, 946, 607 N.E.2d 1050 (1992), cert. den. 507 U.S. 1033, 113 S.Ct. 1854, 123 L.Ed.2d 477 (1993).

398. See, e.g., People v. Davis, 169 A.D.2d 379, 380–81, 564 N.Y.S.2d 320, 321–22 (1st Dep't 1991); People v. Del Giorno, 19 A.D.2d 849, 243 N.Y.S.2d 1010 (4th Dep't 1963); People v. Entrialgo, 19 A.D.2d 509, 511, 245 N.Y.S.2d 850, 852 (2d Dep't 1963), aff'd 14 N.Y.2d 733, 250 N.Y.S.2d 293, 199 N.E.2d 384 (1964); People v. Lombardi, 18 A.D.2d 177, 180–81, 239 N.Y.S.2d 161 (2d Dep't 1963), aff'd 13 N.Y.2d 1014, 245 N.Y.S.2d 595, 195 N.E.2d 306 (1963).

399. People v. Anderson, 16 N.Y.2d 282, 266 N.Y.S.2d 110, 213 N.E.2d 445 (1965); see also People v. Morales, 80 N.Y.2d 450, 455–57, 591 N.Y.S.2d 825, 828–30, 606 N.E.2d 953 (1992).

400. People v. Spotford, 85 N.Y.2d 593, 627 N.Y.S.2d 295, 650 N.E.2d 1296 (1995).

401. People v. Foster, 200 A.D.2d 196, 202–03, 613 N.Y.S.2d 616, 620 (1st Dept. 1994).

prejudiced, and that reasonable alternatives to closure cannot adequately protect that right.[402]

4. The hearing must be conducted by a judge or judicial hearing officer, and decision must be rendered by a judge.[403] Notably, the judge may be the same individual who issued an order that is being attacked in the suppression motion.[404] As at a trial, the judge is not "merely an observer or referee required to play a passive role,"[405] and can both cut off profitless inquiries, and ask questions of witnesses to elicit relevant information.[406]

5. The parties can call witnesses,[407] at least within limitations that are discussed later in this section.

6. The parties are entitled to reasonable continuances to obtain the presence of witnesses, but the granting of such continuances rests in the court's discretion.[408]

7. The parties are entitled to confront the opposing party's witnesses through cross-examination, as at trial.[409] And a defendant is entitled to the aid of such exhibits and documents as are reasonably necessary to assure adequate cross-examination, as at trial.[410] But of course the judge has discretion to limit cross-examination to relevant topics, as at trial.[411]

8. The defendant may testify,[412] and no special cross-examination rule applies when the defendant is the witness. The defendant may be cross-examined concerning matters that go to general credibility, as well as matters material to the suppression proceedings even if they are beyond the scope of a narrow direct examination. The court should, however, prevent cross-examination of the defendant about matters that were not addressed on direct examination, and are not material to the suppression proceedings, even if they might concern other aspects of the case.[413]

402. Associated Press v. Bell, 70 N.Y.2d 32, 517 N.Y.S.2d 444, 510 N.E.2d 313 (1987).

403. See § 10.12, supra; CPL § 255.20(4); see generally People v. Scalza, 76 N.Y.2d 604, 562 N.Y.S.2d 14, 563 N.E.2d 705 (1990).

404. People v. Liberatore, 79 N.Y.2d 208, 216–17, 581 N.Y.S.2d 634, 638–39, 590 N.E.2d 219 (1992).

405. People v. Casado, 83 A.D.2d 385, 386, 444 N.Y.S.2d 920, 920 (1st Dep't 1981).

406. People v. Harrison, 151 A.D.2d 778, 778–79, 543 N.Y.S.2d 108, 108–09 (2d Dep't 1989); People v. Casado, 83 A.D.2d at 386, 444 N.Y.S.2d at 920–21.

407. CPL § 60.15(1).

408. People v. Thomas, 210 A.D.2d 269, 619 N.Y.S.2d 733 (2d Dep't 1994) (defense denied adjournment); People v. Setteroth, 200 A.D.2d 533, 607 N.Y.S.2d 15 (1st Dep't 1994)(same); People v. Patterson, 177 A.D.2d 1042, 578 N.Y.S.2d 55 (4th Dep't 1991) (prosecution denied adjournment).

409. CPL § 60.15(1); People v. Misuis, 47 N.Y.2d 979, 981, 419 N.Y.S.2d 961, 962, 393 N.E.2d 1034 (1979); People v. Whitaker, 79 A.D.2d 668, 433 N.Y.S.2d 849 (2d Dep't 1980); People v. Strever, 73 A.D.2d 1031, 425 N.Y.S.2d 181 (4th Dep't 1980).

410. People v. Robinson, 118 A.D.2d 516, 500 N.Y.S.2d 122 (1st Dep't 1986).

411. People v. Shawcross, 192 A.D.2d 1128, 1129, 596 N.Y.S.2d 622, 624 (4th Dep't 1993); People v. Lourdes, 175 A.D.2d 958, 573 N.Y.S.2d 537 (3d Dep't 1991); People v. Johnson, 129 A.D.2d 815, 514 N.Y.S.2d 805 (2d Dep't 1987).

412. CPL § 60.15(2).

413. People v. Blackwell, 128 Misc.2d 599, 490 N.Y.S.2d 457 (Sup.Ct., N.Y. County, 1985).

9. *Rosario* principles that govern disclosure at trial of the prior, recorded statements of a party's witnesses are generally applicable at suppression hearings.[414] By statute, however, the disclosure obligation is triggered only by the opposing party's request for a witness's statements, and disclosure need not be made before the conclusion of the witness's direct examination.[415] Needless to say, a timely demand for disclosure should be a routine part of every litigant's motion practice.

10. The application of *Brady* principles in suppression proceedings, in which the defendant's guilt or innocence is not the issue, has received little attention in the case law. However, *People v. Geaslen*[416] makes plain that the prosecution's obligation to disclose "exculpatory" information extends to information that would be materially helpful to the defense on a suppression issue:

> This is not to suggest that prosecutors must disclose to the court each and every statement or bit of evidence or the results of every avenue of investigation. Indeed, there are many situations where the prosecution can fairly keep to itself what it alone possesses. But where, as here, there is in the possession of the prosecution evidence of a material nature which if disclosed could affect the ultimate decision on a suppression motion, and that evidence is not disclosed, such nondisclosure denies the defendant due process of law.[417]

The court's language suggests that it may suffice in the suppression context that information be disclosed to the court, which is the trier of fact.

Two subjects deserve more detailed exploration: the attendance of witnesses and the rules of evidence. As to the former, the defendant has a right to call witnesses, and to testify himself or herself.[418] And the subpoena procedures of the CPL are available to the parties at suppression proceedings, enabling them to require attendance by witnesses.[419] But the defense cannot compel the prosecution to present a particular witness at a hearing.[420] And, critically, the defense cannot necessarily compel the presence of an unfriendly witness to testify for the defendant.[421]

In that regard, the "right of compulsory process is essentially a trial

---

414. CPL § 240.44; People v. Banch, 80 N.Y.2d 610, 593 N.Y.S.2d 491, 608 N.E.2d 1069 (1992); People v. Poole, 48 N.Y.2d 144, 422 N.Y.S.2d 5, 397 N.E.2d 697 (1979); People v. Malinsky, 15 N.Y.2d 86, 90–91, 262 N.Y.S.2d 65, 209 N.E.2d 694 (1965). See Chapter 7, § 7.16.

415. CPL § 240.44.

416. 54 N.Y.2d 510, 446 N.Y.S.2d 227, 430 N.E.2d 1280 (1981).

417. 54 N.Y.2d at 516, 446 N.Y.S.2d at 229.

418. CPL § 60.15; see, e.g. People v. Petralia, 62 N.Y.2d 47, 53, 476 N.Y.S.2d 56, 58, 464 N.E.2d 424 (1984).

419. See Matter of Cohen, 144 A.D.2d 605, 534 N.Y.S.2d 1022 (2d Dep't 1988); CPL § 610.20; see also CPL Articles 620, 630, 640, 650.

420. People v. Chipp, 75 N.Y.2d 327, 334, 553 N.Y.S.2d 72, 76, 552 N.E.2d 608 (1990).

421. 75 N.Y.2d at 336–39, 553 N.Y.S.2d at 77–79.

right,"[422] and at a hearing may be outweighed by "countervailing policy concerns, properly within the discretion and control of the hearing Judge."[423] The defendant is entitled to the testimony of a witness at a hearing, even if the witness is a crime victim, if that witness is crucial to the resolution of a substantial suppression issue.[424] Otherwise, however, the defendant has no right to call such a witness. To compel the presence of the witness when the witness's testimony is not needed to resolve a substantial issue will serve only to harass the witness or to provide discovery outside the bounds set in the CPL.[425] Similarly, there is no right to the testimony of an undercover police officer, absent a substantial issue that only the undercover's testimony could resolve.[426]

The trick, then, is to state when a "substantial" issue exists, such that the defendant is entitled to call an unfriendly witness. A defendant is not entitled to call a crime victim simply by speculating that a non-police witness might give testimony about an identification proceeding that would differ from the testimony of the police witnesses.[427] But a defendant is entitled to call a crime victim if only that victim can testify about a particular event relevant to the defendant's contentions.[428]

Helpful in defining when a defendant should be able to call an unfriendly witness are two cases in which the Court of Appeals addressed, not whether the defendant had a right to call witnesses, but whether the prosecution had made a sufficient showing without calling additional witnesses. In *People v. Witherspoon*,[429] the prosecution was obliged to prove that the defendant's statements had been properly obtained, and to do so it presented the testimony of the officer who actually elicited those statements. Neither in his conclusory motion papers, nor at his suppression hearing, had the defendant presented a "bona fide factual predicate" for believing that any other police officer had done anything improper. The Court of Appeals held that the prosecution's burden of proof had been met, and that it was not obliged to call "all police officers who had contact with the defendant from arrest to the time that the challenged statements were elicited."[430]

On the other hand, in *People v. Anderson*,[431] the defendant testified that, before his confession, he had advised a "stocky, white, short" police officer of his desire for counsel. The defendant alleged that he spoke to this officer between his contacts with the two witnesses called by the

422. 75 N.Y.2d at 336, 553 N.Y.S.2d at 77.
423. 75 N.Y.2d at 337, 553 N.Y.S.2d at 78.
424. 75 N.Y.2d at 338, 553 N.Y.S.2d at 78–79.
425. 75 N.Y.2d at 337–38, 553 N.Y.S.2d at 78.
426. People v. Petralia, 62 N.Y.2d 47, 476 N.Y.S.2d 56, 464 N.E.2d 424 (1984).
427. People v. Chipp, footnote 420 supra.
428. People v. Ocasio, 134 A.D.2d 293, 520 N.Y.S.2d 620 (2d Dep't 1987)(whether witnesses spoke to one another in midst of identification procedures), cited with approval in People v. Chipp, 75 N.Y.2d at 338, 553 N.Y.S.2d at 78–79.
429. 66 N.Y.2d 973, 498 N.Y.S.2d 789, 489 N.E.2d 758 (1985).
430. See also People v. Di Stefano, 38 N.Y.2d 640, 652, 382 N.Y.S.2d 5, 12, 345 N.E.2d 548 (1976); People v. Dunlap, 216 A.D.2d 215, 629 N.Y.S.2d 407 (1st Dep't 1995).
431. 69 N.Y.2d 651, 511 N.Y.S.2d 592, 503 N.E.2d 1023 (1986).

§ 10.19   SEARCH WARRANTS & SUPPRESSION   Ch. 10

prosecution—the arresting officer and the officer who took his confession. And the testimony of the prosecution's witnesses lent some support to the claim that the defendant had been alone with an officer other than the witnesses before the confession. The Court of Appeals concluded that the prosecution, by not presenting testimony addressing the scenario defendant had put forward, had failed to show that the defendant's right to counsel had been honored.[432]

While *Witherspoon* and *Anderson* expressly considered whether the prosecution's proof at a suppression hearing was sufficient, there are no better benchmarks as to when a defendant should and should not obtain the aid of the court to compel the presence of unfriendly hearing witnesses on his or her own behalf. Where, as in *Witherspoon*, there is no evidentiary support for a conclusion that additional individuals have knowledge beyond that of the witnesses called by the prosecution, the court need not permit the defendant to compel the presence of additional witnesses. But if, as in *Anderson*, the defendant creates a substantial factual dispute, and the prosecution's witnesses cannot speak to the issue, the defendant is entitled to call witnesses who can.

More stringent rules limit a defendant who seeks to call a confidential informant. When a search or arrest is grounded in an informant's tip, the critical issue at the ensuing *Mapp* hearing may be whether the informant exists and whether the police have correctly reported the informant's tip. In such circumstances the production of the informant may be necessary to resolve the issue, but the defendant has no right to call the confidential informant, or confront him or her.[433] Rather, to protect the identity of the informant, the court can conduct an *in camera* examination of the informant—a *Darden* hearing. While neither the defendant nor defense counsel may attend, the court must endeavor to protect the defendant's interests, and must ask any proper questions submitted on defendant's behalf.[434] If the informant is unavailable, perhaps simply because he or she is too fearful to participate in an inquiry, the prosecution may be able to establish that the informant exists without even making him or her available to the court at a *Darden* hearing.[435]

The Court of Appeals has authorized further divergence from routine suppression procedure in cases in which an informant's identity would be revealed if a warrant application were disclosed to the defense. In such a case, if *in camera* review of the application and of the informant persuades the court both that the existence of probable cause is clear and that disclosure of the application, even with reasonable

432. See also People v. Valerius, 31 N.Y.2d 51, 334 N.Y.S.2d 871, 286 N.E.2d 254 (1972); People v. Harrington, 70 Misc.2d 303, 304, 332 N.Y.S.2d 789, 791 (Allegheny Co.Ct.1972).

433. People v. Darden, 34 N.Y.2d 177, 356 N.Y.S.2d 582, 313 N.E.2d 49 (1974); see People v. Coffey, 12 N.Y.2d 443, 240 N.Y.S.2d 721, 191 N.E.2d 263 (1963), cert. den. 376 U.S. 916, 84 S.Ct. 671, 11 L.Ed.2d 612 (1964). Much different principles govern at trial. See People v. Goggins, 34 N.Y.2d 163, 356 N.Y.S.2d 571, 313 N.E.2d 41, cert. den. 419 U.S. 1012, 95 S.Ct. 332, 42 L.Ed.2d 286 (1974).

434. People v. Darden, 34 N.Y.2d at 182, 356 N.Y.S.2d at 586.

435. People v. Carpenito, 80 N.Y.2d 65, 587 N.Y.S.2d 264, 599 N.E.2d 668 (1992).

redactions, would inevitably reveal the informant's identity, the court may authorize the prosecution not to disclose the application to the defense.[436] But such an order effectively prevents the defense from crafting arguments that probable cause was lacking, and thus the court must be "particularly" diligent about considering all the positions that the defendant would likely take if he or she had full knowledge of the papers.[437]

The second subject deserving of detailed discussion is the law of evidence applicable at hearings. With a single exception, the rules of evidence at suppression hearings are those that apply elsewhere in criminal proceedings.[438] The one exception is that, at a suppression hearing, "hearsay evidence is admissible to establish any material fact."[439]

Before the CPL was enacted, the case law recognized that hearsay was admissible at a suppression hearing to establish probable cause.[440] It has been frequently assumed that the language in the CPL allowing hearsay at suppression hearings was intended solely to let the prosecution establish probable cause for police action through testimony about what the police were told by others.[441] However, the declarations of informants are not introduced at a *Mapp* hearing for their truth, but to establish the reasonableness of police action,[442] and thus such evidence is not properly viewed as hearsay at all.[443]

---

436. People v. Castillo, 80 N.Y.2d 578, 592 N.Y.S.2d 945, 607 N.E.2d 1050 (1992); see People v. Liberatore, 79 N.Y.2d 208, 581 N.Y.S.2d 634, 590 N.E.2d 219 (1992).

437. People v. Castillo, 80 N.Y.2d at 585–86, 592 N.Y.S.2d at 949; see People v. Seychel, 136 Misc.2d 310, 518 N.Y.S.2d 754 (Sup.Ct., N.Y. County, 1987).

438. See CPL Article 60. The rules of evidence applicable in civil proceedings are the rules that apply in criminal proceedings as well. CPL § 60.10. A special provision, CPL § 60.20(2), governs in criminal proceedings as to when witnesses may testify without taking an oath. CPL § 710.60(4) expressly states that this provision applies at suppression hearings.

439. CPL § 710.60(4). The original draft of the CPL had contained a relatively complex statement about the rules of evidence that might apply at hearings. That language would have permitted evidence at a hearing if it was relevant to the suppression issue, even if it was "of a hearsay nature" or "otherwise incompetent by trial standards." The staff comment accompanying the section sheds no light on what the drafters had in mind when they used the words, "otherwise incompetent by trial standards." See Proposed New York Criminal Procedure Law, 375.60(4), p. 421 (Edward Thompson Co.1967).

440. See, e.g., People v. Coffey, 12 N.Y.2d 443, 452, 240 N.Y.S.2d 721, 726, 191 N.E.2d 263 (1963), cert. den. 376 U.S. 916, 84 S.Ct. 671, 11 L.Ed.2d 612 (1964); People v. Loria, 10 N.Y.2d 368, 374, 223 N.Y.S.2d 462, 467, 179 N.E.2d 478 (1961); People v. Entrialgo, 19 A.D.2d 509, 245 N.Y.S.2d 850 (2d Dep't 1963), aff'd 14 N.Y.2d 733, 250 N.Y.S.2d 293, 199 N.E.2d 384 (1964); People v. Melvin, 58 Misc.2d 424, 426, 296 N.Y.S.2d 435, 437 (Dist.Ct., Suffolk County, 1968).

441. See, e.g., People v. Caldwell, 107 Misc.2d 62, 63, 437 N.Y.S.2d 829, 830 (App. Term, 1st Dep't, 1980); People v. Coniglio, 79 Misc.2d 808, 813, 361 N.Y.S.2d 524, 530 (Sup.Ct., Queens County, 1974).

442. See, e.g., People v. Coffey, 12 N.Y.2d 443, 452, 240 N.Y.S.2d 721, 726, 191 N.E.2d 263 (1963), cert. den. 376 U.S. 916, 84 S.Ct. 671, 11 L.Ed.2d 612 (1964).

443. People v. Ward, 95 A.D.2d 233, 237–38, 465 N.Y.S.2d 556, 558–59 (2d Dep't 1983); People v. Sanders, 79 A.D.2d 688, 689–90, 433 N.Y.S.2d 854, 856–57 (2d Dep't 1980). The Ward court distinguished between testimony by the arresting officer about information he received directly from a civilian, which the court considered not to be hearsay, and testimony by the arresting officer about information passed on to him by other officers who had received it from a civilian, which the court considered to be hearsay. 95 A.D.2d at 238, 465 N.Y.S.2d at 559.

§ 10.19   SEARCH WARRANTS & SUPPRESSION   Ch. 10

In any event, the CPL plainly does not limit the receipt of hearsay at hearings to the issue of probable cause; again, "hearsay is admissible to establish any material fact."[444] As a result, the prosecution has been permitted to rely on hearsay to establish probable cause where the hearsay did not involve the declarations of an informant,[445] to demonstrate independent source,[446] to show that an identification proceeding was not police arranged,[447] and to disprove a defendant's claim that a gun was obtained in a search.[448] Moreover, the CPL plainly does not limit the receipt of hearsay to cases in which the prosecution offers the evidence. Thus, the defense has been entitled to rely on hearsay to establish standing,[449] and to prove the nature of a family's efforts to contact a youth who was in custody.[450]

In short, a "hearsay" objection, without more, should not be a ground for excluding evidence at a suppression hearing. However, that hearsay is admissible does not mean that it will necessarily suffice to establish a fact at issue. In *People v. Gonzalez*,[451] the defense presented testimony that the defendant had been taken into custody in his home. The only prosecution witness was a detective who had been told by other detectives that the defendant left his home voluntarily. The Court of Appeals noted that the hearsay testimony of the detective was admissible, but held that it failed to satisfy the prosecution's burden of proving that the defendant consented to accompany the police. The court emphasized that the hearing evidence presented "substantial" questions about the police conduct, and that the prosecution could not eliminate those questions without a witness with first-hand knowledge of the events.

As noted above, whether the prosecution can meet its burden of proof at a hearing without calling additional witnesses may depend on whether the hearing evidence presents a "substantial" issue not yet addressed in the prosecution case. After *Gonzalez*, the sufficiency of hearsay, without more, to establish a material suppression fact would seem to turn on similar considerations. If one party has presented first-hand evidence on a significant point, the other party cannot carry the point with hearsay that bears no particular earmarks of trustworthiness, and would be well advised to supplement the hearsay with first-hand evidence.

444. That rule is consistent with federal law. United States v. Matlock, 415 U.S. 164, 172–75, 94 S.Ct. 988, 993–95, 39 L.Ed.2d 242 (1974).

445. People v. McCreary, 186 A.D.2d 1070, 588 N.Y.S.2d 686 (4th Dep't 1992).

446. People v. Rogers, 85 A.D.2d 843, 446 N.Y.S.2d 497 (3d Dep't 1981).

447. People v. Rose, ___ A.D.2d ___, 631 N.Y.S.2d 354 (1st Dep't 1995).

448. People v. Harrington, 70 Misc.2d 303, 304–05, 332 N.Y.S.2d 789, 791–92 (Allegheny Co.Ct.1972).

449. People v. Gonzalez, 68 N.Y.2d 950, 951, 510 N.Y.S.2d 86, 86, 502 N.E.2d 1001 (1986)(defendant's post-arrest statement as described by prosecution witness).

450. People v. Cavagnaro, 88 A.D.2d 938, 450 N.Y.S.2d 870 (2d Dep't 1982).

451. 80 N.Y.2d 883, 587 N.Y.S.2d 607, 600 N.E.2d 238 (1992).

A discussion of hearsay and suppression hearings would not be complete without reference to *People v. Parris*.[452] Frequently, an officer seizes a defendant because of information transmitted by another officer. The transmitting officer might have based the transmission on his or her own observations of pertinent criminal conduct, or instead on a report received from a civilian informant. In either event, if the transmitting officer had a sufficient basis for seizing the defendant, the officer who received the report was entitled to seize the defendant as well.[453]

For many years it appeared that, if the defendant disputed whether the transmitting officer could justifiably have seized the defendant, the prosecution could not defend the seizure at a *Mapp* hearing by calling only the arresting officer, and having the officer relate what he or she had been told. Rather, the prosecution seemed to be obliged to call the officer who could give a first-hand account of observations of criminal behavior, or of a civilian's report.[454] *Parris* has now made plain that no particular witness must testify. The arresting officer's testimony will suffice—even where he acted on a civilian's report relayed to him by another officer—if at every stage of the chain of information the declarant had a proper basis of knowledge concerning what he or she reported, and was a reliable source.

Four miscellaneous topics concerning the conduct of hearings should be briefly addressed. First, the trial court has discretion to "bifurcate" a *Wade* hearing. That is, the court can elect to limit testimony in the first instance to whether an identification procedure was fatally flawed. Then, should the defendant not establish that the procedure was impermissible, the court will have no occasion to hear evidence concerning an independent source for an in-court identification.[455] Bifurcation has become routine, and has reduced the need for victims of crimes to testify at the suppression stage.

But since *People v. Burts*,[456] bifurcation has entailed some risk. In *Burts*, the Appellate Division found that a photographic identification procedure had been suggestive, but did not order a new trial. Rather, the court ordered that the appeal be held in abeyance, and affirmed after a re-opened *Wade* hearing determined that an independent source for the identification testimony presented at trial rendered the error academic.[457] The Court of Appeals reversed, finding that the defendant was entitled to a new trial. The court concluded that an erroneous decision about an identification proceeding could not be rendered academic by a

---

452. 83 N.Y.2d 342, 610 N.Y.S.2d 464, 632 N.E.2d 870 (1994).

453. People v. Rosario, 78 N.Y.2d 583, 588–89, 578 N.Y.S.2d 454, 456–57, 585 N.E.2d 766 (1991).

454. People v. Havelka, 45 N.Y.2d 636, 412 N.Y.S.2d 345, 384 N.E.2d 1269 (1978); People v. Lypka, 36 N.Y.2d 210, 366 N.Y.S.2d 622, 326 N.E.2d 294 (1975); but see People v. Petralia, 62 N.Y.2d 47, 476 N.Y.S.2d 56, 464 N.E.2d 424 (1984).

455. People v. Jones, 215 A.D.2d 244, 627 N.Y.S.2d 2 (1st Dep't 1995). See People v. Chipp, 75 N.Y.2d 327, 335, 553 N.Y.S.2d 72, 76, 552 N.E.2d 608 (1990). Cf. People v. Dodt, 61 N.Y.2d 408, 417–18, 474 N.Y.S.2d 441, 446–47, 462 N.E.2d 1159 (1984).

456. 78 N.Y.2d 20, 571 N.Y.S.2d 418, 574 N.E.2d 1024 (1991).

457. People v. Burts, 156 A.D.2d 1010, 549 N.Y.S.2d 292 (4th Dep't 1989), after remand 162 A.D.2d 1020, 557 N.Y.S.2d 223 (4th Dep't 1990). Of course, the jury had not learned of the tainted photographic procedure. See People v. Caserta, 19 N.Y.2d 18, 277 N.Y.S.2d 647, 224 N.E.2d 82 (1966).

finding that there was an independent source for the trial testimony, unless that finding preceded the trial.[458] That rule plainly could affect whether, in a particular case, a prosecutor would find it wise to ask the hearing court to bifurcate a *Wade* hearing. Where the legality of an identification proceeding presents a close question, and there would be little cost to expanding the scope of the hearing, it may be sound strategy to avoid the *Burts* rule by establishing independent source before trial.

Second, the attorney who does not present careful legal argument at the end of a suppression hearing, whether orally or in writing, may be doing his or her cause an enormous disservice. Preservation principles have been applied very strictly in the suppression context. An attorney who does not articulate a particular legal argument in the trial court may find that argument precluded on appeal, regardless of its merit, on the theory that the opposing party has not had a fair opportunity to present evidence on the issue.[459] Even the winning party may have to make a record on arguments not endorsed by the trial judge if it wishes to keep those alternative arguments available on appeal.[460]

Third, for the most part, the prosecution has only one chance to introduce evidence on a suppression issue. Unless a ruling by the hearing court wrongly precludes evidence or wrongly suggests that an issue should not be addressed, the prosecution is not entitled to a second opportunity to provide the necessary proof—even after the defendant obtains appellate reversal of a trial court ruling in the prosecution's favor.[461]

Finally, testimony elicited at a suppression hearing is not admissible at trial under the "prior testimony" exception to the hearsay rule, even if the hearing witness has become unavailable.[462]

Library References:

West's Key No. Digests, Criminal Law ☞394.6.

§ 10.20 Suppression Hearings—Burden of Proof

The proposed draft of the CPL contained a provision stating:

---

458. The Burts analysis was sufficiently unpersuasive that it has been read narrowly. See People v. Rosales, ___ A.D.2d ___, 628 N.Y.S.2d 656 (1st Dep't 1995)(mid-trial independent source hearing, held after identification evidence was admitted, cures prior mistaken ruling that identification procedure was not suggestive).

459. See, e.g., People v. Martin, 50 N.Y.2d 1029, 1031, 431 N.Y.S.2d 689, 690, 409 N.E.2d 1363 (1980); People v. Tutt, 38 N.Y.2d 1011, 1012–13, 384 N.Y.S.2d 444, 444, 348 N.E.2d 920 (1976).

460. People v. Parris, 83 N.Y.2d 342, 350–51, 610 N.Y.S.2d 464, 468–69, 632 N.E.2d 870 (1994); People v. Graham, 211 A.D.2d 55, 626 N.Y.S.2d 95, 97 (1st Dep't 1995).

461. See, e.g., People v. Havelka, 45 N.Y.2d 636, 642–44, 412 N.Y.S.2d 345, 348–49, 384 N.E.2d 1269 (1978). See People v. Dodt, 61 N.Y.2d 408, 418, 474 N.Y.S.2d 441, 447, 462 N.E.2d 1159 (1984).

462. CPL § 670.10; People v. Ayala, 75 N.Y.2d 422, 554 N.Y.S.2d 412, 553 N.E.2d 960 (1990). The rule might be different, of course, if the defendant is responsible for the witness's unavailability. See People v. Geraci, 85 N.Y.2d 359, 625 N.Y.S.2d 469, 649 N.E.2d 817 (1995).

> Upon any hearing as prescribed in [section 710.60], the people have the burden of proving by a preponderance of the evidence that the evidence sought to be excluded was not obtained in an unlawful or improper manner or under circumstances precluding admissibility thereof as specified in section [710.20].[463]

That language was stricken before the CPL was adopted by the Legislature. As enacted, the CPL contains no reference at all to evidentiary burdens at suppression hearings, and thus the rules that govern burdens of persuasion in suppression proceedings are entirely the product of case law.

And the case law that has emerged lacks the clarity, and certainly the consistency, of the draft proposal just quoted. The cases establish various and shifting burdens of production and burdens of proof applicable at different types of proceedings, such that an attorney can scarcely be certain who bears the burden of persuasion on an issue of fact until he or she finds a case precisely on point. The case law is discussed below, organized according to the type of suppression proceedings to which the cases apply.

Five rules of general applicability do emerge from the cases, however, and those principles should be noted as an introduction to the discussion of the case law. First, the defendant, as the moving party, generally bears the burden of proof, and that burden is to establish the facts necessary to the motion by a preponderance of the evidence.[464]

Second, where the defendant bears that burden, the prosecution nonetheless has the initial burden of coming forward with proof which, if not rebutted, could defeat the defendant's claim.[465] As stated by the Court of Appeals in a Fourth Amendment case, the task of a hearing judge who must decide whether the prosecution has met its burden is largely the same as that of a judge in passing on an application for an arrest or search warrant.[466] The prosecution's obligation thus is essentially to present a *prima facie* case, one that demonstrates the legality of the acquisition of the challenged evidence if all its evidence is credited.[467] If the prosecution does not satisfy its obligation the defendant will prevail, even though the defendant would otherwise bear the ultimate burden of proof.[468] And the proof adduced by the prosecution in an

---

463. Proposed New York Criminal Procedure Law, CPL § 375.60(6), p. 421 (Edward Thompson Co.1967).

464. See, e.g., People v. Carter, 86 N.Y.2d 721, 631 N.Y.S.2d 116, 655 N.E.2d 157 (1995); People v. Di Stefano, 38 N.Y.2d 640, 651–52, 382 N.Y.S.2d 5, 11–12, 345 N.E.2d 548 (1976); People v. Glen, 30 N.Y.2d 252, 262, 331 N.Y.S.2d 656, 663, 282 N.E.2d 614 (1972).

465. See, e.g., People v. Di Stefano, 38 N.Y.2d at 652, 382 N.Y.S.2d at 12.

466. People v. Dodt, 61 N.Y.2d 408, 415, 474 N.Y.S.2d 441, 445, 462 N.E.2d 1159 (1984).

467. People v. Wise, 46 N.Y.2d 321, 329, 413 N.Y.S.2d 334, 339, 385 N.E.2d 1262 (1978); see People v. Floyd, 41 N.Y.2d 245, 250, 392 N.Y.S.2d 257, 262, 360 N.E.2d 935 (1976).

468. See, e.g., People v. Pettinato, 69 N.Y.2d 653, 654–55, 511 N.Y.S.2d 828, 503 N.E.2d 1365 (1986); People v. Dodt, 61 N.Y.2d 408, 415–16, 474 N.Y.S.2d 441, 445, 462 N.E.2d 1159 (1984); People v. Bouton, 50 N.Y.2d 130, 135–36, 428 N.Y.S.2d 218, 220, 405 N.E.2d 699 (1980); People v. Kemp, 131 A.D.2d 265, 267, 521 N.Y.S.2d 546, 547 (3d Dep't 1987).

§ 10.20   SEARCH WARRANTS & SUPPRESSION   Ch. 10

effort to satisfy the burden of coming forward may be of critical assistance in helping the defendant meet his or her burden of proof.[469]

Third, where the suppression issue turns on whether the defendant voluntarily waived a right, the burden of proof will be on the prosecution, and by a standard greater than proof by a preponderance of the evidence.[470]

Fourth, where the court must resolve whether illegal police action was attenuated by other facts, the burden of proof will be on the prosecution, and by a standard greater than proof by a preponderance of the evidence.[471]

Fifth, where one party is uniquely positioned to provide pertinent information, the burden of proof may be placed on that party.[472]

Mapp. The first two principles control in typical *Mapp* hearings. The prosecution bears the burden of coming forward with evidence establishing that the police action was reasonable under the circumstances and thus did not violate the defendant's Fourth Amendment rights; conclusory testimony that the police were satisfied that action was required will not suffice.[473] If the prosecution makes the necessary showing, the burden shifts, and the defendant must prove by a preponderance of the evidence the facts necessary to make out a violation of his or her rights.[474] In particular, the defendant bears the burden of proving that the seizure of the contested evidence was "causally related" to illegal police action[475] as to which he or she has standing to complain.[476] The evidence presented by the prosecution will sometimes be all that the defendant needs to carry his or her burden.[477]

---

469. People v. Whitfield, 81 N.Y.2d 904, 906, 597 N.Y.S.2d 641, 642, 613 N.E.2d 547 (1993); People v. Wesley, 73 N.Y.2d 351, 359 n. 2, 540 N.Y.S.2d 757, 761 n. 2, 538 N.E.2d 76 (1989); People v. Gonzalez, 68 N.Y.2d 950, 951, 510 N.Y.S.2d 86, 502 N.E.2d 1001 (1986). The prosecution's proof may carry the day for the defendant even where the defendant's own evidence contradicts it. People v. Corona, 206 A.D.2d 305, 614 N.Y.S.2d 722 (1st Dep't 1994).

470. See, e.g., People v. Gonzalez, 39 N.Y.2d 122, 127–28, 383 N.Y.S.2d 215, 218–19, 347 N.E.2d 575 (1976).

471. See, e.g., People v. Knapp, 52 N.Y.2d 689, 697–98, 439 N.Y.S.2d 871, 875–76, 422 N.E.2d 531 (burden on prosecution to establish "inevitable discovery" by showing a "very high degree of probability" that the evidence would have been obtained).

472. See People v. Rosa, 65 N.Y.2d 380, 386–87, 492 N.Y.S.2d 542, 546–47, 482 N.E.2d 21 (1985).

473. People v. Pettinato, 69 N.Y.2d at 654–55, 511 N.Y.S.2d at 828; People v. Dodt, 61 N.Y.2d at 415–16, 474 N.Y.S.2d at 444–45; People v. Bouton, 50 N.Y.2d at 135, 428 N.Y.S.2d at 220; People v. De-Frain, 204 A.D.2d 1002, 613 N.Y.S.2d 303 (4th Dep't 1994).

474. People v. Berrios, 28 N.Y.2d 361, 367–68, 321 N.Y.S.2d 884, 888–89, 270 N.E.2d 709 (1971); People v. Merola, 30 A.D.2d 963, 964, 294 N.Y.S.2d 301, 304 (2d Dep't 1968).

475. People v. Arnau, 58 N.Y.2d 27, 32, 457 N.Y.S.2d 763, 765, 444 N.E.2d 13 (1982).

476. People v. Whitfield, 81 N.Y.2d 904, 905–06, 597 N.Y.S.2d 641, 642, 613 N.E.2d 547 (1993); People v. Wesley, 73 N.Y.2d 351, 355, 540 N.Y.S.2d 757, 759, 538 N.E.2d 76 (1989).

477. See, e.g., People v. Whitfield, 81 N.Y.2d at 906, 597 N.Y.S.2d at 642; People v. Gonzalez, 68 N.Y.2d 950, 951, 510 N.Y.S.2d 86, 86, 502 N.E.2d 1001 (1986); People v. Corona, 206 A.D.2d 305, 306–07, 614 N.Y.S.2d 722, 723–24 (1st Dep't 1994). As a technical matter, it might be more correct to conclude in such a case that the prosecution did not come forward with evidence establishing the propriety of the police action.

But there are exceptions to those basic rules. For example, when the prosecution seeks to justify a warrantless search by citing the existence of exigent circumstances, "the burden of proving the existence of sufficiently exceptional circumstances is placed squarely on the shoulders of the government."[478] Further, in accordance with the third principle, where the prosecution argues that the defendant consented to a search, it bears a "heavy burden" of establishing as much.[479] That "heavy burden" has been equated with an obligation to present "clear and positive" proof, although not proof beyond a reasonable doubt.[480] Similarly, the prosecution bears the burden of proof when the issue is whether a defendant who accompanied the police did so voluntarily and without being taken into custody.[481]

If a court finds that a defendant's Fourth Amendment rights were violated—either because the prosecution did not meet its burden of coming forward, or because the defendant met his or her burden of proof—the fourth principle may become relevant. Evidence obtained after the violation of a defendant's Fourth Amendment rights will be admissible if the prosecution can prove that the evidence was acquired not "by exploitation of" that violation, but by "means sufficiently distinguishable from it to be purged of illegality."[482]

Finally, if a search is conducted pursuant to a warrant, the "*bona fides* of the police will be presumed and the subsequent search upheld in a marginal or doubtful case."[483]

Wade. The first two principles control at the initial stage of a *Wade* hearing. The prosecution bears the burden of coming forward with evidence establishing that a contested identification procedure was not unduly suggestive.[484] The loss of such critical evidence as the photographs that constituted a photo array may create a presumption that the identification procedure was suggestive, but will not necessarily prevent the prosecution from satisfying its burden through other evidence.[485] If the prosecution meets its burden of coming forward the burden shifts, and the defendant must prove the facts necessary to make out undue

---

478. People v. Knapp, 52 N.Y.2d 689, 694, 439 N.Y.S.2d 871, 874, 422 N.E.2d 531 (1981).

479. People v. Gonzalez, 39 N.Y.2d 122, 127–28, 383 N.Y.S.2d 215, 218–19, 347 N.E.2d 575 (1976)(prosecution recognizes its "heavy burden" to prove voluntary consent to search); see also People v. Dodt, 61 N.Y.2d 408, 417, 474 N.Y.S.2d 441, 446, 462 N.E.2d 1159 (1984).

480. People v. Zimmerman, 101 A.D.2d 294, 295, 475 N.Y.S.2d 127, 127 (2d Dep't 1984); see also People v. Corbin, 201 A.D.2d 359, 608 N.Y.S.2d 839 (1st Dep't 1994).

481. People v. Gonzalez, 80 N.Y.2d 883, 885, 587 N.Y.S.2d 607, 607, 600 N.E.2d 238 (1992)(hearsay testimony fails to meet that burden).

482. People v. Johnson, 66 N.Y.2d 398, 407, 497 N.Y.S.2d 618, 624, 488 N.E.2d 439 (1985); but see People v. Arnau, 58 N.Y.2d at 32, 457 N.Y.S.2d at 765. See § 10.10, supra.

483. People v. Hanlon, 36 N.Y.2d 549, 558, 369 N.Y.S.2d 677, 683, 330 N.E.2d 631 (1975).

484. People v. Chipp, 75 N.Y.2d 327, 335, 553 N.Y.S.2d 72, 76, 552 N.E.2d 608 (1990).

485. People v. Green, 188 A.D.2d 385, 591 N.Y.S.2d 175 (1st Dep't 1992); People v. Jackson, 161 Misc.2d 45, 613 N.Y.S.2d 1018 (Sup.Ct., Bronx County, 1994).

§ 10.20   SEARCH WARRANTS & SUPPRESSION   Ch. 10

suggestiveness.[486] Likewise, where the defendant's *Wade* claim turns on whether the right to counsel has attached, the defendant has the burden of proof as to the facts essential to that claim.[487]

If, in accordance with these standards, a court suppresses testimony about a suggestive pretrial identification, the fourth principle becomes relevant. The prosecution can elicit an in-court identification from a witness at trial, despite the prior suggestive identification procedure, if it can establish the existence of an independent source by clear and convincing evidence.[488]

Huntley. When the issue at a *Huntley* hearing is whether the defendant voluntarily made a statement, the third principle controls. The prosecution must prove beyond a reasonable doubt that the defendant's statement was voluntary.[489] Perhaps inconsistently, however, when *Miranda* warnings were required, the defendant must prove that they were not given and understood.[490]

Not all *Huntley* issues involve whether rights were voluntarily waived. When, for example, the issue is whether the defendant's right to counsel has attached, the burden of proof is on the defendant.[491] On the other hand, when the issue is whether the defendant's right to counsel has expired, the burden is on the prosecution.[492] And, despite the fourth principle, where the court must decide whether an improperly

---

486. People v. Chipp, 75 N.Y.2d at 335, 553 N.Y.S.2d at 77.

487. See People v. Green, 188 A.D.2d at 386, 591 N.Y.S.2d at 176 (defendant does not testify that he asked that his attorney attend the lineup).

488. People v. Rahming, 26 N.Y.2d 411, 416–17, 311 N.Y.S.2d 292, 296–97, 259 N.E.2d 727 (1970); People v. Damon, 24 N.Y.2d 256, 261, 299 N.Y.S.2d 830, 834, 247 N.E.2d 651 (1969). See § 10.10, supra. Where identification testimony is suppressed for a reason other than the suggestiveness of the proceeding, the prosecution's obligation to show that later identifications should not be precluded may be particularly easy to satisfy. For example, where a lineup identification is suppressed only because the defendant should have been represented by counsel, or was arrested without probable cause, the fact that the witness was able to identify the defendant in the non-suggestive lineup is, in and of itself, convincing proof that the witness possesses an independent source for identification testimony.

489. People v. Huntley, 15 N.Y.2d 72, 78, 255 N.Y.S.2d 838, 843, 204 N.E.2d 179 (1965); accord People v. Valerius, 31 N.Y.2d 51, 334 N.Y.S.2d 871, 286 N.E.2d 254 (1972). That extremely high burden of proof, so unusual in the suppression context, was imposed by the Huntley court without explanation. In that particular, Huntley is dramatically inconsistent with the federal rule, see Lego v. Twomey, 404 U.S. 477, 92 S.Ct. 619, 30 L.Ed.2d 618 (1972), as the Court of Appeals has itself noted, People v. Pobliner, 32 N.Y.2d 356, 368, 345 N.Y.S.2d 482, 491, 298 N.E.2d 637 (1973), cert. den. 416 U.S. 905, 94 S.Ct. 1609, 40 L.Ed.2d 110 (1974). But the rule survives even in the absence of an explanation, perhaps because it is sufficiently ingrained in New York practice that in every case its continued vitality is assumed. See, e.g., People v. Renis, 94 A.D.2d 728, 462 N.Y.S.2d 266 (2d Dep't 1983).

490. People v. Love, 85 A.D.2d 799, 445 N.Y.S.2d 607 (3d Dep't 1981), aff'd 57 N.Y.2d 998, 457 N.Y.S.2d 238, 443 N.E.2d 486 (1982).

491. People v. West, 81 N.Y.2d 370, 378–79, 599 N.Y.S.2d 484, 489–90, 615 N.E.2d 968 (1993); People v. Rosa, 65 N.Y.2d 380, 387, 492 N.Y.S.2d 542, 547, 482 N.E.2d 21 (1985); People v. Henriquez, 214 A.D.2d 485, 625 N.Y.S.2d 526 (1st Dep't 1995); see People v. Green, 188 A.D.2d 385, 591 N.Y.S.2d 175 (1st Dep't 1992)(defendant does not testify that he asked that his attorney attend lineup); People v. Kemp, 131 A.D.2d 265, 267–68, 521 N.Y.S.2d 546, 547–48 (3d Dep't 1987)(prosecution fails to meet initial burden of coming forward with proof about when officer learned of defendant's pending case).

492. People v. West, 81 N.Y.2d at 378–80, 599 N.Y.S.2d at 490–91.

obtained statement by a defendant taints a later statement, the failure of the defendant who testifies at the hearing to assert that he or she gave the second statement only because the "cat was out of the bag" may resolve the issue in the prosecution's favor.[493]

Other. When the defendant moves to suppress evidence discovered as a result of electronic surveillance, the first two principles apply: the prosecution must come forward with an evidentiary justification for the eavesdropping; and the defendant must then prove that the eavesdropping evidence was improperly obtained.[494] In this context, the prosecution is significantly aided by the presumption that a warrant was properly issued.[495] Should the defendant prove that eavesdropping evidence was improperly obtained, then in accordance with the fourth principle the prosecution can save other evidence by presenting "clear and convincing" proof that this other evidence would have been obtained independently of the eavesdropping.[496]

Similarly, when a defendant moves to suppress the results of a breathalyzer test, the first two principles apply: the prosecution bears the burden of going forward, but the defendant bears the ultimate burden of proof.[497] One court has held that the prosecution need not show that a defendant consented to a breathalyzer test when that test is conducted within two hours of arrest, given the provisions of the Vehicle and Traffic Law that "deem" consent to have been given in that circumstance.[498]

Finally, the courts have not yet resolved which party bears the burden of proof when the defendant claims that evidence was obtained through illegal pen registers or trap and trace devices. Nonetheless, the principles that apply to the resolution of *Mapp* motions and motions to suppress eavesdropping evidence would clearly seem to apply.

Library References:

West's Key No. Digests, Criminal Law ⚖➤394.5(4).

§ 10.21 Suppression Hearings—Decision

Whether or not a hearing has been held, the court that decides a suppression motion must state for the record "its findings of fact, its conclusions of law and the reasons for its determination."[499] A court's

---

493. People v. Tanner, 30 N.Y.2d 102, 106–07, 331 N.Y.S.2d 1, 3–4, 282 N.E.2d 98 (1972); cf. People v. Green, 188 A.D.2d 385, 591 N.Y.S.2d 175 (1st Dep't 1992) (defendant does not testify that he asked that his attorney attend lineup).

494. People v. Floyd, 41 N.Y.2d 245, 250, 392 N.Y.S.2d 257, 262, 360 N.E.2d 935 (1976); People v. Di Stefano, 38 N.Y.2d 640, 651–52, 382 N.Y.S.2d 5, 11–12, 345 N.E.2d 548 (1976). In People v. Frank, 85 A.D.2d 109, 114, 447 N.Y.S.2d 558, 562 (4th Dep't 1982), the court briefly noted how a prosecutor can satisfy the burden of coming forward with evidence that proper minimization procedures were employed.

495. People v. Manuli, 104 A.D.2d 386, 387, 478 N.Y.S.2d 712, 713 (2d Dep't 1984).

496. People v. Pobliner, 32 N.Y.2d 356, 367–68, 345 N.Y.S.2d 482, 491, 298 N.E.2d 637 (1973), cert. den. 416 U.S. 905, 94 S.Ct. 1609, 40 L.Ed.2d 110 (1974).

497. People v. Kelty, 95 Misc.2d 246, 248, 406 N.Y.S.2d 972, 973 (Dist.Ct., Nassau County, 1978).

498. Id.

499. CPL § 710.60(6).

failure to follow that injunction is unlikely itself to provide the basis for successful appellate complaint.[500] Nonetheless, the extent to which the court obeys the statute while resolving questions of law and fact can be extremely significant on appeal.

First, the court's factual findings will virtually always be conclusive at future stages of the litigation. Very occasionally, an appellate court will reject findings on the theory that they are manifestly incorrect.[501] But it is almost inevitable that reviewing courts will accept the findings of fact made by the hearing court.[502] Thus, when the testimony is susceptible to competing inferences, the hearing court's expressed acceptance of a particular inference may have an impact on the conclusions of the reviewing courts.

Second, the hearing court's legal conclusions are often the clearest indicator to the appellate courts of what the parties and the hearing court believed the controlling legal issues to be. The express determination of an issue of law by the hearing court "preserves" that issue for appellate review.[503] In the absence of preservation, the defendant whose position has been rejected by the hearing court will generally find himself or herself limited on appeal to review pursuant to the interest of justice power of the intermediate appellate court.[504] And the prosecutors who wish to advance unpreserved arguments on appeal may find that they have no recourse at all.

Finally, the hearing court's expressed determinations of law and fact may be controlling in other cases pursuant to collateral estoppel principles. A defendant may well be able to invoke the collateral estoppel doctrine when a co-defendant has separately litigated a suppression motion against the same prosecutor's office.[505] The extent to which one prosecutor's office is bound by the unsuccessful litigation efforts of another office, against the same defendant or a co-defendant, is as yet not fully determined. However, in *People v. McGriff*,[506] a suppression ruling against the Queens County District Attorney's Office in a misdemeanor case was considered conclusive in a related felony prosecution brought by New York City's Special Narcotics Prosecutor, despite the arguably differing motives of the two offices to pursue the case.[507]

---

500. See, e.g., People v. Jones, 204 A.D.2d 162, 614 N.Y.S.2d 110 (1st Dep't 1994).

501. See, e.g., People v. Miret–Gonzalez, 159 A.D.2d 647, 649–50, 552 N.Y.S.2d 958, 960 (2d Dep't 1990); People v. Garafolo, 44 A.D.2d 86, 88–89, 353 N.Y.S.2d 500, 502–03 (2d Dep't 1974).

502. See, e.g., People v. Prochilo, 41 N.Y.2d 759, 761, 395 N.Y.S.2d 635, 636, 363 N.E.2d 1380 (1977); People v. Vasquez, ___ A.D.2d ___, 629 N.Y.S.2d 756 (1st Dep't 1995).

503. CPL § 470.05(2). Of course, the parties may also preserve their legal claims for review in their oral and written statements to the hearing court. Id.

504. See People v. Robinson, 36 N.Y.2d 224, 228–29, 367 N.Y.S.2d 208, 210–11, 326 N.E.2d 784 (1975).

505. People v. McGriff, 130 A.D.2d 141, 150–52, 518 N.Y.S.2d 795, 800–02 (1st Dep't 1987).

506. 130 A.D.2d at 150–52, 518 N.Y.S.2d at 800–01.

507. But see People v. Reisman, 29 N.Y.2d 278, 285, 327 N.Y.S.2d 342, 348, 277 N.E.2d 396 (1971), cert. den. 405 U.S. 1041, 92 S.Ct. 1315, 31 L.Ed.2d 582 (1972)("[i]dentity of the prosecuting party is an indispensable precondition" to estoppel).

On the other hand, there is no authority for binding a defendant by a co-defendant's unsuccessful litigation of a suppression position, even against the same prosecutor.[508] Indeed, a defendant will not likely be bound by an adverse suppression ruling in another case against him or her, even when the litigation in both cases concerns the same facts. The defendant can avoid the effects of estoppel simply by identifying strategic concerns that would cause him or her to litigate differently the second time around.[509]

Library References:
West's Key No. Digests, Criminal Law ⇒394.6(5).

§ 10.22 Implications for Subsequent Proceedings

If the trial court determines that a defendant's suppression motion is meritorious, its next step is obvious:

[T]he court must order that the evidence in question be excluded in the criminal action pending against the defendant.[510]

When the evidence to be suppressed is tangible property obtained in an illegal search, the court has discretion to order that the property be restored to the defendant, and presumably will do so if the property is not contraband.[511]

The prosecution has a right to take an interlocutory appeal from a pretrial order suppressing evidence, but in practice that right is severely limited. First, the prosecution cannot appeal an order "precluding" statement or identification evidence on account of the failure to give timely notice as required by CPL § 710.30.[512] Second, the prosecution can appeal an order suppressing evidence only after filing a statement pursuant to CPL § 450.50, certifying that the suppressed evidence is crucial to its case.[513] If the prosecution's appeal is then unsuccessful, it is estopped from proceeding further on any charge contained in the indictment, even one not based on the suppressed evidence.[514] And that rule may not be circumvented by bringing the same charges in a new accusatory instrument.[515] However, the prosecution is not estopped when the prosecution withdraws its appeal.[516]

---

508. People v. Aguilera, 82 N.Y.2d 23, 30–31, 603 N.Y.S.2d 392, 395–96, 623 N.E.2d 519 (1993); People v. McGriff, 130 A.D.2d at 151–52, 518 N.Y.S.2d at 801–02.

509. People v. Aguilera, 82 N.Y.2d at 32–33, 603 N.Y.S.2d at 397–98; People v. Plevy, 52 N.Y.2d 58, 64–66, 436 N.Y.S.2d 224, 227–28, 417 N.E.2d 518 (1980).

510. CPL § 710.70(1).

511. See People v. Gatti, 16 N.Y.2d 251, 253 n. 2, 265 N.Y.S.2d 641, 642 n. 2, 212 N.E.2d 882 (1965).

512. People v. Laing, 79 N.Y.2d 166, 581 N.Y.S.2d 149, 589 N.E.2d 372 (1992); see CPL § 450.20(8); see § 10.29, infra.

513. CPL §§ 450.20(8), 450.50(1).

514. CPL § 450.50(2); Forte v. Supreme Court of the State of New York, 48 N.Y.2d 179, 187, 422 N.Y.S.2d 26, 30, 397 N.E.2d 717 (1979). The Court of Appeals has suggested that a different rule conceivably could apply if new evidence should be discovered after the filing of the prosecution's certification. 48 N.Y.2d at 182 n. 1, 422 N.Y.S.2d at 27 n. 1.

515. 48 N.Y.2d at 186–88, 422 N.Y.S.2d at 29–31.

516. People v. McIntosh, 80 N.Y.2d 87, 587 N.Y.S.2d 568, 600 N.E.2d 199 (1992). The court noted that an appellate court might refuse to allow the prosecution to withdraw an appeal, particularly where it detected bad faith or a pattern of abuse in

§ 10.22   SEARCH WARRANTS & SUPPRESSION   Ch. 10

The obvious—and largely successful—purpose of the certification requirement is to discourage interlocutory appeals. At least in theory, such appeals are practical only in the relatively few cases that are effectively terminated by a suppression order, and in those cases the appeals are in a real sense not "interlocutory" at all.[517] However, the prosecutor and only the prosecutor is the judge of whether an appeal should be taken, and a certificate filed. If the prosecutor chooses to risk estoppel in order to appeal a suppression order of questionable significance, the defendant has no standing to contest that determination with an argument that the prosecution actually has ample additional evidence to introduce at trial.[518]

If, on the other hand, the trial court denies a defendant's suppression motion, the defendant has no right to appeal before trial.[519] Nor may the defendant institute a special proceeding to obtain review of a suppression decision,[520] for the procedure set forth in CPL Article 710 is "the exclusive method" for obtaining a suppression order.[521] Of course, a defendant can move to reargue a suppression order, based perhaps on new information discovered at trial.[522] And the defendant is free to argue to the jurors that the trial proof discloses arguable improprieties in the acquisition of evidence that undermine its probative value.[523]

In one class of cases, the defendant is entitled to go further at trial. A defendant can litigate at trial the voluntariness of his or her statements, with the jury as the trier of fact.[524] And in this context "voluntariness" challenges are not only contentions that a statement was produced by coercion, but also *Miranda* challenges[525] and, arguably, other constitutional challenges.[526] If the trial record contains evidence

the withdrawal of appeals. 80 N.Y.2d at 90, 587 N.Y.S.2d at 569. The court noted as well that if an appeal is withdrawn, the time during which the appeal was pending will be chargeable to the prosecution for statutory speedy trial purposes. Id.

517. See Forte v. Supreme Court of the State of New York, 48 N.Y.2d at 186–87, 422 N.Y.S.2d at 30.

518. People v. Kates, 53 N.Y.2d 591, 596–97, 444 N.Y.S.2d 446, 448–49, 428 N.E.2d 852 (1981).

519. People v. Adler, 50 N.Y.2d 730, 734 n. 1, 431 N.Y.S.2d 412, 413 n. 1, 409 N.E.2d 888 (1980); People v. Richberg, 56 A.D.2d 279, 281, 392 N.Y.S.2d 16, 17 (1st Dep't 1977).

520. Fino v. Johnson, 38 A.D.2d 681, 327 N.Y.S.2d 252 (4th Dep't 1971).

521. CPL § 710.70(3); People v. Hamlin, 71 N.Y.2d 750, 761–62, 530 N.Y.S.2d 74, 78–79, 525 N.E.2d 719 (1988).

522. See § 10.15, supra.

523. People v. Ruffino, 110 A.D.2d 198, 201–03, 494 N.Y.S.2d 8, 11–12 (2d Dep't 1985).

524. CPL § 710.70(3)(final paragraph); People v. Huntley, 15 N.Y.2d 72, 78, 255 N.Y.S.2d 838, 843, 204 N.E.2d 179 (1965).

525. People v. Graham, 55 N.Y.2d 144, 447 N.Y.S.2d 918, 432 N.E.2d 790 (1982).

526. See CPL §§ 60.45, 710.70(3)(last paragraph); cf. People v. Bing, 76 N.Y.2d 331, 346–47, 559 N.Y.S.2d 474, 482–83, 558 N.E.2d 1011 (1990); People v. Griswold, 58 N.Y.2d 633, 635, 458 N.Y.S.2d 513, 513, 444 N.E.2d 977 (1982); People v. Calloway, 171 A.D.2d 1037, 569 N.Y.S.2d 233 (4th Dep't 1991). In People v. Graham, 55 N.Y.2d at 152–53, 447 N.Y.S.2d at 922–23 (Wachtler, J., concurring), three members of the Court of Appeals suggested that there is no rational explanation for the breadth of defendants' statutory right to litigate these suppression claims to the jury, and that it is the product of inadvertence. One commentator has likewise suggested that the statutory right to litigate claims, other than coercion claims, before the jury makes "little sense." Preiser, "Practice Commentary" to CPL § 710.70, McKinney's Cons. Laws of New York, Book 11A, at 350 (1995).

suggesting that a statement by the defendant was improperly obtained, and a pertinent request is made,[527] the judge must upon request advise the jurors to disregard the statement unless the prosecution has persuaded them that the statement was not obtained through violation of the defendant's rights.[528] On the other hand, the defendant is not entitled to a charge that the jurors should disregard physical evidence if they believe it is the indirect fruit of an illegally obtained statement.[529]

While the defendant may not take an interlocutory appeal from an unfavorable suppression ruling, the defendant of course can obtain appellate review if judgment is ultimately entered against him or her.[530] The general rule is that a guilty plea effects a forfeiture of appellate claims, even if the court and the parties intend that the claim remain reviewable after the plea.[531] By statute, however, a defendant is entitled to raise suppression issues on appeal after a guilty plea[532] so long as several conditions are satisfied. First, the suppression motion must have been finally decided by the trial court[533]—although findings of fact and conclusions of law need not yet have been stated by the court.[534] Second, the claim to be presented must be a true suppression claim, not a notice claim[535] or a complaint about the preclusion of a late suppression motion.[536] Third, the suppressed evidence must have been relevant to the action in which the defendant pleaded guilty, not an unrelated action "covered" by the plea.[537] Finally, the defendant must not, as a part of the plea bargain, have waived the right to have the suppression claims considered on appeal.[538]

Library References:

West's Key No. Digests, Criminal Law ⚖1024(1); Searches and Seizures ⚖84.

527. People v. Felder, 186 A.D.2d 1050, 588 N.Y.S.2d 491 (4th Dep't 1992); People v. Betances, 165 A.D.2d 754, 564 N.Y.S.2d 269 (1st Dep't 1990); People v. Estrada, 109 A.D.2d 977, 980, 486 N.Y.S.2d 794, 797 (3d Dep't 1985); People v. Faber, 83 A.D.2d 883, 442 N.Y.S.2d 113 (2d Dep't 1981).

528. People v. Graham, supra; People v. Murray, 130 A.D.2d 773, 774–75, 515 N.Y.S.2d 847, 848–49 (2d Dep't 1987); People v. Sutton, 122 A.D.2d 896, 505 N.Y.S.2d 937 (2d Dep't 1986).

529. People v. Hamlin, 71 N.Y.2d 750, 760–62, 530 N.Y.S.2d 74, 77–78, 525 N.E.2d 719 (1988).

530. CPL § 470.15(1).

531. People v. Thomas, 53 N.Y.2d 338, 441 N.Y.S.2d 650, 424 N.E.2d 537 (1981); see also People v. Prescott, 66 N.Y.2d 216, 495 N.Y.S.2d 955, 486 N.E.2d 813 (1985).

532. CPL § 710.70(2); People v. Di Raffaele, 55 N.Y.2d 234, 239–40, 448 N.Y.S.2d 448, 450, 433 N.E.2d 513 (1982).

533. People v. Fernandez, 67 N.Y.2d 686, 499 N.Y.S.2d 919, 490 N.E.2d 838 (1986); People v. Varon, 168 A.D.2d 349, 562 N.Y.S.2d 673 (1st Dep't 1990)(Darden hearing remained to be conducted); People v. Mitchell, 128 A.D.2d 731, 513 N.Y.S.2d 225 (2d Dep't 1987)(only resolved portion of suppression motions reviewable on appeal); People v. Corti, 88 A.D.2d 345, 453 N.Y.S.2d 439 (2d Dep't 1982).

534. People v. Allman, 133 A.D.2d 638, 519 N.Y.S.2d 747 (2d Dep't 1987).

535. People v. Taylor, 65 N.Y.2d 1, 6–7, 489 N.Y.S.2d 152, 155, 478 N.E.2d 755 (1985).

536. People v. Petgen, 55 N.Y.2d 529, 534, 450 N.Y.S.2d 299, 300, 435 N.E.2d 669 (1982).

537. People v. Dorsey, 122 A.D.2d 393, 394, 505 N.Y.S.2d 210, 210 (3d Dep't 1986).

538. See People v. Seaberg, 74 N.Y.2d 1, 543 N.Y.S.2d 968, 541 N.E.2d 1022 (1989); People v. Esajerre, 35 N.Y.2d 463, 363 N.Y.S.2d 931, 323 N.E.2d 175 (1974).

§ 10.23 Notice—In General

A special notice rule applies when statement evidence or identification evidence is at issue. Under section 710.30, if the prosecution intends to present statement or identification evidence at trial, it generally must serve on the defense, within 15 days of arraignment, notice of its intent to do so, "specifying the evidence intended to be offered."[539] The notice rule is of immense practical significance, for in the absence of timely notice statement or identification evidence will be precluded[540]—and such preclusion can be determinative of the prosecution. The final sections of this Chapter will discuss the notice rule, and in particular when the failure to supply notice will result in the preclusion of evidence.

To begin, however, some discussion should be devoted to the origins of the rule. When the CPL was adopted, section 710.30(2) provided that notice of intent to introduce statement or identification evidence should be provided "before trial."[541] Once notice was given, the defendant was entitled to "reasonable opportunity" to move to suppress the evidence.[542] The section went on to stipulate that "[f]or good cause shown" the prosecution could serve notice during trial; in the case of such late notice, the defendant was entitled to reasonable opportunity to make a mid-trial motion to suppress.[543]

The statute thus provided the prosecution with extraordinary latitude in serving notice, to the point that the defendant could not count on receiving notice of statement or identification evidence until the eve of trial. Not surprisingly, the courts took a dim view of efforts to serve notice even later than authorized. For example, in *People v. Briggs*,[544] "office failure" in the prosecutor's office was held not to be good cause for mid-trial notice of an admission. And in *People v. Spruill*,[545] the failure of one of the arresting officers to notify the prosecutor about the defendant's statement was not good cause for mid-trial notice.

In 1976, as part of a recodification of motion procedure, the Legislature amended section 710.30 to provide that notice of statement and identification evidence should be given defendants within 15 days of arraignment, rather than "before trial."[546] But while the new notice

---

539. CPL § 710.30(1) and (2). The exceptions to that general rule are discussed throughout the remaining portions of this Chapter. A similar, but materially stricter, rule governs in eavesdropping cases. CPL § 700.70; see People v. Capolongo, 85 N.Y.2d 151, 623 N.Y.S.2d 778, 647 N.E.2d 1286 (1995); People v. Schulz, 67 N.Y.2d 144, 501 N.Y.S.2d 12, 492 N.E.2d 120 (1986). The particulars of the eavesdropping rule will be addressed only incidentally in this Chapter.

540. CPL § 710.30(3).

541. L.1970, c.996.

542. Id.

543. Id.

544. 38 N.Y.2d 319, 379 N.Y.S.2d 779, 342 N.E.2d 557 (1975).

545. 47 N.Y.2d 869, 419 N.Y.S.2d 69, 392 N.E.2d 1252 (1979).

546. L.1976, c.194, § 3. See People v. O'Doherty, 70 N.Y.2d 479, 522 N.Y.S.2d 498, 517 N.E.2d 213 (1987). The amendment also provided that the notice had to be provided "before trial," but of course so few trials begin within 15 days of arraignment that this second provision is of little practical consequence. Conforming amendments were made to reflect that a defendant who received late notice could make a suppression motion at any time "thereafter," instead of only "during trial."

rule was dramatically more demanding than the old, no express change was made in the statutory mandate that "good cause" be shown before late notice would be acceptable. Perhaps surprisingly, it was not until 1987 that the Court of Appeals had occasion to decide whether, under the new scheme, a lesser showing of "good cause" might excuse late notice and forestall the preclusion of evidence.

The crucial decision was *People v. O'Doherty*.[547] In *O'Doherty*, the defendant had made a statement to an officer not directly involved in the case, and the prosecutor did not learn of the statement until months after arraignment. The Court of Appeals determined that the prosecutor's lack of knowledge did not constitute good cause for the failure to give notice about the statement within 15 days of arraignment. Of no moment, given the statutory language, was the fact that late notice had worked no prejudice to the defense. The court noted that the Legislature had not amended the "good cause" language in section 710.30 in 1976, and concluded that the Legislature believed that the interests in speedy and orderly motion practice required notice within 15 days—even if later notice did not actually interfere with motion practice. A case decided the same day, *People v. McMullin*,[548] applied the same analysis to late service of notice about identification evidence.

The result, in many cases, is a windfall for defendants, based on a "technicality." That is, when combined with *O'Doherty*'s continued narrow interpretation of the good cause language, the 15-day notice rule provides a basis to suppress—or more correctly to "preclude"—critical statement or identification evidence simply because the defense is formally notified about it 16 or more days after arraignment. And that technicality applies even if there is no doubt that the evidence was legally obtained.[549] An understanding of the particulars of the notice rule is therefore critical to effective criminal practice in New York, for prosecutors and defense counsel alike.

Library References:
West's Key No. Digests, Criminal Law ⟶412(4), 629(10).

§ 10.24 Notice—Timing and Content of Notice

Section 710.30 provides that, within 15 days of arraignment and before trial, the prosecution must give notice of its intent to offer evidence of a statement, made by the defendant to a public servant, which might be suppressible under section 710.20.[550] Likewise, within 15 days of arraignment and before trial, the prosecution must give notice

---

547. 70 N.Y.2d 479, 522 N.Y.S.2d 498, 517 N.E.2d 213 (1987).

548. 70 N.Y.2d 855, 523 N.Y.S.2d 455, 517 N.E.2d 1341 (1987).

549. As Judge Titone wrote in one opinion for the Court of Appeals that reversed a conviction on account of a notice violation:

[I]t should be stressed that the actions taken by the undercover officers here are not in issue. Nor could they be, for their conduct was clearly proper, and indeed commendable. The problem here lies not in regard to what the police did, but solely concerns the People's failure to serve a timely CPL 710.30 notice.

People v. Newball, 76 N.Y.2d 587, 590, 561 N.Y.S.2d 898, 900, 563 N.E.2d 269 (1990).

550. CPL § 710.30(1) and (2).

§ 10.24   SEARCH WARRANTS & SUPPRESSION   Ch. 10

of its intent to offer testimony about an observation of the defendant by a witness who has made an identification of him or her.[551] The "arraignment" that starts the clock in a felony case is the first arraignment on an indictment or superior court information.[552] At least one court has held that, in misdemeanor cases, the clock starts with the first arraignment on an accusatory instrument conveying trial jurisdiction.[553]

If notice is timely given but later withdrawn, it is as if no notice was given at all, and thus in such a case notice cannot be reinstated more than 15 days after arraignment.[554] Moreover, a decision of the Court of Appeals suggests that, once the 15-day deadline is past, the prosecutor cannot evade the consequences of a failure to provide notice by filing new charges against the defendant based on the same facts.[555]

The prosecution's notice, whether written or oral, must "specify[] the evidence intended to be offered."[556] As to statements, it has long been clear that their substance must be described in the notice, if not "word for word," at least to the extent necessary to understand the scope of what the defendant has said. In *People v. Greer*,[557] for example, the defendant was confronted by an officer in the middle of a sex crime, and claimed that the victim was "my woman." The officer asked her name, and the defendant admitted, "I don't know." The prosecution provided notice only of its intent to introduce the defendant's statement that the victim was "my woman," but both statements were admitted at trial. The Court of Appeals held that the failure to include the second statement in the notice was fatal to its admissibility, and reversed the conviction.

The point was underscored in *People v. Lopez*.[558] In that case notice of intent to introduce the defendant's statements about a stabbing was provided at arraignment, but consisted only of checks in boxes on a disclosure form to indicate that the defendant made oral and written statements to a police officer. The court found that notice inadequate:

> The People were required to inform defendant ... of the sum and substance of [his] statements.... Full copies of the state-

---

551. Id.

552. People v. Penasso, 142 A.D.2d 691, 531 N.Y.S.2d 291 (2d Dep't 1988)(notice pursuant to section 700.70).

553. See People v. Alcindor, 157 Misc.2d 725, 598 N.Y.S.2d 449 (N.Y.C.Crim.Ct. 1993).

554. People v. Boughton, 70 N.Y.2d 854, 523 N.Y.S.2d 454, 517 N.E.2d 1340 (1987).

555. People v. Capolongo, 85 N.Y.2d 151, 164–66, 623 N.Y.S.2d 778, 785–86, 647 N.E.2d 1286 (1995). Capolongo is an eavesdropping case. As noted, the notice rules pertaining to eavesdropping, see CPL § 700.70, are to some degree different from those of section 710.30. It is not certain whether the Capolongo holding will be applied by the Court of Appeals outside the eavesdropping context. Compare 85 N.Y.2d at 166 n. 8, 623 N.Y.S.2d at 786 n. 8, with 85 N.Y.2d at 170–72, 623 N.Y.S.2d at 788–79 (Titone, J., dissenting); see also People v. Littlejohn, 184 A.D.2d 790, 585 N.Y.S.2d 495 (2d Dep't 1992).

556. CPL § 710.30(1); see People v. Santana, 191 A.D.2d 174, 594 N.Y.S.2d 189 (1st Dep't 1993); People v. Slater, 166 A.D.2d 828, 562 N.Y.S.2d 985 (3d Dep't 1990).

557. 42 N.Y.2d 170, 397 N.Y.S.2d 613, 366 N.E.2d 273 (1977).

558. 84 N.Y.2d 425, 618 N.Y.S.2d 879, 643 N.E.2d 501 (1994).

ments need not be supplied but they must be described sufficiently so that the defendant can intelligently identify them.[559]

The lack of prejudice to the defendant caused by the abbreviated notice was "irrelevant."[560]

None of this broke new ground. On another front, however, *Lopez* pronounced the unexpected. The *Lopez* court specified that statement notice would not satisfy section 710.30 unless it included "the time and place the oral or written statements were made" as well as the "sum and substance" of the statements. The authorities cited in support of that proposition[561] in fact cannot fairly be read to support it, and how stringently the court will enforce its dictum, particularly in cases in which notice was given before *Lopez* was decided, is yet to be determined.

Lopez created new rules as well for the necessary content of identification notice. In that case the prosecutor had checked a box on his discovery form to indicate that identification testimony would be offered from a witness who had identified the defendant at a lineup. The checked box was not supplemented with additional detail. The Court of Appeals held that this notice had been inadequate, because it did not include the "time, place and manner" in which the lineup identification was made.[562] The court cited no authority for its statement, and again, the extent to which it will be taken literally remains to be determined.

Library References:

West's Key No. Digests, Criminal Law ⟸412(4), 629(10).

§ 10.25 Notice—Statements Within and Without the Rule

The section 710.30 notice requirement applies, not to all statements made by a defendant, but to any statement

> made by a defendant to a public servant, which statement if involuntarily made would render the evidence thereof suppressible upon motion pursuant to [section 710.20(3)].[563]

On its face, then, the statute does not require notice of statements not made to a public servant.[564] In particular, the Legislature excluded from the reach of the notice rule any statements made to a person acting in cooperation with a public servant.[565]

---

559. 84 N.Y.2d at 428, 618 N.Y.S.2d at 881.

560. 84 N.Y.2d at 428, 618 N.Y.S.2d at 881–82.

561. People v. Bennett, 56 N.Y.2d 837, 453 N.Y.S.2d 164, 438 N.E.2d 870 (1982); People v. Laporte, 184 A.D.2d 803, 584 N.Y.S.2d 662 (3d Dep't 1992); People v. Holmes, 170 A.D.2d 534, 566 N.Y.S.2d 93 (2d Dep't 1991).

562. 84 N.Y.2d at 428, 618 N.Y.S.2d at 881.

563. CPL § 710.30(1). As noted, section 710.20(3) provides for the suppression of statements which are "involuntarily made" within the meaning of CPL § 60.45.

564. People v. Smith, ___ A.D.2d ___, 631 N.Y.S.2d 683 (1st Dep't 1995); see People v. Luis M., 83 N.Y.2d 226, 608 N.Y.S.2d 962, 630 N.E.2d 658 (1994).

565. The limitation of the 15-day notice rule to statements made to public servants was intentional. The initial draft of the CPL would have applied the notice rule to

§ 10.25　　SEARCH WARRANTS & SUPPRESSION　　Ch. 10

Also outside the notice rule are some statements that would be presented at trial only upon the occurrence of events outside the prosecution's control. In that regard, section 710.30 requires that notice be given within 15 days of arraignment when the prosecution "intend[s]" to offer evidence of a statement at trial.[566] If, for example, a statement is offered to impeach the defendant only when he or she takes the stand at trial and "opens the door" by giving testimony inconsistent with the statement, the notice rule is not implicated, for there was no true prior "intent" to offer the evidence.[567] The same reasoning would seem to apply when the prosecution introduces a defendant's statement for its truth only on rebuttal, but that has not been established in the case law.[568]

In one of its early notice cases, *People v. Greer*, the Court of Appeals stated that notice "need not be served upon the defendant where there is no question of voluntariness."[569] That does not mean, however, that the prosecution may safely omit notice simply because it is convinced that in a particular case the defendant's statement was voluntary. For example, the failure to give notice is not excused simply because a prosecutor believes it obvious that a statement was spontaneous:

> It is for the court and not the parties to determine whether a statement is truly voluntary or is one in which the actions of the police are the functional equivalent of interrogation.[570]

The correct understanding of the cited language in *Greer* is that there are certain identifiable categories of statement evidence as to which the prospects of suppression are almost impossibly remote, and that there is no notice requirement as to statements in those categories.[571] For example, routine "pedigree" statements taken from a defendant during the booking process need not be preceded by *Miranda* warnings and are otherwise virtually never subject to suppression, and

---

statements made to private individuals acting in cooperation with a public servant. See Proposed New York Criminal Procedure Law, §§ 375.20(3), 375.30(1), pp. 406, 408 (Edward Thompson Co.1967). But before the CPL was enacted the Legislature changed the pertinent language to its present form. While notice of statements made to individuals cooperating with public servants thus are not within the notice rule, such statements are discoverable pursuant to section 240.20(1)(a). And once the defendant learns of such statements, he or she may move to suppress them under the terms of section 710.20(3) and the incorporated language of CPL § 60.45.

566. CPL § 710.30(1).

567. People v. Rahming, 26 N.Y.2d 411, 418, 311 N.Y.S.2d 292, 297, 259 N.E.2d 727 (1970).

568. The Court of Appeals once reversed a conviction in a case in which notice of a defendant's statement apparently was not given, and in which the statement was introduced to rebut an insanity defense.

People v. Hoover, 57 N.Y.2d 908, 456 N.Y.S.2d 756, 442 N.E.2d 1267 (1982). The court's brief opinion does not clearly explain why notice would be required for statements introduced on rebuttal. However, the facts of the case suggest several possibilities, including concern that the statement was in fact part of the prosecution's "case-in-chief" as to insanity.

569. 42 N.Y.2d 170, 178, 397 N.Y.S.2d 613, 618, 366 N.E.2d 273 (1977).

570. People v. Chase, 85 N.Y.2d 493, 500, 626 N.Y.S.2d 721, 724, 650 N.E.2d 379 (1995).

571. In those same categories, a defendant will not be entitled to a hearing if he or she does move to suppress, and thus the cases defining the pertinent categories sometimes discuss whether a motion was correctly denied without a hearing, rather than whether the defendant was entitled to notice.

as to them no notice need be given.[572] Similarly, notice need not be given of a so-called *"res gestae"* statement—a statement made by a defendant, even to a public servant, at the time of the crime.[573]

While the *Greer* concept makes it unnecessary to give notice about a statement within such a category, whether a particular statement may in fact properly be placed in the category may still require factual determinations.[574] If a judge concludes that a defendant's statement was not within a *Greer* category—for example, that the statement was not a response to questions asked for routine booking purposes—the defendant will obtain preclusion of the statement on account of the failure to give notice, even if the propriety of the statement is otherwise obvious. And the judge's decision will not be appealable.[575] The wise prosecutor will not gamble, and will provide notice of a statement within 15 days of arraignment if there is any possible question about whether notice is required.

Library References:
West's Key No. Digests, Criminal Law ⇔412(4).

§ 10.26 Notice—Identifications Within and Without the Rule

There are types of identification testimony, as well, to which the notice rule does not apply. Most obviously, when a witness views an identification procedure and does not identify the defendant, notice need not be supplied—even if it later develops that the witness can make an in-court identification.[576] Further, notice was not required in a case in which the witnesses identified the defendant's shirt, but not the defendant himself.[577] Even where a witness picks out the defendant, however, there are categories of identifications for which the prospects of suppression are so remote that the notice rule, and suppression procedures in general, do not apply.[578]

First, no notice is required about identifications that are not intentionally arranged by the police, for *Wade* motions can succeed only when

---

572. People v. Rodney, 85 N.Y.2d 289, 624 N.Y.S.2d 95, 648 N.E.2d 471 (1995).

573. People v. McCaskell, ___ A.D.2d ___, 630 N.Y.S.2d 66, 68 (1st Dep't 1995); People v. Clark, 198 A.D.2d 46, 603 N.Y.S.2d 450 (1st Dep't 1993).

574. People v. Rodney, 85 N.Y.2d at 293–94, 624 N.Y.S.2d at 98; see People v. Rodriguez, 79 N.Y.2d 445, 453, 583 N.Y.S.2d 814, 819, 593 N.E.2d 268 (1992)(requiring hearing as to whether an identification was "confirmatory," which would in turn control whether a Wade hearing was required).

575. See § 10.29, infra.

576. People v. Trammel, 84 N.Y.2d 584, 620 N.Y.S.2d 754, 644 N.E.2d 1310 (1994). In Trammel, the prosecution apparently learned just before trial that the witness believed he would be able to make an identification, despite his failure to make an identification earlier. The case can also be read to suggest that the prosecution does not have to give notice until it "intend[s]" to call a witness to give identification testimony. But see § 10.27, infra.

577. People v. Anderson, ___ A.D.2d ___, 630 N.Y.S.2d 77 (1st Dep't 1995).

578. Again, in these categories a defendant will not be entitled to a hearing if he or she does move to suppress, and thus the cases defining the pertinent categories sometimes discuss whether a motion was correctly denied without a hearing, rather than whether the defendant was entitled to notice.

§ 10.26   SEARCH WARRANTS & SUPPRESSION   Ch. 10

suggestiveness has been created by the authorities.[579] However, a wise prosecutor will give notice within 15 days if he or she can, for what is a "police arranged" identification may be open to factual dispute. For example, the Court of Appeals has noted that an identification that results from a neighborhood "canvass," during which a crime victim was accompanied by police officers, may be a "police arranged" identification.[580] The First Department since has twice distinguished the case on the facts, finding that a "canvass" will not yield a "police-arranged" identification requiring notice if that canvass is in fact controlled by the witness.[581] But it would be foolish for a prosecutor to take such distinctions for granted.

Second, notice need not be given of police-arranged identifications made by witnesses who know the defendant well—for example, witnesses who are the defendant's family members. There is no realistic prospect that such "confirmatory" identifications could be the product of suggestive circumstances created by the police.[582] In some cases, however, whether the witness actually knows the defendant could be disputed. If notice is not given, the dispute may have to be resolved by a "pre-*Wade*" hearing that may by itself be determinative of whether the evidence is admissible.[583]

Third, the identifications in another category also are referred to as "confirmatory" identifications, and notice need not be given of them. Trained undercover officers who have just purchased contraband often view suspects arrested by their back-up teams, in order to confirm that the correct individuals were arrested. When that process yields an identification within a period of hours after the illegal transaction, the identification is considered to be the ordinary and proper completion of the undercover operation, rather than an independent identification procedure in which suggestiveness might play a part.[584] Accordingly, identification notice and suppression hearings are not required.[585] But that does not mean that notice need not be given about identifications by police officers which do not fit the "confirmatory" pattern.[586]

Fourth, the Court of Appeals has held that notice need not be given that a witness has reviewed a photograph of a lineup during trial preparation.[587] Notably, however, the witness in that case apparently

579. People v. Gissendanner, 48 N.Y.2d 543, 552, 423 N.Y.S.2d 893, 899, 399 N.E.2d 924 (1979).

580. People v. Dixon, 85 N.Y.2d 218, 623 N.Y.S.2d 813, 647 N.E.2d 1321 (1995).

581. People v. Burgos, ___ A.D.2d ___, 631 N.Y.S.2d 336 (1st Dep't 1995); People v. Gillman, ___ A.D.2d ___, 631 N.Y.S.2d 337 (1st Dep't 1995).

582. People v. Collins, 60 N.Y.2d 214, 218–20, 469 N.Y.S.2d 65, 67–68, 456 N.E.2d 1188 (1983); People v. Tas, 51 N.Y.2d 915, 434 N.Y.S.2d 978, 415 N.E.2d 967 (1980).

583. People v. Rodriguez, 79 N.Y.2d 445, 583 N.Y.S.2d 814, 593 N.E.2d 268 (1992).

584. People v. Wharton, 74 N.Y.2d 921, 550 N.Y.S.2d 260, 549 N.E.2d 462 (1989).

585. Id.; People v. Newball, 76 N.Y.2d 587, 592, 561 N.Y.S.2d 898, 901, 563 N.E.2d 269 (1990)(finding that notice had been necessary because officer's identification did not fall within the confirmatory category).

586. People v. Perez, 74 N.Y.2d 637, 541 N.Y.S.2d 976, 539 N.E.2d 1104 (1989); People v. Newball, supra.

587. People v. Herner, 85 N.Y.2d 877, 626 N.Y.S.2d 54, 649 N.E.2d 1198 (1995).

was not asked to make an identification from the photograph, and the "preparation for trial" exception to the notice rule may have turned on that fact.

Finally, notice need not be given, and suppression proceedings need not be conducted, with respect to judicially-supervised identifications, such as those made at pretrial hearings.[588]

Library References:

West's Key No. Digests, Criminal Law ⚖629(10).

§ 10.27 Notice—Good Cause for Lateness

Section 710.30(2) provides that statement and identification notice must be served within 15 days of arraignment, but contains an escape clause:

> For good cause shown, however, the court may permit the People to serve such notice, thereafter.

That escape clause is narrow. As noted in § 10.23, *supra*, the Court of Appeals first construed the "good cause" language when the notice rule was less demanding—when notice could be served until the beginning of trial. Late, *i.e.*, mid-trial notice was likely to prejudice the defense, which would at the least have finalized its trial strategy. The court refused to recognize good cause for mid-trial notice when the arresting officer simply did not report the defendant's statement until he was on the witness stand,[589] or when the delay was attributable to unadorned "office failure" in the prosecutor's office.[590]

After the 15-day notice rule was adopted, the court declined to relax its interpretation of good cause. Indeed, in *People v. O'Doherty*,[591] the court was faced with a practical explanation for late notice, and with disclosure sufficiently before trial that its timing did not prejudice the defense, but nonetheless ruled the explanation inadequate to permit notice beyond the 15-day limit. In *O'Doherty*, the defendant made an admission relevant to a prior robbery at the time of an unrelated arrest, to an officer who had no direct role in the robbery case. Notice was provided only after the officer reported the statement to those on the robbery case, some five months after arraignment. After unsuccessfully protesting the late notice, the defendant moved to suppress the statement. That motion was rejected, without any disruption of the proceedings.

The Court of Appeals reversed the defendant's conviction, finding that the ignorance of those on the case was no excuse for their failure to provide notice within 15 days of arraignment. Further, neither the good faith of the prosecutor, the absence of merit to the suppression claim,

---

588. People v. White, 73 N.Y.2d 468, 541 N.Y.S.2d 749, 539 N.E.2d 577 (1989), cert. den. 493 U.S. 859, 110 S.Ct. 170, 107 L.Ed.2d 127 (1989).

589. People v. Spruill, 47 N.Y.2d 869, 419 N.Y.S.2d 69, 392 N.E.2d 1252 (1979).

590. People v. Briggs, 38 N.Y.2d 319, 379 N.Y.S.2d 779, 342 N.E.2d 557 (1975).

591. 70 N.Y.2d 479, 522 N.Y.S.2d 498, 517 N.E.2d 213 (1987).

nor the absence of prejudice from the late notice, was deemed relevant. The *O'Doherty* ruling was critical, for, as is plainly evident from the case law, belated communication from police officers to prosecutors is virtually always the reason for late notice of statement and identification evidence. According to *O'Doherty*, that explanation does not constitute good cause for late notice, no matter how inconsequential the delay.

Not much has changed since *O'Doherty*. Evidence about statements and about identifications is still subject to preclusion if notice is given more than 15 days after arraignment, and virtually nothing has been held to amount to good cause for late notice. In one case before *O'Doherty*, however, the Court of Appeals did hold that there was good cause for a failure to give notice where a statement was made by the defendant in the presence of his counsel and with the understanding that the statement could be used against the defendant.[592]

A constant refrain since *O'Doherty* is that a lack of prejudice to the defense is irrelevant to a showing of good cause.[593] In that regard, a lack of substantive prejudice has been treated as irrelevant because the notice rule is procedural, and is designed to promote the rapid and orderly disposition of defense motions.[594] But late notice will result in preclusion of evidence even if the delay has no impact on the rapid and orderly disposition of defense motions.

The prosecution's good faith likewise remains irrelevant to good cause.[595] Notably, where notice of statements or identifications is late, only the existence of good cause can save the evidence. Thus, that good faith and the absence of prejudice are irrelevant in good cause analysis renders them completely immaterial to preclusion pursuant to section 710.30(2).

Despite *O'Doherty*'s hard line, there obviously is "good cause" not to give 15-day notice of statements or identifications if they are not even made until more than 15 days after arraignment—if the belated emergence of that evidence does not instead simply make notice unnecessary.[596] Moreover, in *O'Doherty* the court recognized that a police officer could be so "attenuated" from a case that his or her knowledge would not be charged to the prosecution.[597] The court has since suggested more concretely, albeit in the eavesdropping context and in dictum, that inadequate communication among law enforcement officers could consti-

---

592. People v. Michel, 56 N.Y.2d 1014, 453 N.Y.S.2d 639, 439 N.E.2d 355 (1982). The situation might appear to fit better into the rule that notice need not be given of a statement in a category in which it is almost inconceivable that suppression could be warranted. See § 10.25, supra.

593. See, E.g., People v. Trammel, 84 N.Y.2d 584, 591, 620 N.Y.S.2d 754, 757, 644 N.E.2d 1310 (1994)(Kaye, C.J., dissenting); People v. Brown, 140 A.D.2d 266, 528 N.Y.S.2d 565 (1st Dep't 1988).

594. People v. O'Doherty, 70 N.Y.2d at 487–89, 522 N.Y.S.2d at 503–04.

595. See, e.g., People v. Miller, 142 A.D.2d 760, 530 N.Y.S.2d 866 (3d Dep't 1988) (prosecutor did not believe notice had to be given of statements to an off-duty, part-time sheriff from adjoining county).

596. See People v. Trammel, 84 N.Y.2d 584, 620 N.Y.S.2d 754, 644 N.E.2d 1310 (1994)(finding notice unnecessary, and therefore finding good cause irrelevant, as to identification witness who did not report that he recognized the defendant in identification procedures).

597. 70 N.Y.2d at 486, 522 N.Y.S.2d at 502.

tute proper grounds for late notice. Should the New York authorities belatedly learn about eavesdropping by the Canadian police but then speedily give notice, the "untimely acquisition" of the evidence would constitute good cause under the notice provisions of section 700.70.[598]

Library References:

West's Key No. Digests, Criminal Law ⚖︎629.5.

§ 10.28 Notice—Scope of Preclusion

Section 710.30 provides that, where proper notice has not been provided, statement or identification evidence may not be received against the defendant at trial.[599] The preclusion rule is easy to apply when statements are at issue. When the defendant does not receive timely notice of a statement for which notice was required, that statement cannot be used in evidence against the defendant, and its admission at trial is reversible error.[600] When part of a defendant's statement is included in the prosecution's notice, that part is admissible, but the remainder of the statement should be precluded.[601]

The rule for identification testimony has proved more difficult to define, on account of relatively complex statutory provisions. Pursuant to section 710.30(1)(b), notice must be given when testimony will be introduced at trial that the defendant was observed at a time relevant to the case, and when that testimony will be provided by a witness who has already identified the defendant as the individual who was observed. Thus, at issue are both an in-court identification or comparable testimony linking the defendant to the crime, and one or more prior identifications. And, likewise pursuant to section 710.30(1), identification notice must specify "the evidence intended to be offered" at trial. Finally, section 710.30(3) provides that, in the absence of notice, "no evidence of a kind specified in" section 710.30(1) should be received at trial.

Once *O'Doherty* and *McMullin* had continued a strict interpretation of good cause under the 15–day notice rule, the court quickly faced the question of what to preclude when proper identification notice was not provided. In *People v. Bernier*,[602] a critical witness had made a pretrial identification, but the defense had received no identification notice. The trial court nonetheless allowed the witness to make an in-court identification. First the Appellate Division and then the Court of Appeals disagreed, concluding that a failure to give notice about pretrial identifications must be fatal not only to testimony about the pretrial procedures, but to in-court identification testimony as well.[603] Thus, when the

---

598. People v. Capolongo, 85 N.Y.2d 151, 163, 623 N.Y.S.2d 778, 784, 647 N.E.2d 1286 (1995).

599. CPL § 710.30(3).

600. Harmless error principles do apply, see, e.g., People v. Brown, 140 A.D.2d 266, 270, 528 N.Y.S.2d 565, 568 (1st Dep't 1988), and of course the failure to comply with the notice statute is a non-constitutional error.

601. People v. Greer, 42 N.Y.2d 170, 178–79, 397 N.Y.S.2d 613, 618–19, 366 N.E.2d 273 (1977).

602. 73 N.Y.2d 1006, 541 N.Y.S.2d 760, 539 N.E.2d 588 (1989).

603. People v. Bernier, 141 A.D.2d 750, 754, 529 N.Y.S.2d 847, 849 (2d Dep't 1988), aff'd 73 N.Y.2d 1006, 1008, 541 N.Y.S.2d 760, 761, 539 N.E.2d 588 (1989).

statute says "no evidence of a kind specified in" section 710.30(1) can be admitted absent notice, it includes in-court identification testimony.[604]

Not addressed by the court was the proper remedy when the prosecutor has given notice of one of a witness's pretrial identifications, but has not specified every identification procedure in which the witness picked out the defendant. For example, in a particular case the defendant might be notified that a witness identified him or her at a lineup, but not that the witness on an earlier occasion had selected him or her from a showup. In such a circumstance the defendant, citing *Bernier*, might ask the court to preclude all identification testimony by the witness, including the in-court identification. The prosecutor, on the other hand, would certainly suggest that the correct remedy would be to preclude only the evidence about the showup. In that regard, the statute requires only that identification notice specify the evidence that the prosecution intends to offer at trial, and provides for preclusion only "in the absence" of statutory notice.[605] It would seem difficult, under the literal terms of the statute, to find a statutory violation when the prosecution gives notice and introduces no more at trial than what it has specified in its notice. The Court of Appeals has not resolved the issue, but recently the First Department has accepted the argument that the defendant is entitled only to preclusion of testimony about those pre-trial identification procedures that are omitted from the notice.[606]

Also uncertain, initially, was the effect of the preclusion of identification testimony on an eyewitness's ability otherwise to recount at trial what he or she had seen. In question in particular was the ability of a witness whose identification testimony had been precluded to testify about the criminal, his clothing, or his actions, if the jury might be able to associate the descriptions with the defendant. Subsequent decisions by the Court of Appeals hold that such a witness can indeed provide narrative and descriptive testimony about the crime, so long as the record plainly demonstrates that the testimony was based on observations that preceded precluded identifications.[607]

Finally, as noted in § 10.24, the Court of Appeals is not likely to permit a prosecutor to circumvent a preclusion order by bringing related charges against the defendant, and providing notice of the precluded evidence at arraignment in the new prosecution.[608]

Library References:

West's Key No. Digests, Criminal Law ⚖=629.5.

604. The admission of identification testimony despite inadequate notice can be harmless error, see, e.g., People v. Tatum, 205 A.D.2d 397, 613 N.Y.S.2d 391 (1st Dep't 1994), and again the error is statutory rather than constitutional.

605. CPL § 710.30(1) and (3).

606. People v. Bell, 214 A.D.2d 353, 625 N.Y.S.2d 893 (1st Dep't 1995); People v. Tatum, 205 A.D.2d 397, 613 N.Y.S.2d 391 (1st Dep't 1994).

607. People v. Moss, 80 N.Y.2d 857, 587 N.Y.S.2d 593, 600 N.E.2d 224 (1992); People v. Sanders, 66 N.Y.2d 906, 498 N.Y.S.2d 774, 489 N.E.2d 743 (1985); People v. Myrick, 66 N.Y.2d 903, 498 N.Y.S.2d 773, 489 N.E.2d 742 (1985).

608. See People v. Capolongo, 85 N.Y.2d 151, 164–66, 623 N.Y.S.2d 778, 785–86, 647 N.E.2d 1286 (1995).

§ 10.29 Notice—Waiver and Appeal

The notice rules provide windfalls to defendants, but careless defense counsel can waive them. Section 710.30(3), which provides for the preclusion of evidence for lack of notice, goes on to state that evidence should not be precluded if, despite the lack of notice, the defendant has moved to suppress the evidence and that motion has been denied. Under that provision, a defendant's meritorious preclusion motion, even if rejected by the trial court, may be pressed on appeal so long as it was made and denied in advance of the filing and denial of a motion to suppress the same evidence.[609] But the defendant may not invoke the preclusion doctrine as to an item of evidence after a motion to suppress has been filed and denied.[610] Indeed, the Court of Appeals announced in *People v. Merrill*[611] that a preclusion motion will be considered a nullity if it is made simultaneously with a suppression motion, and the suppression motion is then resolved on the merits. Prudent defense counsel will therefore take great pains to consider, and present to the court, any possible claims based on notice deficiencies before proceeding to file suppression motions as to the same evidence.

If a trial judge wrongly grants a preclusion motion—one that was waived or, more likely, one that simply was not meritorious—there is no recourse for the prosecutor. The Court of Appeals has held that the provisions of the CPL authorizing interlocutory appeals from suppression decisions do not apply to preclusion decisions.[612] Once evidence is precluded, therefore, it is out of the case. Of course, an order precluding critical statement or identification evidence can effectively end a prosecution, even if the evidence unquestionably was properly obtained. Ironically, therefore, in holding that a preclusion order is not appealable the court underscored the degree to which its decisions have infused the technical notice rules with a vitality completely independent of the constitutional merits of any suppression claim.[613]

Library References:

West's Key No. Digests, Criminal Law ⚖=412(4), 629.5.

§ 10.30 Practice Summary

A. Application for and Issuance of Search Warrant (*See* §§ 10.2, 10.3, 10.4, 10.5)

1. When a police officer or other applicant applies for a search warrant orally or in writing, the applicant and anyone else providing information in person must be put under oath. An oral application must be memorialized, usually by a tape recording or by a stenographer, then transcribed

---

609. People v. Bernier, 73 N.Y.2d 1006, 541 N.Y.S.2d 760, 539 N.E.2d 588 (1989).

610. See, e.g., People v. Malcolm, 216 A.D.2d 118, 629 N.Y.S.2d 750 (1st Dep't 1995).

611. 87 N.Y.2d 948, ___ N.Y.S.2d ___, ___ N.E.2d ___ (1996), rev'g on dissenting opinion 212 A.D.2d 987, 624 N.Y.S.2d 702 (4th Dep't 1995).

612. People v. Laing, 79 N.Y.2d 166, 581 N.Y.S.2d 149, 589 N.E.2d 372 (1992).

613. People v. Newball, 76 N.Y.2d 587, 590, 561 N.Y.S.2d 898, 900, 563 N.E.2d 269 (1990).

§ 10.30 SEARCH WARRANTS & SUPPRESSION Ch. 10

and certified. The warrant issued upon an oral application must be read back verbatim to the court (see § 10.2).

2. The application must contain allegations of fact providing the court with reasonable cause to believe that there is a substantial probability that the targeted evidence of illegal activity will be found at the time and place of the search and that the property sought constitutes evidence of a crime. The information supporting the warrant application should demonstrate that the designated property was recently in the specified premises (see § 10.3).

3. The issuing judge must personally make a complete inquiry into the sufficiency of the allegations of fact. Warrants may be issued upon hearsay but only if there is a substantial ground for supporting the hearsay's trustworthiness, which may be established by demonstrating the informant's reliability and the basis of his or her knowledge. Only the veracity of the police officer is relevant upon a challenge to the truthfulness of the allegations in a warrant application (see §§ 10.3, 10.4).

4. Only a district court, New York City Criminal Court, or a superior court judge sitting as a local criminal court may issue a warrant to be executed anywhere in the State (provided that the crime occurred within its jurisdiction). Warrants issued by city, town, or village courts can be executed only in the issuing, or in adjoining, counties. Unless a town court has proof that the crime occurred within the town, the court cannot issue a warrant that will be executed outside the town. A village or town court can issue a warrant if another town court is unavailable to do so, and a local criminal court of an adjoining town or village may substitute for the unavailable judge if such court is part of that town or city of the same county (see § 10.2).

5. Because the New York and federal Constitutions prohibit general warrants authorizing indiscriminate and blanket searches and seizures, a properly issued search warrant must contain a description of the targeted property and a designation of the person or the place to be searched specific enough so that the executing officer can reasonably identify the property or premises. A warrant that is overbroad on its face concerning the property to be seized or the place to be searched may be cured by referring to the warrant application and other documents supporting it. The defendant bears the burden of proof in attacking the sufficiency of the warrant application or the propriety of the warrant authorization (see §§ 10.2, 10.3, 10.5).

B. Execution of the Search Warrant (See §§ 10.5, 10.6)

1. The police must execute a search warrant not more than ten days after it is issued and must provide notice that they have a warrant to the occupants of the premises to be searched unless the premises are unoccupied. The police may also enter unannounced if they demonstrate to the issuing court that there is reasonable cause to believe that the property sought will be quickly destroyed or disposed of, or that giving notice will jeopardize their safety; in such cases, the court may

issue a warrant authorizing unnoticed, or "no-knock," entry. The police may use reasonable force to overcome resistance to the entry or to the search authorized by the warrant, but they may not use deadly physical force unless they meet resistance of that nature (*see* § 10.5).

2. The typical warrant may be executed only between 6:00 o'clock in the morning and 9:00 o'clock at night. To grant authorization to execute the warrant at other times, the court must be convinced that there is reasonable cause to believe that the designated property will be removed or destroyed if the warrant is not made executable at any time (*see* § 10.5).

3. The police may search only the premises designated in the warrant and only those places within the premises that are likely to contain the property sought. Similarly, the police may seize only the property, or the type of property, designated in the warrant. They may not frisk or arrest persons not named the warrant who happen to be present when the warrant is executed (*see* § 10.6).

C. **Scope of Suppression Provisions** (*See* §§ 10.8, 10.9, 10.10, 10.11)

1. The availability of the suppression sanction as a penalty for the illegal acquisition of evidence is determined by CPL § 710.20. Under that section, an individual charged in an accusatory instrument may obtain the suppression of physical evidence, statements, and identification testimony through the familiar *Mapp*, *Huntley*, and *Wade* proceedings. Also potentially subject to suppression are intercepted conversations and the images obtained through video surveillance, the results of chemical tests of the blood conducted pursuant to court order, and the products of pen registers and of trap and trace devices. Of course, where the New York or federal Constitution requires the suppression of another category of evidence, the failure to include that category in section 710.20 will not be dispositive (*see* § 10.8).

2. Section 710.20 further provides for the suppression of the indirect fruits of illegal searches, illegally obtained statements, and improper eavesdropping and video surveillance. Also suppressible is any identification testimony that is tainted by illegal identification procedures. And, under standard constitutional "indirect fruits" analysis, even in the absence of these statutory provisions a defendant would be entitled to suppression of the indirect fruits of a violation of his or her constitutional rights. However, the CPL contains no authority for suppressing the indirect fruits of purely statutory violations of the laws governing chemical blood tests and, most importantly, pen registers and trap and trace devices (*see* § 10.9).

3. The suppression of indirect fruits of illegal conduct is limited by "attenuation" principles. Under attenuation rules, the indirect products of illegal conduct are suppressed if they are come at by "exploitation" of the illegality, but not if intervening circumstances "dissipate" the illegality. In particular, evidence will not be suppressed if there is an "independent source" for it, a source other than the illegal conduct.

And evidence will not be suppressed if it would have been "inevitably discovered" had the illegal conduct not taken place. But in New York, neither independent source principles nor inevitable discovery principles can save the direct or "primary" fruits of illegal conduct (see § 10.10).

4. For practical purposes, only a defendant with "standing" can move to suppress evidence. Persons overheard in illegal surveillance, or who own the places or devices surveilled, can move to suppress the results of such surveillance. Otherwise, the general rule is that one has standing to contest the violation of one's own rights, but not another's. In the Fourth Amendment area, a defendant can protest the acquisition of evidence through a violation of his or her own reasonable expectations of privacy. New York does not generally recognize the "automatic standing" rule that would permit a defendant to move to suppress any contraband he or she has been accused of possessing. However, standing is automatically accorded to defendants to move to suppress contraband when the possession charge is based on a statutory presumption (see § 10.11).

D. Where and When to Move to Suppress (See §§ 10.12, 10.13, 10.14, 10.15)

1. Motions to suppress are almost always brought in the court in which the indictment, or the misdemeanor accusatory instrument, is pending. When only a felony complaint has been filed, the motion may be presented to the superior court that would have trial jurisdiction of the felony charge. When a local criminal court has held the defendant for action of a grand jury, the motion may be presented to the superior court that has impanelled or will impanel the grand jury, and also to the County Court if the grand jury has not been impanelled.

2. Occasionally a case is transferred from one court to another after a suppression motion has been made. A decision made in a superior court binds a local criminal court that subsequently obtains jurisdiction of the case. If a motion has been brought in one court but not decided as of the time jurisdiction is obtained by another court, the court considering the motion should not decide it.

3. A judge may entertain a suppression challenge based on an attack on that judge's own earlier order—for example, a search warrant. The judge's earlier order does not control the suppression determination, nor does it bind a determination by a different judge. Finally, a judicial hearing officer can conduct suppression proceedings, but the ultimate decision must be made by a judge (see § 10.12).

4. Suppression motions must be made within 45 days of arraignment, with that period extended if the defendant is without counsel at arraignment or if the prosecution subsequently provides statement, identification, or eavesdropping notice. Moreover, the defendant is entitled to make an untimely motion if, perhaps owing to a lack of critical information, the statutory period was unreasonably short. The court cannot reduce the period made available to the defendant by statute, but has discretion to enlarge it up until the date of sentence (see § 10.13).

Ch. 10 PRACTICE SUMMARY § 10.30

5. Suppression motions made before trial must be decided before trial. A controversial practice is often followed with respect to *Huntley* motions. When the defendant's statement will be offered by the prosecution solely for impeachment purposes, only "classical" voluntariness is at issue. Many judges defer consideration of classical voluntariness issues until the defendant actually takes the stand (*see* § 10.14).

6. Unsuccessful motions may be renewed upon the belated discovery of critical facts not earlier discoverable through the exercise of due diligence. In the absence of a motion to renew, appellate review of the suppression decision will be based only on the facts before the suppression court at the time of its decision. There is authority for liberally granting defendants permission to raise new suppression theories at late stages of the proceedings, where the prosecution is not prejudiced by the delay (*see* § 10.15).

E. Suppression Motion Papers (*See* §§ 10.16, 10.17, 10.18)

1. Suppression motions must generally be made in writing, and must be made on reasonable notice to the prosecution. The defendant's papers must state the legal theory or theories underlying the motion and must allege facts sufficient, if true, to entitle the defendant to relief. Allegations of fact can be based on personal knowledge or on information and belief, but in the latter instance the bases of the information and belief must be stated. Motions are subject to summary denial for failure to satisfy those rules, except that *Huntley* and *Wade* motions cannot be denied on account of inadequate factual pleading (*see* § 10.16).

2. With respect to *Mapp* motions, the courts tend to overlook a failure to attribute allegations of fact to specific sources. But many *Mapp* motions are denied on account of insufficient factual allegations. In general, a defendant must allege facts sufficient to show that he or she has standing to contest the search or seizure at issue, and that property was obtained in violation of the New York or federal Constitutions. When the prosecution's responding papers allege facts under which the search or seizure would be justified, the defendant must offer a rebuttal sufficient at least to create a factual dispute. Exception to those principles is, however, made as to facts that the defendant could not reasonably be expected to know. The same rules presumably apply to the pleadings for all types of suppression motions, other than *Huntley* and *Wade* motions (*see* § 10.17).

3. When the defendant's papers adequately state a basis for suppression, the motion will have to be resolved by a hearing if the prosecution's answering papers create an issue of fact. Except with respect to *Huntley* and *Wade* motions, the prosecution may avoid the need for a hearing if it alleges facts that, if true, render the defendant's allegations legally irrelevant, and the defendant does not offer a factual rebuttal. Even as to *Huntley* and *Wade* motions, the prosecution may avoid the need for a hearing if it can demonstrate that the statement or identification evidence falls within an exceptional category of evidence as to which normal

§ 10.30   SEARCH WARRANTS & SUPPRESSION   Ch. 10

suppression procedures are inapplicable—for example, pedigree statements or confirmatory identifications (*see* § 10.18).

F. Suppression Hearings and their Aftermath (*See* §§ 10.19, 10.20, 10.21, 10.22)

1. When the motion papers create determinative issues of fact, the motion will be resolved at a suppression hearing. Such hearings are formal in nature, with procedures akin to those at a trial. For example, the defendant has a right to be present, the proceedings are presumptively open to the public, a judge or a judicial hearing officer must preside, and the parties have a right to present evidence and confront the witnesses against them.

2. The defendant may subpoena witnesses, but has limited rights to obtain the presence of unfriendly witnesses, such as police officers and crime victims. Such witnesses need not appear unless their testimony is needed to resolve a "substantial" issue created by the evidence. Even when such an issue exists, and as a result a confidential informant must appear, that informant's identity may be protected through special procedures.

3. The rules of evidence that govern at hearings are those that apply at trial. The exception is that hearsay is admissible on any issue at a hearing, including the propriety of action under the "fellow officer" rule. However, hearsay evidence alone will not carry the day for a party whose showing is contradicted by first-hand evidence.

4. A critical component of any suppression proceeding is legal argument. A defendant or a prosecutor who does not preserve his or her suppression theories in the papers or in oral argument may find those theories precluded on appeal, whether he or she becomes the appellant or the respondent (*see* § 10.19).

5. The burden of proof at a suppression hearing is generally on the defendant, the moving party, although the prosecution will have the burden of coming forward with proof that, if not rebutted, would suffice to defeat the defendant's claim. Those principles govern as to most *Mapp* issues, and also apply at *Wade* hearings with respect to whether an identification procedure was unduly suggestive. The burden of proof is on the prosecution when the issue, at a *Huntley* hearing or elsewhere, concerns whether the defendant freely waived his or her rights, or whether the effects of illegal action have been attenuated (*see* § 10.20).

6. Findings on the credibility of witnesses made at the conclusion of the hearing will virtually always be controlling on appeal. On occasion, a court's decision will estop the prosecution in related litigation (*see* § 10.21).

7. Preclusion of evidence on account of a violation of the notice rules is not appealable. Otherwise, the prosecution may appeal a suppression decision if, and only if, it certifies that the case cannot go forward in the absence of the suppressed evidence. The defendant may appeal unfavorable suppression decisions after trial. Absent an express waiver, the

defendant may appeal on suppression grounds after a guilty plea if the court finally resolved an issue against the defendant prior to the plea (*see* § 10.22).

G. Notice (*See* §§ 10.24, 10.25, 10.26, 10.27, 10.28, 10.29)

1. The prosecution must give notice of intent to offer statement and identification evidence within 15 days of arraignment, or that evidence will be precluded even if properly obtained. The notice must describe the time, place, and content of the defendant's statements, or the time, place, and type of prior identification proceedings. The notice rules apply only to statements made to public servants that will not be introduced solely to impeach, and to identifications that are arranged by the police. Additional exceptions to the rules are made out in the case law (*see* §§ 10.24–26).

2. Notice may be given more than 15 days after arraignment when "good cause" for late notice so dictates. However, the "good cause" exception is narrow, and is not satisfied by a lack of communication between the police and the prosecutor, or by "office failure" in the prosecutor's office (*see* § 10.27).

3. When the notice rules apply to statements, a particular statement will be precluded if notice of that statement was not given. When the notice rules apply to a witness's identification testimony, a failure to give any notice will result in preclusion of all that witness's identification testimony. If partial identification notice is given, testimony will be precluded as to pretrial identification procedures not mentioned in the notice. A defendant can waive preclusion by failing to seek it until he or she moves to suppress the evidence. A prosecutor has no appellate remedy when a court precludes evidence under the notice rules (*see* § 10.28–29).

§ 10.31 Forms

§ 10.31.1 Notice of Motion to Suppress Statements

[Caption]

COUNSEL:

PLEASE TAKE NOTICE, that upon the annexed affirmation and all the prior papers and proceedings herein, the undersigned will move this Court, at Part ___ thereof, at the Courthouse at _____, New York, on the ___ day of _____, 19__, at ___ in the forenoon, or as soon thereafter as counsel can be heard, for an order pursuant to section 710.20(3) of the Criminal Procedure Law suppressing statements allegedly made by defendant, and for any other relief that the Court deems proper.

Dated: _____, 19__
  _____, New York

            [Name of defense attorney]
            Attorney for Defendant
            Address
            Tel. No.

TO: HON. _____
District Attorney
_____ County

HON. _____
Clerk of the Court

§ 10.31.2 Affirmation in Support of Motion to Suppress Statements

[Caption]

_____, an attorney duly admitted to practice in the Courts of this State, hereby affirms under penalty of perjury that the following statements are true, and as to those made upon information and belief he [she] believes them to be true:

1. I am the attorney for the defendant herein.

2. On _____, 19__, a[n] [specify accusatory instrument] was filed with this Court charging defendant with the following offense(s): [specify charge(s)]. A copy of [specify accusatory instrument] is attached hereto as Exhibit A.

3. No plea of guilty has been entered as to the offense(s) charged, nor has a trial been commenced thereon.

4. Pursuant to CPL § 710.30, the People have served defendant with notice that they intend to offer at trial evidence of the following statements allegedly made by defendant: [specify statements].

5. Upon information and belief, the aforesaid statements were involuntarily made by defendant because they were obtained in violation of defendant's constitutional rights.

6. No prior application for the relief sought herein has been made.

WHEREFORE, defendant requests that this Court issue an order suppressing the aforesaid statements.

Dated: _____, 19__
_____, New York

[Signature]
_____
[Name of defense attorney]

§ 10.31.3 Notice of Motion to Suppress Identification Evidence

[Caption]

COUNSEL:

PLEASE TAKE NOTICE, that upon the annexed affirmation and all the prior papers and proceedings herein, the undersigned will move this Court, at Part __ thereof, at the Courthouse at _____, New York, on the __ day of _____, 19__, at __ in the forenoon, or as soon thereafter as counsel can be heard, for an order pursuant to section 710.20(6) of the

Criminal Procedure Law, suppressing evidence of an identification allegedly made of the defendant herein, and for any other relief that the Court deems proper.

Dated: _____, 19__
_____, New York

                                    [Name of defense attorney]
                                    Attorney for Defendant
                                    Address
                                    Tel. No.

TO: HON. _____
      District Attorney
      _____ County

      HON. _____
      Clerk of the Court

§ 10.31.4 Affirmation in Support of Motion to Suppress Identification

[Caption]

_____, an attorney duly admitted to practice in the Courts of this State, hereby affirms under penalty of perjury that the following statements are true, and as to those made upon information and belief he [she] believes them to be true:

    1. I am the attorney for the defendant herein.

    2. On _____, 19__, a[n] [specify accusatory instrument] was filed with this Court charging defendant with the following offense(s): [specify charge(s)]. A copy of [specify accusatory instrument] is attached hereto as Exhibit A.

    3. No plea of guilty has been entered as to the offense(s) charged, nor has a trial been commenced thereon.

    4. Pursuant to CPL § 710.30, the People have served defendant with notice of their intention to offer at trial evidence that [specify the alleged identification of defendant].

    5. Upon information and belief, the aforesaid identification violated defendant's constitutional rights because it was conducted in an unduly suggestive manner.

    6. No prior application for the relief sought herein has been made.

WHEREFORE, defendant requests that this Court issue an order suppressing evidence of the aforesaid identification as well as any in-court identification of defendant by [specify name of person who made alleged identification].

Dated: _____, 19__
_____, New York

[Signature]
_____
[Name of defense attorney]

§ 10.31.5 Notice of Motion to Suppress Physical Evidence

[Caption]

COUNSEL:

PLEASE TAKE NOTICE, that upon the annexed affirmation and all the prior papers and proceedings herein, the undersigned will move this Court, at Part ___ thereof, at the Courthouse at _____, New York, on the ___ day of _____, 19__, at ___ in the forenoon, or as soon thereafter as counsel can be heard, for an order pursuant to section 710.20(1) of the Criminal Procedure Law suppressing physical evidence obtained from the defendant herein, and for any other relief that the Court deems proper.

Dated: _____, 19__
_____, New York

[Name of defense attorney]
Attorney for Defendant
Address
Tel. No.

TO: HON. _____
District Attorney
_____ County

HON. _____
Clerk of the Court

§ 10.31.6 Affirmation in Support of Motion to Suppress Physical Evidence

[Caption]

_____, an attorney duly admitted to practice in the Courts of this State, hereby affirms under penalty of perjury that the following statements are true, and as to those made upon information and belief he [she] believes them to be true:

1. I am the attorney for the defendant herein.

2. On _____, 19__, a[n] [specify accusatory instrument] was filed with this Court charging defendant with the following offense(s): [specify charge(s)]. A copy of [specify accusatory instrument] is attached hereto as Exhibit A.

3. No plea of guilty has been entered as to the aforesaid offense(s), nor has a trial been commenced thereon.

4. Upon information and belief, the source of such information being defendant, [specify physical evidence seized from defendant] was

seized from defendant in violation of his [her] rights under the United States and New York Constitutions.

5. [Specify factual allegations in support of claim that evidence was unlawfully seized—*e.g.*: "On June 19, 1993, at 3:00 p.m., defendant was waiting for a bus on the corner of Broadway and 42nd Street in Manhattan when a uniformed police officer approached him stating, 'People like you don't belong in this neighborhood.' The police officer then reached into defendant's jacket pocket and removed a one-inch vial of cocaine."]

6. No prior application for the relief sought herein has been made.

WHEREFORE, defendant requests that this Court issue an order suppressing [specify physical evidence].

Dated: _____, 19__
_____, New York

[Signature]
_____
[Name of defense attorney]

Chapter 11

PLEAS

Table of Sections

11.1	Introduction.
11.2	Pleading Guilty as of Right.
11.3	Guilty Pleas by Permission of the Court and the Consent of the Prosecutor.
11.4	Pleas of Not Responsible by Reason of Mental Disease or Defect.
11.5	Statutory Plea Bargaining Restrictions.
11.6	Withdrawal of Not Guilty Plea by the Defendant.
11.7	Entry of the Guilty Plea—Knowing and Voluntary Waiver of Rights.
11.8	____ Competency of Defendant.
11.9	____ Defendant's Understanding of Collateral Consequences of the Plea.
11.10	____ Factual Basis for the Plea.
11.11	Sentence Promises—In General.
11.12	____ Conditional Nature of Promise.
11.13	____ Special Conditions for Defendants at Liberty Between Plea and Sentence.
11.14	____ Specific Performance.
11.15	Rights Automatically Relinquished by a Defendant Upon Pleading Guilty.
11.16	Claims That Ordinarily Survive a Guilty Plea.
11.17	Bargained-for Waivers of the Right to Appeal.
11.18	Withdrawal of Guilty Plea—Defendant.
11.19	____ Court or Prosecutor.
11.20	Practice Summary—Defense.
11.21	____ Prosecution.
11.22	____ Court.
11.23	Forms.
	11.23.1 Notice of Motion to Withdraw Guilty Plea.
	11.23.2 Affirmation of Attorney Upon Motion to Withdraw Guilty Plea.
	11.23.3 Affidavit of Defendant Upon Motion to Withdraw Guilty Plea.

WESTLAW Electronic Research

See WESTLAW Electronic Research Guide preceding the Summary of Contents.

§ 11.1 Introduction

Once their client agrees to enter a guilty plea, many criminal defense attorneys cease thinking strategically about that case and move their thoughts on to the next one. They do so at their peril. Although most guilty pleas go off smoothly, many do not. And for the defendants, incarceration on the plea often spurs, not acceptance of their condition, but imaginative thoughts of plea withdrawal, post-conviction collateral attacks based upon claimed ineffective assistance of counsel, and of issues to raise on appeal.

Prosecutors and courts, too, have felt the frustration of plea convictions coming undone, not only prior to sentence but also years later, after the prosecution's witnesses have disappeared or their memories have faded.

Increasingly, in an effort to ensure finality, both the prosecutors and the courts have come to rely on "bargained-for" waivers of the right to appeal in plea cases. Many of these waivers are—unbeknown to the parties at the time—defective and subsequently not given effect by the appellate courts. Even otherwise valid waivers have been held ineffective with respect to certain appellate issues, especially the types of issues most likely to prevail on appeal. Since the law regarding appeal waiver is evolving, if not abstruse, many defense practitioners do not have a ready grasp of what appellate issues their clients are being asked to waive. Yet it is defense counsel upon whom the courts rely to explain this matter to the defendants.

The following chapter is not only an overview of CPL Article 220 for practitioners new to the criminal courts, but a ready guide for the experienced—defense attorneys prosecutors, and judges alike—to consult in order to navigate the shoals of plea and sentence procedures. If nothing else, this chapter is a trouble-shooting resource to consult when things—as they are wont to do—go wrong.

Library References:
West's Key No. Digests, Criminal Law ⚖︎267–275.

§ 11.2 Pleading Guilty as of Right

By statute, a defendant has the absolute right to plead guilty only if the plea is to the entire indictment.[1] So long as the plea is knowing and voluntary,[2] and unless the indictment charges first-degree murder as defined in section 125.27 of the Penal Law,[3] the trial court must accept a plea to the entire indictment.[4] In *People v. Moquin*,[5] the Court of Appeals made it clear that this right is to plead to the indictment *as it reads at the time of the plea*, including any judicial modification subsequent to the filing of the indictment.[6]

---

1. CPL § 220.10(2). See People v. Esajerre, 35 N.Y.2d 463, 466, 363 N.Y.S.2d 931, 934, 323 N.E.2d 175 (1974); People v. Rosner, 185 A.D.2d 686, 587 N.Y.S.2d 883 (4th Dep't 1992); People v. Melo, 160 A.D.2d 600, 554 N.Y.S.2d 530 (1st Dep't 1990).

   This right is by statute only. There is no absolute federal constitutional right to have one's guilty plea accepted. Santobello v. New York, 404 U.S. 257, 262, 92 S.Ct. 495, 498, 30 L.Ed.2d 427 (1971).

2. See § 11.7, infra.

3. CPL § 220.10(5)(e). The underlying source of this bar is Art. 1, § 2 of the New York Constitution, which prohibits the waiver of a jury trial where the crime charged is one punishable by death. By extension, this clause forbids a plea to an indictment where the possibility of a death sentence exists if the conviction were after trial.

4. See People v. Moquin, 77 N.Y.2d 449, 453 n. 1, 568 N.Y.S.2d 710, 713 n. 1, 570 N.E.2d 1059 (1991); Matter of Carney v. Feldstein, 193 A.D.2d 1016, 597 N.Y.S.2d 982 (3d Dep't 1993); People v. Rosebeck, 109 A.D.2d 915, 916, 486 N.Y.S.2d 384, 385 (3d Dep't 1985).

5. 77 N.Y.2d 449, 568 N.Y.S.2d 710, 570 N.E.2d 1059.

6. 77 N.Y.2d at 453 n. 1, 568 N.Y.S.2d at 713 n. 1. An automatic stay, however, would be available to any prosecutor aggrieved by the granting of a motion to in-

§ 11.2 PLEAS Ch. 11

A plea of guilty to the entire indictment does not authorize dismissal of its lesser inclusory concurrent counts, as would be the case if there were a conviction on the highest counts after trial.[7]

Although the provisions of CPL § 220.10 are made generally applicable to informations prosecuted in local criminal courts,[8] no authority exists for entering a plea to a felony complaint.[9] In local criminal courts, moreover, a defendant does not have a right to plead to an accusatory instrument charging a misdemeanor where the prosecutor requests an adjournment to present the charges to a grand jury.[10]

Library References:

West's Key No. Digests, Criminal Law ⌲273(2).

§ 11.3 Guilty Pleas by Permission of the Court and the Consent of the Prosecutor

By statute, an indicted defendant needs the permission of the court and the consent of the prosecutor for the entry of a plea to less than the entire indictment,[11] for a plea of "not responsible by reason of mental disease or defect,"[12] and for a plea that covers other accusatory instruments.[13] The same is true for any plea to first-degree murder as defined in P.L. § 125.27; however, such a plea may only be entered when the agreed upon sentence is not one of death.[14]

With respect to a felony complaint, the court may, with the prosecutor's consent, "make inquiry" into the appropriateness of a misdemeanor reduction and plea, and then reduce without the prosecutor's further consent if the court's inquiry reveals no reasonable cause to believe that the defendant committed a felony. If the court's inquiry does reveal reasonable cause to believe the defendant committed a felony, the court

spect and reduce pursuant to CPL § 210.20(1–a). 77 N.Y.2d at 455–56 n. 3, 568 N.Y.S.2d at 714 n. 3.

7. See CPL § 300.40 (3)(b). See also People v. Walton, 41 N.Y.2d 880, 393 N.Y.S.2d 979, 362 N.E.2d 610 (1977).

8. CPL § 340.20(1).

9. See generally CPL Article 180. See also People v. Montanye, 95 A.D.2d 959, 464 N.Y.S.2d 292 (3d Dep't 1983)(no right to plead guilty to felony complaint).

10. People v. Barkin, 49 N.Y.2d 901, 428 N.Y.S.2d 192, 405 N.E.2d 674 (1980). See also People v. Montanye, supra.

11. CPL § 220.10(3) and (4). See People v. Melo, 160 A.D.2d 600, 554 N.Y.S.2d 530 (1st Dep't 1990); People v. Perez, 156 A.D.2d 7, 11, 553 N.Y.S.2d 659, 661 (1st Dep't 1990); Matter of Gold v. Booth, 79 A.D.2d 691, 693, 433 N.Y.S.2d 879, 881 (2d Dep't 1980).

A plea to less than the entire indictment would include a plea to only some counts, CPL § 220.10(4)(a); a plea to a "lesser included offense" with respect to any or all of the counts, § 220.10(3) and (4)(b); or any combination of the above, CPL § 220.10(4)(c).

For the purpose of pleading down, a "lesser included offense" means not only such "lessers" as defined in CPL § 1.20(34), but an expanded list of possibilities as contained in CPL § 220.20.

12. CPL § 220.10(6), 220.15.

13. CPL § 220.30(3). A plea may cover charges in another court with the written consent of the other court and prosecutor. CPL § 220.30(3)(a)(ii).

14. CPL §§ 220.10(5)(e), 220.30(3)(b)(vii). If the prosecutor is seeking the death penalty pursuant to CPL § 250.40, the defendant apparently may not enter a guilty plea to a violation of P.L. § 125.27.

may nonetheless—with two exceptions—reduce to a misdemeanor with the further consent of the prosecutor. The two exceptions are where there is reasonable cause to believe that the defendant has committed a non-drug Class A felony, or an "armed" felony as defined in CPL § 1.20(41).[15]

A prosecutor dissatisfied with the court's decision to reduce a charge in a felony complaint to a misdemeanor may request an immediate adjournment to present the case to the grand jury, and thereby divest the local criminal court of jurisdiction to accept a plea to the misdemeanor charge.[16]

An Article 78 petition in the nature of a writ of prohibition is available to a prosecutor aggrieved by the court's acceptance of a guilty plea to a reduced charge without the prosecutor's consent, at least if the writ is taken prior to entry of judgment and commencement of sentence.[17]

As a general rule, the decision whether to permit a reduced plea is a matter within the court's discretion.[18] The court need not accept a plea, therefore, even if the prosecutor consents. There is some appellate and lower court authority, however, disapproving a trial court's "fixed policy" of not accepting plea bargains.[19]

Prosecutors, too, may attach "reasonable conditions" to their con-

---

15. CPL § 180.50(1) and (2). With respect to informations prosecuted in the local criminal courts, the plea bargaining provisions of section 220.00 regarding indictments are generally applicable. CPL § 340.20.

16. CPL § 170.20(2). Any plea and sentence taken in violation of section 170.20 would be a nullity and subject to vacatur. People v. Phillips, 48 N.Y.2d 1011, 425 N.Y.S.2d 558, 401 N.E.2d 916 (1980); People v. Anderson, 140 A.D.2d 528, 528 N.Y.S.2d 614 (2d Dep't 1988).

17. Matter of McDonald v. Sobel, 272 App.Div. 455, 72 N.Y.S.2d 4 (2d Dep't), aff'd 297 N.Y. 679, 77 N.E.2d 3 (1947); Matter of Gribetz v. Edelstein, 66 A.D.2d 788, 410 N.Y.S.2d 873 (2d Dep't 1978); Matter of Blumberg v. Lennon, 44 A.D.2d 769, 354 N.Y.S.2d 261 (4th Dep't 1974).

While there is some Appellate Division authority for the post-commencement of sentence vacatur by the prosecution, either via Article 78 or on appeal, of a plea to a reduced charge entered without its consent, see Matter of Himelein v. Nenno, 168 A.D.2d 957, 564 N.Y.S.2d 909 (4th Dep't 1990); People v. Perez, 156 A.D.2d 7, 553 N.Y.S.2d 659 (1st Dep't 1990); Matter of Cosgrove v. Kubiniec, 56 A.D.2d 709, 392 N.Y.S.2d 733 (4th Dep't 1977), those holdings predate and appear to run afoul of the holding in People v. Moquin, 77 N.Y.2d 449, 568 N.Y.S.2d 710, 570 N.E.2d 1059 (1991). In Moquin, the Court of Appeals held that the trial court may not vacate a guilty plea in order to remedy a substantive legal error in its acceptance, at least after the defendant has begun serving his or her sentence. 77 N.Y.2d at 452, 568 N.Y.S.2d at 712. See People v. Donnelly, 176 A.D.2d 404, 574 N.Y.S.2d 111 (3d Dep't 1991)(citing Moquin, Third Department refused to vacate plea and sentence where a reduced plea was taken without the prosecutor's consent). See also People v. Smalls, 162 A.D.2d 642, 556 N.Y.S.2d 957 (2d Dep't 1990)(trial court may not vacate sentence upon defendant's failure to keep his plea promise to testify truthfully at the codefendant's trial).

18. People v. Williams, 158 A.D.2d 930, 551 N.Y.S.2d 94 (4th Dep't 1990); People v. Manley, 103 A.D.2d 1024, 478 N.Y.S.2d 400 (4th Dep't 1984); People v. Griffith, 43 A.D.2d 20, 24, 349 N.Y.S.2d 94, 98 (1st Dep't 1973).

19. See People v. Compton, 157 A.D.2d 903, 550 N.Y.S.2d 148 (3d Dep't 1990)(Third Department refuses to "endorse" court's fixed policy of not allowing a negotiated plea on the eve of trial); People v. Glendenning, 127 Misc.2d 880, 881–83, 487 N.Y.S.2d 952, 953–55 (Sup.Ct., Westchester County, 1985)(improper for judge to announce fixed policy of no plea bargaining in DWI cases).

sent to a reduced plea, as such consent is given as "a matter of grace."[20] Thus, a prosecutor may properly require a defendant to testify against a codefendant as a condition of consent to a reduced plea.[21] Similarly, prosecutorial consent may generally be conditioned upon all codefendants pleading guilty,[22] or even conditioned upon a defendant entering a plea more severe than the one offered to the codefendant.[23] While these latter plea conditions can place pressure on the defendant to plead guilty, they do not, in themselves, render a plea involuntary; rather they are simply one factor to weigh in assessing the knowing and voluntary nature of the plea.[24]

A court or prosecutor may also generally condition a reduced plea on the withdrawal of pending motions,[25] or even the right to appeal.[26] Neither the court nor the prosecutor, however, may impose conditions contrary to law or strong public policy.[27]

The refusal of the prosecutor to offer a reduced plea has been held not to be a basis for dismissal in the interest of justice pursuant to CPL § 210.40.[28]

Similarly, a prosecutor's policy of not consenting to reduced pleas has been held not to violate a defendant's right to equal protection.[29]

Library References:

West's Key No. Digests, Criminal Law ⟐273(3), 273.1(2), 286.5, 286.10.

20. People v. Esajerre, 35 N.Y.2d 463, 467, 363 N.Y.S.2d 931, 934, 323 N.E.2d 175 (1974). See also People v. Elliby, 80 A.D.2d 875, 436 N.Y.S.2d 784 (2d Dep't 1981).

21. People v. Cuadrado, 161 A.D.2d 232, 554 N.Y.S.2d 618 (1st Dep't 1990). See also People v. Grant, 99 A.D.2d 536, 471 N.Y.S.2d 325 (2d Dep't 1984) (court may condition acceptance of reduced plea upon defendant's agreement to testify against a codefendant).

22. People v. Antonio, 176 A.D.2d 528, 574 N.Y.S.2d 718 (1st Dep't 1991); People v. Cornielle, 176 A.D.2d 190, 574 N.Y.S.2d 199 (1st Dep't 1991); People v. Bermudez, 157 A.D.2d 533, 549 N.Y.S.2d 1022 (1st Dep't 1990).

23. People v. Fiumefreddo, 82 N.Y.2d 536, 544–46, 605 N.Y.S.2d 671, 676–77, 626 N.E.2d 646 (1993); People v. Keehner, 28 A.D.2d 695, 281 N.Y.S.2d 128 (2d Dep't 1967); People v. Henzey, 24 A.D.2d 764, 263 N.Y.S.2d 678 (2d Dep't 1965).

24. People v. Fiumefreddo, 82 N.Y.2d at 544–46, 605 N.Y.S.2d at 676–77 (plea offer "connected" to more generous plea to defendant's father held voluntarily entered under the particular circumstances surrounding the plea). Cf. People v. Rodriguez, 79 Misc.2d 1002, 362 N.Y.S.2d 116 (Sup.Ct., Bronx County, 1974)("wired" nature of plea offer factor in determination that plea of youthful defendant was involuntary).

25. People v. Esajerre, 35 N.Y.2d 463, 363 N.Y.S.2d 931, 323 N.E.2d 175 (1974); People v. Miller, 79 A.D.2d 687, 434 N.Y.S.2d 36 (2d Dep't 1980), cert. denied 452 U.S. 919, 101 S.Ct. 3056, 69 L.Ed.2d 423 (1981).

26. See § 11.17, infra.

27. See, e.g., People v. Callahan, 80 N.Y.2d 273, 590 N.Y.S.2d 46, 604 N.E.2d 108 (1992)(prosecutor may not condition reduced plea offer upon defendant's waiver of otherwise preserved speedy trial claim); People v. Blakley, 34 N.Y.2d 311, 357 N.Y.S.2d 459, 313 N.E.2d 763 (1974)(same). See also Cowles v. Brownell, 73 N.Y.2d 382, 540 N.Y.S.2d 973, 538 N.E.2d 325 (1989)(city's release from civil liability as a condition of dismissal of criminal charges not enforced); Dziuma v. Korvettes, 61 A.D.2d 677, 403 N.Y.S.2d 269 (1st Dep't 1978)(same); People v. Siragusa, 81 Misc.2d 368, 366 N.Y.S.2d 336 (Dist.Ct., Nassau County, 1975)(prosecutor cannot condition plea on defendant's dropping of lawsuit against county).

28. People v. Molfino, 178 A.D.2d 238, 577 N.Y.S.2d 787 (1st Dep't 1991); People v. Perez, 156 A.D.2d 7, 553 N.Y.S.2d 659 (1st Dep't 1990); People v. Doe, 159 Misc.2d 799, 801, 606 N.Y.S.2d 862, 863 (Sup.Ct., N.Y. County, 1993).

29. People v. Cohen, 186 A.D.2d 843, 588 N.Y.S.2d 211 (3d Dep't 1992).

§ 11.4 Pleas of Not Responsible by Reason of Mental Disease or Defect

A plea of not responsible by reason of mental disease or defect may be entered to the entire indictment with the consent of the prosecutor and the permission of the court.[30] The court need not accept the plea merely because the prosecution consents; rather, it must assure itself that the plea is in the public interest, that it is knowing and voluntary, and that there is a factual basis for the plea.[31] A hearing on the plea is authorized, but not required.[32] In contrast to the lack of a mandatory "catechism" for ensuring the knowing and voluntary nature of regular guilty pleas,[33] the procedures required prior to acceptance of a plea of not guilty by reason of mental disease or defect are mandatory and detailed.[34]

It has been held that the court, in allocating the defendant on such a plea, may use a psychiatric "interpreter" if the defendant's thought processes are too "convoluted" to communicate without one.[35]

Note that while CPL § 220.15(1) speaks in terms of pleas to "indictments," the procedures described in them are applicable to pleas entered in the local criminal courts.[36]

If such a plea is later determined to be the product of the defendant's fraud or misrepresentation, then the court has the inherent power

---

30. CPL § 220.15(1).

31. People v. Behr, 116 Misc.2d 576, 455 N.Y.S.2d 942 (Sup.Ct., N.Y. County, 1982).

32. CPL § 220.15(1).

33. See §§ 11.7, 11.10, infra.

34. CPL § 220.15(1)-(5). Subdivision one requires the prosecution, in writing or orally on the record, to state that it is satisfied that the defendant would prove an "insanity" affirmative defense at trial by a preponderance of the evidence. The prosecution must similarly detail the evidence available to it, both as to the crime elements and as to the affirmative defense, and detail its reasons for recommending the plea.

Per subdivision two, defense counsel must state that, in his or her opinion, the defendant is competent to assist in the defense and understands the consequences of the plea. Similarly, counsel must explain whether, in his or her opinion, the defendant has any viable defense other than the insanity affirmative defense. Finally counsel must set forth the psychiatric evidence available to the defense.

Subdivision three requires the court to orally allocute the defendant, on the record, as to whether the defendant understands (a) the nature of the charges and the consequences of the plea; (b) that he or she may enter a plea of not guilty or continue to press such a plea; (c) that he or she has the right to trial by jury, to the assistance of counsel, to confront and cross-examine witnesses, and against self-incrimination; (d) that the plea constitutes a waiver of the right to trial; (e) that in allocuting about the offense he or she will be waiving the right against self-incrimination; and (f) that the plea is equivalent to a verdict after trial of not responsible by reason of insanity.

Additionally, pursuant to subdivision four, the court must elicit a factual basis for the plea and, on the record, question the defendant as to whether it is knowingly and voluntarily entered.

Finally, subdivision five requires the court to state on the record, in detail, its findings that (a) each element of the crimes charged would be proven at trial; (b) the affirmative defense would be proven at trial; (c) the defendant is competent; (d) the plea has a factual basis and is knowing and voluntary; and (e) acceptance of such a plea is "required in the interest of the public in the effective administration of justice."

35. People v. Johnny P., 112 Misc.2d 647, 651, 445 N.Y.S.2d 1007, 1010 (N.Y.C.Crim.Ct.1981).

36. CPL § 340.20(1). See People v. Johnny P., supra.

§ 11.4 PLEAS Ch. 11

to vacate the plea and return the case to pre-pleading status.[37]

Once such a plea is accepted by the court, all subsequent proceedings are governed by CPL § 330.20, the section relevant to insanity acquitees.[38] Those sections of the CPL dealing with judgments of criminal convictions no longer obtain. Hence, there is no statutory authority for a criminal appeal to the Appellate Division pursuant to Article 450 of the CPL; rather, a defendant unhappy with his or her plea must either move to withdraw the plea in the court that accepted it, or petition for a writ of *habeas corpus* to challenge the legality of the commitment.[39]

Library References:
West's Key No. Digests, Criminal Law ⚖286.5, 286.10.

§ 11.5 Statutory Plea Bargaining Restrictions

The Legislature has set certain floors below which courts and prosecutors cannot go in offering plea bargains to defendants charged with felonies. Pre-indictment, these are contained in CPL §§ 180.50(2) and 180.70(3). Post-indictment, they are set forth in CPL sections 220.10(5)(governing pleas to less than the entire indictment) and 220.30(3)(governing pleas to one accusatory instrument to cover other indictments).

Pre-indictment, a defendant charged in a felony complaint may be permitted, in the "interest of justice", and if the court and prosecutor are so disposed, to plead guilty to a reduced misdemeanor charge, unless the original charge is a Class A non-drug felony or an "armed" felony within the meaning of CPL § 1.20(41).[40] Additionally, a defendant charged in a felony complaint may be permitted, with the prosecutor's consent and prior to indictment, to waive indictment and plead guilty to a superior court information (SCI) containing a lesser included offense of the charge for which the defendant was held for grand jury action.[41]

Once an indictment against the defendant is filed, the pleabargaining restrictions of sections 220.10(5) and 220.30(3) apply. They cannot be evaded merely by having the indicted defendant waive indictment and enter a guilty plea to a superior court information.[42]

---

37. Matter of Lockett v. Juviler, 65 N.Y.2d 182, 490 N.Y.S.2d 764, 480 N.E.2d 378 (1985).

38. CPL § 220.15(6).

39. See People v. Herndon, 191 A.D.2d 248, 595 N.Y.S.2d 8 (1st Dep't 1993).

40. CPL §§ 180.50(1) and (2), 180.70(3).

41. CPL § 195.10. See People v. Menchetti, 76 N.Y.2d 473, 560 N.Y.S.2d 760, 561 N.E.2d 536 (1990). The Menchetti court left open the validity of such a plea bargaining procedure if it is used to bypass section 220.10(5) bargaining restrictions. 76 N.Y.2d at 477, 560 N.Y.S.2d at 762–63.

42. People v. Boston, 75 N.Y.2d 585, 555 N.Y.S.2d 27, 554 N.E.2d 64 (1990); CPL § 195.10(2)(b).

In People v. D'Amico, 76 N.Y.2d 877, 561 N.Y.S.2d 411, 562 N.E.2d 488 (1990), the court upheld a post-indictment prosecution by SCI under slightly different circumstances. Instead of having the indicted defendant simply waive indictment, the prosecutor commenced a new proceeding by filing a new felony complaint containing a new charge. The defendant, after being held for grand jury action on the new complaint, and before indictment, waived indictment and pleaded guilty to an SCI. Although upholding this bypass of section

The restrictions contained in section 220.10(5) are based upon the crimes charged in the indictment. The more salient restrictions are as follows:

Drug Cases. A plea on an indictment charging a Class A–I drug felony must include a plea to a Class A–II drug felony;[43] likewise, a plea on an indictment charging a Class A–II drug felony must include a plea to a Class B felony.[44] If the indictment charges a Class B drug felony, then the plea must be to no less than a Class D felony.[45]

Class A Non-drug Cases. On an indictment charging a Class A non-drug felony, the plea must be to at least a Class C "violent" felony (as "violent" felonies are defined in P.L. § 70.02[1]).[46]

Class B Non-drug Felonies. If the indictment charges a Class B non-drug, non-"violent" felony, then the plea must be to a felony.[47] If it charges a Class B felony which is both "violent" (P.L. § 70.02[1]) and "armed" (CPL § 1.20[41]), the plea must be to at least a Class C "violent" felony.[48] If the Class B felony is "violent" but not "armed," the plea must be to at least a Class D "violent" felony.[49]

Class C Felonies. If the indictment charges a Class C "violent" felony, then the plea must be to at least a Class D "violent" felony.[50] If it charges a non-"violent" C, and the defendant appears to be a predicate felon as defined in P.L. § 70.06, then the plea must be to a felony.[51]

Class D Felonies. If the indictment charges a Class D non-"violent," non-firearm, felony, then no bargaining restriction applies unless the defendant appears to be a predicate felon, in which case the plea must be to a felony.[52]

If the indictment charges a violation of P.L. § 265.02(4)(possession of a loaded firearm outside of home or business), and the defendant is not a predicate, and has not been convicted of a Class A misdemeanor within the previous five years, then the plea must be to either the Class E felony of third-degree attempted criminal possession of a weapon (P.L.

195.10, the D'Amico Court emphasized that the procedure in that case did not violate any section 220.10 plea bargaining restrictions. 76 N.Y.2d at 880, 561 N.Y.S.2d at 413.

In two Appellate Division decisions, People v. Banville, 134 A.D.2d 116, 523 N.Y.S.2d 844 (2d Dep't 1988), and People v. Cook, 93 A.D.2d 942, 463 N.Y.S.2d 59 (3d Dep't 1983), it was expressly held that a post-indictment prosecution by SCI cannot be used to evade section 220.10 plea bargaining restrictions.

43. CPL § 220.10(5)(a)(i). With respect to a youthful offender adjudication, the plea may be to a Class B felony. Id.

44. CPL § 220.10(5)(a)(ii).
45. CPL § 220.10(5)(a)(iii).
46. CPL § 220.10(5)(d)(i).
47. CPL § 220.10(5)(b).
48. CPL § 220.10(5)(d)(i).
49. CPL § 220.10(5)(d)(ii).
50. CPL § 220.10(5)(d)(ii).

51. CPL § 220.10(5)(c). A defendant seemingly barred from a misdemeanor plea based upon subdivision 5(c) may interpose a pre-plea challenge to the predicate, if the purpose is to clear the way to a misdemeanor plea offer. A hearing pursuant to CPL § 400.21 would then be held. If the challenge is successful, then the misdemeanor bargain may ensue. If the challenge is unsuccessful, the post-hearing finding is binding upon the defendant for sentencing purposes. CPL § 220.35.

52. CPL § 220.10(5)(c).

§§ 110.00/265.02(4)), or to the Class A misdemeanor of fourth-degree criminal possession of a weapon (P.L. § 265.01(1)).[53] If it charges a violation of P.L. § 265.02(4), and the defendant has been convicted of a Class A misdemeanor within the previous five years, or if it charges the handgun violation of P.L. § 265.02(5) or P.L. § 265.12, then the plea must be to at least a Class E "violent" felony offense.[54]

All Other Felonies. In all other cases, including indictments charging Class D "violent" felonies other than those mentioned above, and indictments charging Class D and E nonviolent felonies, there is no plea bargaining restriction save for apparent predicate felons, in which case, as noted, the plea must be to a felony.

Separate restrictions or provisions apply where the defendant is a juvenile offender,[55] or where the defendant seeks to enter a plea of not responsible by reason of mental disease or defect.[56]

Section 220.30(3)(b), restricting the use of pleas to one accusatory instrument to "cover" other indictments, mirrors the restrictions contained in section 220.10(5). It bars the parties from evading indirectly, by "covering" an indictment, what they could not evade directly.

The restrictions contained in sections 220.10(5) and 220.30 are—notwithstanding all of the above—often bypassed. This is accomplished, with the consent of all the parties, by the simple expedient of the prosecutor's dismissing top counts of the indictment in contemplation of a disposition.[57] At least one appellate court has ruled, however, that the plea-taking court cannot vacate a *prior* felony conviction to circumvent plea bargaining or sentencing restrictions.[58]

Since the defendant has no right to plead guilty to less than the entire indictment, the statutory plea-down restrictions have been held

---

53. CPL § 220.10(5)(c), (d)(iii). Note that pursuant to P.L. § 70.15(1), the sentence on such a plea-down to P.L. § 265.01(1) must be a definite one-year sentence, absent certain specific court findings, including that such would be unduly harsh.

54. CPL § 220.10(5)(d)(iv).

55. CPL § 220.10(5)(g). Although the plea bargaining restrictions set forth in CPL § 220.10(5)(a)—(d) do not apply to juvenile offenders, other restrictions are set forth in subdivision (5)(g). Under certain circumstances, a juvenile charged with second-degree murder must plead to a crime for which he or she is criminally responsible. Subd. (5)(g)(i). In all other circumstances, the plea must be to a crime for which the defendant is criminally responsible, unless the action is moved to Family Court on the prosecution's recommendation. Subd. 5(g)(ii) and (iii).

56. CPL § 220.10(6). So long as the procedures set forth in CPL § 220.15 (see § 11.4, supra) are followed, the defendant may, with the permission of the court and the consent of the prosecutor, enter a plea of not guilty by reason of mental disease or defect to the entire indictment. There is no provision for such a plea to less than the entire indictment.

57. See People v. Pettway, 131 Misc.2d 20, 497 N.Y.S.2d 279 (Sup.Ct., Kings County, 1985)(court accedes to "common practice" of prosecutor's dismissal of top counts of indictment to circumvent section 220.10 plea bargaining limitations). See also People v. Felman, 137 A.D.2d 341, 347, 529 N.Y.S.2d 395, 399 (3d Dep't 1988)(Levine, J., dissenting). But see People v. Cummings, 159 Misc.2d 1118, 611 N.Y.S.2d 1011 (Sup.Ct., St. Lawrence County, 1994)(Supreme Court disallows prosecutor's dismissal of entire indictment in interest of justice to allow plea to misdemeanor information in town court), aff'd sub nom. Cummings v. Koppell, 212 A.D.2d 11, 627 N.Y.S.2d 480 (3d Dep't 1995).

58. People v. Felman, 137 A.D.2d 341, 529 N.Y.S.2d 395 (3d Dep't 1988).

not to violate the Due Process Clause.[59]

Library References:
West's Key No. Digests, Criminal Law ⇔273.1(2).

§ 11.6 Withdrawal of Not Guilty Plea by the Defendant

A defendant who has pleaded not guilty pursuant to CPL § 220.10(1) may at any time before the rendition of verdict enter any other plea (*i.e.*, "guilty" or "not responsible by reason by reason of mental disease or defect") that he or she was originally authorized to enter,[60] provided the plea is knowing and voluntary.[61]

Library References:
West's Key No. Digests, Criminal Law ⇔301.

§ 11.7 Entry of the Guilty Plea—Knowing and Voluntary Waiver of Rights

As a matter of federal due process, a valid guilty plea must be knowingly, voluntarily, and intelligently entered.[62]

In pleading guilty, the defendant waives his or her so-called "*Boykin*" rights: the constitutional rights to trial by jury, to confront one's accusers, and against compulsory self-incrimination.[63] The court accepting the plea is required "to make sure [that the defendant] has full understanding of what the plea connotes and of its consequences."[64] A "silent record" will not overcome the presumption against waiver by a defendant of these constitutional protections; rather, the plea record must demonstrate "an intentional relinquishment or abandonment" of these rights.[65]

In *People v. Harris*,[66] however, the Court of Appeals expressly held that the Due Process Clause does not go so far as to require the court to expressly advise a pleading defendant that he or she is giving up the right to a jury trial, the right against compulsory self-incrimination, and the right to confront one's accusers.[67] On the contrary, the court has

---

59. People v. Miller, 126 A.D.2d 868, 511 N.Y.S.2d 160 (3d Dep't 1987); People v. Elliby, 80 A.D.2d 875, 436 N.Y.S.2d 784 (2d Dep't 1981). See People v. Felix, 58 N.Y.2d 156, 162 n. 3, 460 N.Y.S.2d 1, 4 n. 3, 446 N.E.2d 757 (1983)(no constitutional violation found in P.L. § 70.02(5), barring definite sentence on reduced plea to a Class D violent felony if indictment originally charged an armed felony). See also People v. Morse, 62 N.Y.2d 205, 226, 476 N.Y.S.2d 505, 515, 465 N.E.2d 12 (1984).

60. See §§ 11.2, 11.5, supra.

61. See §§ 11.7, 11.9, infra.

62. Brady v. United States, 397 U.S. 742, 748, 90 S.Ct. 1463, 1468, 25 L.Ed.2d 747 (1970); Boykin v. Alabama, 395 U.S. 238, 242–43, 89 S.Ct. 1709, 1711–12, 23 L.Ed.2d 274 (1969); Kercheval v. United States, 274 U.S. 220, 223, 47 S.Ct. 582, 583, 71 L.Ed. 1009 (1927).

63. Boykin v. Alabama, 395 U.S. at 243, 89 S.Ct. at 1712.

64. 395 U.S. at 244, 89 S.Ct. at 1712.

65. Johnson v. Zerbst, 304 U.S. 458, 464, 58 S.Ct. 1019, 1023, 82 L.Ed. 1461 (1938); People v. Rodriguez, 50 N.Y.2d 553, 557, 429 N.Y.S.2d 631, 632, 407 N.E.2d 475 (1980).

66. 61 N.Y.2d 9, 471 N.Y.S.2d 61, 459 N.E.2d 170 (1983).

67. 61 N.Y.2d at 17–18, 471 N.Y.S.2d at 64–65.

§ 11.7　　　　　　　　　　PLEAS　　　　　　　　　　Ch. 11

reaffirmed that there is no "uniform mandatory catechism of pleading defendants."[68] Instead, the "key issue" is simply whether "all the relevant circumstances surrounding" the plea reflect that the defendant has knowingly, voluntarily, and intelligently relinquished his or her rights.[69]

As a matter of practice, most pleas taken in superior courts are accompanied by an express advisory of the trilogy of *Boykin* rights being relinquished. This practice, while not constitutionally required under *Harris*, is nonetheless most wise, since it "facilitate[s] subsequent determination on the record of the voluntariness of a guilty plea."[70]

Among the other "relevant circumstances"[71] considered in determining the voluntariness of the plea are "[t]he seriousness of the crime, the competency, experience and actual participation by counsel, the rationality of the 'plea bargain,' and the pace of the proceedings in the particular criminal court."[72]

Library References:

West's Key No. Digests, Criminal Law ⚖273.1.

§ 11.8　Entry of Guilty Plea—Competency of Defendant

To enter a voluntary plea, the pleading defendant must be competent to stand trial. If the defense establishes "sufficient doubt" about defendant's competency, or if the court on its own doubts the defendant's competency, it should order a CPL Article 730 psychiatric examination.[73] While a claim that a pleading defendant was incompetent survives the guilty plea—indeed, it cannot be bargained away[74]—such claims do not generally have any success on appeal.[75]

68. 61 N.Y.2d at 16, 471 N.Y.S.2d at 64, citing People v. Nixon, 21 N.Y.2d 338, 353, 287 N.Y.S.2d 659, 670, 234 N.E.2d 687 (1967), cert. denied sub nom. Robinson v. New York, 393 U.S. 1067, 89 S.Ct. 721, 21 L.Ed.2d 709 (1969).

69. People v. Harris, 61 N.Y.2d at 17, 19, 471 N.Y.S.2d at 64–66.

70. 61 N.Y.2d at 18, 471 N.Y.S.2d at 65. See, e.g., People v. Bates, 204 A.D.2d 473, 614 N.Y.S.2d 163 (2d Dep't 1994).

71. People v. Harris, 61 N.Y.2d at 19, 471 N.Y.S.2d at 66.

72. 61 N.Y.2d at 16, 471 N.Y.S.2d at 64.

73. See People v. Gensler, 72 N.Y.2d 239, 532 N.Y.S.2d 72, 527 N.E.2d 1209, cert. denied 488 U.S. 932, 109 S.Ct. 323, 102 L.Ed.2d 341 (1988); People v. Armlin, 37 N.Y.2d 167, 171, 371 N.Y.S.2d 691, 695, 332 N.E.2d 870 (1975). See also CPL § 730.30(1). Cf. People v. Pringle, 186 A.D.2d 413, 589 N.Y.S.2d 8 (1st Dep't 1992).

74. People v. Seaberg, 74 N.Y.2d 1, 9, 543 N.Y.S.2d 968, 971, 541 N.E.2d 1022 (1989); People v. Armlin, 37 N.Y.2d 167, 171, 371 N.Y.S.2d 691, 695, 332 N.E.2d 870 (1975); People v. Frazier, 114 A.D.2d 1038, 495 N.Y.S.2d 478 (2d Dep't 1985).

75. See, e.g., People v. Rivas, 206 A.D.2d 549, 614 N.Y.S.2d 753 (2d Dep't 1994)(defendant's coherent responses during plea proceedings indicated he was competent to plead); People v. Santiago, 205 A.D.2d 565, 614 N.Y.S.2d 269 (2d Dep't 1994)(recent psychiatric examination resulting in finding of fitness to stand trial was sufficient to demonstrate fitness to plead guilty); People v. Polimeda, 198 A.D.2d 242, 603 N.Y.S.2d 513 (2d Dep't 1993)(defendant's responses during plea allocution indicated fitness); People v. Hall, 168 A.D.2d 310, 562 N.Y.S.2d 641 (1st Dep't 1990)(suicidal defendant's guilty plea upheld, since his answers during the plea allocution were "more than mere monosyllabic responses"); People v. Rogers, 163 A.D.2d 337, 557 N.Y.S.2d 168 (2d Dep't 1990)(same).

In *Godinez v. Moran*,[76] the Supreme Court held that the competency standards for pleading guilty and standing trial are the same. As a matter of State Constitutional due process, the law apparently is no different.[77]

Library References:

West's Key No. Digests, Criminal Law ⚖︎273(2).

§ 11.9 Entry of Guilty Plea—Defendant's Understanding of Collateral Consequences of the Plea

While a plea entered in ignorance of its "direct consequences" is constitutionally invalid,[78] the court need not advise the defendant of the "collateral consequences" of the plea.[79]

Examples of "direct consequences" are the longest possible sentence a defendant might receive pursuant to the plea,[80] as well as the "mandatory minimum sentence," *i.e.*, "the lowest possible maximum" pursuant to the plea.[81]

Even if the court misadvises the defendant as to his or her sentence exposure under the plea, it will not result in plea vacatur unless the record reflects that the defendant would not have pleaded but for the information inaccurately conveyed.[82]

---

76. 509 U.S. 389, 113 S.Ct. 2680, 125 L.Ed.2d 321 (1993).

77. See People v. Reason, 37 N.Y.2d 351, 372 N.Y.S.2d 614, 334 N.E.2d 572 (1975)(no distinction between competency to stand trial and competency to proceed pro se); People v. Schoolfield, 196 A.D.2d 111, 608 N.Y.S.2d 413 (1st Dep't 1994)(same); People v. Sharpe, 72 A.D.2d 572, 420 N.Y.S.2d 736 (2d Dep't 1979)(determination of competency to stand trial satisfied issue of competency to plead guilty).

78. See, e.g., United States ex rel. Leeson v. Damon, 496 F.2d 718 (2d Cir.1974)(maximum possible sentence).

79. See, e.g., Sanchez v. United States, 572 F.2d 210 (9th Cir.1977)(parole revocation).

80. Hart v. Marion Correctional Institution, 927 F.2d 256, 259 (6th Cir.1991); United States ex rel. Leeson v. Damon, 496 F.2d 718; People v. Gotte, 125 A.D.2d 331, 508 N.Y.S.2d 607 (2d Dep't 1986).

Note that it is not error for the court to advise a defendant considering a plea offer of the possible sentence he or she might receive after trial, see, e.g., People v. Safa, 209 A.D.2d 199, 618 N.Y.S.2d 531 (1st Dep't 1994); People v. Grimsley, 193 A.D.2d 618, 598 N.Y.S.2d 964 (2d Dep't 1993); People v. Stephens, 188 A.D.2d 345, 345–46, 591 N.Y.S.2d 25, 25 (1st Dep't 1992), provided the court does so accurately. See People v. Goldfadden, 145 A.D.2d 959, 960, 536 N.Y.S.2d 331, 332 (4th Dep't 1988)(plea vacated where the court erroneously advised defendant that he faced life imprisonment if convicted after trial).

81. Hunter v. Fogg, 616 F.2d 55, 61 (2d Cir.1980). The court need not advise the defendant, however, of the minimum portion of a sentence the court might require him to serve; nor need it advise the defendant that he or she might be kept in prison beyond the mandatory minimum term. Id. See also People v. Ramos, 63 N.Y.2d 640, 643, 479 N.Y.S.2d 510, 511, 468 N.E.2d 692 (1984); People v. Welch, 129 A.D.2d 752, 514 N.Y.S.2d 513 (2d Dep't 1987).

82. Caputo v. Henderson, 541 F.2d 979, 984 (2d Cir.1976); People v. Wright, 196 A.D.2d 700, 601 N.Y.S.2d 618 (1st Dep't 1993); People v. Grimsley, 193 A.D.2d 618, 598 N.Y.S.2d 964 (2d Dep't 1993); People v. Hernandez–Flores, 172 A.D.2d 159, 567 N.Y.S.2d 698 (1st Dep't 1991). See also Hill v. Lockhart, 474 U.S. 52, 106 S.Ct. 366, 88 L.Ed.2d 203 (1985) (guilty plea may be collaterally attacked upon showing that, but for attorney's erroneous advice regarding parole eligibility date, defendant would not have pleaded guilty).

"Collateral consequences," of which the defendant need not be advised are those such as the possibility of deportation,[83] negative parole consequences,[84] the potential forfeiture of assets,[85] the likelihood of an undesirable military discharge,[86] or future civil commitment proceedings.[87] Additionally, the court need not advise the defendant that some other jurisdiction may run the instant sentence consecutively to its own.[88]

By statute, the court must advise a defendant pleading guilty to a felony of the immigration or deportation consequences of the conviction; however, the statute also provides that the failure to so advise the defendant "shall not be deemed to affect the voluntariness" of the plea, nor shall it constitute a bar to deportation.[89]

Finally, there is no requirement that a pleading defendant be advised that *future* convictions could result in a finding of predicate or persistent felony offender status as a consequence of the instant plea.[90]

Note that a defense attorney's off-the-record misadvice to the defendant, as to the amount of time that he or she will have to serve, will not be judicially recognized; however, such misadvice could give rise to a cognizable CPL § 440.10 post-conviction collateral attack based upon ineffective assistance of counsel.[91]

---

83. United States v. Campbell, 778 F.2d 764, 766 (11th Cir.1985); People v. Ford, 86 N.Y.2d 397, 633 N.Y.S.2d 270, 657 N.E.2d 265 (1995); People v. Avila, 177 A.D.2d 426, 576 N.Y.S.2d 534 (1st Dep't 1991). See also United States v. Olvera, 954 F.2d 788, 793 (2d Cir.1992)(deportation is "ordinarily" considered a collateral consequence of a guilty plea).

Nor, it has been held, is a defendant deprived of the effective assistance of counsel by defense counsel's failure to advise him or her of the possible result of deportation. People v. Ford, 205 A.D.2d 798, 613 N.Y.S.2d 688 (2d Dep't 1994). People v. Oditnarian Boodhoo, 191 A.D.2d 448, 593 N.Y.S.2d 882 (2d Dep't 1993); People v. Avila, 177 A.D.2d 426, 576 N.Y.S.2d 534 (1st Dep't 1991).

84. Holmes v. United States, 876 F.2d 1545, 1549 (11th Cir.1989); Sanchez v. United States, 572 F.2d 210, 211 (9th Cir.1977)(parole revocation).

85. United States v. U.S. Currency in the Amount of $228,536.00, 895 F.2d 908 (2d Cir.1990).

86. Redwine v. Zuckert, 317 F.2d 336, 338 (D.C.Cir.1963).

87. George v. Black, 732 F.2d 108, 111 (8th Cir.1984).

88. United States v. Ray, 828 F.2d 399, 418 (7th Cir.1987), cert. denied 485 U.S. 964, 108 S.Ct. 1233, 99 L.Ed.2d 432 (1988); United States v. Degand, 614 F.2d 176, 177 (8th Cir.1980).

89. CPL § 220.50(7). The court must advise the defendant that if he or she is not a U.S. citizen, then the conviction may result in deportation, exclusion, or denial of naturalization. Furthermore, the court must advise a defendant convicted of a felony other than a "violent" felony (P.L. § 70.02) or a non-drug A–I felony that he or she may be paroled to INS for deportation any time after commencement of sentence.

90. People v. Ruscito, 206 A.D.2d 841, 615 N.Y.S.2d 201 (4th Dep't 1994); People v. Barnes, 202 A.D.2d 350, 610 N.Y.S.2d 779 (1st Dep't 1994); People v. Outer, 197 A.D.2d 543, 602 N.Y.S.2d 215 (2d Dep't 1993); People v. Silvers, 163 A.D.2d 71, 558 N.Y.S.2d 25 (1st Dep't 1990); People v. Sirianni, 89 A.D.2d 775, 453 N.Y.S.2d 485 (4th Dep't 1982).

91. People v. Ramos, 63 N.Y.2d 640, 643, 479 N.Y.S.2d 510, 511, 468 N.E.2d 692 (1984). See also Hill v. Lockhart, 474 U.S. 52, 60, 106 S.Ct. 366, 371, 88 L.Ed.2d 203 (1985)(lawyer's erroneous advice as to parole eligibility might give rise to ineffective assistance of counsel claim); Sparks v. Sowders, 852 F.2d 882 (6th Cir.1988)(lawyer's misadvice as to time defendant was facing if he did not plead guilty could constitute ineffective assistance).

Library References:
West's Key No. Digests, Criminal Law ⚖=273.1(4).

§ 11.10 Entry of the Guilty Plea—Factual Basis for the Plea

A valid guilty plea requires, as a matter of federal due process, that the defendant have a complete understanding of the charges against him or her.[92] That is not to say that an explicit admission of guilt as to every element of the crime must be incorporated into the allocution of every valid plea; it does not.[93] Rather, a guilty plea will be sustained in the absence of any factual recitation of the underlying circumstances of the crime if the pleading defendant is represented by able and active counsel, and there is no suggestion in the record that the plea was improvident or baseless.[94] Indeed, the Court of Appeals has squarely held that, where the guilty plea is to a lesser crime than the one charged in the indictment, or covers a second indictment, *no* factual basis for the plea is necessary.[95]

While an inquiry into the factual basis for the guilty plea is not a constitutional requirement,[96] it is nevertheless one means of assuring that a guilty plea is voluntary and intelligent. Hence, it is wise for a court wishing to insulate a plea from subsequent collateral or appellate

---

92. Henderson v. Morgan, 426 U.S. 637, 645, 648 n. 1, 96 S.Ct. 2253, 2257, 2259 n. 1, 49 L.Ed.2d 108 (1976).

93. People v. Nixon, 21 N.Y.2d 338, 287 N.Y.S.2d 659, 234 N.E.2d 687 (1967), cert. denied 393 U.S. 1067, 89 S.Ct. 721, 21 L.Ed.2d 709 (1969).

94. People v. Nixon, 21 N.Y.2d at 350, 287 N.Y.S.2d at 668. See also People v. Doceti, 175 A.D.2d 256, 572 N.Y.S.2d 720 (2d Dep't 1991).

If the defendant is not represented by counsel at the time of the plea, then a higher standard prevails. In such a case, the court must inquire of the pleading defendant as to the details of the crime to satisfy itself of the defendant's factual guilt. People v. Seaton, 19 N.Y.2d 404, 406, 280 N.Y.S.2d 370, 371, 227 N.E.2d 294 (1967).

95. People v. Moore, 71 N.Y.2d 1002, 1006, 530 N.Y.S.2d 94, 96, 525 N.E.2d 740 (1988); People v. Clairborne, 29 N.Y.2d 950, 329 N.Y.S.2d 580, 280 N.E.2d 366 (1972). The historical rationale for holding factual allocutions on pleas to lesser crimes to a lower standard came from the recognition that such plea bargains often entail pleas to hypothetical crimes without objective basis. See People v. Foster, 19 N.Y.2d 150, 154, 278 N.Y.S.2d 603, 606, 225 N.E.2d 200 (1967); People v. Griffin, 7 N.Y.2d 511, 199 N.Y.S.2d 674, 166 N.E.2d 684 (1960). The later Moore and Clairborne decisions, however, make no distinction between pleas to lesser "hypothetical" crimes, such as attempted reckless manslaughter, and lesser "actual" crimes.

Nonetheless, even a plea to a lesser would no doubt fail to pass constitutional muster where the defendant appeared to be ignorant of the nature of the original charges against him. Henderson v. Morgan, 426 U.S. 637, 645 n. 13, 96 S.Ct. 2253, 2257 n. 13, 49 L.Ed.2d 108 (1976). Moreover, such plea would be open to challenge if whatever factual allocution did occur contained statements of the defendant negating an essential element of the crime pleaded to or otherwise "cast[ing] significant doubt on the defendant's guilt." People v. Lopez, 71 N.Y.2d 662, 666, 529 N.Y.S.2d 465, 466, 525 N.E.2d 5 (1988). See, e.g., People v. Thomas, 159 A.D.2d 529, 552 N.Y.S.2d 394 (2d Dep't 1990)(plea down to first-degree manslaughter set aside where defendant denied intent to kill or to cause serious physical injury and claimed self-defense).

96. Willbright v. Smith, 745 F.2d 779, 780 (2d Cir.1984); People v. Winbush, 199 A.D.2d 447, 605 N.Y.S.2d 385 (2d Dep't 1993).

To be distinguished is the practice in federal court, where a valid guilty plea must meet the requirements of Fed.R.Crim. Proc.11. That rule explicitly requires courts to conduct a factual inquiry prior to accepting the guilty plea. No such inquiry, however, is required as a matter of federal due process.

§ 11.10   PLEAS   Ch. 11

attack to elicit the defendant's admission of guilt as to every element of the crime. Indeed, as a matter of practice—at least in the superior courts—most courts, before accepting a guilty plea, will make some inquiry of the defendant as to the factual basis for the plea.[97]

If a factual recitation incorporated into a defendant's guilty plea contains statements casting significant doubts on his or her guilt, or negating an essential element of the crime, then the court must not accept the plea in the absence of further inquiry to ensure that the plea is knowingly and voluntarily entered.[98]

Generally, the court should not accept a guilty plea from a defendant who maintains his or her complete innocence or denies knowledge of the crime.[99] The court is permitted to accept such a plea, however, if it is otherwise knowingly and voluntarily entered by a counseled defendant, if a benefit is conferred on the defendant by virtue of the plea, and if the prosecutor sets forth on the record strong evidence of the defendant's actual guilt.[100]

With "rare" exception, described below, a claimed faulty factual allocution is not considered preserved for appellate review unless the defendant specifically either moves prior to sentencing to withdraw the plea under CPL § 220.60,[101] or makes a post-verdict motion pursuant to CPL § 440.10 to vacate the judgment of conviction.[102] The rare exception, set forth in the Court of Appeals case of *People v. Lopez*, is where the factual allocution "clearly casts significant doubt upon the defendant's guilt or otherwise calls into question the voluntariness of the

---

97. In People v. Serrano, 15 N.Y.2d 304, 308, 258 N.Y.S.2d 386, 388, 206 N.E.2d 330 (1965), the Court of Appeals stated:

Where, as in the usual case today, the trial court, before accepting the plea of guilty, properly inquires of the defendant as to the details of the crime to which he is admitting his guilt, the mere mouthing of the word "guilty" may not be relied upon to establish all the elements of that crime. In such case, the requisite elements should appear from the defendant's own recital and, if the circumstances of the commission of the crime as related by the defendant do not clearly spell out the crime to which the plea is offered, then the court should not proceed, without further inquiry, to accept the guilty plea as a valid one.

To the extent that Serrano might be read to suggest that a factual recitation covering every element of the crime is a prerequisite for any guilty plea, the subsequent holding of People v. Lopez, 71 N.Y.2d 662, 666 n. 2, 529 N.Y.S.2d 465, 467 n. 2, 525 N.E.2d 5 (1988), expressly disapproved of any such interpretation of Serrano. Lopez emphasizes that there is no such requirement. Nonetheless, Serrano's description of the "usual" plea allocution as one involving an inquiry into the factual basis for the plea is still valid today, at least as to those pleas accepted in superior courts.

98. People v. Lopez, 71 N.Y.2d 662, 529 N.Y.S.2d 465, 525 N.E.2d 5 (1988); People v. Serrano, 15 N.Y.2d at 308, 258 N.Y.S.2d at 388; People v. Vasquez, 199 A.D.2d 444, 605 N.Y.S.2d 381 (2d Dep't 1993).

99. People v. Serrano, 15 N.Y.S.2d at 308, 258 N.Y.S.2d at 388–89; People v. Leite, 52 A.D.2d 895, 383 N.Y.S.2d 71 (2d Dep't 1976).

100. North Carolina v. Alford, 400 U.S. 25, 38, 91 S.Ct. 160, 167, 27 L.Ed.2d 162 (1970); People v. Woodson, 176 A.D.2d 186, 574 N.Y.S.2d 310 (1st Dep't 1991). Before accepting an "Alford" plea, however, the court must ensure that the record reflects the defendant's understanding of the nature and character of an Alford plea. See People v. Benton, 143 A.D.2d 526, 533 N.Y.S.2d 32 (4th Dep't 1988).

101. See § 11.18, infra.

102. People v. Lopez, 71 N.Y.2d 662, 666, 529 N.Y.S.2d 465, 466, 525 N.E.2d 5 (1988); People v. Claudio, 64 N.Y.2d 858, 487 N.Y.S.2d 318, 476 N.E.2d 644 (1985); People v. Pellegrino, 60 N.Y.2d 636, 467 N.Y.S.2d 355, 454 N.E.2d 938 (1983).

plea," in which case the court's acceptance of the plea without further inquiry may be challenged on direct appeal, notwithstanding the absence of a defense post-allocution motion.[103] Although Lopez itself makes clear that an allocution that "*negates* an essential element of the crime pleaded to"[104] would perforce cast "significant doubt" on guilt and thus undercut the plea's "voluntariness," it is not entirely settled what other defects in the factual allocution would come under this exception.

Although some post-*Lopez* Appellate Division decisions have held that a factual recitation that raises the possibility of a trial defense comes within the *Lopez* exception,[105] *Lopez* does not directly support these holdings. Moreover, in *People v. Mackey*,[106] the Court of Appeals held the *Lopez* exception inapplicable to a plea allocution claimed to be deficient because it "suggested" an agency defense. The court held that such claim was unpreserved for appellate review in the absence of a post-allocution motion to withdraw or vacate the plea.[107] Also unsettled in the intermediate appellate courts is whether the *Lopez* exception covers *affirmative* defenses suggested by the factual allocution.[108]

Hence, defense attorneys seriously considering an attack on the validity of the factual allocution accompanying a guilty plea would be well advised to move, prior to sentence, to withdraw the plea pursuant to CPL § 220.60—or, if judgment has already been rendered, to immediately move to vacate the judgment pursuant to CPL § 440.10.[109]

---

103. People v. Lopez, 71 N.Y.2d at 666, 529 N.Y.S.2d at 466–67.

104. 71 N.Y.2d at 666, 529 N.Y.S.2d at 467 (emphasis added). See also People v. Lawrence, 192 A.D.2d 332, 595 N.Y.S.2d 764 (1st Dep't 1993); People v. Howard, 183 A.D.2d 916, 584 N.Y.S.2d 150 (2d Dep't 1992).

105. See, e.g., People v. Davis, 176 A.D.2d 1236, 576 N.Y.S.2d 731 (4th Dep't 1991)(agency defense made out in factual allocution; plea vacated despite lack of post-allocution defense motion); People v. Thomas, 159 A.D.2d 529, 552 N.Y.S.2d 394 (2d Dep't 1990)(justification); People v. Goldfadden, 145 A.D.2d 959, 536 N.Y.S.2d 331 (4th Dep't 1988)(intoxication).

106. 77 N.Y.2d 846, 567 N.Y.S.2d 639, 569 N.E.2d 442 (1991).

107. 77 N.Y.2d at 847, 567 N.Y.S.2d at 639–640. Such a claim might nevertheless present an issue of law requiring appellate vacatur of the plea if accompanied by a post-allocution trial court motion to withdraw the plea or vacate the judgment. See People v. Clinton, 179 A.D.2d 670, 579 N.Y.S.2d 895 (2d Dep't 1992)(plea vacated where allocution suggested an agency defense; motion to withdraw the plea had been made).

108. Compare People v. Richardson, 198 A.D.2d 450, 605 N.Y.S.2d 906 (2d Dep't 1993)(factual allocution to first-degree robbery suggested the affirmative defense contained in P.L. § 160.15(4); court erred in accepting plea without further inquiry); People v. Moye, 171 A.D.2d 1036, 569 N.Y.S.2d 38 (4th Dep't 1991)(same); People v. LeGrand, 155 A.D.2d 482, 547 N.Y.S.2d 143 (2d Dep't 1989)(same) with People v. Toxey, 202 A.D.2d 330, 609 N.Y.S.2d 12 (1st Dep't 1994), aff'd 86 N.Y.2d 725, 631 N.Y.S.2d 119, 655 N.E.2d 160 (1995)(Lopez exception held not applicable to the affirmative defense to first-degree robbery, where all defendant said was, "I don't carry weapons"); People v. Rhodes, 176 A.D.2d 828, 575 N.Y.S.2d 156 (2d Dep't 1991)(Lopez exception not applicable to affirmative defense to first-degree robbery). See also Ames v. New York State Division of Parole, 772 F.2d 13, 15 (2d Cir.1985), cert. denied 475 U.S. 1066, 106 S.Ct. 1379, 89 L.Ed.2d 605 (1986)(no constitutional error in court's failure to conduct a further inquiry where defendant's plea allocution raised the affirmative defense to first-degree robbery).

In any event, plea vacatur would hardly be required if the record revealed that the defense decision to forgo the affirmative defense was part of the plea bargain. See People v. Frascone, 176 A.D.2d 128, 574 N.Y.S.2d 15 (1st Dep't 1991).

109. Note that, unless the sentence is one of death, there is no appeal as of right from the denial of a section 440.10 motion.

§ 11.10   PLEAS   Ch. 11

Library References:

West's Key No. Digests, Criminal Law ⚖═273(4.1).

§ 11.11   Sentence Promises—In General

As a general rule, "a guilty plea induced by an unfulfilled promise either must be vacated or the promise honored."[110] Thus, a defendant denied the full benefit of his or her negotiated plea must be allowed to withdraw the guilty plea.[111] A defendant's claim that a sentence promise is not being honored, however, must be judged by an objective reading of the bargain, not the defendant's subjective interpretation, or misinterpretation, of it.[112]

It is not only a court's promise that must be honored, but a prosecutor's as well. Thus, for example, a prosecutor's promise to recommend a certain sentence, or to take no position as to sentence, must be scrupulously honored.[113] Courts frown not only on the *direct* breach of such a promise, but also on an *indirect* breach—for example, by subtly conveying an opinion, at the time of sentence, inconsistent with the promise.[114] Where the prosecution has conditioned its sentence recommendation upon the defendant's providing helpful information leading to the prosecution of others, the prosecution's own assessment of whether that condition has been fulfilled, absent bad faith on its part, has been upheld.[115]

Instead, leave to appeal must be sought from the intermediate appellate court. See CPL § 450.15.

110. People v. Selikoff, 35 N.Y.2d 227, 241, 360 N.Y.S.2d 623, 635, 318 N.E.2d 784 (1974), cert. denied 419 U.S. 1122, 95 S.Ct. 806, 42 L.Ed.2d 822 (1975), citing Santobello v. New York, 404 U.S. 257, 92 S.Ct. 495, 30 L.Ed.2d 427 (1971). See also People v. Rodney E., 77 N.Y.2d 672, 569 N.Y.S.2d 920, 572 N.E.2d 603 (1991); People v. McConnell, 49 N.Y.2d 340, 346, 425 N.Y.S.2d 794, 796, 402 N.E.2d 133 (1980); People v. Frederick, 45 N.Y.2d 520, 410 N.Y.S.2d 555, 382 N.E.2d 1332 (1978).

111. People v. Selikoff, supra. See also People v. Torres, 45 N.Y.2d 751, 408 N.Y.S.2d 487, 380 N.E.2d 313 (1978); People v. John C., 184 A.D.2d 519, 584 N.Y.S.2d 320 (2d Dep't 1992).

112. People v. Cataldo, 39 N.Y.2d 578, 384 N.Y.S.2d 763, 349 N.E.2d 863 (1976); People v. Williams, 195 A.D.2d 1040, 600 N.Y.S.2d 529 (4th Dep't 1993); People v. Acosta, 187 A.D.2d 329, 590 N.Y.S.2d 77 (1st Dep't 1992); People v. Guerra, 157 A.D.2d 500, 549 N.Y.S.2d 691 (1st Dep't 1990).

113. Santobello v. New York, 404 U.S. 257, 92 S.Ct. 495, 30 L.Ed.2d 427 (1971); People v. Gonzalez, 176 A.D.2d 638, 575 N.Y.S.2d 291 (1st Dep't 1991)(judge and prosecutor both renege on plea agreement to recommend concurrent time on upcoming sentence to be imposed by different judge); People v. Ross G., 163 A.D.2d 529, 558 N.Y.S.2d 603 (2d Dep't 1990)(prosecutor renege on agreement to recommend youthful offender adjudication and probation in return for cooperation; Appellate Division modifies sentence to stated term); People v. Coker, 79 A.D.2d 1032, 435 N.Y.S.2d 43 (2d Dep't 1981)(prosecutor contravened plea agreement to take no position on sentence by recommending maximum possible term).

114. People v. Tindle, 61 N.Y.2d 752, 472 N.Y.S.2d 919, 460 N.E.2d 1354 (1984)(resentence ordered before different judge where prosecution officially took no position as to sentence, as per the promise, but made statements implicitly conveying its position); People v. Jasiewicz, 192 A.D.2d 999, 597 N.Y.S.2d 242 (3d Dep't 1993)(prosecutor violated spirit of agreement to support Probation Department's sentence recommendation).

115. See People v. Alzate, 84 N.Y.2d 983, 622 N.Y.S.2d 499, 646 N.E.2d 801 (1994)(absent evidence of bad faith, prosecution's determination that information had not been helpful was sustained); People v. Anonymous, 208 A.D.2d 426, 618 N.Y.S.2d 1009 (1st Dep't 1994)(prosecution's determination that defendant had not fully cooperated was binding where agree-

Note that the imposition of restitution, if not bargained-for, has been held to be a violation of the plea agreement;[116] however, it has been held that the issuance of an order of protection pursuant to CPL § 530.13 need not be part of the bargain in order to be properly imposed.[117]

Except in "the most unusual circumstances," off-the-record sentence promises, even if not directly contradicted by the record, cannot be enforced.[118] Accordingly, a defendant generally may not seek vacatur of the plea based upon alleged off-the-record promises by the court, the prosecutor, or defense counsel.[119] Similarly, the defendant will not be bound by any condition or promise that is not put on the record.[120]

On the one hand, the Court of Appeals has held that the trial court need not even hold a hearing to assess whether a claimed off-the-record promise was, in fact, made.[121] On the other hand, it also has been held that the defendant may use an Article 440 motion to vacate judgment as a vehicle for a claim that the plea was induced by an unfulfilled off-the-record promise.[122]

Moreover, in rare circumstances, appellate courts have given judicial recognition to unfulfilled off-the-record promises. These cases generally involve cooperation agreements, with strong evidence of an unfulfilled off-the-record promise, where the defendant has acted to his or her detriment in reliance on the promise.[123]

---

ment was that the prosecution was to be the sole judge of whether leniency was warranted). But see People v. Kloczkowski, 199 A.D.2d 538, 606 N.Y.S.2d 713 (2d Dep't 1993)(hearing ordered on prosecutor's claim that defendant had failed to cooperate according to the plea agreement).

116. People v. Jackson, 188 A.D.2d 1086, 592 N.Y.S.2d 189 (4th Dep't 1992). As a part of the bargain, however, the defendant may give up his or her right to a hearing on the proper amount of restitution. People v. Oliver, 182 A.D.2d 716, 582 N.Y.S.2d 265 (2d Dep't 1992); People v. Corby, 167 A.D.2d 682, 563 N.Y.S.2d 689 (3d Dep't 1990).

117. People v. Oliver, supra.

118. People v. Huertas, 85 N.Y.2d 898, 626 N.Y.S.2d 750, 650 N.E.2d 408 (1995); People v. Danny G., 61 N.Y.2d 169, 473 N.Y.S.2d 131, 461 N.E.2d 268 (1984); Benjamin S. v. Kuriansky, 55 N.Y.2d 116, 447 N.Y.S.2d 905, 432 N.E.2d 777, reargument denied 56 N.Y.2d 570, 450 N.Y.S.2d 186, 435 N.E.2d 403 (1982); People v. Frederick, 45 N.Y.2d at 520, 410 N.Y.S.2d at 555; People v. Selikoff, 35 N.Y.2d at 244, 360 N.Y.S.2d at 638.

119. See, e.g., People v. Frederick, 45 N.Y.2d 520, 526, 410 N.Y.S.2d 555, 559, 382 N.E.2d 1332. See also People v. Ramos, 63 N.Y.2d 640, 479 N.Y.S.2d 510, 468 N.E.2d 692 (1984)(no judicial recognition afforded to defense counsel's off-the-record promise to client that prison "good time" would be subtracted from minimum sentence).

120. People v. Danny G., 61 N.Y.2d 169, 473 N.Y.S.2d 131, 461 N.E.2d 268.

121. Matter of Benjamin S., 55 N.Y.2d 116, 447 N.Y.S.2d 905, 432 N.E.2d 777. See also People v. Sanchez, 184 A.D.2d 537, 584 N.Y.S.2d 164 (2d Dep't 1992).

122. People v. LaPlaca, 127 A.D.2d 610, 511 N.Y.S.2d 410 (2d Dep't 1987); People v. Smith, 76 A.D.2d 962, 432 N.Y.S.2d 161 (3d Dep't 1980); People v. Wetmore, 51 A.D.2d 591, 379 N.Y.S.2d 114 (2d Dep't 1976). In People v. Harper, 152 A.D.2d 469, 543 N.Y.S.2d 452 (1st Dep't 1989), on an appeal from the denial of such an Article 440 motion, the First Department ordered a hearing to determine the nature of the off-the-record promise made by the prosecutor, in light of the prosecution's concession in its response to the 440 motion that a promise had been made. The court held that, if an off-the-record promise as to a sentence recommendation had indeed been made, it would have to be enforced.

123. See People v. Douglas, 135 A.D.2d 435, 522 N.Y.S.2d 856 (1st Dep't 1987), involving appeals from two Article 440 motion denials, in which the Appellate Division ordered a hearing on the defendants' allegations of an off-the-record unfulfilled

§ 11.11 PLEAS Ch. 11

The Second Circuit has upheld New York's policy of generally refusing to enforce off-the-record promises as reasonable and not inconsistent with the Due Process Clause.[124]

Library References:

West's Key No. Digests, Criminal Law ⚖=273.1(2), 980.

§ 11.12 Sentence Promises—Conditional Nature of Promise

In *People v. Selikoff*,[125] the Court of Appeals held that "any sentence 'promise' at the time of plea is, as a matter of law and strong public policy, conditioned upon its being lawful and appropriate in light of the subsequent presentence report or information obtained from other reliable sources."[126] Thus, the court need not impose a promised sentence that would be illegal.[127] Nor must it impose a promised sentence that it deems "improvident" in light of new facts coming to light after the plea and prior to sentence. Typically, these new facts are contained in the Probation Department's presentence report, but they may also come before the court in any otherwise open and reliable manner.[128] In fact,

promise by an assistant district attorney that the defendants would receive, at worst, concurrent sentences in the state prosecution if they cooperated with the federal prosecution. These allegations were supported by affidavit from the federal prosecutors and not contested by the assistant district attorney. See also People v. Yash Pal Gupta, 80 A.D.2d 743, 437 N.Y.S.2d 175 (4th Dep't 1981), another appeal from a 440 denial in which the Appellate Division ordered a hearing. The defendant alleged an unfulfilled promise that if he cooperated with an investigation of foreign drug suppliers the prosecutor would recommend a 10-year-to-life sentence. There was strong evidence, and insufficient contestation by the prosecutor, that the defendant fully cooperated and that the promise had been made. Similarly, in People v. Argentine, 67 A.D.2d 180, 414 N.Y.S.2d 732 (2d Dep't 1979), the Second Department held the defendant's direct appeal in abeyance pending a hearing on whether there was an unfulfilled off-the-record promise to drop felony charges to a misdemeanor in return for the defendant's cooperation. Affidavits from an assistant district attorney and a detective provided strong evidence that there was such a promise, and that the defendant put himself at risk by cooperating. The appellate court determined that if the hearing bore out an unfulfilled promise, then that promise should be enforced.

124. Siegel v. State of New York, 691 F.2d 620, 624 (2d Cir.1982), cert. denied 459 U.S. 1209, 103 S.Ct. 1201, 75 L.Ed.2d 443 (1983). Likening this policy to a "statute of frauds" rule for plea bargaining, the Second Circuit held that it filled three important policy objectives: increasing the likelihood that the plea was based on factual guilt, enhancing the integrity of the bargaining process, and ensuring the finality of convictions. 691 F.2d at 624.

125. 35 N.Y.2d 227, 360 N.Y.S.2d 623, 318 N.E.2d 784 (1974), cert. denied, 419 U.S. 1122, 95 S.Ct. 806, 42 L.Ed.2d 822 (1975).

126. 35 N.Y.2d at 238, 360 N.Y.S.2d at 633.

127. See People v. DaForno, 53 N.Y.2d 1006, 442 N.Y.S.2d 476, 425 N.E.2d 864 (1981), aff'g 73 A.D.2d 893, 424 N.Y.S.2d 195 (1st Dep't 1980). See also People v. Tullough, 183 A.D.2d 863, 584 N.Y.S.2d 103 (2d Dep't 1992); People v. Bullard, 84 A.D.2d 845, 444 N.Y.S.2d 171 (2d Dep't 1981). Where the promised sentence turns out to be illegal, such as where post-plea information reveals the defendant to be a predicate felon, the defendant will be allowed to withdraw the plea only if he or she was not willfully responsible for the original misapprehension. People v. DaForno, 53 N.Y.2d 1006, 442 N.Y.S.2d 476, 425 N.E.2d 864; People v. Camacho, 102 A.D.2d 728, 476 N.Y.S.2d 566 (1st Dep't 1984); People v. Powell, 105 A.D.2d 761, 481 N.Y.S.2d 188 (2d Dep't 1984).

128. See, e.g., People v. Price, 193 A.D.2d 853, 597 N.Y.S.2d 503 (3d Dep't 1993)(post-plea incident at local county jail justified departure from plea agreement); People v. Richards, 158 A.D.2d 627, 551

668

to depart from the promised sentence, the court need only "conclude[] that it cannot adhere to the promise given,"[129] since the court "retains discretion in fixing an appropriate sentence up until the time of the sentencing."[130]

Should the court decline to impose a promised sentence, "the reasons for departing from the promised sentencing agreement must be placed on the record to ensure effective appellate review of the sentencing court's exercise of discretion."[131] Additionally, the court must ordinarily offer the defendant the opportunity to withdraw his or her plea prior to imposing the higher sentence.[132]

A defendant who wishes to challenge on appeal the soundness of the court's decision to renege on the sentence promise may do so, provided he or she has objected to the court's action and has stood by the plea; if the appellate court agrees that the court's reasons were insufficient, it will modify the sentence to accord with the original offer.[133] At least in the Second Department, a defendant would be entitled to ask for such relief even if the original sentence promise was accompanied by a defendant's routine waiver of the right to appellate review.[134]

If, on the other hand, the defendant accepts the court's offer to withdraw the plea in the face of the court's decision to enhance the sentence upwards, then the defendant has no cause to complain on appeal, since—absent detrimental reliance on the original promise—the court's vacatur of the plea simply restores the defendant to his or her pre-pleading position.[135]

N.Y.S.2d 597 (2d Dep't 1990)(information contained in presentence report was sufficient basis for departure from initial sentencing promise). People v. Sales, 129 Misc.2d 731, 493 N.Y.S.2d 945 (Sup.Ct., Kings County, 1985)(victim's statement at sentencing justified court's reneging on promised sentence).

129. People v. McConnell, 49 N.Y.2d 340, 347, 425 N.Y.S.2d 794, 797, 402 N.E.2d 133 (1980).

130. People v. Schultz, 73 N.Y.2d 757, 758, 536 N.Y.S.2d 46, 47, 532 N.E.2d 1274 (1988). See also Matter of Helbrans v. Owens, 205 A.D.2d 775, 613 N.Y.S.2d 924 (2d Dep't 1994).

131. People v. Schultz, 73 N.Y.2d 757, 758, 536 N.Y.S.2d 46, 47, 532 N.E.2d 1274 (1988).

132. People v. Selikoff, 35 N.Y.2d at 241, 360 N.Y.S.2d at 634. See also People v. Scrivens, 175 A.D.2d 671, 572 N.Y.S.2d 271 (4th Dep't 1991). However, the court in some cases may not need to make that offer in the case of an illegal sentence promise. Additionally, a different analysis would apply if the possibility of a higher sentence for a breached condition was part of the initial sentence bargain (see § 11.13, infra).

133. See, e.g., People v. Brown, 207 A.D.2d 408, 615 N.Y.S.2d 726 (2d Dep't 1994)(court's failure to state reasons for higher sentence required modification to original plea agreement); People v. Alonzo, 155 A.D.2d 233, 546 N.Y.S.2d 617 (1st Dep't 1989)(same); People v. Murray, 63 A.D.2d 708, 404 N.Y.S.2d 692 (2d Dep't 1978)(error not to honor promise merely because defendant was late for sentencing).

One patently inappropriate reason for departing from the promised sentence is that the defendant asserted his or her innocence to the preparer of the Probation Department's presentence report. People v. Stennett, 207 A.D.2d 847, 616 N.Y.S.2d 980 (2d Dep't 1994); People v. Daniels, 132 A.D.2d 667, 518 N.Y.S.2d 37 (2d Dep't 1987); People v. Brunson, 131 A.D.2d 689, 516 N.Y.S.2d 767 (2d Dep't 1987).

134. See People v. Poole, 202 A.D.2d 450, 608 N.Y.S.2d 502 (2d Dep't 1994); People v. Prescott, 196 A.D.2d 599, 601 N.Y.S.2d 325 (2d Dep't 1993). See also § 11.17, infra.

135. People v. Schultz, 73 N.Y.2d 757, 758, 536 N.Y.S.2d 46, 47, 532 N.E.2d 1274 (1988); People v. McConnell, 49 N.Y.2d 340, 347, 425 N.Y.S.2d 794, 797, 402 N.E.2d 133 (1980).

§ 11.12   PLEAS   Ch. 11

Library References:
West's Key No. Digests, Criminal Law ⚖=273.1(2), 980.

§ 11.13   Sentence Promises—Special Conditions for Defendants at Liberty Between Plea and Sentence

In plea bargains contemplating the defendant's liberty between the time of plea and sentence, courts may properly condition the promised sentence on the defendant's (a) appearance on the scheduled sentencing date, (b) cooperation with the Department of Probation, and/or (c) avoidance of any further arrests.[136] If the plea transcript reveals that the defendant was specifically advised that the failure to meet any of those conditions would nullify the sentence promise, then that failure would justify the court's decision to enhance the sentence.[137]

The question arises whether, should the court decide to impose a higher sentence based upon the defendant's violation of the plea promise conditions, the court must first offer the defendant the opportunity to withdraw the plea, or it may act unilaterally in imposing the higher sentence. The answer would appear to depend on whether the plea record unequivocally reveals that the court would impose a higher sentence should any condition be violated. If the bargain contemplates that the court could act unilaterally, then the defendant need not be offered the opportunity to withdraw his or her plea prior to sentence enhancement.[138] On the other hand, should the plea record fail to contain the express condition that a defendant's nonappearance for sentence, lack of cooperation with the Probation Department, or subsequent arrest would result in a higher sentence, then the court cannot impose more than the promised sentence without first offering the defendant the opportunity to withdraw the plea.[139]

---

136. See People v. Outley, 80 N.Y.2d 702, 594 N.Y.S.2d 683, 610 N.E.2d 356 (1993).

137. People v. Wallace, 210 A.D.2d 359, 620 N.Y.S.2d 14 (2d Dep't 1994); People v. K.F. (Anonymous), 208 A.D.2d 948, 618 N.Y.S.2d 98 (2d Dep't 1994); People v. Gwynn, 201 A.D.2d 501, 609 N.Y.S.2d 797 (2d Dep't 1994); People v. Fields, 197 A.D.2d 633, 602 N.Y.S.2d 674 (2d Dep't 1993); People v. Miller, 170 A.D.2d 464, 465, 565 N.Y.S.2d 553, 554 (2d Dep't 1991).

It is apparently not necessary for the court to state at the plea exactly what enhanced sentence would be imposed in order to later impose one. See People v. Yagdis, 201 A.D.2d 521, 607 N.Y.S.2d 407 (2d Dep't 1994). But if the court does specify an exact alternative higher sentence, it cannot exceed that figure. People v. Sepulveda, 151 A.D.2d 335, 542 N.Y.S.2d 591 (1st Dep't 1989).

138. People v. Delano, 208 A.D.2d 644, 618 N.Y.S.2d 236 (2d Dep't 1994); People v. Colon, 200 A.D.2d 492, 606 N.Y.S.2d 644 (1st Dep't 1994); People v. Dukes, 194 A.D.2d 923, 599 N.Y.S.2d 188 (3d Dep't 1993), cert. denied ___ U.S. ___, 114 S.Ct. 1089, 127 L.Ed.2d 403 (1994); People v. Dremeguila, 166 A.D.2d 196, 564 N.Y.S.2d 86 (1st Dep't 1990); People v. Koslow, 160 A.D.2d 954, 555 N.Y.S.2d 627 (2d Dep't 1990); People v. Caridi, 148 A.D.2d 625, 539 N.Y.S.2d 88 (2d Dep't 1989); People v. Betheny, 147 A.D.2d 488, 537 N.Y.S.2d 586 (2d Dep't 1989).

139. Innes v. Dalsheim, 864 F.2d 974 (2d Cir.1988); People v. McKinney, 215 A.D.2d 407, 625 N.Y.S.2d 667 (2d Dep't 1995); People v. Hodge, 207 A.D.2d 845, 616 N.Y.S.2d 978 (2d Dep't 1994); People v. Elliot, 204 A.D.2d 565, 612 N.Y.S.2d 173 (2d Dep't 1994); People v. Moreno, 196 A.D.2d 850, 602 N.Y.S.2d 28 (2d Dep't 1993); People v. Rosa, 194 A.D.2d 755, 599 N.Y.S.2d 608 (2d Dep't 1993); People v. Auslander, 146 A.D.2d 936, 536 N.Y.S.2d 914 (3d Dep't 1989); People v. Annunziata,

The best practice for a court wishing to preserve its option of acting unilaterally, as well as the practice most likely to survive appellate scrutiny, is to unambiguously advise the defendant on the record at the time of plea that the violation of any condition will allow the court to impose a specific sentence higher than the one promised, and that, under that circumstance, the defendant would not be allowed to withdraw his or her plea.[140]

If the defendant apparently breaches the "no-arrest" condition, due process requires some inquiry, upon defense request, into the legitimacy of the new arrest. In *People v. Outley*,[141] the Court of Appeals held that where "an issue is raised concerning the validity of the post-plea charge or there is a denial of any involvement in the underlying crime, the court must conduct an inquiry at which the defendant has an opportunity to show that the arrest is without foundation.... The nature and extent of the inquiry—whether through a summary hearing pursuant to CPL § 400.10 or some other fair means—is within the court's discretion.... the inquiry must be of sufficient depth, however, so that the court can be satisfied—not of the defendant's guilt of the new criminal charge but of the existence of a legitimate basis for the arrest on that charge."[142]

Thus, although no formal hearing as to the new arrest is required, some inquiry must be made; the failure of the court to conduct one, upon request, will invalidate the enhanced sentence.[143] If the defense does not request the inquiry, however, none is required.[144] Moreover, *Outley* suggests, and the Second Department has held, that an indictment on the new charge is in itself assurance of its validity and requires no further inquiry.[145]

In *People v. Avery*,[146] the Court of Appeals squarely upheld the legality of plea agreements that condition a favorable sentence upon the successful completion of a private drug rehabilitation program. In such cases, sentencing may properly be deferred to permit the evaluation of the defendant's progress in the program.[147]

---

105 A.D.2d 709, 481 N.Y.S.2d 148 (2d Dep't 1984).

140. See, e.g., People v. Johnson, 187 A.D.2d 532, 589 N.Y.S.2d 918 (2d Dep't 1992); People v. Black, 187 A.D.2d 517, 589 N.Y.S.2d 911 (2d Dep't 1992).

141. 80 N.Y.2d 702, 594 N.Y.S.2d 683, 610 N.E.2d 356 (1993).

142. 80 N.Y.2d at 713, 594 N.Y.S.2d at 688.

143. People v. McGirt, 198 A.D.2d 101, 603 N.Y.S.2d 164 (1st Dep't 1993); People v. Leslie, 198 A.D.2d 233, 604 N.Y.S.2d 798 (2d Dep't 1993). No inquiry is necessary, however, if the defendant has at the same time breached an additional condition of the plea agreement, such as the provision that the defendant return to the court for sentencing. People v. Figgins, 87 N.Y.2d 840, 637 N.Y.S.2d 684, 661 N.E.2d 156 (1995).

144. People v. Coleman, 211 A.D.2d 562, 621 N.Y.S.2d 578 (1st Dep't 1995); People v. Yu, 204 A.D.2d 129, 612 N.Y.S.2d 116 (1st Dep't 1994).

145. People v. Outley, 80 N.Y.2d at 714, 594 N.Y.S.2d at 688–89; People v. Ruffin, 208 A.D.2d 657, 617 N.Y.S.2d 333 (2d Dep't 1994).

146. 85 N.Y.2d 503, 626 N.Y.S.2d 726, 650 N.E.2d 384 (1995).

147. Id. The court also held that such deferral is not tantamount to "interim probation," which it held illegal in People v. Rodney E., 77 N.Y.2d 672, 569 N.Y.S.2d 920, 572 N.E.2d 603 (1991).

§ 11.13   PLEAS   Ch. 11

Library References:

West's Key No. Digests, Criminal Law ⇔273.1(2).

§ 11.14   Sentence Promises—Specific Performance

Ordinarily, the court's "failure or inability to fulfill a [sentencing] promise requires either that the plea of guilty be vacated or the promise fulfilled, but there is no indicated preference for one course over the other. The choice rests in the discretion of the sentencing court."[148]

In certain instances, however, specific performance is the preferred remedy over plea vacatur. In some cases, specific performance is preferred because keeping the plea intact avoids prejudice to the prosecution. As the Court of Appeals noted in People v. McConnell,[149] "specific performance rather than vacation of the plea works to the benefit of the State in those cases in which the staleness of the indictment would make it difficult if not impossible for the prosecutor to obtain a conviction."[150]

Similarly, the defendant may be entitled to specific performance where the defendant has relied to his or her detriment on the original promise, such as by cooperating with the authorities or testifying against a codefendant. "Once the defendant has been placed in such a 'no-return' position, relegating him to the remedy of vacatur of his plea cannot restore him to the *status quo ante*, and he should therefore receive the benefit of his bargain, absent compelling reasons requiring a different result."[151]

Finally, specific performance is the appropriate appellate remedy for a defendant aggrieved by the court's reneging on a valid sentencing agreement, provided the court's action was taken over defense objection and without just cause, and the defendant has stood by his or her plea.[152] In such circumstance, the defendant is entitled to specific performance on appeal even if he or she had rejected an offer below to have the plea vacated.[153]

---

148. People v. Selikoff, 35 N.Y.2d 227, 239, 360 N.Y.S.2d 623, 634, 318 N.E.2d 784 (1974), cert. denied, 419 U.S. 1122, 95 S.Ct. 806, 42 L.Ed.2d 822 (1975). See also People v. Tesiero, 184 A.D.2d 802, 584 N.Y.S.2d 228 (3d Dep't 1992).

149. 49 N.Y.2d 340, 425 N.Y.S.2d 794, 402 N.E.2d 133 (1980).

150. 49 N.Y.2d at 349, 425 N.Y.S.2d at 798. See, e.g., People v. Annunziata, 105 A.D.2d 709, 481 N.Y.S.2d 148 (2d Dep't 1984)(although defendant entitled to plea vacatur on appeal, because of age of indictment, specific performance of original sentence promise ordered instead).

151. People v. Danny G., 61 N.Y.2d 169, 175–76, 473 N.Y.S.2d 131, 133–34, 461 N.E.2d 268 (1984). See also People v. McConnell, 49 N.Y.2d 340, 425 N.Y.S.2d 794, 402 N.E.2d 133 (1980); People v. Grimaldi, 200 A.D.2d 687, 607 N.Y.S.2d 57 (2d Dep't 1994). Cf. People v. Curdgel, 83 N.Y.2d 862, 611 N.Y.S.2d 827, 634 N.E.2d 199 (1994)(defendant who initially cooperated with prosecution pursuant to plea agreement, but then willfully acted to eliminate his usefulness as a prosecution witness, was not entitled to specific performance).

152. See, e.g., People v. Jones, 99 A.D.2d 1, 472 N.Y.S.2d 460 (3d Dep't 1984).

153. Id. Cf. People v. Walker, 187 A.D.2d 909, 591 N.Y.S.2d 77 (3d Dep't 1992)(where court reneged on sentence promise, its offer to vacate the plea rendered the defendant whole, since the record demonstrated a just basis for the court's departure from the agreement).

§ 11.15 Rights Automatically Relinquished by a Defendant Upon Pleading Guilty

"The pleading process necessarily includes the surrender of many guaranteed rights."[154] Among the rights forfeited by a defendant pleading guilty are those rights associated with a trial. These, the so-called *Boykin* rights,[155] are the right to trial by jury, the right to confront one's accusers, and the right against self-incrimination.[156] *A fortiori*, other rights normally associated with a criminal trial, such as a defendant's right to have one's guilt proven beyond a reasonable doubt, the right to be present at trial, and the right to present evidence on one's own behalf, are also waived by a guilty plea.

In addition to these rights, many more are deemed forfeited as a consequence of a valid guilty plea, in recognition that such a plea "marks the end of a criminal case, not a gateway to further litigation."[157] Indeed, most arguments advanced by the defendant prior to the plea, whether they are based on constitutional, statutory, or decisional law, will be waived in consequence of it.

For example, a guilty plea waives not only most issues relating to the factual guilt or innocence of the defendant, but also those relating to the fairness of the proceedings meant to reach that determination. This is because "where defendant has by his plea admitted commission of the crime with which he was charged, his plea renders irrelevant his contention that the criminal proceedings preliminary to trial were infected with impropriety and error; his conviction rests directly on the sufficiency of his plea, not on the legal or constitutional sufficiency of any proceedings which might have led to his conviction after trial."[158]

Among the trial-related procedural issues forfeited by a guilty plea are: a prosecutor's alleged use of discriminatory peremptory challenges;[159] an *ex post facto* challenge to an evidentiary rule change;[160] adverse rulings on *Sandoval* or *Molineux* applications;[161] whether a proper foundation was laid for the accuracy of a blood alcohol test;[162] an alleged unconstitutional statutory presumption;[163] the applicability of

---

154. People v. Seaberg, 74 N.Y.2d 1, 7, 543 N.Y.S.2d 968, 970, 541 N.E.2d 1022 (1989).

155. See Boykin v. Alabama, 395 U.S. 238, 89 S.Ct. 1709, 23 L.Ed.2d 274 (1969).

156. See People v. Taylor, 65 N.Y.2d 1, 489 N.Y.S.2d 152, 478 N.E.2d 755 (1985).

157. 65 N.Y.2d at 5, 489 N.Y.S.2d at 154.

158. People v. DiRaffaele, 55 N.Y.2d 234, 240, 448 N.Y.S.2d 448, 450, 433 N.E.2d 513 (1982).

159. People v. Green, 75 N.Y.2d 902, 554 N.Y.S.2d 821, 553 N.E.2d 1331 (1990), cert. denied 498 U.S. 860, 111 S.Ct. 165, 112 L.Ed.2d 130 (1990).

160. People v. Latzer, 71 N.Y.2d 920, 528 N.Y.S.2d 533, 523 N.E.2d 820 (1988).

161. People v. Johnson, 141 A.D.2d 848, 530 N.Y.S.2d 189 (2d Dep't 1988); People v. Winchenbaugh, 120 A.D.2d 811, 813, 501 N.Y.S.2d 929, 931 (3d Dep't 1986).

162. People v. Campbell, 73 N.Y.2d 481, 541 N.Y.S.2d 756, 539 N.E.2d 584 (1989).

163. People v. Thomas, 53 N.Y.2d 338, 441 N.Y.S.2d 650, 424 N.E.2d 537 (1981).

§ 11.15 PLEAS Ch. 11

the "merger" doctrine to a kidnapping charge;[164] and motions relating to discovery,[165] the disqualification of a prosecutor,[166] severance or consolidation of defendants,[167] and severance or joinder of offenses.[168]

Also forfeited, by the same token, are the right to litigate on appeal the denials of motions to dismiss in the interest of justice,[169] for preindictment police or prosecutorial misconduct,[170] and for selective prosecution.[171]

A guilty plea forfeits not only those issues related to the factual determination of guilt or innocence, but also all "nonjurisdictional" defects in the accusatory instrument or in the grand jury proceedings. The distinction between "jurisdictional" and "nonjurisdictional" defects is less than obvious in some cases and may only be discerned by a case by case analysis.

The following defects in the accusatory instrument itself have been held to be nonjurisdictional and thus waived by a guilty plea: an indictment's lack of proper form or factual detail;[172] duplicity of counts;[173] the proper interpretation or application of the statutory offense, providing that the indictment alleges all elements and is not facially insufficient;[174] improper joinder of offenses;[175] the lack of, sufficiency of, or failure to timely serve a supporting deposition;[176] the

---

164. People v. Brown, 156 A.D.2d 204, 548 N.Y.S.2d 464 (1st Dep't 1989).

165. People v. Rojas, 169 A.D.2d 464, 564 N.Y.S.2d 341 (1st Dep't 1991); People v. Gill, 164 A.D.2d 867, 559 N.Y.S.2d 376 (2d Dep't 1990); People v. Cusani, 153 A.D.2d 574, 544 N.Y.S.2d 499 (2d Dep't 1989).

The law is unsettled, however, with respect to Brady violations—i.e., the prosecution's failure to turn over exculpatory material prior to plea. The Second Department has held Brady violations waived by a guilty plea. People v. Day, 150 A.D.2d 595, 541 N.Y.S.2d 463 (2d Dep't 1989). The Third Department has held otherwise. People v. Ortiz, 127 A.D.2d 305, 515 N.Y.S.2d 317 (3d Dep't 1987). See also People v. Armer, 119 A.D.2d 930, 501 N.Y.S.2d 203 (3d Dep't 1986)(plea upheld where defendant failed to prove a reasonable probability that he would not have pleaded guilty had the Brady material been furnished). Accord People v. Benard, 163 Misc.2d 176, 620 N.Y.S.2d 242 (Sup.Ct., N.Y. County, 1994). The Second Circuit has held that a Brady violation may result in plea vacatur if the defendant shows such a reasonable probability. Miller v. Angliker, 848 F.2d 1312 (2d Cir.), cert. denied 488 U.S. 890, 109 S.Ct. 224, 102 L.Ed.2d 214 (1988).

166. People v. Cole, 152 A.D.2d 851, 544 N.Y.S.2d 228 (3d Dep't 1989).

167. People v. Marinelli, 148 A.D.2d 550, 540 N.Y.S.2d 185 (2d Dep't 1989).

168. People v. Grant, 140 A.D.2d 623, 528 N.Y.S.2d 993 (2d Dep't 1988).

169. People v. Purcell, 161 A.D.2d 812, 556 N.Y.S.2d 375 (2d Dep't 1990).

170. People v. Di Raffaele, 55 N.Y.2d 234, 240, 448 N.Y.S.2d 448, 450, 433 N.E.2d 513 (1982); People v. D'Angelo, 145 A.D.2d 783, 535 N.Y.S.2d 765 (3d Dep't 1988).

171. People v. Rodriguez, 55 N.Y.2d 776, 447 N.Y.S.2d 246, 431 N.E.2d 972 (1981).

172. People v. Cohen, 52 N.Y.2d 584, 439 N.Y.S.2d 321, 421 N.E.2d 813 (1981); People v. Iannone, 45 N.Y.2d 589, 600–01, 412 N.Y.S.2d 110, 117–18, 384 N.E.2d 656 (1978); People v. Pollay, 145 A.D.2d 972, 538 N.Y.S.2d 714 (4th Dep't 1988).

173. People v. Nicholson, 98 A.D.2d 876, 470 N.Y.S.2d 854 (3d Dep't 1983).

174. People v. Levin, 57 N.Y.2d 1008, 457 N.Y.S.2d 472, 443 N.E.2d 946 (1982).

175. People v. Spears, 106 A.D.2d 417, 482 N.Y.S.2d 340 (2d Dep't 1984).

176. People v. Beattie, 80 N.Y.2d 840, 842–43, 587 N.Y.S.2d 585, 586–87, 600 N.E.2d 216 (1992); People v. Kane, N.Y.L.J. 7/23/85, p. 13, col. 1 (App.Term, 2d & 11th Jud.Dists.); People v. Rodgers, N.Y.L.J. 6/14/82, p. 17, col. 5 (App.Term, 9th & 10th Jud. Dists.); People v. Roby, N.Y.L.J. 4/27/82, p. 12, col. 6 (App.Term, 9th & 10th Jud.Dists.).

prosecution's failure to file a special information pursuant to CPL § 200.60 alleging a prior conviction;[177] any error in allowing the amendment of an indictment;[178] the sufficiency of the evidence supporting an indictment;[179] and lack of venue or geographical jurisdiction.[180]

Those defects in the grand jury proceedings deemed nonjurisdictional, and therefore waived by a guilty plea, are claimed violations of: a defendant's right to transactional or statutory immunity;[181] a defendant's attorney-client or doctor-patient privilege;[182] and a defendant's statutory right to testify before the grand jury.[183] Similarly deemed waived are claims of prosecutorial misconduct in the grand jury,[184] and the denial of motions to remove a case to Family Court.[185]

Also forfeited by a guilty plea are statutory speedy trial claims pursuant to CPL § 30.30;[186] claims that the statute of limitations has been violated, at least where no motion to dismiss pursuant to CPL § 210.20(1)(f) has been made;[187] and statutory double jeopardy claims pursuant to CPL § 40.20.[188]

Claims that are automatically forfeited by a guilty plea cannot be preserved for appellate review by a defendant's reservation of his or her right to appeal, even with the agreement of the court and prosecutor.[189] An appellate court is not authorized to review such claims even in the "interest of justice."[190] However, a defendant who is induced to plead guilty by the mistaken belief that a waived issue could be raised on appeal may collaterally attack the knowing and voluntary nature of the plea.[191]

---

177. People v. DiCarluccio, 168 A.D.2d 509, 562 N.Y.S.2d 750 (2d Dep't 1990).

178. People v. Harris, 117 A.D.2d 752, 498 N.Y.S.2d 475 (2d Dep't 1986).

179. People v. Dunbar, 53 N.Y.2d 868, 440 N.Y.S.2d 613, 423 N.E.2d 36 (1981).

180. People v. Rivera, 156 A.D.2d 177, 548 N.Y.S.2d 439 (1st Dep't 1989); People v. Ianniello, 156 A.D.2d 469, 471, 548 N.Y.S.2d 755, 756 (2d Dep't 1989); People v. Spears, 106 A.D.2d 417, 482 N.Y.S.2d 340 (2d Dep't 1984).

181. People v. Flihan, 73 N.Y.2d 729, 731, 535 N.Y.S.2d 590, 590, 532 N.E.2d 96 (1988); People v. Sobotker, 61 N.Y.2d 44, 48, 471 N.Y.S.2d 78, 80, 459 N.E.2d 187 (1984).

182. People v. Figueroa, 173 A.D.2d 156, 568 N.Y.S.2d 957 (1st Dep't 1991); People v. Buttiglione, 125 A.D.2d 323, 508 N.Y.S.2d 992 (2d Dep't 1986).

183. People v. Rose, 162 A.D.2d 240, 556 N.Y.S.2d 340 (1st Dep't 1990); People v. Ferrara, 99 A.D.2d 257, 472 N.Y.S.2d 407 (2d Dep't 1984).

184. People v. Nelson, 173 A.D.2d 205, 569 N.Y.S.2d 86 (1st Dep't 1991); People v. Bowen, 122 A.D.2d 64, 504 N.Y.S.2d 480 (2d Dep't 1986).

185. People v. Angelo F., 172 A.D.2d 686, 570 N.Y.S.2d 964 (2d Dep't 1991).

186. People v. O'Brien, 56 N.Y.2d 1009, 453 N.Y.S.2d 638, 439 N.E.2d 354 (1982). Similarly, claims of violations of the Interstate Agreement on Detainers (CPL § 580.20) are also waived. People v. Cusick, 111 A.D.2d 251, 489 N.Y.S.2d 96 (2d Dep't 1985).

187. People v. Verkey, 185 A.D.2d 622, 585 N.Y.S.2d 897 (4th Dep't 1992); People v. Dickson, 133 A.D.2d 492, 519 N.Y.S.2d 419 (3d Dep't 1987).

188. People v. Prescott, 66 N.Y.2d 216, 219, 495 N.Y.S.2d 955, 956, 486 N.E.2d 813 (1985), cert. denied 475 U.S. 1150, 106 S.Ct. 1804, 90 L.Ed.2d 349 (1986).

189. People v. Campbell, 73 N.Y.2d 481, 486, 541 N.Y.S.2d 756, 758, 539 N.E.2d 584 (1989); People v. O'Brien, 56 N.Y.2d 1009, 1010, 453 N.Y.S.2d 638, 639, 439 N.E.2d 354 (1982).

190. People v. Morris, 111 A.D.2d 414, 489 N.Y.S.2d 610 (2d Dep't 1985).

191. People v. Brickhouse, 163 A.D.2d 604, 559 N.Y.S.2d 677 (2d Dep't 1990).

Library References:
West's Key No. Digests, Criminal Law ⟶273.4.

§ 11.16 Claims That Ordinarily Survive a Guilty Plea

Certain claims, on the other hand, ordinarily survive a guilty plea, either because they go to the knowing and voluntary nature of the plea itself; are deemed jurisdictional in nature; go to the very power of the prosecution to hail the defendant into court; or else survive by specific statutory provision.

Claims that the plea itself was not entered into knowingly and voluntarily survive a guilty plea.[192] Also surviving such a plea, under the same rationale, are claims relating to the defendant's mental competency,[193] and claims that the incompetence of defense counsel during the plea process compromised the knowing and voluntary nature of the plea.[194]

Deemed "jurisdictional" are fundamental defects in the accusatory instrument such as the failure of the accusatory instrument to adequately charge a criminal offense[195] or to allege that the defendant committed acts constituting every element of a crime,[196] and the procurement of a conviction based upon an indictment supported solely by false evidence.[197]

Also deemed jurisdictional are defects in the grand jury proceedings such as the deprivation of a defendant's right to testify before the grand jury based upon ineffective assistance of counsel,[198] and the resubmission of a case to a second grand jury without having first obtained leave of the court.[199]

---

192. People v. Seaberg, 74 N.Y.2d 1, 10, 543 N.Y.S.2d 968, 972, 541 N.E.2d 1022 (1989).

193. People v. Armlin, 37 N.Y.2d 167, 172, 371 N.Y.S.2d 691, 696, 332 N.E.2d 870 (1975).

194. See People v. Lang, 21 N.Y.2d 338, 354–56, 287 N.Y.S.2d 659, 671–72, 234 N.E.2d 687 (1967); People v. Rosado, 199 A.D.2d 833, 606 N.Y.S.2d 368 (3d Dep't 1993)(guilty plea, even with bargained-for waiver of the right to appeal, cannot waive claim that ineffective assistance of counsel led to entry of plea); People v. Roy, 122 A.D.2d 482, 505 N.Y.S.2d 242 (3d Dep't 1986); People v. Glenn, 59 A.D.2d 724, 398 N.Y.S.2d 364 (2d Dep't 1977). Cf. People v. Petgen, 55 N.Y.2d 529, 535 n. 3, 450 N.Y.S.2d 299, 301 n. 3, 435 N.E.2d 669 (1982)(competency of defense counsel possibly waived by guilty plea where such was "not directly involved" in the plea bargaining process). A claim of incompetence of prior counsel is waived by a guilty plea if the "full measure of asserted derelictions" was known to the attorney who advised the plea. 55 N.Y.2d at 534–35, 450 N.Y.S.2d at 301.

195. People v. Case, 42 N.Y.2d 98, 100, 396 N.Y.S.2d 841, 842, 365 N.E.2d 872 (1977).

196. People v. Iannone, 45 N.Y.2d 589, 600, 412 N.Y.S.2d 110, 117, 384 N.E.2d 656 (1978).

197. People v. Pelchat, 62 N.Y.2d 97, 108, 476 N.Y.S.2d 79, 85, 464 N.E.2d 447 (1984).

198. People v. Johnston, 178 A.D.2d 550, 577 N.Y.S.2d 644 (2d Dep't 1991).

199. People v. Wilkins, 68 N.Y.2d 269, 277 n. 7, 508 N.Y.S.2d 893, 897 n. 7, 501 N.E.2d 542 (1986). People v. Jackson, 212 A.D.2d 732, 622 N.Y.S.2d 808 (2d Dep't 1995)(guilty plea, even with bargained-for appeal waiver, did not foreclose claim that prosecutor resubmitted charges more than 30 days after a CPL § 210.20 reduction order without court permission). Cf. People v. Castillo, 208 A.D.2d 944, 618 N.Y.S.2d 78 (2d Dep't 1994)(bargained-for waiver of right to appeal waived appellate review of motion to dismiss pursuant to CPL § 190.75(3)).

Not ordinarily waived, also, are claims that go to the very power to prosecute: federal constitutional speedy trial[200] or double jeopardy issues;[201] constitutional *ex post facto* claims;[202] the unconstitutionality of the statute under which the defendant is convicted;[203] and the defense of infancy (P.L. § 30.00).[204] The legality of the sentence itself is also deemed so fundamental as to survive a guilty plea.[205]

By statutory provision, an "order finally denying a motion to suppress evidence" pursuant to CPL § 710.20 survives a guilty plea,[206] provided that a final ruling on the motion is obtained prior to the plea.[207] Even an order denying such a motion without a hearing survives the plea.[208] Procedural issues arising from the suppression hearing are also cognizable on appeal.[209] On the other hand, a defendant who pleads guilty while his or her motion to suppress is still pending and undecided has forfeited that claim.[210] Also waived by a guilty plea are ancillary Article 710 claims such as the prosecution's failure to provide the proper notice pursuant to CPL § 710.30 of its intention to introduce identification or statement evidence at trial,[211] or the denial of an application for leave to file a late suppression motion.[212]

Library References:
West's Key No. Digests, Criminal Law ⇔273.4; Double Jeopardy ⇔202.

§ 11.17 Bargained-for Waivers of the Right to Appeal

Ordinarily, a defendant may validly waive his or her right to appeal as part of a plea or sentence bargain.[213] To meet due process concerns,

---

200. People v. Blakley, 34 N.Y.2d 311, 314–15, 357 N.Y.S.2d 459, 461–62, 313 N.E.2d 763 (1974). Even such claims, however, are waived unless preserved by a motion to dismiss adjudicated by the court. People v. Adams, 38 N.Y.2d 605, 381 N.Y.S.2d 847, 345 N.E.2d 318 (1976).

201. Menna v. New York, 423 U.S. 61, 62 n. 2, 96 S.Ct. 241, 242 n. 2, 46 L.Ed.2d 195 (1975). Indeed, such claims may even be raised for the first time on appeal. Id. See also People v. Michael, 48 N.Y.2d 1, 7, 420 N.Y.S.2d 371, 373, 394 N.E.2d 1134 (1979).

202. People v. Rivera, 156 A.D.2d 177, 548 N.Y.S.2d 439 (1st Dep't 1989).

203. People v. Lee, 58 N.Y.2d 491, 462 N.Y.S.2d 417, 448 N.E.2d 1328 (1983).

204. People v. Ennis, 94 A.D.2d 746, 462 N.Y.S.2d 499 (2d Dep't 1983).

205. People v. Seaberg, 74 N.Y.2d 1, 10, 543 N.Y.S.2d 968, 972, 541 N.E.2d 1022 (1989).

206. CPL § 710.70(2).

207. People v. Fernandez, 67 N.Y.2d 686, 688, 499 N.Y.S.2d 919, 919, 490 N.E.2d 838 (1986).

208. See People v. Ramos, 130 A.D.2d 439, 515 N.Y.S.2d 472 (1st Dep't 1987); People v. Patterson, 129 A.D.2d 527, 514 N.Y.S.2d 378 (1st Dep't 1987); People v. Banks, 100 A.D.2d 780, 474 N.Y.S.2d 64 (1st Dep't 1984).

209. People v. White, 184 A.D.2d 676, 587 N.Y.S.2d 178 (2d Dep't 1992); People v. Cruz, 149 A.D.2d 151, 163, 545 N.Y.S.2d 561, 568 (1st Dep't 1989); People v. Robinson, 118 A.D.2d 516, 500 N.Y.S.2d 122 (1st Dep't 1986), judgment rev'd after remand 125 A.D.2d 259, 509 N.Y.S.2d 803 (1st Dep't 1986).

210. People v. Fernandez, 67 N.Y.2d 686, 499 N.Y.S.2d 919, 490 N.E.2d 838 (1986); People v. Paulino, 162 A.D.2d 632, 559 N.Y.S.2d 177 (2d Dep't 1990); People v. Mitchell, 128 A.D.2d 731, 513 N.Y.S.2d 225 (2d Dep't 1987).

211. People v. Taylor, 65 N.Y.2d 1, 489 N.Y.S.2d 152, 478 N.E.2d 755 (1985).

212. People v. Petgen, 55 N.Y.2d 529, 450 N.Y.S.2d 299, 435 N.E.2d 669 (1982).

213. People v. Seaberg, 74 N.Y.2d 1, 543 N.Y.S.2d 968, 541 N.E.2d 1022 (1989).

however, the waiver must be entered into knowingly, voluntarily and intelligently.[214] Relevant factors in evaluating the knowing and voluntary nature of the waiver include "the nature of and terms of the [plea] agreement and the age, experience and background of the accused."[215] Additionally, a waiver that is "unfair" or "coerced to conceal error or misconduct" will not be upheld.[216]

Although "prudence suggests" that the court presiding over the plea "should" require the defendant to state on the record his or her understanding of the waiver,[217] and a valid waiver cannot be inferred from a silent record,[218] no "particular litany" is required.[219]

A defendant may validly waive the right to appeal the excessiveness (as opposed to the legality) of the sentence,[220] but such waiver has not been enforced if the sentence ultimately imposed was greater than the sentence bargained-for at the time of the entry of the waiver.[221] Similarly, a defendant cannot validly waive the right to appeal the length of the sentence if, at the time of the entry of the purported waiver, the court has not yet told the defendant what the imposed sentence will be.[222]

There is no requirement that the waiver be in writing, although many courts insist that the defendant sign a written waiver. Even a written waiver, however, will not be upheld if the court makes no on-the-record inquiry of the defendant regarding whether he or she understands the implications of the waiver, knows the waiver is part of the plea bargain, and voluntarily agrees to it.[223] As part of this inquiry, the court should inform the defendant that the right to appeal being bargained-away is one that ordinarily survives the guilty plea.[224]

The Second Department has refused to uphold appeal waivers where the plea-taking court, in allocuting on the waiver, simply tells the defendant a series of rights automatically given up by pleading guilty, and includes the right to appeal among them so as to suggest that the appeal waiver is an inherent consequence of the plea.[225]

214. People v. Callahan, 80 N.Y.2d 273, 280, 590 N.Y.S.2d 46, 49, 604 N.E.2d 108 (1992); People v. Seaberg, 74 N.Y.2d at 11, 543 N.Y.S.2d at 972.

215. People v. Seaberg, 74 N.Y.2d at 11, 543 N.Y.S.2d at 972.

216. 74 N.Y.2d at 12, 543 N.Y.S.2d at 973.

217. 74 N.Y.2d at 11, 543 N.Y.S.2d at 973.

218. People v. Callahan, 80 N.Y.2d at 283, 590 N.Y.S.2d at 51; People v. Santiago, 194 A.D.2d 468, 599 N.Y.S.2d 964 (1st Dep't 1993).

219. People v. Moissett, 76 N.Y.2d 909, 911, 563 N.Y.S.2d 43, 44, 564 N.E.2d 653 (1990).

220. People v. Allen, 82 N.Y.2d 761, 763, 603 N.Y.S.2d 820, 821, 623 N.E.2d 1170 (1993); People v. Seaberg, 74 N.Y.2d at 9, 543 N.Y.S.2d at 971.

221. People v. Prescott, 196 A.D.2d 599, 601 N.Y.S.2d 325 (2d Dep't 1993). But see People v. Loper, 215 A.D.2d 406, 626 N.Y.S.2d 968 (2d Dep't 1995)(waiver of right to appeal in contemplation of probationary sentence precluded appellate argument that sentence imposed after probation violation was excessive).

222. People v. Leach, 203 A.D.2d 484, 611 N.Y.S.2d 17, 18 (2d Dep't 1994).

223. People v. Callahan, 80 N.Y.2d at 283, 590 N.Y.S.2d at 51; People v. Cohen, 210 A.D.2d 343, 620 N.Y.S.2d 92 (2d Dep't 1994).

224. See People v. Bray, 154 A.D.2d 692, 693, 546 N.Y.S.2d 894, 895 (2d Dep't 1989).

225. People v. Bray, supra.

Issues that ordinarily survive a guilty plea, but that validly may be waived as part of a plea bargain, include the right to appeal the length of the sentence in the interests of justice;[226] the right to appeal a suppression issue ordinarily surviving pursuant to CPL § 710.20;[227] an attack on the procedures used to arrive at a sentencing determination, including the accuracy of the presentence report and procedures used to determine the amount of restitution;[228] the sufficiency of the plea allocution;[229] the court's option of denying youthful offender treatment;[230] the right to appeal from a trial verdict on one indictment that precedes the guilty plea on a second indictment,[231] the denial of a defendant's request to proceed *pro se*,[232] and a constitutional double jeopardy claim.[233]

On the other hand, appellate review of certain issues may not be foreclosed by even an otherwise valid bargained-for waiver, because those issues implicate "society's interest in the integrity of criminal process."[234] These issues include the constitutionally protected right to a speedy trial; the legality of the sentence imposed; the defendant's competency to stand trial; and the knowing and voluntary nature of the plea itself.[235] The Second Department has declined to uphold such a waiver where the prosecutor resubmits charges subject to a CPL

---

226. See People v. Seaberg, 74 N.Y.2d at 7, 543 N.Y.S.2d at 970.

227. People v. Williams, 36 N.Y.2d 829, 830, 370 N.Y.S.2d 904, 905, 331 N.E.2d 684 (1975), cert. denied 423 U.S. 873, 96 S.Ct. 141, 46 L.Ed.2d 104 (1975). Note, however, that the mere "withdrawal of pending motions" at the time of the plea does not result in a forfeiture of the right to appeal other issues that might be contained in the record. People v. Polanco, 201 A.D.2d 410, 609 N.Y.S.2d 772 (1st Dep't 1994).

228. People v. Callahan, 80 N.Y.2d 273, 281, 590 N.Y.S.2d 46, 50, 604 N.E.2d 108 (1992); People v. Brakas, 204 A.D.2d 474, 614 N.Y.S.2d 170 (2d Dep't 1994); People v. Hicks, 201 A.D.2d 831, 608 N.Y.S.2d 543 (3d Dep't 1994); People v. Rosado, 199 A.D.2d 833, 606 N.Y.S.2d 368 (3d Dep't 1993)(challenges to procedural rulings during persistent felony offender hearing forfeited by bargained-for waiver of the right to appeal).

229. People v. Brakas, supra. Where the defect in the factual allocution implicates the very knowing and voluntary nature of the plea, however, the defendant would retain the right to challenge it on appeal despite a purported waiver. People v. Seaberg, 74 N.Y.2d at 10, 543 N.Y.S.2d at 972; People v. Anderson, 203 A.D.2d 373, 612 N.Y.S.2d 909 (2d Dep't 1994); People v. Jackson, 203 A.D.2d 302, 612 N.Y.S.2d 897 (2d Dep't 1994).

230. People v. Williams, 204 A.D.2d 371, 614 N.Y.S.2d 138 (2d Dep't 1994).

231. People v. Korona, 197 A.D.2d 788, 603 N.Y.S.2d 88 (3d Dep't 1993). This situation arose in Korona when the defendant was convicted after trial on one indictment and then entered into a negotiated plea with respect to a second indictment that required a waiver of the right to appeal both indictments. The Court of Appeals has not yet ruled on the validity of such an arrangement. The Third Department upheld the waiver, but only after reviewing the trial transcript and determining that the appeal waiver was not "designed to conceal error or misconduct" occurring during the trial. 197 A.D.2d at 790, 603 N.Y.S.2d at 90.

232. People v. Shields, 205 A.D.2d 833, 613 N.Y.S.2d 281 (3d Dep't 1994), lv granted 84 N.Y.2d 910, 621 N.Y.S.2d 527, 645 N.E.2d 1227 (1994).

233. People v. Allen, 86 N.Y.2d 599, 635 N.Y.S.2d 139, 658 N.E.2d 1012 (1995).

234. People v. Seaberg, 74 N.Y.2d 1, 543 N.Y.S.2d 968, 541 N.E.2d 1022 (1989).

235. People v. Callahan, 80 N.Y.2d 273, 280, 590 N.Y.S.2d 46, 49, 604 N.E.2d 108 (1992); People v. Seaberg, 74 N.Y.2d at 9–10, 543 N.Y.S.2d at 971–72; People v. Kilgore, 199 A.D.2d 1008, 608 N.Y.S.2d 12 (4th Dep't 1993)(right to challenge second felony offender adjudication without hearing cannot be bargained away, as it implicates the legality of the sentence); People v. Clinton, 179 A.D.2d 670, 579 N.Y.S.2d 895 (2d Dep't 1992).

§ 11.17 PLEAS Ch. 11

§ 210.20 reduction order to a grand jury in an untimely manner without court permission.[236]

Note that even a valid waiver does not bar a defendant from filing a notice of appeal, asking for leave to appeal *in forma pauperis*, and filing an appellate brief. Rather, the bargained-for waiver merely forecloses obtaining appellate relief on those issues that were validly bargained away.[237]

Nor does a valid appeal waiver bar a defendant from seeking collateral relief—for example, in the nature of a CPL § 440.10 motion—to review defects in the plea proceedings that might not appear on the record.[238]

Library References:
West's Key No. Digests, Criminal Law ⚖273.1(2), 1026.10(2.1).

§ 11.18 Withdrawal of Guilty Plea—Defendant

At any time prior to imposition of sentence, the court has the discretion to permit a defendant who has pled "guilty," or "not responsible by reason of mental disease or defect," to withdraw that plea and be restored to pre-pleading status.[239] A defendant may want to withdraw the plea if he or she wishes to return the proceedings to the *status quo ante*, *e.g.*, if the plea was improvident or the court's sentence promise is not being kept. There is no requirement that a motion to withdraw a guilty plea be made in writing or on notice to the prosecution.

On a motion to withdraw such a plea, a defendant "should be afforded reasonable opportunity to present his contentions and the court should be enabled to make an informed determination" as to the knowing and voluntary nature of the plea.[240] The nature and extent of the court's factfinding inquiry rests largely within the court's sound discretion and "often a limited interrogation by the court will suffice."[241] Only rarely will an evidentiary hearing be required on the defendant's motion; allowing the defendant to speak—and permitting defense counsel to address the court on the defendant's behalf—normally meets the procedural requirements.[242]

In some instances, however, appellate courts have held that an evidentiary hearing on the defendant's motion to withdraw is required. These cases generally involve a prompt motion to withdraw combined with some confluence of factors suggesting that the plea was not entirely knowing and voluntary, *e.g.*, a claim of innocence that has some support

---

236. People v. Jackson, 212 A.D.2d 732, 622 N.Y.S.2d 808 (2d Dep't 1995).

237. People v. Callahan, 80 N.Y.2d at 284–85, 590 N.Y.S.2d at 52–53.

238. People v. Seaberg, 74 N.Y.2d at 8, 543 N.Y.S.2d at 970; People v. St. John, 163 A.D.2d 687, 558 N.Y.S.2d 294 (3d Dep't 1990).

239. CPL § 220.60(3).

240. People v. Tinsley, 35 N.Y.2d 926, 927, 365 N.Y.S.2d 161, 162, 324 N.E.2d 544 (1974); People v. Williams, 210 A.D.2d 161, 620 N.Y.S.2d 954 (1st Dep't 1994).

241. People v. Tinsley, 35 N.Y.2d 926, 927, 365 N.Y.S.2d 161, 162, 324 N.E.2d 544.

242. Id. See also People v. Wilmer, 191 A.D.2d 850, 595 N.Y.S.2d 123 (3d Dep't 1993).

in the record, a cursory factual allocution, inadequate or coercive representation by counsel, and a nonrecidivist defendant.[243]

A defendant is not entitled to plea withdrawal merely because of a misapprehension of the strength of the prosecution's case.[244] Nor will the defendant's bare allegation of innocence entitle him or her to such relief.[245]

Since the defendant has a right to effective assistance of counsel on the motion to withdraw the plea, it may be necessary under some circumstances for the court to appoint new counsel, either *sua sponte* or in response to a defense request, to litigate the motion.[246] Particularly if the defendant's counsel takes a position adverse to his or her client in response to the defendant's motion, then the court should not decide the motion without first assigning new defense counsel.[247] However, a defendant's unsupported assertions that defense counsel pressured him or her into pleading have been held insufficient to warrant the assignment of new counsel.[248] Moreover, defense counsel has no professional obligation to join in a *pro se* motion to withdraw a plea if the record reflects no basis for the motion.[249]

---

243. See People v. McClain, 32 N.Y.2d 697, 343 N.Y.S.2d 601, 296 N.E.2d 454 (1973); People v. McKennion, 27 N.Y.2d 671, 313 N.Y.S.2d 876, 261 N.E.2d 910 (1970); People v. Britt, 200 A.D.2d 401, 606 N.Y.S.2d 208 (1st Dep't 1994); People v. Derrick, 188 A.D.2d 486, 590 N.Y.S.2d 907 (2d Dep't 1992); People v. Gonzalez, 171 A.D.2d 413, 566 N.Y.S.2d 639 (1st Dep't 1991); People v. Bowers, 45 A.D.2d 241, 357 N.Y.S.2d 563 (4th Dep't 1974). Cf. People v. Miller, 42 N.Y.2d 946, 398 N.Y.S.2d 133, 367 N.E.2d 640 (1977); People v. Dixon, 29 N.Y.2d 55, 323 N.Y.S.2d 825, 272 N.E.2d 329 (1971).

244. See, e.g., People v. Jones, 44 N.Y.2d 76, 404 N.Y.S.2d 85, 375 N.E.2d 41, cert. denied 439 U.S. 846, 99 S.Ct. 145, 58 L.Ed.2d 148 (1978); People v. Junco, 184 A.D.2d 529, 584 N.Y.S.2d 604 (2d Dep't 1992); People v. Lesesne, 173 A.D.2d 407, 570 N.Y.S.2d 40 (1st Dep't 1991).

245. See, e.g., People v. Dixon, 29 N.Y.2d 55, 57, 323 N.Y.S.2d 825, 827, 272 N.E.2d 329 (1971); People v. Rodney Z. Williams, 210 A.D.2d 168, 620 N.Y.S.2d 958 (1st Dep't 1994); People v. Lopez, 209 A.D.2d 545, 619 N.Y.S.2d 623 (2d Dep't 1994); People v. Stone, 193 A.D.2d 838, 597 N.Y.S.2d 538 (3d Dep't 1993); People v. Mercedes, 171 A.D.2d 1044, 579 N.Y.S.2d 601 (4th Dep't 1991).

246. See People v. Boyd, 22 N.Y.2d 707, 291 N.Y.S.2d 816, 238 N.E.2d 923 (1968); People v. Rozzell, 20 N.Y.2d 712, 282 N.Y.S.2d 775, 229 N.E.2d 452 (1967); People v. Brown, 205 A.D.2d 436, 613 N.Y.S.2d 903 (1st Dep't 1994); People v. Santana, 156 A.D.2d 736, 550 N.Y.S.2d 356 (2d Dep't 1989).

247. People v. Rozzell, 20 N.Y.2d 712, 282 N.Y.S.2d 775, 229 N.E.2d 452 (1967); People v. Spearman, 210 A.D.2d 268, 619 N.Y.S.2d 967 (2d Dep't 1994); People v. Santana, 156 A.D.2d 736, 550 N.Y.S.2d 356 (2d Dep't 1989). See Lopez v. Scully, 58 F.3d 38 (2d Cir.1995)(where defendant filed pro se motion to withdraw his plea based upon ineffective assistance of counsel, court should have relieved counsel based on conflict of interest).

248. See People v. Anthony, 208 A.D.2d 637, 618 N.Y.S.2d 247 (2d Dep't 1994); People v. Brown, 126 A.D.2d 898, 900–01, 510 N.Y.S.2d 932, 934–35 (3d Dep't 1987); People v. Sutton, 39 A.D.2d 820, 332 N.Y.S.2d 983 (4th Dep't 1972).

Notably, a defense counsel's advisory to a defendant contemplating a plea offer that the prosecution's case is strong, and that a lengthy sentence will ensue if there is a conviction after trial, has been held not to constitute the sort of "coercion" that renders a plea involuntary. See, e.g., People v. Samuel, 208 A.D.2d 776, 617 N.Y.S.2d 494 (2d Dep't 1994); People v. Anthony, 188 A.D.2d 477, 591 N.Y.S.2d 181 (2d Dep't 1992).

249. See People v. Bourdonnay, 160 A.D.2d 1014, 555 N.Y.S.2d 134 (2d Dep't 1990); People v. Glasper, 151 A.D.2d 692, 542 N.Y.S.2d 747 (2d Dep't 1989); People v. Brown, 126 A.D.2d 898, 900–901, 510 N.Y.S.2d 932, 934–35 (3d Dep't 1987).

§ 11.18 PLEAS Ch. 11

The court should ordinarily offer the defendant the right to withdraw his or her plea if it cannot or will not honor the sentence bargain set forth in the record at the time of the entry of the plea.[250]

Should the court grant a defendant's motion to withdraw the guilty plea, the court then has no power, it has been held, to reinstate the plea over defendant's objection.[251]

The defense must ordinarily either move for plea withdrawal pursuant to section 220.60, or to vacate an already-imposed judgment pursuant to CPL § 440.10, if it wishes to preserve a claimed defect in the plea proceeding for subsequent appellate review.[252]

Library References:

West's Key No. Digests, Criminal Law ⇔274.

§ 11.19 Withdrawal of Guilty Plea—Court or Prosecutor

It is well settled that, as a general rule, in the absence of fraud or misrepresentation the court has no statutory or inherent authority to set aside a guilty plea, once accepted, without the defendant's consent.[253]

One narrow exception is that the court may vacate a plea or sentence to correct a patent "clerical" error or where the judge has merely "misspoken."[254] In that case, the correction would have to be to a plea or sentence that fully comported with the expectation of *all* the parties at the time of the entry of plea or the imposition of sentence.[255]

Another narrow exception is that the court may vacate a plea taken in violation of the plea bargaining restrictions set forth in CPL §§ 220.10(5) or 220.30(3), provided it does so prior to the imposition of sentence.[256] Once sentence has been imposed and commenced, the court may not set aside a plea merely because the plea violated those plea-bargaining restrictions.[257]

---

250. See § 11.11, supra.

251. See People v. Franco, 158 A.D.2d 33, 35, 557 N.Y.S.2d 7, 8 (1st Dep't 1990); People v. Davis, 43 A.D.2d 866, 352 N.Y.S.2d 17 (2d Dep't 1974); People v. Jovet, 41 A.D.2d 608, 340 N.Y.S.2d 409 (1st Dep't 1973).

252. See § 11.10, supra.

253. Matter of Kisloff v. Covington, 73 N.Y.2d 445, 541 N.Y.S.2d 737, 539 N.E.2d 565 (1989); Matter of Lockett v. Juviler, 65 N.Y.2d 182, 186–87, 490 N.Y.S.2d 764, 767, 480 N.E.2d 378 (1985), writ granted sub nom. Warren v. Montemango 618 F.Supp. 147 (E.D.N.Y.1985), rev'd sub nom Lockett v. Montemango, 784 F.2d 78 (2d Cir.), cert. denied, 479 U.S. 832, 107 S.Ct. 120, 93 L.Ed.2d 66 (1986); Matter of Campbell v. Pesce, 60 N.Y.2d 165, 168, 468 N.Y.S.2d 865, 456 N.E.2d 806 (1983); Matter of Crooms v. Corriero, 206 A.D.2d 275, 614 N.Y.S.2d 511 (1st Dep't 1994); Matter of Helbrans v. Owens, 205 A.D.2d 775, 613 N.Y.S.2d 924 (2d Dep't 1994); People v. Donnelly, 176 A.D.2d 404, 574 N.Y.S.2d 111 (3d Dep't 1991).

254. Matter of Campbell v. Pesce, 60 N.Y.2d at 169, 468 N.Y.S.2d at 867.

255. Id.

256. People v. Moquin, 77 N.Y.2d 449, 568 N.Y.S.2d 710, 570 N.E.2d 1059 (1991), reargument denied 78 N.Y.2d 952, 573 N.Y.S.2d 647, 578 N.E.2d 445 (1991); People v. Bartley, 47 N.Y.2d 965, 419 N.Y.S.2d 956, 393 N.E.2d 1029 (1979); Matter of Guzman v. Harrigan, 158 A.D.2d 872, 552 N.Y.S.2d 54 (3d Dep't 1990).

257. People v. Moquin, supra; Matter of Campbell v. Pesce, 60 N.Y.2d 165, 468 N.Y.S.2d 865, 456 N.E.2d 806 (1983); People v. Bartley, supra; People v. Donnelly, 176 A.D.2d at 404, 574 N.Y.S.2d at 113;

It is not within the court's power to vacate a guilty plea, without the defendant's consent, merely because the prosecution has second thoughts about the wisdom—as opposed to legality—of the negotiated plea, or because the sentence involves one more lenient than the one offered by a different trial assistant.[258] However, a different rule obtains where the prosecution's consent to the plea is statutorily required,[259] and where the record establishes that its consent is premised upon the imposition of a negotiated sentence, and the court prior to sentence decides to impose a lesser sentence. In that event, prior to imposing such lesser sentence the court should offer the prosecution an opportunity to withdraw their consent to the plea. Absent the defendant's showing that vacatur of the plea would be prejudicial or inappropriate, such relief would properly be granted.[260]

If the court finds it cannot honor its sentence promise, but instead must impose a higher sentence than the one promised at the time of plea, it cannot *sua sponte* vacate the plea; instead, it must then give the pleading defendant the option of either accepting the higher sentence on the plea or withdrawing the plea and going to trial.[261]

It sometimes happens that, at the sentencing proceeding following a guilty plea, the defendant will assert either that he or she is innocent or that the plea was the product of coercion. Sometimes these assertions will have been recorded in the presentence report rather than in open court. In such cases, the appellate courts have upheld the court's decision to *sua sponte* vacate the plea, provided the defendant concurs or does not object.[262] It is improper for the court to take such action,

---

People v. Latora, 128 A.D.2d 808, 513 N.Y.S.2d 511 (2d Dep't 1987). But see People v. Pena, 169 A.D.2d 392, 564 N.Y.S.2d 135 (1st Dep't 1991)(on prosecution's appeal, Appellate Division vacates plea and sentence where guilty plea that violated Article 220 bargaining restrictions was taken over prosecution's contemporaneous objection). Cf. People ex rel. Leventhal v. Warden, 102 A.D.2d 317, 477 N.Y.S.2d 332 (1st Dep't 1984)(plea and sentence set aside on prosecution's Article 78 petition, where action of Criminal Court in accepting misdemeanor plea was null and void). Leventhal is distinguishable from Moquin because misdemeanor pleas taken in satisfaction of felony complaints, by a local criminal court without jurisdiction to do so, are considered a "nullity" and further prosecution is not barred by double jeopardy provisions. See People v. Anderson, 140 A.D.2d 528, 528 N.Y.S.2d 614 (2d Dep't 1988)(plea void where Criminal Court took a misdemeanor plea to a reduced felony complaint after an indictment had been filed, in violation of CPL § 170.20); People v. Phillips, 66 A.D.2d 696, 411 N.Y.S.2d 259 (1st Dep't 1978), aff'd for reasons stated below 48 N.Y.2d 1011, 425 N.Y.S.2d 558, 401 N.E.2d 916 (1980)(same).

258. Matter of Crooms v. Corriero, 206 A.D.2d 275, 614 N.Y.S.2d 511.

259. For situations where the prosecution's consent to the plea would be required, see § 11.3, supra.

260. People v. Cameron, 83 N.Y.2d 838, 611 N.Y.S.2d 499, 633 N.E.2d 1103 (1994); People v. Farrar, 52 N.Y.2d 302, 307-08, 437 N.Y.S.2d 961, 963, 419 N.E.2d 864 (1981); People v. Saa, 199 A.D.2d 346, 604 N.Y.S.2d 258 (2d Dep't 1993); People v. Gannon, 162 A.D.2d 818, 557 N.Y.S.2d 726 (3d Dep't 1990); People v. Martinez, 124 A.D.2d 505, 508 N.Y.S.2d 180 (1st Dep't 1986).

261. People v. Schultz, 73 N.Y.2d 757, 536 N.Y.S.2d 46, 532 N.E.2d 1274 (1988); People v. Selikoff, 35 N.Y.2d 227, 360 N.Y.S.2d 623, 318 N.E.2d 784 (1974); People v. Easterling, 191 A.D.2d 579, 594 N.Y.S.2d 805 (2d Dep't 1993); Matter of Hoffman v. Fisher, 173 A.D.2d 826, 571 N.Y.S.2d 54 (2d Dep't 1991).

262. People v. Robles, 202 A.D.2d 166, 608 N.Y.S.2d 191 (1st Dep't 1994); People v. Harris, 118 A.D.2d 583, 499 N.Y.S.2d 443 (2d Dep't 1986), aff'd 69 N.Y.2d 850, 514 N.Y.S.2d 719, 507 N.E.2d 312 (1987).

§ 11.19   PLEAS   Ch. 11

however, if the defendant nonetheless wishes to stand by his or her guilty plea.[263]

When the defendant feels aggrieved by the court's setting aside of a guilty plea, over objection, his or her best recourse is to file an Article 78 petition in the nature of a writ of prohibition, which does lie.[264] Alternatively, the defendant may go to trial and, in the event of a conviction, raise the issue on direct appeal.[265] If the defendant merely repleads on the indictment, he or she will probably have effectively waived the right to appellate review of the legality of the court's action.[266]

Library References:

West's Key No. Digests, Criminal Law ⚖274.

§ 11.20   Practice Summary—Defense

A. Prior to Entry of Plea

- Advise the defendant of the rights waived by a guilty plea (*see* §§ 11.15, 11.16).
- Prepare the defendant for the factual allocution that will accompany the plea (*see* § 11.10).
- Discuss with the defendant the possibilities of appeal (*see* § 11.16).
- If the plea will involve an appeal waiver, explain which appellate issues will and will not be encompassed by the waiver (*see* § 11.17).

B. During the Plea Proceeding

- Make sure that all sentence promises, by court or prosecutor, are accurately placed on the record (*see* §§ 11.11–11.13).

C. If the Defendant Seeks Plea Withdrawal

- Evaluate whether there is any merit to defendant's claim (*see* § 11.18).
- Consider the possibility of moving to be relieved if the defendant's motion requires you to take a position adverse to the defendant (*see* § 11.18).
- If the defendant's position is not frivolous, ask the court for a hearing on the defense motion (*see* § 11.18).

---

263. People v. Gamble, 128 A.D.2d 724, 513 N.Y.S.2d 217 (2d Dep't 1987); People v. Ford, 65 A.D.2d 822, 410 N.Y.S.2d 343 (2d Dep't 1978); Matter of Fernandez v. Silbowitz, 59 A.D.2d 837, 398 N.Y.S.2d 896 (1st Dep't 1977); People v. Murphy, 53 A.D.2d 530, 384 N.Y.S.2d 180 (1st Dep't 1976).

264. See, e.g., Matter of Kisloff v. Covington, 73 N.Y.2d 445, 541 N.Y.S.2d 737, 539 N.E.2d 565; Matter of Crooms v. Corriero, 206 A.D.2d 275, 614 N.Y.S.2d 511; Matter of Helbrans v. Owens, 205 A.D.2d 775, 613 N.Y.S.2d 924.

265. See, e.g., People v. Gamble, 128 A.D.2d 724, 513 N.Y.S.2d 217 (2d Dep't 1987); People v. Prato, 89 A.D.2d 860, 453 N.Y.S.2d 40 (2d Dep't 1982); People v. Murphy, 53 A.D.2d 530, 384 N.Y.S.2d 180 (1st Dep't 1976).

266. See People v. Albanese, 163 A.D.2d 482, 558 N.Y.S.2d 168 (2d Dep't 1990); People v. Pacheco, 152 A.D.2d 641, 543 N.Y.S.2d 170 (2d Dep't 1989). But see People v. Damsky, 47 A.D.2d 822, 366 N.Y.S.2d 13 (1st Dep't 1975)(second plea vacated on appeal and first plea reinstated, where first plea had been erroneously vacated on prosecution's motion).

D. If the Court or Prosecutor Reneges on a Sentence Promise
- Discuss with the defendant the option of plea withdrawal (*see* § 11.12).
- If the defendant does not wish to withdraw the plea, ask that the court or prosecutor place on the record the reasons for reneging on the promise (*see* § 11.12).
- If the stated reasons for reneging are insufficient, object to the sentence enhancement and state why the reasons are insufficient (*see* § 11.12).

§ 11.21 Practice Summary—Prosecution

A. Prior to Entry of Plea
- Make sure that the plea comports with statutory plea bargaining restrictions (*see* § 11.15).

B. During the Plea Proceeding
- Make sure the court advises the defendant of his or her *Boykin* rights and the direct consequences of the guilty plea (*see* §§ 11.7, 11.9).
- Make sure the defendant admits guilt as to each element of the crime to which the plea is taken (*see* § 11.10).
- Make sure that all sentence promises or conditions are placed on the record (*see* § 11.11).
- Make sure that the court adequately explains any appeal waiver to the defendant (*see* § 11.17).
- Place on the record any objection the prosecution might have to the court's decision to permit the guilty plea (*see* § 11.3). Consider the option of an immediate Article 78 proceeding in the nature of a writ of prohibition (*see* § 11.3).

C. If the Court Violates the Conditions of the Plea Agreement
- If prosecutorial consent was required for entry of the plea, consider the option of withdrawing that consent (*see* § 11.19).
- If the court reneges on its promise and, over your objection, imposes a sentence lower than that agreed to by the prosecution, consider the possible remedies available to you (*see* § 11.19).

§ 11.22 Practice Summary—Court

A. Prior to Entry of Plea (*See* § 11.5)
- Make sure that the plea comports with statutory plea bargaining restrictions.

B. During the Plea Proceedings
- Advise the defendant of the *Boykin* rights and the direct consequences of the plea (*see* §§ 11.7, 11.9).
- Elicit an admission of guilt as to each element of the crime to which the defendant is pleading (*see* § 11.10).
- Make sure that all sentence promises and conditions are placed on the record (*see* § 11.11).
- Make sure that any appeal waiver is adequately explained to the defendant prior to the entry of the plea (*see* § 11.17).

C. **If the Court Wishes to Depart from the Promised Sentence**
   - If the court wishes to enhance the sentence, it must place its reasons on the record (see § 11.12).
   - Offer the defendant the option of plea withdrawal, unless the record of the plea clearly indicates that unilateral action on the court's part was contemplated by the plea agreement (see § 11.13).
   - If the defendant has violated a "no-arrest" condition, make inquiry, upon defense request, into the validity of the new arrest (see § 11.13).

D. **If the Defendant Seeks to Withdraw the Plea** (See § 11.18)
   - Allow defendant or his counsel to place the reasons for plea withdrawal on the record, and make inquiry into the claim.
   - Relieve defense counsel and assign new counsel if a hearing on the motion is required and that hearing would require counsel to take a position adverse to the defendant.

§ 11.23 Forms

§ 11.23.1 Notice of Motion to Withdraw Guilty Plea

[Caption]

COUNSEL:

PLEASE TAKE NOTICE, that upon the annexed papers and all the prior papers and proceedings herein, the undersigned will move this Court, at Part ___ thereof, to be held at the Courthouse at _____, New York, on the ___ day of _____, at ___ in the forenoon, or as soon thereafter as counsel can be heard for an order, pursuant to section 220.60 of the Criminal Procedural Law, permitting the defendant herein to withdraw his plea of guilty and restoring him to pre-pleading status, together with such other and further relief as the Court deems just and proper.

Dated: _____, 19__.
_____, New York

                              [Name of defense attorney]
                              Attorney for Defendant
                              Address
                              Tel. No.

To: HON. _____
     District Attorney
     _____ County

     HON. _____
     Clerk of the Court
     _____ County

§ 11.23.2 Affirmation of Attorney Upon Motion to Withdraw Guilty Plea

[Caption]

_____, an attorney duly admitted to practice in the Courts of this State, hereby affirms under the penalties of perjury that the following statements are true, except those made on information and belief, which he [she] believes to be true:

1. I am the attorney for the defendant herein.

2. On _____, 199__, the defendant pleaded guilty in this Court to [specify offense(s)].

3. After discussion with the defendant about the circumstances under which he pleaded guilty, I believe that defendant was unaware of the consequences of his guilty plea, that he [she] pleaded guilty not because he [she] was guilty but because [specify reasons defendant pleaded guilty].

4. After discussions with the defendant, and based upon the record of the plea proceedings, I believe that defendant was unaware at the time of the plea that he had a meritorious defense to the prosecution, to wit: [specify meritorious defense].

5. [if appropriate] Upon information and belief, defendant had never previously been convicted of a crime or offense, nor had he had any prior familiarity with the criminal justice system.

WHEREFORE, defendant requests that his [her] guilty plea be vacated and the matter returned to pre-pleading status.

[Signature]

_____

[Name of defense attorney]

Dated: _____, 199__.

§ 11.23.3 Affidavit of Defendant Upon Motion to Withdraw Guilty Plea

[Caption]

STATE OF NEW YORK)
) ss.:
COUNTY OF _____)

_____, being duly sworn, deposes and says:

1. I am the defendant in the above-captioned matter.

2. I was accused by [complainant] of committing the offense(s) of [specify offense(s) charged].

3. [specify defendant's version of events]

4. At my plea proceedings, I pleaded guilty not because I was guilty, but because [specify reasons for guilty plea].

5. I am not guilty of the crime to which I pleaded guilty. [if applicable] I have never before been convicted of any crime and I am not familiar with court procedures. I was confused when I pleaded guilty.

§ 11.23   PLEAS   Ch. 11

WHEREFORE, defendant respectfully requests that he [she] be permitted to withdraw his [her] plea of guilty and to have the charges reinstated as they were prior to the time of guilty plea.

                                   [Signature]
                                   _____
                                   [Name of defendant]

Sworn to before me this ___ day of _____, 199__

_____
Notary Public

TABLE OF STATUTES

NEW YORK, MCKINNEY'S CONSTITUTION

Art.	This Work Sec.	Note
1, § 2	11.2	3
1, § 5	4.1	2
1, § 6	2.1	3
	2.2	10
	5.1	2
	5.8	175
	5.9	194
	5.10	
	5.10	299
	5.11	307
	5.11	311
	5.14	328
	5.20	465
	5.22	568
	5.31	
	9.1	
	9.9	
	9.51	365
	9.56	
	9.58	
1, § 12	10.2	
	10.3	53
	10.5	
6, § 7	1.2	10
	1.2	23
6, § 11	1.2	23
6, § 15(c)	1.2	25
6, § 16(d)	1.2	25
6, § 17(b)	1.2	25
6, § 18(a)	1.8	176
6, § 27	5.2	19
6, § 28	5.2	
6, § 35	1.2	9

NEW YORK, MCKINNEY'S CIVIL PRACTICE LAW AND RULES

Sec.	This Work Sec.	Note
105	4.2	26
207	9.5	17
506(b)	2.11	248
Art. 13–A	1.2	27
	2.10	222
	2.10	233
	4.12	213
1310	4.2	26
1310(8)	2.10	224
1310(10)	4.3	49
1311(1)	2.10	226
1311(1)(a)	2.10	233
1312	4.3	49

NEW YORK, MCKINNEY'S CIVIL PRACTICE LAW AND RULES

Sec.	This Work Sec.	Note
2307	7.8	77
2309(a)	3.6	56
4504	7.30	327
4506	10.11	
4506(2)	10.11	
4508	7.30	328
4510	7.30	332
4518	3.7	
5015	4.12	204
5016(a)	2.2	13
5205	4.2	
5240	4.12	204
5602	4.2	27
Art. 70	3.19	215
	4.13	
7002	4.13	216
7010(b)	4.13	
Art. 78	1.11	
	2.11	
	2.12	
	2.13	
	5.9	210
	5.12	314
	5.27	
	5.27	695
	7.11	128
	11.3	
	11.3	17
	11.19	
	11.19	257
	11.21	
7803(2)	2.11	247
7804(b)	2.11	248

NEW YORK, MCKINNEY'S CIVIL RIGHTS LAW

Sec.	This Work Sec.	Note
12	9.1	
	9.9	68
50–a	7.30	325
	7.30	340
79–h	7.30	330
79–h(b)	7.30	346
79–h(c)	7.30	347

NEW YORK, MCKINNEY'S CODE OF CRIMINAL PROCEDURE

Sec.	This Work Sec.	Note
22(8) (former)	4.13	215

689

TABLE OF STATUTES

NEW YORK, MCKINNEY'S CODE OF CRIMINAL PROCEDURE

Sec.	This Work Sec.	Note
170	3.14	147
279	5.22	562
295–b(2)	5.14	331
395	10.7	138
759 (former)	4.9	116
760 (former)	4.9	116
807	10.7	138
809	10.7	138
813–1	10.7	138
813–c	10.7	138
813–d	10.7	138
813–e	10.7	138
	10.12	245
	10.12	248
	10.12	250
	10.13	277
813–f	10.7	138
813–g	10.7	138
813–h	10.7	138
	10.14	284
813–i	10.7	138
813–m	10.7	138

NEW YORK, MCKINNEY'S CORRECTION LAW

Sec.	This Work Sec.	Note
500–a(2)	3.24	320
500–m	4.2	12
803(1)	6.6	128

NEW YORK, MCKINNEY'S COUNTY LAW

Sec.	This Work Sec.	Note
722	3.24	305
722–a	3.24	296
Art. 18–B	3.24	305
	3.30	407
	9.42	

NEW YORK, MCKINNEY'S CRIMINAL PROCEDURE LAW

Sec.	This Work Sec.	Note
1.20(1)	1.2	26
	9.46	331
1.20(2)	1.5	127
	1.8	163
1.20(3)	5.11	303
	9.37	266
1.20(8)	1.7	155
1.20(9)	1.1	2
	1.1	4
	5.24	632
1.20(11)	2.7	166
	10.14	283
1.20(13)	2.2	12
	4.7	100

NEW YORK, MCKINNEY'S CRIMINAL PROCEDURE LAW

Sec.	This Work Sec.	Note
1.20(13) (Cont'd)	4.9	110
1.20(15)	2.2	15
1.20(16)	1.2	12
	1.8	164
	4.4	50
	9.15	140
	9.46	331
	10.13	280
1.20(17)	1.2	12
	3.1	4
	3.5	50
	9.15	138
	9.15	139
	9.46	331
	10.13	280
1.20(18)	1.2	12
	1.2	27
	4.4	50
	5.6	86
1.20(19)	1.2	8
1.20(20)	1.2	8
1.20(21)	1.2	8
1.20(24)	1.2	14
	5.11	304
1.20(25)	1.2	13
	5.11	304
1.20(26)	4.8	104
1.20(28)	9.37	267
1.20(29)	9.37	267
1.20(30)	4.10	161
1.20(34)	11.3	11
1.20(34–a)	3.12	131
1.20(35)	4.2	12
1.20(37)	5.18	436
	5.27	702
1.20(38)	3.6	56
1.20(39)	1.2	15
	3.2	7
1.20(41)	3.3	27
	3.32	434
	11.3	
	11.5	
1.20(41)(a)	1.10	240
1.20(42)	1.10	214
	3.19	235
	3.33	471
2.20(1)(d)	3.20	241
5.18	5.13	327
Art. 10	1.1	
	2.8	
10.00(6)	5.20	466
10.10(1)	1.2	8
10.10(2)	5.11	303
10.10(3)	1.2	19
10.10(4)	1.2	20
10.10(7)	1.2	26
10.20	1.1	2
	10.20	
10.20(1)	1.2	15
10.20(1)(c)	1.2	24
10.20(2)	1.2	18
10.20(5)	1.2	21

690

TABLE OF STATUTES

NEW YORK, MCKINNEY'S CRIMINAL PROCEDURE LAW

Sec.	This Work Sec.	Note
10.20(6)	1.2	22
10.30	1.1	2
	1.5	125
10.30(1)	1.2	24
10.30(1)(a)	1.2	24
10.30(2)	1.2	25
	3.30	403
	6.7	152
10.30(3)	1.2	18
	1.2	23
Art. 20	1.1	
	1.3	
	1.4	
	1.5	
	2.6	
20.10(1)	1.3	69
20.10(2)	1.4	83
20.10(3)	1.3	47
	2.6	148
20.10(4)	1.3	57
20.20	1.3	39
	1.3	68
	2.7	160
20.20(1)(a)	1.3	40
	1.3	48
20.20(1)(b)	1.3	41
20.20(1)(c)	1.3	42
	1.4	92
20.20(2)(a)	1.3	48
	1.3	49
	2.6	148
20.20(2)(a)—(2)(d)	1.3	45
20.20(2)(b)	1.3	56
20.20(2)(c)	1.3	65
20.20(2)(d)	1.3	66
20.20(3)	1.3	46
20.30	1.3	
	1.3	68
	1.11	
20.30(1)	1.3	68
20.30(2)	1.3	68
20.40	1.1	2
	1.3	35
	2.7	160
	9.6	32
20.40(1)(a)	1.4	85
	1.4	117
	1.4	121
20.40(1)(b)	1.4	91
	1.4	92
20.40(2)(a)	1.4	93
	2.6	148
20.40(2)(b)	1.4	94
20.40(2)(c)	1.4	95
20.40(2)(d)	1.4	96
20.40(2)(e)	1.4	97
20.40(3)	1.4	98
20.40(4)(a)	1.4	100
20.40(4)(a)—(4)(k)	1.4	99
20.40(4)(b)	1.4	101
20.40(4)(c)	1.4	106
	1.4	117

NEW YORK, MCKINNEY'S CRIMINAL PROCEDURE LAW

Sec.	This Work Sec.	Note
20.40(4)(c) (Cont'd)	1.5	139
20.40(4)(d)	1.4	107
20.40(4)(e)	1.4	109
	1.4	117
20.40(4)(f)	1.4	114
	1.4	116
20.40(4)(g)	1.4	110
20.40(4)(h)	1.4	115
20.40(4)(i)	1.4	108
20.40(4)(j)	1.4	102
20.40(4)(k)	1.4	105
20.50	1.2	25
	1.5	137
20.50(1)	1.5	138
20.50(2)	1.5	139
20.60	1.4	116
	1.4	121
	1.4	124
20.60(1)	1.4	118
20.60(2)	1.4	119
20.60(3)	1.4	120
Art. 30	9.1	
30.10	9.1	
	9.2	
	9.3	
	9.6	
	9.6	29
	9.58	
30.10(1)	3.1	5
	9.3	5
30.10(2)	9.3	5
	9.4	
	9.6	
	9.58	
30.10(2)(a)	9.3	6
30.10(2)(b)	9.3	8
30.10(2)(c)	9.3	9
30.10(2)(d)	9.3	10
30.10(3)	9.3	
	9.58	
30.10(3)(a)	9.4	
30.10(3)(b)	9.4	
30.10(3)(c)	9.4	
30.10(3)(d)	9.4	
30.10(4)(a)(i)	9.5	17
30.10(4)(a)(ii)	9.5	18
30.10(4)(b)	9.5	
30.20	9.9	
	9.12	121
	9.13	
	9.51	365
	9.58	
30.20(1)	9.1	
	9.9	
30.20(2)	9.11	
	9.11	111
	9.11	112
30.30	3.25	
	9.1	
	9.10	99
	9.12	
	9.12	121

691

TABLE OF STATUTES

NEW YORK, MCKINNEY'S CRIMINAL PROCEDURE LAW

Sec.	This Work Sec.	Note
30.30 (Cont'd)	9.13	
	9.13	124
	9.13	125
	9.14	
	9.15	
	9.16	
	9.16	151
	9.17	
	9.17	158
	9.18	
	9.19	
	9.20	
	9.20	163
	9.20	165
	9.21	
	9.23	
	9.23	184
	9.24	
	9.30	233
	9.33	
	9.34	256
	9.36	
	9.40	
	9.46	
	9.47	
	9.47	332
	9.47	345
	9.48	
	9.49	
	9.49	356
	9.49	361
	9.49	363
	9.50	
	9.51	
	9.51	365
	9.51	380
	9.52	
	9.52	385
	9.52	387
	9.56	
	9.57	
	11.15	
30.30(1)	3.1	4
	3.11	117
	9.13	
	9.26	
	9.46	331
	9.49	
	9.56	
	9.58	
30.30(1)(a)	9.18	
	9.24	191
	9.58	
30.30(1)(a)—(1)(d)	9.24	189
30.30(1)(b)	9.24	195
30.30(1)(c)	9.24	196
30.30(1)(d)	9.14	135
	9.24	197
30.30(2)	4.10	130
	9.13	
	9.25	
	9.25	198

NEW YORK, MCKINNEY'S CRIMINAL PROCEDURE LAW

Sec.	This Work Sec.	Note
30.30(2) (Cont'd)	9.25	203
	9.26	
	9.49	
	9.49	357
	9.56	
	9.58	
30.30(2)(a)	9.18	
	9.25	199
	9.58	
30.30(2)(b)	9.25	200
30.30(2)(c)	9.25	201
30.30(2)(d)	9.25	202
30.30(3)(a)	9.25	
30.30(3)(b)	9.26	
	9.37	265
	9.47	
	9.48	
	9.51	
30.30(3)(c)(i)	9.25	209
30.30(3)(c)(ii)	9.25	210
30.30(3)(c)(iii)	9.25	211
30.30(4)	9.15	
	9.26	
30.30(4)(a)	6.3	
	9.26	
	9.27	
	9.33	
	9.47	
	9.47	336
30.30(4)(a)—(4)(f)	9.43	
30.30(4)(a)—(4)(j)	9.26	
30.30(4)(b)	9.33	
	9.33	246
	9.34	
	9.42	
	9.43	
	9.44	
	9.47	
	9.47	336
30.30(4)(c)	9.13	129
	9.33	247
	9.35	
	9.36	
	9.37	
	9.37	266
	9.38	273
	9.47	
	9.47	346
	9.51	
30.30(4)(d)	9.40	
30.30(4)(e)	9.41	
	9.47	
30.30(4)(f)	9.34	256
	9.42	
	9.42	297
30.30(4)(g)	9.43	
	9.47	335
30.30(4)(h)	3.29	383
	3.29	384
	9.44	
30.30(4)(h)—(4)(j)	9.43	
30.30(4)(i)	9.45	

692

TABLE OF STATUTES

NEW YORK, MCKINNEY'S CRIMINAL PROCEDURE LAW

Sec.	This Work Sec.	Note
30.30(4)(j)	9.46	
30.30(5)	9.18	
	9.19	
30.30(5)(a)	9.16	
30.30(5)(b)	9.17	
	9.17	158
	9.36	
30.30(5)(c)	9.13	128
	9.18	
	9.19	
	9.19	162
30.30(5)(d)	9.18	
	9.19	
	9.19	162
30.30(5)(e)	9.19	
	9.19	162
30.30(5)(f)	9.19	
	9.19	162
Art. 40	2.1	
	2.6	
	2.10	238
	5.32	
40.10(1)	2.5	93
	2.5	96
40.10(2)	2.5	94
	2.7	156
	5.21	478
	5.22	
	5.22	552
40.10(2)(a)	2.6	115
	2.6	116
40.10(2)(b)	2.6	119
40.20	2.9	209
	11.15	
40.20(1)	2.5	93
	2.5	96
40.20(1)(b)	2.7	166
40.20(2)	2.5	94
	2.6	115
	2.7	
40.20(2)(a)	2.6	125
40.20(2)(a)—(2)(h)	2.6	115
	2.6	124
40.20(2)(b)	2.6	130
40.20(2)(c)	2.6	133
40.20(2)(d)	2.6	137
40.20(2)(e)	2.6	140
	2.7	157
40.20(2)(f)	2.6	144
40.20(2)(g)	2.6	132
	2.6	146
40.20(2)(h)	2.6	150
	2.9	197
	2.9	208
	2.9	209
40.30	2.2	
	2.9	
40.30(1)	1.3	37
	2.2	24
	2.8	175
40.30(1)(a)	2.2	11
40.30(1)(b)	2.2	11

NEW YORK, MCKINNEY'S CRIMINAL PROCEDURE LAW

Sec.	This Work Sec.	Note
40.30(1)(b) (Cont'd)	2.2	16
	2.2	19
	2.4	38
40.30(2)(a)	2.3	28
40.30(2)(b)	2.3	32
40.30(2)(g)	2.6	120
40.30(3)	2.4	37
	2.4	83
40.30(4)	2.4	37
40.40	2.5	95
	2.7	153
40.40(1)	2.7	155
	2.7	159
	5.21	477
40.40(2)	2.7	158
	2.7	161
	2.8	174
40.40(2)(a)	5.21	485
40.40(3)	2.7	167
	5.21	481
40.50	2.9	197
	2.9	209
40.50(1)(a)	2.9	196
	2.9	198
40.50(1)(b)	2.9	199
40.50(1)(c)	2.9	200
40.50(1)(d)	2.9	201
40.50(2)	2.9	202
40.50(3)	2.9	203
	2.9	206
40.50(4)	2.9	206
40.50(5)	2.9	204
40.50(8)	2.9	207
40.50(9)	2.9	208
	2.9	209
50.10	5.9	
	5.9	196
	5.9	210
	5.30	
50.10(1)	5.9	195
	5.9	211
50.10(3)	5.9	
	5.9	229
50.10(4)	5.9	221
Art. 60	10.19	438
60.10	5.6	
	10.19	438
60.10(1)	5.6	
60.15	10.19	418
60.15(1)	10.19	407
	10.19	409
60.15(2)	10.19	412
	3.6	58
	3.33	447
	10.19	438
60.20(3)	5.27	717
60.22	3.6	
	5.27	717
60.45	10.8	143
	10.17	348
	10.22	526
	10.25	563

693

TABLE OF STATUTES

NEW YORK, MCKINNEY'S CRIMINAL PROCEDURE LAW			NEW YORK, MCKINNEY'S CRIMINAL PROCEDURE LAW		
		This Work			This Work
Sec.	Sec.	Note	Sec.	Sec.	Note
60.45 (Cont'd)	10.25	565	100.30(1)(a)	3.6	53
60.50	3.7		100.30(1)(b)	3.6	54
	3.7	79	100.30(1)(c)	3.6	56
	5.27	717	100.30(1)(d)	3.6	57
60.76	7.30	340	100.30(1)(e)	3.6	55
70.10	5.27	714	100.30(2)	3.6	52
70.10(1)	2.4	87	100.35	3.3	30
	2.7	163		3.3	31
	3.7	68		3.3	32
	3.7	80		3.7	
	5.6		100.40	3.7	
	5.27			3.24	287
70.10(2)	3.7	67		3.25	322
	3.18	191		3.27	354
	8.2		100.40(1)	3.2	12
70.20	2.7	163		3.13	134
	5.27	710	100.40(1)(a)	3.7	66
Art. 78	1.4		100.40(1)(b)	3.7	67
	1.8	180	100.40(1)(c)	3.7	68
Art. 100	8.1		100.40(2)	3.7	83
100.05	3.1	1		3.7	84
	3.1	3	100.40(3)	3.7	90
	3.5	49	100.40(4)	3.13	134
	3.5	50	100.40(4)(a)	3.7	87
100.07	9.46	330	100.40(4)(b)	3.7	89
100.10(1)	3.2	11	100.45	8.1	
100.10(2)	3.2	18	100.45(1)	3.5	40
	3.2	19		3.8	91
100.10(3)	3.2	14	100.45(1)(c)	3.4	38
100.10(4)	3.2	7	100.45(2)	3.5	40
	3.2	8		3.8	93
100.10(5)	3.2	9		3.36	
	3.2	10	100.45(3)	3.8	96
100.15	3.7			3.8	101
100.15(1)	3.3	22		3.9	106
	3.3	23		3.36	
	3.3	25	100.45(4)	3.8	92
	3.7	88	100.50(1)	3.9	102
100.15(2)	3.3	27		3.9	103
	3.3	29	100.50(2)	3.2	
100.15(3)	3.3	24		3.2	17
	3.3	26		3.8	101
100.15(4)	3.32	434		3.9	106
100.15(4)(a)	3.3	27		3.9	107
100.20	3.2			3.9	108
	3.4			3.27	366
	3.4	36	100.55	1.2	25
	3.4	37		1.5	126
	3.5			3.13	
100.25	3.5			3.13	138
100.25(1)	3.3	33		3.19	
	3.7			3.19	224
100.25(2)	3.2		100.55(1)	1.5	128
	3.5		100.55(2)	1.5	129
	3.5	39		1.5	136
	3.5	42	100.55(3)	1.5	130
	3.5	44	100.55(5)	1.5	131
	3.5	46		1.5	132
	3.5	47	100.55(6)	1.7	157
	3.7	85	100.55(7)	1.5	133
	3.36		100.55(8)	1.5	135
100.30	3.3		100.55(10)	1.5	137

694

TABLE OF STATUTES

NEW YORK, MCKINNEY'S CRIMINAL PROCEDURE LAW

Sec.	This Work Sec.	Note
110.10	3.10	111
Art. 120	3.10	112
120.10(1)	3.11	116
	3.11	121
	3.15	174
	3.16	175
120.10(2)	3.12	124
	3.12	125
	3.12	129
120.10(3)	3.12	130
120.20	9.45	
120.20(1)	3.2	21
	3.7	65
	3.13	132
	3.13	133
120.20(2)	3.13	134
	3.13	135
120.20(3)	3.13	136
	3.13	137
	3.16	175
	9.45	
	9.45	327
120.30(1)	3.15	166
	3.13	138
	3.13	139
120.40	3.15	167
120.50	3.12	131
120.60(2)	3.14	140
120.60(2)(b)	3.14	141
120.60(3)	3.14	142
120.70(1)	3.14	143
120.70(2)	3.14	141
120.70(2)(a)	3.14	144
120.70(2)(b)	3.14	145
120.80(1)	3.14	146
120.80(2)	3.14	149
	3.14	150
120.80(3)	3.14	151
120.80(4)	3.14	152
	3.14	153
	3.14	157
	3.15	165
	3.18	208
120.80(5)	3.14	158
	3.18	209
120.90(1)	3.15	159
120.90(2)	3.15	162
120.90(3)	3.15	160
	3.15	161
120.90(4)	3.15	164
120.90(5)	1.7	143
	3.15	168
120.90(6)	3.15	169
	3.15	170
Art. 130	3.10	113
	5.23	
130.10	3.16	176
130.10(1)	3.16	177
	3.16	178
130.10(2)	3.16	183
130.20	3.16	177
	3.16	181

NEW YORK, MCKINNEY'S CRIMINAL PROCEDURE LAW

Sec.	This Work Sec.	Note
130.30	3.7	65
	3.16	179
130.40(1)	3.16	184
130.40(2)	3.16	185
130.50	3.16	186
130.50(4–a)	3.5	45
130.60	5.23	
	5.23	631
130.60(1)	3.23	280
130.60(2)	3.23	281
Art. 140	3.10	114
	3.17	
140.10(1)	3.19	216
140.10(1)(a)	3.18	192
140.10(1)(b)	3.18	194
140.10(2)	3.18	196
140.10(2)(b)	3.18	196
140.10(3)	3.18	195
140.10(4)(a)	3.18	198
140.10(4)(b)(i)	3.18	201
140.10(4)(b)(ii)	3.18	202
140.10(4)(c)	3.18	199
140.15(1)	3.18	204
140.15(2)	3.18	205
140.15(3)	3.18	206
140.15(4)	3.18	208
	3.18	209
140.20(1)	1.7	143
	3.15	171
	3.19	
	3.19	210
	3.19	224
	3.36	
140.20(1)(a)	3.19	227
140.20(1)(b)	3.19	229
140.20(1)(c)	3.19	225
140.20(1)(d)	3.19	230
140.20(2)	4.8	104
140.20(3)	3.20	240
	3.19	232
	3.19	233
140.20(4)	3.19	234
140.20(5)	3.23	277
140.20(6)	3.19	236
140.25	3.18	196
140.27	3.18	196
140.27(2)	3.23	277
140.27(4)	4.8	104
140.27(4)(b)	3.20	245
140.30	3.18	196
140.35	3.18	196
140.40	3.18	196
	3.23	277
140.40(1)	3.23	277
140.40(3)(a)	3.20	245
140.40(4)	3.23	277
140.45	3.19	222
	3.19	223
	3.21	262
	3.24	287
	3.30	409
140.50	3.17	188

695

TABLE OF STATUTES

NEW YORK, MCKINNEY'S CRIMINAL PROCEDURE LAW

Sec.	This Work Sec.	Note
140.55	3.18	195
Art. 150	3.10	115
	4.8	104
150.10	3.16	177
	3.20	237
	3.20	242
150.20	3.20	238
150.20(1)	3.20	244
150.20(2)	3.20	244
	3.21	250
150.20(2)(b)	3.20	245
150.20(2)(c)	3.20	245
150.20(3)	3.20	243
150.30	3.21	250
	4.8	106
150.30(1)	3.21	253
150.30(2)	3.21	251
	3.21	252
	4.8	107
150.30(2)(d)	3.22	267
150.30(3)	3.21	255
	3.21	256
	4.8	108
	4.8	109
150.40(2)	3.20	247
150.40(3)	3.20	248
150.40(4)	3.20	249
150.50(1)	3.21	257
150.50(2)	3.21	262
150.60	3.21	260
150.70	3.23	279
150.75	3.22	265
	3.22	266
160.10	3.23	
	3.23	269
	5.23	631
160.10(1)	3.23	277
160.10(1)(a)	3.23	270
160.10(1)(b)	3.23	271
160.10(1)(c)	3.23	272
160.10(1)(d)	3.23	273
160.10(1)(e)	3.23	273
160.10(2)(a)	3.23	274
160.10(2)(b)	3.23	275
160.10(2)(c)	3.23	276
160.10(3)	3.23	269
160.10(4)	5.23	631
160.20	3.23	282
160.30	3.23	282
160.30(2)	3.19	215
160.40	3.23	283
160.40(2)	3.30	426
	3.24	316
	7.15	171
160.50	3.12	122
	5.3	49
	7.30	326
160.50(3)(b)	3.29	384
	3.29	402
160.55	7.30	326
170.05	1.8	167
170.10	3.24	

NEW YORK, MCKINNEY'S CRIMINAL PROCEDURE LAW

Sec.	This Work Sec.	Note
170.10 (Cont'd)	3.32	
170.10(1)(a)	3.24	288
170.10(1)(b)	3.24	289
170.10(2)	3.24	286
170.10(3)	3.24	291
170.10(3)(a)	3.24	292
170.10(3)(b)	3.24	293
170.10(3)(c)	3.24	294
	3.24	296
170.10(4)(a)	3.24	295
170.10(4)(b)	3.24	311
170.10(4)(c)	3.24	310
170.10(4)(d)	3.24	309
170.10(6)	3.24	298
	3.24	312
170.10(7)	3.24	320
	4.4	52
	4.4	53
	4.5	61
170.10(8)	3.24	314
170.15	3.15	168
	3.19	230
	8.1	
170.15(1)	1.7	142
	1.7	156
170.15(2)	1.7	144
	1.7	156
170.15(3)	1.7	146
	1.8	177
	1.8	183
170.15(3)(a)	1.7	147
	1.12	
170.15(3)(b)	1.7	149
	1.12	
170.20	1.8	162
	1.8	172
	1.8	174
	5.20	468
	10.12	251
	11.3	16
	11.19	257
170.20(1)	1.8	163
	1.8	168
170.20(2)	1.8	166
	1.12	
	3.32	
	11.3	16
170.20(2)(a)	1.8	164
	1.8	169
170.25	1.8	171
	1.12	
	5.20	469
170.25(1)	1.8	173
	1.9	188
170.25(2)	1.8	172
170.25(3)	1.8	172
170.25(3)(a)	1.8	172
170.25(3)(b)	1.8	172
170.25(3)(c)	1.8	172
170.25(3)(d)	1.8	172
170.30	3.26	
	3.36	

TABLE OF STATUTES

NEW YORK, MCKINNEY'S CRIMINAL PROCEDURE LAW

Sec.	This Work Sec.	Note
170.30 (Cont'd)	9.51	366
170.30(1)	3.36	
	9.12	
170.30(1)(a)	3.26	343
	3.27	354
170.30(1)(b)	3.26	342
170.30(1)(c)	2.11	239
	2.13	
	3.26	341
170.30(1)(d)	3.26	340
	9.6	23
170.30(1)(e)	3.26	339
	9.12	
	9.49	
	9.49	356
170.30(1)(f)	3.26	345
170.30(1)(g)	3.26	344
	3.36	
170.30(2)	3.26	348
	8.1	17
	9.12	115
	9.12	119
170.30(3)	3.26	349
	3.26	350
170.30(4)	1.8	175
170.30(*l*)(e)	9.12	115
170.35	3.7	64
170.35(1)(b)	3.27	355
170.35(1)(c)	3.27	356
170.35(2)	3.27	357
170.35(3)(a)	3.27	359
170.35(3)(b)	3.27	368
170.40	3.28	369
	3.36	
170.40(1)	3.28	372
	3.36	
170.40(1)(a)—(1)(j)	3.28	373
170.40(1)(e)	1.1	5
170.40(2)	3.28	371
	3.28	374
170.45	3.26	351
	9.51	366
170.50	3.7	64
170.50(1)(a)	3.27	360
170.50(1)(b)	3.27	361
170.50(2)	3.27	362
170.50(3)	3.27	363
170.55	3.29	378
	3.36	
	7.18	217
	9.44	321
170.55(1)	3.29	379
170.55(2)	3.29	380
	3.36	
170.55(3)	3.29	385
	4.10	135
170.55(4)	3.29	386
170.55(5)	3.29	387
170.55(6)	3.29	388
170.55(7)	3.29	389
170.55(8)	3.29	384
	3.29	396

NEW YORK, MCKINNEY'S CRIMINAL PROCEDURE LAW

Sec.	This Work Sec.	Note
170.56	3.29	399
	7.18	217
	9.44	321
170.56(1)	3.29	400
170.56(2)	3.29	401
	3.29	402
170.56(3)	3.29	402
170.65	3.27	
170.65(1)	3.25	321
	3.25	323
170.65(2)	3.25	326
	3.25	328
170.65(3)	3.2	
	3.7	72
	3.25	329
	3.25	333
170.70	3.25	
	3.34	475
	3.36	
170.70(1)	3.25	333
170.70(2)	3.25	334
Art. 180	11.2	9
180.10	3.24	285
180.10(1)	3.30	405
	3.30	412
	3.34	477
180.10(2)	3.30	413
	3.30	416
	3.33	445
180.10(3)	3.30	406
180.10(4)	3.30	407
180.20	1.7	141
	1.7	154
	3.15	168
	3.19	230
180.20(1)	1.7	157
180.20(1–a)	1.7	158
180.20(2)	1.7	160
180.20(6)	4.4	52
	4.4	53
180.30	1.10	220
	5.10	272
	5.10	284
180.30(1)	3.30	419
	3.30	420
180.40	3.31	427
	3.31	428
180.50	1.7	159
	1.10	220
	3.2	
	3.30	
	3.31	
	3.32	431
	3.33	
	9.5	
180.50(1)	3.32	432
	11.3	15
	11.5	40
180.50(2)	11.3	15
	11.5	
	11.5	40
	3.30	421

697

TABLE OF STATUTES

NEW YORK, MCKINNEY'S CRIMINAL PROCEDURE LAW

Sec.	This Work Sec.	Note
180.50(2)(a)	3.3	27
	3.32	433
	3.32	434
	5.10	
180.50(3)	3.33	470
	3.33	471
180.50(3)(a)	3.2	16
	3.32	436
180.50(3)(a)(i)	3.9	109
180.50(3)(b)	3.32	437
180.50(3)(c)	3.32	440
180.50(3)(d)	3.32	438
	3.32	441
180.60(2)	3.33	455
180.60(4)	3.33	447
	3.33	451
180.60(5)	3.33	447
180.60(6)	3.33	452
180.60(7)	3.33	453
180.60(8)	3.33	449
180.60(9)	3.33	464
	3.33	465
	3.36	465
180.70	1.7	159
	1.10	220
	3.2	
180.70(1)	3.33	469
	5.10	285
180.70(2)	3.2	16
	3.33	471
180.70(3)	3.3	27
	3.33	470
	11.5	
	11.5	40
180.70(4)	3.33	472
180.75	1.10	217
180.75(1)	1.10	220
180.75(3)	1.10	221
	3.33	471
180.75(4)	1.10	222
180.75(5)	1.10	223
	1.10	225
	1.10	236
180.75(6)(a)	1.10	228
180.75(6)(b)	1.10	228
180.75(6)(c)	1.10	227
180.75(6)(d)	1.10	226
180.75(6)(f)	1.10	224
	1.10	256
180.80	1.8	163
	3.25	
	3.25	332
	3.25	335
	3.30	
	3.34	
	3.34	474
	3.36	
	4.10	
	5.8	
	5.8	130
180.80(2)(a)	3.34	478
180.80(2)(b)	3.34	479

NEW YORK, MCKINNEY'S CRIMINAL PROCEDURE LAW

Sec.	This Work Sec.	Note
180.80(3)	3.34	481
Art. 182	3.24	
	3.30	426
Art. 190	5.5	
	5.32	
	8.2	
190.05	5.1	
190.10	5.2	
190.15(1)	5.2	21
190.20(1)	5.2	23
190.20(4)	5.3	41
190.20(5)	5.5	62
	5.5	63
190.25	5.2	
	5.3	
190.25(1)	5.8	118
	8.2	
190.25(3)	5.3	
	5.3	33
190.25(3)(h)	5.3	
190.25(4)	5.3	
	5.3	43
	5.27	696
190.25(4)(a)	5.3	46
190.25(6)	5.4	
	5.5	
	5.27	747
	5.27	748
	8.2	
190.30	3.33	
	5.5	
	5.6	95
	5.27	
190.30(1)	5.6	
190.30(2)	3.33	448
	3.35	
190.30(3)	3.33	448
	3.35	
190.30(6)	5.4	
190.30(7)	5.4	
	5.5	65
190.32	5.3	
	7.16	
190.40	5.9	
	5.9	196
	5.9	225
190.40(1)	5.9	192
190.40(2)	5.9	
190.40(2)(b)	5.9	227
190.40(2)(c)	5.9	
	5.9	236
190.45	5.8	
	5.9	
	5.9	246
	5.30	
190.45(1)	5.9	244
	5.9	245
190.45(2)	5.9	243
190.45(4)	5.9	
190.50	3.30	423
	5.8	
	5.8	147

698

TABLE OF STATUTES

NEW YORK, MCKINNEY'S CRIMINAL PROCEDURE LAW

Sec.	This Work Sec.	Note
190.50 (Cont'd)	5.8	165
	5.20	472
	5.26	
	5.27	
	5.32	
	5.33	
	6.3	
	6.7	
190.50(1)	5.8	111
190.50(2)	5.8	113
	5.8	115
	5.8	149
190.50(3)	5.8	
190.50(4)	5.8	119
190.50(5)	5.8	
	5.33	
190.50(5)(a)	3.30	
	3.30	424
	3.35	
	5.8	131
	5.8	137
	5.8	141
	5.8	159
190.50(5)(b)	5.8	177
190.50(5)(c)	5.8	122
	5.8	126
	5.26	645
	8.1	19
190.50(6)	5.8	187
	5.8	188
190.52	5.9	
	5.9	222
	5.9	246
190.52(2)	5.9	254
	5.9	259
	5.9	260
190.60	5.33	
	1.8	164
190.60(2)	1.10	229
190.60(3)	5.21	497
190.65	5.27	
190.65(1)	2.7	164
	3.7	81
	5.10	286
190.65(1)(a)	5.6	
	5.27	713
	8.2	
190.65(1)(b)	5.6	
	5.27	713
	5.27	718
190.70	1.8	164
	1.8	174
	3.2	
	3.27	358
	5.20	470
190.70(1)	3.2	15
	5.20	471
190.71	1.10	217
	1.10	229
190.71(a)	1.10	233
190.71(c)	1.10	230
190.71(d)	1.10	230

NEW YORK, MCKINNEY'S CRIMINAL PROCEDURE LAW

Sec.	This Work Sec.	Note
190.75	5.28	803
190.75(1)	1.10	231
190.75(3)	1.8	165
	5.18	395
	11.16	199
190.80	5.23	623
	5.33	
Art. 195	5.10	
	5.10	287
	5.11	305
	5.31	
195.10	5.10	
	11.5	41
	11.5	42
195.10(1)(b)	5.10	299
195.10(2)	5.10	273
195.10(2)(b)	11.5	42
195.20	5.10	
	5.10	266
	5.31	
195.30	5.10	268
195.40	3.31	429
Art. 200	5.10	295
	5.27	
	5.33	
	8.1	
200.10	1.2	15
	1.8	174
	5.11	306
	5.20	466
200.15	3.31	429
	5.10	269
	5.10	270
	5.10	283
	5.23	618
200.20	3.3	28
	3.8	91
	3.32	439
	5.21	
	5.22	560
200.20(1)(b)	5.22	542
200.20(1)(c)	5.22	543
200.20(2)	5.8	170
	5.33	
200.20(2)(a)	2.7	159
	5.21	
	5.21	475
	5.22	
200.20(2)(b)	5.21	
	5.21	475
	5.21	486
	5.21	491
200.20(2)(c)	5.21	
	5.21	475
	5.21	500
200.20(2)(d)	5.21	476
200.20(3)	5.21	
	5.21	511
	5.21	525
	5.33	
200.20(3)(a)	5.21	515
	5.21	516

699

TABLE OF STATUTES

NEW YORK, MCKINNEY'S CRIMINAL PROCEDURE LAW

Sec.	This Work Sec.	Note
200.20(3)(b)	5.21	
	5.21	511
200.20(3)(b)(i)	5.21	525
200.20(3)(b)(ii)	5.21	
200.20(4)	5.21	479
	5.22	559
	5.33	
200.20(5)	5.21	480
	5.22	559
200.20(6)	1.10	233
200.30	5.12	313
	5.17	
	5.22	531
200.30(2)	5.17	
200.40	3.3	28
	3.8	91
	3.32	439
	5.22	
	5.22	560
200.40(1)	5.22	
	5.22	562
200.40(1)(a)	5.22	
	5.22	544
200.40(1)(b)	5.22	533
	5.22	540
	5.22	545
200.40(2)	5.21	527
	5.22	
	5.22	561
	5.22	563
	5.33	
200.40(2)(b)	5.22	
200.40(2)(c)	5.22	
200.50	3.3	31
	5.12	
	5.13	
	5.14	331
	5.16	345
	5.19	
	5.32	
200.50(6)	5.15	336
200.50(7)	5.12	323
	5.19	450
200.50(7)(a)	5.18	
200.50(7)(b)	5.12	322
200.50(8)	5.29	815
200.60	11.15	
200.70	3.8	93
	5.13	327
	5.18	
	5.19	
	5.21	
	5.33	
200.70(1)	5.18	400
	5.18	402
	5.18	406
200.70(2)	5.18	401
200.70(2)(a)	3.8	94
	5.16	348
200.80	5.18	392
	5.29	811

NEW YORK, MCKINNEY'S CRIMINAL PROCEDURE LAW

Sec.	This Work Sec.	Note
200.90	8.1	
200.95	3.8	92
	5.19	
	5.19	444
	5.19	451
	8.2	
200.95(1)(b)	8.1	15
200.95(2)	3.8	92
	8.1	15
200.95(3)	3.8	92
	5.19	456
	8.1	15
200.95(4)	3.8	92
	5.19	457
	8.1	15
200.95(5)	5.19	460
	5.19	462
200.95(6)	5.19	458
200.95(8)	5.20	464
	5.33	
Art. 210	5.32	
	8.1	
210.05	1.2	16
	5.11	304
	5.11	308
210.10	5.23	
	5.23	619
	5.23	620
	9.45	
210.10(1–a)	3.2	15
210.10(3)	3.11	120
	3.16	176
	5.23	
	5.23	627
	5.23	631
	9.45	
	9.45	327
210.15	3.24	285
	5.24	
210.15(1)	5.24	634
210.15(2)(a)	5.24	636
210.15(3)	5.24	637
210.15(5)	5.24	635
210.15(6)	4.4	52
	4.4	53
210.20	5.2	
	5.25	
	5.27	
	5.32	
	9.19	
	9.49	
	9.49	356
	9.55	
	11.16	199
	11.17	
210.20(1)	5.27	
	9.12	
210.20(1)(a)	5.27	676
	5.33	
210.20(1)(a)—(1)(h)	5.27	753
	5.27	761
	5.27	762

700

TABLE OF STATUTES

NEW YORK, MCKINNEY'S CRIMINAL PROCEDURE LAW

Sec.	This Work Sec.	Note
210.20(1)(b)	5.27	
	5.27	677
210.20(1)(c)	5.27	678
210.20(1)(d)	5.9	208
	5.27	673
	5.33	
210.20(1)(e)	2.11	239
	2.13	
	5.27	674
210.20(1)(f)	5.27	675
	9.6	
	9.6	23
	9.58	
	11.15	
210.20(1)(g)	5.26	646
	5.26	659
	5.27	675
	9.12	
	9.12	115
	9.58	
210.20(1)(h)	5.7	97
	5.27	
	5.27	679
	5.27	729
210.20(1)(i)	5.27	680
	5.33	
210.20(1–a)	5.27	
	5.27	677
	5.27	708
	5.29	
	5.29	814
	11.2	6
210.20(2)	5.26	647
	5.26	655
	8.1	17
	9.6	27
	9.12	115
	9.12	119
	9.49	
	9.49	361
210.20(2)(g)	9.49	
	9.49	356
210.20(2–a)	3.2	
210.20(3)	5.26	658
	9.6	27
210.20(4)	3.27	354
	5.28	802
	5.28	807
	5.29	817
	5.33	
210.20(5)	1.10	217
	1.10	219
	1.10	237
210.20(6)	5.28	
	5.29	
210.20(6)(a)	5.29	
210.20(6)(b)	5.29	
	5.29	816
	5.29	819
210.25	5.27	
	5.28	
210.25(1)	5.21	

NEW YORK, MCKINNEY'S CRIMINAL PROCEDURE LAW

Sec.	This Work Sec.	Note
210.25(1) (Cont'd)	5.33	
210.25(4)	3.27	363
210.30	3.27	362
	5.20	472
	5.27	
	7.4	34
	9.47	
210.30(3)	5.27	
	5.27	699
	8.2	
210.30(6)	5.27	
	5.27	691
210.30(7)	1.10	217
	1.10	219
	1.10	235
210.35	3.27	362
	5.27	
	5.28	
210.35(4)	5.26	
	5.33	
210.35(5)	5.27	737
210.40	1.10	238
	1.10	239
	3.28	369
	5.25	
	5.25	642
	5.27	
	5.27	754
	5.27	757
	5.32	
	5.33	
	6.3	
	11.3	
210.40(1)	1.10	241
210.40(1)(a)	5.27	767
210.40(1)(a)—(1)(j)	5.33	
210.40(1)(b)	5.27	767
210.40(1)(d)	5.27	772
210.40(1)(e)	1.1	5
	1.10	241
210.40(2)	5.27	752
210.43	1.10	217
	1.10	223
	1.10	225
	1.10	236
	1.10	238
	8.1	
210.43(1)(b)	5.12	320
210.43(2)	1.10	222
	1.10	241
210.43(4)	1.10	242
210.43(5)	1.10	242
210.43(b)	1.10	240
210.45	3.26	351
	3.27	362
	5.26	
	9.51	366
	9.55	
210.45(1)	3.26	352
	5.26	660
	8.1	2
	9.12	116

701

TABLE OF STATUTES

NEW YORK, MCKINNEY'S CRIMINAL PROCEDURE LAW		
Sec.	This Work Sec.	Note
210.45(1) (Cont'd)	9.49	359
	9.51	
210.45(3)	5.26	665
210.45(4)	5.26	667
	10.18	385
210.45(4)(c)	5.26	668
	9.51	380
210.45(5)	5.26	667
210.45(5)(c)	9.51	382
210.45(6)	9.51	381
	9.52	
210.45(7)	5.26	670
	9.6	
	9.52	383
210.45(8)	3.27	364
	5.28	808
210.45(9)	3.27	365
	5.28	804
	5.29	820
210.45(9)(d)	5.28	805
	5.28	806
210.46	7.18	217
210.50	3.30	411
	5.24	638
Art. 215	3.29	378
215.10	9.44	321
215.30	7.18	217
Art. 220	5.10	276
	11.1	
	11.19	257
220.00	11.3	15
220.10	1.10	217
	11.2	
	11.5	42
	11.5	57
220.10(1)	5.24	639
	11.6	
220.10(2)	5.24	639
	11.2	1
220.10(3)	11.3	11
220.10(4)	11.3	11
220.10(4)(a)	11.3	11
220.10(4)(b)	11.3	11
220.10(4)(c)	11.3	11
220.10(5)	11.5	
	11.5	41
	11.19	
220.10(5)(a)—(5)(d)	11.5	55
220.10(5)(a)(i)	11.5	43
220.10(5)(a)(ii)	11.5	44
220.10(5)(a)(iii)	11.5	45
220.10(5)(b)	11.5	47
220.10(5)(c)	11.5	51
	11.5	52
	11.5	53
220.10(5)(d)(i)	5.12	318
	11.5	46
	11.5	48
220.10(5)(d)(ii)	11.5	49
	11.5	50
220.10(5)(d)(iii)	11.5	53
220.10(5)(d)(iv)	11.5	54

NEW YORK, MCKINNEY'S CRIMINAL PROCEDURE LAW		
Sec.	This Work Sec.	Note
220.10(5)(e)	5.24	639
	11.2	3
	11.3	14
220.10(5)(g)	1.10	246
	11.5	55
220.10(5)(g)(i)	11.5	55
220.10(5)(g)(ii)	11.5	55
220.10(5)(g)(iii)	11.5	55
220.10(6)	11.3	12
	11.5	56
220.15	2.2	17
	5.24	
	9.16	153
	11.3	12
	11.5	56
220.15(1)	11.4	
	11.4	30
	11.4	32
220.15(1)—(5)	11.4	34
220.15(6)	11.4	38
220.20	11.3	11
220.30	11.5	
220.30(3)	11.3	13
	11.5	
	11.19	
220.30(3)(a)(ii)	11.3	13
220.30(3)(b)	11.5	
220.30(3)(b)(vii)	11.3	14
220.35	11.5	51
220.50	5.16	
220.50(7)	11.9	89
220.60	11.10	
	11.18	
	11.23	
220.60(3)	11.18	239
Art. 230	1.9	
	1.9	189
230.10	1.9	188
230.20	1.9	197
	1.12	
	8.1	
230.20(1)	1.9	188
230.20(2)	1.7	152
	1.9	192
	1.9	198
	1.9	203
	1.12	
	8.1	
230.20(2)(a)	1.9	189
	1.9	204
230.20(2)(b)	1.9	190
	1.9	204
230.20(3)	1.9	192
	1.9	198
230.20(4)	1.9	209
230.30	8.1	
230.30(1)	1.9	188
	1.9	189
	1.9	198
	1.9	201
230.30(2)	1.9	199
230.30(3)	1.9	202

TABLE OF STATUTES

NEW YORK, MCKINNEY'S CRIMINAL PROCEDURE LAW

Sec.	This Work Sec.	Note
230.30(4)	1.9	200
230.40	1.9	210
Art. 240	7.2	
	7.3	
	7.3	18
	7.4	
	7.4	52
	7.6	
	7.7	
	7.15	
	7.20	
	7.33	
	8.1	
	9.47	
240.10(1)	7.3	17
240.10(2)	7.17	206
	7.31	350
240.10(3)	7.3	23
240.20	7.4	
	7.4	51
	7.5	
	7.7	
	7.34	
	7.36	
	7.37	
	8.1	15
	8.2	
240.20 (former)	7.3	16
240.20(1)	7.3	17
	7.3	18
	7.3	21
	7.4	51
240.20(1)(a)	7.4	24
	7.4	43
	10.25	565
240.20(1)(b)	7.4	28
240.20(1)(c)	7.4	30
	7.4	49
240.20(1)(d)	7.4	35
240.20(1)(e)	7.4	37
240.20(1)(f)	7.4	38
240.20(1)(g)	7.4	27
	7.4	42
240.20(1)(h)	7.2	14
	7.14	159
240.20(1)(i)	7.4	44
240.20(1)(j)	7.4	47
240.20(1)(k)	7.4	48
240.20(2)	7.4	52
	8.2	
240.30	7.1	3
	7.11	
	7.35	
	7.36	
	7.37	
240.30(1)	7.3	17
	7.3	18
	7.3	21
240.30(1)(a)	7.5	59
240.30(1)(b)	7.5	60
240.30(2)	7.5	61
	7.5	62

NEW YORK, MCKINNEY'S CRIMINAL PROCEDURE LAW

Sec.	This Work Sec.	Note
240.35	7.5	
	7.6	63
	7.6	65
	7.6	66
	7.37	
240.35(1)(a)	7.5	57
240.40	7.7	
	7.11	
	7.37	
240.40(1)	7.3	18
240.40(1)(a)	7.7	68
	7.7	69
240.40(1)(b)	7.7	70
	7.7	71
240.40(1)(c)	7.2	14
	7.7	72
	7.11	
	7.11	115
240.40(2)	7.3	18
	7.11	127
240.40(2)(a)	7.11	117
240.40(2)(b)	7.11	118
240.40(2)(b)(i)	7.11	120
240.40(2)(b)(ii)	7.11	122
240.40(2)(b)(iii)	7.11	123
240.40(2)(b)(iv)	7.11	124
240.40(2)(b)(v)	7.11	126
240.40(2)(b)(vi)	7.11	125
240.43	7.15	167
	7.15	168
240.44	3.33	
	5.3	51
	6.9	207
	7.2	15
	7.16	
	7.16	177
	7.17	
	7.18	
	7.18	217
	8.2	
	10.19	414
	10.19	415
240.44(1)	6.9	206
	7.16	177
	7.16	181
	7.17	209
240.44(2)	3.33	462
	7.18	217
240.44(3)	3.33	462
	7.18	217
240.45	5.3	51
	7.2	15
	7.16	
	7.16	177
	7.17	
	7.18	
	7.18	217
	8.2	
240.45(1)	7.16	179
	7.18	220
240.45(1)(a)	7.16	177
	7.17	209

703

TABLE OF STATUTES

NEW YORK, MCKINNEY'S CRIMINAL PROCEDURE LAW		
	This Work	
Sec.	Sec.	Note
240.45(1)(b)	7.18	218
240.45(1)(c)	7.18	218
240.45(2)	7.16	181
240.45(2)(a)	7.16	181
240.45(2)(b)	7.18	219
240.45(2)(c)	7.18	219
240.50	7.6	
	7.6	65
	7.6	66
	7.17	
	7.17	206
	7.37	
240.50(1)	7.19	221
	7.19	222
	7.19	227
	7.21	228
240.50(2)	7.19	231
240.50(4)	7.19	229
240.60	7.4	33
	8.2	
240.70	7.7	
	7.7	71
	7.20	
	7.24	
240.70(1)	5.25	643
	7.20	232
240.80(1)	7.3	18
	7.3	19
	7.3	20
	8.1	15
240.80(2)	7.6	63
	7.6	64
	8.1	15
240.80(3)	7.3	22
240.90	7.7	67
240.90(3)	7.6	66
	7.14	
	7.19	
Art. 250	7.25	277
250.10	6.3	63
	7.1	3
	7.5	58
	7.26	
	7.26	288
250.10(1)	7.26	278
250.10(2)	7.26	280
	7.26	281
	7.26	288
250.10(3)	6.4	80
	7.26	282
250.10(4)	7.26	284
250.10(5)	7.26	285
	7.26	286
	7.26	287
250.20	3.24	
	3.35	
	5.26	659
	7.1	3
	7.27	
250.20(1)	7.27	289
	7.27	290
	7.27	293

NEW YORK, MCKINNEY'S CRIMINAL PROCEDURE LAW		
	This Work	
Sec.	Sec.	Note
250.20(2)	7.27	291
	7.27	292
	7.27	293
250.20(3)	7.27	294
	7.27	296
250.20(4)	7.27	295
	7.27	296
250.20(5)	7.27	298
250.30	7.1	3
	7.28	
250.30(1)	7.28	315
250.30(3)	7.28	316
250.40	3.30	407
	11.3	14
250.40(1)	7.29	320
250.40(2)	7.29	321
250.40(3)	7.29	322
250.40(4)	7.29	323
Art. 255	8.1	
	8.1	17
	8.1	18
255.10	5.21	
	5.26	
255.10(1)	8.1	16
255.10(1)(a)	5.27	791
	9.6	27
255.10(1)(e)	1.7	146
	8.1	22
255.10(1)(f)	10.13	257
255.10(1)(g)	5.21	507
255.20	3.26	
	3.26	348
	5.26	
	5.26	655
	7.7	67
	9.6	27
	10.13	
255.20(1)	1.7	146
	1.9	192
	1.9	198
	5.26	
	5.26	644
	5.26	648
	8.1	4
	8.1	5
	8.1	6
	8.1	7
	10.13	
	10.13	257
	10.13	258
	10.13	261
	10.13	270
	10.13	273
255.20(2)	3.26	349
	8.1	9
255.20(3)	1.9	195
	5.26	650
	5.26	652
	8.1	10
	8.1	11
	10.13	
255.20(4)	1.2	32

TABLE OF STATUTES

NEW YORK, MCKINNEY'S CRIMINAL PROCEDURE LAW

Sec.	This Work Sec.	Note
255.20(4) (Cont'd)	10.12	
	10.12	255
	10.19	403
270.35	2.4	58
280.10	2.4	
	2.4	58
280.10(1)	2.4	39
280.10(2)	2.4	46
280.10(3)	2.4	46
280.20	2.4	64
290.10	2.4	65
290.10(1)	2.4	76
	5.27	709
300.10	5.5	
300.40(3)(b)	11.2	7
310.60	2.4	58
	2.4	64
310.60(2)	2.4	
310.70	2.4	68
310.70(2)	2.4	70
310.85	1.10	217
	1.10	233
	1.10	247
Art. 330	5.5	75
330.20	5.27	780
	11.4	
330.25	1.10	217
	1.10	247
340.20	11.3	15
340.20(1)	11.2	8
	11.4	36
340.40(2)	1.7	148
	3.24	288
350.10(3)(d)	9.8	55
380.30(1)	9.8	55
390.10	3.23	284
400.10	11.13	
400.15—400.21	2.10	217
400.21	11.5	51
400.27(13)	7.26	288
410.10(1)	3.29	390
410.60	4.4	55
420.10(1)(e)	4.12	212
420.10(3)	4.4	56
Art. 440	11.11	
	11.11	122
440.10	11.9	
	11.10	
	11.10	109
	11.17	
	11.18	
440.10(1)(f)	7.22	
440.10(1)(h)	10.13	274
Art. 450	9.31	
	11.4	
450.15	11.10	109
450.20	5.29	821
450.20(1)	5.28	798
450.20(2)	2.4	78
450.20(8)	10.14	282
	10.22	512
	10.22	513

NEW YORK, MCKINNEY'S CRIMINAL PROCEDURE LAW

Sec.	This Work Sec.	Note
450.50	10.22	
450.50(1)	10.22	513
450.50(2)	10.22	514
450.60	4.9	122
450.60(6)	2.9	205
450.60(7)	2.9	205
460.20	4.9	128
460.40	5.29	822
460.40(2)	5.28	800
460.50	4.9	
	4.9	111
	4.9	115
460.50(1)(a)	4.9	120
460.50(2)	4.9	122
460.50(5)	4.9	129
460.60	4.9	
460.60(1)	4.9	128
460.60(1)(a)	4.9	120
460.70	4.9	116
470.05(2)	10.21	503
470.15(1)	10.22	530
470.15(2)(c)	4.13	215
470.20(1)	2.4	86
470.20(2)	2.4	88
470.20(3)	2.4	88
470.20(5)	2.4	90
470.55	2.4	
Art. 500	4.1	
	4.2	
	4.15	
500.10(1)	4.2	9
	4.2	16
500.10(2)	4.2	11
500.10(3)	4.2	13
500.10(5)	4.2	14
500.10(6)	4.2	15
500.10(8)	4.2	18
500.10(9)	4.2	17
500.10(10)	4.2	19
500.10(11)	4.2	22
500.10(12)	4.2	22
500.10(13)	4.2	21
500.10(14)	4.2	23
500.10(15)	4.2	23
500.10(16)	4.2	24
500.10(17)	4.2	25
500.10(18)	4.2	32
	4.3	36
500.10(19)	4.2	32
500.10(20)	4.2	10
	4.2	11
Art. 510	4.1	
	4.4	
510.10	4.4	51
	4.4	53
510.15	4.4	54
510.20	4.10	172
	4.13	
510.20(1)	4.5	60
510.20(2)	4.10	
510.30	4.10	130
	4.10	170

705

TABLE OF STATUTES

NEW YORK, MCKINNEY'S CRIMINAL PROCEDURE LAW

Sec.	This Work Sec.	Note
510.30(2)	4.5	79
510.30(2)(a)	4.5	
	4.5	65
	4.5	68
	4.10	156
	4.10	170
	4.15	
510.30(2)(a)(i)	4.5	82
510.30(2)(a)(v)	4.5	66
510.30(2)(a)(viii)	4.5	78
510.30(2)(b)	4.5	69
	4.5	80
	4.9	126
510.40(3)	3.24	320
	4.10	
Art. 520	4.1	
	4.4	
520.10	4.2	20
520.10(2)	4.3	33
	4.3	35
	4.3	48
520.10(3)	4.3	49
520.15(1)	4.3	45
	4.3	46
520.15(2)	3.21	253
	4.2	17
520.20	4.3	40
520.20(1)(b)	4.3	41
520.20(2)	3.21	253
520.20(2)(e)	4.3	42
520.20(2)(f)	4.3	42
520.20(3)	4.3	44
	4.7	103
520.20(4)	4.3	43
520.30	4.11	187
520.30(1)	4.11	178
520.40	4.7	102
Art. 530	4.1	
	4.4	
530.10(2)(a)	4.5	67
530.11	9.46	329
530.11(1)	3.18	
	3.18	199
	3.29	382
	4.10	134
	4.10	136
	4.10	140
530.11(2)	9.46	330
530.11(2)(a)	4.10	140
530.11(2)(h)	9.46	330
530.11(2)(i)	9.46	330
530.11(2-a)	9.46	330
530.12	3.18	
	3.18	200
	3.29	385
	4.10	132
	4.10	144
530.12(1)	4.10	134
	4.10	135
530.12(1)(a)	4.10	138
530.12(1)(a)—(1)(d)	4.10	137
530.12(5)	4.10	135

NEW YORK, MCKINNEY'S CRIMINAL PROCEDURE LAW

Sec.	This Work Sec.	Note
530.12(8)	4.10	141
530.12(11)(a)	4.10	143
530.12(11)(e)	4.10	143
530.12(13)	4.10	134
530.13	3.29	385
	4.10	133
	11.11	
530.13(1)	4.10	135
	4.10	144
530.13(4)	4.10	135
530.13(8)	4.4	57
530.20(1)	3.24	320
	4.2	15
	4.6	90
530.20(2)	4.2	15
	4.7	99
530.20(2)(a)	4.6	91
	4.7	96
530.20(2)(b)(i)	4.6	92
530.20(2)(b)(ii)	4.6	93
	4.6	94
530.30	4.5	63
	4.15	
530.30(1)	4.7	95
	4.7	96
	4.7	97
	4.11	180
	4.13	
530.30(1)(a)—(1)(c)	4.13	214
530.30(2)	4.11	181
530.30(3)	4.7	98
	4.11	182
530.40	4.13	215
	5.23	631
	5.24	
530.40(1)	4.2	15
	4.7	100
530.40(2)	4.2	15
	4.7	100
	4.7	101
530.40(3)	4.7	100
	4.12	203
530.40(4)	5.23	630
530.45	4.9	
	4.9	111
	4.9	124
530.45(1)	4.5	79
530.45(2)(a)	4.9	113
530.45(2)(b)	4.9	114
530.45(5)	4.9	117
530.50	4.9	121
530.60	4.5	63
	4.10	
530.60(1)	4.10	143
	4.10	162
530.60(2)	4.10	165
530.70	3.11	120
	3.12	123
	4.10	161
Art. 540	4.1	
540.10	4.12	
	4.12	200

TABLE OF STATUTES

NEW YORK, MCKINNEY'S CRIMINAL PROCEDURE LAW			NEW YORK, MCKINNEY'S CRIMINAL PROCEDURE LAW		
		This Work			This Work
Sec.	Sec.	Note	Sec.	Sec.	Note
540.10 (Cont'd)	4.12	204	690.05(2) (Cont'd)	10.3	54
540.10(1)	4.12	193		10.3	55
540.10(2)	4.12	196		10.5	121
	4.12	197	690.05(2)(a)	10.1	2
	4.12	198		10.1	3
540.10(3)	4.12	197		10.1	4
540.20	4.12			10.1	5
540.20(2)	4.12	205	690.05(2)(b)	10.1	6
540.30	4.12			10.2	28
	4.12	204		10.6	131
	4.15		690.05(2)(b)(ii)	10.1	6
540.30(1)	4.12	201	690.10(1)	10.1	9
540.30(2)	4.12	205	690.10(2)	10.1	10
Art. 560	3.10	113	690.10(3)	10.1	11
	9.41	293		10.1	13
	9.41	294	690.10(4)	10.1	12
Art. 570	3.10	113		10.1	13
	9.41			10.3	55
	9.55	395	690.15(1)	10.5	
Art. 580	3.10	113	690.15(1)(a)	10.1	2
	9.41		690.15(1)(b)	10.1	3
580.20	9.1		690.15(1)(c)	10.1	4
	9.53		690.15(2)	10.6	129
	9.54		690.20(1)	10.2	28
	9.55		690.20(2)	1.2	25
	9.56			10.2	29
	9.57		690.25(1)	10.2	14
	11.15	186		10.2	46
580.20, Art. II	9.53	388		10.2	47
580.20, Art. III	9.53		690.25(2)	10.5	104
	9.54		690.25(3)	10.5	104
	9.55		690.30(1)	10.3	70
580.20, Art. III(a)	9.54	393		10.5	101
580.20, Art. III(a)—(d)	9.54	390	690.30(2)	10.5	118
580.20, Art. III(d)	9.55	399		10.5	121
580.20, Art. III(e)	9.54	391	690.35	10.2	
580.20, Art. IV	9.53		690.35(1)	10.2	15
	9.55			10.2	17
580.20, Art. IV(a)	9.55	398	690.35(2)	10.2	28
580.20, Art. IV(c)	9.55	396		10.2	29
580.20, Art. IV(e)	9.55	399	690.35(2)(b)	10.2	28
580.20, Art. V(c)	9.54	394		10.3	55
	9.55	397	690.35(2)(ii)	10.2	32
Art. 590	3.10	113		10.2	33
Art. 600	3.10	113	690.35(2)(iii)	10.3	34
600.20	1.1	6	690.35(3)(a)	10.3	52
610.10(3)	7.8	74	690.35(3)(b)	3.14	153
610.20	10.19	419		10.3	54
610.20(3)	7.8		690.35(3)(c)	10.3	59
	7.8	77		10.3	60
610.25	7.8			10.3	61
610.25(2)	7.8	78	690.35(3)(d)	10.3	52
Art. 620	10.19	419	690.35(3)(e)	10.3	55
Art. 630	10.19	419	690.35(4)(a)	10.5	121
Art. 640	10.19	419	690.35(4)(b)	10.5	113
640.10	1.2	27	690.36(1)	10.2	19
Art. 650	10.19	419		10.2	21
670.10	10.19	462	690.36(2)	10.2	20
Art. 690	3.14		690.36(3)	10.2	21
690.05(1)	10.2	14		10.2	22
	10.2	17		10.2	24
690.05(2)	10.1	5	690.40(1)	3.12	122

707

TABLE OF STATUTES

NEW YORK, MCKINNEY'S CRIMINAL PROCEDURE LAW

Sec.	This Work Sec.	Note
690.40(1) (Cont'd)	10.2	40
	10.3	61
690.40(2)	10.1	6
	10.1	9
	10.1	10
	10.1	11
	10.1	12
	10.5	113
	10.5	122
690.40(3)	10.2	25
690.45(1)	10.2	44
690.45(2)	10.2	27
690.45(3)	10.2	46
	10.2	47
690.45(4)	10.2	44
690.45(5)	10.2	44
690.45(6)	10.5	119
	10.5	122
690.45(7)	10.5	115
690.45(8)	10.2	45
690.45(9)	10.3	55
690.50(1)	10.5	105
	10.5	108
	10.5	109
690.50(2)(a)	10.5	105
	10.5	112
690.50(2)(b)	10.5	112
690.50(3)	10.5	108
	10.5	109
690.50(4)	10.6	130
690.50(5)	10.6	131
690.50(6)	10.6	131
690.55(1)	10.6	133
	10.6	134
690.55(2)	10.6	133
	10.6	134
Art. 700	3.12	122
	10.9	
700.05(4)	5.20	473
700.70	8.1	
	10.13	259
	10.13	265
	10.23	539
	10.24	552
	10.24	555
	10.27	
Art. 705	10.8	
	10.9	
Art. 710	8.1	
	8.1	10
	10.7	
	10.8	
	10.11	
	10.15	
	10.17	
	10.18	
	10.22	
	11.16	
710.10(1)	10.8	158
	10.11	201
710.10(5)	10.11	203
	10.11	212

NEW YORK, MCKINNEY'S CRIMINAL PROCEDURE LAW

Sec.	This Work Sec.	Note
710.20	10.8	
	10.8	159
	10.9	
	10.11	
	10.11	201
	10.11	202
	10.16	
	10.24	
	10.20	
	10.30	
	11.16	
	11.17	
710.20(1)	10.8	141
	10.17	347
	10.31	
710.20(2)	10.8	
	10.8	142
	10.9	
710.20(3)	8.2	
	10.8	143
	10.17	
	10.17	346
	10.17	348
	10.25	
	10.25	563
	10.25	565
	10.31	
710.20(4)	10.9	
710.20(5)	10.8	144
	10.8	153
	10.9	
710.20(6)	10.8	145
	10.17	
	10.17	346
	10.31	
710.20(7)	10.8	
	10.8	146
	10.9	
710.30	3.24	
	3.30	
	3.35	
	7.4	24
	8.1	
	8.1	6
	9.47	
	10.13	260
	10.22	
	10.23	
	10.24	
	10.24	555
	10.25	
	10.28	
	10.31	
	11.16	
710.30(1)	10.23	539
	10.24	550
	10.24	551
	10.24	556
	10.25	563
	10.25	566
	10.28	
	10.28	605

TABLE OF STATUTES

NEW YORK, MCKINNEY'S CRIMINAL PROCEDURE LAW

Sec.	This Work Sec.	Note
710.30(1)(b)	10.28	
710.30(2)	10.13	261
	10.13	263
	10.23	
	10.23	539
	10.24	550
	10.24	551
	10.27	
710.30(3)	10.13	265
	10.13	266
	10.23	540
	10.28	
	10.28	599
	10.28	605
	10.29	
710.40	10.13	
	10.14	
710.40(1)	10.13	
	10.13	256
	10.13	271
	10.13	279
710.40(2)	8.1	10
	10.13	
	10.13	261
	10.13	271
710.40(3)	10.14	281
	10.14	289
710.40(4)	10.15	293
	10.15	294
	10.15	302
710.50	5.27	730
	10.12	
	10.12	245
710.50(1)(a)	10.12	240
	10.12	243
	10.12	244
710.50(1)(b)	10.12	242
710.50(1)(c)	10.12	241
710.50(2)	10.12	247
	10.12	249
710.60	10.20	
710.60(1)	10.16	
	10.16	311
	10.16	317
	10.16	321
	10.16	326
	10.16	329
	10.16	330
	10.18	
	10.19	
710.60(2)(a)	10.18	384
710.60(2)(b)	10.18	384
710.60(3)	10.16	322
	10.16	327
	10.17	343
	10.17	365
710.60(3)(b)	10.17	345
710.60(4)	10.19	395
	10.19	438
	10.19	439
710.60(5)	10.16	
	10.16	316

NEW YORK, MCKINNEY'S CRIMINAL PROCEDURE LAW

Sec.	This Work Sec.	Note
710.60(6)	10.21	499
710.70(1)	10.22	510
710.70(2)	10.22	532
	11.16	206
710.70(3)	10.13	274
	10.22	521
	10.22	524
	10.22	526
715.50	5.27	
Art. 720	1.10	214
720.10	3.19	235
720.10(2)	5.12	321
720.25	7.30	326
Art. 725	1.10	218
	3.33	471
725.00	1.10	219
	1.10	248
725.05(1)—(5)	1.10	249
725.05(4–a)	1.10	219
725.05(6)	1.10	250
725.05(7)	1.10	250
725.05(8)	1.10	251
725.10	1.10	254
725.15	7.30	326
725.20	1.10	252
	1.10	253
Art. 730	3.33	
	3.34	
	4.4	58
	5.8	
	5.27	
	5.30	
	6.1	
	6.2	
	6.2	10
	6.3	
	6.6	126
	6.8	
	6.8	178
	6.9	
	6.10	
	6.11	
	9.28	
	11.8	
730.10	6.9	204
730.10(1)	6.1	5
	6.10	218
730.10(2)	6.2	9
	6.2	10
	6.4	66
730.10(4)	6.4	67
730.10(5)	6.4	76
730.10(6)	6.4	77
730.10(8)	6.5	94
730.20(1)	6.4	72
	6.4	79
	6.5	92
	6.9	189
730.20(1) (former)	6.4	74
730.20(2)	6.5	84
	6.5	85
730.20(3)	6.5	86

709

TABLE OF STATUTES

NEW YORK, MCKINNEY'S CRIMINAL PROCEDURE LAW

Sec.	This Work Sec.	Note
730.20(3) (Cont'd)	6.5	87
730.20(4)	6.5	88
	6.5	90
730.20(5)	6.4	78
	6.5	93
730.20(6)	6.3	62
	6.3	65
730.30	6.12	
730.30(1)	6.2	
	6.2	10
	6.2	11
	6.2	37
	11.8	73
730.30(2)	6.6	
	6.6	98
	6.6	99
	6.6	101
	6.6	102
	6.6	120
	6.6	121
	6.7	
	6.7	132
	6.7	133
	6.7	147
	6.7	149
	6.9	187
	6.9	195
730.30(3)	6.6	103
	6.7	134
	6.9	187
730.30(4)	6.6	107
	6.7	137
	6.9	187
730.40	6.3	
730.40(1)	6.7	135
	6.7	136
	6.7	138
	6.7	139
	6.7	143
	6.7	144
	6.7	156
	6.8	181
730.40(2)	6.3	43
	6.7	140
	6.7	143
	6.7	150
	6.7	151
	6.7	156
	6.8	171
	6.8	173
	6.8	181
730.40(3)	5.8	164
	6.3	57
	6.7	153
730.40(4)	6.7	154
730.40(5)	6.7	156
	6.7	157
	6.7	158
730.50	6.6	
	6.6	128
	6.8	
730.50(1)	5.27	778

NEW YORK, MCKINNEY'S CRIMINAL PROCEDURE LAW

Sec.	This Work Sec.	Note
730.50(1) (Cont'd)	6.3	43
	6.6	104
	6.6	105
	6.6	106
	6.6	108
	6.6	109
	6.8	171
730.50(2)	6.6	111
	6.6	112
	6.6	113
	6.6	114
	6.6	115
	6.8	176
730.50(3)	6.6	116
	6.6	117
	6.6	126
	6.6	127
	6.6	129
730.50(4)	5.27	778
	6.6	126
	6.6	131
	6.8	173
730.50(5)	5.27	778
730.60	6.3	
	6.6	97
	6.8	
730.60(1)	6.7	139
	6.7	144
	6.8	159
730.60(2)	6.3	44
	6.6	106
	6.6	110
	6.6	118
	6.6	119
	6.6	122
	6.7	139
	6.7	144
	6.7	145
	6.7	146
	6.7	148
	6.8	159
	6.9	190
	6.9	191
730.60(3)	6.7	141
	6.8	159
	6.8	160
730.60(3)(c)	6.8	163
	6.8	164
	6.8	165
	6.8	166
730.60(4)	5.27	778
	6.3	49
	6.8	159
	6.8	173
730.60(5)	5.27	778
	6.3	52
	6.8	173
730.60(6)	6.6	
	6.7	
	6.8	
730.60(6)(a)	6.8	
	6.8	162

710

TABLE OF STATUTES

NEW YORK, MCKINNEY'S CRIMINAL PROCEDURE LAW

Sec.	This Work Sec.	Note
730.60(6)(a) (Cont'd)	6.8	172
	6.8	178
730.60(6)(b)	6.8	162
730.60(6)(c)	6.8	
	6.8	178
730.60(20)	6.9	
730.70	6.6	130
	6.7	142

NEW YORK, MCKINNEY'S DOMESTIC RELATIONS LAW

Sec.	This Work Sec.	Note
240	3.18	
252	3.18	

NEW YORK, MCKINNEY'S EDUCATION LAW

Sec.	This Work Sec.	Note
Art. 153	6.4	
3212-a(1)	7.9	96

NEW YORK, MCKINNEY'S ENVIRONMENTAL CONSERVATION LAW

Sec.	This Work Sec.	Note
71-27	9.4	
71-2707 to 71-2717	9.4	15

NEW YORK, MCKINNEY'S FAMILY COURT ACT

Sec.	This Work Sec.	Note
166	7.30	326
301.2(1)	1.10	215
	3.35	471
303.2	2.10	237
305.2	10.9	162
306.1	4.5	66
322.1	6.2	10
354.2	4.5	66
Art. 4	3.18	
Art. 5	3.18	
Art. 6	3.18	
Art. 8	3.18	

NEW YORK, MCKINNEY'S GENERAL CONSTRUCTION LAW

Sec.	This Work Sec.	Note
18-a	1.2	26
39	4.2	26
40	4.2	26
46	3.12	123

NEW YORK, MCKINNEY'S GENERAL MUNICIPAL LAW

Sec.	This Work Sec.	Note
99-m	4.12	211
211	1.3	71

NEW YORK, MCKINNEY'S INSURANCE LAW

Sec.	This Work Sec.	Note
6801—6804	4.2	24

NEW YORK, MCKINNEY'S JUDICIARY LAW

Sec.	This Work Sec.	Note
35-b(1)	3.30	407
35-b(2)	3.30	407
35-b(7)	3.30	407
149	5.2	20
177-d	1.4	105
218(5)(a)	3.24	319
	3.30	426
235	5.27	696
Art. 5-B	1.4	105
500	5.2	
500 et seq.	5.2	23
514	5.2	23
750(A)	3.16	187
	4.10	142
849-a	3.29	387

NEW YORK, MCKINNEY'S MENTAL HYGIENE LAW

Sec.	This Work Sec.	Note
19.07(a)(6-a)	3.29	389
33.13(c)	7.30	324

NEW YORK, MCKINNEY'S MUNICIPAL HOME RULE LAW

Sec.	This Work Sec.	Note
10(4)(a)	3.20	242

NEW YORK, MCKINNEY'S NAVIGATION LAW

Sec.	This Work Sec.	Note
49-a(8)	10.8	
710.20(5)	10.8	153

NEW YORK, MCKINNEY'S PARKS, RECREATION AND HISTORIC PRESERVATION LAW

Sec.	This Work Sec.	Note
27.07	3.24	288

TABLE OF STATUTES

NEW YORK, MCKINNEY'S PENAL LAW

Sec.	This Work Sec.	Note
10.00(1)	1.2	17
	3.2	11
	3.18	190
10.00(2)	1.2	15
	9.14	136
10.00(3)	1.2	15
	3.2	7
	4.3	38
	4.4	50
	9.14	134
10.00(4)	1.2	15
	3.2	7
10.00(5)	1.2	15
	3.2	7
10.00(6)	1.2	15
	3.18	193
	3.21	261
	4.4	50
10.00(14)	10.1	3
10.00(18)	1.10	214
20.00	1.4	102
	1.11	
	5.22	529
20.20	1.4	84
30.00	1.10	214
	11.16	
30.00(2)	1.10	214
30.05	5.5	73
	5.5	76
35.30	3.14	151
	3.18	
40.15	6.1	6
	6.1	7
	7.26	278
65.10(2)(*l*)	3.29	390
70.02	11.9	89
70.02(1)	11.5	
70.02(5)	5.12	319
	11.5	59
70.06	3.31	429
	11.5	
70.06—70.10	2.10	217
70.15(1)	11.5	53
70.30(3)	4.4	59
70.30(4)	6.6	128
70.40(1)(b)	6.6	128
70.40(3)(c)	4.4	59
Art. 105	5.22	554
105.20	9.8	
105.25(1)	1.4	96
105.25(2)	1.3	68
105.25(3)	1.3	66
	1.4	92
110.00	1.3	41
	3.18	199
110.00/265.02(4)	11.5	
120.00	3.18	199
120.05	3.18	199
120.10(1)	5.17	377
120.14	3.18	199
120.15	3.18	199
120.20	3.18	199
125.10	9.14	

NEW YORK, MCKINNEY'S PENAL LAW

Sec.	This Work Sec.	Note
125.15	9.14	
125.20	9.14	
125.25	3.30	407
	3.32	434
	9.14	
125.25(1)	5.17	376
125.25(1)(a)	7.26	278
125.25(3)	5.17	376
125.27	3.30	407
	3.32	434
	7.29	319
	9.14	
	11.2	
	11.3	
	11.3	14
125.27(1)(a)(v)	5.17	377
125.27(2)(a)	7.26	278
130.00(8)(a)	5.17	383
130.00(8)(b)	5.17	384
130.16	5.27	717
130.25	3.19	238
	3.20	226
	4.8	104
130.40	3.19	238
	3.20	226
	4.8	104
130.70	5.17	377
135.25	3.32	434
140.00(3)	3.14	152
140.20	5.17	378
140.30	5.17	377
150.20	5.17	377
155.05(2)(a)	1.4	104
155.30	3.18	198
155.45	5.14	334
155.45(1)	5.17	370
Art. 156	7.28	
	7.34	
156.00(6)	7.4	47
156.05	7.4	45
	7.28	310
156.10	7.4	46
	7.28	311
156.20	7.28	312
156.25	7.28	312
156.26	7.28	312
156.27	7.28	312
156.30	7.28	313
156.50	7.28	314
160.15(4)	11.10	108
165.45(1)	5.10	294
165.50	5.10	294
Art. 170	1.4	102
	8.1	
170.35	1.4	103
175.30	1.4	103
205.00(3)	2.6	133
205.10	3.19	238
	3.20	226
	4.8	104
205.17	3.19	238
	3.20	226
	4.8	104

TABLE OF STATUTES

NEW YORK, MCKINNEY'S PENAL LAW

Sec.	This Work Sec.	Note
205.19	3.19	238
	3.20	226
	4.8	104
205.30	3.7	73
210.45	3.6	
	3.6	57
	3.36	
	5.26	644
	10.2	39
210.45(1)	5.26	644
215.50(3)	3.16	187
	3.18	201
215.51	3.18	201
	5.9	192
215.51(b)	4.10	142
215.54	2.5	112
215.55—215.57	4.3	34
	4.10	176
215.56	3.19	238
	3.20	226
	4.8	104
215.58	3.16	187
	3.21	261
215.58(1)	3.21	261
215.70	5.3	43
	5.3	44
	5.3	46
215.75	5.23	627
220.00(1)	2.6	135
220.25(2)	5.17	388
221.05	3.22	263
	3.29	399
221.10	3.29	399
221.15	3.29	399
221.35	3.29	399
221.40	3.29	399
240.25	3.7	75
	3.18	199
240.35(3)	3.23	273
240.37	3.23	273
250.00(1)	10.8	
250.00(2)	10.8	
255.15	1.4	101
260.00	1.4	100
260.05	1.4	100
265.01	2.6	134
265.01(1)	5.10	290
	11.5	
	11.5	53
265.02(4)	2.5	107
	5.10	289
	11.5	
265.02(5)	11.5	
265.03	2.5	109
	5.16	349
265.08	2.6	134
265.09	5.10	280
265.12	11.5	
265.15(3)	10.11	227
410.00	2.10	222
415.00	2.10	222
420.05	2.10	222
450.10	7.4	

NEW YORK, MCKINNEY'S PENAL LAW

Sec.	This Work Sec.	Note
450.10 (Cont'd)	7.4	37
	7.34	
	8.2	
	10.6	
450.10(2)	7.4	37
450.10(4)(c)	7.4	37
Art. 460	2.9	191
460.10(1)	2.9	193
	2.9	194
460.10(3)	2.9	193
460.10(4)	2.9	193
	2.9	195
460.20	2.9	192
460.20(1)(a)	2.9	192
460.20(1)(b)	2.9	192
460.20(1)(c)	2.9	192
460.30	1.2	27
	2.10	221
460.40	2.9	201
460.50	2.9	201
460.60	2.9	201
Art. 480	1.2	27
	2.10	221

NEW YORK, MCKINNEY'S PUBLIC HEALTH LAW

Sec.	This Work Sec.	Note
3388	2.10	222
4143	5.27	757

NEW YORK, MCKINNEY'S PUBLIC OFFICERS LAW

Sec.	This Work Sec.	Note
10	5.3	40
84 et seq.	7.33	366
87(2)(e)	7.33	368
87(2)(f)	7.33	368

NEW YORK, MCKINNEY'S REAL PROPERTY ACTIONS & PROCEEDINGS LAW

Sec.	This Work Sec.	Note
711(5)	2.10	223

NEW YORK, MCKINNEY'S SOCIAL SERVICES LAW

Sec.	This Work Sec.	Note
422(12)	7.30	331
424–a	7.30	331

NEW YORK, MCKINNEY'S VEHICLE AND TRAFFIC LAW

Sec.	This Work Sec.	Note
510	3.5	45

TABLE OF STATUTES

NEW YORK, MCKINNEY'S VEHICLE AND TRAFFIC LAW

Sec.	This Work Sec.	Note
517	3.21	254
1180(d)	7.4	51
1192(2)	3.24	313
1192(3)	3.24	313
	5.27	722
1192(4)	3.24	313
1192(5)	5.27	721
1193(1)(c)	3.23	272
1194	10.8	153
1194(2)	10.8	152
1194(3)	10.8	
	10.8	153
	10.9	
1194–a	10.8	
1195(1)	10.8	153
1195(3)	10.8	153
1800(d)	2.6	151
1805	3.24	288
1806	3.24	288

NEW YORK, ADMINISTRATIVE CODE

Sec.	This Work Sec.	Note
Ch. 46	9.4	
701	2.10	223

NEW YORK LAWS

Year	This Work Sec.	Note
1926, c. 461	5.22	530
1969, c. 1147, § 8	10.11	207
1970, c. 996	5.2	17
	10.23	541
	10.23	542
	10.23	543
1972, c. 784	4.3	35
1973, c. 276	5.27	704
1973, c. 277	5.27	704
1974, c. 762	2.4	71
1974, c. 763, § 8	10.13	268
1976, c. 194, § 3	10.23	546
1977, c. 273, § 1	10.14	291
1978, c. 447	5.9	222
	5.9	257
1978, c. 481	1.10	213
	5.27	705
1979, c. 413, § 3	7.8	75
1979, c. 996	5.27	757
1980, c. 136	1.10	234
1980, c. 549	6.8	168
1980, c. 549, § 2	6.8	161
1980, c. 549, § 3	6.8	161
1980, c. 841	5.27	697
1980, c. 842	5.27	686
	5.27	697
1981, c. 788, § 2	4.10	163
1981, c. 791	6.9	194
1982, c. 558	3.33	460
1983, c. 481, § 2	10.8	150

NEW YORK LAWS

Year	This Work Sec.	Note
1983, c. 481, § 5	10.8	150
1984, c. 672	5.21	514
	5.22	549
1985, c. 257	1.9	205
1986, c. 516, § 15	2.9	209
1986, c. 794, § 3	4.10	164
1986, c. 837, § 2	9.44	320
1987, c. 440, § 2	6.8	172
1987, c. 549	3.20	238
1987, c. 550	3.20	238
1988, c. 47, § 18	10.8	151
1988, c. 744	10.8	157
	10.9	169
1988, c. 744, § 24	10.8	154
	10.8	155
1988, c. 744, § 25	10.8	156
1989, c. 693, § 2	6.4	75
1990, c. 209	5.27	708
1992, c. 316, § 26	4.2	28
1993, c. 446	3.16	176
	5.23	629
1993, c. 446, § 2	9.45	323
1993, c. 446, § 3	9.45	326
1993, c. 446, § 9	9.45	326
1994, c. 222	3.18	197
1994, c. 222, § 29	9.46	328
1994, c. 224	3.18	197
1995, c. 1	5.29	815
1995, c. 3	6.6	128
1995, c. 356	3.18	197

UNITED STATES

UNITED STATES CONSTITUTION

Art.	This Work Sec.	Note
I, § 8	1.4	70
III, § 2	1.3	44
Amend.		
4	3.12	122
	3.36	
	10.2	
	10.3	53
	10.5	
	10.9	
	10.11	
	10.17	
	10.17	349
	10.17	363
	10.20	
5	2.1	
	2.8	
	5.1	1
	5.9	194
	5.9	199
	5.11	309
	6.3	
	7.11	
	7.11	119
	7.17	181
6	1.3	44
	5.11	310
	5.14	328

TABLE OF STATUTES

UNITED STATES CONSTITUTION

Amend.	This Work	
6 (Cont'd)	5.22	
	5.22	568
	7.8	90
	7.24	
	9.1	
	9.8	
	9.51	365
	9.58	
8	4.1	3
14	2.1	
	4.1	2
	9.8	
	9.51	365
	9.58	

UNITED STATES CODE ANNOTATED
18 U.S.C.A.—Crimes and Criminal Procedure

Sec.	This Work Sec.	Note
13	1.3	72
1342(c)	4.10	130
	4.10	157
1342(c)(B)(vii)	4.10	158
1342(c)(B)(x)	4.10	160
3142	4.5	71

UNITED STATES CODE ANNOTATED
18 U.S.C.A.—Crimes and Criminal Procedure

Sec.	This Work Sec.	Note
3142(c)(B)(xiv)	4.10	130
6002	5.9	198

20 U.S.C.A.—Education

Sec.	This Work Sec.	Note
1232g(b)(2)(B)	7.9	96
	7.30	333

28 U.S.C.A.—Judiciary and Judicial Procedure

Sec.	This Work Sec.	Note
1442(a)	1.2	34
2254	9.55	399
2255	9.55	399

42 U.S.C.A.—The Public Health and Welfare

Sec.	This Work Sec.	Note
290dd–2	7.30	329
1983	3.14	154

TABLE OF RULES

NEW YORK RULES OF COURT

Rule	This Work Sec.	Note
111.2(a)	6.4	68
	6.4	69
	6.4	70
	6.4	71
111.3	6.5	91
128.17	5.2	18
200.13	1.2	11
	5.2	18
200.14	1.2	11
200.31	4.9	127

FEDERAL RULES OF CRIMINAL PROCEDURE

Rule	This Work Sec.	Note
8(b)	5.22	
	5.22	547
8(c)	5.22	
11	11.10	96
14	5.22	564
	5.22	601

TABLE OF CASES

Aaron, People v., 201 A.D.2d 574, 607 N.Y.S.2d 950 (N.Y.A.D. 2 Dept.1994)—§ 9.31, n. 234.

Aaron, People v., 172 A.D.2d 842, 569 N.Y.S.2d 206 (N.Y.A.D. 2 Dept.1991)—§ 10.3, n. 54.

Abbamonte, People v., 400 N.Y.S.2d 766, 371 N.E.2d 485 (N.Y.1977)—§ 2.6, n. 120.

Abdullah, People v., 189 A.D.2d 769, 592 N.Y.S.2d 406 (N.Y.A.D. 2 Dept.1993)—§ 5.8, n. 152.

Abdul-Malik, People v., 156 A.D.2d 1023, 549 N.Y.S.2d 304 (N.Y.A.D. 4 Dept. 1989)—§ 6.2, n. 30.

Abedi, People v., 156 Misc.2d 904, 595 N.Y.S.2d 1011 (N.Y.Sup.1993)—§ 1.2, n. 33; § 1.3, n. 64.

Abernathy, People v., 175 A.D.2d 407, 572 N.Y.S.2d 478 (N.Y.A.D. 3 Dept.1991)—§ 10.6, n. 129.

Abraham v. Justices of New York Supreme Court of Bronx County, 376 N.Y.S.2d 79, 338 N.E.2d 597 (N.Y.1975)—§ 2.6, n. 114, 120; § 2.11, n. 245.

Abrams, Matter of, 476 N.Y.S.2d 494, 465 N.E.2d 1 (N.Y.1984)—§ 1.2, n. 27.

A., Carmille v. David A., 162 Misc.2d 22, 615 N.Y.S.2d 584 (N.Y.Fam.Ct.1994)—§ 4.10, n. 142.

Acevedo, People v., 179 A.D.2d 813, 579 N.Y.S.2d 156 (N.Y.A.D. 2 Dept.1992)—§ 10.5, n. 124.

Acevedo, People v., 176 A.D.2d 1007, 575 N.Y.S.2d 174 (N.Y.A.D. 3 Dept.1991)—§ 9.47, n. 336.

Acevedo, People v., 175 A.D.2d 323, 572 N.Y.S.2d 101 (N.Y.A.D. 3 Dept.1991)—§ 10.3, n. 71.

Acevedo, People v., 515 N.Y.S.2d 753, 508 N.E.2d 665 (N.Y.1987)—§ 2.8; § 2.8, n. 180.

Acevedo, People v., 84 Misc.2d 563, 377 N.Y.S.2d 932 (N.Y.Co.Ct.1975)—§ 6.9, n. 186, 193.

Acosta, People v., 187 A.D.2d 329, 590 N.Y.S.2d 77 (N.Y.A.D. 1 Dept.1992)—§ 11.11, n. 112.

Adames, People v., 607 N.Y.S.2d 919, 629 N.E.2d 391 (N.Y.1993)—§ 2.4, n. 40.

Adams, People v., 381 N.Y.S.2d 847, 345 N.E.2d 318 (N.Y.1976)—§ 11.16, n. 200.

Adger, People v., 551 N.Y.S.2d 190, 550 N.E.2d 443 (N.Y.1989)—§ 7.16, n. 184.

Adler, People v., 431 N.Y.S.2d 412, 409 N.E.2d 888 (N.Y.1980)—§ 10.22, n. 519.

Adorno, People v., 628 N.Y.S.2d 426 (N.Y.A.D. 3 Dept.1995)—§ 5.17, n. 391.

Adorno, People v., 128 Misc.2d 389, 489 N.Y.S.2d 441 (N.Y.City Crim.Ct.1984)—§ 3.25, n. 325.

Aguilera, People v., 603 N.Y.S.2d 392, 623 N.E.2d 519 (N.Y.1993)—§ 2.8, n. 190; § 10.21, n. 508.

Agurs, United States v., 427 U.S. 97, 96 S.Ct. 2392, 49 L.Ed.2d 342 (1976)—§ 7.13; § 7.13, n. 143; § 7.22, n. 251.

Ahmed, People v., 496 N.Y.S.2d 984, 487 N.E.2d 894 (N.Y.1985)—§ 1.2, n. 30.

Albanese, People v., 163 A.D.2d 482, 558 N.Y.S.2d 168 (N.Y.A.D. 2 Dept.1990)—§ 11.19, n. 266.

Albarez, People v., 209 A.D.2d 186, 618 N.Y.S.2d 528 (N.Y.A.D. 1 Dept.1994)—§ 2.4, n. 38.

Albelo, People v., 166 A.D.2d 313, 560 N.Y.S.2d 1014 (N.Y.A.D. 1 Dept.1990)—§ 7.23, n. 267.

Albernaz v. United States, 450 U.S. 333, 101 S.Ct. 1137, 67 L.Ed.2d 275 (1981)—§ 2.1, n. 4.

Alcindor, People v., 157 Misc.2d 725, 598 N.Y.S.2d 449 (N.Y.City Crim.Ct.1993)—§ 10.13, n. 257; § 10.24, n. 553.

Alderman v. United States, 394 U.S. 165, 89 S.Ct. 961, 22 L.Ed.2d 176 (1969)—§ 10.11; § 10.11, n. 204.

Alejandro, People v., 517 N.Y.S.2d 927, 511 N.E.2d 71 (N.Y.1987)—§ 3.7, n. 69, 74; § 3.8, n. 99; § 3.9, n. 105; § 3.25, n. 329; § 3.26, n. 350; § 8.1, n. 21.

Alexander, People v., 161 A.D.2d 1035, 558 N.Y.S.2d 200 (N.Y.A.D. 3 Dept.1990)—§ 6.10, n. 219.

Alexander, People v., 88 A.D.2d 749, 451 N.Y.S.2d 473 (N.Y.A.D. 4 Dept.1982)—§ 10.16, n. 335.

Ali, People v., 209 A.D.2d 227, 618 N.Y.S.2d 640 (N.Y.A.D. 1 Dept.1994)—§ 9.41, n. 293.

Ali, People v., 195 A.D.2d 368, 600 N.Y.S.2d 55 (N.Y.A.D. 1 Dept.1993)—§ 9.30, n. 233; § 9.40, n. 287.

Allen, People v., 635 N.Y.S.2d 139, 658 N.E.2d 1012 (N.Y.1995)—§ 11.17, n. 233.

Allen, People v., 204 A.D.2d 973, 614 N.Y.S.2d 949 (N.Y.A.D. 4 Dept.1994)—§ 2.4, n. 52.

TABLE OF CASES

Allen, People v., 203 A.D.2d 582, 611 N.Y.S.2d 221 (N.Y.A.D. 2 Dept.1994)—§ 9.51, n. 380.

Allen, People v., 203 A.D.2d 97, 610 N.Y.S.2d 40 (N.Y.A.D. 1 Dept.1994)—§ 9.10, n. 99, 105.

Allen, People v., 603 N.Y.S.2d 820, 623 N.E.2d 1170 (N.Y.1993)—§ 11.17, n. 220.

Allen, People v., 178 A.D.2d 994, 579 N.Y.S.2d 262 (N.Y.A.D. 4 Dept.1991)—§ 9.55, n. 398.

Allen v. Strojnowski, 129 A.D.2d 700, 514 N.Y.S.2d 463 (N.Y.A.D. 2 Dept.1987)—§ 7.33, n. 371.

Allgood, People v., 523 N.Y.S.2d 431, 517 N.E.2d 1316 (N.Y.1987)—§ 7.23, n. 269; § 7.32, n. 359.

Allman, People v., 133 A.D.2d 638, 519 N.Y.S.2d 747 (N.Y.A.D. 2 Dept.1987)—§ 10.22, n. 534.

Allweiss, People v., 421 N.Y.S.2d 341, 396 N.E.2d 735 (N.Y.1979)—§ 5.21, n. 489.

Alonzo, People v., 155 A.D.2d 233, 546 N.Y.S.2d 617 (N.Y.A.D. 1 Dept.1989)—§ 11.12, n. 133.

Alston, People v., 191 A.D.2d 176, 594 N.Y.S.2d 37 (N.Y.A.D. 1 Dept.1993)—§ 9.38, n. 282.

Altman v. Bradley, 184 A.D.2d 131, 591 N.Y.S.2d 403 (N.Y.A.D. 1 Dept.1992)—§ 2.2, n. 23; § 5.9, n. 240.

Alvarez, People v., 141 Misc.2d 686, 534 N.Y.S.2d 90 (N.Y.City Crim.Ct.1988)—§ 3.7, n. 79.

Alvarez, People v., 94 Misc.2d 334, 404 N.Y.S.2d 509 (N.Y.Sup.1978)—§ 4.12, n. 191.

Alvarez, People v., 88 Misc.2d 709, 389 N.Y.S.2d 980 (N.Y.Sup.1976)—§ 5.22, n. 538.

Alvino, People v., 525 N.Y.S.2d 7, 519 N.E.2d 808 (N.Y.1987)—§ 5.21, n. 489.

Alzate, People v., 622 N.Y.S.2d 499, 646 N.E.2d 801 (N.Y.1994)—§ 11.11, n. 115.

Amato, People v., 173 A.D.2d 717, 570 N.Y.S.2d 1017 (N.Y.A.D. 2 Dept.1991)—§ 5.22, n. 596.

A., Matter of Abe, 452 N.Y.S.2d 6, 437 N.E.2d 265 (N.Y.1982)—§ 5.9, n. 235; § 7.11, n. 128; § 10.9, n. 167.

Amendolara, People v., 135 Misc.2d 170, 514 N.Y.S.2d 598 (N.Y.Sup.1987)—§ 9.16, n. 149.

Ames v. New York State Div. of Parole, 772 F.2d 13 (2nd Cir.1985)—§ 11.10, n. 108.

Ames, People v., 115 A.D.2d 543, 496 N.Y.S.2d 65 (N.Y.A.D. 2 Dept.1985)—§ 5.18, n. 412.

Anderson, People v., 630 N.Y.S.2d 77 (N.Y.A.D. 1 Dept.1995)—§ 10.26, n. 577.

Anderson, People v., 204 A.D.2d 168, 612 N.Y.S.2d 21 (N.Y.A.D. 1 Dept.1994)—§ 5.27, n. 772.

Anderson, People v., 203 A.D.2d 373, 612 N.Y.S.2d 909 (N.Y.A.D. 2 Dept.1994)—§ 11.17, n. 229.

Anderson, People v., 201 A.D.2d 432, 609 N.Y.S.2d 773 (N.Y.A.D. 1 Dept.1994)—§ 9.10, n. 98.

Anderson, People v., 186 A.D.2d 140, 587 N.Y.S.2d 430 (N.Y.A.D. 2 Dept.1992)—§ 2.4, n. 53.

Anderson, People v., 140 A.D.2d 528, 528 N.Y.S.2d 614 (N.Y.A.D. 2 Dept.1988)—§ 11.3, n. 16; § 11.19, n. 257.

Anderson, People v., 511 N.Y.S.2d 592, 503 N.E.2d 1023 (N.Y.1986)—§ 10.19; § 10.19, n. 431.

Anderson, People v., 266 N.Y.S.2d 110, 213 N.E.2d 445 (N.Y.1965)—§ 10.19, n. 399.

Andresen v. Maryland, 427 U.S. 463, 96 S.Ct. 2737, 49 L.Ed.2d 627 (1976)—§ 10.5, n. 82.

Andrews, People v., 176 A.D.2d 530, 574 N.Y.S.2d 719 (N.Y.A.D. 1 Dept.1991)—§ 10.11, n. 232.

Andriani, People v., 67 A.D.2d 20, 414 N.Y.S.2d 159 (N.Y.A.D. 1 Dept.1979)—§ 10.15, n. 303.

Angelillo, People v., 105 Misc.2d 338, 432 N.Y.S.2d 127 (N.Y.Co.Ct.1980)—§ 6.3, n. 61; § 6.9, n. 211.

Annunziata, People v., 105 A.D.2d 709, 481 N.Y.S.2d 148 (N.Y.A.D. 2 Dept.1984)—§ 11.13, n. 139; § 11.14, n. 150.

Anonymous, People v., 208 A.D.2d 426, 618 N.Y.S.2d 1009 (N.Y.A.D. 1 Dept.1994)—§ 11.11, n. 115.

Anonymous, People v., 154 Misc.2d 963, 587 N.Y.S.2d 103 (N.Y.City Crim.Ct.1992)—§ 7.17, n. 194.

Anonymous, People ex rel. v. Waugh, 76 Misc.2d 879, 351 N.Y.S.2d 594 (N.Y.Sup.1974)—§ 6.6, n. 126.

Anonymous A, People v., 118 Misc.2d 427, 460 N.Y.S.2d 864 (N.Y.Sup.1983)—§ 6.8, n. 167, 178.

Anonymous Attorneys v. Bar Ass'n of Erie County, 393 N.Y.S.2d 961, 362 N.E.2d 592 (N.Y.1977)—§ 5.9, n. 199.

Anthony, People v., 208 A.D.2d 637, 618 N.Y.S.2d 247 (N.Y.A.D. 2 Dept.1994)—§ 11.18, n. 248.

Anthony, People v., 188 A.D.2d 477, 591 N.Y.S.2d 181 (N.Y.A.D. 2 Dept.1992)—§ 11.18, n. 248.

Antonio, People v., 176 A.D.2d 528, 574 N.Y.S.2d 718 (N.Y.A.D. 1 Dept.1991)—§ 11.3, n. 22.

Aponte by Gorfinkel, People ex rel. v. Warden, Rikers Island, George Motchan Center, 146 Misc.2d 386, 550 N.Y.S.2d 792 (N.Y.Sup.1990)—§ 5.23, n. 623.

Application of (see name of party)

Arendes, People v., 92 Misc.2d 372, 400 N.Y.S.2d 273 (N.Y.Sup.1977)—§ 6.6, n. 107, 126.

TABLE OF CASES

Argentine, People v., 67 A.D.2d 180, 414 N.Y.S.2d 732 (N.Y.A.D. 2 Dept.1979)—§ 11.11, n. 123.

Argudin, People v., 151 Misc.2d 507, 573 N.Y.S.2d 572 (N.Y.City Crim.Ct.1991)—§ 7.17, n. 194.

Arizona v. Youngblood, 488 U.S. 51, 109 S.Ct. 333, 102 L.Ed.2d 281 (1988)—§ 7.23, n. 254.

Armer, People v., 119 A.D.2d 930, 501 N.Y.S.2d 203 (N.Y.A.D. 3 Dept.1986)—§ 11.15, n. 165.

Armlin, People v., 371 N.Y.S.2d 691, 332 N.E.2d 870 (N.Y.1975)—§ 6.2, n. 13, 16, 38; § 6.4, n. 73; § 6.10, n. 240, 248, 260; § 11.8, n. 73, 74; § 11.16, n. 193.

Arnau, People v., 457 N.Y.S.2d 763, 444 N.E.2d 13 (N.Y.1982)—§ 10.5, n. 93, 99, 121; § 10.9, n. 165; § 10.10; § 10.10, n. 173, 180; § 10.20, n. 475.

Arnold, People v., 177 A.D.2d 633, 576 N.Y.S.2d 339 (N.Y.A.D. 2 Dept.1991)—§ 7.30, n. 342.

Arnold, People v., 113 A.D.2d 101, 495 N.Y.S.2d 537 (N.Y.A.D. 4 Dept.1985)—§ 6.2, n. 14, 40; § 6.10, n. 249, 257.

Arroyo, People v., 209 A.D.2d 328, 618 N.Y.S.2d 783 (N.Y.A.D. 1 Dept.1994)—§ 5.22, n. 576.

Arturo, People v., 122 Misc.2d 1058, 472 N.Y.S.2d 998 (N.Y.City Crim.Ct.1984)—§ 7.3, n. 18.

Ashe v. Swenson, 397 U.S. 436, 90 S.Ct. 1189, 25 L.Ed.2d 469 (1970)—§ 2.8; § 2.8, n. 170.

Associated Press v. Bell, 517 N.Y.S.2d 444, 510 N.E.2d 313 (N.Y.1987)—§ 3.33, n. 466; § 6.9, n. 208; § 10.19, n. 402.

Astacio, People v., 173 A.D.2d 834, 571 N.Y.S.2d 60 (N.Y.A.D. 2 Dept.1991)—§ 7.17, n. 187.

Atkinson v. Barone, 200 A.D.2d 438, 607 N.Y.S.2d 244 (N.Y.A.D. 1 Dept.1994)—§ 2.4, n. 52.

Auer v. Smith, 77 A.D.2d 172, 432 N.Y.S.2d 926 (N.Y.A.D. 4 Dept.1980)—§ 5.21, n. 483, 485.

Augustine, People v., 172 A.D.2d 843, 569 N.Y.S.2d 207 (N.Y.A.D. 2 Dept.1991)—§ 8.2.

Auslander, People v., 168 A.D.2d 759, 563 N.Y.S.2d 912 (N.Y.A.D. 3 Dept.1990)—§ 9.51, n. 380.

Auslander, People v., 146 A.D.2d 936, 536 N.Y.S.2d 914 (N.Y.A.D. 3 Dept.1989)—§ 11.13, n. 139.

Avant, People v., 352 N.Y.S.2d 161, 307 N.E.2d 230 (N.Y.1973)—§ 5.9, n. 206; § 5.27, n. 746.

Avery, People v., 214 A.D.2d 1018, 626 N.Y.S.2d 904 (N.Y.A.D. 4 Dept.1995)—§ 9.22, n. 172.

Avery, People v., 626 N.Y.S.2d 726, 650 N.E.2d 384 (N.Y.1995)—§ 11.13; § 11.13, n. 146, 147.

Avila, People v., 177 A.D.2d 426, 576 N.Y.S.2d 534 (N.Y.A.D. 1 Dept.1991)—§ 11.9, n. 83.

Axentiou, People v., 158 Misc.2d 19, 598 N.Y.S.2d 928 (N.Y.Sup.1993)—§ 1.3, n. 40, 54, 60.

Ayala, People v., 554 N.Y.S.2d 412, 553 N.E.2d 960 (N.Y.1990)—§ 10.19, n. 462.

Azcona, People v., 180 A.D.2d 690, 580 N.Y.S.2d 52 (N.Y.A.D. 2 Dept.1992)—§ 9.43, n. 314.

Baba-Ali, People v., 179 A.D.2d 725, 578 N.Y.S.2d 633 (N.Y.A.D. 2 Dept.1992)—§ 7.21, n. 237.

Babbush, People v., 150 Misc.2d 174, 566 N.Y.S.2d 475 (N.Y.Sup.1991)—§ 1.1, n. 2.

Bacic, People v., 202 A.D.2d 234, 608 N.Y.S.2d 452 (N.Y.A.D. 1 Dept.1994)—§ 6.2, n. 32.

Badolato v. Molinari, 106 Misc. 342, 174 N.Y.S. 512 (N.Y.Sup.1919)—§ 4.2, n. 17.

Baghai-Kermani, People v., 620 N.Y.S.2d 313, 644 N.E.2d 1004 (N.Y.1994)—§ 7.22, n. 248.

Bagley, United States v., 473 U.S. 667, 105 S.Ct. 3375, 87 L.Ed.2d 481 (1985)—§ 7.12, n. 133; § 7.13; § 7.13, n. 146.

Bailey, People v., 630 N.Y.S.2d 499 (N.Y.A.D. 1 Dept.1995)—§ 10.17, n. 374, 375.

Bailey, People v., 537 N.Y.S.2d 111, 534 N.E.2d 28 (N.Y.1988)—§ 7.17, n. 188.

Bailey, People v., 133 A.D.2d 462, 519 N.Y.S.2d 676 (N.Y.A.D. 2 Dept.1987)—§ 1.4, n. 113.

Bailey, People v., 118 Misc.2d 860, 462 N.Y.S.2d 94 (N.Y.Sup.1983)—§ 4.10, n. 168, 173.

Bain, Ex parte, 121 U.S. 1, 7 S.Ct. 781, 30 L.Ed. 849 (1887)—§ 5.18, n. 425.

Baker, People v., 386 N.Y.S.2d 575, 352 N.E.2d 879 (N.Y.1976)—§ 2.4, n. 77.

Baker, People v., 296 N.Y.S.2d 745, 244 N.E.2d 232 (N.Y.1968)—§ 10.6, n. 126.

Baker v. United States, 401 F.2d 958, 131 U.S.App.D.C. 7 (D.C.Cir.1968)—§ 5.21; § 5.21, n. 523, 524.

Ball v. United States, 470 U.S. 856, 105 S.Ct. 1668, 84 L.Ed.2d 740 (1985)—§ 5.17, n. 361.

Ballacchino, People v., 126 Misc.2d 610, 484 N.Y.S.2d 765 (N.Y.City Ct.1984)—§ 2.7, n. 168.

Ballott, People v., 286 N.Y.S.2d 1, 233 N.E.2d 103 (N.Y.1967)—§ 10.7, n. 139; § 10.10, n. 182.

Baltimore City Dept. of Social Services v. Bouknight, 493 U.S. 549, 110 S.Ct. 900, 107 L.Ed.2d 992 (1990)—§ 5.9, n. 239.

Balukas, People v., 95 A.D.2d 813, 463 N.Y.S.2d 534 (N.Y.A.D. 2 Dept.1983)—§ 6.3, n. 58.

TABLE OF CASES

Banch, People v., 593 N.Y.S.2d 491, 608 N.E.2d 1069 (N.Y.1992)—§ 7.22, n. 244; § 7.23, n. 265, 266; § 7.31, n. 351; § 10.19, n. 414.

Bancroft, People v., 110 A.D.2d 773, 488 N.Y.S.2d 215 (N.Y.A.D. 2 Dept.1985)—§ 6.2, n. 33.

Bangert, People v., 292 N.Y.S.2d 900, 239 N.E.2d 644 (N.Y.1968)—§ 6.2, n. 20; § 6.10, n. 241.

Banham, People v., 175 A.D.2d 166, 573 N.Y.S.2d 899 (N.Y.A.D. 2 Dept.1991)—§ 9.38, n. 274.

Banks, People v., 100 A.D.2d 780, 474 N.Y.S.2d 64 (N.Y.A.D. 1 Dept.1984)—§ 11.16, n. 208.

Banville, People v., 134 A.D.2d 116, 523 N.Y.S.2d 844 (N.Y.A.D. 2 Dept.1988)—§ 5.10, n. 276; § 11.5, n. 42.

Baptiste, People v., 533 N.Y.S.2d 853, 530 N.E.2d 377 (N.Y.1988)—§ 2.4, n. 63.

Baquadano, People v., 164 Misc.2d 801, 626 N.Y.S.2d 691 (N.Y.City Crim.Ct.1995)—§ 5.9, n. 253.

Barclift, People v., 97 Misc.2d 994, 412 N.Y.S.2d 991 (N.Y.City Crim.Ct.1979)—§ 3.33, n. 450.

Barker v. Wingo, 407 U.S. 514, 92 S.Ct. 2182, 33 L.Ed.2d 101 (1972)—§ 9.8; § 9.8, n. 37; § 9.9, n. 73; § 9.10, n. 91.

Barkin, People v., 428 N.Y.S.2d 192, 405 N.E.2d 674 (N.Y.1980)—§ 1.8, n. 166; § 11.2, n. 10.

Barnes, People v., 202 A.D.2d 350, 610 N.Y.S.2d 779 (N.Y.A.D. 1 Dept.1994)—§ 11.9, n. 90.

Barnes, People v., 130 Misc.2d 1058, 499 N.Y.S.2d 343 (N.Y.Sup.1986)—§ 9.3, n. 11.

Barnes, People v., 429 N.Y.S.2d 178, 406 N.E.2d 1071 (N.Y.1980)—§ 5.17, n. 381; § 5.18, n. 424.

Barnes, People v., 44 A.D.2d 740, 354 N.Y.S.2d 459 (N.Y.A.D. 3 Dept.1974)—§ 5.14, n. 331.

Barnes, People ex rel. v. N.Y.C. Penitentiary, 75 Misc.2d 291, 347 N.Y.S.2d 383 (N.Y.Sup.1973)—§ 9.6, n. 24.

Barnes v. Tofany, 313 N.Y.S.2d 690, 261 N.E.2d 617 (N.Y.1970)—§ 2.10, n. 232.

Barr v. Albany County, 428 N.Y.S.2d 665, 406 N.E.2d 481 (N.Y.1980)—§ 10.1, n. 6; § 10.6, n. 129.

Barreras, People v., 92 A.D.2d 871, 459 N.Y.S.2d 828 (N.Y.A.D. 2 Dept.1983)—§ 7.12, n. 132.

Bartkus v. People of State of Ill., 359 U.S. 121, 79 S.Ct. 676, 3 L.Ed.2d 684 (1959)—§ 2.2, n. 25.

Bartley, People v., 419 N.Y.S.2d 956, 393 N.E.2d 1029 (N.Y.1979)—§ 2.4, n. 82; § 11.19, n. 256.

Bartok, People v., 209 A.D.2d 530, 619 N.Y.S.2d 626 (N.Y.A.D. 2 Dept.1994)—§ 5.9, n. 251.

Bartolomeo, People v., 126 A.D.2d 375, 513 N.Y.S.2d 981 (N.Y.A.D. 2 Dept.1987)—§ 8.2.

Bashian, People v., 190 A.D.2d 681, 593 N.Y.S.2d 526 (N.Y.A.D. 2 Dept.1993)—§ 10.4, n. 78.

Basir, People v., 141 A.D.2d 745, 529 N.Y.S.2d 841 (N.Y.A.D. 2 Dept.1988)—§ 6.6, n. 98.

Batashure, People v., 552 N.Y.S.2d 896, 552 N.E.2d 144 (N.Y.1990)—§ 5.5; § 5.5, n. 79; § 5.27, n. 716, 751; § 8.2.

Bates, People v., 204 A.D.2d 473, 614 N.Y.S.2d 163 (N.Y.A.D. 2 Dept.1994)—§ 11.7, n. 70.

Batista, People v., 164 Misc.2d 632, 625 N.Y.S.2d 1008 (N.Y.Sup.1995)—§ 5.8, n. 120, 190.

Batista, People v., 128 Misc.2d 1054, 491 N.Y.S.2d 966 (N.Y.City Crim.Ct.1985)—§ 3.23, n. 278.

Battista, People ex rel. v. Christian, 249 N.Y. 314, 164 N.E. 111 (N.Y.1928)—§ 5.11, n. 304.

Battles, People v., 77 A.D.2d 405, 433 N.Y.S.2d 936 (N.Y.A.D. 4 Dept.1980)—§ 9.24, n. 192; § 9.48, n. 355.

Bauer on Behalf of Rhodes, People ex rel. v. McGreevy, 147 Misc.2d 213, 555 N.Y.S.2d 581 (N.Y.Sup.1990)—§ 4.5, n. 75; § 4.7, n. 101.

Baxley, People v., 616 N.Y.S.2d 7, 639 N.E.2d 746 (N.Y.1994)—§ 7.12, n. 134.

Baxley, People v., 140 Misc.2d 516, 531 N.Y.S.2d 491 (N.Y.Sup.1988)—§ 6.3, n. 58.

Baxter, People v., 629 N.Y.S.2d 347 (N.Y.A.D. 4 Dept.1995)—§ 9.49, n. 359.

Beach v. Kunken, 162 Misc.2d 381, 616 N.Y.S.2d 721 (N.Y.Sup.1994)—§ 1.5, n. 136.

Beam, People v., 161 A.D.2d 1153, 556 N.Y.S.2d 181 (N.Y.A.D. 4 Dept.1990)—§ 7.21, n. 234.

Beattie, People v., 587 N.Y.S.2d 585, 600 N.E.2d 216 (N.Y.1992)—§ 3.5, n. 51; § 11.15, n. 176.

Beauchamp, People v., 541 N.Y.S.2d 977, 539 N.E.2d 1105 (N.Y.1989)—§ 5.15, n. 341; § 5.17, n. 358, 365.

Beauvais, People v., 98 A.D.2d 897, 470 N.Y.S.2d 887 (N.Y.A.D. 3 Dept.1983)—§ 5.3, n. 36.

Bebee, People v., 175 A.D.2d 250, 572 N.Y.S.2d 715 (N.Y.A.D. 2 Dept.1991)—§ 5.27, n. 765.

Becher on Behalf of Vadakin v. Dunston, 142 Misc.2d 103, 536 N.Y.S.2d 396 (N.Y.Sup.1988)—§ 4.5, n. 62.

Beck v. State of Ohio, 379 U.S. 89, 85 S.Ct. 223, 13 L.Ed.2d 142 (1964)—§ 3.18, n. 191.

Behr, People v., 116 Misc.2d 576, 455 N.Y.S.2d 942 (N.Y.Sup.1982)—§ 11.4, n. 31.

TABLE OF CASES

Belge, People v., 390 N.Y.S.2d 867, 359 N.E.2d 377 (N.Y.1976)—§ **5.27, n. 755.**

Belkota, People v., 50 A.D.2d 118, 377 N.Y.S.2d 321 (N.Y.A.D. 4 Dept.1975)— § **5.27, n. 764.**

Bell, People v., 214 A.D.2d 353, 625 N.Y.S.2d 893 (N.Y.A.D. 1 Dept.1995)— § **10.28, n. 606.**

Bellach, People v., 58 A.D.2d 613, 395 N.Y.S.2d 673 (N.Y.A.D. 2 Dept.1977)— § **9.11, n. 113.**

Bellamy v. Judges and Justices Authorized to Sit in New York City Criminal Court, 41 A.D.2d 196, 342 N.Y.S.2d 137 (N.Y.A.D. 1 Dept.1973)—§ **4.1, n. 4, 8;** § **4.3, n. 37.**

Bellinger, People v., 269 N.Y. 265, 199 N.E. 213 (N.Y.1935)—§ **5.20, n. 465.**

Bellis v. United States, 417 U.S. 85, 94 S.Ct. 2179, 40 L.Ed.2d 678 (1974)—§ **5.9, n. 237.**

Benard, People v., 163 Misc.2d 176, 620 N.Y.S.2d 242 (N.Y.Sup.1994)—§ **11.15, n. 165.**

Benevento, People v., 59 A.D.2d 1029, 399 N.Y.S.2d 770 (N.Y.A.D. 4 Dept.1977)— § **5.27, n. 764.**

Benjamin, People v., 147 Misc.2d 617, 558 N.Y.S.2d 825 (N.Y.City Crim.Ct.1990)— § **7.18, n. 217.**

Bennett, People v., 583 N.Y.S.2d 825, 593 N.E.2d 279 (N.Y.1992)—§ **7.15, n. 174.**

Bennett, People v., 453 N.Y.S.2d 164, 438 N.E.2d 870 (N.Y.1982)—§ **10.24, n. 561.**

Bentley, People ex rel. Meurer v., 202 A.D.2d 1042, 609 N.Y.S.2d 466 (N.Y.A.D. 4 Dept.1994)—§ **9.25, n. 204.**

Benton v. Maryland, 395 U.S. 784, 89 S.Ct. 2056, 23 L.Ed.2d 707 (1969)—§ **2.1, n. 1;** § **2.2, n. 10.**

Benton, People v., 143 A.D.2d 526, 533 N.Y.S.2d 32 (N.Y.A.D. 4 Dept.1988)— § **11.10, n. 100.**

Benton by Weintraub, People ex rel. v. Warden, 118 A.D.2d 443, 499 N.Y.S.2d 738 (N.Y.A.D. 1 Dept.1986)—§ **4.5, n. 83, 89.**

Berg, People v., 101 Misc.2d 726, 421 N.Y.S.2d 968 (N.Y.Dist.Ct.1979)—§ **1.4, n. 106, 116.**

Berkley, People v., 157 A.D.2d 463, 549 N.Y.S.2d 392 (N.Y.A.D. 1 Dept.1990)— § **7.17, n. 193.**

Berkowitz, People v., 428 N.Y.S.2d 927, 406 N.E.2d 783 (N.Y.1980)—§ **2.8, n. 174, 179;** § **9.26, n. 215;** § **9.51, n. 367.**

Berkowitz, People v., 93 Misc.2d 873, 403 N.Y.S.2d 699 (N.Y.Sup.1978)—§ **6.9, n. 208.**

Bermudez, People v., 157 A.D.2d 533, 549 N.Y.S.2d 1022 (N.Y.A.D. 1 Dept.1990)— § **11.3, n. 22.**

Bernard, People v., 129 Misc.2d 1083, 495 N.Y.S.2d 634 (N.Y.City Crim.Ct.1985)— § **9.20, n. 163.**

Bernier, People v., 541 N.Y.S.2d 760, 539 N.E.2d 588 (N.Y.1989)—§ **10.13, n. 266;** § **10.28;** § **10.28, n. 602;** § **10.29, n. 609.**

Bernier, People v., 141 A.D.2d 750, 529 N.Y.S.2d 847 (N.Y.A.D. 2 Dept.1988)— § **9.34, n. 256;** § **10.28, n. 603.**

Berrios, People v., 321 N.Y.S.2d 884, 270 N.E.2d 709 (N.Y.1971)—§ **10.7, n. 139;** § **10.20, n. 474.**

Berta, People v., 213 A.D.2d 659, 624 N.Y.S.2d 211 (N.Y.A.D. 2 Dept.1995)— § **5.21, n. 504.**

Beslanovics, People v., 454 N.Y.S.2d 976, 440 N.E.2d 1322 (N.Y.1982)—§ **5.18, n. 433.**

Best, People v., 145 A.D.2d 499, 535 N.Y.S.2d 108 (N.Y.A.D. 2 Dept.1988)— § **7.17, n. 216.**

Best, People v., 132 A.D.2d 773, 517 N.Y.S.2d 582 (N.Y.A.D. 3 Dept.1987)— § **5.16, n. 348.**

Betances, People v., 165 A.D.2d 754, 564 N.Y.S.2d 269 (N.Y.A.D. 1 Dept.1990)— § **10.22, n. 527.**

Betancourt, People v., 629 N.Y.S.2d 423 (N.Y.A.D. 1 Dept.1995)—§ **9.51, n. 367, 373.**

Bethea, People v., 502 N.Y.S.2d 713, 493 N.E.2d 937 (N.Y.1986)—§ **10.10, n. 196.**

Betheny, People v., 147 A.D.2d 488, 537 N.Y.S.2d 586 (N.Y.A.D. 2 Dept.1989)— § **11.13, n. 138.**

Betts, People v., 520 N.Y.S.2d 370, 514 N.E.2d 865 (N.Y.1987)—§ **5.8, n. 174;** § **7.15;** § **7.15, n. 173.**

Betts, People v., 90 A.D.2d 641, 456 N.Y.S.2d 278 (N.Y.A.D. 3 Dept.1982)— § **10.6, n. 129.**

Bey, People v., 167 A.D.2d 868, 562 N.Y.S.2d 896 (N.Y.A.D. 4 Dept.1990)— § **6.10, n. 250.**

Bey, People v., 144 A.D.2d 972, 534 N.Y.S.2d 275 (N.Y.A.D. 4 Dept.1988)— § **6.10, n. 248.**

Bey-Allah, People v., 132 A.D.2d 76, 521 N.Y.S.2d 422 (N.Y.A.D. 1 Dept.1987)— § **5.8, n. 125.**

Bialostok, People v., 599 N.Y.S.2d 532, 615 N.E.2d 1016 (N.Y.1993)—§ **10.9, n. 171.**

Bialostok, People v., 594 N.Y.S.2d 701, 610 N.E.2d 374 (N.Y.1993)—§ **10.9, n. 168.**

Bigelow, People v., 497 N.Y.S.2d 630, 488 N.E.2d 451 (N.Y.1985)—§ **10.3, n. 54.**

Billups, People v., 105 A.D.2d 795, 481 N.Y.S.2d 430 (N.Y.A.D. 2 Dept.1984)— § **9.41, n. 294.**

Billups v. Santucci, 151 A.D.2d 663, 542 N.Y.S.2d 726 (N.Y.A.D. 2 Dept.1989)— § **7.33, n. 367.**

Biltsted, People v., 151 Misc.2d 620, 574 N.Y.S.2d 256 (N.Y.City Crim.Ct.1991)— § **5.22, n. 557.**

Bing, People v., 559 N.Y.S.2d 474, 558 N.E.2d 1011 (N.Y.1990)—§ **10.22, n. 526.**

TABLE OF CASES

Bisnett, People v., 144 A.D.2d 567, 534 N.Y.S.2d 424 (N.Y.A.D. 2 Dept.1988)—§ 6.10, n. 235.

Bissereth, People v., 194 A.D.2d 317, 598 N.Y.S.2d 781 (N.Y.A.D. 1 Dept.1993)—§ 9.40, n. 288.

Bizzell, People v., 144 Misc.2d 1000, 545 N.Y.S.2d 528 (N.Y.Sup.1989)—§ 5.8, n. 166.

Black, People v., 632 N.Y.S.2d 823 (N.Y.A.D. 2 Dept.1995)—§ 5.7; § 5.7, n. 107.

Black, People v., 187 A.D.2d 517, 589 N.Y.S.2d 911 (N.Y.A.D. 2 Dept.1992)—§ 11.13, n. 140.

Blackwell, People v., 156 A.D.2d 148, 548 N.Y.S.2d 197 (N.Y.A.D. 1 Dept.1989)—§ 5.21, n. 503.

Blackwell, People v., 128 Misc.2d 599, 490 N.Y.S.2d 457 (N.Y.Sup.1985)—§ 10.19, n. 413.

Blackwell, People v., 128 Misc.2d 584, 490 N.Y.S.2d 456 (N.Y.Co.Ct.1985)—§ 5.8, n. 132.

Blair, People v., 155 A.D.2d 676, 547 N.Y.S.2d 897 (N.Y.A.D. 2 Dept.1989)—§ 10.2, n. 43.

Blake, People v., 133 A.D.2d 549, 520 N.Y.S.2d 92 (N.Y.A.D. 4 Dept.1987)—§ 1.9, n. 197.

Blake, People v., 193 N.Y. 616, 86 N.E. 1129 (N.Y.1908)—§ 9.6, n. 27.

Blakley, People v., 357 N.Y.S.2d 459, 313 N.E.2d 763 (N.Y.1974)—§ 9.7, n. 34; § 9.12, n. 121; § 11.3, n. 27; § 11.16, n. 200.

Bleakley, People v., 515 N.Y.S.2d 761, 508 N.E.2d 672 (N.Y.1987)—§ 2.4, n. 90.

Blockburger v. United States, 284 U.S. 299, 52 S.Ct. 180, 76 L.Ed. 306 (1932)—§ 2.5, n. 97.

Blount, People v., 156 Misc.2d 489, 593 N.Y.S.2d 962 (N.Y.Sup.1993)—§ 1.8, n. 163.

Blowe, People v., 130 A.D.2d 668, 515 N.Y.S.2d 812 (N.Y.A.D. 2 Dept.1987)—§ 10.14, n. 284.

Blumberg v. Lennon, 44 A.D.2d 769, 354 N.Y.S.2d 261 (N.Y.A.D. 4 Dept.1974)—§ 11.3, n. 17.

B., Matter of Tyrell, 177 A.D.2d 375, 576 N.Y.S.2d 127 (N.Y.A.D. 1 Dept.1991)—§ 10.16, n. 339.

Board, People v., 97 A.D.2d 610, 468 N.Y.S.2d 209 (N.Y.A.D. 3 Dept.1983)—§ 4.13, n. 215.

Bogdanoff, People v., 254 N.Y. 16, 171 N.E. 890 (N.Y.1930)—§ 5.14, n. 331.

Bolden, People v., 597 N.Y.S.2d 270, 613 N.E.2d 145 (N.Y.1993)—§ 9.13, n. 129; § 9.26, n. 213; § 9.37; § 9.37, n. 264; § 9.51, n. 372.

Bonet, People v., 176 A.D.2d 641, 575 N.Y.S.2d 294 (N.Y.A.D. 1 Dept.1991)—§ 7.21, n. 234.

Bongarzone, People v., 515 N.Y.S.2d 227, 507 N.E.2d 1083 (N.Y.1987)—§ 5.21, n. 491, 509.

Bonilla, People v., 604 N.Y.S.2d 937, 624 N.E.2d 1032 (N.Y.1993)—§ 10.16, n. 340.

Bonilla, People v., 193 A.D.2d 362, 597 N.Y.S.2d 46 (N.Y.A.D. 1 Dept.1993)—§ 10.16, n. 335.

Bonterre, People v., 87 Misc.2d 243, 384 N.Y.S.2d 351 (N.Y.City Crim.Ct.1976)—§ 9.43, n. 316.

Boone, People v., 194 A.D.2d 407, 599 N.Y.S.2d 540 (N.Y.A.D. 1 Dept.1993)—§ 7.19, n. 223.

Boose v. City of Rochester, 71 A.D.2d 59, 421 N.Y.S.2d 740 (N.Y.A.D. 4 Dept. 1979)—§ 3.12, n. 126.

Booth v. Clary, 613 N.Y.S.2d 110, 635 N.E.2d 279 (N.Y.1994)—§ 2.2, n. 27.

Boots, People v., 106 Misc.2d 522, 434 N.Y.S.2d 850 (N.Y.Co.Ct.1980)—§ 1.3, n. 73.

Bornholdt, People v., 350 N.Y.S.2d 369, 305 N.E.2d 461 (N.Y.1973)—§ 5.22; § 5.22, n. 612.

Borrello v. Balbach, 112 A.D.2d 1051, 492 N.Y.S.2d 822 (N.Y.A.D. 2 Dept.1985)—§ 5.8, n. 125.

Borzuko v. City of New York Police Dept. Property Clerk, 136 Misc.2d 758, 519 N.Y.S.2d 491 (N.Y.Sup.1987)—§ 1.3, n. 41, 43.

Boston, People v., 555 N.Y.S.2d 27, 554 N.E.2d 64 (N.Y.1990)—§ 5.10; § 5.10, n. 271, 275; § 5.18, n. 425, 442; § 11.5, n. 42.

Botta, People v., 100 A.D.2d 311, 474 N.Y.S.2d 72 (N.Y.A.D. 2 Dept.1984)—§ 1.4, n. 121, 124.

Boudin, People v., 90 A.D.2d 253, 457 N.Y.S.2d 302 (N.Y.A.D. 2 Dept.1982)—§ 1.9, n. 194; § 8.1, n. 23.

Boudin, People v., 114 Misc.2d 523, 452 N.Y.S.2d 496 (N.Y.Sup.1982)—§ 7.11, n. 128.

Boughton, People v., 523 N.Y.S.2d 454, 517 N.E.2d 1340 (N.Y.1987)—§ 10.24, n. 554.

Bourdonnay, People v., 160 A.D.2d 1014, 555 N.Y.S.2d 134 (N.Y.A.D. 2 Dept. 1990)—§ 11.18, n. 249.

Bourjaily v. United States, 483 U.S. 171, 107 S.Ct. 2775, 97 L.Ed.2d 144 (1987)—§ 5.22, n. 591.

Bouton, People v., 428 N.Y.S.2d 218, 405 N.E.2d 699 (N.Y.1980)—§ 10.20, n. 468.

Bowen, People v., 122 A.D.2d 64, 504 N.Y.S.2d 480 (N.Y.A.D. 2 Dept.1986)—§ 11.15, n. 184.

Bowers, People v., 92 A.D.2d 669, 461 N.Y.S.2d 900 (N.Y.A.D. 3 Dept.1983)—§ 10.3, n. 59.

Bowers, People v., 45 A.D.2d 241, 357 N.Y.S.2d 563 (N.Y.A.D. 4 Dept.1974)—§ 11.18, n. 243.

TABLE OF CASES

Boyd, People v., 189 A.D.2d 433, 596 N.Y.S.2d 760 (N.Y.A.D. 1 Dept.1993)—§ 9.32, n. 237, 239; § 9.43, n. 309.

Boyd, People v., 164 A.D.2d 800, 560 N.Y.S.2d 15 (N.Y.A.D. 1 Dept.1990)—§ 7.19, n. 223.

Boyd, People v., 123 A.D.2d 638, 506 N.Y.S.2d 904 (N.Y.A.D. 2 Dept.1986)—§ 9.32, n. 238.

Boyd, People v., 116 A.D.2d 978, 498 N.Y.S.2d 932 (N.Y.A.D. 4 Dept.1986)—§ 9.42, n. 303.

Boyd, People v., 59 A.D.2d 558, 397 N.Y.S.2d 150 (N.Y.A.D. 2 Dept.1977)—§ 5.18, n. 422.

Boyd, People v., 291 N.Y.S.2d 816, 238 N.E.2d 923 (N.Y.1968)—§ 11.18, n. 246.

Boykin v. Alabama, 395 U.S. 238, 89 S.Ct. 1709, 23 L.Ed.2d 274 (1969)—§ 11.7, n. 62; § 11.15, n. 155.

Boyle v. Kelley, 396 N.Y.S.2d 834, 365 N.E.2d 866 (N.Y.1977)—§ 10.6, n. 135.

Boyne, People v., 174 A.D.2d 103, 579 N.Y.S.2d 338 (N.Y.A.D. 1 Dept.1992)—§ 7.23, n. 254.

Bracken, People v., 129 Misc.2d 1048, 494 N.Y.S.2d 1021 (N.Y.City Crim.Ct. 1985)—§ 3.20, n. 246.

Brackley v. Donnelly, 53 A.D.2d 849, 385 N.Y.S.2d 587 (N.Y.A.D. 2 Dept.1976)—§ 2.4, n. 38.

Bradley, People v., 181 A.D.2d 316, 586 N.Y.S.2d 119 (N.Y.A.D. 1 Dept.1992)—§ 10.4, n. 78.

Bradley, People v., 119 A.D.2d 993, 500 N.Y.S.2d 892 (N.Y.A.D. 4 Dept.1986)—§ 7.17, n. 195.

Bradley, People v., 74 A.D.2d 850, 425 N.Y.S.2d 382 (N.Y.A.D. 2 Dept.1980)—§ 9.10, n. 103.

Brady v. Maryland, 373 U.S. 83, 83 S.Ct. 1194, 10 L.Ed.2d 215 (1963)—§ 7.2, n. 10; § 7.12; § 7.12, n. 131; § 7.30, n. 334; § 8.2.

Brady v. United States, 397 U.S. 742, 90 S.Ct. 1463, 25 L.Ed.2d 747 (1970)—§ 11.7, n. 62.

Brakas, People v., 204 A.D.2d 474, 614 N.Y.S.2d 170 (N.Y.A.D. 2 Dept.1994)—§ 11.17, n. 228.

Branch, People v., 612 N.Y.S.2d 365, 634 N.E.2d 966 (N.Y.1994)—§ 5.9, n. 255.

Brancoccio, People v., 612 N.Y.S.2d 353, 634 N.E.2d 954 (N.Y.1994)—§ 1.8, n. 170; § 2.3; § 2.3, n. 30.

Brandon's Estate, Matter of, 448 N.Y.S.2d 436, 433 N.E.2d 501 (N.Y.1982)—§ 5.22, n. 536.

Brannon, People v., 58 A.D.2d 34, 394 N.Y.S.2d 974 (N.Y.A.D. 4 Dept.1977)—§ 5.17; § 5.17, n. 366.

Braswell v. United States, 487 U.S. 99, 108 S.Ct. 2284, 101 L.Ed.2d 98 (1988)—§ 5.9, n. 237.

Bratton, People v., 491 N.Y.S.2d 623, 481 N.E.2d 255 (N.Y.1985)—§ 9.36; § 9.36, n. 261, 262; § 9.38; § 9.38, n. 279, 280.

Bray, People v., 154 A.D.2d 692, 546 N.Y.S.2d 894 (N.Y.A.D. 2 Dept.1989)—§ 11.17, n. 224.

Brazeau, People v., 162 A.D.2d 979, 557 N.Y.S.2d 205 (N.Y.A.D. 4 Dept.1990)—§ 9.38, n. 276, 277.

Breed v. Jones, 421 U.S. 519, 95 S.Ct. 1779, 44 L.Ed.2d 346 (1975)—§ 2.10, n. 236.

Brensic, People v., 136 A.D.2d 169, 526 N.Y.S.2d 968 (N.Y.A.D. 2 Dept.1988)—§ 1.9, n. 193; § 8.1, n. 23.

Brensic, People v., 517 N.Y.S.2d 120, 509 N.E.2d 1226 (N.Y.1987)—§ 5.22, n. 590.

Brewster, People v., 482 N.Y.S.2d 724, 472 N.E.2d 686 (N.Y.1984)—§ 5.6; § 5.6, n. 93; § 5.27, n. 745.

Brewster, People v., 100 A.D.2d 134, 473 N.Y.S.2d 984 (N.Y.A.D. 2 Dept.1984)—§ 5.6; § 5.6, n. 91.

B., Ricardo, People v., 538 N.Y.S.2d 796, 535 N.E.2d 1336 (N.Y.1989)—§ 5.22; § 5.22, n. 593.

Brickhouse, People v., 163 A.D.2d 604, 559 N.Y.S.2d 677 (N.Y.A.D. 2 Dept.1990)—§ 11.15, n. 191.

Brigante, People v., 115 A.D.2d 547, 496 N.Y.S.2d 70 (N.Y.A.D. 2 Dept.1985)—§ 10.15, n. 301.

Briggs, People v., 136 Misc.2d 687, 519 N.Y.S.2d 294 (N.Y.Town Ct.1987)—§ 7.4, n. 50.

Briggs, People v., 379 N.Y.S.2d 779, 342 N.E.2d 557 (N.Y.1975)—§ 10.23; § 10.23, n. 544; § 10.27, n. 590.

Brinson, People v., 177 A.D.2d 1019, 578 N.Y.S.2d 38 (N.Y.A.D. 4 Dept.1991)—§ 10.2, n. 23.

Britt, People v., 200 A.D.2d 401, 606 N.Y.S.2d 208 (N.Y.A.D. 1 Dept.1994)—§ 11.18, n. 243.

Britt, People ex rel. Fraser v., 289 N.Y. 614, 43 N.E.2d 836 (N.Y.1942)—§ 4.1, n. 4.

Broccolo, People v., 130 Misc.2d 606, 497 N.Y.S.2d 816 (N.Y.Co.Ct.1985)—§ 6.9, n. 200.

Bronson, People v., 115 A.D.2d 484, 495 N.Y.S.2d 716 (N.Y.A.D. 2 Dept.1985)—§ 6.6, n. 98; § 6.10, n. 224.

Brooks, People v., 199 A.D.2d 275, 604 N.Y.S.2d 219 (N.Y.A.D. 2 Dept.1993)—§ 7.30, n. 342.

Brooks, People v., 105 A.D.2d 977, 481 N.Y.S.2d 914 (N.Y.A.D. 3 Dept.1984)—§ 9.51, n. 365.

Brooks, People v., 54 A.D.2d 333, 388 N.Y.S.2d 450 (N.Y.A.D. 4 Dept.1976)—§ 10.5, n. 88, 93, 94.

Brothers, People v., 429 N.Y.S.2d 558, 407 N.E.2d 405 (N.Y.1980)—§ 9.23, n. 184; § 9.26, n. 214; § 9.33, n. 240; § 9.43, n. 317.

TABLE OF CASES

Brown v. City of New York, 470 N.Y.S.2d 573, 458 N.E.2d 1250 (N.Y.1983)—§ 2.8, n. 177.

Brown v. Illinois, 422 U.S. 590, 95 S.Ct. 2254, 45 L.Ed.2d 416 (1975)—§ 10.10, n. 190.

Brown v. Ohio, 432 U.S. 161, 97 S.Ct. 2221, 53 L.Ed.2d 187 (1977)—§ 2.5, n. 99, 105.

Brown, People v., 207 A.D.2d 556, 616 N.Y.S.2d 389 (N.Y.A.D. 2 Dept.1994)—§ 9.33, n. 241; § 9.49, n. 360; § 9.51, n. 373.

Brown, People v., 207 A.D.2d 408, 615 N.Y.S.2d 726 (N.Y.A.D. 2 Dept.1994)—§ 11.12, n. 133.

Brown, People v., 206 A.D.2d 326, 615 N.Y.S.2d 16 (N.Y.A.D. 1 Dept.1994)—§ 9.33, n. 245.

Brown, People v., 205 A.D.2d 436, 613 N.Y.S.2d 903 (N.Y.A.D. 1 Dept.1994)—§ 11.18, n. 246.

Brown, People v., 204 A.D.2d 789, 611 N.Y.S.2d 707 (N.Y.A.D. 3 Dept.1994)—§ 5.27, n. 733.

Brown, People v., 202 A.D.2d 266, 609 N.Y.S.2d 2 (N.Y.A.D. 1 Dept.1994)—§ 7.15, n. 170.

Brown, People v., 159 Misc.2d 11, 603 N.Y.S.2d 256 (N.Y.Sup.1993)—§ 5.17, n. 364; § 9.3, n. 11.

Brown, People v., 195 A.D.2d 310, 600 N.Y.S.2d 53 (N.Y.A.D. 1 Dept.1993)—§ 9.34, n. 256; § 9.42, n. 297.

Brown, People v., 194 A.D.2d 548, 598 N.Y.S.2d 88 (N.Y.A.D. 2 Dept.1993)—§ 5.27, n. 758, 784.

Brown, People v., 167 A.D.2d 847, 562 N.Y.S.2d 254 (N.Y.A.D. 4 Dept.1990)—§ 7.14, n. 165.

Brown, People v., 156 A.D.2d 204, 548 N.Y.S.2d 464 (N.Y.A.D. 1 Dept.1989)—§ 11.15, n. 164.

Brown, People v., 140 A.D.2d 266, 528 N.Y.S.2d 565 (N.Y.A.D. 1 Dept.1988)—§ 10.27, n. 593; § 10.28, n. 600.

Brown, People v., 126 A.D.2d 898, 510 N.Y.S.2d 932 (N.Y.A.D. 3 Dept.1987)—§ 11.18, n. 248, 249.

Brown, People v., 505 N.Y.S.2d 574, 496 N.E.2d 663 (N.Y.1986)—§ 7.4, n. 36; § 7.13, n. 152; § 7.21, n. 235.

Brown, People v., 117 A.D.2d 978, 499 N.Y.S.2d 529 (N.Y.A.D. 4 Dept.1986)—§ 9.10, n. 103.

Brown, People v., 113 A.D.2d 812, 493 N.Y.S.2d 568 (N.Y.A.D. 2 Dept.1985)—§ 9.34, n. 250.

Brown, People v., 104 Misc.2d 157, 427 N.Y.S.2d 722 (N.Y.City Crim.Ct.1980)—§ 7.4, n. 40.

Brown, People v., 96 Misc.2d 127, 408 N.Y.S.2d 927 (N.Y.Sup.1978)—§ 4.12, n. 194.

Brown, People v., 386 N.Y.S.2d 359, 352 N.E.2d 545 (N.Y.1976)—§ 10.2, n. 18, 39.

Brown, People v., 386 N.Y.S.2d 848, 353 N.E.2d 811 (N.Y.1976)—§ 2.1, n. 8; § 2.4, n. 77.

Brown, People v., 46 A.D.2d 590, 364 N.Y.S.2d 512 (N.Y.A.D. 1 Dept.1975)—§ 10.5, n. 113, 121.

Brown, People v., 356 N.Y.S.2d 571, 313 N.E.2d 41 (N.Y.1974)—§ 7.10, n. 106.

Brown, People ex rel. Maxian v., p. 26, col. 6 (Sup.Ct., N.Y.County 1990)—§ 3.19, n. 217.

Brown, People ex rel. Maxian on Behalf of Roundtree v., 568 N.Y.S.2d 575, 570 N.E.2d 223 (N.Y.1991)—§ 3.15, n. 172; § 3.19; § 3.19, n. 211; § 3.36.8; § 5.23, n. 625.

Brown, People ex rel. Maxian on Behalf of Roundtree v., 164 A.D.2d 56, 561 N.Y.S.2d 418 (N.Y.A.D. 1 Dept.1990)—§ 3.19, n. 218.

Browning–Ferris Industries of Vermont, Inc. v. Kelco Disposal, Inc., 492 U.S. 257, 109 S.Ct. 2909, 106 L.Ed.2d 219 (1989)—§ 4.1, n. 3.

Brunetti v. Scotti, 77 Misc.2d 388, 353 N.Y.S.2d 630 (N.Y.Sup.1974)—§ 4.5, n. 67, 76.

Brunskill, People v., 192 A.D.2d 666, 597 N.Y.S.2d 89 (N.Y.A.D. 2 Dept.1993)—§ 9.37, n. 265.

Brunson, People v., 131 A.D.2d 689, 516 N.Y.S.2d 767 (N.Y.A.D. 2 Dept.1987)—§ 11.12, n. 133.

Bruton v. United States, 391 U.S. 123, 88 S.Ct. 1620, 20 L.Ed.2d 476 (1968)—§ 5.22; § 5.22, n. 567.

Bryan, People v., 191 A.D.2d 1029, 595 N.Y.S.2d 150 (N.Y.A.D. 4 Dept.1993)—§ 10.3, n. 72.

Bryant, People v., 153 A.D.2d 636, 544 N.Y.S.2d 661 (N.Y.A.D. 2 Dept.1989)—§ 9.51, n. 372, 380.

Bryant, People v., 79 A.D.2d 867, 434 N.Y.S.2d 558 (N.Y.A.D. 4 Dept.1980)—§ 9.10, n. 85.

Bryant, People v., 65 A.D.2d 333, 411 N.Y.S.2d 932 (N.Y.A.D. 2 Dept.1978)—§ 9.10, n. 89.

Bryce, People ex rel. v. Infante, 144 A.D.2d 898, 535 N.Y.S.2d 215 (N.Y.A.D. 3 Dept. 1988)—§ 4.10, n. 159.

B. T. Productions, Inc. v. Barr, 405 N.Y.S.2d 9, 376 N.E.2d 171 (N.Y.1978)—§ 10.1, n. 7; § 10.2, n. 14.

Buckley, People v., 552 N.Y.S.2d 912, 552 N.E.2d 160 (N.Y.1990)—§ 5.17, n. 364.

Buckson v. Harris, 145 A.D.2d 883, 536 N.Y.S.2d 219 (N.Y.A.D. 3 Dept.1988)—§ 4.10, n. 153.

Bugayong, People v., 182 A.D.2d 450, 582 N.Y.S.2d 175 (N.Y.A.D. 1 Dept.1992)—§ 7.30, n. 342.

TABLE OF CASES

Bullard, People v., 84 A.D.2d 845, 444 N.Y.S.2d 171 (N.Y.A.D. 2 Dept.1981)—§ 11.12, n. 127.

Bundy, People v., 186 A.D.2d 1042, 590 N.Y.S.2d 829 (N.Y.A.D. 4 Dept.1992)—§ 9.55, n. 401.

Bundy, People v., 186 A.D.2d 357, 588 N.Y.S.2d 167 (N.Y.A.D. 1 Dept.1992)—§ 5.8, n. 138, 145.

Burgos, People v., 631 N.Y.S.2d 336 (N.Y.A.D. 1 Dept.1995)—§ 10.26, n. 581.

Burke, People v., 105 Misc.2d 722, 432 N.Y.S.2d 832 (N.Y.Sup.1980)—§ 5.10, n. 282.

Burkett v. Cunningham, 826 F.2d 1208 (3rd Cir.1987)—§ 9.8, n. 56.

Burks v. United States, 437 U.S. 1, 98 S.Ct. 2141, 57 L.Ed.2d 1 (1978)—§ 2.4, n. 89.

Burnette, People v., 160 Misc.2d 1005, 612 N.Y.S.2d 774 (N.Y.Sup.1994)—§ 7.8, n. 82, 89.

Burr, People v., 520 N.Y.S.2d 739, 514 N.E.2d 1363 (N.Y.1987)—§ 10.10, n. 189.

Burse v. Bristol, 203 A.D.2d 962, 612 N.Y.S.2d 990 (N.Y.A.D. 4 Dept.1994)—§ 5.27, n. 731.

Burton, People v., 191 A.D.2d 451, 594 N.Y.S.2d 300 (N.Y.A.D. 2 Dept.1993)—§ 5.8, n. 182.

Burton, People v., 150 Misc.2d 214, 569 N.Y.S.2d 861 (N.Y.Sup.1990)—§ 4.2, n. 30.

Burton, People v., 148 Misc.2d 716, 561 N.Y.S.2d 328 (N.Y.Sup.1990)—§ 4.2; § 4.2, n. 29.

Burts, People v., 571 N.Y.S.2d 418, 574 N.E.2d 1024 (N.Y.1991)—§ 10.15; § 10.15, n. 309; § 10.19; § 10.19, n. 456.

Burts, People v., 156 A.D.2d 1010, 549 N.Y.S.2d 292 (N.Y.A.D. 4 Dept.1989)—§ 10.19, n. 457.

Buszak, People v., 185 A.D.2d 621, 587 N.Y.S.2d 52 (N.Y.A.D. 4 Dept.1992)—§ 5.8, n. 121, 190.

Butchino, People v., 13 A.D.2d 183, 215 N.Y.S.2d 321 (N.Y.A.D. 3 Dept.1961)—§ 6.3, n. 65.

Buthy v. Ward, 34 A.D.2d 884, 312 N.Y.S.2d 119 (N.Y.A.D. 4 Dept.1970)—§ 4.5, n. 62.

Butler, People v., 161 Misc.2d 980, 615 N.Y.S.2d 843 (N.Y.Sup.1994)—§ 5.17, n. 367.

Butor, People v., 75 Misc.2d 558, 348 N.Y.S.2d 89 (N.Y.Co.Ct.1973)—§ 10.18, n. 383.

Buttiglione, People v., 125 A.D.2d 323, 508 N.Y.S.2d 992 (N.Y.A.D. 2 Dept.1986)—§ 11.15, n. 182.

Buxton, People v., 189 A.D.2d 996, 593 N.Y.S.2d 87 (N.Y.A.D. 3 Dept.1993)—§ 7.14, n. 166.

Byrdsong, People v., 133 A.D.2d 164, 518 N.Y.S.2d 828 (N.Y.A.D. 2 Dept.1987)—§ 5.27, n. 681.

Caban, People v., 123 Misc.2d 943, 475 N.Y.S.2d 330 (N.Y.Sup.1984)—§ 7.4, n. 55.

Cabon, People v., 148 Misc.2d 260, 560 N.Y.S.2d 370 (N.Y.City Crim.Ct.1990)—§ 7.8, n. 82, 89.

Cade, People v., 548 N.Y.S.2d 137, 547 N.E.2d 339 (N.Y.1989)—§ 5.18; § 5.18, n. 394, 398; § 5.29, n. 818.

Calandra, People v., 164 A.D.2d 638, 565 N.Y.S.2d 467 (N.Y.A.D. 1 Dept.1991)—§ 1.2, n. 33.

Calandra, People v., 120 Misc.2d 1059, 467 N.Y.S.2d 141 (N.Y.Sup.1983)—§ 7.31, n. 353.

Calandra, United States v., 414 U.S. 338, 94 S.Ct. 613, 38 L.Ed.2d 561 (1974)—§ 10.10, n. 199.

Calbud, Inc., People v., 426 N.Y.S.2d 238, 402 N.E.2d 1140 (N.Y.1980)—§ 5.5; § 5.5, n. 66; § 5.6, n. 87; § 5.27, n. 749.

Caldwell, People v., 107 Misc.2d 62, 437 N.Y.S.2d 829 (N.Y.Sup.1980)—§ 10.19, n. 441.

Calero, People v., 163 Misc.2d 13, 618 N.Y.S.2d 996 (N.Y.Sup.1994)—§ 5.6, n. 95; § 5.27, n. 718, 746.

California v. Trombetta, 467 U.S. 479, 104 S.Ct. 2528, 81 L.Ed.2d 413 (1984)—§ 7.23, n. 254.

Callahan, People v., 590 N.Y.S.2d 46, 604 N.E.2d 108 (N.Y.1992)—§ 9.12, n. 121; § 11.3, n. 27; § 11.17, n. 214, 228, 235.

Calloway, People v., 171 A.D.2d 1037, 569 N.Y.S.2d 233 (N.Y.A.D. 4 Dept.1991)—§ 10.22, n. 526.

Calloway, People ex rel. v. Skinner, 347 N.Y.S.2d 178, 300 N.E.2d 716 (N.Y. 1973)—§ 4.1, n. 4; § 4.4, n. 50.

Caltabiano, People v., 154 Misc.2d 860, 586 N.Y.S.2d 714 (N.Y.Just.Ct.1992)—§ 1.7, n. 143.

Camacho, People v., 102 A.D.2d 728, 476 N.Y.S.2d 566 (N.Y.A.D. 1 Dept.1984)—§ 11.12, n. 127.

Camargo, People v., 135 Misc.2d 987, 516 N.Y.S.2d 1004 (N.Y.Sup.1986)—§ 5.27, n. 775.

Camarre, People v., 171 A.D.2d 1003, 569 N.Y.S.2d 224 (N.Y.A.D. 4 Dept.1991)—§ 10.2, n. 23; § 10.6, n. 132.

Cameron, People v., 611 N.Y.S.2d 499, 633 N.E.2d 1103 (N.Y.1994)—§ 11.19, n. 260.

Cammilleri, People v., 123 Misc.2d 851, 475 N.Y.S.2d 228 (N.Y.Sup.1984)—§ 7.8, n. 81.

Campbell v. Adams, 206 Misc. 673, 133 N.Y.S.2d 876 (N.Y.Sup.1954)—§ 3.23, n. 268.

TABLE OF CASES

Campbell, People v., 541 N.Y.S.2d 756, 539 N.E.2d 584 (N.Y.1989)—§ **11.15, n. 162, 189.**

Campbell, People v., 535 N.Y.S.2d 580, 532 N.E.2d 86 (N.Y.1988)—§ **5.18, n. 441.**

Campbell, People v., 91 A.D.2d 1075, 458 N.Y.S.2d 322 (N.Y.A.D. 3 Dept.1983)—§ **9.47, n. 332.**

Campbell, People ex rel. Ferguson v., 175 A.D.2d 959, 573 N.Y.S.2d 539 (N.Y.A.D. 3 Dept.1991)—§ **9.47, n. 338.**

Campbell, People ex rel. Robinson v., 184 A.D.2d 988, 585 N.Y.S.2d 604 (N.Y.A.D. 3 Dept.1992)—§ **4.5, n. 85.**

Campbell v. Pesce, 468 N.Y.S.2d 865, 456 N.E.2d 806 (N.Y.1983)—§ **2.4, n. 82;** § **3.32, n. 443;** § **11.19, n. 253, 257.**

Campbell, United States v., 778 F.2d 764 (11th Cir.1985)—§ **11.9, n. 83.**

Canales, People v., 75 A.D.2d 875, 427 N.Y.S.2d 879 (N.Y.A.D. 2 Dept.1980)—§ **7.10, n. 110.**

Cannon, People v., 194 A.D.2d 496, 599 N.Y.S.2d 809 (N.Y.A.D. 1 Dept.1993)—§ **1.2, n. 33;** § **5.17, n. 370.**

Cantave v. Supreme Court, 193 A.D.2d 277, 603 N.Y.S.2d 591 (N.Y.A.D. 3 Dept. 1993)—§ **2.10, n. 220.**

Canty, People v., 153 A.D.2d 640, 544 N.Y.S.2d 857 (N.Y.A.D. 2 Dept.1989)—§ **5.27, n. 718.**

Capital Newspapers Div. of Hearst Corp. v. Lee, 139 A.D.2d 31, 530 N.Y.S.2d 872 (N.Y.A.D. 3 Dept.1988)—§ **3.33, n. 466.**

Capitello, People v., 139 Misc.2d 618, 528 N.Y.S.2d 263 (N.Y.Co.Ct.1988)—§ **5.21, n. 508.**

Capolongo, People v., 623 N.Y.S.2d 778, 647 N.E.2d 1286 (N.Y.1995)—§ **10.23, n. 539;** § **10.24, n. 555;** § **10.27, n. 598;** § **10.28, n. 608.**

Capuano, People v., 68 Misc.2d 481, 327 N.Y.S.2d 17 (N.Y.Sup.1971)—§ **1.7, n. 153;** § **1.9, n. 197.**

Caputo v. Henderson, 541 F.2d 979 (2nd Cir.1976)—§ **11.9, n. 82.**

Caputo, People v., 175 A.D.2d 290, 572 N.Y.S.2d 922 (N.Y.A.D. 2 Dept.1991)—§ **7.27, n. 297.**

Caracciola, People v., 576 N.Y.S.2d 74, 581 N.E.2d 1329 (N.Y.1991)—§ **5.5, n. 81;** § **5.27, n. 750.**

Caracciola, People v., 164 A.D.2d 755, 560 N.Y.S.2d 133 (N.Y.A.D. 1 Dept.1990)—§ **8.2.**

Cardwell, People v., 194 A.D.2d 550, 598 N.Y.S.2d 319 (N.Y.A.D. 2 Dept.1993)—§ **9.10, n. 105.**

Cardwell, People v., 575 N.Y.S.2d 267, 580 N.E.2d 753 (N.Y.1991)—§ **5.22, n. 605.**

Carey v. Kitson, 93 A.D.2d 50, 461 N.Y.S.2d 876 (N.Y.A.D. 2 Dept.1983)—§ **5.9, n. 226.**

Caridi, People v., 148 A.D.2d 625, 539 N.Y.S.2d 88 (N.Y.A.D. 2 Dept.1989)—§ **11.13, n. 138.**

Carkner, People v., 213 A.D.2d 735, 623 N.Y.S.2d 350 (N.Y.A.D. 3 Dept.1995)—§ **6.6, n. 96.**

Carlson v. Landon, 342 U.S. 524, 72 S.Ct. 525, 96 L.Ed. 547 (1952)—§ **4.1, n. 3.**

Carney v. Feldstein, 193 A.D.2d 1016, 597 N.Y.S.2d 982 (N.Y.A.D. 3 Dept.1993)—§ **11.2, n. 4.**

Carpenito, People v., 199 A.D.2d 522, 606 N.Y.S.2d 24 (N.Y.A.D. 2 Dept.1993)—§ **9.30, n. 232.**

Carpenito, People v., 587 N.Y.S.2d 264, 599 N.E.2d 668 (N.Y.1992)—§ **10.19, n. 435.**

Carroll, United States v., 582 F.2d 942 (5th Cir.1978)—§ **5.18, n. 428.**

Carson, People v., 99 A.D.2d 664, 472 N.Y.S.2d 68 (N.Y.A.D. 4 Dept.1984)—§ **10.5, n. 110.**

Carswell, People v., 120 Misc.2d 274, 465 N.Y.S.2d 687 (N.Y.Sup.1983)—§ **9.16, n. 150.**

Cartagena, People v., 92 A.D.2d 901, 459 N.Y.S.2d 896 (N.Y.A.D. 2 Dept.1983)—§ **6.2, n. 40;** § **6.10, n. 255.**

Carter, People v., 631 N.Y.S.2d 116, 655 N.E.2d 157 (N.Y.1995)—§ **10.17, n. 377;** § **10.20, n. 464.**

Carter, People v., 564 N.Y.S.2d 992, 566 N.E.2d 119 (N.Y.1990)—§ **5.3, n. 36.**

Carter, People v., 56 A.D.2d 948, 392 N.Y.S.2d 712 (N.Y.A.D. 3 Dept.1977)—§ **10.5, n. 98.**

Caruso, People v., 174 A.D.2d 1051, 572 N.Y.S.2d 216 (N.Y.A.D. 4 Dept.1991)—§ **10.5, n. 84, 91.**

Caruso, People v., 125 A.D.2d 403, 509 N.Y.S.2d 361 (N.Y.A.D. 2 Dept.1986)—§ **5.8, n. 176.**

Casado, People v., 83 A.D.2d 385, 444 N.Y.S.2d 920 (N.Y.A.D. 1 Dept.1981)—§ **10.19, n. 405.**

Casdia, People v., 576 N.Y.S.2d 75, 581 N.E.2d 1330 (N.Y.1991)—§ **5.10;** § **5.10, n. 277.**

Case, People v., 396 N.Y.S.2d 841, 365 N.E.2d 872 (N.Y.1977)—§ **11.16, n. 195.**

Caserta, People v., 277 N.Y.S.2d 647, 224 N.E.2d 82 (N.Y.1966)—§ **10.19, n. 457.**

Cassidy, People v., 133 A.D.2d 374, 519 N.Y.S.2d 275 (N.Y.A.D. 2 Dept.1987)—§ **5.27, n. 681.**

Castillo, People v., 208 A.D.2d 944, 618 N.Y.S.2d 78 (N.Y.A.D. 2 Dept.1994)—§ **11.16, n. 199.**

Castillo, People v., 592 N.Y.S.2d 945, 607 N.E.2d 1050 (N.Y.1992)—§ **7.10, n. 101;** § **7.30, n. 349;** § **10.4, n. 76;** § **10.19, n. 397, 436.**

Castillo, People v., 417 N.Y.S.2d 915, 391 N.E.2d 997 (N.Y.1979)—§ **5.21, n. 498.**

Castillo, People v., 62 A.D.2d 938, 403 N.Y.S.2d 746 (N.Y.A.D. 1 Dept.1978)—§ **5.21, n. 498.**

Castro, People v., 119 Misc.2d 787, 464 N.Y.S.2d 650 (N.Y.Sup.1983)—§ **4.2, n. 17, 22.**

TABLE OF CASES

Castro–Restrepo, People v., 169 A.D.2d 454, 565 N.Y.S.2d 461 (N.Y.A.D. 1 Dept. 1991)—§ 5.22, n. 608.

Cataldo, People v., 384 N.Y.S.2d 763, 349 N.E.2d 863 (N.Y.1976)—§ 11.11, n. 112.

Catten, People v., 516 N.Y.S.2d 186, 508 N.E.2d 920 (N.Y.1987)—§ 2.4, n. 39, 44.

Catterson v. Rohl, 202 A.D.2d 420, 608 N.Y.S.2d 696 (N.Y.A.D. 2 Dept.1994)—§ 7.16, n. 178.

Causeway Const. Co., Inc., People v., 164 Misc.2d 393, 625 N.Y.S.2d 856 (N.Y.City Crim.Ct.1995)—§ 1.1, n. 6.

Caussade, People v., 162 A.D.2d 4, 560 N.Y.S.2d 648 (N.Y.A.D. 2 Dept.1990)—§ 9.22, n. 171.

Cavagnaro, People v., 88 A.D.2d 938, 450 N.Y.S.2d 870 (N.Y.A.D. 2 Dept.1982)—§ 10.19, n. 450.

Ceccolini, United States v., 435 U.S. 268, 98 S.Ct. 1054, 55 L.Ed.2d 268 (1978)—§ 10.9, n. 164; § 10.10, n. 173, 175.

Cedeno, People v., 437 N.Y.S.2d 72, 418 N.E.2d 665 (N.Y.1981)—§ 9.12, n. 122; § 9.51, n. 365.

Celestino, People v., 201 A.D.2d 91, 615 N.Y.S.2d 346 (N.Y.A.D. 1 Dept.1994)—§ 9.29, n. 227; § 9.43, n. 308.

Cephas, People v., 207 A.D.2d 903, 616 N.Y.S.2d 668 (N.Y.A.D. 2 Dept.1994)—§ 9.47, n. 346.

C., Gregory, People v., 158 Misc.2d 872, 602 N.Y.S.2d 492 (N.Y.Sup.1993)—§ 1.10, n. 245.

Chaitin, People v., 472 N.Y.S.2d 597, 460 N.E.2d 1082 (N.Y.1984)—§ 1.4, n. 78.

Chakwin on Behalf of Ford, People ex rel. v. Warden, 480 N.Y.S.2d 719, 470 N.E.2d 146 (N.Y.1984)—§ 9.25, n. 203, 204; § 9.49, n. 358.

Chambers, People v., 134 Misc.2d 688, 512 N.Y.S.2d 631 (N.Y.Sup.1987)—§ 7.33, n. 361.

Chang v. Rotker, 155 A.D.2d 49, 552 N.Y.S.2d 676 (N.Y.A.D. 2 Dept.1990)—§ 2.2, n. 10.

Channer, People v., 209 A.D.2d 1056, 619 N.Y.S.2d 1013 (N.Y.A.D. 4 Dept.1994)—§ 9.51, n. 375.

Chapman, People v., 185 A.D.2d 892, 587 N.Y.S.2d 379 (N.Y.A.D. 2 Dept.1992)—§ 9.30, n. 230; § 9.33, n. 245.

Chapman, People v., 516 N.Y.S.2d 159, 508 N.E.2d 894 (N.Y.1987)—§ 5.8, n. 175; § 5.9, n. 247, 251.

Chapple, People v., 378 N.Y.S.2d 682, 341 N.E.2d 243 (N.Y.1975)—§ 10.10; § 10.10, n. 194.

Charles, People v., 180 A.D.2d 868, 580 N.Y.S.2d 99 (N.Y.A.D. 3 Dept.1992)—§ 9.10, n. 94, 103, 104, 110.

Charles, People v., 576 N.Y.S.2d 81, 581 N.E.2d 1336 (N.Y.1991)—§ 5.22, n. 574, 581.

Charles, People v., 473 N.Y.S.2d 941, 462 N.E.2d 118 (N.Y.1984)—§ 5.17, n. 372, 390.

Charlton, People v., 192 A.D.2d 757, 596 N.Y.S.2d 210 (N.Y.A.D. 3 Dept.1993)—§ 6.2, n. 35; § 6.10, n. 224.

Charon, People v., 113 A.D.2d 950, 493 N.Y.S.2d 847 (N.Y.A.D. 2 Dept.1985)—§ 6.2, n. 22.

Chase, People v., 626 N.Y.S.2d 721, 650 N.E.2d 379 (N.Y.1995)—§ 10.25, n. 570.

Chavis, People v., 190 A.D.2d 683, 593 N.Y.S.2d 271 (N.Y.A.D. 2 Dept.1993)—§ 7.17, n. 206.

Chavis, People v., 113 A.D.2d 896, 493 N.Y.S.2d 613 (N.Y.A.D. 2 Dept.1985)—§ 7.10, n. 110.

Cheswick, People v., 166 A.D.2d 88, 570 N.Y.S.2d 318 (N.Y.A.D. 2 Dept.1991)—§ 5.22, n. 596.

Chicas, People v., 204 A.D.2d 476, 611 N.Y.S.2d 873 (N.Y.A.D. 2 Dept.1994)—§ 5.16, n. 349.

Chimel v. California, 395 U.S. 752, 89 S.Ct. 2034, 23 L.Ed.2d 685 (1969)—§ 10.6, n. 126.

Chipp, People v., 553 N.Y.S.2d 72, 552 N.E.2d 608 (N.Y.1990)—§ 7.8, n. 90; § 10.15, n. 304; § 10.19, n. 420, 455; § 10.20, n. 484.

Chisolm, People v., 162 A.D.2d 267, 556 N.Y.S.2d 625 (N.Y.A.D. 1 Dept.1990)—§ 6.2, n. 26.

Choi, People v., 210 A.D.2d 495, 620 N.Y.S.2d 131 (N.Y.A.D. 2 Dept.1994)—§ 5.8, n. 134.

Christian, People ex rel. Battista v., 249 N.Y. 314, 164 N.E. 111 (N.Y.1928)—§ 5.11, n. 304.

Christopher, People v., 492 N.Y.S.2d 566, 482 N.E.2d 45 (N.Y.1985)—§ 6.9; § 6.9, n. 188, 196; § 6.10; § 6.10, n. 258.

Churba, People v., 76 Misc.2d 1028, 353 N.Y.S.2d 130 (N.Y.City Crim.Ct.1974)—§ 7.23, n. 272.

Church, People v., 630 N.Y.S.2d 16 (N.Y.A.D. 1 Dept.1995)—§ 10.15, n. 298.

Churchill, People v., 417 N.Y.S.2d 221, 390 N.E.2d 1146 (N.Y.1979)—§ 1.4, n. 104.

Cibro Oceana Terminal Corp., People v., 148 Misc.2d 149, 559 N.Y.S.2d 782 (N.Y.City Crim.Ct.1990)—§ 3.9, n. 105.

Cierra, People v., 178 A.D.2d 303, 577 N.Y.S.2d 607 (N.Y.A.D. 1 Dept.1991)—§ 7.17, n. 216.

Ciola, People v., 136 A.D.2d 557, 523 N.Y.S.2d 553 (N.Y.A.D. 2 Dept.1988)—§ 7.23, n. 268.

Cirillo v. Justices of Supreme Court In and For Kings County, 43 A.D.2d 4, 349 N.Y.S.2d 129 (N.Y.A.D. 2 Dept.1973)—§ 2.6, n. 136.

Cirillo, People v., 100 Misc.2d 502, 419 N.Y.S.2d 820 (N.Y.Sup.1979)—§ 5.18, n. 399.

TABLE OF CASES

City of (see name of city)

C., John, People v., 184 A.D.2d 519, 584 N.Y.S.2d 320 (N.Y.A.D. 2 Dept.1992)—§ 11.11, n. 111.

Clairborne, People v., 329 N.Y.S.2d 580, 280 N.E.2d 366 (N.Y.1972)—§ 11.10, n. 95.

Clapper, People v., 131 Misc.2d 1079, 502 N.Y.S.2d 919 (N.Y.Co.Ct.1986)—§ 4.9, n. 118.

Clark v. New York, 459 U.S. 1090, 103 S.Ct. 577, 74 L.Ed.2d 937 (1982)—§ 7.21, n. 235.

Clark, People v., 198 A.D.2d 46, 603 N.Y.S.2d 450 (N.Y.A.D. 1 Dept.1993)—§ 10.25, n. 573.

Clark, People v., 194 A.D.2d 868, 598 N.Y.S.2d 847 (N.Y.A.D. 3 Dept.1993)—§ 7.18, n. 217.

Clark, People v., 120 Misc.2d 365, 466 N.Y.S.2d 211 (N.Y.City Crim.Ct.1983)—§ 3.29, n. 393, 395; § 9.44, n. 322.

Clark, People v., 89 A.D.2d 820, 453 N.Y.S.2d 525 (N.Y.A.D. 4 Dept.1982)—§ 7.14, n. 161; § 7.21, n. 235.

Clarke, People v., 160 Misc.2d 1018, 611 N.Y.S.2d 1006 (N.Y.City Crim.Ct. 1994)—§ 3.6, n. 61.

Clarke, People v., 173 A.D.2d 550, 570 N.Y.S.2d 305 (N.Y.A.D. 2 Dept.1991)—§ 10.3, n. 72.

Claron, People v., 103 Misc.2d 841, 427 N.Y.S.2d 146 (N.Y.Sup.1980)—§ 6.9, n. 217; § 6.10, n. 224.

Claud, People v., 181 A.D.2d 830, 581 N.Y.S.2d 387 (N.Y.A.D. 2 Dept.1992)—§ 2.3, n. 35.

Claud, People v., 563 N.Y.S.2d 720, 565 N.E.2d 469 (N.Y.1990)—§ 2.6; § 2.6, n. 128, 131.

Claudio, People v., 183 A.D.2d 945, 583 N.Y.S.2d 563 (N.Y.A.D. 3 Dept.1992)—§ 6.2, n. 25.

Claudio, People v., 487 N.Y.S.2d 318, 476 N.E.2d 644 (N.Y.1985)—§ 11.10, n. 102.

Claxton, People v., 160 Misc.2d 550, 610 N.Y.S.2d 735 (N.Y.City Crim.Ct.1994)—§ 3.6, n. 61.

Clayton, People v., 41 A.D.2d 204, 342 N.Y.S.2d 106 (N.Y.A.D. 2 Dept.1973)—§ 3.28, n. 370; § 5.27, n. 754.

Clemente, People v., 150 A.D.2d 709, 541 N.Y.S.2d 583 (N.Y.A.D. 2 Dept.1989)—§ 9.10, n. 87, 88, 109.

Clickner, People v., 128 A.D.2d 917, 512 N.Y.S.2d 572 (N.Y.A.D. 3 Dept.1987)—§ 6.2, n. 20, 24, 30, 32.

Clifford Howard, People v. (N.Y.1996)—§ 7.17, n. 193.

Clinton, People v., 179 A.D.2d 670, 579 N.Y.S.2d 895 (N.Y.A.D. 2 Dept.1992)—§ 11.10, n. 107; § 11.17, n. 235.

Clinton, People v., 65 A.D.2d 692, 409 N.Y.S.2d 739 (N.Y.A.D. 1 Dept.1978)—§ 10.5, n. 107.

Clinton, People v., 59 A.D.2d 854, 399 N.Y.S.2d 131 (N.Y.A.D. 1 Dept.1977)—§ 10.5, n. 113.

Close, People ex rel. Hirschberg v., 152 N.Y.S.2d 1, 134 N.E.2d 818 (N.Y.1956)—§ 3.33, n. 473; § 5.1, n. 15.

C., Matter of Gina, 138 A.D.2d 77, 531 N.Y.S.2d 86 (N.Y.A.D. 1 Dept.1988)—§ 7.17, n. 193, 194.

C., Matter of Richard, 115 Misc.2d 314, 453 N.Y.S.2d 366 (N.Y.Fam.Ct.1982)—§ 3.29, n. 395.

Cobey, People v., 184 A.D.2d 1002, 584 N.Y.S.2d 244 (N.Y.A.D. 4 Dept.1992)—§ 5.19, n. 458.

Codey on Behalf of State of N.J. v. Capital Cities, American Broadcasting Corp., Inc., 605 N.Y.S.2d 661, 626 N.E.2d 636 (N.Y.1993)—§ 1.2, n. 27.

Coffey, People v., 240 N.Y.S.2d 721, 191 N.E.2d 263 (N.Y.1963)—§ 10.19, n. 433, 440, 442.

Cohen, Matter of, 144 A.D.2d 605, 534 N.Y.S.2d 1022 (N.Y.A.D. 2 Dept.1988)—§ 10.19, n. 419.

Cohen, People v., 210 A.D.2d 343, 620 N.Y.S.2d 92 (N.Y.A.D. 2 Dept.1994)—§ 11.17, n. 223.

Cohen, People v., 186 A.D.2d 843, 588 N.Y.S.2d 211 (N.Y.A.D. 3 Dept.1992)—§ 11.3, n. 29.

Cohen, People v., 439 N.Y.S.2d 321, 421 N.E.2d 813 (N.Y.1981)—§ 5.13, n. 325; § 5.14, n. 334; § 5.16, n. 347; § 11.15, n. 172.

Coker, People v., 134 A.D.2d 507, 521 N.Y.S.2d 96 (N.Y.A.D. 2 Dept.1987)—§ 7.17, n. 212.

Coker, People v., 131 A.D.2d 585, 516 N.Y.S.2d 293 (N.Y.A.D. 2 Dept.1987)—§ 9.29, n. 227.

Coker, People v., 79 A.D.2d 1032, 435 N.Y.S.2d 43 (N.Y.A.D. 2 Dept.1981)—§ 11.11, n. 113.

Colas, People v., 206 A.D.2d 183, 619 N.Y.S.2d 702 (N.Y.A.D. 1 Dept.1994)—§ 9.16, n. 151.

Colcloughley, People ex rel. v. Montanye, 49 A.D.2d 1034, 374 N.Y.S.2d 504 (N.Y.A.D. 4 Dept.1975)—§ 5.18, n. 432.

Cole, People v., 196 A.D.2d 634, 601 N.Y.S.2d 352 (N.Y.A.D. 2 Dept.1993)—§ 5.9, n. 249.

Cole, People v., 152 A.D.2d 851, 544 N.Y.S.2d 228 (N.Y.A.D. 3 Dept.1989)—§ 11.15, n. 166.

Cole, People v., 540 N.Y.S.2d 984, 538 N.E.2d 336 (N.Y.1989)—§ 5.26, n. 668; § 9.22, n. 173; § 9.51, n. 375.

Cole, People v., 90 A.D.2d 27, 457 N.Y.S.2d 589 (N.Y.A.D. 3 Dept.1982)—§ 9.29, n. 228.

Cole v. State of Ark., 333 U.S. 196, 68 S.Ct. 514, 92 L.Ed. 644 (1948)—§ 5.11, n. 310.

TABLE OF CASES

Coleman v. Alabama, 399 U.S. 1, 90 S.Ct. 1999, 26 L.Ed.2d 387 (1970)—§ 3.33, n. 463.

Coleman, People v., 211 A.D.2d 562, 621 N.Y.S.2d 578 (N.Y.A.D. 1 Dept.1995)—§ 11.13, n. 144.

Coleman, People v., 191 A.D.2d 390, 595 N.Y.S.2d 431 (N.Y.A.D. 1 Dept.1993)—§ 10.17; § 10.17, n. 355.

Coleman, People v., 178 A.D.2d 842, 577 N.Y.S.2d 900 (N.Y.A.D. 3 Dept.1991)—§ 7.9, n. 94.

Coleman, People v., 115 A.D.2d 488, 496 N.Y.S.2d 41 (N.Y.A.D. 2 Dept.1985)—§ 3.19, n. 223.

Coles, People v., 141 Misc.2d 965, 535 N.Y.S.2d 897 (N.Y.Sup.1988)—§ 5.9, n. 199.

Collado, People v., 125 A.D.2d 584, 509 N.Y.S.2d 839 (N.Y.A.D. 2 Dept.1986)—§ 9.30, n. 231.

Collier, People v., 532 N.Y.S.2d 718, 528 N.E.2d 1191 (N.Y.1988)—§ 5.2; § 5.2, n. 27; § 8.2.

Collins, People v., 604 N.Y.S.2d 11, 624 N.E.2d 139 (N.Y.1993)—§ 9.26; § 9.26, n. 216; § 9.30, n. 231; § 9.52, n. 386.

Collins, People v., 154 A.D.2d 901, 545 N.Y.S.2d 959 (N.Y.A.D. 4 Dept.1989)—§ 6.10, n. 219.

Collins, People v., 98 A.D.2d 947, 472 N.Y.S.2d 796 (N.Y.A.D. 4 Dept.1983)—§ 9.47, n. 332.

Collins, People v., 469 N.Y.S.2d 65, 456 N.E.2d 1188 (N.Y.1983)—§ 10.26, n. 582.

Collins v. Quinones, 200 A.D.2d 569, 606 N.Y.S.2d 306 (N.Y.A.D. 2 Dept.1994)—§ 2.4, n. 52.

Colloca, People v., 57 A.D.2d 1039, 395 N.Y.S.2d 811 (N.Y.A.D. 4 Dept.1977)—§ 5.14, n. 331.

Colombo, People v., 341 N.Y.S.2d 97, 293 N.E.2d 247 (N.Y.1972)—§ 2.5, n. 112.

Colon, People v., 209 A.D.2d 254, 620 N.Y.S.2d 935 (N.Y.A.D. 1 Dept.1994)—§ 5.27; § 5.27, n. 766, 770, 781.

Colon, People v., 200 A.D.2d 492, 606 N.Y.S.2d 644 (N.Y.A.D. 1 Dept.1994)—§ 11.13, n. 138.

Colon, People v., 180 A.D.2d 876, 580 N.Y.S.2d 95 (N.Y.A.D. 3 Dept.1992)—§ 8.1, n. 12.

Colon, People v., 466 N.Y.S.2d 319, 453 N.E.2d 548 (N.Y.1983)—§ 9.17, n. 156; § 9.22, n. 171; § 9.33, n. 244; § 9.36, n. 258; § 9.38, n. 276, 278.

Colon, People v., 318 N.Y.S.2d 929, 267 N.E.2d 577 (N.Y.1971)—§ 1.4, n. 88.

Commack, People v., 194 A.D.2d 619, 599 N.Y.S.2d 56 (N.Y.A.D. 2 Dept.1993)—§ 9.47, n. 345.

Communiello, People v., 180 A.D.2d 809, 580 N.Y.S.2d 420 (N.Y.A.D. 2 Dept. 1992)—§ 5.21, n. 527.

Compton, People v., 157 A.D.2d 903, 550 N.Y.S.2d 148 (N.Y.A.D. 3 Dept.1990)—§ 11.3, n. 19.

Coniglio, People v., 79 Misc.2d 808, 361 N.Y.S.2d 524 (N.Y.Sup.1974)—§ 10.19, n. 441.

Conlan, People v., 146 A.D.2d 319, 541 N.Y.S.2d 347 (N.Y.A.D. 1 Dept.1989)—§ 7.12, n. 140.

Connor, People v., 137 A.D.2d 701, 524 N.Y.S.2d 791 (N.Y.A.D. 2 Dept.1988)—§ 9.10, n. 85.

Connor, People v., 479 N.Y.S.2d 197, 468 N.E.2d 35 (N.Y.1984)—§ 3.25, n. 331.

Connors, People v., 83 A.D.2d 640, 441 N.Y.S.2d 523 (N.Y.A.D. 2 Dept.1981)—§ 5.21, n. 527.

Conrad, People v., 407 N.Y.S.2d 694, 379 N.E.2d 220 (N.Y.1978)—§ 9.33, n. 240.

Consolazio, People v., 387 N.Y.S.2d 62, 354 N.E.2d 801 (N.Y.1976)—§ 2.4, n. 77; § 7.16, n. 183; § 7.17, n. 196, 203, 205.

Consolidated Edison Co., People v., 161 Misc.2d 907, 615 N.Y.S.2d 978 (N.Y.City Crim.Ct.1994)—§ 1.1, n. 2, 6; § 3.21, n. 259.

Consolidated Edison Co., People v., 159 Misc.2d 354, 604 N.Y.S.2d 482 (N.Y.City Crim.Ct.1993)—§ 1.1, n. 6; § 3.21, n. 259.

Consolidated Edison Co. of New York, Inc., People v., 153 Misc.2d 595, 582 N.Y.S.2d 614 (N.Y.City Crim.Ct.1992)—§ 1.1, n. 6; § 3.21, n. 258.

Constantine v. Leto, 157 A.D.2d 376, 557 N.Y.S.2d 611 (N.Y.A.D. 3 Dept.1990)—§ 7.8, n. 76, 86.

Conte, People v., 159 A.D.2d 993, 552 N.Y.S.2d 743 (N.Y.A.D. 4 Dept.1990)—§ 10.5, n. 99.

Cook, People v., 193 A.D.2d 366, 596 N.Y.S.2d 822 (N.Y.A.D. 1 Dept.1993)—§ 5.26, n. 664; § 9.49, n. 360.

Cook, People v., 93 A.D.2d 942, 463 N.Y.S.2d 59 (N.Y.A.D. 3 Dept.1983)—§ 11.5, n. 42.

Cook, People v., 71 A.D.2d 801, 419 N.Y.S.2d 350 (N.Y.A.D. 4 Dept.1979)—§ 9.41, n. 296.

Coolidge v. New Hampshire, 403 U.S. 443, 91 S.Ct. 2022, 29 L.Ed.2d 564 (1971)—§ 10.5, n. 82; § 10.6, n. 126.

Cooper, People v., 162 Misc.2d 192, 616 N.Y.S.2d 442 (N.Y.Just.Ct.1994)—§ 10.16, n. 324.

Cooper, People v., 139 Misc.2d 44, 526 N.Y.S.2d 910 (N.Y.Co.Ct.1988)—§ 5.9, n. 252.

Cooper, People v., 101 A.D.2d 1, 475 N.Y.S.2d 660 (N.Y.A.D. 4 Dept.1984)—§ 3.19, n. 223.

Cooper v. Sheindlin, 154 A.D.2d 288, 546 N.Y.S.2d 589 (N.Y.A.D. 1 Dept.1989)—§ 2.5, n. 111.

TABLE OF CASES

Copeland, People v., 127 A.D.2d 846, 511 N.Y.S.2d 949 (N.Y.A.D. 2 Dept.1987)—§ 2.4, n. 41.

Copicotto, People v., 428 N.Y.S.2d 649, 406 N.E.2d 465 (N.Y.1980)—§ 7.1, n. 1, 3; § 7.11, n. 119.

Coppola, People v., 123 Misc.2d 31, 472 N.Y.S.2d 558 (N.Y.Sup.1984)—§ 5.9, n. 253.

Corbin v. Hillery, 545 N.Y.S.2d 71, 543 N.E.2d 714 (N.Y.1989)—§ 2.2, n. 16; § 2.3; § 2.3, n. 33; § 2.6, n. 152; § 2.11, n. 246.

Corbin, People v., 201 A.D.2d 359, 608 N.Y.S.2d 839 (N.Y.A.D. 1 Dept.1994)—§ 10.20, n. 480.

Corby, People v., 167 A.D.2d 682, 563 N.Y.S.2d 689 (N.Y.A.D. 3 Dept.1990)—§ 11.11, n. 116.

Cordero, People v., 124 Misc.2d 43, 475 N.Y.S.2d 973 (N.Y.Sup.1983)—§ 10.5, n. 103.

Corley, People v., 124 A.D.2d 390, 507 N.Y.S.2d 491 (N.Y.A.D. 3 Dept.1986)—§ 7.4, n. 50; § 7.21, n. 236.

Cornielle, People v., 176 A.D.2d 190, 574 N.Y.S.2d 199 (N.Y.A.D. 1 Dept.1991)—§ 11.3, n. 22.

Corona, People v., 206 A.D.2d 305, 614 N.Y.S.2d 722 (N.Y.A.D. 1 Dept.1994)—§ 10.20, n. 469, 477.

Corona, People v., 149 Misc.2d 581, 567 N.Y.S.2d 353 (N.Y.Sup.1991)—§ 5.8, n. 147.

Correa, People v., 200 A.D.2d 415, 608 N.Y.S.2d 802 (N.Y.A.D. 1 Dept.1994)—§ 10.14, n. 285.

Correa, People v., 197 A.D.2d 430, 602 N.Y.S.2d 839 (N.Y.A.D. 1 Dept.1993)—§ 5.8, n. 154, 156.

Correa, People v., 188 A.D.2d 542, 591 N.Y.S.2d 447 (N.Y.A.D. 2 Dept.1992)—§ 10.3, n. 68.

Correa, People v., 569 N.Y.S.2d 601, 572 N.E.2d 42 (N.Y.1991)—§ 9.26, n. 219; § 9.33, n. 242; § 9.45, n. 324, 325.

Corrigan, People v., 590 N.Y.S.2d 174, 604 N.E.2d 723 (N.Y.1992)—§ 5.8, n. 183; § 5.9, n. 207.

Corsino, People v., 91 Misc.2d 46, 397 N.Y.S.2d 342 (N.Y.City Crim.Ct.1977)—§ 1.3, n. 60.

Corso, People v., 135 A.D.2d 551, 521 N.Y.S.2d 773 (N.Y.A.D. 2 Dept.1987)—§ 10.15, n. 300.

Cortes, People v., 590 N.Y.S.2d 9, 604 N.E.2d 71 (N.Y.1992)—§ 9.22, n. 170; § 9.24, n. 192; § 9.26, n. 213; § 9.33, n. 241; § 9.34, n. 250; § 9.40, n. 286; § 9.42; § 9.42, n. 299; § 9.43; § 9.43, n. 318; § 9.47, n. 338; § 9.48, n. 352; § 9.51, n. 367.

Cortez, People v., 140 Misc.2d 267, 531 N.Y.S.2d 676 (N.Y.City Crim.Ct.1988)—§ 3.6, n. 59, 60.

Corti, People v., 88 A.D.2d 345, 453 N.Y.S.2d 439 (N.Y.A.D. 2 Dept.1982)—§ 10.22, n. 533.

Cortijo, People v., 523 N.Y.S.2d 463, 517 N.E.2d 1349 (N.Y.1987)—§ 7.14, n. 160, 161; § 7.21, n. 233, 235.

Cosgrove v. Kubiniec, 56 A.D.2d 709, 392 N.Y.S.2d 733 (N.Y.A.D. 4 Dept.1977)—§ 11.3, n. 17.

Costa, People v., 121 Misc.2d 864, 469 N.Y.S.2d 545 (N.Y.Sup.1983)—§ 1.3, n. 60.

Cotroneo, People v., 199 A.D.2d 670, 604 N.Y.S.2d 979 (N.Y.A.D. 3 Dept.1993)—§ 10.5, n. 106.

Counselman v. Hitchcock, 142 U.S. 547, 12 S.Ct. 195, 35 L.Ed. 1110 (1892)—§ 5.9; § 5.9, n. 200.

County of (see name of county)

Cousart, People v., 458 N.Y.S.2d 507, 444 N.E.2d 971 (N.Y.1982)—§ 9.8, n. 53, 54.

Covington, People v., 144 A.D.2d 238, 533 N.Y.S.2d 433 (N.Y.A.D. 1 Dept.1988)—§ 10.17, n. 349.

Cowles v. Brownell, 540 N.Y.S.2d 973, 538 N.E.2d 325 (N.Y.1989)—§ 3.29, n. 391; § 11.3, n. 27.

Cox v. New York City Housing Authority, 105 A.D.2d 663, 482 N.Y.S.2d 5 (N.Y.A.D. 1 Dept.1984)—§ 7.30, n. 340.

Cox, People v., 196 A.D.2d 596, 601 N.Y.S.2d 175 (N.Y.A.D. 2 Dept.1993)—§ 6.9, n. 213.

Cox, People v., 127 Misc.2d 336, 486 N.Y.S.2d 143 (N.Y.Sup.1985)—§ 1.3, n. 61, 68.

Cox, People v., 286 N.Y. 137, 36 N.E.2d 84 (N.Y.1941)—§ 5.17, n. 364.

CPL Inquiry, In re, 78 Misc.2d 244, 356 N.Y.S.2d 749 (N.Y.Sup.1974)—§ 4.11, n. 188.

Cramer, People v., 166 A.D.2d 316, 560 N.Y.S.2d 777 (N.Y.A.D. 1 Dept.1990)—§ 7.14, n. 163.

Crean, People v., 115 Misc.2d 996, 454 N.Y.S.2d 943 (N.Y.Sup.1982)—§ 1.3, n. 55.

Crean, People v., 115 Misc.2d 526, 454 N.Y.S.2d 231 (N.Y.Sup.1982)—§ 7.8, n. 81.

Crews, United States v., 445 U.S. 463, 100 S.Ct. 1244, 63 L.Ed.2d 537 (1980)—§ 10.10, n. 178.

Crispell, People v., 110 A.D.2d 926, 487 N.Y.S.2d 174 (N.Y.A.D. 3 Dept.1985)—§ 10.5, n. 121.

Crooms v. Corriero, 206 A.D.2d 275, 614 N.Y.S.2d 511 (N.Y.A.D. 1 Dept.1994)—§ 11.19, n. 253, 258, 264.

Cropper, People v., 202 A.D.2d 603, 609 N.Y.S.2d 288 (N.Y.A.D. 2 Dept.1994)—§ 9.47, n. 346.

Crosby, People v., 140 Misc.2d 904, 531 N.Y.S.2d 753 (N.Y.Dist.Ct.1988)—§ 9.5, n. 21.

TABLE OF CASES

Cross, Application of, 275 A.D. 719, 87 N.Y.S.2d 338 (N.Y.A.D.1949)—§ **1.8, n. 180.**

Cruz v. New York, 481 U.S. 186, 107 S.Ct. 1714, 95 L.Ed.2d 162 (1987)—§ **5.22;** § **5.22, n. 584.**

Cruz, People v., 161 A.D.2d 1182, 555 N.Y.S.2d 523 (N.Y.A.D. 4 Dept.1990)— § **3.26, n. 353.**

Cruz, People v., 149 A.D.2d 151, 545 N.Y.S.2d 561 (N.Y.A.D. 1 Dept.1989)— § **11.16, n. 209.**

Cruz, People v., 495 N.Y.S.2d 14, 485 N.E.2d 221 (N.Y.1985)—§ **5.22, n. 583, 604.**

Cruz, People v., N.Y.L.J., p. 25, col. 5 (N.Y.C.Crim.Ct.1990)—§ **7.8, n. 81.**

Cuadrado, People v., 161 A.D.2d 232, 554 N.Y.S.2d 618 (N.Y.A.D. 1 Dept.1990)— § **11.3, n. 21.**

Cuevas, People v., 67 A.D.2d 219, 414 N.Y.S.2d 520 (N.Y.A.D. 1 Dept.1979)— § **7.27, n. 299, 303.**

Cullen, People v., 428 N.Y.S.2d 456, 405 N.E.2d 1021 (N.Y.1980)—§ **1.4, n. 90, 112.**

Cummings, People v., 159 Misc.2d 1118, 611 N.Y.S.2d 1011 (N.Y.Sup.1994)— § **11.5, n. 57.**

Cummings, People v., 109 A.D.2d 748, 485 N.Y.S.2d 847 (N.Y.A.D. 2 Dept.1985)— § **3.33, n. 456.**

Cunningham v. Nadjari, 383 N.Y.S.2d 590, 347 N.E.2d 915 (N.Y.1976)—§ **1.2, n. 27.**

Cunningham, People v., 189 A.D.2d 821, 592 N.Y.S.2d 447 (N.Y.A.D. 2 Dept. 1993)—§ **7.21, n. 234.**

Cupp v. Murphy, 412 U.S. 291, 93 S.Ct. 2000, 36 L.Ed.2d 900 (1973)—§ **7.11, n. 119.**

Curdgel, People v., 611 N.Y.S.2d 827, 634 N.E.2d 199 (N.Y.1994)—§ **11.14, n. 151.**

Curry, People v., 153 Misc.2d 61, 579 N.Y.S.2d 1000 (N.Y.Sup.1992)—§ **5.1, n. 13.**

Cusani, People v., 153 A.D.2d 574, 544 N.Y.S.2d 499 (N.Y.A.D. 2 Dept.1989)— § **11.15, n. 165.**

Cusick, People v., 111 A.D.2d 251, 489 N.Y.S.2d 96 (N.Y.A.D. 2 Dept.1985)— § **11.15, n. 186.**

Cuyler v. Adams, 449 U.S. 433, 101 S.Ct. 703, 66 L.Ed.2d 641 (1981)—§ **9.54, n. 389;** § **9.55, n. 395, 402.**

Cwikla, People v., 414 N.Y.S.2d 102, 386 N.E.2d 1070 (N.Y.1979)—§ **7.12, n. 138, 139;** § **7.13, n. 152.**

Dabbs, People v., 192 A.D.2d 932, 596 N.Y.S.2d 893 (N.Y.A.D. 3 Dept.1993)— § **5.21, n. 506.**

Dabbs v. State, 464 N.Y.S.2d 428, 451 N.E.2d 186 (N.Y.1983)—§ **3.12, n. 127.**

Da Forno, People v., 442 N.Y.S.2d 476, 425 N.E.2d 864 (N.Y.1981)—§ **11.12, n. 127.**

Dagata, People v., 629 N.Y.S.2d 186, 652 N.E.2d 932 (N.Y.1995)—§ **7.4, n. 29, 32.**

D'Alessio, People v., 134 Misc.2d 1005, 513 N.Y.S.2d 906 (N.Y.City Crim.Ct.1986)— § **3.21, n. 258.**

D'Amico, People v., 561 N.Y.S.2d 411, 562 N.E.2d 488 (N.Y.1990)—§ **5.10;** § **5.10, n. 279, 301;** § **11.5, n. 42.**

D'Amico, People v., 147 Misc.2d 731, 556 N.Y.S.2d 456 (N.Y.Sup.1990)—§ **2.2, n. 14.**

D'Amico, People v., 136 Misc.2d 16, 517 N.Y.S.2d 881 (N.Y.Co.Ct.1987)—§ **7.4, n. 25, 26.**

Damon, People v., 299 N.Y.S.2d 830, 247 N.E.2d 651 (N.Y.1969)—§ **10.20, n. 488.**

Damon, United States ex rel. Leeson v., 496 F.2d 718 (2nd Cir.1974)—§ **11.9, n. 78, 80.**

Damsky, People v., 47 A.D.2d 822, 366 N.Y.S.2d 13 (N.Y.A.D. 1 Dept.1975)— § **11.19, n. 266.**

D'Angelo, People v., 145 A.D.2d 783, 535 N.Y.S.2d 765 (N.Y.A.D. 3 Dept.1988)— § **11.15, n. 170.**

Daniels, People v., 630 N.Y.S.2d 5 (N.Y.A.D. 1 Dept.1995)—§ **9.51, n. 369;** § **9.52, n. 386.**

Daniels, People v., 132 A.D.2d 667, 518 N.Y.S.2d 37 (N.Y.A.D. 2 Dept.1987)— § **11.12, n. 133.**

Danielson, People v., 184 A.D.2d 723, 585 N.Y.S.2d 78 (N.Y.A.D. 2 Dept.1992)— § **1.4, n. 87, 88.**

Danylocke, People v., 150 A.D.2d 480, 541 N.Y.S.2d 84 (N.Y.A.D. 2 Dept.1989)— § **5.27, n. 681.**

Darby, People v., 554 N.Y.S.2d 426, 553 N.E.2d 974 (N.Y.1990)—§ **5.5, n. 78;** § **5.27, n. 732, 738.**

Darden, People v., 356 N.Y.S.2d 582, 313 N.E.2d 49 (N.Y.1974)—§ **7.10;** § **7.10, n. 99;** § **10.4, n. 76;** § **10.19, n. 433.**

Darling, People v., 50 A.D.2d 1038, 377 N.Y.S.2d 718 (N.Y.A.D. 3 Dept.1975)— § **1.2, n. 23.**

Darling, People v., 81 Misc.2d 487, 366 N.Y.S.2d 982 (N.Y.Sup.1975)—§ **1.7, n. 144.**

Davis, People v., 162 Misc.2d 662, 618 N.Y.S.2d 194 (N.Y.Sup.1994)—§ **1.2, n. 28;** § **5.4, n. 59.**

Davis, People v., 205 A.D.2d 697, 613 N.Y.S.2d 668 (N.Y.A.D. 2 Dept.1994)— § **9.38, n. 275, 277, 282;** § **9.41, n. 292.**

Davis, People v., 195 A.D.2d 1, 606 N.Y.S.2d 899 (N.Y.A.D. 1 Dept.1994)—§ **9.16;** § **9.16, n. 152.**

Davis, People v., 199 A.D.2d 61, 605 N.Y.S.2d 244 (N.Y.A.D. 1 Dept.1993)— § **5.22, n. 576.**

Davis, People v., 194 A.D.2d 473, 599 N.Y.S.2d 559 (N.Y.A.D. 1 Dept.1993)— § **1.4, n. 81, 88.**

TABLE OF CASES

Davis, People v., 193 A.D.2d 885, 597 N.Y.S.2d 780 (N.Y.A.D. 3 Dept.1993)—§ 7.27, n. 297.

Davis, People v., 598 N.Y.S.2d 156, 614 N.E.2d 719 (N.Y.1993)—§ 7.12, n. 135.

Davis, People v., 184 A.D.2d 575, 584 N.Y.S.2d 638 (N.Y.A.D. 2 Dept.1992)—§ 9.38, n. 276; § 9.39, n. 283; § 9.51, n. 382.

Davis, People v., 176 A.D.2d 1236, 576 N.Y.S.2d 731 (N.Y.A.D. 4 Dept.1991)—§ 11.10, n. 105.

Davis, People v., 169 A.D.2d 379, 564 N.Y.S.2d 320 (N.Y.A.D. 1 Dept.1991)—§ 10.15, n. 299; § 10.19, n. 398.

Davis, People v., 146 A.D.2d 942, 537 N.Y.S.2d 93 (N.Y.A.D. 3 Dept.1989)—§ 10.5, n. 96.

Davis, People v., 530 N.Y.S.2d 529, 526 N.E.2d 20 (N.Y.1988)—§ 5.17, n. 355.

Davis, People v., 133 Misc.2d 1031, 509 N.Y.S.2d 257 (N.Y.Sup.1986)—§ 5.8, n. 153.

Davis, People v., 119 Misc.2d 1013, 465 N.Y.S.2d 404 (N.Y.Sup.1983)—§ 5.9, n. 261.

Davis, People v., 93 A.D.2d 970, 463 N.Y.S.2d 67 (N.Y.A.D. 3 Dept.1983)—§ 10.2, n. 47; § 10.3, n. 73; § 10.5, n. 102; § 10.6, n. 132.

Davis, People v., 86 A.D.2d 956, 448 N.Y.S.2d 315 (N.Y.A.D. 4 Dept.1982)—§ 7.30, n. 349.

Davis, People v., 105 Misc.2d 409, 432 N.Y.S.2d 350 (N.Y.City Ct.1980)—§ 7.14, n. 158.

Davis, People v., 394 N.Y.S.2d 865, 363 N.E.2d 572 (N.Y.1977)—§ 5.19; § 5.19, n. 452.

Davis, People v., 43 A.D.2d 866, 352 N.Y.S.2d 17 (N.Y.A.D. 2 Dept.1974)—§ 11.18, n. 251.

Dawkins, People v., 604 N.Y.S.2d 34, 624 N.E.2d 162 (N.Y.1993)—§ 2.4, n. 45.

Dawson, People v., 101 A.D.2d 816, 475 N.Y.S.2d 454 (N.Y.A.D. 2 Dept.1984)—§ 10.14, n. 286.

Dawson, People v., 428 N.Y.S.2d 914, 406 N.E.2d 771 (N.Y.1980)—§ 2.4, n. 58.

Day, People v., 150 A.D.2d 595, 541 N.Y.S.2d 463 (N.Y.A.D. 2 Dept.1989)—§ 11.15, n. 165.

Dean, People v., 542 N.Y.S.2d 512, 540 N.E.2d 707 (N.Y.1989)—§ 5.26, n. 657.

Dean, People v., 80 A.D.2d 695, 436 N.Y.S.2d 455 (N.Y.A.D. 3 Dept.1981)—§ 5.20, n. 472.

Dean, People v., 412 N.Y.S.2d 353, 384 N.E.2d 1277 (N.Y.1978)—§ 2.8, n. 182; § 9.26, n. 212; § 9.30, n. 229; § 9.31, n. 236.

Dean, People v., 96 Misc.2d 781, 409 N.Y.S.2d 647 (N.Y.Sup.1978)—§ 1.8, n. 186.

Dean, People v., 56 A.D.2d 242, 392 N.Y.S.2d 134 (N.Y.A.D. 4 Dept.1977)—§ 2.7, n. 154; § 5.21, n. 483.

De Frain, People v., 204 A.D.2d 1002, 613 N.Y.S.2d 303 (N.Y.A.D. 4 Dept.1994)—§ 10.20, n. 473.

Degand, United States v., 614 F.2d 176 (8th Cir.1980)—§ 11.9, n. 88.

Degro, People v., 141 Misc.2d 810, 535 N.Y.S.2d 330 (N.Y.City Crim.Ct.1988)—§ 9.37, n. 271.

De Jesus, People v., 190 A.D.2d 1012, 593 N.Y.S.2d 633 (N.Y.A.D. 4 Dept.1993)—§ 9.43, n. 308.

De Jesus, People v., 125 Misc.2d 963, 480 N.Y.S.2d 807 (N.Y.Sup.1984)—§ 10.5, n. 102.

Delacruz, People v., 189 A.D.2d 717, 592 N.Y.S.2d 732 (N.Y.A.D. 1 Dept.1993)—§ 9.37, n. 265; § 9.38, n. 277.

De Lago, People v., 266 N.Y.S.2d 353, 213 N.E.2d 659 (N.Y.1965)—§ 10.3, n. 51; § 10.5, n. 94, 95.

Delaney, People v., 125 Misc.2d 928, 481 N.Y.S.2d 229 (N.Y.Co.Ct.1984)—§ 7.4, n. 34.

Delano, People v., 208 A.D.2d 644, 618 N.Y.S.2d 236 (N.Y.A.D. 2 Dept.1994)—§ 11.13, n. 138.

Delgado, People v., 209 A.D.2d 218, 618 N.Y.S.2d 311 (N.Y.A.D. 1 Dept.1994)—§ 9.22, n. 171.

Delgado, People v., 202 A.D.2d 299, 610 N.Y.S.2d 770 (N.Y.A.D. 1 Dept.1994)—§ 6.2, n. 23, 32; § 6.9, n. 216.

Del Giorno, People v., 19 A.D.2d 849, 243 N.Y.S.2d 1010 (N.Y.A.D. 4 Dept.1963)—§ 10.19, n. 398.

DeLong, People v., 206 A.D.2d 914, 615 N.Y.S.2d 168 (N.Y.A.D. 4 Dept.1994)—§ 9.3, n. 11.

De Luna v. United States, 308 F.2d 140 (5th Cir.1962)—§ 5.22, n. 608.

De Meo, People v., 123 A.D.2d 879, 507 N.Y.S.2d 658 (N.Y.A.D. 2 Dept.1986)—§ 10.5, n. 87.

Dentine, People v., 27 A.D.2d 139, 276 N.Y.S.2d 963 (N.Y.A.D. 1 Dept.1967)—§ 10.10; § 10.10, n. 174.

De Pillo, People v., 168 A.D.2d 899, 565 N.Y.S.2d 650 (N.Y.A.D. 4 Dept.1990)—§ 9.3, n. 27; § 9.7, n. 35.

Derisi, People v., 110 Misc.2d 718, 442 N.Y.S.2d 908 (N.Y.Dist.Ct.1981)—§ 4.10, n. 146.

De Rosa, People v., 397 N.Y.S.2d 780, 366 N.E.2d 868 (N.Y.1977)—§ 9.12, n. 116.

Derrick, People v., 188 A.D.2d 486, 590 N.Y.S.2d 907 (N.Y.A.D. 2 Dept.1992)—§ 11.18, n. 243.

Dery, People v., 115 A.D.2d 996, 497 N.Y.S.2d 560 (N.Y.A.D. 4 Dept.1985)—§ 9.40, n. 288.

Devone, People v., 163 Misc.2d 581, 620 N.Y.S.2d 927 (N.Y.Sup.1994)—§ 5.8, n. 174.

TABLE OF CASES

Diaz, People v., 211 A.D.2d 402, 621 N.Y.S.2d 36 (N.Y.A.D. 1 Dept.1995)—§ 5.9, n. 256.

Diaz, People v., 201 A.D.2d 580, 607 N.Y.S.2d 959 (N.Y.A.D. 2 Dept.1994)—§ 5.27, n. 733.

Diaz, People v., 170 A.D.2d 395, 566 N.Y.S.2d 283 (N.Y.A.D. 1 Dept.1991)—§ 7.17, n. 216.

DiCarluccio, People v., 168 A.D.2d 509, 562 N.Y.S.2d 750 (N.Y.A.D. 2 Dept.1990)—§ 11.15, n. 177.

Dickson, People v., 133 A.D.2d 492, 519 N.Y.S.2d 419 (N.Y.A.D. 3 Dept.1987)—§ 9.6, n. 24; § 9.7, n. 33, 35; § 11.15, n. 187.

DiFabio, People v., 580 N.Y.S.2d 182, 588 N.E.2d 80 (N.Y.1992)—§ 5.4; § 5.4, n. 54.

Di Falco, People v., 406 N.Y.S.2d 279, 377 N.E.2d 732 (N.Y.1978)—§ 5.3; § 5.3, n. 35; § 5.8, n. 115.

Diggs, People v., 140 Misc.2d 794, 531 N.Y.S.2d 723 (N.Y.Dist.Ct.1988)—§ 3.33, n. 461.

Dillard, People v., 214 A.D.2d 1028, 627 N.Y.S.2d 184 (N.Y.A.D. 4 Dept.1995)—§ 5.7, n. 102.

Di Napoli, People v., 316 N.Y.S.2d 622, 265 N.E.2d 449 (N.Y.1970)—§ 5.3; § 5.3, n. 32, 45; § 5.27, n. 696.

Di Noia, People v., 105 A.D.2d 799, 481 N.Y.S.2d 738 (N.Y.A.D. 2 Dept.1984)—§ 5.27, n. 681.

Dionisio, United States v., 410 U.S. 1, 93 S.Ct. 764, 35 L.Ed.2d 67 (1973)—§ 5.9, n. 232; § 7.11, n. 119.

Di Pasquale, People v., 161 A.D. 196, 146 N.Y.S. 523 (N.Y.A.D. 3 Dept.1914)—§ 9.5, n. 22.

Di Raffaele, People v., 448 N.Y.S.2d 448, 433 N.E.2d 513 (N.Y.1982)—§ 10.22, n. 532; § 11.15, n. 158, 170.

Dishaw, People v., 54 A.D.2d 1122, 388 N.Y.S.2d 795 (N.Y.A.D. 4 Dept.1976)—§ 2.3, n. 36.

Di Stefano, People v., 382 N.Y.S.2d 5, 345 N.E.2d 548 (N.Y.1976)—§ 1.3, n. 41; § 10.19, n. 430; § 10.20, n. 464, 494.

District Attorney of Kings County v. Iadarola, 164 Misc.2d 204, 623 N.Y.S.2d 999 (N.Y.Sup.1995)—§ 2.10, n. 234.

District Attorney of Suffolk County, Matter of, 461 N.Y.S.2d 773, 448 N.E.2d 440 (N.Y.1983)—§ 5.3, n. 47, 48.

Dixon, People v., 623 N.Y.S.2d 813, 647 N.E.2d 1321 (N.Y.1995)—§ 10.26, n. 580.

Dixon, People v., 154 Misc.2d 454, 584 N.Y.S.2d 735 (N.Y.Sup.1992)—§ 5.8, n. 138.

Dixon, People v., 323 N.Y.S.2d 825, 272 N.E.2d 329 (N.Y.1971)—§ 2.2, n. 16; § 11.18, n. 243, 245.

Dixon, United States v., 509 U.S. 688, 113 S.Ct. 2849, 125 L.Ed.2d 556 (1993)—§ 2.3, n. 33; § 2.5, n. 98, 112; § 2.6, n. 152.

D., Terry, Matter of, 601 N.Y.S.2d 452, 619 N.E.2d 389 (N.Y.1993)—§ 7.8, n. 76, 86; § 7.9; § 7.9, n. 95.

Dobbs, People v., 156 A.D.2d 990, 549 N.Y.S.2d 283 (N.Y.A.D. 4 Dept.1989)—§ 6.9, n. 200.

Doceti, People v., 175 A.D.2d 256, 572 N.Y.S.2d 720 (N.Y.A.D. 2 Dept.1991)—§ 11.10, n. 94.

Dodson, People v., 421 N.Y.S.2d 47, 396 N.E.2d 194 (N.Y.1979)—§ 2.11, n. 241.

Dodt, People v., 474 N.Y.S.2d 441, 462 N.E.2d 1159 (N.Y.1984)—§ 10.19, n. 455, 461; § 10.20, n. 466, 468, 479.

Doe, People v., 159 Misc.2d 799, 606 N.Y.S.2d 862 (N.Y.Sup.1993)—§ 5.27, n. 768, 787; § 11.3, n. 28.

Doe, People v., 158 Misc.2d 863, 602 N.Y.S.2d 507 (N.Y.City Crim.Ct.1993)—§ 3.28, n. 377; § 5.27, n. 772.

Doe, People v., 151 Misc.2d 829, 574 N.Y.S.2d 453 (N.Y.Sup.1991)—§ 5.1, n. 4, 7.

Doe, People v., 148 Misc.2d 286, 560 N.Y.S.2d 177 (N.Y.Co.Ct.1990)—§ 5.8, n. 116.

Doe, People v., 90 A.D.2d 669, 455 N.Y.S.2d 866 (N.Y.A.D. 4 Dept.1982)—§ 5.9, n. 241.

Doe, People v., 47 Misc.2d 975, 263 N.Y.S.2d 607 (N.Y.Co.Ct.1965)—§ 5.3, n. 43.

Doe, United States v., 465 U.S. 605, 104 S.Ct. 1237, 79 L.Ed.2d 552 (1984)—§ 5.9; § 5.9, n. 238.

Doggett v. United States, 505 U.S. 647, 112 S.Ct. 2686, 120 L.Ed.2d 520 (1992)—§ 5.23, n. 624; § 9.8; § 9.8, n. 43.

Dolan, People v., 184 A.D.2d 892, 585 N.Y.S.2d 549 (N.Y.A.D. 3 Dept.1992)—§ 5.27, n. 793.

Donnelly, People v., 176 A.D.2d 404, 574 N.Y.S.2d 111 (N.Y.A.D. 3 Dept.1991)—§ 11.3, n. 17; § 11.19, n. 253.

Doran, People v., 246 N.Y. 409, 159 N.E. 379 (N.Y.1927)—§ 5.22, n. 565.

Dorsey, People v., 122 A.D.2d 393, 505 N.Y.S.2d 210 (N.Y.A.D. 3 Dept.1986)—§ 10.22, n. 537.

Douglas, People v., 209 A.D.2d 161, 617 N.Y.S.2d 765 (N.Y.A.D. 1 Dept.1994)—§ 9.33, n. 240, 247.

Douglas, People v., 156 A.D.2d 173, 548 N.Y.S.2d 217 (N.Y.A.D. 1 Dept.1989)—§ 9.30, n. 233.

Douglas, People v., 135 A.D.2d 435, 522 N.Y.S.2d 856 (N.Y.A.D. 1 Dept.1987)—§ 11.11, n. 123.

Douglass, People v., 469 N.Y.S.2d 56, 456 N.E.2d 1179 (N.Y.1983)—§ 3.26, n. 346, 347; § 5.25, n. 641; § 5.27, n. 756.

Dowdy, People ex rel. v. Smith, 423 N.Y.S.2d 862, 399 N.E.2d 894 (N.Y.1979)—§ 2.8, n. 178, 187.

TABLE OF CASES

Dowling v. United States, 493 U.S. 342, 110 S.Ct. 668, 107 L.Ed.2d 708 (1990)—§ **2.8, n. 173, 181.**

Doyle v. Hofstader, 257 N.Y. 244, 177 N.E. 489 (N.Y.1931)—§ **5.9, n. 199.**

Drake, People v., 205 A.D.2d 996, 613 N.Y.S.2d 961 (N.Y.A.D. 3 Dept.1994)—§ **9.42, n. 304.**

Drake, People v., 474 N.Y.S.2d 276, 462 N.E.2d 376 (N.Y.1984)—§ **9.8, n. 55.**

Drapala, People v., 93 A.D.2d 956, 463 N.Y.S.2d 70 (N.Y.A.D. 3 Dept.1983)—§ **10.5, n. 107.**

Draper, People v., 278 A.D. 298, 104 N.Y.S.2d 703 (N.Y.A.D. 4 Dept.1951)—§ **6.3, n. 65.**

Draxler, People ex rel. Yannarilli v., 41 A.D.2d 684, 340 N.Y.S.2d 755 (N.Y.A.D. 3 Dept.1973)—§ **4.5, n. 83.**

Dremeguila, People v., 166 A.D.2d 196, 564 N.Y.S.2d 86 (N.Y.A.D. 1 Dept.1990)—§ **11.13, n. 138.**

Drope v. Missouri, 420 U.S. 162, 95 S.Ct. 896, 43 L.Ed.2d 103 (1975)—§ **6.1, n. 2; § 6.2, n. 18.**

Drummond, People v., 215 A.D.2d 579, 627 N.Y.S.2d 55 (N.Y.A.D. 2 Dept.1995)—§ **5.26, n. 671; § 9.37, n. 269; § 9.51, n. 367.**

Dudasik, People v., 112 A.D.2d 20, 490 N.Y.S.2d 385 (N.Y.A.D. 4 Dept.1985)—§ **6.10, n. 219.**

Duignan, People v., 104 Misc.2d 351, 432 N.Y.S.2d 291 (N.Y.City Crim.Ct.1980)—§ **4.10, n. 149.**

Duke, People v., 158 Misc.2d 647, 606 N.Y.S.2d 516 (N.Y.Sup.1993)—§ **3.28, n. 377.**

Dukes, People v., 194 A.D.2d 923, 599 N.Y.S.2d 188 (N.Y.A.D. 3 Dept.1993)—§ **11.13, n. 138.**

Dukes, People v., 156 A.D.2d 203, 548 N.Y.S.2d 462 (N.Y.A.D. 1 Dept.1989)—§ **7.14, n. 163.**

Dumas, People v., 506 N.Y.S.2d 319, 497 N.E.2d 686 (N.Y.1986)—§ **3.7, n. 89; § 5.27, n. 727.**

Dunbar, People v., 440 N.Y.S.2d 613, 423 N.E.2d 36 (N.Y.1981)—§ **5.3, n. 36; § 11.15, n. 179.**

Dunkley, People v., 200 A.D.2d 499, 606 N.Y.S.2d 638 (N.Y.A.D. 1 Dept.1994)—§ **10.10, n. 197.**

Dunlap, People v., 629 N.Y.S.2d 407 (N.Y.A.D. 1 Dept.1995)—§ **5.27, n. 758, 794; § 10.19, n. 430.**

Dunn, People v., 155 A.D.2d 75, 553 N.Y.S.2d 257 (N.Y.A.D. 4 Dept.1990)—§ **10.13, n. 276.**

Durante, People v., 97 A.D.2d 851, 469 N.Y.S.2d 18 (N.Y.A.D. 2 Dept.1983)—§ **5.8, n. 181.**

Dusky v. United States, 362 U.S. 402, 80 S.Ct. 788, 4 L.Ed.2d 824 (1960)—§ **6.1, n. 4.**

Dwork, People v., 116 Misc.2d 411, 453 N.Y.S.2d 319 (N.Y.Co.Ct.1982)—§ **10.6, n. 126.**

Dziuma v. Korvettes, 61 A.D.2d 677, 403 N.Y.S.2d 269 (N.Y.A.D. 1 Dept.1978)—§ **11.3, n. 27.**

Earl, People v., 632 N.Y.S.2d 689 (N.Y.A.D. 3 Dept.1995)—§ **6.10, n. 238; § 7.33, n. 363.**

Earl, People v., 138 A.D.2d 839, 525 N.Y.S.2d 952 (N.Y.A.D. 3 Dept.1988)—§ **10.6, n. 132.**

Easterling, People v., 191 A.D.2d 579, 594 N.Y.S.2d 805 (N.Y.A.D. 2 Dept.1993)—§ **11.19, n. 261.**

Easterling, People v., 59 A.D.2d 537, 397 N.Y.S.2d 125 (N.Y.A.D. 2 Dept.1977)—§ **2.7, n. 162.**

Eastern Ambulance Service, Inc., People v., 106 A.D.2d 867, 483 N.Y.S.2d 508 (N.Y.A.D. 4 Dept.1984)—§ **9.3, n. 11.**

Ebbecke, People v., 99 Misc.2d 1, 414 N.Y.S.2d 977 (N.Y.Sup.1979)—§ **5.23, n. 624.**

Ebron, People v., 116 Misc.2d 774, 456 N.Y.S.2d 308 (N.Y.Sup.1982)—§ **1.3, n. 35; § 1.4, n. 113, 116.**

Edjardo, People v., N.Y.L.J., p. 31, col. 1 (Sup.Ct., N.Y.County 1995)—§ **5.27, n. 713.**

Edwards, People v., 513 N.Y.S.2d 960, 506 N.E.2d 530 (N.Y.1987)—§ **10.3, n. 49, 54; § 10.5, n. 89.**

Edwards, People v., 485 N.Y.S.2d 252, 474 N.E.2d 612 (N.Y.1984)—§ **1.3, n. 73.**

Eiffel, People v., 139 Misc.2d 340, 527 N.Y.S.2d 347 (N.Y.Sup.1988)—§ **5.8, n. 160.**

Einhorn, People v., 365 N.Y.S.2d 171, 324 N.E.2d 551 (N.Y.1974)—§ **5.9, n. 260.**

Einhorn, People v., 45 A.D.2d 75, 356 N.Y.S.2d 620 (N.Y.A.D. 1 Dept.1974)—§ **5.19, n. 447.**

Eldridge, People v., 173 A.D.2d 975, 569 N.Y.S.2d 482 (N.Y.A.D. 3 Dept.1991)—§ **10.5, n. 122.**

Eleby, People v., 137 A.D.2d 708, 525 N.Y.S.2d 51 (N.Y.A.D. 2 Dept.1988)—§ **7.21, n. 234.**

Elliby, People v., 80 A.D.2d 875, 436 N.Y.S.2d 784 (N.Y.A.D. 2 Dept.1981)—§ **11.3, n. 20; § 11.5, n. 59.**

Elliot, People v., 204 A.D.2d 565, 612 N.Y.S.2d 173 (N.Y.A.D. 2 Dept.1994)—§ **11.13, n. 139.**

Ellis, People v., 188 A.D.2d 1043, 592 N.Y.S.2d 200 (N.Y.A.D. 4 Dept.1992)—§ **7.16, n. 185.**

Ellis, People ex rel. v. Koehler, 165 A.D.2d 848, 560 N.Y.S.2d 226 (N.Y.A.D. 2 Dept. 1990)—§ **9.25, n. 208.**

Ellis, People ex rel. v. Koehler, 151 A.D.2d 309, 542 N.Y.S.2d 578 (N.Y.A.D. 1 Dept. 1989)—§ **3.34, n. 476, 486.**

TABLE OF CASES

Emery, People v., 159 A.D.2d 992, 552 N.Y.S.2d 746 (N.Y.A.D. 4 Dept.1990)—§ 7.21, n. 234.

Emmons, People v., 99 Misc.2d 941, 417 N.Y.S.2d 432 (N.Y.Co.Ct.1979)—§ 7.23, n. 262.

England, People v., 613 N.Y.S.2d 854, 636 N.E.2d 1387 (N.Y.1994)—§ 5.23, n. 623; § 9.21, n. 169; § 9.33, n. 241.

English, People v., 103 A.D.2d 979, 480 N.Y.S.2d 56 (N.Y.A.D. 3 Dept.1984)—§ 7.4, n. 50.

Ennis, People v., 94 A.D.2d 746, 462 N.Y.S.2d 499 (N.Y.A.D. 2 Dept.1983)—§ 11.16, n. 204.

Ennis v. Slade, 179 A.D.2d 558, 579 N.Y.S.2d 59 (N.Y.A.D. 1 Dept.1992)—§ 7.33, n. 370.

Enright v. Siedlecki, 464 N.Y.S.2d 418, 451 N.E.2d 176 (N.Y.1983)—§ 2.4, n. 48, 49.

Entrialgo, People v., 19 A.D.2d 509, 245 N.Y.S.2d 850 (N.Y.A.D. 2 Dept.1963)—§ 10.19, n. 398, 440.

Epstein, People v., 47 A.D.2d 661, 364 N.Y.S.2d 38 (N.Y.A.D. 2 Dept.1975)—§ 1.2, n. 25.

Erber, People v., 210 A.D.2d 250, 619 N.Y.S.2d 344 (N.Y.A.D. 2 Dept.1994)—§ 5.7, n. 109.

Erickson, People v., 302 N.Y. 461, 99 N.E.2d 240 (N.Y.1951)—§ 9.3, n. 11.

E., Rodney, People v., 569 N.Y.S.2d 920, 572 N.E.2d 603 (N.Y.1991)—§ 11.11, n. 110; § 11.13, n. 147.

Esajerre, People v., 363 N.Y.S.2d 931, 323 N.E.2d 175 (N.Y.1974)—§ 10.22, n. 538; § 11.2, n. 1; § 11.3, n. 20, 25.

Escalera v. Coombe, 852 F.2d 45 (2nd Cir. 1988)—§ 7.24, n. 274.

Escobar v. Roberts, 324 N.Y.S.2d 318, 272 N.E.2d 898 (N.Y.1971)—§ 2.10, n. 232.

Esquivel, People v., 158 Misc.2d 720, 601 N.Y.S.2d 541 (N.Y.Sup.1993)—§ 4.11; § 4.11, n. 184.

Essner, People v., 125 Misc.2d 908, 480 N.Y.S.2d 857 (N.Y.Sup.1984)—§ 7.17, n. 206.

Estelle v. Smith, 451 U.S. 454, 101 S.Ct. 1866, 68 L.Ed.2d 359 (1981)—§ 6.3, n. 61.

Estrada, People v., 142 A.D.2d 512, 530 N.Y.S.2d 148 (N.Y.A.D. 1 Dept.1988)—§ 7.10, n. 110.

Estrada, People v., 109 A.D.2d 977, 486 N.Y.S.2d 794 (N.Y.A.D. 3 Dept.1985)—§ 10.22, n. 527.

Evans, People v., 583 N.Y.S.2d 358, 592 N.E.2d 1362 (N.Y.1992)—§ 3.34, n. 484; § 5.8, n. 112, 142, 167.

Ewell, United States v., 383 U.S. 116, 86 S.Ct. 773, 15 L.Ed.2d 627 (1966)—§ 9.8, n. 38.

Ex parte (see name of party)

Faber, People v., 83 A.D.2d 883, 442 N.Y.S.2d 113 (N.Y.A.D. 2 Dept.1981)—§ 10.22, n. 527.

Fagan, People v., 498 N.Y.S.2d 335, 489 N.E.2d 222 (N.Y.1985)—§ 2.8, n. 187.

Fahrenkopf, People v., 191 A.D.2d 903, 595 N.Y.S.2d 139 (N.Y.A.D. 3 Dept.1993)—§ 10.5, n. 89, 94.

Faieta, People v., 109 Misc.2d 841, 440 N.Y.S.2d 1007 (N.Y.Dist.Ct.1981)—§ 4.10, n. 146.

Falcon, People v., 204 A.D.2d 181, 612 N.Y.S.2d 130 (N.Y.A.D. 1 Dept.1994)—§ 5.7; § 5.7, n. 106.

Familia–Morel, People v., 151 Misc.2d 55, 570 N.Y.S.2d 895 (N.Y.City Crim.Ct. 1991)—§ 9.43, n. 308.

F., Angelo, People v., 172 A.D.2d 686, 570 N.Y.S.2d 964 (N.Y.A.D. 2 Dept.1991)—§ 11.15, n. 185.

Fargher, People v., 112 A.D.2d 599, 492 N.Y.S.2d 123 (N.Y.A.D. 3 Dept.1985)—§ 9.55, n. 399, 400, 401.

Farmer, People v., 198 A.D.2d 805, 604 N.Y.S.2d 391 (N.Y.A.D. 4 Dept.1993)—§ 10.6, n. 126.

Farrar, People v., 437 N.Y.S.2d 961, 419 N.E.2d 864 (N.Y.1981)—§ 11.19, n. 260.

Fata, People v., 184 A.D.2d 206, 586 N.Y.S.2d 780 (N.Y.A.D. 1 Dept.1992)—§ 5.18, n. 409, 431.

Faust, People v., 537 N.Y.S.2d 118, 534 N.E.2d 35 (N.Y.1988)—§ 5.22, n. 586.

Fazio, People ex rel. v. McNeill, 4 A.D.2d 686, 164 N.Y.S.2d 156 (N.Y.A.D. 2 Dept. 1957)—§ 6.10, n. 221, 232.

F., Charles, People v., 470 N.Y.S.2d 342, 458 N.E.2d 801 (N.Y.1983)—§ 1.8, n. 186; § 5.20, n. 472.

Fea, People v., 416 N.Y.S.2d 778, 390 N.E.2d 286 (N.Y.1979)—§ 1.3, n. 58.

Felder, People v., 186 A.D.2d 1050, 588 N.Y.S.2d 491 (N.Y.A.D. 4 Dept.1992)—§ 10.22, n. 527.

Feldman, People v., 429 N.Y.S.2d 602, 407 N.E.2d 448 (N.Y.1980)—§ 5.18, n. 410.

Feliciano, People v., 207 A.D.2d 803, 616 N.Y.S.2d 529 (N.Y.A.D. 2 Dept.1994)—§ 5.8, n. 134.

Felix, People v., 460 N.Y.S.2d 1, 446 N.E.2d 757 (N.Y.1983)—§ 11.5, n. 59.

Felix, United States v., 503 U.S. 378, 112 S.Ct. 1377, 118 L.Ed.2d 25 (1992)—§ 2.5, n. 110.

Felman, People v., 137 A.D.2d 341, 529 N.Y.S.2d 395 (N.Y.A.D. 3 Dept.1988)—§ 11.5, n. 57, 58.

Ferguson, People v., 502 N.Y.S.2d 972, 494 N.E.2d 77 (N.Y.1986)—§ 2.4, n. 42.

Ferguson, People ex rel. v. Campbell, 175 A.D.2d 959, 573 N.Y.S.2d 539 (N.Y.A.D. 3 Dept.1991)—§ 9.47, n. 338.

Ferlito v. Judges of County Court, Suffolk County, 340 N.Y.S.2d 635, 292 N.E.2d 779 (N.Y.1972)—§ 2.4, n. 57.

TABLE OF CASES

Fernandez, People v., 499 N.Y.S.2d 919, 490 N.E.2d 838 (N.Y.1986)—§ **10.22, n. 533**; § **11.16, n. 207, 210.**

Fernandez v. Silbowitz, 59 A.D.2d 837, 398 N.Y.S.2d 896 (N.Y.A.D. 1 Dept.1977)— § **11.19, n. 263.**

Ferrara, People v., 99 A.D.2d 257, 472 N.Y.S.2d 407 (N.Y.A.D. 2 Dept.1984)— § **5.8, n. 145, 165; § 11.15, n. 183.**

Ferrari, People v., 155 Misc.2d 749, 589 N.Y.S.2d 983 (N.Y.Co.Ct.1992)—§ **9.5, n. 17; § 9.6, n. 25.**

Fex v. Michigan, 507 U.S. 43, 113 S.Ct. 1085, 122 L.Ed.2d 406 (1993)—§ **9.54, n. 392.**

Fici, People v., 114 A.D.2d 468, 494 N.Y.S.2d 377 (N.Y.A.D. 2 Dept.1985)— § **10.2, n. 38.**

Fidler v. Murphy, 203 Misc. 51, 113 N.Y.S.2d 388 (N.Y.Sup.1952)—§ **3.23, n. 268.**

Field, People v., 161 A.D.2d 660, 555 N.Y.S.2d 437 (N.Y.A.D. 2 Dept.1990)— § **5.27, n. 792.**

Fields, People v., 214 A.D.2d 332, 625 N.Y.S.2d 483 (N.Y.A.D. 1 Dept.1995)— § **9.22, n. 172; § 9.51, n. 373; § 9.52, n. 386.**

Fields, People v., 197 A.D.2d 633, 602 N.Y.S.2d 674 (N.Y.A.D. 2 Dept.1993)— § **11.13, n. 137.**

Fields, People v., 146 A.D.2d 505, 537 N.Y.S.2d 157 (N.Y.A.D. 1 Dept.1989)— § **7.17, n. 193.**

Fields, People v., 413 N.Y.S.2d 112, 385 N.E.2d 1040 (N.Y.1978)—§ **2.4, n. 77.**

Figgins, People v., 637 N.Y.S.2d 684, 661 N.E.2d 156 (N.Y.1995)—§ **11.13, n. 143.**

Figliolo, People v., 207 A.D.2d 679, 616 N.Y.S.2d 367 (N.Y.A.D. 1 Dept.1994)— § **10.15, n. 301.**

Figueroa, People v., 203 A.D.2d 72, 610 N.Y.S.2d 25 (N.Y.A.D. 1 Dept.1994)— § **5.27, n. 768.**

Figueroa, People v., 173 A.D.2d 156, 568 N.Y.S.2d 957 (N.Y.A.D. 1 Dept.1991)— § **11.15, n. 182.**

Fikaris, People v., 101 Misc.2d 460, 421 N.Y.S.2d 179 (N.Y.Sup.1979)—§ **4.9, n. 112.**

Finch, People v., 57 A.D.2d 641, 393 N.Y.S.2d 222 (N.Y.A.D. 3 Dept.1977)— § **10.3, n. 63.**

Fink v. Lefkowitz, 419 N.Y.S.2d 467, 393 N.E.2d 463 (N.Y.1979)—§ **7.33, n. 372.**

Fino v. Johnson, 38 A.D.2d 681, 327 N.Y.S.2d 252 (N.Y.A.D. 4 Dept.1971)— § **10.22, n. 520.**

Fiore, People v., 356 N.Y.S.2d 38, 312 N.E.2d 174 (N.Y.1974)—§ **5.22, n. 537, 555.**

First Meridian Planning Corp., People v., 635 N.Y.S.2d 144, 658 N.E.2d 1017 (N.Y. 1995)—§ **5.17, n. 363.**

First Meridian Planning Corp., People v., 201 A.D.2d 145, 614 N.Y.S.2d 811 (N.Y.A.D. 3 Dept.1994)—§ **5.16, n. 348; § 5.17, n. 362.**

Fisher, People v., 199 A.D.2d 279, 604 N.Y.S.2d 223 (N.Y.A.D. 2 Dept.1993)— § **3.19, n. 223.**

Fisher, People v., 97 A.D.2d 651, 469 N.Y.S.2d 187 (N.Y.A.D. 3 Dept.1983)— § **1.3, n. 71.**

Fisher, People v., 249 N.Y. 419, 164 N.E. 336 (N.Y.1928)—§ **5.21, n. 513.**

Fisher v. United States, 425 U.S. 391, 96 S.Ct. 1569, 48 L.Ed.2d 39 (1976)—§ **5.9, n. 237.**

Fishman, People v., 532 N.Y.S.2d 739, 528 N.E.2d 1212 (N.Y.1988)—§ **7.17, n. 195.**

Fishman, People v., 387 N.Y.S.2d 1003, 356 N.E.2d 475 (N.Y.1976)—§ **10.2, n. 30.**

Fitzgerald v. Cawley, 368 F.Supp. 677 (S.D.N.Y.1973)—§ **9.8, n. 50.**

Fitzgerald, People v., 412 N.Y.S.2d 102, 384 N.E.2d 649 (N.Y.1978)—§ **5.12, n. 323; § 5.14, n. 331; § 5.16, n. 345; § 5.19, n. 449.**

Fiumefreddo, People v., 605 N.Y.S.2d 671, 626 N.E.2d 646 (N.Y.1993)—§ **11.3, n. 23.**

Fletcher, People v., 140 Misc.2d 389, 530 N.Y.S.2d 768 (N.Y.Sup.1988)—§ **5.8, n. 133.**

Flihan, People v., 535 N.Y.S.2d 590, 532 N.E.2d 96 (N.Y.1988)—§ **5.9, n. 209; § 11.15, n. 181.**

Floyd, People v., 392 N.Y.S.2d 257, 360 N.E.2d 935 (N.Y.1976)—§ **10.20, n. 467, 494.**

Fluellen, People v., 160 A.D.2d 219, 553 N.Y.S.2d 670 (N.Y.A.D. 1 Dept.1990)— § **9.40, n. 289.**

Flynn, People v., 581 N.Y.S.2d 160, 589 N.E.2d 383 (N.Y.1992)—§ **7.4, n. 53, 54; § 7.17, n. 190.**

F., Matter of Lionel, 559 N.Y.S.2d 228, 558 N.E.2d 30 (N.Y.1990)—§ **2.4, n. 79.**

Forbes, People v., 203 A.D.2d 609, 609 N.Y.S.2d 961 (N.Y.A.D. 3 Dept.1994)— § **5.22, n. 602.**

Ford v. Kreindler, 206 A.D.2d 425, 614 N.Y.S.2d 439 (N.Y.A.D. 2 Dept.1994)— § **7.11, n. 121.**

Ford, People v., 633 N.Y.S.2d 270, 657 N.E.2d 265 (N.Y.1995)—§ **11.9, n. 83.**

Ford, People v., 205 A.D.2d 798, 613 N.Y.S.2d 688 (N.Y.A.D. 2 Dept.1994)— § **11.9, n. 83.**

Ford, People v., 476 N.Y.S.2d 783, 465 N.E.2d 322 (N.Y.1984)—§ **5.10, n. 298; § 5.18; § 5.18, n. 437.**

Ford, People v., 65 A.D.2d 822, 410 N.Y.S.2d 343 (N.Y.A.D. 2 Dept.1978)— § **11.19, n. 263.**

Forest, People v., 50 A.D.2d 260, 377 N.Y.S.2d 492 (N.Y.A.D. 1 Dept.1975)— § **5.21; § 5.21, n. 520.**

Forman, People v., 145 Misc.2d 115, 546 N.Y.S.2d 755 (N.Y.City Crim.Ct.1989)— § **4.5, n. 64; § 4.10; § 4.10, n. 131, 145.**

TABLE OF CASES

Forrest, People v., 573 N.Y.S.2d 458, 577 N.E.2d 1050 (N.Y.1991)—**§ 7.21, n. 240.**

Forte v. Supreme Court of State of N. Y., 422 N.Y.S.2d 26, 397 N.E.2d 717 (N.Y. 1979)—**§ 2.11, n. 245; § 10.22, n. 514.**

Foster, People v., 200 A.D.2d 196, 613 N.Y.S.2d 616 (N.Y.A.D. 1 Dept.1994)—**§ 10.19, n. 401.**

Foster, People v., 197 A.D.2d 411, 602 N.Y.S.2d 395 (N.Y.A.D. 1 Dept.1993)—**§ 10.16; § 10.16, n. 336, 339.**

Foster, People v., 127 A.D.2d 684, 511 N.Y.S.2d 677 (N.Y.A.D. 2 Dept.1987)—**§ 5.27, n. 765.**

Foster, People v., 278 N.Y.S.2d 603, 225 N.E.2d 200 (N.Y.1967)—**§ 5.10, n. 298; § 5.18, n. 439; § 11.10, n. 95.**

Foucha v. Louisiana, 504 U.S. 71, 112 S.Ct. 1780, 118 L.Ed.2d 437 (1992)—**§ 6.8, n. 179.**

$405,089.23 U.S. Currency, United States v., 33 F.3d 1210 (9th Cir.1994)—**§ 2.10, n. 231.**

Francabandera, People v., 354 N.Y.S.2d 609, 310 N.E.2d 292 (N.Y.1974)—**§ 6.1, n. 5; § 6.10; § 6.10, n. 227.**

Francine CC, People v., 112 A.D.2d 531, 491 N.Y.S.2d 470 (N.Y.A.D. 3 Dept.1985)—**§ 1.4, n. 113.**

Francis, Matter of, 1995 WL 761944 (N.Y. 1995)—**§ 6.8, n. 179.**

Francis, People v., 149 Misc.2d 693, 566 N.Y.S.2d 486 (N.Y.Sup.1991)—**§ 7.30, n. 345.**

Franco, People v., 196 A.D.2d 357, 612 N.Y.S.2d 591 (N.Y.A.D. 2 Dept.1994)—**§ 5.18, n. 392.**

Franco, People v., 158 A.D.2d 33, 557 N.Y.S.2d 7 (N.Y.A.D. 1 Dept.1990)—**§ 11.18, n. 251.**

Frank, People v., 166 Misc.2d 277, 631 N.Y.S.2d 1014 (N.Y.City Crim.Ct. 1995)—**§ 2.10, n. 235.**

Frank, People v., 85 A.D.2d 109, 447 N.Y.S.2d 558 (N.Y.A.D. 4 Dept.1982)—**§ 10.20, n. 494.**

Frank, People v., 363 N.Y.S.2d 953, 323 N.E.2d 191 (N.Y.1974)—**§ 3.14, n. 155, 156.**

Frankel, People v., 129 Misc.2d 95, 492 N.Y.S.2d 671 (N.Y.City Crim.Ct.1985)—**§ 1.3, n. 68.**

Franks v. Delaware, 438 U.S. 154, 98 S.Ct. 2674, 57 L.Ed.2d 667 (1978)—**§ 10.3, n. 48; § 10.4, n. 78; § 10.5, n. 99.**

Frascone, People v., 176 A.D.2d 128, 574 N.Y.S.2d 15 (N.Y.A.D. 1 Dept.1991)—**§ 11.10, n. 108.**

Fraser, People ex rel. v. Britt, 289 N.Y. 614, 43 N.E.2d 836 (N.Y.1942)—**§ 4.1, n. 4.**

Frazier, People v., 200 A.D.2d 510, 606 N.Y.S.2d 682 (N.Y.A.D. 1 Dept.1994)—**§ 5.7, n. 99.**

Frazier, People v., 114 A.D.2d 1038, 495 N.Y.S.2d 478 (N.Y.A.D. 2 Dept.1985)—**§ 6.2, n. 40; § 11.8, n. 74.**

Freckelton, People ex rel. Washor on Behalf of Lopez v., 187 A.D.2d 406, 590 N.Y.S.2d 203 (N.Y.A.D. 1 Dept.1992)—**§ 4.5, n. 86.**

Frederick, People v., 410 N.Y.S.2d 555, 382 N.E.2d 1332 (N.Y.1978)—**§ 11.11, n. 110, 119.**

Fredericks, People v., 157 Misc.2d 822, 598 N.Y.S.2d 682 (N.Y.Sup.1993)—**§ 9.25, n. 206.**

Freeman v. People, 4 Denio 1 (N.Y.Sup.Ct. 1847)—**§ 6.1, n. 3.**

Freitag, People v., 148 A.D.2d 544, 538 N.Y.S.2d 872 (N.Y.A.D. 2 Dept.1989)—**§ 10.3, n. 72.**

Friedman, People v., 384 N.Y.S.2d 408, 348 N.E.2d 883 (N.Y.1976)—**§ 10.19, n. 396.**

Friess v. Morgenthau, 86 Misc.2d 852, 383 N.Y.S.2d 784 (N.Y.Sup.1975)—**§ 3.30, n. 417.**

Friscia, People v., 433 N.Y.S.2d 754, 413 N.E.2d 1168 (N.Y.1980)—**§ 9.12, n. 121.**

Friscia, People v., 73 A.D.2d 702, 422 N.Y.S.2d 538 (N.Y.A.D. 3 Dept.1979)—**§ 9.33, n. 246.**

Fromen, People v., 125 A.D.2d 987, 510 N.Y.S.2d 384 (N.Y.A.D. 4 Dept.1986)—**§ 10.3, n. 60.**

Fruchtman, People ex rel. v. Ossakow, 335 N.Y.S.2d 301, 286 N.E.2d 736 (N.Y. 1972)—**§ 4.5, n. 76.**

Fuentes, People v., 74 A.D.2d 753, 425 N.Y.S.2d 589 (N.Y.A.D. 1 Dept.1980)—**§ 10.15, n. 303.**

Fuentes-Borda, People v., 186 A.D.2d 405, 589 N.Y.S.2d 5 (N.Y.A.D. 1 Dept.1992)—**§ 10.17, n. 381.**

Fuggazzatto, People v., 477 N.Y.S.2d 619, 466 N.E.2d 159 (N.Y.1984)—**§ 9.38; § 9.38, n. 281, 282.**

Fulcher, People v., 97 Misc.2d 239, 411 N.Y.S.2d 167 (N.Y.City Crim.Ct.1978)—**§ 3.31, n. 430.**

Fuller, People v., 200 A.D.2d 498, 606 N.Y.S.2d 640 (N.Y.A.D. 1 Dept.1994)—**§ 10.17, n. 349.**

Fuller, People v., 455 N.Y.S.2d 253, 441 N.E.2d 563 (N.Y.1982)—**§ 9.10, n. 109; § 9.12, n. 121.**

Fuller v. Plumadore, 88 A.D.2d 674, 450 N.Y.S.2d 918 (N.Y.A.D. 3 Dept.1982)—**§ 2.6; § 2.6, n. 127.**

Fusco on Behalf of Wells, People ex rel. v. Sera, 123 Misc.2d 19, 472 N.Y.S.2d 564 (N.Y.Sup.1984)—**§ 6.2, n. 10.**

Fysekis, People v., 164 Misc.2d 627, 625 N.Y.S.2d 861 (N.Y.City Crim.Ct.1995)—**§ 1.1, n. 2; § 9.17, n. 158.**

Gadsden, People v., 139 A.D.2d 925, 528 N.Y.S.2d 955 (N.Y.A.D. 4 Dept.1988)—**§ 5.21, n. 499, 527.**

Gaffney, People v., N.Y.L.J., p. 23, col. 1 (Sup.Ct.N.Y.County 1993)—**§ 5.8, n. 148.**

TABLE OF CASES

Gager v. White, 442 N.Y.S.2d 463, 425 N.E.2d 851 (N.Y.1981)—§ **1.1, n. 2.**

Gaggi, People v., 104 A.D.2d 422, 478 N.Y.S.2d 732 (N.Y.A.D. 2 Dept.1984)—§ **9.34, n. 250.**

Gagnon v. Scarpelli, 411 U.S. 778, 93 S.Ct. 1756, 36 L.Ed.2d 656 (1973)—§ **9.8, n. 52.**

Gaines, People v., 199 A.D.2d 335, 604 N.Y.S.2d 272 (N.Y.A.D. 2 Dept.1993)—§ **7.12, n. 140.**

Gaines, People v., 547 N.Y.S.2d 620, 546 N.E.2d 913 (N.Y.1989)—§ **5.17, n. 379.**

Gaines, People v., 136 A.D.2d 731, 524 N.Y.S.2d 70 (N.Y.A.D. 2 Dept.1988)—§ **3.24, n. 303.**

Galamison, People v., 42 Misc.2d 387, 248 N.Y.S.2d 358 (N.Y.Sup.1964)—§ **1.8, n. 184.**

Galatro, People v., 615 N.Y.S.2d 650, 639 N.E.2d 7 (N.Y.1994)—§ **5.27, n. 714.**

Gallardo, People v., 173 A.D.2d 636, 570 N.Y.S.2d 222 (N.Y.A.D. 2 Dept.1991)—§ **7.16, n. 185.**

Gallishaw, People v., 143 A.D.2d 198, 531 N.Y.S.2d 816 (N.Y.A.D. 2 Dept.1988)—§ **5.21, n. 494.**

Gamble, People v., 128 A.D.2d 724, 513 N.Y.S.2d 217 (N.Y.A.D. 2 Dept.1987)—§ **11.19, n. 263, 265.**

Ganci, People v., 318 N.Y.S.2d 484, 267 N.E.2d 263 (N.Y.1971)—§ **10.14, n. 290.**

Gannon, People v., 162 A.D.2d 818, 557 N.Y.S.2d 726 (N.Y.A.D. 3 Dept.1990)—§ **11.19, n. 260.**

Gans, People v., 119 Misc.2d 843, 465 N.Y.S.2d 147 (N.Y.Sup.1983)—§ **6.4, n. 74; § 6.9, n. 204.**

Garafolo, People v., 44 A.D.2d 86, 353 N.Y.S.2d 500 (N.Y.A.D. 2 Dept.1974)—§ **10.21, n. 501.**

Garcia, People v., 161 A.D.2d 796, 556 N.Y.S.2d 667 (N.Y.A.D. 2 Dept.1990)—§ **6.10, n. 237.**

Gardner, People v., 162 A.D.2d 466, 556 N.Y.S.2d 163 (N.Y.A.D. 2 Dept.1990)—§ **7.14, n. 163.**

Garfinkel, People v., 112 A.D.2d 949, 492 N.Y.S.2d 630 (N.Y.A.D. 2 Dept.1985)—§ **9.34, n. 250.**

Garnes, People v., 134 Misc.2d 39, 510 N.Y.S.2d 409 (N.Y.Sup.1986)—§ **5.22, n. 617.**

Garrity v. State of N. J., 385 U.S. 493, 87 S.Ct. 616, 17 L.Ed.2d 562 (1967)—§ **5.9, n. 205.**

Garrow, People v., 91 A.D.2d 699, 457 N.Y.S.2d 611 (N.Y.A.D. 3 Dept.1982)—§ **10.2, n. 30.**

Gaskins, People v., 171 A.D.2d 272, 575 N.Y.S.2d 564 (N.Y.A.D. 2 Dept.1991)—§ **7.17, n. 200.**

Gatling, People v., 160 Misc.2d 886, 611 N.Y.S.2d 762 (N.Y.Sup.1994)—§ **9.42, n. 297.**

Gatti, People v., 265 N.Y.S.2d 641, 212 N.E.2d 882 (N.Y.1965)—§ **10.22, n. 511.**

Gault, Application of, 387 U.S. 1, 87 S.Ct. 1428, 18 L.Ed.2d 527 (1967)—§ **9.8, n. 48.**

G., Danny, People v., 473 N.Y.S.2d 131, 461 N.E.2d 268 (N.Y.1984)—§ **11.11, n. 118, 120; § 11.14, n. 151.**

Geaslen, People v., 446 N.Y.S.2d 227, 430 N.E.2d 1280 (N.Y.1981)—§ **10.19; § 10.19, n. 416.**

Gelikkaya, People v., 618 N.Y.S.2d 895, 643 N.E.2d 517 (N.Y.1994)—§ **6.2, n. 12, 29; § 6.3, n. 60; § 6.9, n. 214.**

Gensler, People v., 532 N.Y.S.2d 72, 527 N.E.2d 1209 (N.Y.1988)—§ **6.3, n. 46; § 6.6, n. 98, 120; § 6.9, n. 203; § 11.8, n. 73.**

George v. Black, 732 F.2d 108 (8th Cir. 1984)—§ **11.9, n. 87.**

George, United States v., 975 F.2d 72 (2nd Cir.1992)—§ **10.5, n. 83.**

Geraci, People v., 625 N.Y.S.2d 469, 649 N.E.2d 817 (N.Y.1995)—§ **10.19, n. 462.**

Germaine, People v., 87 A.D.2d 848, 449 N.Y.S.2d 508 (N.Y.A.D. 2 Dept.1982)—§ **10.5, n. 87, 96.**

Germosen, People v., 633 N.Y.S.2d 472, 657 N.E.2d 493 (N.Y.1995)—§ **5.8, n. 178, 182.**

Gerstein v. Pugh, 420 U.S. 103, 95 S.Ct. 854, 43 L.Ed.2d 54 (1975)—§ **3.19, n. 219; § 3.24, n. 287; § 3.30, n. 409.**

Geyer, People v., 196 N.Y. 364, 90 N.E. 48 (N.Y.1909)—§ **5.18, n. 415.**

Gibbs, People v., 210 A.D.2d 4, 618 N.Y.S.2d 813 (N.Y.A.D. 1 Dept.1994)—§ **10.13, n. 276.**

Giglio v. United States, 405 U.S. 150, 92 S.Ct. 763, 31 L.Ed.2d 104 (1972)—§ **7.12, n. 133, 140.**

Gilbert v. California, 388 U.S. 263, 87 S.Ct. 1951, 18 L.Ed.2d 1178 (1967)—§ **7.11, n. 119, 120; § 10.10, n. 182.**

Gilbert, People v., 149 Misc.2d 411, 565 N.Y.S.2d 690 (N.Y.Sup.1991)—§ **5.3, n. 34.**

Giles, People v., 543 N.Y.S.2d 37, 541 N.E.2d 37 (N.Y.1989)—§ **10.15; § 10.15, n. 295.**

Giles, People v., 137 A.D.2d 1, 527 N.Y.S.2d 409 (N.Y.A.D. 1 Dept.1988)—§ **10.15, n. 296.**

Gill, People v., 164 A.D.2d 867, 559 N.Y.S.2d 376 (N.Y.A.D. 2 Dept.1990)—§ **11.15, n. 165.**

Gillman, People v., 631 N.Y.S.2d 337 (N.Y.A.D. 1 Dept.1995)—§ **10.26, n. 581.**

Gingello, People v., 84 Misc.2d 63, 374 N.Y.S.2d 276 (N.Y.Co.Ct.1975)—§ **2.2, n. 22.**

Gini, People v., 72 A.D.2d 752, 421 N.Y.S.2d 269 (N.Y.A.D. 2 Dept.1979)—§ **5.8, n. 138, 160.**

TABLE OF CASES

Giordano, People v., 211 A.D.2d 814, 622 N.Y.S.2d 89 (N.Y.A.D. 2 Dept.1995)—§ 1.4, n. 124.

Giordano, People v., 72 A.D.2d 550, 420 N.Y.S.2d 719 (N.Y.A.D. 2 Dept.1979)—§ 10.5, n. 83.

Giordano, People v., 449 N.Y.S.2d 955, 434 N.E.2d 1333 (N.Y.1982)—§ 9.47, n. 332.

Giordano, People v., 1995 WL 761939 (N.Y. 1995)—§ 1.4, n. 74, 90, 121, 124.

Gipson, United States v., 553 F.2d 453 (5th Cir.1977)—§ 5.17, n. 375.

Gissendanner, People v., 423 N.Y.S.2d 893, 399 N.E.2d 924 (N.Y.1979)—§ 7.8, n. 76, 86; § 7.9, n. 97; § 7.14, n. 154; § 7.30; § 7.30, n. 337; § 10.26, n. 579.

G., John v. Dubin, 89 A.D.2d 839, 452 N.Y.S.2d 907 (N.Y.A.D. 2 Dept.1982)—§ 1.10, n. 245, 255.

Glasper, People v., 151 A.D.2d 692, 542 N.Y.S.2d 747 (N.Y.A.D. 2 Dept.1989)—§ 11.18, n. 249.

Glass on Behalf of Ryan, People ex rel. v. McGreevy, 134 Misc.2d 1085, 514 N.Y.S.2d 622 (N.Y.Sup.1987)—§ 4.10, n. 154.

Glen, People v., 331 N.Y.S.2d 656, 282 N.E.2d 614 (N.Y.1972)—§ 10.3, n. 56, 71; § 10.4, n. 74; § 10.5, n. 103; § 10.20, n. 464.

Glen, People v., 173 N.Y. 395, 66 N.E. 112 (N.Y.1903)—§ 5.4, n. 53.

Glendenning, People v., 127 Misc.2d 880, 487 N.Y.S.2d 952 (N.Y.Sup.1985)—§ 1.7, n. 146, 151; § 11.3, n. 19.

Glenn, People v., 632 N.Y.S.2d 188 (N.Y.A.D. 2 Dept.1995)—§ 5.7, n. 108.

Glenn, People v., 59 A.D.2d 724, 398 N.Y.S.2d 364 (N.Y.A.D. 2 Dept.1977)—§ 11.16, n. 194.

Glover, People v., 453 N.Y.S.2d 660, 439 N.E.2d 376 (N.Y.1982)—§ 5.18, n. 438; § 5.27, n. 702.

Glowa, People v., 87 Misc.2d 471, 384 N.Y.S.2d 673 (N.Y.Sup.1976)—§ 9.2, n. 4; § 9.4, n. 16.

Godinez v. Moran, 509 U.S. 389, 113 S.Ct. 2680, 125 L.Ed.2d 321 (1993)—§ 6.3, n. 46; § 11.8; § 11.8, n. 76.

Goggins, People v., 356 N.Y.S.2d 571, 313 N.E.2d 41 (N.Y.1974)—§ 7.2, n. 13; § 7.10; § 7.10, n. 102; § 7.30, n. 336; § 10.19, n. 433.

Goins, People v., 540 N.Y.S.2d 994, 538 N.E.2d 346 (N.Y.1989)—§ 7.21, n. 239.

Gold v. Booth, 79 A.D.2d 1013, 435 N.Y.S.2d 325 (N.Y.A.D. 2 Dept.1981)—§ 5.8, n. 170.

Gold v. Booth, 79 A.D.2d 691, 433 N.Y.S.2d 879 (N.Y.A.D. 2 Dept.1980)—§ 11.3, n. 11.

Gold v. Menna, 307 N.Y.S.2d 33, 255 N.E.2d 235 (N.Y.1969)—§ 5.9, n. 193, 199.

Gold v. Shapiro, 62 A.D.2d 62, 403 N.Y.S.2d 906 (N.Y.A.D. 2 Dept.1978)—§ 4.9, n. 112.

Goldfadden, People v., 145 A.D.2d 959, 536 N.Y.S.2d 331 (N.Y.A.D. 4 Dept.1988)—§ 11.9, n. 80; § 11.10, n. 105.

Goldswer, People v., 385 N.Y.S.2d 274, 350 N.E.2d 604 (N.Y.1976)—§ 1.3, n. 44; § 1.9, n. 187.

Gomez, People v., 210 A.D.2d 14, 619 N.Y.S.2d 561 (N.Y.A.D. 1 Dept.1994)—§ 9.49, n. 364.

Gomez, People v., 193 A.D.2d 882, 597 N.Y.S.2d 815 (N.Y.A.D. 3 Dept.1993)—§ 10.5, n. 108.

Gomez, People v., 501 N.Y.S.2d 650, 492 N.E.2d 778 (N.Y.1986)—§ 10.17, n. 364, 380; § 10.18, n. 388.

Gomez v. United States, 490 U.S. 858, 109 S.Ct. 2237, 104 L.Ed.2d 923 (1989)—§ 1.2, n. 29.

Gonzales, People v., 96 A.D.2d 847, 465 N.Y.S.2d 694 (N.Y.A.D. 2 Dept.1983)—§ 5.18, n. 432.

Gonzalez, People v., 214 A.D.2d 451, 625 N.Y.S.2d 203 (N.Y.A.D. 1 Dept.1995)—§ 10.14, n. 285.

Gonzalez, People v., 201 A.D.2d 414, 607 N.Y.S.2d 670 (N.Y.A.D. 1 Dept.1994)—§ 5.8, n. 182.

Gonzalez, People v., 201 A.D.2d 667, 609 N.Y.S.2d 824 (N.Y.A.D. 2 Dept.1994)—§ 7.27, n. 302.

Gonzalez, People v., 587 N.Y.S.2d 607, 600 N.E.2d 238 (N.Y.1992)—§ 10.19; § 10.19, n. 451; § 10.20, n. 481.

Gonzalez, People v., 176 A.D.2d 638, 575 N.Y.S.2d 291 (N.Y.A.D. 1 Dept.1991)—§ 11.11, n. 113.

Gonzalez, People v., 176 A.D.2d 109, 573 N.Y.S.2d 689 (N.Y.A.D. 1 Dept.1991)—§ 5.8, n. 127.

Gonzalez, People v., 171 A.D.2d 413, 566 N.Y.S.2d 639 (N.Y.A.D. 1 Dept.1991)—§ 11.18, n. 243.

Gonzalez, People v., 169 A.D.2d 646, 565 N.Y.S.2d 466 (N.Y.A.D. 1 Dept.1991)—§ 5.22; § 5.22, n. 607.

Gonzalez, People v., 168 A.D.2d 568, 562 N.Y.S.2d 785 (N.Y.A.D. 2 Dept.1990)—§ 6.2, n. 27.

Gonzalez, People v., 510 N.Y.S.2d 86, 502 N.E.2d 1001 (N.Y.1986)—§ 10.19, n. 449; § 10.20, n. 469, 477.

Gonzalez, People v., 132 Misc.2d 1004, 506 N.Y.S.2d 276 (N.Y.Sup.1986)—§ 6.7, n. 155; § 6.9, n. 200.

Gonzalez, People v., 116 A.D.2d 735, 497 N.Y.S.2d 778 (N.Y.A.D. 2 Dept.1986)—§ 9.51, n. 375.

Gonzalez, People v., 471 N.Y.S.2d 847, 459 N.E.2d 1285 (N.Y.1983)—§ 5.18, n. 433.

Gonzalez, People v., 447 N.Y.S.2d 145, 431 N.E.2d 630 (N.Y.1981)—§ 10.15, n. 299.

TABLE OF CASES

Gonzalez, People v., 383 N.Y.S.2d 215, 347 N.E.2d 575 (N.Y.1976)—§ **10.20, n. 470, 479.**

Gonzalez, People v., 282 N.Y.S.2d 538, 229 N.E.2d 220 (N.Y.1967)—§ **6.10, n. 248.**

Goode, People v., 628 N.Y.S.2d 727 (N.Y.A.D. 2 Dept.1995)—§ **9.39, n. 283.**

Goodell, People v., 164 A.D.2d 321, 565 N.Y.S.2d 929 (N.Y.A.D. 4 Dept.1990)—§ **6.10, n. 232; § 7.21, n. 234.**

Gooden, People v., 151 A.D.2d 773, 542 N.Y.S.2d 757 (N.Y.A.D. 2 Dept.1989)—§ **9.55, n. 401.**

Goodman, People v., 511 N.Y.S.2d 565, 503 N.E.2d 996 (N.Y.1986)—§ **2.8, n. 182.**

Goodman, People v., 393 N.Y.S.2d 985, 362 N.E.2d 615 (N.Y.1977)—§ **9.43, n. 305, 308.**

Goodwine, People v., 142 Misc.2d 1080, 539 N.Y.S.2d 273 (N.Y.City Crim.Ct.1989)—§ **3.25, n. 337.**

Gordon, People v., 214 A.D.2d 1029, 626 N.Y.S.2d 601 (N.Y.A.D. 4 Dept.1995)—§ **5.27, n. 729.**

Gordon, People v., 125 A.D.2d 257, 509 N.Y.S.2d 543 (N.Y.A.D. 1 Dept.1986)—§ **9.14, n. 133.**

Gordon, People v., 125 A.D.2d 587, 509 N.Y.S.2d 651 (N.Y.A.D. 2 Dept.1986)—§ **6.9, n. 216.**

Gotte, People v., 125 A.D.2d 331, 508 N.Y.S.2d 607 (N.Y.A.D. 2 Dept.1986)—§ **11.9, n. 80.**

Grady v. Corbin, 495 U.S. 508, 110 S.Ct. 2084, 109 L.Ed.2d 548 (1990)—§ **2.5, n. 98; § 2.6, n. 113; § 3.24; § 3.24, n. 315.**

Grafton, People v., 536 N.Y.S.2d 738, 533 N.E.2d 668 (N.Y.1988)—§ **9.31, n. 234.**

Graham, People v., 211 A.D.2d 55, 626 N.Y.S.2d 95 (N.Y.A.D. 1 Dept.1995)—§ **10.19, n. 460.**

Graham, People v., 135 A.D.2d 563, 521 N.Y.S.2d 783 (N.Y.A.D. 2 Dept.1987)—§ **9.10, n. 99, 101.**

Graham, People v., 117 A.D.2d 832, 498 N.Y.S.2d 730 (N.Y.A.D. 3 Dept.1986)—§ **7.30, n. 341.**

Graham, People v., 447 N.Y.S.2d 918, 432 N.E.2d 790 (N.Y.1982)—§ **10.22, n. 525.**

Grand Jury ex rel. Riley, 98 Misc.2d 454, 414 N.Y.S.2d 441 (N.Y.Sup.1979)—§ **5.9, n. 258.**

Grand Jury, New York County, Matter of, 125 Misc.2d 918, 480 N.Y.S.2d 998 (N.Y.Sup.1984)—§ **5.3, n. 50.**

Grand Jury of Supreme Court of Rensselaer County, Matter of, 98 A.D.2d 284, 471 N.Y.S.2d 378 (N.Y.A.D. 3 Dept.1983)—§ **5.13, n. 326.**

Grant, People v., 188 A.D.2d 1052, 592 N.Y.S.2d 206 (N.Y.A.D. 4 Dept.1992)—§ **6.2, n. 31; § 6.10, n. 225.**

Grant, People v., 140 A.D.2d 623, 528 N.Y.S.2d 993 (N.Y.A.D. 2 Dept.1988)—§ **11.15, n. 168.**

Grant, People v., 127 A.D.2d 965, 512 N.Y.S.2d 747 (N.Y.A.D. 4 Dept.1987)—§ **9.51, n. 381.**

Grant, People v., 99 A.D.2d 536, 471 N.Y.S.2d 325 (N.Y.A.D. 2 Dept.1984)—§ **11.3, n. 21.**

Grant, People v., 262 N.Y.S.2d 106, 209 N.E.2d 723 (N.Y.1965)—§ **1.1, n. 3.**

Graves, People v., 630 N.Y.S.2d 972, 654 N.E.2d 1220 (N.Y.1995)—§ **7.17, n. 216.**

Graves, People v., 556 N.Y.S.2d 16, 555 N.E.2d 268 (N.Y.1990)—§ **5.17, n. 379.**

Gray, People v., 158 Misc.2d 597, 601 N.Y.S.2d 526 (N.Y.Sup.1993)—§ **5.8, n. 157.**

Gray, People v., 190 A.D.2d 1057, 593 N.Y.S.2d 681 (N.Y.A.D. 4 Dept.1993)—§ **6.10, n. 260.**

Gray, People v., 146 Misc.2d 470, 551 N.Y.S.2d 154 (N.Y.City Crim.Ct.1990)—§ **3.34, n. 479.**

Graydon, People v., 59 Misc.2d 330, 298 N.Y.S.2d 555 (N.Y.Sup.1969)—§ **1.8, n. 183.**

Green, People v., 188 A.D.2d 385, 591 N.Y.S.2d 175 (N.Y.A.D. 1 Dept.1992)—§ **10.20, n. 485, 491, 493.**

Green, People v., 187 A.D.2d 528, 589 N.Y.S.2d 916 (N.Y.A.D. 2 Dept.1992)—§ **5.8, n. 136, 139.**

Green, People v., 554 N.Y.S.2d 821, 553 N.E.2d 1331 (N.Y.1990)—§ **11.15, n. 159.**

Green, People v., 139 A.D.2d 760, 527 N.Y.S.2d 509 (N.Y.A.D. 2 Dept.1988)—§ **9.10, n. 98; § 9.31, n. 235.**

Green, People v., 110 A.D.2d 1035, 489 N.Y.S.2d 129 (N.Y.A.D. 4 Dept.1985)—§ **5.8, n. 130.**

Green, People v., 90 A.D.2d 705, 455 N.Y.S.2d 368 (N.Y.A.D. 1 Dept.1982)—§ **9.30, n. 232.**

Green, People v., 80 A.D.2d 650, 436 N.Y.S.2d 420 (N.Y.A.D. 3 Dept.1981)—§ **5.8, n. 180, 181.**

Green, People v., 354 N.Y.S.2d 933, 310 N.E.2d 533 (N.Y.1974)—§ **10.5, n. 98; § 10.6, n. 125.**

Green v. United States, 355 U.S. 184, 78 S.Ct. 221, 2 L.Ed.2d 199 (1957)—§ **2.1, n. 2.**

Greene, People v., 134 A.D.2d 612, 521 N.Y.S.2d 507 (N.Y.A.D. 2 Dept.1987)—§ **9.34, n. 256; § 9.42, n. 302.**

Greene, People v., 203 Misc. 191, 116 N.Y.S.2d 561 (N.Y.Co.Ct.1952)—§ **6.9, n. 217.**

Greenwaldt, People v., 103 A.D.2d 933, 479 N.Y.S.2d 781 (N.Y.A.D. 3 Dept.1984)—§ **9.16, n. 151.**

Greer, People v., 397 N.Y.S.2d 613, 366 N.E.2d 273 (N.Y.1977)—§ **10.24; § 10.24, n. 557; § 10.25; § 10.25, n. 569; § 10.28, n. 601.**

TABLE OF CASES

Gribetz, Matter of, 66 A.D.2d 788, 410 N.Y.S.2d 873 (N.Y.A.D. 2 Dept.1978)—§ 11.3, n. 17.

Griffin, People v., 163 Misc.2d 43, 619 N.Y.S.2d 931 (N.Y.City Crim.Ct.1994)—§ 3.34, n. 482.

Griffin, People v., 142 Misc.2d 41, 536 N.Y.S.2d 386 (N.Y.Sup.1988)—§ 1.8, n. 176.

Griffin, People v., 137 A.D.2d 558, 524 N.Y.S.2d 298 (N.Y.A.D. 2 Dept.1988)—§ 5.21, n. 478.

Griffin, People v., 138 Misc.2d 279, 524 N.Y.S.2d 153 (N.Y.Sup.1988)—§ 7.33, n. 363.

Griffin, People v., 100 A.D.2d 659, 473 N.Y.S.2d 851 (N.Y.A.D. 3 Dept.1984)—§ 6.6, n. 98.

Griffin, People v., 425 N.Y.S.2d 547, 401 N.E.2d 905 (N.Y.1980)—§ 5.22, n. 587.

Griffin, People v., 99 Misc.2d 874, 420 N.Y.S.2d 824 (N.Y.Sup.1979)—§ 1.5, n. 139.

Griffin, People v., 199 N.Y.S.2d 674, 166 N.E.2d 684 (N.Y.1960)—§ 11.10, n. 95.

Griffith, People v., 43 A.D.2d 20, 349 N.Y.S.2d 94 (N.Y.A.D. 1 Dept.1973)—§ 11.3, n. 18.

Grimaldi, People v., 200 A.D.2d 687, 607 N.Y.S.2d 57 (N.Y.A.D. 2 Dept.1994)—§ 11.14, n. 151.

Grimes, People v., 51 A.D.2d 625, 378 N.Y.S.2d 978 (N.Y.A.D. 3 Dept.1976)—§ 10.3, n. 50.

Griminger, People v., 529 N.Y.S.2d 55, 524 N.E.2d 409 (N.Y.1988)—§ 10.3, n. 68; § 10.4, n. 76.

Grimsley, People v., 193 A.D.2d 618, 598 N.Y.S.2d 964 (N.Y.A.D. 2 Dept.1993)—§ 11.9, n. 80, 82.

Grisset, People v., 118 Misc.2d 450, 460 N.Y.S.2d 987 (N.Y.Sup.1983)—§ 6.3, n. 61, 64; § 6.9, n. 209.

Grissom, People v., 128 Misc.2d 246, 490 N.Y.S.2d 110 (N.Y.City Crim.Ct.1985)—§ 7.4, n. 55.

Griswold, People v., 458 N.Y.S.2d 513, 444 N.E.2d 977 (N.Y.1982)—§ 10.22, n. 526.

Groff, People v., 524 N.Y.S.2d 13, 518 N.E.2d 908 (N.Y.1987)—§ 5.4, n. 55.

Gronachan, People v., 162 A.D.2d 852, 557 N.Y.S.2d 753 (N.Y.A.D. 3 Dept.1990)—§ 6.2, n. 15.

G., Ross, People v., 163 A.D.2d 529, 558 N.Y.S.2d 603 (N.Y.A.D. 2 Dept.1990)—§ 11.11, n. 113.

Gross, People v., 148 Misc.2d 232, 560 N.Y.S.2d 227 (N.Y.City Crim.Ct.1990)—§ 1.1, n. 2; § 9.6, n. 27.

Grosunor, People v., 108 Misc.2d 932, 439 N.Y.S.2d 243 (N.Y.City Crim.Ct.1981)—§ 7.4, n. 55.

Gruden, People v., 397 N.Y.S.2d 704, 366 N.E.2d 794 (N.Y.1977)—§ 5.26, n. 668; § 9.51, n. 375; § 10.16, n. 334; § 10.18, n. 383, 385.

Guerra, People v., 157 A.D.2d 500, 549 N.Y.S.2d 691 (N.Y.A.D. 1 Dept.1990)—§ 11.11, n. 112.

Guerra, People v., 489 N.Y.S.2d 718, 478 N.E.2d 1319 (N.Y.1985)—§ 10.9, n. 168; § 10.12, n. 254.

Guest, People v., 53 A.D.2d 892, 385 N.Y.S.2d 376 (N.Y.A.D. 2 Dept.1976)—§ 5.14, n. 331.

Guidice, People v., 612 N.Y.S.2d 350, 634 N.E.2d 951 (N.Y.1994)—§ 1.4, n. 84, 86.

Guido v. Berkman, 116 A.D.2d 439, 501 N.Y.S.2d 827 (N.Y.A.D. 1 Dept.1986)—§ 2.4, n. 69.

Gunning v. Codd, 427 N.Y.S.2d 209, 403 N.E.2d 1208 (N.Y.1980)—§ 2.2, n. 15.

Gurney, People v., 129 Misc.2d 712, 493 N.Y.S.2d 957 (N.Y.City Crim.Ct.1985)—§ 3.33, n. 450.

Gushlaw, People v., 112 A.D.2d 792, 492 N.Y.S.2d 292 (N.Y.A.D. 4 Dept.1985)—§ 9.51, n. 367.

Gutkaiss, People v., 206 A.D.2d 628, 614 N.Y.S.2d 599 (N.Y.A.D. 3 Dept.1994)—§ 7.33, n. 363.

Guzman v. Harrigan, 158 A.D.2d 872, 552 N.Y.S.2d 54 (N.Y.A.D. 3 Dept.1990)—§ 11.19, n. 256.

Guzman, People v., 180 A.D.2d 469, 579 N.Y.S.2d 386 (N.Y.A.D. 1 Dept.1992)—§ 5.27, n. 733.

Guzman, People v., 168 A.D.2d 154, 570 N.Y.S.2d 827 (N.Y.A.D. 2 Dept.1991)—§ 5.27, n. 756.

Guzman, People v., 469 N.Y.S.2d 916, 457 N.E.2d 1143 (N.Y.1983)—§ 5.2; § 5.2, n. 24.

Gwynn, People v., 201 A.D.2d 501, 609 N.Y.S.2d 797 (N.Y.A.D. 2 Dept.1994)—§ 11.13, n. 137.

Haas, People v., 55 A.D.2d 683, 390 N.Y.S.2d 202 (N.Y.A.D. 2 Dept.1976)—§ 10.6, n. 126.

Hall, People v., 213 A.D.2d 558, 624 N.Y.S.2d 58 (N.Y.A.D. 2 Dept.1995)—§ 9.52, n. 386.

Hall, People v., 181 A.D.2d 1008, 581 N.Y.S.2d 951 (N.Y.A.D. 4 Dept.1992)—§ 7.21, n. 234.

Hall, People v., 168 A.D.2d 310, 562 N.Y.S.2d 641 (N.Y.A.D. 1 Dept.1990)—§ 11.8, n. 75.

Hall, People v., 425 N.Y.S.2d 56, 401 N.E.2d 179 (N.Y.1979)—§ 3.7, n. 76; § 3.25, n. 329.

Hall, People v., 61 A.D.2d 1050, 403 N.Y.S.2d 112 (N.Y.A.D. 2 Dept.1978)—§ 9.43, n. 308.

Hall v. Potoker, 427 N.Y.S.2d 211, 403 N.E.2d 1210 (N.Y.1980)—§ 2.4, n. 52.

Halper, People v., 209 A.D.2d 637, 619 N.Y.S.2d 308 (N.Y.A.D. 2 Dept.1994)—§ 4.10, n. 142.

TABLE OF CASES

Halper, United States v., 490 U.S. 435, 109 S.Ct. 1892, 104 L.Ed.2d 487 (1989)—§ 2.10, n. 227.

Hameed v. Jones, 750 F.2d 154 (2nd Cir. 1984)—§ 2.4, n. 62.

Hamilton, People v., 187 A.D.2d 451, 590 N.Y.S.2d 731 (N.Y.A.D. 2 Dept.1992)—§ 9.15, n. 144.

Hamilton, People v., 528 N.Y.S.2d 532, 523 N.E.2d 819 (N.Y.1988)—§ 7.21, n. 239.

Hamilton, People v., 415 N.Y.S.2d 208, 388 N.E.2d 345 (N.Y.1979)—§ 9.13, n. 125; § 9.23, n. 184.

Hamlin, People v., 530 N.Y.S.2d 74, 525 N.E.2d 719 (N.Y.1988)—§ 5.22, n. 585; § 10.22, n. 521, 529.

Hammpud, People v., 161 A.D.2d 179, 554 N.Y.S.2d 567 (N.Y.A.D. 1 Dept.1990)—§ 9.51, n. 382.

Handley, People v., 105 Misc.2d 215, 431 N.Y.S.2d 982 (N.Y.Sup.1980)—§ 7.11, n. 128, 130.

Hanlon, People v., 369 N.Y.S.2d 677, 330 N.E.2d 631 (N.Y.1975)—§ 10.3, n. 49, 67; § 10.20, n. 483.

Hansel, People v., 208 A.D.2d 1112, 617 N.Y.S.2d 542 (N.Y.A.D. 3 Dept.1994)—§ 5.26, n. 664.

Hansen, People v., 377 N.Y.S.2d 461, 339 N.E.2d 873 (N.Y.1975)—§ 10.5, n. 99.

Harden, People v., 151 A.D.2d 777, 543 N.Y.S.2d 947 (N.Y.A.D. 2 Dept.1989)—§ 9.55, n. 400.

Harder, People v., 146 A.D.2d 286, 540 N.Y.S.2d 557 (N.Y.A.D. 3 Dept.1989)—§ 7.30, n. 349.

Hardy, People v., 199 A.D.2d 49, 605 N.Y.S.2d 23 (N.Y.A.D. 1 Dept.1993)—§ 9.32, n. 237.

Hardy, on Behalf of Miller, People ex rel. v. Sielaff, 584 N.Y.S.2d 742, 595 N.E.2d 817 (N.Y.1992)—§ 4.2, n. 31.

Harmon, People v., 181 A.D.2d 34, 586 N.Y.S.2d 922 (N.Y.A.D. 1 Dept.1992)—§ 5.27; § 5.27, n. 758, 765, 770.

Harper, People v., 152 A.D.2d 469, 543 N.Y.S.2d 452 (N.Y.A.D. 1 Dept.1989)—§ 11.11, n. 122.

Harper, People v., 137 Misc.2d 357, 520 N.Y.S.2d 892 (N.Y.City Crim.Ct.1987)—§ 1.1, n. 2.

Harper, People v., 371 N.Y.S.2d 467, 332 N.E.2d 336 (N.Y.1975)—§ 3.8, n. 97; § 5.11, n. 304.

Harrington, People v., 111 Misc.2d 648, 444 N.Y.S.2d 848 (N.Y.Co.Ct.1981)—§ 3.20, n. 246.

Harrington, People v., 70 Misc.2d 303, 332 N.Y.S.2d 789 (N.Y.Co.Ct.1972)—§ 10.19, n. 432, 448.

Harris v. Justices of Supreme Court, Kings County, 407 N.Y.S.2d 478, 378 N.E.2d 1048 (N.Y.1978)—§ 2.4, n. 43.

Harris v. Oklahoma, 433 U.S. 682, 97 S.Ct. 2912, 53 L.Ed.2d 1054 (1977)—§ 2.5, n. 104.

Harris, People v., 604 N.Y.S.2d 918, 624 N.E.2d 1013 (N.Y.1993)—§ 5.27, n. 698; § 9.49, n. 363.

Harris, People v., 148 Misc.2d 408, 560 N.Y.S.2d 926 (N.Y.City Crim.Ct.1990)—§ 1.8, n. 184.

Harris, People v., 150 A.D.2d 723, 541 N.Y.S.2d 593 (N.Y.A.D. 2 Dept.1989)—§ 5.8, n. 136, 139.

Harris, People v., 130 A.D.2d 939, 516 N.Y.S.2d 554 (N.Y.A.D. 4 Dept.1987)—§ 7.21, n. 240.

Harris, People v., 121 A.D.2d 788, 504 N.Y.S.2d 552 (N.Y.A.D. 3 Dept.1986)—§ 7.30, n. 344.

Harris, People v., 118 A.D.2d 583, 499 N.Y.S.2d 443 (N.Y.A.D. 2 Dept.1986)—§ 11.19, n. 262.

Harris, People v., 117 A.D.2d 752, 498 N.Y.S.2d 475 (N.Y.A.D. 2 Dept.1986)—§ 11.15, n. 178.

Harris, People v., 103 A.D.2d 891, 478 N.Y.S.2d 188 (N.Y.A.D. 3 Dept.1984)—§ 9.12, n. 121.

Harris, People v., 471 N.Y.S.2d 61, 459 N.E.2d 170 (N.Y.1983)—§ 11.7; § 11.7, n. 66.

Harris, People v., 85 A.D.2d 742, 445 N.Y.S.2d 801 (N.Y.A.D. 2 Dept.1981)—§ 3.24, n. 302.

Harris, People v., 303 N.Y.S.2d 71, 250 N.E.2d 349 (N.Y.1969)—§ 10.14, n. 286.

Harrison, People v., 151 A.D.2d 778, 543 N.Y.S.2d 108 (N.Y.A.D. 2 Dept.1989)—§ 10.19, n. 406.

Harrison, People v., 122 A.D.2d 223, 505 N.Y.S.2d 3 (N.Y.A.D. 2 Dept.1986)—§ 10.5, n. 121.

Hart v. Marion Correctional Inst., 927 F.2d 256 (6th Cir.1991)—§ 11.9, n. 80.

Hart, People v., 205 A.D.2d 943, 613 N.Y.S.2d 762 (N.Y.A.D. 3 Dept.1994)—§ 6.10, n. 224.

Harvall, People v., 196 A.D.2d 553, 601 N.Y.S.2d 146 (N.Y.A.D. 2 Dept.1993)—§ 9.49, n. 359.

Harvin, People v., 126 Misc.2d 775, 483 N.Y.S.2d 913 (N.Y.City Crim.Ct.1984)—§ 3.25, n. 325.

Haskins, People v., 107 Misc.2d 480, 435 N.Y.S.2d 261 (N.Y.City Crim.Ct.1981)—§ 3.7, n. 78.

Haupt, People v., 528 N.Y.S.2d 808, 524 N.E.2d 129 (N.Y.1988)—§ 7.23, n. 255.

Havelka, People v., 412 N.Y.S.2d 345, 384 N.E.2d 1269 (N.Y.1978)—§ 10.15, n. 292; § 10.19, n. 454, 461.

Hawley, People v., 192 A.D.2d 742, 596 N.Y.S.2d 205 (N.Y.A.D. 3 Dept.1993)—§ 10.3, n. 72; § 10.4, n. 79.

Hayday, People v., 144 A.D.2d 207, 534 N.Y.S.2d 521 (N.Y.A.D. 3 Dept.1988)—§ 4.10, n. 139, 148.

Healy, In re, 161 Misc. 582, 293 N.Y.S. 584 (N.Y.Co.Ct.1937)—§ 5.1, n. 7.

TABLE OF CASES

Heasley, People v., 133 A.D.2d 977, 521 N.Y.S.2d 128 (N.Y.A.D. 3 Dept.1987)— § 6.6, n. 120.

Heath v. Alabama, 474 U.S. 82, 106 S.Ct. 433, 88 L.Ed.2d 387 (1985)—§ 2.2, n. 25.

Helbrans v. Owens, 205 A.D.2d 775, 613 N.Y.S.2d 924 (N.Y.A.D. 2 Dept.1994)— § 11.12, n. 130; § 11.19, n. 253, 264.

Helfman, People v., 91 A.D.2d 1034, 458 N.Y.S.2d 628 (N.Y.A.D. 2 Dept.1983)— § 6.7, n. 142; § 6.8, n. 178.

Heller v. Doe by Doe, 509 U.S. 312, 113 S.Ct. 2637, 125 L.Ed.2d 257 (1993)— § 6.8, n. 169.

Heller, People v., 120 A.D.2d 612, 502 N.Y.S.2d 498 (N.Y.A.D. 2 Dept.1986)— § 9.33, n. 247.

Helm, People v., 178 A.D.2d 656, 577 N.Y.S.2d 889 (N.Y.A.D. 2 Dept.1991)— § 6.2, n. 25, 30.

Helm, People v., 69 A.D.2d 198, 419 N.Y.S.2d 287 (N.Y.A.D. 3 Dept.1979)— § 5.8, n. 146.

Helmsley, People v., 170 A.D.2d 209, 566 N.Y.S.2d 223 (N.Y.A.D. 1 Dept.1991)— § 2.6, n. 121.

Henderson v. Morgan, 426 U.S. 637, 96 S.Ct. 2253, 49 L.Ed.2d 108 (1976)— § 11.10, n. 92, 95.

Henderson, People v., 629 N.Y.S.2d 239 (N.Y.A.D. 1 Dept.1995)—§ 10.17, n. 349, 371, 374.

Henderson, People v., 391 N.Y.S.2d 563, 359 N.E.2d 1357 (N.Y.1976)—§ 5.18, n. 435.

Hendricks, People v., 303 N.Y.S.2d 33, 250 N.E.2d 323 (N.Y.1969)—§ 10.3, n. 51.

Henriquez, People v., 214 A.D.2d 485, 625 N.Y.S.2d 526 (N.Y.A.D. 1 Dept.1995)— § 10.20, n. 491.

Henzey, People v., 24 A.D.2d 764, 263 N.Y.S.2d 678 (N.Y.A.D. 2 Dept.1965)— § 11.3, n. 23.

Hernandez, People v., 636 N.Y.S.2d 45 (N.Y.A.D. 1 Dept.1996)—§ 5.8, n. 133.

Hernandez, People v., 198 A.D.2d 375, 603 N.Y.S.2d 187 (N.Y.A.D. 2 Dept.1993)— § 1.4, n. 76.

Hernandez, People v., 190 A.D.2d 752, 593 N.Y.S.2d 335 (N.Y.A.D. 2 Dept.1993)— § 9.10, n. 105.

Hernandez, People v., 145 Misc.2d 491, 546 N.Y.S.2d 958 (N.Y.City Crim.Ct.1989)— § 3.25, n. 338.

Hernandez, People v., 131 A.D.2d 509, 516 N.Y.S.2d 254 (N.Y.A.D. 2 Dept.1987)— § 10.6, n. 132.

Hernandez, People v., 15 A.D.2d 798, 224 N.Y.S.2d 703 (N.Y.A.D. 2 Dept.1962)— § 4.12, n. 191.

Hernandez-Flores, People v., 172 A.D.2d 159, 567 N.Y.S.2d 698 (N.Y.A.D. 1 Dept. 1991)—§ 11.9, n. 82.

Herndon, People v., 191 A.D.2d 248, 595 N.Y.S.2d 8 (N.Y.A.D. 1 Dept.1993)— § 11.4, n. 39.

Herne, People v., 110 Misc.2d 152, 441 N.Y.S.2d 936 (N.Y.Co.Ct.1981)—§ 5.10, n. 287.

Herner, People v., 626 N.Y.S.2d 54, 649 N.E.2d 1198 (N.Y.1995)—§ 10.26, n. 587.

Herrara, People v., 112 A.D.2d 315, 491 N.Y.S.2d 763 (N.Y.A.D. 2 Dept.1985)— § 10.2, n. 30.

Herrera, People v., 131 Misc.2d 96, 499 N.Y.S.2d 311 (N.Y.Sup.1985)—§ 7.30, n. 340, 345.

Hess, People v., 140 A.D.2d 895, 528 N.Y.S.2d 921 (N.Y.A.D. 3 Dept.1988)— § 7.21, n. 234.

Hetrick, People v., 590 N.Y.S.2d 183, 604 N.E.2d 732 (N.Y.1992)—§ 10.2, n. 38; § 10.3, n. 68.

Hewitt, In re Application of, 81 Misc.2d 202, 365 N.Y.S.2d 760 (N.Y.Co.Ct. 1975)—§ 1.8, n. 181, 185.

HH, Matter of Mary Jane, 120 A.D.2d 906, 502 N.Y.S.2d 827 (N.Y.A.D. 3 Dept. 1986)—§ 5.9, n. 219.

Hibbler, People v., 111 A.D.2d 67, 489 N.Y.S.2d 191 (N.Y.A.D. 1 Dept.1985)— § 10.14, n. 284.

Hickey, People v., 390 N.Y.S.2d 42, 358 N.E.2d 868 (N.Y.1976)—§ 1.2, n. 25; § 10.2, n. 30.

Hicks, People v., 201 A.D.2d 831, 608 N.Y.S.2d 543 (N.Y.A.D. 3 Dept.1994)— § 11.17, n. 228.

Hicks, People v., 85 Misc.2d 649, 381 N.Y.S.2d 794 (N.Y.City Crim.Ct.1976)— § 7.23, n. 261.

Higgins, People ex rel. McCoy v., 177 A.D.2d 1052, 578 N.Y.S.2d 70 (N.Y.A.D. 4 Dept.1991)—§ 4.9, n. 118.

Hightower, People v., 629 N.Y.S.2d 164, 652 N.E.2d 910 (N.Y.1995)—§ 10.17; § 10.17, n. 372.

Hightower, People v., 206 A.D.2d 253, 614 N.Y.S.2d 407 (N.Y.A.D. 1 Dept.1994)— § 10.17, n. 373.

Higley, People v., 518 N.Y.S.2d 778, 512 N.E.2d 299 (N.Y.1987)—§ 5.9, n. 248.

Hill v. Lockhart, 474 U.S. 52, 106 S.Ct. 366, 88 L.Ed.2d 203 (1985)—§ 11.9, n. 82, 91.

Hilton, People v., 151 A.D.2d 364, 542 N.Y.S.2d 990 (N.Y.A.D. 1 Dept.1989)— § 9.47, n. 346.

Himelein v. Nenno, 168 A.D.2d 957, 564 N.Y.S.2d 909 (N.Y.A.D. 4 Dept.1990)— § 11.3, n. 17.

Hines, People v., 284 N.Y. 93, 29 N.E.2d 483 (N.Y.1940)—§ 9.3, n. 12.

Hinestrosa, People v., 121 A.D.2d 469, 503 N.Y.S.2d 155 (N.Y.A.D. 2 Dept.1986)— § 1.4, n. 77.

TABLE OF CASES

Hinsman, People v., 182 Misc. 61, 43 N.Y.S.2d 89 (N.Y.Co.Ct.1943)—§ **6.10, n. 222.**
Hinson, People v., 203 A.D.2d 480, 610 N.Y.S.2d 578 (N.Y.A.D. 2 Dept.1994)— § **9.43, n. 313.**
Hinton, People v., 181 A.D.2d 696, 581 N.Y.S.2d 65 (N.Y.A.D. 2 Dept.1992)— § **9.41, n. 296.**
Hipp, People v., 197 A.D.2d 590, 602 N.Y.S.2d 428 (N.Y.A.D. 2 Dept.1993)— § **5.27, n. 783.**
Hirsch, People v., 85 A.D.2d 902, 447 N.Y.S.2d 80 (N.Y.A.D. 4 Dept.1981)— § **5.27, n. 759.**
Hirschberg, People ex rel. v. Close, 152 N.Y.S.2d 1, 134 N.E.2d 818 (N.Y.1956)— § **3.33, n. 473; § 5.1, n. 15.**
Hodge, People v., 207 A.D.2d 845, 616 N.Y.S.2d 978 (N.Y.A.D. 2 Dept.1994)— § **11.13, n. 139.**
Hodge, People v., 441 N.Y.S.2d 231, 423 N.E.2d 1060 (N.Y.1981)—§ **3.30, n. 414; § 3.33, n. 446, 454, 457.**
Hoff, People v., 110 A.D.2d 782, 487 N.Y.S.2d 851 (N.Y.A.D. 2 Dept.1985)— § **9.10, n. 83, 85.**
Hoffman v. Fisher, 173 A.D.2d 826, 571 N.Y.S.2d 54 (N.Y.A.D. 2 Dept.1991)— § **11.19, n. 261.**
Hohmeyer, People v., 517 N.Y.S.2d 448, 510 N.E.2d 317 (N.Y.1987)—§ **3.5, n. 41.**
Holley, People v., 191 A.D.2d 401, 595 N.Y.S.2d 206 (N.Y.A.D. 1 Dept.1993)— § **9.34, n. 256; § 9.42, n. 297.**
Holley, People v., 56 A.D.2d 684, 391 N.Y.S.2d 482 (N.Y.A.D. 3 Dept.1977)— § **10.6, n. 125.**
Hollman, People v., 581 N.Y.S.2d 619, 590 N.E.2d 204 (N.Y.1992)—§ **10.8, n. 140; § 10.9, n. 161.**
Holmes, People v., 206 A.D.2d 542, 615 N.Y.S.2d 52 (N.Y.A.D. 2 Dept.1994)— § **9.23, n. 181; § 9.29, n. 228; § 9.31, n. 235.**
Holmes, People v., 170 A.D.2d 534, 566 N.Y.S.2d 93 (N.Y.A.D. 2 Dept.1991)— § **10.24, n. 561.**
Holmes, People v., 105 A.D.2d 803, 481 N.Y.S.2d 741 (N.Y.A.D. 2 Dept.1984)— § **9.16, n. 151; § 9.43, n. 310.**
Holmes v. United States, 876 F.2d 1545 (11th Cir.1989)—§ **11.9, n. 84.**
Holtzman v. Goldman, 528 N.Y.S.2d 21, 523 N.E.2d 297 (N.Y.1988)—§ **3.26, n. 347; § 3.28, n. 377; § 5.25, n. 641; § 5.27, n. 756.**
Hood, People v., 194 A.D.2d 556, 598 N.Y.S.2d 569 (N.Y.A.D. 2 Dept.1993)— § **5.18, n. 409.**
Hooray v. Cummings, 89 A.D.2d 790, 453 N.Y.S.2d 521 (N.Y.A.D. 4 Dept.1982)— § **4.9, n. 119.**
Hoover, People v., 456 N.Y.S.2d 756, 442 N.E.2d 1267 (N.Y.1982)—§ **10.25, n. 568.**

Horney, People v., 99 A.D.2d 886, 472 N.Y.S.2d 477 (N.Y.A.D. 3 Dept.1984)— § **9.24, n. 192.**
Horonzy, People v., 597 N.Y.S.2d 622, 613 N.E.2d 528 (N.Y.1993)—§ **10.15, n. 301.**
Horton, People v., 32 A.D.2d 707, 300 N.Y.S.2d 15 (N.Y.A.D. 3 Dept.1969)— § **10.6, n. 125.**
Hoskins, People v., 95 A.D.2d 899, 464 N.Y.S.2d 55 (N.Y.A.D. 3 Dept.1983)— § **9.10, n. 109.**
Howard, People v., 183 A.D.2d 916, 584 N.Y.S.2d 150 (N.Y.A.D. 2 Dept.1992)— § **11.10, n. 104.**
Howard, People v., 151 A.D.2d 253, 542 N.Y.S.2d 172 (N.Y.A.D. 1 Dept.1989)— § **5.27, n. 758, 765, 770.**
Howell v. McGinity, 129 A.D.2d 60, 516 N.Y.S.2d 694 (N.Y.A.D. 2 Dept.1987)— § **4.4, n. 51.**
Howell, People v., 426 N.Y.S.2d 477, 403 N.E.2d 182 (N.Y.1980)—§ **3.20, n. 239.**
Hoy, People ex rel. Modica v., 51 Misc.2d 579, 273 N.Y.S.2d 634 (N.Y.Sup.1966)— § **4.13, n. 220.**
Hudson, People v., 217 A.D.2d 53, 634 N.Y.S.2d 752 (N.Y.A.D. 2 Dept.1995)— § **5.27, n. 758; § 6.3, n. 59.**
Hudson, People v., 205 A.D.2d 367, 613 N.Y.S.2d 374 (N.Y.A.D. 1 Dept.1994)— § **9.49, n. 362.**
Hudson, People v., 167 A.D.2d 950, 561 N.Y.S.2d 1014 (N.Y.A.D. 4 Dept.1990)— § **9.38, n. 280.**
Hudson, People v., 278 N.Y.S.2d 593, 225 N.E.2d 193 (N.Y.1967)—§ **6.10; § 6.10, n. 246.**
Hudson, United States v., 14 F.3d 536 (10th Cir.1994)—§ **2.10, n. 231.**
Huertas, People v., 626 N.Y.S.2d 750, 650 N.E.2d 408 (N.Y.1995)—§ **11.11, n. 118.**
Hughes, People v., 632 N.Y.S.2d 585 (N.Y.A.D. 2 Dept.1995)—§ **9.5, n. 22.**
Hughes, People v., 159 Misc.2d 663, 606 N.Y.S.2d 499 (N.Y.Sup.1992)—§ **5.5, n. 82.**
Hughes, People v., 24 A.D.2d 884, 264 N.Y.S.2d 874 (N.Y.A.D. 2 Dept.1965)— § **5.24, n. 636.**
Hulsen, People v., 178 A.D.2d 189, 577 N.Y.S.2d 48 (N.Y.A.D. 1 Dept.1991)— § **10.5, n. 85.**
Hults, People v., 557 N.Y.S.2d 270, 556 N.E.2d 1077 (N.Y.1990)—§ **10.13, n. 276; § 10.14, n. 287.**
Hunt, People v., 574 N.Y.S.2d 178, 579 N.E.2d 208 (N.Y.1991)—§ **2.10, n. 219.**
Hunt, People v., 65 A.D.2d 246, 412 N.Y.S.2d 208 (N.Y.A.D. 3 Dept.1979)— § **1.3, n. 50.**
Hunt v. Roth, 648 F.2d 1148 (8th Cir. 1981)—§ **4.1, n. 6.**
Hunter v. Fogg, 616 F.2d 55 (2nd Cir. 1980)—§ **11.9, n. 81.**
Huntley, People v., 255 N.Y.S.2d 838, 204 N.E.2d 179 (N.Y.1965)—§ **10.7, n. 139;**

TABLE OF CASES

§ 10.8, n. 148; § 10.20, n. 489; § 10.22, n. 524.

Huntzinger v. Siedlecki, 59 N.Y.2d 195, 464 N.Y.S.2d 418, 451 N.E.2d 176—§ 2.4, n. 50.

Hurtado v. People of State of Cal., 110 U.S. 516, 4 S.Ct. 111, 28 L.Ed. 232 (1884)—§ 5.1, n. 3.

Hurtado v. People of State of California, 110 U.S. 516, 4 S.Ct. 292, 28 L.Ed. 232 (1884)—§ 5.11, n. 309.

Hussain, People v., 165 A.D.2d 538, 568 N.Y.S.2d 966 (N.Y.A.D. 2 Dept.1991)—§ 5.22, n. 578.

Hutchenson, People v., 136 A.D.2d 737, 524 N.Y.S.2d 76 (N.Y.A.D. 2 Dept.1988)—§ 9.16, n. 149.

Hyde, People v., 172 A.D.2d 305, 568 N.Y.S.2d 388 (N.Y.A.D. 1 Dept.1991)—§ 7.23, n. 264.

Hylton, People v., 139 Misc.2d 645, 529 N.Y.S.2d 412 (N.Y.Sup.1988)—§ 5.8, n. 120, 190.

Hynes v. George, 561 N.Y.S.2d 538, 562 N.E.2d 863 (N.Y.1990)—§ 3.26, n. 347; § 5.25, n. 641.

Hynes v. Lerner, 405 N.Y.S.2d 649, 376 N.E.2d 1294 (N.Y.1978)—§ 5.1, n. 16.

Ianniello, People v., 156 A.D.2d 469, 548 N.Y.S.2d 755 (N.Y.A.D. 2 Dept.1989)—§ 1.4, n. 77; § 11.15, n. 180.

Ianniello, People v., 288 N.Y.S.2d 462, 235 N.E.2d 439 (N.Y.1968)—§ 5.9, n. 262.

Iannone, People v., 412 N.Y.S.2d 110, 384 N.E.2d 656 (N.Y.1978)—§ 1.1, n. 7; § 3.7, n. 76; § 5.11, n. 309, 311; § 5.14; § 5.14, n. 329; § 5.16, n. 345; § 11.15, n. 172; § 11.16, n. 196.

Ilardo, People v., 103 Misc.2d 454, 426 N.Y.S.2d 212 (N.Y.City Ct.1980)—§ 9.10, n. 82.

Illinois v. Vitale, 447 U.S. 410, 100 S.Ct. 2260, 65 L.Ed.2d 228 (1980)—§ 2.5, n. 102.

Imbesi, People v., 381 N.Y.S.2d 862, 345 N.E.2d 333 (N.Y.1976)—§ 9.10, n. 95; § 9.11, n. 111, 113.

Indemnity Ins. Co. of North America v. People, 133 A.D.2d 345, 519 N.Y.S.2d 244 (N.Y.A.D. 2 Dept.1987)—§ 4.12, n. 191.

Infante, People ex rel. Bryce v., 144 A.D.2d 898, 535 N.Y.S.2d 215 (N.Y.A.D. 3 Dept. 1988)—§ 4.10, n. 159.

Infante, People ex rel. Moquin v., 134 A.D.2d 764, 521 N.Y.S.2d 580 (N.Y.A.D. 3 Dept.1987)—§ 4.5, n. 75; § 4.10, n. 153; § 4.13, n. 218.

Ingram, People v., 74 Misc.2d 635, 345 N.Y.S.2d 441 (N.Y.City Crim.Ct.1973)—§ 9.3, n. 11.

Innes v. Dalsheim, 864 F.2d 974 (2nd Cir. 1988)—§ 11.13, n. 139.

Innis, People v., 182 A.D.2d 641, 582 N.Y.S.2d 245 (N.Y.A.D. 2 Dept.1992)—§ 2.2, n. 20.

In re (see name of party)

Insignares, People v., 109 A.D.2d 221, 491 N.Y.S.2d 166 (N.Y.A.D. 1 Dept.1985)—§ 5.27, n. 758.

International Fidelity Ins. Co. (Bailey) v. People, 208 A.D.2d 838, 618 N.Y.S.2d 399 (N.Y.A.D. 2 Dept.1994)—§ 4.12, n. 204.

International Fidelity Ins. Co. (Brown) v. People, 208 A.D.2d 837, 618 N.Y.S.2d 566 (N.Y.A.D. 2 Dept.1994)—§ 4.12, n. 199.

Irizarry, People v., 611 N.Y.S.2d 807, 634 N.E.2d 179 (N.Y.1994)—§ 5.22, n. 595.

Irvin v. Dowd, 366 U.S. 717, 81 S.Ct. 1639, 6 L.Ed.2d 751 (1961)—§ 1.9, n. 187.

Isaacson, People v., 406 N.Y.S.2d 714, 378 N.E.2d 78 (N.Y.1978)—§ 2.4, n. 75.

Isla, People v., 96 A.D.2d 789, 466 N.Y.S.2d 16 (N.Y.A.D. 1 Dept.1983)—§ 5.7, n. 99.

Israel, People v., 161 A.D.2d 730, 555 N.Y.S.2d 865 (N.Y.A.D. 2 Dept.1990)—§ 10.5, n. 121.

Izsak, People v., 99 Misc.2d 543, 416 N.Y.S.2d 1004 (N.Y.City Crim.Ct. 1979)—§ 3.28, n. 377.

Izzo, People v., 50 A.D.2d 905, 377 N.Y.S.2d 558 (N.Y.A.D. 2 Dept.1975)—§ 10.5, n. 117.

Jackson v. Denno, 378 U.S. 368, 84 S.Ct. 1774, 12 L.Ed.2d 908 (1964)—§ 10.7, n. 136.

Jackson v. Indiana, 406 U.S. 715, 92 S.Ct. 1845, 32 L.Ed.2d 435 (1972)—§ 6.3, n. 50; § 6.6; § 6.6, n. 123; § 6.8, n. 174, 182.

Jackson, People v., 212 A.D.2d 732, 622 N.Y.S.2d 808 (N.Y.A.D. 2 Dept.1995)—§ 5.29, n. 812; § 11.16, n. 199; § 11.17, n. 236.

Jackson, People v., 161 Misc.2d 45, 613 N.Y.S.2d 1018 (N.Y.Sup.1994)—§ 10.20, n. 485.

Jackson, People v., 203 A.D.2d 302, 612 N.Y.S.2d 897 (N.Y.A.D. 2 Dept.1994)—§ 11.17, n. 229.

Jackson, People v., 188 A.D.2d 1086, 592 N.Y.S.2d 189 (N.Y.A.D. 4 Dept.1992)—§ 11.11, n. 116.

Jackson, People v., 154 Misc.2d 718, 593 N.Y.S.2d 410 (N.Y.Sup.1992)—§ 7.14, n. 157.

Jackson, People v., 578 N.Y.S.2d 483, 585 N.E.2d 795 (N.Y.1991)—§ 7.22, n. 245.

Jackson, People v., 178 A.D.2d 305, 577 N.Y.S.2d 609 (N.Y.A.D. 1 Dept.1991)—§ 9.10, n. 105.

Jackson, People v., 178 A.D.2d 438, 577 N.Y.S.2d 299 (N.Y.A.D. 2 Dept.1991)—§ 5.22, n. 571.

TABLE OF CASES

Jackson, People v., 153 Misc.2d 270, 582 N.Y.S.2d 336 (N.Y.Sup.1991)—**§ 5.18, n. 397, 404.**

Jackson, People v., 174 A.D.2d 444, 572 N.Y.S.2d 891 (N.Y.A.D. 1 Dept.1991)— **§ 5.18, n. 415.**

Jackson, People v., 150 A.D.2d 609, 541 N.Y.S.2d 478 (N.Y.A.D. 2 Dept.1989)— **§ 9.38, n. 278.**

Jackson, People v., 144 A.D.2d 488, 534 N.Y.S.2d 203 (N.Y.A.D. 2 Dept.1988)— **§ 5.21, n. 493.**

Jackson, People v., 134 A.D.2d 521, 521 N.Y.S.2d 294 (N.Y.A.D. 2 Dept.1987)— **§ 5.8, n. 146.**

Jackson, People v., 103 A.D.2d 858, 477 N.Y.S.2d 1011 (N.Y.A.D. 3 Dept.1984)— **§ 9.51, n. 375.**

Jackson, People v., 88 A.D.2d 604, 449 N.Y.S.2d 759 (N.Y.A.D. 2 Dept.1982)— **§ 6.10, n. 234.**

Jackson, People v., 413 N.Y.S.2d 369, 385 N.E.2d 1296 (N.Y.1978)—**§ 5.14; § 5.14, n. 332.**

Jackson, People v., 277 N.Y.S.2d 263, 223 N.E.2d 790 (N.Y.1966)—**§ 5.27, n. 689, 690, 703.**

Jacobowitz, People v., 89 A.D.2d 625, 452 N.Y.S.2d 679 (N.Y.A.D. 2 Dept.1982)— **§ 10.5, n. 102.**

Jacquin, People v., 127 Misc.2d 241, 485 N.Y.S.2d 477 (N.Y.Co.Ct.1985)—**§ 9.33, n. 243.**

Jaffe v. Scheinman, 417 N.Y.S.2d 241, 390 N.E.2d 1165 (N.Y.1979)—**§ 5.27; § 5.27, n. 691, 695.**

James, People v., 193 A.D.2d 694, 598 N.Y.S.2d 38 (N.Y.A.D. 2 Dept.1993)— **§ 7.16, n. 185.**

James, People v., 187 A.D.2d 672, 591 N.Y.S.2d 784 (N.Y.A.D. 2 Dept.1992)— **§ 9.38, n. 277.**

Jarrells, People v., 190 A.D.2d 120, 597 N.Y.S.2d 305 (N.Y.A.D. 1 Dept.1993)— **§ 7.21, n. 239.**

Jasiewicz, People v., 192 A.D.2d 999, 597 N.Y.S.2d 242 (N.Y.A.D. 3 Dept.1993)— **§ 11.11, n. 114.**

Jefferson, People v., 181 A.D.2d 1007, 581 N.Y.S.2d 501 (N.Y.A.D. 4 Dept.1992)— **§ 7.10, n. 110.**

Jemmott, People v., 144 A.D.2d 694, 535 N.Y.S.2d 84 (N.Y.A.D. 2 Dept.1988)— **§ 7.14, n. 161.**

Jencks v. United States, 353 U.S. 657, 77 S.Ct. 1007, 1 L.Ed.2d 1103 (1957)— **§ 7.2, n. 11.**

Jenkins, People v., 184 A.D.2d 585, 584 N.Y.S.2d 643 (N.Y.A.D. 2 Dept.1992)— **§ 10.4, n. 79.**

Jenkins, People v., 392 N.Y.S.2d 587, 360 N.E.2d 1288 (N.Y.1977)—**§ 7.10, n. 111.**

Jenkins, People v., 47 A.D.2d 832, 365 N.Y.S.2d 870 (N.Y.A.D. 1 Dept.1975)— **§ 5.21, n. 498.**

Jennings, People v., 512 N.Y.S.2d 652, 504 N.E.2d 1079 (N.Y.1986)—**§ 3.26, n. 353; § 5.26, n. 661; § 5.27, n. 711; § 8.1, n. 25; § 9.49, n. 360.**

Jensen, People v., 203 A.D.2d 820, 611 N.Y.S.2d 363 (N.Y.A.D. 3 Dept.1994)— **§ 5.27, n. 733.**

Jhirad v. Ferrandina, 536 F.2d 478 (2nd Cir.1976)—**§ 9.8, n. 51.**

Johnson v. Andrews, 179 A.D.2d 417, 579 N.Y.S.2d 332 (N.Y.A.D. 1 Dept.1992)— **§ 1.8, n. 166.**

Johnson v. Crane, 171 A.D.2d 537, 568 N.Y.S.2d 22 (N.Y.A.D. 1 Dept.1991)— **§ 4.11, n. 183, 189.**

Johnson v. Louisiana, 406 U.S. 356, 92 S.Ct. 1620, 32 L.Ed.2d 152 (1972)— **§ 10.10; § 10.10, n. 177.**

Johnson v. Morgenthau, 512 N.Y.S.2d 797, 505 N.E.2d 240 (N.Y.1987)—**§ 2.5; § 2.5, n. 106.**

Johnson v. Oval Pharmacy, 165 A.D.2d 587, 569 N.Y.S.2d 49 (N.Y.A.D. 1 Dept. 1991)—**§ 2.8, n. 186.**

Johnson, People v., 213 A.D.2d 791, 623 N.Y.S.2d 418 (N.Y.A.D. 3 Dept.1995)— **§ 1.4, n. 84.**

Johnson, People v., 209 A.D.2d 986, 619 N.Y.S.2d 452 (N.Y.A.D. 4 Dept.1994)— **§ 9.47, n. 338.**

Johnson, People v., 204 A.D.2d 188, 612 N.Y.S.2d 26 (N.Y.A.D. 1 Dept.1994)— **§ 6.2, n. 33.**

Johnson, People v., 611 N.Y.S.2d 496, 633 N.E.2d 1100 (N.Y.1994)—**§ 10.8, n. 160.**

Johnson, People v., 191 A.D.2d 709, 595 N.Y.S.2d 515 (N.Y.A.D. 2 Dept.1993)— **§ 9.32, n. 237; § 9.34, n. 257; § 9.38, n. 276; § 9.43, n. 308; § 9.48, n. 355.**

Johnson, People v., 187 A.D.2d 532, 589 N.Y.S.2d 918 (N.Y.A.D. 2 Dept.1992)— **§ 11.13, n. 140.**

Johnson, People v., 155 Misc.2d 791, 590 N.Y.S.2d 153 (N.Y.Sup.1992)—**§ 5.8, n. 122.**

Johnson, People v., 184 A.D.2d 862, 585 N.Y.S.2d 111 (N.Y.A.D. 3 Dept.1992)— **§ 9.49, n. 363.**

Johnson, People v., 167 A.D.2d 422, 561 N.Y.S.2d 830 (N.Y.A.D. 2 Dept.1990)— **§ 9.43, n. 314.**

Johnson, People v., 159 A.D.2d 725, 553 N.Y.S.2d 206 (N.Y.A.D. 2 Dept.1990)— **§ 9.8, n. 52.**

Johnson, People v., 157 A.D.2d 855, 550 N.Y.S.2d 430 (N.Y.A.D. 2 Dept.1990)— **§ 7.14, n. 163.**

Johnson, People v., 141 A.D.2d 848, 530 N.Y.S.2d 189 (N.Y.A.D. 2 Dept.1988)— **§ 11.15, n. 161.**

Johnson, People v., 134 A.D.2d 284, 520 N.Y.S.2d 455 (N.Y.A.D. 2 Dept.1987)— **§ 3.26, n. 353.**

Johnson, People v., 129 A.D.2d 815, 514 N.Y.S.2d 805 (N.Y.A.D. 2 Dept.1987)— **§ 10.19, n. 411.**

TABLE OF CASES

Johnson, People v., 133 Misc.2d 721, 507 N.Y.S.2d 791 (N.Y.Sup.1986)—§ **5.9, n. 199.**

Johnson, People v., 115 A.D.2d 794, 496 N.Y.S.2d 306 (N.Y.A.D. 3 Dept.1985)—§ **9.41, n. 296.**

Johnson, People v., 497 N.Y.S.2d 618, 488 N.E.2d 439 (N.Y.1985)—§ **3.7, n. 67;** § **3.18, n. 191;** § **10.20, n. 482.**

Johnson, People v., 112 A.D.2d 1, 490 N.Y.S.2d 399 (N.Y.A.D. 4 Dept.1985)—§ **9.23, n. 188.**

Johnson, People v., 112 Misc.2d 578, 447 N.Y.S.2d 380 (N.Y.Co.Ct.1982)—§ **8.1, n. 18.**

Johnson, People v., 88 Misc.2d 749, 389 N.Y.S.2d 766 (N.Y.Co.Ct.1976)—§ **3.23, n. 268.**

Johnson, People v., 379 N.Y.S.2d 735, 342 N.E.2d 525 (N.Y.1975)—§ **9.10, n. 80.**

Johnson, People v., 44 A.D.2d 451, 355 N.Y.S.2d 601 (N.Y.A.D. 1 Dept.1974)—§ **10.2, n. 30.**

Johnson v. Zerbst, 304 U.S. 458, 58 S.Ct. 1019, 82 L.Ed. 1461 (1938)—§ **9.12, n. 121;** § **11.7, n. 65.**

Johnson Newspaper Corp. v. Parker, 101 A.D.2d 708, 475 N.Y.S.2d 951 (N.Y.A.D. 4 Dept.1984)—§ **3.33, n. 467.**

Johnston, People v., 178 A.D.2d 550, 577 N.Y.S.2d 644 (N.Y.A.D. 2 Dept.1991)—§ **11.16, n. 198.**

Johnston, People v., 111 A.D.2d 262, 489 N.Y.S.2d 99 (N.Y.A.D. 2 Dept.1985)—§ **9.10, n. 86.**

Jones, People v., 215 A.D.2d 244, 627 N.Y.S.2d 2 (N.Y.A.D. 1 Dept.1995)—§ **10.19, n. 455.**

Jones, People v., 214 A.D.2d 1051, 626 N.Y.S.2d 617 (N.Y.A.D. 4 Dept.1995)—§ **1.9, n. 196.**

Jones, People v., 498 N.Y.S.2d 119, 488 N.E.2d 1231 (N.Y.1985)—§ **5.23, n. 622;** § **9.41, n. 292;** § **9.47;** § **9.47, n. 332, 340.**

Jones, People v., 206 A.D.2d 82, 618 N.Y.S.2d 319 (N.Y.A.D. 1 Dept.1994)—§ **5.18, n. 392.**

Jones, People v., 204 A.D.2d 162, 614 N.Y.S.2d 110 (N.Y.A.D. 1 Dept.1994)—§ **10.21, n. 500.**

Jones, People v., 523 N.Y.S.2d 53, 517 N.E.2d 865 (N.Y.1987)—§ **7.22, n. 243.**

Jones, People v., 134 A.D.2d 701, 521 N.Y.S.2d 194 (N.Y.A.D. 3 Dept.1987)—§ **6.2, n. 23, 26, 30.**

Jones, People v., 506 N.Y.S.2d 315, 497 N.E.2d 682 (N.Y.1986)—§ **9.47, n. 347.**

Jones, People v., 105 A.D.2d 179, 483 N.Y.S.2d 345 (N.Y.A.D. 2 Dept.1984)—§ **9.24, n. 193;** § **9.29, n. 228;** § **9.48, n. 353.**

Jones, People v., 103 A.D.2d 973, 479 N.Y.S.2d 819 (N.Y.A.D. 3 Dept.1984)—§ **9.12, n. 122.**

Jones, People v., 99 A.D.2d 1, 472 N.Y.S.2d 460 (N.Y.A.D. 3 Dept.1984)—§ **11.14, n. 152, 153.**

Jones, People v., 91 A.D.2d 1175, 459 N.Y.S.2d 144 (N.Y.A.D. 4 Dept.1983)—§ **7.31, n. 352.**

Jones, People v., 114 Misc.2d 31, 449 N.Y.S.2d 409 (N.Y.Sup.1982)—§ **6.8, n. 182.**

Jones, People v., 85 A.D.2d 50, 448 N.Y.S.2d 543 (N.Y.A.D. 3 Dept.1982)—§ **7.14, n. 158.**

Jones, People v., 404 N.Y.S.2d 85, 375 N.E.2d 41 (N.Y.1978)—§ **7.12, n. 132;** § **11.18, n. 244.**

Jones, People v., 56 Misc.2d 884, 290 N.Y.S.2d 771 (N.Y.Sup.1968)—§ **5.23, n. 623.**

Jones v. United States, 463 U.S. 354, 103 S.Ct. 3043, 77 L.Ed.2d 694 (1983)—§ **6.8, n. 169.**

Jones v. United States, 362 U.S. 257, 80 S.Ct. 725, 4 L.Ed.2d 697 (1960)—§ **10.11;** § **10.11, n. 209.**

Jordan, People v., 153 A.D.2d 263, 550 N.Y.S.2d 917 (N.Y.A.D. 2 Dept.1990)—§ **5.8, n. 153.**

Jordan, People v., 141 A.D.2d 886, 528 N.Y.S.2d 951 (N.Y.A.D. 3 Dept.1988)—§ **9.10, n. 86, 108.**

Jordan, People v., 477 N.Y.S.2d 605, 466 N.E.2d 145 (N.Y.1984)—§ **9.12, n. 118.**

Joseph, People v., 635 N.Y.S.2d 123, 658 N.E.2d 996 (N.Y.1995)—§ **7.17, n. 202.**

Jovet, People v., 41 A.D.2d 608, 340 N.Y.S.2d 409 (N.Y.A.D. 1 Dept.1973)—§ **11.18, n. 251.**

Juhans, People v., 126 Misc.2d 868, 484 N.Y.S.2d 432 (N.Y.Sup.1984)—§ **9.16, n. 149.**

Junco, People v., 184 A.D.2d 529, 584 N.Y.S.2d 604 (N.Y.A.D. 2 Dept.1992)—§ **11.18, n. 244.**

Kaatsiz, People v., 156 Misc.2d 898, 595 N.Y.S.2d 648 (N.Y.Sup.1992)—§ **5.22;** § **5.22, n. 534, 541.**

Kaltenbach, People v., 469 N.Y.S.2d 685, 457 N.E.2d 791 (N.Y.1983)—§ **3.24, n. 299, 300, 302.**

Kaminiski, People v., 143 Misc.2d 1089, 542 N.Y.S.2d 923 (N.Y.City Crim.Ct.1989)—§ **3.7, n. 79.**

Kaminski, People v., 151 Misc.2d 664, 573 N.Y.S.2d 394 (N.Y.Just.Ct.1991)—§ **1.4, n. 109.**

Kaminski, People v., 460 N.Y.S.2d 495, 447 N.E.2d 43 (N.Y.1983)—§ **5.17;** § **5.17, n. 382;** § **5.18, n. 421.**

Kane, People v., N.Y.L.J., p. 13, col. 1 (App. Term, 2d & 11th Jud.Dists.1985)—§ **11.15, n. 176.**

Kaplan v. Ritter, 525 N.Y.S.2d 1, 519 N.E.2d 802 (N.Y.1987)—§ **2.6, n. 142.**

TABLE OF CASES

Karmye, People v., 164 Misc.2d 746, 624 N.Y.S.2d 743 (N.Y.Sup.1995)—§ **5.3, n. 42.**

Karp, People v., 158 A.D.2d 378, 551 N.Y.S.2d 503 (N.Y.A.D. 1 Dept.1990)— § **5.8, n. 182.**

Karpeles, People v., 146 Misc.2d 53, 549 N.Y.S.2d 903 (N.Y.City Crim.Ct.1989)— § **7.32, n. 358.**

Kase, People v., 76 A.D.2d 532, 431 N.Y.S.2d 531 (N.Y.A.D. 1 Dept.1980)— § **9.3, n. 13.**

Kastigar v. United States, 406 U.S. 441, 92 S.Ct. 1653, 32 L.Ed.2d 212 (1972)— § **5.9;** § **5.9, n. 197, 202;** § **10.10, n. 183.**

Kates, People v., 444 N.Y.S.2d 446, 428 N.E.2d 852 (N.Y.1981)—§ **10.22, n. 518.**

Kato, People v., 178 A.D.2d 381, 578 N.Y.S.2d 143 (N.Y.A.D. 1 Dept.1991)— § **9.43, n. 309.**

Katz v. United States, 389 U.S. 347, 88 S.Ct. 507, 19 L.Ed.2d 576 (1967)— § **10.11;** § **10.11, n. 215.**

Kay, People v., 125 Misc.2d 833, 480 N.Y.S.2d 171 (N.Y.Town Ct.1984)— § **5.20, n. 474.**

Keefer, People v., 197 A.D.2d 915, 602 N.Y.S.2d 268 (N.Y.A.D. 4 Dept.1993)— § **1.9, n. 206, 211.**

Keehner, People v., 28 A.D.2d 695, 281 N.Y.S.2d 128 (N.Y.A.D. 2 Dept.1967)— § **11.3, n. 23.**

Keenan v. Gigante, 417 N.Y.S.2d 226, 390 N.E.2d 1151 (N.Y.1979)—§ **5.9, n. 191.**

Keeper of City Prison, People ex rel. Shapiro v., 290 N.Y. 393, 49 N.E.2d 498 (N.Y. 1943)—§ **4.1, n. 4.**

Keindl, People v., 509 N.Y.S.2d 790, 502 N.E.2d 577 (N.Y.1986)—§ **5.15, n. 341;** § **5.17, n. 358, 362;** § **9.3, n. 11.**

Kellerman, People v., 102 A.D.2d 629, 479 N.Y.S.2d 815 (N.Y.A.D. 3 Dept.1984)— § **1.3, n. 66;** § **1.4, n. 77, 121, 124.**

Kelley, People v., 141 A.D.2d 764, 529 N.Y.S.2d 855 (N.Y.A.D. 2 Dept.1988)— § **3.28, n. 377.**

Kellman, People v., 156 Misc.2d 179, 592 N.Y.S.2d 214 (N.Y.Sup.1992)—§ **5.8, n. 142.**

Kellog, People v., 53 Misc.2d 560, 279 N.Y.S.2d 104 (N.Y.Co.Ct.1967)—§ **10.12, n. 252.**

Kelly, People v., 209 A.D.2d 439, 618 N.Y.S.2d 821 (N.Y.A.D. 2 Dept.1994)— § **7.17, n. 193.**

Kelly, People v., 478 N.Y.S.2d 834, 467 N.E.2d 498 (N.Y.1984)—§ **7.4, n. 39;** § **7.23;** § **7.23, n. 253.**

Kelly, People v., 382 N.Y.S.2d 1, 345 N.E.2d 544 (N.Y.1976)—§ **9.11, n. 111.**

Kelly, People v., 40 A.D.2d 624, 336 N.Y.S.2d 514 (N.Y.A.D. 4 Dept.1972)— § **10.12, n. 252.**

Kelty, People v., 95 Misc.2d 246, 406 N.Y.S.2d 972 (N.Y.Dist.Ct.1978)— § **10.20, n. 497, 498.**

Kemp, People v., 131 A.D.2d 265, 521 N.Y.S.2d 546 (N.Y.A.D. 3 Dept.1987)— § **10.20, n. 468, 491.**

Kendzia, People v., 486 N.Y.S.2d 888, 476 N.E.2d 287 (N.Y.1985)—§ **9.23;** § **9.23, n. 178, 179.**

Keneston, People v., 105 Misc.2d 440, 432 N.Y.S.2d 355 (N.Y.Co.Ct.1980)—§ **1.7, n. 150.**

Kennedy v. Mendoza-Martinez, 372 U.S. 144, 83 S.Ct. 554, 9 L.Ed.2d 644 (1963)—§ **2.10, n. 226.**

Kennedy, People v., 151 A.D.2d 831, 542 N.Y.S.2d 806 (N.Y.A.D. 3 Dept.1989)— § **6.10, n. 260.**

Keppler, People v., 92 A.D.2d 1032, 461 N.Y.S.2d 513 (N.Y.A.D. 3 Dept.1983)— § **7.21, n. 235.**

Kercheval v. United States, 274 U.S. 220, 47 S.Ct. 582, 71 L.Ed. 1009 (1927)— § **11.7, n. 62.**

Kern, People v., 149 A.D.2d 187, 545 N.Y.S.2d 4 (N.Y.A.D. 2 Dept.1989)— § **10.10, n. 197.**

Kersch, People v., 135 A.D.2d 570, 521 N.Y.S.2d 788 (N.Y.A.D. 2 Dept.1987)— § **10.10, n. 198;** § **10.12, n. 246.**

Kesselbrenner v. Anonymous, 75 Misc.2d 289, 347 N.Y.S.2d 369 (N.Y.Sup.1973)— § **6.6, n. 126.**

Kessler v. Sherman, 393 N.Y.S.2d 703, 362 N.E.2d 254 (N.Y.1977)—§ **2.6, n. 131.**

Key, People v., 408 N.Y.S.2d 16, 379 N.E.2d 1147 (N.Y.1978)—§ **2.3, n. 31;** § **2.4, n. 77, 78, 80;** § **3.3, n. 34;** § **3.5, n. 43, 51;** § **9.12, n. 116.**

K.F., People v., 208 A.D.2d 948, 618 N.Y.S.2d 98 (N.Y.A.D. 2 Dept.1994)— § **11.13, n. 137.**

Khadaidi, People v., 201 A.D.2d 585, 608 N.Y.S.2d 471 (N.Y.A.D. 2 Dept.1994)— § **7.21, n. 240.**

Khan, People v., 200 A.D.2d 129, 613 N.Y.S.2d 198 (N.Y.A.D. 2 Dept.1994)— § **5.22, n. 578.**

Khan, People v., 172 A.D.2d 231, 568 N.Y.S.2d 367 (N.Y.A.D. 1 Dept.1991)— § **9.40, n. 289.**

Kilgore, People v., 199 A.D.2d 1008, 608 N.Y.S.2d 12 (N.Y.A.D. 4 Dept.1993)— § **11.17, n. 235.**

Kinchen, People v., 469 N.Y.S.2d 680, 457 N.E.2d 786 (N.Y.1983)—§ **6.10, n. 243.**

Kindlon, People v., 629 N.Y.S.2d 827 (N.Y.A.D. 3 Dept.1995)—§ **5.17, n. 360.**

King, People v., 137 Misc.2d 1087, 523 N.Y.S.2d 748 (N.Y.City Crim.Ct.1988)— § **3.6, n. 62.**

King, People v., 114 A.D.2d 650, 494 N.Y.S.2d 484 (N.Y.A.D. 3 Dept.1985)— § **9.10, n. 93.**

TABLE OF CASES

Kirby v. Illinois, 406 U.S. 682, 92 S.Ct. 1877, 32 L.Ed.2d 411 (1972)—§ **7.11, n. 120.**

Kisloff on Behalf of Wilson v. Covington, 541 N.Y.S.2d 737, 539 N.E.2d 565 (N.Y. 1989)—§ **2.4, n. 82; § 11.19, n. 253, 264.**

Klaus, People v., 104 A.D.2d 566, 479 N.Y.S.2d 273 (N.Y.A.D. 2 Dept.1984)— § **9.52, n. 385.**

Klein v. Murtagh, 360 N.Y.S.2d 416, 318 N.E.2d 606 (N.Y.1974)—§ **2.6; § 2.6, n. 145.**

Klein, People v., 130 Misc.2d 549, 496 N.Y.S.2d 889 (N.Y.Co.Ct.1985)—§ **3.19, n. 223.**

Klein, People v., 30 Misc.2d 334, 217 N.Y.S.2d 885 (N.Y.Sup.1961)—§ **6.2, n. 24, 27.**

Klein, People ex rel. v. Krueger, 307 N.Y.S.2d 207, 255 N.E.2d 552 (N.Y. 1969)—§ **4.1, n. 2, 4, 7; § 4.13, n. 217.**

Klipfel, People v., 160 N.Y. 371, 54 N.E. 788 (N.Y.1899)—§ **5.17, n. 357.**

Kloczkowski, People v., 199 A.D.2d 538, 606 N.Y.S.2d 713 (N.Y.A.D. 2 Dept.1993)— § **11.11, n. 115.**

Klopfer v. State of N. C., 386 U.S. 213, 87 S.Ct. 988, 18 L.Ed.2d 1 (1967)—§ **9.8, n. 36.**

Knapp, People v., 439 N.Y.S.2d 871, 422 N.E.2d 531 (N.Y.1981)—§ **10.10, n. 188; § 10.20, n. 471, 478.**

Knight, People v., 163 A.D.2d 583, 558 N.Y.S.2d 967 (N.Y.A.D. 2 Dept.1990)— § **9.34, n. 256; § 9.39, n. 283; § 9.41, n. 292.**

Knowell, People v., 127 A.D.2d 794, 512 N.Y.S.2d 190 (N.Y.A.D. 2 Dept.1987)— § **7.30, n. 343.**

Kobryn, People v., 294 N.Y. 192, 61 N.E.2d 441 (N.Y.1945)—§ **1.3, n. 71.**

Koehler, People ex rel. Ellis v., 151 A.D.2d 309, 542 N.Y.S.2d 578 (N.Y.A.D. 1 Dept. 1989)—§ **3.34, n. 476, 486.**

Koehler, People ex rel. Ellis on Behalf of Robinson v., 165 A.D.2d 848, 560 N.Y.S.2d 226 (N.Y.A.D. 2 Dept.1990)— § **9.25, n. 208.**

Kohut, People v., 331 N.Y.S.2d 416, 282 N.E.2d 312 (N.Y.1972)—§ **9.6, n. 23; § 9.7, n. 35.**

Konits, People v., 159 A.D.2d 590, 552 N.Y.S.2d 448 (N.Y.A.D. 2 Dept.1990)— § **6.2, n. 41.**

Kopciowski, People v., 505 N.Y.S.2d 52, 496 N.E.2d 211 (N.Y.1986)—§ **9.34, n. 255.**

Kornegay, People v., 55 A.D.2d 462, 390 N.Y.S.2d 666 (N.Y.A.D. 3 Dept.1977)— § **9.11, n. 112.**

Korona, People v., 197 A.D.2d 788, 603 N.Y.S.2d 88 (N.Y.A.D. 3 Dept.1993)— § **11.17, n. 231.**

Koslow, People v., 160 A.D.2d 954, 555 N.Y.S.2d 627 (N.Y.A.D. 2 Dept.1990)— § **11.13, n. 138.**

Kotteakos v. United States, 328 U.S. 750, 66 S.Ct. 1239, 90 L.Ed. 1557 (1946)— § **5.22, n. 547.**

Kroemer, People v., 204 A.D.2d 1017, 613 N.Y.S.2d 304 (N.Y.A.D. 4 Dept.1994)— § **5.18, n. 407.**

Kronberg, In re, 95 A.D.2d 714, 464 N.Y.S.2d 466 (N.Y.A.D. 1 Dept.1983)— § **5.8, n. 114.**

Krueger, People ex rel. Klein v., 307 N.Y.S.2d 207, 255 N.E.2d 552 (N.Y. 1969)—§ **4.1, n. 2, 4, 7; § 4.13, n. 217.**

Kuberka, People v., 215 A.D.2d 592, 626 N.Y.S.2d 855 (N.Y.A.D. 2 Dept.1995)— § **10.15, n. 294.**

Kuriansky v. Seewald, 148 A.D.2d 238, 544 N.Y.S.2d 336 (N.Y.A.D. 1 Dept.1989)— § **5.8, n. 115.**

Kurtz, People v., 434 N.Y.S.2d 200, 414 N.E.2d 699 (N.Y.1980)—§ **2.4, n. 77, 81.**

Kurtz, People v., 71 Misc.2d 493, 336 N.Y.S.2d 322 (N.Y.Co.Ct.1972)—§ **6.9, n. 193.**

Kyles v. Whitley, ___ U.S. ___, 115 S.Ct. 1555, 131 L.Ed.2d 490 (1995)—§ **7.14, n. 157.**

LaBelle, Matter of, 582 N.Y.S.2d 970, 591 N.E.2d 1156 (N.Y.1992)—§ **4.4, n. 58; § 4.5, n. 61; § 4.10, n. 177; § 5.24, n. 637.**

La Belle, People v., 276 N.Y.S.2d 105, 222 N.E.2d 727 (N.Y.1966)—§ **5.22, n. 582.**

La Bello, People v., 301 N.Y.S.2d 544, 249 N.E.2d 412 (N.Y.1969)—§ **5.9, n. 199, 223.**

LaBounty, People v., 127 A.D.2d 989, 512 N.Y.S.2d 950 (N.Y.A.D. 4 Dept.1987)— § **5.8, n. 130.**

Lacher, People v., 59 A.D.2d 725, 398 N.Y.S.2d 363 (N.Y.A.D. 2 Dept.1977)— § **6.10, n. 220.**

LaCongo, People v., 30 A.D.2d 757, 292 N.Y.S.2d 214 (N.Y.A.D. 4 Dept.1968)— § **10.14, n. 284.**

LaDolce, People v., 196 A.D.2d 49, 607 N.Y.S.2d 523 (N.Y.A.D. 4 Dept.1994)— § **7.12, n. 137.**

Ladson, People v., 626 N.Y.S.2d 999, 650 N.E.2d 846 (N.Y.1995)—§ **9.51; § 9.51, n. 377, 378.**

Ladson, People v., 202 A.D.2d 212, 608 N.Y.S.2d 966 (N.Y.A.D. 1 Dept.1994)— § **9.38, n. 276.**

LaForce, People ex rel. v. Skinner, 65 Misc.2d 884, 319 N.Y.S.2d 10 (N.Y.Sup. 1971)—§ **4.5, n. 73, 76.**

Laing, People v., 581 N.Y.S.2d 149, 589 N.E.2d 372 (N.Y.1992)—§ **10.13, n. 264; § 10.22, n. 512; § 10.29, n. 612.**

Laino, People v., 218 N.Y.S.2d 647, 176 N.E.2d 571 (N.Y.1961)—§ **5.9, n. 224.**

Lalli, People v., 401 N.Y.S.2d 489, 372 N.E.2d 330 (N.Y.1977)—§ **10.3, n. 66.**

TABLE OF CASES

Lamar, People v., 86 A.D.2d 751, 447 N.Y.S.2d 772 (N.Y.A.D. 4 Dept.1982)—§ 7.10, n. 110.
Lancaster, People v., 511 N.Y.S.2d 559, 503 N.E.2d 990 (N.Y.1986)—§ 5.1, n. 8; § 5.5; § 5.5, n. 72; § 5.7; § 5.7, n. 96, 103, 109; § 5.8, n. 164, 186; § 5.27, n. 745; § 6.3, n. 57.
Landy, People v., 125 A.D.2d 703, 510 N.Y.S.2d 190 (N.Y.A.D. 2 Dept.1986)—§ 5.15, n. 337; § 9.3, n. 11.
Lane, People v., 143 Misc.2d 385, 540 N.Y.S.2d 664 (N.Y.Sup.1989)—§ 5.29, n. 818.
Lane, People v., 451 N.Y.S.2d 6, 436 N.E.2d 456 (N.Y.1982)—§ 5.21; § 5.21, n. 487, 509, 522.
Lang, People v., 287 N.Y.S.2d 659, 234 N.E.2d 687—§ 11.16, n. 194.
Lange, Ex parte, 85 U.S. 163, 21 L.Ed. 872 (1873)—§ 2.10, n. 210.
La Placa, People v., 127 A.D.2d 610, 511 N.Y.S.2d 410 (N.Y.A.D. 2 Dept.1987)—§ 7.11, n. 121; § 11.11, n. 122.
La Porte, People v., 184 A.D.2d 803, 584 N.Y.S.2d 662 (N.Y.A.D. 3 Dept.1992)—§ 10.24, n. 561.
LaRocca, People v., 172 A.D.2d 628, 568 N.Y.S.2d 431 (N.Y.A.D. 2 Dept.1991)—§ 7.14, n. 164; § 9.10, n. 83.
Larry Smith, a/k/a Keith Gates, a/k/a Edwin Kevin Fischer, People v. (N.Y.1996)—§ 5.6, n. 86; § 5.8, n. 17.
Lashway, People v., 187 A.D.2d 747, 589 N.Y.S.2d 687 (N.Y.A.D. 3 Dept.1992)—§ 9.43, n. 310; § 9.51, n. 367.
Latham, People v., 609 N.Y.S.2d 141, 631 N.E.2d 83 (N.Y.1994)—§ 2.5, n. 99; § 2.6; § 2.6, n. 138.
Latora, People v., 128 A.D.2d 808, 513 N.Y.S.2d 511 (N.Y.A.D. 2 Dept.1987)—§ 11.19, n. 257.
Latzer, People v., 528 N.Y.S.2d 533, 523 N.E.2d 820 (N.Y.1988)—§ 11.15, n. 160.
Lawrence, People v., 192 A.D.2d 332, 595 N.Y.S.2d 764 (N.Y.A.D. 1 Dept.1993)—§ 11.10, n. 104.
Lawrence, People v., 166 A.D.2d 164, 563 N.Y.S.2d 794 (N.Y.A.D. 1 Dept.1990)—§ 10.6, n. 128.
Lawrence, People v., 485 N.Y.S.2d 233, 474 N.E.2d 593 (N.Y.1984)—§ 5.26; § 5.26, n. 647, 654; § 8.1, n. 1; § 9.12, n. 115; § 9.49, n. 359.
Lawson, People v., 198 A.D.2d 71, 603 N.Y.S.2d 311 (N.Y.A.D. 1 Dept.1993)—§ 5.27, n. 771.
Lazer on Behalf of Palmieri, People ex rel. v. Warden, 173 A.D.2d 425, 571 N.Y.S.2d 441 (N.Y.A.D. 1 Dept.1991)—§ 4.10, n. 152.
Leach, People v., 203 A.D.2d 484, 611 N.Y.S.2d 17 (N.Y.A.D. 2 Dept.1994)—§ 11.17, n. 222.
Leach, People v., 414 N.Y.S.2d 121, 386 N.E.2d 1088 (N.Y.1978)—§ 2.4, n. 78.

Lebron, People v., 211 A.D.2d 208, 628 N.Y.S.2d 54 (N.Y.A.D. 1 Dept.1995)—§ 6.3, n. 54; § 9.28; § 9.28, n. 225.
Lee v. County Court of Erie County, 318 N.Y.S.2d 705, 267 N.E.2d 452 (N.Y. 1971)—§ 6.4, n. 80; § 7.24, n. 276.
Lee v. Illinois, 476 U.S. 530, 106 S.Ct. 2056, 90 L.Ed.2d 514 (1986)—§ 5.22, n. 569.
Lee, People v., 100 A.D.2d 357, 474 N.Y.S.2d 308 (N.Y.A.D. 1 Dept.1984)—§ 5.18; § 5.18, n. 434.
Lee, People v., 462 N.Y.S.2d 417, 448 N.E.2d 1328 (N.Y.1983)—§ 11.16, n. 203.
Leeson, United States ex rel. v. Damon, 496 F.2d 718 (2nd Cir.1974)—§ 11.9, n. 78, 80.
Lefkowitz v. Turley, 414 U.S. 70, 94 S.Ct. 316, 38 L.Ed.2d 274 (1973)—§ 5.9, n. 206.
Legal Aid Soc. of Sullivan County, Inc. v. Scheinman, 439 N.Y.S.2d 882, 422 N.E.2d 542 (N.Y.1981)—§ 1.8, n. 178.
Lego v. Twomey, 404 U.S. 477, 92 S.Ct. 619, 30 L.Ed.2d 618 (1972)—§ 10.20, n. 489.
LeGrand, People v., 155 A.D.2d 482, 547 N.Y.S.2d 143 (N.Y.A.D. 2 Dept.1989)—§ 11.10, n. 108.
Leisner, People v., 538 N.Y.S.2d 517, 535 N.E.2d 647 (N.Y.1989)—§ 5.22, n. 532; § 9.3, n. 12; § 9.6; § 9.6, n. 30.
Leite, People v., 52 A.D.2d 895, 383 N.Y.S.2d 71 (N.Y.A.D. 2 Dept.1976)—§ 11.10, n. 99.
Lemon, People ex rel. v. Supreme Court of State of New York, 245 N.Y. 24, 156 N.E. 84 (N.Y.1927)—§ 7.2, n. 8.
Lennertz, People v., 156 Misc.2d 88, 591 N.Y.S.2d 955 (N.Y.City Crim.Ct.1992)—§ 9.5, n. 18.
Lent v. New York & M. Ry. Co., 130 N.Y. 504, 29 N.E. 988 (N.Y.1892)—§ 2.2, n. 13.
Leon, People v., 134 Misc.2d 757, 512 N.Y.S.2d 991 (N.Y.Co.Ct.1987)—§ 7.7, n. 73; § 7.19, n. 224.
Leonardo, People v., 141 Misc.2d 526, 533 N.Y.S.2d 660 (N.Y.Co.Ct.1988)—§ 9.49, n. 356.
Lerman, People v., 116 A.D.2d 665, 497 N.Y.S.2d 733 (N.Y.A.D. 2 Dept.1986)—§ 5.8, n. 181.
Lesesne, People v., 173 A.D.2d 407, 570 N.Y.S.2d 40 (N.Y.A.D. 1 Dept.1991)—§ 11.18, n. 244.
Lesiuk, People v., 600 N.Y.S.2d 931, 617 N.E.2d 1047 (N.Y.1993)—§ 9.9, n. 75; § 9.10, n. 85.
Leslie, People v., 198 A.D.2d 233, 604 N.Y.S.2d 798 (N.Y.A.D. 2 Dept.1993)—§ 11.13, n. 143.
Lester, People v., 135 Misc.2d 205, 514 N.Y.S.2d 861 (N.Y.Sup.1987)—§ 5.3, n. 49.

TABLE OF CASES

Letizia, People v., 159 A.D.2d 1010, 552 N.Y.S.2d 732 (N.Y.A.D. 4 Dept.1990)—§ 7.17, n. 193.

Letterio, People v., 266 N.Y.S.2d 368, 213 N.E.2d 670 (N.Y.1965)—§ 3.24, n. 296.

Lev, People v., 91 Misc.2d 241, 398 N.Y.S.2d 593 (N.Y.Sup.1977)—§ 5.9, n. 219.

Leventhal on Behalf of Agosta, People ex rel. v. Warden, Rikers Island, 102 A.D.2d 317, 477 N.Y.S.2d 332 (N.Y.A.D. 1 Dept.1984)—§ 3.32, n. 442; § 11.19, n. 257.

Levin, People v., 457 N.Y.S.2d 472, 443 N.E.2d 946 (N.Y.1982)—§ 5.14, n. 334; § 11.15, n. 174.

Lewis, People v., 150 Misc.2d 886, 578 N.Y.S.2d 393 (N.Y.City Crim.Ct.1991)—§ 9.37, n. 271.

Leyva, People v., 379 N.Y.S.2d 30, 341 N.E.2d 546 (N.Y.1975)—§ 7.10, n. 110.

Liberatore, People v., 581 N.Y.S.2d 634, 590 N.E.2d 219 (N.Y.1992)—§ 1.2, n. 28; § 7.10, n. 98, 101; § 10.19, n. 404, 436.

Liberatore, People v., 96 A.D.2d 1047, 466 N.Y.S.2d 683 (N.Y.A.D. 2 Dept.1983)—§ 9.10, n. 108.

Lieberman, People v., 419 N.Y.S.2d 946, 393 N.E.2d 1019 (N.Y.1979)—§ 9.51, n. 365.

Liller, United States v., 999 F.2d 61 (2nd Cir.1993)—§ 2.5, n. 100, 101.

Lincoln, People v., 80 A.D.2d 877, 436 N.Y.S.2d 782 (N.Y.A.D. 2 Dept.1981)—§ 5.8, n. 144, 145.

Lindsly, People v., 99 A.D.2d 99, 472 N.Y.S.2d 115 (N.Y.A.D. 2 Dept.1984)—§ 2.7, n. 161; § 5.21, n. 484.

Liotta, People v., 580 N.Y.S.2d 184, 588 N.E.2d 82 (N.Y.1992)—§ 9.34; § 9.34, n. 249.

Lippman, People v., 156 Misc.2d 333, 601 N.Y.S.2d 365 (N.Y.Sup.1993)—§ 3.5, n. 45.

Little v. Savarese, 156 A.D.2d 564, 550 N.Y.S.2d 715 (N.Y.A.D. 2 Dept.1989)—§ 7.11, n. 121.

Littlejohn, People v., 184 A.D.2d 790, 585 N.Y.S.2d 495 (N.Y.A.D. 2 Dept.1992)—§ 10.24, n. 555.

Littles, People v., 192 A.D.2d 314, 595 N.Y.S.2d 463 (N.Y.A.D. 1 Dept.1993)—§ 7.16, n. 178.

Littles, People v., 188 A.D.2d 255, 591 N.Y.S.2d 2 (N.Y.A.D. 1 Dept.1992)—§ 5.26, n. 664.

Livoti, People v., 632 N.Y.S.2d 425 (N.Y.Sup.1995)—§ 5.18, n. 398.

Lloyd, People v., 141 A.D.2d 669, 529 N.Y.S.2d 801 (N.Y.A.D. 2 Dept.1988)—§ 9.41, n. 293.

Lobel, People v., 298 N.Y. 243, 82 N.E.2d 145 (N.Y.1948)—§ 5.22, n. 565.

Lo Cicero, People v., 251 N.Y.S.2d 953, 200 N.E.2d 622 (N.Y.1964)—§ 2.8, n. 176.

Lockett v. Juviler, 490 N.Y.S.2d 764, 480 N.E.2d 378 (N.Y.1985)—§ 2.2, n. 9, 16, 18; § 11.4, n. 37; § 11.19, n. 253.

Lockhart v. Nelson, 488 U.S. 33, 109 S.Ct. 285, 102 L.Ed.2d 265 (1988)—§ 2.4, n. 78, 89.

Lohnes, People v., 76 Misc.2d 507, 351 N.Y.S.2d 279 (N.Y.Sup.1973)—§ 9.5, n. 22.

Lo-Ji Sales, Inc. v. New York, 442 U.S. 319, 99 S.Ct. 2319, 60 L.Ed.2d 920 (1979)—§ 10.5, n. 82.

Lomax, People v., 428 N.Y.S.2d 937, 406 N.E.2d 793 (N.Y.1980)—§ 3.7, n. 77; § 3.9, n. 110; § 3.27, n. 354; § 9.10, n. 100; § 9.15; § 9.15, n. 139, 141; § 9.51, n. 370.

Lombard, People ex rel. Shaw v., 95 Misc.2d 664, 408 N.Y.S.2d 664 (N.Y.Co.Ct. 1978)—§ 4.5, n. 70, 73; § 4.10, n. 131, 155.

Lombardi, People v., 18 A.D.2d 177, 239 N.Y.S.2d 161 (N.Y.A.D. 2 Dept.1963)—§ 10.19, n. 398.

London, People v., 164 Misc.2d 575, 624 N.Y.S.2d 786 (N.Y.Sup.1995)—§ 5.23, n. 621.

Longwood, People v., 116 A.D.2d 590, 497 N.Y.S.2d 450 (N.Y.A.D. 2 Dept.1986)—§ 5.27, n. 792.

Loper, People v., 215 A.D.2d 406, 626 N.Y.S.2d 968 (N.Y.A.D. 2 Dept.1995)—§ 11.17, n. 221.

Lopez, People v., 618 N.Y.S.2d 879, 643 N.E.2d 501 (N.Y.1994)—§ 10.24; § 10.24, n. 558.

Lopez, People v., 209 A.D.2d 545, 619 N.Y.S.2d 623 (N.Y.A.D. 2 Dept.1994)—§ 11.18, n. 245.

Lopez, People v., 185 A.D.2d 285, 585 N.Y.S.2d 797 (N.Y.A.D. 2 Dept.1992)—§ 3.19, n. 223.

Lopez, People v., 583 N.Y.S.2d 356, 592 N.E.2d 1360 (N.Y.1992)—§ 5.6; § 5.6, n. 88.

Lopez, People v., 160 A.D.2d 335, 554 N.Y.S.2d 98 (N.Y.A.D. 1 Dept.1990)—§ 6.10, n. 225.

Lopez, People v., 529 N.Y.S.2d 465, 525 N.E.2d 5 (N.Y.1988)—§ 11.10, n. 95, 97, 98, 102.

Lopez, People v., 134 A.D.2d 456, 521 N.Y.S.2d 78 (N.Y.A.D. 2 Dept.1987)—§ 10.2, n. 42.

Lopez, People v., 126 Misc.2d 1072, 484 N.Y.S.2d 974 (N.Y.Sup.1985)—§ 6.4, n. 76.

Lopez, People v., 77 A.D.2d 287, 433 N.Y.S.2d 569 (N.Y.A.D. 1 Dept.1980)—§ 9.43, n. 313.

Lopez v. Scully, 58 F.3d 38 (2nd Cir.1995)—§ 11.18, n. 247.

LoPizzo, People v., 151 A.D.2d 614, 543 N.Y.S.2d 88 (N.Y.A.D. 2 Dept.1989)—§ 9.33, n. 246.

TABLE OF CASES

Loria, People v., 214 A.D.2d 1043, 626 N.Y.S.2d 941 (N.Y.A.D. 4 Dept.1995)—**§ 5.27, n. 794.**

Loria, People v., 223 N.Y.S.2d 462, 179 N.E.2d 478 (N.Y.1961)—**§ 10.19, n. 440.**

Loud Hawk, United States v., 474 U.S. 302, 106 S.Ct. 648, 88 L.Ed.2d 640 (1986)—**§ 9.8, n. 59; § 9.9, n. 72.**

Lourdes, People v., 175 A.D.2d 958, 573 N.Y.S.2d 537 (N.Y.A.D. 3 Dept.1991)—**§ 10.19, n. 411.**

Lourens, People v., 208 A.D.2d 768, 617 N.Y.S.2d 779 (N.Y.A.D. 2 Dept.1994)—**§ 9.34, n. 252.**

Lovacco, People v., 147 A.D.2d 592, 537 N.Y.S.2d 886 (N.Y.A.D. 2 Dept.1989)—**§ 1.4, n. 86.**

Lovasco, United States v., 431 U.S. 783, 97 S.Ct. 2044, 52 L.Ed.2d 752 (1977)—**§ 9.8, n. 58; § 9.9, n. 73; § 9.10, n. 85.**

Love, People v., 85 A.D.2d 799, 445 N.Y.S.2d 607 (N.Y.A.D. 3 Dept.1981)—**§ 10.20, n. 490.**

Lovejoy, People v., 197 A.D.2d 353, 602 N.Y.S.2d 126 (N.Y.A.D. 1 Dept.1993)—**§ 10.17, n. 363, 380.**

Lovejoy, People v., 66 Misc.2d 1003, 323 N.Y.S.2d 95 (N.Y.Co.Ct.1971)—**§ 1.8, n. 184, 185.**

Lowe, People v., 109 A.D.2d 300, 491 N.Y.S.2d 529 (N.Y.A.D. 4 Dept.1985)—**§ 6.2, n. 38; § 6.5, n. 96; § 6.10, n. 256.**

Lowen, People v., 100 A.D.2d 518, 473 N.Y.S.2d 22 (N.Y.A.D. 2 Dept.1984)—**§ 1.4, n. 75; § 5.12, n. 314.**

Lowman, People v., 102 A.D.2d 896, 476 N.Y.S.2d 937 (N.Y.A.D. 2 Dept.1984)—**§ 9.43, n. 311.**

Luciano, People v., 277 N.Y. 348, 14 N.E.2d 433 (N.Y.1938)—**§ 5.21, n. 492; § 5.22, n. 539.**

Luna, People v., 127 Misc.2d 608, 486 N.Y.S.2d 839 (N.Y.Sup.1985)—**§ 5.8, n. 132.**

Lunney, People v., 84 Misc.2d 1090, 378 N.Y.S.2d 559 (N.Y.Sup.1975)—**§ 7.23, n. 260.**

Luongo, People v., 418 N.Y.S.2d 365, 391 N.E.2d 1341 (N.Y.1979)—**§ 2.6; § 2.6, n. 141.**

Luperon, People v., 623 N.Y.S.2d 735, 647 N.E.2d 1243 (N.Y.1995)—**§ 9.26, n. 215; § 9.37; § 9.37, n. 266, 268; § 9.51, n. 367.**

Lupo, People v., 74 Misc.2d 679, 345 N.Y.S.2d 348 (N.Y.City Crim.Ct.1973)—**§ 3.30, n. 418.**

Luster v. Howard, 123 Misc.2d 410, 473 N.Y.S.2d 750 (N.Y.Co.Ct.1984)—**§ 4.10, n. 150.**

Lydon, People v., 197 A.D.2d 640, 603 N.Y.S.2d 771 (N.Y.A.D. 2 Dept.1993)—**§ 5.22, n. 596.**

Lynch, People v., 145 Misc.2d 354, 546 N.Y.S.2d 538 (N.Y.City Crim.Ct.1989)—**§ 3.25, n. 325.**

Lypka, People v., 366 N.Y.S.2d 622, 326 N.E.2d 294 (N.Y.1975)—**§ 10.19, n. 454.**

MacCall, People v., 122 A.D.2d 79, 504 N.Y.S.2d 227 (N.Y.A.D. 2 Dept.1986)—**§ 5.8, n. 139.**

MacDonald, United States v., 456 U.S. 1, 102 S.Ct. 1497, 71 L.Ed.2d 696 (1982)—**§ 9.8, n. 59.**

Mace, People v., 206 A.D.2d 296, 614 N.Y.S.2d 416 (N.Y.A.D. 1 Dept.1994)—**§ 9.37, n. 265; § 9.51, n. 372.**

Machado v. Donalty, 107 A.D.2d 1079, 486 N.Y.S.2d 544 (N.Y.A.D. 4 Dept.1985)—**§ 1.4, n. 121, 124.**

Mack by Padden, People ex rel. v. Warden, Ann M. Kross Center, 145 Misc.2d 1016, 549 N.Y.S.2d 558 (N.Y.Sup.1989)—**§ 3.25, n. 338.**

Mackey, People v., 567 N.Y.S.2d 639, 569 N.E.2d 442 (N.Y.1991)—**§ 11.10; § 11.10, n. 106.**

Mackey, People v., 425 N.Y.S.2d 288, 401 N.E.2d 398 (N.Y.1980)—**§ 5.18, n. 423.**

MacLachlan, People v., 58 A.D.2d 586, 395 N.Y.S.2d 106 (N.Y.A.D. 2 Dept.1977)—**§ 5.9, n. 241.**

Maddicks, People v., 118 A.D.2d 437, 499 N.Y.S.2d 93 (N.Y.A.D. 1 Dept.1986)—**§ 6.6, n. 100, 101, 102.**

Mahboubian, People v., 544 N.Y.S.2d 769, 543 N.E.2d 34 (N.Y.1989)—**§ 5.22; § 5.22, n. 530, 565, 582, 598.**

Mahones, People v., 136 A.D.2d 745, 524 N.Y.S.2d 84 (N.Y.A.D. 2 Dept.1988)—**§ 7.17, n. 199.**

Mahoney, People v., 462 N.Y.S.2d 410, 448 N.E.2d 1321 (N.Y.1983)—**§ 10.5, n. 110, 112.**

Mai, People v., 175 A.D.2d 692, 573 N.Y.S.2d 90 (N.Y.A.D. 1 Dept.1991)—**§ 7.26, n. 288.**

Malcolm, People v., 629 N.Y.S.2d 750 (N.Y.A.D. 1 Dept.1995)—**§ 10.29, n. 610.**

Maldonado, People v., 210 A.D.2d 259, 619 N.Y.S.2d 730 (N.Y.A.D. 2 Dept.1994)—**§ 9.38, n. 280.**

Maldonado, People v., 95 Misc.2d 113, 407 N.Y.S.2d 393 (N.Y.City Crim.Ct.1978)—**§ 4.5, n. 77, 84.**

Malinsky, People v., 262 N.Y.S.2d 65, 209 N.E.2d 694 (N.Y.1965)—**§ 10.19, n. 414.**

Maneiro, People v., 426 N.Y.S.2d 471, 403 N.E.2d 176 (N.Y.1980)—**§ 7.10, n. 113.**

Manley, People v., 103 A.D.2d 1024, 478 N.Y.S.2d 400 (N.Y.A.D. 4 Dept.1984)—**§ 11.3, n. 18.**

Manuli, People v., 104 A.D.2d 386, 478 N.Y.S.2d 712 (N.Y.A.D. 2 Dept.1984)—**§ 10.16, n. 319; § 10.20, n. 495.**

Manzanillo, People v., 145 Misc.2d 504, 546 N.Y.S.2d 954 (N.Y.City Crim.Ct.1989)—**§ 7.30, n. 349.**

TABLE OF CASES

Mapp v. Ohio, 367 U.S. 643, 81 S.Ct. 1684, 6 L.Ed.2d 1081 (1961)—§ **10.7, n. 136;** § **10.8, n. 147.**

Mara, United States v., 410 U.S. 19, 93 S.Ct. 774, 35 L.Ed.2d 99 (1973)—§ **5.9, n. 231.**

Marinelli, People v., 148 A.D.2d 550, 540 N.Y.S.2d 185 (N.Y.A.D. 2 Dept.1989)—§ **11.15, n. 167.**

Marini, People v., 173 A.D.2d 742, 570 N.Y.S.2d 360 (N.Y.A.D. 2 Dept.1991)—§ **5.27, n. 733.**

Marino, People v., 135 A.D.2d 573, 521 N.Y.S.2d 791 (N.Y.A.D. 2 Dept.1987)—§ **10.10, n. 193.**

Marion, United States v., 404 U.S. 307, 92 S.Ct. 455, 30 L.Ed.2d 468 (1971)—§ **9.8, n. 38, 57;** § **9.10, n. 91.**

Marrin, People v., 187 A.D.2d 284, 589 N.Y.S.2d 874 (N.Y.A.D. 1 Dept.1992)—§ **9.38, n. 280.**

Marron v. United States, 275 U.S. 192, 48 S.Ct. 74, 72 L.Ed. 231 (1927)—§ **10.6, n. 126.**

Marshall, People v., 170 A.D.2d 463, 565 N.Y.S.2d 551 (N.Y.A.D. 2 Dept.1991)—§ **7.27, n. 297.**

Marshall, People v., 241 N.Y.S.2d 417, 191 N.E.2d 798 (N.Y.1963)—§ **10.6, n. 125.**

Marte, People v., 207 A.D.2d 314, 615 N.Y.S.2d 678 (N.Y.A.D. 1 Dept.1994)—§ **10.17, n. 371.**

Marte, People v., 177 A.D.2d 347, 576 N.Y.S.2d 122 (N.Y.A.D. 1 Dept.1991)—§ **9.34, n. 257.**

Martin, People v., 163 A.D.2d 536, 558 N.Y.S.2d 192 (N.Y.A.D. 2 Dept.1990)—§ **10.2, n. 14.**

Martin, People v., 431 N.Y.S.2d 689, 409 N.E.2d 1363 (N.Y.1980)—§ **10.19, n. 459.**

Martin, People v., 54 A.D.2d 624, 387 N.Y.S.2d 434 (N.Y.A.D. 1 Dept.1976)—§ **7.10, n. 110.**

Martinez v. CPC Intern. Inc., 88 A.D.2d 656, 450 N.Y.S.2d 528 (N.Y.A.D. 2 Dept. 1982)—§ **5.3, n. 52.**

Martinez, People v., 607 N.Y.S.2d 610, 628 N.E.2d 1320 (N.Y.1993)—§ **5.17;** § **5.17, n. 387.**

Martinez, People v., 595 N.Y.S.2d 376, 611 N.E.2d 277 (N.Y.1993)—§ **5.18, n. 441.**

Martinez, People v., 592 N.Y.S.2d 628, 607 N.E.2d 775 (N.Y.1992)—§ **10.3, n. 69.**

Martinez, People v., 528 N.Y.S.2d 813, 524 N.E.2d 134 (N.Y.1988)—§ **7.21, n. 238;** § **7.23, n. 254, 263.**

Martinez, People v., 126 A.D.2d 942, 511 N.Y.S.2d 988 (N.Y.A.D. 4 Dept.1987)—§ **9.12, n. 118.**

Martinez, People v., 124 A.D.2d 505, 508 N.Y.S.2d 180 (N.Y.A.D. 1 Dept.1986)—§ **11.19, n. 260.**

Martinez, People v., 111 Misc.2d 67, 443 N.Y.S.2d 576 (N.Y.Sup.1981)—§ **5.8, n. 135, 151.**

Maryland v. Garrison, 480 U.S. 79, 107 S.Ct. 1013, 94 L.Ed.2d 72 (1987)—§ **10.5, n. 96.**

Mason, People v., 176 A.D.2d 356, 574 N.Y.S.2d 589 (N.Y.A.D. 2 Dept.1991)—§ **5.8, n. 125, 128.**

Mason, People v., 125 A.D.2d 595, 509 N.Y.S.2d 842 (N.Y.A.D. 2 Dept.1986)—§ **9.10, n. 96, 108.**

Mason v. Rothwax, 152 A.D.2d 272, 548 N.Y.S.2d 926 (N.Y.A.D. 1 Dept.1989)—§ **2.9, n. 209.**

Massachusetts v. Morash, 490 U.S. 107, 109 S.Ct. 1668, 104 L.Ed.2d 98 (1989)—§ **1.2, n. 33.**

Masters, People v., 33 A.D.2d 637, 305 N.Y.S.2d 132 (N.Y.A.D. 4 Dept.1969)—§ **10.5, n. 82.**

Mastrangelo, People v., 100 A.D.2d 914, 474 N.Y.S.2d 572 (N.Y.A.D. 2 Dept.1984)—§ **9.47, n. 332.**

Materon, People v., 107 A.D.2d 408, 487 N.Y.S.2d 334 (N.Y.A.D. 2 Dept.1985)—§ **1.3, n. 71.**

Mathews, People v., 173 A.D.2d 565, 570 N.Y.S.2d 814 (N.Y.A.D. 2 Dept.1991)—§ **7.17, n. 216.**

Matlock, United States v., 415 U.S. 164, 94 S.Ct. 988, 39 L.Ed.2d 242 (1974)—§ **10.19, n. 444.**

Mato, People v., 160 A.D.2d 435, 554 N.Y.S.2d 121 (N.Y.A.D. 1 Dept.1990)—§ **10.11, n. 230.**

Matos, People v., 195 A.D.2d 287, 599 N.Y.S.2d 598 (N.Y.A.D. 1 Dept.1993)—§ **5.27, n. 733.**

Matt v. Larocca, 524 N.Y.S.2d 180, 518 N.E.2d 1172 (N.Y.1987)—§ **5.9, n. 205.**

Matter of (see name of party)

Matthews, People v., 154 Misc.2d 848, 585 N.Y.S.2d 948 (N.Y.Sup.1992)—§ **6.3, n. 51.**

Matute, People v., 141 Misc.2d 988, 535 N.Y.S.2d 524 (N.Y.City Crim.Ct.1988)—§ **9.14, n. 137;** § **9.20, n. 163.**

Mauceri, People v., 74 A.D.2d 833, 425 N.Y.S.2d 346 (N.Y.A.D. 2 Dept.1980)—§ **5.7, n. 97.**

Mauro, People v., 147 Misc.2d 381, 555 N.Y.S.2d 533 (N.Y.City Crim.Ct.1990)—§ **3.7, n. 79.**

Maxian on Behalf of Roundtree, People ex rel. v. Brown, 568 N.Y.S.2d 575, 570 N.E.2d 223 (N.Y.1991)—§ **3.15, n. 172;** § **3.19;** § **3.19, n. 211;** § **3.36.8;** § **5.23, n. 625.**

Maxian on Behalf of Roundtree, People ex rel. v. Brown, 164 A.D.2d 56, 561 N.Y.S.2d 418 (N.Y.A.D. 1 Dept.1990)—§ **3.19, n. 218.**

Maxian, People ex rel. Brown v., N.Y.L.J., p. 26, col. 6 (Sup.Ct., N.Y.County, 1990)—§ **3.19, n. 217.**

Maye, People v., 584 N.Y.S.2d 1011, 596 N.E.2d 409 (N.Y.1992)—§ **2.4;** § **2.4, n. 84.**

TABLE OF CASES

Mayo, People v., 201 A.D.2d 412, 607 N.Y.S.2d 654 (N.Y.A.D. 1 Dept.1994)—§ 5.22, n. 615.

Mayo, People v., 422 N.Y.S.2d 361, 397 N.E.2d 1166 (N.Y.1979)—§ 2.4; § 2.4, n. 66, 92.

McAllister, People v., 77 Misc.2d 142, 352 N.Y.S.2d 360 (N.Y.City Crim.Ct.1974)—§ 9.2, n. 3; § 9.3, n. 11.

McArthur, People v., 118 Misc.2d 665, 461 N.Y.S.2d 173 (N.Y.Sup.1983)—§ 6.8, n. 178.

McCabe, People v., 87 A.D.2d 852, 449 N.Y.S.2d 245 (N.Y.A.D. 2 Dept.1982)—§ 6.2, n. 38.

McCaffery, People v., 78 A.D.2d 1003, 433 N.Y.S.2d 909 (N.Y.A.D. 4 Dept.1980)—§ 9.33, n. 245.

McCants, People v., 59 A.D.2d 999, 399 N.Y.S.2d 715 (N.Y.A.D. 3 Dept.1977)—§ 10.3, n. 71; § 10.5, n. 102.

McCaskell, People v., 630 N.Y.S.2d 66 (N.Y.A.D. 1 Dept.1995)—§ 10.25, n. 573.

McClain, People v., 343 N.Y.S.2d 601, 296 N.E.2d 454 (N.Y.1973)—§ 11.18, n. 243.

McCloskey, People ex rel. Van Der Beek v., 18 A.D.2d 205, 238 N.Y.S.2d 676 (N.Y.A.D. 1 Dept.1963)—§ 5.8, n. 116.

McConnell, People v., 425 N.Y.S.2d 794, 402 N.E.2d 133 (N.Y.1980)—§ 11.11, n. 110; § 11.12, n. 129, 135; § 11.14; § 11.14, n. 149, 151.

McCowan, People v., 629 N.Y.S.2d 163, 652 N.E.2d 909 (N.Y.1995)—§ 4.10, n. 141.

McCoy, People v., 71 Misc.2d 381, 337 N.Y.S.2d 49 (N.Y.Sup.1972)—§ 10.16, n. 333.

McCoy, People ex rel. v. Higgins, 177 A.D.2d 1052, 578 N.Y.S.2d 70 (N.Y.A.D. 4 Dept.1991)—§ 4.9, n. 118.

McCreary, People v., 186 A.D.2d 1070, 588 N.Y.S.2d 686 (N.Y.A.D. 4 Dept.1992)—§ 10.19, n. 445.

McCullough, People v., 141 A.D.2d 856, 530 N.Y.S.2d 198 (N.Y.A.D. 2 Dept.1988)—§ 5.8, n. 122.

McCummings, People v., 203 A.D.2d 656, 610 N.Y.S.2d 634 (N.Y.A.D. 3 Dept.1994)—§ 9.10, n. 94, 99, 105.

McDermott, People v., 515 N.Y.S.2d 225, 507 N.E.2d 1081 (N.Y.1987)—§ 2.6, n. 133.

McDonald v. Burrows, 731 F.2d 294 (5th Cir.1984)—§ 9.8, n. 51.

McDonald, People ex rel. v. Warden, 354 N.Y.S.2d 939, 310 N.E.2d 537 (N.Y.1974)—§ 4.13, n. 219.

McDonald v. Sobel, 272 A.D. 455, 72 N.Y.S.2d 4 (N.Y.A.D. 2 Dept.1947)—§ 11.3, n. 17.

McDonnell, People v., 277 N.Y.S.2d 257, 223 N.E.2d 785 (N.Y.1966)—§ 10.11, n. 206.

McElvaine, People v., 125 N.Y. 596, 26 N.E. 929 (N.Y.1891)—§ 6.2, n. 13, 22.

McFarlan, People v., 89 Misc.2d 905, 396 N.Y.S.2d 559 (N.Y.Sup.1975)—§ 5.9; § 5.9, n. 216, 226.

McGee, People v., 508 N.Y.S.2d 927, 501 N.E.2d 576 (N.Y.1986)—§ 5.22; § 5.22, n. 609.

McGee, People v., 131 Misc.2d 770, 501 N.Y.S.2d 1002 (N.Y.Sup.1986)—§ 5.18, n. 440.

McGee, People v., 424 N.Y.S.2d 157, 399 N.E.2d 1177 (N.Y.1979)—§ 1.3, n. 42; § 1.4, n. 92.

McGirt, People v., 198 A.D.2d 101, 603 N.Y.S.2d 164 (N.Y.A.D. 1 Dept.1993)—§ 11.13, n. 143.

McGrath v. Gold, 369 N.Y.S.2d 62, 330 N.E.2d 35 (N.Y.1975)—§ 2.8, n. 183.

McGrath, People v., 412 N.Y.S.2d 801, 385 N.E.2d 541 (N.Y.1978)—§ 10.10, n. 200.

McGraw, People v., 158 A.D.2d 719, 552 N.Y.S.2d 166 (N.Y.A.D. 2 Dept.1990)—§ 5.27, n. 765.

McGreevy, People ex rel. Bauer on Behalf of Rhodes v., 147 Misc.2d 213, 555 N.Y.S.2d 581 (N.Y.Sup.1990)—§ 4.5, n. 75; § 4.7, n. 101.

McGreevy, People ex rel. Glass on Behalf of Ryan v., 134 Misc.2d 1085, 514 N.Y.S.2d 622 (N.Y.Sup.1987)—§ 4.10, n. 154.

McGriff, People v., 142 A.D.2d 934, 530 N.Y.S.2d 360 (N.Y.A.D. 4 Dept.1988)—§ 10.2, n. 24, 40.

McGriff, People v., 139 Misc.2d 361, 526 N.Y.S.2d 712 (N.Y.City Crim.Ct.1988)—§ 3.25, n. 324.

McGriff, People v., 130 A.D.2d 141, 518 N.Y.S.2d 795 (N.Y.A.D. 1 Dept.1987)—§ 10.21; § 10.21, n. 505.

McIntosh, People v., 587 N.Y.S.2d 568, 600 N.E.2d 199 (N.Y.1992)—§ 9.26; § 9.26, n. 218; § 9.31, n. 234; § 10.22, n. 516.

McIntosh, People v., 184 A.D.2d 662, 587 N.Y.S.2d 165 (N.Y.A.D. 2 Dept.1992)—§ 7.23, n. 264.

McIntosh, People v., 173 A.D.2d 490, 570 N.Y.S.2d 298 (N.Y.A.D. 2 Dept.1991)—§ 9.10, n. 98.

McIntyre v. State, 142 A.D.2d 856, 530 N.Y.S.2d 898 (N.Y.A.D. 3 Dept.1988)—§ 3.12, n. 128.

McKay, People v., 101 A.D.2d 960, 479 N.Y.S.2d 87 (N.Y.A.D. 3 Dept.1984)—§ 7.4, n. 40.

McKenna, People v., 556 N.Y.S.2d 514, 555 N.E.2d 911 (N.Y.1990)—§ 9.22, n. 177; § 9.47; § 9.47, n. 338, 343.

McKennion, People v., 313 N.Y.S.2d 876, 261 N.E.2d 910 (N.Y.1970)—§ 11.18, n. 243.

McKinney, People v., 215 A.D.2d 407, 625 N.Y.S.2d 667 (N.Y.A.D. 2 Dept.1995)—§ 11.13, n. 139.

McKinney, People v., 145 Misc.2d 460, 546 N.Y.S.2d 927 (N.Y.City Crim.Ct.1989)—§ 3.7, n. 79.

TABLE OF CASES

McKoy v. North Carolina, 494 U.S. 433, 110 S.Ct. 1227, 108 L.Ed.2d 369 (1990)—§ 5.17, n. 372.

McLaughlin, People v., 591 N.Y.S.2d 966, 606 N.E.2d 1357 (N.Y.1992)—§ 1.3, n. 36, 38; § 9.6, n. 32.

McLaurin, People v., 196 A.D.2d 511, 601 N.Y.S.2d 139 (N.Y.A.D. 2 Dept.1993)—§ 5.5, n. 64.

McLees, People v., 166 Misc.2d 260, 631 N.Y.S.2d 990 (N.Y.Sup.1995)—§ 2.10, n. 235.

McMickens, People ex rel. Neufeld on Behalf of Garcia v., 520 N.Y.S.2d 744, 514 N.E.2d 1368 (N.Y.1987)—§ 3.25, n. 336.

McMillan, People v., 212 A.D.2d 445, 622 N.Y.S.2d 935 (N.Y.A.D. 1 Dept.1995)—§ 6.9, n. 199.

McMillan, People v., 125 Misc.2d 177, 479 N.Y.S.2d 449 (N.Y.City Crim.Ct.1984)—§ 3.25, n. 324.

McMoore, People v., 203 A.D.2d 612, 609 N.Y.S.2d 964 (N.Y.A.D. 3 Dept.1994)—§ 5.8, n. 129.

McMullin, People v., 523 N.Y.S.2d 455, 517 N.E.2d 1341 (N.Y.1987)—§ 10.23; § 10.23, n. 548.

McNamee, People v., 145 Misc.2d 187, 547 N.Y.S.2d 519 (N.Y.Sup.1989)—§ 6.3, n. 64; § 6.4, n. 82.

McNeill, People ex rel. Fazio v., 4 A.D.2d 686, 164 N.Y.S.2d 156 (N.Y.A.D. 2 Dept. 1957)—§ 6.10, n. 221, 232.

McPhee, People v., 161 Misc.2d 660, 614 N.Y.S.2d 884 (N.Y.Sup.1994)—§ 6.9, n. 206.

McRay, People v., 435 N.Y.S.2d 679, 416 N.E.2d 1015 (N.Y.1980)—§ 3.18, n. 191.

M., David v. Dwyer, 107 A.D.2d 884, 484 N.Y.S.2d 323 (N.Y.A.D. 3 Dept.1985)—§ 7.11, n. 128.

Mead v. Walker, 839 F.Supp. 1030 (S.D.N.Y.1993)—§ 6.3, n. 50.

Medina v. California, 505 U.S. 437, 112 S.Ct. 2572, 120 L.Ed.2d 353 (1992)—§ 6.1, n. 1.

Medina, People v., 208 A.D.2d 771, 617 N.Y.S.2d 491 (N.Y.A.D. 2 Dept.1994)—§ 2.4, n. 41.

Medina, People v., 198 A.D.2d 146, 603 N.Y.S.2d 858 (N.Y.A.D. 1 Dept.1993)—§ 9.37, n. 270.

Meierdiercks, People v., 505 N.Y.S.2d 51, 496 N.E.2d 210 (N.Y.1986)—§ 9.34, n. 255.

Meldish v. Braatz, 99 A.D.2d 316, 472 N.Y.S.2d 699 (N.Y.A.D. 2 Dept.1984)—§ 5.21, n. 478.

Melendez, People v., 141 A.D.2d 860, 530 N.Y.S.2d 202 (N.Y.A.D. 2 Dept.1988)—§ 10.14, n. 285.

Melendez, People v., 92 A.D.2d 904, 459 N.Y.S.2d 900 (N.Y.A.D. 2 Dept.1983)—§ 9.41, n. 296.

Melillo, People v., 112 Misc.2d 1004, 448 N.Y.S.2d 108 (N.Y.Sup.1982)—§ 8.1, n. 13.

Melo, People v., 160 A.D.2d 600, 554 N.Y.S.2d 530 (N.Y.A.D. 1 Dept.1990)—§ 11.2, n. 1; § 11.3, n. 11.

Melville, People v., 62 Misc.2d 366, 308 N.Y.S.2d 671 (N.Y.City Crim.Ct.1970)—§ 4.5, n. 76.

Melvin, People v., 58 Misc.2d 424, 296 N.Y.S.2d 435 (N.Y.Dist.Ct.1968)—§ 10.19, n. 440.

Menchetti, People v., 560 N.Y.S.2d 760, 561 N.E.2d 536 (N.Y.1990)—§ 5.10; § 5.10, n. 288; § 11.5, n. 41.

Mendez, People v., 320 N.Y.S.2d 39, 268 N.E.2d 778 (N.Y.1971)—§ 10.10, n. 174.

Mendoza, People v., 604 N.Y.S.2d 922, 624 N.E.2d 1017 (N.Y.1993)—§ 5.26, n. 651; § 10.16, n. 322, 328, 334, 344; § 10.17; § 10.17, n. 344, 349, 358; § 10.18; § 10.18, n. 386.

Mendoza, People v., 186 A.D.2d 458, 589 N.Y.S.2d 35 (N.Y.A.D. 1 Dept.1992)—§ 10.17, n. 363.

Menna v. New York, 423 U.S. 61, 96 S.Ct. 241, 46 L.Ed.2d 195 (1975)—§ 2.11, n. 243; § 11.16, n. 201.

Mercedes, People v., 171 A.D.2d 1044, 579 N.Y.S.2d 601 (N.Y.A.D. 4 Dept.1991)—§ 11.18, n. 245.

Meredith, People v., 152 Misc.2d 387, 578 N.Y.S.2d 79 (N.Y.Sup.1991)—§ 4.9, n. 123; § 4.11, n. 190.

Merlo, People v., 195 A.D.2d 576, 600 N.Y.S.2d 494 (N.Y.A.D. 2 Dept.1993)—§ 5.27, n. 797.

Merola, People v., 30 A.D.2d 963, 294 N.Y.S.2d 301 (N.Y.A.D. 2 Dept.1968)—§ 10.20, n. 474.

Merrill, People v., 123 Misc.2d 498, 474 N.Y.S.2d 198 (N.Y.Sup.1984)—§ 6.8, n. 178.

Merrill, People v. — N.Y.S.2d —, 1996 WL 65059 (N.Y.1996)—§ 10.13, n. 266; § 10.29; § 10.29, n. 611.

Mesa v. California, 489 U.S. 121, 109 S.Ct. 959, 103 L.Ed.2d 99 (1989)—§ 1.2, n. 34.

Meurer, People v., 184 A.D.2d 1067, 584 N.Y.S.2d 370 (N.Y.A.D. 4 Dept.1992)—§ 6.5, n. 96.

Meurer, People ex rel. v. Bentley, 202 A.D.2d 1042, 609 N.Y.S.2d 466 (N.Y.A.D. 4 Dept.1994)—§ 9.25, n. 204.

Meyers, People v., 114 A.D.2d 861, 494 N.Y.S.2d 897 (N.Y.A.D. 2 Dept.1985)—§ 9.43, n. 310.

Mezon, People v., 589 N.Y.S.2d 838, 603 N.E.2d 943 (N.Y.1992)—§ 3.26, n. 353; § 5.26, n. 661; § 8.1, n. 25; § 9.49, n. 360; § 10.16, n. 312, 313.

Michael, People v., 420 N.Y.S.2d 371, 394 N.E.2d 1134 (N.Y.1979)—§ 2.4, n. 47, 56; § 2.11, n. 240; § 11.16, n. 201.

TABLE OF CASES

Michallow, People v., 201 A.D.2d 915, 607 N.Y.S.2d 781 (N.Y.A.D. 4 Dept.1994)—§ 2.4, n. 43.
Michel, People v., 453 N.Y.S.2d 639, 439 N.E.2d 355 (N.Y.1982)—§ 10.27, n. 592.
Michelson v. Clyne, 84 A.D.2d 883, 444 N.Y.S.2d 331 (N.Y.A.D. 3 Dept.1981)—§ 1.2, n. 24.
Michigan v. Lucas, 500 U.S. 145, 111 S.Ct. 1743, 114 L.Ed.2d 205 (1991)—§ 7.1, n. 3; § 7.24, n. 275.
Michigan v. Tucker, 417 U.S. 433, 94 S.Ct. 2357, 41 L.Ed.2d 182 (1974)—§ 10.10, n. 175.
Middlemiss, People v., 198 A.D.2d 755, 604 N.Y.S.2d 308 (N.Y.A.D. 3 Dept.1993)—§ 5.23, n. 622.
Middleton, People v., 444 N.Y.S.2d 581, 429 N.E.2d 100 (N.Y.1981)—§ 1.2, n. 18; § 5.9, n. 235.
Midland Ins. Co., People v., 97 Misc.2d 341, 411 N.Y.S.2d 521 (N.Y.Sup.1978)—§ 4.12, n. 194.
Mikolasko, People v., 144 A.D.2d 760, 535 N.Y.S.2d 167 (N.Y.A.D. 3 Dept.1988)—§ 10.5, n. 111.
Miles, People v., 192 A.D.2d 781, 596 N.Y.S.2d 482 (N.Y.A.D. 3 Dept.1993)—§ 2.10, n. 214.
Miles, People v., 485 N.Y.S.2d 747, 475 N.E.2d 118 (N.Y.1984)—§ 3.2, n. 13.
Millan, People v., 516 N.Y.S.2d 168, 508 N.E.2d 903 (N.Y.1987)—§ 10.11; § 10.11, n. 225.
Millan, United States v., 2 F.3d 17 (2nd Cir.1993)—§ 2.10, n. 233.
Miller v. Angliker, 848 F.2d 1312 (2nd Cir. 1988)—§ 11.15, n. 165.
Miller, Application of, 46 A.D.2d 177, 362 N.Y.S.2d 628 (N.Y.A.D. 4 Dept.1974)—§ 4.5, n. 70.
Miller, People v., 197 A.D.2d 925, 602 N.Y.S.2d 272 (N.Y.A.D. 4 Dept.1993)—§ 5.15, n. 341.
Miller, People v., 183 A.D.2d 790, 583 N.Y.S.2d 517 (N.Y.A.D. 2 Dept.1992)—§ 7.17, n. 207.
Miller, People v., 170 A.D.2d 464, 565 N.Y.S.2d 553 (N.Y.A.D. 2 Dept.1991)—§ 11.13, n. 137.
Miller, People v., 167 A.D.2d 958, 562 N.Y.S.2d 300 (N.Y.A.D. 4 Dept.1990)—§ 6.4, n. 74.
Miller, People v., 144 A.D.2d 94, 537 N.Y.S.2d 318 (N.Y.A.D. 3 Dept.1989)—§ 5.8, n. 179.
Miller, People v., 142 A.D.2d 760, 530 N.Y.S.2d 866 (N.Y.A.D. 3 Dept.1988)—§ 10.27, n. 595.
Miller, People v., 126 A.D.2d 868, 511 N.Y.S.2d 160 (N.Y.A.D. 3 Dept.1987)—§ 11.5, n. 59.
Miller, People v., 493 N.Y.S.2d 96, 482 N.E.2d 892 (N.Y.1985)—§ 2.10, n. 213; § 10.15; § 10.15, n. 305.
Miller, People v., 106 A.D.2d 787, 484 N.Y.S.2d 183 (N.Y.A.D. 3 Dept.1984)—§ 7.9, n. 94.
Miller, People v., 120 Misc.2d 30, 465 N.Y.S.2d 120 (N.Y.Town Ct.1983)—§ 1.5, n. 132.
Miller, People v., 79 A.D.2d 687, 434 N.Y.S.2d 36 (N.Y.A.D. 2 Dept.1980)—§ 11.3, n. 25.
Miller, People v., 78 A.D.2d 817, 433 N.Y.S.2d 130 (N.Y.A.D. 1 Dept.1980)—§ 9.28, n. 221.
Miller, People v., 398 N.Y.S.2d 133, 367 N.E.2d 640 (N.Y.1977)—§ 11.18, n. 243.
Miller, People v., 84 Misc.2d 310, 376 N.Y.S.2d 393 (N.Y.City Crim.Ct.1975)—§ 6.10, n. 220.
Miller, People v., 75 Misc.2d 1, 346 N.Y.S.2d 144 (N.Y.Co.Ct.1973)—§ 5.12, n. 316.
Miller v. Schwartz, 532 N.Y.S.2d 354, 528 N.E.2d 507 (N.Y.1988)—§ 7.2, n. 9; § 7.4, n. 51.
Mills, People v., 154 A.D.2d 405, 545 N.Y.S.2d 792 (N.Y.A.D. 2 Dept.1989)—§ 5.10, n. 274.
Mills, People v., 142 A.D.2d 653, 530 N.Y.S.2d 593 (N.Y.A.D. 2 Dept.1988)—§ 7.17, n. 207.
Millson, People v., 93 A.D.2d 899, 461 N.Y.S.2d 586 (N.Y.A.D. 3 Dept.1983)—§ 5.8, n. 179.
Mincey v. Arizona, 437 U.S. 385, 98 S.Ct. 2408, 57 L.Ed.2d 290 (1978)—§ 10.14, n. 287.
Min Chi Ma, People v., 161 Misc.2d 542, 615 N.Y.S.2d 222 (N.Y.Sup.1994)—§ 5.26, n. 668.
Miner, People v., 126 A.D.2d 798, 510 N.Y.S.2d 300 (N.Y.A.D. 3 Dept.1987)—§ 10.6, n. 129.
Minnesota v. Olson, 495 U.S. 91, 110 S.Ct. 1684, 109 L.Ed.2d 85 (1990)—§ 10.11; § 10.11, n. 236.
Miranda v. Isseks, 41 A.D.2d 176, 341 N.Y.S.2d 541 (N.Y.A.D. 2 Dept.1973)—§ 5.27, n. 691.
Miranda, People v., 115 Misc.2d 533, 455 N.Y.S.2d 247 (N.Y.Sup.1982)—§ 7.8, n. 79.
Miret–Gonzalez, People v., 159 A.D.2d 647, 552 N.Y.S.2d 958 (N.Y.A.D. 2 Dept. 1990)—§ 10.21, n. 501.
Missouri v. Hunter, 459 U.S. 359, 103 S.Ct. 673, 74 L.Ed.2d 535 (1983)—§ 2.10, n. 216.
Misuis, People v., 419 N.Y.S.2d 961, 393 N.E.2d 1034 (N.Y.1979)—§ 10.19, n. 409.
Mitchell, People v., 605 N.Y.S.2d 655, 626 N.E.2d 630 (N.Y.1993)—§ 5.6; § 5.6, n. 89; § 5.7; § 5.7, n. 98; § 5.27, n. 744.
Mitchell, People v., 189 A.D.2d 900, 592 N.Y.S.2d 988 (N.Y.A.D. 2 Dept.1993)—§ 5.27, n. 797.

TABLE OF CASES

Mitchell, People v., 128 A.D.2d 731, 513 N.Y.S.2d 225 (N.Y.A.D. 2 Dept.1987)—§ 10.22, n. 533; § 11.16, n. 210.

Mitchell, People v., 106 A.D.2d 478, 482 N.Y.S.2d 574 (N.Y.A.D. 2 Dept.1984)—§ 9.39, n. 283.

Mitchell, People v., 99 A.D.2d 609, 472 N.Y.S.2d 166 (N.Y.A.D. 3 Dept.1984)—§ 5.27, n. 759.

Mitchell, People ex rel. Sykes on Behalf of Rodriguez v., 184 A.D.2d 466, 586 N.Y.S.2d 937 (N.Y.A.D. 1 Dept.1992)—§ 9.25, n. 206; § 9.47, n. 339.

M., Matter of Luis, 608 N.Y.S.2d 962, 630 N.E.2d 658 (N.Y.1994)—§ 10.25, n. 564.

Mobley, People v., 190 A.D.2d 821, 593 N.Y.S.2d 839 (N.Y.A.D. 2 Dept.1993)—§ 7.17, n. 209.

Mobley, People v., 162 A.D.2d 305, 558 N.Y.S.2d 1 (N.Y.A.D. 1 Dept.1990)—§ 7.19, n. 223.

Modica, People ex rel. v. Hoy, 51 Misc.2d 579, 273 N.Y.S.2d 634 (N.Y.Sup.1966)—§ 4.13, n. 220.

Mohler v. State, 84 Md.App. 431, 579 A.2d 1208 (Md.App.1990)—§ 9.55, n. 402.

Moissett, People v., 563 N.Y.S.2d 43, 564 N.E.2d 653 (N.Y.1990)—§ 11.17, n. 219.

Molfino, People v., 178 A.D.2d 238, 577 N.Y.S.2d 787 (N.Y.A.D. 1 Dept.1991)—§ 5.27, n. 788; § 11.3, n. 28.

Molineux, People v., 168 N.Y. 264, 61 N.E. 286 (N.Y.1901)—§ 5.21; § 5.21, n. 488; § 7.15, n. 172.

Monaco, People v., 121 Misc.2d 976, 469 N.Y.S.2d 863 (N.Y.Sup.1983)—§ 9.5, n. 22.

Mondon, People v., 129 Misc.2d 13, 492 N.Y.S.2d 344 (N.Y.Sup.1985)—§ 7.4, n. 31.

Monroe, People v., 125 Misc.2d 550, 480 N.Y.S.2d 259 (N.Y.Sup.1984)—§ 5.1, n. 7.

Monserrate v. Upper Court St. Book Store, Inc., 425 N.Y.S.2d 304, 401 N.E.2d 414 (N.Y.1980)—§ 10.3, n. 65.

Montana Department of Revenue v. Kurth Ranch, ___ U.S. ___, 114 S.Ct. 1937, 128 L.Ed.2d 767 (1994)—§ 2.10, n. 230.

Montanye, People v., 95 A.D.2d 959, 464 N.Y.S.2d 292 (N.Y.A.D. 3 Dept.1983)—§ 3.30, n. 410; § 11.2, n. 9.

Montanye, People ex rel. Colcloughley v., 49 A.D.2d 1034, 374 N.Y.S.2d 504 (N.Y.A.D. 4 Dept.1975)—§ 5.18, n. 432.

Montgomery, People v., 205 A.D.2d 543, 614 N.Y.S.2d 277 (N.Y.A.D. 2 Dept. 1994)—§ 4.12, n. 204.

Moore, People v., 213 A.D.2d 352, 624 N.Y.S.2d 412 (N.Y.A.D. 1 Dept.1995)—§ 10.17, n. 371.

Moore, People v., 530 N.Y.S.2d 94, 525 N.E.2d 740 (N.Y.1988)—§ 11.10, n. 95.

Moore, People v., 412 N.Y.S.2d 795, 385 N.E.2d 535 (N.Y.1978)—§ 1.4, n. 74, 81, 106, 111, 122.

Moore v. Santucci, 151 A.D.2d 677, 543 N.Y.S.2d 103 (N.Y.A.D. 2 Dept.1989)—§ 7.33, n. 367.

Moorhead, People v., 473 N.Y.S.2d 967, 462 N.E.2d 144 (N.Y.1984)—§ 9.43, n. 317.

Moquin, People v., 568 N.Y.S.2d 710, 570 N.E.2d 1059 (N.Y.1991)—§ 2.4, n. 82; § 3.32, n. 443; § 5.28, n. 801; § 5.29, n. 822; § 11.2; § 11.2, n. 4, 5; § 11.3, n. 17; § 11.19, n. 256.

Moquin, People ex rel. v. Infante, 134 A.D.2d 764, 521 N.Y.S.2d 580 (N.Y.A.D. 3 Dept.1987)—§ 4.5, n. 75; § 4.10, n. 153; § 4.13, n. 218.

Morales, People v., 591 N.Y.S.2d 825, 606 N.E.2d 953 (N.Y.1992)—§ 10.19, n. 399.

Morales, People v., 97 Misc.2d 733, 412 N.Y.S.2d 310 (N.Y.City Crim.Ct.1979)—§ 7.30, n. 340.

Morbelli, People v., 144 Misc.2d 482, 544 N.Y.S.2d 442 (N.Y.City Crim.Ct.1989)—§ 1.3, n. 63.

Mordkofsky, People ex rel. v. Stancari, 93 A.D.2d 826, 460 N.Y.S.2d 830 (N.Y.A.D. 2 Dept.1983)—§ 4.5, n. 88.

Moreno, People v., 196 A.D.2d 850, 602 N.Y.S.2d 28 (N.Y.A.D. 2 Dept.1993)—§ 11.13, n. 139.

Morgan, People v., 638 N.Y.S.2d 942, 662 N.E.2d 260 (N.Y.1995)—§ 6.2, n. 13, 14, 22, 30, 41; § 6.10, n. 223.

Morgan, People v., 162 A.D.2d 723, 558 N.Y.S.2d 88 (N.Y.A.D. 2 Dept.1990)—§ 10.6, n. 132.

Morgenthau v. Altman, 462 N.Y.S.2d 629, 449 N.E.2d 409 (N.Y.1983)—§ 5.1, n. 11; § 5.4; § 5.4, n. 57; § 5.8, n. 171.

Morgenthau v. Roberts, 492 N.Y.S.2d 21, 481 N.E.2d 561 (N.Y.1985)—§ 9.49, n. 356.

Morgenthau v. Rosenberger, 633 N.Y.S.2d 473, 657 N.E.2d 494 (N.Y.1995)—§ 4.9, n. 125.

Morrell, People v., 97 A.D.2d 703, 468 N.Y.S.2d 127 (N.Y.A.D. 1 Dept.1983)—§ 9.47, n. 332.

Morris, People v., 204 A.D.2d 973, 613 N.Y.S.2d 66 (N.Y.A.D. 4 Dept.1994)—§ 5.7, n. 102.

Morris, People v., 153 A.D.2d 984, 545 N.Y.S.2d 427 (N.Y.A.D. 3 Dept.1989)—§ 7.17, n. 193.

Morris, People v., 111 A.D.2d 414, 489 N.Y.S.2d 610 (N.Y.A.D. 2 Dept.1985)—§ 11.15, n. 190.

Morris, People v., 473 N.Y.S.2d 769, 461 N.E.2d 1256 (N.Y.1984)—§ 5.11, n. 311; § 5.14, n. 330; § 5.15, n. 341.

Morrison, People v., 148 Misc.2d 61, 559 N.Y.S.2d 1013 (N.Y.City Crim.Ct. 1990)—§ 7.8, n. 81, 83.

Morse, People v., 476 N.Y.S.2d 505, 465 N.E.2d 12 (N.Y.1984)—§ 11.5, n. 59.

Moschelle, People v., 96 Misc.2d 1030, 410 N.Y.S.2d 764 (N.Y.Sup.1978)—§ 5.9, n. 219.

TABLE OF CASES

Moselle, People v., 454 N.Y.S.2d 292, 439 N.E.2d 1235 (N.Y.1982)—§ 10.9, n. 167.
Moskowicz, People v., 192 A.D.2d 317, 595 N.Y.S.2d 464 (N.Y.A.D. 1 Dept.1993)— § 5.8, n. 129, 145.
Mosley, People v., 508 N.Y.S.2d 931, 501 N.E.2d 580 (N.Y.1986)—§ 10.11, n. 225.
Moss, People v., 587 N.Y.S.2d 593, 600 N.E.2d 224 (N.Y.1992)—§ 10.28, n. 607.
Mossow, People v., 118 Misc.2d 522, 461 N.Y.S.2d 191 (N.Y.Co.Ct.1983)—§ 1.8, n. 185.
Moulton, People v., 172 A.D.2d 1001, 569 N.Y.S.2d 220 (N.Y.A.D. 3 Dept.1991)— § 9.33, n. 245.
Moye, People v., 171 A.D.2d 1036, 569 N.Y.S.2d 38 (N.Y.A.D. 4 Dept.1991)— § 11.10, n. 108.
Muhanimac, People v., 181 A.D.2d 464, 581 N.Y.S.2d 301 (N.Y.A.D. 1 Dept.1992)— § 9.34, n. 257; § 9.37, n. 271.
Mulholland, People v., 129 A.D.2d 857, 514 N.Y.S.2d 135 (N.Y.A.D. 3 Dept.1987)— § 6.10, n. 260.
Mullins, People v., 137 A.D.2d 227, 528 N.Y.S.2d 698 (N.Y.A.D. 3 Dept.1988)— § 6.2, n. 38; § 6.4, n. 73.
Mullooly, People v., 37 A.D.2d 6, 322 N.Y.S.2d 7 (N.Y.A.D. 1 Dept.1971)— § 6.10, n. 254.
Mulvaney v. Dubin, 80 A.D.2d 566, 435 N.Y.S.2d 761 (N.Y.A.D. 2 Dept.1981)— § 7.2, n. 9.
Mundhenk, People v., 141 Mjsc.2d 795, 534 N.Y.S.2d 843 (N.Y.Co.Ct.1988)—§ 1.7, n. 153.
Munger, People v., 301 N.Y.S.2d 39, 248 N.E.2d 882 (N.Y.1969)—§ 5.21, n. 492.
Muniz, People v., 129 Misc.2d 456, 493 N.Y.S.2d 241 (N.Y.City Crim.Ct.1985)— § 3.25, n. 324.
Munnelly, People v., 158 Misc.2d 340, 601 N.Y.S.2d 204 (N.Y.Dist.Ct.1993)—§ 3.6, n. 61.
Munoz, People v., 207 A.D.2d 418, 615 N.Y.S.2d 730 (N.Y.A.D. 2 Dept.1994)— § 5.8, n. 130.
Munoz, People v., 205 A.D.2d 452, 613 N.Y.S.2d 892 (N.Y.A.D. 1 Dept.1994)— § 10.3, n. 72.
Murphy, People v., 188 A.D.2d 742, 591 N.Y.S.2d 860 (N.Y.A.D. 3 Dept.1992)— § 7.30, n. 341.
Murphy, People v., 154 Misc.2d 777, 586 N.Y.S.2d 716 (N.Y.Co.Ct.1992)—§ 4.10, n. 151.
Murphy, People v., 525 N.Y.S.2d 834, 520 N.E.2d 552 (N.Y.1988)—§ 1.10, n. 240.
Murphy, People v., 99 A.D.2d 613, 472 N.Y.S.2d 202 (N.Y.A.D. 3 Dept.1984)— § 9.11, n. 112.
Murphy, People v., 53 A.D.2d 530, 384 N.Y.S.2d 180 (N.Y.A.D. 1 Dept.1976)— § 11.19, n. 263, 265.
Murphy v. Waterfront Commission of New York Harbor, 378 U.S. 52, 84 S.Ct. 1594, 12 L.Ed.2d 678 (1964)—§ 5.9; § 5.9, n. 203, 218; § 10.10, n. 183.
Murray, People v., 634 N.Y.S.2d 985 (N.Y.Sup.1995)—§ 5.27, n. 775.
Murray, People v., 172 A.D.2d 437, 569 N.Y.S.2d 12 (N.Y.A.D. 1 Dept.1991)— § 10.16, n. 323; § 10.17; § 10.17, n. 354; § 10.18, n. 387.
Murray, People v., 140 A.D.2d 949, 529 N.Y.S.2d 628 (N.Y.A.D. 4 Dept.1988)— § 7.14, n. 164.
Murray, People v., 130 A.D.2d 773, 515 N.Y.S.2d 847 (N.Y.A.D. 2 Dept.1987)— § 10.22, n. 528.
Murray, People v., 127 A.D.2d 704, 512 N.Y.S.2d 111 (N.Y.A.D. 2 Dept.1987)— § 9.15, n. 144.
Murray, People v., 63 A.D.2d 708, 404 N.Y.S.2d 692 (N.Y.A.D. 2 Dept.1978)— § 11.12, n. 133.
Murray, People ex rel. v. New York State Bd. of Parole, 70 A.D.2d 918, 417 N.Y.S.2d 286 (N.Y.A.D. 2 Dept.1979)— § 3.29, n. 398.
Murray v. United States, 487 U.S. 533, 108 S.Ct. 2529, 101 L.Ed.2d 472 (1988)— § 10.10, n. 181, 188.
Muwwakkil v. Hoke, 968 F.2d 284 (2nd Cir.1992)—§ 9.8, n. 54.
Myers, People v., 171 A.D.2d 148, 575 N.Y.S.2d 152 (N.Y.A.D. 2 Dept.1991)— § 9.26, n. 220.
Myles, People v., 107 Misc.2d 960, 436 N.Y.S.2d 134 (N.Y.Co.Ct.1981)—§ 1.7, n. 145.
Myrick, People v., 498 N.Y.S.2d 773, 489 N.E.2d 742 (N.Y.1985)—§ 10.28, n. 607.

Nadeau v. Sullivan, 204 A.D.2d 913, 612 N.Y.S.2d 501 (N.Y.A.D. 3 Dept.1994)— § 4.10, n. 148.
Nardone v. United States, 308 U.S. 338, 60 S.Ct. 266, 84 L.Ed. 307 (1939)—§ 10.10, n. 173.
Nash v. United States, 54 F.2d 1006 (2nd Cir.1932)—§ 5.22, n. 577.
Nassau, County of v. Sullivan, 194 A.D.2d 236, 606 N.Y.S.2d 249 (N.Y.A.D. 2 Dept. 1993)—§ 7.14, n. 156; § 7.17, n. 193.
Natal, People v., 553 N.Y.S.2d 650, 553 N.E.2d 239 (N.Y.1990)—§ 7.8, n. 78.
Natarelli, People v., 154 A.D.2d 769, 546 N.Y.S.2d 219 (N.Y.A.D. 3 Dept.1989)— § 5.27, n. 758, 765.
Neal, People v., 160 Misc.2d 173, 607 N.Y.S.2d 866 (N.Y.Sup.1994)—§ 9.38, n. 276.
Neely v. Hogan, 62 Misc.2d 1056, 310 N.Y.S.2d 63 (N.Y.Sup.1970)—§ 6.3, n. 50.
Negron, People v., 105 Misc.2d 492, 432 N.Y.S.2d 348 (N.Y.Sup.1980)—§ 5.21, n. 502, 508; § 8.1, n. 18.

TABLE OF CASES

Nelson v. Mollen, 175 A.D.2d 518, 573 N.Y.S.2d 99 (N.Y.A.D. 3 Dept.1991)—§ 5.3, n. 52.

Nelson v. O'Neil, 402 U.S. 622, 91 S.Ct. 1723, 29 L.Ed.2d 222 (1971)—§ 5.22, n. 571, 587.

Nelson, People v., 151 Misc.2d 951, 574 N.Y.S.2d 144 (N.Y.Sup.1991)—§ 7.33, n. 363.

Nelson, People v., 173 A.D.2d 205, 569 N.Y.S.2d 86 (N.Y.A.D. 1 Dept.1991)—§ 11.15, n. 184.

Neufeld on Behalf of Garcia, People ex rel. v. McMickens, 520 N.Y.S.2d 744, 514 N.E.2d 1368 (N.Y.1987)—§ 3.25, n. 336.

Neulist, People v., 43 A.D.2d 150, 350 N.Y.S.2d 178 (N.Y.A.D. 2 Dept.1973)—§ 10.6, n. 126.

Newball, People v., 561 N.Y.S.2d 898, 563 N.E.2d 269 (N.Y.1990)—§ 10.23, n. 549; § 10.26, n. 585; § 10.29, n. 613.

New Jersey v. Portash, 440 U.S. 450, 99 S.Ct. 1292, 59 L.Ed.2d 501 (1979)—§ 6.9, n. 210.

New York City, People ex rel. Tannuzzo v., 174 A.D.2d 443, 571 N.Y.S.2d 230 (N.Y.A.D. 1 Dept.1991)—§ 4.10, n. 152.

New York City Human Resources Administration-Department of Social Services v. Carey, 107 A.D.2d 625, 484 N.Y.S.2d 10 (N.Y.A.D. 1 Dept.1985)—§ 6.10, n. 233.

New York, City of v. Wright, 162 Misc.2d 572, 618 N.Y.S.2d 938 (N.Y.Sup.1994)—§ 2.10, n. 234.

New York State Bd. of Parole, People ex rel. Murray v., 70 A.D.2d 918, 417 N.Y.S.2d 286 (N.Y.A.D. 2 Dept.1979)—§ 3.29, n. 398.

Nibur, People v., 113 A.D.2d 957, 493 N.Y.S.2d 855 (N.Y.A.D. 2 Dept.1985)—§ 10.5, n. 91, 96.

Nicely, United States v., 922 F.2d 850, 287 U.S.App.D.C. 322 (D.C.Cir.1991)—§ 5.22, n. 550.

Nicholas, People v., 157 Misc.2d 947, 599 N.Y.S.2d 779 (N.Y.Sup.1993)—§ 7.33, n. 364.

Nicholas, People v., 35 A.D.2d 18, 312 N.Y.S.2d 645 (N.Y.A.D. 3 Dept.1970)—§ 5.17, n. 372.

Nichols, United States v., 56 F.3d 403 (2nd Cir.1995)—§ 6.2, n. 22.

Nicholson, People v., 98 A.D.2d 876, 470 N.Y.S.2d 854 (N.Y.A.D. 3 Dept.1983)—§ 11.15, n. 173.

Nielson, People v., 115 A.D.2d 972, 497 N.Y.S.2d 537 (N.Y.A.D. 4 Dept.1985)—§ 7.31, n. 352.

Niemczycki, People v., 67 A.D.2d 442, 415 N.Y.S.2d 258 (N.Y.A.D. 2 Dept.1979)—§ 10.5, n. 86, 99, 100.

Nieves, People v., 205 A.D.2d 173, 617 N.Y.S.2d 751 (N.Y.A.D. 1 Dept.1994)—§ 1.3, n. 39, 40.

Nieves, People v., 369 N.Y.S.2d 50, 330 N.E.2d 26 (N.Y.1975)—§ 10.5, n. 84, 90; § 10.6, n. 129.

Nitzberg, People v., 289 N.Y. 523, 47 N.E.2d 37 (N.Y.1943)—§ 5.27, n. 688.

Nix v. Williams, 467 U.S. 431, 104 S.Ct. 2501, 81 L.Ed.2d 377 (1984)—§ 10.10; § 10.10, n. 187.

Nixon, People v., 287 N.Y.S.2d 659, 234 N.E.2d 687 (N.Y.1967)—§ 11.7, n. 68; § 11.10, n. 93.

Nixon, United States v., 418 U.S. 683, 94 S.Ct. 3090, 41 L.Ed.2d 1039 (1974)—§ 7.8, n. 90.

Nocerino, People v., 159 A.D.2d 358, 553 N.Y.S.2d 2 (N.Y.A.D. 1 Dept.1990)—§ 9.10, n. 89.

Norman, People v., 150 Misc.2d 583, 569 N.Y.S.2d 573 (N.Y.City Crim.Ct.1991)—§ 9.5; § 9.5, n. 20.

North Carolina v. Alford, 400 U.S. 25, 91 S.Ct. 160, 27 L.Ed.2d 162 (1970)—§ 2.4, n. 73; § 11.10, n. 100.

North Carolina v. Pearce, 395 U.S. 711, 89 S.Ct. 2072, 23 L.Ed.2d 656 (1969)—§ 2.10, n. 211.

North Street Book Shoppe, Inc., People v., 139 A.D.2d 118, 530 N.Y.S.2d 869 (N.Y.A.D. 3 Dept.1988)—§ 2.6, n. 117.

Nova, People v., 198 A.D.2d 193, 603 N.Y.S.2d 863 (N.Y.A.D. 1 Dept.1993)—§ 10.10, n. 197.

Novoa, People v., 522 N.Y.S.2d 504, 517 N.E.2d 219 (N.Y.1987)—§ 7.12, n. 137, 140; § 7.22, n. 247.

Nuccio, People v., 571 N.Y.S.2d 693, 575 N.E.2d 111 (N.Y.1991)—§ 1.8, n. 165; § 3.3, n. 35; § 3.7, n. 86; § 3.27, n. 354.

Nunez, People v., 157 Misc.2d 793, 598 N.Y.S.2d 917 (N.Y.Sup.1993)—§ 5.29, n. 810.

Nunez, People v., 136 Misc.2d 1062, 519 N.Y.S.2d 623 (N.Y.Sup.1987)—§ 5.1, n. 7.

N.Y.C. Penitentiary, People ex rel. Barnes v., 75 Misc.2d 291, 347 N.Y.S.2d 383 (N.Y.Sup.1973)—§ 9.6, n. 24.

Oakes, People v., 168 A.D.2d 893, 565 N.Y.S.2d 648 (N.Y.A.D. 4 Dept.1990)—§ 7.26, n. 288.

Oakley, People v., 321 N.Y.S.2d 596, 270 N.E.2d 318 (N.Y.1971)—§ 5.7, n. 97; § 5.27, n. 728; § 10.10, n. 198; § 10.12, n. 246.

O'Brien, People v., 453 N.Y.S.2d 638, 439 N.E.2d 354 (N.Y.1982)—§ 9.12, n. 121; § 9.49, n. 361; § 11.15, n. 186, 189.

Ocasio, People v., 160 Misc.2d 422, 609 N.Y.S.2d 523 (N.Y.Sup.1994)—§ 5.8, n. 138, 151, 157.

Ocasio, People v., 134 A.D.2d 293, 520 N.Y.S.2d 620 (N.Y.A.D. 2 Dept.1987)—§ 10.19, n. 428.

TABLE OF CASES

O'Connell, People v., 133 A.D.2d 970, 521 N.Y.S.2d 121 (N.Y.A.D. 3 Dept.1987)—**§ 9.26, n. 219; § 9.49, n. 359.**

Oditnarian Boodhoo, People v., 191 A.D.2d 448, 593 N.Y.S.2d 882 (N.Y.A.D. 2 Dept. 1993)—**§ 11.9, n. 83.**

O'Doherty, People v., 522 N.Y.S.2d 498, 517 N.E.2d 213 (N.Y.1987)—**§ 10.13, n. 267, 275; § 10.23; § 10.23, n. 546, 547; § 10.27; § 10.27, n. 591.**

O'Donnell, People v., 146 A.D.2d 923, 536 N.Y.S.2d 889 (N.Y.A.D. 3 Dept.1989)—**§ 10.3, n. 68.**

Ohio v. Roberts, 448 U.S. 56, 100 S.Ct. 2531, 65 L.Ed.2d 597 (1980)—**§ 5.22, n. 589.**

Ohrenstein, People v., 563 N.Y.S.2d 744, 565 N.E.2d 493 (N.Y.1990)—**§ 5.23, n. 628.**

Okafore, People v., 531 N.Y.S.2d 762, 527 N.E.2d 245 (N.Y.1988)—**§ 2.5; § 2.5, n. 108; § 5.15, n. 343.**

Okun, People v., 135 A.D.2d 1064, 522 N.Y.S.2d 991 (N.Y.A.D. 3 Dept.1987)—**§ 10.5, n. 110; § 10.15, n. 307; § 10.16, n. 325.**

Oliver v. Justices of New York Supreme Court of New York County, 364 N.Y.S.2d 874, 324 N.E.2d 348 (N.Y. 1974)—**§ 2.4, n. 69.**

Oliver, People v., 182 A.D.2d 716, 582 N.Y.S.2d 265 (N.Y.A.D. 2 Dept.1992)—**§ 11.11, n. 116.**

Oliver, People v., 171 N.Y.S.2d 811, 148 N.E.2d 874 (N.Y.1958)—**§ 5.16; § 5.16, n. 352.**

Olvera, United States v., 954 F.2d 788 (2nd Cir.1992)—**§ 11.9, n. 83.**

Omaro, People v., 201 A.D.2d 324, 607 N.Y.S.2d 44 (N.Y.A.D. 1 Dept.1994)—**§ 10.17, n. 370.**

O'Neal, People v., 99 A.D.2d 844, 472 N.Y.S.2d 449 (N.Y.A.D. 2 Dept.1984)—**§ 9.43, n. 315.**

One Assortment of 89 Firearms, United States v., 465 U.S. 354, 104 S.Ct. 1099, 79 L.Ed.2d 361 (1984)—**§ 2.10, n. 225.**

Ordine, People v., 177 A.D.2d 734, 575 N.Y.S.2d 977 (N.Y.A.D. 3 Dept.1991)—**§ 7.4, n. 41.**

Oreckinto, People v., 178 A.D.2d 562, 577 N.Y.S.2d 470 (N.Y.A.D. 2 Dept.1991)—**§ 5.27, n. 733.**

Oregon v. Elstad, 470 U.S. 298, 105 S.Ct. 1285, 84 L.Ed.2d 222 (1985)—**§ 10.10, n. 196.**

Oregon v. Kennedy, 456 U.S. 667, 102 S.Ct. 2083, 72 L.Ed.2d 416 (1982)—**§ 2.4, n. 40.**

Orse, People v., 118 A.D.2d 816, 500 N.Y.S.2d 173 (N.Y.A.D. 2 Dept.1986)—**§ 9.41, n. 294.**

Ortega, People v., 152 Misc.2d 84, 575 N.Y.S.2d 247 (N.Y.City Crim.Ct.1991)—**§ 1.3, n. 62, 67.**

Ortiz, People v., 209 A.D.2d 332, 619 N.Y.S.2d 12 (N.Y.A.D. 1 Dept.1994)—**§ 9.14, n. 132.**

Ortiz, People v., 611 N.Y.S.2d 500, 633 N.E.2d 1104 (N.Y.1994)—**§ 10.11, n. 239.**

Ortiz, People v., 127 A.D.2d 305, 515 N.Y.S.2d 317 (N.Y.A.D. 3 Dept.1987)—**§ 11.15, n. 165.**

Ortiz, People v., 75 Misc.2d 997, 349 N.Y.S.2d 944 (N.Y.City Crim.Ct.1973)—**§ 4.4, n. 50.**

Ortlieb, People v., 622 N.Y.S.2d 501, 646 N.E.2d 803 (N.Y.1994)—**§ 3.19, n. 223.**

Osgood, People v., 436 N.Y.S.2d 213, 417 N.E.2d 507 (N.Y.1980)—**§ 3.7, n. 77; § 3.9, n. 110; § 3.27, n. 354; § 9.15; § 9.15, n. 139, 143; § 9.16, n. 146.**

Ossakow, People ex rel. Fruchtman v., 335 N.Y.S.2d 301, 286 N.E.2d 736 (N.Y. 1972)—**§ 4.5, n. 76.**

O'Sullivan, People v., 121 A.D.2d 658, 504 N.Y.S.2d 49 (N.Y.A.D. 2 Dept.1986)—**§ 9.14, n. 132.**

Otero, People v., 177 A.D.2d 284, 575 N.Y.S.2d 862 (N.Y.A.D. 1 Dept.1991)—**§ 10.5, n. 96.**

Outer, People v., 197 A.D.2d 543, 602 N.Y.S.2d 215 (N.Y.A.D. 2 Dept.1993)—**§ 11.9, n. 90.**

Outley, People v., 594 N.Y.S.2d 683, 610 N.E.2d 356 (N.Y.1993)—**§ 11.13; § 11.13, n. 136, 141.**

Owen v. Stroebel, 491 N.Y.S.2d 611, 481 N.E.2d 243 (N.Y.1985)—**§ 2.4, n. 61.**

Owens, People v., 291 N.Y.S.2d 313, 238 N.E.2d 715 (N.Y.1968)—**§ 5.22, n. 611, 614.**

Pacheco, People v., 152 A.D.2d 641, 543 N.Y.S.2d 170 (N.Y.A.D. 2 Dept.1989)—**§ 11.19, n. 266.**

Pacifico, People v., 105 Misc.2d 396, 432 N.Y.S.2d 588 (N.Y.City Crim.Ct.1980)—**§ 3.8, n. 98.**

Padilla, People v., 627 N.Y.S.2d 914 (N.Y.A.D. 1 Dept.1995)—**§ 9.51, n. 377.**

Padilla, People v., 132 A.D.2d 578, 517 N.Y.S.2d 299 (N.Y.A.D. 2 Dept.1987)—**§ 10.6, n. 127.**

Pagano, People v., 207 A.D.2d 685, 616 N.Y.S.2d 366 (N.Y.A.D. 1 Dept.1994)—**§ 9.51, n. 377.**

Pagano, People v., 40 Misc.2d 930, 244 N.Y.S.2d 214 (N.Y.Sup.1963)—**§ 10.12, n. 245.**

Pagnotta, People v., 305 N.Y.S.2d 484, 253 N.E.2d 202 (N.Y.1969)—**§ 5.26, n. 672.**

P., In re Dora, 68 A.D.2d 719, 418 N.Y.S.2d 597 (N.Y.A.D. 1 Dept.1979)—**§ 9.8, n. 48.**

Palacios, People v., 581 N.Y.S.2d 661, 590 N.E.2d 246 (N.Y.1992)—**§ 9.33, n. 242.**

TABLE OF CASES

Palumbo, People v., N.Y.L.J., p. 25, col. 6 (Sup.Ct., Bronx County, 1994)—§ **7.30, n. 345.**

Panibianci, People v., 134 Misc.2d 274, 510 N.Y.S.2d 801 (N.Y.Sup.1986)—§ **5.27, n. 795.**

Papa, People v., 96 A.D.2d 601, 465 N.Y.S.2d 295 (N.Y.A.D. 2 Dept.1983)—§ **9.43, n. 315; § 9.49, n. 363.**

Papa, People v., 47 A.D.2d 902, 366 N.Y.S.2d 205 (N.Y.A.D. 2 Dept.1975)—§ **5.22, n. 566.**

Pappas, People v., 128 A.D.2d 556, 512 N.Y.S.2d 493 (N.Y.A.D. 2 Dept.1987)—§ **9.34, n. 250; § 9.39, n. 285.**

Parker, People v., 191 A.D.2d 717, 595 N.Y.S.2d 519 (N.Y.A.D. 2 Dept.1993)—§ **6.2, n. 30.**

Parker, People v., 186 A.D.2d 593, 588 N.Y.S.2d 390 (N.Y.A.D. 2 Dept.1992)—§ **9.37, n. 270; § 9.42, n. 302.**

Parker, People v., 186 A.D.2d 157, 587 N.Y.S.2d 718 (N.Y.A.D. 2 Dept.1992)—§ **5.18, n. 408.**

Parker, People v., 132 A.D.2d 629, 517 N.Y.S.2d 783 (N.Y.A.D. 2 Dept.1987)—§ **6.10, n. 236.**

Parker, People v., 468 N.Y.S.2d 870, 456 N.E.2d 811 (N.Y.1983)—§ **1.9, n. 195.**

Parker v. Randolph, 442 U.S. 62, 99 S.Ct. 2132, 60 L.Ed.2d 713 (1979)—§ **5.22, n. 583.**

Parliman, People v., 56 A.D.2d 966, 393 N.Y.S.2d 94 (N.Y.A.D. 3 Dept.1977)—§ **10.5, n. 116.**

Parris, People v., 610 N.Y.S.2d 464, 632 N.E.2d 870 (N.Y.1994)—§ **10.19; § 10.19, n. 452, 460.**

Parris, People v., 580 N.Y.S.2d 167, 588 N.E.2d 65 (N.Y.1992)—§ **9.17; § 9.17, n. 158.**

Parris, People v., 113 Misc.2d 1066, 450 N.Y.S.2d 721 (N.Y.City Crim.Ct.1982)—§ **3.8, n. 100.**

Parsons, People v., 82 Misc.2d 1090, 371 N.Y.S.2d 840 (N.Y.Co.Ct.1975)—§ **6.10, n. 226.**

Pasquino, People v., 65 A.D.2d 629, 409 N.Y.S.2d 518 (N.Y.A.D. 2 Dept.1978)—§ **9.51, n. 365.**

Passero, People v., 96 A.D.2d 721, 465 N.Y.S.2d 360 (N.Y.A.D. 4 Dept.1983)—§ **9.16, n. 151.**

Pate v. Robinson, 383 U.S. 375, 86 S.Ct. 836, 15 L.Ed.2d 815 (1966)—§ **6.1, n. 2; § 6.10; § 6.10, n. 242, 244.**

Patterson, People v., 189 A.D.2d 733, 593 N.Y.S.2d 8 (N.Y.A.D. 1 Dept.1993)—§ **5.8, n. 150, 154.**

Patterson, People v., 579 N.Y.S.2d 617, 587 N.E.2d 255 (N.Y.1991)—§ **3.12, n. 122.**

Patterson, People v., 177 A.D.2d 1042, 578 N.Y.S.2d 55 (N.Y.A.D. 4 Dept.1991)—§ **10.19, n. 408.**

Patterson, People v., 148 Misc.2d 528, 561 N.Y.S.2d 502 (N.Y.City Crim.Ct.1990)—§ **5.18, n. 398.**

Patterson, People v., 129 A.D.2d 527, 514 N.Y.S.2d 378 (N.Y.A.D. 1 Dept.1987)—§ **11.16, n. 208.**

Patton v. Yount, 467 U.S. 1025, 104 S.Ct. 2885, 81 L.Ed.2d 847 (1984)—§ **1.9, n. 187.**

Paul, People v., 139 A.D.2d 916, 527 N.Y.S.2d 905 (N.Y.A.D. 4 Dept.1988)—§ **10.18, n. 383.**

Paul, People v., 133 Misc.2d 234, 506 N.Y.S.2d 834 (N.Y.City Crim.Ct.1986)—§ **3.25, n. 324.**

Paulides, People v., 88 Misc.2d 1061, 389 N.Y.S.2d 1018 (N.Y.Co.Ct.1976)—§ **6.7, n. 140.**

Paulino, People v., 162 A.D.2d 632, 559 N.Y.S.2d 177 (N.Y.A.D. 2 Dept.1990)—§ **11.16, n. 210.**

Pavlak, People ex rel. Pulver v., 71 Misc. 95, 335 N.Y.S.2d 721 (N.Y.Co.Ct.1972)—§ **3.30, n. 417.**

Paxhia, People v., 140 A.D.2d 962, 529 N.Y.S.2d 638 (N.Y.A.D. 4 Dept.1988)—§ **6.6, n. 98.**

Payne, People v., 358 N.Y.S.2d 701, 315 N.E.2d 762 (N.Y.1974)—§ **5.21, n. 513; § 5.22, n. 569, 587.**

Payne v. Virginia, 468 U.S. 1062, 104 S.Ct. 3573, 82 L.Ed.2d 801 (1984)—§ **2.5, n. 104.**

Payton v. New York, 445 U.S. 573, 100 S.Ct. 1371, 63 L.Ed.2d 639 (1980)—§ **3.11, n. 119; § 3.18, n. 207; § 10.11, n. 237.**

Payton, People v., 408 N.Y.S.2d 395, 380 N.E.2d 224 (N.Y.1978)—§ **10.10; § 10.10, n. 184, 185.**

Pearl, People v., 272 A.D. 563, 74 N.Y.S.2d 108 (N.Y.A.D. 1 Dept.1947)—§ **2.2, n. 21.**

Pearson v. Northeast Airlines, Inc., 309 F.2d 553 (2nd Cir.1962)—§ **1.3, n. 44.**

Pearson, People v., 179 A.D.2d 786, 579 N.Y.S.2d 150 (N.Y.A.D. 2 Dept.1992)—§ **10.2, n. 14.**

Peerless Ins. Co., People v., 21 A.D.2d 609, 253 N.Y.S.2d 91 (N.Y.A.D. 1 Dept. 1964)—§ **4.12; § 4.12, n. 191, 207.**

Pelchat, People v., 476 N.Y.S.2d 79, 464 N.E.2d 447 (N.Y.1984)—§ **5.1, n. 5, 14; § 5.7, n. 100, 108; § 5.27, n. 742; § 11.16, n. 197.**

Pellegrino, People v., 467 N.Y.S.2d 355, 454 N.E.2d 938 (N.Y.1983)—§ **11.10, n. 102.**

Peltak, People v., 411 N.Y.S.2d 4, 383 N.E.2d 556 (N.Y.1978)—§ **7.10, n. 108.**

Pena, People v., 169 A.D.2d 392, 564 N.Y.S.2d 135 (N.Y.A.D. 1 Dept.1991)—§ **11.19, n. 257.**

Pena, People v., 376 N.Y.S.2d 452, 339 N.E.2d 149 (N.Y.1975)—§ **7.10, n. 98, 109.**

TABLE OF CASES

Penasso, People v., 142 A.D.2d 691, 531 N.Y.S.2d 291 (N.Y.A.D. 2 Dept.1988)—§ 10.13, n. 257; § 10.24, n. 552.

Pender, People v., 156 Misc.2d 325, 593 N.Y.S.2d 447 (N.Y.Sup.1992)—§ 5.27, n. 774.

Pennsylvania v. Ritchie, 480 U.S. 39, 107 S.Ct. 989, 94 L.Ed.2d 40 (1987)—§ 7.8, n. 90; § 7.30, n. 335, 349.

People v. _____ (see opposing party)

People ex rel. v. _____ (see opposing party and relator)

Pepin, People v., 6 A.D.2d 992, 176 N.Y.S.2d 15 (N.Y.A.D. 4 Dept.1958)—§ 5.22, n. 562.

Pepper, People v., 465 N.Y.S.2d 850, 452 N.E.2d 1178 (N.Y.1983)—§ 1.9, n. 211.

Peralta, People v., 127 A.D.2d 803, 512 N.Y.S.2d 201 (N.Y.A.D. 2 Dept.1987)—§ 7.27, n. 297.

Perel, People v., 358 N.Y.S.2d 383, 315 N.E.2d 452 (N.Y.1974)—§ 10.1, n. 1.

Perez, People v., 609 N.Y.S.2d 564, 631 N.E.2d 570 (N.Y.1994)—§ 5.13, n. 326; § 5.18; § 5.18, n. 397.

Perez, People v., 158 Misc.2d 956, 602 N.Y.S.2d 307 (N.Y.Sup.1993)—§ 5.8, n. 156, 163.

Perez, People v., 189 A.D.2d 625, 592 N.Y.S.2d 349 (N.Y.A.D. 1 Dept.1993)—§ 9.43, n. 317.

Perez, People v., 156 A.D.2d 7, 553 N.Y.S.2d 659 (N.Y.A.D. 1 Dept.1990)—§ 5.27, n. 785; § 11.3, n. 11, 17, 28.

Perez, People v., 145 Misc.2d 446, 551 N.Y.S.2d 1021 (N.Y.Sup.1990)—§ 9.20, n. 164.

Perez, People v., 541 N.Y.S.2d 976, 539 N.E.2d 1104 (N.Y.1989)—§ 10.26, n. 586.

Perez, People v., 490 N.Y.S.2d 747, 480 N.E.2d 361 (N.Y.1985)—§ 7.17, n. 186, 210, 211; § 7.21, n. 233; § 7.22, n. 241.

Perez, People v., 104 A.D.2d 454, 478 N.Y.S.2d 968 (N.Y.A.D. 2 Dept.1984)—§ 10.15, n. 301.

Perez v. Sullivan, 793 F.2d 249 (10th Cir. 1986)—§ 9.8, n. 45, 56.

Perico, People v., 143 Misc.2d 961, 542 N.Y.S.2d 911 (N.Y.Dist.Ct.1989)—§ 9.6, n. 27.

Perkins, People v., 161 Misc.2d 502, 614 N.Y.S.2d 709 (N.Y.Sup.1994)—§ 2.7, n. 160; § 5.21, n. 484.

Perkins, People v., 166 A.D.2d 737, 562 N.Y.S.2d 244 (N.Y.A.D. 3 Dept.1990)—§ 6.4, n. 81; § 6.9, n. 200.

Perri, People v., 441 N.Y.S.2d 444, 424 N.E.2d 278 (N.Y.1981)—§ 5.9, n. 226.

Perri, People v., 72 A.D.2d 106, 423 N.Y.S.2d 674 (N.Y.A.D. 2 Dept.1980)—§ 5.9, n. 233.

Perry, People v., 639 N.Y.S.2d 307, 662 N.E.2d 787 (N.Y.1996)—§ 3.5, n. 42, 50.

Perry, People v., 199 A.D.2d 889, 605 N.Y.S.2d 790 (N.Y.A.D. 3 Dept.1993)—§ 5.2, n. 29.

Perry, People v., 187 A.D.2d 678, 590 N.Y.S.2d 251 (N.Y.A.D. 2 Dept.1992)—§ 5.7, n. 102.

Perry, United States v., 788 F.2d 100 (3rd Cir.1986)—§ 4.1, n. 6.

Perry, United States v., 731 F.2d 985, 235 U.S.App.D.C. 283 (D.C.Cir.1984)—§ 5.22, n. 550.

Peterson, People v., 194 A.D.2d 124, 605 N.Y.S.2d 542 (N.Y.A.D. 3 Dept.1993)—§ 1.4, n. 81.

Peterson, People v., 115 A.D.2d 497, 496 N.Y.S.2d 231 (N.Y.A.D. 2 Dept.1985)—§ 9.38, n. 278.

Peterson, People v., 96 A.D.2d 871, 465 N.Y.S.2d 743 (N.Y.A.D. 2 Dept.1983)—§ 7.27, n. 297, 304.

Peterson, People v., 391 N.Y.S.2d 530, 359 N.E.2d 1325 (N.Y.1976)—§ 6.2, n. 40; § 6.10; § 6.10, n. 251.

Petgen, People v., 450 N.Y.S.2d 299, 435 N.E.2d 669 (N.Y.1982)—§ 10.22, n. 536; § 11.16, n. 194, 212.

Petralia, People v., 476 N.Y.S.2d 56, 464 N.E.2d 424 (N.Y.1984)—§ 10.19, n. 418, 426, 454.

Pettinato, People v., 511 N.Y.S.2d 828, 503 N.E.2d 1365 (N.Y.1986)—§ 10.20, n. 468.

Pettway, People v., 131 Misc.2d 20, 497 N.Y.S.2d 279 (N.Y.Sup.1985)—§ 11.5, n. 57.

Phears, People v., 441 N.Y.S.2d 666, 424 N.E.2d 553 (N.Y.1981)—§ 2.8, n. 176.

Phelps, People v., 550 N.Y.S.2d 259, 549 N.E.2d 461 (N.Y.1989)—§ 6.4, n. 74; § 6.10, n. 243.

Phillipe, People v., 142 Misc.2d 574, 538 N.Y.S.2d 400 (N.Y.City Crim.Ct.1989)—§ 3.6, n. 63; § 3.7, n. 70, 71.

Phillips, People v., 88 A.D.2d 672, 450 N.Y.S.2d 925 (N.Y.A.D. 3 Dept.1982)—§ 5.8, n. 150.

Phillips, People v., 425 N.Y.S.2d 558, 401 N.E.2d 916 (N.Y.1980)—§ 11.3, n. 16.

Phillips, People v., 66 A.D.2d 696, 411 N.Y.S.2d 259 (N.Y.A.D. 1 Dept.1978)—§ 11.19, n. 257.

Phipps, People v., 631 N.Y.S.2d 853 (N.Y.A.D. 1 Dept.1995)—§ 6.9, n. 217.

Picozzi, People v., 106 A.D.2d 413, 482 N.Y.S.2d 335 (N.Y.A.D. 2 Dept.1984)—§ 6.2, n. 21, 34, 41.

Pierce, People ex rel. v. Thomas, 70 Misc.2d 629, 334 N.Y.S.2d 666 (N.Y.Sup.1972)—§ 3.33, n. 453.

Pierre, People v., 140 Misc.2d 623, 533 N.Y.S.2d 170 (N.Y.City Crim.Ct.1988)—§ 3.6, n. 59, 60.

Pilgrim, People v., 436 N.Y.S.2d 265, 417 N.E.2d 559 (N.Y.1980)—§ 1.4, n. 76, 89.

TABLE OF CASES

Pilon, People v., 30 A.D.2d 365, 293 N.Y.S.2d 393 (N.Y.A.D. 3 Dept.1968)—§ 5.22, n. 566.

Pimental, People v., 182 A.D.2d 80, 587 N.Y.S.2d 365 (N.Y.A.D. 2 Dept.1992)—§ 10.4, n. 77.

Pimentel, People v., 140 A.D.2d 270, 528 N.Y.S.2d 568 (N.Y.A.D. 1 Dept.1988)—§ 10.16, n. 318.

Pinchback, People v., 609 N.Y.S.2d 158, 631 N.E.2d 100 (N.Y.1993)—§ 10.3, n. 54.

Pinkas, People v., 156 A.D.2d 485, 548 N.Y.S.2d 767 (N.Y.A.D. 2 Dept.1989)—§ 5.21, n. 502.

Pischetola, People v., 63 A.D.2d 687, 404 N.Y.S.2d 658 (N.Y.A.D. 2 Dept.1978)—§ 10.5, n. 106.

Pisco, People v., 69 Misc.2d 675, 330 N.Y.S.2d 542 (N.Y.Co.Ct.1972)—§ 6.10, n. 232.

Pizzichillo, People v., 144 A.D.2d 589, 534 N.Y.S.2d 432 (N.Y.A.D. 2 Dept.1988)—§ 10.5, n. 99.

Pizzuto, People v., 101 A.D.2d 1024, 476 N.Y.S.2d 696 (N.Y.A.D. 4 Dept.1984)—§ 10.2, n. 44.

P., Johnny, People v., 112 Misc.2d 647, 445 N.Y.S.2d 1007 (N.Y.City Crim.Ct. 1981)—§ 11.4, n. 35.

P.J. Video, Inc., People v., 508 N.Y.S.2d 907, 501 N.E.2d 556 (N.Y.1986)—§ 10.3, n. 65.

P., Johnny, People v., 112 Misc.2d 647, 445 N.Y.S.2d 1007 (N.Y.City Crim.Ct. 1981)—§ 11.4, n. 35.

P.J. Video, Inc., People v., 493 N.Y.S.2d 988, 483 N.E.2d 1120 (N.Y.1985)—§ 1.2, n. 28.

Pleasant, People v., 446 N.Y.S.2d 29, 430 N.E.2d 905 (N.Y.1981)—§ 10.10, n. 174.

Pleban, People v., 108 A.D.2d 880, 485 N.Y.S.2d 377 (N.Y.A.D. 2 Dept.1985)—§ 9.12, n. 122.

Plevy, People v., 436 N.Y.S.2d 224, 417 N.E.2d 518 (N.Y.1980)—§ 2.8, n. 190; § 10.21, n. 509.

Plummer v. Rothwax, 481 N.Y.S.2d 657, 471 N.E.2d 429 (N.Y.1984)—§ 2.4, n. 59, 60.

Pobliner, People v., 345 N.Y.S.2d 482, 298 N.E.2d 637 (N.Y.1973)—§ 10.20, n. 489, 496.

Polanco, People v., 201 A.D.2d 410, 609 N.Y.S.2d 772 (N.Y.A.D. 1 Dept.1994)—§ 11.17, n. 227.

Polanco, People v., 174 A.D.2d 468, 571 N.Y.S.2d 710 (N.Y.A.D. 1 Dept.1991)—§ 7.21, n. 240.

Polimeda, People v., 198 A.D.2d 242, 603 N.Y.S.2d 513 (N.Y.A.D. 2 Dept.1993)—§ 11.8, n. 75.

Polito, People v., 128 Misc.2d 71, 488 N.Y.S.2d 593 (N.Y.City Ct.1985)—§ 3.7, n. 79.

Pollard v. United States, 352 U.S. 354, 77 S.Ct. 481, 1 L.Ed.2d 393 (1957)—§ 9.8, n. 56.

Pollay, People v., 145 A.D.2d 972, 538 N.Y.S.2d 714 (N.Y.A.D. 4 Dept.1988)—§ 11.15, n. 172.

Pomales, People v., 159 A.D.2d 451, 553 N.Y.S.2d 131 (N.Y.A.D. 1 Dept.1990)—§ 9.43, n. 312.

Ponder, People v., 445 N.Y.S.2d 57, 429 N.E.2d 735 (N.Y.1981)—§ 10.11; § 10.11, n. 224.

Poole, People v., 202 A.D.2d 450, 608 N.Y.S.2d 502 (N.Y.A.D. 2 Dept.1994)—§ 11.12, n. 134.

Poole, People v., 422 N.Y.S.2d 5, 397 N.E.2d 697 (N.Y.1979)—§ 7.16, n. 184; § 10.19, n. 414.

Portelli, People v., 257 N.Y.S.2d 931, 205 N.E.2d 857 (N.Y.1965)—§ 10.11, n. 214.

Porter, People v., 157 Misc.2d 879, 599 N.Y.S.2d 436 (N.Y.Sup.1993)—§ 5.21, n. 528.

Potwora, People v., 421 N.Y.S.2d 850, 397 N.E.2d 361 (N.Y.1979)—§ 10.3, n. 65.

Powell, People v., 148 Misc.2d 966, 564 N.Y.S.2d 663 (N.Y.Sup.1990)—§ 5.29, n. 811.

Powell, People v., 153 A.D.2d 54, 549 N.Y.S.2d 276 (N.Y.A.D. 4 Dept.1989)—§ 5.18; § 5.18, n. 429.

Powell, People v., 105 A.D.2d 761, 481 N.Y.S.2d 188 (N.Y.A.D. 2 Dept.1984)—§ 11.12, n. 127.

Powers, People v., 173 A.D.2d 886, 570 N.Y.S.2d 362 (N.Y.A.D. 3 Dept.1991)—§ 10.6, n. 126.

Prato, People v., 89 A.D.2d 860, 453 N.Y.S.2d 40 (N.Y.A.D. 2 Dept.1982)—§ 11.19, n. 265.

Prescott, People v., 196 A.D.2d 599, 601 N.Y.S.2d 325 (N.Y.A.D. 2 Dept.1993)—§ 11.12, n. 134; § 11.17, n. 221.

Prescott, People v., 495 N.Y.S.2d 955, 486 N.E.2d 813 (N.Y.1985)—§ 2.5, n. 103, 104; § 2.11, n. 244; § 10.22, n. 531; § 11.15, n. 188.

Press–Enterprise Co. v. Superior Court of California, Riverside County, 464 U.S. 501, 104 S.Ct. 819, 78 L.Ed.2d 629 (1984)—§ 3.33, n. 466.

Pressley, People v., 115 A.D.2d 228, 496 N.Y.S.2d 147 (N.Y.A.D. 4 Dept.1985)—§ 9.43, n. 308.

Prest, People v., 105 A.D.2d 1078, 482 N.Y.S.2d 172 (N.Y.A.D. 4 Dept.1984)—§ 5.8, n. 129, 145.

Price, People v., 204 A.D.2d 753, 611 N.Y.S.2d 675 (N.Y.A.D. 3 Dept.1994)—§ 10.2, n. 25.

Price, People v., 193 A.D.2d 853, 597 N.Y.S.2d 503 (N.Y.A.D. 3 Dept.1993)—§ 11.12, n. 128.

Price, People v., 145 A.D.2d 445, 535 N.Y.S.2d 398 (N.Y.A.D. 2 Dept.1988)—§ 9.12, n. 123.

TABLE OF CASES

Primmer, People v., 59 A.D.2d 221, 399 N.Y.S.2d 478 (N.Y.A.D. 3 Dept.1977)— **§ 9.55, n. 400, 402.**

Pringle, People v., 186 A.D.2d 413, 589 N.Y.S.2d 8 (N.Y.A.D. 1 Dept.1992)— **§ 6.2, n. 31; § 6.10, n. 225; § 11.8, n. 73.**

Prisco, People v., 68 Misc.2d 493, 326 N.Y.S.2d 758 (N.Y.Co.Ct.1970)— **§ 1.8, n. 179, 183.**

Prochilo, People v., 395 N.Y.S.2d 635, 363 N.E.2d 1380 (N.Y.1977)— **§ 10.21, n. 502, 503.**

Property Clerk, New York City Police Dept. v. Famiglietti, 160 A.D.2d 542, 554 N.Y.S.2d 519 (N.Y.A.D. 1 Dept.1990)— **§ 3.29, n. 397.**

Prosser, People v., 309 N.Y. 353, 130 N.E.2d 891 (N.Y.1955)— **§ 9.9, n. 74, 75; § 9.10, n. 106.**

Public Service Mut. Ins. Co., People v., 376 N.Y.S.2d 421, 339 N.E.2d 128 (N.Y. 1975)— **§ 4.2, n. 21; § 4.12, n. 202, 206.**

Pugh, People v., 207 A.D.2d 503, 615 N.Y.S.2d 912 (N.Y.A.D. 2 Dept.1994)— **§ 5.8, n. 160.**

Puig, People v., 85 Misc.2d 228, 378 N.Y.S.2d 925 (N.Y.Sup.1976)— **§ 1.3, n. 43, 44, 51, 52; § 5.12, n. 314; § 5.29, n. 818.**

Pulver, People ex rel. v. Pavlak, 71 Misc.2d 95, 335 N.Y.S.2d 721 (N.Y.Co.Ct.1972)— **§ 3.30, n. 417.**

Punter, People v., 150 Misc.2d 136, 566 N.Y.S.2d 1005 (N.Y.Sup.1991)— **§ 5.8, n. 136.**

Purcell, People v., 161 A.D.2d 812, 556 N.Y.S.2d 375 (N.Y.A.D. 2 Dept.1990)— **§ 5.27, n. 797; § 11.15, n. 169.**

Pymm, People v., 561 N.Y.S.2d 687, 563 N.E.2d 1 (N.Y.1990)— **§ 1.2, n. 33.**

Quackenbush, People v., 98 A.D.2d 875, 470 N.Y.S.2d 855 (N.Y.A.D. 3 Dept.1983)— **§ 1.3, n. 40.**

Quartararo, People v., 200 A.D.2d 160, 612 N.Y.S.2d 635 (N.Y.A.D. 2 Dept.1994)— **§ 1.9, n. 187, 207, 212.**

Quinones, People v., 540 N.Y.S.2d 993, 538 N.E.2d 345 (N.Y.1989)— **§ 7.17, n. 204.**

Quinones, People v., 139 A.D.2d 404, 527 N.Y.S.2d 5 (N.Y.A.D. 1 Dept.1988)— **§ 7.17, n. 198.**

Quiroz, People v., 192 A.D.2d 730, 597 N.Y.S.2d 106 (N.Y.A.D. 2 Dept.1993)— **§ 9.10, n. 109.**

R., People v., 160 Misc.2d 142, 607 N.Y.S.2d 887 (N.Y.Sup.1994)— **§ 1.4, n. 122.**

Rahming, People v., 311 N.Y.S.2d 292, 259 N.E.2d 727 (N.Y.1970)— **§ 10.7, n. 139; § 10.20, n. 488; § 10.25, n. 567.**

Rainey, People v., 248 N.Y.S.2d 33, 197 N.E.2d 527 (N.Y.1964)— **§ 10.5, n. 82, 89, 90, 93.**

Rakas v. Illinois, 439 U.S. 128, 99 S.Ct. 421, 58 L.Ed.2d 387 (1978)— **§ 10.8, n. 158; § 10.11; § 10.11, n. 211, 217.**

Ralys, Matter of, 156 Misc.2d 268, 592 N.Y.S.2d 572 (N.Y.Co.Ct.1992)— **§ 4.3, n. 47.**

Ramjit, People v., 203 A.D.2d 488, 612 N.Y.S.2d 600 (N.Y.A.D. 2 Dept.1994)— **§ 5.7, n. 109; § 5.22; § 5.22, n. 556.**

Ramos, People v., 130 A.D.2d 439, 515 N.Y.S.2d 472 (N.Y.A.D. 1 Dept.1987)— **§ 11.16, n. 208.**

Ramos, People v., 479 N.Y.S.2d 510, 468 N.E.2d 692 (N.Y.1984)— **§ 11.9, n. 81, 91; § 11.11, n. 119.**

Randall, People v., 214 N.Y.S.2d 417, 174 N.E.2d 507 (N.Y.1961)— **§ 5.16, n. 353.**

Randall v. Rothwax, 577 N.Y.S.2d 211, 583 N.E.2d 924 (N.Y.1991)— **§ 2.4; § 2.4, n. 72.**

Ranghelle, People v., 511 N.Y.S.2d 580, 503 N.E.2d 1011 (N.Y.1986)— **§ 7.4, n. 53, 54; § 7.16, n. 182; § 7.17, n. 187, 197, 205, 215; § 7.21, n. 238; § 7.22, n. 242.**

Ranieri, People v., 127 Misc.2d 132, 485 N.Y.S.2d 495 (N.Y.City Crim.Ct.1985)— **§ 3.25, n. 324.**

Rawlings v. Kentucky, 448 U.S. 98, 100 S.Ct. 2556, 65 L.Ed.2d 633 (1980)— **§ 10.11, n. 223.**

Ray, People v., 527 N.Y.S.2d 740, 522 N.E.2d 1037 (N.Y.1988)— **§ 5.16, n. 349.**

Ray, State ex rel. v. Warden, 184 A.D.2d 477, 585 N.Y.S.2d 424 (N.Y.A.D. 1 Dept. 1992)— **§ 4.5, n. 87.**

Ray, United States v., 828 F.2d 399 (7th Cir.1987)— **§ 11.9, n. 88.**

Reason, People v., 372 N.Y.S.2d 614, 334 N.E.2d 572 (N.Y.1975)— **§ 6.3, n. 46; § 11.8, n. 77.**

Redwine v. Zuckert, 317 F.2d 336, 115 U.S.App.D.C. 130 (D.C.Cir.1963)— **§ 11.9, n. 86.**

Reed v. Farley, ___ U.S. ___, 114 S.Ct. 2291, 129 L.Ed.2d 277 (1994)— **§ 9.41, n. 294; § 9.54, n. 389.**

Reedy, People v., 523 N.Y.S.2d 438, 517 N.E.2d 1324 (N.Y.1987)— **§ 7.17, n. 192; § 7.33, n. 360.**

Reets, People v., 157 Misc.2d 515, 597 N.Y.S.2d 577 (N.Y.Sup.1993)— **§ 5.27, n. 772.**

Reeves, People v., 406 N.Y.S.2d 36, 377 N.E.2d 480 (N.Y.1978)— **§ 10.5, n. 87.**

Reibman, People ex rel. v. Warden of County Jail at Salem, 242 A.D. 282, 275 N.Y.S. 59 (N.Y.A.D. 3 Dept.1934)— **§ 9.2, n. 3.**

Reichbach, People v., 131 A.D.2d 515, 515 N.Y.S.2d 891 (N.Y.A.D. 2 Dept.1987)— **§ 10.6, n. 125.**

TABLE OF CASES

Reid, People v., 214 A.D.2d 396, 625 N.Y.S.2d 171 (N.Y.A.D. 1 Dept.1995)— § 9.37, n. 269.

Reid, People v., 192 A.D.2d 1117, 596 N.Y.S.2d 282 (N.Y.A.D. 4 Dept.1993)— § 5.22, n. 592.

Reid, People v., 190 A.D.2d 575, 593 N.Y.S.2d 521 (N.Y.A.D. 1 Dept.1993)— § 10.13, n. 269, 276.

Reilly, People v., 136 A.D.2d 355, 527 N.Y.S.2d 234 (N.Y.A.D. 2 Dept.1988)— § 9.55, n. 399.

Reilly v. Warden, FCI Petersburg, 947 F.2d 43 (2nd Cir.1991)—§ 9.55, n. 403.

Reisman, People v., 327 N.Y.S.2d 342, 277 N.E.2d 396 (N.Y.1971)—§ 2.8, n. 176; § 10.21, n. 507.

Relin v. Maloy, 182 A.D.2d 1142, 583 N.Y.S.2d 103 (N.Y.A.D. 4 Dept.1992)— § 5.8, n. 189.

Renis, People v., 94 A.D.2d 728, 462 N.Y.S.2d 266 (N.Y.A.D. 2 Dept.1983)— § 10.20, n. 489.

Respeto v. McNab, 469 N.Y.S.2d 695, 457 N.E.2d 802 (N.Y.1983)—§ 2.4, n. 55.

Reyes, People v., 193 A.D.2d 452, 597 N.Y.S.2d 685 (N.Y.A.D. 1 Dept.1993)— § 5.22, n. 604.

Reyes, People v., 174 A.D.2d 87, 579 N.Y.S.2d 34 (N.Y.A.D. 1 Dept.1992)— § 5.27, n. 786.

Reyes, People v., 148 Misc.2d 227, 564 N.Y.S.2d 954 (N.Y.Sup.1990)—§ 3.28, n. 377.

Reynolds, People v., 528 N.Y.S.2d 15, 523 N.E.2d 291 (N.Y.1988)—§ 10.17; § 10.17, n. 357.

Rhee, People v., 111 A.D.2d 655, 490 N.Y.S.2d 215 (N.Y.A.D. 1 Dept.1985)— § 9.24, n. 192.

Rhoades, People v., 126 A.D.2d 774, 510 N.Y.S.2d 718 (N.Y.A.D. 3 Dept.1987)— § 10.5, n. 106; § 10.6, n. 128.

Rhodes, People v., 176 A.D.2d 828, 575 N.Y.S.2d 156 (N.Y.A.D. 2 Dept.1991)— § 11.10, n. 108.

Rhone v. United States, 365 F.2d 980, 125 U.S.App.D.C. 47 (D.C.Cir.1966)—§ 5.22, n. 601.

Ribowsky, People v., 567 N.Y.S.2d 392, 568 N.E.2d 1197 (N.Y.1991)—§ 1.4, n. 79; § 5.17, n. 356, 363, 375.

Riccelli, People v., 149 A.D.2d 941, 540 N.Y.S.2d 74 (N.Y.A.D. 4 Dept.1989)— § 5.27, n. 758.

Rice, People v., 148 Misc.2d 204, 560 N.Y.S.2d 105 (N.Y.City Ct.1990)— § 3.33, n. 450.

Rice, People v., 76 Misc.2d 632, 351 N.Y.S.2d 888 (N.Y.Co.Ct.1974)—§ 6.4, n. 81.

Richards, People v., 158 A.D.2d 627, 551 N.Y.S.2d 597 (N.Y.A.D. 2 Dept.1990)— § 11.12, n. 128.

Richardson v. Marsh, 481 U.S. 200, 107 S.Ct. 1702, 95 L.Ed.2d 176 (1987)— § 5.22, n. 573.

Richardson, People v., 198 A.D.2d 450, 605 N.Y.S.2d 906 (N.Y.A.D. 2 Dept.1993)— § 11.10, n. 108.

Richberg, People v., 56 A.D.2d 279, 392 N.Y.S.2d 16 (N.Y.A.D. 1 Dept.1977)— § 10.22, n. 519.

Richetti, People v., 302 N.Y. 290, 97 N.E.2d 908 (N.Y.1951)—§ 6.9, n. 205.

Richlin, People v., 74 Misc.2d 906, 346 N.Y.S.2d 698 (N.Y.Co.Ct.1973)—§ 5.17, n. 371, 376.

Rickert, People v., 459 N.Y.S.2d 734, 446 N.E.2d 419 (N.Y.1983)—§ 3.28, n. 374; § 5.27, n. 760.

Ridley, People v., 65 Misc.2d 547, 318 N.Y.S.2d 331 (N.Y.Co.Ct.1971)—§ 4.9, n. 116.

Riedd, People v., 160 Misc.2d 733, 609 N.Y.S.2d 997 (N.Y.Sup.1993)—§ 5.12, n. 312; § 5.13, n. 326.

Riley, People v., 58 A.D.2d 816, 396 N.Y.S.2d 271 (N.Y.A.D. 2 Dept.1977)— § 1.4, n. 106.

Rios, People v., 203 A.D.2d 491, 610 N.Y.S.2d 871 (N.Y.A.D. 2 Dept.1994)— § 5.29, n. 812.

Rios, People v., 126 A.D.2d 860, 510 N.Y.S.2d 923 (N.Y.A.D. 3 Dept.1987)— § 6.2, n. 24, 27, 34.

Rios, People v., 469 N.Y.S.2d 670, 457 N.E.2d 776 (N.Y.1983)—§ 7.10, n. 110.

Rios, People v., 78 A.D.2d 642, 432 N.Y.S.2d 120 (N.Y.A.D. 2 Dept.1980)—§ 1.10, n. 232.

Ritter v. Surles, 144 Misc.2d 945, 545 N.Y.S.2d 962 (N.Y.Sup.1988)—§ 6.7, n. 141; § 6.8, n. 183.

Rivas, People v., 206 A.D.2d 549, 614 N.Y.S.2d 753 (N.Y.A.D. 2 Dept.1994)— § 11.8, n. 75.

Rivera, People v., 622 N.Y.S.2d 671, 646 N.E.2d 1098 (N.Y.1995)—§ 5.18, n. 411, 422; § 5.19, n. 444.

Rivera, People v., 161 Misc.2d 237, 612 N.Y.S.2d 782 (N.Y.Sup.1994)—§ 5.5, n. 84.

Rivera, People v., 185 A.D.2d 152, 586 N.Y.S.2d 114 (N.Y.A.D. 1 Dept.1992)— § 7.23, n. 264.

Rivera, People v., 156 A.D.2d 177, 548 N.Y.S.2d 439 (N.Y.A.D. 1 Dept.1989)— § 11.15, n. 180; § 11.16, n. 202.

Rivera, People v., 144 Misc.2d 1007, 545 N.Y.S.2d 455 (N.Y.City Crim.Ct.1989)— § 1.8, n. 164, 169.

Rivera, People v., 151 A.D.2d 789, 543 N.Y.S.2d 120 (N.Y.A.D. 2 Dept.1989)— § 9.28, n. 222.

Rivera, People v., 138 A.D.2d 169, 530 N.Y.S.2d 802 (N.Y.A.D. 1 Dept.1988)— § 7.30, n. 343.

TABLE OF CASES

Rivera, People v., 132 Misc.2d 903, 505 N.Y.S.2d 798 (N.Y.Sup.1986)—**§ 3.34, n. 480.**

Rivera, People v., 119 A.D.2d 517, 501 N.Y.S.2d 38 (N.Y.A.D. 1 Dept.1986)—**§ 7.9, n. 92.**

Rivera, People v., 468 N.Y.S.2d 601, 456 N.E.2d 492 (N.Y.1983)—**§ 2.5, n. 104; § 2.6, n. 139; § 2.7, n. 165.**

Rivera, People v., 72 A.D.2d 922, 422 N.Y.S.2d 211 (N.Y.A.D. 4 Dept.1979)—**§ 9.29, n. 228.**

Rivera, People v., 58 A.D.2d 147, 396 N.Y.S.2d 26 (N.Y.A.D. 1 Dept.1977)—**§ 10.16, n. 332.**

Riverside, County of v. McLaughlin, 500 U.S. 44, 111 S.Ct. 1661, 114 L.Ed.2d 49 (1991)—**§ 3.19, n. 220; § 3.24, n. 287; § 3.30, n. 409; § 3.36.8.**

R., Matter of Jose, 610 N.Y.S.2d 937, 632 N.E.2d 1260 (N.Y.1994)—**§ 2.10, n. 238.**

Roberson, People v., 149 A.D.2d 926, 540 N.Y.S.2d 60 (N.Y.A.D. 4 Dept.1989)—**§ 5.8, n. 130.**

Roberson, People v., 99 A.D.2d 619, 472 N.Y.S.2d 157 (N.Y.A.D. 3 Dept.1984)—**§ 9.42, n. 303.**

Roberts, People v., 204 A.D.2d 974, 613 N.Y.S.2d 67 (N.Y.A.D. 4 Dept.1994)—**§ 5.18, n. 412.**

Roberts, People v., 178 A.D.2d 622, 577 N.Y.S.2d 672 (N.Y.A.D. 2 Dept.1991)—**§ 7.17, n. 206; § 7.23, n. 268.**

Roberts, People v., 176 A.D.2d 1200, 576 N.Y.S.2d 698 (N.Y.A.D. 4 Dept.1991)—**§ 9.47, n. 336.**

Roberts, People v., 163 A.D.2d 690, 558 N.Y.S.2d 296 (N.Y.A.D. 3 Dept.1990)—**§ 5.18, n. 419.**

Roberts, People v., 162 A.D.2d 729, 557 N.Y.S.2d 127 (N.Y.A.D. 2 Dept.1990)—**§ 5.17; § 5.17, n. 380.**

Roberts, People v., 534 N.Y.S.2d 647, 531 N.E.2d 279 (N.Y.1988)—**§ 5.17, n. 386; § 5.18; § 5.18, n. 414, 416; § 5.19; § 5.19, n. 443.**

Roberts, People v., 95 Misc.2d 41, 406 N.Y.S.2d 432 (N.Y.Co.Ct.1978)—**§ 1.7, n. 153.**

Robinson, People v., 200 A.D.2d 693, 606 N.Y.S.2d 908 (N.Y.A.D. 2 Dept.1994)—**§ 7.19, n. 223.**

Robinson, People v., 199 A.D.2d 345, 606 N.Y.S.2d 998 (N.Y.A.D. 2 Dept.1993)—**§ 2.4, n. 41.**

Robinson, People v., 187 A.D.2d 296, 589 N.Y.S.2d 453 (N.Y.A.D. 1 Dept.1992)—**§ 5.8, n. 139, 162.**

Robinson, People v., 171 A.D.2d 475, 567 N.Y.S.2d 401 (N.Y.A.D. 1 Dept.1991)—**§ 9.22, n. 174; § 9.42, n. 302.**

Robinson, People v., 510 N.Y.S.2d 837, 503 N.E.2d 485 (N.Y.1986)—**§ 5.21, n. 496; § 10.1, n. 12; § 10.3, n. 55.**

Robinson, People v., 119 A.D.2d 598, 500 N.Y.S.2d 768 (N.Y.A.D. 2 Dept.1986)—**§ 5.18, n. 407.**

Robinson, People v., 118 A.D.2d 516, 500 N.Y.S.2d 122 (N.Y.A.D. 1 Dept.1986)—**§ 10.19, n. 410; § 11.16, n. 209.**

Robinson, People v., 65 A.D.2d 896, 410 N.Y.S.2d 409 (N.Y.A.D. 3 Dept.1978)—**§ 2.6, n. 118.**

Robinson, People v., 367 N.Y.S.2d 208, 326 N.E.2d 784 (N.Y.1975)—**§ 10.21, n. 504.**

Robinson, People ex rel. v. Campbell, 184 A.D.2d 988, 585 N.Y.S.2d 604 (N.Y.A.D. 3 Dept.1992)—**§ 4.5, n. 85.**

Robles, People v., 202 A.D.2d 166, 608 N.Y.S.2d 191 (N.Y.A.D. 1 Dept.1994)—**§ 11.19, n. 262.**

Robles, People v., 139 A.D.2d 781, 527 N.Y.S.2d 527 (N.Y.A.D. 2 Dept.1988)—**§ 9.49, n. 364.**

Robustelli, People v., 189 A.D.2d 668, 592 N.Y.S.2d 704 (N.Y.A.D. 1 Dept.1993)—**§ 6.5, n. 89.**

Roby, People v., N.Y.L.J., p. 17, col. 6 (App. Term, 9th & 10th Jud.Dists., 1984)—**§ 11.15, n. 176.**

Rodgers, People v., N.Y.L.J., p. 17, col. 5 (App.Term, 9th & 10th Jud.Dists. 1982)—**§ 11.15, n. 176.**

Rodney, People v., 624 N.Y.S.2d 95, 648 N.E.2d 471 (N.Y.1995)—**§ 10.18, n. 392; § 10.25, n. 572.**

Rodriguez v. Grajales, 188 A.D.2d 474, 591 N.Y.S.2d 66 (N.Y.A.D. 2 Dept.1992)—**§ 1.10, n. 256.**

Rodriguez v. Morgenthau, 121 Misc.2d 694, 468 N.Y.S.2d 833 (N.Y.Sup.1983)—**§ 5.8, n. 115.**

Rodriguez, People v., 214 A.D.2d 347, 625 N.Y.S.2d 20 (N.Y.A.D. 1 Dept.1995)—**§ 9.30, n. 230; § 9.43, n. 314.**

Rodriguez, People v., 212 A.D.2d 368, 622 N.Y.S.2d 243 (N.Y.A.D. 1 Dept.1995)—**§ 9.42, n. 302; § 9.43, n. 308, 309.**

Rodriguez, People v., 205 A.D.2d 417, 613 N.Y.S.2d 398 (N.Y.A.D. 1 Dept.1994)—**§ 9.10, n. 90.**

Rodriguez, People v., 193 A.D.2d 363, 596 N.Y.S.2d 824 (N.Y.A.D. 1 Dept.1993)—**§ 9.49, n. 359.**

Rodriguez, People v., 188 A.D.2d 565, 591 N.Y.S.2d 461 (N.Y.A.D. 2 Dept.1992)—**§ 10.5, n. 96.**

Rodriguez, People v., 184 A.D.2d 317, 584 N.Y.S.2d 831 (N.Y.A.D. 1 Dept.1992)—**§ 9.40, n. 287.**

Rodriguez, People v., 583 N.Y.S.2d 814, 593 N.E.2d 268 (N.Y.1992)—**§ 10.17, n. 350, 382; § 10.18, n. 391; § 10.25, n. 574; § 10.26, n. 583.**

Rodriguez, People v., 180 A.D.2d 517, 580 N.Y.S.2d 24 (N.Y.A.D. 1 Dept.1992)—**§ 9.38, n. 276, 277.**

Rodriguez, People v., 152 Misc.2d 501, 577 N.Y.S.2d 760 (N.Y.City Crim.Ct.1991)—**§ 1.8, n. 163.**

TABLE OF CASES

Rodriguez, People v., 155 A.D.2d 257, 546 N.Y.S.2d 861 (N.Y.A.D. 1 Dept.1989)—§ 7.17, n. 187.

Rodriguez, People v., 150 A.D.2d 265, 541 N.Y.S.2d 423 (N.Y.A.D. 1 Dept.1989)—§ 9.15, n. 144.

Rodriguez, People v., 150 A.D.2d 622, 541 N.Y.S.2d 491 (N.Y.A.D. 2 Dept.1989)—§ 10.2, n. 17.

Rodriguez, People v., 148 A.D.2d 320, 538 N.Y.S.2d 535 (N.Y.A.D. 1 Dept.1989)—§ 5.22, n. 566.

Rodriguez, People v., 513 N.Y.S.2d 75, 505 N.E.2d 586 (N.Y.1987)—§ 10.11, n. 235.

Rodriguez, People v., 91 A.D.2d 591, 457 N.Y.S.2d 268 (N.Y.A.D. 1 Dept.1982)—§ 5.22, n. 610.

Rodriguez, People v., 449 N.Y.S.2d 962, 434 N.E.2d 1340 (N.Y.1982)—§ 6.2, n. 23.

Rodriguez, People v., 447 N.Y.S.2d 246, 431 N.E.2d 972 (N.Y.1981)—§ 11.15, n. 171.

Rodriguez, People v., 81 A.D.2d 840, 438 N.Y.S.2d 845 (N.Y.A.D. 2 Dept.1981)—§ 9.10, n. 87, 88, 101.

Rodriguez, People v., 79 A.D.2d 576, 434 N.Y.S.2d 347 (N.Y.A.D. 1 Dept.1980)—§ 6.9, n. 192.

Rodriguez, People v., 79 A.D.2d 539, 433 N.Y.S.2d 584 (N.Y.A.D. 1 Dept.1980)—§ 5.26, n. 666.

Rodriguez, People v., 429 N.Y.S.2d 631, 407 N.E.2d 475 (N.Y.1980)—§ 9.12, n. 121; § 11.7, n. 65.

Rodriguez, People v., 79 Misc.2d 1002, 362 N.Y.S.2d 116 (N.Y.Sup.1974)—§ 11.3, n. 24.

Rodriquez, People v., 387 N.Y.S.2d 110, 354 N.E.2d 850 (N.Y.1976)—§ 2.4, n. 45.

Roe, People v., 191 A.D.2d 844, 595 N.Y.S.2d 121 (N.Y.A.D. 3 Dept.1993)—§ 5.10, n. 297; § 5.16, n. 346; § 5.18, n. 441.

Roesch, People v., 163 A.D.2d 429, 558 N.Y.S.2d 144 (N.Y.A.D. 2 Dept.1990)—§ 5.27, n. 790.

Rogelio, People v., 160 A.D.2d 359, 553 N.Y.S.2d 743 (N.Y.A.D. 1 Dept.1990)—§ 7.17; § 7.17, n. 213.

Rogers v. Leff, 45 A.D.2d 630, 360 N.Y.S.2d 652 (N.Y.A.D. 1 Dept.1974)—§ 4.9, n. 112.

Rogers, People v., 195 A.D.2d 977, 601 N.Y.S.2d 755 (N.Y.A.D. 4 Dept.1993)—§ 9.38, n. 274.

Rogers, People v., 163 A.D.2d 337, 557 N.Y.S.2d 168 (N.Y.A.D. 2 Dept.1990)—§ 6.2, n. 32, 41; § 11.8, n. 75.

Rogers, People v., 85 A.D.2d 843, 446 N.Y.S.2d 497 (N.Y.A.D. 3 Dept.1981)—§ 10.19, n. 446.

Rogers, People v., 314 N.Y.S.2d 1000, 263 N.E.2d 396 (N.Y.1970)—§ 5.24, n. 640.

Rogers, People v., 32 A.D.2d 756, 300 N.Y.S.2d 868 (N.Y.A.D. 1 Dept.1969)—§ 6.2, n. 14, 16, 27, 29.

Rogha, People v., 213 A.D.2d 266, 624 N.Y.S.2d 125 (N.Y.A.D. 1 Dept.1995)—§ 6.2, n. 32.

Rojas, People v., 169 A.D.2d 464, 564 N.Y.S.2d 341 (N.Y.A.D. 1 Dept.1991)—§ 11.15, n. 165.

Romanello, United States v., 726 F.2d 173 (5th Cir.1984)—§ 5.22, n. 601.

Ronald Colavito, People v. (N.Y.1996)—§ 7.2, n. 8; § 7.5, n. 52; § 7.8, n. 73.

Rooney, People v., 455 N.Y.S.2d 595, 441 N.E.2d 1113 (N.Y.1982)—§ 5.17, n. 390.

Rosa, People v., 194 A.D.2d 755, 599 N.Y.S.2d 608 (N.Y.A.D. 2 Dept.1993)—§ 11.13, n. 139.

Rosa, People v., 492 N.Y.S.2d 542, 482 N.E.2d 21 (N.Y.1985)—§ 10.20, n. 472, 491.

Rosado, People v., 199 A.D.2d 833, 606 N.Y.S.2d 368 (N.Y.A.D. 3 Dept.1993)—§ 11.16, n. 194; § 11.17, n. 228.

Rosado, People v., 153 Misc.2d 477, 583 N.Y.S.2d 130 (N.Y.Sup.1992)—§ 7.27, n. 300, 306.

Rosales, People v., 628 N.Y.S.2d 656 (N.Y.A.D. 1 Dept.1995)—§ 10.15, n. 308; § 10.19, n. 458.

Rosario, People v., 578 N.Y.S.2d 454, 585 N.E.2d 766 (N.Y.1991)—§ 10.19, n. 453.

Rosario, People v., 213 N.Y.S.2d 448, 173 N.E.2d 881 (N.Y.1961)—§ 5.3, n. 51; § 7.2, n. 11; § 7.16, n. 176.

Rose, People v., 631 N.Y.S.2d 354 (N.Y.A.D. 1 Dept.1995)—§ 10.19, n. 447.

Rose, People v., 162 A.D.2d 240, 556 N.Y.S.2d 340 (N.Y.A.D. 1 Dept.1990)—§ 11.15, n. 183.

Rose, People v., 122 A.D.2d 484, 505 N.Y.S.2d 244 (N.Y.A.D. 3 Dept.1986)—§ 7.33, n. 365.

Rose, People v., 82 Misc.2d 429, 368 N.Y.S.2d 387 (N.Y.Co.Ct.1975)—§ 1.8, n. 182.

Rosebeck, People v., 109 A.D.2d 915, 486 N.Y.S.2d 384 (N.Y.A.D. 3 Dept.1985)—§ 11.2, n. 4.

Roselle, People v., 618 N.Y.S.2d 753, 643 N.E.2d 72 (N.Y.1994)—§ 2.8, n. 188.

Rosenberg, People v., 59 Misc. 342, 112 N.Y.S. 316 (N.Y.Gen.Sess.1908)—§ 1.8, n. 181.

Rosenthal, People v., 207 A.D.2d 364, 616 N.Y.S.2d 199 (N.Y.A.D. 2 Dept.1994)—§ 5.22, n. 616.

Rosenthal on Behalf of Kolman, People ex rel. v. Wolfson, 422 N.Y.S.2d 55, 397 N.E.2d 745 (N.Y.1979)—§ 4.13, n. 218.

Rosich, People v., 170 A.D.2d 703, 567 N.Y.S.2d 749 (N.Y.A.D. 2 Dept.1991)—§ 9.3, n. 11.

Rosner, People v., 185 A.D.2d 686, 587 N.Y.S.2d 883 (N.Y.A.D. 4 Dept.1992)—§ 11.2, n. 1.

Ross, People v., 185 A.D.2d 661, 586 N.Y.S.2d 75 (N.Y.A.D. 4 Dept.1992)—§ 6.2, n. 29, 30.

TABLE OF CASES

Ross, People v., 502 N.Y.S.2d 693, 493 N.E.2d 917 (N.Y.1986)—§ **3.24, n. 297, 298.**

Ross, People v., 50 A.D.2d 1064, 375 N.Y.S.2d 714 (N.Y.A.D. 4 Dept.1975)—§ **6.2, n. 38; § 6.4, n. 73.**

Rossi, People v., 154 Misc.2d 616, 587 N.Y.S.2d 511 (N.Y.Just.Ct.1992)—§ **3.5, n. 48.**

Roth, People v., 129 Misc.2d 381, 492 N.Y.S.2d 971 (N.Y.Co.Ct.1985)—§ **5.17, n. 364.**

Roth, United States ex rel. v. Zelker, 455 F.2d 1105 (2nd Cir.1972)—§ **6.2, n. 13, 29.**

Roviaro v. United States, 353 U.S. 53, 77 S.Ct. 623, 1 L.Ed.2d 639 (1957)—§ **7.2, n. 12; § 7.10, n. 98; § 7.30, n. 335.**

Rowley, People v., 119 Misc.2d 86, 462 N.Y.S.2d 366 (N.Y.City Crim.Ct.1983)—§ **5.22, n. 561.**

Roy, People v., 122 A.D.2d 482, 505 N.Y.S.2d 242 (N.Y.A.D. 3 Dept.1986)—§ **11.16, n. 194.**

Rozzell, People v., 282 N.Y.S.2d 775, 229 N.E.2d 452 (N.Y.1967)—§ **11.18, n. 246, 247.**

Rubin, People v., 101 A.D.2d 71, 474 N.Y.S.2d 348 (N.Y.A.D. 4 Dept.1984)—§ **5.18, n. 426.**

Ruffin, People v., 208 A.D.2d 657, 617 N.Y.S.2d 333 (N.Y.A.D. 2 Dept.1994)—§ **11.13, n. 145.**

Ruffino, People v., 110 A.D.2d 198, 494 N.Y.S.2d 8 (N.Y.A.D. 2 Dept.1985)—§ **10.22, n. 523.**

Ruiz, People v., 207 A.D.2d 917, 616 N.Y.S.2d 658 (N.Y.A.D. 2 Dept.1994)—§ **5.22, n. 578.**

Ruiz, People v., 130 Misc.2d 191, 496 N.Y.S.2d 612 (N.Y.Sup.1985)—§ **5.22; § 5.22, n. 538, 551.**

Ruiz, People v., 107 A.D.2d 770, 484 N.Y.S.2d 136 (N.Y.A.D. 2 Dept.1985)—§ **9.12, n. 118.**

Rupp, People v., 75 Misc.2d 683, 348 N.Y.S.2d 649 (N.Y.Sup.1973)—§ **1.2, n. 11; § 5.12, n. 317.**

Ruscito, People v., 206 A.D.2d 841, 615 N.Y.S.2d 201 (N.Y.A.D. 4 Dept.1994)—§ **11.9, n. 90.**

Rush v. Mordue, 509 N.Y.S.2d 493, 502 N.E.2d 170 (N.Y.1986)—§ **5.9, n. 210.**

Russell, People v., 549 N.Y.S.2d 646, 548 N.E.2d 1297 (N.Y.1989)—§ **6.2, n. 24.**

Russo, People v., 128 Misc.2d 876, 491 N.Y.S.2d 951 (N.Y.Co.Ct.1985)—§ **7.3, n. 18.**

Russo, People v., 109 A.D.2d 855, 486 N.Y.S.2d 769 (N.Y.A.D. 2 Dept.1985)—§ **7.14, n. 156.**

Russo, People v., 99 A.D.2d 498, 470 N.Y.S.2d 447 (N.Y.A.D. 2 Dept.1984)—§ **9.52, n. 385.**

Ruzas, People v., 54 A.D.2d 1083, 389 N.Y.S.2d 205 (N.Y.A.D. 4 Dept.1976)—§ **2.7, n. 160; § 5.21, n. 481, 484.**

Ryback, People v., 168 N.Y.S.2d 945, 146 N.E.2d 680 (N.Y.1957)—§ **5.20, n. 471.**

Saa, People v., 199 A.D.2d 346, 604 N.Y.S.2d 258 (N.Y.A.D. 2 Dept.1993)—§ **11.19, n. 260.**

Sabatier v. Dabrowski, 586 F.2d 866 (1st Cir.1978)—§ **9.8, n. 51.**

Sable, People v., 138 A.D.2d 234, 525 N.Y.S.2d 45 (N.Y.A.D. 1 Dept.1988)—§ **5.21, n. 502, 519.**

Sabol v. People, 203 A.D.2d 369, 610 N.Y.S.2d 93 (N.Y.A.D. 2 Dept.1994)—§ **7.30, n. 349.**

Saccoccio v. Lange, 194 A.D.2d 794, 599 N.Y.S.2d 306 (N.Y.A.D. 2 Dept.1993)—§ **2.8, n. 177.**

Saddler, People v., 166 A.D.2d 878, 560 N.Y.S.2d 539 (N.Y.A.D. 4 Dept.1990)—§ **5.22, n. 586.**

Saddy, People v., 84 A.D.2d 175, 445 N.Y.S.2d 601 (N.Y.A.D. 2 Dept.1981)—§ **7.23, n. 259.**

Safa, People v., 209 A.D.2d 199, 618 N.Y.S.2d 531 (N.Y.A.D. 1 Dept.1994)—§ **11.9, n. 80.**

Safian, People v., 413 N.Y.S.2d 118, 385 N.E.2d 1046 (N.Y.1978)—§ **5.22, n. 583.**

Sage, People v., 204 A.D.2d 746, 612 N.Y.S.2d 648 (N.Y.A.D. 2 Dept.1994)—§ **5.18, n. 409.**

Sailor, People v., 491 N.Y.S.2d 112, 480 N.E.2d 701 (N.Y.1985)—§ **2.8, n. 184; § 2.10, n. 217.**

Salabarria, People v., 121 A.D.2d 438, 503 N.Y.S.2d 411 (N.Y.A.D. 2 Dept.1986)—§ **4.12, n. 192, 204.**

Saldana, People v., 161 A.D.2d 441, 556 N.Y.S.2d 534 (N.Y.A.D. 1 Dept.1990)—§ **5.8, n. 139.**

Salerno, People v., 164 N.Y.S.2d 729, 143 N.E.2d 917 (N.Y.1957)—§ **5.18, n. 393.**

Salerno, United States v., 481 U.S. 739, 107 S.Ct. 2095, 95 L.Ed.2d 697 (1987)—§ **4.1, n. 3; § 4.5, n. 72.**

Sales, People v., 169 A.D.2d 411, 563 N.Y.S.2d 825 (N.Y.A.D. 1 Dept.1991)—§ **5.27, n. 769.**

Sales, People v., 129 Misc.2d 731, 493 N.Y.S.2d 945 (N.Y.Sup.1985)—§ **11.12, n. 128.**

Salgado, People v., 454 N.Y.S.2d 69, 439 N.E.2d 878 (N.Y.1982)—§ **10.5, n. 97.**

Salladeen, People v., 50 A.D.2d 765, 377 N.Y.S.2d 63 (N.Y.A.D. 1 Dept.1975)—§ **6.2, n. 24, 27, 33.**

Salvucci, United States v., 448 U.S. 83, 100 S.Ct. 2547, 65 L.Ed.2d 619 (1980)—§ **10.11, n. 220.**

Sampson, People v., 539 N.Y.S.2d 288, 536 N.E.2d 617 (N.Y.1989)—§ **3.12, n. 122.**

TABLE OF CASES

Samuel, People v., 208 A.D.2d 776, 617 N.Y.S.2d 494 (N.Y.A.D. 2 Dept.1994)—§ 11.18, n. 248.
Samuels, People v., 424 N.Y.S.2d 892, 400 N.E.2d 1344 (N.Y.1980)—§ 3.11, n. 118; § 3.15, n. 173; § 5.9, n. 250.
Sanchez, People v., 618 N.Y.S.2d 887, 643 N.E.2d 509 (N.Y.1994)—§ 5.13, n. 324; § 5.15, n. 342.
Sanchez, People v., 184 A.D.2d 537, 584 N.Y.S.2d 164 (N.Y.A.D. 2 Dept.1992)—§ 11.11, n. 121.
Sanchez, People v., 144 Misc.2d 262, 543 N.Y.S.2d 878 (N.Y.Sup.1989)—§ 5.12, n. 317.
Sanchez, People v., 128 A.D.2d 816, 513 N.Y.S.2d 521 (N.Y.A.D. 2 Dept.1987)—§ 1.10, n. 243.
Sanchez v. United States, 572 F.2d 210 (9th Cir.1977)—§ 11.9, n. 79, 84.
Sanders, People v., 528 N.Y.S.2d 819, 524 N.E.2d 140 (N.Y.1988)—§ 2.8, n. 184.
Sanders, People v., 498 N.Y.S.2d 774, 489 N.E.2d 743 (N.Y.1985)—§ 10.28, n. 607.
Sanders, People v., 451 N.Y.S.2d 30, 436 N.E.2d 480 (N.Y.1982)—§ 5.22, n. 591.
Sanders, People v., 79 A.D.2d 688, 433 N.Y.S.2d 854 (N.Y.A.D. 2 Dept.1980)—§ 10.19, n. 443.
Sandoval, People v., 357 N.Y.S.2d 849, 314 N.E.2d 413 (N.Y.1974)—§ 7.15, n. 169; § 8.1, n. 20; § 10.19, n. 396.
Sanin, People v., 467 N.Y.S.2d 38, 454 N.E.2d 119 (N.Y.1983)—§ 10.5, n. 98.
Santana, People v., 191 A.D.2d 174, 594 N.Y.S.2d 189 (N.Y.A.D. 1 Dept.1993)—§ 10.24, n. 556.
Santana, People v., 587 N.Y.S.2d 570, 600 N.E.2d 201 (N.Y.1992)—§ 6.3, n. 53; § 7.26, n. 283; § 9.28; § 9.28, n. 223.
Santana, People v., 156 A.D.2d 736, 550 N.Y.S.2d 356 (N.Y.A.D. 2 Dept.1989)—§ 11.18, n. 246, 247.
Santarelli, People v., 425 N.Y.S.2d 77, 401 N.E.2d 199 (N.Y.1980)—§ 5.21, n. 502.
Santiago, People v., 209 A.D.2d 885, 618 N.Y.S.2d 925 (N.Y.A.D. 3 Dept.1994)—§ 9.9, n. 75; § 9.10, n. 97.
Santiago, People v., 205 A.D.2d 565, 614 N.Y.S.2d 269 (N.Y.A.D. 2 Dept.1994)—§ 11.8, n. 75.
Santiago, People v., 194 A.D.2d 468, 599 N.Y.S.2d 964 (N.Y.A.D. 1 Dept.1993)—§ 11.17, n. 218.
Santiago, People v., 127 A.D.2d 619, 511 N.Y.S.2d 415 (N.Y.A.D. 2 Dept.1987)—§ 9.51, n. 382.
Santiago, People v., N.Y.L.J., p. 27, col. 2 (Sup.Ct., N.Y.County, 1995)—§ 5.27, n. 684.
Santobello v. New York, 404 U.S. 257, 92 S.Ct. 495, 30 L.Ed.2d 427 (1971)—§ 11.2, n. 1; § 11.11, n. 110, 113.
Santos, People v., 508 N.Y.S.2d 411, 501 N.E.2d 19 (N.Y.1986)—§ 9.26, n. 213; § 9.41, n. 295, 296; § 9.51, n. 367, 374.

Santos, People v., 485 N.Y.S.2d 524, 474 N.E.2d 1192 (N.Y.1984)—§ 1.2, n. 27.
Santucci v. Di Tucci, 124 A.D.2d 850, 514 N.Y.S.2d 640 (N.Y.A.D. 2 Dept.1986)—§ 5.22, n. 617.
Sardino v. State Com'n on Judicial Conduct, 461 N.Y.S.2d 229, 448 N.E.2d 83 (N.Y.1983)—§ 5.24, n. 637.
Sargeant, People v., 128 A.D.2d 914, 512 N.Y.S.2d 570 (N.Y.A.D. 3 Dept.1987)—§ 10.6, n. 128.
Saulnier, People v., 129 Misc.2d 151, 492 N.Y.S.2d 897 (N.Y.Sup.1985)—§ 4.10, n. 169.
Sawyer, People v., 453 N.Y.S.2d 418, 438 N.E.2d 1133 (N.Y.1982)—§ 3.24, n. 301.
Sayavong, People v., 613 N.Y.S.2d 343, 635 N.E.2d 1213 (N.Y.1994)—§ 5.3; § 5.3, n. 37; § 5.27, n. 739, 743.
S., Benjamin v. Kuriansky, 447 N.Y.S.2d 905, 432 N.E.2d 777 (N.Y.1982)—§ 11.11, n. 118, 121.
Scala, People v., 128 Misc.2d 831, 491 N.Y.S.2d 555 (N.Y.Sup.1985)—§ 7.26, n. 279.
Scalise, People v., 105 A.D.2d 869, 482 N.Y.S.2d 362 (N.Y.A.D. 3 Dept.1984)—§ 4.12, n. 192.
Scalza, People v., 562 N.Y.S.2d 14, 563 N.E.2d 705 (N.Y.1990)—§ 1.2, n. 32; § 10.12, n. 255; § 10.19, n. 403.
Scalzo, People v., 176 A.D.2d 363, 574 N.Y.S.2d 782 (N.Y.A.D. 2 Dept.1991)—§ 7.23, n. 273.
Schad v. Arizona, 501 U.S. 624, 111 S.Ct. 2491, 115 L.Ed.2d 555 (1991)—§ 5.17; § 5.17, n. 373.
Schaffer, People v., 634 N.Y.S.2d 22, 657 N.E.2d 1305 (N.Y.1995)—§ 5.27; § 5.27, n. 777; § 6.3, n. 50, 59; § 6.6, n. 125.
Scharton, United States v., 285 U.S. 518, 52 S.Ct. 416, 76 L.Ed. 917 (1932)—§ 9.2, n. 3.
Schiavo, People v., 162 A.D.2d 639, 556 N.Y.S.2d 954 (N.Y.A.D. 2 Dept.1990)—§ 10.3, n. 54.
Schiavo, B & B Salvage, People v., 212 A.D.2d 816, 623 N.Y.S.2d 273 (N.Y.A.D. 2 Dept.1995)—§ 9.49, n. 364.
Schildhaus on Behalf of Weinstein, People ex rel. v. Warden, 37 Misc.2d 660, 235 N.Y.S.2d 531 (N.Y.Sup.1962)—§ 6.1, n. 3; § 6.2, n. 36; § 6.5, n. 85, 87.
Schlatter, People v., 55 A.D.2d 922, 390 N.Y.S.2d 441 (N.Y.A.D. 2 Dept.1977)—§ 1.3, n. 53.
Schmerber v. California, 384 U.S. 757, 86 S.Ct. 1826, 16 L.Ed.2d 908 (1966)—§ 5.9, n. 230; § 7.11, n. 119.
Schmidt on Behalf of McNell v. Roberts, 549 N.Y.S.2d 633, 548 N.E.2d 1284 (N.Y. 1989)—§ 2.6, n. 120, 129, 131, 147.
Schonfeld, People v., 547 N.Y.S.2d 266, 546 N.E.2d 395 (N.Y.1989)—§ 4.12, n. 199, 204, 210.

TABLE OF CASES

Schoolfield, People v., 196 A.D.2d 111, 608 N.Y.S.2d 413 (N.Y.A.D. 1 Dept.1994)—§ 11.8, n. 77.
Schultz, People v., 536 N.Y.S.2d 46, 532 N.E.2d 1274 (N.Y.1988)—§ 11.12, n. 130, 131, 135; § 11.19, n. 261.
Schulz, People v., 501 N.Y.S.2d 12, 492 N.E.2d 120 (N.Y.1986)—§ 10.23, n. 539.
Schupf, People ex rel. Wayburn v., 385 N.Y.S.2d 518, 350 N.E.2d 906 (N.Y. 1976)—§ 4.5, n. 75.
Schweizer, People ex rel. v. Welch, 40 A.D.2d 621, 336 N.Y.S.2d 556 (N.Y.A.D. 4 Dept.1972)—§ 4.5, n. 75.
Schwenk, People v., 92 Misc.2d 331, 400 N.Y.S.2d 291 (N.Y.Co.Ct.1977)—§ 9.6, n. 29.
Schwimmer, People v., 66 A.D.2d 91, 411 N.Y.S.2d 922 (N.Y.A.D. 2 Dept.1978)—§ 5.22, n. 554.
Sciacca, People v., 408 N.Y.S.2d 22, 379 N.E.2d 1153 (N.Y.1978)—§ 10.5, n. 92; § 10.6, n. 126.
Scott v. Illinois, 440 U.S. 367, 99 S.Ct. 1158, 59 L.Ed.2d 383 (1979)—§ 3.24, n. 297, 298.
Scott, People v., 141 Misc.2d 623, 533 N.Y.S.2d 799 (N.Y.Sup.1988)—§ 5.8, n. 133.
Scrivens, People v., 175 A.D.2d 671, 572 N.Y.S.2d 271 (N.Y.A.D. 4 Dept.1991)—§ 11.12, n. 132.
Seaberg, People v., 543 N.Y.S.2d 968, 541 N.E.2d 1022 (N.Y.1989)—§ 10.22, n. 538; § 11.8, n. 74; § 11.15, n. 154; § 11.16, n. 192, 205; § 11.17, n. 213, 234.
Seager, People v., 147 A.D.2d 932, 537 N.Y.S.2d 392 (N.Y.A.D. 4 Dept.1989)—§ 10.3, n. 61, 66.
Searles, People v., 135 Misc.2d 881, 517 N.Y.S.2d 370 (N.Y.City Ct.1987)—§ 3.33, n. 450.
Searles, People v., 79 Misc.2d 850, 361 N.Y.S.2d 568 (N.Y.Sup.1974)—§ 6.3, n. 58.
Seaton, People v., 280 N.Y.S.2d 370, 227 N.E.2d 294 (N.Y.1967)—§ 11.10, n. 94.
Segal, People v., 444 N.Y.S.2d 588, 429 N.E.2d 107 (N.Y.1981)—§ 7.24, n. 276.
Seidman, People v., 206 A.D.2d 257, 613 N.Y.S.2d 875 (N.Y.A.D. 1 Dept.1994)—§ 6.2, n. 14, 26.
Seifert, People v., 113 A.D.2d 80, 495 N.Y.S.2d 543 (N.Y.A.D. 4 Dept.1985)—§ 1.4, n. 86.
Selby, People v., 148 Misc.2d 447, 561 N.Y.S.2d 123 (N.Y.Sup.1990)—§ 5.10, n. 267.
Selikoff, People v., 360 N.Y.S.2d 623, 318 N.E.2d 784 (N.Y.1974)—§ 2.2, n. 16; § 11.11, n. 110; § 11.12; § 11.12, n. 125; § 11.14, n. 148; § 11.19, n. 261.
Senisi, People v., 196 A.D.2d 376, 610 N.Y.S.2d 542 (N.Y.A.D. 2 Dept.1994)—§ 5.17, n. 359.

Sepulveda, People v., 151 A.D.2d 335, 542 N.Y.S.2d 591 (N.Y.A.D. 1 Dept.1989)—§ 11.13, n. 137.
Sera, People ex rel. Fusco on Behalf of Wells v., 123 Misc.2d 19, 472 N.Y.S.2d 564 (N.Y.Sup.1984)—§ 6.2, n. 10.
Serfass v. United States, 420 U.S. 377, 95 S.Ct. 1055, 43 L.Ed.2d 265 (1975)—§ 2.2, n. 9.
Serrando, People v., 184 A.D.2d 1094, 583 N.Y.S.2d 245 (N.Y.A.D. 1 Dept.1992)—§ 7.30, n. 341.
Serrano, People v., 163 A.D.2d 497, 558 N.Y.S.2d 593 (N.Y.A.D. 2 Dept.1990)—§ 5.27, n. 758.
Serrano, People v., 258 N.Y.S.2d 386, 206 N.E.2d 330 (N.Y.1965)—§ 11.10, n. 97.
Sessa, People v., 43 Misc.2d 24, 250 N.Y.S.2d 193 (N.Y.City Crim.Ct.1964)—§ 1.1, n. 5.
Setteroth, People v., 200 A.D.2d 533, 607 N.Y.S.2d 15 (N.Y.A.D. 1 Dept.1994)—§ 10.19, n. 408.
Settles, People v., 412 N.Y.S.2d 874, 385 N.E.2d 612 (N.Y.1978)—§ 3.1, n. 6.
Sexton, People v., 187 N.Y. 495, 80 N.E. 396 (N.Y.1907)—§ 5.27, n. 687.
Seychel, People v., 136 Misc.2d 310, 518 N.Y.S.2d 754 (N.Y.Sup.1987)—§ 10.19, n. 437.
Sgro v. United States, 287 U.S. 206, 53 S.Ct. 138, 77 L.Ed. 260 (1932)—§ 10.3, n. 70.
Shannon, People v., 127 A.D.2d 863, 512 N.Y.S.2d 242 (N.Y.A.D. 2 Dept.1987)—§ 5.16, n. 353.
Shannon, People v., 129 Misc.2d 289, 488 N.Y.S.2d 348 (N.Y.Sup.1985)—§ 5.16, n. 351.
Shapard, People v., 199 A.D.2d 888, 606 N.Y.S.2d 103 (N.Y.A.D. 3 Dept.1993)—§ 6.2, n. 29.
Shapiro, People v., 474 N.Y.S.2d 470, 462 N.E.2d 1188 (N.Y.1984)—§ 3.2, n. 20.
Shapiro, People v., 431 N.Y.S.2d 422, 409 N.E.2d 897 (N.Y.1980)—§ 5.21; § 5.21, n. 502, 512, 517.
Shapiro, People ex rel. v. Keeper of City Prison, 290 N.Y. 393, 49 N.E.2d 498 (N.Y.1943)—§ 4.1, n. 4.
Sharpe, People v., 72 A.D.2d 572, 420 N.Y.S.2d 736 (N.Y.A.D. 2 Dept.1979)—§ 11.8, n. 77.
Sharpton, People v., 141 Misc.2d 322, 533 N.Y.S.2d 230 (N.Y.City Crim.Ct.1988)—§ 5.21, n. 480; § 5.22, n. 560.
Sharpton v. Turner, 169 A.D.2d 947, 565 N.Y.S.2d 255 (N.Y.A.D. 3 Dept.1991)—§ 5.12, n. 314.
Shaw, People v., 196 A.D.2d 558, 601 N.Y.S.2d 151 (N.Y.A.D. 2 Dept.1993)—§ 7.16, n. 185.
Shaw, People ex rel. v. Lombard, 95 Misc.2d 664, 408 N.Y.S.2d 664 (N.Y.Co.Ct. 1978)—§ 4.5, n. 70, 73; § 4.10, n. 131, 155.

TABLE OF CASES

Shawcross, People v., 192 A.D.2d 1128, 596 N.Y.S.2d 622 (N.Y.A.D. 4 Dept.1993)—§ 10.19, n. 411.

Shedrick, People v., 83 A.D.2d 988, 443 N.Y.S.2d 716 (N.Y.A.D. 4 Dept.1981)—§ 8.1, n. 23.

Shelton, People v., 209 A.D.2d 963, 619 N.Y.S.2d 436 (N.Y.A.D. 4 Dept.1994)—§ 5.22, n. 586.

Sherman, People v., 156 A.D.2d 889, 550 N.Y.S.2d 109 (N.Y.A.D. 3 Dept.1989)—§ 7.4, n. 26.

Shields, People v., 205 A.D.2d 833, 613 N.Y.S.2d 281 (N.Y.A.D. 3 Dept.1994)—§ 11.17, n. 232.

Shore Realty Corp., People v., 127 Misc.2d 419, 486 N.Y.S.2d 124 (N.Y.Dist.Ct. 1984)—§ 5.26, n. 672.

Sian, People v., 167 A.D.2d 435, 561 N.Y.S.2d 791 (N.Y.A.D. 2 Dept.1990)—§ 5.7, n. 97.

Sides, People v., 552 N.Y.S.2d 555, 551 N.E.2d 1233 (N.Y.1990)—§ 3.24, n. 308.

Siegel v. State of N.Y., 691 F.2d 620 (2nd Cir.1982)—§ 11.11, n. 124.

Sielaff, People ex rel. Hardy, on Behalf of Miller v., 584 N.Y.S.2d 742, 595 N.E.2d 817 (N.Y.1992)—§ 4.2, n. 31.

Sierra, People v., 149 Misc.2d 588, 566 N.Y.S.2d 818 (N.Y.Sup.1990)—§ 5.27, n. 776.

Silver, People v., 354 N.Y.S.2d 915, 310 N.E.2d 520 (N.Y.1974)—§ 6.2, n. 12.

Silvers, People v., 163 A.D.2d 71, 558 N.Y.S.2d 25 (N.Y.A.D. 1 Dept.1990)—§ 11.9, n. 90.

Silverstein, People v., 545 N.Y.S.2d 86, 543 N.E.2d 729 (N.Y.1989)—§ 10.5, n. 123.

Silverthorne Lumber Co. v. United States, 251 U.S. 385, 40 S.Ct. 182, 64 L.Ed. 319 (1920)—§ 10.10, n. 179.

Silvestri, People v., 132 Misc.2d 1015, 506 N.Y.S.2d 251 (N.Y.Sup.1986)—§ 4.10, n. 166, 169.

Simmons, People v., 178 A.D.2d 972, 579 N.Y.S.2d 499 (N.Y.A.D. 4 Dept.1991)—§ 5.8, n. 130, 133.

Simmons, People v., 365 N.Y.S.2d 812, 325 N.E.2d 139 (N.Y.1975)—§ 7.12, n. 142.

Simmons v. United States, 390 U.S. 377, 88 S.Ct. 967, 19 L.Ed.2d 1247 (1968)—§ 5.21, n. 525; § 10.11, n. 221; § 10.16, n. 331.

Simon, People v., 202 A.D.2d 302, 610 N.Y.S.2d 769 (N.Y.A.D. 1 Dept.1994)—§ 9.51, n. 365.

Simon, People v., 187 A.D.2d 740, 590 N.Y.S.2d 533 (N.Y.A.D. 2 Dept.1992)—§ 5.8, n. 170.

Simon, People v., 180 A.D.2d 866, 580 N.Y.S.2d 493 (N.Y.A.D. 3 Dept.1992)—§ 7.30, n. 349.

Simonson v. Cahn, 313 N.Y.S.2d 97, 261 N.E.2d 246 (N.Y.1970)—§ 5.10; § 5.10, n. 264.

Simpson, People v., 109 A.D.2d 461, 492 N.Y.S.2d 609 (N.Y.A.D. 1 Dept.1985)—§ 7.15, n. 172.

Sinatra, People v., 102 A.D.2d 189, 476 N.Y.S.2d 913 (N.Y.A.D. 2 Dept.1984)—§ 10.5, n. 87.

Singer, People v., 405 N.Y.S.2d 17, 376 N.E.2d 179 (N.Y.1978)—§ 9.8, n. 66; § 9.9, n. 69.

Singh, People v., 190 A.D.2d 640, 594 N.Y.S.2d 165 (N.Y.A.D. 1 Dept.1993)—§ 2.4, n. 38.

Singh, People v., 131 Misc.2d 1094, 503 N.Y.S.2d 228 (N.Y.Sup.1986)—§ 5.8, n. 160.

Singleton, People v., 531 N.Y.S.2d 798, 527 N.E.2d 281 (N.Y.1988)—§ 5.12, n. 322.

Singleton, People v., 398 N.Y.S.2d 871, 368 N.E.2d 1237 (N.Y.1977)—§ 5.25, n. 642; § 5.26, n. 663; § 7.10, n. 107; § 8.1, n. 25; § 9.49, n. 360.

Sinistaj, People v., 501 N.Y.S.2d 793, 492 N.E.2d 1209 (N.Y.1986)—§ 3.7, n. 77; § 9.15, n. 145.

Siragusa, People v., 81 Misc.2d 368, 366 N.Y.S.2d 336 (N.Y.Dist.Ct.1975)—§ 11.3, n. 27.

Sirianni, People v., 89 A.D.2d 775, 453 N.Y.S.2d 485 (N.Y.A.D. 4 Dept.1982)—§ 11.9, n. 90.

Skinner, People ex rel. Calloway v., 347 N.Y.S.2d 178, 300 N.E.2d 716 (N.Y. 1973)—§ 4.1, n. 4; § 4.4, n. 50.

Skinner, People ex rel. LaForce v., 65 Misc.2d 884, 319 N.Y.S.2d 10 (N.Y.Sup. 1971)—§ 4.5, n. 73, 76.

Skrynski, People v., 397 N.Y.S.2d 707, 366 N.E.2d 797 (N.Y.1977)—§ 1.8, n. 186.

Slater, People v., 166 A.D.2d 828, 562 N.Y.S.2d 985 (N.Y.A.D. 3 Dept.1990)—§ 10.24, n. 556.

Slaughter, People v., 376 N.Y.S.2d 114, 338 N.E.2d 622 (N.Y.1975)—§ 10.4, n. 78.

Sledge, People v., 90 A.D.2d 588, 456 N.Y.S.2d 198 (N.Y.A.D. 3 Dept.1982)—§ 5.10, n. 300.

Slowe, People v., 125 Misc.2d 591, 479 N.Y.S.2d 962 (N.Y.Co.Ct.1984)—§ 7.4, n. 32.

Smalis v. Pennsylvania, 476 U.S. 140, 106 S.Ct. 1745, 90 L.Ed.2d 116 (1986)—§ 2.4, n. 77.

Smalley, People v., 64 Misc.2d 363, 314 N.Y.S.2d 924 (N.Y.Co.Ct.1970)—§ 5.19, n. 447.

Smalls, People v., 162 A.D.2d 642, 556 N.Y.S.2d 957 (N.Y.A.D. 2 Dept.1990)—§ 11.3, n. 17.

Smalls, People v., 111 A.D.2d 38, 488 N.Y.S.2d 712 (N.Y.A.D. 1 Dept.1985)—§ 5.8, n. 124.

Smays, People v., 156 Misc.2d 621, 594 N.Y.S.2d 101 (N.Y.Sup.1993)—§ 5.9, n. 259, 260.

TABLE OF CASES

S., Mitchell, People v., 151 Misc.2d 208, 573 N.Y.S.2d 124 (N.Y.City Crim.Ct.1991)—§ 5.17, n. 371.

Smith v. Hooey, 393 U.S. 374, 89 S.Ct. 575, 21 L.Ed.2d 607 (1969)—§ 9.8, n. 49.

Smith v. Maryland, 442 U.S. 735, 99 S.Ct. 2577, 61 L.Ed.2d 220 (1979)—§ 10.9, n. 168.

Smith, People v., 631 N.Y.S.2d 683 (N.Y.A.D. 1 Dept.1995)—§ 10.25, n. 564.

Smith, People v., 630 N.Y.S.2d 84 (N.Y.A.D. 2 Dept.1995)—§ 5.27, n. 765.

Smith, People v., 211 A.D.2d 586, 622 N.Y.S.2d 19 (N.Y.A.D. 1 Dept.1995)—§ 9.34, n. 257.

Smith, People v., 622 N.Y.S.2d 507, 646 N.E.2d 809 (N.Y.1994)—§ 5.8, n. 178.

Smith, People v., 601 N.Y.S.2d 466, 619 N.E.2d 403 (N.Y.1993)—§ 9.34; § 9.34, n. 251.

Smith, People v., 191 A.D.2d 598, 594 N.Y.S.2d 799 (N.Y.A.D. 2 Dept.1993)—§ 5.8, n. 161; § 5.27, n. 794.

Smith, People v., 155 Misc.2d 596, 589 N.Y.S.2d 254 (N.Y.Co.Ct.1992)—§ 5.8, n. 134, 156.

Smith, People v., 540 N.Y.S.2d 987, 538 N.E.2d 339 (N.Y.1989)—§ 9.41, n. 296.

Smith, People v., 143 Misc.2d 100, 539 N.Y.S.2d 663 (N.Y.City Crim.Ct.1989)—§ 3.34, n. 485.

Smith, People v., 145 A.D.2d 517, 535 N.Y.S.2d 110 (N.Y.A.D. 2 Dept.1988)—§ 10.3, n. 54.

Smith, People v., 141 Misc.2d 568, 533 N.Y.S.2d 801 (N.Y.City Crim.Ct.1988)—§ 3.7, n. 78; § 3.8, n. 98.

Smith, People v., 138 A.D.2d 932, 526 N.Y.S.2d 682 (N.Y.A.D. 4 Dept.1988)—§ 10.6, n. 128.

Smith, People v., 127 A.D.2d 864, 512 N.Y.S.2d 243 (N.Y.A.D. 2 Dept.1987)—§ 7.12, n. 132.

Smith, People v., 113 A.D.2d 905, 493 N.Y.S.2d 623 (N.Y.A.D. 2 Dept.1985)—§ 5.27, n. 681.

Smith, People v., 479 N.Y.S.2d 706, 468 N.E.2d 879 (N.Y.1984)—§ 7.13, n. 151; § 7.14, n. 162; § 7.21, n. 235.

Smith, People v., 97 A.D.2d 485, 468 N.Y.S.2d 129 (N.Y.A.D. 2 Dept.1983)—§ 9.24, n. 192, 193; § 9.48, n. 353.

Smith, People v., 91 A.D.2d 928, 457 N.Y.S.2d 822 (N.Y.A.D. 1 Dept.1983)—§ 9.42, n. 297; § 9.49, n. 360.

Smith, People v., 76 A.D.2d 962, 432 N.Y.S.2d 161 (N.Y.A.D. 3 Dept.1980)—§ 11.11, n. 122.

Smith, People v., 53 A.D.2d 652, 384 N.Y.S.2d 488 (N.Y.A.D. 2 Dept.1976)—§ 9.14, n. 132.

Smith, People ex rel. Dowdy v., 423 N.Y.S.2d 862, 399 N.E.2d 894 (N.Y. 1979)—§ 2.8, n. 178, 187.

Smolen, People v., 186 A.D.2d 292, 588 N.Y.S.2d 312 (N.Y.A.D. 2 Dept.1992)—§ 9.36, n. 262.

Smyers, People v., 167 A.D.2d 773, 562 N.Y.S.2d 1017 (N.Y.A.D. 3 Dept.1990)—§ 5.21, n. 526.

Smyth, People v., 164 N.Y.S.2d 737, 143 N.E.2d 922 (N.Y.1957)—§ 6.2, n. 17.

Sniadach v. Family Finance Corp. of Bay View, 395 U.S. 337, 89 S.Ct. 1820, 23 L.Ed.2d 349 (1969)—§ 4.10, n. 147.

Snyder, People v., 99 A.D.2d 83, 471 N.Y.S.2d 430 (N.Y.A.D. 4 Dept.1984)—§ 2.3, n. 35.

Snyder, People v., 246 N.Y. 491, 159 N.E. 408 (N.Y.1927)—§ 5.22, n. 530.

Sobotker, People v., 471 N.Y.S.2d 78, 459 N.E.2d 187 (N.Y.1984)—§ 5.9, n. 199, 209; § 11.15, n. 181.

Soler, People v., 92 A.D.2d 280, 460 N.Y.S.2d 537 (N.Y.A.D. 1 Dept.1983)—§ 10.5, n. 114.

Solimine, People v., 276 N.Y.S.2d 882, 223 N.E.2d 341 (N.Y.1966)—§ 10.4, n. 78.

Solomon, People v., 172 A.D.2d 781, 569 N.Y.S.2d 101 (N.Y.A.D. 2 Dept.1991)—§ 1.9, n. 206.

Sommersell, People v., 638 N.Y.S.2d 272 (N.Y.Sup.1995)—§ 9.20, n. 168.

Sosnik, People v., 568 N.Y.S.2d 340, 569 N.E.2d 1019 (N.Y.1991)—§ 1.4, n. 79.

Soto, People v., 189 A.D.2d 712, 592 N.Y.S.2d 721 (N.Y.A.D. 1 Dept.1993)—§ 6.2, n. 34.

Soto, People v., 76 Misc.2d 491, 352 N.Y.S.2d 144 (N.Y.City Crim.Ct.1974)—§ 9.5, n. 21; § 9.7, n. 33.

Soto, People v., 68 Misc.2d 629, 327 N.Y.S.2d 669 (N.Y.Co.Ct.1972)—§ 6.10, n. 232.

South, People v., 393 N.Y.S.2d 695, 362 N.E.2d 246 (N.Y.1977)—§ 9.8, n. 55.

Souvenir, People v., 83 Misc.2d 1038, 373 N.Y.S.2d 824 (N.Y.City Crim.Ct.1975)—§ 6.10, n. 238.

Spadafora, People v., 131 A.D.2d 40, 519 N.Y.S.2d 979 (N.Y.A.D. 1 Dept.1987)—§ 9.43, n. 312.

Spann, People v., 452 N.Y.S.2d 869, 438 N.E.2d 402 (N.Y.1982)—§ 5.18; § 5.18, n. 403, 413.

Sparks v. Sowders, 852 F.2d 882 (6th Cir. 1988)—§ 11.9, n. 91.

Spearman, People v., 210 A.D.2d 268, 619 N.Y.S.2d 967 (N.Y.A.D. 2 Dept.1994)—§ 11.18, n. 247.

Spears, People v., 106 A.D.2d 417, 482 N.Y.S.2d 340 (N.Y.A.D. 2 Dept.1984)—§ 11.15, n. 175, 180.

Spence, People v., 139 Misc.2d 77, 526 N.Y.S.2d 747 (N.Y.Sup.1988)—§ 5.8, n. 138.

Spivey, People v., 599 N.Y.S.2d 477, 615 N.E.2d 961 (N.Y.1993)—§ 7.23, n. 268.

TABLE OF CASES

Spotford, People v., 627 N.Y.S.2d 295, 650 N.E.2d 1296 (N.Y.1995)—§ **10.19, n. 400.**

Sprague, People v., 47 A.D.2d 510, 367 N.Y.S.2d 598 (N.Y.A.D. 3 Dept.1975)—§ **10.5, n. 90.**

Spruill, People v., 419 N.Y.S.2d 69, 392 N.E.2d 1252 (N.Y.1979)—§ **10.23; § 10.23, n. 545; § 10.27, n. 589.**

Stack v. Boyle, 342 U.S. 1, 72 S.Ct. 1, 96 L.Ed. 3 (1951)—§ **4.1, n. 3.**

Stafford, People v., 215 A.D.2d 212, 626 N.Y.S.2d 763 (N.Y.A.D. 1 Dept.1995)—§ **10.15, n. 301.**

Stafford, People v., 79 A.D.2d 435, 437 N.Y.S.2d 195 (N.Y.A.D. 4 Dept.1981)—§ **8.1, n. 14.**

Staley, People v., 396 N.Y.S.2d 339, 364 N.E.2d 1111 (N.Y.1977)—§ **9.9, n. 69, 72; § 9.10, n. 86.**

Stancari, People ex rel. Mordkofsky v., 93 A.D.2d 826, 460 N.Y.S.2d 830 (N.Y.A.D. 2 Dept.1983)—§ **4.5, n. 88.**

Stanton, People v., 71 A.D.2d 932, 419 N.Y.S.2d 717 (N.Y.A.D. 2 Dept.1979)—§ **9.43, n. 311.**

Star Supermarkets, Inc., People v., 40 A.D.2d 946, 339 N.Y.S.2d 262 (N.Y.A.D. 4 Dept.1972)—§ **5.20, n. 466.**

State ex rel. v. _____ **(see opposing party and relator)**

Stateikin, People v., 163 Misc.2d 517, 620 N.Y.S.2d 903 (N.Y.City Crim.Ct.1994)—§ **9.20, n. 168.**

Staton, People v., 209 A.D.2d 652, 619 N.Y.S.2d 667 (N.Y.A.D. 2 Dept.1994)—§ **9.51, n. 381.**

Staton, People v., 94 Misc.2d 1002, 406 N.Y.S.2d 242 (N.Y.City Crim.Ct.1978)—§ **3.33, n. 448.**

Steadman, People v., 603 N.Y.S.2d 382, 623 N.E.2d 509 (N.Y.1993)—§ **7.12, n. 140; § 7.14, n. 160.**

Steagald v. United States, 451 U.S. 204, 101 S.Ct. 1642, 68 L.Ed.2d 38 (1981)—§ **3.14, n. 153; § 3.18, n. 208; § 10.1, n. 6.**

Steele v. United States, 267 U.S. 498, 45 S.Ct. 414, 69 L.Ed. 757 (1925)—§ **10.5, n. 83, 89.**

Stefano, People v., 159 A.D.2d 1016, 552 N.Y.S.2d 727 (N.Y.A.D. 4 Dept.1990)—§ **9.42, n. 303.**

Steinberg, People v., 170 A.D.2d 50, 573 N.Y.S.2d 965 (N.Y.A.D. 1 Dept.1991)—§ **7.16, n. 178.**

Steingut v. Gold, 397 N.Y.S.2d 765, 366 N.E.2d 854 (N.Y.1977)—§ **1.3, n. 59; § 1.4, n. 80, 82; § 5.12, n. 314.**

Steingut v. Gold, 54 A.D.2d 481, 388 N.Y.S.2d 622 (N.Y.A.D. 2 Dept.1976)—§ **2.3, n. 29.**

Stennett, People v., 207 A.D.2d 847, 616 N.Y.S.2d 980 (N.Y.A.D. 2 Dept.1994)—§ **11.12, n. 133.**

Stephens, People v., 188 A.D.2d 345, 591 N.Y.S.2d 25 (N.Y.A.D. 1 Dept.1992)—§ **11.9, n. 80.**

Stepteau, People v., 595 N.Y.S.2d 371, 611 N.E.2d 272 (N.Y.1993)—§ **5.4, n. 58; § 5.8, n. 172.**

Stern, People v., 171 N.Y.S.2d 265, 148 N.E.2d 400 (N.Y.1958)—§ **5.1, n. 15.**

Steuding, People v., 189 N.Y.S.2d 166, 160 N.E.2d 468 (N.Y.1959)—§ **5.9; § 5.9, n. 220.**

Stevens, People v., 151 A.D.2d 704, 542 N.Y.S.2d 754 (N.Y.A.D. 2 Dept.1989)—§ **5.8, n. 129, 145.**

Stevens, People v., 133 Misc.2d 407, 506 N.Y.S.2d 995 (N.Y.City Ct.1986)—§ **4.10, n. 175.**

S. T. Grand, Inc. v. City of New York, 344 N.Y.S.2d 938, 298 N.E.2d 105 (N.Y. 1973)—§ **2.8, n. 185.**

Stiles, People v., 520 N.Y.S.2d 745, 514 N.E.2d 1368 (N.Y.1987)—§ **9.24, n. 194; § 9.48, n. 350, 351.**

Stirone v. United States, 361 U.S. 212, 80 S.Ct. 270, 4 L.Ed.2d 252 (1960)—§ **5.18, n. 425.**

Stith, People v., 514 N.Y.S.2d 201, 506 N.E.2d 911 (N.Y.1987)—§ **10.10, n. 188.**

St. John, People v., 163 A.D.2d 687, 558 N.Y.S.2d 294 (N.Y.A.D. 3 Dept.1990)—§ **11.17, n. 238.**

Stone, People v., 193 A.D.2d 838, 597 N.Y.S.2d 538 (N.Y.A.D. 3 Dept.1993)—§ **11.18, n. 245.**

Stone, People v., 128 Misc.2d 1009, 491 N.Y.S.2d 921 (N.Y.City Crim.Ct.1985)—§ **3.20, n. 240, 246.**

Strever, People v., 73 A.D.2d 1031, 425 N.Y.S.2d 181 (N.Y.A.D. 4 Dept.1980)—§ **10.19, n. 409.**

Strunk v. United States, 412 U.S. 434, 93 S.Ct. 2260, 37 L.Ed.2d 56 (1973)—§ **9.8, n. 37.**

Stubbs, People v., 183 A.D.2d 178, 590 N.Y.S.2d 539 (N.Y.A.D. 3 Dept.1992)—§ **7.30, n. 344.**

Stukes, People v., 211 A.D.2d 565, 621 N.Y.S.2d 79 (N.Y.A.D. 1 Dept.1995)—§ **9.51, n. 370.**

Sturgis, People v., 381 N.Y.S.2d 860, 345 N.E.2d 331 (N.Y.1976)—§ **9.17; § 9.17, n. 156; § 9.36; § 9.36, n. 258, 259; § 9.38, n. 278; § 9.43, n. 316.**

Stuyvesant Ins. Co., People v., 24 A.D.2d 989, 265 N.Y.S.2d 268 (N.Y.A.D. 2 Dept. 1965)—§ **4.12, n. 191, 208.**

Suarez, People v., 103 Misc.2d 910, 427 N.Y.S.2d 187 (N.Y.Sup.1980)—§ **5.8, n. 133.**

Suffolk County Dept. of Social Services on Behalf of Michael V. v. James M., 608 N.Y.S.2d 940, 630 N.E.2d 636 (N.Y. 1994)—§ **2.8, n. 189.**

Sullivan v. Grupposo, 77 Misc.2d 833, 355 N.Y.S.2d 55 (N.Y.City Civ.Ct.1974)—§ **2.6, n. 133.**

TABLE OF CASES

Sullivan, People v., 452 N.Y.S.2d 373, 437 N.E.2d 1130 (N.Y.1982)—§ 10.2, n. 39.

Supreme Court of State of New York, People ex rel. Lemon v., 245 N.Y. 24, 156 N.E. 84 (N.Y.1927)—§ 7.2, n. 8.

Sutton, People v., 149 Misc.2d 672, 564 N.Y.S.2d 646 (N.Y.Sup.1990)—§ 5.5, n. 83.

Sutton, People v., 122 A.D.2d 896, 505 N.Y.S.2d 937 (N.Y.A.D. 2 Dept.1986)—§ 10.22, n. 528.

Sutton, People v., 91 A.D.2d 522, 456 N.Y.S.2d 771 (N.Y.A.D. 1 Dept.1982)—§ 10.17; § 10.17, n. 351.

Sutton, People v., 39 A.D.2d 820, 332 N.Y.S.2d 983 (N.Y.Sup.1972)—§ 11.18, n. 248.

Swamp, People v., 622 N.Y.S.2d 472, 646 N.E.2d 774 (N.Y.1995)—§ 5.7, n. 97; § 5.27; § 5.27, n. 711, 718, 724.

Swan, People v., 158 A.D.2d 158, 557 N.Y.S.2d 791 (N.Y.A.D. 4 Dept.1990)—§ 6.2, n. 29; § 6.9, n. 212.

Sweeney, People v., 143 Misc.2d 175, 539 N.Y.S.2d 677 (N.Y.City Crim.Ct.1989)—§ 3.34, n. 483.

Sykes on Behalf of Rodriguez, People ex rel. v. Mitchell, 184 A.D.2d 466, 586 N.Y.S.2d 937 (N.Y.A.D. 1 Dept.1992)—§ 9.25, n. 206; § 9.47, n. 339.

Szychulda, People v., 454 N.Y.S.2d 705, 440 N.E.2d 790 (N.Y.1982)—§ 5.25, n. 643.

Taggart, People v., 51 A.D.2d 863, 380 N.Y.S.2d 168 (N.Y.A.D. 4 Dept.1976)—§ 10.5, n. 88, 95.

Taibi, People v., 174 A.D.2d 585, 571 N.Y.S.2d 88 (N.Y.A.D. 2 Dept.1991)—§ 5.27, n. 769.

Talham, People v., 41 A.D.2d 354, 342 N.Y.S.2d 921 (N.Y.A.D. 3 Dept.1973)—§ 3.30, n. 420.

Tambe, People v., 527 N.Y.S.2d 372, 522 N.E.2d 448 (N.Y.1988)—§ 10.3, n. 66; § 10.4, n. 79; § 10.12, n. 253.

Tanner, People v., 331 N.Y.S.2d 1, 282 N.E.2d 98 (N.Y.1972)—§ 10.10, n. 191, 192; § 10.20, n. 493.

Tannuzzo, People ex rel. v. New York City, 174 A.D.2d 443, 571 N.Y.S.2d 230 (N.Y.A.D. 1 Dept.1991)—§ 4.10, n. 152.

Tarallo, People v., 48 A.D.2d 611, 367 N.Y.S.2d 286 (N.Y.A.D. 1 Dept.1975)—§ 10.5, n. 105.

Taranovich, People v., 373 N.Y.S.2d 79, 335 N.E.2d 303 (N.Y.1975)—§ 9.8, n. 37; § 9.10; § 9.10, n. 78.

Tardbania, People v., 130 A.D.2d 954, 515 N.Y.S.2d 936 (N.Y.A.D. 4 Dept.1987)—§ 5.21, n. 494.

Tas, People v., 434 N.Y.S.2d 978, 415 N.E.2d 967 (N.Y.1980)—§ 10.26, n. 582.

Tate, People v., 128 A.D.2d 652, 513 N.Y.S.2d 38 (N.Y.A.D. 2 Dept.1987)—§ 1.3, n. 71.

Tateo, United States v., 377 U.S. 463, 84 S.Ct. 1587, 12 L.Ed.2d 448 (1964)—§ 2.4, n. 85.

Tatum, People v., 205 A.D.2d 397, 613 N.Y.S.2d 391 (N.Y.A.D. 1 Dept.1994)—§ 10.28, n. 604, 606.

Taylor v. Illinois, 484 U.S. 400, 108 S.Ct. 646, 98 L.Ed.2d 798 (1988)—§ 7.1, n. 3; § 7.24, n. 274.

Taylor, People v., 181 A.D.2d 408, 580 N.Y.S.2d 337 (N.Y.A.D. 1 Dept.1992)—§ 5.26, n. 653.

Taylor, People v., 165 A.D.2d 800, 564 N.Y.S.2d 60 (N.Y.A.D. 1 Dept.1990)—§ 5.8, n. 139, 160.

Taylor, People v., 543 N.Y.S.2d 357, 541 N.E.2d 386 (N.Y.1989)—§ 3.12, n. 122; § 10.2, n. 18, 40, 43.

Taylor, People v., 124 A.D.2d 843, 509 N.Y.S.2d 46 (N.Y.A.D. 2 Dept.1986)—§ 9.41, n. 293.

Taylor, People v., 489 N.Y.S.2d 152, 478 N.E.2d 755 (N.Y.1985)—§ 5.27, n. 683; § 10.22, n. 535; § 11.15, n. 156; § 11.16, n. 211.

Taylor, People v., 97 A.D.2d 381, 467 N.Y.S.2d 590 (N.Y.A.D. 1 Dept.1983)—§ 10.17; § 10.17, n. 352, 353.

Taylor, People v., 83 A.D.2d 595, 441 N.Y.S.2d 116 (N.Y.A.D. 2 Dept.1981)—§ 7.10, n. 110.

Taylor, People v., 74 A.D.2d 177, 427 N.Y.S.2d 439 (N.Y.A.D. 2 Dept.1980)—§ 5.19; § 5.19, n. 445.

Taylor v. United States, 504 U.S. 991, 112 S.Ct. 2982, 119 L.Ed.2d 599 (1992)—§ 9.55, n. 399.

Teicher, People v., 439 N.Y.S.2d 846, 422 N.E.2d 506 (N.Y.1981)—§ 10.1, n. 12; § 10.8, n. 155.

Tejada, People v., 597 N.Y.S.2d 626, 613 N.E.2d 532 (N.Y.1993)—§ 10.11, n. 231.

Telesco, People v., 207 A.D.2d 920, 616 N.Y.S.2d 773 (N.Y.A.D. 2 Dept.1994)—§ 10.3, n. 71; § 10.5, n. 88.

Terrero, People v., 139 A.D.2d 830, 527 N.Y.S.2d 135 (N.Y.A.D. 3 Dept.1988)—§ 3.22, n. 264.

Tesiero, People v., 184 A.D.2d 802, 584 N.Y.S.2d 228 (N.Y.A.D. 3 Dept.1992)—§ 11.14, n. 148.

Testa, People v., 48 A.D.2d 691, 367 N.Y.S.2d 838 (N.Y.A.D. 2 Dept.1975)—§ 7.17, n. 187.

Texas v. McCullough, 475 U.S. 134, 106 S.Ct. 976, 89 L.Ed.2d 104 (1986)—§ 2.10, n. 215.

Theard, People v., 155 Misc.2d 475, 588 N.Y.S.2d 754 (N.Y.Sup.1992)—§ 5.8, n. 151.

Thomas, People v., 213 A.D.2d 73, 628 N.Y.S.2d 707 (N.Y.A.D. 2 Dept.1995)—§ 5.8, n. 185.

Thomas, People v., 210 A.D.2d 736, 620 N.Y.S.2d 555 (N.Y.A.D. 3 Dept.1994)—§ 9.43, n. 310.

TABLE OF CASES

Thomas, People v., 210 A.D.2d 269, 619 N.Y.S.2d 733 (N.Y.A.D. 2 Dept.1994)—§ 10.10, n. 408.

Thomas, People v., 200 A.D.2d 419, 606 N.Y.S.2d 217 (N.Y.A.D. 1 Dept.1994)—§ 9.51, n. 370.

Thomas, People v., 160 Misc.2d 39, 607 N.Y.S.2d 871 (N.Y.Sup.1994)—§ 5.4; § 5.4, n. 60.

Thomas, People v., 188 A.D.2d 431, 592 N.Y.S.2d 586 (N.Y.A.D. 1 Dept.1992)—§ 6.2, n. 25, 31; § 6.10, n. 225.

Thomas, People v., 159 A.D.2d 529, 552 N.Y.S.2d 394 (N.Y.A.D. 2 Dept.1990)—§ 11.10, n. 95, 105.

Thomas, People v., 147 A.D.2d 725, 538 N.Y.S.2d 330 (N.Y.A.D. 2 Dept.1989)—§ 7.17, n. 195.

Thomas, People v., 441 N.Y.S.2d 650, 424 N.E.2d 537 (N.Y.1981)—§ 10.22, n. 531; § 11.15, n. 163.

Thomas, People v., 107 Misc.2d 947, 436 N.Y.S.2d 153 (N.Y.Dist.Ct.1981)—§ 3.9, n. 109.

Thomas, People v., 434 N.Y.S.2d 941, 415 N.E.2d 931 (N.Y.1980)—§ 5.22, n. 616.

Thomas, People v., 106 Misc.2d 64, 432 N.Y.S.2d 317 (N.Y.City Crim.Ct.1980)—§ 5.19, n. 463.

Thomas, People v., 93 Misc.2d 961, 404 N.Y.S.2d 254 (N.Y.City Ct.1978)—§ 1.5, n. 139.

Thomas, People v., 77 Misc.2d 1095, 355 N.Y.S.2d 909 (N.Y.Sup.1974)—§ 6.4, n. 80.

Thomas, People ex rel. Pierce v., 70 Misc.2d 629, 334 N.Y.S.2d 666 (N.Y.Sup.1972)—§ 3.33, n. 453.

Thompson, People v., 611 N.Y.S.2d 470, 633 N.E.2d 1074 (N.Y.1994)—§ 5.27, n. 796.

Thompson, People v., 161 A.D.2d 1203, 555 N.Y.S.2d 993 (N.Y.A.D. 4 Dept.1990)—§ 5.22, n. 586.

Thompson, People v., 116 A.D.2d 377, 501 N.Y.S.2d 381 (N.Y.A.D. 2 Dept.1986)—§ 5.8, n. 184.

Thompson v. Weinstein, 150 A.D.2d 782, 542 N.Y.S.2d 33 (N.Y.A.D. 2 Dept. 1989)—§ 7.33, n. 369.

Thornton, People v., 130 A.D.2d 78, 517 N.Y.S.2d 807 (N.Y.A.D. 3 Dept.1987)—§ 7.14, n. 165.

Tibbs v. Florida, 457 U.S. 31, 102 S.Ct. 2211, 72 L.Ed.2d 652 (1982)—§ 2.4, n. 91.

Tindle, People v., 472 N.Y.S.2d 919, 460 N.E.2d 1354 (N.Y.1984)—§ 11.11, n. 114.

Tinsley, People v., 461 N.Y.S.2d 1005, 448 N.E.2d 790 (N.Y.1983)—§ 2.4, n. 51.

Tinsley, People v., 365 N.Y.S.2d 161, 324 N.E.2d 544 (N.Y.1974)—§ 11.18, n. 240, 241, 242.

Tirado, People v., 197 A.D.2d 927, 602 N.Y.S.2d 273 (N.Y.A.D. 4 Dept.1993)—§ 5.8, n. 130.

Tissois, People v., 531 N.Y.S.2d 228, 526 N.E.2d 1086 (N.Y.1988)—§ 7.17, n. 189; § 7.30, n. 349.

Titus v. Hill, 134 A.D.2d 911, 521 N.Y.S.2d 932 (N.Y.A.D. 4 Dept.1987)—§ 3.12, n. 124.

Tomassetti, People v., 159 Misc.2d 969, 607 N.Y.S.2d 588 (N.Y.Sup.1993)—§ 9.5, n. 21.

Tompkins, Matter of, 146 Misc.2d 754, 553 N.Y.S.2d 69 (N.Y.Co.Ct.1990)—§ 6.2, n. 10.

Tonnele v. Wetmore, 195 N.Y. 436, 88 N.E. 1068 (N.Y.1909)—§ 1.1, n. 1.

Tootick, United States v., 952 F.2d 1078 (9th Cir.1991)—§ 5.22, n. 606.

Toro, People v., 198 A.D.2d 532, 604 N.Y.S.2d 189 (N.Y.A.D. 2 Dept.1993)—§ 7.27, n. 297.

Toro, People v., 151 A.D.2d 142, 546 N.Y.S.2d 842 (N.Y.A.D. 1 Dept.1989)—§ 9.37, n. 270; § 9.39, n. 284.

Torres, People v., 214 A.D.2d 401, 625 N.Y.S.2d 166 (N.Y.A.D. 1 Dept.1995)—§ 9.34, n. 255.

Torres, People v., 194 A.D.2d 488, 599 N.Y.S.2d 561 (N.Y.A.D. 1 Dept.1993)—§ 6.10, n. 239.

Torres, People v., 190 A.D.2d 52, 597 N.Y.S.2d 492 (N.Y.A.D. 3 Dept.1993)—§ 7.23, n. 270.

Torres, People v., 173 A.D.2d 284, 569 N.Y.S.2d 676 (N.Y.A.D. 1 Dept.1991)—§ 7.17, n. 216.

Torres, People v., 164 A.D.2d 923, 559 N.Y.S.2d 584 (N.Y.A.D. 2 Dept.1990)—§ 7.9, n. 93; § 7.19, n. 223.

Torres, People v., 534 N.Y.S.2d 914, 531 N.E.2d 635 (N.Y.1988)—§ 1.2, n. 31.

Torres, People v., 468 N.Y.S.2d 606, 456 N.E.2d 497 (N.Y.1983)—§ 9.55, n. 398.

Torres, People v., 112 Misc.2d 145, 446 N.Y.S.2d 969 (N.Y.Sup.1981)—§ 4.5, n. 76; § 4.10, n. 169, 174.

Torres, People v., 408 N.Y.S.2d 487, 380 N.E.2d 313 (N.Y.1978)—§ 11.11, n. 111.

Toussie v. United States, 397 U.S. 112, 90 S.Ct. 858, 25 L.Ed.2d 156 (1970)—§ 9.2, n. 1.

Townes, People v., 390 N.Y.S.2d 893, 359 N.E.2d 402 (N.Y.1976)—§ 10.10; § 10.10, n. 176.

Townsend, People v., 127 A.D.2d 505, 511 N.Y.S.2d 858 (N.Y.A.D. 1 Dept.1987)—§ 5.7, n. 99.

Townsend, People v., 38 A.D.2d 569, 328 N.Y.S.2d 333 (N.Y.A.D. 2 Dept.1971)—§ 9.10, n. 90.

Toxey, People v., 202 A.D.2d 330, 609 N.Y.S.2d 12 (N.Y.A.D. 1 Dept.1994)—§ 11.10, n. 108.

Traficante, People v., 147 A.D.2d 843, 538 N.Y.S.2d 331 (N.Y.A.D. 3 Dept.1989)—§ 9.39, n. 283; § 9.41, n. 292; § 9.47, n. 346.

TABLE OF CASES

Trammel, People v., 620 N.Y.S.2d 754, 644 N.E.2d 1310 (N.Y.1994)—§ **10.26, n. 576; § 10.27, n. 593, 596.**

Trocchio, People v., 107 Misc.2d 610, 435 N.Y.S.2d 639 (N.Y.Co.Ct.1980)—§ **7.33, n. 363.**

Troiano, People v., 127 Misc.2d 738, 486 N.Y.S.2d 991 (N.Y.Co.Ct.1985)—§ **7.30, n. 348.**

Tullo, People v., 356 N.Y.S.2d 861, 313 N.E.2d 340 (N.Y.1974)—§ **1.4, n. 81, 86.**

Tullough, People v., 183 A.D.2d 863, 584 N.Y.S.2d 103 (N.Y.A.D. 2 Dept.1992)—§ **11.12, n. 127.**

Turcios-Umana, People v., 153 A.D.2d 707, 544 N.Y.S.2d 682 (N.Y.A.D. 2 Dept. 1989)—§ **7.21, n. 235.**

Tutt, People v., 384 N.Y.S.2d 444, 348 N.E.2d 920 (N.Y.1976)—§ **10.19, n. 459.**

Twine, People v., 121 Misc.2d 762, 468 N.Y.S.2d 559 (N.Y.City Crim.Ct.1983)—§ **3.9, n. 105.**

Tychanski, People v., 573 N.Y.S.2d 454, 577 N.E.2d 1046 (N.Y.1991)—§ **9.13, n. 128; § 9.16, n. 147; § 9.18; § 9.18, n. 160, 161; § 9.20, n. 167, 168.**

United States v. _____ (see opposing party)

United States ex rel. v. _____ (see opposing party and relator)

Updike, People v., 125 A.D.2d 735, 509 N.Y.S.2d 158 (N.Y.A.D. 3 Dept.1986)—§ **5.24, n. 638.**

Uplinger, People v., 460 N.Y.S.2d 514, 447 N.E.2d 62 (N.Y.1983)—§ **3.23, n. 273.**

Urraea, People v., 214 A.D.2d 378, 625 N.Y.S.2d 163 (N.Y.A.D. 1 Dept.1995)—§ **9.33, n. 246; § 9.34, n. 252; § 9.47, n. 339.**

Ursery, United States v., 59 F.3d 568 (6th Cir.1995)—§ **2.10, n. 231.**

U.S. Currency in the Amount of $228,536.00, United States v., 895 F.2d 908 (2nd Cir.1990)—§ **11.9, n. 85.**

Valentine, People v., 182 A.D.2d 655, 583 N.Y.S.2d 168 (N.Y.A.D. 2 Dept.1992)—§ **7.17, n. 216.**

Valerius, People v., 334 N.Y.S.2d 871, 286 N.E.2d 254 (N.Y.1972)—§ **10.19, n. 432; § 10.20, n. 489.**

Vallen, People v., 128 Misc.2d 397, 488 N.Y.S.2d 994 (N.Y.Co.Ct.1985)—§ **6.3, n. 45.**

Valles, People v., 476 N.Y.S.2d 50, 464 N.E.2d 418 (N.Y.1984)—§ **5.5; § 5.5, n. 69; § 5.7; § 5.7, n. 96, 104; § 5.27, n. 706.**

Valvano, People v., 131 A.D.2d 615, 516 N.Y.S.2d 507 (N.Y.A.D. 2 Dept.1987)—§ **5.8, n. 176.**

Van Buren, People v., 187 A.D.2d 925, 590 N.Y.S.2d 362 (N.Y.A.D. 4 Dept.1992)—§ **5.27; § 5.27, n. 719.**

Van Der Beek, People ex rel. v. McCloskey, 18 A.D.2d 205, 238 N.Y.S.2d 676 (N.Y.A.D. 1 Dept.1963)—§ **5.8, n. 116.**

Vanderbilt (Rosner-Hickey), Matter of, 453 N.Y.S.2d 662, 439 N.E.2d 378 (N.Y. 1982)—§ **5.9, n. 242.**

Van Pelt, People v., 556 N.Y.S.2d 984, 556 N.E.2d 423 (N.Y.1990)—§ **2.10, n. 212.**

Vara, People v., 117 A.D.2d 1013, 499 N.Y.S.2d 296 (N.Y.A.D. 4 Dept.1986)—§ **10.5, n. 120.**

Varela, People v., 106 A.D.2d 339, 483 N.Y.S.2d 13 (N.Y.A.D. 1 Dept.1984)—§ **5.27, n. 758, 771.**

Varela, People v., 124 Misc.2d 992, 479 N.Y.S.2d 116 (N.Y.Sup.1984)—§ **4.12, n. 200, 210.**

Varon, People v., 168 A.D.2d 349, 562 N.Y.S.2d 673 (N.Y.A.D. 1 Dept.1990)—§ **10.22, n. 533.**

Vasquez, People v., 629 N.Y.S.2d 756 (N.Y.A.D. 1 Dept.1995)—§ **10.21, n. 502, 503.**

Vasquez, People v., 200 A.D.2d 344, 613 N.Y.S.2d 595 (N.Y.A.D. 1 Dept.1994)—§ **5.26, n. 651; § 10.17; § 10.17, n. 369.**

Vasquez, People v., 199 A.D.2d 444, 605 N.Y.S.2d 381 (N.Y.A.D. 2 Dept.1993)—§ **11.10, n. 98.**

Vasquez, People v., 172 A.D.2d 435, 569 N.Y.S.2d 11 (N.Y.A.D. 1 Dept.1991)—§ **6.2, n. 34, 41.**

Vasquez, People v., 108 A.D.2d 701, 485 N.Y.S.2d 1008 (N.Y.A.D. 1 Dept.1985)—§ **3.12, n. 122.**

Vaughan, United States v., 682 F.2d 290 (2nd Cir.1982)—§ **1.3, n. 72.**

Vega v. Bell, 419 N.Y.S.2d 454, 393 N.E.2d 450 (N.Y.1979)—§ **1.10, n. 224, 238; § 3.33, n. 446; § 5.27; § 5.27, n. 782.**

Vega, People v., 80 A.D.2d 867, 436 N.Y.S.2d 748 (N.Y.A.D. 2 Dept.1981)—§ **5.7, n. 97.**

Vega, People v., 73 Misc.2d 857, 342 N.Y.S.2d 693 (N.Y.City Crim.Ct.1973)—§ **6.9, n. 213.**

Vega v. Rubin, 73 A.D.2d 658, 423 N.Y.S.2d 193 (N.Y.A.D. 2 Dept.1979)—§ **2.7, n. 160; § 5.21, n. 484.**

Velasquez, People v., 147 A.D.2d 726, 538 N.Y.S.2d 949 (N.Y.A.D. 2 Dept.1989)—§ **5.22, n. 571.**

Velasquez, United States v., 772 F.2d 1348 (7th Cir.1985)—§ **5.22, n. 547.**

Velez, People v., 161 A.D.2d 823, 556 N.Y.S.2d 147 (N.Y.A.D. 2 Dept.1990)—§ **7.17, n. 209.**

Velez, People v., 118 A.D.2d 116, 504 N.Y.S.2d 404 (N.Y.A.D. 1 Dept.1986)—§ **7.12, n. 134.**

Veloz v. Rothwax, 493 N.Y.S.2d 452, 483 N.E.2d 127 (N.Y.1985)—§ **5.26, n. 649; § 8.1, n. 8; § 10.13, n. 272.**

Veloz v. Rothwax, 103 A.D.2d 715, 478 N.Y.S.2d 14 (N.Y.A.D. 1 Dept.1984)—§ **10.13, n. 257.**

TABLE OF CASES

Ventimiglia, People v., 438 N.Y.S.2d 261, 420 N.E.2d 59 (N.Y.1981)—**§ 5.21, n. 482, 496; § 7.15, n. 172; § 10.19, n. 396.**

Ventresca, United States v., 380 U.S. 102, 85 S.Ct. 741, 13 L.Ed.2d 684 (1965)—**§ 10.3, n. 50, 62, 67.**

Verardi, People v., 158 Misc.2d 1039, 602 N.Y.S.2d 318 (N.Y.City Crim.Ct.1993)—**§ 3.29, n. 392.**

Verkey, People v., 185 A.D.2d 622, 585 N.Y.S.2d 897 (N.Y.A.D. 4 Dept.1992)—**§ 9.7, n. 33; § 11.15, n. 187.**

Vescur, People v., 134 Misc.2d 574, 511 N.Y.S.2d 997 (N.Y.City Crim.Ct.1987)—**§ 9.17, n. 158.**

Vesprey, People v., 183 A.D.2d 212, 590 N.Y.S.2d 91 (N.Y.A.D. 1 Dept.1992)—**§ 2.6, n. 122, 143.**

Vidal, People v., 180 A.D.2d 447, 580 N.Y.S.2d 13 (N.Y.A.D. 1 Dept.1992)—**§ 9.30, n. 230, 231; § 9.40, n. 290, 291.**

Vidal, People v., 161 A.D.2d 313, 555 N.Y.S.2d 233 (N.Y.A.D. 1 Dept.1990)—**§ 9.51, n. 381.**

Vientos, People v., 164 A.D.2d 122, 561 N.Y.S.2d 443 (N.Y.A.D. 1 Dept.1990)—**§ 10.10, n. 197.**

Vilardi, People v., 556 N.Y.S.2d 518, 555 N.E.2d 915 (N.Y.1990)—**§ 7.2, n. 10; § 7.8; § 7.8, n. 87; § 7.13, n. 148; § 7.30, n. 334; § 8.2.**

Villanueva, People v., 161 A.D.2d 552, 556 N.Y.S.2d 293 (N.Y.A.D. 1 Dept.1990)—**§ 10.3, n. 72.**

Virag v. Hynes, 446 N.Y.S.2d 196, 430 N.E.2d 1249 (N.Y.1981)—**§ 5.8, n. 117.**

Vivenzio, People v., 477 N.Y.S.2d 318, 465 N.E.2d 1254 (N.Y.1984)—**§ 3.24, n. 299.**

Vogler, People v., 92 Misc.2d 462, 400 N.Y.S.2d 315 (N.Y.Sup.1977)—**§ 9.4, n. 14.**

Vollick, People v., 148 A.D.2d 950, 539 N.Y.S.2d 187 (N.Y.A.D. 4 Dept.1989)—**§ 5.27; § 5.27, n. 720.**

Von Wolfersdorf, People v., 69 Misc.2d 896, 330 N.Y.S.2d 813 (N.Y.Co.Ct.1972)—**§ 6.3, n. 52.**

Vrlaku, People v., 537 N.Y.S.2d 24, 533 N.E.2d 1053 (N.Y.1988)—**§ 9.55, n. 398.**

Wade, United States v., 388 U.S. 218, 87 S.Ct. 1926, 18 L.Ed.2d 1149 (1967)—**§ 7.11, n. 119, 120; § 10.7, n. 136; § 10.8, n. 149; § 10.9, n. 166.**

Walker, People v., 187 A.D.2d 909, 591 N.Y.S.2d 77 (N.Y.A.D. 3 Dept.1992)—**§ 11.14, n. 153.**

Walker, People v., 133 A.D.2d 2, 518 N.Y.S.2d 392 (N.Y.A.D. 1 Dept.1987)—**§ 9.38, n. 278.**

Wallace, People v., 210 A.D.2d 359, 620 N.Y.S.2d 14 (N.Y.A.D. 2 Dept.1994)—**§ 11.13, n. 137.**

Wallace, People v., 563 N.Y.S.2d 722, 565 N.E.2d 471 (N.Y.1990)—**§ 7.23, n. 257.**

Wallace, People v., 153 A.D.2d 59, 549 N.Y.S.2d 515 (N.Y.A.D. 2 Dept.1989)—**§ 5.22, n. 596.**

Wallace, People v., 310 N.Y.S.2d 484, 258 N.E.2d 904 (N.Y.1970)—**§ 9.10, n. 82.**

Waller v. Florida, 397 U.S. 387, 90 S.Ct. 1184, 25 L.Ed.2d 435, 52 O.O.2d 320 (1970)—**§ 2.2, n. 26.**

Wallert, People v., 98 A.D.2d 47, 469 N.Y.S.2d 722 (N.Y.A.D. 1 Dept.1983)—**§ 7.12, n. 136.**

Walsh, People v., 123 Misc.2d 1042, 476 N.Y.S.2d 408 (N.Y.Sup.1984)—**§ 9.7, n. 33.**

Walsh, People v., 407 N.Y.S.2d 472, 378 N.E.2d 1041 (N.Y.1978)—**§ 2.4, n. 71.**

Walston, People v., 60 Misc.2d 531, 303 N.Y.S.2d 239 (N.Y.Sup.1969)—**§ 9.11, n. 114.**

Walter v. United States, 447 U.S. 649, 100 S.Ct. 2395, 65 L.Ed.2d 410 (1980)—**§ 10.6, n. 125.**

Walters, People v., 127 A.D.2d 870, 511 N.Y.S.2d 957 (N.Y.A.D. 2 Dept.1987)—**§ 9.39, n. 284.**

Walton, People v., 98 A.D.2d 842, 470 N.Y.S.2d 831 (N.Y.A.D. 3 Dept.1983)—**§ 9.12, n. 118.**

Walton, People v., 393 N.Y.S.2d 979, 362 N.E.2d 610 (N.Y.1977)—**§ 11.2, n. 7.**

W., Andre People v., 404 N.Y.S.2d 578, 375 N.E.2d 758 (N.Y.1978)—**§ 7.9; § 7.9, n. 91.**

Ward, People v., 95 A.D.2d 233, 465 N.Y.S.2d 556 (N.Y.A.D. 2 Dept.1983)—**§ 10.19, n. 443.**

Ward, United States v., 448 U.S. 242, 100 S.Ct. 2636, 65 L.Ed.2d 742 (1980)—**§ 2.10, n. 226.**

Warden, People v., 170 A.D.2d 469, 565 N.Y.S.2d 828 (N.Y.A.D. 2 Dept.1991)—**§ 5.27, n. 682.**

Warden, People v., 113 A.D.2d 116, 495 N.Y.S.2d 373 (N.Y.A.D. 1 Dept.1985)—**§ 4.10, n. 167.**

Warden, Ann M. Kross Center, People ex rel. Mack by Padden v., 145 Misc.2d 1016, 549 N.Y.S.2d 558 (N.Y.Sup. 1989)—**§ 3.25, n. 338.**

Warden, People ex rel. Benton by Weintraub v., 118 A.D.2d 443, 499 N.Y.S.2d 738 (N.Y.A.D. 1 Dept.1986)—**§ 4.5, n. 83, 89.**

Warden, People ex rel. Chakwin on Behalf of Ford v., 480 N.Y.S.2d 719, 470 N.E.2d 146 (N.Y.1984)—**§ 9.25, n. 203, 204; § 9.49, n. 358.**

Warden, People ex rel. Lazer on Behalf of Palmieri v., 173 A.D.2d 425, 571 N.Y.S.2d 441 (N.Y.A.D. 1 Dept.1991)—**§ 4.10, n. 152.**

Warden, People ex rel. McDonald v., 354 N.Y.S.2d 939, 310 N.E.2d 537 (N.Y. 1974)—**§ 4.13, n. 219.**

TABLE OF CASES

Warden, People ex rel. Schildhaus on Behalf of Weinstein v., 37 Misc.2d 660, 235 N.Y.S.2d 531 (N.Y.Sup.1962)—**§ 6.1, n. 3; § 6.2, n. 36; § 6.5, n. 85, 87.**

Warden of County Jail at Salem, People ex rel. Reibman v., 242 A.D. 282, 275 N.Y.S. 59 (N.Y.A.D. 3 Dept.1934)—**§ 9.2, n. 3.**

Warden, People ex rel. Weisenfeld v., 374 N.Y.S.2d 631, 337 N.E.2d 140 (N.Y. 1975)—**§ 4.5, n. 81.**

Warden, Rikers Island, People ex rel. Leventhal on Behalf of Agosta v., 102 A.D.2d 317, 477 N.Y.S.2d 332 (N.Y.A.D. 1 Dept.1984)—**§ 3.32, n. 442; § 11.19, n. 257.**

Warden, Rikers Island, George Motchan Center, People ex rel. Aponte by Gorfinkel v., 146 Misc.2d 386, 550 N.Y.S.2d 792 (N.Y.Sup.1990)—**§ 5.23, n. 623.**

Warden, State ex rel. Ray v., 184 A.D.2d 477, 585 N.Y.S.2d 424 (N.Y.A.D. 1 Dept. 1992)—**§ 4.5, n. 87.**

Wardius v. Oregon, 412 U.S. 470, 93 S.Ct. 2208, 37 L.Ed.2d 82 (1973)—**§ 7.27, n. 309; § 7.28; § 7.28, n. 317.**

Waring, People v., 206 A.D.2d 329, 615 N.Y.S.2d 21 (N.Y.A.D. 1 Dept.1994)—**§ 9.34, n. 257; § 9.49, n. 363.**

Warren, People v., 85 A.D.2d 747, 445 N.Y.S.2d 797 (N.Y.A.D. 2 Dept.1981)—**§ 9.43, n. 316.**

Washington, People v., 630 N.Y.S.2d 693, 654 N.E.2d 967 (N.Y.1995)—**§ 7.17, n. 191.**

Washington, People v., 433 N.Y.S.2d 745, 413 N.E.2d 1159 (N.Y.1980)—**§ 10.8, n. 160.**

Washington, People v., 401 N.Y.S.2d 1007, 372 N.E.2d 795 (N.Y.1977)—**§ 9.43, n. 315.**

Washor on Behalf of Lopez, People ex rel. v. Freckelton, 187 A.D.2d 406, 590 N.Y.S.2d 203 (N.Y.A.D. 1 Dept.1992)—**§ 4.5, n. 86.**

Washpun, People v., 134 A.D.2d 858, 521 N.Y.S.2d 915 (N.Y.A.D. 4 Dept.1987)—**§ 5.21, n. 493.**

Watkins, People v., 189 A.D.2d 623, 592 N.Y.S.2d 347 (N.Y.A.D. 1 Dept.1993)—**§ 7.23, n. 271.**

Watkins, People v., 157 A.D.2d 301, 556 N.Y.S.2d 541 (N.Y.A.D. 1 Dept.1990)—**§ 7.17, n. 209.**

Watt, People v., 593 N.Y.S.2d 782, 609 N.E.2d 135 (N.Y.1993)—**§ 5.15, n. 338, 339, 340.**

Watts, People v., 456 N.Y.S.2d 677, 442 N.E.2d 1188 (N.Y.1982)—**§ 9.10, n. 94.**

Waugh, People ex rel. Anonymous v., 76 Misc.2d 879, 351 N.Y.S.2d 594 (N.Y.Sup. 1974)—**§ 6.6, n. 126.**

Wayburn, People ex rel. v. Schupf, 385 N.Y.S.2d 518, 350 N.E.2d 906 (N.Y. 1976)—**§ 4.5, n. 75.**

Weaver, People v., 162 A.D.2d 486, 556 N.Y.S.2d 173 (N.Y.A.D. 2 Dept.1990)—**§ 9.16, n. 150.**

Weaver, People v., 157 A.D.2d 983, 550 N.Y.S.2d 467 (N.Y.A.D. 3 Dept.1990)—**§ 1.3, n. 66.**

Weaver, People v., 112 A.D.2d 782, 492 N.Y.S.2d 280 (N.Y.A.D. 4 Dept.1985)—**§ 5.27, n. 793.**

Webb, People v., 105 Misc.2d 660, 432 N.Y.S.2d 826 (N.Y.City Crim.Ct.1980)—**§ 7.3, n. 18.**

Weech, People v., 105 A.D.2d 1085, 482 N.Y.S.2d 174 (N.Y.A.D. 4 Dept.1984)—**§ 6.10; § 6.10, n. 261.**

Weeks, People v., 126 A.D.2d 857, 510 N.Y.S.2d 920 (N.Y.A.D. 3 Dept.1987)—**§ 5.16, n. 351; § 9.43, n. 310.**

Weinberg, People v., 358 N.Y.S.2d 357, 315 N.E.2d 434 (N.Y.1974)—**§ 3.25, n. 330.**

Weirich, People v., 429 N.Y.S.2d 635, 407 N.E.2d 479 (N.Y.1980)—**§ 9.30, n. 229; § 9.33, n. 246.**

Weisenfeld, People ex rel. v. Warden, 374 N.Y.S.2d 631, 337 N.E.2d 140 (N.Y. 1975)—**§ 4.5, n. 81.**

Welch, People v., 129 A.D.2d 752, 514 N.Y.S.2d 513 (N.Y.A.D. 2 Dept.1987)—**§ 11.9, n. 81.**

Welch, People ex rel. Schweizer v., 40 A.D.2d 621, 336 N.Y.S.2d 556 (N.Y.A.D. 4 Dept.1972)—**§ 4.5, n. 75.**

Welkes v. Brennan, 79 A.D.2d 644, 433 N.Y.S.2d 817 (N.Y.A.D. 2 Dept.1980)—**§ 6.2, n. 10.**

Wells, People v., 133 A.D.2d 385, 519 N.Y.S.2d 553 (N.Y.A.D. 2 Dept.1987)—**§ 7.4, n. 26.**

Welsh, People v., 124 A.D.2d 301, 508 N.Y.S.2d 278 (N.Y.A.D. 3 Dept.1986)—**§ 5.8, n. 160, 163.**

Wesley, People v., 540 N.Y.S.2d 757, 538 N.E.2d 76 (N.Y.1989)—**§ 10.11; § 10.11, n. 213, 226; § 10.17, n. 376, 380; § 10.20, n. 469, 476.**

West, People v., 599 N.Y.S.2d 484, 615 N.E.2d 968 (N.Y.1993)—**§ 10.20, n. 491.**

West, People v., 184 A.D.2d 743, 585 N.Y.S.2d 467 (N.Y.A.D. 2 Dept.1992)—**§ 7.17, n. 216.**

West, People v., 171 A.D.2d 1026, 569 N.Y.S.2d 33 (N.Y.A.D. 4 Dept.1991)—**§ 6.9, n. 200.**

West, People v., 160 A.D.2d 301, 553 N.Y.S.2d 721 (N.Y.A.D. 1 Dept.1990)—**§ 5.21, n. 494.**

West, People v., 533 N.Y.S.2d 50, 529 N.E.2d 418 (N.Y.1988)—**§ 5.22, n. 586.**

Westchester Rockland Newspapers, Inc. v. Leggett, 423 N.Y.S.2d 630, 399 N.E.2d 518 (N.Y.1979)—**§ 3.33, n. 465; § 6.9, n. 208.**

Wetmore, People v., 51 A.D.2d 591, 379 N.Y.S.2d 114 (N.Y.A.D. 2 Dept.1976)—**§ 11.11, n. 122.**

TABLE OF CASES

Wharton, People v., 550 N.Y.S.2d 260, 549 N.E.2d 462 (N.Y.1989)—§ 10.26, n. 584, 585.

Wheeler, People v., 176 A.D.2d 1133, 575 N.Y.S.2d 951 (N.Y.A.D. 3 Dept.1991)—§ 5.8, n. 145.

Wheeler, People v., 478 N.Y.S.2d 254, 466 N.E.2d 846 (N.Y.1984)—§ 5.22; § 5.22, n. 570, 574, 579.

Wheeler, United States v., 435 U.S. 313, 98 S.Ct. 1079, 55 L.Ed.2d 303 (1978)—§ 2.2, n. 26.

Whelan, People v., 165 A.D.2d 313, 567 N.Y.S.2d 817 (N.Y.A.D. 2 Dept.1991)—§ 10.3, n. 67, 68.

Whitaker, People v., 79 A.D.2d 668, 433 N.Y.S.2d 849 (N.Y.A.D. 2 Dept.1980)—§ 10.19, n. 409.

White v. Illinois, 502 U.S. 346, 112 S.Ct. 736, 116 L.Ed.2d 848 (1992)—§ 5.22, n. 589.

White, People v., 184 A.D.2d 676, 587 N.Y.S.2d 178 (N.Y.A.D. 2 Dept.1992)—§ 11.16, n. 209.

White, People v., 541 N.Y.S.2d 749, 539 N.E.2d 577 (N.Y.1989)—§ 10.26, n. 588.

White, People v., 451 N.Y.S.2d 57, 436 N.E.2d 507 (N.Y.1982)—§ 3.24, n. 299.

White, People v., 390 N.Y.S.2d 405, 358 N.E.2d 1031 (N.Y.1976)—§ 7.19, n. 225; § 7.32, n. 355.

Whitehurst, People v., 306 N.Y.S.2d 673, 254 N.E.2d 905 (N.Y.1969)—§ 10.7, n. 139.

Whitfield, People v., 597 N.Y.S.2d 641, 613 N.E.2d 547 (N.Y.1993)—§ 10.20, n. 469, 476.

Whitney, People v., 167 A.D.2d 254, 561 N.Y.S.2d 754 (N.Y.A.D. 1 Dept.1990)—§ 10.14, n. 288.

Whysong, People v., 187 A.D.2d 1037, 591 N.Y.S.2d 103 (N.Y.A.D. 4 Dept.1992)—§ 6.10, n. 250.

Whysong, People v., 175 A.D.2d 576, 572 N.Y.S.2d 243 (N.Y.A.D. 4 Dept.1991)—§ 6.5, n. 96; § 6.10, n. 248.

Wicks, People v., 556 N.Y.S.2d 970, 556 N.E.2d 409 (N.Y.1990)—§ 3.33, n. 458.

Wiggans, People v., 140 Misc.2d 1011, 532 N.Y.S.2d 42 (N.Y.City Crim.Ct.1988)—§ 3.6, n. 63.

Wiggins, People v., 634 N.Y.S.2d 747 (N.Y.A.D. 2 Dept.1995)—§ 5.8, n. 145.

Wiggins, People v., 197 A.D.2d 802, 603 N.Y.S.2d 81 (N.Y.A.D. 3 Dept.1993)—§ 9.51, n. 372.

Wiggins, People v., 194 A.D.2d 840, 598 N.Y.S.2d 391 (N.Y.A.D. 3 Dept.1993)—§ 9.37, n. 265; § 9.51, n. 381.

Wiley v. Altman, 438 N.Y.S.2d 490, 420 N.E.2d 371 (N.Y.1981)—§ 2.6, n. 131, 132; § 2.7, n. 168.

Wilkins, People v., 188 A.D.2d 320, 591 N.Y.S.2d 18 (N.Y.A.D. 1 Dept.1992)—§ 5.8, n. 127.

Wilkins, People v., 508 N.Y.S.2d 893, 501 N.E.2d 542 (N.Y.1986)—§ 5.18, n. 395; § 5.27, n. 740, 741; § 8.2; § 11.16, n. 199.

Willbright v. Smith, 745 F.2d 779 (2nd Cir. 1984)—§ 11.10, n. 96.

Williams v. Florida, 399 U.S. 78, 90 S.Ct. 1893, 26 L.Ed.2d 446 (1970)—§ 7.1, n. 3; § 7.27; § 7.27, n. 307.

Williams, People v., 626 N.Y.S.2d 1002, 650 N.E.2d 849 (N.Y.1995)—§ 6.6, n. 98; § 6.9, n. 201.

Williams, People v., 210 A.D.2d 168, 620 N.Y.S.2d 958 (N.Y.A.D. 1 Dept.1994)—§ 11.18, n. 245.

Williams, People v., 210 A.D.2d 161, 620 N.Y.S.2d 954 (N.Y.A.D. 1 Dept.1994)—§ 11.18, n. 240.

Williams, People v., 204 A.D.2d 77, 611 N.Y.S.2d 849 (N.Y.A.D. 1 Dept.1994)—§ 6.9, n. 202; § 6.10, n. 254.

Williams, People v., 204 A.D.2d 371, 614 N.Y.S.2d 138 (N.Y.A.D. 2 Dept.1994)—§ 11.17, n. 230.

Williams, People v., 195 A.D.2d 1040, 600 N.Y.S.2d 529 (N.Y.A.D. 4 Dept.1993)—§ 11.11, n. 112.

Williams, People v., 165 A.D.2d 839, 560 N.Y.S.2d 220 (N.Y.A.D. 2 Dept.1990)—§ 7.17, n. 207.

Williams, People v., 158 A.D.2d 930, 551 N.Y.S.2d 94 (N.Y.A.D. 4 Dept.1990)—§ 11.3, n. 18.

Williams, People v., 538 N.Y.S.2d 222, 535 N.E.2d 275 (N.Y.1989)—§ 5.2; § 5.2, n. 22; § 5.27, n. 735; § 8.2.

Williams, People v., 142 A.D.2d 310, 536 N.Y.S.2d 814 (N.Y.A.D. 2 Dept.1988)—§ 5.22, n. 610.

Williams, People v., 144 A.D.2d 402, 533 N.Y.S.2d 963 (N.Y.A.D. 2 Dept.1988)—§ 6.10, n. 226.

Williams, People v., 143 A.D.2d 959, 533 N.Y.S.2d 742 (N.Y.A.D. 2 Dept.1988)—§ 3.24, n. 303.

Williams, People v., 141 A.D.2d 402, 529 N.Y.S.2d 991 (N.Y.A.D. 1 Dept.1988)—§ 9.20, n. 164.

Williams, People v., 136 Misc.2d 294, 518 N.Y.S.2d 751 (N.Y.City Crim.Ct.1987)—§ 1.3, n. 71.

Williams, People v., 130 A.D.2d 697, 515 N.Y.S.2d 622 (N.Y.A.D. 2 Dept.1987)—§ 9.14, n. 133.

Williams, People v., 134 Misc.2d 860, 512 N.Y.S.2d 1007 (N.Y.Co.Ct.1987)—§ 4.12, n. 195.

Williams, People v., 132 Misc.2d 549, 504 N.Y.S.2d 364 (N.Y.Sup.1986)—§ 9.43, n. 310.

Williams, People v., 119 A.D.2d 606, 500 N.Y.S.2d 778 (N.Y.A.D. 2 Dept.1986)—§ 10.3, n. 64; § 10.4, n. 80.

Williams, People v., 123 Misc.2d 165, 473 N.Y.S.2d 689 (N.Y.Sup.1984)—§ 5.21, n. 484.

TABLE OF CASES

Williams, People v., 452 N.Y.S.2d 571, 438 N.E.2d 104 (N.Y.1982)—§ 9.36, n. 258.
Williams, People v., 81 A.D.2d 418, 440 N.Y.S.2d 935 (N.Y.A.D. 2 Dept.1981)—§ 5.9; § 5.9, n. 212.
Williams, People v., 433 N.Y.S.2d 94, 412 N.E.2d 1320 (N.Y.1980)—§ 7.27, n. 305.
Williams, People v., 72 A.D.2d 950, 422 N.Y.S.2d 237 (N.Y.A.D. 4 Dept.1979)—§ 9.16, n. 149.
Williams, People v., 370 N.Y.S.2d 904, 331 N.E.2d 684 (N.Y.1975)—§ 11.17, n. 227.
Williams, People v., 248 N.Y.S.2d 659, 198 N.E.2d 45 (N.Y.1964)—§ 1.4, n. 77.
Williams, United States v., 504 U.S. 36, 112 S.Ct. 1735, 118 L.Ed.2d 352 (1992)—§ 5.1, n. 10; § 5.7, n. 100; § 5.27, n. 701.
Wills, People v., 201 A.D.2d 519, 607 N.Y.S.2d 409 (N.Y.A.D. 2 Dept.1994)—§ 9.41, n. 296.
Wilmer, People v., 191 A.D.2d 850, 595 N.Y.S.2d 123 (N.Y.A.D. 3 Dept.1993)—§ 11.18, n. 242.
Wilson, Matter of, 89 Misc.2d 1046, 393 N.Y.S.2d 275 (N.Y.Fam.Ct.1977)—§ 4.5, n. 76.
Wilson v. Arkansas, ___ U.S. ___, 115 S.Ct. 1914, 131 L.Ed.2d 976 (1995)—§ 3.14, n. 155, 156.
Wilson, People v., 631 N.Y.S.2d 127, 655 N.E.2d 168 (N.Y.1995)—§ 9.23; § 9.23, n. 185, 186.
Wilson, People v., 210 A.D.2d 666, 619 N.Y.S.2d 884 (N.Y.A.D. 3 Dept.1994)—§ 5.27, n. 733.
Wilson, People v., 188 A.D.2d 671, 591 N.Y.S.2d 513 (N.Y.A.D. 2 Dept.1992)—§ 9.16, n. 151.
Wilson, People v., 153 Misc.2d 784, 583 N.Y.S.2d 125 (N.Y.Sup.1992)—§ 5.8, n. 168.
Winbush, People v., 199 A.D.2d 447, 605 N.Y.S.2d 385 (N.Y.A.D. 2 Dept.1993)—§ 11.10, n. 96.
Winchenbaugh, People v., 120 A.D.2d 811, 501 N.Y.S.2d 929 (N.Y.A.D. 3 Dept.1986)—§ 11.15, n. 161.
Winley, People v., 105 Misc.2d 474, 432 N.Y.S.2d 429 (N.Y.Sup.1980)—§ 1.3, n. 40, 68.
Wirchansky, People v., 391 N.Y.S.2d 70, 359 N.E.2d 666 (N.Y.1976)—§ 10.3, n. 68.
Wirtschafter, People v., 305 N.Y. 515, 114 N.E.2d 18 (N.Y.1953)—§ 4.12, n. 203.
Wise, People v., 204 A.D.2d 133, 612 N.Y.S.2d 117 (N.Y.A.D. 1 Dept.1994)—§ 10.15, n. 298.
Wise, People v., 141 Misc.2d 409, 532 N.Y.S.2d 833 (N.Y.Dist.Ct.1988)—§ 9.20, n. 165.
Wise, People v., 413 N.Y.S.2d 334, 385 N.E.2d 1262 (N.Y.1978)—§ 10.20, n. 467.

Witherspoon, People v., 498 N.Y.S.2d 789, 489 N.E.2d 758 (N.Y.1985)—§ 10.19; § 10.19, n. 429.
Witte v. United States, ___ U.S. ___, 115 S.Ct. 2199, 132 L.Ed.2d 351 (1995)—§ 2.10, n. 218.
Wittmann, People v., 73 A.D.2d 1053, 425 N.Y.S.2d 416 (N.Y.A.D. 4 Dept.1980)—§ 9.38, n. 282.
Wolf, People v., 176 A.D.2d 1070, 575 N.Y.S.2d 726 (N.Y.A.D. 3 Dept.1991)—§ 6.10, n. 225.
Wolfson, People ex rel. Rosenthal on Behalf of Kolman v., 422 N.Y.S.2d 55, 397 N.E.2d 745 (N.Y.1979)—§ 4.13, n. 218.
Wong Sun v. United States, 371 U.S. 471, 83 S.Ct. 407, 9 L.Ed.2d 441 (1963)—§ 10.9, n. 163; § 10.10, n. 173.
Wood v. Hughes, 212 N.Y.S.2d 33, 173 N.E.2d 21 (N.Y.1961)—§ 5.11, n. 306.
Wood, People v., 64 A.D.2d 767, 407 N.Y.S.2d 271 (N.Y.A.D. 3 Dept.1978)—§ 6.4, n. 81.
Woods, People v., 150 Misc.2d 1070, 572 N.Y.S.2d 279 (N.Y.City Crim.Ct.1991)—§ 9.26, n. 220; § 9.47, n. 346.
Woods, People v., 143 A.D.2d 1068, 533 N.Y.S.2d 888 (N.Y.A.D. 2 Dept.1988)—§ 1.10, n. 243, 244.
Woodson, People v., 176 A.D.2d 186, 574 N.Y.S.2d 310 (N.Y.A.D. 1 Dept.1991)—§ 9.55, n. 401; § 11.10, n. 100.
Woolnough, People v., 180 A.D.2d 837, 580 N.Y.S.2d 776 (N.Y.A.D. 2 Dept.1992)—§ 10.4, n. 75.
Woolson, People v., 195 A.D.2d 949, 600 N.Y.S.2d 587 (N.Y.A.D. 4 Dept.1993)—§ 5.10, n. 300.
Worley, People v., 201 A.D.2d 520, 607 N.Y.S.2d 408 (N.Y.A.D. 2 Dept.1994)—§ 9.41, n. 293.
Worley, People v., 498 N.Y.S.2d 116, 488 N.E.2d 1228 (N.Y.1985)—§ 9.33, n. 247; § 9.34, n. 255; § 9.47, n. 336.
Wright, Vicki-Crystal People v., 635 N.Y.S.2d 136, 658 N.E.2d 1009 (N.Y.1995)—§ 7.13, n. 152; § 7.14, n. 157.
Wright, People v., 163 Misc.2d 139, 619 N.Y.S.2d 525 (N.Y.City Ct.1994)—§ 1.5, n. 138.
Wright, People v., 196 A.D.2d 700, 601 N.Y.S.2d 618 (N.Y.A.D. 1 Dept.1993)—§ 11.9, n. 82.
Wright, People v., 192 A.D.2d 875, 596 N.Y.S.2d 896 (N.Y.A.D. 3 Dept.1993)—§ 3.24, n. 303.
Wright, People v., 124 A.D.2d 1015, 508 N.Y.S.2d 1017 (N.Y.A.D. 4 Dept.1986)—§ 6.10, n. 250.
Wright, People v., 105 A.D.2d 1088, 482 N.Y.S.2d 591 (N.Y.A.D. 4 Dept.1984)—§ 6.10, n. 248, 260.
Wyatt, People v., 60 A.D.2d 958, 401 N.Y.S.2d 890 (N.Y.A.D. 3 Dept.1978)—§ 10.3, n. 57.

TABLE OF CASES

Yagdis, People v., 201 A.D.2d 521, 607 N.Y.S.2d 407 (N.Y.A.D. 2 Dept.1994)—§ 11.13, n. 137.

Yanez, People v., 128 Misc.2d 716, 490 N.Y.S.2d 971 (N.Y.Sup.1985)—§ 9.5, n. 17; § 9.6, n. 25.

Yannarilli, People ex rel. v. Draxler, 41 A.D.2d 684, 340 N.Y.S.2d 755 (N.Y.A.D. 3 Dept.1973)—§ 4.5, n. 83.

Yash Pal Gupta, People v., 80 A.D.2d 743, 437 N.Y.S.2d 175 (N.Y.A.D. 4 Dept. 1981)—§ 11.11, n. 123.

Yattaw, People v., 106 A.D.2d 679, 484 N.Y.S.2d 140 (N.Y.A.D. 3 Dept.1984)—§ 7.10, n. 110.

Ybarra v. Illinois, 444 U.S. 85, 100 S.Ct. 338, 62 L.Ed.2d 238 (1979)—§ 10.6, n. 129.

Ylda, United States v., 653 F.2d 912 (5th Cir.1981)—§ 5.18, n. 427.

Young, People v., 163 Misc.2d 36, 620 N.Y.S.2d 223 (N.Y.Sup.1994)—§ 5.6, n. 95.

Young, People v., 582 N.Y.S.2d 977, 591 N.E.2d 1163 (N.Y.1992)—§ 7.17, n. 201.

Young, People v., 138 A.D.2d 764, 526 N.Y.S.2d 577 (N.Y.A.D. 2 Dept.1988)—§ 5.8, n. 138.

Young, People v., 137 Misc.2d 400, 520 N.Y.S.2d 924 (N.Y.Sup.1987)—§ 5.8, n. 165.

Young, People v., 123 Misc.2d 486, 473 N.Y.S.2d 715 (N.Y.City Crim.Ct.1984)—§ 3.9, n. 109.

Yourdon, People v., 142 A.D.2d 998, 530 N.Y.S.2d 419 (N.Y.A.D. 4 Dept.1988)—§ 7.14, n. 166.

Yu, People v., 204 A.D.2d 129, 612 N.Y.S.2d 116 (N.Y.A.D. 1 Dept.1994)—§ 11.13, n. 144.

Yuk Bui Yee, People v., 94 Misc.2d 628, 405 N.Y.S.2d 386 (N.Y.Sup.1978)—§ 5.21, n. 482, 508.

Zaccaro, People v., 132 A.D.2d 589, 517 N.Y.S.2d 567 (N.Y.A.D. 2 Dept.1987)—§ 1.3, n. 55; § 2.6, n. 149.

Zackowitz, People v., 254 N.Y. 192, 172 N.E. 466 (N.Y.1930)—§ 5.21, n. 495.

Zafiro v. United States, 506 U.S. 534, 113 S.Ct. 933, 122 L.Ed.2d 317 (1993)—§ 5.22, n. 601.

Zambito, People v., 153 A.D.2d 975, 545 N.Y.S.2d 414 (N.Y.A.D. 3 Dept.1989)—§ 9.51, n. 365; § 9.55, n. 400.

Zanghi, People v., 580 N.Y.S.2d 179, 588 N.E.2d 77 (N.Y.1991)—§ 5.10; § 5.10, n. 287, 293.

Zarate, People v., 160 A.D.2d 466, 554 N.Y.S.2d 137 (N.Y.A.D. 1 Dept.1990)—§ 10.17, n. 378; § 10.18, n. 389.

Zehner, People v., 112 A.D.2d 465, 490 N.Y.S.2d 879 (N.Y.A.D. 3 Dept.1985)—§ 1.9, n. 206.

Zeigler v. Morgenthau, 488 N.Y.S.2d 633, 477 N.E.2d 1087 (N.Y.1985)—§ 2.4, n. 54.

Zelker, United States ex rel. Roth v., 455 F.2d 1105 (2nd Cir.1972)—§ 6.2, n. 13, 29.

Zelkowitz, People v., 84 Misc.2d 746, 375 N.Y.S.2d 1005 (N.Y.Sup.1975)—§ 5.23, n. 624.

Zimmer, People v., 112 A.D.2d 500, 490 N.Y.S.2d 912 (N.Y.A.D. 3 Dept.1985)—§ 10.2, n. 16, 18.

Zimmerman, People v., 157 Misc.2d 293, 596 N.Y.S.2d 307 (N.Y.Co.Ct.1993)—§ 10.16, n. 320.

Zimmerman, People v., 101 A.D.2d 294, 475 N.Y.S.2d 127 (N.Y.A.D. 2 Dept.1984)—§ 10.20, n. 480.

Zirpola, People v., 454 N.Y.S.2d 702, 440 N.E.2d 787 (N.Y.1982)—§ 9.26, n. 215; § 9.43, n. 305, 310; § 9.52, n. 384.

Zisis, People v., 113 Misc.2d 998, 450 N.Y.S.2d 655 (N.Y.City Crim.Ct.1982)—§ 7.3, n. 18.

Zlochevsky, People v., 196 A.D.2d 701, 603 N.Y.S.2d 433 (N.Y.A.D. 1 Dept.1993)—§ 7.21, n. 236.

Zolin, United States v., 491 U.S. 554, 109 S.Ct. 2619, 105 L.Ed.2d 469 (1989)—§ 5.21, n. 526.

Z., Robert, People v., 134 Misc.2d 555, 511 N.Y.S.2d 473 (N.Y.Co.Ct.1986)—§ 5.20, n. 472.

Zupan, People v., 184 A.D.2d 888, 585 N.Y.S.2d 545 (N.Y.A.D. 3 Dept.1992)—§ 5.7, n. 99.

Zurcher v. Stanford Daily, 436 U.S. 547, 98 S.Ct. 1970, 56 L.Ed.2d 525 (1978)—§ 10.1, n. 8; § 10.3, n. 58; § 10.5, n. 85.

Zvonik, People v., 40 A.D.2d 840, 337 N.Y.S.2d 336 (N.Y.A.D. 2 Dept.1972)—§ 5.19, n. 458.

INDEX

References are to Sections

ABSENCE OR UNAVAILABILITY OF DEFENDANT
Absent defendant, § 9.38
Bench warrants, § 9.37
Definitions, § 9.35
Readiness rule,
    Causation of prosecution's unreadiness, § 9.36
Unavailable defendant, § 9.39

ACCUSATORY INSTRUMENTS
Complaints, generally, this index
Defective instruments,
    Jurisdictional defects,
        Guilty pleas, survival of claim, § 11.16
        Omnibus motion, exception, § 8.1
    Motion to dismiss, §§ 3.26, 3.27
    Nonjurisdictional defects,
        Guilty pleas, waiver, § 11.15
Facial sufficiency, § 3.7
Indictment, generally, this index
Information, § 3.2
Joinder,
    Defendants, of, § 3.3
    Offenses, of, § 3.3
Limitation of Actions, generally, this index
Misdemeanor complaints. Complaints, this index
Motion to dismiss,
    Affirmation in support, form, § 3.36.10
    Defective instrument, §§ 3.26, 3.27
    Double jeopardy, § 2.11
        Affirmation in support, form, § 2.13.2
        Notice of motion, form, § 2.13.1
    Notice of motion, form, § 3.36.9
Prosecutor's Information, generally, this index
Simplified information, § 3.2
Summary, § 3.35(A)
Superior court information,
    Chargeable offenses, § 5.10
    Waiver of indictment, § 5.10
        Summary, § 5.31

ADJOURNMENT IN CONTEMPLATION OF DISMISSAL
Motion to Dismiss, this index

ALCOHOL AWARENESS PROGRAMS
Adjournment in contemplation of dismissal,
    Conditions on defendant, § 3.29

ALIBI, NOTICE
Defenses, this index

AMENDMENT
Arrest warrants, § 3.12

INDEX

AMENDMENT—Continued
Bill of particulars, § 5.19
   Notice of motion, form, § 5.33.15
   Summary, § 5.32(D)
Indictment, § 5.13
   Affirmation in support, form, § 5.33.14
   Defects, curing, § 5.18
   Lesser included offenses, § 5.18
   Notice of motion, form, § 5.33.13
   Summary, §§ 5.32(A), 5.32(C)
Information, § 3.8
   Motion to amend,
      Affirmation in support, form, § 3.36.7
      Notice of motion, form, § 3.36.6
Prosecutor's information, § 3.8
   Motion to amend,
      Affirmation in support, form, § 3.36.5
      Notice of motion, form, § 3.36.4

AMNESIA
Competency, § 6.10

APPEALS
Bail and recognizance, § 4.9
   Excessive bail, superior courts, §§ 4.6, 4.13
   Remission, denial of application, § 4.12
Delay in process,
   Speedy trial, federal constitutional rights inapplicable, § 9.8
Double jeopardy,
   Attachment of jeopardy,
      Reversal on appeal, § 2.4
      Summary, § 2.12(A)
   Raising claim, § 2.11
      Summary, § 2.12(H)
   Reversal on appeal,
      Attachment of jeopardy, § 2.4
      Increased sentence, § 2.10
Guilty pleas,
   Reservation of rights, waiver, § 11.15
   Suppression of evidence, § 10.22
   Voluntariness, bargained for waiver of right to appeal, § 11.17
Indictment,
   Following dismissal, § 5.28
      Murder charge, § 5.29
      Summary, § 5.32(I)
Notice,
   Suppression of evidence, § 10.29
      Summary, § 10.30(E)
Plea bargaining,
   Waiver of right to appeal, voluntariness, § 11.17
Prosecutors,
   Readiness rule, excludable periods, § 9.31
   Suppression of evidence, § 10.22
Reversal on appeal,
   Commencement of criminal action,
      Recommencement rule, § 9.16
Suppression of evidence,
   Guilty pleas, following, § 10.22
   Interlocutory, § 10.22
   Notice, § 10.29
      Summary, § 10.30(E)
   Prosecution, by, § 10.22

APPEARANCE TICKET
Arraignment, this index

ARRAIGNMENT
Appearance ticket, § 3.20

INDEX

ARRAIGNMENT—Continued
Appearance ticket—Continued
    Commencement of criminal action,
        Recommencement rule, § 9.17
    Facially sufficient, § 3.21
    Failure to appear, § 3.21
    Marihuana, § 3.22
    Pre-arraignment bail, § 3.21
    Return, § 3.21
Arrest warrant,
    Securing defendant's appearance, § 5.23
    Summary, § 5.32(G)
Bail and recognizance, § 3.24
Compelling defendant's appearance, § 3.10
Court's duty to inform defendant of rights, §§ 3.24, 5.24
    Summary, § 5.32(G)
Electronic arraignment,
    Defendant's consent required, § 3.24
Failure to appear,
    Bench warrants, § 5.23
Felony complaints, § 3.30
    Court's duty to inform defendant of rights, § 3.30
    Not guilty pleas, § 3.30
    Reasonable cause determination, § 3.30
    Summary, § 3.35(F)
Fingerprinting, § 5.23
    Summary, § 5.32(G)
Guilty pleas, § 5.24
Hearing, notice, § 5.23
Non-felony accusatory instruments, § 3.24
    Summary, § 3.35(C)
Not guilty pleas, § 5.24
Not responsible by reason of mental disease or defect, § 5.24
Pre-arraignment bail, § 4.8
    Appearance ticket, § 3.21
Prosecutor's direction to appear,
    Time excludable, § 9.45
Securing defendant's appearance, § 5.23
Summons,
    Securing defendant's appearance, § 5.23
Suppression of evidence, time for filing motion, § 10.13
Television coverage, consent of parties required, § 3.24
Traffic offenses,
    Court's duty to inform defendant of rights, § 3.24
"Without unnecessary delay" standard, § 3.19

ARREST
Warrantless Arrest, generally, this index
Warrants. Arrest Warrants, generally, this index

ARREST WARRANTS
Amendment, § 3.12
Appearance ticket, failure to appear, § 3.21
Arraignment,
    Securing defendant's appearance, § 5.23
    Summary, § 5.32(G)
Commencement of criminal action required, § 3.11
Content, § 3.12
Execution, § 3.14
Force, use, § 3.14
Form, § 3.12
Issuance, §§ 3.11, 3.13
"John Doe" or "Jane Doe" warrants, § 3.12
"Knock and announce" rule, § 3.14
Post-arrest procedure, § 3.15
    "Without unnecessary delay" standard, § 3.15
Reasonable cause determination, § 3.13

INDEX

ARREST WARRANTS—Continued
Simplified information,
    Traffic ticket, arrest warrant precluded, § 3.13
Summary, § 3.35(B)
Summons, failure to appear, § 3.16
Third party dwelling, search warrant required, § 3.14
Traffic ticket, arrest warrant precluded, § 3.13

ATTORNEYS
Ineffective Assistance of Counsel, generally, this index
Prosecutors, generally, this index
Right to Counsel, generally, this index
Work product rule,
    Privileged information,
        Discovery, § 7.31
            In camera review, § 7.31
        Waiver, § 7.31

BAIL AND RECOGNIZANCE
    Generally, § 4.1 et seq.
Affirmation in support of application, form, § 4.15.2
Appeal, § 4.9
    Excessive bail, superior courts, §§ 4.6, 4.13
    Remission, denial of application, § 4.12
Appearance ticket. Arraignment, this index
Application, § 4.5
Arraignment, § 3.24
Arrest warrant,
    Post-arrest procedure, § 3.15
Bail bonds, § 4.2
    Appearance bonds, §§ 4.2, 4.3
    Insurance company bail bond, § 4.3
    Partially secured bonds, §§ 4.2, 4.3
    Secured bonds, §§ 4.2, 4.3
    Surety bonds, § 4.3
    Termination, § 4.3
    Unsecured bonds, §§ 4.2, 4.3
Cash bail, § 4.3
Commitment to custody of sheriff, § 4.2
    Juveniles, § 4.4
Competency determination, imprisonment without bail, § 4.4
Conditions, § 4.10
    Improper restrictions, § 4.10
    Summary, § 4.14(B)
    Temporary protection orders, § 4.10
        Hearings, § 4.10
        Summary, § 4.14(B)
Definitions, § 4.2
Excessive bail,
    Appeal, superior courts, §§ 4.6, 4.13
    Habeas corpus, § 4.13
        Form, § 4.15.3
    Summary, § 4.14(F)
Fines, failure to pay, imprisonment without bail, § 4.4
Fixing bail, § 4.2
    Authority, § 4.4
    Factors to consider, § 4.5
        Summary, § 4.14(A)
    Local criminal courts, § 4.6
    Superior courts, § 4.7
Forfeiture, § 4.12
    Summary, § 4.14(E)
Habeas corpus, § 4.13
    Form, § 4.15.3
Imprisonment without bail, § 4.4
Improper restrictions, § 4.10
Local criminal courts, fixing bail, § 4.6

INDEX

BAIL AND RECOGNIZANCE—Continued
Modification, § 4.10
Notice of application, form, § 4.15.1
Order of protection, violation, imprisonment without bail, § 4.4
Post-conviction bail, § 4.9
Pre-arraignment bail, § 4.8
    Appearance ticket, § 3.21
Preliminary hearings,
    Failure to commence hearing timely,
        Release of defendant from custody, § 3.34
            Summary, § 3.35(I)
Pretrial service programs, § 4.4
Preventive detention improper, § 4.5
Readiness rule,
    Readiness to avoid release on bail or recognizance,
        Affirmation in support, form, § 9.58.8
        Calculation of time, § 9.25
            Summary, defense, § 9.56(B)
        Motion for bail or recognizance, form, § 9.58.7
Release on own recognizance, § 4.2
Remission,
    Affirmation in support of application, form, § 4.15.4
    Denial of application, appeal, § 4.12
    Limitation of actions, § 4.12
    Notice of application, form, § 4.15.4
Revocation,
    Hearing, § 4.10
    Summary, § 4.14(D)
Securing order, §§ 4.2, 5.24
    Summary, § 5.32(G)
"Stationhouse" bail, § 4.8
Sufficiency, § 4.11
    Summary, § 4.14(C)
Summary, § 4.14(B)
Superior courts,
    Appeal. excessive bail, §§ 4.6, 4.13
    Fixing bail, § 4.7
Temporary protection orders, § 4.10
    Hearings, § 4.10
    Summary, § 4.14(B)
Traffic tickets, credit card posting, § 4.3

BENCH TRIALS
Double jeopardy,
    Attachment of jeopardy, § 2.2
        Summary, § 2.12(A)

BENCH WARRANTS
Absence or unavailability of defendant, § 9.37
Failure to appear,
    Arraignment, § 5.23
        Summary, § 5.32(G)

BILL OF PARTICULARS
Amendment, § 5.19
    Affirmation in support, form, § 5.33.16
    Notice of motion, form, § 5.33.15
    Summary, § 5.32(D)
Complaints, misdemeanor, § 3.8
Contents, § 5.19
Indictment,
    Summary, § 5.32(A)
    Supplementing defects, § 5.13
Information, § 3.8
Notice, § 5.14
    Summary, § 5.32(A)

INDEX

BILL OF PARTICULARS—Continued
Omnibus motion, § 5.19
    Exception, § 8.1
Prosecutor's information, § 3.8
Request, service of process, § 5.19

BLOOD
Scientific tests,
    Defendant's right to test physical evidence, § 7.32
        Order compelling blood sample from complainant, § 7.33
    Suppression of evidence, § 10.8
Withdrawal from defendant,
    Prosecution's motion to compel, § 7.11

"BRADY" EVIDENCE
Discovery, this index

BURDEN OF PROOF
Limitation of actions, § 9.6
Preliminary hearings, § 3.33
Procedural requirements, §§ 9.50, 9.52
    Summary, defense, § 9.56(C)
    Summary, prosecution, § 9.57
Search warrants, § 10.4
Suppression of evidence, hearing, § 10.20

CAPITAL PUNISHMENT
Death Penalty, generally, this index

CHANGE OF VENUE
Geographical jurisdiction, generally. Jurisdiction, this index

CHILD ABUSE
Privileged information, discovery, § 7.30

CHILDREN
Juveniles, generally, this index
Minors, generally, this index

COLLATERAL ESTOPPEL
Double jeopardy, §§ 2.5, 2.8
    Summary, § 2.12(E)

COMMENCEMENT OF CRIMINAL ACTION
Arrest warrant, § 3.11
Filing of accusatory instrument, § 9.15
Recommencement rule,
    Appeals, reversal, § 9.16
    Appearance ticket, arraignment, § 9.17
    Guilty pleas, withdrawal, § 9.16
    Mistrials, retrial following, § 9.16
    Not responsible by reason of mental disease or defect, withdrawal of plea, § 9.16
Reduction of original charges,
    Inspection and reduction of indicted felony, § 9.19
    Misdemeanors, § 9.20
    Reduction of felony complaint, § 9.18
Summons, § 3.16

COMMUNITY SERVICE
Adjournment in contemplation of dismissal,
    Conditions on defendant, § 3.29

COMPETENCY
    Generally, § 6.1 et seq.
Amnesia, § 6.10
Deafness, § 6.10
Developmental disabilities, § 6.10
Discharge from commitment, § 6.8
Due process, discharge from commitment, § 6.8
Duration of commitment, § 6.6

INDEX

COMPETENCY—Continued
Grand jury,
    Effect of mental examination, § 6.3
Guilty pleas,
    Mental examination, § 11.8
Hearings,
    Discharge from commitment, § 6.8
    Mental examination, § 6.6
    Procedure, § 6.9
Local criminal court,
    Post-examination procedure, § 6.7
Mental examinations, this index
Mild retardation, § 6.10
Motion to dismiss,
    Furtherance of justice, not proper basis, § 6.3
Paranoia, § 6.10
Presumption of competency, § 6.2
Readiness rule, excludable periods, § 9.28
Refusal to cooperate, waiver of hearing, § 6.10
Retardation, mild, § 6.10
Schizophrenia, § 6.10
Speedy trial,
    Effect of mental examination, § 6.3
Summary, § 6.11
Superior court,
    Post-examination procedure, § 6.6
Synthetic competence, § 6.10
Verification,
    Mentally ill person's capacity to testify under oath, § 3.6
    Minor's capacity to testify under oath, § 3.6
Waiver, § 6.10

COMPLAINTS
Felony complaints, § 3.2
    Arraignment, § 3.30
        Court's duty to inform defendant of rights, § 3.30
        Not guilty pleas, § 3.30
        Reasonable cause determination, § 3.30
        Summary, § 3.35(F)
    Commencement of criminal action,
        Reduction of charges, § 9.18
    Content, § 3.3
    Facial sufficiency, § 3.7
    Form, § 3.3
    Limitation of actions, generally, this index
    Petition for return of felony complaint to local criminal court, § 3.31
    Plea Bargaining, generally, this index
    Reduction of charges, § 3.32
        Guilty pleas, § 11.3
        Plea bargaining, § 11.3
        Summary, § 3.35(G)
    Verification, § 3.6
Misdemeanor complaints, § 3.2
    Bill of particulars, § 3.8
    Commencement of criminal action,
        Reduction of original charges, § 9.20
    Content, § 3.3
    Conversion or replacement with information, § 3.25
        Motion for order releasing defendant from custody,
            Affirmation in support, form, § 3.36.16
            Notice of motion, form, § 3.36.15
        Summary, § 3.35(D)
    Facial sufficiency, § 3.7
    Form, § 3.3
    Joinder, § 3.8
    Plea Bargaining, generally, this index
    Severance, § 3.8

INDEX

COMPLAINTS—Continued
Misdemeanor complaints—Continued
    Verification, § 3.6
    Waiver of prosecution by information, §§ 3.2, 3.25

COMPUTERS
Computer tampering,
    Defenses, notice, § 7.28
Computer trespass and unauthorized use,
    Defenses, notice, § 7.28
    Discovery,
        Demand disclosure, § 7.4
Unlawful duplication of computer related material,
    Defenses, notice, § 7.28

CONFIDENTIAL INFORMANTS
Informants, generally, this index

CONFIDENTIAL INFORMATION
Privileged Information, generally, this index

CONFRONTATION RIGHTS
    See also Cross-Examination, generally, this index
Guilty pleas, waiver of rights, § 11.15
Severance,
    Statements by co-defendant, § 5.22
    Summary, § 5.32(F)

CONSOLIDATION
Joinder, generally, this index

CONSTITUTION
Discovery rights, § 7.2
Double Jeopardy, generally, this index

CONSTITUTIONALITY
Guilty pleas, survival of claim, § 11.16

CONTINUANCES
Discovery sanction, § 7.21
Readiness rule, excludable periods, § 9.34

CORRUPTION
Organized Crime Control Act,
    Enterprise corruption,
        Double jeopardy, § 2.9
            Summary, § 2.12(F)

COUNTY COURTS
Jurisdiction, generally. Superior Courts, this index

CREDIBILITY
Impeachment, generally, this index

CRIMINAL COURTS, LOCAL
Local Criminal Courts, generally, this index

CROSS-EXAMINATION
Grand jury,
    Defendant's right to testify, § 5.8
Impeachment, generally, this index
Omnibus motion, exception, § 8.1
Preliminary hearings,
    Limitation by court, § 3.33
"Sandoval" motion,
    Omnibus motion, exception, § 8.1
Suppression of evidence, hearing, § 10.19

DEAFNESS
Competency, § 6.10

INDEX

DEATH PENALTY
Indictment, waiver prohibited, § 5.10
Notice, § 7.29

DEFECTIVE INSTRUMENTS
Accusatory Instruments, this index

DEFENSES
Alibi, notice,
    Demand for, form, § 7.37.12
    Form, § 7.37.13
    Pretrial, § 7.27
    Rebuttal witnesses of prosecution, § 7.27
    Sanctions, § 7.27
    Self-incrimination, not violating, § 7.27
Computer related offenses,
    Pretrial notices, § 7.28
Grand jury,
    Presentation for consideration, § 5.5
    Summary, § 5.30(C)
Infancy,
    Guilty pleas, survival of claim, § 11.16
Limitation of Actions, generally, this index
Notice,
    Alibi, notice, generally, ante
    Pretrial, § 7.25
        Alibi, § 7.27
        Summary, defense, § 7.34(F)
        Summary, prosecution, § 7.35(E)
    Sanctions on defense for failure to comply,
        Summary, court, § 7.36(E)
Psychiatric evidence,
    Pretrial notices, § 7.26
Severance,
    Defendants,
        Mutually antagonistic defenses, § 5.22
        Summary, § 5.32(F)

DEFINITIONS
Absence of defendant, § 9.35
Bail, § 4.2
Bail bonds, § 4.2
Commitment to custody of sheriff, § 4.2
Conviction, § 2.2
Criminal act, § 2.9
Criminal enterprise, § 2.9
Criminal transaction, § 5.21
Genuine readiness, § 9.22
Judgment, § 2.2
Obligor, § 4.2
Pattern of criminal activity, § 2.9
Principal, § 4.2
Readiness, § 9.21
Release on own recognizance, § 4.2
Securing order, § 4.2
Surety, § 4.2
Unavailability of defendant, § 9.35
Valid communication of present readiness, § 9.23

DEMAND DISCLOSURE
Discovery, this index

DEPOSITIONS, SUPPORTING
Supporting Depositions, generally, this index

DEVELOPMENTAL DISABILITIES
Competency, § 6.10

INDEX

DISCOVERY
    Generally, § 7.1 et seq.
"Brady" evidence, §§ 7.2, 7.12
  Credibility of prosecution's witnesses, § 7.12
  Materiality, § 7.13
  Prosecution's promises in exchange for testimony, § 7.12
  Sanctions for failure to disclose, § 7.22
  Subpoenas, § 7.8
  Suppression of evidence, § 10.19
Child abuse,
  Privileged information, § 7.30
Co-defendants, property recovered from, § 7.4
Computer trespass and unauthorized use, § 7.4
Constitutional rights, § 7.2
Continuing duty to disclose, § 7.4
  Summary, prosecution, § 7.35(H)
Defendant, by, § 7.4
  Form, § 7.37.1
Defendant's duties, § 7.5
Demand disclosure, § 7.3
  Co-defendants, property recovered from, § 7.4
  Computer trespass and unauthorized use, § 7.4
  Continuing duty to disclose, § 7.4
    Summary, prosecution, § 7.35(H)
  Defendant, by, § 7.4
    Form, § 7.37.1
  Defendant's duties, § 7.5
  Driving while intoxicated,
    Breathalyzer, calibration records, § 7.4
  Motion,
    Statutory authority, § 7.7
    Summary, court, § 7.36(B)
    Summary, defense, § 7.34(C)
    Summary, prosecution, § 7.35(C)
  Motion for discovery beyond that required under demand,
    Affirmation in support, form, § 7.37.7
    Notice of motion, form, § 7.37.6
  Motion in response to refusal,
    Affirmation in support, form, § 7.37.5
    Notice of motion, form, § 7.37.4
  Photographs, §§ 7.4, 7.5
  Physical and mental examination reports, § 7.4
  Prosecution, by, § 7.5
    Form, § 7.37.2
  Prosecutor's duties, § 7.4
  Records and reports, §§ 7.4, 7.5
  Refusal, § 7.6
    Form, § 7.37.3
    Summary, defense, § 7.34(B)
    Summary, prosecution, § 7.35(B)
  Scientific test or experiment reports, § 7.4
  Statements, § 7.4
  Stolen property, § 7.4
  Summary, defense, § 7.34(A)
  Summary, prosecution, § 7.35(A)
  Tape recordings, § 7.4
  Videotape recordings, § 7.4
Driving while intoxicated,
  Breathalyzer, calibration records, § 7.4
Drug treatment records, privileged information, § 7.30
Education records, privileged information, § 7.30
Exculpatory material. "Brady" evidence, generally, ante
Grand jury, disclosure, § 5.3
In camera review, privileged information, § 7.30
Indictment,
  Summary, § 5.32(A)

INDEX

DISCOVERY—Continued
Indictment—Continued
    Supplementing defects, § 5.13
Law enforcement personnel records, privileged information, § 7.30
Law enforcement records, Freedom of Information Law, § 7.33
Loss or destruction of discoverable material,
    Adverse inference jury instruction, § 7.23
    Sanctions, § 7.23
Medical records, privileged information, § 7.30
News reporting, privileged information, § 7.30
Non-testimonial evidence,
    Motion by prosecutor,
        Affirmation in support, form, § 7.37.9
        Form, § 7.37.8
Omnibus motion, exception, § 8.1
Photographs, §§ 7.4, 7.5
Physical and mental examination reports, § 7.4
Prior recorded statements. "Rosario" material, generally, post
Prosecutors,
    Duties, § 7.4
        Summary, prosecution, § 7.35(F)
    Obligation to obtain demanded property,
        Summary, prosecution, § 7.35(G)
Protective orders, § 7.19
    Affirmation in support of motion, § 7.37.11
    Notice of motion, § 7.37.10
    Summary, court, § 7.36(C)
    Summary, prosecution, § 7.35(I)
Psychiatric records, privileged information, § 7.30
Rape crisis counselor's records, privileged information, § 7.30
Readiness rule, excludable periods, § 9.29
Records and reports, §§ 7.4, 7.5
Request for disclosure of defense witnesses' statements, § 7.16
    Summary, prosecution, § 7.35(D)
"Rosario" material, § 7.16
    Witnesses' statements, § 7.2
        Automatic reversal rule, § 7.16
        Duplicative equivalent exception, § 7.17
        Preliminary hearings, § 3.33
        Sanctions for failure to disclose, § 7.22
        Waiver, § 7.17
        Within prosecution's possession and control, § 7.17
Sanctions, § 7.20 et seq.
    "Brady" evidence, § 7.22
    Continuances, § 7.21
    Defendant, against, § 7.24
    Delay in disclosure, § 7.21
    Failure to disclose, § 7.22
    Loss or destruction of discoverable material, § 7.23
        Adverse inference jury instruction, § 7.23
    Per se rule, § 7.22
    Prejudicial effect, § 7.21
    "Rosario" material, § 7.22
    Summary, court, § 7.36(D)
    Summary, defense, § 7.34(G)
    Waiver, § 7.23
Scientific test or experiment reports, § 7.4
Sealed court records, privileged information, § 7.30
Social worker records, privileged information, § 7.30
Statements, § 7.4
Statutory authority, § 7.2
Stolen property, § 7.4
Subpoena duces tecum, § 7.8
    Summary, defense, § 7.34(E)
Summary, court, § 7.36(A)
Tape recordings, § 7.4

INDEX

DISCOVERY—Continued
Uncharged prior bad acts,
    Disclosure by prosecution, § 7.15
Videotape recordings, § 7.4
Witnesses,
    Criminal histories, § 7.18
    Identity of police informant,
        Motion for, § 7.10
        Suppression of evidence, § 10.19
    Identity of prosecution witnesses, motion for, § 7.9
    Statements. "Rosario" material, ante
Work product rule, privileged information, § 7.31

DISMISS, MOTION TO
Motion to Dismiss, generally, this index

DISPUTE RESOLUTION
Adjournment in contemplation of dismissal,
    Conditions on defendant, § 3.29

DISTRICT ATTORNEYS
Prosecutors, generally, this index

DISTRICT COURTS
Local criminal courts, § 1.2

DOMESTIC VIOLENCE
Duty to arrest, § 3.18
Family Offenses, generally, this index
Protection orders, temporary,
    Condition of bail, § 4.10
Warrantless arrest,
    Duty to arrest, § 3.18

DOUBLE JEOPARDY
    Generally, § 2.1 et seq.
Appeals, this index
Attachment of jeopardy, § 2.2 et seq.
    Guilty pleas, § 2.2
    Jury trials,
        Hung juries, § 2.4
    Lack of jurisdiction exception, § 2.3
    Mistrials, § 2.4
    Not responsible by reason of mental disease or defect, § 2.2
    Procurement exception, § 2.3
    Reversal on appeal, § 2.4
    Summary, § 2.12(A)
    Vacation of plea, § 2.4
"Blockburger" test, § 2.5
Collateral estoppel, §§ 2.5, 2.8
    Summary, § 2.12(E)
Constitution, § 2.1
    Summary, § 2.12(B)
Consummated result offense, § 2.6
Continuing offense provision, § 2.5
Contraband exception, § 2.6
Delayed death exception, § 2.6
Different victim exception, § 2.6
Enterprise corruption, § 2.9
    Summary, § 2.12(F)
Forfeiture, § 2.10
Guilty pleas,
    Survival of claim, § 11.16
    Waiver, § 11.15
Joinder,
    Mandatory, § 2.7
        Summary, § 2.12(D)
Juvenile proceedings, § 2.10

INDEX

DOUBLE JEOPARDY—Continued
Mistrials,
    Attachment of jeopardy, § 2.4
        Summary, § 2.12(A)
    Manifest necessity, § 2.4
Motion to dismiss, §§ 2.11, 3.26
    Accusatory instruments,
        Affirmation in support, form, § 2.13.2
        Notice of motion, form, § 2.13.1
Multiple punishments, § 2.10
    Summary, § 2.12(G)
Prohibition, § 2.11
    Form, § 2.13.3
    Summary, § 2.12(H)
Recidivist sentencing, § 2.10
Reversal on appeal,
    Attachment of jeopardy, § 2.4
    Increased sentence, § 2.10
Same criminal transaction, exceptions, § 2.6
Same offense provision, § 2.5
Statutory authority, § 2.1
    Summary, § 2.12(C)

DRIVING WHILE INTOXICATED
Arraignment,
    Guilty plea, prosecutor's consent required, § 3.24
Breathalyzer,
    Calibration records, discovery, § 7.4
    Refusal to test,
        Denial of appearance test coercive, § 3.20

DRUG OFFENSES
Marihuana,
    Adjournment in contemplation of dismissal, § 3.29
    Arraignment,
        Appearance ticket, § 3.22
Plea bargaining restrictions, § 11.5

DRUG TREATMENT PROGRAMS
Plea bargaining,
    Sentence promises,
        Favorable sentence for successful completion, § 11.13
Records and reports,
    Privileged information, discovery, § 7.30

DUE PROCESS
Competency, discharge from commitment, § 6.8
Federal constitutional rights, speedy trial, § 9.8
Motion to dismiss,
    Procedural requirements, § 9.12
        Summary, defense, § 9.56(C)
Readiness Rule, generally, this index
State constitutional rights,
    Speedy trial, § 9.9
        "Taranovich" factors, § 9.10

ENTERPRISE CORRUPTION
Organized Crime Control Act,
    Double jeopardy, § 2.9
        Summary, § 2.12(F)

ENVIRONMENTAL CONSERVATION LAW
Limitation of actions, extensions, § 9.4
Simplified information, § 3.2
    Form, § 3.3

EQUAL PROTECTION
Grand jury,
    Fair cross-section of community, § 5.2

INDEX

EVIDENCE
Blood, generally, this index
Burden of Proof, generally, this index
Discovery, generally, this index
Fingerprinting, generally, this index
Hair Samples, generally, this index
Handwriting Samples, generally, this index
Hearsay, generally, this index
Photographs, generally, this index
Privileged Information, generally, this index
Saliva, generally, this index
Scientific Tests, generally, this index
Statements, generally, this index
Suppression of Evidence, generally, this index

EXCLUSIONARY RULE
Generally, § 10.7

EXTRADITION
Interstate Agreement on Detainers, generally, this index

FAMILY COURT
Removal from local criminal court, § 1.10

FAMILY OFFENSES
Accusatory instrument,
    Filing commencing criminal action, § 9.46
Educational program on family violence issues,
    Condition of adjournment in contemplation of dismissal, § 3.29
Motion to dismiss,
    Adjournment in contemplation of dismissal, § 3.29
Protection orders, temporary,
    Condition of bail, § 4.10
Warrantless arrest,
    Duty to arrest, § 3.18

FELONY COMPLAINTS
Complaints, this index

FIDUCIARIES
Limitation of actions, extensions, § 9.4

FINES
Bail and recognizance,
    Imprisonment without bail,
        Failure to pay fines, § 4.4

FINGERPRINTING
Arraignment, § 5.23
    Summary, § 5.32(G)
Arrest warrant,
    Post-arrest procedure, § 3.15
Discovery,
    Prosecution's motion to compel, § 7.11
Loitering for purpose of engaging in prostitution, § 3.23
Loitering for purpose of soliciting or engaging in deviate sexual behavior, § 3.23
Refusal to submit to,
    Court order compelling submission, § 3.23
Statutory authority, § 3.23
Transmission of copies to State Division of Criminal Justice Services, § 3.23
Warrantless arrest,
    Post-arrest procedure, § 3.19

FORFEITURE
Double jeopardy, § 2.10

FORMS
Accusatory instruments,
    Complaint, § 3.3

INDEX

FORMS—Continued
Accusatory instruments—Continued
  Motion to dismiss,
    Double jeopardy,
      Affirmation in support, § 2.13.2
      Notice of motion, § 2.13.1
Amendment,
  Indictment,
    Affirmation in support, § 5.33.14
    Notice of motion, § 5.33.13
Arrest warrants, § 3.12
Bail and recognizance,
  Affirmation in support of application, § 4.15.2
  Excessive bail, § 4.15.3
  Habeas corpus, § 4.15.3
  Notice of application, § 4.15.1
  Readiness rule,
    Readiness to avoid release on bail or recognizance,
      Affirmation in support, § 9.58.8
      Motion for bail or recognizance, § 9.58.7
  Remission,
    Affirmation in support of application, § 4.15.4
    Notice of application, § 4.15.4
Bill of particulars,
  Amendment,
    Affirmation in support, § 5.33.16
    Notice of motion, § 5.33.15
Competency,
  Mental examinations,
    Order of examination,
      Affirmation in support, § 6.12.2
      Notice of motion, § 6.12.1
Defendant's request for supporting deposition, § 3.36.2
Defenses,
  Alibi,
    Notice of alibi, § 7.37.13
      Demand for, § 7.37.12
Discovery,
  Demand disclosure,
    Defendant, by, § 7.37.1
    Motion for discovery beyond that required under demand, affirmation in support, § 7.37.7
    Motion for discovery beyond that required under demand, notice, § 7.37.6
    Motion in response to refusal, affirmation in support, § 7.37.5
    Motion in response to refusal, notice, § 7.37.4
    Prosecution, by, § 7.37.2
    Refusal, § 7.37.3
  Non-testimonial evidence,
    Motion by prosecutor,
      Affirmation in support, § 7.37.9
      Notice of motion, § 7.37.8
Double jeopardy,
  Prohibition, § 2.13.3
Environmental conservation law,
  Simplified information, § 3.3
Grand jury,
  Automatic immunity,
    Affirmation in support, § 5.33.20
    Notice of motion, § 5.33.19
  Defendant's right to testify,
    Motion to dismiss,
      Affirmation in support, § 5.33.4
      Notice of motion, § 5.33.3
  Failure of timely grand jury action,
    Affirmation in support, § 5.33.2
    Notice of motion, § 5.33.1

INDEX

FORMS—Continued
Grand jury—Continued
  Transactional immunity,
    Affirmation in support, § 5.33.20
    Notice of motion, § 5.33.19
  Use immunity,
    Affirmation in support, § 5.33.20
    Notice of motion, § 5.33.20
Guilty pleas,
  Withdrawal,
    Affidavit of defendant, § 11.23.3
    Affirmation of attorney, § 11.23.2
    Notice of motion, § 11.23.1
Habeas corpus,
  Bail and recognizance,
    Excessive bail, § 4.15.3
  Petition for writ,
    Warrantless arrest, § 3.36.8
Immunity from prosecution,
  Automatic immunity,
    Grand jury,
      Affirmation in support, § 5.33.20
      Notice of motion, § 5.33.19
    Motion to dismiss,
      Affirmation in support, § 3.33.20
      Notice of motion, § 3.33.20
  Transactional immunity,
    Grand jury,
      Affirmation in support, § 5.33.20
      Notice of motion, § 5.33.19
  Use immunity,
    Grand jury,
      Affirmation in support, § 5.33.20
      Notice of motion, § 5.33.19
Indictment,
  Defects,
    Motion to dismiss,
      Affirmation in support, § 5.33.18
      Notice of motion, § 5.33.17
  Motion to dismiss,
    Furtherance of justice,
      Affirmation in support, § 5.33.22
      Notice of motion, § 5.33.21
  Resubmission,
    Affirmation in support, § 5.33.24
    Notice of motion, § 5.33.23
Information,
  Motion to amend,
    Affirmation in support, § 3.36.7
    Notice of motion, § 3.36.6
Joinder,
  Co-defendants, of,
    Motion to consolidate indictments against different defendants,
      Affirmation in support, § 5.33.12
      Notice of motion, § 5.33.11
  Offenses, of,
    Motion to consolidate indictments against same defendant,
      Affirmation in support, § 5.33.8
      Notice of motion, § 5.33.7
Jurisdiction,
  Motion by defendant to remove misdemeanor charge to superior court,
    Affirmation in support, § 1.12.6
    Notice of motion, § 1.12.5
  Motion by prosecutor to remove action for grand jury consideration,
    Affirmation in support, § 1.12.4
    Notice of motion, § 1.12.3

INDEX

FORMS—Continued
Jurisdiction—Continued
  Motion for change of venue,
    Affirmation in support, § 1.12.8
    Notice of motion, § 1.12.7
  Motion to remove action to another local criminal court,
    Affirmation in support, § 1.12.2
    Notice of motion, § 1.12.1
Limitation of actions,
  Motion to dismiss,
    Affirmation in support, § 9.58.2
    Notice of motion, § 9.58.1
Misdemeanor complaints,
  Conversion or replacement with information,
    Motion for order releasing defendant from custody,
      Affirmation in support, § 3.36.16
      Notice of motion, § 3.36.15
Motion to dismiss,
  Accusatory instrument,
    Affirmation in support, § 3.36.10
    Notice of motion, § 3.36.9
  Adjournment in contemplation of dismissal,
    Motion to restore proceedings,
      Affirmation in support, § 3.36.14
      Notice of motion, § 3.36.13
  Furtherance of justice,
    Affirmation in support, §§ 3.36.12, 5.33.22
    Notice of motion, §§ 3.36.11, 5.33.21
  Grand jury,
    Defendant's right to testify,
      Affirmation in support, § 5.33.4
      Notice of motion, § 5.33.3
  Indictment,
    Defective instrument,
      Affirmation in support, § 5.33.18
      Notice of motion, § 5.33.17
    Furtherance of justice,
      Affirmation in support, § 5.33.22
      Notice of motion, § 5.33.21
  Limitation of actions,
    Affirmation in support, § 9.58.2
    Notice of motion, § 9.58.1
  Readiness rule,
    Affirmation in support, § 9.58.6
    Notice of motion, § 9.58.5
  Speedy trial,
    Affirmation in support, § 9.58.4
    Notice of motion, § 9.58.3
Navigation law,
  Simplified information, § 3.3
Omnibus motion,
  Affirmation in support, § 8.2.2
  Notice of motion, § 8.2.1
Parks and recreation law,
  Simplified information, § 3.3
Preliminary hearings,
  Failure to commence hearing timely,
    Motion for release of defendant from custody,
      Affirmation in support, § 3.36.18
      Notice of motion, § 3.36.17
    Release of defendant from custody,
      Affirmation in support, § 3.36.16
      Notice of motion, § 3.36.17
Prohibition,
  Double jeopardy, § 2.13.3
Prosecutor's information, § 3.3

INDEX

FORMS—Continued
Prosecutor's information—Continued
    Motion to amend,
        Affirmation in support, § 3.36.5
        Notice of motion, § 3.36.4
Readiness rule,
    Motion to dismiss,
        Affirmation in support, § 9.58.6
        Notice of motion, § 9.58.5
    Readiness to avoid release on bail or recognizance,
        Motion for bail or recognizance, § 9.58.7
Severance,
    Defendants, of,
        Motion for severance of trials of jointly indicted defendants,
            Affirmation in support, § 5.33.10
            Notice of motion, § 5.33.9
    Offenses, of,
        Affirmation in support, § 5.33.6
        Notice of motion, § 5.33.5
Simplified information,
    Supporting deposition, § 3.36.3
Speedy trial,
    Motion to dismiss,
        Affirmation in support, § 9.58.4
        Notice of motion, § 9.58.3
Supporting depositions, § 3.36.1
    Simplified information, § 3.36.3
Suppression of evidence,
    Identification,
        Affirmation in support, § 10.31.4
        Notice of motion, § 10.31.3
    Motion to suppress,
        Affirmation in support, § 10.31.2
        Notice of motion, § 10.31.1
    Notice,
        Physical evidence, § 10.31.5
    Physical evidence,
        Affirmation in support, § 10.31.6
        Notice of motion, § 10.31.5
Traffic tickets, simplified information, § 3.3

FREEDOM OF INFORMATION LAW
Law enforcement records,
    Discovery, § 7.33

GEOGRAPHICAL JURISDICTION
Jurisdiction, this index

GRAND JURY
Attendance rules, § 5.3
    Summary, § 5.30(B)
Automatic immunity, § 5.9
    Affirmation in support, form, § 5.33.20
    Notice of motion, form, § 5.33.19
    Summary, § 5.30(E)
Competency,
    Mental examination order, effect, § 6.3
Defendant's right to testify. Witnesses, post
Defenses,
    Presentation for consideration, § 5.5
    Summary, § 5.30(C)
Disclosure,
    Court order, § 5.3
        Summary, § 5.30(B)
    Discovery, § 5.3
Due process,
    Fair cross-section of community, § 5.2

INDEX

GRAND JURY—Continued
Due process—Continued
  Fair cross-section of community—Continued
    Summary, § 5.30(A)
Equal protection,
  Fair cross-section of community, § 5.2
    Summary, § 5.30(A)
Exculpatory evidence,
  Presentation for consideration, § 5.7
    Summary, § 5.30(C)
Failure of timely grand jury action,
  Affirmation in support, form, § 5.33.2
  Notice of motion, form, § 5.33.1
Immunity,
  Automatic immunity, generally, ante
  Transactional immunity, generally, post
  Use immunity, generally, post
  Waiver of immunity, generally, post
Impaneling, § 5.2
  Summary, § 5.30(A)
Indictment, generally, this index
Ineffective assistance of counsel,
  Defendant's right to testify,
    Guilty pleas, survival of claim, § 11.16
Instructions, § 5.5
  Summary, § 5.30(C)
Jurisdiction,
  Motion by prosecutor to remove action for grand jury consideration,
    Affirmation in support, form, § 1.12.4
    Notice of motion, form, § 1.12.3
Jurisdictional defects,
  Guilty pleas, survival of claim, § 11.16
Legal advisors, §§ 5.4, 5.30(C)
Minutes,
  Motion to inspect, § 5.27
    Summary, § 5.30(B)
Motion to dismiss,
  Defective proceedings, § 5.27
    Summary, § 5.32(H)
Nonjurisdictional defects,
  Guilty pleas, waiver, § 11.15
Notice,
  Cross-grand jury notice, § 5.8
  Defendant's right to testify, § 5.8
    Summary, § 5.30(D)
  Failure of timely grand jury action, form, § 5.33.1
Prosecutor's information,
  Defective instrument, § 3.27
  Grand jury directing filing, § 3.2
  Resubmission to grand jury, § 3.27
Quorum, § 5.2
  Summary, § 5.30(A)
Release of defendant,
  Failure of timely grand jury action,
    Affirmation in support, form, § 5.33.2
    Notice of motion, form, § 5.33.1
Removal from local criminal court, § 1.8
Removal to family court, § 1.10
Rules of evidence, applicability, § 5.6
  Summary, § 5.30(C)
Secrecy, § 5.3
  Summary, § 5.30(B)
Special,
  Supreme court, § 5.2
Term, § 5.2
  Summary, § 5.30(A)

INDEX

GRAND JURY—Continued
Transactional immunity, § 5.9
    Affirmation in support, form, § 5.33.20
    Non-testimonial evidence, § 5.9
    Notice of motion, form, § 5.33.19
    Records and reports, § 5.9
    Summary, § 5.30(E)
    Waiver, § 5.9
        Summary, § 5.30(F)
Unlawful grand jury disclosure, § 5.3
    Summary, § 5.30(B)
Use immunity, § 5.9
    Affirmation in support, form, § 5.33.20
    Notice of motion, form, § 5.33.19
    Summary, § 5.30(E)
    Waiver, § 5.9
        Summary, § 5.30(F)
Waiver of immunity, § 5.8
    Right to counsel, § 5.9
        Summary, § 5.30(G)
    Summary, § 5.30(F)
Witnesses,
    Defendant's right to testify, § 5.8
        Affirmation in support, form, § 5.33.4
        Cross-examination, § 5.8
        Impeachment, § 5.8
        Notice of motion, form, § 5.33.3
        Summary, § 5.30(D)
        Waiver, § 5.8
            Summary, § 5.30(F)
    Grand jury summoning, § 5.8
        Limitations, § 5.8
    Notice, § 5.8
        Summary, § 5.30(D)
    Prosecution's duties, § 5.8
    Waiver of immunity, § 5.8
        Summary, § 5.30(F)

GUILTY PLEAS
Absolute right to plead guilty, § 11.2
Accusatory instruments,
    Defective instrument,
        Jurisdictional defects, survival of claim, § 11.16
        Nonjurisdictional defects, waiver, § 11.15
Appeals,
    Reservation of rights, waiver, § 11.15
    Suppression of evidence, § 10.22
    Voluntariness, bargained for waiver of right to appeal, § 11.17
Arraignment, § 5.24
    Summary, § 5.32(G)
"Boykin" rights, waiver, §§ 11.7, 11.15
Competency,
    Mental examinations, § 11.8
    Survival of claim, § 11.16
Confrontation rights, waiver, § 11.15
Consent of prosecutor, § 11.3
Constitutionality, survival of claim, § 11.16
Court's discretion, § 11.3
Determination of guilt, waiver, § 11.15
Double jeopardy,
    Attachment of jeopardy, § 2.2
        Summary, § 2.12(A)
    Survival of claim, § 11.16
    Waiver, § 11.15
Driving while intoxicated,
    Arraignment, prosecutor's consent required, § 3.24
Factual basis, § 11.10

INDEX

GUILTY PLEAS—Continued
Felony complaints,
    Reduction of charges, § 11.3
        Conditions, § 11.3
        Refusal to offer, § 11.3
        Restrictions, § 11.5
        Voluntariness, § 11.3
        Writ of prohibition, § 11.3
Grand jury,
    Jurisdictional defects, survival of claim, § 11.16
    Nonjurisdictional defects, waiver, § 11.15
Indictment,
    Guilty plea as waiver of defects, § 5.13
    Summary, § 5.32(A)
Ineffective assistance of counsel,
    Survival of claim, § 11.16
Infancy defense, survival of claim, § 11.16
Joinder,
    Defendants, waiver, § 11.15
    Offenses, waiver, § 11.15
Jury trial, waiver, § 11.15
Kidnapping,
    Merger doctrine, waiver, § 11.15
Lesser included offenses, § 11.3
    Factual basis, § 11.10
Limitation of actions,
    Waiver, §§ 9.7, 11.15
Motion to dismiss,
    Furtherance of justice,
        Denial, waiver, § 11.15
Peremptory challenges,
    Discriminatory use by prosecutor, waiver, § 11.15
Prosecutors,
    Disqualification, waiver, § 11.15
    Misconduct, waiver, § 11.15
Right to present evidence, waiver, § 11.15
Self-incrimination, waiver, § 11.15
Sentence promises,
    Court departing from, §§ 11.12, 11.13
        Summary, § 11.22(C)
    Reneging,
        Summary, defense, § 11.20(D)
    Vacation of plea, § 11.11
    Withdrawal, § 11.11
Severance,
    Defendants, waiver, § 11.15
    Offenses, waiver, § 11.15
Speedy trial,
    Survival of claim, § 11.16
    Waiver, § 11.15
Summary,
    Conditions of plea bargain, violation, § 11.21(C)
    During plea proceedings,
        Court, § 11.22(B)
        Defense, § 11.20(B)
        Prosecution, § 11.21(B)
    Prior to entry of plea,
        Court, § 11.22(A)
        Defense, § 11.20(A)
        Prosecution, § 11.21(A)
    Sentence promises,
        Court departing from, § 11.22(D)
        Prosecution reneging, § 11.20(D)
    Withdrawal,
        Court, § 11.22(D)
        Defense, § 11.20(C)

INDEX

GUILTY PLEAS—Continued
Suppression of evidence,
    Appeal following, § 10.22
    Denial, survival of claim, § 11.16
    Pending, waiver, § 11.16
Vacation of plea,
    Double jeopardy, § 2.4
    Sentence promises, § 11.11
Voluntariness, § 11.7
    Bargained for waiver of right to appeal, § 11.17
    Survival of claim, § 11.16
Waiver, readiness rule, § 9.13
    Summary, defense, § 9.56(C)
Withdrawal, § 11.18
    Affidavit of defendant, form, § 11.23.3
    Affirmation of attorney, form, § 11.23.2
    Clerical error, § 11.19
    Commencement of criminal action,
        Recommencement rule, § 9.16
    Court, by, § 11.19
    Notice of motion, form, § 11.23.1
    Plea bargain restrictions, violation, § 11.19
    Sentence promises, § 11.11
    Summary,
        Court, § 11.22(D)
        Defense, § 11.20(C)

HABEAS CORPUS
Bail and recognizance,
    Excessive bail, § 4.13
        Form, § 4.15.3
Petition for writ,
    Not responsible by reason of mental disease or defect, § 11.4
    Warrantless arrest, form, § 3.36.8
Preliminary hearings, failure to commence hearing timely, § 3.34

HAIR SAMPLES
Withdrawal from defendant,
    Prosecution's motion to compel, § 7.11

HANDWRITING SAMPLES
Prosecution's motion to compel, § 7.11

HEARINGS
Arraignment,
    Notice, § 5.23
        Summary, § 5.32(G)
Bail and recognizance,
    Revocation, § 4.10
    Temporary protection orders, § 4.10
Competency,
    Discharge from commitment, § 6.8
    Mental examination, § 6.6
    Procedure, § 6.9
Indictment,
    Motion to dismiss, § 5.26
        Summary, § 5.32(H)
Motion to dismiss,
    Indictment, § 5.26
        Summary, § 5.32(H)
Not responsible by reason of mental disease or defect, § 11.4
Preliminary Hearings, generally, this index
Suppression of evidence,
    "Brady" evidence, § 10.19
    Burden of proof, § 10.20
        Summary, § 10.30(D)
    Cross-examination, § 10.19
    Defendant's right to be present, § 10.19

INDEX

HEARINGS—Continued
Suppression of evidence—Continued
    Hearsay, § 10.19
    Identification, bifurcation of hearing, § 10.19
    Judge's duties, § 10.19
    Judicial hearing officer's duties, § 10.19
    Public's right to be present, § 10.19
    "Rosario" material, § 10.19
    Subpoenas, § 10.19
    Summary, § 10.30(D)
    Witnesses, § 10.19

HEARSAY
Information, exceptions to non-hearsay requirement, § 3.7
Search warrants, § 10.3
Suppression of evidence, hearing, § 10.19

IDENTIFICATION
Confirmatory identification, § 10.26
Fingerprinting, generally, this index
Handwriting samples, prosecution's motion to compel, § 7.11
Lineup, prosecution's motion to compel, § 7.11
Neighborhood canvassing identification, § 10.26
Notice,
    Appeals, § 10.29
    Arraignment, service of process at, § 3.30
    Confirmatory identification, § 10.26
    Content of notice, § 10.24
    Neighborhood canvassing identification, § 10.26
    Notice by prosecution of intent to use,
        Arraignment, service of process at, § 3.30
    Police arranged identifications, § 10.26
    Preclusion rule, § 10.28
    Show-up identification, § 10.26
    Suppression of evidence, § 10.23
        Scope, § 10.26
    Timing, § 10.23
        Good cause for late notice, § 10.27
    Waiver, § 10.29
Police arranged identifications, § 10.26
Preclusion rule, § 10.28
Show-up identification, § 10.26
Suppression of evidence, § 10.8
    Affirmation in support, form, § 10.31.4
    Bifurcation of hearing, § 10.19
    Notice, § 10.23
        Form, § 10.31.3
        Scope, § 10.26

IMMUNITY FROM PROSECUTION
Automatic immunity,
    Grand jury, § 5.9
        Affirmation in support, form, § 5.33.20
        Notice of motion, form, § 5.33.19
        Summary, § 5.30(E)
Motion to dismiss, § 3.26
    Affirmation in support, form, § 3.33.20
    Notice of motion, form, § 3.33.19
Non-testimonial evidence, § 5.9
Records and reports,
    Grand jury, § 5.9
Transactional immunity,
    Grand jury, § 5.9
        Affirmation in support, form, § 5.33.20
        Notice of motion, form, § 5.33.19
Use immunity,
    Grand jury, § 5.9

INDEX

IMMUNITY FROM PROSECUTION—Continued
  Use immunity—Continued
    Grand jury—Continued
      Affirmation in support, form, § 5.33.20
      Notice of motion, form, § 5.33.19
  Waiver of immunity,
    Grand jury, § 5.8
      Right to counsel, § 5.9
        Summary, § 5.30(G)

IMPEACHMENT
Grand jury, defendant's right to testify, § 5.8
Prior convictions, disclosure by prosecution, § 7.15
Suppression of evidence, § 10.14

IN PERSONAM JURISDICTION
  Generally, § 1.1
See also Jurisdiction, generally, this index

INDICTMENT
  Generally, § 5.10 et seq.
Accusatory Instruments, generally, this index
Amendment, § 5.13
  Affirmation in support, form, § 5.33.14
  Defects, curing, § 5.18
  Lesser included offenses, § 5.18
  Notice of motion, form, § 5.33.13
  Summary, §§ 5.32(A), 5.32(C)
Appeal following dismissal, § 5.28
  Murder charge, § 5.29
  Summary, § 5.32(I)
Bill of particulars,
  Summary, § 5.32(A)
  Supplementing defects, § 5.13
Competency,
  Temporary order of observation, indictment nullifying, § 6.7
Content, § 5.12
  Summary, § 5.32(A)
Defects,
  Bill of particulars supplementing, § 5.13
  Curing,
    Amendment, § 5.18
    Summary, § 5.32(C)
    Superseding indictments, § 5.18
  Discovery supplementing, § 5.13
  Failure to object as waiver, § 5.13
  Guilty plea as waiver, § 5.13
  Motion to dismiss, § 5.27
    Affirmation in support, form, § 5.33.18
    Notice of motion, form, § 5.33.17
  Prejudice test, § 5.18
  Summary, § 5.32(A)
  Surprise test, § 5.18
  Variance, § 5.18
Dismissal. Motion to dismiss, generally, post
Duplicitous counts, § 5.17
  Summary, § 5.32(B)
Grand jury minutes, motion to inspect, § 5.27
Hearing, motion to dismiss, § 5.26
Joinder,
  Defendants, 5.22
    Common scheme or plan, § 5.22
    Motion to consolidate indictments against different defendants,
      Affirmation in support, form, § 5.33.12
      Notice of motion, form, § 5.33.11
    Prosecutor's discretion to file motion, § 5.22
    Same offense, § 5.22

INDEX

INDICTMENT—Continued
Joinder—Continued
  Defendants—Continued
    Same transaction, § 5.22
    Summary, § 5.32(F)
  Offenses, § 5.21
    Motion to consolidate indictments against same defendant,
      Affirmation in support, form, § 5.33.8
      Notice of motion, form, § 5.33.7
    Summary, § 5.32(E)
Jurisdiction, § 5.11
  Summary, § 5.32(A)
Jurisdictional defects, § 5.16
  Summary, §§ 5.32(A), 5.32(C)
  Waiver prohibited, § 5.18
Lesser included offenses,
  Amendment, § 5.18
  Misdemeanor offenses, § 5.20
  Summary, § 5.32(C)
Motion to dismiss, § 5.25 et seq.
  Appeal following dismissal, § 5.28
    Murder charge, § 5.29
    Summary, § 5.32(I)
  Defective instrument, § 5.27
    Affirmation in support, form, § 5.33.18
    Notice of motion, form, § 5.33.17
  Furtherance of justice, §§ 5.25, 5.27
    Affirmation in support, form, § 5.33.22
    Notice of motion, form, § 5.33.21
  Grounds, § 5.27
  Hearing, § 5.26
    Summary, § 5.32(H)
  Insufficiency, § 5.27
  Lesser included offenses, § 5.27
  Notice, § 5.26
  Omnibus motion, § 5.26
    Time, § 5.26
  Reduction of charges, § 5.27
  Statutory authority, § 5.25
Multiplicitous counts, § 5.17
  Summary, § 5.32(B)
Notice, § 5.14
  Date of offense, § 5.15
  Summary, § 5.32(A)
Plea bargaining,
  Restrictions, § 11.5
Resubmission, § 5.28
  Affirmation in support, form, § 5.33.24
  Murder charge, § 5.29
  Notice of motion, form, § 5.33.23
  Summary, § 5.32(I)
Statutory reference, § 5.16
  Summary, § 5.32(A)
Suppression of evidence,
  Subsequent suppression of evidence not invalidating indictment, § 10.10
Waiver, § 5.10
  Reduction of charges in local criminal court prohibited, § 5.10
  Summary, § 5.31
  Superior court information, § 5.10
  Timing, § 5.10
  Waiver of death penalty or life imprisonment cases prohibited, § 5.10

INEFFECTIVE ASSISTANCE OF COUNSEL
Grand jury,
  Defendant's right to testify, § 11.16
Guilty pleas,
  Survival of claim, § 11.16

INDEX

INEFFECTIVE ASSISTANCE OF COUNSEL—Continued
Guilty pleas—Continued
    Withdrawal, § 11.18

INFANCY
Defenses,
    Guilty pleas, survival of claim, § 11.16

INFORMANTS
Discovery,
    Identity of police informant,
        Motion for, § 7.10
        Suppression of evidence, § 10.19

INFORMATION
Amendment, § 3.8
    Motion to amend,
        Affirmation in support, form, § 3.36.7
        Notice of motion, form, § 3.36.6
Bill of particulars, § 3.8
Facial sufficiency, § 3.7
    Jurisdictional defect, not waivable, § 3.7
Misdemeanor complaints. Complaints, this index
Non-hearsay requirement, exceptions, § 3.7
Plea Bargaining, generally, this index
Prosecutor's Information, generally, this index
Severance, § 3.8
Simplified Information, generally, this index
Superior Court Information, generally, this index
Superseding information, § 3.9
    Speedy trial, effect on, § 3.9
Verification, § 3.6
Waiver of prosecution by information,
    Misdemeanor complaint, § 3.2

INSANITY
Not Responsible by Reason of Mental Disease or Defect, generally, this index

INTERSTATE AGREEMENT ON DETAINERS
    Generally, § 9.53 et seq.
Anti-shuttling provisions, § 9.55
Motion to dismiss, § 9.55
Prisoner's request, § 9.54
Receiving state's request, § 9.55
Summary, defense, § 9.56(C)
Summary, prosecution, § 9.57
Time limits, § 9.55
Uniform Criminal Extradition Act, § 9.55

"JOHN DOE" OR "JANE DOE" WARRANTS
Arrest warrants, § 3.12

JOINDER
Complaints, misdemeanor, § 3.8
Defendants, of,
    Accusatory instruments, § 3.3
    Co-defendants,
        Excludability of reasonable delay, § 9.40
        Motion to consolidate indictments against different defendants,
            Affirmation in support, form, § 5.33.12
            Notice of motion, form, § 5.33.11
    Common scheme or plan, § 5.22
    Guilty pleas, waiver, § 11.15
    Information, § 3.8
    Prosecutor's discretion to file motion, § 5.22
    Same offense, § 5.22
    Same transaction, § 5.22
    Summary, § 5.32(F)

INDEX

JOINDER—Continued
Mandatory,
    Double jeopardy, § 2.7
        Summary, § 2.12(D)
    Offenses, of, § 5.21
        Summary, § 5.32(E)
Offenses, of,
    Accusatory instruments, § 3.3
    Common evidence, § 5.21
    Guilty pleas, waiver, § 11.15
    Indictment, § 5.21
    Information, § 3.8
    Mandatory, § 5.21
    Motion to consolidate indictments against same defendant,
        Affirmation in support, form, § 5.33.8
        Notice of motion, form, § 5.33.7
    Permissive, § 5.21
    Same or similar offenses, § 5.21
    Same transaction, § 5.21
    Summary, § 5.32(E)
Prosecutor's information, § 3.8
Severance, generally, this index

JURISDICTION
    Generally, § 1.1 et seq.
Attempt, § 1.3
Conspiracy, § 1.3
Extraterritorial, § 1.3
Geographical jurisdiction, § 1.1
    County, § 1.3
        Conduct establishing element of offense, § 1.4
        Waiver, § 1.4
    Local criminal courts, § 1.5
    Special rules, § 1.4
    State, § 1.3
    Waiver, § 1.4
In personam, § 1.1
Indictment, § 5.11
    Summary, § 5.32(A)
Information,
    Facial sufficiency, defect not waivable, § 3.7
Local criminal courts, § 1.2
Particular effect, § 1.3
Preemption by federal law, § 1.2
Result offense, §§ 1.3, 1.4
Subject matter, § 1.1
    Preliminary jurisdiction, § 1.2
    Trial jurisdiction, § 1.2
Summary, § 1.11
Superior courts. Superior Courts, this index

JURY INSTRUCTIONS
Discovery,
    Loss or destruction of discoverable material,
        Adverse inference jury instruction, § 7.23

JURY TRIALS
Double jeopardy,
    Attachment of jeopardy, § 2.2
        Summary, § 2.12(A)
Guilty pleas,
    Waiver of rights, § 11.15
Hung juries,
    Double jeopardy,
        Attachment of jeopardy, § 2.4
            Summary, § 2.12(A)

INDEX

JUVENILES
Bail and recognizance,
    Commitment to custody of sheriff, § 4.4
Double jeopardy, § 2.10
Plea bargaining restrictions, § 11.5
Speedy trial, federal constitutional rights, § 9.8
Verification, capacity to testify under oath, § 3.6
Warrantless arrest,
    Notice to parent or guardian, § 3.19

KIDNAPPING
Merger doctrine,
    Guilty pleas, waiver, § 11.15

"KNOCK AND ANNOUNCE" RULE
Arrest warrants, § 3.14

LAWYERS
Attorneys, generally, this index

LESSER INCLUDED OFFENSES
Guilty pleas, § 11.3
    Factual basis, § 11.10
Indictment,
    Amendment, § 5.18
    Misdemeanor offenses, § 5.20
    Summary, § 5.32(C)
Motion to dismiss,
    Indictment, § 5.27
        Summary, § 5.32(H)

LIMITATION OF ACTIONS
    Generally, § 9.2 et seq.
Bail and recognizance,
    Remission, § 4.12
Burden of proof, § 9.6
Environmental conservation law, extensions, § 9.4
Extensions, § 9.4
Fiduciaries, extensions, § 9.4
Guilty pleas, waiver, §§ 9.7, 11.15
Motion to dismiss, §§ 3.26, 9.6
    Affirmation in support, form, § 9.58.2
    Notice of motion, form, § 9.58.1
    Pre-accusatory delay,
        Summary, defense, § 9.56(A)
Public servants, extensions, § 9.4
Relevant time periods, § 9.3
Taxation, extensions, § 9.4
Tolling, § 9.5

LINEUPS
Photographic lineup,
    Discovery,
        Demand disclosure, § 7.4
        Prosecution's motion to compel, § 7.11
Prosecution's motion to compel, § 7.11

LOCAL CRIMINAL COURTS
    Generally, § 3.1 et seq.
Bail and recognizance,
    Fixing bail, § 4.6
City court, § 1.2
Competency,
    Post-examination procedure, § 6.7
District courts, § 1.2
Jurisdiction, § 1.2
New York city criminal court, § 1.2
Petition for return of felony complaint to local criminal court, § 3.31
Prosecutor's information, local criminal court directing filing, § 3.2

INDEX

LOCAL CRIMINAL COURTS—Continued
Removal to another local criminal court, § 1.7
Removal to family court, § 1.10
Removal to superior court, § 1.8
Town courts, § 1.2
Village courts, § 1.2

MARIHUANA
Drug Offenses, this index

MEDICAL RECORDS
Privileged information, discovery, § 7.30

MENTAL EXAMINATIONS
Competency,
    Confinement, duration, § 6.5
    Discharge from commitment, § 6.8
    Duration of commitment, § 6.6
    Final order of observation, § 6.6
    Guilty pleas, § 11.8
        Survival of claim, § 11.16
    Hearing, § 6.6
    Initial examination, § 6.4
    Location of examination, § 6.5
    Order of commitment, § 6.6
    Order of examination, § 6.2
        Affirmation in support, form, § 6.12.2
        Effect, § 6.3
        Notice of motion, form, § 6.12.1
    Order of observation, § 6.7
    Order of retention, § 6.6
    Readiness rule, excludable periods, § 9.28
    Reports, § 6.5
    Retrospective examination, § 6.10
    Right to counsel, § 6.4
    Summary, § 6.11
    Superior court,
        Post-examination procedure, § 6.6
    Temporary order of observation, § 6.7
        Indictment nullifying order, § 6.7
Defendant's refusal to cooperate, sanctions, § 7.26
Defenses,
    Pretrial notices, § 7.26
Discovery,
    Demand disclosure,
        Reports, §§ 7.4, 7.5
Prosecution's examination of defendant, § 7.26
Psychiatric records,
    Privileged information, discovery, § 7.30

MENTALLY ILL PERSONS
Bail and recognizance,
    Imprisonment without bail,
        Competency determination, § 4.4
Examinations. Mental Examinations, generally, this index
Motion to dismiss,
    Furtherance of justice,
        "Clayton" motion, § 5.27
        Summary, § 5.32(H)
Not Responsible by Reason of Mental Disease or Defect, generally, this index
Verification, capacity to testify under oath, § 3.6

MENTALLY RETARDED PERSONS
Competency, § 6.10

MINORS
Child abuse,
    Privileged information, discovery, § 7.30

INDEX

MINORS—Continued
Juveniles, generally, this index
Verification,
    Capacity to testify under oath, § 3.6

MISDEMEANOR COMPLAINTS
Complaints, this index

MISTRIALS
Double jeopardy,
    Attachment of jeopardy, § 2.4
        Summary, § 2.12(A)
    Manifest necessity, § 2.4
Retrial,
    Commencement of criminal action,
        Recommencement rule, § 9.16

MOTION, OMNIBUS
Omnibus Motions, generally, this index

MOTION TO DISMISS
Accusatory instruments,
    Affirmation in support, form, § 3.36.10
    Defective instrument, §§ 3.26, 3.27
    Double jeopardy, § 2.11
        Affirmation in support, form, § 2.13.2
        Notice of motion, form, § 2.13.1
    Notice of motion, form, § 3.36.9
Adjournment in contemplation of dismissal, § 3.29
    Conditions on defendant, § 3.29
    Domestic violence, § 3.29
    Marihuana offenses, § 3.29
    Motion to restore proceedings,
        Affirmation in support, form, § 3.36.14
        Notice of motion, form, § 3.36.13
    Restoration of charges, § 3.29
    Speedy trial time tolled, § 3.29
    Time excludable, § 9.44
Double jeopardy, §§ 2.11, 3.26
    Summary, § 2.12(H)
Due process,
    Procedural requirements, § 9.12
        Summary, defense, § 9.56(C)
Furtherance of justice, §§ 3.26, 5.27
    Affirmation in support, form, §§ 3.36.12, 5.33.22
    "Clayton" motion, §§ 3.28, 5.27
    Denial,
        Guilty pleas, waiver, § 11.15
    Factors to be considered, § 3.28
    Incompetency not proper basis, § 6.3
    Indictment, § 5.25
    Notice, § 5.27
        Form, §§ 3.36.11, 5.33.21
    Summary, § 5.32(H)
Grand jury, defective proceedings, § 5.27
Hearing, indictment, § 5.26
    Summary, § 5.32(H)
Indictment, § 5.25 et seq.
    Appeal following dismissal, § 5.28
        Murder charge, § 5.29
        Summary, § 5.32(I)
    Defective instrument, § 5.27
        Affirmation in support, form, § 5.33.18
        Notice of motion, form, § 5.33.17
    Furtherance of justice, §§ 5.25, 5.27
        Affirmation in support, form, § 5.33.22
        Notice of motion, form, § 5.33.21
    Grounds, § 5.27

INDEX

MOTION TO DISMISS—Continued
Indictment—Continued
  Hearing, § 5.26
    Summary, § 5.32(H)
  Insufficiency, § 5.27
  Lesser included offenses, § 5.27
  Notice, § 5.26
  Omnibus motion, § 5.26
    Time, § 5.26
  Reduction of charges, § 5.27
  Statutory authority, § 5.25
Interstate agreement on detainers, § 9.55
Limitation of actions, § 9.6
  Affirmation in support, form, § 9.58.2
  Notice of motion, form, § 9.58.1
  Pre-accusatory delay,
    Summary, defense, § 9.56(A)
Non-felony accusatory instruments, § 3.26
  Defective instrument, §§ 3.26, 3.27
Notice, § 3.26
  Waiver by prosecution for failure to object, § 3.26
Procedural requirements, § 9.49
  Summary, defense, § 9.56(C)
  Summary, prosecution, § 9.57
Readiness rule,
  Affirmation in support, form, § 9.58.6
  Notice of motion, form, § 9.58.5
Speedy trial,
  Affirmation in support. form, § 9.58.4
  Notice of motion, form, § 9.58.3
  Procedural requirements, §§ 9.12, 9.49
    Summary, defense, § 9.56(C)
    Summary, prosecution, § 9.57
Sufficiency of motion papers,
  Procedural requirements, §§ 9.50, 9.51
    Summary, defense, § 9.56(C)
    Summary, prosecution, § 9.57
Summary, § 3.35(E)
Timing, § 3.26

MOTION TO SUPPRESS EVIDENCE
Suppression of Evidence, generally, this index

MOTIONS IN LIMINE
Omnibus motion, exception, § 8.1

MURDER
Death Penalty, generally, this index

NAVIGATION LAW
Simplified information, § 3.2
  Form, § 3.3

NEWSPAPERS
News reporting sources,
  Privileged information, discovery, § 7.30

NOT GUILTY PLEAS
Arraignment, § 5.24
  Felony complaints, § 3.30
  Summary, § 5.32(G)
Withdrawal, § 11.6

NOT RESPONSIBLE BY REASON OF MENTAL DISEASE OR DEFECT
Acceptance by court, § 11.4
Arraignment, § 5.24
  Summary, § 5.32(G)
Double jeopardy, attachment of jeopardy, § 2.2
Habeas corpus writ, § 11.4

INDEX

NOT RESPONSIBLE BY REASON OF MENTAL DISEASE OR DEFECT—Continued
Hearing, § 11.4
Plea bargaining restrictions, § 11.5
Withdrawal, § 11.4
    Commencement of criminal action,
        Recommencement rule, § 9.16

NOTICE
Appeals,
    Suppression of evidence, § 10.29
        Summary, § 10.30(E)
Arraignment,
    Hearing, § 5.23
        Summary, § 5.32(G)
Bill of particulars, § 5.14
    Amendment, form, § 5.33.15
    Summary, § 5.32(A)
Competency,
    Discharge from commitment, § 6.8
    Mental examination order, form, § 6.12.1
Death penalty specification, § 7.29
Defendant's statements, notice by prosecution of intent to use,
    Arraignment, service of process at, § 3.30
Defenses,
    Alibi,
        Notice of alibi,
            Demand for, form, § 7.37.12
        Pretrial notices, § 7.27
        Rebuttal witnesses of prosecution, § 7.27
        Sanctions, § 7.27
        Self incrimination, not violating, § 7.27
    Pretrial notices, § 7.25 et seq.
        Alibi, § 7.27
        Computer related offenses, § 7.28
        Psychiatric evidence, § 7.26
        Summary, court, § 7.36(E)
        Summary, defense, § 7.34(F)
        Summary, prosecution, § 7.35(E)
    Sanctions on defense for failure to comply,
Grand jury,
    Cross-grand jury notice, § 5.8
    Defendant's right to testify, § 5.8
        Summary, § 5.30(D)
Identification,
    Appeals, § 10.29
    Confirmatory identification, § 10.26
    Content of notice, § 10.24
    Neighborhood canvassing identification, § 10.26
    Notice by prosecution of intent to use,
        Arraignment, service of process at, § 3.30
    Police arranged identifications, § 10.26
    Preclusion rule, § 10.28
    Show-up identification, § 10.26
    Suppression of evidence, § 10.23
        Scope, § 10.26
    Timing, § 10.23
        Good cause for late notice, § 10.27
    Waiver, § 10.29
Indictment, § 5.14
    Date of offense, § 5.15
    Summary, § 5.32(A)
Motion to dismiss, § 3.26
    Furtherance of justice, § 5.27
        Summary, § 5.32(H)
    Indictment, § 5.26
        Summary, § 5.32(H)
    Waiver by prosecution for failure to object, § 3.26

INDEX

NOTICE—Continued
Omnibus motion, § 8.1
Search warrants, § 10.5
Statement evidence,
 Appeals, § 10.29
 Arraignment, service of process at, § 3.30
 Impeachment, outside scope of rule, § 10.25
 Pedigree statements excluded, § 10.25
 Preclusion rule, § 10.28
 Res gestae statements excluded, § 10.25
 Timing, § 10.23
  Good cause for late notice, § 10.27
 Voluntariness, § 10.25
 Waiver, § 10.29
Suppression of Evidence, this index
Warrantless arrest,
 Juveniles, notice to parent or guardian, § 3.19

OATHS
Competency,
 Mentally ill person's capacity to testify under oath, § 3.6
 Minor's capacity to testify under oath, § 3.6
Search warrants, § 10.2

OBJECTIONS
Indictment,
 Failure to object as waiver of defects, § 5.13
 Summary, §§ 5.32(A), 7.25

OMNIBUS MOTIONS
 Generally, § 8.1 et seq.
Accusatory instruments,
 Jurisdictional defects, § 8.1
Affirmation in support, form, § 8.2.2
Bill of particulars, §§ 5.19, 8.1
 Summary, § 5.32(D)
Cross-examination, § 8.1
 "Sandoval" motion, § 8.1
Discovery, § 8.1
Joinder of offenses, § 5.21
 Summary, § 5.32(E)
Motion to dismiss,
 Indictment, § 5.26
  Summary, § 5.32(H)
  Time, § 5.26
Motions in limine, § 8.1
Notice of motion, form, § 8.2.1
Service of process, § 8.1
Severance, § 5.21
Speedy trial, § 8.1
Suppression of evidence, § 8.1

ORDERS OF PROTECTION
Adjournment in contemplation of dismissal,
 Conditions on defendant, § 3.29
Domestic violence, condition of bail, § 4.10
Family offenses, condition of bail, § 4.10
Temporary,
 Bail and recognizance,
  Condition of bail, § 4.10
  Summary, § 4.14(B)
Violations, imprisonment without bail, § 4.4
Warrantless arrest, duty to arrest, § 3.18

ORGANIZED CRIME CONTROL ACT
Definitions, § 2.9
Enterprise corruption,
 Double jeopardy, § 2.9

INDEX

ORGANIZED CRIME CONTROL ACT—Continued
Enterprise corruption—Continued
    Double jeopardy—Continued
        Summary, § 2.12(F)

PARANOIA
Competency, § 6.10

PARKS AND RECREATION LAW
Simplified information, § 3.2

PEREMPTORY CHALLENGES
Discriminatory use by prosecutor,
    Guilty pleas, waiver, § 11.15

PHOTOGRAPHS
Arrest warrant,
    Post-arrest procedure, § 3.15
Discovery,
    Demand disclosure, §§ 7.4, 7.5
Photographic lineup,
    Discovery,
        Demand disclosure, § 7.4
        Prosecution's motion to compel, § 7.11
Warrantless arrest,
    Post-arrest procedure, § 3.15

PLEA BARGAINING
Drug offenses, restrictions, § 11.5
Felony complaints,
    Reduction of charges, § 11.3
        Commencement of criminal action, § 9.18
        Conditions, § 11.3
        Refusal to offer, § 11.3
        Writ of prohibition, § 11.3
Juveniles, restrictions, § 11.5
Not responsible by reason of mental disease or defect, restrictions, § 11.5
Post-indictment restrictions, § 11.5
Pre-indictment restrictions, § 11.5
Sentence promises, § 11.11 et seq.
    Conditional nature of promise, § 11.12
    Conditions, § 11.11
        Drug treatment programs, favorable sentence, § 11.13
        Special conditions for defendants at liberty between plea and sentence, § 11.13
        Summary, prosecution, § 11.21(C)
        Violations, increased sentence, § 11.13
    Guilty pleas,
        Reneging, summary, § 11.20(D)
        Vacation of plea, §§ 11.11, 11.19
    "Off the record" promises unenforceable, § 11.11
    Specific performance, § 11.14
Waiver of right to appeal, voluntariness, § 11.17

PLEAS
    Generally, § 11.1 et seq.
Guilty Pleas, generally, this index
Not Guilty Pleas, generally, this index
Not responsible by reason of mental disease or defect, § 11.4
Sentence promises, generally. Plea Bargaining, this index
Voluntariness, § 11.7

POLICE
Law enforcement records, Freedom of Information Law, § 7.33
Personnel records,
    Privileged information, discovery, § 7.30

POLICE INFORMANTS
Informants, generally, this index

INDEX

PREEMPTION
Jurisdiction, § 1.2

PRELIMINARY HEARINGS
Burden of proof, § 3.33
Closure, court's discretion, § 3.33
Cross-examination, limitation by court, § 3.33
Failure to commence hearing timely,
    Habeas corpus, § 3.34
    Motion for release of defendant from custody,
        Affirmation in support, form, § 3.36.18
        Notice of motion, form, § 3.36.17
    Release of defendant from custody, § 3.34
        Summary, § 3.35(I)
Reasonable cause determination, § 3.33
Right to counsel, § 3.33
Subpoenas, § 3.33
Summary, § 3.35(H)
Waiver, § 3.30
Witness statements,
    "Rosario" material, § 3.33

PRIOR CONVICTIONS
Impeachment, § 7.15

PRIVILEGED INFORMATION
Discovery,
    Child abuse, § 7.30
    Drug treatment records, § 7.30
    Education records, § 7.30
    In camera review, § 7.30
    Law enforcement personnel records, § 7.30
    Medical records, § 7.30
    News reporting, § 7.30
    Psychiatric records, § 7.30
    Rape crisis counselor's records, § 7.30
    Sealed court records, § 7.30
    Social worker records, § 7.30
    Work product rule, § 7.31

PROHIBITION
Double jeopardy, § 2.11
    Form, § 2.13.3
    Summary, § 2.12(H)
Guilty pleas,
    Felony complaints, reduction of charges, § 11.3
Plea bargaining,
    Felony complaints, reduction of charges, § 11.3

PROSECUTORS
Appeals,
    Readiness rule, excludable periods, § 9.31
    Suppression of evidence, § 10.22
Discovery, this index
Disqualification,
    Guilty pleas, waiver, § 11.15
Grand jury, legal advisor to, § 5.4
Guilty Pleas, generally, this index
Plea Bargaining, generally, this index
Prosecutorial misconduct,
    Guilty pleas, waiver, § 11.15
Prosecutor's Information, generally, this index
Readiness Rule, generally, this index

PROSECUTOR'S INFORMATION
    Generally, § 3.2
Amendment, § 3.8
Bill of particulars, § 3.8

INDEX

PROSECUTOR'S INFORMATION—Continued
Content, § 3.3
Defective instrument, motion to dismiss, § 3.27
Facial sufficiency, § 3.7
Form, § 3.3
Grand jury,
    Directing filing, § 3.2
    Resubmission to grand jury, § 3.27
Joinder, § 3.8
    Defendants, of, § 3.3
    Offenses, of, § 3.3
Local criminal court directing filing, § 3.2
Motion to amend,
    Affirmation in support, form, § 3.36.5
    Notice of motion, form, § 3.36.4
Plea Bargaining, generally, this index
Severance, § 3.8
Superior court directing filing, § 3.2
Superseding information, § 3.9
    Speedy trial, effect on, § 3.9
Supporting deposition not required, § 3.4
Verification, § 3.6

PROSTITUTION
Loitering for purpose of,
    Fingerprinting, § 3.23

PROTECTIVE ORDERS
Discovery, § 7.19
    Affirmation in support, form, § 7.37.11
    Notice of motion, form, § 7.37.10
    Summary, court, § 7.36(C)
    Summary, prosecution, § 7.35(I)

PSYCHIATRIC EXAMINATIONS
Mental Examinations, generally, this index

PUBLIC SERVANTS
Limitation of actions, extensions, § 9.4

RACKETEERING
Organized Crime Control Act, generally, this index

RADIO
News reporting sources,
    Privileged information, discovery, § 7.30

RAPE
Crisis counselor's records,
    Privileged information, discovery, § 7.30

READINESS RULE
    See also Speedy Trial, generally, this index
Applicability, § 9.14
Excludable periods, § 9.26 et seq.
    Absence or unavailability of defendant,
        Absent defendant, § 9.38
        Absent defined, § 9.35
        Bench warrants, § 9.37
        Causation of prosecution's unreadiness, § 9.36
        Unavailable defendant, § 9.39
        Unavailable defined, § 9.35
    Adjournment in contemplation of dismissal, § 9.44
    Appeals, § 9.31
    Arraignment, prosecutor's direction to appear, § 9.45
    Competency, § 9.28
    Consideration of matters by court, § 9.33
    Continuances, § 9.34
    Defendant without counsel, § 9.42

INDEX

READINESS RULE—Continued
Excludable periods—Continued
    Discovery, § 9.29
    Domestic violence, § 9.46
    Exceptional circumstances, § 9.43
    Family offenses, § 9.46
    Incarcerated defendants, § 9.41
    Joinder of co-defendants, § 9.40
    Other proceedings concerning defendant, § 9.27
    Post-readiness excludable delays, § 9.26
    Post-readiness prosecutorial delay, § 9.47
    Pre-readiness excludable delays, § 9.26
    Pretrial motions, § 9.30
    Trial of other charges, § 9.32
Genuine readiness defined, § 9.22
Guilty plea as waiver, § 9.13
Motion to dismiss,
    Affirmation in support, form, § 9.58.6
    Notice of motion, form, § 9.58.5
Readiness defined, § 9.21
Readiness to avoid dismissal,
    Calculation of time, § 9.24
        Summary, defense, § 9.56(B)
Readiness to avoid release on bail or recognizance,
    Affirmation in support, form, § 9.58.8
    Calculation of time, § 9.25
        Summary, defense, § 9.56(B)
    Motion for bail or recognizance, form, § 9.58.7
    Notice of motion, form, § 9.58.7
Sanctions, § 9.13
Summary, defense, § 9.56(C)
Summary, prosecution, § 9.57

RECONSIDERATION
Motion to suppress, § 10.15

RECORDS AND REPORTS
Competency,
    Mental examination, § 6.5
Discovery,
    Demand disclosure, § 7.4
Drug treatment programs,
    Privileged information, discovery, § 7.30
Education records,
    Privileged information, discovery, § 7.30
Immunity from prosecution,
    Grand jury, § 5.9
Law enforcement personnel records,
    Privileged information, discovery, § 7.30
Medical records,
    Privileged information, discovery, § 7.30
Psychiatric records,
    Privileged information, discovery, § 7.30
Rape crisis counselor's records,
    Privileged information, discovery, § 7.30
Sealed court records,
    Privileged information, discovery, § 7.30
Social worker records,
    Privileged information, discovery, § 7.30

REMOVAL
    Generally, § 1.6 et seq.
Family court, removal to, § 1.10
Local criminal courts,
    Removal from one criminal court to another, § 1.7
    Removal to superior court, § 1.8

INDEX

REMOVAL—Continued
Motion by defendant to remove misdemeanor charge to superior court,
    Affirmation in support, form, § 1.12.6
    Notice of motion, form, § 1.12.5
Motion by prosecutor to remove action for grand jury consideration,
    Affirmation in support, form, § 1.12.4
    Notice of motion, form, § 1.12.3
Motion to remove action to another local criminal court,
    Affirmation in support, form, § 1.12.2
    Notice of motion, form, § 1.12.1
Summary, § 1.11
Superior courts,
    Removal from local criminal court to superior court, § 1.8
    Removal from one superior court to another, § 1.9

RIGHT TO COUNSEL
Arraignment,
    Court's duty to inform defendant of rights, § 3.24
        Felony complaints, § 3.30
    Waiver, § 3.24
Assignment of counsel, reasonable delay excludable, § 9.42
Competency,
    Mental examination, § 6.4
Grand jury,
    Waiver of immunity, § 5.9
        Summary, § 5.30(G)
Preliminary hearings, § 3.33

"ROSARIO" MATERIAL
Discovery, this index

SALIVA
Scientific tests,
    Defendant's right to test physical evidence,
        Order compelling saliva sample from complainant, § 7.33
Withdrawal from defendant, prosecution's motion to compel, § 7.11

SANCTIONS
Discovery, this index

SCHIZOPHRENIA
Competency, § 6.10

SCHOOLS
Education records,
    Privileged information, discovery, § 7.30

SCIENTIFIC TESTS
Defendant's right to test physical evidence, § 7.32
    Order compelling blood sample from complainant, § 7.33
    Order compelling saliva sample from complainant, § 7.33
Discovery,
    Demand disclosure,
        Scientific test or experiment reports, § 7.4
    Summary, defense, § 7.34(D)
Suppression of evidence, § 10.8

SEARCH WARRANTS
    Generally, § 10.1 et seq.
Affirmation in support, § 10.2
Application, § 10.2
Arrest warrant, execution,
    Third party dwelling, § 3.14
Blanket searches prohibited, § 10.5
Burden of proof, § 10.4
Execution, § 10.5
Extent of search, § 10.6
Facial sufficiency, § 10.3
Hearsay, § 10.3

INDEX

SEARCH WARRANTS—Continued
Informants, § 10.3
Issuance, § 10.2
Nighttime search, § 10.5
"No knock" provision, § 10.5
Notice, § 10.5
Oaths, § 10.2
Reasonable cause requirement, § 10.3
Return, § 10.5
Scope, § 10.6
Seizure of personal property, § 10.1
Severability of invalid clause, § 10.5
Stale information, § 10.3
Validity, § 10.3
Warrantless arrest, execution,
    Third party dwelling, § 3.18

SELF INCRIMINATION
Grand Jury, generally, this index
Guilty pleas, waiver of rights, § 11.15
Immunity from prosecution, generally, this index
Notice,
    Defenses,
        Alibi, not violating, § 7.27

SENTENCES
Promises. Sentence promises, generally. Plea Bargaining, this index

SERVICE OF PROCESS
Appearance ticket, § 3.20
Bill of particulars,
    Request, § 5.19
    Summary, § 5.32(D)
Omnibus motion, § 8.1
Simplified information,
    Supporting depositions, § 3.5
Summons, § 3.16
Supporting depositions,
    Simplified information, § 3.5

SEVERANCE
Complaints, misdemeanor, § 3.8
Defendants,
    Co-defendant as witness, § 5.22
    Good cause for severance, § 5.22
    Guilty pleas, waiver, § 11.15
    Interlocking confession exception, § 5.22
    Motion for severance of trials of jointly indicted defendants,
        Affirmation in support, form, § 5.33.10
        Notice of motion, form, § 5.33.9
    Mutually antagonistic defenses, § 5.22
    Statements by co-defendant, § 5.22
    Summary, § 5.32(F)
Information, § 3.8
Joinder, generally, this index
Offenses,
    Affirmation in support, form, § 5.33.6
    Good cause for severance, § 5.21
    Guilty pleas, waiver, § 11.15
    Need to refrain test, § 5.21
    Notice of motion, form, § 5.33.5
    Omnibus motion, § 5.21
    Summary, § 5.32(E)
Prosecutor's information, § 3.8

SEX OFFENSES
Loitering for purpose of engaging in prostitution,
    Fingerprinting, § 3.23

INDEX

SEX OFFENSES—Continued
Loitering for purpose of soliciting or engaging in deviate sexual behavior,
    Fingerprinting, § 3.23

SIMPLIFIED INFORMATION
    Generally, § 3.2
Environmental conservation law violation, § 3.2
    Form, § 3.3
Facial sufficiency, § 3.7
Navigation law violation, § 3.2
    Form, § 3.3
Parks and recreation law violations, § 3.2
    Form, § 3.3
Plea Bargaining, generally, this index
Supporting deposition, §§ 3.2, 3.5
    Form, § 3.36.3
Traffic ticket, § 3.2
    Arrest warrant precluded, § 3.13
    Form, § 3.3
    Summons precluded, § 3.16
Verification, § 3.6

SOCIAL WORKERS
Records and reports,
    Privileged information, discovery, § 7.30

SPEEDY TRIAL
Competency,
    Mental examination, order, effect, § 6.3
Criminal trial preference over civil trials, § 9.11
Federal constitutional rights,
    "Barker" factors, § 9.8
    Due process rights, § 9.8
    Juveniles, § 9.8
    Pre-accusatory delay, inapplicable, § 9.8
Guilty pleas,
    Survival of claim, § 11.16
    Waiver, § 11.15
Mental examination to determine competency, effect, § 6.3
Motion to dismiss, § 3.26
    Adjournment in contemplation of dismissal, time tolled, § 3.29
    Affirmation in support, form, § 9.58.4
    Notice of motion, form, § 9.58.3
    Procedural requirements, §§ 9.12, 9.49
        Summary, defense, § 9.56(C)
        Summary, prosecution, § 9.57
    Sufficiency of motion papers,
        Procedural requirements, §§ 9.50, 9.51
            Summary, defense, § 9.56(C)
            Summary, prosecution, § 9.57
Omnibus motion, exception, § 8.1
Readiness rule,
    Applicability, § 9.14
    Excludable periods, § 9.26 et seq.
        Absence or unavailability of defendant,
            Absent defendant, § 9.38
            Absent defined, § 9.35
            Bench warrants, § 9.37
            Causation of prosecution's unreadiness, § 9.36
            Unavailable defendant, § 9.39
            Unavailable defined, § 9.35
        Adjournment in contemplation of dismissal, § 9.44
        Appeals, § 9.31
        Arraignment, prosecutor's direction to appear, § 9.45
        Competency, § 9.28
        Consideration of matters by court, § 9.33
        Continuances, § 9.34

INDEX

SPEEDY TRIAL—Continued
Readiness rule—Continued
    Excludable periods—Continued
        Defendant without counsel, § 9.42
        Discovery, § 9.29
        Domestic violence, § 9.46
        Exceptional circumstances, § 9.43
        Family offenses, § 9.46
        Incarcerated defendants, § 9.41
        Joinder of co-defendants, § 9.40
        Other proceedings concerning defendant, § 9.27
        Post-readiness excludable delays, § 9.26
        Post-readiness prosecutorial delay, § 9.47
        Pre-readiness excludable delays, § 9.26
        Pretrial motions, § 9.30
        Trial of other charges, § 9.32
    Genuine readiness defined, § 9.22
    Guilty plea as waiver, § 9.13
    Motion to dismiss,
        Affirmation in support, form, § 9.58.6
        Notice of motion, form, § 9.58.5
    Readiness defined, § 9.21
    Readiness to avoid dismissal,
        Calculation of time, § 9.24
            Summary, defense, § 9.56(B)
    Readiness to avoid release on bail or recognizance,
        Affirmation in support, form, § 9.58.8
        Calculation of time, § 9.25
            Summary, defense, § 9.56(B)
        Motion for bail or recognizance, form, § 9.58.7
        Notice of motion, form, § 9.58.7
    Sanctions, § 9.13
    Summary, defense, § 9.56(C)
    Summary, prosecution, § 9.57
Sixth Amendment, § 9.8
State constitutional rights,
    Due process, § 9.9
        "Taranovich" factors, § 9.10
    Post-accusatory delay, § 9.8
    Pre-accusatory delay, § 9.8
Superseding information, effect, § 3.9

STANDING
Suppression of evidence, § 10.11
    Summary, § 10.30

STATEMENTS
Appeals,
    Suppression of evidence, § 10.29
        Summary, § 10.30(E)
Co-defendant, by,
    Severance, § 5.22
        Summary, § 5.32(F)
Defendant, by,
    Notice by prosecution of intent to use,
        Arraignment, service of process at, § 3.30
Discovery, demand disclosure, § 7.4
Notice of statements,
    Appeals, § 10.29
    Arraignment, service of process at, § 3.30
    Impeachment, outside scope of rule, § 10.25
    Pedigree statements excluded, § 10.25
    Preclusion rule, § 10.28
    Res gestae statements excluded, § 10.25
    Timing, § 10.23
        Good cause for late notice, § 10.27
    Voluntariness, § 10.25

INDEX

STATEMENTS—Continued
Notice of statements—Continued
    Waiver, § 10.29
Witnesses,
    "Rosario" material,
        Automatic reversal rule, § 7.16
        Discovery, § 7.2
        Duplicative equivalent exception, § 7.17
        Preliminary hearings, § 3.33
        Request for disclosure of defense witnesses' statements, § 7.16
        Sanctions for failure to disclose, § 7.22
        Suppression of evidence, hearing, § 10.19
        Waiver, § 7.17
        Within prosecution's possession and control, § 7.17

STATUTE OF LIMITATIONS
Limitation of Actions, generally, this index

STOLEN PROPERTY
Discovery,
    Demand disclosure, § 7.4

SUBPOENAS
Discovery,
    Exculpatory material, § 7.8
    Subpoena duces tecum, § 7.8
        Summary, defense, § 7.34(E)
Preliminary hearings, § 3.33
Subpoena duces tecum,
    Discovery, § 7.8
        Summary, defense, § 7.34(E)
Suppression of evidence,
    Hearing, § 10.19
        Summary, § 10.30(D)

SUBSTANCE ABUSE TREATMENT
Drug Treatment Programs, generally, this index

SUMMONS
Appearance ticket, failure to appear, § 3.21
Arraignment,
    Securing defendant's appearance, § 5.23
    Summary, § 5.32(G)
Arrest warrant for failure to appear, § 3.16
Commencement of criminal action required, § 3.16
Issuance, § 3.16
Service of process, § 3.16
Simplified information,
    Traffic ticket, summons precluded, § 3.16

SUPERIOR COURT INFORMATION
Chargeable offenses, § 5.10
Waiver of indictment, § 5.10
    Summary, § 5.31

SUPERIOR COURTS
Bail and recognizance,
    Excessive bail, appeal, §§ 4.6, 4.13
    Fixing bail, § 4.6
    Notice of application, form, § 4.15.1
Competency,
    Post-examination procedure, § 6.6
County courts, § 1.2
Information,
    Chargeable offenses, § 5.10
    Waiver of indictment, § 5.10
        Summary, § 5.31
Jurisdiction, § 1.2
    Exclusive trial jurisdiction of felonies, § 1.2

INDEX

SUPERIOR COURTS—Continued
Jurisdiction—Continued
    Motion by defendant to remove misdemeanor charge to superior court,
        Affirmation in support, form, § 1.12.6
        Notice of motion, form, § 1.12.5
    Motion for change of venue,
        Affirmation in support, form, § 1.12.8
        Notice of motion, form, § 1.12.7
Prosecutor's information,
    Superior court directing filing, § 3.2
Removal from local criminal court, § 1.8
Removal to another superior court, § 1.9
Removal to family court, § 1.10
Supreme court, § 1.2

SUPPORTING DEPOSITIONS
    Generally, § 3.4
Defendant's request for, form, § 3.36.2
Form, § 3.36.1
Prosecutor's information, deposition not required, § 3.4
Simplified information, §§ 3.2, 3.5
    Defense request required, § 3.5
    Form, § 3.36.3
    Police officer issuing, § 3.5
    Public servant issuing, § 3.5
    Service of process, § 3.5
    Waiver, § 3.5
Verification, § 3.6

SUPPRESSION OF EVIDENCE
    Generally, § 10.7 et seq.
Aggrieved person, § 10.11
Appeal by prosecution, § 10.22
Appeals,
    Guilty pleas, following, § 10.22
    Interlocutory, § 10.22
    Notice, § 10.29
        Summary, § 10.30(E)
    Prosecution, by, § 10.22
Attenuation principles, §§ 10.9, 10.10
    Summary, § 10.30(A)
Beepers, § 10.8
Blood tests, § 10.8
Chemical tests, § 10.8
Confessions, § 10.8
Denial,
    Guilty pleas, survival of claim, § 11.16
Eavesdropping, § 10.8
    Indirect fruits, § 10.9
    Standing to challenge, § 10.11
Exclusionary rule, § 10.7
Expectation of privacy, § 10.11
Fourth Amendment rights, § 10.11
Hearing,
    "Brady" evidence, § 10.19
    Burden of proof, § 10.20
        Summary, § 10.30(D)
    Cross-examination, § 10.19
    Defendant's right to be present, § 10.19
    Hearsay, § 10.19
    Identification, bifurcation of hearing, § 10.19
    Judge's duties, § 10.19
    Judicial hearing officer's duties, § 10.19
    Public's right to be present, § 10.19
    "Rosario" material, § 10.19
    Subpoenas, § 10.19
    Summary, § 10.30(D)

INDEX

SUPPRESSION OF EVIDENCE—Continued
Hearing—Continued
    Witnesses, § 10.19
Hearsay,
    Hearing, § 10.19
Identification, § 10.8
    Affirmation in support, form, § 10.31.4
    Bifurcation of hearing, § 10.19
    Notice, § 10.23
        Form, § 10.31.3
        Scope, § 10.26
Illegal surveillance, § 10.8
Impeachment, § 10.14
Independent source doctrine, § 10.10
Indictment,
    Subsequent suppression of evidence not invalidating indictment, § 10.10
Indirect fruits, § 10.9
    Summary, § 10.30(A)
Inevitable discovery doctrine, § 10.10
Informants,
    Identity of police informant, § 10.19
Involuntary statements, § 10.8
Judicial hearing officers, § 10.12
Motion to suppress,
    Affirmation in support, form, § 10.31.2
    Appellate review, § 10.15
    Arraignment, § 10.13
    Defendant's motion papers, § 10.16
        Pleading requirements, § 10.17
    Filing, § 10.12
    Legal grounds for motion, § 10.16
    Notice, § 10.13
        Form, § 10.31.1
    Preclusion motion, § 10.13
    Prosecution's motion papers, § 10.18
    Reconsideration, motion for, § 10.15
    Summary, §§ 10.30(B), 10.30(C)
    Sworn factual allegations, § 10.16
        Exceptions, § 10.17
        Pleading requirements, § 10.17
    Time of decision, § 10.14
    Timing, § 10.13
    Writing requirement, § 10.16
Notice,
    Appeals, § 10.29
        Summary, § 10.30(E)
    Content, § 10.24
    Form, § 10.31.1
    Identification, § 10.23
        Form, § 10.31.3
        Scope, § 10.26
    Physical evidence, form, § 10.31.5
    Preclusion rule, § 10.28
    Scope, § 10.25
    Statement evidence, § 10.23
    Time for filing motion, § 10.13
    Timing, § 10.24
        Good cause for late notice, § 10.27
    Waiver, § 10.29
Omnibus motion, exception, § 8.1
Pagers, § 10.8
Pen register, § 10.8
    Indirect fruits, § 10.9
    Standing to challenge, § 10.11
Pending,
    Guilty pleas, waiver, § 11.16

INDEX

SUPPRESSION OF EVIDENCE—Continued
Physical evidence,
    Affirmation in support, form, § 10.31.6
    Notice of motion, form, § 10.31.5
Pronounced break test, § 10.10
Standing to challenge, § 10.11
    Summary, § 10.30(A)
Statement evidence,
    Appeals, § 10.29
    Arraignment, service of process at, § 3.30
    Impeachment, outside scope of rule, § 10.25
    Pedigree statements excluded, § 10.25
    Preclusion rule, § 10.28
    Res gestae statements excluded, § 10.25
    Timing, § 10.23
        Good cause for late notice, § 10.27
    Voluntariness, § 10.25
    Waiver, § 10.29
Trap and trace device, § 10.8
    Indirect fruits, § 10.9
    Standing to challenge, § 10.11
Unlawful search, § 10.8

SUPREMACY CLAUSE
Preemption,
    Jurisdiction, § 1.2

TAMPERING
Computer tampering,
    Defenses, notice, § 7.28

TAPE RECORDINGS
Discovery,
    Demand disclosure, § 7.4

TAXATION
Limitation of actions, extensions, § 9.4

TELEVISION
Arraignment,
    Consent of parties required, § 3.24
News reporting sources,
    Privileged information, discovery, § 7.30

TERRITORIAL JURISDICTION
Geographical jurisdiction, generally. Jurisdiction, this index

TIME
    Generally, § 9.1 et seq.
Arraignment,
    Suppression of evidence, filing motion, § 10.13
Bail and recognizance,
    Preliminary hearings,
        Failure to commence hearing timely, release of defendant from custody, § 3.34
            Summary, § 3.35(I)
Calculation, § 9.48
Commencement of criminal action,
    Arrest warrant, § 3.11
    Filing of accusatory instrument, § 9.15
    Recommencement rule,
        Appeals, reversal, § 9.16
        Appearance ticket, arraignment, § 9.17
        Guilty pleas, withdrawal, § 9.16
        Mistrials, retrial following, § 9.16
        Not responsible by reason of mental disease or defect, withdrawal of plea, § 9.16
    Reduction of original charges,
        Inspection and reduction of indicted felony, § 9.19
        Misdemeanors, § 9.20
        Reduction of felony complaint, § 9.18

INDEX

TIME—Continued
Commencement of criminal action—Continued
    Summons, § 3.16
Excludable periods, generally. Readiness Rule, this index
Indictment,
    Motion to dismiss,
        Omnibus motion, § 5.26
        Summary, § 5.32(H)
    Waiver, § 5.10
Interstate agreement on detainers, § 9.55
Limitation of Actions, generally, this index
Motion to dismiss, § 3.26
Preliminary hearings,
    Failure to commence hearing timely,
        Bail and recognizance, release of defendant from custody, § 3.34
            Summary, § 3.35(I)
        Habeas corpus, § 3.34
        Motion for release of defendant from custody,
            Affirmation in support, form, § 3.36.18
            Notice of motion, form, § 3.36.17
Readiness Rule, generally, this index
Speedy Trial, generally, this index
Suppression of evidence,
    Filing motion, § 10.13
    Notice, § 10.24
        Good cause for late notice, § 10.27

TRAFFIC TICKETS
Arraignment,
    Court's duty to inform defendant of rights, § 3.24
Bail and recognizance,
    Credit card posting, § 4.3
Simplified information, § 3.2
    Form, § 3.3

TRESPASS
Computer trespass and unauthorized use,
    Defenses, notice, § 7.28
    Discovery,
        Demand disclosure, § 7.4

USE OF FORCE
Arrest warrant, execution, § 3.14

VENUE
Geographical jurisdiction, generally. Jurisdiction, this index

VERIFICATION
Child witness' capacity to testify under oath, § 3.6
Complaints, § 3.6
Information, § 3.6
Mentally ill witness' capacity to testify under oath, § 3.6
Prosecutor's information, § 3.6
Search warrants, § 10.2
Simplified information, § 3.6
Supporting depositions, § 3.6

VIDEOTAPE RECORDINGS
Discovery,
    Demand disclosure, § 7.4

WARRANTLESS ARREST
    Generally, § 3.17 et seq.
Authority to arrest, § 3.18
Duty to arrest,
    Domestic violence, § 3.18
    Family offenses, § 3.18
    Protection orders, § 3.18
Dwelling, entry to effectuate arrest,

INDEX

WARRANTLESS ARREST—Continued
Dwelling—Continued
    Consent required, § 3.18
    Exigent circumstances required, § 3.18
Execution, § 3.18
    Third party dwelling, search warrant required, § 3.18
Habeas corpus,
    Petition for writ, form, § 3.36.8
Juveniles, notice to parent or guardian, § 3.19
Post-arrest procedure, § 3.19
    "Without unnecessary delay" standard, §§ 3.15, 3.19
"Reasonable cause" standard, §§ 3.18, 3.19

WARRANTS
Arrest Warrants, generally, this index
Bench Warrants, generally, this index
Search Warrants, generally, this index

WITNESSES
Criminal histories, discovery, § 7.18
Discovery, this index
Grand Jury, this index
Statements, this index

WORDS AND PHRASES
Definitions, generally, this index

WORK PRODUCT RULE
Attorneys, this index

WRITS
Habeas Corpus, generally, this index
Prohibition, generally, this index

†